The Art of the Critic

The Art of the Critic
Literary Theory and Criticism from the Greeks to the Present

Volume 5
Early Romantics

EDITED WITH AN INTRODUCTION BY

HAROLD BLOOM

Sterling Professor of the Humanities, Yale University

1988
CHELSEA HOUSE PUBLISHERS
NEW YORK   NEW HAVEN   PHILADELPHIA

Project Editor: James Uebbing
Editorial Coordinator: Karyn Gullen Browne
Copy Chief: Richard Fumosa
Editorial Staff: Neal Dolan, Stephen Mudd
Design: Susan Lusk

Printed and bound in the United States of America

Library of Congress Cataloging in Publication Data
Main entry under title:

The Art of the Critic

    Includes bibliographies and index.
    Contents: v. 1. Classical and medieval—   —v. 5.
Early romantics.
    1. Criticism—Collected works. 2. Literature—
Philosophy—Collected works. I. Bloom, Harold.
PN86.A77 1985   809   84–15547
ISBN 0–87754–493–X (set)
    0–87754–498–0 (vol. 5)

Contents

Index and Glossary are contained in Volume 11

Coleridge and Hazlitt:
Two Modes of Romantic Criticism

Harold Bloom

1

COLERIDGE, THE YOUNGEST of fourteen children of a country clergyman, was a precocious and lonely child, a kind of changeling in his own family. Early a dreamer and (as he said) a "character," he suffered the loss of his father (who had loved him best of all the children) when he was only nine. At Christ's Hospital in London, soon after his father's death, he found an excellent school that gave him the intellectual nurture he needed, as well as a lifelong friend in the future essayist Charles Lamb. Early a poet, he fell deeply in love with Mary Evans, a schoolfellow's sister, but sorrowfully nothing came of it.

At Jesus College, Cambridge, Coleridge started well, but temperamentally he was not suited to academic discipline and failed of distinction. Fleeing Cambridge, and much in debt, he enlisted in the cavalry under the immortal name of Silas Tomkyn Comberback but kept falling off his horse. Though he proved useful to his fellow dragoons at writing love letters, he was good for little else but stable-cleaning, and the cavalry allowed his brothers to buy him out. He returned to Cambridge, but his characteristic guilt impeded academic labor and when he abandoned Cambridge in 1794 he had no degree.

A penniless young poet, radical in politics, original in religion, he fell in with the then equally radical bard Robert Southey, remembered today as the Conservative Laureate constantly savaged in Byron's satirical verse. Like our contemporary communards, the two poetical youths projected what they named a "pantisocracy." With the right young ladies and, hopefully, other choice spirits, they would found a communistic agrarian-literary settlement on the banks of the Susquehanna in exotic Pennsylvania. At Southey's urging, Coleridge made a pantisocratic engagement to the not very brilliant Miss Sara Fricker, whose sister Southey was to marry. Pantisocracy died aborning, and Coleridge in time woke up miserably to find himself unsuitably married, the greatest misfortune of his life.

He turned to Wordsworth, whom he had met early in 1795. His poetry influenced Wordsworth's and helped the latter attain his characteristic mode. It is not too much to say that Coleridge's poetry disappeared into Wordsworth's. We remember *Lyrical Ballads* (1798) as Wordsworth's book, yet about a third of it (in length) was Coleridge's, and "Tintern Abbey," the crown of the volume except for "The Rime of the Ancient Mariner," is immensely indebted to Coleridge's "Frost at Midnight." Not is there much evidence of Wordsworth admiring or encouraging his friend's poetry; toward "The Ancient Mariner" he was always very grudging, and he was discomfited (but inevitably so) by both "Dejection: An Ode" and "To William Wordsworth." Selfless where Wordsworth's poetry was concerned, Coleridge had to suffer his closest friend's neglect of his own poetic ambitions.

This is not an easy matter to be fair about, since literature necessarily is as much a matter of personality as it is of character. Coleridge, like Keats (and to certain readers, Shelley), is lovable. Byron is at least always fascinating, and Blake in his lonely magnificence is a hero of the imagination. But Wordsworth's personality, like Milton's or Dante's, does not stimulate affection for the poet in the common reader. Coleridge has, as Walter Pater observed, a "peculiar charm"; he seems to lend himself to myths of failure, which is astonishing when the totality of his work is contemplated.

Yet it is his life, and his self-abandonment of his poetic ambitions, that continue to convince us that we ought to find in him parables of the failure of genius. His best poetry was all written in the year and a half in which he saw Wordsworth daily (1797–8), yet even his best poetry, with the single exception of "The Ancient Mariner," is fragmentary. The pattern of his life is fragmentary also. When he received an annuity from the Wedgwoods, he left Wordsworth and Dorothy to study language and philosophy in Germany (1798–9). Soon after returning, his miserable middle years began, though he was only twenty-seven. He moved near the Wordsworths again and fell in love, permanently and unhappily, with Sara Hutchinson, whose sister Mary was to become Wordsworth's wife in 1802. His own marriage was hopeless, and his health rapidly deteriorated, perhaps for psychological reasons. To help endure the pain he began to drink laudanum, liquid opium, and thus contracted an addiction he never entirely cast off. In 1804, seeking better health, he went to Malta but returned two years later in the worst condition of his life. Separating from Mrs. Coleridge, he moved to London and began another career as lecturer, general man-of-letters, and periodical editor, while his miseries augmented. The inevitable quarrel with Wordsworth in 1810 was ostensibly reconciled in 1812, but real friendship was not reestablished until 1828.

From 1816 on, Coleridge lived in the household of a physician, James Gillman, so as to be able to keep working and thus avoid total breakdown. Prematurely aged, his poetry period over, Coleridge entered into a major last phase as critic and philosopher, upon which his historical importance depends; but this, like his earlier prose achievements, is beyond the scope of an introduction to his poetry. It remains to ask, What was his achievement as a poet, and extraordinary as that was, why did his poetry effectively cease after about 1807? Wordsworth went on with poetry after 1807 but mostly very badly. The few poems Coleridge wrote, from the age of thirty-five on, are powerful but occasional. Did the poetic will not fail in him, since his imaginative powers did not?

Coleridge's large poetic ambitions included the writing of a philosophic epic on the origin of evil and a sequence of hymns to the sun, moon, and elements. These high plans died, slowly but definitively, and were replaced by the dream of a philosophic *Opus Maximum*, a huge work of synthesis that would reconcile German idealist philosophy with the orthodox truths of Christianity. Though only fragments of this work were ever written, much was done in its place—speculations on theology, political theory, and criticism that were to influence profoundly conservative British thought in the Victorian period and, in quite another way, the American transcendentalism led by Emerson and Theodore Parker.

Walter Pater's essay of 1866 on "Coleridge's Writings" seems to me still the best short treatment of Coleridge, and this after a century of commentary. Pater, who knew his debt to Coleridge, knew also the anxiety Coleridge caused him, and Pater therefore came to a further and subtler knowing. In the Organic analogue, against which the entire soul of the great Epicurean critic rebelled, Pater recognized the product of Coleridge's profound anxieties as a creator. I begin therefore with Pater on Coleridge, and then will move immediately deep into the Coleridgean interior, to look upon Coleridge's fierce refusal to take on the ferocity of the strong poet.

This ferocity, as both Coleridge and Pater well knew, expresses itself as a near-solipsism, and Egotistical Sublime, or Miltonic godlike stance. From 1795 on, Coleridge knew, loved, envied, was both cheered and darkened by the largest instance of that Sublime since Milton himself. He studied constantly, almost involuntarily, the glories of the truly modern strong poet, Wordsworth. Whether he gave Wordsworth rather more than he received, we cannot be certain; we know only that he wanted more from Wordsworth than he received, but then it was his endearing though exasperating weakness that he always needed more love than he could get, no matter how much he got: "To be beloved is all I need, / And whom I love, I love indeed."

Pater understood what he called Coleridge's "peculiar charm," but he resisted it in the sacred name of what he called the "relative" spirit against Coleridge's archaizing "absolute" spirit. In gracious but equivocal tribute to Coleridge he observed:

> The literary life of Coleridge was a disinterested struggle against the application of the relative spirit to moral and religious questions. Everywhere he is restlessly scheming to apprehend the absolute; to affirm it effectively; to get it acknowledged. Coleridge failed in that attempt, happily even for him, for it was a struggle against the increasing life of the mind itself. . . . How did his choice of a controversial interest, his determination to affirm the absolute, weaken or modify his poetic gift?

To affirm the absolute, Pater says—or, as we might say, to reject all dualisms except those sanctioned by orthodox Christian thought—is not *materia poetica* for the start of the nineteenth century, and if we think of a poem like the "Hymn before Sun-Rise, in the Vale of Chamouni," we are likely to agree with Pater. We will agree also when he contrasts Wordsworth favorably with Coleridge, and even with Goethe, commending Wordsworth for "that flawless temperament . . . which keeps his conviction of a latent intelligence in nature within the limits of sentiment or instinct, and confines it to those delicate and subdued shades of expression which perfect art allows." Pater goes on to say that Coleridge's version of Wordsworth's instinct is a philosophical idea, which means that Coleridge's poetry had to be "more dramatic, more self-conscious" than Wordsworth's. But this in turn, Pater insists, means that for aesthetic success ideas must be held loosely, in the relative spirit. One idea that Coleridge did not hold loosely was the Organic analogue, and it becomes clearer as we proceed in Pater's essay that the aesthetic critic is building toward a passionate assault upon the Organic principle. He quotes Coleridge's description of Shakespeare as "a nature humanized, a genial understanding, directing self-consciously a power and an implicit wisdom deeper even than our consciousness." "There," Pater comments, with bitter eloquence, "'the absolute' has been affirmed in the sphere of art; and thought begins to congeal." With great dignity Pater adds that Coleridge has "obscured the true interest of art." By likening the work of art to a living organism, Coleridge does justice to the impression the work may give us, but he "does not express the process by which that work was produced."

M. H. Abrams, in his *The Mirror and the Lamp*, defends Coleridge against Pater by insisting that Coleridge knew his central problem "was to use analogy with organic growth to account for the spontaneous, the inspired, and the self-evolving in the psychology of invention, yet not to commit himself as far to the elected figure as to minimize the supervention of the antithetic qualities of foresight and choice." Though Abrams calls Pater "short-sighted," I am afraid the critical palms remain with the relative spirit, for Pater's point was not that Coleridge had no awareness of the dangers of using the Organic analogue but rather that awareness, here as elsewhere, was no salvation for Coleridge. The issue is whether Coleridge, not Shakespeare, was able to direct "self-consciously a power and an implicit wisdom deeper than consciousness." Pater's complaint is valid because Coleridge, in describing Shakespeare, Dante, Milton, keeps repeating his absolute formula that poems grow from within themselves, that their "wholeness is not in vision or conception, but in an inner feeling of totality and absolute being." As Pater says, "that exaggerated inwardness is barren" because it "withdraws us too far from what we can see, hear, and feel," because it cheats the senses and emotions of their triumph. I urge Pater's wisdom here not only against Coleridge, though I share Pater's love for Coleridge, but against the formalist criticism that continued in Coleridge's absolute spirit.

What is the imaginative source of Coleridge's disabling hunger for the Absolute? On August 9, 1831, about three years before he died, he wrote in his Notebook: "From my earliest recollection I have had a consciousness of Power without Strength—a perception, an experience, of more than ordinary power with an inward sense of Weakness. . . . More than ever do I feel this now, when all my fancies still in their integrity are, as it were, drawn *inward* and by their suppression and compression rendered a mock substitute for Strength—" Here again is Pater's barren and exaggerated inwardness, but in a darker context than the Organic principle provided.

This context is Milton's "universe of death," where Coleridge apprehended death-in-life as being "the wretchedness of *division*." If we stand in that universe, then "we think of ourselves as separated beings, and place nature in antithesis to the mind, as object to subject, thing to thought, death to life." To be so separated is to become, Coleridge says, "a soul-less fixed star, receiving no rays nor influences into my Being, *a Solitude which I so tremble at, that I cannot attribute it even to the Divine Nature*." This, we can say, is Coleridge's Counter-Sublime, his answer to the anxiety of influence, in strong poets. The fear of solipsism is greater in him than the fear of not individuating his own imagination.

As with every other major Romantic, the prime precursor poet for Coleridge was Milton. There is a proviso to be entered here; for all these poets—Blake, Wordsworth, Shelley, Coleridge (only Keats is an exception)— there is a greater Sublime poetry behind Milton, but as its author is a people and not a single poet, and as it is far removed in time, its greatness does not inhibit a new imagination—not unless it is taken as the work of the Prime Precursor Himself, to whom all creation belongs. Only Coleridge, among these poets, acquired a double Sublime anxiety of influence. Beyond the beauty that has terror in it of Milton, was beauty more terrible. In a letter to Thelwall, December 17, 1796, Coleridge wrote: "Is not Milton a *sublimer* poet than Homer or Virgil? Are not his Personages more sublimely cloathed? And do you not know, that there is not perhaps *one* page in Milton's *Paradise Lost*, in which he has not borrowed his imagery from the *Scriptures*?—I allow, and rejoice that *Christ* appealed only to the understanding & the affections; but I affirm that, after reading Isaiah, or St. Paul's Epistle to the Hebrews, Homer & Virgil are disgustingly *tame* to me, & Milton himself barely tolerable." Yet these statements are rare in Coleridge. Frequently, Milton seems to blend with the ultimate influence, which I think is a normal enough procedure. In 1796, Coleridge also says, in his review of Burke's *Letter to a Noble Lord:* "It is lucky for poetry, that Milton did not live in our days. . . ." Here Coleridge moves toward the center of his concern, and we should remember his formula: "Shakespeare was all men, potentially, except Milton." This leads to a more ambiguous formula, reported to us of a lecture that Coleridge gave on November 28, 1811: "Shakespeare became all things well into which he infused himself, while all forms, all things became Milton—the poet ever present to our minds and more than gratifying us for the loss of the distinct individuality of what he represents." Though Coleridge truly professes himself more than gratified, he admits loss. Milton's greatness is purchased at the cost of something dear to Coleridge, a principle of difference he knows may be flooded out by his monistic yearnings. For Milton, to Coleridge, is a mythic monad in himself. Commenting upon the apostrophe to light at the commencement of the third book of *Paradise Lost*, Coleridge notes: "In all modern poetry in Christendom there is an under consciousness of a sinful nature, a fleeting away of external things, the mind or subject greater than the object, the reflective character predominant. In the *Paradise Lost* the sublimest parts are the revelations of Milton's own mind, producing itself and evolving its own greatness; and this is truly so, that when that which is merely entertaining for its objective beauty is introduced, it at first seems a discord." This might be summarized as: where Milton is not, nature is barren, and its significance is that Milton is permitted just such a solitude as Coleridge trembles to imagine for the Divine Being.

Pater thought that Coleridge had succumbed to the Organic analogue because he hungered too intensively for eternity, as Lamb had said of his old school-friend. Pater also quoted De Quincey's summary of Coleridge: "He wanted better bread than can be made with wheat." I would add that Coleridge hungered also for an eternity of generosity between poets, as between people—a generosity that is not allowed in a world where each poet must struggle to individuate his own breath and this at the expense of his forebears as much as of his contemporaries. Perhaps also, to modify De Quincey, Coleridge wanted better poems than can be made without misprision.

I suggest then that the Organic analogue, with all its pragmatic neglect of the processes by which poems have to be produced, appealed so overwhelmingly to Coleridge because it seemed to preclude the anxiety of influence and to obviate the poet's necessity not just to unfold like a natural growth but to develop at the expense of others. Whatever the values of the Organic analogue for literary criticism—and I believe, with Pater, that it does more harm than good—it provided Coleridge with a rationale for a dangerous evasion of the inner steps he had to take for his own poetic development. As Blake might have said, Coleridge's imagination insisted upon slaying itself on the stems of generation—or, to invoke another Blakean image, Coleridge lay down to sleep upon the Organic analogue as though it were a Beulah-couch of soft, moony repose.

I would maintain that the finest achievement of the High Romantic poets of England was their humanization of the Miltonic Sublime. But when we attend deeply to the works where this humanization is most strenuously accomplished—Blake's *Milton* and *Jerusalem*, Wordsworth's *Prelude*, Shelley's *Prometheus Unbound,* Keats's two *Hyperions,* even in a way Byron's *Don Juan*—we sense at last a quality lacking, a quality in which Milton abounds for all his severity. This quality, though not in itself a tenderness, made Milton's Eve possible, and we miss such a figure in all her Romanic descendants. More than the other five great Romantic poets, Coleridge was able, by temperament and by subtly shaded intellect, to have given us a High Romantic Eve, a total humanization of the tenderest and most appealing element in the Miltonic Sublime. Many anxieties blocked Coleridge from that rare accomplishment, and of these the anxiety of influence was not the least.

2

David Bromwich, Hazlitt's best critic, shrewdly says of Hazlitt's key word *gusto* that it "accords nicely with the belief that taste adds to our nature instead

of correcting it." I take it that Hazlitt's *gusto* is an aesthetic displacement of the
Dissenting Protestant version of grace, which corrects our nature without
abolishing it. The son of a radical Dissenting Minister, Hazlitt himself was
always a Jacobin with a faith in Napoleon as the true heir of the Revolution.
Unswerving in his politics, Hazlitt also remained an unreconstructed early
Wordsworthian, unlike Wordsworth himself, a difference that Hazlitt bitterly
kept in mind, as here in his observations on Wordsworth's *The Excursion:*

> In the application of these memorable lines, we should, perhaps,
> differ a little from Mr. Wordsworth; nor can we indulge with him in the
> fond conclusion afterwards hinted at, that one day *our* triumph, the
> triumph of humanity and liberty, may be complete. For this purpose,
> we think several things necessary which are impossible. It is a
> consummation which cannot happen till the nature of things is
> changed, till the many become as united as the *one*, till romantic
> generosity shall be as common as gross selfishness, till reason shall
> have acquired the obstinate blindness of prejudice, till the love of
> power and of change shall no longer goad man on to restless action, till
> passion and will, hope and fear, love and hatred, and the objects proper
> to excite them, that is, alternate good and evil, shall no longer sway the
> bosoms and businesses of men. All things move, not in progress, but
> in a ceaseless round; our strength lies in our weakness; our virtues are
> built on our vices; our faculties are as limited as our being; nor can we
> lift man above his nature more than above the earth he treads. But
> though we cannot weave over again the airy, unsubstantial dream,
> which reason and experience have dispelled,
>
> > What though the radiance, which was once so bright,
> > Be now for ever taken from our sight,
> > Though nothing can bring back the hour
> > Of glory in the grass, of splendour in the flower:
>
> yet we will never cease, nor be prevented from returning on the
> wings of imagination to that bright dream of our youth; that glad dawn
> of the day-star of liberty; that spring-time of the world, in which the
> hopes and expectations of the human race seemed opening in the
> same gay career with our own; when France called her children to
> partake her equal blessings beneath her laughing skies; when the
> stranger was met in all her villages with dance and festive songs, in
> celebration of a new and golden era; and when, to the retired and
> contemplative student, the prospects of human happiness and glory
> were seen ascending like the steps of Jacob's ladder, in bright and
> never-ending succession. The dawn of that day was suddenly overcast;
> that season of hope is past; it is fled with the other dreams of our
> youth, which we cannot recall, but has left behind it traces, which are
> not to be effaced by Birthday and Thanksgiving odes, or the chaunting
> of *Te Deums* in all the churches of Christendom. To those hopes

eternal regrets are due; to those who maliciously and wilfully blasted them, in the fear that they might be accomplished, we feel no less what we owe—hatred and scorn as lasting!

In effect, the aesthetic loss of Wordsworth's visionary gleam is associated here with the spiritual loss of revolutionary hope. All loss, for the critic Hazlitt, is ultimately a loss of gusto, since *gusto* is Hazlitt's version of Blake's "exuberance," as in: "Exuberance is Beauty." One sees this clearly when he transfers the term *gusto* from painters to writers:

> The infinite quantity of dramatic invention in Shakespeare takes from his gusto. The power he delights to shew is not intense, but discursive. He never insists on any thing as much as he might, except a quibble. Milton has great gusto. He repeats his blow twice; grapples with and exhausts his subject. His imagination has a double relish of its objects, an inveterate attachment to the things he describes, and to the words describing them.

> > ——Or where Chineses drive
> > With sails and wind their *cany* waggons *light*.

> Wild above rule or art, *enormous* bliss.

> There is a gusto in Pope's compliments, in Dryden's satires, and Prior's tales; and among prose-writers, Boccaccio and Rabelais had the most of it. We will only mention one other work which appears to us to be full of gusto, and that is the *Beggar's Opera*. If it is not, we are altogether mistaken in our notions on this delicate subject.

Shakespeare's gusto is in his exuberance of invention, Milton's in his exhaustive tenacity at battering the object, as it were. An aesthetic category comprehensive enough to include also Pope, Dryden, and Prior, on the one side, and Boccaccio, Rabelais, and John Gay, on the other, is perhaps too broad to be of use to practical criticism. Hazlitt's own gusto or critical exuberance proved capable of overcoming this difficulty, and he gave us a poetics of power still unsurpassed in its potential:

> The language of poetry naturally falls in with the language of power. The imagination is an exaggerating and exclusive faculty; it takes from one thing to add to another: it accumulates circumstances together to give the greatest possible effect to a favourite object. The understanding is a dividing and measuring faculty, it judges of things not according to their immediate impression on the mind, but according to their relations to one another. The one is a monopolising faculty, which seeks the greatest quantity of present excitement by inequality and dispro-portion; the other is a distributive faculty, which seeks the greatest quantity of ultimate good, by justice and proportion. The one is an aristocratical, the other a republican faculty. The principle of poetry is a very anti-levelling principle. It aims at effect, it exists by contrast. It admits of no medium. It is everything by excess. It rises above the

ordinary standard of sufferings and crimes. It presents a dazzling appearance. It shows its head turretted, crowned, and crested. Its front is gilt and bloodstained. Before it "it carries noise, and behind it leaves tears." It has its altars and its victims, sacrifices, human sacrifices. Kings, priests, nobles, are its train-bearers, tyrants and slaves its executioners.—"Carnage is its daughter."—Poetry is right-royal. It puts the individual for the species, the one above the infinite-many, might before right. A lion hunting a flock of sheep or a herd of wild asses is a more poetical object than they; and we even take part with the lordly beast, because our vanity or some other feeling makes us disposed to place ourselves in the situation of the strongest party. So we feel some concern for the poor citizens of Rome when they meet together to compare their wants and grievances, till Coriolanus comes in and with blows and big words drives this set of "poor rats," this rascal scum, to their homes and beggary before him. There is nothing heroical in a multitude of miserable rogues not wishing to be starved, or complaining that they are like to be so; but when a single man comes forward to brave their cries and to make them submit to the last indignities, from mere pride and self-will, our admiration of his prowess is immediately converted into contempt for their pusillanimity. The insolence of power is stronger than the plea of necessity. The tame submission to usurped authority or even the natural resistance to it has nothing to excite or flatter the imagination: it is the assumption of a right to insult or oppress others that carries an imposing air of superiority with it. We had rather be the oppressor than the oppressed. The love of power in ourselves and the admiration of it in others are both natural to man: the one makes him a tyrant, the other a slave.

This is from Hazlitt's discussion of *Coriolanus* in his *Characters of Shakespear's Plays*. The quality of excess is central to Hazlitt's insight here, which tells us that meaning gets started (rather than being merely repeated) by excess, by overflow, and by a sense of potential, a sense of something evermore about to be. The dialectic of this poetics of power depends upon an interplay of Shakespearean and Wordsworthian influences upon Hazlitt. From Shakespeare, Hazlitt takes an awareness that character may be fate, yet only personality bestows some measure of freedom. From Wordsworth, Hazlitt received a new consciousness of how a writer could begin again despite the strength and persistence of cultural traditions. The freedom of personality, in Falstaff, *is* freedom because ego ceases to be persecuted by superego. The originality of writing, in Wordsworth, is the disappearance of subject matter, and its replacement by subjectivity. Taken together, the ego of free wit and the triumph of a fresh subjectivity make up the manner and matter of Hazlitt's characteristic achievement, an essay at once familiar and critical, firmly literary yet also discursive and speculative.

In his loving meditation, "On the Periodical Essayists," Hazlitt lists his precursors: Montaigne, Steele (rather than Addison), Johnson (despite

Hazlitt's dislike of his style), Goldsmith. Had Edmund Burke been a familiar essayist rather than an orator, Burke certainly would be Hazlitt's nearest ancestor. Instead, Hazlitt makes a second to Johnson in a great procession of critical essayists that goes on to Carlyle, Emerson, Ruskin, Pater, and Wilde. (I omit Coleridge because of his obsession with method, and Arnold because of his authentic incompetence.) The procession ceases in our century because the mode now seems inadequate, not so much to the apparent complexities of modernist literature (after all, many of those now resolve themselves into more complications), but to the waning of the self, with all the perplexities attendant upon that waning. A curious irony of modern literature made Freud, the analyst of such waning, also the only twentieth-century essayist worthy to be the coda of the long tradition that went from Montaigne on through Johnson, Hazlitt, and Emerson until it culminated in Freud's older contemporaries, Ruskin, Nietzsche, and Pater.

   Hazlitt's poetics of power seems to me more Freudian than any of the psychopoetics—orthodox or Lacanian—that currently drift uselessly in Freud's wake. Like Freud, Hazlitt knows that the poets—Shakespeare, Milton, Wordsworth—were there before him, which is a very different realization than any that penetrate the blindnesses of what now passes for "Freudian literary criticism." The poets are still there before Freud, better guides to the interpretation of Freud than he could ever be to the reading of consciousnesses even more comprehensive and coherent than his own. Hazlitt, in his best theoretical essay, "On Poetry in General," begins with the fine realization: "Poetry then is an imitation of Nature, but the imagination and the passions are a part of man's nature." Passion, or pathos, or sublimity, or power (the four are rightly one, according to Hazlitt) remove poetry from the domain of all conventional considerations of psychology and morality:

> We are as fond of indulging our violent passions as of reading a description of those of others. We are as prone to make a torment of our fears, as to luxuriate in our hopes of good. If it be asked, Why do we do so? the best answer will be, Because we cannot help it. The sense of power is as strong a principle in the mind as the love of pleasure. Objects of terror and pity exercise the same despotic control over it as those of love or beauty. It is as natural to hate as to love, to despise as to admire, to express our hatred or contempt, as our love or admiration.
>
>   Masterless passion sways us to the mood
>   Of what it likes or loathes.
>
> Not that we like what we loathe; but we like to indulge our hatred and scorn of it; to dwell upon it, to exasperate our idea of it by every refinement of ingenuity and extravagance of illustration; to make it a bugbear to ourselves, to point it out to others in all the splendour of deformity, to embody it to the senses, to stigmatize it by name, to grapple with it in thought, in action, to sharpen our intellect, to arm our will against it, to know the worst we have to contend with, and to

contend with it to the utmost. Poetry is only the highest eloquence of passion, the most vivid form of expression that can be given to our conception of anything, whether pleasurable or painful, mean or dignified, delightful or distressing. It is the perfect coincidence of the image and the words with the feeling we have, and of which we cannot get rid in any other way, that gives an instant "satisfaction to the thought." This is equally the origin of wit and fancy, of comedy and tragedy, of the sublime and pathetic. When Pope says of the Lord Mayor's show,—

> Now night descending, the proud scene is o'er,
> But lives in Settle's numbers one day more!

—when Collins makes Danger, "with limbs of giant mould,"

> —Throw him on the steep
> Of some loose hanging rock asleep:

when Lear calls out in extreme anguish,

> Ingratitude, thou marble-hearted fiend,
> How much more hideous shew'st in a child
> Than the sea-monster!

—the passion of contempt in the one case, of terror in the other, and of indignation in the last, is precisely satisfied. We see the thing ourselves, and shew it to others as we feel it to exist, and as, in spite of ourselves, we are compelled to think of it. The imagination, by thus embodying and turning them to shape, gives an obvious relief to the indistinct and importunate cravings of the will.—We do not wish the thing to be so; but we wish it to appear such as it is. For knowledge is conscious power; and the mind is no longer, in this case, the dupe, though it may be the victim of vice or folly.

To speak of poetry as giving "an obvious relief to the indistinct and importunate cravings of the will" is to have more than anticipated Freud. Hazlitt's quotation from *The Merchant of Venice* is the center of one of Shylock's great speeches:

> Some men there are love not a gaping pig;
> Some that are mad if they hold a cat;
> And others, when the bagpipe sings i' th' nose,
> Cannot contain their urine; for affection,
> Mistress of passion, sways it to the mood
> Of what it likes or loathes.

"Masterless passion" is as likely a reading as "Mistress of passion," the text being uncertain, and better suits Hazlitt's emphasis upon the cravings of the will. Hazlittian exuberance, *gusto*, teaches us to admire Shylock even as we admire Coriolanus. Few passages even in Hazlitt are as superbly memorable as when he shows us how the grandest poetry can be the most immoral, here in *Coriolanus:*

> This is but natural, it is but natural for a mother to have more regard for her son than for a whole city; but then the city should be left to take some care of itself. The care of the state cannot, we here see, be safely entrusted to maternal affection, or to the domestic charities of high life. The great have private feelings of their own, to which the interests of humanity and justice must courtesy. Their interests are so far from being the same as those of the community, that they are in direct and necessary opposition to them; their power is at the expense of *our* weakness; their riches of *our* poverty; their pride of *our* degradation; their splendour of *our* wretchedness; their tyranny of *our* servitude. If they had the superior knowledge ascribed to them (which they have not) it would only render them so much more formidable; and from Gods would convert them into Devils. The whole dramatic moral of *Coriolanus* is that those who have little shall have less, and that those who have much shall take all that others have left. The people are poor; therefore they ought to be starved. They are slaves; therefore they ought to be beaten. They work hard; therefore they ought not to be treated like beasts of burden. They are ignorant; therefore they ought not to be allowed to feel that they want food, or clothing, or rest, that they are enslaved, oppressed, and miserable. This is the logic of the imagination and the passions; which seek to aggrandize what excites admiration, and to heap contempt on misery, to raise power into tyranny, and to make tyranny absolute; to thrust down that which is low still lower, and to make wretches desperate; to exult magistrates into kings, kings into gods; to degrade subjects to the rank of slaves, and slaves to the condition of brutes. The history of mankind is a romance, a mask, a tragedy, constructed upon the principles of *poetical justice;* it is a noble or royal hunt, in which what is sport to the few is death to the many, and in which the spectators halloo and encourage the strong to set upon the weak, and cry havoc in the chase though they do not share in the spoil. We may depend upon it that what men delight to read in books, they will put in practice in reality.

Though Hazlitt is an intellectual of the permanent Left, of the French Revolution, he is too great a critic not to see that poetry worships power without regard to the morality of power. Indeed, his poetics of power compels us to see more than that, which is that Plato was right in fearing Homer's effect upon society. Poetical justice is antithetical to societal justice, and the noble or royal hunt of the imagination does not make us better citizens or better human beings, and very likely may make us worse.

Hazlitt, like Johnson before him, and the great progression of Carlyle, Emerson, Ruskin, Pater, and Wilde after him, teaches us several unfashionable truths as to the nature of authentically *literary* criticism. It must be experiential; it must be at least somewhat empirical or pragmatic; it must be informed by love for its subject; above all it must follow no method except the personality of the critic himself. Coleridge never ceased to quest for method, and lost the critical gift in consequence, while Matthew Arnold drowned what gift he had by assuring himself that they handled these matters better on the Continent. Hazlitt is a literary critic; our contemporary imitators of Continental philosophy may be human scientists or ideological rebels or what they will, but they are not literary critics. Hume's philosophy teaches the critic to fall back upon personality because every other possibility has been collapsed by skepticism. German thought persuaded Coleridge to posit an "organic" unity in imaginative works, but such organicism and its resultant unities can be seen now as banal fictions. Hazlitt, like Johnson, refuses to carry philosophical aesthetics into the pragmatic realms of criticism. I read Coleridge when and as I have to, but I read Hazlitt for pleasure and insight. Whether he writes on "The Indian Jugglers" or "On Going a Journey" or "On a Sun-Dial," Hazlitt reminds us always that life and literature are, for him, the one interpenetrated reality.

I remember "The Indian Jugglers" partly for its vivid celebration of the jugglers' skill:

> Coming forward and seating himself on the ground in his white dress and tightened turban, the chief of the Indian Jugglers begins with tossing up two brass balls, which is what any of us could do, and concludes with keeping up four at the same time, which is what none of us could do to save our lives, nor if we were to take our whole lives to do it in. Is it then a trifling power we see at work, or is it not something next to miraculous? It is the utmost stretch of human ingenuity, which nothing but the bending the faculties of body and mind to it from the tenderest infancy with incessant, ever-anxious application up to manhood, can accomplish or make even a slight approach to. Man, thou art a wonderful animal, and thy ways past finding out! Thou canst do strange things, but thou turnest them to little account!—To conceive of this effort of extraordinary dexterity distracts the imagination and makes admiration breathless. Yet it costs nothing to the performer, any more than if it were a mere mechanical deception with which he had nothing to do but to watch and laugh at the astonishment of the spectators. A single error of a hair's-breadth, of the smallest conceivable portion of time, would be fatal: the precision of the movements must be like a mathematical truth, their rapidity is like lightning. To catch four balls in succession in less than a second of time, and deliver them back so as to return with seeming consciousness to the hand again, to make them revolve round him at certain intervals, like the planets in their spheres, to make them chase one another like sparkles of fire, or shoot up like flowers or meteors, to throw them behind his back and twine them round his neck like ribbons or like serpents, to do what appears an impossibility, and to do

it with all the ease, the grace, the carelessness imaginable, to laugh at, to play with the glittering mockeries, to follow them with his eye as if he could fascinate them with its lambent fire, or as if he had only to see that they kept time with the music on the stage—there is something in all this which he who does not admire may be quite sure he never really admired anything in the whole course of his life. It is skill surmounting difficulty, and beauty triumphing over skill.

Remarkable as descriptive writing, this acquires hidden power when subsequently it is revealed as a literary paradigm, leading Hazlitt to the profound observation: "No act terminating in itself constitutes greatness." The act of writing *Paradise Lost* is precisely one that does not terminate in itself. Hazlitt's insight is that the canon is constituted by works that engender further works that do not terminate in themselves. "On Going a Journey" begins by advising that "the soul of a journey is liberty, perfect liberty, to think, feel, do just as one pleases." A few pages later the essay achieves perceptions into our involuntary perspectivism that both anticipate and correct Nietzsche:

There is hardly anything that shows the short-sightedness or capriciousness of the imagination more than travelling does. With change of place we change our ideas; nay, our opinions and feelings. We can by an effort indeed transport ourselves to old and long-forgotten scenes, and then the picture of the mind revives again, but we forget those that we have just left. It seems that we can think but of one place at a time. The canvas of the fancy has only a certain extent, and if we paint one set of objects upon it, they immediately efface every other. We cannot enlarge our conceptions; we only shift our point of view. The landscape bares its bosom to the enraptured eye; we take our fill of it; and seem as if we could form no other image of beauty or grandeur. We pass on, and think no more of it; the horizon that shuts it from our sight also blots it from our memory like a dream. In travelling through a wild barren country, I can form no idea of a woody and cultivated one. It appears to me that all the world must be barren, like what I see of it. In the country we forget the town, and in town we despise the country. "Beyond Hyde Park," says Sir Fopling Flutter, "all is a desert." All that part of the map that we do not see before us is a blank. The world in our conceit of it is not much bigger than a nutshell. It is not one prospect expanded into one another, county joined to county, kingdom to kingdom, lands to seas, making an image voluminous and vast; the mind can form no larger idea of space than the eye can take in at a single glance. The rest is a name written on a map, a calculation of arithmetic. For instance, what is the true signification of that immense mass of territory and population, known by the name of China to us? An inch of paste-board on a wooden globe, of no more account than a China orange! Things near us are seen of the size of life: things at a distance are diminished to the size of the understanding. We measure the universe by ourselves, and even comprehend the texture of our own being only piece-meal.

"On a Sun-Dial" is a nostalgic reverie explaining why Hazlitt has never bothered to own a watch or a clock. In the midst of this brief study of the nostalgias, we are suddenly given a memorable theory of romance, as applicable to Hawthorne as to Wordsworth:

> Surely, if there is anything with which we should not mix up our vanity and self-consequence, it is with Time, the most independent of all things. All the sublimity, all the superstition that hang upon this palpable mode of announcing its flight, are chiefly attracted to this circumstance. Time would lose its abstracted character, if we kept it like a curiosity or a jack-in-a-box: its prophetic warnings would have no effect, if it obviously spoke only at our prompting, like a paltry ventriloquism. The clock that tells the coming, dreaded hour—the castle bell, that "with its brazen throat and iron tongue, sounds one unto the drowsy ear of night"—the curfew, "swinging slow with sullen roar" o'er wizard stream or fountain, are like a voice from other worlds, big with unknown events. The last sound, which is still kept up as an old custom in many parts of England, is a great favourite with me. I used to hear it when a boy. It tells a tale of other times. The days that are past, the generations that are gone, the tangled forest glades and hamlets brown of my native country, the woodsman's art, the Norman warrior armed for the battle or in his festive hall, the conqueror's iron rule and peasant's lamp extinguished, all start up at the clamorous peal, and fill my mind with fear and wonder. I confess, nothing at present interests me but what has been—the recollection of the impressions of my early life, or events long past, of which only the dim traces remain in a smouldering ruin or half-obsolete custom. That *things should be that are now no more,* creates in my mind the most unfeigned astonishment. I cannot solve the mystery of the past, nor exhaust my pleasure in it.

One sees, after reading this, why Wordsworth's "Ode: Intimations of Immortality" was Hazlitt's poem-of-poems, as it was Emerson's and Ruskin's. Hazlitt's regret is hardly for actual immortality, which he dismisses with splendid vigor in his "On the Fear of Death." It is rather what he adumbrates in his superb "On the Feeling of Immortality in Youth":

> Objects, on our first acquaintance with them, have that singleness and integrity of impression that it seems as if nothing could destroy or obliterate them, so firmly are they stamped and rivetted on the brain. We repose on them with a sort of voluptuous indolence, in full faith and boundless confidence. We are absorbed in the present moment, or return to the same point—idling away a great deal of time in youth, thinking we have enough and to spare. There is often a local feeling in

the air, which is as fixed as if it were of marble; we loiter in dim cloisters, losing ourselves in thought and in their glimmering arches; a winding road before us seems as long as the journey of life, and as full of events. Time and experience dissipate this illusion; and by reducing them to detail, circumscribe the limits of our expectations. It is only as the pageant of life passes by and the masques turn their backs upon us, that we see through the deception, or believe that the train will have an end. In many cases, the slow progress and monotonous texture of our lives, before we mingle with the world and are embroiled in its affairs, has a tendency to aid the same feeling. We have a difficulty, when left to ourselves, and without the resource of books or some more lively pursuit, to "beguile the slow and creeping hours of time," and argue that if it moves on always at this tedious snail's-pace, it can never come to an end. We are willing to skip over certain portions of it that separate us from favourite objects, that irritate ourselves at the unnecessary delay. The young are prodigal of life from a superabundance of it; the old are tenacious on the same score, because they have little left, and cannot enjoy even what remains of it.

As a commentary upon our common experience, both when young and when old, this compels the chill of a self-recognition beyond illusion and delusion alike. But it is also a powerfully implicit commentary upon Wordsworth's Great Ode, and upon very nearly everything else in Wordsworth that truly matters. Hazlitt's strength, matched among critics in the language only by Johnson and by Ruskin, is that he never allows us to forget the dark and antithetical relationship between the power of the imagination and the power of human experience. Imaginative gain and experiential loss are identical in Hazlitt, who, unlike Wordsworth, understands that there is no knowledge that is not purchased by the loss of power, no power that is not purchased at the expense both of others and of the self.

The Art of the Critic

Immanuel Kant

1724–1804

Immanuel Kant was born at Königsberg in East Prussia on April 22, 1724. He later claimed that his grandfather had emigrated from Scotland many years earlier. His father was a saddler, his mother uneducated but intelligent. He attended a local school run by Pietists, then went to the University of Königsberg in 1740. His earliest work, *Thoughts on the True Estimation of Living Forces*, was written in 1746.

After leaving the university, Kant worked as a private tutor, then returned to the university as a teacher in 1755. For fifteen years he taught a wide range of subjects in science, mathematics, and philosophy. In the 1760s he became acquainted with many of the major contemporary German thinkers, including Moses Mendelssohn, Johann Heinrich Lambert, Johann George Hamann, and Johann Gottfried von Herder. In 1770 Kant was elected professor of logic and metaphysics at the university and remained active in this role until a few years before his death.

Kant's major work, *The Critique of Pure Reason*, was published in 1781. It represented a Copernican revolution in the history of philosophy. It was both enthusiastically praised and resoundingly criticized, and Kant devoted many years to defending his ideas. He wrote prolifically during the 1780s, most notably the *Prolegomena to Every Future Metaphysic* (1783), the *Critique of Practical Reason* (1788), and the *Critique of Judgment* (1790).

Kant was criticized by the authorities for the seeming unorthodoxy of his religious opinions; his rationalism was viewed by Frederick Wilhelm II as a distortion and deprecation of Christianity, and for many years he was in effect prevented from writing on religious topics. Only in his last major essay, *The Conflict of the Faculties* (1798), did he return to the subject. Kant was in ill health for several years at the end of his life and died on February 12, 1804.

In the highly influential *Critique of Judgment* Kant offers his aesthetic theory. According to Kantian thought we can never know directly things in themselves; our sensibility organizes raw data according to prior categories of perception, such as space and time. On the basis of these schema, we impose teleological judgments upon phenomena, considering objects in terms of their purposes. For Kant, aesthetic judgments are different from teleological judgments because they do not consider the object in terms of its outer purpose. There are two kinds of aesthetic judgments—those of the beautiful and those of the sublime—and both are subjective. For Kant, the beautiful implies form and boundary, while the sublime object is limitless. Sublime experiences can be pleasurable even when they elicit fear; they are always characterized by deep feeling. The beautiful, on the other hand, invites disinterested contemplation.

No object viewed aesthetically can be judged in terms of an external purpose, in Kant's view. Thus the standard of accuracy in making aesthetic judgments implied by the Platonic idea of imitation is irrelevant. Because no exterior purpose or ideal of beauty is permissible, the work of art must generate its own standard and its own internal purpose. The *Critique of Judgment* influenced the thought of many Romantic writers, particularly Coleridge, and continues to be important in the twentieth century, having affected the work of Valéry, Cassirer, and the New Critics.

THE BEAUTIFUL AND THE SUBLIME

The two different feelings of pleasure and annoyance are not so much based upon the quality of the external things when exciting them as upon the sentiment, peculiar to each man, of being moved to pleasure or displeasure. . . .

The finer sentiment which we propose to consider here is primarily of two kinds: the sentiment of the *lofty* or *sublime (Erhabenen)* and the sentiment of the *beautiful*. Being moved by either is agreeable, but in a very different way. A view of a mountain, the snowy peaks of which rise above the clouds, a description of a raging storm or a description by Milton of the Kingdom of Hell cause pleasure, but it is mixed with awe; on the other hand, a view of flower-filled meadows, valleys with winding brooks and the herds upon them, the description of *elysium* or Homer's description of the belt of Venus cause an agreeable feeling which is gay and smiling. We must have a sense of the sublime to receive the first impression adequately, and a sense of the beautiful to enjoy the latter fully. Great oak trees and lovely spots in a sacred grove are sublime. Beds of flowers, low hedges and trees trimmed into shape are beautiful. The night is sublime while the day is beautiful. Temperaments which have a sense for the sublime will be drawn toward elevated sentiments regarding friendship, contempt for the world and toward eternity, by the quiet silence of a summer evening when the twinkling light of the stars breaks through the shadows of the night and a lovely moon is visible. The glowing day inspires busy effort and a sense of joy. The sublime *moves;* the expression of a person experiencing the full sense of the sublime is serious, at times rigid and amazed. On the other hand, the vivid sense of the beautiful reveals itself in the shining gaiety of the eyes, by smiling and even by noisy enjoyment. The sublime, in turn, is at times accompanied by some terror or melancholia, in some cases merely by quiet admiration and in still others by the beauty which is spread over a sublime place. The first I want to call the terrible sublime, the second the noble, and the third the magnificent. Deep loneliness is sublime, but in a terrifying way.

The sublime must always be large; the beautiful may be small. The sublime must be simple; the beautiful may be decorated and adorned. A very great height is sublime as well as a very great depth; but the latter is accompanied by the sense of terror, the former by admiration. Hence the one may be terrible sublime, the other noble.

A long duration is sublime. If it concerns past time it is noble; if anticipated as an indeterminable future, it has something terrifying.

TRANSCENDENTAL AESTHETIC

Sensation is the actual affection of our sensibility, or capacity of receiving impressions, by an object. The perception which refers itself to an object through sensation, is *empirical perception*. The undetermined object of such a perception is a *phenomenon* (Erscheinung).

That element in the phenomenon which corresponds to sensation I call the *matter*, while that element which makes it possible that the various determinations of the phenomenon should be arranged in certain ways relatively to one another, is its *form*. Now, sensations cannot possibly give order or form to themselves. The matter of a phenomenon is given to us entirely *a posteriori*, but its form must lie *a priori* in the mind, ready to be applied to all sensations as they arise, and hence it must be capable of being considered by itself apart from sensation.

This pure form of sensibility is also called *pure perception*. Thus, if from the consciousness of a body, I separate all that the understanding has thought into it, as substance, force, divisibility, etc., and all that is due to sensation, as impenetrability, hardness, colour, etc.; what is left over are extension and figure. These, therefore, belong to pure perception, which exists in the mind *a priori*, as a mere form of sensibility, even when no sensation or object of sense is actually present.

The science of all the *a priori* principles of sensibility I call *Transcendental Aesthetic*, in contradistinction from the science of the principles of pure thought, which I call *Transcendental Logic*.

In Transcendental Aesthetic we shall first of all isolate sensibility, abstracting from all that the understanding contributes through its conceptions, so that we may have nothing before us but empirical perception. In the next place, we shall separate from empirical perception all that belongs to sensation; when there will remain only pure perception, or the mere form of phenomena, the sole element that sensibility can yield *a priori*. If this is done, it will be found that there are two pure forms of sensible perception, which constitute principles of *a priori* knowledge, namely, Space and Time. With these it will now be our business to deal.

Section I

Metaphysical Exposition of Space

In external sense we are conscious of objects as outside of ourselves, and as all without exception in space. In space their shape, size, and relative position are marked out, or are capable of being marked out. Inner sense, in which we are conscious of ourselves, or rather of our own state, gives us, it is true, no direct perception of the soul itself as an object; but it nevertheless is the one single form in which our own state comes before us as a definite object of perception; and hence all inner determinations appear to us as related to one another in time. We cannot be conscious of time as external, any more than we can be conscious of space as something within us. What, then, are space and time? Are they in themselves real things? Are they only determinations, or perhaps merely relations of things, which yet would belong to things in themselves even if those things were not perceived by us? Or, finally, have space and time no meaning except as forms of perception, belonging to the subjective constitution of our own mind, apart from which they cannot be predicated of anything whatever? To answer these questions I shall begin with a metaphysical exposition of space. An *exposition* I call it, because it gives a distinct although not a detailed, statement of what is implied in the idea of space; and the exposition is *metaphysical,* because it brings forward the reasons we have for regarding space as given *a priori.*

(1) Space is not an empirical conception, which has been derived from external experiences. For I could not be conscious that certain of my sensations are relative to something outside of me, that is, to something in a different part of space from that in which I myself am; nor could I be conscious of them as outside of and beside one another, were I not at the same time conscious that they not only are different in content, but are in different places. The consciousness of space is, therefore, necessarily presupposed in external perception. No experience of the external relations of sensible things could yield the idea of space, because without the consciousness of space there would be no external experience whatever.

(2) Space is a necessary *a priori* idea, which is presupposed in all external perceptions. By no effort can we think space to be away, although we can quite readily think of space as empty of objects. Space we therefore regard as a condition of the possibility of phenomena, and not as a determination dependent on phenomena. It is thus *a priori,* and is necessarily presupposed in external phenomena.

(3) Space is not a discursive or general conception of the relations of things, but a pure perception. For we can be conscious only of a single space. It is true that we speak as if there were many spaces, but we really mean only parts of one and the same identical space. Nor can we say that these parts exist *before* the one all-embracing space, and are put together to form a whole; but we can think of them only as *in* it. Space is essentially single; by the plurality of spaces, we merely mean that because space can be limited in many ways, the general conception of spaces presupposes such limitations as its foundation. From this it follows, that an *a priori* perception, and not an empirical perception, underlies all conceptions of pure space. Accordingly, no geometrical proposition, as, for instance, that any two sides of a triangle are greater than the third side, can ever be derived from the general conceptions of line and triangle, but only from perception. From the perception, however, it can be derived *a priori,* and with demonstrative certainty.

(4) Space is *presented* before our consciousness as an infinite magnitude. Now, in every conception we certainly think of a certain attribute as common to an infinite number of possible objects, which are subsumed *under* the conception; but, from its very nature, no conception can possibly be supposed to contain an infinite number of determinations *within* it. But it is just in this way that space is thought of, all its parts being conceived to co-exist *ad infinitum*. Hence the original consciousness of space is an *a priori* perception, not a conception.

Transcendental Exposition of Space

A transcendental exposition seeks to show how, from a certain principle, the possibility of other *a priori* synthetic knowledge may be explained. To be successful, it must prove (1) that there really are synthetic propositions which can be derived from the principle in question, (2) that they can be so derived only if a certain explanation of that principle is adopted.

Now, geometry is a science that determines the properties of space synthetically, and yet *a priori*. What, then, must be the nature of space, in order that such knowledge of it may be possible? Our original consciousness of it must be perception, for no new truth, such as we have in the propositions of geometry, can be obtained from the mere analysis of a given conception. And this perception must be *a priori,* or, in other words, must be found in us before we actually observe an object, and hence it must be pure, not empirical perception. For all geometrical propositions, as, for instance, that space has but three dimensions, are of demonstrative certainty, or present themselves in consciousness as necessary; and such propositions cannot be empirical, nor can they be derived from judgments of experience.

How, then, can there be in the mind an external perception, which is antecedent to objects themselves, and in which the conception of those objects may be determined *a priori*? Manifestly, only if that perception has its seat in the subject, that is, if it belongs to the formal constitution of the subject, in virtue of which it is so affected by objects as to have a direct consciousness or perception of them; therefore, only if perception is the universal *form* of outer sense.

Our explanation is, therefore, the only one that makes the possibility of geometry intelligible, as a mode of *a priori* synthetic knowledge. All other explanations fail to do so, and, although they may have an external resemblance to ours, may readily be distinguished from it by this criterion.

Inferences

(*a*) Space is in no sense a property of things in themselves, nor is it a relation of things in themselves to one another. It is not a determination that still belongs to objects even when abstraction has been made from all the subjective conditions of perception. For we never could perceive *a priori* any determination of things, whether belonging to them individually or in relation to one another, antecedently to our perception of those things themselves.

(*b*) Space is nothing but the form of all the phenomena of outer sense. It is the subjective condition without which no external perception is possible for us. The receptivity of the subject, or its capability of being affected by objects, necessarily exists before there is any perception of objects. Hence it is easy to understand, how the form of all phenomena may exist in the mind *a priori*, antecedently to actual observation, and how, as a pure perception in which all objects must be determined, it may contain the principles that determine beforehand the relations of objects when they are met with in experience.

It is, therefore, purely from our human point of view that we can speak of space, of extended things, etc. Suppose the subjective conditions to be taken away, without which we cannot have any external perception, or be affected by objects, and the idea of space ceases to have any meaning. We cannot predicate spatial dimensions of things, except in so far as they appear in our consciousness. The unalterable form of this receptivity, which we call sensibility, is a necessary condition of all the relations in which objects are perceived as outside of us, and this form, when it is viewed in abstraction from objects, is the pure perception that is known by the name of space. We are not entitled to regard the conditions that are proper to our sensibility as conditions of the possibility of things, but only of things as they appear to us. Hence, while it is correct to say, that space embraces all things that are capable of appearing to us as external, we cannot say, that it embraces all things as they are in themselves, no matter what subject may perceive them, and, indeed, whether they are perceived or not. For we have no means of judging whether other thinking beings are in their perceptions bound down by the same conditions as ourselves, and which for us hold universally. If we state the limitations under which a judgment holds of a given subject, the judgment is then unconditionally true. The proposition, that all things are side by side in space, is true only under the limitation that we are speaking of our own sensible perception. But, if we more exactly define the subject of the proposition by saying, that all things as external phenomena are side by side in space, it will be true universally and without any exception. Our exposition, therefore, establishes the *reality*, or objective truth of space, as a determination of every object that can possibly come before us as external; but, at the same time, it proves the *ideality* of space, when space is considered by reason relatively to things in themselves, that is, without regard to the constitution of our sensibility. We, therefore, affirm the *empirical reality* of space, as regards all possible external experience; but we also maintain its *transcendental ideality*, or, in other words, we hold that space is nothing at all, if its limitation to possible experience is ignored, and it is treated as a necessary condition of things in themselves.

Section II

Metaphysical Exposition of Time

(1) Time is not an empirical conception, which has been derived from any experience. For we should not observe things to co-exist or to follow one another, did we not possess the idea of time *a priori*. It is, therefore, only under the presupposition of time, that we can be conscious of certain things as existing at the same time (simultaneously), or at different times (successively).

(2) Time is a necessary idea, which is presupposed in all perceptions. We cannot be conscious of phenomena if time is taken away, although we can quite readily suppose phenomena to be absent from time. Time is, therefore, given *a priori*. No phenomenon can exist at all that is not in time. While, therefore, phenomena may be supposed to vanish completely out of time, time itself, as the universal condition of their possibility, cannot be supposed away.

(3) Time is not a discursive, or general conception, but a pure form of sensible perception. Different times are but parts of the very same time. Now, the consciousness of that which is presented as one single object, is perception. Moreover, the proposition, that no two moments of time can co-exist, cannot be derived from a general conception. The proposition is synthetic, and cannot originate in mere conceptions. It therefore rests upon the direct perception and idea of time.

(4) The infinity of time simply means, that every definite quantity of time is possible only as a limitation of one single time. There must, therefore, be originally a consciousness of time as unlimited. Now, if an object presents itself as a whole, so that its parts and every quantity of it can be represented only by limiting that whole, such an object cannot be given in conception, for conceptions contain only partial determinations of a thing. A direct perception must therefore be the foundation of the idea of time.

Transcendental Exposition of Time

Apodictic principles which determine relations in time, or axioms of time in general, are possible only because time is the necessary *a priori* condition of all phenomena. Time has but one dimension; different times do not co-exist but follow one another, just as different spaces do not follow one another but co-exist. Such propositions cannot be derived from experience, which never yields strict universality or demonstrative certainty. If they were based upon experience, we could say only, that it has ordinarily been observed to be so, not that it must be so. Principles like these have the force of rules, that lay down the conditions without which no experience whatever is possible: they are not learned from experience, but anticipate what experience must be.

Let me add here that change, including motion or change of place, is conceivable only in and through the idea of time. Were time not an inner *a priori* perception, we could not form the least idea how there should be any such thing as change. Take away time, and change combines in itself absolutely contradictory predicates. Motion, or change of place, for instance, must then be thought of as at once the existence and the non-existence of one and the same thing in the same place. The contradiction disappears, only when it is seen that the thing has those opposite determinations one after the other. Our conception of time as an *a priori* form of perception, therefore explains the possibility of the whole body of *a priori* synthetic propositions in regard to motion that are contained in the pure part of physics, and hence it is not a little fruitful in results.

Inferences

(*a*) Time is not an independent substance nor an objective determination of things, and hence it does not survive when abstraction has been made from all the subjective conditions of perception. Were it an independent thing, it would be real without being a real object of consciousness. Were it a determination or order of things as they are in themselves, it could not precede our perception of those things as its necessary condition, nor could it be known by means of synthetic judgments. But the possibility of such judgments becomes at once intelligible if time is nothing but the subjective condition, without which we can have no perception whatever. For in that case we may be conscious of this form of inner perception before we are conscious of objects, and therefore *a priori*.

(*b*) Time is nothing but the form of inner sense, that is, of the perception of ourselves and our own inner state. As it has no influence on the shape or position of an object, time cannot be a determination of outer phenomena as such; what it does determine is the relation of ideas in our own inner state. And just because this inner perception has no shape of its own, we seek to make up for this want by analogies drawn from space. Thus, we figure the series of time as a line that proceeds to infinity, the parts of which form a series; and we reason from the properties of this line to all the properties of time, taking care to allow for the one point of difference, that the parts of the spatial line all exist at once, while the parts of the temporal line all follow one after the other. Even from this fact alone, that all the relations of time may thus be presented in an external perception, it would be evident that time is itself a perception.

(*c*) Time is the formal *a priori* condition of all phenomena without exception. Space, as the pure form of all external phenomena, is the *a priori* condition only of external phenomena. But all objects of perception, external as well as internal, are determinations of the mind, and, from that point of view, belong to our inner state. And as this inner state comes under time, which is the formal condition of inner perception, time is an *a priori* condition of all phenomena: it is the immediate condition of inner phenomena, and so the mediate condition of outer phenomena. Just as I can say, *a priori,* that all external phenomena are in space, and are determined *a priori* in conformity with the relations of space, so, from the principle of the inner sense, I can say quite generally that all phenomena are in time, and stand necessarily in relations of time.

If we abstract from the manner in which we immediately perceive our own inner state, and mediately all external phenomena, and think of objects in themselves, we find that in relation to them time is nothing at all. It is objectively true in relation to phenomena, because we are conscious of phenomena as *objects of our senses;* but it is no longer objective, if we abstract from our sensibility, and therefore from the form proper to our perceptive consciousness, and speak of *things as such.* Time is therefore a purely subjective condition of human perception, and in itself, or apart from the subject, it is nothing at all. Nevertheless, it is necessarily objective in relation to all phenomena, and therefore also to everything that can possibly enter into our experience. We cannot say that all things are in time, because when we speak of things in this unqualified way, we are thinking of things in abstraction from the manner in which we perceive them, and therefore in abstraction from the condition under which alone we can say that they are in time. But, if we qualify our assertion by adding that condition, and say that all things as phenomena, or objects of sensible perception, are in time, the proposition is, in the strictest sense of the word, objective, and is universally true *a priori.*

We see, then, that time is empirically real, or is objectively true in relation to all objects that are capable of being presented to our senses. And as our perception always is sensuous, no object can ever be presented to us in experience, which does not conform to time as its condition. On the other hand, we deny to time all claim to absolute reality, because such a claim, in paying no heed to the form of sensible perception, assumes time to be an absolute condition or property of things. Such properties, as supposed to belong to things in themselves, can never be presented to us in sense. From this we infer the *transcendental ideality* of time; by which we mean that, in abstraction from the subjective conditions of sensible perception, time is simply nothing, and cannot be said either to subsist by itself, or to inhere in things that do so subsist.

Explanatory Remarks

To this doctrine, which admits the empirical reality of time, but denies its absolute or transcendental reality, there is one objection so commonly made, that I must suppose it to occur spontaneously to everybody who is new to the present line of thought. It runs thus: No one can doubt that there are real changes, for, even if it is denied that we perceive the external world, together with the changes in it, we are at least conscious of a change in our own ideas. Now, changes can take place only in time. Therefore time is real.

There is no difficulty in meeting this objection. I admit all that is said. Certainly time is real: it is the real form of inner perception. It has reality for me relatively to my inner experience; in other words, I actually am conscious of time, and of my own determinations as in it. Time is therefore real, not as an object beyond consciousness, but as the manner in which I exist for myself as an object of consciousness. But, if I could be perceived by myself or by any other being without the condition of sensibility, the very same determinations, which now appear as changes, would not be known as in time, and therefore would not be known as changes. The empirical reality of time thus remains, on our theory, the condition of all our experience. It is only its absolute reality that we refuse to admit. Time is therefore nothing but the form of our inner perception. If we take away from it the peculiar condition of our sensibility, the idea of time also vanishes; for time does not belong to objects as they are in themselves, but only to the subject that perceives them.

Time and space are two sources of knowledge from which a variety of *a priori* synthetic judgments may be derived. Mathematics, especially, supplies a splendid instance of such judgments, in the science of space and the relations of space. Time and space are the two pure forms of all sensible perception, and as such they make *a priori* synthetic propositions possible. And just because they are mere conditions of sensibility, they mark out their own limits as sources of *a priori* knowledge. Applying only to objects regarded as phenomena, they do not present things as they are in themselves. Beyond the phenomenal world, which is their legitimate domain, they cannot be employed in determination of objects. But this limitation in no way lessens the stability of our empirical knowledge; for, such knowledge, as depending upon necessary forms of the perception of things, is just as certain as if it rested upon necessary forms of things in themselves.

Transcendental Aesthetic cannot contain more than these two elements. This is plain, if we reflect that all other conceptions belonging to sensibility presuppose something empirical. Even the idea of motion, in which both elements are united, presupposes the observation of something that moves. Now, there is nothing movable in space considered purely by itself; hence that which is movable can be found in space only by experience, and is therefore an empirical datum. Similarly the idea of change cannot be put among the *a priori* data of transcendental æsthetic. Time itself does not change, but only something that is in time; hence the idea of change must be derived from the observation of some actual object with its successive determinations—that is, from experience.

General Remarks on the Transcendental Aesthetic

(1) A distinction is commonly drawn between what belongs essentially to an object, and is perceived by every one to belong to it, and what is accidental, being perceived only from a certain position, or when a special organ is affected in a particular way. In the one case, we are said to know the object as it is in itself; in the other case, to know it only as it appears to us. This, however, is merely an empirical distinction. For, it must be remembered, that the empirical object which is here called the thing, is itself but an appearance. If this were all, our transcendental distinction would be altogether lost sight of, and we might imagine ourselves to know things in themselves when we knew only phenomena. For the truth is, that, however far we may carry our investigations into the world of sense, we never can come into contact with aught but appearances. For instance, we call the rainbow in a sun-shower a

mere appearance, and the rain the thing itself. Nor is there any objection to this, if we mean to state merely the physical truth, that from whatever position it is viewed the rain will appear to our senses as a real object of experience. But, if we go beyond the fact, that the sensible object is here the same for every one, and ask whether the object is known as it is in itself, we pass to the transcendental point of view, and the question now is in regard to the relation of our consciousness of the object to the object as it exists apart from our consciousness. In this point of view, not merely the rain-drops, but their round shape, and even the space in which they fall, must be regarded as mere appearances, not as things in themselves. Every aspect of the phenomenon, in short, is but a modification or a permanent form of our sensible perception, while the transcendental object remains to us unknown.

(2) It is recognized in natural theology, not only that God cannot be an object of perception to us, but that He can never be an object of *sensuous* perception to Himself. At the same time, His knowledge must be *perception*, and not thought, for thought always involves limitations. Now, the natural theologian is very careful to say, that God, in His perception, is free from the limits of space and time. But, how can this possibly be maintained, if it has previously been assumed, that space and time are forms of things in them-selves? It must then be held that, even if those things were annihilated, space and time would continue to be *a priori* conditions of their existence. And if they are conditions of all existence, they must be conditions of the existence even of God. We can avoid this conclusion only by saying that space and time are not objective forms of all things, but subjective forms of our outer as well as of our inner perceptions. In fact our perception is sensuous, just because it is *not original*. Were it original, the very existence of the object would be given in the perception, and such a perception, so far as we can see, can belong only to the Original Being. Our perception is dependent upon the existence of the object, and therefore it is possible only if our perceptive consciousness is affected by the presence of the object.

Nor is it necessary to say, that man is the only being who perceives objects under the forms of space and time; it may be that all finite thinking beings agree with man in that respect, although of this we cannot be certain. But, however universal this mode of perception may be, it cannot be other than sensuous, simply because it is derivative (*intuitus derivativus*) and not original (*intuitus originarius*), and therefore is not an intellectual perception. An intellectual perception, as we have already seen reason to believe, is the prerogative of the Original Being, and never can belong to a being which is dependent in its existence as well as in its perception, and in fact is conscious of its own existence only in relation to given objects.

Conclusion of the Transcendental Aesthetic

We have, then, in the Transcendental Aesthetic, one of the elements required in the solution of the general problem of transcendental philosophy: *How are a priori synthetic propositions possible?* Such propositions rest upon space and time, which are pure *a priori* perceptions. To enable us to go beyond a given conception, in an *a priori* judgment, we have found that something is needed, which is not contained in the conception, but in the perception corresponding to it, something therefore that may be connected with that conception synthetically. But such judgments, as based upon perception, can never extend beyond objects of sense, and therefore hold true only for objects of possible experience.

Gotthold Ephraim Lessing

1729–1781

Gotthold Ephraim Lessing, the son of a pastor, was born on January 22, 1729, in Kamenz, Upper Lusatia, Saxony. He received a classical education at the Fürstenschule in Meissen, then entered the University of Leipzig in 1746, where he concentrated on theology and medicine. He became interested in the theatre in Leipzig and, encouraged by the actress Caroline Neuber, wrote a series of comedies that were performed locally by her company. Forced to leave Leipzig because of debt, in the fall of 1748 Lessing settled in Berlin to work as a journalist. He soon became a respected critic of the *Berlinische Zeitung*. He also produced translations of English and French history, and founded two periodicals devoted to the theatre. Lessing then spent two years in Wittenberg (1751–52), where he received a medical degree.

Returning to Berlin in 1753, he published a six-volume collection of his works, including the domestic tragedy *Miss Sara Sampson,* which was performed to a positive reception in Frankfurt an der Oder. His critical writings at this time included *Vindications* and other essays that advanced the progressive thought of the Enlightenment, especially the demand for religious toleration.

Over the next few years, Lessing lived in both Leipzig and Berlin. He continued to write critical essays, particularly on the theatre, calling for a new national drama no longer dependent upon French conventions. In 1760 he went to Breslau as secretary to a Prussian general, continued to study philosophy and aesthetics, and wrote what has become his best-known work, *Laocoön: An Essay on the Limits of Painting and Poetry* (1766). Lessing was a lucid, witty stylist, and a formidable opponent in print. He relentlessly attacked some of the prominent academic critics of his day, incisively deflating several bloated reputations.

Lessing worked briefly in Hamburg as an adviser to a group of merchants who tried unsuccessfully to establish a national theatre, then went to Wolfenbüttel as librarian to the Duke of Brunswick. Late in life he married a longtime friend, Eva Konig, who died giving birth to their first child. Despite the solitude, poverty, and sadness of his last years, Lessing continued to write, and produced a number of important critical essays on literature and drama, as well as several plays. His last work was the essay *The Education of the Human Race* (1780), in which he affirms his belief in human progress and in the classical ideals of truth and reason. He died on February 15, 1781.

LAOKOON

Preface

The first person who compared painting and poetry with one another was a man of refined feeling, who became aware of a similar effect produced upon himself by both arts. He felt that both represent what is absent as if it were present, and appearance as if it were reality; that both deceive, and that the deception of both is pleasing.

A second observer sought to penetrate below the surface of this pleasure, and discovered that in both it flowed from the same source. Beauty, the idea of which we first deduce from bodily objects, possesses universal laws, applicable to more things than one; to actions and to thoughts as well as to forms.

A third reflected upon the value and distribution of these universal laws, and noticed that some are more predominant in painting, others in poetry; that thus, in the latter case, poetry will help to explain and illustrate painting; in the former, painting will do the same for poetry.

The first was the amateur, the second the philosopher, the third the critic.

The two first could not easily make a wrong use of either their feelings or conclusions. On the other hand, the value of the critic's observations mainly depends upon the correctness of their application to the individual case; and since for one clear-sighted critic there have always been fifty ingenious ones, it would have been a wonder if this application had always been applied with all that caution which is required to hold the balance equally between the two arts.

If Apelles and Protogenes, in their lost writings on painting, affirmed and illustrated its laws by the previously established rules of poetry, we may feel sure that they did it with that moderation and accuracy with which we now see, in the works of Aristotle, Cicero, Horace, and Quintilian, the principles and experience of painting applied to eloquence and poetry. It is the privilege of the ancients never in any matter to do too much or too little.

But in many points we moderns have imagined that we have advanced far beyond them, because we have changed their narrow lanes into highways, even though the shorter and safer highways contract into footpaths as they lead through deserts.

The dazzling antithesis of the Greek Voltaire, "Painting is dumb poetry, and poetry speaking painting," can never have been found in any didactic work; it was an idea, amongst others, of Simonides, and the truth it contains is so evident that we feel compelled to overlook the indistinctness and error which accompany it.

And yet the ancients did not overlook them. They confined the expression of Simonides to the effect of either art, but at the same time forgot not to inculcate that, notwithstanding the complete similarity of this effect, the two were different, both in the objects which they imitated and in their mode of imitation (ὕλη καὶ τρόποις μιμήσεως).

But, just as though no such difference existed, many recent critics have drawn from this harmony of poetry and painting the most ill-digested conclusions. At one time they compress poetry into the narrower limits of painting; at another they allow painting to occupy the whole wide sphere of poetry. Everything, say they, that the one is entitled to should be conceded to the other; everything that pleases or displeases in the one is necessarily pleasing or displeasing in the other. Full of this idea, they give utterance in the most confident tone to the most shallow decisions; when, criticizing the works of a poet and painter upon the same subject, they set down as faults any divergences they may observe, laying the blame upon the one or other accordingly as they may have more taste for poetry or for painting.

Indeed, this false criticism has misled in some degree the professors of art. It has produced the love of description in poetry, and of allegory in painting: while the critics strove to reduce poetry to a speaking painting, without properly knowing what it could and ought to paint; and painting to a dumb poem, without having considered in what degree it could express general ideas, without alienating itself from its destiny, and degenerating into an arbitrary method of writing.

The counteraction of this false taste and these groundless judgments is the principal aim of the following essay.

It originated casually, and has grown up rather in consequence of my reading than through the systematic development of general principles. It is accordingly rather to be regarded as unarranged collectanea for a book than as a book itself.

Still I flatter myself that even as such it will not be altogether deserving of contempt. We Germans have in general no want of systematic books. At deducing everything we wish, in the most beautiful order, from a few adopted explanations of words, we are the most complete adepts of any nation in the world.

Baumgarten acknowledged that he was indebted to Gesner's Dictionary for a great part of the examples in his work on Æsthetic. If my reasoning is not so cogent as Baumgarten's, my illustrations will at least taste more freshly of the well-spring.

Since I have, as it were, set out from the Laokoon, and several times return to it, I have wished to give it a share also in the title. Other short digressions on different points in the history of ancient art contribute less to my end, and only stand where they do because I can never hope to find a more suitable place for them.

Calling to mind, as I do, that under the term Painting I comprehend the plastic arts generally, I give no pledge that under the name of Poetry I may not take a glance at those other arts in which the method of imitation is progressive.

Chapter I

Herr Winckelmann has pronounced a noble simplicity and quiet grandeur, displayed in the posture no less than in the expression, to be the characteristic features common to all the Greek masterpieces of Painting and Sculpture. "As," says he, "the depths of the sea always remain calm, however much the surface may be raging, so the expression in the figures of the Greeks, under every form of passion, shows a great and self-collected soul.

"This spirit is portrayed in the countenance of Laokoon, and not in the countenance alone, under the most violent suffering; the pain discovers itself in every muscle and sinew of his body, and the beholder, whilst looking at the agonized contraction of the abdomen, without viewing the face and the other parts, believes that he almost feels the pain himself. This pain expresses itself, however, without any violence, both in the features and in the whole posture. He raises no terrible shriek, such as Virgil makes his Laokoon utter, for the opening of the mouth does not admit it; it is rather an anxious and suppressed sigh, as described by Sadoleto. The pain of body and grandeur of soul are, as it were, weighed out, and distributed, with equal strength, through the whole frame of the figure. Laokoon suffers, but he suffers as the Philoktetes of Sophokles; his misery pierces us to the very soul, but inspires us with a wish that we could endure misery like that great man.

"The expressing of so great a soul is far higher than the painting of beautiful nature. The artist must have felt within himself that strength of spirit which he imprinted upon his marble. Greece had philosophers and artists in one person, and more than one Metrodorus. Philosophy gave her hand to art, and breathed into its figures more than ordinary souls."

The observation on which the foregoing remarks are founded, "that the pain in the face of Laokoon does not show itself with that force which its intensity would have led us to expect," is perfectly correct. Moreover, it is indisputable that it is in this very point where the half-connoisseur would have decided that the artist had fallen short of Nature, and had not reached the true pathos of pain, that his wisdom is particularly conspicuous.

But I confess I differ from Winckelmann as to what is in his opinion the basis of this wisdom, and as to the universality of the rule which he deduces from it.

I acknowledge that I was startled, first by the glance of disapproval which he casts upon Virgil, and secondly by the comparison with Philoktetes. From this point then I shall set out, and write down my thoughts as they were developed in me.

"Laokoon suffers as Sophokles' Philoktetes." But how does the latter suffer? It is curious that his sufferings should leave such a different impression behind them. The cries, the shrieking, the wild imprecations, with which he filled the camp, and interrupted all the sacrifices and holy rites, resound no less horribly through his desert island, and were the cause of his being banished to it. The same sounds of despondency, sorrow, and despair fill the theatre in the poet's imitation. It has been observed that the third act of this piece is shorter than the others: from this it may be gathered, say the critics, that the ancients took little pains to preserve a uniformity of length in the different acts. I quite agree with them, but I should rather ground my opinion upon another example than this. The sorrowful exclamations, the moanings, the interrupted $\hat{α}$! $\hat{α}$! φεῦ! ἀτταταῖ! ὤ μοι μοι! the whole lines full of πάπα πάπα! of which this act consists, must have been pronounced with tensions and breakings off altogether different from those required in a continuous speech, and doubtless made this act last quite as long in the representation as the others. It appears much shorter to the reader, when seen on paper, than it must have done to the audience in a theatre.

A cry is the natural expression of bodily pain. Homer's wounded heroes frequently fall with cries to the ground. He makes Venus, when merely scratched, shriek aloud; not that he may thereby paint the effeminacy of the goddess of pleasure, but rather that he may give suffering Nature her due; for even the iron Mars, when he feels the lance of Diomedes, shrieks so horribly that his cries are like those of ten thousand furious warriors, and fill both armies with horror. Though Homer, in other respects, raises his heroes above human nature, they always remain faithful to it in matters connected with the feeling of pain and insult, or its expression through cries, tears, or reproaches. In their actions they are beings of a higher order, in their feelings true men.

I know that we more refined Europeans, of a wiser and later age, know how to keep our mouths and eyes under closer restraint. We are forbidden by courtesy and propriety to cry and weep; and with us the active bravery of the first rough age of the world has been changed into a passive. Yet even our own ancestors, though barbarians, were greater in the latter than in the former. To suppress all pain, to meet the stroke of death with unflinching eye, to die laughing under the bites of adders, to lament neither their sins nor the loss of their dearest friends: these were the characteristics of the old heroic courage of the north. Palnatoki forbade his Jomsburgers either to fear or so much as to mention the name of fear.

Not so the Greek. He felt and feared. He gave utterance to his pain and sorrow. He was ashamed of no human weaknesses; only none of them must hold him back from the path of honour, or impede him in the fulfilment of his duty. What in the barbarian sprang from habit and ferocity arose from principle in the Greek. With him heroism was as the spark concealed in flint, which, so long as no external force awakens it, sleeps in quiet, nor robs the stone either of its clearness or its coldness. With the barbarian it was a bright consuming flame, which was ever roaring, and devoured, or at least blackened, every other good quality. Thus when Homer makes the Trojans march to the combat with wild cries, the Greeks, on the contrary, in resolute silence, the critics justly observe that the poet intended to depict the one as barbarians, the other as a civilized people. I wonder that they have not remarked a similar contrast of character in another passage. The hostile armies have made a truce; they are busied with burning their dead; and these rites are accompanied on both sides with the warm flow of tears (δάκρυα θέρμα χέοντες). But Priam forbids the

Trojans to weep (οὐδ᾽ εἴα κλαίειν Πρίαμος μέγας). He forbade them to weep, says Dacier, because he feared the effect would be too softening, and that on the morrow they would go with less courage to the battle. True! But why, I ask, should Priam only fear this result? Why does not Agamemnon also lay the same prohibition on the Greeks? The poet has a deeper meaning; he wishes to teach us that the civilized Greek could be brave at the same time that he wept, while in the uncivilized Trojan all human feelings were to be previously stifled. Νεμέσσωμαί γε μὲν οὐδὲν κλαίειν, is the remark which, elsewhere, Homer puts in the mouth of the intelligent son of Nestor.

It is worth observing that among the few tragedies which have come down to us from antiquity, two are found in which bodily pain constitutes not the lightest part of the misfortune which befalls the suffering heroes—the Philoktetes and the dying Hercules. Sophokles paints the last also, as moaning and shrieking, weeping and crying. Thanks to our polite neighbours, those masters of propriety, no such ridiculous and intolerable characters as a moaning Philoktetes or a shrieking Hercules will ever again appear upon the stage. One of their latest poets has indeed ventured upon a Philoktetes, but would he have dared to exhibit the true one?

Even a Laokoon is found among the lost plays of Sophokles. Would that Fate had spared it to us! The slight mention which some old grammarians have made of it affords us no ground for concluding how the poet had handled his subject; but of this I feel certain, that Laokoon would not have been drawn more stoically than Philoktetes and Hercules. All stoicism is undramatical; and our sympathy is always proportioned to the suffering expressed by the object which interests us. It is true, if we see him bear his misery with a great soul, this grandeur of soul excites our admiration; but admiration is only a cold emotion, and its inactive astonishment excludes every warmer passion as well as every distinct idea.

I now come to my inference; if it be true that a cry at the sensation of bodily pain, particularly according to the old Greek way of thinking, is quite compatible with greatness of soul, it cannot have been for the sake of expressing such greatness that the artist avoided imitating this shriek in marble. Another reason therefore must be found for his here deviating from his rival, the poet, who expresses it with the highest purpose.

Chapter II

Be it fable or history that Love made the first essay in the plastic arts, it is certain that it never wearied of guiding the hands of the great masters of old. Painting, as now carried out in its whole compass, may be defined generally as the art of imitating figures on a flat surface; but the wise Greek allotted it far narrower limits, and confined it to the imitation of beautiful figures only; his artist painted nothing but the beautiful. Even the commonly beautiful, the beautiful of a lower order, was only his accidental subject, his exercise, his relaxation. It was the perfection of the object itself that was to make his work exquisite; and he was too great to ask beholders to be satisfied with the mere cold pleasure which arises from a striking resemblance, or the consideration of his ability. In his art nothing was dearer, nothing seemed nobler to him than its proper end.

"Who would paint you when nobody will look at you?" asks an old epigrammatist of an exceedingly deformed man. Many modern artists would say, "However misshapen you are, I will paint you; and although no one could look at you with pleasure, they will look with pleasure at my picture; not because it is your likeness, but because it will be an evidence of my skill in knowing how to delineate such a horror so faithfully."

It is true the propensity to this wanton boasting, united to fair abilities, not ennobled by exalted subjects, is too natural for even the Greeks not to have had their Pauson and their Pyricus. They had them, but they rendered them strict justice. Pauson, who kept below the beautiful of common nature, whose low taste loved to portray all that is faulty and ugly in the human form, lived in the most contemptible poverty. And Pyricus, who painted barbers' rooms, dirty workshops, apes, and kitchen herbs, with all the industry of a Dutch artist (as though things of that kind possessed such charm in nature, or could so rarely be seen), acquired the surname of Rhyparographer, or "Dirt-Painter!" although the luxurious rich man paid for his works with their weight in gold, as if to assist their intrinsic worthlessness by this imaginary value.

The state itself did not deem it beneath its dignity to confine the artist within his proper sphere by an exercise of its power. The law of the Thebans recommending him to use imitation as a means of arriving at ideal beauty; and prohibiting, on pain of punishment, its use for the attainment of ideal ugliness, is well known. This was no law against bunglers, as most writers, and among them even Junius, have supposed. It was in condemnation of the Greek Ghezzi, of that unworthy device which enables an artist to obtain a likeness by the exaggeration of the uglier parts of his original, i.e. by caricature.

From the self-same spirit of the beautiful sprang the following regulation of the Olympic judges (ἑλλανοδίχαι). Every winner obtained a statue, but only to him who had been thrice a conqueror was a portrait statue (ἄγαλμα εἰκωνικόν) erected. Too many indifferent portraits were not allowed to find a place among the productions of art; for although a portrait admits of the ideal, this last must be subordinate to the likeness; it is the ideal of an individual man, and not the ideal of man in the abstract.

We laugh when we hear that among the ancients even the arts were subjected to municipal laws, but we are not always in the right when we laugh. Unquestionably law must not assume the power of laying any constraint on knowledge; for the aim of knowledge is truth; truth is necessary to the soul, and it becomes tyranny to do it the smallest violence in the gratification of this essential need. The aim of art, on the contrary, is pleasure, which is not indispensable; and it may therefore depend upon the lawgiver to decide what kind of pleasure, and what degree of every kind, he would allow.

The plastic arts especially, besides the infallible influence which they exercise upon the national character, are capable of an effect which demands the closest inspection of the law. As beautiful men produced beautiful statues, so the latter reacted upon the former, and the state became indebted to beautiful statues for beautiful men. But with us the tender imaginative power of the mother is supposed to show itself only in the production of monsters.

In this point of view I think I can detect some truth in certain stories, which are generally rejected as pure inventions. The mothers of Aristomenes, Aristodamas, Alexander the Great, Scipio, Augustus, and Galerius, all dreamed, while pregnant, that they had intercourse with a serpent. The serpent was a token of divinity, and the beautiful statues and paintings of Bacchus, Apollo, Mercury, or Hercules were seldom without one. These honourable wives had by day feasted their eyes upon the god, and the confusing dream recalled the reptile's form. Thus I at the same time maintain the dream and dispose of the interpretation, which the pride of their sons and the shamelessness of the flatterer put upon it: for there must have been a reason why the adulterous phantasy should always have been a serpent.

But I am digressing; all I want to establish is, that among the ancients beauty was the highest law of the plastic arts. And this, once proved, it is a necessary consequence that everything else over which their range could be at the same time extended, if incompatible with beauty, gave way entirely to it; if compatible, was at least subordinate. I will abide by my expression. There are passions, and degrees of passion, which are expressed by the ugliest possible contortions of countenance, and throw the whole body into such a forced position that all the beautiful lines which cover its surface in a quiet attitude are lost. From all such emotions the ancient masters either abstained entirely, or reduced them to that lower degree in which they are capable of a certain measure of beauty.

Rage and despair disgraced none of their productions; I dare maintain that they have never painted a Fury.

Indignation was softened down to seriousness. In poetry it was the indignant Jupiter who hurled the lightning, in art it was only the serious. Grief was lessened into mournfulness; and where this softening could find no place, where mere grief would have been as lowering as disfiguring, what did Timanthes? His painting of the sacrifice of Iphigeneia is known, in which he has imparted to all the bystanders that peculiar degree of sorrow which becomes them, but has concealed the face of the father, which should have shown the most profound of all. On this many clever criticisms have been passed. He had, says one, so exhausted his powers in the sorrowful faces of the bystanders that he despaired of being able to give a more sorrowful one to the father. By so doing he confessed, says another, that the pain of a father under such circumstances is beyond all expression. For my part, I see no incapacity of either artist or art in it. With the degree of passion the corresponding lines of countenance are also strengthened; in the highest degree they are most decided, and nothing in art is easier than their expression. But Timanthes knew the limits within which the Graces had confined his art. He knew that the grief which became Agamemnon, as a father, must have been expressed by contortions, at all times ugly; but so far as dignity and beauty could be combined with the expression of such a feeling, so far he pushed it. True, he would fain have passed over the ugly, fain have softened it; but since his piece did not admit either of its omission or diminution, what was left him but its concealment? He left to conjecture what he might not paint. In short, this concealment is a sacrifice which the artist made to beauty, and is an instance, not how expression may exceed the capacity of art, but how it should be subjected to art's first law, the law of beauty.

And now, if we apply this to the Laokoon, the principle for which I am searching is clear. The master aimed at the highest beauty compatible with the adopted circumstances of bodily pain. The latter, in all its disfiguring violence, could not be combined with the former; therefore he must reduce it; he must soften shrieks into sighs, not because a shriek would have betrayed an ignoble soul, but because it would have produced a hideous contortion of countenance. For only imagine the mouth of Laokoon to be forced open, and then judge! Let him shriek, and look at him! It *was* a form which inspired compassion, for it displayed beauty and pain at once. It has become an ugly and horrible shape from which we gladly avert our eyes; for the sight of pain excites annoyance, unless the beauty of the suffering object change that annoyance into the sweet emotion of pity.

The mere wide opening of the mouth, setting aside the forced and disagreeable manner in which the other parts of the face are displaced and distorted by it, is in painting a spot, and in sculpture a cavity; both which produce the worst possible effect. Montfaucon displayed little taste when he pronounced an old bearded head with a gaping mouth to be a bust of Jupiter, uttering oracles. Is a god obliged to shout when he divulges the future? Would a pleasing outline of the mouth have cast suspicion on his utterance? Neither do I believe Valerius when he says, merely from memory, that in that picture of Timanthes, Ajax was represented as shrieking. Even far worse masters, in a period when art was already degenerate, did not think of allowing the wildest barbarians, when filled with affright, and the terrors of death beneath the victor's sword, to open their mouths and shriek.

It is certain that this softening down of extreme bodily pain to a lower degree of feeling is perceptible in several productions of ancient art. The suffering Hercules in the poisoned garment, the work of an unknown old master, was not the Hercules of Sophokles, whose shrieks are so horrible that the rocks of Lokris and headlands of Euboia resound therewith. He was gloomy rather than wild. The Philoktetes of Pythagoras Leontinus appeared to impart his pain to the beholder, yet this effect would have been destroyed by the least ugliness of feature. I may be asked how I know that this master executed a statue of Philoktetes? From a passage in Pliny, so manifestly either interpolated or mutilated that it ought not to have awaited my amendment.

Chapter III

But, as has been already mentioned, art has in modern times been allotted a far wider sphere. "Its imitations, it is said, extend over the whole of visible nature, of which the beautiful is but a small part: truth and expression is its first law; and as nature herself is ever ready to sacrifice beauty to higher aims, so likewise the artist must render it subordinate to his general design, and not pursue it farther than truth and expression permit. Enough that, through these two, what is most ugly in nature has been changed into a beauty of art."

But even if we should leave this idea, whatever its value, for the present undisputed, would there not arise other considerations independent of it, which would compel the artist to put certain limits to expression, and prevent him from ever drawing it at its highest intensity?

I believe the fact, that it is to a single moment that the material limits of art confine all its imitations, will lead us to similar views.

If the artist, out of ever-varying nature, can only make use of a single moment, and the painter especially can only use this moment from one point of view, whilst their works are intended to stand the test not only of a passing glance, but of long and repeated contemplation, it is clear that this moment, and the point from which this moment is viewed, cannot be chosen with too great a regard to results. Now that only is a happy choice which allows the imagination free scope. The longer we gaze, the more must our imagination add; and the more our imagination adds, the more we must believe we see. In the whole course of an emotion there is no moment which possesses this advantage so little as its highest stage. There is nothing beyond this; and the presentation of extremes to the eye clips the wings of fancy, prevents her from soaring beyond the impression of the senses, and compels her to occupy herself with weaker images; further than these she ventures not, but shrinks from the visible fulness of expression as her limit. Thus, if Laokoon sighs, the imagination can hear him shriek; but if he shrieks, it can neither rise a step higher above nor descend a step below this representation, without seeing him in a condition which, as it will be more endurable, becomes less interesting. It either hears him merely moaning, or sees him already dead.

Furthermore, this single moment receives through art an unchangeable duration; therefore it must not express anything, of which we can think only as transitory. All appearances, to whose very being, according to our ideas, it is essential that they suddenly break forth and as suddenly vanish, that they can be what they are but for a moment,—all such appearances, be they pleasing or be they horrible, receive, through the prolongation which art gives them, such an unnatural character, that at every repeated glance the impression they make grows weaker and weaker, and at last fills us with dislike or disgust of the whole object. La Mettrie, who got himself painted and engraved as a second Demokritus, laughs only the first time we look at him. Look at him oftener, and he changes from a philosopher into a fool. His laugh becomes a grin. So it is with shrieks; the violent pain which compels their utterance soon either subsides, or destroys its suffering subject altogether. If, therefore, even the most patient and resolute man shrieks, he does not do so unremittingly; and it is only the seeming continuance of his cries in art which turns them into effeminate impotence or childish petulance. This, at least, the artist of the Laokoon must needs have avoided, even if beauty were not injured by a shriek, and even had his art allowed of his expressing suffering without beauty.

Among the ancient painters, Timomachus seems to have delighted in selecting subjects suited to the display of extreme passion. His raving Ajax and infanticide Medea were celebrated paintings; but, from the descriptions we possess of them, it is plain that he thoroughly understood and judiciously combined that point at which the beholder is rather led to the conception of the extreme than actually sees it with that appearance with which we do not associate the idea of transitoriness so inseparably as to be displeased by its continuance in art. He did not paint Medea at the instant when she was actually murdering her children, but a few moments before, whilst her motherly love was still struggling with her jealousy. We see the end of the contest beforehand; we tremble in the anticipation of soon recognizing her as simply cruel, and our imagination carries us far beyond anything which the painter could have portrayed in that terrible moment itself. But, for that very reason, the irresolution of Medea, which art has made perpetual, is so far from giving offence, that we are rather inclined to wish that it could have remained the same in nature, that the contest of passions had never been decided, or at least had continued so long that time and reflexion had gained the mastery over fury, and assured the victory to the feelings of the mother. This wisdom of Timomachus has called forth great and frequent praise, and raised him far above another unknown painter, who was foolish enough to draw Medea at the very height of her frenzy, and thus to impart to this fleeting, transient moment of extreme madness a duration that disgusts all nature. The poet, who censures him, says very sensibly, whilst addressing the figure itself: "Thirstest thou then ever for the blood of thy children? Is there ever a new Jason, a new Kreusa there to exasperate thee unceasingly?" "Away with thee, even in painting!" he adds, in a tone of vexation.

Of the frenzied Ajax of Timomachus we can form some judgment from the account of Philostratus. Ajax did not appear raging among the herds, and binding and slaughtering oxen and rams instead of men; but the master exhibits him sitting, wearied with these heroic deeds of insanity, and conceiving the design of suicide; and that is really the raging Ajax: not because he is just then raging, but because we see that he has been; because we can form the most lively idea of the extremity of his frenzy from the shame and despair which he himself feels at the thoughts of it. We see the storm in the wrecks and corpses with which it has strewn the beach.

Chapter IV

I have passed under review the reasons alleged for the artist of the Laokoon being obliged to set certain bounds to the expression of bodily pain;

and I find that they are altogether derived from the peculiar conditions of his art, and its necessary limits and wants. Perhaps hardly any of them would be found equally applicable to poetry.

We will not here examine how far the poet can succeed in depicting physical beauty. It is undeniable, that as the whole infinite realm of the perfectly excellent lies open to his imitation, this outward visible garb, the perfect form of which is beauty, is only one of the least of the means by which he can interest us in his characters. Often he neglects this means entirely, feeling certain, if his hero has once won our regard, of so preoccupying our minds with his nobler qualities that we shall not bestow a thought upon his bodily form; or that if we do think of it, it will be with such favourable prepossessions that we shall, of ourselves, attribute to him an exterior, if not handsome, at least not unpleasing; at any rate he will not permit himself to pay any regard to the sense of sight, in any trait, which is not expressly intended to appeal to it. When Virgil's Laokoon shrieks, does it occur to any one that a widely opened mouth is the necessary accompaniment of a shriek, and that this open mouth is ugly? It is enough that "clamores horrendos ad sidera tollit," whatever it may be to the eyes, is a powerful appeal to the ears. If any one here feels the want of a beautiful picture, the poet has failed to make a due impression on him.

Moreover, the poet is not compelled to concentrate his picture into the space of a single moment. He has it in his power to take up every action of his hero at its source, and pursue it to its issue, through all possible variations. Each of these, which would cost the artist a separate work, costs the poet but a single trait; and should this trait, if viewed by itself, offend the imagination of the hearer, either such preparation has been made for it by what has preceded, or it will be so softened and compensated by what follows that its solitary impression is lost, and the combination produces the best possible effect. Thus, were it really unbecoming in a man to shriek under the violence of bodily pain, what prejudice could this slight and transitory impropriety excite in us against one in whose favour we are already prepossessed by his other virtues? Virgil's Laokoon shrieks, but this shrieking Laokoon is the same man whom we already know and love as a far-sighted patriot and affectionate father. We attribute his cries not to his character, but solely to his intolerable suffering. It is this alone that we hear in them, and by them alone could the poet have brought it home to us.

Who, then, still censures him? Who is not rather forced to own that whilst the artist has done well in not allowing him to shriek, the poet has done equally well in causing him to do so?

But Virgil is here merely a narrative poet: will his justification include the dramatic poet also? One impression is produced by the relation of a person's shriek, another by the shriek itself. The drama designed for the living art of the actor should, perhaps, for that very reason be compelled to confine itself more strictly within the limits of material art. In it we do not merely believe that we see and hear a shrieking Philoktetes, we actually do see and hear him. The nearer the actor approaches to nature, the more will our eyes and ears be offended; for it is indisputable that they are so in nature itself when we meet with such loud and violent expressions of pain. Besides, bodily pain generally is not capable of exciting that sympathy which other ills awaken. Our imagination can discern too little in it for the mere sight of it to arouse in us anything of an equivalent emotion. Sophokles, therefore, in making Philoktetes and Hercules moan and cry, shriek and howl, to such an excess, may easily have offended not a merely conventional sense of propriety, but one grounded upon the very existence of our feelings. It is impossible that the coactors in the scene should share his sufferings in the high degree that these unmeasured outbreaks seem to demand. These coactors would appear to us, their spectators, comparatively cold; and yet we cannot but regard their sympathies as the measure of our own. If we add, that it is with difficulty, if at all, that the actor can succeed in carrying the representation of bodily pain as far as positive illusion, it becomes a question whether the modern dramatic poets should not rather be praised than blamed for having completely avoided this rock, or at all events doubled it in but a light craft.

How many things would appear incontestable in theory, if genius had not succeeded in proving them to be the contrary by fact. None of the above considerations are groundless, and still the Philoktetes remains one of the masterpieces of the stage: for a part of them are not applicable to Sophokles, and only by rising superior to the rest has he attained to that beauty of which the timid critic, without this example, would never have dreamt. The following remarks will demonstrate this more exactly.

1. What wonderful skill has the poet shown in strengthening and enlarging the idea of bodily pain. He chose a wound (for the circumstances of the story may also be considered as depending on his choice, inasmuch as he selected the whole legend for the sake of the circumstances favourable to him which it contained); he chose, I say, a wound, and not an internal malady; because the former admits of a more lively representation than the latter, however painful it may be. For this reason, the inward sympathetic fire which consumes Meleager as his mother sacrifices him to her sisterly fury by means of the fatal brand, would be less dramatic than a wound. This wound, moreover, was a punishment divinely decreed. A supernatural poison incessantly raged therein, and only a more violent attack of pain had its periodical duration, at the expiration of which the unhappy man always fell into a benumbing sleep, during which exhausted nature recovered strength to tread again the same path of suffering. Chateaubrun makes him wounded merely by the poisoned arrow of a Trojan. What extraordinary issue was to be expected from so ordinary an occurrence? In the ancient wars every one was exposed to it: how came it, then, that in Philoktetes' case only it was followed by such dreadful consequences? Besides, is not a natural poison, that works for nine whole years, far more improbable than all the fabled wonders with which the Greek has adorned his piece?

2. Sophokles felt full well that, however great and terrible he made the bodily pain of his hero, it would not be sufficient, by itself, to excite any remarkable degree of sympathy. He therefore combined it with other evils,

which likewise could not greatly move us of themselves, but which, from this combination, receive the same melancholy colouring, which they in their turn impart to the bodily pain. These evils were a complete absence of human society, hunger, and all the hardships of life, to which a man under such privations and an inclement climate is exposed. Imagine a man in these circumstances, but give him health, strength, and industry, and he becomes a Robinson Crusoe, whose lot, though not indifferent to us, has certainly no great claim upon our sympathy. For we are seldom so contented with human society, that the quiet we enjoy when secluded from it seems without a charm for us; especially under the idea, which flatters every individual, that he can gradually learn to dispense with all external aid. On the other hand, imagine a man afflicted by the most painful and incurable disease, but at the same time surrounded by kind friends who take care that he suffers no want, who as far as it lies in their power alleviate his calamity, and before whom he may freely vent his complaints and sorrows—for such a one we shall undoubtedly feel sympathy; but this sympathy will not endure throughout; and at last we shrug our shoulders and recommend patience. Only when both cases are combined—when the solitary one possesses no control over his own body, when the sick man receives as little assistance from others as he can render himself, and his complaints are wafted away on the desert winds; then, and then only, do we see every misery that can afflict human nature close over the head of the unfortunate one; and then only does every fleeting thought, in which we picture ourselves in his situation, excite shrinking and horror. We see nothing save despair in its most horrible form before us; and no sympathy is so strong, none melts our whole soul so much, as that which entwines itself with the idea of despair. Of this kind is the sympathy that we feel for Philoktetes, and feel most strongly at the moment when we see him deprived of his bow, the only means he still possessed of prolonging his mournful existence. Oh, the Frenchman who had no understanding to consider this, no heart to feel it; or if he had, was mean enough to sacrifice it all to the wretched taste of his nation! Chateaubrun gives Philoktetes society. He makes a young princess come to him in his desert island; and even she does not come alone, but is accompanied by her governess, whom I know not whether princess or poet needed most. He has left out the whole of the striking scene where Philoktetes plays with his bow; and in its stead has introduced the play of beautiful eyes. Bows and arrows, I suppose, would have appeared but a merry sport to the hero youth of France; nothing, on the contrary, more serious than the scorn of beautiful eyes. The Greek racks us with the shocking apprehension that the miserable Philoktetes will be left on the island without his bow, and pitiably perish. The Frenchman knows a surer road to our hearts: he fills us with fear that the son of Achilles may have to depart without his princess. This the Parisian critics called triumphing over the ancients; and one of them proposed to name Chateaubrun's piece "La difficulté vaincue."

3. After considering the effect of the whole piece, we must pass on to the single scenes, in which Philoktetes no longer appears as the abandoned sick man, but is in hopes of soon leaving the cheerless desert island and again

reaching his kingdom; in which, therefore, the whole of his misfortune centres in his painful wound. He moans, he shrieks, he falls into the most horrible convulsions. Against this the objection of offended propriety is properly urged. It is an Englishman who raises it; a man therefore not lightly to be suspected of a false delicacy: and, as already hinted, he adduces very good reasons for his opinion. All feelings and passions, he says, with which others can but little sympathize become offensive if expressed with too much violence. "It is for the same reason that to cry out with bodily pain, how intolerable soever, appears always unmanly and unbecoming. There is, however, a good deal of sympathy even with bodily pain. If I see a stroke aimed, and just ready to fall upon the leg or arm of another person, I naturally shrink, and draw back my own leg or my own arm; and when it does fall, I feel it in some measure, and am hurt by it, as well as the sufferer. My hurt, however, is no doubt exceedingly slight, and upon that account, if he makes any violent outcry, as I cannot go along with him, I never fail to despise him." Nothing is more deceitful than laying down general laws for our feelings. Their web is so fine and complicated, that it is scarcely possible even for the most cautious speculation to take up clearly a single thread and follow it amidst all those which cross it. But if speculation does succeed, is any advantage gained? There are in nature no simple unmodified feelings; together with each a thousand others arise, the least of which is sufficient entirely to change the original sensation, so that exceptions multiply upon exceptions, until at last a supposed general law is reduced to a mere experience in some single cases. We despise a man, says the English-man, if we hear him cry out violently under bodily pain. But not always; not for the first time; not when we see that the sufferer makes every possible effort to suppress it; not when we know that he is in other respects a man of firmness; still less when we see him even in the midst of his distress afford proofs of his constancy; when we see that his pain can indeed compel him to shriek, but cannot force him a step further; when we see that he had rather subject himself to a prolongation of this pain than suffer his mode of thought or resolution to undergo the slightest alteration, even though he has reason to hope that by this change his pain would be brought altogether to an end. All this is found in the case of Philoktetes. Moral greatness consisted, among the Greeks, in an unalterable love of their friends, and undying hatred of their foes; and this greatness Philoktetes preserved through all his troubles. His eyes were not so dried up with pain that they had no tears to bestow upon the fate of his former friends; neither was his spirit so subdued by it that to obtain a release from it he could forgive his enemies and willingly lend himself to all their selfish ends. And were the Athenians to despise this rock of a man because the waves which were powerless to shake him could at least wring from him some sound? I confess I think that Cicero generally displays but little taste in his philosophy, and least of all in that part of the second book of the Tusculan Questions, where he puffs up the endurance of bodily pain. One would think he wanted to train a gladiator, so hot is his zeal against any expression of pain; in which he appears to find only a want of patience, without reflecting that it is often anything but voluntary, while true bravery can be exhibited in voluntary actions only. In Sophokles' play he hears nothing but Philoktetes' complaints and shrieks, and entirely overlooks his steadfast bearing in other respects. How else would he have found occasion for his rhetorical sally against the poets? "Their object surely is to render us effeminate, when they introduce the bravest men weeping." They must let them weep, for the theatre is no arena. It became the condemned or mercenary gladiator to do and suffer all with propriety. From him no sound of complaint was to be heard, in him no painful convulsions seen; for since his wounds and death were intended to afford delight to the spectators, it was part of his art to conceal all pain. The least expression of it would have awakened sympathy; and sympathy, frequently awakened, would soon have put an end to these cold revolting spectacles. But to awaken the sensation, which was there forbidden, is the sole aim of the tragic stage. Its heroes must exhibit feeling, must express their pain, and let simple nature work within them. If they betray training and constraint, they leave our hearts cold, and prize fighters in the cothurnus at the most do but excite our wonder. Yet this epithet is merited by all the characters in the so-called tragedies of Seneca; and I am firmly convinced that the gladiatorial shows were the principal cause why the Romans always remained so far below mediocrity in the tragic art. The spectators learnt to misapprehend all nature at the bloody spectacles of the amphitheatre, where perhaps a Ktesias might have studied his art, but a Sophokles never could. The most truly tragic genius accustomed to these artificial scenes of death could not have failed to degenerate into bombast and rhodomontade: but such rhodomontade is as little capable of inspiring true heroism as Philoktetes' complaints of producing effeminacy. The complaints are those of a man, the actions those of a hero. The two combined constitute the human hero, who is neither effeminate nor hard, but now the one, now the other, as now nature, now principle and duty, require. He is the noblest production of wisdom, the highest object for the imitation of art.

4. Sophokles was not contented with having secured his sensitive Philoktetes from all contempt, but has wisely forestalled every objection which Adam Smith's remarks would warrant being raised against him. For although we do not always despise a man for crying out at bodily pain, it is indisputable that we do not feel so much sympathy for him as his cry appears to demand. How then ought the actors who are on the stage with the shrieking Philoktetes to demean themselves? Should they appear deeply moved, it would be contrary to nature; should they show themselves as cold and embarrassed as we are actually wont to be in such cases, an effect in the highest degree inharmonious would be produced upon the spectators. But, as it has been said, Sophokles has provided against this also; he has imparted to the bystanders an interest of their own; the impression which Philoktetes' cry makes upon them is not the only thing which occupies them: the attention of the spectators, therefore, is not so much arrested by the disproportion of their sympathy with this cry as by the change which, through this sympathy, be it weak or strong, takes place, or ought to take place, in the sentiments and designs of these bystanders. Neoptolemus and the chorus have deceived the unfortunate Philoktetes. They

see into what despair their deceit may plunge him; then his terrible malady assails him before their very eyes. Though this seizure may not be capable of exciting any remarkable degree of sympathy in them, it may induce them to look into their own conduct, to pay some regard to so much misery, and to feel reluctance to heighten it by their treachery. This the spectator expects, and his expectations are not deceived by the noble-spirited Neoptolemus. Philoktetes, if he had been master of his pain, would have confirmed Neoptolemus in his dissimulation: Philoktetes, rendered by pain incapable of all dissimulation, however necessary it may seem, to prevent his fellow-travellers from too soon repenting of their promise to take him home with them, by his naturalness brings back Neoptolemus to his nature. This conversion is excellent, and the more moving because it is brought about by mere humanity. In the Frenchman's drama, the beautiful eyes again play their part in it. But I will think no more of this parody. In the Trachiniæ, Sophokles has resorted to the same artifice of uniting some other emotion in the bystanders with the sympathy which should be called out by hearing a cry of pain. The pain of Hercules is not merely a wearing one. It drives him to madness in which he pants after nothing but revenge. Already he has in this fury seized Lichas, and dashed him to pieces against the rocks. The chorus is composed of women, and for that reason is naturally filled with fear and horror. These, and the suspense arising from the doubt whether a god will yet hasten to the aid of Hercules, or whether he will be left to sink under his misfortunes, here create that proper universal interest to which sympathy imparts but a light shading. As soon as the event is decided by the assistance of the oracle, Hercules becomes quiet, and admiration at the resolution he has finally displayed occupies the place of all other emotions. But, in the general comparison of the suffering Hercules with the suffering Philoktetes, we must not forget that the one is a demi-god, the other only a man. The man is ashamed of no complaints, while the demi-god is indignant at finding that his mortal part has such power over his immortal, that it can compel him to weep and moan like a girl. We moderns do not believe in demi-gods, and yet expect that the commonest hero should act and feel like one.

That an actor can carry imitation of the shrieks and convulsions of pain as far as illusion I do not venture either positively to deny or assert. If I found that our actors could not, I should first inquire whether Garrick also would find it impossible; and if my question were answered in the affirmative, I should still be at liberty to suppose that the acting and declamation of the ancients attained a perfection of which we can at this day form no conception.

Chapter X

I go on to notice an expression of surprise in Spence, which most significantly proves how little reflexion he can have bestowed upon the nature of the limits of Art and Painting.

"As to the muses in general," he says, "it is remarkable that the poets say so little of them in a descriptive way; much less indeed than might be expected for deities to whom they are so particularly indebted."

What does this mean, if not that he feels surprised that, when the poet speaks of the deities, he does not do it in the dumb speech of the painter? Urania, with the poets, is the muse of astronomy; from her name and her performances we at once recognize her office. The artist, in order to render it palpable, represents her pointing with a wand to a globe of the heavens. This wand, this celestial globe, and this posture are, as it were, his letters, from which he leaves us to spell out the name Urania. But when the poet wishes to say that "Urania had long ago foreseen his death in the aspect of the stars"—

> *Ipsa diu positis lethum prædixerat astris*
> *Uranie*

> Statius

—why should he, out of respect to the painter, subjoin, "Urania, wand in hand, and heavenly globe before her"? Would it not be as though a man who could and might speak clearly should still make use of those signs which the mutes in the seraglios of the Turks, from an inability to articulate, have adopted among themselves?

Spence again expresses the same surprise at the moral beings, or those divinities, to whom the ancients allotted the superintendence of virtues, or whom they supposed to preside over the conduct and events of human life. "It is observable," he says, "that the Roman poets say less of the best of these moral beings than might be expected. The artists are much fuller on this head; and one who would settle what appearances each of them made should go to the medals of the Roman emperors. The poets, in fact, speak of them very often as persons; but of their attributes, their dress, and the rest of their figure they generally say but little."

When the poet personifies abstractions, they are sufficiently characterized by their names and the actions which he represents them as performing.

The artist does not command these means. He is therefore compelled to add to his personified abstractions some emblems by which they may be easily recognised. These emblems, since they are different and have different significations, constitute them allegorical figures.

A female form, with a bridle in her hand; another, leaning against a pillar, are, in art, allegorical beings. On the contrary, with the poets, Temperance and Constancy are not allegorical beings, but personified abstractions.

The invention of these emblems was forced upon artists by necessity. For thus only they make it understood what this or that figure is intended to signify. But why should the poet allow that to be forced upon him to which the artists have only been driven by a necessity, in which he himself has no share?

What causes Spence so much surprise deserves to be prescribed, as a general law, to poets. They must not convert the necessities of painting into a part of their own wealth. They must not look upon the instruments which art has invented for the sake of following poetry as perfections of which they have any cause to be envious. When an artist clothes an image with symbols, he exalts a mere statue to a higher being. But if the poet makes use of these artistic decorations, he degrades a higher being into a puppet.

As this rule is confirmed by the practice of the ancients, so is its intentional violation the favourite fault of modern poets. All their imaginary beings appear masqued, and the artists who are most familiar with the details of this masquerade generally understand least of the principal work, viz. how to make their beings act, and act in such a way as to indicate their characters.

Still, among the attributes with which the artists characterize their abstractions, there is a class which is more capable and more deserving of being adopted by the poets. I mean those which possess nothing properly allegorical, but are to be considered less as emblems than as instruments, of which the beings to whom they are attributed, should they be called upon to act as real persons, would or could make use. The bridle in the hand of Temperance, the pillar against which Constancy is leaning, are entirely allegorical, and therefore of no use whatever to the poet. The scales in the hand of Justice are somewhat less so because the right use of the scales is really a part of justice. But the lyre or flute in the hand of a Muse, the lance in the hand of Mars, the hammer and tongs in the hands of Vulcan, are in reality not symbols, but simply instruments, without which these beings could not produce the results which we ascribe to them. Of this class are those attributes which the ancient poets sometimes introduce in their descriptions, and which, on that account, I might, in contradistinction to the allegorical, term the poetical. The latter signify the thing itself, the former only something similar to it.

Chapter XI

Count Caylus also appears to desire that the poet should clothe his imaginary beings with allegorical symbols. The Count understood painting far better than he did poetry.

Yet, in the work in which he expresses this desire, I have found occasion for some weightier reflexions, the most important of which I now notice, in order to afford it a maturer consideration.

The artist, according to the Count's view, should make himself more closely acquainted with the greatest of descriptive poets, Homer—that second nature. He shows him what rich and hitherto unemployed materials for the most excellent pictures the story written by the Greek affords, and that the more closely he adheres even to the most trifling circumstances mentioned by the poet the more likely he is to succeed in the execution of his work.

In this proposition, the two kinds of imitation which I distinguished above are again confounded. The painter shall not only represent what the poet has represented, but the details of his representation shall be the same. He shall make use of the poet, not only as a relater, but as a poet.

But why is not this second kind of imitation, which is so degrading to a poet, equally so to an artist? If a series of such pictures as Count Caylus has adduced from Homer had existed in the poet's time, and we knew that he had derived his work from them, would he not be immeasurably lowered in our admiration? How then does it happen that we withdraw none of our high esteem from the artist, when he really does nothing more than express the words of the poet in form and colour?

The following seems to be the cause. In the artist's case the execution appears to be more difficult than the invention; in the poet's this is reversed, and execution seems easier to him than invention. If Virgil had borrowed the connexion of Laokoon and his children by the serpent-folds from the group of statuary, the merit which we now esteem the greater and more difficult of attainment in this picture of his would at once fall to the ground, and only the more trifling one be left. For the first creation of this connexion in the imagination is far greater than the expression of it in words. On the contrary, had the artist borrowed this connexion from the poet, he would still have always retained sufficient merit in our eyes, although he would have been entirely deprived of the credit of the invention. For expression in marble is far more difficult than expression in words; and, when we weigh invention and representation against one another, we are always inclined to yield to the master on one side, just as much as we think we have received in excess on the other.

There are even cases where it is a greater merit for artists to have imitated nature through the medium of the imitation of the poet, than without it. The painter who executes a beautiful landscape after the description of a Thomson has done more than he who takes it directly from nature. This latter sees his original before him, while the former must exert his imagination until he believes he has it before him. The latter produces something beautiful from a lively and sensible impression; the former from the indefinite and weak representation of arbitrary signs.

But, as a consequence of this natural readiness in us to dispense with the merit of invention in the artist, there arose on his part an equally natural indifference to it. For, when we saw that invention could not be his strong point, but that his highest merit depended on execution, it became of no importance to him whether his original matter were old or new, used once or a thousand times; whether it belonged to himself or another. He confined himself, therefore, within the narrow circle of a few subjects, already become familiar to himself and the public, and expended his whole inventive power upon variations of materials already known, upon fresh combinations of old objects. That is in fact the idea which most of the elementary books on painting attach to the word invention; for, although they divide it into the artistic and poetical, the latter does not extend to the production of objects themselves, but is solely confined to arrangement and expression. It is invention, yet not the invention of a whole, but of single parts, and of their position in respect to one another; it is invention, but of that lower kind which Horace recommends to his tragic poet!

Tuque
Rectius Iliacum carmen deducis in actus,
Quam si proferres ignota indictaque primus.

Recommends, I repeat, not enjoins. Recommends as more easy, convenient, and advantageous, but does not prescribe as better and nobler in itself.

In fact, the poet who treats a well-known story or a well-known character, has already made considerable progress towards his object. He can afford to pass over a hundred cold details, which would otherwise be indispensable to the understanding of his whole; and the more quickly his audience comprehends this, the sooner their interest will be awakened. This advantage the painter also enjoys, when his subject is not new to us, and we recognize, at the first glance, the intention and meaning of his whole composition; at once not only see that his characters are speaking, but hear what they are saying. The most important effect depends on the first glance, and, if this involves us in laborious thought and reflexion, our longing to have our feelings roused cools down, and, in order to avenge ourselves on the unintelligible artist, we harden ourselves against the expression, and woe to him if he has sacrificed beauty to expression. We find in that case nothing to induce us to linger before his work. What we see does not please us; and what to think meanwhile we do not know.

Let us now consider together, firstly, *That invention and novelty in his subjects are far from being the principal things we look for in an artist;* secondly, *That a familiar subject furthers and renders more easy the effect of his art.* And I think that we shall not look, with Count Caylus, for the reasons why the artist so seldom determines upon a new subject, either in his indolence, in his ignorance, or in the difficulty of the mechanical part of his art, which demands all his industry and all his time; but we shall find them more deeply founded, and shall perhaps be inclined to praise as an act of self-restraint, wise, and useful to ourselves, what at first sight appeared limitation of art, and curtailment of our pleasure. I do not fear that experience will contradict me; the painters will thank the Count for his good intentions, but will scarcely make such general use of him as he seems to expect. But even if they should, still in another hundred years a fresh Caylus would be necessary to bring the ancient subjects again into remembrance, and lead back the artist into that field where others before him had already gathered such undying laurels. Or do we desire that the public should be as learned as is the connoisseur from his books, that it should be acquainted and familiar with every scene of history and of fable which can yield a beautiful picture? I quite allow that the artists would have done better if, since the time of Raphael, they had made Homer their text-book instead of Ovid. But since it has happened otherwise, let them not attempt to divert the public from its old track, nor surround its enjoyment with greater difficulties than those which enjoyment must have in order to be what it is supposed to be.

Protogenes painted the mother of Aristotle. I do not know how much the philosopher paid him for the portrait. But whether it was instead of payment, or in addition to it, he imparted to him a piece of advice more valuable than the price itself. For I cannot imagine that it could have been intended for mere flattery, but believe that it was out of an especial regard to that necessity of art, namely of being intelligible to all, that he counselled him to paint the exploits of Alexander; exploits with the fame of which, at that time, the whole world was ringing; and which he could well foresee would never be erased from the memory of future generations. But Protogenes had not sufficient steadiness to act upon this advice. "Impetus animi," says Pliny, "et quædam artis libido." Too great a buoyancy of spirits (as it were) in art and a kind of craving after the curious and unknown, impelled him towards an entirely different class of subjects. He chose rather to paint the story of an Ialysus, or a Kydippe; and, in consequence, we can no longer even guess what they represented.

Chapter XII

Homer elaborates two kinds of beings and actions, visible and invisible. This distinction cannot be indicated by painting: in it everything is visible, and visible in but one way.

When, therefore, Count Caylus continues the pictures of invisible actions in an unbroken series with those of the visible; and when, in pictures of mixed actions, in which both visible and invisible beings take part, he does not, and perhaps cannot, specify how these last (which we only who are contemplating the picture ought to see in it) are to be introduced, so that the persons in the painting itself should not see them, or at least should not appear as if they necessarily did so—when, I say, Caylus does this, the whole series, as well as many single pieces, necessarily becomes in the highest degree confused, incomprehensible, and contradictory.

Still, ultimately, it would be possible, with book in hand, to remedy this fault: only the worst of it is this: when painting wipes away the distinction between visible and invisible beings, it at the same time destroys all those characteristic traits by which the latter and higher order is elevated above the former and lower.

For instance, when the gods, after disputing over the destiny of the Trojans, at length appeal to arms, the whole of this contest, according to the poet, is waged invisibly; and this invisibility permits the imagination to magnify the scene, and allows it free scope to fancy the persons and actions of the gods, as great and as far exalted above those of ordinary humanity as ever it will. But painting must adopt a visible scene, the various necessary parts of which become the standard for the persons who take part in it: this standard the eye has ready at hand, and by its want of proportion to the higher beings, these last, which in the poet were great, upon the artist's canvas become monsters.

Minerva, against whom, in this contest, Mars assays the first assault, steps backwards; and, with mighty hand, seizes from the ground a large, black, rough stone, which in olden times the united hands of men had rolled there for a landmark.—Iliad, xxi. 403.

> ἡ δ᾽ ἀναχασσαμένη λίθον εἵλετο χειρὶ παχείῃ,
> κείμενον ἐν πεδίῳ, μέλανα, τρηχύν τε, μέγαν τε,
> τὸν ῥ᾽ ἄνδρες πρότεροι θέσαν, ἔμμεναι οὖρον ἀρούρης.

In order fully to realize the size of this stone, we must recollect that, though Homer describes his heroes as being as strong again as the strongest men of his own time, he tells us that even they were still further surpassed by the men whom Nestor had known in his youth. Now, I ask, if Minerva hurls a stone which no single man, even of the younger days of Nestor, could set up for a landmark—if, I ask, Minerva hurls such a stone as this at Mars, of what stature ought the goddess herself to be represented? If her stature is proportioned to the size of the stone, the marvellous disappears at once. A man who is three times the size that I am naturally can hurl a stone three times as great as I can. On the other hand, should the stature of the goddess not be proportionate to the size of the stone, there arises in the painting an evident improbability, the offensiveness of which will not be removed by the cold reflexion that a goddess must be possessed of superhuman strength. Where I see a greater effect, there I expect to see more powerful causes.

And Mars, overthrown by this mighty stone—

> ἑπτὰ δ᾽ ἐπέσχε πέλεθρα,

covered seven hides. It is impossible for the painter to invest the god with this extraordinary size; but, if he does not, then it is not Mars who is lying on the ground; at least, not the Mars of Homer, but a common warrior.

Longinus says that he often felt that Homer appeared to raise his men to gods, and reduce his gods to men. Painting effects this reduction. In it everything that in the poet raises the gods above god-like men utterly vanishes. The strength, size, and swiftness, of which Homer always bestowed upon his deities a much higher and more extraordinary degree than he attributes to his most eminent heroes, must sink, in the painting, to the common level of humanity; and Jupiter and Agamemnon, Apollo and Achilles, Ajax and Mars, become exactly the same beings, and can be recognized by nothing but their outward conventional symbols.

The means used by painters of giving us to understand that this or that object in their compositions must be considered as invisible is a thin cloud, with which they surround it on the side that is turned towards the other persons in the sccnc. This cloud appears to be borrowed from Homer. For if, in the tumult of the fight, one of the more important heroes falls into a danger from which none but divine power can save him, the poet represents him as being enveloped by the rescuing divinity in a thick cloud, or in night, and so carried off—as Paris is by Venus, Idaeus by Neptune, and Hector by Apollo. And Caylus, when he designs paintings of such occurrences, never fails to recommend to the artist the introduction of this mist and cloud. Yet surely it is manifest to all that in the poet concealment in mist and night is nothing more than a poetical expression for rendering invisible. I have always, therefore, been astonished to find this poetical expression realized, and an actual cloud introduced into the painting, behind which, as behind a Spanish cloak, the hero stands concealed from his enemy. Such was not the intention of the poet. It is stepping beyond the limits of painting. For the cloud is here a real hieroglyphic, a mere symbolical token, which does not make the rescued hero invisible, but says to the beholders, You must represent him to yourself as invisible. It is here no better than the labels with inscriptions which are placed in the mouths of the figures in old Gothic paintings.

It is true that when Hector is being carried off by Apollo, Homer represents Achilles as making three thrusts with his lance into the thick mist at him—τρὶς δ' ἠέρα τύψε βαθεῖαν. But in the language of the poet this means nothing more than that Achilles had become so furious that he made three thrusts with his lance before he perceived that his enemy was no longer in his presence. Achilles saw no actual mist; and the power which the gods possessed of rendering the objects of their protection invisible lay not in a mist, but in the rapidity with which they bore them away. But in order to express, at the same time, that this abduction was performed with such celerity that no human eye could follow the body so disappearing, the poet previously conceals it in a mist. Not that a mist appeared in the place of the body which had been carried off, but because we think of what is enveloped in a mist as invisible. Accordingly, Homer sometimes inverts the case, and, instead of describing the object as rendered invisible, makes the subject struck with blindness. Thus Neptune darkens the eyes of Achilles when he rescues Æneas from his murderous hand, and, snatching him out of the midst of the melée, places him at once in the rear. In fact, however, the eyes of Achilles are here no more blinded than, in the former passage, the rescued heroes were concealed in a cloud. But in both cases the poet has made these additions in order to render more palpable to our senses that extreme swiftness of disappearance which we call vanishing.

But painters have appropriated the Homeric mist, not only in those cases where Homer has himself used it, viz. when persons become invisible, or disappear; but also in all those where it is intended that the spectator should be able to perceive, in a painting, anything which the characters themselves, either all or part of them, cannot see. Minerva was visible to Achilles alone when she prevented him from coming to actual blows with Agamemnon. I know no other way, says Caylus, to express this than by concealing her, on the side nearest to the rest of the council, by a cloud. This is in complete opposition to the spirit of the poet. Invisibility is the natural condition of his divinities. There was needed no dazzling to render them invisible—no cutting off of the ordinary beams of light; while, on the contrary, to render them visible, an enlightenment and enlargement of mortal vision was required. Thus it is not enough that in painting the cloud is an arbitrary and not a natural sign; this arbitrary symbol has not even the single, definite meaning which, as such, it could have; for it is used indiscriminately, either to represent the visible as invisible, or the invisible as visible.

Chapter XVI

However, I will endeavour to trace the matter from its first principles.

I reason thus: if it is true that painting and poetry in their imitations make use of entirely different means or symbols—the first, namely, of form and colour in space, the second of articulated sounds in time—if these symbols indisputably require a suitable relation to the thing symbolized, then it is clear that symbols arranged in juxtaposition can only express subjects of which the wholes or parts exist in juxtaposition; while consecutive symbols can only express subjects of which the wholes or parts are themselves consecutive.

Subjects whose wholes or parts exist in juxtaposition are called bodies. Consequently, bodies with their visible properties are the peculiar subjects of painting.

Subjects whose wholes or parts are consecutive are called actions. Consequently, actions are the peculiar subject of poetry.

Still, all bodies do not exist in space only, but also in time. They endure, and in each moment of their duration may assume a different appearance, or stand in a different combination. Each of these momentary appearances and combinations is the effect of a preceding one, may be the cause of a subsequent one, and is therefore, as it were, the centre of an action. Consequently, painting too can imitate actions, but only indicatively, by means of bodies.

On the other hand, actions cannot exist by themselves, they must depend on certain beings. So far, therefore, as these beings are bodies, or are regarded as such, poetry paints bodies, but only indicatively, by means of actions.

In its coexisting compositions painting can only make use of a single instant of the action, and must therefore choose the one which is most pregnant, and from which what precedes and what follows can be most easily gathered.

In like manner, poetry, in its progressive imitations, is confined to the use of a single property of bodies, and must therefore choose that which calls up the most sensible image of the body in the aspect in which she makes use of it.

From this flows the rule as to the unity of descriptive epithets and moderation in the depiction of bodily objects.

I should put but little confidence in this dry chain of reasoning did I not find it completely confirmed by the practice of Homer, or rather had it not been the practice of Homer himself which led me to it. It is only on these principles that the sublime style of the Greek poet can be determined and explained, and at the same time a due value assigned to the directly opposite style of so many modern poets who have endeavoured to rival the painter in a department in which he must necessarily vanquish them.

I find that Homer describes nothing but progressive actions, and that when he paints bodies and single objects he does it only as contributory to such, and then generally only by a single touch. It is no wonder, then, that where Homer paints, the artist finds least to employ his pencil, and that his harvest is only to be found where the story assembles a number of beautiful bodies in beautiful attitudes, and in a space advantageous to art, however little the poet himself may depict these forms, these attitudes, and this space. If we go through the whole series of paintings, as Caylus proposes them, piece by piece, we shall find in each a proof of this remark.

I here quit the Count, who would make the palette of the artist the touchstone of the poet, in order to explain the style of Homer more closely.

For one thing, I say that Homer has generally but a single characteristic; a ship is for him now the black ship, now the hollow ship, now the swift ship, at most the well-rowed black ship. Farther than this he does not enter into any description of the ship. But of the sailing, the setting out, and hauling up of the ship he draws a detailed picture enough, of which, if the artist wished to transfer the whole of it to his canvas, he would be compelled to make five or six different paintings.

If, indeed, special circumstances compel Homer to fix our attention longer upon a single object, he nevertheless makes no picture which could be an object of imitation to an artist; but by innumerable devices he contrives to set before our eyes a single object, as it would appear at distinct and successive instants, in each of which it is in a different stage, and in the last of which the artist must await the poet, in order to show us complete that which we have seen the poet forming. For instance, when Homer wants to show us the chariot of Juno, Hebe puts it together, piece by piece, before our eyes. We see the wheels, the axle, the seat, the pole, the traces and straps, not as they are when all fitted together, but rather as they are being put together under the hands of Hebe. Of the wheel alone does the poet give us more than a single feature; there he points out, one by one, the eight bronze spokes, the golden felloes, the tires of bronze, and the silver naves. One might almost say that, because there was more than one wheel, he felt bound to spend as much more time in their description as putting them on separately would have taken in reality.

> Ἥβη δ' ἀμφ' ὀχέεσσι θοῶς βάλε καμπύλα κύκλα,
> χάλκεα ὀκτάκνημα, σιδηρέῳ ἄξονι ἀμφίς·
> τῶν ἦτοι χρυσέη ἴτυς ἄφθιτος, αὐτὰρ ὕπερθεν
> χάλκε' ἐπίσσωτρα, προσαρηρότα, θαῦμα ἰδέσθαι.
> πλῆμναι δ' ἀργύρου εἰσὶ περίδρομοι ἀμφοτέρωθεν.
> δίφρος δὲ χρυσέοισι καὶ ἀργυρέοισιν ἱμᾶσιν
> ἐντέταται· δοιαὶ δὲ περίδρομοι ἄντυγές εἰσιν·
> τοῦ δ' ἐξ ἀργύρεος ῥυμὸς πέλεν· αὐτὰρ ἐπ' ἄκρῳ
> δῆσε χρύσειον καλὸν ζυγόν, ἐν δὲ λέπαδνα
> κάλ' ἔβαλε, χρύσεια.

Again, when Homer would show us how Agamemnon was clad, the king dons each article of his dress, separately, in our presence; his soft under-coat, his great mantle, his beautiful half-boots, and his sword. Now he is ready, and grasps his sceptre. We see the garments whilst the poet is describing the operation of putting them on; but another would have described the robes themselves, down to the smallest fringe, and we should have seen nothing whatever of the action.

> μαλακὸν δ᾽ ἔνδυνε χιτῶνα,
> καλον, νηγάτεον, περὶ δὲ μέγα βάλλετο φᾶρος.
> ποσσὶ δ᾽ ὑπὸ λιπαροῖσιν ἐδήσατο καλὰ πέδιλα·
> ἀμφὶ δ᾽ ἄρ᾽ ὤμοισιν βάλετο ξίφος ἀργυρόηλον,
> εἵλετο δὲ σκῆπτρον πατρῷον, ἄφθιτον αἰεί.

This sceptre is here styled "the paternal," "the imperishable," as elsewhere one like it is described merely as χρυσέοις ἥ λοισι πεπαρμένον, "golden-studded." But when a closer and more complete picture of this important sceptre is required, what does Homer do then? In addition to the golden studs, does he describe the wood and the carved head? He might have done so if he had intended to draw an heraldic description, from which, in after-times, another sceptre exactly like it could be made. And I am sure that many a modern poet would have given us such a description in the king-of-arms style, believing in the simplicity of his heart that he himself had painted the sceptre, because he had supplied the artist with the materials for so doing. But what does Homer care how far he leaves the painter in his rear? Instead of the appearance he gives us the history of the sceptre; first, it is being formed by the labour of Vulcan; next, it glitters in the hands of Jupiter; now it betokens the dignity of Mercury; now it is the martial wand of the warlike Pelops; now the shepherd's staff of the peaceful Atreus.

> σκῆ πτρον, . . . τὸ μὲν Ἥφαιστος κάμε τεύχων·
> Ἥφαιστος μὲν ἐδῶκε Διῒ Κρονίωνι ἄνακτι.
> αὐτὰρ ἄρα Ζεὺς δῶκε διακτόρῳ Ἀργειφόντῃ·
> Ἑρμείας δὲ ἄναξ δῶκεν Πέλοπι πληξίππῳ,
> αὐτὰρ ὁ αὖτε Πέλοψ δῶκ᾽ Ἀτρέϊ, ποιμένι λαῶν·
> Ἀτρεὺς δὲ θνήσκων ἔλιπεν πολύαρνι Θυέστῃ·
> αὐτὰρ ὁ αὖτε Θυέστ᾽ Ἀγαμέμνονι λεῖπε φορῆναι,
> πολλῆσιν νήσοισι καὶ Ἄργεϊ παντὶ ἀνάσσειν.

Now I am better acquainted with this sceptre than if a painter were to place it before my eyes or a second Vulcan give it into my hands. I should not be surprised to find that one of the old commentators of Homer had admired this passage as the most perfect allegory of the origin, progress, establishment, and final hereditary succession of kingly power among men. I should indeed smile if I read that Vulcan, who made the sceptre, represented fire, which is indispensable to man's support, and that alleviation of his wants generally which persuaded the men of early times to submit themselves to the authority of an individual; that the first king, a son of Time (Ζεὺς Κρονίων), was a venerable patriarch, who was willing to share his power with a man remarkable for his eloquence and ability, with a Hermes (Διακτόρῳ Ἀργειφόντῃ), or to deliver it over entirely to him; that in course of time the clever orator, as the young state was threatened by foreign enemies, resigned his power into the

hands of the bravest warrior (Πέλοπι πληξίππῳ); that the brave warrior, after
he had exterminated his foes and assured the safety of the kingdom, artfully
contrived to establish his son in his place; who, as a peace-loving ruler, and
benevolent shepherd of his people (ποιμὴν λαῶν), first rendered them familiar
with a life of pleasure and superfluity; at his death, therefore, the way was
paved for the richest of his connexions (πολύαρνι Θυοέστῃ) to acquire by gifts
and bribery, and afterwards secure to his family, as a purchased possession,
that power which hitherto confidence only had bestowed, and merit had
esteemed a burden rather than a dignity. I should smile, but nevertheless I
should be strengthened in my esteem for the poet to whom so much meaning
could be lent. All this, however, is a digression from my subject; and I merely
view the history of the sceptre as a device of art by which the poet causes us
to linger over a single object, without entering into a cold description of its
parts. Even when Achilles swears by his sceptre to revenge the neglect with
which Agamemnon had treated him, Homer gives us the history of this
sceptre. We see it putting forth leaves upon the hill; the steel divides it from the
stem, strips it of its leaves and bark, and renders it fit to serve the judges of the
people, as an emblem of their godlike dignity.

> ναὶ μὰ τόδε σκῆπτρον, τὸ μὲν οὔποτε φύλλα καὶ ὄζους
> φύσει, ἐπειδὴ πρῶτα τομὴν ἐν ὄρεσσι λέλοιπεν,
> οὐδ' ἀναθηλήσει· περὶ γάρ ῥά ἑ χαλκὸς ἔλεψεν
> φύλλα τε καὶ φλοιόν· νῦν αὐτέ μεν υἷες Ἀχαιῶν
> ἐν παλάμῃς φορέουσι δικασπόλοι, οἵ τε θέμιστας
> πρὸς Διὸς εἰρύαται.

It was not so much Homer's desire to describe two sceptres of different
material and shape as to convey to our minds a clear and comprehensive image
of that difference of power of which they were the emblems—the one the work
of Vulcan, the other cut by some unknown hand upon the hill; the one an
ancient possession of a noble house, the other destined for the hand of any to
whom it might chance to fall; the one extended by a monarch over many isles
and the whole of Argos, the other borne by one from the midst of the Greeks,
to whom, with others, the maintenance of the laws had been entrusted. This
was the real difference which existed between Agamemnon and Achilles: and
which Achilles, in spite of all his blind rage, could not but confess.

But it is not only where he combines such further aims with his
descriptions that Homer disperses the picture of the object over a kind of
history of it; he follows the same course, where the picture itself is the only end
in view, in order that its parts, which, naturally, are seen beside each other,
may, by following upon one another, be seen as naturally in his description,
and, as it were, keep pace with the progress of the narrative; e.g. he wishes to
paint us the bow of Pandarus; a bow of horn, of such and such a length, well
polished, and tipped with gold at either end. What does he? Enumerate all
these dry details one after the other? Not at all: that might be called a
specification or description of such a bow, but could never be called painting

it. He begins with the chase of the wild goat out of whose horns the bow was made. Pandarus himself had laid in wait for and killed it among the rocks; its horns were of an extraordinary size, and for that reason were destined by him to be turned into a bow. Then comes their manufacture; the craftsman joins them, polishes them, and tips them. And thus, as I said before, in the poet we see the making of that which, in the artist, we only see as made.

> τόξον ἐΰξοον ἰξάλου αἰγὸς
> ἀγρίου, ὅν ῥά ποτ' αὐτὸς ὑπὸ στέρνοιο τυχήσας,
> πέτρης ἐκβαίνοντα, δεδεγμένος ἐν προδοκῆσιν
> βεβλήκει πρὸς στῆθος· ὁ δ' ὕπτιος ἔμπεσε πέτρῃ·
> τοῦ κέρα ἐκ κεφαλῆς ἑκκαιδεκάδωρα πεφύκει·
> καὶ τὰ μὲν ἀσκήσας κεραοξόος ἤραρε τέκτων,
> πᾶν δ' εὖ λειήνας, χρυσέην ἐπέθηκε κορώνην.

I should never come to an end if I were to transcribe all the examples of this kind. They will occur, without number, to every one who is familiar with Homer.

Chapter XVII

But, it will be answered, symbols of poetry are not merely progressive, but are also arbitrary; and, as arbitrary symbols, are certainly capable of representing bodies as they exist in space. Examples of this might be cited from Homer himself, whose shield of Achilles one need only call to mind in order to have the most decisive instance how comprehensively, and yet poetically, a single object may be described by its parts placed in juxtaposition.

I will reply to this twofold objection. I call it twofold because a justly drawn conclusion must stand even without an example; and, on the other hand, an example of Homer would be of great weight with me, even if I did not know any argument by which to justify it.

It is true that, since the symbols of speech are arbitrary, it is quite possible that by it the parts of a body may be made to follow upon one another just as easily as they stand side by side in nature. But this is a peculiarity of language and its signs generally, and not in so far forth as they are most adapted to the aim of poetry. The poet does not merely wish to be intelligible; the prose writer is contented with simply rendering his descriptions clear and distinct, but not the poet. He must awaken in us conceptions so lively, that, from the rapidity with which they arise, the same impression should be made upon our senses which the sight of the material objects that these conceptions represent would produce. In this moment of illusion we should cease to be conscious of the instruments—his words—by which this effect is obtained. This was the source of the explanation of poetical painting which we have given. But a poet should always produce a picture; and we will now proceed to inquire how far bodies, according to their parts in juxtaposition, are adapted for this painting.

How do we attain to a distinct conception of an object in space? First, we look at its parts singly; then at their combination; and, lastly, at the whole. The different operations are performed by our senses with such astonishing rapidity that they appear to us to be but one; and this rapidity is indispensable, if we are to form an idea of the whole, which is nothing more than the resultant of the ideas of the parts and of their combination. Supposing, therefore, that the poet could lead us, in the most beautiful order, from one part of the object to another; supposing that he knew how to make the combination of these parts ever so clear to us; still, how much time would be spent in the process? What the eye takes in at a glance he enumerates slowly and by degrees; and it often happens that we have already forgotten the first traits before we come to the last; yet from these traits we are to form our idea of the whole. To the eye the parts once seen are continually present; it can run over them time after time, while the ear, on the contrary, entirely loses those parts it has heard, if they are not retained in the memory. And even if they are thus retained, what trouble and effort it costs us to renew their whole impression in the same order, and with the same liveliness; to pass them at one time under review with but moderate rapidity, in order to attain any possible idea of the whole!

I will illustrate this position by an example, which may be called a masterpiece of its kind.

> There towers the noble gentian's lofty head
>   Far o'er the common herd of vulgar plants,
> A whole flower people 'neath his flag is led,
>   E'en his blue brother bends and fealty grants.
> In circled rays his flowers of golden sheen
>   Tower on the stem, and crown its vestment grey;
> His glossy leaves of white bestreak'd with green
>   Gleam with the watery diamond's varied ray.
> O law most just! that Might consort with Grace,
> In body fair a fairer soul has place.
> Here, like grey mist, a humble earth-plant steals,
>   Its leaf by Nature like a cross disposed;
> The lovely flower two gilded bills reveals,
>   Borne by a bird of amethyst composed.
> There finger-shaped a glancing leaf endues
>   A crystal stream with its reflexion green:
> The flower's soft snow, stain'd with faint purple hues,
>   Clasps a striped star its blanchèd rays within.
> On trodden heath the rose and emerald bloom,
> And craggy hills a purple robe assume.

These are herbs and flowers, which the learned poet describes with great art, and faithfulness to nature; paints, but paints without illusion. I will not say that any one who had never seen these herbs and flowers could form little better than no conception of them therefrom; it may be that all poetical descriptions require a previous acquaintance with their object; nor will I deny that, if any one has the advantage of such acquaintance, the poet might awaken in him a more lively idea of some of the parts. I only ask him what is the case with respect to the conception of the whole? If this also is to be vivid, no individual prominence must be given to single parts, but the higher light must seem distributed to all alike; and our imagination must have the power of running over all with the same speed, that it may at once construct from them that which can be at once seen in nature. Is this the case here? And if it is not, how can it have been said that "the most faithful delineation of a painter would prove weak and dull in comparison with this poetical description"? It is far below the expression of which lines and colours upon a surface are capable; and the critic who bestowed this exaggerated praise upon it must have contemplated it from an entirely false point of view; he must have looked to the foreign ornaments which the poet has interwoven with it, to its elevation above vegetable life, and to the development of those inner perfections for which external beauty serves merely as the shell, more than to this beauty itself, and the degree of liveliness and faithfulness in the representation of it which the painter and poet can respectively preserve. Yet it is the latter only with which we have any concern here; and any one who would say that the mere lines—

> In circled rays his flowers of golden sheen
>   Tower on the stem, and crown its vestment grey;
> His glossy leaves of white bestreak'd with green
>   Gleam with the watery diamond's varied ray

—that these lines, in regard to the impression they create, can vie with the imitation of a Huysum, must either have never questioned his feelings, or be deliberately prepared to belie them. They are verses that might be very beautiful, recited with the flower before us, but which by themselves express little or nothing. In each word I hear the elaborating poet, but I am very far from seeing the object itself.

Once more, therefore, I do not deny to language generally the power of depicting a corporeal whole according to its parts. It can do so, because its symbols, although consecutive, are still arbitrary; but I do deny it to language, as the means of poetry, because such verbal descriptions are entirely deficient in that illusion which is the principal end of poetry. And this illusion, I repeat, cannot fail to be wanting to them, because the coexistence of the body comes into collision with the consecutiveness of language, and though, during the solution of the former into the latter, the division of the whole into its parts is certainly made easy to us, the ultimate recomposition of these parts into their whole is rendered extremely difficult, and often impossible.

Everywhere, therefore, where illusion is not the question, where the writer appeals only to the understanding of his readers, and merely aims at conveying distinct and, as far as it is possible, complete ideas, these descriptions of bodies, so justly excluded from poetry, are quite in place; and not only the prose writer, but even the didactic poet (for where he is didactic he ceases to be a poet), may make use of them with great advantage. Thus, for instance, in his Georgics, Virgil describes a cow fit for breeding—

> *Optima torvæ*
> *Forma bovis, cui turpe caput, cui plurima cervix,*
> *Et crurum tenus a mento palearia pendent.*
> *Tum longo nullus lateri modus: omnia magna,*
> *Pes etiam; et camuris hirtæ sub cornibus aures.*
> *Nec mihi displiceat maculis insignis et albo,*
> *Aut juga detrectans, interdumque aspera cornu*
> *Et faciem tauro propior, quæque ardua tota,*
> *Et gradiens ima verrit vestigia cauda.*

Or a beautiful colt:—

> *Illi ardua cervix,*
> *Argutumque caput, brevis alvus obesaque terga;*
> *Luxuriatque toris animosum pectus,*

Here it is plain that the poet thought more about the discrimination of the different parts than about the whole. His object is to enumerate the points of a beautiful colt, or useful cow, in such a manner that on meeting with one or more of them we should be enabled to form a judgment of their respective values. But whether or not these good points can be recomposed into an animated picture is a matter of perfect indifference to him.

With the exception of this use of it, the detailed description of corporeal objects, without the above-mentioned device of Homer for changing what is coexisting in them into what is really successive, has always been acknowledged by the finest judges to be mere cold, insignificant work, to which little or no genius can be attributed. When the poetaster, says Horace, can do nothing more, he at once begins to paint a grove, an altar, a brook meandering through pleasant meads, a rushing stream, or a rainbow:—

> *Lucus et ara Dianæ,*
> *Et properantis aquæ per amœnos ambitus agros,*
> *Aut flumen Rhenum, aut pluvius describitur arcus.*

Pope, when a man, looked back with great contempt upon the descriptive efforts of his poetic childhood. He expressly desires that he who would worthily bear the name of poet should renounce description as early as possible, and declares that a purely descriptive poem is like a banquet consisting of nothing but sauces. On Von Kleist's own authority I can assert that he took little pride in his 'Spring.' Had he lived longer, he would have thrown it into a totally different form. He intended to methodize it, and reflected upon the means of causing the multitude of images, which he appears to have taken at random, now here, now there, from revivified creation, to arise and follow one another in a natural order before his eyes. He would at the same time have followed the advice which Marmontel, doubtlessly referring to his eclogues, had bestowed on several German poets. He would have converted a series of images, thinly interspersed with feelings, into a succession of feelings but sparingly interwoven with images.

Chapter XVIII

And yet could even Homer be said to have fallen into this cold description of material objects?

I venture to hope that there are but few passages which can be cited in support of this; and I feel assured that these will prove to be of such a kind as to confirm the rule from which they appear to be exceptions.

I maintain that succession of time is the department of the poet, as space is that of the painter.

To introduce two necessarily distant points of time into one and the same painting, as Fr. Mazzuoli has the rape of the Sabine women and their subsequent reconciliation of their husbands and relations, or as Titian has the whole history of the prodigal son, his disorderly life, his misery, and his repentance, is an encroachment by the painter upon the sphere of the poet which good taste could never justify.

To enumerate one by one to the reader, in order to afford him an idea of the whole, several parts or things, which, if they are to produce a whole, I must necessarily in nature take in at one glance, is an encroachment by the poet upon the sphere of the painter, whereby he squanders much imagination to no purpose.

Yet just as two equitable neighbouring powers, while not allowing either to presume to take unbecoming freedom within the heart of the dominions of the other, yet on their frontiers practise a mutual forbearance, by which both sides render a peaceful compensation for those slight aggressions which, in haste or from the force of circumstances, they have found themselves compelled to make on one another's privileges; so do painting and poetry.

In support of this view I will not cite the fact that in great historical pictures the single moment is almost always extended; and that perhaps there is scarcely any piece very rich in figures in which every one of them is in the same motion and attitude in which he would have been at the moment of the main action; some being represented in the posture of a little earlier, others in that of a little later, period. This freedom the master must rectify by a certain refinement in the arrangement, by bringing his several characters either prominently forwards, or placing them in the background, which allows them to take a more or less momentary share in what is passing. I will merely avail myself of a remark which Herr Mengs has made upon Raphael's drapery: "There is a cause," he says, "for all his folds, either in their own weight or in

the motion of the limbs. We can often tell from them how they have been
before. Herein Raphael has even sought to give significance. We can see from
the folds whether a leg or arm, previously to its movement, was in a backward
or forward posture; whether a bent limb had been, or was in the act of being,
straightened; or whether it had been straight and was being contracted." It is
indisputable that in this case the artist combines two different moments in one.
For, as that part of the drapery which rested upon the hinder foot would, unless
the material were very stiff and entirely unsuitable for painting, immediately
follow it in its motion forwards, there is no moment at which the garment can
form any other folds than those which the present attitude of the limb requires;
and, if it is made to fall in other folds, the limb is represented at the present
moment and the drapery at the one previous to it. Yet in spite of this, who
would be punctilious with the artist who has seen good to present us with both
these moments at once? Who would not much rather praise him for having
had the understanding and courage to fall into a slight error for the sake of
attaining greater perfection of expression?

The poet deserves similar indulgence. His progressive imitation properly
permits him to deal with only one side, one property of his material object, at
a time. But, when the happy arrangement of his language enables him to do
this with a single word, why should he not now and then venture to subjoin a
second? Why not, if it requires the trouble, a third, or even a fourth? I have
already remarked that in Homer, for example, a ship is only the black ship, or
the hollow ship, or the swift ship: at the very most, the well-manned black ship.
I wish, however, to be understood as speaking of his style generally; here and
there a passage may be found where he adds the third descriptive epithet,
καμπύλα κύκλα, χάλκεα, ὀκτάκνημα, round, bronze, eight-spoked wheels.
Also where the fourth ἀσπίδα πάντοσε ἐΐσην, καλὴν, χαλκείην, ἐξήλατον,
"a beautiful, brazen, wrought, all-even shield." Who would censure him for it?
who is not rather grateful to him for this little luxuriancy, when he feels what
a good effect it may produce in some few suitable passages.

But I will not allow the actual justification either of the poet or the painter
to rest upon the above-mentioned analogy of two friendly neighbours. A mere
analogy proves and justifies nothing. Their real justification is the fact that in
the work of the painter the two different moments border so closely upon one
another that, without hesitating, we count them as one; and that in the poet
the several features, representing the various parts and properties in space,
follow one another with such speed and condensed brevity that we fancy that
we hear all at once.

And herein, I maintain, Homer is aided in an unusual degree by the
excellence of his language. It not only allows him all possible freedom in the
accumulation and combination of epithets, but its arrangement of these
multiplied epithets is so happy that we are relieved from the prejudicial delay
of the noun to which they refer. In one or more of these advantages the modern
languages fail entirely. Some which, as the French, for instance, must convert
the καμπύλα κύκλα, χάλκεα, ὀκτάκνημα into such a periphrasis as "the round
wheels, which were made of brass and had eight spokes," express the sense,

but annihilate the picture; yet here the picture is everything and the sense nothing; and the one without the other turns a very lively poet into a most tedious twaddler. This fate has often befallen Homer under the pen of the conscientious Dacier. Our German tongue, on the other hand, though it can replace the epithets by equivalent adjectives quite as short, has not the power of imitating the advantageous arrangement of the Greek. We say, indeed, "the round, brazen, eight-spoked" (*die runden ehernen, achtspeichigten*), but "wheels" (*Räder*) drags behind. Who does not feel that three distinct predicates, before we learn the subject, can only produce a weak and confused picture? The Greek joins the subject at once to the first predicate, and leaves the others to follow. He says, "round wheels, brazen, eight-spoked." Thus we know at once what he is speaking of, and become acquainted, conformably with the natural order of thought, first with the thing of which he speaks, and afterwards what is accidental to it. This advantage our language has not; or, perhaps, I should say possesses, but can rarely use without being equivocal. It comes to the same thing. For, if we place the epithets after the substantive, they must stand *in statu absoluto;* we must say, "round wheels, brazen, and eight-spoked" (*runde Räder, ehern und achtspeichigt*). Now, in this *statu,* our adjectives are just the same as adverbs; and, if we construe them as such with the next verb that is predicated of the subject, must produce not unfrequently a completely false and at all events a very ambiguous meaning.

But I am wasting my time on trifles, and appear as if I meant to forget the shield—that famous picture, the shield of Achilles, in respect of which especially, Homer, in ancient times, was regarded as a master of painting. A shield at any rate, it will be said, is a single material object, which a poet cannot be allowed to describe according to its parts in juxtaposition. And yet Homer, in more than a hundred splendid lines, has described its material, its form, and all the figures which filled its enormous surface, so circumstantially and closely, that modern artists have not found it difficult to produce a drawing of it corresponding in all points.

My reply to this particular objection is, that I have already answered it. Homer does not describe the shield as finished and complete, but as it is being wrought. Thus he here also makes use of that knack of art which I have commended; changing that which, in his subject, is coexistent into what is consecutive, and thereby converting a tedious painting of a body into a vivid picture of an action. We see, not the shield, but the divine craftmaster as he executes it. He steps with hammer and tongs before his anvil, and, after he has forged the plates out of the raw material, the figures which he destines for the ornament of the shield rise, one after another, out of the bronze, under our eyes, beneath the finer strokes of his hammer. We never lose sight of him until all is ready; and when it is complete, we feel indeed astonishment at the work, but it is the confident astonishment of an eye-witness, who has seen it produced.

This cannot be said of the shield of Æneas in Virgil. The Roman poet either did not here feel the refinement of his model, or the objects which he wished to introduce upon his shield appeared to him of such a kind as not well

to admit of being executed before our eyes. They were prophecies, in respect
to which it would certainly have been inappropriate if the god had uttered them
in our presence as distinctly as the poet has afterwards explained them.
Prophecies, as such, require a darker language, in which the real names of the
persons of futurity, of whom they speak, are out of place; yet, apparently, these
real names were all-important to the courtier poet. But if this defence justifies
him, it does not do away with the bad effect which his deviation from Homer's
style here produces. All readers of refined taste will allow that I am right. The
preparations which Vulcan makes for his work are nearly the same in Virgil as
in Homer. But, whilst in Homer not only the preparations for labour, but the
labour itself, is seen, Virgil, after he has given us a general view of the god
employed with his Cyclopes—

> *Ingentem clypeum informant . . .*
> *Alii ventosis follibus auras*
> *Accipiunt, redduntque; alii stridentia tingunt*
> *Æra lacu; gemit impositis incudibus antrum;*
> *Illi inter sese multa vi brachia tollunt*
> *In numerum, versantque tenaci forcipe massam,*

lets the curtain fall at once, and transports us to quite a different scene,
whence he gradually conducts us to the valley, in which Venus comes to
Æneas with the arms, that have been, in the meantime, completed. She sets
them against the trunk of an oak, and, after the hero has sufficiently gazed at,
admired, felt, and tried them, the description, or rather the painting, of the
shield begins, which by the everlasting "Here is" and "There is," "Next there
stands" and "Not far off is seen," grows so cold and tedious that all the poetic
ornament which a Virgil could bestow on it is required to prevent its becoming
intolerable. Since this picture, in the next place, is not delineated by Æneas,
being, as he is, amused with the mere figures, and knowing nothing about
their meaning—

> *Rerumque ignarus imagine gaudet;*

nor by Venus, although she must presumably have known just as much of the
future destinies of her beloved progeny as did her easy-going husband; but
since the explanation is given by the mouth of the poet himself, therefore the
action of the poem is manifestly at a standstill whilst it lasts. Not one of his
characters takes any part in it; nor is the sequel in the least affected, whether
this or anything else is represented on the shield; the clever courtier, who
adorns his subject with every kind of flattering allusion, is transparent in it all,
but not the great genius, which relies entirely upon the intrinsic merit of his
work, and rejects all external means of being interesting. The shield of Æneas
is, in consequence, really an interpolation, simply and solely designed to flatter
the national pride of the Roman people. It is a foreign stream turned by the
poet into his main river to make the latter a little more stirring. The shield of
Achilles, on the contrary, is the growth of its own fruitful soil: for a shield was

to be made; and, since nothing that is necessary comes from the hand of the divinity without grace also, it must needs have ornament. But the art lay in treating these decorations merely as such; in interweaving them into the main subject, and making it furnish the opportunity of showing them to us: all this could only be accomplished in the style of Homer. Homer makes Vulcan expend his skill in decoration because he has to produce, and whilst he does produce, a shield that is worthy of him. Virgil, on the other hand, appears to make him forge the shield for the sake of its decorations, since he considers them of sufficient importance to be described particularly, long after the shield has been completed.

Johann Wolfgang von Goethe

1749–1832

Johann Wolfgang von Goethe was born in Frankfurt am Main on August 28, 1749, the son of a lawyer. He was educated privately by tutors, introduced to Italian culture as a youth by his father, and sent to the University of Leipzig in 1765 to study law. After an interlude at home because of illness, Goethe resumed his law studies at the University of Strasbourg and became friendly with the daughter of a country pastor, who inspired many of his poems, including "Mailied" and "Willkommen und Abschied." He also became acquainted with J. G. Herder, who directed his attention to the study of Shakespeare, Ossian, and German folk literature. Goethe's association with Herder inspired a series of major works, including the lengthy prose drama *Götz von Berlichingen* (1771–73), an attempt at a German version of a Shakespearean history play. Another major work, *The Sorrows of Young Werther* (1774), an epistolary novel based on Goethe's unrequited love for Charlotte Buff, made Goethe famous throughout Europe. Also during this period (1771–75) Goethe began an early version of *Faust*, the completion of which became a life-long endeavor.

In 1775, following a broken engagement to a socially prominent young woman in Frankfurt, Goethe traveled in Switzerland. He then went to Weimar to serve the duke, Karl August, as companion and adviser. Goethe remained in Weimar in various official posts for the remainder of his life. During his early years there he worked on two major blank verse dramas, *Iphigenie auf Tauris* and *Torquato Tasso,* and completed the historical prose drama *Egmont*. In 1786–88 Goethe made his famous trip through Italy, spending most of his time in Rome viewing the great art works of classical antiquity. Upon his return to Weimar he wrote the *Romische Elegien* (1788), a set of poems in classical meters based upon his experiences in Rome. At this time he broke off a long-standing relationship with an older woman, Charlotte von Stein, and began his long relationship with Christiane Vulpius, a simple, uneducated girl who eventually bore him five children and whom he married late in life.

Soon afterwards Goethe returned to Italy briefly, this time to Venice, and published the *Venezianische Epigramme* in 1790. *Faust: Ein Fragment,* which included most of the first part of Goethe's masterpiece, also appeared in 1790. In 1792 Goethe accompanied Duke Karl August into the Rhineland during the invasion of France by the German states, and was present at the siege of Mainz. During the 1790s his interest in science grew; he added botany, optics, anatomy, and geology to an already astonishing range of intellectual interests.

In 1794 Goethe began his close association with the poet and dramatist Friedrich Schiller, then a lecturer at the University of Jena. The association was extremely fruitful for Goethe; he credited Schiller with rescuing him from distracting social responsibilities and returning his attention to poetry. The two men shared a commitment to furthering a serious German national literature, and by all accounts they were enormously successful. By the turn of the century Goethe had become a revered figure in Germany and the idol of the Romantic school, despite the fact that he was no longer an enthusiastic supporter of its major tenets. From 1791 to 1817 he served as director of the Weimar Court Theatre, producing both his and Schiller's dramas and setting a high standard of artistic excellence.

In his later years Goethe continued to write prolifically, producing not only plays and poems but a scientific study of color, *Die Farbenlehre;* a continuation of the story of Wilhelm Meister, *Wilhelm Meisters Wanderjahre;* and his autobiography, *Dichtung und Wahrheit. Faust,* Part II, was completed a year before his death and published posthumously. Goethe's recurring romantic attachments continued to inspire some of his best work, including the *Marienbader Elegie* (1823). He died on March 22, 1832, following a brief illness.

SHAKESPEARE AD INFINITUM

There has already been so much said about Shakespeare that it would seem as if there was nothing left to say; and yet it is the characteristic of genius ever to be stimulating other men's genius. In the present case I wish to consider Shakespeare from more than one point of view,—first as a poet in general, then in comparison with the classic and modern writers, and finally as a writer of poetic drama. I shall attempt to work out what the imitation of his art has meant to us, and what it can mean in the future. I shall express my agreement with what has been written by reiterating it, and express my dissent briefly and positively, without involving myself in conflict and contradiction. I proceed to the first topic.

Shakespeare as Poet in General

The highest achievement possible to a man is the full consciousness of his own feelings and thoughts, for this gives him the means of knowing intimately the hearts of others. Now there are men who are born with a natural talent for this and who cultivate it by experience towards practical ends. From this talent springs the ability to profit in a higher sense by the world and its opportunities. Now the poet is born with the same talent, only he cultivates it not for his immediate worldly purposes but for a loftier spiritual and universal purpose. If we call Shakespeare one of the greatest poets, we mean that few have perceived the world as accurately as he, that few who have expressed their inner contemplation of it have given the reader deeper insight into its meaning and consciousness. It becomes for us completely transparent: we find ourselves at once in the most intimate touch with virtue and vice, greatness and meanness, nobility and infamy, and all this through the simplest of means. If we ask what these means are, it seems as if they were directed towards our visual apprehension. But we are mistaken; Shakespeare's works are not for the physical vision. I shall attempt to explain what I mean.

The eye, the most facile of our organs of receptivity, may well be called the clearest of the senses; but the inner sense is still clearer, and to it by means of words belongs the most sensitive and clear receptivity. This is particularly obvious when what we apprehend with the eye seems alien and unimpressive considered in and for itself. But Shakespeare speaks always to our inner sense. Through this, the picture-world of imagination becomes animated, and a complete effect results, of which we can give no reckoning. Precisely here lies the ground for the illusion that everything is taking place before our eyes. But if we study the works of Shakespeare enough, we find that they contain much more of spiritual truth than of spectacular action. He makes happen what can easily be conceived by the imagination, indeed what can be better imagined than seen. Hamlet's ghost, Macbeth's witches, many fearful incidents, get

57

their value only through the power of the imagination, and many of the minor scenes get their force from the same source. In reading, all these things pass easily through our minds, and seem quite appropriate, whereas in representation on the stage they would strike us unfavorably and appear not only unpleasant but even disgusting.

Shakespeare gets his effect by means of the living word, and it is for this reason that one should hear him read, for then the attention is not distracted either by a too adequate or a too inadequate stage-setting. There is no higher or purer pleasure than to sit with closed eyes and hear a naturally expressive voice recite, not declaim, a play of Shakespeare's. According to the delineation of the characters we can picture to ourselves certain forms, but more particularly are we able by the succession of words and phrases to learn what is passing in their souls; the characters seem to have agreed to leave us in the dark, in doubt, about nothing. To that end conspire heroes and lackeys, gentlemen and slaves, kings and heralds; indeed even the subordinate characters are often more expressive in this way than the leading figures. Everything which in an affair of great importance breathes only secretly through the air, or lies hidden in the hearts of men, is here openly expressed. What the soul anxiously conceals and represses is here brought freely and abundantly to the light. We experience the truth of life,—how, we do not know!

Shakespeare associates himself with the World-Spirit; like it, he explores the world; from neither is anything hidden. But whereas it is the business of the World-Spirit to keep its secrets both before and after the event, it is the work of the poet to tell them, and take us into his confidence before the event or in the very action itself. The depraved man of power, the well-intentioned dullard, the passionate lover, the quiet scholar, all carry their heart in their hand, often contrary to verisimilitude. Every one is candid and loquacious. It is enough that the secret must out, and even the stones would publish it. The inanimate insists upon speaking; the elements, the phenomena of sky, earth and sea, thunder and lightning, wild animals, lift their voice, often apparently symbolically, but all joining in the revelation.

The whole civilized world too brings its treasures to Shakespeare; Art and Science, Commerce and Industry, all bear him their gifts. Shakespeare's poems are a great animated fair; and it is to his own country that he owes his riches.

For back of him is England, the sea-encircled and mist-covered country, whose enterprise reaches all the parts of the earth. The poet lives at a noble and important epoch, and presents all its glory and its deficiencies with great vivacity; indeed, he would hardly produce such an effect upon us were it not just his own life-epoch that he was representing. No one despised the outer costume of men more than he; but he understood well the inner man, and here all are similar. It is said that he has delineated the Romans with wonderful skill. I cannot see it. They are Englishmen to the bone; but they are human, thoroughly human, and thus the Roman toga presumably fits them. When one takes this into consideration, one finds his anachronisms entirely admirable; indeed, it is just his neglect of the outer form that makes his works so vital.

Enough of these slight words, which cannot begin to sound the praises of Shakespeare. His friends and worshipers will have to add many a word to them. But one more remark:—it would be hard to find a poet each of whose works was more thoroughly pervaded by a definite and effective idea than his.

Thus *Coriolanus* is permeated by the idea of anger at the refusal of the lower classes to recognize the superiority of their betters. In *Julius Cæsar* everything hinges on the idea that the upper classes are not willing to see the highest place in the State occupied, since they wrongly imagine that they are able to act together. *Antony and Cleopatra* expresses with a thousand tongues the idea that pleasure and action are ever incompatible. And so one will ever find, in searching his works, new cause for astonishment and admiration.

Shakespeare Compared with the Ancients and the Moderns

The interests which vitalize Shakespeare's great genius are interests which centre in this world. For if prophecy and madness, dreams, omens, portents, fairies and gnomes, ghosts, imps, and conjurers introduce a magical element which so beautifully pervades his poems, yet these figures are in no way the basic elements of his works, but rest on a broad basis of the truth and fidelity of life, so that everything that comes from his pen seems to us genuine and sound. It has already been suggested that he belongs not so much to the poets of the modern era, which has been called "romantic," but much more to the "naturalistic" school, since his work is permeated with the reality of the present, and scarcely touches the emotions of unsatisfied desire, except at his highest points.

Disregarding this, however, he is, from a closer point of view, a decidedly modern poet, separated from the ancients by an enormous gulf, not perhaps with regard to his outer form, which is here beside our point, but with regard to his inner and most profound spirit.

Here let me say that it is not my idea to use the following terminology as exhaustive or exclusive; it is an attempt not so much to add another new antithesis to those already recognized, as to indicate that it is already contained in these. These are the antitheses:—

Ancient	Modern
Natural	Sentimental
Pagan	Christian
Classic	Romantic
Realistic	Idealistic
Necessity	Freedom
Duty (*sollen*)	Will (*wollen*)

The greatest ills to which men are exposed, as well as the most numerous, arise from a certain inner conflict between duty and will, as well as between duty and its accomplishment, and desire and its accomplishment; and it is these conflicts which bring us so often into trouble in the course of our lives. Little difficulties, springing from a slight error which, though taking us by surprise, can be solved easily, give the clue to situations of comedy. The great difficulties, on the other hand, unresolved and unresolvable, give us tragedy.

Predominating in the old poems is the conflict between duty and performance, in the new between desire and accomplishment. Let us put this decided divergency among the other antitheses and see if it does not prove suggestive. In both epochs, I have said, there predominates now this side, now that; but since duty and desire are not radically separated in men's characters, both will be found together, even if one prevails and the other is subordinate. Duty is imposed upon men; "must" is a bitter pill. The Will man imposes upon himself; man's will is his kingdom of heaven. A long-continued obligation is burdensome, the inability to perform it even terrible; but a constant will is pleasurable, and with a firm will men can console themselves for their inability to accomplish their desire.

Let us consider a game of cards as a kind of poem; it consists of both those elements. The form of the game, bound up with chance, plays here the rôle of necessity, just as the ancients knew it under the form of Fate; the will, bound up with the skill of the player, works in the other direction. In this sense I might call whist "classic." The form of play limits the operation of chance, and even of the will itself. I have to play, in company with definite partners and opponents, with the cards which come into my hand, make the best of a long series of chance plays, without being able to control or parry them. In Ombre and similar games, the contrary is the case. Here are many openings left for skill and daring. I can disavow the cards that fall to my hand, make them count in different ways, half or completely discard them, get help by luck, and in the play get the best advantage out of the worst cards. Thus this kind of game resembles perfectly the modern mode of thought and literature.

Ancient tragedy was based on unescapable necessity, which was only sharpened and accelerated by an opposing will. Here is the seat of all that is fearful in the oracles, the region in which Œdipus lords it over all. Less tragic appears necessity in the guise of duty in the "Antigone"; and in how many forms does it not appear! But all necessity is despotic, whether it belong to the realm of Reason, like custom and civil law, or to Nature, like the laws of Becoming, and Growing and Passing-away, of Life and of Death. Before all these we tremble, without realizing that it is the good of the *whole* that is aimed at. The will, on the contrary, is free, appears free, and is advantageous to the *individual*. Thus the will is a flatterer, and takes possession of men as soon as they learn to recognize it. It is the god of the modern world. Dedicated to it, we are afraid of opposing doctrines, and here lies the crux of that eternal division which separates our art and thought from the ancients. Through the motive of Necessity, tragedy became mighty and strong; through the motive of Will, weak and feeble. Out of the latter arose the so-called Drama, in which dread Necessity is overcome and dissolved through the Will. But just because this comes to the aid of our weakness we feel moved when, after painful tension, we are at last a little encouraged and consoled.

As I turn now, after these preliminaries, to Shakespeare, I must express the hope that the reader himself will make the proper comparisons and applications. It is Shakespeare's unique distinction that he has combined in such remarkable fashion the old and the new. In his plays Will and Necessity struggle to maintain an equilibrium; both contend powerfully, yet always so that Will remains at a disadvantage.

No one has shown perhaps better than he the connection between Necessity and Will in the individual character. The person, considered as a character, is under a certain necessity; he is constrained, appointed to a certain particular line of action; but as a human being he has a will, which is unconfined and universal in its demands. Thus arises an inner conflict, and Shakespeare is superior to all other writers in the significance with which he endows this. But now an outer conflict may arise, and the individual through it may become so aroused that an insufficient will is raised through circumstance to the level of irremissible necessity. These motives I have referred to earlier in the case of Hamlet; but the motive is repeated constantly in Shakespeare,—Hamlet through the agency of the ghost; Macbeth through the witches, Hecate, and his wife; Brutus through his friends gets into a dilemma and situation to which they were not equal; even in Coriolanus the same motive is found. This Will, which reaches beyond the power of the individual, is decidedly modern. But since in Shakespeare it does not spring from within, but is developed through external circumstance, it becomes a sort of Necessity, and approaches the classical motive. For all the heroes of ancient poetry willed only what was possible to men, and from this arose that beautiful balance between Necessity, Will, and Accomplishment. Still their Necessity is a little too severe for it really to be able to please us, even though we may wonder at and admire it. A Necessity which more or less, or even completely, excludes human freedom does not chime with our views any longer. It is true that Shakespeare in his own way has approximated this, but in making this Necessity a moral necessity he has, to our pleasure and astonishment, united the spirit of the ancient and the modern worlds. If we are to learn anything from him, here is the point where we must study in his school. Instead of singing the praises of our Romanticism so exclusively, and sticking to it so uncritically,—our Romanticism, which need not be chidden or rejected,—and thus mistaking and obscuring its strong, solid practical aspect, we should rather attempt to make this great fusion between the old and the new, even though it does seem inconsistent and paradoxical; and all the more should we make the attempt, because a great and unique master, whom we value most highly, and, often without knowing why, give homage to above all others, has already most effectively accomplished this miracle. To be sure, he had the advantage of living in a true time of harvest, and of working in a vigorous Protestant country, where the madness of bigotry was silent for a time, so that freedom was given to a true child of nature, such as Shakespeare was, to develop religiously his own pure inner nature, without reference to any established religion.

The preceding words were written in the summer of 1813; I ask that the reader will not now find fault with me, but simply recall what was said above,— that this is merely an individual attempt to show how different poetic geniuses have tried to reconcile and resolve that tremendous antithesis which has appeared in their works in so many forms. To say more would be superfluous, since interest has been centred in this question for the past few years, and excellent explanations have been given us. Above all I wish to mention Blümner's highly valuable treatise, *On the Idea of Fate in the Tragedies of Æschylus*, and the excellent criticism of it in the supplement of the *Jenaische Literaturzeitung*. Therefore, I come without further comment to my third point, which relates immediately to the German theatre and to Schiller's efforts to establish it for the future.

Shakespeare as Playwright

When lovers of art wish to enjoy any work, they contemplate and delight in it as a whole, that is, they try to feel and apprehend the unity which the artist can bring to them. Whoever, on the other hand, wishes to judge such works theoretically, to assert some judgment about them, or instruct some one about them, must use his discriminating and analytic faculty. This we attempted to carry out when we discussed Shakespeare, first, as poet in general, and then compared him with the ancient and modern poets. Now we intend to close the matter by considering him as a playwright, or poet of the theatre.

Shakespeare's fame and excellence belong to the history of poetry; but it is an injustice towards all playwrights of earlier and more recent times to give him his entire merit in the annals of the theatre.

A universally recognized talent may make of its capacities some use which is problematical. Not everything which the great do is done in the best fashion. So Shakespeare belongs by necessity in the annals of poetry; in the annals of the theatre he appears only by accident. Since we can honor him so unreservedly in the first case, it behooves us in the second to explain the conditions to which he had to accommodate himself, but not therefore to extol these conditions as either admirable or worthy of imitation.

We must distinguish closely-related poetic *genres*, however often they may be confused and merged together in actual treatment,—epic, dialogue, drama, play. *Epic* requires the verbal delivery to the crowd, through the mouth of an individual; *dialogue*, conversation in a narrow circle, where the crowd may eventually listen; *drama*, conversation bound up with action, even if enacted only before the imagination; *play*, all three together, in so far as they appeal to the sense of vision, and can be embodied under certain conditions of personal presence and stage-setting.

Shakespeare's works are in this sense highly dramatic; by his treatment, his revelation of the inner life, he wins the reader; the theatrical demands appear to him unimportant, and so he takes it easy, and we, spiritually speaking, take it easy with him. We pass with him from place to place; our power of imagination provides all the episodes which he omits. We even feel grateful to him for arousing our imagination in so profitable a way. Since he exhibits everything in dramatic form, he renders easy the working of our imaginations; for with the "stage that signifies the world," we are more familiar than with the world itself, and we can read and hear the most phantastic things, and still imagine that they might pass before our eyes on the stage. This accounts for the frequently bungling dramatizations of favorite novels.

Strictly speaking, nothing is theatrical except what is immediately symbolical to the eye: an important action, that is, which signifies a still more important one. That Shakespeare knew how to attain this summit, that moment witnesses where the son and heir in *Henry IV* takes the crown from the side of the slumbering king, who lies sick unto death,—takes the crown and marches proudly away with it. But these are only moments, scattered jewels, separated by much that is untheatrical. Shakespeare's whole method finds in the stage itself something unwieldy and hostile. His great talent is that of a universal interpreter, or "epitomizer" *(Epitomator)*, and since the poet in essence appears as universal interpreter of Nature, so we must recognize Shakespeare's great genius as lying in this realm; it would be only falsehood— and in no sense is this to his dishonor—were we to say that the stage was a worthy field for his genius. These limitations of the stage, however, have forced upon him certain limitations of his own. But he does not, like other poets, pick out disconnected materials for his separate works, but puts an idea at the centre, and to it relates the world and the universe. As he works over and boils down ancient and modern history, he can often make use of the material of old chronicles; indeed, he often adapts them word for word. With romances he does not deal so conscientiously, as *Hamlet* shows us. *Romeo and Juliet* is truer to the original; still he almost destroys the tragic content of it by his two comic characters, Mercutio and the old nurse, played apparently by two favorite actors, the nurse perhaps originally by a male performer. If one examines the construction of the piece carefully, however, one notices that these two figures, and what surrounds them, come in only as farcical interludes, and must be as unbearable to the minds of the lovers on the stage as they are to us.

But Shakespeare appears most remarkable when he revises and pieces together already existing plays. In *King John* and *Lear* we can make this comparison, for the older plays are extant. But in these cases, too, he turns out to be more of a poet than playwright.

In closing, let us proceed to the solution of the riddle. The primitiveness of the English stage has been brought to our attention by scholars. There is no trace in it of that striving after realism, which we have developed with the improvement of machinery and the art of perspective and costuming, and from which we should find it hard to turn back to that childlike beginning of the stage,—a scaffolding, where one saw little, where everything was *signified,* where the audience was content to assume a royal chamber behind a green curtain; and the trumpeter, who always blew his trumpet at a certain place, and all the rest of it. Who would be content to-day to put up with such a stage? But amid such surroundings, Shakespeare's plays were highly interesting stories, only told by several persons, who, in order to make somewhat more of an impression, had put on masks, and, when it was necessary, moved back and forth, entered and left the stage; but left to the spectator nevertheless the task of imagining at his pleasure Paradise and palaces on the empty stage.

How else then did Schroeder acquire the great distinction of bringing Shakespeare's plays to the German stage, except by the fact that he was the "epitomizer" of the "epitomizer"!

Schroeder confined himself exclusively to effect; everything else he discarded, even many necessary things, if they seemed to injure the effect which he wanted to produce on his country and his time. Thus by the omission, for instance, of the first scenes of *King Lear,* he annulled the character of the play. And he was right, for in this scene Lear seems so absurd that we are not able, in what follows, to ascribe to his daughters the entire guilt. We are sorry for the old man, but we do not feel real pity for him; and it is pity that Schroeder wishes to arouse, as well as abhorrence for the daughters, who are indeed unnatural, but not wholly blameworthy.

In the old play, which Shakespeare revised, this scene produces in the course of the action the loveliest effect. Lear flees to France; the daughters and the stepson, from romantic caprice, make a pilgrimage over the sea, and meet the old man, who does not recognize them. Here everything is sweet, where Shakepeare's loftier tragic genius has embittered us. A comparison of these plays will give the thoughtful reader ever fresh pleasure.

Many years ago the superstition crept into Germany that Shakespeare must be given literally word for word, even if actors and audience were murdered in the process. The attempts, occasioned by an excellent and exact translation, were nowhere successful, of which fact the painstaking and repeated endeavors of the stage at Weimar are the best witness. If we wish to see a Shakespearean play, we must take up again Schroeder's version; but the notion that in the staging of Shakespeare not an iota may be omitted, senseless as it is, one hears constantly repeated. If the defenders of this opinion maintain the upper hand, in a few years Shakespeare will be quite driven from the stage, which for that matter would be no great misfortune; for then the reader, whether he be solitary or sociable, will be able to get so much the purer pleasure out of him.

They have, however, with the idea of making an attempt along the lines of which we have spoken in detail above, revised *Romeo and Juliet* for the theatre at Weimar. The principles according to which this was done we shall develop before long, and it will perhaps become apparent why this version, whose staging is by no means difficult, although it must be handled artistically and carefully, did not take on the German stage. Attempts of a similar kind are going on, and perhaps something is preparing for the future, for frequent endeavors do not always show immediate effects.

ANCIENT AND MODERN

I have been obliged, in what precedes, to say so much in favor of antiquity, and particularly of the plastic artists of those times, that I may possibly be misunderstood, which so often happens where the reader, instead of preserving a just balance, throws himself at once into the opposite scale. I therefore seize the present opportunity to explain my meaning, using plastic art as a symbol of the never-ceasing life of human actions and affairs.

A young friend, Karl Ernst Schubarth, in his pamphlet, *A Critique on Goethe,* which in every respect calls for my esteem and thanks, says: "I do not agree with those worshipers of the ancients, among whom is Goethe himself, who maintain that in high and complete development of humanity nothing has ever been arrived at to compare with the Greeks." Fortunately, Schubarth's own words give us an opportunity to adjust this difference, where he says, "As to our Goethe, let me say that I prefer Shakespeare to him, for this reason,— that in Shakespeare I seem to find a strong, unconscious man, who is able, with perfect certainty, and without reasoning, reflecting, subtilizing and classifying, to seize with never-failing hand the true and false in man, and express it quite naturally; whilst in Goethe, though I recognize the same ultimate aim, I am always fighting with obstacles, and must be always taking heed lest I accept for plain truth what is only an exhibition of plain error."

Here our friend hits the nail on the head; for in that very point where he places me below Shakespeare do we stand below the ancients. And what is it we advance concerning the ancients? Any talent, the development of which is not favored by time and circumstances, and must on that account work its way through a thousand obstacles, and get rid of a thousand errors, must always be at a disadvantage, when compared with a contemporary one that has the opportunity to cultivate itself with facility and act to the extent of its capacity without opposition.

It often happens that people who are no longer young are able, out of the fullness of their experience, to furnish an illustration that will explain or strengthen an assertion; and this is my excuse for relating the following anecdote. A practised diplomatist who had desired my acquaintance, after the first interview, when he had had but little opportunity of seeing or conversing with me, remarked to his friends: "Voilà un homme qui a eu de grands chagrins!" These words set me to thinking. The skilful physiognomist's eye did not deceive him, only he laid to the effect of suffering the phenomenon that should also have been ascribed to opposition. An observant, straightforward German might have said, "Here is a man who has had a very hard time of it." Since, then, the signs of past endurance and of persevering activity do not disappear from the face, it is no wonder if all that remains of us and our strivings should bear the same impress, and indicate, to the attentive observer, a mode of being whose aim has been to preserve its balance alike under circumstances of happiest development or narrowest limitation, and to maintain the stubbornness, if it could not always the highest dignity, of human existence.

But letting pass old and new, past and present, we may in general assert that every artistic production places us in the same state of mind the author was in. If that was clear and bright, we shall feel free; if that was narrow, timid, or anxious, we shall feel limited in the same proportion.

Upon reflection, we should add that this refers only to treatment. Material and import do not enter into consideration. If we bear in mind this principle, and look around in the world of art, we maintain that every work will afford us pleasure which the artist himself produced with ease and facility. What amateur does not rejoice in the possession of a successful drawing or etching of our Chodowiecki? We see in them such an immediate apprehension of nature, as we know it, that they leave nothing to wish for. But he would not be able to go beyond his mark and line, without losing all the advantage he derived from his peculiar qualifications.

We shall even go farther, and confess that we have derived great pleasure from Mannerists, when the manner has not been carried too far, and that we are pleased with the possession of their works. The artists who have received this name have been gifted with uncommon talent, but became early aware that, in the state of the times as well as of the schools into which they were cast by fate, there was no room for minute labor, but that they must choose their part, and perfect themselves speedily. They therefore made themselves a language, into which they could, without farther trouble, translate with ease and dexterity all visible subjects, and exhibit to us representations of all sorts of scenes with greater or less success. Thus whole nations have been entertained and hoodwinked for long periods of time, until at last one or another artist has found the way back to nature and a higher feeling of art.

We may perceive, by the Herculanean antiquities, how the ancients also fell into this kind of manner; only their models were too great, too present, fresh, and well preserved, for their second and third rate artists to be able to lose themselves entirely in insignificance.

Let us now assume a higher and more agreeable point of view, and consider the talent with which Raphael was so singularly gifted. Born with the happiest natural gifts, at a time when art combined the most conscientious labor, attention, industry, and truth, the young man was already led by excellent masters to the threshold, and had only to raise his foot to enter the temple. Disciplined by Perugino in the most careful elaboration, his genius was developed by Leonardo da Vinci and Michelangelo. Neither of these artists, in spite of their long life and the cultivation of their powers, seems ever to have reached the true enjoyment of artistic production. The former, if we look closely, wearied himself with thought, and dissipated his powers in mechanical inquiries; and we have to blame the latter for spending his fairest years among stone quarries, getting out marble blocks and slabs, so that, instead of carrying out his intention of carving all the heroes of the Old and New Testament, he has left only his Moses as an example of what he could and should have done. Raphael, however, during his whole life, ever increased in the even facility of his work. We see in him the development of the intellectual and active powers, which preserve such remarkable balance that it may be affirmed that no modern artist has possessed such purity and completeness of thought and such clearness of expression. In him we have another instance of a talent that pours out to us the freshest water from the purest source. He never affects a Greek manner, but feels, thinks, works like a Greek. We see the fairest talent developed in the most favorable hours. The same thing occurred, under like conditions and circumstances, in the time of Pericles.

It may therefore always be maintained that native talent is indeed indispensable to production, but equally indispensable is a commensurate development in the provinces of nature and art. Art cannot dispense with its prerogatives, and cannot achieve perfection without favorable outward circumstances.

Consider the school of the Caracci. Here was a ground-work of talent, earnestness, industry, and consistent development; here was an element for the natural and artistic development of admirable powers. We see a whole dozen of excellent artists produced by it, each practising and cultivating his peculiar talent according to the same general idea, so that it hardly seems possible that after times should produce anything similar.

Let us consider the immense stride made by the highly gifted Rubens into the world of art! He too was no son of earth; look at the rich inheritance he was heir to, from the old masters of the fourteenth and fifteenth centuries, through all the admirable artists of the sixteenth, at the close of which he was born.

Again, think of the crowd of Dutch painters of the seventeenth century, whose great abilities found development now at home, now south, now north, until we can no longer deny the incredible sagacity with which their eye pierced into nature, and the facility with which they have succeeded in expressing her legitimate charm, so as to enchant us everywhere. Nay, in proportion as we possess their productions, we are willing to limit ourselves for long stretches of time to their study and admiration, and are far from blaming those amateurs who are contented with the possession and enjoyment of this class of pictures exclusively.

In the same way, we could bring a hundred examples in support of our assertion. To see distinctly, to apprehend clearly, to impart with facility,—these are the qualities that enchant us; and when we maintain that all these are to be found in the genuine Greek words, united with the noblest subjects, the most unerring and perfect execution, it will be seen why it is we always begin and end with them. Let each one be a Greek in his own way, but let him be a *Greek!*

The same is true of literary merit. What is comprehensible is always the first to attract us and give us complete satisfaction. If we even take the works of one and the same poet, we shall find some that seem to indicate a degree of laborious effort, and others again affect us like natural products, because the talent was commensurate with the form and import. And once more, it is our firm belief that although any age may give birth to the fairest talent, it is not given to all to be able to develop it in its perfect proportions.

ON CRITICISM

I

Criticism is either destructive or constructive. The former is very easy; for one need only set up some imaginary standard, some model or other, however foolish this may be, and then boldly assert that the work of art under consideration does not measure up to that standard, and therefore is of no value. That settles the matter, and one can without any more ado declare that the poet has not come up to one's requirements. In this way the critic frees himself of all obligations of gratitude toward the artist.

Constructive criticism is much harder. It asks: What did the author set out to do? Was his plan reasonable and sensible, and how far did he succeed in carrying it out? If these questions are answered with discernment and sympathy, we may be of real assistance to the author in his later works, for even in his first attempts he has undoubtedly taken certain preliminary steps which approach the level of our criticism.

Perhaps we should call attention to another point which is altogether too frequently overlooked, namely, that the critic must judge a work of art more for the sake of the author than of the public. Every day we see how, without the least regard for the opinions of reviewers, some drama or novel is received by men and women in the most divers individual ways, is praised, found fault with, given or refused a place in the heart, merely as it happens to appeal to the personal idiosyncrasy of each reader.

II

Criticism is a practice of the Moderns. What does this mean? Just this: If you read a book and let it work upon you, and yield yourself up entirely to its influence, then, and only then, will you arrive at a correct judgment of it.

III

Some of my admiring readers have told me for a long time that instead of expressing a judgment on books, I describe the influence which they have had on me. And at bottom this is the way all readers criticize, even if they do not communicate an opinion or formulate ideas about it to the public. The scholar finds nothing new in a book, and therefore cannot praise it, while the young student, eager for knowledge, finds that knowledge increased, and a stimulus given to his culture. The one is stirred, while the other remains cold. This explains why the reception of books is so varied.

IV

I am more and more convinced that whenever one has to express an opinion on the actions or on the writings of others, unless this be done from a certain one-sided enthusiasm, or from a loving interest in the person and the work, the result is hardly worth considering. Sympathy and enjoyment in what we see are in fact the only reality; and from such reality, reality as a natural product follows. All else is vanity.

ARISTOTLE'S POETICS

SUPPLEMENT

Every one who has concerned himself at all about the theory of poetic art—and of tragedy in particular—will remember a passage in Aristotle which has caused the commentators much difficulty, without their ever having been able to convince themselves wholly of its meaning. In his definition of tragedy this great writer seems to demand of it that, through the representation of stirring deeds and events, which should arouse pity and fear, the soul of the spectator should be purified of these passions.

My thoughts and convictions in regard to this passage I can best impart by a translation of it:—

"Tragedy is the imitation of a significant and complete action, which has a certain extension in time and is portrayed in beautiful language by separate individuals, each of whom plays a rôle, instead of having all represented by one person as in the narration of a story or epic. After a course of events arousing pity and fear, the action closes with the equilibration of these passions."

In the foregoing translation, I believe I have made this hitherto dubious passage clear; it will only be necessary to add the following remarks: Could Aristotle, notwithstanding his always objective manner,—as, for instance, here, where he seems to be speaking exclusively of the technique of tragedy,—be really thinking of the effect, indeed the distant effect, upon the *spectator*? By no means! He speaks clearly and definitely: When the course of action is one arousing pity and fear, the tragedy must close *on the stage* with an equilibration, a reconciliation, of these emotions.

By "catharsis," he understands this reconciling culmination, which is demanded of all drama, indeed of all poetical works.

This occurs in the tragedy through a kind of human sacrifice, whether it be rigidly worked out with the death of the victim, or, under the influence of a favoring divinity, be satisfied by a substitute, as in the case of Abraham and Agamemnon. But this reconciliation, this release, is necessary at the end if the tragedy is to be a perfect work of art. This release, on the other hand, when effected through a favorable or desirable outcome, rather makes the work resemble an intermediate species of art, as in the return of Alcestis. In comedy, on the contrary, for the clearing up of all complications, which in themselves are of little significance from the point of view of arousing fear and hope, a marriage is usually introduced; and this, even if it does not end life completely, does make in it an important and serious break. Nobody wants to die, everybody to marry; and in this lies the half-jocose, half-serious difference between tragedy and comedy in practical æsthetics.

We shall perceive further that the Greeks did make use of their "trilogy" for such a purpose; for there is no loftier "catharsis" than the *Œdipus of Kolonus*, where a half-guilty delinquent,—a man who, through a demonic strain in his nature, through the sombre vehemence as well as greatness of his character, and through a headstrong course of action, puts himself at the mercy of the ever-inscrutable, unalterable powers,—plunges himself and his family into the deepest, irreparable misery, and yet finally, after having made atonement and reparation, is raised to the company of the gods, as the auspicious protecting spirit of a region, revered with special sacrifices and services.

Here we find the principle of the great master, that the hero of a tragedy must be regarded and represented neither as wholly guilty nor as wholly innocent. In the first case the catharsis would merely result from the nature of the story, and the murdered wretch would appear only to have escaped the common justice which would have fallen upon him anyway by law. In the second case, it is not feasible either; for then there would seem to fall on human power or fate the weight of an all too heavy burden of injustice.

But on this subject I do not wish to wax polemical, any more than on any other; I have only to point out here how up to the present time people have been inclined to put up with a dubious interpretation of this passage. Aristotle had said in the *Politics* that music could be made use of in education for ethical purposes, since by means of the sacred melodies the minds of those raised to frenzy by the orgies were quieted and soothed again; thus he thought other emotions and passions could be calmed and equilibrated. That the argument here is from analogous cases we cannot deny; yet we think they are not identical. The effect of music depends on its particular character, as Handel has worked out in his "Alexander's Feast," and as we can see evidenced at every ball, where perhaps after a chaste and dignified polonaise, a waltz is played and whirls the whole company of young people away in a bacchic frenzy.

For music, like all the arts, has little power directly to influence morality, and it is always wrong to demand such results from them. Philosophy and Religion alone can accomplish this. If piety and duty must be stimulated, the arts can only casually effect this stimulation. What they can accomplish, however, is a softening of crude manners and morals; yet even this may, on the other hand, soon degenerate into effeminacy.

Whoever is on the path of a truly moral and spiritual self-cultivation, will feel and acknowledge that tragedy and tragic romance do not quiet and satisfy the mind, but rather tend to unsettle the emotions and what we call the heart, and induce a vague, unquiet mood. Youth is apt to love this mood and is for that reason passionately devoted to such productions.

We now return to our original point, and repeat: Aristotle speaks of the *technique* of tragedy, in the sense that the poet, making it the object of his attention, contrives to create something pleasing to eye and ear in a course of a completed action.

If the poet has fulfilled this purpose and his duty on his side, tying together his knots of meaning and unraveling them again, the same process will pass before the mind of the spectator; the complications will perplex him, the solution enlighten him, but he will not go home any the better for it all. He will be inclined perhaps, if he is given to reflection, to be amazed at the state of mind in which he finds himself at home again—just as frivolous, as obstinate, as zealous, as weak, as tender or as cynical as he was when he went out. On this point we believe we have said all we can until a further working out of the whole subject makes it possible to understand it more clearly.

CONVERSATIONS WITH ECKERMANN

The Universality of Poetry

Within the last few days I have read many and various things; especially a Chinese novel, which occupies me still, and seems to me very remarkable. The Chinese think, act, and feel almost exactly like ourselves; and we soon find that we are perfectly like them, excepting that all they do is more clear, more pure and decorous than with us.

With them all is orderly, simple, without great passion or poetic flight; and there is a strong resemblance to my *Hermann and Dorothea,* as well as to the English novels of Richardson. They differ from us, however, inasmuch as with them external nature is always associated with human figures. You always hear the goldfish splashing in the pond, the birds are always singing on the bough, the day is always serene and sunny, the night is always clear. There is much talk about the moon, but it does not alter the landscape, its light is conceived to be as bright as day itself; and the interior of the houses is as neat and elegant as their pictures. For instance, "I heard the lovely girls laughing, and when I got a sight of them, they were sitting on cane chairs." There you have, at once, the prettiest situation; for cane chairs are necessarily associated with the greatest lightness and elegance. Then there is an infinite number of legends which are constantly introduced into the narrative, and are applied almost like proverbs; as, for instance, one of a girl, who was so light and graceful on her feet that she could balance herself on a flower without breaking it; and then another, of a young man so virtuous and brave that in his thirtieth year he had the honor to talk with the Emperor; then there is another of two lovers who showed such great purity during a long acquaintance that when they were on one occasion obliged to pass the night in the same chamber, they occupied the time with conversation, and did not approach one another.

And in the same way, there are innumerable other legends, all turning upon what is moral and proper. It is by this severe moderation in everything that the Chinese Empire has sustained itself for thousands of years, and will endure hereafter.

I am more and more convinced that poetry is the universal possession of mankind, revealing itself everywhere, and at all times, in hundreds and hundreds of men. One makes it a little better than another, and swims on the surface a little longer than another—that is all. Herr von Matthisson must not think he is the man, nor must I think that I am the man; but each must say to himself that the gift of poetry is by no means so very rare, and that nobody need think very much of himself because he has written a good poem.

But, really, we Germans are very likely to fall too easily into this pedantic conceit, when we do not look beyond the narrow circle which surrounds us. I therefore like to look about me in foreign nations, and advise every one to do the same. National literature is now rather an unmeaning term; the epoch of World Literature is at hand, and every one must strive to hasten its approach. But, while we thus value what is foreign, we must not bind ourselves to anything in particular, and regard it as a model. We must not give this value to the Chinese, or the Servian, or Calderon, or the Nibelungen; but if we really want a pattern, we must always return to the ancient Greeks, in whose works the beauty of mankind is constantly represented. All the rest we must look at only historically, appropriating to ourselves what is good, so far as it goes.

Poetry and Patriotism

To write military songs, and sit in a room! That would have suited me! To have written them in the bivouac, when the horses at the enemy's outposts are heard neighing at night, would have been well enough; however, that was not my life and not my business, but that of Theodor Körner. His war-songs suit him perfectly. But to me, who am not of a warlike nature, and who have no warlike sense, war-songs would have been a mask which would have fitted my face very badly.

I have never affected anything in my poetry. I have never uttered anything which I have not experienced, and which has not urged me to production. I have only composed love-songs when I have loved. How could I write songs of hatred without hating! And, between ourselves, I did not hate the French, although I thanked God that we were free from them. How could I, to whom culture and barbarism are alone of importance, hate a nation which is among the most cultivated of the earth, and to which I owe so great a part of my own culture?

Altogether, national hatred is something peculiar. You will always find it strongest and most violent where there is the lowest degree of culture. But there is a degree where it vanishes altogether, and where one stands to a certain extent *above* nations, and feels the weal or woe of a neighboring people, as if it had happened to one's own. This degree of culture was conformable to my nature, and I had become strengthened in it long before I had reached my sixtieth year. . . .

It is better for us moderns to say with Napoleon, "Politics are Destiny." But let us beware of saying, with our latest literati, that politics are poetry, or a suitable subject for the poet. The English poet Thomson wrote a very good poem on the Seasons, but a very bad one on Liberty, and that not from want of poetry in the poet, but from want of poetry in the subject.

If a poet would work politically, he must give himself up to a party; and so soon as he does that he is lost as a poet; he must bid farewell to his free spirit, his unbiased view, and draw over his ears the cap of bigotry and blind hatred.

The poet, as a man and citizen, will love his native land; but the native land of his *poetic* powers and poetic action is the good, noble, and beautiful, which is confined to no particular province or country, and which he seizes upon and forms wherever he finds it. Therein is he like the eagle, who hovers with free gaze over whole countries, and to whom it is of no consequence whether the hare on which he pounces is running in Prussia or in Saxony.

And, then, what is meant by love of one's country? what is meant by patriotic deeds? If the poet has employed a life in battling with pernicious prejudices, in setting aside narrow views, in enlightening the minds, purifying the tastes, ennobling the feelings and thoughts of his countrymen, what better could he have done? how could he have acted more patriotically?

Poetry and History

Manzoni wants nothing except to know what a good poet he is, and what rights belong to him as such. He has too much respect for history, and on this account always adds explanations to his pieces, in which he shows how faithful he has been to detail. Now, though his facts may be historical, his characters are not so, any more than my Thoas and Iphigenia. No poet has ever known the historical characters which he has painted; if he had, he could scarcely have made use of them. The poet must know what effects he wishes to produce, and regulate the nature of his characters accordingly. If I had tried to make Egmont as history represents him, the father of a dozen children, his light-minded proceedings would have appeared very absurd. I needed an Egmont more in harmony with his own actions and my poetic views; and this is, as Clara says, *my* Egmont.

What would be the use of poets, if they only repeated the record of the historian? The poet must go further, and give us, if possible, something higher and better. All the characters of Sophocles bear something of that great poet's lofty soul; and it is the same with the characters of Shakespeare. This is as it ought to be. Nay, Shakespeare goes farther, and makes his Romans Englishmen; and there, too, he is right; for otherwise his nation would not have understood him.

Here again the Greeks were so great that they regarded fidelity to historic facts less than the treatment of them by the poet. We have a fine example in Philoctetes, which subject has been treated by all three of the great tragic poets, and lastly and best by Sophocles. This poet's excellent play has, fortunately, come down to us entire, while of the Philoctetes of Æschylus and Euripides only fragments have been found, although sufficient to show how they have managed the subject. If time permitted, I would restore these pieces, as I did the Phäeton of Euripides; it would be to me no unpleasant or useless task.

In this subject the problem was very simple, namely, to bring Philoctetes, with his bow, from the island of Lemnos. But the manner of doing this was the business of the poet, and here each could show the power of his invention, and one could excel another. Ulysses must fetch him; but shall he be recognized by Philoctetes or not? and if not, how shall he be disguised? Shall Ulysses go alone, or shall he have companions, and who shall they be? In Æschylus the companion is unknown; in Euripides, it is Diomed; in Sophocles, the son of

Achilles. Then, in what situation is Philoctetes to be found? Shall the island be inhabited or not? and, if inhabited, shall any sympathetic soul have taken compassion on him or not? And so with a hundred other things, which are all at the discretion of the poet, and in the selection and omission of which one may show his superiority in wisdom to another. This is the important point, and the poets of to-day should do like the ancients. They should not be always asking whether a subject has been used before, and look to south and north for unheard-of adventures, which are often barbarous enough, and merely make an impression as incidents. But to make something of a simple subject by a masterly treatment requires intellect and great talent, and these we do not find.

Originality

The Germans cannot cease to be Philistines. They are now squabbling about some distichs, which are printed both in Schiller's works and mine, and fancy it is important to ascertain which really belong to Schiller and which to me; as if anything could be gained by such investigation—as if the existence of such things were not enough. Friends like Schiller and myself, intimate for years, with the same interests, in habits of daily intercourse, and under reciprocal obligations, live so completely in one another that it is hardly possible to decide to which of the two the particular thoughts belong.

We have made many distiches together; sometimes I gave the thought, and Schiller made the verse; sometimes the contrary was the case; sometimes he made one line, and I the other. What matters the mine and thine? One must be a thorough Philistine, indeed, to attach the slightest importance to the solution of such questions.

We are indeed born with faculties; but we owe our development to a thousand influences of the great world, from which we appropriate to ourselves what we can, and what is suitable to us. I owe much to the Greeks and French; I am infinitely indebted to Shakespeare, Sterne, and Goldsmith; but in saying this I do not exhaust the sources of my culture; that would be an endless as well as an unnecessary task. We might as well question a strong man about the oxen, sheep, and swine which he has eaten, and which have given him strength. What is important is to have a soul which loves truth, and receives it wherever it finds it.

Besides, the world is now so old, so many eminent men have lived and thought for thousands of years, that there is little new to be discovered or expressed. Even my theory of colors is not entirely new. Plato, Leonardo da Vinci, and many other excellent men, have before me found and expressed the same thing in a detached form: my merit is that I have found it also, that I have said it again, and that I have striven to bring the truth once more into a confused world.

The truth must be repeated over and over again, because error is repeatedly preached among us, not only by individuals, but by the masses. In periodicals and cyclopedias, in schools and universities, everywhere, in fact, error prevails, and is quite easy in the feeling that it has a decided majority on its side. . . .

People are always talking about originality; but what do they mean? As soon as we are born, the world begins to work upon us, and this goes on to the end. And, after all, what can we call our own except energy, strength, and will? If I could give an account of all that I owe to great predecessors and contemporaries, there would be but a small balance in my favor.

However, the time of life in which we are subjected to a new and important personal influence is, by no means, a matter of indifference. That Lessing, Winckelmann, and Kant were older than I, and that the first two acted upon my youth, the latter on my advanced age,—this circumstance was for me very important. Again, that Schiller was so much younger than I, and engaged in his freshest strivings just as I began to be weary of the world—just, too, as the brothers von Humboldt and Schlegel were beginning their career under my eye—was of the greatest importance. I derived from it unspeakable advantages.

What seduces young people is this. We live in a time in which so much culture is diffused that it has communicated itself, as it were, to the atmosphere which a young man breathes. Poetical and philosophic thoughts live and move within him, he has sucked them in with his very breath, but he thinks they are his own property, and utters them as such. But after he has restored to the time what he has received from it, he remains poor. He is like a fountain which plays for a while with the water with which it is supplied, but which ceases to flow as soon as the liquid treasure is exhausted. . . .

The critic of *Le Temps* has not been so wise. He presumes to point out to the poet the way he should go. This is a great fault; for one cannot thus make him better. After all, there is nothing more foolish than to say to a poet: "You should have done this in this way—and that in that." I speak from long experience. One can never make anything of a poet but what nature has intended him to be. If you force him to be another, you will destroy him. Now, the gentlemen of the *Globe,* as I said before, act very wisely. They print a long list of all the commonplaces which M. Arnault has picked up from every hole and corner; and by doing this they very cleverly point out the rock which the author has to avoid in future. It is almost impossible, in the present day, to find a situation which is thoroughly new. It is merely the manner of looking at it, and the art of treating and representing it, which can be new, and one must be the more cautious of every imitation.

Personality in Art

You have before you the works of very fair talents, who have learned something, and have acquired no little taste and art. Still, something is wanting in all these pictures—the *Manly*. Take notice of this word, and underscore it. The pictures lack a certain urgent power, which in former ages was generally expressed, but in which the present age is deficient, and that with respect not only to painting, but to all the other arts. We have a more weakly race, of which we cannot say whether it is so by its origin, or by a more weakly training and diet.

Personality is everything in art and poetry; nevertheless, there are many weak personages among the modern critics who do not admit this, but look upon a great personality in a work of poetry or art merely as a kind of trifling appendage.

However, to feel and respect a great personality one must be something oneself. All those who denied the sublime to Euripides were either poor wretches incapable of comprehending such sublimity, or shameless charlatans, who, by their presumption, wished to make more of themselves, and really did make more of themselves than they were.

The Subject-Matter of Poetry

The world is so great and rich, and life so full of variety, that you can never want occasions for poems. But they must all be occasional poems; that is to say, reality must give both impulse and material for their production. A particular case becomes universal and poetic by the very circumstance that it is treated by a poet. All my poems are occasional poems, suggested by real life, and having therein a firm foundation. I attach no value to poems snatched out of the air.

Let no one say that reality wants poetical interest; for in this the poet proves his vocation, that he has the art to win from a common subject an interesting side. Reality must give the motive, the points to be expressed, the kernel, as I may say; but to work out of it a beautiful, animated whole, belongs to the poet. You know Fürnstein, called the Poet of Nature; he has written the prettiest poem possible on the cultivation of hops. I have now proposed to him to make songs for the different crafts of working-men, particularly a weaver's song, and I am sure he will do it well, for he has lived among such people from his youth; he understands the subjects thoroughly, and is therefore master of his material. That is exactly the advantage of small works; you need only choose those subjects of which you are master. With a great poem, this cannot be: no part can be evaded; all which belongs to the animation of the whole, and is interwoven into the plan, must be represented with precision. In youth, however, the knowledge of things is only one-sided. A great work requires many-sidedness, and on that rock the young author splits. . . .

I especially warn you against great inventions of your own; for then you would try to give a view of things, and for that purpose youth is seldom ripe. Further, character and views detach themselves as sides from the poet's mind, and deprive him of the fullness requisite for future productions. And, finally, how much time is lost in invention, internal arrangement, and combination, for which nobody thanks us, even supposing our work is happily accomplished.

With a *given* material, on the other hand, all goes easier and better. Facts and characters being provided, the poet has only the task of animating the whole. He preserves his own fullness, for he needs to part with but little of himself, and there is much less loss of time and energy, since he has only the trouble of execution. Indeed, I would advise the choice of subjects which have been worked before. How many Iphigenias have been written! yet they are all different, for each writer considers and arranges the subject differently; namely, after his own fashion. . . .

The majority of our young poets have no fault but this, that their subjectivity is not important, and that they cannot find matter in the objective. At best, they only find a material which is similar to themselves, which corresponds to their own subjectivity; but as for taking the material on its own account, merely because it is poetical, even when it is repugnant to their subjectivity, such a thing is never thought of. . . .

Our German æstheticians are always talking about poetical and unpoetical objects; and, in one respect, they are not quite wrong; yet, at bottom, no real object is unpoetical, if the poet knows how to use it properly.

The Influence of Environment

If a talent is to be speedily and happily developed, the great point is that a great deal of intellect and sound culture should be current in a nation.

We admire the tragedies of the ancient Greeks; but, to take a correct view of the case, we ought rather to admire the period and the nation in which their production was possible than the individual authors; for though these pieces differ a little from each other, and one of these poets appears somewhat greater and more finished than the other, still, taking all things together, only one decided character runs through the whole.

This is the character of grandeur, fitness, soundness, human perfection, elevated wisdom, sublime thought, clear, concrete vision, and whatever other qualities one might enumerate. But when we find all these qualities, not only in the dramatic works that have come down to us, but also in lyrical and epic works, in the philosophers, the orators, and the historians, and in an equally high degree in the works of plastic art that have come down to us, we must feel convinced that such qualities did not merely belong to individuals, but were the current property of the nation and the whole period.

Now, take up Burns. How is he great, except through the circumstance that the old songs of his predecessors lived in the mouth of the people,—that they were, so to speak, sung at his cradle; that, as a boy, he grew up amongst them, and the high excellence of these models so pervaded him that he had therein a living basis on which he could proceed further? Again, why is he great, but from this, that his own songs at once found susceptible ears amongst his compatriots; that, sung by reapers and sheaf-binders, they at once greeted him in the field; and that his boon-companions sang them to welcome him at the alehouse? Something was certainly to be done in this way.

On the other hand, what a pitiful figure is made by us Germans! Of our old songs—no less important than those of Scotland—how many lived among the people in the days of my youth? Herder and his successors first began to collect them and rescue them from oblivion; then they were at least printed in the libraries. Then, more lately, what songs have not Bürger and Voss composed! Who can say that they are more insignificant or less popular than those of the excellent Burns? but which of them so lives among us that it greets us from the mouth of the people?—they are written and printed, and they remain in the libraries, quite in accordance with the general fate of German poets. Of my own songs, how many live? Perhaps one or another of them may be sung by a pretty girl at the piano; but among the people, properly so called, they have no sound. With what sensations must I remember the time when passages from Tasso were sung to me by Italian fishermen!

We Germans are of yesterday. We have indeed been properly cultivated for a century; but a few centuries more must still elapse before so much mind and elevated culture will become universal amongst our people that they will appreciate beauty like the Greeks, that they will be inspired by a beautiful song, and that it will be said of them "it is long since they were barbarians."

Culture and Morals

The audacity and grandeur of Byron must certainly tend towards Culture. We should take care not to be always looking for it in only what is decidedly pure and moral. Everything that is great promotes cultivation as soon as we are aware of it.

Classic and Romantic

A new expression occurs to me which does not ill define the state of the case. I call the classic *healthy,* the romantic *sickly.* In this sense, the *Nibelungenlied* is as classic as the *Iliad,* for both are vigorous and healthy. Most modern productions are romantic, not because they are new, but because they are weak, morbid, and sickly; and the antique is classic, not because it is old, but because it is strong, fresh, joyous, and healthy. If we distinguish "classic" and "romantic" by these qualities, it will be easy to see our way clearly. . . .

This is a pathological work; a superfluity of sap is bestowed on some parts which do not require it, and drawn out of those which stand in need of it. The subject was good, but the scenes which I expected were not there; while others, which I did not expect, were elaborated with assiduity and love. This is what I call pathological, or "romantic," if you would rather speak according to our new theory. . . .

The French now begin to think justly of these matters. Both classic and romantic, say they, are equally good. The only point is to use these forms with judgment, and to be capable of excellence. You can be absurd in both, and then one is as worthless as the other. This, I think, is rational enough, and may content us for a while. . . .

The idea of the distinction between classical and romantic poetry, which is now spread over the whole world, and occasions so many quarrels and divisions, came originally from Schiller and myself. I laid down the maxim of objective treatment in poetry, and would allow no other; but Schiller, who worked quite in the subjective way, deemed his own fashion the right one, and to defend himself against me, wrote the treatise upon *Naïve and Sentimental Poetry.* He proved to me that I myself, against my will, was romantic, and that my *Iphigenia,* through the predominance of sentiment, was by no means so classical and so much in the antique spirit as some people supposed.

The Schlegels took up this idea, and carried it further, so that it has now been diffused over the whole world; and every one talks about classicism and romanticism—of which nobody thought fifty years ago.

Taste

This is the way to cultivate what we call taste. Taste is only to be educated by contemplation, not of the tolerably good, but of the truly excellent. I therefore show you only the best works; and when you are grounded in these, you will have a standard for the rest, which you will know how to value, without overrating them. And I show you the best in each class, that you may perceive that no class is to be despised, but that each gives delight when a man of genius attains its highest point. For instance, this piece, by a French artist, is *galant,* to a degree which you see nowhere else, and is therefore a model in its way.

Style

On the whole, philosophical speculation is injurious to the Germans, as it tends to make their style abstract, difficult, and obscure. The stronger their attachment to certain philosophical schools, the worse they write. Those Germans who, as men of business and actual life, confine themselves to the practical, write the best. Schiller's style is most noble and impressive whenever he leaves off philosophizing, as I observe every day in his highly interesting letters, with which I am now busy.

There are also among the German women talented beings who write a really excellent style, and, indeed, in that respect surpass many of our celebrated male writers.

The English almost always write well, being born orators and practical men, with a tendency to the real.

The French, in their style, remain true to their general character. They are of a social nature, and therefore never forget the public whom they address; they strive to be clear, that they may convince their reader—agreeable, that they may please him.

Altogether, the style of a writer is a faithful representative of his mind; therefore, if any man wishes to write a clear style, let him first be clear in his thoughts: and if any would write in a noble style, let him first possess a noble soul.

Intellect and Imagination

I wonder what the German critics will say [of this poetic inconsistency]. Will they have freedom and boldness enough to get over this? Intellect will stand in the way of the French; they will not consider that the imagination has its own laws, to which the intellect cannot, and should not, penetrate.

If imagination did not originate things which must ever be problems to the intellect, there would be but little for the imagination to do. It is this which separates poetry from prose; and it is in the latter that the intellect always is, and always should be, at home.

Definition of Poetry

What need of much definition? Lively feeling of situations, and power to express them, make the poet.

Definition of Beauty

I cannot help laughing at the æstheticians, who torment themselves in endeavoring, by some abstract words, to reduce to a conception that inexpressible thing to which we give the name of beauty. Beauty is a primeval phenomenon, which itself never makes its appearance, but the reflection of which is visible in a thousand different utterances of the creative mind, and is as various as nature herself.

Architecture and Music

I have found a paper of mine among some others, in which I call architecture "petrified music." Really there is something in this; the tone of mind produced by architecture approaches the effect of music.

Primitive Poetry

From these old-German gloomy times we can obtain as little as from the Servian songs, and similar barbaric popular poetry. We can read it and be interested about it for a while, but merely to cast it aside, and let it lie behind us. Generally speaking, a man is quite sufficiently saddened by his own passions and destiny, and need not make himself more so by the darkness of a barbaric past. He needs enlightening and cheering influences, and should therefore turn to those eras in art and literature, during which remarkable men obtained perfect culture, so that they were satisfied with themselves, and able to impart to others the blessings of their culture.

Weltliteratur

We [Germans] are weakest in the æsthetic department, and may wait long before we meet such a man as Carlyle. It is pleasant to see that intercourse is now so close between the French, English, and Germans, that we shall be able to correct one another. This is the greatest use of a World Literature, which will show itself more and more.

Carlyle has written a life of Schiller, and judged him as it would be difficult for a German to judge him. On the other hand, we are clear about Shakespeare and Byron, and can, perhaps, appreciate their merits better than the English themselves.

French Critics

I am now really curious to know what the gentlemen of the *Globe* will say of this novel. They are clever enough to perceive its excellencies; and the whole tendency of the work is so much grist to the mill of these liberals, although Manzoni has shown himself very moderate. Nevertheless, the French seldom receive a work with such pure kindliness as we; they cannot readily adapt themselves to the author's point of view, but, even in the best, always find something which is not to their mind, and which the author should have done otherwise. . . .

What men these writers in the *Globe* are! One has scarcely a notion how much greater and more remarkable they become every day, and how much, as it were, they are imbued with one spirit. Such a paper would be utterly impossible in Germany. We are mere individuals; harmony and concert are not to be thought of; each has the opinions of his province, his city, and his own idiosyncrasy; and it will be a long while before we have attained an universal culture.

The Construction of a Good Play

When a piece makes a deep impression on us in reading, we think that it will do the same on the stage, and that such a result can be obtained with little trouble. But this is by no means the case. A piece that is not originally, by the intent and skill of the poet, written for the boards, will not succeed; but whatever is done to it will always remain something unmanageable. What trouble have I taken with my *Goetz von Berlichingen!* Yet it will not quite do as an acting play; it is too long; and I have been forced to divide it into two parts, of which the last is indeed theatrically effective, while the first is to be looked upon as a mere introduction. If the first part were given only once as an introduction, and then the second repeatedly, it might succeed. It is the same with *Wallenstein;* the *Piccolomini* does not bear repetition, but *Wallenstein's Death* is always seen with delight.

The construction of a play must be symbolical; that is to say, each incident must be significant in itself, and lead to another still more important. The *Tartuffe* of Molière is, in this respect, a great example. Only think what an introduction is the first scene! From the very beginning everything is highly significant, and leads us to expect something still more important which is to come. The beginning of Lessing's *Minna von Barnhelm* is also admirable; but that of *Tartuffe* is absolutely unique: it is the greatest and best thing that exists of the kind.

In Calderon you find the same perfect adaptation to the theatre. His pieces are throughout fit for the boards; there is not a touch in them which is not directed towards the required effect. Calderon is a genius who had also the finest understanding.

Shakespeare wrote his plays direct from his own nature. Then, too, his age and the existing arrangements of the stage made no demands upon him; people were forced to put up with whatever he gave them. But if Shakespeare had written for the court of Madrid, or for the theatre of Louis XIV, he would probably have adapted himself to a severer theatrical form. This, however, is by no means to be regretted, for what Shakespeare has lost as a theatrical poet he has gained as a poet in general. Shakespeare is a great psychologist, and we learn from his pieces what really moves the hearts of men.

Dramatic Unities

He [Byron] understood the purpose of this law no better than the rest of the world. Comprehensibility [*das Fassliche*] is the purpose, and the three unities are only so far good as they conduce to this end. If the observance of them hinders the comprehension of a work, it is foolish to treat them as laws, and to try to observe them. Even the Greeks, from whom the rule was taken, did not always follow it. In the *Phaethon* of Euripides, and in other pieces, there is a change of place, and it is obvious that good representation of their subject was with them more important than blind obedience to law, which, in itself, is of no great consequence. The pieces of Shakespeare deviate, as far as possible, from the unities of time and place; but they are comprehensible— nothing more so—and on this account the Greeks would have found no fault in them. The French poets have endeavored to follow most rigidly the laws of the three unities, but they sin against comprehensibility, inasmuch as they solve a dramatic law, not dramatically, but by narration.

The Theatre

Any one who is sufficiently young, and who is not quite spoiled, could not easily find any place that would suit him so well as a theatre. No one asks you any questions: you need not open your mouth unless you choose; on the contrary, you sit quite at your ease like a king, and let everything pass before you, and recreate your mind and senses to your heart's content. There is poetry, there is painting, there are singing and music, there is acting, and what not besides. When all these arts, and the charm of youth and beauty heightened to an important degree, work in concert on the same evening, it is a bouquet to which no other can compare. But even when part is bad and part is good, it is still better than looking out of the window, or playing a game of whist in a close party amid the smoke of cigars.

Acting

It is a great error to think that an indifferent piece may be played by indifferent actors. A second or third rate play can be incredibly improved by the employment of first-rate talents, and be made something really good. But if a second or third rate play be performed by second or third rate actors, no one can wonder if it is utterly ineffective.

Second-rate actors are excellent in great plays. They have the same effect that the figures in half shade have in a picture; they serve admirably to show off more powerfully those which have the full light.

Dramatic Situations

Gozzi maintained that there are only thirty-six tragical situations. Schiller took the greatest pains to find more, but he did not find even so many as Gozzi.

Management of the Theatre

The Grand Duke disclosed to me his opinion that a theatre need not be of architectural magnificence, which could not be contradicted. He further said that it was after all but a house for the purpose of getting money. This view appears at first sight rather material; but rightly considered, it is not without a higher purport. For if a theatre is not only to pay its expenses, but is, besides, to make and save money, everything about it must be excellent. It must have the best management at its head; the actors must be of the best; and good pieces must continually be performed, that the attractive power required to draw a full house every evening may never cease. But that is saying a great deal in a few words—almost what is impossible.

Even Shakespeare and Molière had no other view. Both of them wished, above all things, to make money out of their theatres. In order to attain this, their principal aim, they necessarily strove that everything should be as good as possible, and that, besides good old plays, there should be some worthy novelty to please and attract.

Nothing is more dangerous to the well-being of a theatre than when the director is so placed that a greater or less receipt at the treasury does not affect him personally, and he can live on in careless security, knowing that, however the receipts at the treasury may fail in the course of the year, at the end of that time he will be able to indemnify himself from another source. It is a property of human nature soon to relax when not impelled by personal advantage or disadvantage.

Menander

I know no one, after Sophocles, whom I love so well. He is thoroughly pure, noble, great, and cheerful, and his grace is inimitable. It is certainly to be lamented that we possess so little of him, but that little is invaluable, and highly instructive to gifted men.

Calderon

The great point is that he from whom we would learn should be congenial to our nature. Now, Calderon, for instance, great as he is, and much as I admire him, has exerted no influence over me for good or for ill. But he would have been dangerous to Schiller—he would have led him astray; and hence it is fortunate that Calderon was not generally known in Germany till after Schiller's death. Calderon is infinitely great in the technical and theatrical; Schiller, on the contrary, far more sound, earnest, and great in his intention, and it would have been a pity if he had lost any of these virtues, without, after all, attaining the greatness of Calderon in other respects.

Molière

Molière is so great that one is astonished anew every time one reads him. He is a man by himself—his pieces border on tragedy; they are apprehensive; and no one has the courage to imitate them. His *Miser,* where the vice destroys all the natural piety between father and son, is especially great, and in a high sense tragic. But when, in a German paraphrase, the son is changed into a relation, the whole is weakened, and loses its significance. They feared to show the vice in its true nature, as he did; but what is tragic there, or indeed anywhere, except what is intolerable?

I read some pieces of Molière's every year, just as, from time to time, I contemplate the engravings after the great Italian masters. For we little men are not able to retain the greatness of such things within ourselves; we must therefore return to them from time to time, and renew our impressions. . . .

If we, for our modern purposes, wish to learn how to conduct ourselves upon the theatre, Molière is the man to whom we should apply.

Do you know his *Malade Imaginaire?* There is a scene in it which, as often as I read the piece, appears to me the symbol of a perfect knowledge of the boards. I mean the scene where the "malade imaginaire" asks his little daughter Louison if there has not been a young man in the chamber of her eldest sister.

Now, any other who did not understand his craft so well would have let the little Louison plainly tell the fact at once, and there would have been the end of the matter.

But what various motives for delay are introduced by Molière into this examination, for the sake of life and effect. He first makes the little Louison act as if she did not understand her father; then she denies that she knows anything; then, threatened with the rod, she falls down as if dead; then, when her father bursts out in despair, she springs up from her feigned swoon with roguish hilarity, and at last, little by little, she confesses all.

My explanation can only give you a very meagre notion of the animation of the scene; but read this scene yourself till you become thoroughly impressed with its theatrical worth, and you will confess that there is more practical instruction contained in it than in all the theories in the world.

I have known and loved Molière from my youth, and have learned from him during my whole life. I never fail to read some of his plays every year, that I may keep up a constant intercourse with what is excellent. It is not merely the perfectly artistic treatment which delights me; but particularly the amiable nature, the highly-formed mind, of the poet. There is in him a grace and a feeling for the decorous, and a tone of good society, which his innate beautiful nature could only attain by daily intercourse with the most eminent men of his age. Of Menander, I only know the few fragments; but these give me so high an idea of him that I look upon this great Greek as the only man who could be compared to Molière.

Shakespeare

We cannot talk about Shakespeare; everything is inadequate. I have touched upon the subject in my *Wilhelm Meister,* but that is not saying much. He is not a theatrical poet; he never thought of the stage; it was far too narrow for his great mind: nay, the whole visible world was too narrow.

He is even too rich and too powerful. A productive nature ought not to read more than one of his dramas in a year if it would not be wrecked entirely. I did well to get rid of him by writing *Goetz* and *Egmont,* and Byron did well by not having too much respect and admiration for him, but going his own way. How many excellent Germans have been ruined by him and Calderon!

Shakespeare gives us golden apples in silver dishes. We get, indeed, the silver dishes by studying his works; but, unfortunately, we have only potatoes to put into them. . . .

Macbeth is Shakespeare's best acting play, the one in which he shows most understanding with respect to the stage. But would you see his mind unfettered, read *Troilus and Cressida,* where he treats the materials of the *Iliad* in his own fashion.

A. W. Schlegel's Lectures
On Dramatic Art and Literature

It is not to be denied that Schlegel knows a great deal, and one is almost terrified at his extraordinary attainments and his extensive reading. But this is not enough. Learning in itself does not constitute judgment. His criticism is completely one-sided, because in all theatrical pieces he merely regards the skeleton of the plot and arrangement, and only points out small points of resemblance to great predecessors, without troubling himself in the least as to what the author brings forward of graceful life and the culture of a high soul. But of what use are all the arts of genius, if we do not find in a theatrical piece an amiable or great personality of the author? This alone influences the cultivation of the people.

I look upon the manner in which Schlegel has treated the French drama as a sort of recipe for the formation of a bad critic, who is wanting in every organ for the veneration of excellence, and who passes over an able personality and a great character as if they were chaff and stubble.

The French Romanticists

Extremes are never to be avoided in any revolution. In a political one nothing is generally desired in the beginning but the abolition of abuses; but before people are aware, they are deep in bloodshed and horror. Thus the French, in their present literary revolution, desired nothing at first but a freer form; however, they will not stop there, but will reject the traditional contents together with the form. They begin to declare the representation of noble sentiments and deeds as tedious, and attempt to treat of all sorts of abominations. Instead of the beautiful subjects from Grecian mythology, there are devils, witches, and vampires, and the lofty heroes of antiquity must give place to jugglers and galley slaves. This is piquant! This is effective! But after the public has once tasted this highly seasoned food, and has become accustomed to it, it will always long for more, and that stronger. A young man of talent, who would produce an effect and be acknowledged, and who is great enough to go his own way, must accommodate himself to the taste of the day—nay, must seek to outdo his predecessors in the horrible and frightful. But in this chase after outward means of effect, all profound study, and all gradual and thorough development of the talent and the man from within, is entirely neglected. And this is the greatest injury which can befall a talent, although literature in general will gain by this tendency of the moment.

The extremes and excrescences which I have described will gradually disappear; but this great advantage will finally remain—besides a freer form, richer and more diversified subjects will have been attained, and no object of the broadest world and the most manifold life will be any longer excluded as unpoetical. I compare the present literary epoch to a state of violent fever, which is not in itself good and desirable, but of which improved health is the happy consequence. That abomination which now often constitutes the whole subject of a poetical work will in future only appear as a useful expedient; aye, the pure and the noble, which is now abandoned for the moment, will soon be resought with additional ardor.

Mérimée has treated these things very differently from his fellow-authors. These poems, it is true, are not deficient in various horrible motifs, such as churchyards, nocturnal crossroads, ghosts and vampires; but the repulsive themes do not touch the intrinsic merit of the poet. On the contrary, he treats them from a certain objective distance, and, as it were, with irony. He goes to work with them like an artist, to whom it is an amusement to try anything of the sort. He has, as I have said before, quite renounced himself, nay, he has even renounced the Frenchman, and that to such a degree that at first these poems of Guzla were deemed real Illyrian popular poems, and thus little was wanting for the success of the imposition he had intended.

Mérimée, to be sure, is a splendid fellow! Indeed, more power and genius are generally required for the objective treatment of a subject than is supposed. So Lord Byron, also, notwithstanding his predominant personality, has sometimes had the power of renouncing himself altogether, as may be seen in some of his dramatic pieces, particularly in his *Marino Faliero*. In this piece one quite forgets that Lord Byron, or even an Englishman, wrote it. We live entirely in Venice, and entirely in the time in which the action takes place. The personages speak quite from themselves, and from their own condition, without having any of the subjective feelings, thoughts, and opinions of the poet. That is as it should be. Of our young French romantic writers of the exaggerating sort, one cannot say as much. What I have read of them—poems, novels, dramatic works—have all borne the personal coloring of the author, and none of them ever make me forget that a Parisian—that a Frenchman— wrote them. Even in the treatment of foreign subjects one still remains in France and Paris, quite absorbed in all the wishes, necessities, conflicts, and fermentations of the present day.

Victor Hugo

He has a fine talent, but quite entangled in the unhappy romantic tendency of his time, by which he is seduced to represent, together with what is beautiful, also that which is most insupportable and hideous. I have lately been reading his *Notre Dame de Paris,* and required no little patience to support the horror with which this reading has inspired me. It is the most abominable book that ever was written! Besides, one is not even indemnified for the torture one has to endure by the pleasure one might receive from a truthful representation of human nature or human character. His book is, on the contrary, utterly destitute of nature and truth! The so-called characters whom he brings forward are not human beings with living flesh and blood, but miserable wooden puppets, which he deals with as he pleases, and which he causes to make all sorts of contortions and grimaces just as he needs them for his desired effects. But what an age it must be which not only renders such a book possible and calls it into existence, but even finds it endurable and delightful.

The "Idea" of
Goethe's Tasso and Faust

Idea! as if I knew anything about it. I had the life of Tasso, I had my own life; and whilst I brought together two odd figures with their peculiarities, the image of Tasso arose in my mind, to which I opposed, as a prosaic contrast, that of Antonio, for whom also I did not lack models. The further particulars of court life and love affairs were at Weimar as they were in Ferrara; and I can truly say of my production, *it is bone of my bone, and flesh of my flesh.*

The Germans are, certainly, strange people. By their deep thoughts and ideas, which they seek in everything and fix upon everything, they make life much more burdensome than is necessary. Only have the courage to give yourself up to your impressions, allow yourself to be delighted, moved, elevated, nay, instructed and inspired for something great; but do not imagine all is vanity, if it is not abstract thought and idea.

Then they come and ask what idea I meant to embody in my *Faust.* As if I knew myself and could inform them. *From heaven, through the world, to hell,* would indeed be something; but this is no idea, only a course of action. And further, that the devil loses the wager, and that a man, continually struggling from difficult errors towards something better, should be redeemed, is an effective, and to many, a good enlightening thought; but it is no idea which lies at the foundation of the whole and of every individual scene. It would have been a fine thing, indeed, if I had strung so rich, varied, and highly diversified a life as I have brought to view in *Faust* upon the slender string of one pervading idea.

It was, on the whole, not in my line, as a poet, to strive to embody anything *abstract.* I received in my mind *impressions,* and those of a sensuous, animated, charming, varied, hundredfold kind, just as a lively imagination presented them; and I had, as a poet, nothing more to do than artistically to round off and elaborate such views and impressions, and by means of a lively representation so to bring them forward that others might receive the same impression in hearing or reading my representation of them.

If I however wished, as a poet, to represent any idea, I did it in short poems, where a decided unity could prevail, as, for instance, in the *Metamorphosis of Animals,* that of *Plants,* the poem *Legacy,* and many others. The only production of greater extent, in which I am conscious of having labored to set forth a pervading idea, is probably my *Elective Affinities.* This novel has thus become comprehensible to the intellect; but I will not say that it is therefore better. I am rather of the opinion that the more incommensurable, and the more incomprehensible to the intellect, a poetic production is, so much the better it is.

Schiller

Yes, everything else about him was proud and majestic, only the eyes were soft. And his talent was like his outward form. He seized boldly on a great subject, and turned it this way and that, and handled it this way and that. But he saw his object, as it were, only from the outside; a quiet development from within was not his province. His talent was desultory. Thus he was never decided—could never have done. He often changed a part just before a rehearsal.

And, as he went so boldly to work, he did not take sufficient pains about *motives.* I recollect what trouble I had with him when he wanted to make

Gessler, in *Tell*, abruptly break an apple from the tree, and have it shot from the boy's head. This was quite against my nature, and I urged him to give at least some motive to this barbarity, by making the boy boast to Gessler of his father's dexterity, and say that he could shoot an apple from a tree at a hundred paces. Schiller, at first, would have nothing of the sort: but at last he yielded to my arguments and intentions, and did as I advised him. I, on the other hand, by too great attention to *motives*, kept my pieces from the theatre. My *Eugenie* is nothing but a chain of *motives*, and this cannot succeed on the stage.

Schiller's genius was really made for the theatre. With every piece he progressed, and became more finished; but, strange to say, a certain love for the horrible adhered to him from the time of the *Robbers*, which never quite left him even in his prime. I still recollect perfectly well that in the prison scene in my *Egmont*, where the sentence is read to him, Schiller would have made Alva appear in the background, masked and muffled in a cloak, enjoying the effect which the sentence would produce on Egmont. Thus Alva was to show himself insatiable in revenge and malice. I, however, protested, and prevented the apparition. He was a singular, great man.

Every week he became different and more finished; each time that I saw him he seemed to me to have advanced in learning and judgment. His letters are the fairest memorials of him which I possess, and they are also among the most excellent of his writings.

Edinburgh Review

It is a pleasure to me to see the elevation and excellence to which the English critics now rise. There is not a trace of their former pedantry, but its place is occupied by great qualities. In the last article—the one on German literature—you will find the following remark:—"There are some poets who have a tendency always to occupy themselves with things which another likes to drive from his mind." What say you to this? There we know at once where we are, and how we have to classify a great number of our most modern literati.

Byron

Lord Byron is to be regarded as a man, as an Englishman, and as a great genius. His good qualities belong chiefly to the man, his bad to the Englishman and the peer, his talent is incommensurable.

All Englishmen, as such, are without reflection, properly so called; distractions and party spirit will not permit them to perfect themselves in quiet. But they are great as practical men.

Thus Lord Byron could never attain reflection concerning himself, and on this account his maxims in general are not successful, as is shown by his creed, "much money and no authority," for much money always paralyzes authority.

But where he creates he always succeeds; and we may truly say that with him inspiration supplies the place of reflection. Something within him ever drove him to poetry, and then everything that came from the man, especially from his heart, was excellent. He produced his best things, as women do pretty children, without thinking about it or knowing how it was done.

He is a great talent, a born talent, and I never saw the true poetical power greater in any man than in him. In the apprehension of external objects, and a clear penetration into past situations, he is quite as great as Shakespeare. But as a pure individuality, Shakespeare is his superior. This was felt by Byron, and on this account he does not say much of Shakespeare, although he knows whole passages by heart. He would willingly have denied him altogether; for Shakespeare's serenity is in his way, and he feels that he is no match for it. Pope he does not deny, for he had no cause to fear him. On the contrary, he mentions him, and shows him respect when he can, for he knows well enough that Pope is a mere foil to himself.

His high rank as an English peer was very injurious to Byron; for every talent is oppressed by the outer world,—how much more, then, when there is such high birth and so great a fortune. A certain middle rank is much more favorable to talent, on which account we find all great artists and poets in the middle classes. Byron's predilection for the unbounded could not have been nearly so dangerous with more humble birth and smaller means. But as it was, he was able to put every fancy into practice, and this involved him in innumerable scrapes. Besides, how could one of such high rank be inspired with awe and respect by any rank whatever? He expressed whatever he felt, and this brought him into ceaseless conflict with the world. . . .

Moreover, his perpetual negation and fault-finding is injurious even to his excellent works. For not only does the discontent of the poet infect the reader, but the end of all opposition is negation; and negation is nothing. If I call *bad* bad, what do I gain? But if I call *good* bad, I do a great deal of mischief. He who will work aright must never rail, must not trouble himself at all about what is ill done, but only strive to do well himself. For the great point is not to pull down, but to build up, and in this humanity finds pure joy. . . .

I could not make use of any man as the representative of the modern poetical era except him, who undoubtedly is to be regarded as the greatest genius of our century. Byron is neither antique nor romantic, but like the present day itself. This was the sort of man I required. Then he suited me on account of his unsatisfied nature and his warlike tendency, which led to his death at Missolonghi. . . .

Lord Byron is only great as a poet; as soon as he reflects, he is a child.

Scott

Walter Scott's *Fair Maid of Perth* is excellent, is it not? There is finish! there is a hand! What a firm foundation for the whole, and in particular not a touch which does not lead to the goal! Then, what details of dialogue and description, both of which are excellent. His scenes and situations are like pictures by Teniers; in the arrangement they show the summit of art, the individual figures have a speaking truth, and the execution is extended with artistic love to the minutest details, so that not a stroke is lost.

You find everywhere in Walter Scott a remarkable security and thoroughness in his delineation, which proceeds from his comprehensive knowledge of the real world, obtained by life-long studies and observations, and a daily discussion of the most important relations. Then come his great talent and his comprehensive nature. You remember the English critic who compares the poets to the voices of singers, of which some can command only a few fine tones, while others have the whole compass, from the highest to the lowest, completely in their power. Walter Scott is one of this last sort. In the *Fair Maid of Perth* you will not find a single weak passage to make you feel as if his knowledge and talent were insufficient. He is equal to his subject in every direction in which it takes him; the king, the royal brother, the prince, the head of the clergy, the nobles, the magistracy, the citizens and mechanics, the Highlanders, are all drawn with the same sure hand, and hit off with equal truth.

The passage where the prince, sitting on horseback, makes the pretty minstrel girl step upon his foot, that he may raise her up for a kiss, is in the boldest English style. But you ladies are wrong always to take sides. Usually, you read a book to find nutrition for the heart, to find a hero whom you could love. This is not the way to read; the great point is not whether this or that character pleases, but whether the whole book pleases.

But, when you have finished the *Fair Maid of Perth,* you must at once read *Waverley,* which is written from quite a different point of view, but which may, without hesitation, be set beside the best works that have ever been written in this world. We see that it is the same man who wrote the *Fair Maid of Perth,* but that he has yet to gain the favor of the public, and therefore collects his forces so that he may not give a touch that is short of excellence. The *Fair Maid of Perth,* on the other hand, is from a freer pen; the author is now sure of his public, and he proceeds more at liberty. After reading *Waverley,* you will understand why Walter Scott still designates himself the author of that work; for there he showed what he could do, and he has never since written anything to surpass, or even equal, that first published novel. . . .

Walter Scott is a great genius; he has not his equal; and we need not wonder at the extraordinary effect he produces on the whole reading world. He gives me much to think of; and I discover in him a wholly new art, with laws of its own. . . .

We read far too many poor things, thus losing time, and gaining nothing. We should only read what we admire, as I did in my youth, and as I now experience with Sir Walter Scott. I have just begun *Rob Roy,* and will read his best novels in succession. All is great—material, import, characters, execution; and then what infinite diligence in the preparatory studies! what truth of detail in the execution! We see, too, what English history is; and what a thing it is when such an inheritance falls to the lot of a clever poet. Our German history, in five volumes, is, on the other hand, sheer poverty. . . .

It is a peculiarity of Walter Scott's that his great talent in representing details often leads him into faults. Thus, in *Ivanhoe*, there is a scene where they are seated at a table in a castle-hall at night, and a stranger enters. Now, he is quite right in describing the stranger's appearance and dress, but it is a fault that he goes to the length of describing his feet, shoes, and stockings. When we sit down in the evening, and some one comes in, we see only the upper part of his body. If I describe the feet, daylight enters at once, and the scene loses its nocturnal character.

Johann Gottfried von Herder

1744–1803

Johann Gottfried von Herder was born to a poor family on August 25, 1744, in Mohrungen, East Prussia. In 1762 he began the study of theology, philosophy, and literature at Königsberg, where he came into close contact with Kant and Hamann. In late 1764, Herder went to Riga to teach and preach, and several years later, he published his first works, *Über die Neuere deutsche Literatur* (1767) and *Kritische Wälder* (1769).

During a visit to Strasbourg in 1770 Herder met the young Goethe, who was greatly impressed by Herder's observations on literature, particularly on Homer, Pindar, Shakespeare, and Ossian. The following year, Herder went to Bückeburg as Court Preacher, where he wrote and published a series of books and essays that played a significant role in bringing about the *Sturm und Drang* movement. Through the influence of Goethe, Herder received an appointment as a government councilor at Weimar in 1776. There he published a series of works on philosophy, including the unfinished *Ideen zur Philosophie der Geschichte der Menschheit* (1784–91), a work strongly influenced by his association with Goethe.

A combination of factors, including differences of opinion over the French Revolution as well as Herder's probable inability to tolerate the continued presence of a gifted contemporary, led to an estrangement between Herder and Goethe, and to Herder's strong and often bitter opposition to the classical movement in German poetry and philosophy. His later works, particularly his *Briefe zur Beforderung der Humanitat* (1794–97), argue that poetry has a didactic purpose—a point of view that contradicts his earlier belief in the autonomy of art—and in his last writings he attacks the philosophy of Kant. Herder died at Weimar on December 18, 1803.

ON THE ORIGIN OF LANGUAGE

Section I

While still an animal, man already has language. All violent sensations of his body, and among the violent the most violent, those which cause him pain, and all strong passions of his soul express themselves directly in screams, in sounds, in wild inarticulate tones. A suffering animal, no less than the hero Philoctetus, will whine, will moan when pain befalls it, even though it be abandoned on a desert island, without sight or trace or hope of a helpful fellow creature. It is as though it could breathe more freely as it vents its burning, frightened spirit. It is as though it could sigh out part of its pain and at least draw in from the empty air space new strength of endurance as it fills the unhearing winds with its moans. So little did nature create us as severed blocks of rock, as egotistic monads! Even the most delicate chords of animal feeling—I must use this image because I know none better for the mechanics of sentient bodies—even the chords whose sound and strain do not arise from choice and slow deliberation, whose very nature the probing of reason has not as yet been able to fathom, even they—though there be no awareness of sympathy from outside—are aligned in their entire performance for a going out toward other creatures. The plucked chord performs its natural duty: it sounds! It calls for an echo from one that feels alike, even if none is there, even if it does not hope or expect that such another might answer.

Should physiology ever progress to a point where it can demonstrate psychology—which I greatly doubt—it would derive many a ray of light for this phenomenon, though it might also divide it in individual, excessively small, and obtuse filaments. Let us accept it at present as a whole, as a shining law of nature: "Here is a sentient being which can enclose within itself none of its vivid sensations; which must, in the very first moment of surprise, utter each one aloud, apart from all choice and purpose." It was, as it were, the last motherly touch of the formative hand of nature that it gave to all, to take out into the world, the law, "Feel not for yourself alone. But rather: your feeling resound!" And since this last creative touch was, for all of one species, of one kind, this law became a blessing: "The sound of your feeling be of one kind to your species and be thus perceived by all in compassion as by one!" Do not now touch this weak, this sentient being. However lonesome and alone it may seem to be, however exposed to every hostile storm of the universe, yet is it not alone: It stands allied with all nature! Strung with delicate chords; but nature hid sounds in these chords which, when called forth and encouraged, can arouse other beings of equally delicate build, can communicate, as though along an invisible chain, to a distant heart a spark that makes it feel for this unseen being. These sighs, these sounds are language. There is, then, a language of feeling which is—underived—a law of nature.

That man has such a language, has it originally and in common with the animals, is nowadays evident, to be sure, more through certain remains than through full-fledged manifestations. But these remains, too, are incontrovertible. However much we may want to insist that our artful language has displaced the language of nature, that our civilized way of life and our social urbanity have dammed in, dried out, and channeled off the torrent and the ocean of our passions, the most violent moment of feeling—wherever, however rarely, it may occur—still time and again reclaims its right, sounding in its maternal language, without mediation, through accents. The surging storm of a passion, the sudden onslaught of joy or pleasure, pain or distress, which cut deep furrows into the soul, an overpowering feeling of revenge, despair, rage, horror, fright, and so forth, they all announce themselves, each differently after its kind. As many modes of sensitivity as are slumbering in our nature, so many tonal modes too.—And thus I note that the less human nature is akin to an animal species, the more the two differ in their nervous structures, the less shall we find the natural language of that animal species comprehensible to us. We, as animals of the earth, understand the animal of the earth better than the creature of the waters; and on the earth, the herd animal better than the creature of the forest; and among the herd animals, those best that stand closest to us. Though in the case of these latter, contact and custom too contribute their greater or lesser share. It is natural that the Arab, who is of one piece with his horse, understands it better than a man who mounts a horse for the first time—almost as well as Hector in the Iliad was able to speak with the ones that were his. The Arab in the desert, who sees no life about except his camel and perhaps a flight of erring birds, can more easily understand the camel's nature and imagine that he understands the cry of the birds than we in our dwellings. The son of the forest, the hunter, understands the voice of the hart, and the Lapp that of his reindeer—. But all that follows logically or is an exception. The rule remains that this language of nature is a group language for the members of each species among themselves. And thus man too has a language of nature all his own.

Now, to be sure, these tones are very simple, and when they are articulated and spelled out on paper as interjections, the most contrary sensations may have almost a single expression. A dull "ah!" is as much the sound of languid love as of sinking despair; the fiery "oh!" as much the outburst of sudden joy as of boiling rage, of rising awe as of surging commiseration. But are these sounds meant to be marked down on paper as interjections? The tear which moistens this lusterless and extinguished, this solace-starved eye—how moving is it not in the total picture of a face of sorrow. Take it by itself and it is a cold drop of water. Place it under the microscope, and—I do not care to learn what it may be there. This weary breath—half a sigh—which dies away so movingly on pain-distorted lips, isolate it from its living helpmeets, and it is an empty draft of air. Can it be otherwise with the sounds of feeling? In their living contexts, in the total picture of pulsating nature, accompanied by so many other phenomena, they are moving and sufficient unto themselves. Severed from everything else, torn away, deprived of their life, they are, to be sure, no more than ciphers, and the voice of nature turns into an arbitrarily penciled symbol. Few in number are, it is true, the sounds of this language. But sentient nature, in so far as it suffers only mechanically, has likewise fewer chief varieties of feeling than our psychologies chalk up or invent as passions of the soul. But in that state every feeling is the more a mightily attracting bond, the less it is divided in separate threads. These sounds do not speak much, but what they speak is strong. Whether a plaintive sound bewails the wounds of the soul or of his body, whether it was fear or pain that forced out this scream, whether this soft "ah" clings to the bosom of the beloved in a kiss or in a tear—to establish all such distinctions was not the task of this language. It was to call attention to the picture as a whole. Leave it to that picture to speak for itself. That language was meant to sound, not to depict. Indeed, as the fable of Socrates has it, pain and pleasure touch. In feeling, nature shows its extremes interlinked, and what then can the language of feeling do but show such points of contact?—Now I may proceed with the application.

In all aboriginal languages, vestiges of these sounds of nature are still to be heard, though, to be sure, they are not the principal fiber of human speech. They are not the roots as such; they are the sap that enlivens the roots of language.

A refined, late-invented metaphysical language, a variant—perhaps four times removed—of the original wild mother of the human race, after thousands of years of variation again in its turn refined, civilized, and humanized for hundreds of years of its life: such a language, the child of reason and of society, cannot know much or anything of the childhood of its earliest forebear. But the old, the wild languages, the nearer they are to their origin, the more they retain of it. Here I cannot yet speak of a formation of language that might to any extent be regarded as human. I can only consider the raw materials going into it. Not a single word exists for me as yet, only the sounds fit for a word of feeling. But behold! in the languages I mentioned, in their interjections, in the roots of their nouns and verbs, how much has not been retained of these sounds! The oldest Oriental languages are full of exclamations for which we peoples of latter-day cultures have nothing but gaps or obtuse and deaf miscomprehension. In their elegies—as among the savages in their burial grounds—those howling and wailing tones resound that are a continuous interjection of the language of nature; in their psalms of praise, the shouts for joy and the recurrent hallelujahs, which Shaw explains from the mouths of lamenting women and which, with us, are so often solemn nonsense. In the flow and the rhythm of the poems and songs of other ancient peoples echoes the tone which still animates the dances of war and of religion, the songs of mourning and the songs of joy of all savages, whether they live at the foot of the Andes or in the snows of the Iroquois, in Brazil or on the Caribbean Islands. The roots of the simplest, most effective among their earliest verbs are, finally, those initial exclamations of nature, which came to be molded only at a later time; which explains why the languages of all the old and all the savage peoples are forever—in this inner living tone—outside the powers of enunciation of the foreign-born.

The explanation of most of these phenomena must wait for a later context. Here I note only this: One of the upholders of the divine origin of language[1] discerns and admires divine order in the fact that all the sounds of all the languages known to us can be reduced to some twenty odd letters. Unfortunately the fact is wrong, and the conclusion still wronger. There is no language whose living tones can be totally reduced to letters, let alone to twenty. All languages—one and all—bear witness to this fact. The modes of articulation of our speech organs are so numerous. Every sound can be pronounced in so many ways that for instance Lambert in the second part of his Organon has been able to demonstrate, and rightly so, how we have far fewer letters than sounds and how imprecise therefore the latter's expression by the former must needs remain. And that demonstration was done only for German—a language that has not even begun to accept into its written form the differences and multiplicity of tones of its dialects. What then, when the whole language is nothing but such a living dialect? What explains all the peculiarities, all of the idiosyncrasies of orthography if not the awkward difficulty of writing as one speaks? What living language can be learned in its tones from bookish letters? And hence what dead language can be called to life? The more alive a language is—the less one has thought of reducing it to letters, the more spontaneously it rises to the full unsorted sounds of nature—the less, too, is it writeable, the less writeable in twenty letters; and for outsiders, indeed, often quite unpronounceable.

Father Rasles, who spent ten years among the Abnaki in North America, complained bitterly that with the greatest care he would often not manage to repeat more than one half of a word and was laughed at. How much more laughable would it have been for him to spell out such an expression with his French letters? Father Chaumont, who spent fifty years among the Hurons and who took on the task of writing a grammar of their language, still complained about their guttural letters and their unpronounceable accents: "Often two words consisting entirely of the same letters had the most different meanings." Garcilaso de la Vega complained that the Spaniards distorted, mutilated, and falsified the Peruvian language in the sounds of its words, attributing to the Peruvians the most dreadful things in consequence of nothing but errors of rendition. De la Condamine says of a small nation living on the Amazon River: "Some of their words could not be written, not even most imperfectly. One would need at least nine or ten syllables where in their pronunciation they appear to utter hardly three." And la Loubere of the language of Siam: "Of ten words pronounced by a European, a native Siamese understands perhaps no single one, try as one may to express their language in our letters."

But why go to peoples in such remote corners of the world? What little we have left of savage peoples of Europe, the Estonians and the Lapps and their like have sounds which in many cases are just as half articulated and unwriteable as those of the Hurons and the Peruvians. The Russians and the Poles—however long their languages may have been written and molded by writing—still aspirate to such an extent that the true tone of their sounds cannot be depicted by letters. And the Englishman, how he struggles to write his sounds, and how little is one a speaking Englishman when one understands written English! The Frenchman, who draws up less from the throat, and that half Greek, the Italian, who speaks as it were in a higher region of the mouth, in a more refined ether, still retains a living tone. His sounds must remain within the organs where they are formed: As drawn characters they are—however convenient and uniform long usage in writing has made them— no more than mere shadows!

Thus the fact is wrong and the conclusion wronger: It does not lead to a divine but—quite on the contrary—to an animal origin. Take the so-called divine, the first language, Hebrew, of which the greater part of the world has inherited its letters: That in its beginnings it was so full of living sounds that it could be written only most imperfectly, is made quite evident by the entire structure of its grammar, its frequent confusion of similar letters, and especially the total lack of vowels in it. What explains this peculiarity that its letters are exclusively consonants and that precisely those elements of the words on which everything depends, the self-sounding vowels, were originally not written at all? This manner of writing is so contrary to the course of sound reason—of writing the nonessential and omitting the essential—that it would be incomprehensible to the grammarians, if the grammarians were accustomed to comprehend. With us, vowels are the first, the most vital things, the hinges of language, as it were. With the Hebrews, they are not written. Why? Because they could not be written. Their pronunciation was so alive and finely articulated, their breath so spiritual and etherlike that it evaporated and eluded containment in letters. It was only with the Greeks that these living aspirations were pinned down in formal vowels, though these still required a seconding by the spiritus signs and the like, whereas with the Orientals speech as it were was a continuous breath, nothing but spiritus, the spirit of the mouth—as they so often call it in their depictive poems. What the ear caught was the breath of God, was wafting air; and the dead characters they drew out were only the inanimate body which the act of reading had to animate with the spirit of life.

This is not the place to speak about the tremendous importance of such facts for an understanding of their language, but that this wafting reveals the origin of their language is evident. What is more unwriteable than the inarticulate sounds of nature? And if it is true that language is the more inarticulate the nearer it is to its origins, it follows—does it not?—that it was surely not invented by some superior being to fit the twenty-four letters which were invented together with it, that these letters were a much later and only imperfect attempt to provide memory with a few markers, and that language did not arise from the letters of a grammar of God but from the untutored sounds of free organs.[2] Otherwise it would be strange that precisely the letters from which and for which God invented language, by means of which He taught language to the earliest of men, are the most imperfect in the world, that they reveal nothing of the spirit of language but admit through their entire structure that they are not trying to reveal anything of it.

Judged by its worth, this hypothesis of letters would merit no more than a hint, but because of its ubiquity and the numerous attempts to cover up its shortcomings I had to unmask its baselessness and simultaneously show therein a peculiarity for which I for one know no explanation. . . .

Section III

The focal point has been found where Prometheus' divine spark ignites in the human soul—with the first characteristic mark there was language. But what were the first characteristic marks to serve as elements of language?

Sounds

Cheselden's blind man[3] shows how slowly the sense of vision evolves, how difficult it is for the soul to establish the concepts of space, of form, and of color, and how many trials are needed and what geometric art must be acquired in order to use these characteristic marks with clarity. That therefore was not the most appropriate of the senses to be used in language. Furthermore, its phenomena were so cold and mute while the sensations received by the coarser senses were so indistinct and so intermingled that, by the very nature of things, it was either nothing or the ear that had to become the first teacher of language.

There is for instance the sheep. As an image it looms before the eye with all things and images and colors on a great canvas of nature. How much is there and how difficult to distinguish! All the characteristic marks are finely interwoven, placed together, and all still ineffable! Who can speak shapes? Who can sound colors? Let him take the sheep under his probing hand. This sensation is more secure and fuller, but it is so full and so obscure, with one thing within the other. Who can say what he is thus feeling? But listen! The sheep bleats! Now one distinguishing mark separates by itself from the canvas of the colors wherein so little was to be distinguished. One distinguishing mark has penetrated deeply and clearly into the soul. "Oh," says the learning beginner, like Cheselden's blind man when given the power of sight, "now I shall know you again—you bleat!" The dove coos, the dog barks! Three words have arisen because he tried three distinct ideas. The latter go into his logic as the former into his vocabulary. Reason and language together took a timid step and nature came to meet them halfway—through the power of hearing. Nature did not merely ring out the characteristic mark, it rang it in, deep into the soul. There was a sound, the soul grasped for it, and there it had a ringing word.

So man is a listening, a noting creature, naturally formed for language, and even a blind and a mute man—we understand—would have to invent language if he is not without feeling and is not deaf. Place him at ease and in comfort on a deserted island: Nature will reveal itself to him through the ear. A thousand creatures that he cannot see will still appear to speak to him, and though his mouth and his eye remain closed forever, his soul is not wholly without language. When the leaves of the tree rustle refreshing coolness down upon the poor man in his solitude, when the passing waters of the murmuring brook rock him to sleep, when the whispering west wind fans his burning cheeks—the bleating sheep gives him milk, the flowing brook water, the rustling tree fruit—enough of interest for him to *know* the beneficent beings; enough of urgency, without eyes and without speech, for him to *name* them in his soul. The tree will be called the rustler, the west wind the fanner, the brook the murmurer—and there, all finished and ready, is a little dictionary, waiting for the imprint of the speech organs. But how poor and how strange would the conceptions be which this mutilated individual could associate with such sounds![4]

But now grant man the freedom of all his senses: let him see and touch and feel simultaneously all the beings which speak into his ear—Heavens! What a lecture hall of ideas and of language! Do not bother to bring down from the clouds a Mercury or Apollo as operatic *Dei ex machina*.—The entire, multisonant, divine nature is man's teacher of language and man's muse. Past him it leads a procession of all creatures: Each one has its name on its tongue and introduces itself to this concealed yet visible god as a vassal and servant. It delivers to him its distinguishing word to be entered, like a tribute, into the book of his dominion so that he may, by virtue of its name, remember it, call it in future, and enjoy it. I ask if ever this truth—the truth that "the very power of reason by which man rules over nature was the father of the living language which he abstracted from the tones of sounding beings as characteristic marks of differentiation"—I ask whether in the style of the Orient this sober truth could ever be expressed more nobly and more beautifully than in the words, "And God brought the animals unto the man to see what he would call them; and whatsoever the man called every living creature, that was the name thereof." Where, in the poetic manner of the Orient, could there be a more definite statement that man invented language for himself—from the tones of living nature—as characteristic marks of his ruling reason!—And that is what I prove.

If an angel or a heavenly spirit had invented language, how could its entire structure fail to bear the imprint of the manner of thinking of that spirit, for through what could I know the picture of an angel in a painting if not through its angelic and supernatural features? But where does the like occur in our language? Structure and design and even the earliest cornerstone of this palace reveals humanity!

In what language are celestial and spiritual concepts the first? Those concepts which, according to the principles of our thinking mind, too, ought to be the first—subjects, *notiones communes*, the germinal seeds of our cognition, the centers about which everything revolves and to which everything leads back—are these living centers to be found as elements of language? It would appear natural that the subjects should have preceded the predicates, that the simplest subjects should have preceded the composed ones, the thing that acts and does the acts and doings of it, essentials and certainties the uncertain and accidental. How much more could one not conclude in this manner, yet—in our original language it is clearly the very opposite that holds true. A hearing, a listening creature is evident, but no celestial spirit, for—

Sounding verbs are the first elements of power. Sounding verbs? Actions and nothing as yet that acts? Predicates and no subject as yet? The celestial genius would have to blush for it but not the sensuous human being, for what—as we have seen—could move this being more profoundly than those sounding actions? And what else, after all, is the entire structure of language but a manner of growth of his spirit, a history of his discoveries? The divine origin explains nothing and allows nothing to be explained from it. It is—as Bacon said of another thing—a holy vestal, dedicated to the gods but infertile, pious but of no use!

The first vocabulary was thus collected from the sounds of the world. From every sounding being echoed its name: The human soul impressed upon it its image, thought of it as a distinguishing mark.—How could it be otherwise than that these sounding interjections came first? And so, for example, the Oriental languages are full of verbs as basic roots of the language. The thought of the thing itself was still hovering between the actor and the action: The sound had to designate the thing as the things gave forth the sound. From the verbs it was that the nouns grew and not from the nouns the verbs. The child names the sheep, not as a sheep, but as a bleating creature, and hence makes of the interjection a verb. In the gradual progress of human sensuousness, this state of affairs is explicable; but not in the logic of a higher spirit.

All the old unpolished languages are replete with this origin, and in a philosophical dictionary of the Orientals every stem word with its family—rightly placed and soundly evolved—would be a chart of the progress of the human spirit, a history of its development, and a complete dictionary of that kind would be a most remarkable sample of the inventive skill of the human soul. Also of God's method of language and of teaching? I doubt it!

Since all of nature sounds, nothing is more natural to a sensuous human being than to think that it lives, that it speaks, that it acts. That savage saw the tall tree with its mighty crown and sensed the wonder of it: the crown rustled! There the godhead moves and stirs! The savage falls down in adoration! Behold, that is the story of sensuous man, the dark link by which nouns are fashioned from verbs—and a faint move toward abstraction! With the savages of North America, for instance, everything is still animated: Every object has it genius, its spirit, and that the same held true with the Greeks and Orientals is attested by their oldest vocabulary and grammar. They are what all of nature was to their inventor: a pantheon, a realm of animated, of acting beings!

But as man referred everything to himself, as everything appeared to speak to him and indeed acted for or against him; as he thus engaged himself with or against it, as he loved or hated and conceived of everything in human terms—all these traces of humanity appear impressed in the first names! They, too, spoke love or hatred, curse or blessing, tenderness or adversity, and in particular there arose from this feeling, in many languages, the articles!

Everything was personified in human terms, as woman and man. Everywhere gods, goddesses, acting beings of evil or of good. The howling storm and the sweet zephyr, the clear source and the mighty ocean—their entire mythology lies in the treasure trove, the verbs and nouns of the old languages, and the oldest dictionary was thus a sounding pantheon, an assembly of both sexes, as was nature to the senses of the first inventor. Here the language of an old unpolished nation appears as a study in the aberrations of human fantasy and passion as does its mythology. Every family of words is a tangled underbrush around a sensuous central idea, around a sacred oak, still bearing traces of the impression received by the inventor from this dryad. Feelings are interwoven in it: What moves is alive; what sounds speaks; and since it sounds for or against you, it is friend or foe: god or goddess, acting from passion as are you!

What I love in this manner of thinking is the humanity of it, the sensuous being in it: Everywhere I see the weak, timid, sensitive being who must love or hate, trust or fear and longs to spread over all existence these sensations in his heart. I see everywhere the weak yet mighty being that is in need of the entire universe and involves everything in war or peace with itself; that depends on everything and yet rules over everything. The poetry and the attribution of sex through language are thus an interest of mankind, and the genitals of speech are, as it were, the means of its propagation. But what, if some higher genius had brought it down from the stars? How would that be? Was this genius from among the stars involved on our earth under the moon in such passions of love and weakness, of hate and fear that he entwined everything in affection and hate, that he imbued all words with fear and joy, that in fine he built everything on acts of copulation? Did he so see and feel as a man sees and feels that the nouns, to him, had to join in the sex and gender, that he brought together the verbs in action and suffering, that he ascribed to them so many true and promiscuous children, in short, that he built all of language on the feeling of human weaknesses? Did he thus see and feel?

To an upholder of the supernatural origin of language it is a matter of divine order "that most stem words are monosyllabic, that the verbs are mostly bisyllabic, and that language is thus divided according to criteria of memory."[5] The fact is not accurate and the conclusion is uncertain. In the remains of the language considered to be the oldest, the roots are all bisyllabic verbs, a fact I can well explain on the basis of the foregoing, while the opposite hypothesis finds no reason for it. Those verbs are built directly on the tones and interjections of sounding nature. They often continue to echo in them, and here and there they are preserved as interjections. Mostly, to be sure, being half-inarticulate sounds, they were bound to be lost as the formation of language progressed. The first attempts of the stammering tongue are thus lacking in the Oriental languages, but the very fact that they are lacking and that only their regularized remnants echo in the verbs, bears witness to the originality and—humanity of language. Are these stems treasures and abstractions from the reason of God, or are they the first sounds of the listening ear, the first tones of the stammering tongue? The human race in its childhood formed language for itself precisely as it is stammered by the immature: it is the babbling vocabulary of the nursery. Where does it survive in the mouth of the adult?

What was said by so many of the Ancients, what in modern times has so often been repeated without understanding, derives from this its living reality: "That poetry is older than prose!" For what was this first language of ours other than a collection of elements of poetry? Imitation it was of sounding, acting, stirring nature! Taken from the interjections of all beings and animated by the interjections of human emotion! The natural language of all beings fashioned by reason into sounds, into images of action, passion, and living impact! A dictionary of the soul that was simultaneously mythology and a marvelous epic of the actions and the speech of all beings! Thus a continuous fabulation with passion and interest!—What else is poetry?

And then: The tradition of Antiquity says that the first language of the human race was song, and many good musical people have hence imagined that man may well have learned that song from the birds.—That indeed is imagining a great deal! A great ponderous clock with all its sharp wheels and newly tensed springs and hundred-pound weights can well produce a carillon of tones; but to put down newly created man with his active mainsprings, with his needs, with his strong emotions, with his almost blindly preoccupied attention, and finally with his brute throat, and to have him ape the nightingale and derive language from singing after it—no matter how many histories of music and poetry say so—is more than I can understand. To be sure, a language through musical tones would be possible—as Leibnitz,[6] too, has thought of it—but for our earliest forebears, still in the state of nature, this language was not possible. It is too artful and refined. In the procession of beings each has its own voice and a language after its own voice. The language of love in the nest of the nightingale is sweet song; in the cave of the lion it is a roar; in the forest it is the troating of the buck deer and in the hiding place of cats a caterwaul. Every species speaks its own language of love, not for man, but for itself, a language as pleasant to itself as was Petrarch's song to his Laura. As little, then, as the nightingale sings—as some imagine—to entertain man, so little can man ever be minded to invent for himself a language by trilling the trills of the nightingale. And what a monstrosity: A human nightingale in a cave or out in the forest with the hunt!

If then the first language of man was song, it was song as natural to him, as commensurate with his organs and his natural drives as the nightingale's song is to the nightingale which is, as it were, a winged lung; and that was— that was precisely our sounding language. Here, Condillac, Rousseau, and others did halfway find the road in that they derived the prosody and the song of the oldest languages from outcries of emotion, and there can be no doubt that emotion did indeed animate and elevate the first tones. But as mere tones of emotion could never be the origin of human language (which, after all, was what this song was), something is still wanting to produce it, and that, once again, was the naming of every creature after its own language. There then all of nature sang and sounded its recital, and the song of man was a concert of all those voices as far as his reason had use for them, as far as his emotions grasped them, as far as his organs could express them.—It was song, but it was neither the song of the nightingale nor the musical language of Leibnitz, nor a mere screaming of animal emotion. It was an expression of the language of all creatures within the natural scale of the human voice!

Even when subsequently language became more regular, more unisonant, and more orderly, it still remained a kind of song, as the accents of so many savages attest. And that this song—eventually sublimated and refined—gave rise to the oldest poetry and music, has by now been proven by more than one. The philosophical Englishman,[7] who in our century took up this matter of the origin of poetry and music, would have been able to progress farthest if he had not excluded the spirit of language from his investigation and if, instead of concerning himself so much with his system of bringing poetry and music to a single focus (in which neither can show itself properly), he had concerned himself more with the origin of both from the full nature of man. In any event, since the best samples of the poetry of the Ancients are remnants from the times of the sung language, there are bound to be innumerable instances of misapprehension, of falsifications, and of misalignment and bad taste spelled out from the continuity of the oldest poems, of the tragedies of the Greeks, and of their declamation. How much remains to be said on this point for a philosopher who has learned, among the savages amongst whom that age is still alive, the right tone for reading those pieces! Otherwise and commonly one see nothing but the texture of the wrong side of a tapestry! *Disiecti membra poetae!*—But I might go endlessly afield if I were to allow myself to make individual linguistic comments. So back to the high road of the invention of language! . . .

If now at this point I could gather up all the loose ends and make at once visible the woven texture called human nature—in all its parts a texture for language! For that, we have seen, space and sphere were assigned to this positive power of thought: for that its substance and its matter were meted out; for that its shape and its form were created; for that its senses organized and aligned—for language! That is why man thinks neither more brightly nor more darkly; why he sees not and feels not more keenly, more lastingly, more vividly; why he has these and not more and not other senses. All things are balanced against one another. In economy and substitution! Laid out and distributed with a purpose! Unity and coherence! Proportion and order! A whole! A system! A creature of reflection and language, of the power to reflect and to create language! If anyone, after all these observations, were still ready to deny man's being destined to be a creature of language, he first would have to turn from being an observer of nature into being its destroyer! Would have to break into dissonance all the harmonies shown; lay waste the whole splendid structure of human forces, corrupt his sensuousness, and sense instead of nature's masterpiece a creature full of wants and lacunae, full of weaknesses and convulsions! And if now, on the other hand, language is precisely as it arose of necessity and in accordance with the plan and the might of the creature described?

I shall proceed to prove this last point, although I might take this occasion for a most pleasant excursus and calculate according to the rules of Sulzer's theory of pleasure what advantages and conveniences a language through the sense of hearing has for us in comparison with the language of the other senses.—But the excursus would take me too far afield and I must forsake it, while the main road still needs to be secured and rectified.—So then firstly

I. "The older and the more original languages are, the more is this analogy of the senses noticeable in their roots."

Where with later languages we characterize wrath in its roots as a phenomenon of the face or as an abstract concept—for instance through the sparkle of the eyes or a glowing of the cheeks and the like—and hence merely see or think it, the Oriental hears it, hears it roar, hears it burst out in burning smoke and storming sparks! That became the stem of the word: the nostrils the seat of wrath; the whole family of words and metaphors of wrath snort out their origin.

If to us life manifests itself through the pulse beat, through surging blood and delicate marks of characterization also in language, to him it revealed itself through audible breathing. Man lived while he respired; he died as he expired. And the root of the word could be heart as the first animated Adam was heard to respire.

While we characterize child-bearing in our way, he again hears in the corresponding designations the screams of the frightened mother or again in animals the emptying of the amniotic sac. All his images revolve about this central idea.

Where in the word dawn we faintly hear an element of beauty, brilliance, and freshness, a lingering wanderer in the Orient feels in the very root of the word the first quick delightful ray of light which the like of us has never seen or at least has never felt with full feeling.—Examples from old and unsophisticated languages, showing how warmly and with what strong emotion they characterize from hearing and feeling, are numberless. And a work of the kind that would thoroughly trace the basic feeling of such ideas in various peoples, would be a full demonstration of my postulate and of the human invention of language.

II. "The older and the more original languages are, the more the feelings intertwine in the roots of the words!"

Open at random an Oriental dictionary, and you will see the urge to express! How these inventors tore ideas away from one feeling to use them in the expression of another! How they did this borrowing most extensively from the heaviest, coldest, keenest senses! How everything had to turn into feeling and sound before it could turn into expression! Hence those powerful bold metaphors in the roots of the words! Hence the transpositions from feeling to feeling until the significations of a stem word, and still more of its branches seen side by side, form a most colorful, motley array. The genetic cause of this lies in the poverty of the human soul and in the convergence of all sensations in the unrefined individual. We see clearly his need to express himself: We see it the more, the more remote the idea was from the feeling and the tone of sensation, so that it is no longer possible to doubt the human origin of language. For how would the protagonists of another genesis explain this intertwining of ideas in the roots of the words? Was God so lacking in ideas and words that he had to have recourse to that kind of confusing word usage? Or was he so enamored of hyperbole, of far-fetched metaphors that he impressed this spirit upon the very roots of his language?

The so-called language of God, Hebrew, is totally imbued with such boldnesses, and rightly does the Orient claim the honor of designating it with its name. But beware of calling this spirit of metaphors Asian, as though it were not to be found anywhere else! It is alive in all unpolished languages, though, to be sure, according to the degree of each nation's culture and the specific character of its way of thinking. A people not wont to subject its feelings to thorough and keen differentiation, a people not endowed with the ardor to express itself and to take hold with sovereign unconcern of expressions wherever they might be found—such a people will not worry much about fine shades of feeling and will make do with slow-paced half-expressions. A fiery people reveals its boldness in its metaphors, whether it inhabits the Orient or North America. But where in the deepest depths such transplantations are to be found in the greatest numbers, there the language was by far the least endowed, was the oldest and most original, and that—without doubt—takes us to the Orient.

It is apparent what a difficult undertaking a true etymological survey would be in such a language. Those varied significations of one root that are to be traced and reduced to their origin in its genealogical tree are interrelated by no more than vague feelings, transient side associations, and perceptional echoes which arise from the depth of the soul and can hardly be covered by rules. Furthermore, their interrelations are so specifically national, so much in conformity with the manner of thinking and seeing of the people, of the inventor, in a particular country, in a particular time, under particular circumstances, that it is exceedingly difficult for a Northerner and Westerner to strike them right and that they must suffer greatly in long-winded and cold-hearted circumlocutions. And since they were demanded by necessity and invented in a state of feeling and arousal to satisfy an expressive want— what rare good luck would not be needed to strike the very same note? And since finally in a dictionary of this kind the words and the significations of a word are to be gathered from such diverse times, occasions, and ways of thinking, and since thus these momentary determinations appear infinitely augmented—how then is not the difficulty multiplied! What keen insight is needed to penetrate into those circumstances and into those requirements and what moderation to avoid all excess in the interpretation of various times! How much knowledge, how much adaptability of mind is not needed to acquire fully the native wit, the bold imagination, the national feelings of such remote ages, and to modernize them in accordance with ours! Yet the venture would not simply elucidate the history, the forms of thought, and the literature of a particular country, it would quite universally carry a torch to the dark recesses of the human soul where concepts commingle and intertwine, where the most diverse feelings engender one another, where an urgent occasion musters all forces of the soul, revealing the whole range of inventive powers with which it is endowed. Every step in that endeavor would mark a discovery and every new observation would represent the most complete proof of the human origin of language.

Schultens has the great merit of having elaborated a number of such origins in the Hebrew language. And each of his elaborations provides proof of my thesis. But for a variety of reasons, I do not believe that the origins of the first human language, even though it were Hebrew, can ever be completely elaborated.

I must still argue out a note which is too general and too important to be omitted. The basis and the cause of such bold verbal metaphors lay in their original invention. But what when much later, with the need long since satisfied, such species of words and of imagery survive or, indeed, are extended and increased in sheer imitation or for the love of things past? Then, oh yes, then the product turns out to be sublime nonsense, a turgid play with words which, in the beginning, it most certainly was not. In the beginning it was bold and virile acuity, which doubtless was the least intent upon playing where it seemed the most to play. It was unschooled sublimity of imagination that worked out such feelings in such words. But now, as used by stale imitators without such feeling and without such occasion, alas, they are vials of words which the spirit has left; and that, in later times, has been the fate of all the languages in which the first forms were so bold. French writers of later times cannot lose themselves in the clouds because the first inventors of their language did not lose themselves in the clouds. Their entire language is prose of sound reason and has, by origin, almost no poetic word, almost none that would be peculiar to the poet. But the Orientals? The Greeks? The British? And we Germans?

From this it follows that, the older a language and the more such boldnesses in its roots—if it has lived a long time and has evolved a long time—the less is it permissible to jump at every original boldness as though each one of all those mutually intertwined concepts were always consciously present in every later application. The metaphor of the beginning was the urge to speak. If later, when the word is current and its keenness blunted, the combination of such disparities is regarded as proof of fertility and energy—what miserable specimens are not then spawned in whole schools in the Oriental languages!

And one more thing. If now such bold verbal labors, such transpositions of feelings into a term, such ruleless and lineless meshings of ideas appear as the basis, or are made to be the basis, on which the refined concepts of a dogma or a system are to be tacked or in which such concepts are to be studied—heavens! how little were these verbal trials of a nascent or immature language definitions of a system and how often is one led to create word idols of which the inventor and subsequent usage knew nothing!—But such comments could go on forever. I proceed with another canon.

III. "The more original a language and the more frequently such feelings appear intertwined in it, the less is it possible for them to be subordinated to one another with precision and logic. Language is rich in synonyms. With all its inadequacies in essentials, it has the greatest unnecessary abundance."

The upholders of the divine origin, who manage to discover divine order in everything, are hard put to it to find it here, and they deny that there are synonyms.[8] They deny? Well now, let it be assumed that among the fifty words which the Arabs have for the lion, among the two hundred which they have for the snake, or the eighty for honey and the more than a thousand which they have for the sword, nice differences can be found, that is, were once present and have since vanished—why if they had to vanish were they present? Why did God invent an unnecessary wealth of words which, as the Arabs claim, only a divine prophet could grasp in its entire range? Was he inventing into a vacuum of oblivion? Relatively speaking, these words are still synonyms, considering the numerous other ideas for which words are totally missing. Now trace, if you can, divine order in the fact that a god, who saw the plan of language as a whole, invented seventy words for the stone and none for all the indispensable ideas, innermost feelings, and abstractions, that in one case he drowned us in unnecessary abundance while leaving us in the other in the direst need which obliged us to steal and usurp metaphors and talk half nonsense, etc.

In human terms the thing is easily explained. While difficult and rare ideas had to be expressed indirectly, those that were at hand and easy could find frequent expression. The more unfamiliar man was with nature, that is, the more numerous the angles under which in his inexperience he looked at it, hardly able to recognize it again, and the less he invented *a priori* but instead in accordance with sensuous circumstances, the more synonyms had to arise! The more numerous the individuals who did the inventing and the more they did so roaming by themselves and in isolation, inventing in general terms only within their own circle for identical things; when later on they foregathered, when their languages streamed out into an ocean of vocabulary, the more synonyms there were. None could be rejected, for which should have been? They were in use with this tribe, this clan, this singer. And so, as the Arab compiler of a dictionary put it when he had enumerated four hundred words for misery, it was a four hundred first misery to be obliged to list the words for misery. Such a language is rich because it is poor, because its inventors did not have plan enough to grow poor. And we are to believe that the idle inventor of such an outstandingly imperfect language was God?

The analogies of all languages still in the state of nature confirm my thesis: Each in its own way is both lavish and lacking, but, to be sure, each in its own way. If the Arabs have so many words for stone, camel, sword, snake (things amongst which they live), the language of Ceylon, in accordance with the inclination of its people, is rich in flatteries, titles, and verbal décor. For the term "woman" it has, according to rank and class, twelve different names, while we discourteous Germans, for example, are forced in this to borrow from our neighbors. According to class, rank, and number, you is rendered in sixteen different ways, and this as well in the language of the journeyman as in that of the courtier. Profusion is the style of the language. In Siam there are eight different ways of saying I and we, depending on whether the master speaks to the servant or the servant to the master. The language of the savage Caribs is virtually divided in two, one for women and one for men, and the most common objects—bed, moon, sun, bow—are named differently in the two. What a superfluity of synonyms! And yet these same Caribs have only four words for colors, to which they must refer all others. What paucity!—The Hurons have consistently double verbs for animate and inanimate things, so that to see, when it is "to see a stone" and to see, when it is "to see a man" are two different terms. Pursue this through all of nature. What wealth! To make use of a thing one owns or to make use of a thing owned by him to whom one is speaking is always expressed by two different words. What wealth!—In the main language of Peru, blood relations are termed in such remarkable segmentation that the sister of the brother and the sister of the sister, the child of the father and the child of the mother have quite different designations, and yet this same language has not really a plural.—Each one of these synonymies is linked to custom, character, and origin of the people; and everywhere the inventive human spirit reveals itself.—Still another canon:

IV. "As the human soul can recall no abstraction from the realm of the spirits to which it did not advance through opportunities and arousals of the senses, so no language has an abstract term to which it was not led through tone and feeling. And the more original a language, the fewer its abstractions and the more numerous its feelings." Once again, I can in this limitless field do no more than gather flowers:

The entire structure of the Oriental languages bears witness to the fact that all their abstracts were once sensates. Spirit was wind, breath, nocturnal storm. Sacred was called set-off, solitudinous. The soul was called breathing, wrath the snorting of the nose, etc. The more general concepts were thus evolved in them only later on through abstraction, perception, fantasy, simile, analogy, etc.—None lies in the deepest depths of language.

Among all savages the same holds true according to their level of culture. In the language of Barantola no word for sacred and among the Hottentots no word for spirit could be found. All missionaries throughout the world complain about the difficulty of communicating Christian concepts to the natives, in the language of the natives; and yet such communications are doubtless not concerned with scholastic dogma but only with common concepts of common reason. As one reads here and there translated specimens of versions made for natives or even for speakers of the unpolished languages of Europe—such as the languages of the Lapps, the Finns, the Esthonians— and compares the grammars and dictionaries of such peoples, the difficulties are plain to see.

And if one prefers not to believe the missionaries, then one can read the philosophers, de la Condamine in Peru and along the Amazon, Maupertuis in Lapland, etc. Time, duration, space, essence, substance, body, virtue, justice, freedom, appreciation are not to be heard from the mouths of the Peruvians, even though they show by their manner of reasoning that they conclude according to such concepts and by their actions that they possess such virtues.

As long as an idea has not become clear to them, has not been used by them as a distinguishing mark, they have no corresponding word.

Wherever such words have entered the language, they clearly show their origin. The Church language of the Russian nation is primarily Greek. The Christian concepts of the Letts are German words or German concepts Lettified. The Mexican wishing to express his idea of a poor sinner depicts him as a person kneeling in auricular confession and his trinity as three faces with halos. We all know by what pathways most abstractions came into our languages of science, of theology, and jurisprudence, of philosophy and the like. We all know how often scholasticists and polemicists were unable to carry out their fights with words of their own language and therefore had to go and borrow their weapons (hypostasis and substance, homoousios and homoiousios) from those languages in which the concepts had been abstracted, in which the weapons had been tempered! Our entire psychology, however refined and defined it may be, has not a single word of its own.

This is so true that even the illuminati in their frenzy do not find it possible to characterize their new secrets from nature or heaven and hell by means other than imagery and sensuous conceptions. Swedenborg, in piecing together his angels and spirits, could not but use snippets from all the senses, and the sublime Klopstock, the greatest antithesis of the former, could not but build his heaven and hell from sensuous materials. The Negro scents the presence of his gods from the treetops, the Chinghailese finds his devil by hearing him in the rustling of the forests. I have stalked some of these abstractions in various languages among various peoples and have found the most remarkable inventive tricks of the human mind. The subject is much too vast. The base, however, is always the same. When the savage surmises that this particular thing has a spirit, then a particular sensuous thing must exist from which he can abstract that spirit. Though, to be sure, abstraction has diverse varieties, stages, and methods. The simplest example to show that no nation has in its language more words and words other than it has learned to abstract is to be seen in the no doubt easy abstraction of the numerals. How few do most savages possess, no matter how rich, how excellent, and elaborate their languages may be. Never more than their needs call for. The trading Phoenican was the first to invent the art of numeration. The herdsman checking his herd learns naturally how to count. Nations of hunters, never involved in concerns of multiple numbers, know how to describe an army only as being like the hair on the head. Who can count hair? Who, without ever having counted that far, has words to do so?

Is it possible to look away from all these traces of the roaming, language-making spirit, and to seek the origin of language in the clouds? What proof is there of the existence of a single word which only God could invent? Is there in any language anywhere a single, pure and universal concept that was handed down to man from Heaven? Where is even the possibility for such a concept?[9]—But a hundred thousand reasons and analogies and proofs of the genesis of language in the human soul, in accordance with human senses, human ways of perception! Proofs of the advance of language with reason, of its development from reason among all peoples, in all zones, under all conditions! What ear can fail to hear this universal voice of nations?

And yet I see with amazement that once again Herr Süssmilch comes to meet me, discovering divine order where I see the most human.[10] "That so far no language has been discovered that was totally unfit for the arts and the sciences," what else does this prove but that no language is bestial and that all languages are human? Where has a human being been found quite unfit for the arts and the sciences? And was that cause for wonder or was it the most ordinary thing because he was a human being? "All missionaries have been able to talk to the most savage peoples and have been able to convince them. That could not be done without conclusions and without arguments. Hence their languages had to contain abstract terms, etc." And if so, was it divine order? Or was it not simply a most human thing to produce terms by abstraction where they were needed? And what people has ever had a single abstraction in its language that was not acquired by that people itself? And were there equal numbers of them for all peoples? Did missionaries find it everywhere equally easy to express themselves or have we not read the opposite from all parts of the world? And how did they express themselves other than by molding their new concepts by analogy to the contours of the language before them? And was this done everywhere in the same way?— Much, very much could be said about the fact as such! The conclusion states the very opposite of what it has been made out to be. Precisely because human reason cannot be without abstraction and because no abstraction can be performed without language, it follows that in every people language must of necessity contain abstractions, that is, must of necessity be a copy of the power of reason by which it was used as a tool. But as each language contains only as many abstractions as its speakers were able to make and none that was made without senses (as is apparent from their originally sensuous expression), divine order is nowhere to be seen, except—except in so far as language in all its aspects is human.

V. Finally: "Since every grammar is only a philosophy of language and a method for its use, it follows that, the more primordial a language is, the less grammar must there be in it, and the oldest language is no more than the aforementioned dictionary of nature." I outline a few striking illustrations.

1. Declensions and conjugations are merely shortcuts and identifications in the use of nouns and verbs according to number, tense, mode, and person. Therefore, the less refined a language is, the less regular is it in these determinations, reflecting at every turn the course of human reason. In fine, without the art of usage, it is a simple dictionary.

2. As the verbs of a language are earlier than the nouns roundly abstracted from them, so also were there originally the more conjugations the less numerous the concepts one had learned to place in subordination to one another. How numerous are those the Orientals have! And yet there are really none, for how numerous everywhere are not the transpositions and translocations of verbs from one conjugation to another! The thing is quite natural. Since nothing concerns man or, at least, since nothing affects him in terms of

language as deeply as what he is about to relate, deeds and acts and events, there must be gathered together, in the beginning, such a mass of deeds and events that a new verb arises for almost every state. "In the language of the Hurons everything is conjugated. An art which cannot be explained permits in it the distinction of verbs, nouns, pronouns, and adjectives. The simple verbs have a double conjugation, one for themselves and one relating to other things. The third persons have forms for the two sexes. As for the tenses, the same nice distinctions exist that are to be noted for instance in Greek. Indeed, in relating a journey, the expression differs depending on whether it was by land or by water. The active forms are multiplied as often as there are things to be covered by the doing. The term for to eat changes from one edible substance to another. Acts performed by an animate being are expressed differently from those done by an inanimate thing. Making use of one's own property and of that of the person with whom one speaks has two forms of expression, etc."

Imagine this multiplicity of verbs, modes, tenses, persons, states, genders, etc.—What trouble and what art to keep all that somehow straightened out, to evolve somehow a grammar from what was no more than a vocabulary!—The grammar of Father Leri of the Topinambuans in Brazil shows just that.—For as the first vocabulary of the human soul was a living epic of sounding and acting nature, so the first grammar was almost nothing but a philosophical attempt to develop that epic into a more regularized history. Thus it works itself down with verbs and more verbs and keeps working in a chaos which is inexhaustible for poetry, which is very rich—when subjected to a little more order—for the fixing of history, and which becomes usable only much later for axioms and demonstrations.

3. The word which in imitation followed directly upon a sound of nature followed a thing that was past. Preterits are therefore the roots of verbs, but these are preterits which are still almost valid for the present. This fact must, *a priori,* seem strange and inexplicable, since the present time ought to be the first, as indeed it came to be in all languages of later development. According to the history of the invention of language it could not be otherwise. The present is something one shows; the past is something one must relate. And since it could be related in so many ways, and since—in the beginning, in the need to find words—it had to be done in many ways, there came into being, in all the old languages, many preterits but only one present or none at all. This then, in more civilized ages, was greatly to the advantage of poetry and history but very little to that of philosophy, for philosophy has no love of confusingly rich supplies.—Here again the Hurons, the Brazilians, the Orientals, and the Greeks are alike: Everywhere traces of the development of the human mind.

4. All the more recent philosophical languages have modified the noun in greater refinement, the verb less so but more regularly, for these languages adapted themselves more and more to the needs of a detached contemplation of what is and in fact has been and ceased to be irregularly stammering mixtures of things that possibly were and perhaps persist. The habit arose to state one after the other the things that are and in fact have been and hence to define them through numbers and articles and cases, etc. The early

inventors wanted to say everything at once, not just what appeared to have been done but also who did it and when and how and where it happened.[11] They thus carried into the noun the state; into every form of the verb the gender; they distinguished—by pre- and adformatives, by affixes and suffixes—the verb and the adverb, the verb and the noun, and all things flowed together. But later there came to be more and more differentiation, more and more enumerations: From breaths evolved articles, from starting clicks persons, from prestatements modes or adverbs. The parts of speech separated. Gradually grammar evolved. Thus the art of speech, this philosophy of language, evolved but slowly and gradually down through the centuries and ages, and the mind that was the first to think of a true philosophy of grammar, of "the art of speech," must of necessity have begun by thinking over, down through the generations and down its stages, its history. If only we had such a history! It would be, with all its deviations and excursuses, a charter of the humanity of language.

5. But how was it possible for a language to exist entirely without grammar? As a mere confluence of images and sensations without coherence and definition?—Both were cared for: It was a living language. In it the great harmonizing power of gestures provided, as it were, the order and sphere where things belonged; and the great wealth of delimitations inherent in the vocabulary itself replaces the art of grammar. Consider the old script of the Mexicans! They drew whole sequences of individual pictures. And where no picture came to mind, they agreed on strokes, and the coherence of it all must be supplied by the world in which it belonged and from which it was being divined. This art of divination, of surmising coherence from detached signs, how far is it not still being mastered by individual mute and deaf persons! And if this art is an intrinsic part of the language, if it is learned, as language and with language, from childhood up, if through tradition in the succession of generations it becomes simplified and perfected, I see in it nothing incomprehensible.—But then, the more it becomes simplified, the more it declines; the more it turns into grammar—and that is the stepwise progression of the human mind.

Exemplifications of this are for instance the notes of la Loubere on the language of Siam. How much it still resembles the continuity of the Oriental languages, especially before a later development carried more structure into it. The Siamese who wants to say, "If I were in Siam, I would be pleased," says in fact, "If I be city Siam, I well heart much."—He wants to recite the Lord's Prayer and must say, "Father, us be Heaven. Name God want sacred all place, etc." How Oriental and how primordial! Quite as coherent as Mexican picture writing or the stammering of the unsophisticated in a foreign language.

6. There is still another peculiarity which I must explain here, and again one which I find to have been misunderstood in Süssmilch's divine order, namely "the multiplicity of significations of a single word in accordance with the differentiation of minor aspects of articulation." I find this skill among almost all the savages; Garcilaso de la Vega, for instance, notes it for the Peruvians, Condamine for the Brazilians, la Loubere for the Siamese, Resnel

for the North Americans. I find it likewise in the ancient languages, Chinese for instance, and the languages of the Orient, especially Hebrew, where a minor sound, accent, breath changes the whole meaning, and yet I find in this nothing I would not call very human, nothing but inadequacy and inertia of the inventors! They required a new word, and since leisurely invention from an empty head is difficult, they took a similar one with perhaps just a change of breath. This was a law of economy, quite natural to them with their pervading feelings, yet with their powerful enunciation of words, convenient. But for an outsider—whose ear is not accustomed to it from childhood on and who now gets something in that language hissed into his face, with half the sounds phlegmatically held back in the mouth—this law of economic expediency makes the language impossible to understand and to pronounce. The more a wholesome grammar makes for order in the household of a language, the less will such parsimony be necessary.—Hardly a hallmark of divine invention, that the inventor, for lack of ingenuity, had to fall back on such devices.

7. Most evident, finally, is the progress of language through reason and of reason through language when the latter has already taken some steps forward, when there are in it already works of art, such as poems, when a system of writing has been invented, when literary genres begin to evolve one after another. Then no step can be taken, no new word can be invented, no new felicitous form can be put to use which does not carry the imprint of the human soul. Then, through poetry, come into being syllabic meter, choice of expressive words and of colors, order and impact of imagery; then, through history, come differentiation of tenses, precision of expression; then, through oratory, comes finally the perfect rounding of periodic speech. If now, before the moment of such an addition, nothing like it lay in the language but was carried into it and could be carried into it by the human soul, where then would one set limits to this productivity, to this fertility? Where would one say: Here a human soul began to act but not before? If it proved able to invent the finest, the most difficult, why not the easiest? If it was able to accomplish, why was it not able to try, why not to begin? For what was the beginning other than the production of one single word, as a sign of reason? And this was for it an inescapable necessity, however blind and mute it was within, as truly as it was endowed with reason.

I believe that through the things I have said—proceeding, internally, from within the human soul and arguing, externally, on the basis of the organization of man and by the analogy of all languages and all peoples, partly in the component parts of all speech, partly with respect to the grandiose overall progress of language in correlation with reason—man's ability to invent language for himself has been demonstrated to such an extent that no one can doubt it for one moment if he does not deny man's reason or, which amounts to the same thing, if he but knows what reason is, if, furthermore, he has ever concerned himself philosophically with the elements of language and has, with the eyes of an observer, considered the nature and the history of the languages on earth. The genesis of language in the human soul is as conclusively evident as any philosophical demonstration could be, and the external analogy of all ages, languages, and peoples imparts to it as high a degree of probability as is possible with the most certain events in history.

NOTES

1. Süssmilch, *Beweis, dass der Ursprung der Menschlichen Sprache Göttlich sey* [*Proof that the Origin of the Language of Man Is Divine*], Berlin, 1766, p. 21.

2. The best book on this matter, which so far has not been worked out in all its parts, is Wachter's *Naturae et scripturae concordia* [*Concordance of Nature and Scripture*], Hafn. 1752, which differs from the dreams of Kircher and numerous others as a history of antiquity differs from fairy tales.

3. *Philosophical Transactions*, abridgment. Also in *Cheselden's Anatomy*, in Smith-Kästner's optics, in Buffon's natural history, in the encyclopedia, and in a dozen small French dictionaries under the key word "*aveugle.*"

4. Diderot in his entire letter *Sur les sourds et muets* [*On the Deaf and Mute*] hardly got around to discussing this central point, for he spent his time with inversions and a hundred other details.

5. Süssmilch, §8 [actually, §7, note].

6. *Oeuvres philosophiques*, publiées p. Raspe [*Philosophical Works*, ed. Raspe], p. 232.

7. Brown.

8. Süssmilch, §9.

9. The best treatise I have seen on this subject is by an Englishman: *Things divine & supernatural conceived by analogy with things natural and human*, London, 1755, by the author of *the procedure, extent and limits of human understanding.*

10. Süssmilch, §11.

11. Rousseau divined this postulate in his hypothesis. I define and prove it.

William Blake

1757–1827

William Blake, the son of a hosier, was born in London on November 28, 1757. As a small child he showed artistic talent and at the age of ten he was sent to a drawing school in the Strand; at fifteen he was apprenticed to an engraver. In 1779 he enrolled at the Royal Academy as an engraving student, but appears to have been at odds with the faculty. He later wrote of his contempt for Sir Joshua Reynolds and other Establishment figures. He was soon earning his living by producing engravings for publishers and by teaching drawing. In 1782 Blake married Catherine Boucher, the illiterate daughter of a poor shopkeeper; she remained a source of strength and support to him throughout his life.

Blake educated himself by reading widely not only in the history of art but also in literature. He began writing verses and songs as a youth, and he later reported having many visions, rich in biblical imagery. Blake's first collection of verse, *Poetical Sketches,* includes poems written between ages twelve and twenty and was printed privately by a group of his admirers in 1783. In the 1780s Blake emerged as a well-known figure in progressive literary and political circles, and became part of a group that included Thomas Paine, Mary Wollstonecraft, and Josiah Wedgwood. After his father's death in 1784 Blake opened a print shop in London, taking his younger brother Robert on as an assistant.

Following Robert's death in February 1787, William claimed to have had a vision of his brother who, he said, revealed to him a new method of engraving. In this method, which Blake called "illuminated printing," both text and illustration were engraved on a single plate, rather than having the text set separately by a printer. All of Blake's subsequent work, following the *Poetical Sketches,* was produced in this manner.

About this time Blake and his wife moved to Poland Street, Soho, where Blake established his studio. Here he produced his first two works by "illuminated printing": *There Is No Natural Religion* and *All Religions Are One* (1788), two short tracts which set forth the ideas that were to be central to his work and life. In them he refutes the prevailing materialistic philosophies based on Lockean empiricism, proclaiming that what man knows is not bounded by his organs of perception. Imagination, Blake argues, enables men to perceive the Infinite that is God, and the "Poetic Genius" of the imagination is the "true Man." These tracts were followed by a burst of creative activity that saw the production of six masterpieces in a five-year period: *Songs of Innocence* and *The Book of Thel* (both 1789); *The French Revolution* (1791), *The Marriage of Heaven and Hell* (1794), *Visions of the Daughters of Albion*

(1793), and *Songs of Innocence and Experience* (1794). Blake was a strong supporter of the French Revolution and like his literary and political friends was strongly opposed to the Establishment, both Church and State. But Blake's profound religious sensibility made him at the same time an opponent of atheism, deism, and materialism.

Blake moved again in 1793, this time to a house and garden in Lambeth, where he remained for seven years and enjoyed relative prosperity. Here he produced some of his most memorable pictures, among them "God Calling Adam," and a series of poetry volumes known as "the Lambeth Books": *America, A Prophecy* (1793), *Europe, A Prophecy* (1794), *The Book of Urizen* (1794), *The Book of Ahania, The Book of Los,* and *The Song of Los* (all 1795). At the end of this creative period Blake was spiritually exhausted; he had lost faith in the Revolution as a regenerating force. He engraved no more books for nearly a decade, but he did continue to produce art to illustrate the works of other writers.

Beginning in 1795 Blake worked for nine years on what became his first full-length epic poem, *The Four Zoas, The Torments of Love & Jealousy in the Death and Judgement of Albion the Ancient Man.* The work, which used Milton's *Paradise Lost* and *Paradise Regained* as its models, was never engraved by Blake, and was not printed in its entirety until 1925.

In 1803 the Blakes moved again, this time to South Moulton Street, where they remained until 1821. Here Blake composed and engraved his major epics: *Milton* (1804–1808), a vision of the fall and regeneration of an ideal England (Albion); and *Jerusalem* (completed about 1808), in which Albion, enmeshed in abstract materialism, is reunited with Jerusalem, the Divine Womanhood. During this period Blake had few worldly successes. He received few commissions, and he had to resort to engraving advertisements to pay his bills. In 1809 he saw an exhibition of his paintings dismissed as a failure. A description by Blake to accompany one of the paintings in the exhibition, "The Last Judgment" (now lost), was preserved in a notebook known as the Rossetti Manuscript. This description, a collection of notes later entitled "A Vision of the Last Judgement," is valued today because it sets forth key aspects of Blake's critical theory, including his distinction between "Fable or Allegory" on the one hand and "Vision or Imagination" on the other. It also presents his theory of aesthetic perception; the sun was not a mere disk, he wrote, but "an innumerable company of the Heavenly host crying, 'Holy, Holy, Holy is the Lord God Almighty,'" and his eye was a window, "I look thro' it & not with it."

Around 1819 the painter John Linnell became Blake's patron and introduced him to a group of young artists; together they formed what became known as the "Ancients" and revered Blake as their master. In 1821 the Blakes moved for the last time, to Fountain Court, off the Strand, where the poet was frequently visited by Henry Crabb Robinson, whose account of their conversations and those with other early Romantics was published posthumously (*The Remains . . .* , 1922). Blake's last notable poetic work was *The Everlasting Gospel,* written about 1818, an unfinished narrative that reinterprets the character and teachings of Christ. His last years were devoted mainly to pictorial art, including the production of his only wood engravings, illustrations for Thornton's *Pastorals of Virgil*. He also produced a series of watercolors inspired by the Book of Job that include many of his best-known pictures. Left unfinished at his death was a series of watercolors for an edition of the *Divine Comedy*.

Blake died at his home in Fountain Court on August 12, 1827, and was buried as a pauper in Bunhill Fields. Not widely read in his lifetime, he was regarded for many years after his death as a mad eccentric on the fringes of both literature and painting. Only in the twentieth century has he been recognized as a major English poet and painter whose ideas anticipated those of Nietzsche, Freud, and D. H. Lawrence.

THE MARRIAGE OF HEAVEN AND HELL

Plates 5–6

Those who restrain desire, do so because theirs is weak enough to be restrained; and the restrainer or reason usurps its place & governs the unwilling.

And being restrain'd, it by degrees becomes passive, till it is only the shadow of desire.

The history of this is written in Paradise Lost, & the Governor or Reason is call'd Messiah.

And the original Archangel, or possessor of the command of the heavenly host, is call'd the Devil or Satan, and his children are call'd Sin & Death.

But in the Book of Job, Milton's Messiah is call'd Satan.

For this history has been adopted by both parties.

It indeed appear'd to Reason as if Desire was cast out; but the Devil's account is, that the Messiah fell, & formed a heaven of what he stole from the Abyss.

This is shewn in the Gospel, where he prays to the Father to send the comforter, or Desire, that Reason may have Ideas to build on; the Jehovah of the Bible being no other than he who dwells in flaming fire.

Know that after Christ's death, he became Jehovah.

But in Milton, the Father is Destiny, the Son a Ratio of the five senses, & the Holy-ghost Vacuum!

Note: The reason Milton wrote in fetters when he wrote of Angels & God, and at liberty when of Devils & Hell, is because he was a true Poet and of the Devil's party without knowing it.

Plate 10

The head Sublime, the heart Pathos, the genitals Beauty, the hands & feet Proportion.

As the air to a bird or the sea to a fish, so is contempt to the contemptible.

The crow wish'd every thing was black, the owl that every thing was white.

Exuberance is Beauty.

If the lion was advised by the fox, he would be cunning.

Improve[me]nt makes strait roads; but the crooked roads without Improvement are roads of Genius.

Sooner murder an infant in its cradle than nurse unacted desires.
Where man is not, nature is barren.
Truth can never be told so as to be understood, and not be believ'd.
Enough! or Too much.

Plate 11

The ancient Poets animated all sensible objects with Gods or Geniuses, calling them by the names and adorning them with the properties of woods, rivers, mountains, lakes, cities, nations, and whatever their enlarged & numerous senses could percieve.

And particularly they studied the genius of each city & country, placing it under its mental deity;

Till a system was formed, which some took advantage of, & enslav'd the vulgar by attempting to realize or abstract the mental deities from their objects: thus began Priesthood;

Choosing forms of worship from poetic tales.

And at length they pronounc'd that the Gods had order'd such things.

Thus men forgot that All deities reside in the human breast.

Plates 12–13

A Memorable Fancy

The Prophets Isaiah and Ezekiel dined with me, and I asked them how they dared so roundly to assert that God spoke to them; and whether they did not think at the time that they would be misunderstood, & so be the cause of imposition.

Isaiah answer'd: "I saw no God, nor heard any, in a finite organical perception; but my senses discover'd the infinite in every thing, and as I was then perswaded, & remain confirm'd, that the voice of honest indignation is the voice of God, I cared not for consequences, but wrote."

Then I asked: "does a firm perswasion that a thing is so, make it so?"

He replied: "All poets believe that it does, & in ages of imagination this firm perswasion removed mountains; but many are not capable of a firm perswasion of any thing."

Then Ezekiel said: "The philosophy of the east taught the first principles of human perception: some nations held one principle for the origin, & some another: we of Israel taught that the Poetic Genius (as you now call it) was the first principle and all the others merely derivative, which was the cause of our despising the Priests & Philosophers of other countries, and prophecying that all Gods would at last be proved to originate in ours & to be the tributaries of the Poetic Genius; it was this that our great poet, King David, desired so fervently & invokes so pathetic'ly, saying by this he conquers enemies & governs kingdoms; and we so loved our God, that we cursed in his name all the deities of surrounding nations, and asserted that they had rebelled: from these opinions the vulgar came to think that all nations would at last be subject to the jews."

"This," said he, "like all firm perswasions, is come to pass; for all nations believe the jews' code and worship the jews' god, and what greater subjection can be?"

I heard this with some wonder, & must confess my own conviction. After dinner I ask'd Isaiah to favour the world with his lost works; he said none of equal value was lost. Ezekiel said the same of his.

I also asked Isaiah what made him go naked and barefoot three years? he answer'd: "the same thing that made our friend Diogenes, the Grecian."

I then asked Ezekiel why he eat dung, & lay so long on his right & left side? he answer'd, "the desire of raising other men into a perception of the infinite: this the North American tribes practise, & is he honest who resists his genius or conscience only for the sake of present ease or gratification?"

Plate 14

The ancient tradition that the world will be consumed in fire at the end of six-thousand years is true, as I have heard from Hell.

For the cherub with his flaming sword is hereby commanded to leave his guard at tree of life; and when he does, the whole creation will be consumed and appear infinite and holy, whereas it now appears finite & corrupt.

This will come to pass by an improvement of sensual enjoyment.

But first the notion that man has a body distinct from his soul is to be expunged; this I shall do by printing in the infernal method, by corrosives, which in Hell are salutary and medicinal, melting apparent surfaces away, and displaying the infinite which was hid.

If the doors of perception were cleansed every thing would appear to man as it is, infinite.

For man has closed himself up, till he sees all things thro' narrow chinks of his cavern.

Plates 15–17

A Memorable Fancy

I was in a Printing house in Hell, & saw the method in which knowledge is transmitted from generation to generation.

In the first chamber was a Dragon-Man, clearing away the rubbish from a cave's mouth; within, a number of Dragons were hollowing the cave.

In the second chamber was a Viper folding round the rock & the cave, and others adorning it with gold, silver and precious stones.

In the third chamber was an Eagle with wings and feathers of air: he caused the inside of the cave to be infinite; around were numbers of Eagle-like men who built palaces in the immense cliffs.

In the fourth chamber were Lions of flaming fire, raging around & melting the metals into living fluids.

In the fifth chamber were Unnam'd forms, which cast the metals into the expanse.

There they were reciev'd by Men who occupied the sixth chamber, and took the forms of books & were arranged in libraries.

The Giants who formed this world into its sensual existence, and now seem to live in it in chains, are in truth the causes of its life & the sources of all activity; but the chains are the cunning of weak and tame minds which have power to resist energy; according to the proverb, the weak in courage is strong in cunning.

Thus one portion of being is the Prolific, the other the Devouring: to the Devourer it seems as if the producer was in his chains; but it is not so, he only takes portions of existence and fancies that the whole.

But the Prolific would cease to be Prolific unless the Devourer, as a sea, reciev'd the excess of his delights.

Some will say: "Is not God alone the Prolific?" I answer: "God only Acts & Is, in existing beings or Men."

These two classes of men are always upon earth, & they should be enemies: whoever tries to reconcile them seeks to destroy existence.

Religion is an endeavour to reconcile the two.

Note: Jesus Christ did not wish to unite, but to seperate them, as in the Parable of sheep and goats! & he says: "I came not to send Peace, but a Sword."

Messiah or Satan or Tempter was formerly thought to be one of the Antediluvians who are our Energies.

Plates 17–20

A Memorable Fancy

An Angel came to me and said: "O pitiable foolish young man! O horrible! O dreadful state! consider the hot burning dungeon thou art preparing for thyself to all eternity, to which thou art going in such career."

I said: "Perhaps you will be willing to shew me my eternal lot, & we will contemplate together upon it, and see whether your lot or mine is most desirable."

So he took me thro' a stable & thro' a church & down into the church vault, at the end of which was a mill: thro' the mill we went, and came to a cave: down the winding cavern we groped our tedious way, till a void boundless as a nether sky appear'd beneath us, & we held by the roots of trees and hung over this immensity; but I said: "if you please, we will commit ourselves to this void, and see whether providence is here also: if you will not, I will:" but he answer'd: "do not presume, O young man, but as we here remain, behold thy lot which will soon appear when the darkness passes away."

So I remain'd with him, sitting in the twisted root of an oak; he was suspended in a fungus, which hung with the head downward into the deep.

By degrees we beheld the infinite Abyss, fiery as the smoke of a burning city; beneath us, at an immense distance, was the sun, black but shining; round it were fiery tracks on which revolv'd vast spiders, crawling after their prey, which flew, or rather swum, in the infinite deep, in the most terrific shapes of animals sprung from corruption; & the air was full of them, & seem'd composed of them: these are Devils, and are called Powers of the air. I now asked my companion which was my eternal lot? he said: "between the black & white spiders."

But now, from between the black & white spiders, a cloud and fire burst and rolled thro' the deep, black'ning all beneath, so that the nether deep grew black as a sea, & rolled with a terrible noise; beneath us was nothing now to be seen but a black tempest, till looking east between the clouds & the waves, we saw a cataract of blood mixed with fire, and not many stones' throw from us appear'd and sunk again the scaly fold of a monstrous serpent; at last, to the east, distant about three degrees, appear'd a fiery crest above the waves; slowly it reared like a ridge of golden rocks, till we discover'd two globes of crimson fire, from which the sea fled away in clouds of smoke; and now we saw it was the head of Leviathan; his forehead was divided into streaks of green & purple like those on a tyger's forehead: soon we saw his mouth & red gills hang just above the raging foam, tinging the black deep with beams of blood, advancing toward us with all the fury of a spiritual existence.

My friend the Angel climb'd up from his station into the mill: I remain'd alone; & then this appearance was no more, but I found myself sitting on a pleasant bank beside a river by moonlight, hearing a harper, who sung to the harp; & his theme was: "The man who never alters his opinion is like standing water, & breeds reptiles of the mind."

But I arose and sought for the mill, & there I found my Angel, who, surprised, asked me how I escaped?

I answer'd: "All that we saw was owing to your metaphysics; for when you ran away, I found myself on a bank by moonlight hearing a harper. But now we have seen my eternal lot, shall I shew you yours?" he laugh'd at my proposal; but I by force suddenly caught him in my arms, & flew westerly thro' the night, till we were elevated above the earth's shadow; then I flung myself with him directly into the body of the sun; here I clothed myself in white, & taking in my hand Swedenborg's volumes, sunk from the glorious clime, and passed all the planets till we came to saturn: here I stay'd to rest, & then leap'd into the void between saturn & the fixed stars.

"Here," said I, "is your lot, in this space—if space it may be call'd." Soon we saw the stable and the church, & I took him to the altar and open'd the Bible, and lo! it was a deep pit, into which I descended, driving the Angel before me; soon we saw seven houses of brick; one we enter'd; in it were a number of monkeys, baboons, & all of that species, chain'd by the middle, grinning and snatching at one another, but withheld by the shortness of their chains: however, I saw that they sometimes grew numerous, and then the weak were caught by the strong, and with a grinning aspect, first coupled with, & then devour'd, by plucking off first one limb and then another, till the body was left a helpless trunk; this, after grinning & kissing it with seeming fondness, they devour'd too; and here & there I saw one savourily picking the flesh off his own tail; as the stench terribly annoy'd us both, we went into the mill, & I in my hand brought the skeleton of a body, which in the mill was Aristotle's Analytics.

So the Angel said: "thy phantasy has imposed upon me, & thou oughtest to be ashamed."

I answer'd: "we impose on one another, & it is but lost time to converse with you whose works are only Analytics."

Opposition is true Friendship.

Plates 21–22

I have always found that Angels have the vanity to speak of themselves as the only wise; this they do with a confident insolence sprouting from systematic reasoning.

Thus Swedenborg boasts that what he writes is new; tho' it is only the Contents or Index of already publish'd books.

A man carried a monkey about for a shew, & because he was a little wiser than the monkey, grew vain, and conciev'd himself as much wiser than seven men. It is so with Swedenborg: he shews the folly of churches, & exposes hypocrites, till he imagines that all are religious, & himself the single one on earth that ever broke a net.

Now hear a plain fact: Swedenborg has not written one new truth. Now hear another: he has written all the old falsehoods.

And now hear the reason. He conversed with Angels who are all religious, & conversed not with Devils who all hate religion, for he was incapable thro' his conceited notions.

Thus Swedenborg's writings are a recapitulation of all superficial opinions, and an analysis of the more sublime—but no further.

Have now another plain fact. Any man of mechanical talents may, from the writings of Paracelsus or Jacob Behmen, produce ten thousand volumes of equal value with Swedenborg's, and from those of Dante or Shakespear an infinite number.

But when he has done this, let him not say that he knows better than his master, for he only holds a candle in sunshine.

Plates 22–24

A Memorable Fancy

Once I saw a Devil in a flame of fire, who arose before an Angel that sat on a cloud, and the Devil utter'd these words: "The worship of God is: Honouring his gifts in other men, each according to his genius, and loving the greatest men best: those who envy or calumniate great men hate God; for there is no other God."

The Angel hearing this became almost blue; but mastering himself he grew yellow, & at last white, pink, & smiling, and then replied:

"Thou Idolater! is not God One? & is not he visible in Jesus Christ? and has not Jesus Christ given his sanction to the law of ten commandments? and are not all other men fools, sinners, & nothings?"

The Devil answer'd: "bray a fool in a morter with wheat, yet shall not his folly be beaten out of him; if Jesus Christ is the greatest man, you ought to love him in the greatest degree; now hear how he has given his sanction to the law of ten commandments: did he not mock at the sabbath, and so mock the sabbath's God? murder those who were murder'd because of him? turn away the law from the woman taken in adultery? steal the labor of others to support him? bear false witness when he omitted making a defence before Pilate? covet when he pray'd for his disciples, and when he bid them shake off the dust of their feet against such as refused to lodge them? I tell you, no virtue can exist without breaking these ten commandments. Jesus was all virtue, and acted from impulse, not from rules."

When he had so spoken, I beheld the Angel, who stretched out his arms, embracing the flame of fire, & he was consumed and arose as Elijah.

Note: This Angel, who is now become a Devil, is my particular friend; we often read the Bible together in its infernal or diabolical sense, which the world shall have if they behave well.

I have also The Bible of Hell, which the world shall have whether they will or no.

One Law for the Lion & Ox is Oppression.

ANNOTATIONS

TO BOYD'S TRANSLATION
OF DANTE'S INFERNO

In "A Comparative View of the Inferno, With some other Poems relative to the Original Principles of Human Nature."

> *Page 35.*
> *But* the most daring flights of fancy, the most accurate delineations of character, and the most artful conduct of fable, are *not, even* when combined together, sufficient of themselves to make a poem interesting. [*The italicized words have been strongly deleted by Blake*].
> *Pages 35–36.*
> The discord of Achilles and Agamemnon may produce the most tragical consequences; but if we, who are cool and impartial in the affair . . . cannot enter warmly into the views of either party, the story, though adorned with all the genius of an Homer, will be read by us with some degree of nonchalance. The superstitions that led the Crusaders to rescue the Holy Land from the Infidels, instead of interesting us, appears frigid, if not ridiculous. We cannot be much concerned for the fate of such a crew of fanatics, notwithstanding the magic numbers of a Tasso . . . we cannot sympathise with Achilles for the loss of his Mistress, when we feel that he gained her by the massacre of her family.

nobody considers these things when they read Homer or Shakespear or Dante.

> *Page 37.*
> When a man, where no interest is concerned, no provocation given, lays a whole nation in blood merely for his glory; we, to whom his glory is indifferent, cannot enter into his resentment.

false: All poetry gives the lie to this.

> *Pages 37–38.*
> Such may be good poetical characters, of that mixt kind that Aristotle admits; but the most beautiful mixture of light and shade has no attraction unless it warms *or freezes* the heart. [*The words italicized inserted by Blake*] It must have something that engages the sympathy, something that appeals to the *moral sense* [*These two words deleted by Blake and altered to:* passions & senses]; for nothing can thoroughly captivate the fancy, however artfully delineated, that does not awake the sympathy and interest the passions *that enlist on the side of Virtue* [*words deleted*] and appeal to our native notions of right and wrong.
> *Pages 38–39.*
> It is this that sets the Odyssey, in point of sentiment, so far above the Iliad. We feel the injuries of Ulysses; . . . we seem to feel the generous indignation of the young Telemachus, and we tremble at the dangers of the fair Penelope . . . we can go along with the resentment of Ulysses, because it is just, but our feelings must tell us that Achilles carries his resentment to a savage length, a length where we cannot follow him.

If Homer's merit was only in these Historical combinations & Moral sentiments he would be no better than Clarissa.

> *Pages 39–40.*
> *Iliacos extra muros peccatur; et intra.* It is a contest between barbarians,
> equally guilty of injustice, rapine, and bloodshed; and we are not sorry to see
> the vengeance of Heaven equally inflicted on both parties.

Homer meant this.

> Aeneas indeed is a more amiable personage than Achilles; he seems meant for
> a perfect character. But compare his conduct with respect to Dido with the
> self-denial of Dryden's Cleomenes, or with the conduct of Titus in the
> Berenice of Racine, we will then see what is meant by making a character
> interesting.

Every body naturally hates a perfect character because they are all greater
Villains than the imperfect, as Eneas is here shewn a worse man than Achilles
in leaving Dido.

> *Pages 45–46.*
> Antecedent to and independent of all laws, a man may learn to argue on the
> nature of moral obligation, and the duty of universal benovolence, from
> Cumberland, Wollaston, Shaftesbury, Hutcheson; but would he feel what vice
> is in itself . . . let him enter into the passions of Lear, when he feels the
> ingratitude of his children; of Hamlet, when he learns the story of his father's
> murder; . . . and he will know the difference of right and wrong much more
> clearly than from all the moralists that ever wrote.

the grandest Poetry is Immoral, the Grandest characters Wicked, Very Satan—
Capanius, Othello a murderer, Prometheus, Jupiter, Jehovah, Jesus a wine
bibber. Cunning & Morality are not Poetry but Philosophy; the Poet is
Independent & Wicked; the Philosopher is Dependent & Good.

Poetry is to excuse Vice & shew its reason & necessary purgation.

> *Page 49.*
> The industrious knave cultivates the soil; the indolent good man leaves it
> uncultivated. Who ought to reap the harvest? . . . The natural course of things
> decides in favour of the villain; the natural sentiments of men in favour of the
> man of virtue.

false.

> *Pages 56–57.*
> As to those who think the notion of a future Life arose from the descriptions
> and inventions of the Poets, they may just as well suppose that eating and
> drinking had the same original . . . The Poets indeed altered the genuine
> sentiments of nature, and tinged the Light of Reason by introducing the wild
> conceits of Fancy . . . But still the root was natural, though the fruit was wild.
> All that *nature teaches* [*underlined by Blake*] is, that there is a future life,
> distinguished into different states of happiness and misery.

False.

Nature Teaches nothing of Spiritual Life but only of Natural Life.

> *Page 74.*
> [On a blank page at the end of "A Comparative View"]

Every Sentiment & Opinion as well as Every Principle in Dante is in these Preliminary Essays Controverted & proved Foolish by his Translator, If I have any Judgment in Such Things as Sentiments Opinions & Principles.

> In "Historical Essay of the State of Affairs in the thirteenth and fourteenth centuries: With Respect to the History of Florence."
> *Page 118.*
> [Concerning the quarrel between Guilielmo and Bertaccio, the heads of two branches of the family of Cancelieri]. Dante was at this time Prior of Florence, and it was he who gave the advice, *ruinous to himself*, and *pernicious to his native country*, of calling in the heads of the two factions to Florence. [*Italicized words underlined by Blake*]

Dante was a Fool or his Translator was Not: That is, Dante was Hired or Tr. was Not. It appears to Me that Men are hired to Run down Men of Genius under the Mask of Translators, but Dante gives too much Caesar: he is not a Republican.
[*at the top of the page*] Dante was an Emperor's, a Caesar's Man; Luther also left the Priest & join'd the Soldier.

> *Pages 129–130.*
> The fervours of religion have often actuated the passions to deeds of the wildest fanaticism. The booted Apostles of Germany, and the Crusards of Florence, carried their zeal to a very guilty degree. But the passion for any thing laudable will hardly carry men to a proper pitch, unless it be so strong as sometimes to push them beyond the golden mean.

How very Foolish all this Is.

> *Page 131.*
> Such were the effects of intolerance even in the extreme. In a more moderate degree, every well-regulated government, both ancient and modern, were *so far intolerant*, as not to admit the pollutions of every superstition and *every pernicious opinion*. It was from regard to the morals of the people, that the Roman Magistrates expelled the Priests of Bacchus, in the first and most virtuous ages of the republic. It was on this principle that the *Persians* destroyed the *temples of Greece wherever they came*. [*Italicized words underlined by Blake*]

If Well regulated Governments act so who can tell so well as the hireling Writer whose praise is contrary to what he Knows to be true. Persians destroy the Temples & are praised for it.

> *Pages 133–134.*
> The Athenians and Romans kept a watchful eye, not only over the grosser superstitions, but over impiety . . . Polybius plainly attributes the fall of freedom in Greece to the prevalence of atheism . . . It was not till the republic was verging to its fall, that Caesar dared in open senate to laugh at the speculative opinion of a future state. These were the times of universal

toleration, when every pollution, from every clime, flowed to Rome, whence they had carefully been kept out before.

What is Liberty without Universal Toleration?

Pages 135–136.

I leave it to these who are best acquainted with the spirit of antiquity, to determine whether a species of religion . . . had or had not a very principal share in raising those celebrated nations to the summit of their glory: their decline and fall, at least, may be fairly attributed to irreligion, and to the want of some general standard of morality, whose authority they all allowed and to which they all appealed. The want of this pole-star left them adrift in the boundless ocean of conjecture; the disputes of their philosophers were endless, and their opinions of the grounds of morality were as different as their conditions, their tastes and their pursuits.

Yet simple country Hinds are Moral Enthusiasts, Indignant against Knavery, without a Moral criterion other than Native Honesty untaught, while other country Hinds are as indignant against honesty & Enthusiasts for Cunning & Artifice.

Page 148.

. . . but there are certain *bounds* even to *liberty* [*Italicized words underlined by Blake*]

If it is thus, the extreme of black is white & of sweet sower & of good Evil & of Nothing Something.

PUBLIC ADDRESS

Chaucer's Canterbury Pilgrims
Being a Complete Index of Human Characters
As They Appear Age after Age

This day is Publish'd Advertizements to Blake's Canterbury Pilgrims from Chaucer, Containing Anecdotes of Artists. Price 6ᵈ.

P. 1. If Men of weak capacities [in Art *del.*] have alone the Power of Execution in Art, Mʳ B. has now put to the test. If to Invent & to draw well hinders the Executive Power in Art, & his strokes are still to be Condemn'd because they are unlike those of Artists who are Unacquainted with Drawing [& the accompanying *del.*], is now to be Decided by The Public. Mʳ B.'s Inventive Powers & his Scientific Knowledge of Drawing is on all hands acknowledg'd; it only remains to be Certified whether [The Fool's hand or the *del.*] Physiognomic Strength & Power is to give Place to Imbecillity, [and whether (*several words illegible*) an unabated study & practise of forty Years (for I devoted myself to engraving in my Earliest Youth) are sufficient to elevate me above the Mediocrity to which I have hitherto been the victim. *del.*] In a work of Art it is not fine tints that are required, but Fine Forms. Fine Tints without, are nothing. Fine Tints without Fine Forms are always the Subterfuge of the Blockhead.

I account it a Public Duty respectfully to address myself to The Chalcographic Society & to Express to them my opinion (the result of the incessant Practice & Experience of Many Years) That Engraving as an art is Lost in England owing to an artfully propagated [in a most wretched state of injury from an *del.*] opinion that Drawing spoils an Engraver, [which opinion has been held out to me by such men as Flaxman, Romney, Stothard *del.*]. I request the Society to inspect my Print, of which drawing is the Foundation & indeed the Superstructure: it is drawing on copper, as Painting ought to be drawing on canvas or any other [table *del.*] surface, & nothing Else. I request likewise that the Society will compare the Prints of Bartolozzi, Woolett, Strange &c. with the old English Portraits, that is, compare the Modern Art with the Art as it Existed Previous to the Enterance of Vandyke and Rubens into this Country, since which English Engraving is Lost, & I am sure [of *del.*] the Result of the comparison will be that the Society must be of my Opinion that Engraving, by Losing drawing, has Lost all the character & all Expression, without which The Art is Lost.

Pp. 51–57. In this Plate Mʳ B. has resumed the style with which he set out in life, of which Heath & Stothard were the awkward imitators at that time; it is the style of Alb. Durer's Histories & the old Engravers, which cannot be imitated by any one who does not understand drawing, & which, according to

Heath & Stothard, Flaxman, & even Romney, spoils an Engraver; for Each of these Men have repeatedly asserted this Absurdity to me in Condemnation of my Work & approbation of Heath's lame imitation, Stothard being such a fool as to suppose that his blundering blurs can be made out & delineated by any Engraver who knows how to cut dots & lozenges equally well with those little prints which I engraved after him five & twenty years ago & by which he got his reputation as a draughtsman.

The manner in which my Character has been blasted these thirty years, both as an artist & a Man, may be seen particularly in a Sunday Paper cal'd the Examiner, Publish'd in Beaufort Buildings (We all know that Editors of Newspapers trouble their heads very little about art & science, & that they are always paid for what they put in upon these ungracious Subjects), & the manner in which I have routed out the nest of villains will be seen in a Poem concerning my Three years' Herculean Labours at Felpham, which I will soon Publish. Secret Calumny & open Professions of Friendship are common enough all the world over, but have never been so good an occasion of Poetic Imagery. When a Base Man means to be your Enemy he always begins with being your Friend. Flaxman cannot deny that one of the very first Monuments he did, I gratuitously design'd for him; at the same time he was blasting my character as an Artist to Macklin, my Employer, as Macklin told me at the time; how much of his Homer & Dante he will allow to be mine I do not know, as he went far enough off to Publish them, even to Italy, but the Public will know & Posterity will know.

Many People are so foolish [as] to think that they can wound Mr Fuseli over my Shoulder; they will find themselves mistaken; they could not wound even Mr Barry so.

A certain Portrait Painter said To me in a boasting way, "Since "I have Practised Painting I have lost all idea of drawing." Such a Man must know that I look'd upon him with contempt; he did not care for this any more than West did, who hesitated & equivocated with me upon the same subject, at which time he asserted that Woolett's Prints were superior to Basire's because they had more Labour & Care; now this is contrary to the truth. Woolett did not know how to put so much labour into a head or a foot as Basire did; he did not know how to draw the Leaf of a tree; all his study was clean strokes & mossy tints—how then should he be able to make use of either Labour or Care, unless the Labour & Care of Imbecillity? The Life's Labour of Mental Weakness scarcely Equals one Hour of the Labour of Ordinary Capacity, like the full Gallop of the Gouty Man to the ordinary walk of youth & health. I allow that there is such a thing as high finish'd Ignorance, as there may be a fool or a knave in an Embroider'd Coat; but I say that the Embroidery of the Ignorant finisher is not like a Coat made by another, but is an Emanation from Ignorance itself, & its finishing is like its master—The Life's Labour of Five Hundred Idiots, for he never does the Work Himself.

What is Call'd the English Style of Engraving, such as proceeded from the Toilettes of Woolett & Strange (for theirs were Fribble's Toilettes) can never produce Character & Expression. I knew the Men intimately, from their

Intimacy with Basire, my Master, & knew them both to be heavy lumps of Cunning & Ignorance, as their works shew to all the Continent, who Laugh at the Contemptible Pretences of Englishmen to Improve Art before they even know the first [lines *del.*] Beginnings of Art. I hope this Print will redeem my Country from this Coxcomb situation & shew that it is only some Englishmen, and not All, who are thus ridiculous in their Pretences. Advertisements in Newspapers are no proof of Popular approbation, but often the Contrary. A Man who Pretends to Improve Fine Art does not know what Fine Art is. Ye English Engravers must come down from your high flights; ye must condescend to study Marc Antonio & Albert Durer. Ye must begin before you attempt to finish or improve, & when you have begun you will know better than to think of improving what cannot be improv'd. It is very true, what you have said for these thirty two Years. I am Mad or Else you are so; both of us cannot be in our right senses. Posterity will judge by our Works. Woolett's & Strange's works are like those of Titian & Correggio: the Life's Labour of Ignorant Journeymen, Suited to the Purposes of Commerce no doubt, for Commerce Cannot endure Individual Merit; its insatiable Maw must be fed by What all can do Equally well; at least it is so in England, as I have found to my Cost these Forty Years.

Commerce is so far from being beneficial to Arts, or to Empires, that it is destructive of both, as all their History shews, for the above Reason of Individual Merit being its Great hatred. Empires flourish till they become Commercial, & then they are scatter'd abroad to the four winds.

Wooletts best works were Etch'd by Jack Brown. Woolett Etch'd very bad himself. Strange's Prints were, when I knew him, all done by Aliamet & his french journeymen whose names I forget.

"The Cottagers," & "Jocund Peasants," the "Views in Kew Gardens," "Foots Cray," & "Diana," & "Acteon," & in short all that are Call'd Woolett's were Etch'd by Jack Browne, & in Woolett's works the Etching is All, tho' even in these, a single leaf of a tree is never correct.

Such Prints as Woolett & Strange produc'd will do for those who choose to purchase the Life's labour of Ignorance & Imbecillity, in Preference to the Inspired Moments of Genius & Animation.

P. 60. I also knew something of Tom Cooke who Engraved after Hogarth. Cooke wished to Give to Hogarth what he could take from Rafael, that is Outline & Mass & Colour, but he could not [& Hogarth with all his Merit . . . *del.*].

P. 57. I do not pretend to Paint better than Rafael or Mich. Angelo or Julio Romano or Alb. Durer, but I do Pretend to Paint finer than Rubens or Remb^t. or Correggio or Titian. I do not Pretend to Engrave finer than Alb. Durer, Goltzius, Sadeler or Edelinck, but I do pretend to Engrave finer than Strange, Woolett, Hall or Bartolozzi, & all because I understand drawing which They understood not.

P. 58. In this manner the English Public have been imposed upon for many years under the impression that Engraving & Painting are somewhat Else besides drawing. Painting is drawing on Canvas, & Engraving is drawing on Copper, & Nothing Else; & he who pretends to be either Painter or Engraver without being a Master of drawing is an Imposter. We may be Clever as Pugilists, but as Artists we are & have long been the Contempt of the Continent. [*word del.*] Gravelot once said to My Master, Basire, "[*you del.*] de "English may be very clever in [*your del.*] deir own opinions, but "[*you del.*] dey do not draw de [the *written over*] draw."

Resentment for Personal Injuries has had some share in this Public Address, But Love to My Art & Zeal for my Country a much Greater.

P. 59. Men think they can Copy Nature as Correctly as I copy Imagination; this they will find Impossible, & all the Copies or Pretended Copiers of Nature, from Rembrandt to Reynolds, Prove that Nature becomes [*word del.*] to its Victim nothing but Blots & Blurs. Why are Copiers of Nature Incorrect, while Copiers of Imagination are Correct? this is manifest to all.

Pp. 60–62. The Originality of this Production makes it necessary to say a few words.

While the Works [of Imitators *del.*] of Pope & Dryden are look'd upon as [in the same class of *del.*] the same Art with those of Milton & Shakespeare, while the works of Strange & Woollett are look'd upon as the same Art with those of Rafael & Albert Durer, there can be no Art in a Nation but such as is Subservient to the interest of the Monopolizing Trader [*words del.*] [who Manufactures Art by the Hands of Ignorant Journeymen till at length Christian Charity is held out as a Motive to encourage a Blockhead, & he is Counted the Greatest Genius who can sell a Good-for-Nothing Commodity for a Great Price. Obedience to the Will of the Monopolist is call'd Virtue, and the really Industrious, Virtuous & Independent Barry is driven out to make room for a pack of Idle Sychophants with whitlows on their fingers. *mostly del.*]. Englishmen, rouze yourselves from the fatal Slumber into which Booksellers & Trading Dealers have thrown you, Under the artfully propagated pretence that a Translation or a Copy of any kind can be as honourable to a Nation as An Original, [Belying *del.*] Be-lying the English Character in that well known Saying, 'Englishmen Improve what others Invent.' This Even Hogarth's Works Prove a detestable Falshood. No Man Can Improve An Original Invention. [Since Hogarth's time we have had very few Efforts of Originality *del.*] Nor can an Original Invention Exist without Execution, Organized & minutely delineated & Articulated, Either by God or Man. I do not mean smooth'd up & Niggled & Poco-Pen'd, and all the beauties pick'd out [*word del.*] & blurr'd & blotted, but Drawn with a firm & decided hand at once [with all its Spots & Blemishes which are beauties & not faults *del.*], like Fuseli & Michael Angelo, Shakespeare & Milton.

> Dryden in Rhyme cries, "Milton only Planned."
> Every Fool shook his bells throughout the Land.
> Tom Cooke cut Hogarth down with his clean Graving.
> How many thousand Connoisseurs with joy ran raving!
> Some blush at what others can see no crime in,
> But Nobody at all sees harm in Rhyming.

Thus Hayley on his toilette seeing the sope
Says, "Homer is very much improv'd by Pope."
While I looking up to my umbrella,
Resolv'd to be a very Contrary Fellow,
Cry, "Tom Cooke proves, from Circumference to Center,
No one can finish so high as the original inventor."

I have heard many People say, 'Give me the Ideas. It is no matter 'what Words you put them into,' & others say, 'Give me the Design, 'it is no matter for the Execution.' These People know Enough of Artifice, but Nothing Of Art. Ideas cannot be Given but in their minutely Appropriate Words, nor Can a Design be made without its minutely Appropriate Execution. The unorganized Blots & Blurs of Rubens & Titian are not Art, nor can their Method ever express Ideas or Imaginations any more than Pope's Metaphysical Jargon of Rhyming. Unappropriate Execution is the Most nauseous of all affectation & foppery. He who copies does not Execute; he only Imitates what is already Executed. Execution is only the result of Invention.

P. 63. Whoever looks at any of the Great & Expensive Works of Engraving that have been Publish'd by English Traders must feel a Loathing & disgust, & accordingly most Englishmen have a Contempt for Art, [which will *del.*] which is the Greatest Curse that can fall upon a Nation.

He who could represent Christ uniformly like a Drayman must have Queer Conceptions; consequently his Execution must have been as Queer, & those must be Queer fellows who give great sums for such nonsense & think it fine Art.

The Modern Chalcographic Connoisseurs & Amateurs admire only the work of the journeyman, Picking out of whites & blacks in what is call'd Tints; they despise drawing, which despises them in return. They see only whether every thing is toned down but one spot of light.

Mr B. submits to a more severe tribunal; he invites the admirers of old English Portraits to look at his Print.

P. 64. I do not know whether Homer is a Liar & that there is no such thing as Generous Contention: I know that all those with whom I have Contended in Art have strove not to Excell, but to Starve me out by Calumny & the Arts of Trading Combination.

P. 66. It is Nonsense for Noblemen & Gentlemen to offer Premiums for the Encouragement of Art when such Pictures as these can be done without Premiums; let them Encourage what Exists Already, & not endeavour to counteract by tricks; let it no more be said that Empires Encourage Arts, for it is Arts that Encourage Empires. Arts & Artists are Spiritual & laugh at Mortal Contingencies. It is in their Power to hinder Instruction but not to Instruct, just as it is in their Power to Murder a Man but not to make a Man.

Let us teach Buonaparte, & whomsoever else it may concern, That it is not Arts that follow & attend upon Empire, but Empire that attends upon & follows [where Art leads *del.*] The Arts.

P. 67. No Man of Sense can think that an Imitation of the Objects of

Nature is The Art of Painting, or that such Imitation, which any one may easily
perform, is worthy of Notice, much less that such an Art should be the Glory
& Pride of a Nation [& that the man who does this is *del.*]. The Italians laugh
at English Connoisseurs, who are [All *del.*] most of them such silly Fellows as
to believe this.

A Man sets himself down with Colours & with all the Articles of Painting;
he puts a Model before him & he copies that so neat as to make it a deception:
now let any Man of Sense ask himself one Question: Is this Art? can it be
worthy of admiration to any body of Understanding? Who could not do this?
what man who has eyes and an ordinary share of patience cannot do this
neatly? Is this Art? Or is it glorious to a Nation to produce such contemptible
Copies? Countrymen, Countrymen, do not suffer yourselves to be disgraced!

P. 66. The English Artist may be assured that he is doing an injury &
injustice to his Country while he studies & imitates the Effects of Nature.
England will never rival Italy while we servilely copy what the Wise Italians,
Rafael & Michael Angelo, scorned, nay abhorred, as Vasari tells us.

> Call that the Public Voice which is their Error,
> Like [to *del.*] as a Monkey peeping in a Mirror
> Admires all his colours brown & warm
> And never once percieves his ugly form.

What kind of Intellects must he have who sees only the Colours of things & not
the Forms of Things.

P. 71. A Jockey that is anything of a Jockey will never buy a Horse by the
Colour, & a Man who has got any brains will never buy a Picture by the Colour.

When I tell any Truth it is not for the sake of Convincing those who do not
know it, but for the sake of defending those who do.

P. 76. No man of Sense ever supposes that Copying from Nature is the Art
of Painting; if the Art is no more than this, it is no better than any other Manual
Labour; any body may do it & the fool often will do it best as it is a work of no
Mind.

P. 78. The Greatest part of what are call'd in England Old Pictures are Oil
Colour Copies from Fresco Originals; the Comparison is Easily made & the
copy detected. Note, I mean Fresco, Easel, or Cabinet Pictures on Canvas &
Wood & Copper &c.

P. 86. The Painter hopes that his Friends Anytus, [& *del.*] Melitus & Lycon
will perceive that they are not now in Ancient Greece, & tho' they can use the
Poison of Calumny, the English Public will be convinc'd that such a Picture as
this Could never be Painted by a Madman or by one in a State of Outrageous
manners, as these [Villains *del.*] Bad Men both Print & Publish by all the
means in their Power; the Painter begs Public Protection & all will be well.

P. 17. I wonder who can say, Speak no Ill of the dead when it is asserted
in the Bible that the name of the Wicked shall Rot. It is Deistical Virtue, I
suppose, but as I have none of this I will pour Aqua fortis on the Name of the
Wicked & turn it into an Ornament & an Example to be Avoided by Some and
Imitated by Others if they Please.

Columbus discover'd America, but American Vesputius finish'd & smooth'd it over like an English Engraver or Corregio & Titian.

Pp. 18–19. What Man of Sense will lay out his Money upon the Life's Labours of Imbecillity & Imbecillity's Journeymen, or think to Educate a Fool how to build a Universe with Farthing Balls? The Contemptible Idiots who have been call'd Great Men of late Years ought to rouze the Public Indignation of Men of Sense in all Professions.

There is not, because there cannot be, any difference of Effect in the Pictures of Rubens & Rembrandt: when you have seen one of their Pictures you have seen all. It is not so with Rafael, Julio Roman[o], Alb. d[urer], Mich. Ang. Every Picture of theirs has a different & appropriate Effect.

Yet I do not shrink from the comparison, in Either Relief or Strength of Colour, with either Rembrandt or Rubens; on the contrary I court the Comparison & fear not the Result, but not in a dark corner; their Effects are in Every Picture the same. Mine are in every Picture different.

I hope my Countrymen will Excuse me if I tell them a Wholesome truth. Most Englishmen, when they look at a Picture, immediately set about searching for Points of Light & clap the Picture into a dark corner. This, when done by [this in *del.*] Grand Works, is like looking for Epigrams in Homer. A point of light is a Witticism; many are destructive of all Art. One is an Epigram only & no Grand Work can have them.

Rafael, Mich. Ang., Alb. d., Jul. Rom. are accounted ignorant of that Epigrammatic Wit in Art because they avoid it as a destructive Machine, as it is.

That Vulgar Epigram in Art, Rembrandt's "Hundred Guelders," has entirely put an End to all Genuine & Appropriate Effect; all, both Morning & Night, is now a dark cavern. It is the Fashion; they Produce System & Monotony. When you view a Collection of Pictures painted since Venetian Art was the Fashion, or Go into a Modern Exhibition, with a very few Exceptions, Every Picture has the same Effect, a Piece of Machinery of Points of Light to be put into a dark hole.

M[r] B. repeats that there is not one Character or Expression in this Print which could be Produced with the Execution of Titian, Rubens, Coreggio, Rembrandt, or any of that Class. Character & Expression can only be Expressed by those who Feel Them. Even Hogarth's Execution cannot be Copied or Improved. Gentlemen of Fortune who give Great Prices for Pictures should consider the following. Rubens's Luxembourg Gallery is Confessed on all hands [because it bears the evidence at first view *del.*] to be the work of a Blockhead: it bears this Evidence in its face; how can its Execution be any other than the Work of a Blockhead? Bloated [Creatures & *del.*] Gods, Mercury, Juno, Venus, & the rattle traps of Mythology & the lumber of an [old *del.*] awkward French Palace are thrown together around Clumsy & Ricketty Princes & Princesses higgledy piggledy. On the Contrary, Julio Rom[ano's] Palace of T at Mantua, is allow'd on all hands to be the Product of a Man of the Most Profound sense & Genius, & yet his Execution is pronounc'd by English Connoisseurs & Reynolds, their doll, to be unfit for the Study of the Painter.

Can I speak with too great Contempt of such Contemptible fellows? If all the Princes in Europe, like Louis XIV & Charles the first, were to Patronize such Blockheads, I, William Blake, a Mental Prince, should decollate & Hang their Souls as Guilty of Mental High Treason.

Who that has Eyes cannot see that Rubens & Corregio must have been very weak & Vulgar fellows? & we are [we *del.*] to imitate their Execution. This is [as if *del.*] like what Sr Francis Bacon [should downright assert *del.*] says, that a healthy Child should be taught & compell'd to walk like a Cripple, while the Cripple must be taught to walk like healthy people. O rare wisdom!

I am really sorry to see my Countrymen trouble themselves about Politics. If Men were Wise, the Most arbitrary Princes could not hurt them. If they are not wise, the Freest Government is compell'd to be a Tyranny. Princes appear to me to be Fools. Houses of Commons & Houses of Lords appear to me to be fools; they seem to me to be something Else besides Human Life.

Pp. 20–21. The wretched State of the Arts in this Country & in Europe, originating in the wretched State of Political Science, which is the Science of Sciences, Demands a firm & determinate conduct on the part of Artists to Resist the Contemptible Counter Arts [set on foot *del.*] Establish'd by such contemptible Politicians as Louis XIV & [but *del.*] originally set on foot by Venetian Picture traders, Music traders, & Rhime traders, to the destruction of all true art as it is this Day. To recover Art has been the business of my life to the Florentine Original & if possible to go beyond that Original; this I thought the only pursuit worthy of [an Englishman *del.*] a Man. To Imitate I abhor. I obstinately adhere to the true Style of Art such as Michael Angelo, Rafael, Jul. Rom., Alb. Durer left it, [the Art of Invention, not of Imitation. Imagination is My World; this world of Dross is beneath my Notice & beneath the Notice of the Public. *del.*] I demand therefore of the Amateurs of art the Encouragement which is my due; if they continue to refuse, theirs is the loss, not mine, & theirs is the Contempt of Posterity. I have Enough in the Approbation of fellow labourers; this is my glory & exceeding great reward. I go on & nothing can hinder my course:

> and in Melodious Accents I
> Will sit me down & Cry, I, I.

P. 20 (sideways). An Example of these Contrary Arts is given us in the Characters of Milton & Dryden as they are written in a Poem signed with the name of Nat Lee, which perhaps he never wrote & perhaps he wrote in a paroxysm of insanity, In which it is said that Milton's Poem is a rough Unfinish'd Piece & Dryden has finish'd it. Now let Dryden's Fall & Milton's Paradise be read, & I will assert that every Body of Understanding [will *del.*] must cry out Shame on such Niggling & Poco-Pen as Dryden has degraded Milton with. But at the same time I will allow that Stupidity will Prefer Dryden, because it is in Rhyme [but for no other cause *del.*] & Monotonous Sing Song, Sing Song from beginning to end. Such are Bartolozzi, Woolett & Strange.

P. 23. [*Four lines del.*] The Painters of England are unemploy'd in Public

Works, while the Sculptors have continual & superabundant employment. Our Churches & Abbeys are treasures of [*words del.*] their producing for ages back, While Painting is excluded. Painting, the Principal Art, has no place [in our *del.*] among our almost only public works. [While *del.*] Yet it is more adapted to solemn ornament than [*word del.*] Marble can be, as it is capable of being Placed on any heighth & indeed would make a Noble finish Placed above the Great Public Monuments in Westminster, St Pauls & other Cathedrals. To the Society for Encouragement of Arts I address myself with [duty & *del.*] Respectful duty, requesting their Consideration of my Plan as a Great Public [*word del.*] means of advancing Fine Art in Protestant Communities. Monuments to the dead, Painted by Historical & Poetical Artists, like Barry & Mortimer (I forbear to name living Artists tho' equally worthy), I say, Monuments so Painted must make England What Italy is, an Envied Storehouse of Intellectual Riches.

Pp. 24–25. It has been said of late years The English Public have no Taste for Painting. This is a Falsehood. The English are as Good Judges of Painting as of Poetry, & they prove it in their Contempt for Great Collections of all the Rubbish of the Continent brought here by Ignorant Picture dealers. An Englishman may well say, 'I am no 'Judge of Painting,' when he is sold these Smears & Dawbs at an immense price & told that such is the Art of Painting. I say the English Public are true Encouragers of real Art, while they discourage and look with Contempt on False Art.

In a Commercial Nation Impostors are abroad in all Professions; these are the greatest Enemies of Genius [Mr B. thinks it his duty to Caution the Public against a Certain Impostor who *del.*] In [our Art *del.*] the Art of Painting these Impostors sedulously propogate an Opinion that Great Inventors Cannot Execute. This Opinion is as destructive of the true Artist as it is false by all Experience. Even Hogarth cannot be either Copied or Improved. Can Anglus never Discern Perfection but in the Journeyman's Labour?

Pp. 24–25 (sideways). I know my Execution is not like Any Body Else. I do not intend it should be so; none but Blockheads Copy one another. My Conception & Invention are on all hands allow'd to be Superior. My Execution will be found so too. To what is it that Gentleman of the first Rank both in Genius & Fortune have subscribed their Names? To My Inventions: the Executive part they never disputed; the Lavish praise I have received from all Quarters for Invention & drawing has Generally been accompanied by this: "he can concieve "but he cannot Execute"; this Absurd assertion has done me, & may still do me, the greatest mischief. I call for Public protection against these Villains. I am, like others, Just Equal in Invention & in Execution as my works shew. I, in my own defence, Challenge a Competition with the finest Engravings & defy the most critical judge to make the Comparison Honestly, asserting in my own Defence that This Print is the Finest that has been done or is likely to be done in England, where drawing, its foundation, is Contemn'd, and absurd Nonsense about dots & Lozenges & Clean Strokes made to occupy the attention to the Neglect of all real Art. I defy any Man to Cut Cleaner Strokes than I do, or rougher where I please, & assert that he who thinks he can Engrave, or Paint either, without being a Master of drawing, is a Fool. Painting is drawing on Canvas, & Engraving is drawing on Copper, & nothing Else. Drawing is Execution, & nothing Else, & he who draws best must be the best Artist; to this I subscribe my name as a Public Duty.

William Blake

P.S.—I do not believe that this Absurd opinion ever was set on foot till in my Outset into life it was artfully publish'd, both in whispers & in print, by Certain persons whose robberies from me made it necessary to them that I should be [left *del.*] hid in a corner; it never was supposed that a Copy could be better than an original, or near so Good, till a few Years ago it became the interest of certain envious Knaves.

ADDITIONAL PASSAGES

P. 38. There is just the same Science in Lebrun or Rubens, or even Vanloo, that there is in Rafael or Mich. Angelo, but not the same Genius. Science is soon got; the other never can be acquired, but must be Born.

P. 39. I do not condemn Rubens, Rembrandt or Titian because they did not understand drawing, but because they did not Understand Colouring; how long shall I be forced to beat this into Men's Ears? I do not condemn [Bartolozzi *del.*] Strange or Woolett because they did not understand drawing, but because they did not understand Graving. I do not condemn Pope or Dryden because they did not understand Imagination, but because they did not understand Verse. Their Colouring, Graving & Verse can never be applied to Art—That is not either Colouring, Graving or Verse which is Unappropriate to the Subject. He who makes a design must know the Effect & Colouring Proper to be put to that design & will never take that of Rubens, Rembrandt or Titian to [put *del.*] turn that which is Soul & Life into a Mill or Machine.

P. 44. Let a Man who has made a drawing go on & on & he will produce a Picture or Painting, but if he chooses to leave it before he has spoil'd it, he will do a Better Thing.

Pp. 46–47. They say there is no Strait Line in Nature; this Is a Lie, like all that they say. For there is Every Line in Nature. But I will tell them what is Not in Nature. An Even Tint is not in Nature; it produces Heaviness. Nature's Shadows are Ever varying, & a Ruled Sky that is quite Even never can Produce a Natural Sky; the same with every Object in a Picture, its Spots are its beauties. Now, Gentlemen Critics, how do you like this? You may rage, but what I say, I will prove by Such Practise & have already done, so that you will rage to your own destruction. Woolett I knew very intimately by his intimacy with Basire, & I knew him to be one of the most ignorant fellows that I ever knew. A Machine is not a Man nor a Work of Art; it is destructive of Humanity & of Art; the word Machination [*word del.*]. Woolett I know did not know how to Grind his Graver. I know this; he has often proved his Ignorance before me at Basire's by laughing at Basire's knife tools & ridiculing the Forms of Basire's other Gravers till Basire was quite dash'd & out of Conceit with what he himself knew, but his Impudence had a Contrary Effect on me. Englishmen have been so used to Journeymen's undecided bungling that they cannot bear the firmness of a Master's Touch.

Every Line is the Line of Beauty; it is only fumble & Bungle which cannot draw a Line; this only is Ugliness. That is not a Line which doubts & Hesitates in the Midst of its Course.

ON HOMER'S
POETRY & ON VIRGIL

ON HOMER'S POETRY

Every Poem must necessarily be a perfect Unity, but why Homer's is peculiarly so, I cannot tell; he has told the story of Bellerophon & omitted the Judgment of Paris, which is not only a part, but a principal part, of Homer's subject.

But when a Work has Unity, it is as much in a Part as in the Whole: the Torso is as much a Unity as the Laocoon.

As Unity is the cloke of folly, so Goodness is the cloke of knavery. Those who will have Unity exclusively in Homer come out with a Moral like a sting in the tail. Aristotle says Characters are either Good or Bad; now Goodness or Badness has nothing to do with Character: an Apple tree, a Pear tree, a Horse, a Lion are Characters, but a Good Apple tree or a Bad is an Apple tree still; a Horse is not more a Lion for being a Bad Horse: that is its Character: its Goodness or Badness is another consideration.

It is the same with the Moral of a whole Poem as with the Moral Goodness of its parts. Unity & Morality are secondary considerations, & belong to Philosophy & not to Poetry, to Exception & not to Rule, to Accident & not to Substance; the Ancients call'd it eating of the tree of good & evil.

The Classics! it is the Classics, & not Goths nor Monks, that Desolate Europe with Wars.

ON VIRGIL

Sacred Truth has pronounced that Greece & Rome, as Babylon & Egypt, so far from being parents of Arts & Sciences as they pretend, were destroyers of all Art. Homer, Virgil & Ovid confirm this opinion & make us reverence The Word of God, the only light of antiquity that remains unperverted by War. Virgil in the Eneid, Book VI, line 848, says "Let others study Art: Rome has somewhat better to do, "namely War & Dominion."

Rome & Greece swept Art into their maw & destroy'd it; a Warlike State never can produce Art. It will Rob & Plunder & accumulate into one place, & Translate & Copy & Buy & Sell & Criticise, but not Make. Grecian is Mathematic Form: Gothic is Living Form, Mathematic Form is Eternal in the Reasoning Memory: Living Form is Eternal Existence.

ANNOTATIONS

TO "POEMS" BY WILLIAM WORDSWORTH
VOL. I, LONDON, MDCCCXV

[Blake's annotations are here printed in larger type after the passages from Wordsworth to which they refer.]

Page viii.
The powers requisite for the production of poetry are, first, those of observation and description . . . 2dly, Sensibility.

One Power alone makes a Poet: Imagination, The Divine Vision.

Page 1.
[*Sub-title*]: "Poems Referring to the Period of Childhood."

I see in Wordsworth the Natural Man rising up against the Spiritual Man Continually, & then he is No Poet but a Heathen Philosopher at Enmity against all true Poetry or Inspiration.

Page 3.

> And I could wish my days to be
> Bound each to each by natural piety.

There is no such Thing as Natural Piety Because The Natural Man is at Enmity with God.

Page 43.

> "To H. C. Six Years Old."

This is all in the highest degree Imaginative & equal to any Poet, but not Superior. I cannot think that Real Poets have any competition. None are greatest in the Kingdom of Heaven; it is so in Poetry.

Page 44.

> "Influence of Natural Objects
> "In calling forth and strengthening the Imagination
> "in Boyhood and early Youth."

Natural Objects always did & now do weaken, deaden & obliterate Imagination in Me. Wordsworth must know that what he Writes Valuable is Not to be found in Nature. Read Michael Angelo's Sonnet, vol. 2, p. 179:

> [Heaven-born, the Soul a heaven-ward course must hold;
> Beyond the visible world She soars to seek,

146

> (For what delights the sense is false and weak)
> Ideal Form, the universal mould.]

Page 341.

"Essay, Supplementary to the Preface."

I do not know who wrote these Prefaces: they are very mischievous & direct contrary to Wordsworth's own Practise.

Pages 364–5.
In Macpherson's work it is exactly the reverse; every thing (that is not stolen) is in this manner defined, insulated, dislocated, deadened,—yet nothing distinct . . . Yet, much as these pretended treasures of antiquity have been admired, they have been wholly uninfluential upon the literature of the country . . . no Author in the least distinguished, has ventured formally to imitate them—except the Boy, Chatterton, on their first appearance.

I believe both Macpherson & Chatterton, that what they say is Ancient Is so. I own myself an admirer of Ossian equally with any other Poet whatever, Rowley & Chatterton also.

Pages 374–5.
Is it the result of the whole that, in the opinion of the Writer, the judgment of the People is not to be respected? The thought is most injurious; . . . to the People . . . his devout respect, his reverence, is due. He . . . takes leave of his Readers by assuring them—that if he were not persuaded that the Contents of these Volumes, and the Work to which they are subsidiary, evinced something of the "Vision and the Faculty divine," . . . he would not, if a wish could do it, save them from immediate destruction.

It appears to me as if the last Paragraph beginning "Is it the result" Was writ by another hand & mind from the rest of these Prefaces. Perhaps they are the opinions of a Portrait or Landscape painter. Imagination is the Divine Vision not of The World, or of Man, nor from Man as he is a Natural Man, but only as he is a Spiritual Man. Imagination has nothing to do with Memory.

ANNOTATIONS

TO "THE EXCURSION"
BY WILLIAM WORDSWORTH,

[together with a manuscript copy in Blake's
hand of the poetical portion of Wordsworth's
Preface and his prefatory sentences; the relevant
passages are here followed by Blake's notes in larger
type. Words underlined by Blake are printed in italic.]

Page xi.

> All strength—all terror, single or in bands,
> That ever was put forth in personal form;
> Jehovah—with his thunder, and the choir
> Of shouting Angels, and the empyreal thrones,
> I pass them, unalarmed . . .

Solomon, when he Married Pharaoah's daughter & became a Convert to the Heathen Mythology, Talked exactly in this way of Jehovah as a Very inferior object of Man's Contemplation; he also passed him by unalarm'd & was permitted. Jehovah dropped a tear & follow'd him by his Spirit into the Abstract Void; it is called the Divine Mercy. Satan dwells in it, but Mercy does not dwell in him; he knows not to Forgive.

Pages xii–xiii.

> How exquisitely the individual Mind
> (And the progressive powers perhaps no less
> Of the whole species) to the external World
> Is fitted:—& how exquisitely, too,
> Theme this but little heard of among Men,
> The external World is fitted to the Mind.

You shall not bring me down to believe such fitting & fitted. I know better & please your Lordship.

> Such grateful haunts foregoing, if I oft
> Must turn elsewhere—to travel near the tribes
> And fellowships of Men, & see ill sights
> Of madding passions mutually inflamed;
> Must hear *Humanity in fields & groves*
> *Pipe solitary anguish;* or must hang
> Brooding above the fierce confederate storm
> Of Sorrow, barricadoed evermore

> With the walls of cities; may these sounds
> Have their authentic comment,—that, even these
> Hearing, I be not downcast or forlorn!

Does not this Fit, & is it not Fitting most Exquisitely too, but to what?—not to Mind, but to the Vile Body only & to its Laws of Good & Evil & its Enmities against Mind.

NOTES

ON THE ILLUSTRATIONS TO DANTE

On design no. 7, a map of the classical conception of the Universe, written in the circles surrounding the central figure of Homer.

Every thing in Dante's Comedia shews That for Tyrannical Purposes he has made This World the Foundation of All, & the Goddess Nature Mistress; [Nature *del.*] is his Inspirer & not . . . the Holy Ghost. As poor Churchill said: "Nature, thou art my Goddess."

Round Purgatory is Paradise, & round Paradise is Vacuum or Limbo, so that Homer is the Center of All—I mean the Poetry of the Heathen, Stolen & Perverted from the Bible, not by Chance but by design, by the Kings of Persia & their Generals, The Greek Heroes & lastly by the Romans.

Swedenborg does the same in saying that in this World is the Ultimate of Heaven. This is the most damnable Falshood of Satan & his Antichrist.

On design no. 16, The Goddess Fortune.

The hole of a Shit-house.
The Goddess Fortune is the devil's servant, ready to Kiss any one's Arse.

On design no. 101, a diagram of the Circles of Hell.

It seems as if Dante's supreme Good was something Superior to the Father or Jesus; for if he gives his rain to the Evil & the Good, & his Sun to the Just & the Unjust, He could never have Built Dante's Hell, nor the Hell of the Bible neither, in the way our Parsons explain it—It must have been originally Formed by the devil Himself; & So I understand it to have been.

Whatever Book is for Vengeance for Sin & whatever Book is Against the Forgiveness of Sins is not of the Father, but of Satan the Accuser & Father of Hell.

This [*the diagram*] is Upside Down When view'd from Hell's gate, which ought to be at top, But right When View'd from Purgatory after they have passed the Center.
In Equivocal Worlds Up & Down are Equivocal.

In the circles from below upwards

1. Limbo. Charon.
2. Minos.

3. Cerberus.
4. Phitus & Phlegyas.
5. City of Dis. Queen of Endless Woe. furies & . . . Lesser Circle Point of the Universe. Canto Eleventh Line 68.
6. Minotaur. The City of Dis seems to occupy the Space between the Fifth and Sixth Circles or perhaps it occupies both Circles with its Environs.
7. Centaurs. Most likely Dante describes the 7, 8 & 9 Circles in Canto XI, v. 18.
   3 Compartments.
   Dante calls them Cerchietti.
8. Malebolge. Geryon. Containing 10 gulfs.
9. Lucifer. Containing 9 Rounds.

Friedrich Schiller

1759–1805

Johann Christoph Friedrich Schiller was born at Marbach on November 10, 1759, the son of an army officer. He was educated at local schools, then sent to a military academy on the orders of his father's supervisor, the Duke of Wurttemberg. Here he studied first law, then medicine. At twenty-one, he was appointed assistant medical officer of a regiment in Stuttgart. Schiller was not happy with the regimentation of his schooling, however, and his resentment was expressed in his early poems, published in the *Anthologie auf das Jahr 1782*, and in his first play, *Die Rauber* (1781)—a protest against social convention and corruption among the powerful. It was first performed in January 1782 at the National Theatre in Mannheim, and was an immediate success. Schiller attended the premiere of his play against the wishes of the Duke, and was ordered to stop writing. His response was to leave the army and settle in Mannheim, where he lived in poverty and continued writing plays. He eventually received an appointment as resident playwright with the Mannheim Theatre and saw his tragedy *Kabale und Liebe* performed successfully, but had to leave the post after one year. Schiller then moved to Leipzig to live with friends and completed *Don Carlos,* his first play in blank verse, published in 1787.

Schiller moved to Weimar, Goethe's home city and the literary capital of Germany, in 1787, but it was not until 1794 that he met the older poet. Meanwhile, Schiller had been developing his talents as an historian, and his scholarly account of the revolt of the Netherlands secured him—with the help of Goethe—an unsalaried position as professor of history at the University of Jena. His history of the Thirty Years' War further enhanced his reputation as a scholar, and provided him with the background material for what is considered his greatest drama, *Wallenstein* (1800).

Beginning in the early 1790s Schiller's health began to decline under the pressures of overwork—he had married in 1790 and soon had four children to support. Two Danish noblemen, hearing of his plight, granted him a generous pension for three years, and despite continuing ill-health Schiller was able to continue his writing. He spent part of the time studying the philosophy of Kant, which inspired him to write a series of essays—among them the well-known *Briefe über die aesthetische Erziehung des Menschen* (1795) and *Über das Erhabene* (1801)—which examined the nature of aesthetic activity and its relation to society. He also wrote his well-known essay *Über naïve and sentimentalische Dichtung* (1795–96), in which he distinguishes several types of poetic creativity.

During this period Schiller wrote a group of popular ballads as well as the famous *Lied von der Glocke*, all of which illustrate his belief that poetry can be made accessible to ordinary men without debasing it. In his last five years Schiller produced adaptations of *Macbeth* and of Gozzi's *Turandot* for the German stage, a translation of Racine's *Phèdre*, and four more plays: *Maria Stuart, Die Jungfrau von Orleans, Die Braut von Messina,* and the famous *Wilhelm Tell.* He died at Weimar on May 9, 1805.

ON SIMPLE AND SENTIMENTAL POETRY

T here are moments in life when nature inspires us with a sort of love and respectful emotion, not because she is pleasing to our senses, or because she satisfies our mind or our taste (it is often the very opposite that happens), but merely because she is nature. This feeling is often elicited when nature is considered in her plants, in her mineral kingdom, in rural districts; also in the case of human nature, in the case of children, and in the manners of country people and of the primitive races. Every man of refined feeling, provided he has a soul, experiences this feeling when he walks out under the open sky, when he lives in the country, or when he stops to contemplate the monuments of early ages; in short, when escaping from factitious situations and relations, he finds himself suddenly face to face with nature. This interest, which is often exalted in us so as to become a want, is the explanation of many of our fancies for flowers and for animals, our preference for gardens laid out in the natural style, our love of walks, of the country, and those who live there, of a great number of objects proceeding from a remote antiquity, etc. It is taken for granted that no affectation exists in the matter, and moreover that no accidental interest comes into play. But this sort of interest which we take in nature is only possible under two conditions. First the object that inspires us with this feeling must be really *nature,* or something we take for nature; secondly this object must be in the full sense of the word *simple,* that is, presenting the entire contrast of nature with art, all the advantage remaining on the side of nature. Directly this second condition is united to the first, but no sooner, nature assumes the character of simplicity.

Considered thus, nature is for us nothing but existence in all its freedom; it is the constitution of things taken in themselves; it is existence itself according to its proper and immutable laws.

It is strictly necessary that we should have this idea of nature to take an interest in phenomena of this kind. If we conceive an artificial flower so perfectly imitated that it has all the appearance of nature and would produce the most complete illusion, or if we imagine the imitation of simplicity carried out to the extremest degree, the instant we discover it is only an imitation, the feeling of which I have been speaking is completely destroyed. It is, therefore, quite evident that this kind of satisfaction which nature causes us to feel is not a satisfaction of the æsthetical taste, but a satisfaction of the moral sense; for it is produced by means of a conception and not immediately by the single fact of intuition: accordingly it is by no means determined by the different degrees of beauty in forms. For, after all, is there anything so specially charming in a flower of common appearance, in a spring, a moss-covered stone, the warbling of birds, or the buzzing of bees, etc.? What is it that can give these objects a claim to our love? It is not these objects in themselves; it is an idea represented by them that we love in them. We love in them life and its latent action, the effects peacefully produced by beings of themselves, existence under its proper laws, the inmost necessity of things, the eternal unity of their nature.

These objects which captivate us *are* what we *were*, what we *must be* again some day. We were nature as they are; and culture, following the way of reason and of liberty, must bring us back to nature. Accordingly, these objects are an image of our infancy irrevocably past—of our infancy which will remain eternally very dear to us, and thus they infuse a certain melancholy into us; they are also the image of our highest perfection in the ideal world, whence they excite a sublime emotion in us.

But the perfection of these objects is not a merit that belongs to them, because it is not the effect of their free choice. Accordingly they procure quite a peculiar pleasure for us, by being our models without having anything humiliating for us. It is like a constant manifestation of the divinity surrounding us, which refreshes without dazzling us. The very feature that constitutes their character is precisely what is lacking in ours to make it complete; and what distinguishes us from them is precisely what they lack to be divine. We are free and they are necessary; we change and they remain identical. Now it is only when these two conditions are united, when the will submits freely to the laws of necessity, and when, in the midst of all the changes of which the imagination is susceptible, reason maintains its rule—it is only then that the divine or the ideal is manifested. Thus we perceive eternally *in them* that which we have not, but which we are continually forced to strive after; that which we can never reach, but which we can hope to approach by continual progress. And we perceive *in ourselves* an advantage which they lack, but in which some of them—the beings deprived of reason—cannot absolutely share, and in which the others, such as children, can only one day have a share by following *our* way. Accordingly, they procure us the most delicious feeling of our human nature, as an idea, though in relation to each *determinate* state of our nature they cannot fail to humble us.

As this interest in nature is based on an idea, it can only manifest itself in a soul capable of ideas, that is, in a moral soul. For the immense majority it is nothing more than pure affectation; and this taste of *sentimentality* so widely diffused in our day, manifesting itself, especially since the appearance of certain books, by sentimental excursions and journeys, by sentimental gardens, and other fancies akin to these—this taste by no means proves that true refinement of sense has become general. Nevertheless, it is certain that nature will always produce something of this impression, even on the most insensible hearts, because all that is required for this is the moral disposition or aptitude, which is common to all men. For all men, however contrary their acts may be to simplicity and to the truth of nature are brought back to it in their ideas. This sensibility in connection with nature is specially and most strongly manifested, in the greater part of persons, in connection with those sort of objects which are closely related to us, and which, causing us to look closer into ourselves, show us more clearly what in us departs from nature; for example, in connection with children, or with nations in a state of infancy. It is an error to suppose that it is only the idea of their weakness that, in certain moments, makes us dwell with our eyes on children with so much emotion. This may be true with those who, in the presence of a feeble being, are used to feel nothing but their own superiority. But the feeling of which I speak is only experienced in a very peculiar moral disposition, nor must it be confounded with the feeling awakened in us by the joyous activity of children. The feeling of which I speak is calculated rather to humble than to flatter our self-love; and if it gives us the idea of some advantage, this advantage is at all events not on our side.

We are moved in the presence of childhood, but it is not because from the height of our strength and of our perfection we drop a look of pity on it; it is, on the contrary, because from the depths of our impotence, of which the feeling is inseparable from that of the real and determinate state to which we have arrived, we raise our eyes to the child's determinableness and pure innocence. The feeling we then experience is too evidently mingled with sadness for us to mistake its source. In the child, all is *disposition* and *destination;* in us, all is in the state of a *completed, finished* thing, and the completion always remains infinitely below the destination. It follows that the child is to us like the representation of the ideal; not, indeed, of the ideal as we have realised it, but such as our destination admitted; and, consequently, it is not at all the idea of its indigence, of its hinderances, that makes us experience emotion in the child's presence; it is, on the contrary, the idea of its pure and free force, of the integrity, the infinity of its being. This is the reason why, in the sight of every moral and sensible man, the child will always be a *sacred* thing; I mean an object which, by the grandeur of an idea, reduces to nothingness all grandeur realised by experience; an object which, in spite of all it may lose in the judgment of the understanding, regains largely the advantage before the judgment of reason.

Now it is precisely this contradiction between the judgment of reason and that of the understanding which produces in us this quite special phenome-non, this mixed feeling, called forth in us by the sight of the simple—I mean the simple in the manner of thinking. It is at once the idea of a childlike simplicity and of a childish simplicity. By what it has of childish simplicity it exposes a weak side to the understanding, and provokes in us that smile by which we testify our superiority (an entirely speculative superiority). But directly we have reason to think that childish simplicity is at the same time a childlike simplicity—that it is not consequently a want of intelligence, an infirmity in a theoretical point of view, but a superior force (practically), a heart-full of truth and innocence, which is its source, a heart that has despised the help of art because it was conscious of its real and internal greatness— directly this is understood, the understanding no longer seeks to triumph. Then raillery, which was directed against simpleness, makes way for the admiration inspired by noble simplicity. We feel ourselves obliged to esteem this object, which at first made us smile, and directing our eyes to ourselves, to feel ourselves unhappy in not resembling it. Thus is produced that very special phenomenon of a feeling in which good-natured raillery, respect, and sadness are confounded. It is the condition of the simple that nature should triumph over art, either unconsciously to the individual and against his inclination, or with his full and entire cognisance. In the former case it is *simplicity* as a *surprise* and the impression resulting from it is one of gaiety; in the second case, it is simplicity of *feeling,* and we are moved.

With regard to simplicity as a surprise, the person must be *morally* capable of denying nature. In simplicity of feeling the person may be morally incapable of this, but we must not think him physically incapable, in order that it may make upon us the impression of the simple. This is the reason why the acts and words of children only produce the impression of simplicity upon us when we forget that they are physically incapable of artifice, and in general only when we are exclusively impressed by the contrast between their natural character and what is artificial in us. Simplicity is a *childlike ingenuousness* which is encountered when it is not *expected;* and it is for this very reason that, taking the word in its strictest sense, simplicity could not be attributed to childhood properly speaking.

But in both cases, in simplicity as a surprise and simplicity as a feeling, nature must always have the upper hand, and art succumb to her.

Until we have established this distinction we can only form an incomplete idea of simplicity. The affections are also something natural, and the rules of decency are artificial; yet the triumph of the affections over decency is anything but simple. But when affection triumphs over artifice, over false decency, over dissimulation, we shall have no difficulty in applying the word simple to this. Nature must therefore triumph over art, not by its blind and brutal force as a *dynamical power,* but in virtue of its form as a *moral magnitude;* in a word, not as a want, but as an *internal necessity.* It must not be *insufficiency,* but the inopportune character of the latter that gives nature her victory; for insufficiency is only a want and a defect, and nothing that results from a want or defect could produce esteem. No doubt in the simplicity resulting from surprise, it is always the predominance of affection and a want of reflection that causes us to appear natural. But this want and this predominance do not by any means suffice to constitute simplicity; they merely give occasion to nature to *obey without let or hinderance* her *moral constitution,* that is, the *law of harmony.*

The simplicity resulting from surprise can only be encountered in man, and that only in as far as at the moment he ceases to be a pure and innocent nature. This sort of simplicity implies a will that is not in harmony with that which nature does of her own accord. A person simple after this fashion, when recalled to himself, will be the first to be alarmed at what he is; on the other hand, a person in whom simplicity is found as a *feeling,* will only wonder at one thing, that is, at the way in which men feel astonishment. As it is not the moral subject as a person, but only his natural character set free by affection, that confesses the truth, it follows from this that we shall not attribute this sincerity to man as a merit, and that we shall be entitled to laugh at it, our raillery not being held in check by any personal esteem for his character. Nevertheless, as it is still the sincerity of nature which, even in the simplicity caused by surprise, pierces suddenly through the veil of dissimulation, a satisfaction of a superior order is mixed with the mischievous joy we feel in having caught any one in the act. This is because nature, opposed to affectation, and truth, opposed to deception, must in every case inspire us with esteem. Thus we experience, even in the presence of simplicity originating in surprise, a really moral pleasure, though it be not in connection with a moral object.

I admit that in simplicity proceeding from surprise we always experience a feeling of esteem for *nature*, because we must esteem truth; whereas in the simplicity of feeling we esteem the *person* himself, enjoying in this way not only a moral satisfaction, but also a satisfaction of which the object is moral. In both cases nature is *right*, since she speaks the truth; but in the second case not only nature is right, but there is also an act that does *honour* to the person. In the first case the sincerity of nature always puts the person to the blush, because it is involuntary; in the second it is always a merit which must be placed to the credit of the person, even when what he confesses is of a nature to cause a blush.

We attribute simplicity of feeling to a man, when, in the judgments he pronounces on things, he passes, without seeing them, over all the factitious and artificial sides of an object, to keep exclusively to simple nature. We require of him all the judgments that can be formed of things without departing from a sound nature; and we only hold him entirely free in what presupposes a departure from nature in his mode of thinking or feeling.

If a father relates to his son that such and such a person is dying of hunger, and if the child goes and carries the purse of his father to this unfortunate being, this is a simple action. It is in fact a healthy nature that acts in the child; and in a world where healthy nature would be the law, he would be perfectly right to act so. He only sees the misery of his neighbour and the speediest means of relieving him. The extension given to the right of property, in consequence of which part of the human race might perish, is not based on mere nature. Thus the act of this child puts to shame real society, and this is acknowledged by our heart in the pleasure it experiences from this action.

If a good-hearted man, inexperienced in the ways of the world, confides his secrets to another, who deceives him, but who is skilful in disguising his perfidy, and if by his very sincerity he furnishes him with the means of doing him injury, we find his conduct simple. We laugh at him, yet we cannot avoid esteeming him, precisely on account of his simplicity. This is because his trust in others proceeds from the rectitude of his own heart; at all events, there is simplicity here only as far as this is the case.

Simplicity in the mode of thinking cannot then ever be the act of a depraved man; this quality only belongs to children, and to men who are children in heart. It often happens to these in the midst of the artificial relations of the great world to act or to think in a simple manner. Being themselves of a truly good and humane nature, they forget that they have to do with a depraved world; and they act, even in the courts of kings, with an ingenuousness and an innocence that are only found in the world of pastoral idyls.

Nor is it always such an easy matter to distinguish exactly childish candour from childlike candour, for there are actions that are on the skirts of both. Is a certain act foolishly simple, and must we laugh at it? or is it nobly simple, and must we esteem the actors the higher on that account? It is difficult to know which side to take in some cases. A very remarkable example of this is found in the history of the government of Pope Adrian VI., related by Mr. Schröckh with all the solidity and the spirit of practical truth which distinguish him. Adrian, a Netherlander by birth, exerted the pontifical sway at one of the most critical moments for the hierachy—at a time when an exasperated party laid bare without any scruple all the weak sides of the Roman Church, while the opposite party was interested in the highest degree in covering them over. I do not entertain the question how a man of a truly simple character ought to act in such a case, if such a character were placed in the papal chair. But, we ask, how could this simplicity of feeling be compatible with the part of a Pope? This question gave indeed very little embarrassment to the predecessors and successors of Adrian. They followed uniformly the system adopted once for all by the court of Rome, not to make any concessions anywhere. But Adrian had preserved the upright character of his nation and the innocence of his previous condition. Issuing from the humble sphere of literary men to rise to this eminent position, he did not belie at that elevation the primitive simplicity of his character. He was moved by the abuses of the Roman Church, and he was much too sincere to dissimulate publicly what he confessed privately. It was in consequence of this manner of thinking that, in his instruction to his legate in Germany, he allowed himself to be drawn into avowals hitherto unheard of in a sovereign pontiff, and diametrically contrary to the principles of that court: "We know well," he said, among other things, "that for many years many abominable things have taken place in this holy chair; it is not, therefore, astonishing that the evil has been propagated from the head to the members, from the Pope to the prelates. We have all gone astray from the good road, and for a long time there is none of us, not one, who has done anything good." Elsewhere he orders his legate to declare in his name "that he, Adrian, cannot be blamed for what other Popes have done before him; that he himself, when he occupied a comparatively mediocre position, had always condemned these excesses." It may easily be conceived how such simplicity in a Pope must have been received by the Roman clergy. The smallest crime of which he was accused was that of betraying the Church and delivering it over to heretics. Now this proceeding, supremely imprudent in a Pope, would yet deserve our esteem and admiration if we could believe it was real simplicity; that is, that Adrian, without fear of consequences, had made such an avowal moved by his natural sincerity, and that he would have persisted in acting thus, though he had understood all the drift of his clumsiness. Unhappily we have some reason to believe that he did not consider his conduct as altogether impolitic, and that in his candour he went so far as to flatter himself that he had served very usefully the interests of his Church by his indulgence to his adversaries. He did not even imagine that he ought to act thus in his quality as an honest man; he thought also as a Pope to be able to justify himself, and forgetting that the most artificial of structures could only be supported by continuing to deny the truth, he committed the unpardonable fault of having recourse to means of safety, excellent, perhaps, in a natural situation, but here applied to entirely contrary circumstances. This necessarily modifies our judgment very much, and although we cannot refuse our esteem for the honesty of heart in which the act originates, this esteem is greatly lessened when we reflect that nature on this occasion was too easily mistress of art, and that the heart too easily overruled the head.

True genius is of necessity simple, or it is not genius. Simplicity alone gives it this character, and it cannot belie in the moral order what it is in the intellectual and æsthetical order. It does not know those rules, the crutches of feebleness, those pedagogues which prop up slippery spirits; it is only guided by nature and instinct, its guardian angel; it walks with a firm, calm step across all the snares of false taste, snares in which the man without genius, if he have not the prudence to avoid them the moment he detects them, remains infallibly imbedded. It is therefore the part only of genius to issue from the known without ceasing to be at home, or to enlarge the circle of nature without *overstepping* it. It does indeed sometimes happen that a great genius oversteps it; but only because geniuses have their moments of frenzy, when nature, their protector, abandons them, because the force of example impels them, or because the corrupt taste of their age leads them astray.

The most intricate problems must be solved by genius with simplicity, without pretension, with ease; the egg of Christopher Columbus is the emblem of all the discoveries of genius. It only justifies its character as genius by triumphing through simplicity over all the complications of art. It does not proceed according to known principles, but by feelings and inspiration. The sallies of genius are the inspirations of a God (all that healthy nature produces is divine); its feelings are laws for all time, for all human generations.

This childlike character imprinted by genius on its works is also shown by it in its private life and manners. It is *modest,* because nature is always so; but it is not *decent,* because corruption alone is decent. It is *intelligent,* because nature cannot lack intelligence; but it is not *cunning,* because art only can be cunning. It is *faithful* to its character and inclinations, but this is not so much because it has principles as because nature, notwithstanding all its oscillations, always returns to its equilibrium, and brings back the same wants. It is *modest* and even timid, because genius remains always a secret to itself; but it is not anxious, because it does not know the dangers of the road in which it walks. We know little of the private life of the greatest geniuses; but the little that we know of it—what tradition has preserved, for example, of Sophocles, of Archimedes, of Hippocrates, and in modern times of Ariosto, of Dante, of Tasso, of Raphael, of Albert Dürer, of Cervantes, of Shakespeare, of Fielding, of Sterne, etc.—confirms this assertion.

Nay, more; though this admission seems more difficult to support, even the greatest philosophers and great commanders, if great by their genius, have simplicity in their character. Among the ancients I need only name Julius Cæsar and Epaminondas; among the moderns Henry IV. in France, Gustavus

Adolphus in Sweden, and the Czar Peter the Great. The Duke of Marlborough, Turenne, and Vendôme all present this character. With regard to the other sex, nature proposes to it simplicity of character as the supreme perfection to which it should reach. Accordingly, the love of pleasing in women strives after nothing so much as the appearance of *simplicity;* a sufficient proof, if it were the only one, that the greatest power of the sex reposes in this quality. But, as the principles that prevail in the education of women are perpetually struggling with this character, it is as difficult for them in the moral order to reconcile this magnificent gift of nature with the advantages of a good education as it is difficult for men to preserve them unchanged in the intellectual order: and the woman who knows how to join a knowledge of the world to this sort of simplicity of manners is as deserving of respect as a scholar who joins to the strictness of scholastic rules the freedom and orginality of thought.

Simplicity in our mode of thinking brings with it of necessity simplicity in our mode of expression, simplicity in terms as well as movement; and it is in this that grace especially consists. Genius expresses its most sublime and its deepest thoughts with this simple grace; they are the divine oracles that issue from the lips of a child; while the scholastic spirit, always anxious to avoid error, tortures all its words, all its ideas, and makes them pass through the crucible of grammar and logic, hard and rigid, in order to keep from vagueness, and uses few words in order not to say too much, enervates and blunts thought in order not to wound the reader who is not on his guard—genius gives to its expression, with a single and happy stroke of the brush, a precise, firm, and yet perfectly free form. In the case of grammar and logic, the sign and the thing signified are always heterogenous and strangers to each other: with genius, on the contrary, the expression gushes forth spontaneously from the idea, the language and the thought are one and the same, so that even though the expression thus gives it a body the spirit appears as if disclosed in a nude state. This fashion of expression, when the sign disappears entirely in the thing signified, when the tongue, so to speak, leaves the thought it translates naked, whilst the other mode of expression cannot represent thought without veiling it at the same time. This is what is called originality and inspiration in style.

This freedom, this natural mode by which genius expresses itself in works of intellect, is also the expression of the innocence of heart in the intercourse of life. Every one knows that in the world men have departed from simplicity, from the rigorous veracity of language, in the same proportion as they have lost the simplicity of feelings. The guilty conscience easily wounded, the imagination easily seduced, made an anxious decency necessary. Without telling what is false, people often speak differently from what they think; we are obliged to make circumlocutions to say certain things, which, however, can never afflict any but a sickly self-love, and that have no danger except for a depraved imagination. The ignorance of these laws of propriety (conventional laws), coupled with a natural sincerity which despises all kinds of bias and all appearance of falsity (sincerity I mean, not coarseness, for coarseness dispenses with forms because it is hampered), gives rise in the intercourse of life to a simplicity of expression that consists in naming things by their proper name without circumlocution. This is done because we do not venture to designate them as they are, or only to do so by artificial means. The ordinary expressions of children are of this kind. They make us smile because they are in opposition to received manners; but men would always agree in the bottom of their hearts that the child is right.

It is true that simplicity of feeling cannot properly be attributed to the child any more than to the man,—that is, to a being not absolutely subject to nature, though there is still no simplicity, except on the condition that it is pure nature that acts through him. But by an effort of the imagination, which likes to poetise things, we often carry over these attributes of a rational being to beings destitute of reason. It is thus that, on seeing an animal, a landscape, a building, and nature in general, from opposition to what is arbitrary and fantastic in the conceptions of man, we often attribute to them a simple character. But that implies always that in our thought we attribute a will to these things that have none, and that we are struck to see it directed rigorously according to the laws of necessity. Discontented as we are that we have ill employed our own moral freedom, and that we no longer find moral harmony in our conduct, we are easily led to a certain disposition of mind, in which we willingly address ourselves to a being destitute of reason, as if it were a person. And we readily view it as if it had really had to struggle against the temptation of acting otherwise, and proceed to make a merit of its eternal uniformity, and to envy its peaceable constancy. We are quite disposed to consider in those moments reason, this prerogative of the human race, as a pernicious gift and as an evil; we feel so vividly all that is imperfect in our conduct that we forget to be just to our destiny and to our aptitudes.

We see, then, in nature, destitute of reason, only a sister who, more fortunate than ourselves, has remained under the maternal roof, while in the intoxication of our freedom we have fled from it to throw ourselves into a stranger world. We regret this place of safety, we earnestly long to come back to it as soon as we have begun to feel the bitter side of civilisation, and in the totally artificial life in which we are exiled we hear in deep emotion the voice of our mother. While we were still only children of nature we were happy, we were perfect: we have become free, and we have lost both advantages. Hence a twofold and very unequal longing for nature: the longing for happiness and the longing for the perfection that prevails there. Man, as a sensuous being, deplores sensibly the loss of the former of these goods; it is only the moral man who can be afflicted at the loss of the other.

Therefore, let the man with a sensible heart and a loving nature question himself closely. Is it your indolence that longs for its repose, or your wounded moral sense that longs for its harmony? Ask yourself well, when, disgusted with the artifices, offended by the abuses that you discover in social life, you feel yourself attracted toward inanimate nature, in the midst of solitude ask yourself what impels you to fly the world. Is it the privation from which you suffer, its loads, its troubles? or is it the moral anarchy, the caprice, the disorder that prevail there? Your heart ought to plunge into these troubles with joy, and to find in them the compensation in the liberty of which they are the consequence. You can, I admit, propose as your aim, in a distant future, the calm and the happiness of nature; but only that sort of happiness which is the reward of your dignity. Thus, then, let there be no more complaint about the loads of life, the inequality of conditions, or the hampering of social relations, or the uncertainty of possession, ingratitude, oppression, and persecution. You must submit to all these *evils* of civilisation with a free resignation; it is the natural condition of good, *par excellence,* of the only good, and you ought to respect it under this head. In all these *evils* you ought only to deplore what is *morally evil* in them, and you must do so not with cowardly tears only. Rather watch to remain pure yourself in the midst of these impurities, free amidst this slavery, constant with yourself in the midst of these capricious changes, a faithful observer of the law amidst this anarchy. Be not frightened at the disorder that is without you, but at the disorder which is within; aspire after unity, but seek it not in uniformity; aspire after repose, but through equilibrium, and not by suspending the action of your faculties. This nature which you envy in the being destitute of reason deserves no esteem: it is not worth a wish. You have passed beyond it; it ought to remain for ever behind you. The ladder that carried you having given way under your foot, the only thing for you to do is to seize again on the moral law freely, with a free consciousness, a free will, or else to roll down, hopeless of safety, into a bottomless abyss.

But when you have consoled yourself for having lost the *happiness* of nature, let its *perfection* be a model to your heart. If you can issue from the circle in which art keeps you enclosed and find nature again, if it shows itself to you in its greatness and in its calm, in its simple beauty, in its childlike innocence and simplicity, oh! then pause before its image, cultivate this feeling lovingly. It is worthy of you, and of what is noblest in man. Let it no more come into your mind to *change* with it; rather embrace it, absorb it into your being, and try to associate the infinite advantage it has over you with that infinite prerogative that is peculiar to you, and let the divine issue from this sublime union. Let nature breathe around you like a lovely *idyl,* where far from artifice and its wanderings you may always find yourself again, where you may go to draw fresh courage, a new confidence, to resume your course, and kindle again in your heart the flame of the *ideal,* so readily extinguished amidst the tempests of life.

If we think of that beautiful nature which surrounded the ancient Greeks, if we remember how intimately that people, under its blessed sky, could live with that free nature; how their mode of imagining, and of feeling, and their manners, approached far nearer than ours to the simplicity of nature, how faithfully the works of their poets express this; we must necessarily remark, as a strange fact, that so few traces are met among them of that *sentimental* interest that we moderns ever take in the scenes of nature and in natural characters. I admit that the Greeks are superiorly exact and faithful in their descriptions of nature. They reproduce their details with care, but we see that they take no more interest in them and more heart in them than in describing a vestment, a shield, armour, a piece of furniture, or any production of the mechanical arts. In their love for the object it seems that they make no difference between what exists in itself and what owes its existence to art, to the human will. It seems that nature interests their minds and their curiosity more than moral feeling. They do not attach themselves to it with that depth of feeling, with that gentle melancholy, that characterise the moderns. Nay, more, by personifying nature in its particular phenomena, by deifying it, by representing its effects as the acts of free being, they take from it that character of calm necessity which is precisely what makes it so attractive to us. Their impatient imagination only traverses nature to pass beyond it to the drama of human life. It only takes pleasure in the spectacle of what is living and free; it requires characters, acts, the accidents of fortune and of manners; and whilst it happens with *us,* at least in certain moral dispositions, to curse our prerogative, this free will, which exposes us to so many combats with ourselves, to so many anxieties and errors, and to wish to exchange it for the condition of beings destitute of reason, for that fatal existence that no longer admits of any choice, but which is so calm in its uniformity,—while we do this, the Greeks, on the contrary, only have their imagination occupied in retracing human nature in the inanimate world, and in giving to the will an influence where blind necessity rules.

Whence can arise this difference between the spirit of the ancients and the modern spirit? How comes it that, being, for all that relates to nature, incomparably below the ancients, we are superior to them precisely on this point, that we render a more complete homage to nature; that we have a closer attachment to it; and that we are capable of embracing even the inanimate world with the most ardent sensibility? It is because nature, in our time, is no longer in man, and that we no longer encounter it in its primitive truth, except out of humanity, in the inanimate world. It is not because we are more *comfortable to nature*—quite the contrary; it is because in our social relations, in our mode of existence, in our manners, we are in *opposition with nature.* This is what leads us, when the instinct of truth and of simplicity is awakened—this instinct which, like the moral aptitude from which it pro-ceeds, lives incorruptible and indelible in every human heart—to procure for it in the physical world the satisfaction which there is no hope of finding in the moral order. This is the reason why the feeling that attaches us to nature is connected so closely with that which makes us regret our infancy, for ever flown, and our primitive innocence. Our childhood is all that remains of nature in humanity, such as civilisation has made it, of untouched, unmutilated nature. It is, therefore, not wonderful, when we meet out of us the impress of nature, that we are always brought back to the idea of our childhood.

It was quite different with the Greeks in antiquity. Civilisation with them did not degenerate, nor was it carried to such an excess that it was necessary to break with nature. The entire structure of their social life reposed on feelings, and not on a factitious conception, on a work of art. Their very theology was the inspiration of a simple spirit, the fruit of a joyous imagination, and not, like the ecclesiastical dogmas of modern nations, subtle combinations of the understanding. Since, therefore, the Greeks had not lost sight of nature in humanity, they had no reason, when meeting it out of man, to be surprised at their discovery, and they would not feel very imperiously the need of objects in which nature could be retraced. In accord with themselves, happy in feeling themselves men, they would of necessity keep to humanity as to what was greatest to them, and they must needs try to make all the rest approach it; while we, who are not in accord with ourselves—we who are discontented with the experience we have made of our humanity—have no more pressing interest than to fly out of it and to remove from our sight a so ill-fashioned form. The feeling of which we are treating here is, therefore, not that which was known by the ancients; it approaches far more nearly that *which we ourselves experience for the ancients*. The ancients felt naturally; we, on our part, feel what is natural. It was certainly a very different inspiration that filled the soul of Homer, when he depicted his divine cowherd giving hospitality to Ulysses, from that which agitated the soul of the young Werther at the moment when he read the "Odyssey" on issuing from an assembly in which he had only found tedium. The feeling we experience for nature resembles that of a sick man for health.

As soon as nature gradually vanishes from human life—that is, in proportion as it ceases to be *experienced* as a *subject* (active and passive)—we see it dawn and increase in the poetical world in the guise of an *idea* and as an *object*. The people who have carried farthest the want of nature, and at the same time the reflections on that matter, must needs have been the people who at the same time were most struck with this phenomenon of the *simple,* and gave it a name. If I am not mistaken, this people was the French. But the feeling of the simple, and the interest we take in it, must naturally go much farther back, and it dates from the time when the moral sense and the æsthetical sense began to be corrupt. This modification in the manner of feeling is exceedingly striking in Euripides, for example, if compared with his predecessors, especially Æschylus; and yet Euripides was the favourite poet of his time. The same revolution is perceptible in the ancient historians. Horace, the poet of a cultivated and corrupt epoch, praises, under the shady groves of Tibur, the calm and happiness of the country, and he might be termed the true founder of this sentimental poetry, of which he has remained the unsurpassed model. In Propertius, Virgil, and others, we also find traces of this mode of feeling; less of it is found in Ovid, who would have required for that more abundance of heart, and who in his exile at Tomes sorrowfully regrets the happiness that Horace so readily dispensed with in his villa at Tibur.

It is the fundamental idea of poetry that the poet is everywhere the *guardian* of nature. When he can no longer entirely fill this part, and has already in himself suffered the deleterious influence of arbitrary and factitious forms, or has had to struggle against this influence, he presents himself as the *witness* of nature and as its avenger. The poet will, therefore, be the *expression* of nature itself, or his part will be to *seek* it, if men have lost sight of it. Hence arise two kinds of poetry, which embrace and exhaust the entire field of poetry. All poets—I mean those who are really so—will belong, according to the time when they flourish, according to the accidental circumstances that have influenced their education generally, and the different dispositions of mind through which they pass, will belong, I say, to the order of the *sentimental* poetry or to *simple* poetry.

The poet of a young world, simple and inspired, as also the poet who at an epoch of artifical civilisation approaches nearest to the primitive bards, is austere and prudish, like the virginal Diana in her forests. Wholly unconfiding, he hides himself from the heart that seeks him, from the desire that wishes to embrace him. It is not rare for the dry truth with which he treats his subject to resemble insensibility. The whole object possesses him, and to reach his heart it does not suffice, as with metals of little value, to stir up the surface; as with pure gold, you must go down to the lowest depths. Like the Deity behind this universe, the simple poet hides himself behind his work; he is *himself* his work, and his work is *himself.* A man must be no longer worthy of the work, nor understand it, or be tired of it, to be even anxious to learn who is its author.

Such appears to us, for instance, Homer in antiquity, and Shakespeare among moderns: two natures infinitely different and separated in time by an abyss, but perfectly identical as to this trait of character. When, at a very youthful age, I became first acquainted with Shakespeare, I was displeased with his coldness, with his insensibility, which allows him to jest even in the most pathetic moments, to disturb the impression of the most harrowing scenes in "Hamlet," in "King Lear," and in "Macbeth," etc., by mixing with them the buffooneries of a madman. I was revolted by his insensibility, which allowed him to pause sometimes at places where my sensibility would bid me hasten and bear me along, and which sometimes carried him away with indifference when my heart would be so happy to pause. Though I was accustomed, by the practice of modern poets, to seek at once the poet in his works, to meet his heart, to reflect with him in his theme—in a word, to see the object in the subject—I could not bear that the poet could in Shakespeare never be seized, that he would never give me an account of himself. For some years Shakespeare had been the object of my study and of all my respect before I had learned to love his personality. I was not yet able to comprehend nature at first hand. All that my eyes could bear was its image only, reflected by the understanding and arranged by rules: and on this score the sentimental poetry of the French, or that of the Germans, of 1750 to 1780, was what suited me best. For the rest, I do not blush at this childish judgment: adult critics pronounced in that day in the same way, and carried their simplicity so far as to publish their decisions to the world.

The same thing happened to me in the case of Homer, with whom I made acquaintance at a later date. I remember now that remarkable passage of the sixth book of the "Iliad," where Glaucus and Diomed meet each other in the strife, and then, recognising each other as host and guest, exchange presents. With this touching picture of the piety with which the laws of *hospitality* were observed even in war, may be compared a picture of chivalrous generosity in Ariosto. The knights, rivals in love, Ferragus and Rinaldo,—the former a Saracen, the latter a Christian,—after having fought to extremity, all covered with wounds, make peace together, and mount the same horse to go and seek the fugitive Angelica. These two examples, however different in other respects, are very similar with regard to the impression produced on our heart: both represent the noble victory of moral feeling over passion, and touch us by the simplicity of feeling displayed in them. But what a difference in the way in which the two poets go to work to describe two such analogous scenes! Ariosto, who belongs to an advanced epoch, to a world where simplicity of manners no longer existed, in relating this trait, cannot conceal the astonishment, the admiration, he feels at it. He measures the distance from those manners to the manners of his own age, and this feeling of astonishment is too strong for him. He abandons suddenly the painting of the object, and comes himself on the scene in person. This beautiful stanza is well known, and has been always specially admired at all times:

"Oh, nobleness, oh, generosity of the ancient manners of chivalry! These were rivals, separated by their faith, suffering bitter pain throughout their frames in consequence of a desperate combat; and, without any suspicion, behold them riding in company along dark and winding paths. Stimulated by four spurs, the horse hastens his pace till they arrive at the place where the road divides."

Now let us turn to old Homer. Scarcely has Diomed learned by the story of Glaucus, his adversary, that the latter has been, from the time of their fathers, the host and friend of his family, when he drives his lance into the ground, converses familiarly with him, and both agree henceforth to avoid each other in the strife. But let us hear Homer himself:

"Thus, then, I am for thee a faithful host in Argos, and thou to me in Lycia, when I shall visit that country. We shall, therefore, avoid our lances meeting in the strife. Are there not for me other Trojans or brave allies to kill when a god shall offer them to me and my steps shall reach them? And for thee, Glaucus, are there not enough Achæans, that thou mayest immolate whom thou wishest? But let us exchange our arms, in order that others may also see that we boast of having been hosts and guests at the time of our fathers." Thus they spoke, and, rushing from their chariots, they seized each other's hands, and swore friendship the one to the other.

It would have been difficult for a *modern* poet (at least to one who would be modern in the moral sense of the term) even to wait as long as this before expressing his joy in the presence of such an action. We should pardon this in him the more easily, because we also, in reading it, feel that our heart makes a pause here, and readily turns aside from the object to bring back its thoughts on itself. But there is not the least trace of this in Homer. As if he had been relating something that is seen every day—nay, more, as if he had no heart beating in his breast—he continues, with his dry truthfulness:

"Then the son of Saturn blinded Glaucus, who, exchanging his armour with Diomed, gave him golden arms of the value of one hecatomb, for brass arms only worth nine beeves."

The poets of this order,—the genuinely simple poets, are scarcely any longer in their place in this artificial age. Accordingly they are scarcely possible in it, or at least they are only possible on the condition of *traversing* their age, like *scared persons,* at a *running* pace, and of being preserved by a happy star from the influence of their age, which would mutilate their genius. Never, for aye and for ever, will society produce these poets; but out of society they still appear sometimes at intervals, rather, I admit, as strangers, who excite wonder, or as ill-trained children of nature, who give offence. These apparitions, so very comforting for the artist who studies them, and for the real connoisseur, who knows how to appreciate them, are, as a general conclusion, in the age when they are begotten, to a very small degree preposterous. The seal of empire is stamped on their brow, and we,—we ask the Muses to cradle us, to carry us in their arms. The critics, as regular constables of art, detest these poets as *disturbers of rules or of limits.* Homer himself may have been only indebted to the testimony of ten centuries for the reward these aristarchs are kindly willing to concede him. Moreover, they find it a hard matter to maintain their rules against his example, or his authority against their rules.

SENTIMENTAL POETRY

I have previously remarked that the poet *is* nature, or he *seeks* nature. In the former case, he is a simple poet, in the second case, a sentimental poet.

The poetic spirit is immortal, nor can it disappear from humanity; it can only disappear with humanity itself, or with the aptitude to be a man, a human being. And actually, though man by the freedom of his imagination and of his understanding departs from simplicity, from truth, from the necessity of nature, not only a road always remains open to him to return to it, but, moreover, a powerful and indestructible instinct, the moral instinct, brings him incessantly back to nature, and it is precisely the poetical faculty that is united to this instinct by the ties of the closest relationship. Thus man does not lose the poetic faculty directly he parts with the simplicity of nature; only this faculty acts out of him in another direction.

Even at present nature is the only flame that kindles and warms the poetic soul. From nature alone it obtains all its force; to nature alone it speaks in the artificial culture-seeking man. Any other form of displaying its activity is remote from the poetic spirit. Accordingly it may be remarked that it is incorrect to apply the expression poetic to any of the so-styled productions of wit, though the high credit given to French literature has led people for a long period to class them in that category. I repeat that at present, even in the existing phase of culture, it is still nature that powerfully stirs up the poetic spirit, only its present relation to nature is of a different order from formerly.

As long as man dwells in a state of pure nature (I mean pure and not coarse nature), all his being acts at once like a simple sensuous unity, like a harmonious whole. The senses and reason, the receptive faculty and the spontaneously active faculty, have not been as yet separated in their respective functions: *à fortiori* they are not yet in contradiction with each other. Then the feelings of man are not the formless play of chance; nor are his thoughts an empty play of the imagination, without any value. His feelings proceed from the law of necessity; his *thoughts* from *reality*. But when man enters the state of civilisation, and art has fashioned him, this *sensuous* harmony which was in him disappears, and henceforth he can only manifest himself as a *moral unity*, that is, as aspiring to unity. The harmony that existed as a *fact* in the former state, the harmony of feeling and thought, only exists now in an *ideal* state. It is no longer in him, but out of him; it is a conception of thought which he must begin by realising in himself; it is no longer a fact, a reality of his life. Well, now let us take the idea of poetry, which is nothing else than *expressing humanity as completely as possible,* and let us apply this idea to these two states. We shall be brought to infer that, on the one hand, in the state of natural simplicity, when all the faculties of man are exerted together, his being still manifests itself in a harmonious unity, where, consequently, the *totality* of his nature expresses itself in reality itself, the part of the *poet* is necessarily to imitate the

170

real as completely as is possible. In the state of civilisation, on the contrary, when this harmonious competition of the whole of human nature is no longer anything but an idea, the part of the poet is necessarily to raise reality to the ideal, or what amounts to the same thing, *to represent the ideal*. And, actually, these are the only two ways in which, in general, the poetic genius can manifest itself. Their great difference is quite evident, but though there be great opposition between them, a higher idea exists that embraces both, and there is no cause to be astonished if this idea coincides with the very idea of humanity.

This is not the place to pursue this thought any further, as it would require a separate discussion to place it in its full light. But if we only compare the modern and ancient poets together, not according to the accidental forms which they may have employed, but according to their spirit, we shall be easily convinced of the truth of this thought. The thing that touches us in the ancient poets is nature; it is the truth of sense, it is a present and a living reality: modern poets touch us through the medium of ideas.

The path followed by modern poets is moreover that necessarily followed by man generally, individuals as well as the species. Nature reconciles man with himself; art divides and disunites him; the ideal brings him back to unity. Now, the ideal being an infinite that he never succeeds in reaching, it follows that civilised man can never become perfect in his kind, while the man of nature can become so in his. Accordingly in relation to perfection one would be infinitely below the other, if we only considered the relation in which they are both to their own kind and to their maximum. If, on the other hand, it is the kinds that are compared together, it is ascertained that the end to which man tends by civilisation is infinitely superior to that which he reaches through nature. Thus one has his reward, because, having for object a finite magnitude, he completely reaches this object; the merit of the other is to approach an object that is of infinite magnitude. Now, as there are only degrees, and as there is only progress in the second of these evolutions, it follows that the relative merit of the man engaged in the ways of civilisation is never determinable in general, though this man, taking the individuals separately, is necessarily at a disadvantage, compared with the man in whom nature acts in all its perfection. But we know also that humanity cannot reach its final end except by *progress*, and that the man of nature cannot make progress save through culture, and consequently by passing himself through the way of civilisation. Accordingly there is no occasion to ask with which of the two the advantage must remain, considering this last end.

All that we say here of the different forms of humanity may be applied equally to the two orders of poets who correspond to them.

Accordingly it would have been desirable not to compare at all the ancient and the modern poets, the simple and the sentimental poets, or only to compare them by referring them to a higher idea (since there is really only one) which embraces both. For, sooth to say, if we begin by forming a specific idea of poetry, merely from the ancient poets, nothing is easier, but also nothing is more vulgar, than to depreciate the moderns by this comparison. If persons wish to confine the name of poetry to that which has in all times produced the same impression in simple nature, this places them in the necessity of contesting the title of poet in the moderns precisely in that which constitutes their highest beauties, their greatest originality and sublimity; for precisely in the points where they excel the most, it is the child of civilisation whom they address, and they have nothing to say to the simple child of nature.

To the man who is not disposed beforehand to issue from reality in order to enter the field of the ideal, the richest and most substantial poetry is an empty appearance, and the sublimest flights of poetic inspiration are an exaggeration. Never will a reasonable man think of placing alongside Homer, in his grandest episodes, any of our modern poets; and it has a discordant and ridiculous effect to hear Milton or Klopstock honoured with the name of a "new Homer." But take in modern poets what characterises them, what makes their special merit, and try to compare any ancient poet with them in this point, they will not be able to support the comparison any better, and Homer less than any other. I should express it thus: the power of the ancients consists in compressing objects into the finite, and the moderns excel in the art of the infinite.

What we have said here may be extended to the fine arts in general, except certain restrictions that are self-evident. If, then, the strength of the artists of antiquity consists in determining and limiting objects, we must no longer wonder that in the field of the plastic arts the ancients remain so far superior to the moderns, nor especially that poetry and the plastic arts with the moderns, compared respectively with what they were among the ancients, do not offer the same relative value. This is because an object that addresses itself to the eyes is only perfect in proportion as the object is clearly limited in it; whilst a work that is addressed to the imagination can also reach the perfection which is proper to it by means of the ideal and the infinite. This is why the superiority of the moderns in what relates to ideas is not of great aid to them in the plastic arts, where it is necessary for them to *determine* in *space,* with the greatest precision, the image which their imagination has conceived, and where they must therefore measure themselves with the ancient artist just on a point where his superiority cannot be contested. In the matter of poetry it is another affair, and if the advantage is still with the ancients on that ground, as respects the simplicity of forms,—all that can be represented by sensuous features, all that is something *bodily,*—yet, on the other hand, the moderns have the advantage over the ancients as regards fundamental wealth, and all that can neither be represented nor translated by sensuous signs; in short, for all that is called mind and idea in the works of art.

From the moment that the simple poet is content to follow simple nature and feeling, that he is contented with the imitation of the real world, he can only be placed, with regard to his subject, in a single relation. And in this respect he has no choice as to the manner of treating it. If simple poetry produces different impressions,—I do not, of course, speak of the impressions that are connected with the nature of the subject, but only of those that are dependent on poetic execution,—the whole difference is in the *degree;* there is only one way of feeling, which varies from more to less; even the diversity of external forms changes nothing in the quality of æsthetic impressions. Whether the form be lyric or epic, dramatic or descriptive, we can receive an impression either stronger or weaker, but if we remove what is connected with the nature of the subject, we shall always be affected in the same way. The feeling we experience is absolutely identical; it proceeds entirely from one single and the same element to such a degree that we are unable to make any distinction. The very difference of tongues and that of times does not here occasion any diversity, for their strict unity of origin and of effect is precisely a characteristic of simple poetry.

It is quite different with sentimental poetry. The sentimental poet *reflects* on the impression produced on him by objects; and it is only on this reflection that his poetic force is based. It follows that the sentimental poet is always concerned with two opposite forces, has two modes of representing objects to himself, and of feeling them; these are, the real or limited, and the ideal or infinite; and the mixed feeling that he will awaken will always testify to this duality of origin. Sentimental poetry thus admitting more than one principle, it remains to know which of the two will be *predominant* in the poet, both in his fashion of feeling and in that of representing the object; and consequently a difference in the mode of treating it is possible. Here, then, a new subject is presented; shall the poet attach himself to the real or the ideal? to the real as an object of aversion and of disgust, or to the ideal as an object of inclination? The poet will therefore be able to treat the same subject either in its *satirical aspect* or in its *elegiac* aspect,—taking these words in a larger sense, which will be explained in the sequel: every sentimental poet will of necessity become attached to one or the other of these two modes of feeling.

ON THE SUBLIME

"Man is never obliged to say, *I must—must*," says the Jew Nathan to the dervish; and this expression is true in a wider sense than man might be tempted to suppose. The will is the specific character of man, and reason itself is only the eternal rule of his will. All nature acts reasonably; all our prerogative is to act reasonably, with consciousness and with will. All other objects obey necessity; man is the being who wills.

It is exactly for this reason that there is nothing more inconsistent with the dignity of man than to suffer violence, for violence effaces him. He who does violence to us disputes nothing less than our humanity; he who submits in a cowardly spirit to the violence abdicates his quality of man. But this pretension to remain absolutely free from all that is violence seems to imply a being in possession of a force sufficiently great to keep off all other forces. But if this pretension is found in a being who, in the order of forces, cannot claim the first rank, the result is an unfortunate contradiction between his instinct and his power.

Man is precisely in this case. Surrounded by numberless forces, which are all superior to him and hold sway over him, he aspires by his nature not to have to suffer any injury at their hands. It is true that by his intelligence he adds artificially to his natural forces, and that up to a certain point he actually succeeds in reigning physically over everything that is physical. The proverb says, "There is a remedy for everything except death;" but this exception, if it is one in the strictest acceptation of the term, would suffice to entirely ruin the very idea of our nature. Never will man be the cause that wills, if there is a case, *a single case,* in which, with or without his consent, he is forced to do what he does not wish. This single terrible exception, to be or to do what is necessary and not what he wishes, this idea will pursue him as a phantom; and as we see in fact among the greater part of men, it will give him up a prey to the blind terrors of imagination. His boasted liberty is nothing, if there is a single point where he is under constraint and bound. It is education that must give back liberty to man, and help him to complete the whole idea of his nature. It ought, therefore, to make him capable of making his will prevail, for, I repeat it, man is the being who wills.

It is possible to reach this end in two ways: either *really,* by opposing force to force, by commanding nature, as nature yourself; or by the *idea,* issuing from nature, and by thus destroying in relation to self the very idea of violence. All that helps man really to hold sway over nature is what is styled physical education. Man cultivates his understanding and develops his physical force, either to convert the forces of nature, according to their proper laws, into the instruments of his will, or to secure himself against their effects when he cannot direct them. But the forces of nature can only be directed or turned aside up to a certain point; beyond that point they withdraw from the influence of man and place him under theirs.

Thus beyond the point in question his freedom would be lost, were he only susceptible of physical education. But he must be man in the full sense of the term, and consequently he must have nothing to endure, in any case, *contrary* to his will. Accordingly, when he can no longer oppose to the physical forces any proportional physical force, only one resource remains to him to avoid suffering any violence: that is, to cause to *cease entirely that relation* which is so fatal to him. It is, in short, to *annihilate* as an *idea* the violence he is obliged to suffer in fact. The education that fits man for this is called moral education.

The man fashioned by moral education, and he only, is entirely free. He is either superior to nature as a power, or he is in harmony with her. None of the actions that she brings to bear upon him is violence, for before reaching him it has become an *act of his own will*, and dynamic nature could never touch him, because he spontaneously keeps away from all to which she can reach. But to attain to this state of mind, which morality designates as resignation to necessary things, and religion styles absolute submission to the counsels of Providence, to reach this by an effort of his free will and with reflection, a certain clearness is required in thought, and a certain energy in the will, superior to what man commonly possesses in active life. Happily for him, man finds here not only in his rational nature a moral aptitude that can be developed by the understanding, but also in his reasonable and sensible nature—that is, in his human nature—an *æsthetic* tendency which seems to have been placed there expressly: a faculty awakens of itself in the presence of certain sensuous objects, and which, after our feelings are purified, can be cultivated to such a point as to become a powerful ideal development. This aptitude, I grant, is *idealistic* in its principle and in its essence, but one which even the realist allows to be seen clearly enough in his conduct, though he does not acknowledge this in theory. I am now about to discuss this faculty.

I admit that the sense of the beautiful, when it is developed by culture, suffices of itself even to make us, in a certain sense, independent of nature as far as it is a force. A mind that has ennobled itself sufficiently to be more sensible of the form than of the matter of things, contains in itself a plenitude of existence that nothing could make it lose, especially as it does not trouble itself about the possession of the things in question, and finds a very liberal pleasure in the mere contemplation of the phenomenon. As this mind has no want to appropriate the objects in the midst of which it lives, it has no fear of being deprived of them. But it is nevertheless necessary that these phenomena should have a body, through which they manifest themselves; and, consequently, as long as we feel the want even only of finding a beautiful appearance or a beautiful phenomenon, this want implies that of the existence of certain objects; and it follows that our satisfaction still depends on nature, considered as a force, because it is nature who disposes of all existence in a sovereign manner. It is a different thing, in fact, to feel in yourself the want of objects endowed with beauty and goodness, or simply to require that the objects which surround us are good and beautiful. This last desire is compatible with the most perfect freedom of the soul; but it is not so with the other. We are entitled to require that the object before us should be beautiful and good, but we can only wish that the beautiful and the good should be realised objectively before us. Now the disposition of mind is, *par excellence*, called grand and sublime, in which no attention is given to the question of knowing if the beautiful, the good, and the perfect exist; but when it is rigorously required that that which exists should be good, beautiful, and perfect, this character of mind is called sublime, because it contains in it positively all the characteristics of a fine mind without sharing its negative features.

A sign by which beautiful and good minds, but having weaknesses, are recognised, is the aspiring always to find their moral ideal realised in the world of facts, and their being painfully affected by all that places an obstacle to it. A mind thus constituted is reduced to a sad state of dependence in relation to chance, and it may always be predicted of it, without fear of deception, that it will give too large a share to the matter in moral and æsthetical things, and that it will not sustain the more critical trials of character and taste. Moral imperfections ought not to be to us a cause of *suffering* and of pain: suffering and pain bespeak rather an ungratified wish than an unsatisfied moral want. An unsatisfied moral want ought to be accompanied by a more manly feeling, and fortify our mind and confirm it in its energy rather than make us unhappy and pusillanimous.

Nature has given to us two genii as companions in our life in this lower world. The one, amiable and of good companionship, shortens the troubles of the journey by the gaiety of its plays. It makes the chains of necessity light to us, and leads us, amidst joy and laughter, to the most perilous spots, where we must act as pure spirits and strip ourselves of all that is body, on the knowledge of the true and the practice of duty. Once when we are there, it abandons us, for its realm is limited to the world of sense; its earthly wings could not carry it beyond. But at this moment the other companion steps upon the stage, silent and grave, and with his powerful arm carries us beyond the precipice that made us giddy.

In the former of these genii we recognise the feeling of the beautiful, in the other the feeling of the sublime. No doubt the beautiful itself is already an expression of liberty. This liberty is not the kind that raises us above the power of nature, and that sets us free from all bodily influence, but it is only the liberty which we enjoy as men, without issuing from the limits of nature. In the presence of beauty we feel ourselves free, because the sensuous instincts are in harmony with the laws of reason. In presence of the sublime we feel ourselves sublime, because the sensuous instincts have no influence over the jurisdiction of reason, because it is then the pure spirit that acts in us as if it were not absolutely subject to any other laws than its own.

The feeling of the sublime is a mixed feeling. It is at once a *painful state*, which in its paroxysm is manifested by a kind of shudder, and a *joyous state*, that may rise to rapture, and which, without being properly a pleasure, is greatly preferred to every kind of pleasure by delicate souls. This union of two contrary sensations in one and the same feeling proves in a peremptory manner our moral independence. For as it is absolutely impossible that the same object should be with us in two opposite relations, it follows that it is we *ourselves* who sustain two different relations with the object. It follows that these two opposed natures should be united in us, which, on the idea of this object, are brought into play in two perfectly opposite ways. Thus we experience by the feeling of the beautiful that the state of our spiritual nature is not necessarily determined by the state of our sensuous nature; that the laws of nature are not necessarily our laws; and that there is in us an autonomous principle independent of all sensuous impressions.

The sublime object may be considered in two lights. We either represent it to our *comprehension,* and we try in vain to make an image or idea of it, or we refer it to our *vital force,* and we consider it as a power before which ours is nothing. But though in both cases we experience in connection with this object the painful feeling of *our limits,* yet we do not seek to avoid it; on the contrary we are attracted to it by an irresistible force. Could this be the case if the limits of our imagination were at the same time those of our comprehension? Should we be willingly called back to the feeling of the omnipotence of the forces of nature if we had not in us something that cannot be a prey of these forces? We are pleased with the spectacle of the sensuous infinite, because we are able to attain by thought what the senses can no longer embrace and what the understanding cannot grasp. The sight of a terrible object transports us with enthusiasm, because we are capable of willing what the instincts reject with horror, and of rejecting what they desire. We willingly allow our imagination to find something in the world of phenomena that passes beyond it; because, after all, it is only one sensuous force that triumphs over another sensuous force, but nature, notwithstanding all her infinity, cannot attain to the absolute grandeur which is in ourselves. We submit willingly to physical necessity both our well-being and our existence. This is because the very power reminds us that there are in us principles that escape its empire. Man is in the hands of nature, but the will of man is in his own hands.

Nature herself has actually used a sensuous means to teach us that we are something more than mere sensuous natures. She has even known how to make use of our sensations to put us on the track of this discovery—that we are by no means subject as slaves to the violence of the sensations. And this is quite a different effect from that which can be produced by the beautiful; I mean the beautiful of the *real* world, for the sublime itself is surpassed by the *ideal.* In the presence of beauty, reason and sense are in harmony, and it is only on account of this harmony that the beautiful has attraction for us. Consequently, beauty alone could never teach us that our destination is to act as pure intelligences, and that we are capable of showing ourselves such. In the presence of the sublime, on the contrary, reason and the sensuous are not in harmony, and it is precisely this contradiction between the two which makes the charm of the sublime,—its irresistible action on our minds. Here the physical man and the moral man separate in the most marked manner; for it is exactly in the presence of objects that make us feel at once how limited the former is that the other makes the experience of its force. The very thing that lowers one to the earth is precisely that which raises the other to the infinite.

Let us imagine a man endowed with all the virtues of which the union constitutes a *fine* character. Let us suppose a man who finds his delight in practising justice, beneficence, moderation, constancy, and good faith. All the duties whose accomplishment is prescribed to him by circumstances are only a play to him, and I admit that fortune favours him in such wise that none of the actions which his good heart may demand of him will be hard to him. Who would not be charmed with such a delightful harmony between the instincts of nature and the prescriptions of reason? and who could help admiring such a man? Nevertheless, though he may inspire us with affection, are we quite sure that he is really virtuous? or in general that he has anything that corresponds to the idea of virtue? If this man had only in view to obtain agreeable sensations, unless he were mad he could not act in any other possible way; and he would have to be his own enemy to wish to be vicious. Perhaps the principle of his actions is pure, but this is a question to be discussed between himself and his conscience. For *our* part, we see nothing of it; we do not see him do anything more than a simply clever man would do who had no other god than pleasure. Thus all his virtue is a phenomenon that is explained by reasons derived from the sensuous order, and we are by no means driven to seek for reasons beyond the world of sense.

Let us suppose that this same man falls suddenly under misfortune. He is deprived of his possessions; his reputation is destroyed; he is chained to his bed by sickness and suffering; he is robbed by death of all those he loves; he is forsaken in his distress by all in whom he had trusted. Let us under these circumstances again seek him, and demand the practice of the same virtues under trial as he formerly had practised during the period of his prosperity. If he is found to be absolutely the same as before, if his poverty has not deteriorated his benevolence, or ingratitude his kindly offices of good-will, or bodily suffering his equanimity, or adversity his joy in the happiness of others; if his change of fortune is perceptible in externals, but not in his habits, in the matter but not in the form of his conduct; then, doubtless, his virtue could not be explained by any reason drawn from the physical order; *the idea of nature*— which always necessarily supposes that actual phenomena rest upon some anterior phenomenon, as effects upon cause—this idea no longer suffices to enable us to comprehend this man; because there is nothing more contradictory than to admit that effect can remain the same when the cause has changed to its contrary. We must then give up all natural explanation or thought of finding the reason of his acts in his condition; we must of necessity go beyond the physical order, and seek the principle of his conduct in quite another world, to which the reason can indeed raise itself with its ideas, but which the understanding cannot grasp by its conceptions. It is this revelation of the absolute moral power which is subjected to no condition of nature, it is this which gives to the melancholy feeling that seizes our heart at the sight of such a man that peculiar, inexpressible charm, which no delight of the senses, however refined, could arouse in us to the same extent as the sublime.

Thus the sublime opens to us a road to overstep the limits of the world of sense, in which the feeling of the beautiful would for ever imprison us. It is not little by little (for between absolute dependence and absolute liberty there is no possible transition), it is suddenly and by a shock that the sublime wrenches our spiritual and independent nature away from the net which feeling has spun round us, and which enchains the soul the more tightly because of its subtle texture. Whatever may be the extent to which feeling has gained a mastery over men by the latent influence of a softening taste, when even it should have succeeded in penetrating into the most secret recesses of moral jurisdiction under the deceptive envelope of spiritual beauty, and there poisoning the holiness of principle at its source—one single sublime emotion often suffices to break all this tissue of imposture, at one blow to give freedom to the fettered elasticity of spiritual nature, to reveal its true destination, and to oblige it to conceive, for one instant at least, the feeling of its liberty. Beauty, under the shape of the divine Calypso, bewitched the virtuous son of Ulysses, and the power of her charms held him long a prisoner in her island. For long he believed he was obeying an immortal divinity, whilst he was only the slave of sense; but suddenly an impression of the sublime in the form of Mentor seizes him; he remembers that he is called to a higher destiny—he throws himself into the waves, and is free.

The sublime, like the beautiful, is spread profusely throughout nature, and the faculty to feel both one and the other has been given to all men; but the germ does not develop equally; it is necessary that art should lend its aid. The aim of nature supposes already that we ought spontaneously to advance toward the beautiful, although we still avoid the sublime: for the beautiful is like the nurse of our childhood, and it is for her to refine our soul in withdrawing it from the rude state of nature. But though she is our first affection, and our faculty of feeling is first developed for her, nature has so provided, nevertheless, that this faculty ripens slowly and awaits its full development until the understanding and the heart are formed. If taste attains its full maturity before truth and morality have been established in our heart by a better road than that which taste would take, the sensuous world would remain the limit of our aspirations. We should not know, either in our ideas or in our feelings, how to pass beyond the world of sense, and all that imagination failed to represent would be without reality to us. But happily it enters into the plan of nature, that taste, although it first comes into bloom, is the last to ripen of all the faculties of the mind. During this interval, man has time to store up in his mind a provision of ideas, a treasure of principles in his heart, and then to develop especially, in drawing from reason, his feeling for the great and the sublime.

As long as man was only the slave of physical necessity, while he had found no issue to escape from the narrow circle of his appetites, and while he as yet felt none of that superior liberty which connects him with the *angels*, nature, so far as she is *incomprehensible*, could not fail to impress him with the insufficiency of his imagination, and again, as far as she is a destructive force, to recall his physical powerlessness. He is forced then to pass timidly toward one, and to turn away with affright from the other. But scarcely has free contemplation assured him against the blind oppression of the forces of nature—scarcely has he recognised amidst the tide of phenomena something permanent in his own being—than at once the coarse agglomeration of nature that surrounds him begins to speak in another language to his heart, and the relative grandeur which is without becomes for him a mirror in which he contemplates the absolute greatness which is within himself. He approaches without fear, and with a thrill of pleasure, those pictures which terrified his imagination, and intentionally makes an appeal to the whole strength of that faculty by which we represent the infinite perceived by the senses, in order if she fails in this attempt, to feel all the more vividly how much these ideas are superior to all that the highest sensuous faculty can give. The sight of a distant infinity—of heights beyond vision, this vast ocean which is at his feet, that other ocean still more vast which stretches above his head, transport and ravish his mind beyond the narrow circle of the real, beyond this narrow and oppressive prison of physical life. The simple majesty of nature offers him a less circumscribed measure for estimating its grandeur, and, surrounded by the grand outlines which it presents to him, he can no longer bear anything mean in his way of thinking. Who can tell how many luminous ideas, how many heroic resolutions, which would never have been conceived in the dark study of the imprisoned man of science, nor in the saloons where the people of society elbow each other, have been inspired on a sudden during a walk, only by the contact and the generous struggle of the soul with the great spirit of nature? Who knows if it is not owing to a less frequent intercourse with this sublime spirit that we must partially attribute the narrowness of mind so common to the dwellers in towns, always bent under the minutiæ which dwarf and wither their soul, whilst the soul of the nomad remains open and free as the firmament beneath which he pitches his tent?

But it is not only the unimaginable or the sublime in quantity, it is also the incomprehensible, that which escapes the understanding and that which *troubles* it, which can serve to give us an idea of the supersensuous infinity. As soon as this element attains the grandiose and announces itself to us as the work of nature (for otherwise it is only despicable), it then aids the soul to represent to itself the ideal, and imprints upon it a noble development. Who does not prefer the eloquent disorder of natural scenery to the insipid regularity of a French garden? Who does not admire in the plains of Sicily the marvellous combat of nature with herself—of her creative force and her destructive power? Who does not prefer to feast his eyes upon the wild streams and waterfalls of Scotland, upon its misty mountains, upon that romantic nature from which Ossian drew his inspiration—rather than to grow enthusiastic in this stiff Holland, before the laborious triumph of patience over the most stubborn of elements? No one will deny that in the rich grazing-grounds of Holland, things are not better ordered for the wants of physical man than upon the perfervid crater of Vesuvius, and that the understanding which likes to comprehend and arrange all things does not find its requirements rather in the regularly planted farm-garden than in the uncultivated beauty of natural scenery. But man has requirements which go beyond those of natural life and comfort or well-being; he has another destiny than merely to comprehend the phenomena which surround him.

In the same manner as for the observant traveller the strange wildness of nature is so attractive in physical nature—thus, and for the same reason, every soul capable of enthusiasm finds even in the regrettable anarchy found in the moral world a source of singular pleasure. Without doubt he who sees the grand economy of nature only from the impoverished light of the understanding; he who has never any other thought than to reform its defiant disorder and to substitute harmony, such a one could not find pleasure in a world which seems given up to the caprice of chance rather than governed according to a wise ordination, and where merit and fortune are for the most part in opposition. He desires that the whole world throughout its vast space should be ruled like a house well regulated; and when this much-desired regularity is not found, he has no other resource than to defer to future life, and to another and better nature, the satisfaction which is his due, but which neither the present nor the past afford him. On the contrary, he renounces willingly the pretension of restoring this chaos of phenomena to one single notion; he regains on another side, and with interest, what he loses on this side. Just this want of connection, this anarchy, in the phenomena, making them useless to the understanding, is what makes them valuable to reason. The more they are disorderly the more they represent the freedom of nature. In a sense, if you suppress all connection, you have independence. Thus, under the idea of liberty, reason brings back to *unity of thought* that which the understanding could not bring to unity of notion. It thus shows its superiority over the understanding, as a faculty subject to the conditions of a sensuous order. When we consider of what value it is to a rational being to be independent of natural laws we see how much man finds in the liberty of sublime objects as a set-off against the checks of his cognitive faculty. Liberty, with all its drawbacks, is everywhere vastly more attractive to a noble soul than good social order without it—than society like a flock of sheep, or a machine working like a watch. This mechanism makes of man only a product; liberty makes him the citizen of a better world.

It is only thus viewed that history is sublime to me. The world, as a historic object, is only the strife of natural forces; with one another and with man's freedom. History registers more actions referable to nature than to free-will; it is only in a few cases, like Cato and Phocion, that reason has made its power felt. If we expect a treasury of knowledge in history, how we are deceived! All attempts of philosophy to reconcile what the moral world demands with what the real world gives is belied by experience, and nature seems as illogical in history as she is logical in the organic kingdoms.

But if we give up explanation it is different. Nature, in being capricious and defying logic, in pulling down great and little, in crushing the noblest works of man, taking centuries to form—nature, by deviating from intellectual laws, proves that you cannot explain nature by nature's laws *themselves*, and this sight drives the mind to the world of ideas, to the absolute.

But though nature as a sensuous activity drives us to the ideal, it throws us still more into the world of ideas by the terrible. Our highest aspiration is to be in good relations with physical nature, without violating morality. But it is not always convenient to serve two masters; and though duty and the appetites should never be at strife, physical necessity is peremptory, and nothing can save men from evil destiny. Happy is he who learns to bear what he cannot change! There are cases where fate overpowers all ramparts, and where the only resistance is, like a pure spirit, to throw freely off all interest of sense, and strip yourself of your body. Now this force comes from sublime emotions, and a frequent commerce with destructive nature. Pathos is a sort of artificial misfortune, and brings us to the spiritual law that commands our soul. Real misfortune does not always choose its time opportunely, while pathos finds us armed at all points. By frequently renewing this exercise of its own activity the mind controls the sensuous, so that when real misfortune comes, it can treat it as an artificial suffering, and make it a sublime emotion. Thus pathos takes away some of the malignity of destiny, and wards off its blows.

Away then with that false theory which supposes falsely a harmony binding well being and well doing. Let evil destiny show its face. Our safety is not in blindness, but in facing our dangers. What can do so better than familiarity with the splendid and terrible evolution of events, or than pictures showing man in conflict with chance; evil triumphant, security deceived— pictures shown us throughout history, and placed before us by tragedy? Whoever passes in review the terrible fate of Mithridates, of Syracuse, and Carthage, cannot help keeping his appetite in check, at least for a time, and, seeing the vanity of things, strive after that which is permanent. The capacity of the sublime is one of the noblest aptitudes of man. Beauty is useful, but does not go beyond man. The sublime applies to the pure spirit. The sublime must be joined to the beautiful to complete the *aesthetic education,* and to enlarge man's heart beyond the sensuous world.

Without the beautiful there would be an eternal strife between our natural and rational destiny. If we only thought of our vocation as spirits we should be strangers to this sphere of life. Without the sublime, beauty would make us forget our dignity. Enervated—wedded to this transient state, we should lose sight of our true country. We are only perfect citizens of nature when the sublime is wedded to the beautiful.

Many things in nature offer man the beautiful and sublime. But here again he is better served at secondhand. He prefers to have them ready-made in art rather than seek them painfully in nature. This instinct for imitation in art has the advantage of being able to make those points essential that nature has made secondary. While nature *suffers* violence in the organic world, or exercises violence, working with power upon man, though she can only be æsthetical as an object of pure contemplation, art, plastic art, is fully free because it throws off all accidental restrictions and leaves the mind free, because it imitates the appearance, not the reality of objects. As all sublimity and beauty consists in the appearance, and not in the value of the object, it follows that art has all the advantages of nature without her shackles.

Madame De Staël

1766–1817

Madame de Staël was born Anne Louise Germaine Necker in Paris on April 22, 1766, the daughter of Swiss parents. Her father was a Geneva banker who became Louis XVI's finance minister; her mother was known for her literary and political salon, in which the young Germaine participated as a child.

In 1786 she was married to the Swedish ambassador in Paris, Baron Eric de Staël-Holstein, and before the age of twenty-one she had written several plays that were later published. She was influenced at an early age by both Rousseau and Montesquieu, and in 1788 published *Lettres sur les ouvrages et le caractère de J.-J. Rousseau*, which gained considerable attention. Her political views, which favored the English parliamentarian form of government, led her to support the Revolution and she was identified with the Jacobin cause. Unsatisfied with her first marriage, she became the mistress of Louis de Narbonne, one of Louis XVI's ministers, and joined him in exile in England in 1793. The following year she returned to France and began a salon that flourished. She also published political and literary essays, including *De l'influence des passions* (1796), which became an important document in European Romanticism. At this time she also began reading German writers, particularly Humboldt and the Schlegels, under the tutelage of her new lover, Henri Benjamin Constant de Rebecque, who is believed to have fathered her daughter, Albertine de Staël, born in 1796.

Madame de Staël's literary importance was established with the publication in 1800 of *De la littérature considérée dans ses rapports avec les institutions sociales*, described by Chateaubriand as "a prospectus of Romanticism." Its central idea is that a successful work of art must express the *Zeitgeist,* the unique moral and historical spirit, of the nation in which it is conceived. She also expressed the belief that Nordic and Classical ideas were basically opposed, and declared herself in favor of the Nordic. Her two novels, *Delphine* (1802) and *Corinne* (1807), can be read as illustrations of her literary theories.

Madame de Staël disliked Napoleon, and with Constant and a group of friends formed a liberal group that opposed him. In 1803 he had her banished from Paris, and she thenceforth made the family home in Coppet, Switzerland, outside Geneva, her headquarters. In 1803–1804 she traveled through Germany, visiting Weimar and Berlin, where she met A. W. Schlegel, who later became her traveling companion. The following year she traveled to Italy; from experiences there she wrote her two novels.

Madame de Staël's most important work is *De l'Allemagne*, published in 1810. In this work, based on her travels through Germany, she describes for her contemporaries German Romanticism in the years 1770–80. Napoleon, interpreting the work as anti-French, seized the French edition and had it destroyed. It was published in England in 1813.

In 1811, Madame de Staël married a young Swiss officer. In 1812, persecuted by the police, she fled to Austria, traveled to Russia, Finland, and Sweden, and then went to England in June 1813. In general, she was received with enthusiasm. She returned to Paris after the Bourbon restoration in 1814 but was disillusioned by the new regime. During the Hundred Days she fled to Coppet, then spent the next few years travelling in Italy and Switzerland. Toward the end of her life she became friendly with Byron, who was also in exile. In failing health she returned to Paris for the winter of 1816–17 and briefly resumed her salon. She died in Paris on July 14, 1817.

GERMANY

PART II

Chapter II

Of the Judgment Formed by the English on the Subject
of German Literature

German literature is much better known in England than in France. In England, the foreign languages are more studied, and the Germans are more naturally connected with the English, than with the French; nevertheless, prejudices exist even in England, both against the philosophy and the literature of Germany. It may be interesting to examine the cause of them.

The minds of the people of England are not formed by a taste for society, by the pleasure and interest excited by conversation. Business, parliament, the administration, fill all heads, and political interests are the principal objects of their meditations. The English wish to discover consequences immediately applicable to every subject, and from thence arises their dislike of a philosophy, which has for its object the beautiful rather than the useful.

The English, it is true, do not separate dignity from utility, and they are always ready, when it is necessary, to sacrifice the useful to the honorable; but they are not of those, who, as it is said in Hamlet, "with the incorporal air do hold discourse"—a sort of conversation of which the Germans are very fond. The philosophy of the English is directed towards results beneficial to the cause of humanity: the Germans pursue truth for its own sake, without thinking on the advantages which men may derive from it. The nature of their different governments having offered them no great or splendid opportunity of attaining glory, or of serving their country, they attach themselves to contemplation of every kind; and, to indulge it, seek in heaven that space which their limited destiny denies to them on earth. They take pleasure in the ideal, because there is nothing in the actual state of things which speaks to their imagination. The English, with reason, pride themselves in all they possess, in all they are, and in all that they may become; they place their admiration and love on their laws, their manners, and their forms of worship. These noble sentiments give to the soul more strength and energy; but thought, perhaps, takes a bolder flight, when it has neither limit nor determinate aim, and when incessantly connecting itself with the immense and the infinite, no interest brings it back to the affairs of this world.

Whenever an idea is consolidated, or, in other words, when it is changed into effect, nothing can be better than to examine attentively its consequences and conclusions, and then to circumscribe and fix them; but when it is merely in theory, it should be considered in itself alone. Neither practice nor utility are the objects of inquiry; and the pursuit of truth in philosophy, like imagination in poetry, should be free from all restraint.

The Germans are to the human mind what pioneers are to an army: they try new roads, they try unknown means: how can we avoid being curious to know what they say on their return from their excursions into the infinite? The English, who have so much originality of character, have nevertheless generally a dread of new systems. Justness of thought has been so beneficial to them in the affairs of life, that they like to discover it even in intellectual studies; and yet it is in these that boldness is inseparable from genius. Genius, provided it respect religion and morality, should be free to take any flight it chooses: it aggrandizes the empire of thought.

Literature, in Germany, is so impressed with the reigning philosophy, that the repugnance felt for the one will influence the judgment we form of the other. The English have, how ever, for some time, translated the German poets with pleasure, and do not fail to perceive that analogy which ought to result from one common origin. There is more sensibility in the English poetry, and more imagination in that of Germany. Domestic affections holding great sway over the hearts of the English, their poetry is impressed with the delicacy and permanency of those affections: the Germans, more independent in all things, because they bear the impress of no political institution, paint sentiments as well as ideas through a cloud: it might be said that the universe vacillates before their eyes; and even, by the uncertainty of their sight, those objects are multiplied, which their talent renders useful to its own purposes.

The principle of terror, which is employed as one of the great means in German poetry, has less ascendency over the imagination of the English in our days. They describe nature with enthusiasm, but it no longer acts as a formidable power which incloses phantoms and presages within its breast; and holds, in modern times, the place held by destiny among the ancients. Imagination in England is almost always inspired by sensibility; the imaginations of the Germans is sometimes rude and wild: the religion of England is more austere, that of Germany more vague; and the poetry of the two nations must necessarily bear the impression of their religious sentiments. In England conformity to rule does not reign in the arts, as it does in France; nevertheless, public opinion holds a greater sway there than in Germany. National unity is the cause of it. The English wish, in all things, to make principles and actions accord with each other. Theirs is a wise and well-regulated nation, which comprises glory in wisdom, and liberty in order: the Germans, with whom these are only subjects of reverie, have examined ideas independent of their application, and have thus attained a higher elevation in theory.

It will appear strange, that the present men of literature in Germany, have shown themselves more averse than the English to the introduction of philosophical reflections in poetry. It is true, that men of the highest genius in English literature, Shakspeare, Milton, Dryden in his Odes, etc., are poets, who do not give themselves up to a spirit of argumentation; but Pope, and many others, must be considered as didactic poets and moralists. The Germans have renewed their youth, the English are become mature. The Germans profess a doctrine which tends to revive enthusiasm in the arts as well as in philosophy, and they will merit applause if they succeed; for this age lays restraints also on them, and there was never a period in which there existed a greater inclination to despise all that is merely beautiful; none in which the most common of all questions, *What is it good for?* has been more frequently repeated.

Chapter X

Of Poetry

That which is truly divine in the heart of man cannot be defined; if there be words for some of its features, there are none to express the whole together, particularly the mystery of true beauty in all its varieties. It is easy to say what poetry is not; but if we would comprehend what it is, we must call to our assistance the impressions excited by a fine country, harmonious music, the sight of a favored object, and, above all, a religious sentiment which makes us feel within ourselves the presence of the Deity. Poetry is the natural language of all worship. The Bible is full of poetry; Homer is full of religion: not that there are fictions in the Bible, or doctrines in Homer; but enthusiasm concentrates different sentiments in the same focus; enthusiasm is the incense offered by earth to heaven; it unites the one to the other.

The gift of revealing by speech the internal feelings of the heart is very rare; there is, however, a poetical spirit in all beings who are capable of strong and lively affections: expression is wanting to those who have not exerted themselves to find it. It may be said, that the poet only disengages the sentiment that was imprisoned in his soul. Poetic genius is an internal disposition, of the same nature with that which renders us capable of a generous sacrifice. The composition of a fine ode is a heroic trance. If genius were not versatile, it would as often inspire fine actions as affecting expressions: for they both equally spring from a consciousness of the beautiful which is felt within us.

A man of superior talent said that "prose was factitious, and poetry natural;" and, in fact, nations little civilized begin always with poetry; and whenever a strong passion agitates the soul, the most common of men make use, unknown to themselves, of images and metaphors; they call exterior nature to their assistance, to express what is inexpressible within themselves. Common people are much nearer being poets, than men accustomed to good society; the rules of politeness, and delicate raillery, are fit only to impose limits, they cannot impart inspiration.

In this world there is an endless contest between poetry and prose; but pleasantry must always place itself on the side of prose, for to jest is to descend. The spirit of society is, however, very favorable to that gay and graceful poetry of which Ariosto, La Fontaine, and Voltaire are the most brilliant models. Dramatic poetry is admirable in our first writers; descriptive, and, above all, didactic poetry have been carried by the French to a very high degree of perfection; but it does not appear that they have hitherto been called on to distinguish themselves in lyric or epic poetry, such as it was formerly conceived by the ancients, and at present by foreigners.

Lyric poetry is expressed in the name of the author himself; he no longer assumes a character, but experiences in his own person, the various emotions he describes. J. B. Rousseau, in his devotional odes, and Racine, in his Athalie, have shown themselves lyric poets. They were imbued with a love of psalmody, and penetrated with a lively faith. Nevertheless, the difficulties of the language and of French versification are frequently obstacles to this delirium of enthusiasm. We may quote admirable strophes in some of our odes, but have we any complete ode in which the Muse has not abandoned the poet? Fine verses are not always poetry; inspiration in the arts is an inexhaustible source, which vivifies the whole, from the first word to the last. Love, country, faith, all are divinities in an ode. It is the apotheosis of sentiment. In order to conceive the true grandeur of lyric poetry, we must wander in thought into the ethereal regions, forget the tumult of earth in listening to celestial harmony, and consider the whole universe as a symbol of the emotions of the soul.

The enigma of human destiny is nothing to the generality of men; the poet has it always present to his imagination. The idea of death, which depresses vulgar minds, gives to genius additional boldness; and the mixture of the beauties of nature with the terrors of dissolution, excites an indescribable delirium of happiness and terror, without which we can neither comprehend nor describe the spectacle of this world. Lyric poetry relates nothing, is not confined to the succession of time, or the limits of space; it spreads its wings over countries and over ages; it gives duration to the sublime moment in which man rises superior to the pains and pleasures of life. Amid the wonders of the world, he feels himself a being at once creator and created; who must die, and yet cannot cease to be, and whose heart, trembling, yet at the same time powerful, takes pride in itself, yet prostrates itself before God.

The Germans, at once uniting the powers of imagination and reflection (qualities which very rarely meet), are more capable of lyric poetry than most other nations. The moderns cannot give up a certain profundity of ideas, to which they have been habituated by a religion completely spiritual; and yet, nevertheless, if this profundity were not invested with images, it would not be poetry: nature then must be aggrandized in the eyes of men, before they can employ it as the emblem of their thoughts. Groves, flowers, and rivers were sufficient for the poets of paganism; but the solitude of forests, the boundless ocean, the starry firmament, can scarcely express the eternal and the infinite, which pervade and fill the soul of Christians.

The Germans possess no epic poem any more than ourselves: this admirable species of composition does not appear to be granted to the moderns, and perhaps the Iliad alone completely answers our ideas of it. To form an epic poem, a particular combination of circumstances, such as occurred only among the Greeks, is requisite, together with the imagination displayed in heroic times, and the perfection of language peculiar to more civilized periods. In the middle ages, imagination was strong, but the language imperfect; in our days, language is pure, but the imagination defective. The Germans have much boldness in their ideas and style, but little invention in the plan of their subject: their essays in the epic almost always resemble the character of lyric poetry; those of the French bear a stronger affinity to the dramatic, and we discover in them more of interest than of grandeur. When the object is to please on the stage, the art of circumscribing one's self within a given space, of guessing at the taste of spectators, and bending to it with address, forms a part of the success; but in the composition of an epic poem, nothing must depend on external and transient circumstances. It exacts absolute beauties— beauties which may strike the solitary reader, even when his sentiments are most natural, and his imagination most emboldened. He who hazards too much in an epic poem would possibly incur severe censure from the good taste of the French; but he who hazards nothing would not be the less condemned.

It must be acknowledged, that in improving the taste and language of his country, Boileau has given to French genius a disposition very unfavorable to poetic composition. He has spoken only of that which ought to be avoided, he has dwelt only on precepts of reason and wisdom, which have introduced into literature a sort of pedantry, very prejudicial to the sublime energy of the arts. In French, we have masterpieces of versification; but how can we call mere versification poetry! To render into verse what should have remained in prose, to express, in lines of ten syllables, like Pope, the minutest details of a game at cards: or, as in some poems which have lately appeared among us, draughts, chess, and chemistry, is a trick of legerdemain in words: it is composing with words what we call a poem, in the same manner as, with notes of music, we compose a sonata.

A great knowledge of the poetic art is, however, necessary to enable an author thus admirably to describe objects which yield so little scope to the imagination, and we have reason to admire some detached pieces in those galleries of pictures; but the intervals by which they are separated are necessarily prosaic, like that which passes in the mind of the writer. He says to himself, "I will make verses on this subject, then on that, and afterwards on this also;" and, without perceiving it, he intrusts us with a knowledge of the manner in which he pursues his work. The true poet, it may be said, conceives his whole poem at once in his soul, and, were it not for the difficulties of language, would pour forth his extemporaneous effusions, the sacred hymns of genius, as the sibyls and prophets did in ancient times. He is agitated by his conceptions as by a real event of his life; a new world is opened to him; the sublime image of every various situation and character, of every beauty in nature, strikes his eye; and his heart pants for that celestial happiness, the idea of which, like lightning, gives a momentary splendor to the obscurity of his fate. Poetry is a momentary possession of all our soul desires; genius makes the boundaries of existence disappear, and transforms into brilliant images the uncertain hope of mortals.

It would be easier to describe the symptoms of genius than to give precepts for the attainment of it. Genius, like love, is felt by the strong emotions with which it penetrates him who is endowed with it; but if we dared to advise where nature should be the only guide, it is not merely literary counsel that we should give. We should speak of poets, as to citizens and heroes; we should say to them, Be virtuous, be faithful, be free; respect what is dear to you, seek immortality in love, and the Deity in nature; in short, sanctify your soul as a temple, and the angel of noble thoughts will not disdain to appear in it.

Chapter XI

Of Classic and Romantic Poetry

The word *romantic* has been lately introduced in Germany to designate that kind of poetry which is derived from the songs of the Troubadours; that which owes its birth to the union of chivalry and Christianity. If we do not admit that the empire of literature has been divided between paganism and Christianity, the North and the South, antiquity and the middle ages, chivalry and the institutions of Greece and Rome, we shall never succeed in forming a philosophical judgment of ancient and of modern taste.

We sometimes consider the word classic as synonymous with perfection. I use it at present in a different acceptation, considering classic poetry as that of the ancients, and romantic, as that which is generally connected with the traditions of chivalry. This division is equally suitable to the two eras of the world,—that which preceded, and that which followed the establishment of Christianity.

In various German works, ancient poetry has also been compared to sculpture, and romantic to painting; in short, the progress of the human mind has been characterized in every manner, passing from material religions to those which are spiritual, from nature to the Deity.

The French nation, certainly the most cultivated of all that are derived from Latin origin, inclines towards classic poetry imitated from the Greeks and Romans. The English, the most illustrious of the Germanic nations, is more attached to that which owes its birth to chivalry and romance; and it prides itself on the admirable compositions of this sort which it possesses. I will not, in this place, examine which of these two kinds of poetry deserves the preference; it is sufficient to show, that the diversities of taste on this subject do not merely spring from accidental causes, but are derived also from the primitive sources of imagination and thought.

There is a kind of simplicity both in the epic poems and tragedies of the ancients; because at that time men were completely the children of nature, and believed themselves controlled by fate, as absolutely as nature herself is controlled by necessity. Man, reflecting but little, always bore the action of his soul without; even conscience was represented by external objects, and the torch of the Furies shook the horrors of remorse over the head of the guilty. In ancient times, men attended to events alone, but among the moderns, character is of greater importance; and that uneasy reflection, which, like the vulture of Prometheus, often internally devours us, would have been folly amid circumstances and relations so clear and decided, as they existed in the civil and social state of the ancients.

When the art of sculpture began in Greece, single statues alone were formed; groups were composed at a later period. It might be said with equal truth, that there we no groups in any art: objects were represented in succession, as in bas-reliefs, without combination, without complication of any kind. Man personified nature; nymphs inhabited the waters, hamadryads the forests; but nature, in turn, possessed herself of man; and, it might be said, he resembled the torrent, the thunderbolt, the volcano, so wholly did he act from involuntary impulse, and so insufficient was reflection in any respect, to alter the motives or the consequences of his actions. The ancients, thus to speak, possessed a corporeal soul, and its emotions were all strong, decided, and consistent; it is not the same with the human heart as developed by Christianity: the moderns have derived from Christian repentance a constant habit of self-reflection.

But in order to manifest this kind of internal existence, a great variety of outward facts and circumstances must display, under every form, the innumerable shades and gradations of that which is passing in the soul. If in our days the fine arts were confined to the simplicity of the ancients, we should never attain that primitive strength which distinguishes them, and we should lose those intimate and multiplied emotions of which our souls are susceptible. Simplicity in the arts would, among the moderns, easily degenerate into coldness and abstraction, while that of the ancients was full of life and animation. Honor and love, valor and pity, were the sentiments which distinguished the Christianity of chivalrous ages; and those dispositions of the soul could only be displayed by dangers, exploits, love, misfortunes—that romantic interest, in short, by which pictures are incessantly varied. The sources from which art derives its effect are then very different in classic poetry and in that of romance; in one it is fate which reigns, in the other it is Providence. Fate counts the sentiments of men as nothing; but Providence judges of actions according to those sentiments. Poetry must necessarily create a world of a very different nature, when its object is to paint the work of destiny, which is both blind and deaf, maintaining an endless contest with mankind; and when it attempts to describe that intelligent order, over which the Supreme Being continually presides,—that Being whom our hearts supplicate, and who mercifully answers their petitions!

The poetry of the pagan world was necessarily as simple and well defined as the objects of nature; while that of Christianity requires the various colors of the rainbow to preserve it from being lost in the clouds. The poetry of the ancients is more pure as an art; that of the moderns more readily calls forth our tears. But our present object is not so much to decide between classic and romantic poetry, properly so called, as between the imitation of the one and the inspiration of the other. The literature of the ancients is, among the moderns, a transplanted literature; that of chivalry and romance is indigenous, and flourishes under the influence of our religion and our institutions. Writers, who are imitators of the ancients, have subjected themselves to the rules of strict taste alone; for, not being able to consult either their own nature or their own recollections, it is necessary for them to conform to those laws by which the *chefs-d'œuvre* of the ancients may be adapted to our taste; though the circumstances both political and religious, which gave birth to these *chefs-d'œuvre* are all entirely changed. But the poetry written in imitation of the ancients, however perfect in its kind, is seldom popular, because, in our days, it has no connection whatever with our national feelings.

The French being the most classical of all modern poetry, is of all others least calculated to become familiar among the lower orders of the people. The stanzas of Tasso are sung by the gondoliers of Venice; the Spaniards and Portugese, of all ranks, know by heart the verses of Calderon and Camoëns. Shakspeare is as much admired by the populace in England as by those of a higher class. The poems of Goethe and Bürger are set to music, and repeated from the banks of the Rhine to the shores of the Baltic. Our French poets are admired wherever there are cultivated minds, either in our own nation, or in the rest of Europe; but they are quite unknown to the common people, and even to the class of citizens in our towns, because the arts, in France, are not, as elsewhere, natives of the very country in which their beauties are displayed.

Some French critics have asserted that German literature is still in its infancy. This opinion is entirely false; men who are best skilled in the knowledge of languages and the works of the ancients, are certainly not ignorant of the defects and advantages attached to the species of literature which they either adopt or reject; but their character, their habits, and their modes of reasoning, have led them to prefer that which is founded on the recollection of chivalry, on the wonders of the middle ages, to that which has for its basis the mythology of the Greeks. Romantic literature is alone capable of further improvement, because, being rooted in our own soil, that alone can continue to grow and acquire fresh life: it expresses our religion; it recalls our history; its origin is ancient, although not of classical antiquity.

Classic poetry, before it comes home to us, must pass through our recollections of paganism: that of the Germans is the Christian era of the fine arts; it employs our personal impressions to excite strong and vivid emotions; the genius by which it is inspired addresses itself immediately to our hearts, and seems to call forth the spirit of our own lives, of all phantoms at once the most powerful and the most terrible.

Chapter XIII

Of German Poetry

The detached pieces of poetry among the Germans are, it appears to me, still more remarkable than their poems, and it is particularly on that species of writing that the stamp of originality is impressed; it is also true that the authors who have written most in this manner, Goethe, Schiller, Bürger, etc., are of the modern school, which alone bears a truly national character. Goethe has most imagination, and Schiller most sensibility; but Bürger is more popular than either. By successively examining some poetical pieces of each of these authors, we shall the better be able to form an idea of the qualities which distinguish them. The productions of Schiller bear some analogy to the French taste, yet we do not find in his detached poems any thing that resembles the fugitive pieces of Voltaire; that elegance of conversation, and almost of manners, transfused into French poetry, belongs to France alone; and Voltaire, in point of gracefulness, was the first of French writers. It would be interesting to compare Schiller's stanzas on the loss of youth, entitled the *Ideal,* with those of Voltaire, beginning,

> *Si vous voulez que j'aime encore,*
> *Rendez moi l'age des amours, etc.*

We see in the French poet the expression of a pleasing regret, which has for its object the pleasures of love and the joys of life; the German poet laments the loss of that enthusiasm and innocent purity of thought peculiar to early age, and flatters himself that his decline in life will still be embellished by the charms of poetry and of reflection. The stanzas of Schiller do not possess that easy and brilliant clearness which is generally so striking and attractive; but we may draw from them consolations which intimately affect the soul. Schiller never presents to us a serious or profound reflection without investing it with noble images; he speaks to man as nature herself would speak to him, for nature is also contemplative and poetical. To paint the idea of time, she brings before us an ever-flowing stream; and lest, through her eternal youth, we should forget our own transient existence, she adorns herself with flowers which quickly fade, and strips the trees in autumn of those leaves which spring beheld in all their beauty. Poetry should be the terrestrial mirror of this divinity, and by colors, sounds, and rhythm, reflect all the beauties of the universe.

The poem entitled *The Song of the Bell,* consists of two distinct parts: the alternate stanzas express the labor which is performed at a forge, and between each of these there are charming verses on the solemn circumstances and extraordinary events commonly announced by the ringing of bells, such as birth, marriage, death, fire, insurrection, etc. We may translate into French the fine and affecting images which Schiller derives from those great epochs of human life; but it is impossible properly to imitate the strophes in short verse, and composed of words whose rough and quick sound almost conveys to our ears the repeated blows and rapid steps of the workmen who direct the boiling metal. Can a prose translation give any just idea of a poem of this sort? It is reading music instead of hearing it; and yet it is easier to conceive the effect of instruments which are known to us, than of the concords and contrasts of a rhythm and a language we are ignorant of. Sometimes the regular shortness of the metre gives us an idea of the activity of the workmen, the limited but regular force which they exert in their principal operations; and sometimes, immediately after this harsh and strong sound, we hear the aerial strains of enthusiasm and melancholy.

The originality of this poem is lost, if we separate it from the effect of a versification skilfully chosen, where the rhymes answer each other like intelligent echoes modified by thought; and nevertheless, these picturesque effects of sound would be bold and hazardous in French. The vulgarity in point of style continually threatens us: we have not like almost every other nation, two languages, that of prose and that of verse; and it is with words as with persons—wherever ranks are confounded familiarity is dangerous.

Cassandra, another piece of Schiller's, might more easily be translated into French, although its poetical language is extremely bold. At the moment when the festival to celebrate the marriage of Polyxena and Achilles is beginning, Cassandra is seized with a presentiment of the misfortunes which will result from it; she walks sad and melancholy in the grove of Apollo, and laments that knowledge of futurity which troubles all her enjoyments. We see in this ode what a misfortune it would be to a human being, could he possess the prescience of a divinity. Is not the sorrow of the prophetess experienced by all persons of strong passions and superior minds? Schiller has given us a fine moral idea under a very poetical form, namely, that true genius, that of sentiment, even if it escape suffering from its commerce with the world, is frequently the victim of its own feelings. Cassandra never marries, not that she is either insensible or rejected; but her penetrating soul in a moment passes the boundaries of life and death, and finds repose only in heaven.

I should never end if I were to mention all the poetical pieces of Schiller which contain new thoughts and new beauties. He has composed a hymn on the departure of the Greeks after the siege of Troy, which might be supposed the production of a poet then living, so faithfully has he adhered to the complexion of those times. I shall examine, under the subject of dramatic art, the admirable skill with which the Germans transport themselves into ages, countries, and characters, different from their own,—a superior faculty, without which the personages produced on the stage would resemble puppets moved by the same wire, and made to speak in the same voice, namely, that of the author. Schiller deserves particularly to be admired as a dramatic poet: Goethe stands unrivalled in the art of composing elegies, ballads, stanzas, etc.; his detached pieces have a very different merit from those of Voltaire. The French poet has transfused into his verse the spirit of the most brilliant society; the German, by a few slight touches, awakens in the soul profound and contemplative impressions.

Goethe is to the highest degree natural in this species of composition; and not only so when he speaks from his own impressions, but even when he transports himself to new climates, customs, and situations, his poetry easily assimilates itself with foreign countries; he seizes, with a talent perfectly unique, all that pleases in the national songs of each nation; he becomes, when he chooses it, a Greek, an Indian, or a Morlachian. We have often mentioned that melancholy and meditation which characterizes the poets of the North: Goethe, like all other men of genius, unites in himself most astonishing contrasts; we find in his works many traces of character peculiar to the inhabitants of the South; they are more awakened to the pleasures of existence, and have at once a more lively and tranquil enjoyment of nature than those of the North; their minds have not less depth, but their genius has more vivacity; we find in it a certain sort of *naïveté*, which awakens at once the remembrance of ancient simplicity with that of the middle ages: it is not the *naïveté* of innocence, but that of strength. We perceive in Goethe's poetical compositions, that he disdains the crowd of obstacles, criticisms, and obser-vations, which may be opposed to him. He follows his imagination wherever it leads him, and a certain predominant pride frees him from the scruples of self-love. Goethe is in poetry an absolute master of nature, and most admirable when he does not finish his pictures; for all his sketches contain the germ of a fine fiction, but his finished fictions do not always equally convey the idea of a good sketch.

In his elegies, composed at Rome, we must not look for descriptions of Italy: Goethe scarcely does whatever is expected from him, and when there is any thing pompous in an idea it displeases him; he wishes to produce effect by an untrodden path hitherto unknown both to himself and to the reader. His elegies describe the effect of Italy on his whole existence, that delirium of happiness resulting from the influence of a serene and beautiful sky. He relates his pleasures, even of the most common kind, in the manner of Propertius; and from time to time some fine recollections of that city, which was once the mistress of the world, give an impulse to the imagination, the more lively because it was not prepared for it.

He relates, that he once met in the Campagna of Rome a young woman suckling her child and seated on the remains of an ancient column; he wished to question her on the subject of the ruins with which her hut was surrounded; but she was ignorant of every thing concerning them, wholly devoted to the affections which filled her soul; she loved, and to her the present moment was the whole of existence.

We read in a Greek author, that a young girl, skilful in the art of making nosegays of flowers, entered into a contest with her lover, Pausias, who knew how to paint them. Goethe has composed a charming idyl on that subject. The author of that idyl is also the author of *Werther*. Goethe has run through all the shades and gradations of love, from the sentiment which confers grace and tenderness, to that despair which harrows up the soul, but exalts genius.

After having made himself a Greek in Pausias, Goethe conducts us to Asia in a most charming ballad, called *the God and the Bayaderé*. An Indian deity (Mahadoch) clothes himself in a mortal form, in order to judge of the pleasures and pains of men from his own experience. He travels through Asia, observes both the great and the lower classes of people; and as one evening, on leaving a town, he was walking on the banks of the Ganges, he is stopped by a Bayadere, who persuades him to rest himself in her habitation. There is so much poetry, colors so truly oriental in his manner of painting the dances of this Bayadere, the perfumes and flowers with which she is surrounded, that we cannot, from our own manners, judge of a picture so perfectly foreign to them. The Indian deity inspires this erring female with true love, and touched with that return towards virtue which sincere affection should always inspire, he resolves to purify the soul of the Bayadere by the trials of misfortune.

When she awakes, she finds her lover dead by her side. The priests of Brahma carry off the lifeless body to consume it on the funeral pile. The Bayadere endeavors to throw herself on it with him she loves, but is repulsed by the priests, because, not being his wife, she has no right to die with him. After having felt all the anguish of love and of shame, she throws herself on the pile, in spite of the Brahmins. The god receives her in his arms; he darts through the flames, and carries the object of his tenderness, now rendered worthy of his choice, with him to heaven.

Zelter, an original musician, has set this romance to an air, by turns voluptuous and solemn, which suits the words extremely well. When we hear it, we think ourselves in India, surrounded with all its wonders; and let it not be said, that a ballad is too short a poem to produce such an effect. The first notes of an air, the first verse of a poem, transports the imagination to any distant age or country; but, if a few words are thus powerful, a few words can also destroy the enchantment. Magicians formerly could perform or prevent prodigies by the help of a few magical words. It is the same with the poet; he may call up the past, or make the present appear again, according as the expressions he makes use of are, or are not, comfortable to the time or country which is the subject of his verse, according as he observes or neglects local coloring, and those little circumstances so ingeniously invented, which, both in fiction and reality, exercise the mind in the endeavor to discover truth where it is not specifically pointed out to us.

Another ballad of Goethe's produces a delightful effect by the most simple means; it is *the Fisherman*. A poor man, on a summer's evening, seats himself on the bank of a river, and, as he throws his line, contemplates the clear and limpid tide, which gently flows and bathes his naked feet. The nymph of the stream invites him to plunge himself into it; she describes to him the delightful freshness of the water during the heat of summer, the pleasure which the sun takes in cooling itself at night in the sea, the calmness of the moon when its rays repose and sleep on the bosom of the stream. At length, the fisherman, attracted, seduced, drawn on, advances near the nymph, and forever disappears. The story on which this ballad is founded is trifling; but what is delightful in it, is the art of making us feel the mysterious power which may proceed from the phenomena of nature. It is said there are persons who discover springs, hidden under the earth, by the nervous agitation which they cause in them: in German poetry, we often think we discover this miraculous

sympathy between man and the elements. The German poet comprehends
nature not only as a poet, but as a brother; and we might almost say, that the
bonds of family union connect him with the air, the water, flowers, trees, in
short, with all the primary beauties of the creation.

There is no one who has not felt the undefinable attraction which we
experience when looking on the waves of the sea, whether from the charm of
their freshness, or from the ascendency which a uniform and perpetual motion
insensibly acquires over our transient and perishable existence. This ballad of
Goethe's admirably expresses the increasing pleasure we derive from contemplating the pure waters of a flowing stream: the measure of the rhythm and
harmony is made to imitate the motion of the waves, and produces an
analogous effect on the imagination. The soul of nature discovers itself to us in
every place, and under a thousand different forms. The fruitful country and the
unpeopled desert, the sea as well as the stars, are all subjected to the same
laws; and man contains within himself sensations and occult powers, which
correspond with the day, with the night, and with the storm; it is this secret
alliance of our being with the wonders of the universe, which gives to poetry
its true grandeur. The poet knows how to restore the union between the
natural and the moral world: his imagination forms a connecting tie between
the one and the other.

There is much gayety in several of Goethe's pieces; but we seldom find in
them that sort of pleasantry to which we have been accustomed: he is sooner
struck by the imagery of nature, than by ridiculous circumstances; with a
singular instinct, he points out the originality of animals, always new, yet never
varying. *Lili's Park* and *the Wedding song in the Old Castle,* describe animals,
not like men, in La Fontaine's manner, but, like fantastic creatures, the sports
of Nature. Goethe also finds in the marvellous a source of pleasantry, the more
gratifying, because we discover in it no serious aim.

A song, entitled *the Magician's Apprentice,* also deserves to be mentioned.
The apprentice of a magician having heard his master mutter some magical
words, by the help of which he gets a broomstick to tend on him, recollects
those words, and commands the broomstick to go and fetch him water from the
river, to wash his house. The broomstick sets off and returns, brings one
bucket, then another, and then another, and so on without ceasing. The
apprentice wants to stop it, but he has forgot the words necessary for that
purpose: the broomstick, faithful to its office, still goes to the river, and still
draws up water, which is thrown on the house at the risk of inundating it. The
apprentice, in his fury, takes an axe and cuts the broomstick in two; the two
parts of the stick then become two servants instead of one, and go for water,
which they throw into the apartments, as if in emulation of each other, with
more zeal than ever. In vain the apprentice scolds these stupid sticks; they
continue their business without ceasing, and the house would have been lost,
had not the master arrived in time to assist his apprentice, at the same time
laughing heartily at his ridiculous presumption. An awkward imitation of the
great secrets of art is very well depicted in this little scene.

We have not yet spoken of an inexhaustible source of poetical effect in

Germany, which is terror; stories of apparitions and sorcerers are equally well received by the populace and by men of more enlightened minds: it is a relic of the northern mythology—a disposition naturally inspired by the long nights of a northern climate; and besides, though Christianity opposes all groundless fears, yet popular superstitions have always some sort of analogy to the prevailing religion. Almost every true opinion has its attendant error, which, like a shadow, places itself in the imagination at the side of the reality; it is a luxuriance or excess of belief, which is commonly attached both to religion and to history, and I know not why we should disdain to avail ourselves of it. Shakspeare has produced wonderful effects from the introduction of spectres and magic; and poetry cannot be popular when it despises that which exercises a spontaneous empire over the imagination. Genius and taste may preside over the arrangement of these tales, and in proportion to the commonness of the subject, the more skill is required in the manner of treating it: perhaps it is in this union alone that the great force of a poem consists. It is probable that the great events recorded in the Iliad and Odyssey were sung by nurses, before Homer rendered them the *chefs-d'œuvre* of the poetical art.

Of all German writers, Bürger has made the best use of this vein of superstition which carries us so far into the recesses of the heart. His romances are therefore well known throughout Germany. *Lenore*, which is most generally admired, is not, I believe, translated into French, or, at least, it would be very difficult to relate it circumstantially either in our prose or verse. A young girl is alarmed at not hearing from her lover who is gone to the army; peace is made, and the soldiers return to their habitations. Mothers again meet their sons, sisters their brothers, and husbands their wives; the warlike trumpet accompanies the songs of peace, and joy reigns in every heart. Lenore in vain surveys the ranks of the soldiers; she sees not her lover, and no one can tell her what has become of him. She is in despair; her mother attempts to calm her; but the youthful heart of Lenore revolts against the stroke of affliction, and in its frenzy she accuses Providence. From the moment in which the blasphemy is uttered, we are sensible that the story is to have something fatal in it, and this idea keeps the mind in constant agitation.

At midnight, a knight stops at the door of Lenore's house; she hears the neighing of the horse and the clinking of the spurs; the knight knocks, she goes down and beholds her lover. He tells her to follow him instantly, having not a moment to lose, he says, before he returns to the army. She presses forward; he places her behind him on his horse, and sets off with the quickness of lightning. During the night he gallops through the barren and desert countries; his youthful companion is filled with terror, and continually asks him why he goes so fast; the knight still presses on his horse by his hoarse and hollow cries, and in a low voice says, "The dead ride quick, the dead ride quick!" Lenore answers, "Ah! leave the dead in peace!" but whenever she addresses to him any anxious question, he repeats the same appalling words.

In approaching the church, where he says he is carrying her to complete their union, the frosts of winter seem to change nature herself into a frightful omen: priests carry a coffin in great pomp, and their black robes train slowly on the snow, the winding-sheet of the earth; Lenore's terror increases, and her lover cheers her with a mixture of irony and carelessness which makes one shudder. All that he says is pronounced with a monotonous precipitation, as if already, in his language, the accents of life were no longer heard; he promises to bring her to that narrow and silent abode where their union was to be accomplished. We see, at a distance, the church-yard by the side of the church: the knight knocks, and the door opens; he pushes forward with his horse, making him pass between the tombstones; he then, by degrees, loses the appearance of a living being, is changed into a skeleton, and the earth opens to swallow up both him and his mistress.

I certainly do not flatter myself that I have been able, in this abridged recital, to give a just idea of the astonishing merit of this romance; all the imagery, all the sounds connected with the situation of the soul, are wonderfully expressed by the poetry; the syllables, the rhymes, all the art of language is employed to excite terror. The rapidity of the horse's pace seems more solemn and more appalling than even the slowness of a funeral procession. The energy with which the knight quickens his course, that petulance of death, causes an inexpressible emotion; and we feel ourselves carried off by the phantom, as well as the poor girl whom he drags with him into the abyss.

There are four English translations of this tale of Lenore, but the best beyond comparison is that of Wm. Spencer, who of all English poets is best acquainted with the true spirit of foreign languages. The analogy between the English and German, allows a complete transfusion of the originality of style and versification of Bürger; and we not only find in the translation, the same ideas as in the original, but also the same sensations; and nothing is more necessary than this to convey the true knowledge of a literary production. It would be difficult to obtain the same result in French, where nothing strange or odd seems natural.

Bürger has written another romance, less celebrated, but also extremely original, entitled *the Wild Huntsman.* Followed by his servants and a large pack of hounds, he set out for the chase on a Sunday, just as the village bell announces divine service. A knight in white armor presents himself, and conjures him not to profane the Lord's day; another knight, arrayed in black armor, makes him ashamed of subjecting himself to prejudices, which are suitable only to old men and children: the huntsman yields to these evil suggestions; he sets off, and reaches the field of a poor widow; she throws herself at his feet, imploring him not to destroy her harvest by trampling down her corn with his attendants; the knight in white armor entreats the huntsman to listen to the voice of pity; the black knight laughs at a sentiment so puerile; the huntsman mistakes ferocity for energy, and his horses trample on the hope of the poor and the orphan. At length the stag, pursued, seeks refuge in the hut of an old hermit; the huntsman wishes to set it on fire in order to drive out his prey; the hermit embraces his knees, and endeavors to soften the ferocious being who thus threatens his humble abode: for the last time, the good genius, under the form of the white knight, again speaks to him; the evil genius, under that of the black knight triumphs; the huntsman kills the hermit, and is at once changed into a phantom, pursued by his own dogs, who seek to devour him. This story is derived from a popular superstition: it is said, that at midnight, in certain seasons of the year, a huntsman is seen in the clouds, just over the forest where this event is supposed to have passed, and that he is pursued by a furious pack of hounds till daybreak.

What is truly fine in this poem of Bürger's, is his description of the ardent will of the huntsman; it was at first innocent, as are all the faculties of the soul; but it becomes more and more depraved, as often as he resists the voice of conscience and yields to his passions. His headstrong purpose was at first only the intoxication of power; it soon becomes that of guilt, and the earth can no longer sustain him. The good and evil inclinations of men are well character-ized by the white and black knights; the words, always the same, which are pronounced by the white knight to stop the career of the huntsman, are also very ingeniously combined. The ancients, and the poets of the middle ages, were well acquainted with the kind of terror caused in certain circumstances by the repetition of the same words; it seems to awaken the sentiment of inflexible necessity. Apparitions, oracles—all supernatural powers, must be monotonous; what is immutable is uniform; and in certain fictions it is a great art to imitate by words that solemn fixedness which imagination assigns to the empire of darkness and of death.

We also remark in Bürger a certain familiarity of expression, which does not lessen the dignity of the poetry, but, on the contrary, singularly increases its effect. When we succeed in exciting both terror and admiration without weakening either, each of those sentiments is necessarily strengthened by the union: it is mixing, in the art of painting, what we see continually with what we never see; and from what we know, we are led to believe what astonishes us.

Goethe has also made trial of his talents in those subjects which are at the same time terrifying both to children and men; but he has treated them with a depth of thought that leaves us also a wide field for reflection. I will endeavor to give an account of one of his poems on apparitions which is the most admired in Germany; it is called *the Bride of Corinth*. I certainly do not mean in any respect to defend this fiction either as considered in itself, or in its tendency; but it seems to me scarcely possible not to be struck with the warmth of imagination which it indicates.

Two friends, one of Athens and the other of Corinth, had resolved to unite their son and daughter to each other. The young man sets out for Corinth to see her who had been promised to him, and whom he had never yet beheld: it was at the time when Christianity was first established. The family of the Athenian adhered to the old religion, but that of the Corinthian had adopted the new faith; and the mother, during a lingering illness, had devoted her daughter to the altar. The youngest sister is destined to fill the place of the eldest, who is thus consecrated to religion.

The young man arrives late at the house; all the family had retired to rest; the servants bring some supper to his apartment, and leave him alone; but he is soon afterwards joined by a very singular guest: he sees, advancing to the middle of the room, a young girl clothed in a veil and a white robe, her forehead bound with a black and gold ribbon; and when she perceives the young man she draws back with timidity, and, lifting her white hands to heaven, cries out:

> Is a stranger here, and nothing told me?
> Am I then forgotten even in name?
> Ah! 'tis thus within my cell they hold me,
> And I now am cover'd o'er with shame!

She attempts to retire, but the young man holds her back; he learns that she is the person who was destined to be his wife. Their fathers had sworn to unite them, and therefore every other vow appeared to him without effect.

> "Maiden—darling! Stay, O stay!" and, leaping
> From the couch before her stands the boy:
> "Ceres—Bacchus, here their gifts are heaping,
> And thou bringest Amor's gentle joy!
>   Why with terror pale?
>   Sweet one, let us hail
> These bright gods—their festive gifts employ."

The young man conjurs his youthful companion to yield herself to his wishes.

> Oh, no—no! Young stranger, come not nigh me;
>   Joy is not for me, nor festive cheer.
> Ah! such bliss may ne'er be tasted by me,
>   Since my mother, in fantastic fear,
>   By long sickness bow'd,
>   To Heaven's service vow'd
> Me, and all the hopes that warm'd me here.
> They have left our hearth, and left it lonely—
>   The old gods, that bright and jocund train.
> One, unseen, in heaven, is worshipp'd only,
>   And upon the cross a Savior slain;
>   Sacrifice is here,
>   Not of lamb nor steer,
> But of human woe and human pain. . . .
> But, alas! these limbs of mine would chill thee:
>   Love! they mantle not with passion's glow;
>   Thou wouldst be afraid,
>   Didst thou find the maid
> Thou hast chosen, cold as ice or snow.

At midnight, which is called the hour of spectres, the young girl seems more unconstrained; she eagerly drinks wine of the color of blood, like that which is taken by the ghosts in the Odyssey to renew their lost memory; but she obstinately refuses to taste a bit of bread: she gives a chain of gold to him

whom she was to have married, and asks in return a lock of his hair: the young
man, charmed with the beauty of his companion, presses her with transport in
his arms, but he feels no heart beat responsive against his bosom; her limbs are
frozen.

> Round her waist his eager arms he bended,
>   With the strength that youth and love inspire;
> Wert thou even from the grave ascended,
>   I could warm thee well with my desire!

And then begins a scene as extraordinary as the frenzied imagination can
possibly conceive,—a mixture of love and terror, a formidable union of life and
death. There is, as it were, a funereal voluptuousness in this picture where love
forms an alliance with the grave, where beauty itself seems only a terrifying
apparition.

At length the mother arrives, and convinced that one of her slaves has
been introduced to the stranger, she gives way to her just indignation; but
immediately the young girl increases in size, till like a shadow she reaches the
vaulted ceiling, and then reproaches her mother with having caused her death
by obliging her to take the veil:

> Mother! mother! wherefore thus deprive me
>   Of such joy as I this night have known?
> Wherefore from these warm embraces drive me?
>   Was I waken'd up to meet thy frown?
>   Did it not suffice
>   That, in virgin guise,
>   To an early grave you brought me down?
>
> Fearful is the weird that forced me hither,
>   From the dark-heap'd chamber where I lay;
> Powerless are your drowsy anthems, neither
>   Can your priests prevail, howe'er they pray.
>   Salt nor lymph can cool,
>   Where the pulse is full;
>   Love must still burn on, though wrapp'd in clay.
>
> To this youth my early troth was plighted,
>   While yet Venus ruled within the land;
> Mother! and that vow ye falsely slighted,
>   At your new and gloomy faith's command.
>   But no god will hear,
>   If a mother swear
>   Pure from love to keep her daughter's hand.
>
> Nightly from my narrow chamber driven,
>   Come I to fulfil my destined part,
> Him to seek to whom my troth was given,
>   And to draw the life-blood from his heart.
>   He hath served my will;

> More I yet must kill,
> For another prey I now depart.
>
> Fair young man! thy thread of life is broken,
> Human skill can bring no aid to thee.
> There thou hast my chain—a ghastly token—
> And this lock of thine I take with me.
> Soon must thou decay,
> Soon wilt thou be gray,
> Dark although to-night thy tresses be!
>
> Mother! hear, oh hear my last entreaty!
> Let the funeral-pile arise once more;
> Open up my wretched tomb for pity,
> And in flames our souls to peace restore.
> When the ashes glow,
> When the fire-sparks flow,
> To the ancient gods aloft we soar.

Without doubt, a pure and chastened taste will find many things to blame in this piece; but when it is read in the original, it is impossible not to admire the art with which every word is made to produce an increasing degree of terror; every word indicates, without explaining, the astonishing horror of this situation. A history, of which nothing in nature could have given the idea, is related in striking and natural details, as if the subject of it had really taken place; and curiosity is constantly excited, without our being willing to sacrifice a single circumstance, in order to satisfy it the sooner.

This piece, nevertheless, is the only one among the detached poems of celebrated German authors against which French taste can find any thing to object: in all the others the two nations appear to agree. In the verses of Jacobi we almost discover the brilliancy and lightness of Gresset. Matthisson has given to descriptive poetry (the features of which are frequently too vague) the character of a picture as striking in its coloring as in its resemblance. The charm which pervades the poetry of Salis makes us love its author as if he were our friend. Tiedge is a moral poet, whose writings lead the soul to the purest devotional feelings. We should still, in short, have to mention a crowd of other poets, if it were possible to point out every name deserving of applause, in a country where poetry is so natural to all cultivated minds.

A. W. Schlegel, whose literary opinions have made so much noise in Germany, has not, in any of his poems, allowed himself the slightest expression which can attract censure from the most severe taste. His elegies on the death of a young person; his stanzas on the union of the church with the fine arts; his elegy on Rome, are written throughout with delicacy and dignity. The two specimens I am about to give of his poetry will convey but a very imperfect idea of it; but they will serve, at least, to render the character of the poet better known. The sonnet, entitled *Attachment to the World*, appears to me charming.

Oft will the soul her wings unfold,
Invigorated by contemplation of purer things;
To her seems, in the narrow circle she traverses,
Her doing vain, and her knowing illusive.

She feels deeply an irresistible longing
For higher worlds, for freer spheres of action,
And believes, at the close of her earthly career,
First lifted is the curtain revealing brighter scenes.

Yet let death touch her body, so that she must leave it,
Then she shudders, and looks back with longing
On earthly pleasures and mortal companions:

As once Proserpine, from Enna's meads
In Pluto's arms borne off, childish in her complaints,
For the flowers wept, which from her bosom fell.

The following piece of verses must lose even more by a translation than the sonnet; it is called *the Melodies of Life:* the swan is placed in opposition to the eagle,—the former as the emblem of contemplative existence, the latter as the image of active existence; the rhythm of the verse changes when the swan speaks, and when the eagle answers her; and the strains of both are nevertheless comprised in the same stanza united by the rhyme; the true beauties of harmony are also found in this piece, not imitative harmony, but the internal music of the soul. Our emotion discovers it without having recourse to reflection; and reflecting genius converts it into poetry.

THE SWAN
In the waters is pass'd my tranquil life,
It traces only a slight furrow that vanishes,
And never fail me in the watery mirror
The curving neck and rounded form.

THE EAGLE
I dwell in the rocky cliffs,
I sail in the stormy air,
Trusting to the beating wings,
In chase and battle and peril.

THE SWAN
Me delights the blue of the sky serene,
Me sweetly intoxicates the spicewort's perfume,
When I, in the glow of the evening-red,
Rock my feather'd breast.

THE EAGLE
I triumph in tempests,
When they root up the forests,
I ask the lightning, whether it kills,
With glad annihilating pleasure.

The Swan
  By a glance from Apollo invited,
Dare I bathe in harmony's tide,
At his feet reposing, when the songs
Resound in Tempé's vale.

The Eagle
  I enthrone myself by Jupiter's seat;
He winks and I bring him the lightning,
Then drop I in sleep my wings
Over his ruling sceptre.

The Swan
  With the blessed power of the gods penetrated,
Have I myself in Leda's bosom entwined;
Flatteringly caress'd me her tender hands,
As she her sense in rapture lost.

The Eagle
  I came out of the clouds like an arrow,
Tore him from his feeble companions:
I bore in my talons the youthful
Ganymede to Olympus on high.

The Swan
  So bore she friendly natures,
Helena and you, ye Dioscuri,
Wild stars, whose brother-virtue,
Changing, shadow-world and heaven share.

The Eagle
  Now hands the nectar-beeker
The youth to drinkers immortal;
Never brown'd is the fair young cheek,
As endlessly time hurries on.

The Swan
  Prophetically contemplate I oft the stars,
In the water-mirror the deep-arch'd immensity,
And me draws an inner tender longing
Towards my home in a heavenly land.

The Eagle
  I spread my wings with joy,
In my youth, towards the deathless sun,
Can never to the dust myself accustom,
I am akin to the gods.

The Swan
  Willingly yields to death a peaceful life;
When the web of existence is unwoven,
Loos'd is the tongue: melodiously celebrates
Each breath the holy moment.

THE EAGLE
The torch of the dead makes young again:
A blooming phœnix, rises
The soul free and unveil'd,
And greets its god-like fortune.

It is a circumstance worthy of observation, that national taste in general differs much more in the dramatic art than in any other branch of literature. We will analyze the cause of this difference in the following chapters; but before we enter on the examination of the German theatre, some general observations on taste appear to me necessary. I shall not consider it abstractedly as an intellectual faculty; several writers, and Montesquieu in particular, have exhausted this subject. I will only point out why literary taste is understood in so different a manner by the French and the nations of Germany.

Chapter XIV

Of Taste

Those who think themselves in possession of taste are more proud of it than those who believe that they possess genius. Taste is in literature what *bon ton* is in society; we consider it as a proof of fortune and of birth, or at least of the habits which are found in connection with them; while genius may spring from the head of an artisan, who has never had any intercourse with good company. In every country where there is vanity, taste will be placed in the highest rank of qualifications, because it separates different classes, and serves as a rallying-point to all the individuals of the first class. In every country where the power of ridicule is felt, taste will be reckoned as one of the first advantages; for, above all things, it teaches us what we ought to avoid. A sense of the fitness of things, and of propriety, peculiarly belongs to taste; and it is an excellent armor to ward off the blows of the various contending kinds of self-love, which we have to deal with; in short, it may so happen, that a whole nation shall, with respect to other nations, form itself into an aristocracy of good taste; and this may be applied to France, where the spirit of society reigned in so eminent a manner, that it had some excuse for such a pretension.

But taste, in its application to the fine arts, differs extremely from taste as applied to the relations of social life; when the object is to force men to grant us a reputation, ephemeral as our own lives, what we omit doing is at least as necessary as what we do; for the higher orders of society are naturally so hostile to all pretension, that very extraordinary advantages are requisite to compensate that of not giving occasion to the world to speak about us. Taste in poetry depends on nature, and, like nature, should be creative; the principles of this taste are therefore quite different from those which depend on our social relations.

It is by confounding these two kinds of taste that we find such opposite judgments formed on subjects of literature; the French judge of the fine arts by the rules of social fitness and propriety, and the Germans judge of these as they would of the fine arts: in the relations of society we must study how to defend ourselves, but in those of poetry, we should yield ourselves up without reserve. If you consider surrounding objects as a man of the world, you will not be sensible to the charms of nature; if you survey them as an artist, you will lose that tact which society alone can give. If we are to subject the arts to the regulations of good company, the French alone are truly capable of it; but greater latitude of composition is necessary, in order strongly to affect the imagination and the soul. I know it may be objected to me, and with reason, that our three best dramatic authors are elevated to the most sublime height, without offending any established rule. Some men of genius, reaping a field before uncultivated, have indeed rendered themselves illustrious in spite of the difficulties they had to conquer; but is not the cessation of all progress in the art, since that time, a strong proof that there are too many obstacles in the road which they followed?

"Good taste in literature is in some respects like order under despotism; it is of consequence that we should know at what price we purchase it." In a political point of view, M. Necker said: The utmost degree of liberty should be granted which is consistent with order. I would change the maxim, by saying, that in literature, we should have all the taste which is consistent with genius; for if in a state of society the chief object be order and quietness, that which is of most importance in literature is, on the contrary, interest, curiosity, and that sort of emotion which taste alone would frequently disapprove.

A treaty of peace might be proposed between the different modes of judgment adopted by artists and men of the world, by Germans and Frenchmen. The French ought to abstain from condemning even a violation of rule, if an energetic thought or a true sentiment can be pleaded in its excuse. The Germans ought to prohibit all that is offensive to natural taste, all that retraces images repulsive to our feelings: no philosophical theory, however ingenious it may be, can compensate for this defect; as, on the contrary, no established rule in literature can prevent the effect of involuntary emotions. In vain do the most intelligent German writers contend, that, in order to understand the conduct of Lear's daughters towards their father, it is necessary to show the barbarity of the times in which they lived, and therefore tolerate the action of the Duke of Cornwall, who, excited by Regan, treads out the eye of Gloucester with his heel on the stage: our imaginations will always revolt at such a sight, and will demand other means of attaining the great beauties of composition. But, were the French to direct the utmost force of their literary criticisms against the prediction of the witches in Macbeth, the ghost of Banquo, etc., we should not the less feel, with the most lively emotion, the terrific effect which it is their endeavor to proscribe.

We cannot teach good taste in the arts as we can *bon ton* in society; for the knowledge of *bon ton* assists us to hide the points in which we fail, while in the arts it is above all things necessary to possess a creative spirit. Good taste cannot supply the place of genius in literature, for the best proof of taste, when there is no genius, would be, not to write at all. If we dared to speak our opinion on this subject, perhaps we should say, that in France there are too many curbs for coursers that have so little mettle, and that in Germany, great literary independence has not yet produced effects proportionably striking and brilliant.

FROM

Chapter XXVIII

Of Romances

Of all fictions, romances being the easiest, there is no career in which the writers of modern nations have more generally essayed themselves. The romance constitutes what may be called the transition between real and imaginary existence. The history of every individual is, with some modifications, a romance sufficiently similar to those which are printed, and personal recollections often, in this respect, take place of invention. It has been attempted to give more importance to this species of compositions, by mixing with it poetry, history, and philosophy; but it seems to me that this is to alter its nature. Moral reflections and impassioned eloquence may find room in romances, but the interest of situations ought always to be the first princple of action in this sort of writings, and nothing can ever properly supply its place. If theatrical effect is the indispensable condition for all pieces for representation, it is equally true that a romance can be neither a good work, nor a happy fiction, unless it inspires a lively curiosity; it is in vain that we would supply the want of this by ingenious digressions: the expectation of amusement frustrated would cause an insurmountable fatigue.

The multitude of love romances published in Germany has somewhat turned into ridicule the light of the moon, the harps that resound at evening through the valley, in short, all known and approved methods of softly soothing the soul; and yet we have a natural disposition that is delighted with these easy sorts of reading, and it is the part of genius to avail itself of a disposition which it would be in vain to think of combating. It is so sweet to love and to be loved, that this hymn of life is susceptible of infinite modulation, without the heart experiencing any lassitude; thus we return with pleasure to the first melody of a song embellished by brilliant variations. I shall not however dissemble that romances, even those which are most pure, do mischief; they have too well discovered to us the most secret recesses of sentiment. Nothing can be experienced that we do not remember to have read before, and all the veils of the heart have been rent. The ancients would never thus have made of the human soul a subject of fiction; it remained a sanctuary for them, into which their own looks would have feared to penetrate; but in fine, the class of romances once admitted, there must be interest in it; and it is, as Cicero said of action in the Orator, the condition trebly necessary.

The Germans, like the English, are very fertile in romances descriptive of domestic life. The delineation of manners is more elegant in the English, but more diversified in the German. There is in England, notwithstanding the independence of characters, a generality of manner inspired by good company; in Germany nothing of this sort is matter of convention. Many of these romances, founded on our sentiments and manners, which hold among books the rank of dramas in the theatre, deserve to be cited; but that which is without equal and without parallel is *Werther;* there we behold all that the genius of Goethe was capable of producing when impassioned. It is said that he now attaches little value to this work of his youth; the effervescence of imagination, which inspired him almost with enthusiasm for suicide, may now appear to him deserving of censure. In youth, the degradation of existence not having yet any commencement, the tomb appears only a poetical image, a sleep surrounded with figures weeping for us on their knees; it is no longer the same in middle life, and we then learn why religion, that science of the soul, has mingled the horror of murder with the attempt upon one's own existence.

Nevertheless, Goethe would be much in the wrong did he despise the admirable talent that manifests itself in *Werther*; it is not only the sufferings of love, but the maladies of the imagination, so prevalent in our times, of which he has painted the picture; those thoughts that press into the mind, without our being able to change them into acts of the will; the singular contrast of a life much more monotonous than that of the ancients, and of an internal existence much more tumultuous, cause a sort of dizziness like that which we experience on the brink of a precipice, when the very fatigue of long contemplating the abyss below may urge us to throw ourselves into it. Goethe has been able to join to this picture of the inquietudes of the soul, so philosophical in its result, a fiction, simple, but of prodigious interest. If it has been thought necessary in all the sciences to strike the eyes by outward images, is it not natural to interest the heart, in order to impress it with great thoughts?

Romances by means of letters, always suppose more of sentiment than of fact; the ancients would never have thought of giving this form to their fictions; and it is only for two centuries past that philosophy has been sufficiently directed within ourselves, to enable the analysis of our feelings to hold so great a place in our books. This manner of conceiving romances is certainly not so poetical as that which consists entirely in narration; but the human mind is now much less disposed to be gratified by events even the best combined, than by observations on what passes within the heart. This disposition is the consequence of those great intellectual changes that have taken place in man; he has in general a much greater tendency to fall back upon himself, and to seek religion, love, and sentiment, in the most inward recesses of his being.

Many German writers have composed tales of ghosts and witches, and think that there is more genius in these inventions, than in a romance founded on the circumstances of ordinary life: it is very well for those who are led to it by natural inclination; but, in general, verse is necessary for the marvelous, prose is inadequate to it. When ages and countries, very different from those we live in, are represented in fiction, the charm of poetry must supply the want of that pleasure which the resemblance to ourselves would make us experience. Poetry is the winged mediator that transports times past and foreign nations into a sublime region, where admiration fills the place of sympathy.

Romances of chivalry abound in Germany; but they should have been more scrupulous in fastening them to ancient traditions: at present, they take the trouble of investigating these precious sources, and in a book called *the Book of Heroes*, they have found a number of adventures related with force and *naïveté;* it is of importance to preserve the color of this ancient style and of these ancient manners, and not to prolong, by the analysis of sentiments, the recitals of times in which honor and love acted on the heart of man, like the fatality of the ancients, without their reflecting on the motives of actions, or admitting any uncertainty into their operations.

Philosophical romance has, for some time past, taken the lead, in Germany, of all other sorts; it does not resemble that of the French; it is not, like Voltaire's, a general idea expressed by a fact in form of apologue, but it is a picture of human life altogether impartial, a picture in which no impassioned interest predominates; different situations succeed each other in all ranks, in all conditions, in all circumstances, and the writer is present to relate them. It is upon these principles that Goethe has conceived his *Wilhelm Meister*, a work greatly admired in Germany, but little known elsewhere.

Wilhelm Meister is full of ingenious and lively discussions; it would make a philosophical work of the first order, if the intrigue of romance were not introduced into it, the interest of which is not worth what is sacrificed to it; we find in it very fine and minute pictures of a certain class of society, more numerous in Germany than in other countries; a class in which artists, players, and adventurers mix with those of the bourgeois who love an independent life, and with those of the nobility who esteem themselves the protectors of the arts: every picture, taken separately, is charming; but there is no other interest in the *tout-ensemble* but what we may feel in knowing the opinion of Goethe on every subject: the hero of his novel is an intruding third person whom he has placed, we know not why, between himself and his reader.

Amid all these personages in *Wilhelm Meister*, more intelligent than important, and these situations so much more natural than prominent, a charming episode is scattered through many parts of the work, in which is united all that the warmth and originality of genius of Goethe is capable of producing of most animated. A young Italian girl is the child of love, and of a criminal and frightful love, which has taken hold of a man consecrated by oath to the worship of the divinity; the lovers, already so culpable, discover after their marriage that they are brother and sister, and that incest has been rendered for them the punishment of perjury. The mother loses her reason, and the father runs over the world like an unhappy wanderer who refuses any shelter. The unfortunate fruit of this fatal love, without support from its birth, is carried away by a troop of rope-dancers; they exercise it to the age of ten years, in the wretched play which constitutes their own subsistence: the cruel treatment they make it undergo excites the interest of Wilhelm, and he takes into his service this young girl, in the dress of a boy, which she has worn ever since her birth.

There is developed in this extraordinary creature, a singular mixture of childishness and depth of understanding, of seriousness and imagination; ardent like the women of Italy, silent and persevering like a person of reflection, speech does not seem to be her natural language. The few words she utters, however, are solemn, and answerable to sentiments much stronger than those natural to her age, and of which she does not herself possess the secret. She becomes attached to Wilhelm with love and reverence; she serves him as a faithful domestic, she loves him as an impassioned wife: her life having been always unhappy, it seems as if she had never known childhood, and as if having been doomed to suffering in an age which nature has destined only for enjoyments, she existed only for one solitary affection with which the beatings of her heart begin and end.

The character of Mignon (this is the young girl's name) is mysterious like a dream; she expresses her longing for Italy in some enchanting verses which all people know by heart in Germany: "Dost thou know the land where citron-trees flourish?" etc. In the end, jealousy, that passion too strong for so tender organs, breaks the heart of the poor girl, who becomes a prey to grief before age has given her strength to struggle against it. To comprehend all the effect of this admirable picture, it would be necessary to enter into all the details of it. We cannot represent to ourselves without emotion the least of the feelings that agitate this young girl; there is in her I know not what of magic simplicity, that supposes abysses of thought and feeling; we think we hear the tempest moaning at the bottom of her soul, even while we are unable to fix upon a word or a circumstance to account for the inexpressible uneasiness she makes us feel.

Notwithstanding this beautiful episode, we perceive in *Wilhelm Meister* the singular system that has developed itself of late in the German school. The recitals of the ancients, even their poems, however internally animated, are calm in form; and we are persuaded that the moderns would do well to imitate the tranquillity of the ancient authors; but, in respect of imagination, what is not prescribed in theory seldom succeeds in practice. Events like those of the Illiad interest of themselves, and the less the author's own sentiments are brought forward, the greater is the impression made by the picture; but if we set ourselves to describe romantic situations with the impartial calmness of Homer, the result would not be very alluring.

Goethe has just produced a romance called *the Elective Affinities,* which is extremely obnoxious to the censure I have been remarking. A happy family has retired into the country; the husband and wife invite the one his friend, the other her niece, to partake their solitude; the friend falls in love with the wife, and the husband with the young girl, her niece. He abandons himself to the idea of recurring to a divorce in order to procure a union with the object of his attachment; the young girl is ready to consent: unfortunate events happen to bring her back to the feeling of duty; but as soon as she is brought to the acknowledge the necessity of sacrificing her love, she dies of grief, and her lover shortly follows her.

The translation of *the Elective Affinities* has not met with success in France, because there is nothing characteristic in the general effect of the fiction, and it is difficult to comprehend with what view it was conceived: this uncertainty is not a matter for censure in Germany, as the events of this world often furnish only undecided results, people are satisfied to find in romances which pretend to describe them the same contradictions and the same doubts. Goethe's work contains a number of refined sentiments and observations; but it is true that the interest often languishes, and that we find almost as many vacancies in the novel as in the ordinary course of human life. A romance, however, ought not to resemble the memoirs of individuals; for every thing interests in what has really existed, while fiction can only equal the effect of truth by surpassing it, that is, by possessing greater strength, more unity, and more action.

The description of the Baron's garden, and the embellishments made in it by the Baroness, absorbs more than a third part of the whole story, and it does not dispose the reader to be moved by a tragic catastrophe: the death of the hero and heroine seems no more than a fortuitous accident, because the heart is not prepared long beforehand to feel and to partake the pain they suffer. This work affords a singular mixture of a life of convenience with stormy passions; an imagination full of grace and strength draws near to the production of grand effects to let them go all of a sudden, as if it were not worth the pain to produce them; one would say that the author has been injured by his own emotion, and that, by mere cowardice of heart, he lays aside the one half of his talent for fear of making himself suffer in trying to move his readers.

A more important question is, whether such a work is moral, that is, whether the impression derived from it is favorable to the improvement of the soul? The mere events of a fiction have nothing to do with this question; we so well know their dependence on the will of the author, that they can awaken the conscience of no man: the morality of a novel consists, therefore, in the sentiments it inspires. It cannot be denied that there is in Goethe's book a profound knowledge of the human heart, but it is a discouraging knowledge; it represents life as at best very indifferent, in whatever manner it passes; when probed to the bottom, sad and mournful, only tolerably agreeable when slightly skimmed over, liable to moral diseases which must be cured if possible, and must kill if they cannot be cured.

The passions exist, the virtues also exist; there are some who asssure us that the first must be counteracted by the second; others pretend that this cannot be; see and judge, says the writer who sums up with impartiality the arguments which fate may furnish for and against each method of viewing the subject.

It would be wrong to imagine, however, that this skepticism was inspired by the materialistic tendency of the eighteenth century; the opinions of Goethe are much more profound, but they do not present any greater consolation to the soul. His writings offer to us a contemptuous philosophy, that says to good as well as to evil: "It ought to be so because it is so;" a wonderful imagination, which rules over all the other faculties, and grows tired of genius itself, as having in it something too involuntary and too partial. In fine, what is most of all defective in this romance, is a firm and positive feeling of religion; the principal personages are more accessible to superstition than to faith; and we perceive that in their hearts religion, like love, is only the effect of circumstances, and liable to vary with them.

In the progress of this work, the author displays too much uncertainty; the forms he draws, and the opinions he indicates, leave only doubtful recollections: it must be agreed that, to think a great deal sometimes leads to the total unsettling of our fundamental ideas; but a man of genius like Goethe should serve as a guide to his admirers in an ascertained road. It is no longer time to doubt, it is no longer time to place, on every possible subject, ingenious ideas in each scale of the balance; we should now abandon ourselves to confidence, to enthusiasm, to the admiration which the immortal youth of the soul may always keep alive within us; this youth springs forth again out of the very ashes of the passions; it is the golden bough that can never fade, and which gives entrance to the Sibyl into the Elysian fields.

Tieck deserves to be mentioned in many different styles of composition; he is the author of a novel called *Sternbald,* which it is delightful to read; the events are but few, and even those few are not conducted to the *dénoûment;* but we can nowhere else, I believe, meet with so pleasing a picture of the life of an artist. The author places his hero in the fine age of the arts, and supposes him to be a scholar of Albert Durer, the contemporary of Raphael. He makes him travel in different countries of Europe, and paints with the charm of novelty the pleasure that must be caused by external objects when we belong to no country and no station exclusively, but are at liberty to range through all nature in search of inspiration and example. This state of existence, wandering and at the same time contemplative, is thoroughly understood nowhere but in Germany. In French romances we always describe social manners and the intercourse of society; yet there is a great secret of enjoyment in this sort of imagination, which seems to hover over the earth while it traverses, and mixes not at all in the active interests of the world.

Unhappy mortals hardly ever receive from fate the blessing of a destiny in which the events succeed each other in the regular concatenation they desire; but insulated impressions are for the most part sufficiently gentle, and the present, when it can be contemplated apart from recollections and apprehensions, is still the happiest moment of life. There is a sort of poetical philosophy, then, of great wisdom in those instantaneous enjoyments which compose the artist's existence; the new points of view, the accidents of light which embellish them, are for him so many events that have their beginning and ending in the same day, and have nothing to do with the past or the future; the affections of the heart unveil the face of nature, and we are astonished, in reading Tieck's novel, by all the wonders that surround us without our perceiving it.

The author has mingled in his work several detached pieces of poetry, some of which are extremely fine. When verses are introduced into a French novel, they almost always interrupt the interest, and destroy the harmony of the whole. It is not so in *Sternbald;* the story is so poetical in itself, that the prose seems like a recitative which follows the verse, or prepares the way for it. Among others, there are some stanzas on the spring, as enchanting as nature herself at that season. Infancy is represented in them under a thousand different shapes; man, the plants, the earth, the heaven, all things there are so young, all things so rich in hope, that the poet appears to be celebrating the first fine days, and the first flowers that ever attired the world.

We have, in French, several comic romances, and one of the most remarkable is *Gil Blas*. I do not think any work can be mentioned among the Germans, in which the affairs of life are so agreeably sported with. The Germans have hardly yet attained a real world, how can they be supposed capable already of laughing at it? That serious kind of gayety which turns nothing into ridicule, but amuses without intending it, and makes others laugh without laughing itself—that gayety which the English call *humor*—is to be found also in many of the German writers; but it is almost impossible to translate them. When the pleasantry consists in a philosophical sentiment happily expressed, as in Swift's *Gulliver*, the change of language is of no importance; but Sterne's *Tristram Shandy* loses almost all its beauty in French. Pleasantries, which consist in the forms of language, speak to the mind a thousand times more, perhaps, than ideas; and yet these impressions so lively, excited by shades so fine, are incapable of being transmitted to foreigners.

Claudius is one of the German authors who have most of that national gayety, the exclusive property of every foreign literature. He has published a collection of various detached pieces on different subjects; some are in bad taste, others unimportant, but there reigns in all of them an originality and a truth which render the least things attractive. This writer, whose style is clothed in a simple, and sometimes even in a vulgar habit, penetrates to the bottom of the heart by the sincerity of his sentiments. He makes you weep, as he makes you laugh, by exciting sympathy, and by giving you to recognize a fellow-creature and a friend in all he feels. Nothing can be extracted from the writings of Claudius; his talent acts like sensation, and to speak of it, it is necessary to have felt it. He resembles those Flemish painters who sometimes rise to the representation of what is most noble in nature, or to the Spanish Murillo, who paints poor beggars with the utmost exactness, and yet often gives them, unconsciously, some traits of a noble and profound impression. To mix the comic and the pathetic with success, it is necessary to be eminently natural in both; as soon as the artificial makes its appearance, all contrast vanishes; but a great genius full of simplicity may successfully represent a union, of which the only charm is on the countenance of childhood, a smile in the midst of tears.

Another writer, of later date and greater celebrity than Claudius, has acquired great reputation in Germany by works which might be called romances, if any known denomination could suit productions so extraordinary. Jean Paul Richter is possessed of powers certainly more than sufficient to compose a work that would be as interesting to foreigners as to his own countrymen, and yet nothing that he has published can ever extend beyond the limits of Germany. His admirers will say that this results from the originality even of his genius; I think that his faults are as much the cause of it as his excellencies. In these modern times, the mind should be European; the Germans encourage their authors too much in that wandering spirit of enterprise, which, daring as it seems, is not always void of affectation. Madame de Lambert said to her son: "My friend, indulge yourself in no follies that will not afford you a very high degree of pleasure." We might beg Jean Paul never to be singular except in spite of himself: whatever is said involuntarily always hits some natural feeling; but when natural originality is spoiled by the pretension to originality, the reader has no perfect enjoyment even of what is true, from the remembrance and the dread of what is otherwise.

Some admirable beauties are to be found, nevertheless, in the works of Jean Paul; but the arrangement and frame of his pictures are so defective, that the most luminous traits of genius are lost in the general confusion. The writings of Jean Paul deserve to be considered in two points of view, the humorous and the serious, for he constantly mixes both together. His manner of observing the human heart is full of delicacy and vivacity, but his knowledge of it is merely such as may be acquired in the little towns of Germany; and in his delineation of manners, confined as it is, there is frequently something too innocent for the age in which we live. Observations so delicate, and almost minute, on the moral affections, recall a little to our recollection the personage in the fairy tales who went by the name of *Fine-Ear,* because he could hear the grass grow. In this respect Sterne bears some analogy to Jean Paul; but if Jean Paul is very superior to him in the serious and poetical part of his works, Sterne has more taste and elegance in his humor, and we see that he has lived in societies less confined and more brilliant.

Thoughts extracted from the writings of Jean Paul would, however, form a very remarkable work; but we perceive, in reading them, his singular custom of collecting from every quarter, from obsolete books, scientific works, etc., his metaphors and allusions. The resemblances thus produced are almost always very ingenious; but when study and attention are required to enable us to find out a jest, scarcely any but the Germans would consent thus to laugh after a serious study, and give themselves as much trouble to understand what amuses them as what is calculated for their instruction.

At the bottom of all this we find a mine of new ideas, and if we reach it, we are enriched; but the author has neglected the stamp which should have been given to those treasures. The gayety of the French is derived from the spirit of society; that of the Italians from the imagination; that of the English from originality of character; the gayety of the Germans is philosophic. They jest with things and with books, rather than with men. Their heads contain a chaos of knowledge, which an independent and fantastic imagination combines in a thousand different ways, sometimes original, sometimes confused, but in which we always perceive great vigor of intellect and of soul.

The genius of Jean Paul frequently resembles that of Montaigne. The French authors of former times are in general more like the Germans, than writers of the age of Louis XIV; for it is since that time that French literature has taken a classical direction.

Jean Paul Richter is often sublime in the serious parts of his works, but the continued melancholy of his language sometimes moves till it fatigues us. When the imagination is kept too long in the clouds, the colors are confused, the outlines are effaced, and we retain of all that we have read rather a reverberation of the sound than a recollection of the substance. The sensibility of Jean Paul affects the soul, but does not sufficiently strengthen it. The poetry of his style resembles the sounds of a harmonica, which delight us at first, but give us pain a few minutes afterwards, because the exaltation excited by them has no determinate object. We give too great an advantage to cold and insipid characters, when we represent sensibility to them as a disease, while, on the contrary, it is the most energetic of all our moral faculties, since it imparts both the desire and ability to devote ourselves to others.

Among the affecting episodes which abound in the writings of Jean Paul, where the principal subjects are seldom more than slight pretexts to introduce the episodes, I will now quote three, taken by chance, to give an idea of the rest. An English lord is blind in consequence of a double cataract; he has an operation performed on one of his eyes; it fails, and that eye is irretrievably lost. His son, without informing him of it, studies with an oculist, and at the end of a year he is judged capable of operating on the eye, which may yet be preserved. The father, ignorant of his son's intention, thinks he is placing himself in the hands of a stranger, and prepares himself with fortitude for the moment which is to decide whether the rest of his life is, or is not, to be passed in darkness; he even directs that his son should be sent from his chamber, that he may not be too much affected by being present at so important a decision. The son approaches his father in silence; his hand does not tremble, for the circumstance is too momentuous to admit of the common signs of tenderness. All his soul is concentered in a simple thought, and even the excess of his sensibility gives that supernatural presence of mind, which would be succeeded by phrensy, if hope were lost. At length the operation succeeds, and the father, in recovering his sight, beholds the instrument of its restoration in the hand of his own son!

Another romance by the same author also presents a very affecting situation. A young blind man requests a description of the setting of the sun, whose mild and pure rays, he says he feels in the atmosphere, like the farewell of a friend. The person whom he interrogates describes nature to him in all its beauty; but he mingles in his painting an impression of melancholy, calculated to console the unfortunate being who is deprived of sight. He incessantly appeals to the Deity, as to the living source of the wonders of the world; and bringing every thing within the scope of that intellectual sight which the blind man probably enjoys in a more perfect manner than we do, he makes his soul perceive what his eyes can no longer behold. . . .

Chapter XXXI

Of the Literary Treasures of Germany, and
of Its Most Renowned Critics, A. W. and F. Schlegel

In the picture which I have now given of German literature, I have endeavored to point out the principal works; but I have been obliged to omit naming a great number of men, whose writings, being less known, conduce more to the instruction of those who read them, than to the reputation of the authors themselves.

Treatises on the fine arts, works of erudition and philosophy, though they do not immediately belong to literature, must, however, be counted among its treasures. There is in Germany a fund of ideas and knowledge which the other nations of Europe will not for a long time be able to exhaust.

The poetical genius, if Heaven ever restores it to us, may also receive a happy impulse from the love of nature, of arts, and philosophy, which is kindled in the countries of Germany; but at least, I dare affirm that any man who now wishes to devote himself to a serious work of whatever sort, whether history, philosophy, or antiquities, cannot excuse himself from becoming acquainted with the German writers, who have been occupied with the study of those subjects.

France may boast of a great number of learned men of the first rank, but they have seldom united knowledge and philosophical sagacity, while in Germany they are now almost inseparable. Those who plead in favor of ignorance, as a pledge of grace, mention many very sensible men who have had no instruction; but they forget that those men have deeply studied the human heart, such as it shows itself in the world, and that their ideas are derived from that source. But if those men, learned in society, would judge of literature without being acquainted it, they would be as tiresome as citizens are when they talk of the court.

When I began the study of German literature, it seemed as if I was entering on a new sphere, where the most striking light was thrown on all that I had before perceived only in a confused manner. For some time past, little has been read in France except memoirs and novels, and it is not wholly from frivolity that we are become less capable of more serious reading, but because the events of the revolution have accustomed us to value nothing but the knowledge of men and things: we find in German books, even on the most abstract subjects, that kind of interest which confers their value upon good novels, and which is excited by the knowledge which they teach us of our own hearts. The peculiar character of German literature is to refer every thing to an interior existence; and as that is the mystery of mysteries, it awakens an unbounded curiosity.

Before we proceed to philosophy, which always makes a part of learning in countries where the empire of literature is free and powerful, I will say a few words on what may be considered as the legislation of that empire—I mean criticism. There is no branch of German literature which has been carried to a greater extent, and as in certain cities there are more physicians than sick people, there are sometimes in Germany more critics than authors; but the analyses of Lessing, who was the creator of style in German prose, are made in such a manner, that they may themselves be considered as works.

Kant, Goethe, J. von Müller, the greatest German writers of every kind, have inserted in the periodicals, what they call *recensions* of different publications, and these *recensions* contain the most profound philosophical theory, and positive knowledge. Among the younger writers, Schiller and the two Schlegels have shown themselves very superior to all other critics. Schiller is the first among the disciples of Kant who applied his philosophy to literature; and indeed, to judge from the soul, of exterior objects, or from exterior objects to know what passes in the soul, is so different a progress, that all connected with either, must be sensible of it. Schiller has written two treatises *on the naif and the sentimental,* in which, genius unconscious of its own powers, and genius which is self-observant, are analyzed with great sagacity; but in his *Essay on Grace and Dignity,* and in his letters on *Æsthetics,* that is, the theory of the beautiful, there is too much of metaphysics. When we mean to speak of that enjoyment of the arts of which all men are susceptible, we should dwell on the impressions they have received, instead of permitting the use of abstract forms, which make us lose the trace of those impressions. Schiller was a man of literature by his genius, and a philosopher by his inclination to reflection; his prose writings border on the confines of the two regions; but he often treads a little forward on the highest, and returning incessantly to what is more abstract in theory, he disdains the application as a useless consequence of the principles he has laid down.

Animated descriptions of the *chefs-d'œuvre* of literature give much more interest to criticism, than general ideas which skim over all subjects without characterizing any. Metaphysics may be termed the science of what is immutable; but all that is subjected to the course of time, is explained only by the mixture of facts and reflections: the Germans would attain complete theories, independent of circumstances, on all subjects; but as that is impossible, we must not give up facts from a fear lest they should circumscribe ideas; and examples alone in theory, as well as in practice, engrave precepts deeply in the memory.

The quintessence of thoughts which some German works present to us, does not, like that of flowers, concentrate the most odoriferous perfumes; on the contrary, we may say with greater truth, that it is only a cold remnant of emotions that were full of life. We might, however, extract from those works a multitude of very interesting observations; but they are confounded with each other. The author, by great exertion of mind, leads his readers to that point where his ideas are too fine and delicate for him to attempt transmitting them to others.

The writings of A. W. Schlegel are less abstracted than those of Schiller; as his knowledge of literature is uncommon even in Germany, he is led continually to application by the pleasure which he finds in comparing different languages and different poems with each other; so general a point of view ought almost to be considered as infallible, if partiality did not sometimes impair it; but this partiality is not of an arbitrary kind, and I will point out both the progress and aim of it; nevertheless, as there are subjects in which it is not perceived, it is of those that I shall first speak.

W. Schlegel has given a course of dramatic literature at Vienna, which comprises every thing remarkable that has been composed for the theatre from the time of the Grecians to our own days: it is not a barren nomenclature of the works of the various authors; he seizes the spirit of their different sorts of literature with all the imagination of a poet; we are sensible that to produce such consequences extraordinary studies are required; but learning is not perceived in this work except by his perfect knowledge of the *chefs-d'œuvre* of composition. In a few pages we reap the fruit of the labor of a whole life; every opinion formed by the author, every epithet given to the writers of whom he speaks, is beautiful and just, concise and animated. W. Schlegel has found the art of treating the finest pieces of poetry as so many wonders of nature, and of painting them in lively colors which do not injure the justness of the outline; for we cannot repeat too often, that imagination, far from being an enemy to truth, brings it forward more than any other faculty of the mind, and all those who depend upon it as an excuse for indefinite terms or exaggerated expressions, are at least as destitute of poetry as of good sense.

An analysis of the principles on which both tragedy and comedy are founded, is treated in W. Schlegel's course of dramatic literature with much depth of philosophy; this kind of merit is often found among the German writers; but Schlegel has no equal in the art of inspiring enthusiasm for the great geniuses he admires; in general he shows himself attached to a simple taste, sometimes bordering on rusticity, but he deviates from his usual opinons in favor of the opinions of the inhabitants of the South. Their *jeux de mots* and their *concetti* are not the objects of his censure; he detests the affectation which owes its existence to the spirit of society, but that which is excited by the luxury of imagination pleases him in poetry as the profusion of colors and perfumes would do in nature. Schlegel, after having acquired a great reputation by his translation of Shakspeare, became equally enamored of Calderon, but with a very different sort of attachment from that with which Shakspeare had inspired him; for while the English author is deep and gloomy in his knowledge of the human heart, the Spanish poet gives himself up with pleasure and delight to the beauty of life, to the sincerity of faith, and to all the brilliancy of those virtues which derive their coloring from the sunshine of the soul.

I was at Vienna when W. Schlegel gave his public course of lectures. I expected only good sense and instruction where the object was only to convey information; I was astonished to hear a critic as eloquent as an orator, and who, far from falling upon defects, which are the eternal food of mean and little jealousy, sought only the means of reviving a creative genius.

Spanish literature is but little known, and it was the subject of one of the finest passages delivered during the sitting at which I attended. W. Schlegel gave us a picture of that chivalrous nation, whose poets were all warriors, and whose warriors were poets. He mentioned that Count Ercilla, "who composed his poem of the Araucana in a tent, as now on the shores of the ocean, now at the foot of the Cordilleras, while he made war on the devoted savages. Garcilasso, one of the descendants of the Incas, wrote love-poems on the ruins of Carthage, and perished at the siege of Tunis. Cervantes was dangerously wounded at the battle of Lepanto; Lope de Vega escaped miraculously at the defeat of the Invincible Armada; and Calderon served as an intrepid soldier in the wars of Flanders and Italy.

"Religion and war were more frequently united among the Spaniards than in any other nation; it was they who, by perpetual combats, drove out the Moors from the bosom of their country, and who may be considered as the vanguard of European christendom; they conquered their churches from the Arabians, an act of their worship was a trophy for their arms, and their triumphant religion, sometimes carried to fanaticism, was allied to the sentiment of honor, and gave to their character an impressive dignity. That gravity tinctured with imagination, even that gayety which loses nothing of what is serious in the warmest affections, show themselves in Spanish literature, which is wholly composed of fictions and of poetry, of which religion, love, and warlike exploits are constantly the object. It might be said, that when the new world was discovered, the treasures of another hemisphere contributed to enrich the imagination as much as the state; and that in the empire of poetry as well as in that of Charles V, the sun never ceased to enlighten the horizon."

All who heard W. Schlegel, were much struck with this picture, and the German language, which he spoke with elegance, added depth of thought and affecting expression to those high-sounding Spanish names, which can never be pronounced without presenting to our imaginations the orangetrees of the kingdom of Grenada, and the palaces of its Moorish sovereigns.

We may compare W. Schlegel's manner of speaking of poetry, to that of Winkelmann in describing statues; and it is only by such a method of estimating talents, that it is honorable to be a critic: every artist or professional man can point out faults and inaccuracies which ought to be avoided, but the ability to discover genius and to admire it, is almost equal to the possession of genius itself.

Frederick Schlegel being much engaged in philosophical pursuits, devoted himself less exclusively to literature than his brother; yet the piece he wrote on the intellectual culture of the Greeks and Romans, contains in small compass perceptions and conclusions of the first order. F. Schlegel has more originality of genius than almost any other celebrated man in Germany; but far from depending on that originality, though it promised him much success, he endeavored to assist it by extensive study. It is a great proof of our respect for the human species, when we dare not address it from the suggestions of our own minds, without having first conscientiously examined into all that has been left to us by our predecessors as an inheritance. The Germans, in those acquired treasures of the human mind, are true proprietors: those who depend on their own natural understandings alone, are mere sojourners in comparison with them.

After having done justice to the uncommon talents of the two Schlegels, we will now examine in what that partiality consists of which they are accused, and from which it is certain all their writings are not exempt. They are evidently prepossessed in favor of the middle ages, and the opinions that were then prevalent; chivalry without spot, unbounded faith, and unstudied poetry, appear to them inseparable; and they apply themselves to all that may enable them to direct the minds and understandings of others to the same preference. W. Schlegel expresses his admiration for the middle ages in several of his writings, and particularly in two stanzas of which I will now give a translation.

"In those distinguished ages Europe was sole and undivided, and the soil of that universal country was fruitful in those generous thoughts which are calculated to serve as guides through life and in death. Knighthood converted combatants into brethren in arms: they fought in defence of the same faith; the same love inspired all hearts, and the poetry which sung that alliance, expressed the same sentiment in different languages.

"Alas! the noble energy of ancient times is lost: our age is the inventor of a narrow-minded wisdom, and what weak men have no ability to conceive, is in their eyes only a chimera; surely nothing truly great can succeed if undertaken with a grovelling heart. Our times, alas! no longer know either faith or love; how then can hope be expected to remain with them?"

Opinions, whose tendency is so strongly marked, must necessarily affect impartiality of judgment on works of art: without doubt, as I have continually repeated during the whole course of this work, it is much to be desired that modern literature should be founded on our history and our religion; it does not, however, follow that the literary productions of the middle ages should be considered as absolutely good. The energetic simplicity, the pure and loyal character which is displayed in them, interests us warmly; but on the other hand, the knowledge of antiquity and the progress of civilization have given us advantages which are not to be despised. The object is not to trace back the arts to remote times, but to unite, as much as we can, all the various qualities which have been developed in the human mind at different periods.

The Schlegels have been strongly accused of not doing justice to French literature; there are, however, no writers who have spoken with more enthusiasm of the genius of our troubadours, and of that French chivalry which was unequalled in Europe, when it united in the highest degree, spirit and loyalty, grace and frankness, courage and gayety, the most affecting simplicity with the most ingenuous candor; but the German critics affirm that those distinguished traits of the French character were effaced during the course of the reign of Louis XIV; literature, they say, in ages which are called classical, loses in originality what it gains in correctness; they have attacked our poets, particularly, in various ways, and with great strength of argument. The general spirit of those critics is the same with that of Rousseau in his letter against French music. They think they discover in many of our tragedies that kind of pompous affectation, of which Rousseau accuses Lully and Rameau, and they affirm that the same taste which gives the preference to Coypel and Boucher in painting, and to the Chevalier Bernini in sculpture, forbids in poetry that rapturous ardor which alone renders it a divine enjoyment; in short, they are tempted to apply to our manner of conceiving and of loving the fine arts, the verses so frequently quoted from Corneille:

> Othon à la princesse a fait un compliment,
> Plus un homme d'esprit qu'en véritable amant.

W. Schlegel pays due homage, however, to most of our great authors; but what he chiefly endeavors to prove, is, that from the middle of the seventeenth century, a constrained and affected manner has prevailed throughout Europe, and that this prevalence has made us lose those bold flights of genius which animated both writers and artists in the revival of literature. In the pictures and bas-reliefs where Louis XIV is sometimes represented as Jupiter, and sometimes as Hercules, he is naked, or clothed only with the skin of a lion, but always with a great wig on his head. The writers of the new school tell us that this great wig may be applied to the physiognomy of the fine arts in the seventeenth century: an affected sort of politeness, derived from factitious greatness, is always to be discovered in them.

It is interesting to examine the subject in this point of view, in spite of the innumerable objections which may be opposed to it; it is however certain that these German critics have succeeded in the object aimed at, as, of all writers since Lessing, they have most essentially contributed to discredit the imitation of French literature in Germany; but from the fear of adopting French taste, they have not sufficiently improved that of their own country, and have often rejected just and striking observations, merely because they had before been made by our writers.

They know not how to make a book in Germany, and scarcely ever adopt that methodical order which classes ideas in the mind of the reader; it is not, therefore, because the French are impatient, but because their judgment is just and accurate, that this defect is so tiresome to them; in German poetry fictions are not delineated with those strong and precise outlines which insure the effect, and the uncertainty of the imagination corresponds to the obscurity of the thought. In short, if taste be found wanting in those strange and vulgar pleasantries which constitute what is called *comic* in some of their works, it is not because they are natural, but because the affectation of energy is at least as ridiculous as that of gracefulness. "I am making myself lively," said a German as he jumped out of window: when we attempt to make ourselves any thing, we are nothing: we should have recourse to the good taste of the French to secure us from the excessive exaggeration of some German authors, as on the other hand we should apply to the solidity and depth of the Germans to guard us against the dogmatic frivolity of some men in France.

Different nations ought to serve as guides to each other, and all would do wrong to deprive themselves of the information they may mutually receive and impart. There is something very singular in the difference which subsists between nations; the climate, the aspect of nature, the language, the government, and above all, the events of history, which have in themselves powers more extraordinary than all the others united, all combine to produce those diversities; and no man, however superior he may be, can guess at that which is naturally developed in the mind of him who inhabits another soil and breathes another air: we should do well then, in all foreign countries, to welcome foreign thoughts and foreign sentiments, for hospitality of this sort makes the fortune of him who exercises it.

G. W. F. Hegel
1770–1831

Georg Wilhelm Friedrich Hegel was born at Stuttgart on August 27, 1770, the son of a revenue officer. He was tutored in Latin by his mother, then attended the grammar school in Stuttgart where he remained until 1788, when he entered the University of Tübingen with the ultimate objective of taking holy orders. He concentrated in philosophy and classics, receiving a Ph.D. in 1790. He also studied theology, but he was never ordained.

Upon leaving college in 1793 Hegel became a private tutor in Berne. In his ample spare time he studied the Greek and Roman classics, as well as Gibbon, Montesquieu, and Kant. He was particularly interested in Kant's thoughts on religion, which prompted him to write several essays on the development of Christianity. In 1796 Hegel moved to Frankfurt am Main, where his friend J. C. F. Hölderlin had secured another tutorship for him. Hegel continued his study of Christianity, attacking orthodoxy while maintaining a belief in the basic tenets of Christian theology. In his essay *The Spirit of Christianity*, written in 1798, he expressed the main ideas of what became his philosophical system. In contrast to Kant's argument that man could have knowledge only of a world of finite appearances, Hegel argues that man is a union of flesh and spirit, and that as spirit he is capable of comprehending God. The theory of love as a unity of opposites which Hegel works out in this book prefigures his later notion of *Geist* as a synthesis of contradictions.

In 1801 Hegel left Frankfurt to embark upon an academic career at the University of Jena, where he began giving lectures on logic and metaphysics. He was promoted to extraordinary professor in July 1806, only a few months before Napoleon's victory at Jena. He is said to have completed his masterwork, *The Phenomenology of Mind*, with the sounds of battle coming through his window. He served briefly as editor of the *Bamberger Zeitung*, then became rector of a *Gymnasium* in Nuremberg from 1808 to 1816, during which time he published his two-part *Science of Logic*. Hegel then spent two years at Heidelberg, during which time he published his *Encyclopedia of the Philosophical Sciences*. In 1818 he assumed the chair of philosophy at the University of Berlin. The last major work published during his lifetime was the *Philosophy of Right*, which appeared in 1821; thereafter Hegel devoted himself to his lectures. In the 1820s he began to cultivate an interest in the fine arts, attending the theatre, concerts, and picture galleries. One result of his new concern was the preparation of a series of lectures on aesthetics, delivered in 1820, 1823, and 1826.

Art, for Hegel, is one of three modes of apprehension of the Absolute, along with religion and philosophy. Man satisfies in works of art his need to increase his self-awareness. Art "imprints the seal of his inner life" on man and thus frees the external world of its "stubborn alienation from himself." The basic function of art is to reveal truth under the mode of a material configuration. A work of art achieves beauty when it reconciles matter and content; thus the excellence of a work of art is judged by the degree to which "idea and configuration appear together in elaborated fusion."

Hegel lived to see a Hegelian school begin to form, and received much adulation toward the end of his life. In the year prior to his death—on November 14, 1831, from cholera—he served as rector of the university. The influence of his philosophy declined in the nineteenth century, but beginning early in the twentieth interest in him revived with the publication of new editions and even first printings of many of his essays and lectures, and the appearance of English translations of his work. A renewed interest in his early theological writings spawned critical interest on the Continent, while political thinkers, mindful of his influence on Karl Marx, reinvestigated his political writings.

ON ART

The present course of lectures deals with aesthetics. Their subject is the wide *realm of the beautiful*, and, more particularly, their province is *art*—we may restrict it, indeed, *to fine art*.

The name "aesthetics" in its natural sense is not quite appropriate to this subject. "Aesthetics" means more precisely the science of sensation or feeling. Thus understood, it arose as a new science, or rather as something that was to become a branch of philosophy for the first time, in the school of Wolff, at the epoch when works of art were being considered in Germany in the light of the feelings which they were supposed to evoke—feelings of pleasure, admiration, fear, pity, etc. The name was so inappropriate, or, strictly speaking, so superficial, that for this reason it was attempted to form other names, e.g. "Kallistic." But this name, again, is unsatisfactory, for the science to be designated does not treat of beauty in general, but merely of *artistic* beauty. We shall, therefore, permit the name Aesthetics to stand, because it is nothing but a name, and so is indifferent to us, and, moreover, has up to a certain point passed into common language. As a name, therefore, it may be retained. The proper expression, however, for our science is the "Philosophy of Art," or, more definitely, the "Philosophy of Fine Art."

By the above expression we at once exclude the *beauty of nature*. Such a limitation of our subject may appear to be an arbitrary demarcation resting on the principle that every science has the prerogative of marking out its bound-aries at pleasure. But this is not the sense in which we are to understand the limitation of Aesthetics to *the beauty of art*. It is true that in common life we are in the habit of speaking of beautiful colour, a beautiful sky, a beautiful river, and, moreover, of beautiful flowers, beautiful animals, and, above all, of beautiful human beings. We will not just now enter into the controversy of how far such objects can justly have the attribute of beauty ascribed to them, or how far, speaking generally, natural beauty ought to be recognized as existing besides artistic beauty. We may, however, begin at once by asserting that artistic beauty stands *higher* than nature. For the beauty of art is the beauty that is born—born again, that is—of the mind; and by as much as the mind and its products are higher than nature and its appearances, by so much is the beauty of art higher than the beauty of nature. Indeed, if we look at it *formally*—i.e. only considering in what way it exists, not what there is in it— even a silly fancy such as may pass through a man's head is *higher* than any product of nature; for such a fancy must at least be characterized by intel-lectual being and by freedom. In respect of its content, on the other hand, the sun, for instance, appears to us to be an absolutely necessary factor in the universe, while a blundering notion passes away as accidental and transient; but yet, in its own being, a natural existence such as the sun is indifferent, is not free or self-conscious, while if we consider it in its necessary connection with other things we are not regarding it by itself or for its own sake, and, therefore, not as beautiful.

To say, as we have said in general terms, that mind and its artistic beauty stand *higher* than natural beauty is no doubt to determine almost nothing. For "higher" is an utterly indefinite expression, which designates the beauty of nature and that of art as if merely standing side by side in the space of the imagination and states the difference between them as purely quantitative and, therefore, purely external. But the mind and its artistic beauty, in being *"higher"* as compared with nature, have a distinction which is not simply relative. Mind, and mind only, is capable of truth, and comprehends in itself all that is, so that whatever is beautiful can only be really and truly beautiful as it partakes in this higher element and as it is created thereby. In this sense the beauty of nature reveals itself as but a reflection of the beauty that belongs to the mind, as an imperfect, incomplete mode of being, as a mode whose really substantial element is contained in the mind itself.

Moreover, we shall find the restriction to fine art very natural, for, however much has been and is said—though less by the ancients than by ourselves—of the beauties of nature, yet no one has taken it into his head to emphasize the point of view of the *beauty* of natural objects, and to attempt to make a science, a systematic account of these beauties. The aspect of *utility,* indeed, has been accentuated, and a science, e.g. of natural things useful against diseases, a materia medica, has been compiled, consisting in a description of minerals, chemical products, plants, and animals that are of use for curative purposes. But the realm of nature has not been arrayed and estimated under the aspect of beauty. In dealing with natural beauty we find ourselves too open to vagueness and too destitute of a criterion, for which reason such a review would have little interest.

The above prefatory remarks upon beauty in nature and in art, upon the relation between the two, and the exclusion of the former from the region of the subject proper, are meant to remove any idea that the limitation of our science is owing merely to choice and to caprice. But this is not the place to *demonstrate* the above relation, for the consideration of it falls within our science itself, and therefore it cannot be discussed and demonstrated till later.

Supposing that for the present we have limited ourselves to the beauty of art, this first step brings us at once into contact with fresh difficulties.

The first thing that may suggest itself to us is the question of whether fine art shows itself to *deserve* a scientific treatment. Beauty and art, no doubt, pervade all the business of life like a kindly genius, and form the bright adornment of all our surroundings, both mental and material, soothing the sadness of our condition and the embarrassments of real life, killing time in entertaining fashion, and where there is nothing good to be achieved, occupying the place of what is vicious, better, at any rate, than vice. Yet although art presses in with its pleasing shapes on every possible occasion, from the rude adornments of the savage to the splendour of the temple with its untold wealth of decoration, still these shapes themselves appear to fall outside the real purposes of life. And even if the creations of art do not prove detrimental to our graver purposes, if they appear at times actually to further them by keeping evil at a distance, still it is so far true that art belongs rather to the relaxation and leisure of the mind, while the substantive interests of life demand its exertion. Hence it may seem unsuitable and pedantic to treat with scientific seriousness what is not in itself of a serious nature. In any case, upon such a view art appears as a superfluity, even if the softening of the mental temper which preoccupation with beauty has power to produce does not turn out a detrimental, because effeminating, influence. In this aspect of the matter, the fine arts being granted to be a *luxury*, it has been thought necessary in various ways to take up their defence with reference to their relation towards *practical* necessities, and more especially towards morality and piety, and, as it is impossible to demonstrate their harmlessness, at least to make it credible that the mental luxury in question afforded a larger sum of advantages than of disadvantages. With this view very serious aims have been ascribed to art, and it has been recommended in various ways as a mediator between reason and sensuousness, between inclination and duty, as the reconciler of these elements in the obstinate conflict and repulsion which their collision generates. But the opinion may be maintained that, assuming such aims of art, more serious though they are, nothing is gained for reason and duty by the attempt at mediation, because these principles, as essentially incapable of intermixture, can be parties to no such compromise but demand in their manifestation the same purity which they have in themselves. And it might be said that art itself is not made any more worthy of scientific discussion by such treatment, seeing that it is still doubly a servant—to higher aims, no doubt, on the one hand, but none the less to vacuity and frivolity on the other; and in such service can at best only display itself as a means, instead of being an end pursued for its own sake.

Finally, art, considered as a means, seems to labour under this defect of form: that, supposing it to be subordinated to serious ends and to produce results of importance, still the means employed by art for such purposes is *deception*. For beauty has its being in appearance. Now, it will readily be admitted that an aim which is real and true in itself ought not to be attained by deception, and if it does here and there achieve some success in this way, that can only be the case to a limited extent, and even then deception cannot approve itself as the right means. For the means should correspond to the dignity of the end, and only what is real and true, not semblance or deception, has power to create what is real and true; just as science, for instance, has to consider the true interests of the mind in accordance with the truth of reality and the true way of conceiving it.

In all these respects it may appear as if fine art were *unworthy* of scientific consideration, because, as is alleged, it is at best a pleasing amusement, and even if it pursues more serious aims is in contradiction with their nature, but is at best the mere servant alike of amusement and of serious aims, and yet has at command, whether as the element of its being or as the vehicle of its action, nothing beyond deception and semblance.

But, in the second place, it is a still more probable aspect of the question that, even if fine art were to form a subject of philosophical reflections in a general way, it would be no *appropriate* matter for strictly scientific treatment. The beauty of art presents itself to sense, to feeling, to perception, to imagination; its sphere is not that of thought, and the apprehension of its activity and its production demand another organ than that of the scientific intelligence. Moreover, what we enjoy in the beauty of art is precisely the *freedom* of its productive and plastic energy. In the origination, as in the contemplation, of its creations we appear to escape wholly from the fetters of rule and regularity. In the forms of art we seek repose and animation in place of the austerity of the reign of law and the sombre self-concentration of thought; we would exchange the shadowland of the Idea for cheerful vigorous reality. And lastly, the source of artistic creations is the free activity of fancy, which in her imagination is more free than nature's self. Not only has art at command the whole wealth of natural forms in the brilliant variety of their appearance, but also the creative imagination has power to expatiate inexhaustibly beyond their limit in products of *its own*. It may be supposed that, in presence of this immeasurable abundance of inspiration and its free creations, thought will necessarily lose the courage to bring them *completely* before it, to criticize them, and to array them under its universal formulas.

Science, on the contrary, everyone admits, is compelled by its form to busy itself with thought, which abstracts from the mass of particulars. For this reason, on the one hand, imagination with its contingency and caprice—that is, the organ of artistic activity and enjoyment—is of necessity excluded from science. And on the other hand, seeing that art is what cheers and animates the dull and withered dryness of the notion, reconciles with reality its abstraction and its dissociation therefrom, and supplies out of the real world what is lacking to the notion, it follows, we may think, that a *purely* intellectual treatment of art destroys this very means of supplementation, annihilates it, and reduces the notion once more to its simplicity, devoid of reality, and to its shadowy abstractness. And further, it is objected that science, as a matter of *content*, occupies itself with what is *necessary*. Now, if Aesthetics puts aside the beauty of nature, we not only gain nothing in respect of necessity but to all appearance have got further away from it. For the expression *nature* at once gives us the idea of necessity and uniformity—that is to say, of a behaviour which may be hoped to be akin to science and capable of submitting thereto. But in the mind generally, and more particularly in the imagination, compared with nature, caprice and lawlessness are supposed to be peculiarly at home; and these withdraw themselves as a matter of course from all scientific explanation.

Thus in all these aspects—in origin, in effect, and in range—fine art, instead of showing itself fitted for scientific study, seems rather in its own right to resist the regulating activity of thought and to be unsuitable for strict scientific discussion.

These and similar objections against a genuinely scientific treatment of fine art are drawn from common ideas, points of view, and considerations, which may be read *ad nauseam* in full elaboration in the older writers on beauty and the fine arts, especially in the works of French authors. And in part they contain facts which have a certain truth; in part, too, the argumentation based upon these facts appears plausible at first sight. Thus, for example, there is the fact that the forms of beauty are as manifold as the phenomenon of beauty is omnipresent; and from this, if we choose, we may proceed to conclude to a universal *impulse of beauty* in human nature, and then go on to the further inference: that because ideas of beauty are so endlessly various, and therefore, as seems obvious, are something *particular,* it follows that there can be no universal laws of beauty and of taste.

Before it is possible for us to turn from such considerations to our subject proper, it is our business to devote a brief introductory discussion to the objections and doubts which have been raised. In the first place, as regards the *worthiness* of art to be scientifically considered, it is no doubt the case that art can be employed as a fleeting pastime, to serve the ends of pleasure and entertainment, to decorate our surroundings, to impart pleasantness to the external conditions of our life, and to emphasize other objects by means of ornament. In this mode of employment art is indeed not independent, not free, but servile. But what *we* mean to consider, is the art which is *free* in its end as in its means.

That art is in the abstract capable of serving other aims, and of being a mere pastime, is moreover a relation which it shares with thought. For, on the one hand, science, in the shape of the subservient understanding, submits to be used for finite purposes, and as an accidental means, and in that case is not self-determined but determined by alien objects and relations; but, on the other hand, science liberates itself from this service to rise in free independence to the attainment of truth, in which medium, free from all interference, it fulfils itself in conformity with its proper aims.

Fine art is not real art till it is in this sense free, and only achieves its highest task when it has taken its place in the same sphere with religion and philosophy and has become simply a mode of revealing to consciousness and bringing to utterance the divine nature, the deepest interests of humanity, and the most comprehensive truths of the mind. It is in works of art that nations have deposited the profoundest intuitions and ideas of their hearts; and fine art is frequently the key—with many nations there is no other—to the understanding of their wisdom and of their religion.

This is an attribute which art shares with religion and philosophy, only in this peculiar mode, that it represents even the highest ideas *in sensuous forms,* thereby bringing them nearer to the character of natural phenomena, to the senses, and to feeling. The world, into whose depths *thought* penetrates, is a suprasensuous world, which is thus, to begin with, erected as a *beyond* over against immediate consciousness and present sensation; the power which thus rescues itself from the *here,* that consists in the actuality and finiteness of sense, is the freedom of thought in cognition. But the mind is able to heal this schism which its advance creates; it generates out of itself the works of fine art as the first middle term of reconciliation between pure thought and what is external, sensuous, and transitory, between nature with its finite actuality and the infinite freedom of the reason that comprehends.

The *element* of art was said to be in its general nature an *unworthy* element, as consisting in appearance and deception. The censure would be not devoid of justice if it were possible to class appearance as something that ought not to exist. An appearance or show, however, is essential to existence. Truth could not be if it did not appear and reveal itself, were it not truth *for* someone or something, *for* itself as also *for* mind. Therefore, there can be objection not against appearance in general, but, if at all, against the particular mode of appearance in which art gives actuality to what is in itself real and true. If, in this aspect, the *appearance* with which art gives its conceptions life as determinate existences is to be termed a *deception,* this is a criticism which primarily receives its meaning by comparison with the external world of phenomena and its immediate contact with us as *matter,* and in like manner by the standard of our own world of feeling, that is, the inner world of *sense.* These are the two worlds to which, in the life of daily experience, in our own phenomenal life, we are accustomed to attribute the value and the title of actuality, reality, and truth, in contrast to art, which we set down as lacking such reality and truth. Now, this whole sphere of the empirical inner and outer world is just what is not the world of genuine reality, but is to be entitled a mere appearance more strictly than is true of art, and a crueller deception. Genuine reality is only to be found beyond the immediacy of feeling and of external objects. Nothing is genuinely real but that which is actual in its own right, that which is the substance of nature and of mind, fixing itself indeed in present and definite existence, but in this existence still obtaining its essential and self-centered being, and thus and no otherwise attaining genuine reality. The dominion of these universal powers is exactly what art accentuates and reveals. The common outer and inner worlds also no doubt present to us this essence of reality, but in the shape of a chaos of accidental matters, encumbered by the immediateness of sensuous presentation, and by arbitrary states, events, characters, etc. Art liberates the real import of appearances from the semblance and deception of this bad and fleeting world and imparts to phenomenal semblances a higher reality, born of mind. The appearances of art, therefore, far from being mere semblances, have the higher reality and the more genuine existence in comparison with the realities of common life.

Just as little can the representations of art be called a deceptive semblance in comparison with the representations of historical narrative, as if that had the more genuine truth. For history has not even immediate existence, but only the intellectual presentation of it, for the element of its portrayals, and its content remains burdened with the whole mass of contingent matter formed by common reality with its occurrences, complications, and individualities. But the work of art brings before us the eternal powers that hold dominion in history, without any such superfluity in the way of immediate sensuous presentation and its unstable semblances.

Again, the mode of appearance of the shapes produced by art may be called a deception in comparison with philosophic thought, with religious or moral principles. Beyond a doubt the mode of revelation which a content attains in the realm of thought is the truest reality; but in comparison with the show or semblance of immediate sensuous existence or of historical narrative, the artistic semblance has the advantage that in itself it points beyond itself and refers us away from itself to something spiritual that it is meant to bring before the mind's eye. Whereas immediate appearance does not give itself out to be deceptive, but rather to be real and true, though all the time its truth is contaminated and infected by the immediate sensuous element. The hard rind of nature and the common world give the mind more trouble in breaking through to the idea than do the products of art.

But if, on the one side, we assign this high position to art, we must no less bear in mind, on the other hand, that art is not, either in content or in form, the supreme and absolute mode of bringing the mind's genuine interests into consciousness. The form of art is enough to limit it to a restricted content. Only a certain circle and grade of truth is capable of being represented in the medium of art. Such truth must have in its own nature the capacity to go forth into sensuous form and be adequate to itself therein if it is to be a genuinely artistic content, as is the case with the gods of Greece. There is, however, a deeper form of truth, in which it is no longer so closely akin and so friendly to sense as to be adequately embraced and expressed by that medium.

Of such a kind is the Christian conception of truth; and more especially the spirit of our modern world, or, to come closer, of our religion and our intellectual culture, reveals itself as beyond the stage at which art is the highest mode assumed by man's consciousness of the absolute. The peculiar mode to which artistic production and works of art belong no longer satisfies our supreme need. We are above the level at which works of art can be venerated as divine, and actually worshipped; the impression which they make is of a more considerate kind, and the feelings which they stir within us require a higher test and a further confirmation. Thought and reflection have taken their flight above fine art. Those who delight in grumbling and censure may set down this phenomenon for a corruption and ascribe it to the predominance of passion and selfish interests, which scare away at once the seriousness and the cheerfulness of the art. Or we may accuse the troubles of the present time and the complicated condition of civil and political life as hindering the feelings, entangled in minute preoccupations, from freeing themselves and rising to the higher aims of art, the intelligence itself being subordinate to petty needs and interests, in sciences which only subserve such purposes and are seduced into making this barren region their home.

However all this may be, it certainly is the case that art no longer affords that satisfaction of spiritual wants which earlier epochs and peoples have sought therein, and have found therein only; a satisfaction which, at all events on the religious side, was most intimately and profoundly connected with art. The beautiful days of Greek art and the golden time of the later Middle Ages are gone by. The reflective culture of our life of today makes it a necessity for us, in respect of our will no less than of our judgment, to adhere to general points of view and to regulate particular matters according to them, so that general forms, laws, duties, rights, maxims are what have validity as grounds of determination and are the chief regulative force. But what is required for artistic interest as for artistic production is, speaking generally, a living creation, in which the universal is not present as law and maxim, but acts as if at one with the mood and the feelings, just as, in the imagination, the universal and rational is contained only as brought into unity with a concrete sensuous phenomenon. Therefore, our present in its universal condition is not favourable to art. As regards the artist himself, it is not merely that the reflection which finds utterance all round him and the universal habit of having an opinion and passing judgment about art infect him and mislead him into putting more abstract thought into his works themselves, but also the whole spiritual culture of the age is of such a kind that he himself stands within this reflective world and its conditions, and it is impossible for him to abstract from it by will and resolve, or to contrive for himself and to bring to pass, by means of peculiar education or removal from the relations of life, a peculiar solitude that would replace all that is lost.

In all these respects art is, and remains for us, on the side of its highest destiny, a thing of the past. Herein it has further lost for us its genuine truth and life, and is transferred into our *ideas* more than it asserts its former necessity, or assumes its former place, in reality. What is now aroused in us by works of art is our immediate enjoyment, and together with it, our judgment; in that we subject the content and the means of representation of the work of art and the suitability or unsuitability of the two to our intellectual consideration. Therefore, the *science* of art is a much more pressing need in our day than it was in times in which art, simply as art, was enough to furnish a full satisfaction. Art invites us to consideration of it by means of thought, not to the end of stimulating art production, but in order to ascertain scientifically what art is.

As soon as we propose to accept this invitation we are met by the difficulty which has already been touched upon in the suggestion that, though art is a suitable subject for philosophical reflection in the general sense, yet it is not so for systematic and scientific discussion. In this objection there lies the false idea that a philosophical consideration may, nevertheless, be unscientific. On this point it can only be remarked here with brevity that, whatever ideas others may have of philosophy and philosophizing, I regard the pursuit of philosophy as utterly incapable of existing apart from a scientific procedure. Philosophy has to consider its object in its necessity, not, indeed, in its subjective necessity or external arrangement, classification, etc., but it has to unfold and demonstrate the object out of the necessity of its own inner nature. Until this explication is brought to pass the scientific element is lacking to the treatment. Insofar, however, as the objective necessity of an object lies essentially in its logical and metaphysical nature, the isolated treatment of art must be conducted with a certain relaxation of scientific stringency. For art involves the most complex presuppositions, partly in reference to its content, partly in respect of its medium and element, in which art is constantly on the borders of the arbitrary or accidental. Thus it is only as regards the essential innermost progress of its content and of its media of expression that we must call to mind the outline prescribed by its necessity.

The objection that works of fine art elude the treatment of scientific thought because they originate out of the unregulated fancy and out of the feelings, are of a number and variety that defy the attempt to gain a conspectus, and therefore take effect only on feeling and imagination, raises a problem which appears still to have importance. For the beauty of art does in fact appear in a form which is expressly contrasted with abstract thought, and which the latter is forced to destroy in exerting the activity which is its nature. This idea coheres with the opinion that reality as such, the life of nature and of mind, is disfigured and slain by comprehension; that, so far from being brought close to us by the thought which comprehends, it is by it that such life is absolutely dissociated from us, so that, by the use of thought as the *means* of grasping what has life, man rather cuts himself off from this his purpose. We cannot speak fully on this subject in the present passage, but only indicate the point of view from which the removal of this difficulty, or impossibility depending on maladaptation, might be effected.

It will be admitted, to begin with, that the mind is capable of contemplating itself and of possessing a consciousness, and a *thinking* consciousness, of itself and all that is generated by itself. Thought—to think—is precisely that in which the mind has its innermost and essential nature. In gaining this thinking consciousness concerning itself and its products, the mind is behaving according to its essential nature, however much freedom and caprice those products may display, supposing only that in real truth they have mind in them.

Now art and its works as generated and created by the mind (spirit) are themselves of a spiritual nature, even if their mode of representation admits into itself the semblance of sensuous being and pervades what is sensuous with mind. In this respect art is, to begin with, nearer to mind and its thinking activity than is mere external unintelligent nature; in works of art, mind has to do but with its own. And even if artistic works are not abstract thought and notion, but are an evolution of the notion *out of* itself, an alienation from itself towards the sensuous, still the power of the thinking spirit (mind) lies herein, *not merely* to grasp *itself only* in its peculiar form of the self-conscious spirit (mind), but just as much to recognise itself in its alienation in the shape of feeling and the sensuous, in its other form, by transmuting the metamorphosed thought back into definite thoughts, and so restoring it to itself. And in this preoccupation with the other of itself the thinking spirit is not to be held untrue to itself as if forgetting or surrendering itself therein, nor is it so weak as to lack strength to comprehend what is different from itself, but it comprehends both itself and its opposite. For the notion is the universal, which preserves itself in its particularizations, dominates alike itself and its "other," and so becomes the power and activity that consists in undoing the alienation which it had evolved.

And thus the work of art in which thought alienates itself belongs, like thought itself, to the realm of comprehending thought, and the mind, in subjecting it to scientific consideration, is thereby but satisfying the need of its own inmost nature. For because thought is its essence and notion, it can in the last resort only be satisfied when it has succeeded in imbuing all the products of its activity with thought, and has thus for the first time made them genuinely its own. But, as we shall see more definitely below, art is far from being the highest form of mind and receives its true ratification only from science.

Just as little does art elude philosophical consideration by unbridled caprice. As has already been indicated, it is its true task to bring to consciousness the highest interests of the mind. Hence it follows at once with respect to the *content* that fine art cannot rove in the wildness of unfettered fancy, for these spiritual interests determine definite bases for its content, however manifold and inexhaustible its forms and shapes may be. The same holds true for the forms themselves. They, again, are not at the mercy of mere chance. Not every plastic shape is capable of being the expression and representation of those spiritual interests, of absorbing and of reproducing them; every definite content determines a form suitable to it.

In this aspect too, then, we are in a position to find our bearings according to the needs of thought in the apparently unmanageable mass of works and types of art.

Thus, I hope, we have begun by defining the content of our science, to which we propose to confine ourselves, and have seen that neither is fine art unworthy of a philosophical consideration, nor is a philosophical consideration incompetent to arrive at a knowledge of the essence of fine art.

II

If we now investigate *the required mode of scientific consideration,* we here again meet with two opposite ways of treating the subject, each of which appears to exclude the other, and so to hinder us from arriving at *any true result.*

On one side we see the science of art merely, so to speak, busying itself about the actual productions of art from the outside, arranging them in series as a history of art, initiating discussions about extant works, or sketching out theories intended to provide the general points of view that are to govern both criticism and artistic production.

On the other side we see science abandoning itself independently to reflection upon the beautiful and producing mere generalities which do not touch the work of art in its peculiarity, creating, in short, an abstract philosophy of the beautiful.

1. As regards the former mode of treatment, which starts from the empirical side, it is the indispensable road for anyone who means to become a student of art. And just as in the present day every one, even though he is not busied with natural science, yet pretends to be equipped with the essentials of

physical knowledge, so it has become more or less obligatory for a cultivated man to possess some acquaintance with art, and the pretension to display oneself as a dilettante and connoisseur is pretty universal.

If such information is really to be recognised as art scholarship, it must be of various kinds and of wide range. The first necessity is an exact acquaintance with the immeasurable region of individual works of art of ancient and modern times, works which in part have actually perished, in part belong to distant countries or portions of the world, or which adverse fortune has withdrawn from one's own observation. Moreover, every work belongs to its *age*, to its *nation*, and to its environment, and depends upon particular historical and other ideas and aims. For this reason art scholarship further requires a vast wealth of historical information of a very special kind, seeing that the individualized nature of the work of art is related to individual detail and demands special matter to aid in its comprehension and elucidation. And lastly, this kind of scholarship needs, like every other, not only a memory for information, but a vivid imagination in order to retain distinctly the images of artistic forms in all their different features, and especially in order to have them present to the mind for purposes of comparison with other works.

Within this kind of consideration, which is primarily historical, there soon emerge various points of view which cannot be lost sight of in contemplating a work of art, inasmuch as our judgments must be derived from them. Now these points of view, as in other sciences which have an empirical starting point, when extracted and put together form universal criteria and rules, and, in a still further stage of formal generalization, *theories of the arts*. This is not the place to go into detail about literature of this kind, and it may, therefore, suffice to mention a few writings in the most general way. For instance, there is Aristotle's "Poetics," the theory of tragedy contained in which is still of interest; and to speak more particularly, among the ancients, Horace's "Ars Poetica" and Longinus's "Treatise on the Sublime" suffice to give a general idea of the way in which this kind of theorizing has been carried on. The general formulas that were abstracted by such writers were meant to stand especially as precepts and rules, according to which, particularly in times of degeneration of poetry and art, works of art were meant to be produced. The prescriptions, however, compiled by these physicians of art had even less assured success than those of physicians whose aim was the restoration of health.

Respecting theories of this kind, I propose merely to mention that, though *in detail* they contain much that is instructive, yet their remarks were abstracted from a very limited circle of artistic productions, which passed for *the* genuinely beautiful ones, but yet always belonged to a but narrow range of art. And again, such formulas are in part very trivial reflections which in their generality proceed to no establishment of particulars, although this is the matter of chief concern.

The above-mentioned Horatian epistle is full of these reflections, and, therefore, is a book for all men, but one which for this very reason contains much that amounts to nothing, e.g.:

Omne tulit punctum qui miscuit utile dulci
Lectorem delectando pariterque monendo—

"He carries all votes, who has mingled the pleasant and the useful, by at once charming and instructing his reader." This is just like so many copybook headings, e.g. "Stay at home and earn an honest livelihood," which are right enough as generalities but lack the concrete determinations on which action depends.

Another kind of interest was found, not in the express aim of directly causing the production of genuine works of art, but in the purpose which emerged of influencing men's judgment upon works of art by such theories, in short of *forming taste*. In this aspect, Hume's "Elements of Criticism," the writings of Batteux, and Ramler's "Introduction to the Fine Arts," were works much read in their day. Taste in this sense has to do with arrangement and treatment, the harmony and finish of what belongs to the external aspect of a work of art. Besides, they brought in among the principles of taste views that belonged to the psychology that was then in vogue, and that had been drawn from empirical observation of capacities and activities of the soul, of the passions and their probable heightening, succession, etc. But it remains invariably the case that every man judges works of art, or characters, actions, and incidents according to the measure of his insight and his feelings; and as that formation of taste only touched what was meagre and external, and moreover drew its precepts only from a narrow range of works of art and from a *borné* culture of intellect and feelings, its whole sphere was inadequate, and incapable of seizing the inmost and the true, and of sharpening the eye for the apprehension thereof.

Such theories proceed in general outline, as do the remaining non-philosophic sciences. The content that they subject to consideration is borrowed from our ordinary idea of it, as something found there; then further questions are asked about the nature of this idea, inasmuch as a need reveals itself for closer determinations, which are also found in our idea of the matter, and drawn from it to be fixed in definitions. But in so doing, we find ourselves at once on uncertain and debatable ground. It might indeed appear at first as if the beautiful were a perfectly simple idea. But it soon becomes evident that manifold sides may be found in it, one of which is emphasized by one writer and another by another, or, even if the same points of view are adopted, a dispute arises on the question which side after all is to be regarded as the essential one.

With a view to such questions it is held a point of scientific completeness to adduce and to criticize the various definitions of the beautiful. We will do this neither with historical *exhaustiveness*, so as to learn all the subtleties which have emerged in the defining process, nor for the sake of the *historical* interest, but we will simply produce by way of illustration, some of the more interesting modern views which come pretty close in their purport to what in fact the Idea of the beautiful does involve. For such purpose we have chiefly to mention Goethe's account of the beautiful, which Meyer embodied in his

"History of the Fine Arts in Greece," on which occasion he also brings forward Hirt's view, though without mentioning him.

Hirt, one of the greatest of genuine connoisseurs in the present day, in his brochure about artistic beauty (*Horen,* 1797, seventh number), after speaking of the beautiful in the several arts, sums up his ideas in the result that the basis of a just criticism of beauty in art and of the formation of taste is the conception of the *characteristic*. That is to say, he defines the beautiful as the "perfect, which is or can be an object of eye, ear, or imagination." Then he goes on to define the perfect as "that which is adequate to its aim, that which nature or art aimed at producing within the given genus and species in the formation of the object." For which reason, in order to form our judgment on a question of beauty, we ought to direct our observation as far as possible to the individual marks which constitute a definite essence. For it is just these marks that form its characteristics. And so by *character* as the law of art he means "that determinate individual modification whereby forms, movement and gesture, bearing and expression, local colour, light and shade, chiaroscuro and attitude distinguish themselves, in conformity, of course, with the requirements of an object previously selected."

This formula gives us at once something more significant than the other definitions. If we go on to ask what "the characteristic" is, we see that it involves in the first place *a content,* as, for instance, a particular feeling, situation, incident, action, individual; and secondly, the *mode* and *fashion* in which this content is embodied in a representation. It is to this, the mode of representation, that the artistic law of the "characteristic" refers, inasmuch as it requires that every particular element in the mode of expression shall subserve the definite indication of its content and be a member in the expression of that content. The abstract formula of the characteristic thus has reference to the degree of appropriateness with which the particular detail of the artistic form sets in relief the content that it is intended to represent. If we desire to illustrate this conception in a quite popular way, we may explain the limitation which it involves as follows: In a dramatic work, for instance, an action forms the content; the drama is to represent how this action takes place. Now, men and women do all sorts of things; they speak to each other from time to time, at intervals they eat, sleep, put on their clothes, say one thing and another, and so forth. But in all this, whatever does not stand in immediate connection with that particular action considered as the content proper is to be excluded, so that in reference to it nothing may be without import. So, too, a picture, that only represented a single phase of that action might yet include in it—so wide are the ramifications of the external world—a multitude of circumstances, persons, positions, and other matters which at that moment have no reference to the action in question and are not subservient to its distinctive character.

But according to the rule of the characteristic, only so much ought to enter into the work of art as belongs to the display and, essentially, to the expression of that content and no other; for nothing must appear as otiose and superfluous.

This is a very important rule, which may be justified in a certain aspect. Meyer, however, in his above-mentioned work, gives it as his opinion that this view has vanished and left no trace, and, in his judgment, to the benefit of art. For he thinks that the conception in question would probably have *led* to caricature. This judgment at once contains the perversity of implying that such a determination of the beautiful had to do with *leading*. The philosophy of art does not trouble itself about precepts for artists, but it has to ascertain what beauty in general is, and how it has displayed itself in actual productions, in works of art, without meaning to give rules for guidance. Apart from this, if we examine the criticism, we find it to be true, no doubt, that Hirt's definition includes caricature, for even a caricature may be characteristic; but, on the other hand, it must be answered at once that in caricature the definite character is intensified to exaggeration, and is, so to speak, a superfluity of the characteristic. But a superfluity ceases to be what is properly required in order to be characteristic, and becomes an offensive iteration, whereby the characteristic itself may be made unnatural. Moreover, what is of the nature of caricature shows itself in the light of the characteristic representation of what is ugly, which ugliness is, of course, a distortion.

Ugliness, for its part, is closely connected with the content, so that it may be said that the principle of the characteristic involves as a fundamental property both ugliness and the representation of what is ugly. Hirt's definition, of course, gives no more precise information as to what is to be characterized and what is not, in the artistically beautiful, or about the content of the beautiful, but it furnishes in this respect a mere formal rule, which nevertheless contains some truth, although stated in abstract shape.

Then follows the further question—what Meyer opposes to Hirt's artistic principle, i.e. what he himself prefers. He is treating, in the first place, exclusively the principle shown in the artistic works of the ancients, which principle, however, must include the essential attribute of beauty. In dealing with this subject he is led to speak of Mengs and Winckelmann's principle of the Ideal, and pronounces himself to the effect that he desires neither to reject nor wholly to accept this law of beauty, but, on the other hand, has no hesitation in attaching himself to the opinion of an enlightened judge of art (Goethe), as it is definite, and seems to solve the enigma more precisely.

Goethe says: "The highest principle of the ancients was the *significant,* but the highest result of successful *treatment,* the *beautiful.*"

If we look closer at what this opinion implies, we find in it again two elements: the content or matter in hand and the mode and fashion of representation. In looking at a work of art we begin with what presents itself immediately to us, and after that go on to consider what is its significance or content.

The former, the external element, has no value for us simply as it stands; we assume something further behind it, something inward, a significance, by which the external semblance has a soul breathed into it. It is this, its soul, that the external appearance indicates. For an appearance which means something does not present to the mind's eye itself and that which it is qua external, but something else; as does the *symbol,* for instance, and still more obviously the *fable,* whose moral and precept constitutes its meaning. Indeed every *word* points to a meaning and has no value in itself. Just so the human eye, a man's face, flesh, skin, his whole figure, are a revelation of mind and soul, and in this case the meaning is always something other than what shows itself within the immediate appearance. This is the way in which a work of art should have its meaning, and not appear as exhausted in these mere particular lines, curves, surfaces, borings, reliefs in the stone, in these colours, tones, sounds, of words, or whatever other medium is employed; but it should reveal life, feeling, soul, import, and mind, which is just what we mean by the significance of a work of art.

Thus this requirement of *significance* in a work of art amounts to hardly anything beyond or different from Hirt's principle of the *characteristic.*

According to this notion, then, we find distinguished as the elements of the beautiful something inward, a content, and something outer which has that content as its significance; the inner shows itself in the outer and gives itself to be known by its means, inasmuch as the outer points away from itself to the inner.

We cannot go into detail on this matter.

But the earlier fashion alike of rules and of theories has already been violently thrown aside in Germany—especially owing to the appearance of genuine living poetry—and the rights of genius, its works and their effects, have had their value asserted against the encroachment of such legalities and against the wide, watery streams of theory. From this foundation both of an art which is itself genuinely spiritual and of a general sympathy and communion with it, have arisen the receptivity and freedom which enabled us to enjoy and to recognise the great works of art which have long been in existence, whether those of the modern world, of the Middle Ages, or even of peoples of antiquity quite alien to us (e.g. the Indian productions); works which by reason of their antiquity or of their alien nationality have, no doubt, a foreign element in them, yet in view of their content—common to all humanity and dominating their foreign character—could not have been branded as products of bad and barbarous taste except by the prejudices of theory. This recognition, so to speak generally, of works of art which depart from the sphere and form of those upon which more especially the abstractions of theory were based led, in the first instance, to the recognition of a peculiar kind of art—that is, of romantic art—and it therefore became necessary to apprehend the idea and the nature of the beautiful in a deeper way than was possible for those theories. With this influence there cooperated another, viz. that the idea in its self-conscious form, the thinking mind, attained at this time, on its side, a deeper self-knowledge in philosophy, and was thereby directly impelled to understand the essence of art, too, in a profounder fashion.

Thus, then, even judging by the phases of this more general evolution of ideas, the theoretical mode of reflection upon art which we were considering has become antiquated alike in its principles and in its particulars. Only the *scholarship* of the history of art has retained its permanent value, and cannot but retain it, all the more that the advance of intellectual receptivity, of which we spoke, has extended its range of vision on every side. Its business and vocation consists in the aesthetic appreciation of individual works of art and in acquaintance with the historical circumstances that externally condition such works; an appreciation which, if made with sense and mind, supported by the requisite historical information, is the only power that can penetrate the entire individuality of a work of art. Thus Goethe, for instance, wrote much about art and particular works of art. Theorizing proper is not the purpose of this mode of consideration, although no doubt it frequently busies itself with abstract principles and categories and may give way to this tendency without being aware of it. But for a reader who does not let this hinder him, but keeps before him the concrete accounts of works of art, which we spoke of just now, it at all events furnishes the philosophy of art with the perceptible illustrations and instances, into the particular historical details of which philosophy cannot enter.

This, then, may be taken to be the first mode of the study of art, starting from particular and extant works.

2. There is an essential distinction between this and the opposite aspect, the wholly theoretical reflection, which made an effort to understand beauty as such out of itself alone and to get to the bottom of its idea.

It is well known that Plato was the first to require of philosophical study, in a really profound sense, that its objects should be apprehended not in their *particularity* but in their *universality,* in their genus, in their own nature and its realization: inasmuch as he affirmed that the truth of things did not consist in individual good actions, true opinions, beautiful human beings, or works of art, but in *goodness, beauty, truth* themselves. Now, if the beautiful is in fact to be known according to its essence and conception, this is only possible with the help of the thinking idea, by means of which the logico-metaphysical nature of the *idea as such,* as also that of the *particular Idea of the beautiful,* enters into the thinking consciousness. But the study of the beautiful in its separate nature and in its own Idea may itself turn into an abstract Metaphysic, and even though Plato is accepted in such an inquiry as foundation and as guide, still the Platonic abstraction must not satisfy us, even for the logical Idea of beauty. We must understand this Idea more profoundly and more in the concrete, for the emptiness of content which characterizes the Platonic Idea is no longer satisfactory to the fuller philosophical wants of the mind of today. Thus it is, no doubt, the case that we, too, in modern times, must in our philosophy of art start from the Idea of the beautiful, but we ought not to abide by the fashion of Platonic Ideas, which was purely abstract and the mere beginning of the philosophic study of beauty.

3. The philosophic conception of the beautiful, to indicate its true nature at least by anticipation, must contain, reconciled within it, the two extremes which have been mentioned, by combining metaphysical universality with the determinateness of real particularity. Only thus is it apprehended in its truth,

in its real and explicit nature. It is then fertile out of its own resources, in contrast to the barrenness of one-sided reflection. For it has in accordance with its own conception to develop into a totality of attributes, while the conception itself as well as its detailed exposition contains the necessity of its particulars, as also of their progress and transition one into another. On the other hand, again, these particulars, to which the transition is made, carry in themselves the universality and essentiality of the conception as the particulars of which they appear. The modes of consideration of which we have so far been treating lack both these qualities, and for this reason it is only the complete conception of which we have just spoken that can lead to substantive, necessary, and self-complete determinations.

III

After the above prefatory remarks, we approach closer to our subject, the philosophy of artistic beauty. Inasmuch as we are undertaking to treat it scientifically we must begin with its *conception* or notion. Not till we have established this conception can we map out the division, and with it the plan of the entirety of the science; for a division, if it is not, as is the case with unphilosophical inquiries, taken in hand in a purely external manner, must find its principle in the conception of the object itself.

In presence of such a demand we are at once met by the question, "Whence do we get this conception?" If we begin with the given conception of artistic beauty itself, that is enough to make it a *presupposition* and mere assumption; now, mere assumptions are not admitted by the philosophical method, but whatever it allows to pass must have its truth demonstrated, i.e. displayed as necessary.

We will devote a few words to coming to an understanding upon this difficulty, which concerns the introduction to every philosophical branch of study when taken in hand by itself.

The object of every science presents prima facie two aspects: in the first place, that such an object *is;* in the second place, *what* it is.

In ordinary science little difficulty attaches to the first of these points. It might even, at first sight, look ridiculous if the requirement were presented that in astronomy and physics it should be demonstrated that there was a sun, heavenly bodies, magnetic phenomena, etc. In these sciences, which have to do with what is given to sense, the objects are taken from external experience, and instead of demonstrating them (*beweisen*) it is thought sufficient to show them (*weisen*). Yet even within the nonphilosophical sciences, doubts may arise about the existence of their objects, as, for example, in psychology, the science of mind, it may be doubted if there *is* a soul, a mind, i.e. something subjective, separate, and independent, distinct from what is material; or in theology, whether a God *is*. If, moreover, the objects are of subjective kind, i.e. are given only in the mind, and not as external sensuous objects, we are confronted by our conviction that there is nothing in the mind but what its own activity has produced. This brings up the accidental question whether men have produced this inner idea or perception in their minds or not, and even if the former is actually the case, whether they have not made the idea in question vanish again, or at any rate degraded it to a merely *subjective idea,* whose content has no natural and independent being. So, for instance, the beautiful has often been regarded not as naturally and independently necessary in our ideas but as a mere subjective pleasure or accidental sense. Our external intuitions, observations, and perceptions are often deceptive and erroneous, but still more is this the case with the inner ideas, even if they have in themselves the greatest vividness and are forcible enough to transport us irresistibly into passion.

This doubt whether an object of inward ideas and inward perception as such is or is not, as also the accidental question whether the subjective consciousness has produced it in itself, and whether the act or mode in which it brought it before itself was in its turn adequate to the object in its essential and independent nature—all this is just what arouses in men the higher scientific need, which demands that, even if we have an idea that an object is, or that there is such an object, the object must yet be displayed or demonstrated in terms of its necessity.

This proof, if it is developed in a really scientific way, must also satisfy the further question of *what* an object is. But to expound this relation would carry us too far in this place, and we can only make the following remarks on the point.

If we are to display the necessity of our object, the beautiful in art, we should have to prove that art or beauty was a result of antecedents such as, when considered in their true conception, to lead us on with scientific necessity to the conception of fine art. But in as far as we begin with *art,* and propose to treat of the essence of *its* conception and of the realization of that conception, not of antecedents which go before it *as demanded by* its nature, so far art, as a peculiar scientific object, has, for us, a presupposition which lies beyond our consideration, and which, being a different content, belongs in scientific treatment to a different branch of philosophical study. We have thus no other alternative than to presuppose the conception of art, something that is the case with all philosophical sciences when considered individually and in isolation. For it is nothing short of the whole of philosophy that is the knowledge of the universe as in itself *one single* organic totality which develops itself out of its own conception and which, returning into itself so as to form a whole in virtue of the necessity in which it is placed towards itself, binds itself together with itself into *one single* world of truth. In the coronal of this scientific necessity, each individual part is just as much a circle that returns into itself, as it has, at the same time, a necessary connection with other parts. This connection is a backward out of which it derives itself, as well as a forward, to which in its own nature it impels itself on and on, in as far as it is fertile by creating fresh matter out of itself, and issuing it into the further range of scientific knowledge.

Therefore, it is not our present aim to demonstrate the Idea of beauty from which we set out—that is, to derive it according to its necessity from the presuppositions which are its antecedents in science. This task belongs to an encyclopedic development of philosophy as a whole and of its particular branches. For us, the conception of beauty and of art is a presupposition given in the system of philosophy. But as we cannot in this place discuss this system, and the connection of art with it, we have not yet the conception of the beautiful before us *in a scientific form*. What we have at command are merely the elements and aspects of it, as they are or have at former periods been presented, in the diverse ideas of the beautiful and of art in the mere common consciousness.

Having started from this point, we shall subsequently pass to the more profound consideration of the views in question, in order thereby to gain the advantage of, in the first place, obtaining a general idea of our object, and further, by a brief criticism effecting a preliminary acquaintance with its higher principles, with which we shall have to do in the sequel. By this mode of treatment our final introduction will act, so to speak, as the overture to the account of the subject itself, and will serve the purpose of a general collection and direction of our thoughts towards the proper subject matter of our discussion.

What we know, to begin with, as a current idea of the work of art, comes under the three following general predicates:

1. We suppose the work of art to be no natural product, but brought to pass by means of human activity.

2. To be essentially made *for* man, and, indeed, to be more or less borrowed from the sensuous and addressed to man's sense.

3. To contain an *end*.

1. As regards the first point, that a work of art is taken to be a product of human activity, this view has given rise to the view that this activity, being the *conscious* production of an external object, can also be *known,* and *expounded,* and learnt, and prosecuted by others. For, what one can do, it might seem, another can do, or imitate, as soon as he is acquainted with the mode of procedure; so that, supposing universal familiarity with the rules of artistic production, it would only be a matter of any one's will and pleasure to carry out the process in a uniform way, and so to produce works of art. It is thus that the above-mentioned rule-providing theories and their precepts, calculated for practical observance, have arisen. But that which can be executed according to such instruction can only be something formally regular and mechanical. For only what is mechanical is of such an external kind that no more than a purely empty exercise of will and dexterity is required to receive it among our ideas and put it in act, such an exercise not needing to be supplemented by anything concrete or anything that goes beyond the precepts conveyed in general rules. This is most vividly displayed when precepts of the kind in question do not limit themselves to what is purely external and mechanical, but extend to the meaning-laden spiritual activity of true art. In this region the rules contain nothing but indefinite generalities; e.g. "The theme ought to be interesting, and each individual ought to be made to speak according to his rank, age, sex, and position." But if rules are meant to be adequate on this

subject, their precepts ought to have been drawn up with such determinateness that they could be carried out just as they are expressed, without further and original activity of mind. Being abstract, however, in their content, such rules reveal themselves, in respect of their pretension of being adequate to fill the consciousness of the artist, as wholly inadequate, inasmuch as artistic production is not formal activity in accordance with given determinations. For it is bound as spiritual activity to work by drawing on its own resources, and to bring before the mind's eye a quite other and richer content and ampler individual creations than any abstract formulas can dictate. Such rules may furnish guidance in case of need, if they contain anything really definite, and therefore of practical utility, but their directions can apply only to purely external circumstances.

The tendency that we have just indicated has therefore been abandoned, and, in place of it, the opposite principle has been pursued to no less lengths. For the work of art came to be regarded no longer as the product of a *general activity* in mankind, but as the work of a mind endowed with wholly peculiar gifts. This mind, it is thought, has then nothing to do but *simply* to give free play to its particular gift, as though it were a specific force of nature, and is to be entirely released from attention to laws of universal validity, as also from the interference of reflection in its instinctively creative operation. And, indeed, it is to be guarded therefrom, inasmuch as its productions could only be infected and tainted by such a consciousness. In this aspect the work of art was pronounced to be the product of *talent* and *genius,* and stress was laid on the natural element which talent and genius contain. The view was partly right. Talent is specific, and genius universal capability, with which a man has not the power to endow himself simply by his own self-conscious activity. We shall treat this point more fully in the sequel.

In this place we have only to mention the aspect of falsity in the view before us, in that all consciousness respecting the man's own activity was held, in the case of artistic production, not merely superfluous, but even injurious. Production on the part of talent and genius then appears, in general terms, as a *state,* and, in particular, as a state of *inspiration.* To such a state, it is said, genius is in part excited by a given object, and in part it has the power of its own free will to place itself therein, in which process, moreover, the good service of the champagne bottle is not forgotten. This notion became prominent in Germany in the so-called epoch of genius, which was introduced by the early poetical production of Goethe, and subsequently sustained by those of Schiller. In their earliest works these poets began everything anew, in scorn of all the rules which had then been fabricated, transgressed these rules of set purpose, and, while doing so, distanced all rivals by a long interval.

I will not enter more closely into the confusions which have prevailed respecting the conception of inspiration and genius, and which prevail even at the present day respecting the omnipotence of inspiration as such. We need only lay down as essential the view that, though the artist's talent and genius contains a natural element, yet it is essentially in need of cultivation by thought, and of reflection on the mode in which it produces, as well as of

practice and skill in producing. A main feature of such production is unquestionably external workmanship, inasmuch as the work of art has a purely
technical side, which extends into the region of handicraft, especially in
architecture and sculpture, less so in painting and music, least of all in poetry.
Skill in this comes not by inspiration, but solely by reflection, industry, and
practice. And such skill is indispensable to the artist, in order that he may
master his external material and not be thwarted by its stubbornness.

Moreover, the higher an artist ranks, the more profoundly ought he to
represent the depths of heart and mind; and these are not known without
learning them, but are only to be fathomed by the direction of a man's own
mind to the inner and outer world. So here, too, *study* is the means whereby
the artist brings this content into his consciousness, and wins the material and
substance of his conceptions.

In this respect one art may need the consciousness and cognition of such
substance more than others. Music, for instance, which concerns itself only
with the undefined movement of the inward spiritual nature, and deals with
musical sounds as, so to speak, feeling without thought, needs little or no
spiritual content to be present in consciousness. It is for this reason that
musical talent generally announces itself in very early youth, while the head is
still empty and the heart has been but little moved, and is capable of attaining
to a very considerable height in early years, before mind and life have
experience of themselves. And again, as a matter of fact, we often enough see
very great expertness in musical composition, as also in execution, subsist
along with remarkable barrenness of mind and character.

The reverse is the case with poetry. In poetry all depends on the
representation—which must be full of matter and thought—of man, of his
profounder interests, and of the powers that move him; and therefore mind and
heart themselves must be richly and profoundly educated by life, experience,
and reflection before genius can bring to pass anything mature, substantial,
and self-complete. Goethe's and Schiller's first productions are of an immatu-
rity, and even of a rudeness and barbarism, that are really shocking. This
phenomenon, that the greater part of those attempts display a predominant
mass of thoroughly prosaic and in part of frigid and commonplace elements,
furnishes the chief objection to the common opinion, that inspiration is
inseparable from youth and youthful fire. Those two men of genius, it may be
said, were the first to give our nation works of true poetry, and yet it was only
their mature manhood that presented us with creations profound, substantial,
and the outcome of genuine inspiration, while no less thoroughly perfect in
form. Thus, too, it was not till his old age that Homer devised and uttered his
immortal songs.

A third view, which concerns the idea of the work of art as a product of
human activity, refers to the position of such a work in relation to the external
appearances of nature. It was an obvious opinion for the common consciousness to adopt on this matter that the work of art made by man ranked *below* the
product of nature. The work of art has no feeling in itself, and is not through
and through a living thing, but, regarded as an external object, is dead. But we

are wont to prize the living more than the dead. We must admit, of course, that
the work of art has not in itself movement and life. An animated being in
nature is within and without an organization appropriately elaborated down to
all its minutest parts, while the work of art attains the semblance of animation
on its surface only, but within is common stone, or wood and canvas, or, as in
the case of poetry, is idea, uttering itself in speech and letters. But this aspect,
viz. its external existence, is not what makes a work into a production of fine
art; it is a work of art only insofar as, being the offspring of mind, it continues
to belong to the realm of mind, has received the baptism of the spiritual, and
only represents that which has been moulded in harmony with mind. A human
interest, the spiritual value which attaches to an incident, to an individual
character, to an action in its plot and in its denouement, is apprehended in the
work of art, and exhibited more purely and transparently than is possible on
the soil of common unartistic reality. This gives the work of art a higher rank
than anything produced by nature, which has not sustained this passage
through the mind. So, for instance, by reason of the feeling and insight of
which a landscape as depicted by an artist is a manifestation, such a work of
mind assumes a higher rank than the mere natural landscape. For everything
spiritual is better than anything natural. At any rate, no existence in nature is
able, like art, to represent divine ideals.

Upon that which, in works of art, the mind borrows from its own inner life
it is able, even on the side of external existence, to confer *permanence;*
whereas the individual living thing of nature is transient, vanishing, and
mutable in its aspect, while the work of art persists. Though, indeed, it is not
mere permanence, but the accentuation of the character which animation by
mind confers, that constitutes its genuine pre-eminence as compared with
natural reality.

Nevertheless, this higher rank assigned to the work of art is in turn
disputed by another idea of the common consciousness. It is said that nature
and its products are a work of God, created by his goodness and wisdom,
whereas the work of art is *merely* a human production, made after man's
devising by man's hands. In this antithesis between natural production as a
divine creation and human activity as a merely finite creation, we at once come
upon the misconception that God does *not* work in man and through man, but
limits the range of his activity to nature alone. This false opinion is to be
entirely abandoned if we mean to penetrate the true conception of art. Indeed,
in opposition to such an idea, we must adhere to the very reverse, believing
that God is more honoured by what mind does or makes than by the
productions or formations of nature. For not only is there a divinity in man, but
in him it is operative under a form that is appropriate to the essence of God, in
a mode quite other and higher than in nature. God is a Spirit, and it is only in
man that the medium through which the divine element passes has the form
of conscious spirit and actively realizes itself. In nature the corresponding
medium is the unconscious, sensible, and external, which is far below
consciousness in value. In the products of art God is operative neither more nor
less than in the phenomena of nature; but the divine element, as it makes itself

known in the work of art, has attained, as being generated out of the mind, an adequate thoroughfare for its existence; while existence in the unconscious sensuousness of nature is not a mode of appearance adequate to the Divine Being.

Granting, then, that the work of art is made by man as a creation of mind, we come to the last question, which will enable us to draw a deeper result from what has been said. What is man's need to produce works of art? On the one hand the production may be regarded as a mere toy of chance and of man's fancies, which might just as well be let alone as pursued. For, it may be said, there are other and better means for effecting that which is the aim of art, and man bears in him interests that are yet higher and of more import than art has power to satisfy. But, on the other hand, art appears to arise from the higher impulse and to satisfy the higher needs, at times, indeed, even the highest, the absolute need of man, being wedded to the religious interests of whole epochs and peoples and to their most universal intuitions respecting the world. This inquiry concerning the not contingent but absolute need of art we cannot as yet answer completely, seeing that it is more concrete than any shape which could here be given to the answer. We must, therefore, content ourselves for the present with merely establishing the following points.

The universal and absolute need out of which art, on its formal side, arises has its source in the fact that man is a *thinking* consciousness, i.e. that he draws out of himself, and makes explicit *for himself,* that which he is, and, generally, whatever is. The things of nature are only *immediate and single,* but man as mind *reduplicates* himself, inasmuch as prima facie he *is* like the things of nature, but in the second place just as really is *for* himself, perceives himself, has ideas of himself, thinks himself, and only thus is active self-realizedness. This consciousness of himself man obtains in a two-fold way: *in the first place theoretically,* insofar as he has inwardly to bring himself into his own consciousness, with all that moves in the human breast, all that stirs and works therein, and, generally, to observe and form an idea of himself, to fix before himself what thought ascertains to be his real being, and, in what is summoned out of his inner self as in what is received from without, to recognise only himself.

Secondly, man is realised for himself by *practical* activity, inasmuch as he has the impulse, in the medium which is directly given to him, to produce himself, and therein at the same time to recognise himself. This purpose he achieves by the modification of external things upon which he impresses the seal of his inner being, and then finds repeated in them his own characteristics. Man does this in order as a free subject to strip the outer world of its stubborn foreignness, and to enjoy in the shape and fashion of things a mere external reality of himself. Even the child's first impulse involves this practical modification of external things. A boy throws stones into the river, and then stands admiring the circles that trace themselves on the water, as an effect in which he attains the sight of something that is his own doing. This need traverses the most manifold phenomena, up to the mode of self-production in the medium of external things as it is known to us in the work of art. And it is not only external things that man treats in this way, but himself no less, i.e. his own natural form, which he does not leave as he finds it but alters of set purpose. This is the cause of all ornament and decoration, though it may be as barbarous, as tasteless, as utterly disfiguring, or even as destructive as crushing Chinese ladies' feet, or as slitting the ears and lips. It is only among cultivated men that change of the figure, of behaviour, and of every kind and mode of self-utterance emanates from spiritual education.

The universal need for expression in art lies, therefore, in man's rational impulse to exalt the inner and outer world into a spiritual consciousness for himself, as an object in which he recognises his own self. He satisfies the need of this spiritual freedom when he makes all that exists explicit for himself *within,* and in a corresponding way realises this his explicit self *without,* evoking thereby, in this reduplication of himself, what is in him into vision and into knowledge for his own mind and for that of others. This is the free rationality of man, in which, as all action and knowledge, so also art has its ground and necessary origin. The specific need of art, however, in contradistinction to other action, political or moral, to religious imagination and to scientific cognition, we shall consider later.

2. We have so far been considering that aspect of the work of art in which it is made by man. We have now to pass on to its second characteristic, that it is made for man's *sense* and for this reason is more or less borrowed from the sensuous.

This reflection has furnished occasion for the consideration to be advanced that fine art is intended to arouse feeling, and indeed more particularly the feeling which we find suits us—that is, pleasant feeling. Looking at the question thus, men have treated the investigation of fine art as an investigation of the feelings and have asked what feelings it must be held that art ought to evoke—fear, for example, and compassion; and then, how these could be pleasant—how, for example, the contemplation of misfortune could produce satisfaction. This tendency of reflection is traceable particularly to Moses Mendelssohn's times, and many such discussions are to be found in his writings. Yet such an investigation did not lead men far, for feeling is the indefinite dull region of the mind; what is felt remains wrapped in the form of the most abstract individual subjectivity, and therefore the distinctions of the actual subject matter itself. For instance, fear, anxiety, alarm, terror, are no doubt of one and the same sort of feeling variously modified, but in part are mere quantitative heightenings, in part are forms which in themselves have nothing to do with their content itself, but are indifferent to it. In the case of fear, for instance, an existence is given in which the subject (i.e. a person) has an interest but at the same time sees approaching the negative that threatens to annihilate this existence, and so finds immediately in himself, as a contradictory affection of his subjectivity, the two at once, this interest and that negative.

Now, such fear considered in itself is not enough to condition any content but is capable of receiving into itself the most diverse and opposite matters. Feeling, as such, is a thoroughly empty form of subjective affection. No doubt this form may in some cases be manifold in itself, as are hope, grief, joy, or pleasure; and, again, may in such diversity comprehend varied contents, as there is a feeling of justice, moral feeling, sublime religious feeling, and so forth. But the fact that such content is forthcoming in different forms of feeling is not enough to bring to light its essential and definite nature; they remain purely subjective affections of myself, in which the concrete matter vanishes, as though narrowed into a circle of the utmost abstraction. Therefore, the inquiry into the feelings which art arouses, or ought to arouse, comes utterly to a standstill in the indefinite and is a mode of study which precisely abstracts from the content proper and from its concrete essence and notion. For reflection upon feeling contents itself with the observation of the subjective affection in its isolation, instead of diving into and fathoming the matter in question itself, the work of art, and, while engaged with it, simply letting go the mere subjectivity and its states. In feeling it is just this empty subjectivity that is not merely retained, but given the first place, and that is why men are so fond of having emotions. And for the same reason such a study becomes tedious from its indefiniteness and emptiness, and repulsive from its atten-tiveness to little subjective peculiarities.

Now, as a work of art does not merely do in general something of the nature of arousing emotion—for this is a purpose which it would have in common, without specific difference, with eloquence, historical composition, religious edification, and so forth—but is beautiful, reflection hit upon the idea, seeing that beauty was the object, of searching out a *peculiar feeling of beauty* to correspond to it and of discovering a particular *sense of beauty*. In this search it soon appeared that such a sense is no blind instinct made rigidly definite by nature, and capable from the beginning in its own independent essence of discerning beauty. Hence it followed that education came to be demanded for this sense, and the educated sense of beauty came to be called *taste,* which, although an educated appreciation and apprehension of the beautiful, was yet supposed to retain the nature of immediate feeling. We have already mentioned how abstract theories undertook to educate such a sense of taste, and how external and one-sided that sense remained. The criticism of the time when those views prevailed was not only defective in *universal* principles but also, in its particular references to individual works of art, was less directed to justifying a *definite* judgment—the power to make one not having at that time been acquired—than to advancing the general education of taste.

For this reason such education in its turn came to a standstill in the indefinite, and merely endeavoured so to equip feeling with a sense of beauty by help of reflection, that there might thenceforth be capacity to find out beauty whenever and wherever it should exist. Yet the depths of the matter remained a sealed book to mere taste, for these depths demand not only sensibility and abstract reflection, but the undivided reason and the mind in its solid vigour, while taste was only directed to the external surface about which the feelings play and on which one-sided maxims may pass for valid. But for this very reason what is called good taste takes fright at all more profound effects of art and is silent where the reality comes in question and where externalities and trivialities vanish. For when great passions and the movements of a profound soul are unveiled, we are no longer concerned with the finer distinctions of taste and its pettifogging particularities. Taste feels that genius strides contemptuously over such ground as this, and, shrinking before its power, becomes uneasy, and knows not which way to turn.

And thus, as we should expect, men have abandoned the tendency to consider works of art solely with an eye to the education of taste and with the purpose of merely displaying taste. The connoisseur, or scholar of art, has replaced the art judge, or man of taste. The positive side of art scholarship, so far as it concerns a thorough acquaintance with the entire circumference of the individual character in a given work of art, we have already pronounced to be essential to the study of art. For a work of art, owing to its nature as at once material and individual, is essentially originated by particular conditions of the most various kinds, to which belong especially the time and place of its production, then the peculiar individuality of the artist, and in particular the grade of technical development attained by his art. Attention to all these aspects is indispensable to distinct and thorough insight and cognition, and even to the enjoyment of a work of art; it is with them that connoisseurship, or art scholarship, is chiefly occupied, and all that it can do for us in its own way is to be accepted with gratitude. Yet, though such scholarship is entitled to rank as something essential, still it ought not to be taken for the sole or supreme element in the relation which the mind adopts towards a work of art, and towards art in general. For art scholarship (and this is its defective side) is capable of resting in an acquaintance with purely external aspects, such as technical or historical details, etc., and of guessing but little, or even knowing absolutely nothing, of the true and real nature of a work of art. It may even form a disparaging estimate of the value of more profound considerations in comparison with purely positive, technical, and historical information. Still, even so, art scholarship, if only it is of a genuine kind, at least strives after definite grounds and information, and an intelligent judgment, with which is closely conjoined the more precise distinction of the different, even if partly external, aspects in a work of art, and the estimation of their importance.

After these remarks upon the modes of study which have arisen out of that aspect of a work of art in which, being a sensuous object, it is invested with a relation to man as a sensuous being, we will now consider this aspect in its more essential relations to art as such, and so partly as regards the work of art as object, partly with respect to the subjectivity of the artist, his genius, talent, and so on, but without entering into matter relative to these points that can only proceed from the knowledge of art in its universal concept. For we are not yet on genuinely scientific ground, but have only reached the province of external reflection.

The work of art then, of course, presents itself to sensuous apprehension. It is addressed to sensuous feeling, outer or inner, to sensuous perception and imagination, just as is the nature that surrounds us without, or our own sensitive nature within. Even a speech, for instance, may be addressed to sensuous imagination and feeling. Notwithstanding, the work of art is not only for the *sensuous* apprehension as sensuous object, but its position is of such a kind that as sensuous it is at the same time essentially addressed to the *mind,* that the mind is meant to be affected by it, and to find some sort of satisfaction in it.

This intention of the work of art explains how it is in no way meant to be a natural product and to possess natural life, whether a natural product is to be ranked higher or lower than a *mere* work of art, as it is often called in a depreciatory sense.

For the sensuous aspect of the work of art has a right to existence only in as far as it exists for man's mind, but not in as far as qua sensuous thing it has separate existence by itself. If we examine more closely in what way the sensuous is presented to man, we find that what is sensuous may bear various relations to the mind.

The lowest mode of apprehension, and that least appropriate to the mind, is purely sensuous apprehension. It consists naturally in mere looking, listening, feeling, just as in seasons of mental fatigue it may often be entertaining to go about without thought and just to hear and look around us. The mind, however, does not rest in the mere apprehension of external things by sight and hearing; it makes them objects for its own inner nature, which then is itself impelled in a correspondingly sensuous form to realize itself in the things and relates itself to them as *desire.* In this appetitive relation to the outer world, the man stands as a sensuous particular over against the things as likewise particulars. He does not open his mind to them with general ideas as a thinking being but has relations dictated by particular impulses and interests to the objects as themselves particulars, and preserves himself in them, inasmuch as he uses them, consumes them, and puts in act his self-satisfaction by sacrificing them to it. In this negative relation desire requires for itself not merely the superficial appearance of external things, but themselves in their concrete sensuous existence. Mere pictures of the wood that it wants to use, or of the animals that it wants to eat, would be of no service to desire. Just as little is it possible for desire to let the object subsist in its freedom. For its impulse urges it just precisely to destroy this independence and freedom of external things and to show that they are only there to be destroyed and consumed. But at the same time the subject himself, as entangled in the particular limited and valueless interests of his desires, is neither free in himself, for he does not determine himself out of the essential universality and rationality of his will, nor free in relation to the outer world, for his desire remains essentially determined by things and related to them.

This relation of desire is not that in which man stands to the work of art. He allows it to subsist as an object, free and independent, and enters into relation with it apart from desire, as with an object which only appeals to the theoretic side of the mind. For this reason the work of art, although it has sensuous existence, yet, in this point of view, does not require concrete sensuous existence and natural life; indeed, it even *ought* not to remain on such a level, seeing that it has to satisfy only the interests of mind, and is bound to exclude from itself all desire. Hence it is, indeed, that practical desire rates individual things in nature, organic and inorganic, which are serviceable to it, higher than works of art, which reveal themselves to be useless for its purpose and enjoyable only for other modes of mind.

A second mode in which the externally present may be related to the mind is, in contrast with singular sensuous perception and desire, the purely theoretical relation to the intelligence. The theoretic contemplation of things has no interest in consuming them as particulars, in satisfying itself sensuously, and in preserving itself by their means, but rather in becoming acquainted with them in their universality, in finding their inner being and law, and in conceiving them in terms of their notion. Therefore the theoretical interest lets the single things be and holds aloof from them as sensuous particulars, because this sensuous particularity is not what the contemplation exercised by the intelligence looks for. For the rational intelligence does not belong, as do the desires, to the individual subject as such, but only to the individual as at the same time in his nature universal. Insofar as man has relation to things in respect of this universality, it is his universal reason which attempts to find itself in nature, and thereby to reproduce the inner essence of things, which sensuous existence, though having its ground therein, cannot immediately display. But again, this theoretic interest, the satisfaction of which is the work of science, is in the scientific form no more shared by art than the latter makes common cause with the impulse of the purely practical desires. Science may, no doubt, start from the sensuous thing in its individuality, and may possess a sensuous idea of the way in which such an individual presents itself in its individual colour, shape, size, etc. Still, this isolated sensuous thing, as such, has no further relation to the mind, inasmuch as the intelligence aims at the universal, the law, the thought and notion of the object. Not only, therefore, does it abandon all intercourse with the thing as a given individual, but it transforms the thing within the mind, making a concrete object of sense into an abstract matter of thought, and so into something quite other than the same object qua sensuous phenomenon. The artistic interest, as distinguished from science, does not act thus. Artistic contemplation accepts the work of art just as it displays itself qua external object, in immediate determinateness and sensuous individuality clothed in colour, figure, and sound, or as a single isolated perception, etc., and does not go so far beyond the immediate appearance of objectivity which is presented before it, as to aim, like science, at apprehending the notion of such an objective appearance as a universal notion.

Thus, the interest of art distinguishes itself from the practical interest of *desire* by the fact that it permits its object to subsist freely and in independence, while desire utilizes it in its own service by its destruction. On the other hand, artistic contemplation differs from theoretical consideration by the scientific intelligence, in cherishing interest for the object as an individual existence, and not setting to work to transmute it into its universal thought and notion.

It follows, then, from the above, that though the sensuous must be present

in a work of art, yet it must only appear as surface and *semblance* of the
sensuous. For, in the sensuous aspect of a work of art, the mind seeks neither
the concrete framework of matter, that empirically thorough completeness and
development of the organism which desire demands, nor the universal and
merely ideal thought. What it requires is sensuous presence, which, while not
ceasing to be sensuous, is to be liberated from the apparatus of its merely
material nature. And thus the sensuous in works of art is exalted to the rank
of a mere *semblance* in comparison with the immediate existence of things in
nature, and the work of art occupies the mean between what is immediately
sensuous and ideal thought. It is not as yet pure thought, but despite the
sensuousness it is also no longer simple material existence, like stones, plants,
and organic life. Rather the sensuous in the work of art is itself something
ideal, not, however, the ideal of thought but as thing still in an external way.
This semblance of the sensuous presents itself to the mind externally as the
shape, the visible look, and the sonorous vibration of things—supposing that
the mind leaves the objects uninterfered with (physically), but yet does not
descend into their inner essence (by abstract thought), for if it did so, it would
entirely destroy their external existence as separate individuals *for it*. For this
reason the sensuous aspect of art only refers to the two *theoretical* senses of
sight and *hearing*, while smell, taste, and feeling remain excluded from being
sources of artistic enjoyment. For smell, taste, and feeling have to do with
matter as such, and with its immediate sensuous qualities; smell with material
volatilization in air, taste with the material dissolution of substance, and
feeling with warmth, coldness, smoothness, etc. On this account these senses
cannot have to do with the objects of art, which are destined to maintain
themselves in their actual independent existence, and admit of no purely
sensuous relation. The pleasant for these latter senses is not the beautiful in
art.

Thus art on its sensuous side purposely produces no more than a shadow
world of shapes, sounds, and imaginable ideas; and it is absolutely out of the
question to maintain that it is owing to simple powerlessness and to the
limitations on his actions that man, when evoking worlds of art into existence,
fails to present more than the mere surface of the sensuous, than mere
schemata. In art, these sensuous shapes and sounds present themselves, not
simply for their own sake and for that of their immediate structure, but with
the purpose of affording in that shape satisfaction to higher spiritual interests,
seeing that they are powerful to call forth a response and echo in the mind
from all the depths of consciousness. It is thus that, in art, the sensuous is
spiritualized, i.e. the *spiritual* appears in sensuous shape.

But for this very reason we have a product of art only in so far as it has
found a passage through the mind and has been generated by spiritually
productive activity. This leads us to the other question which we have to
answer—how, that is, the sensuous side, which is indispensable to art, is
operative in the artist as a productive state of the subject or person.

This, the method and fashion of production, contains in itself as a
subjective activity just the same properties which we found objectively present

in the work of art; it must be a spiritual activity which, nevertheless, at the same time has in itself the element of sensuousness and immediateness. It is neither, on the one hand, purely mechanical work, as mere unconscious skill in sensuous sleight of hand, or a formal activity according to fixed rules learnt by rote. Nor is it, on the other hand, a scientific productive process, which passes from sense to abstract ideas and thoughts, or exercises itself exclusively in the element of pure thinking. Rather the spiritual and the sensuous side must in artistic production be as one. For instance, it would be possible in poetical creation to try and proceed by first apprehending the theme to be treated as a prosaic thought, and by then putting it into pictorial ideas, and into rhyme, and so forth; so that the pictorial element would simply be hung upon the abstract reflections as an ornament or decoration. Such a process could only produce bad poetry, for in it there would be operative as two *separate activities* that which in artistic production has its right place only as undivided unity.

This genuine mode of production constitutes the activity of artistic *imagination*. It is the rational element which, qua spirit, only exists in as far as it actively extrudes itself into consciousness, but yet does not array before it what it bears within itself till it does so in sensuous form. This activity has, therefore, a spiritual import, which, however, it embodies in sensuous shape. Such a process may be compared with the habit even of a man with great experience of the world, or, again, with that of a man of *esprit* or wit, who, although he has complete knowledge of the main stakes of life, of the substantive interests that hold men together, of what moves them, and of what is the power that they recognize, yet neither has himself apprehended this content in the form of general rules, nor is able to explain it to others in general reflections, but makes plain to himself and to others what occupies his consciousness always in particular cases, whether real or invented, in adequate instances, and the like. For in his ideas, everything shapes itself into concrete images, determinate in time and place, to which, therefore, names and other external circumstances of all kinds must not be wanting. Yet such a kind of imagination rather rests on the recollection of states that he has gone through, and of experiences that have befallen him, than is creative in its own strength. His recollection preserves and reproduces the individuality and external fashion of occurrences that had such and such results with all their external circumstances, and prevents the universal from emerging in its own shape. But the productive imagination of the *artist* is the imagination of a great mind and heart, the apprehension and creation of ideas and of shapes, and, indeed, the exhibition of the profoundest and most universal human interests in the definite sensuous mould of pictorial representation.

From this it follows at once, that in one aspect imagination unquestionably rests on natural gifts—speaking generally, on talent—because its mode of production requires a sensuous medium. It is true that we speak in the same way of scientific "talent," but the sciences only presuppose the universal capacity of thought, which has not, like imagination, a natural mode (as well as an intellectual one), but abstracts just precisely from all that is natural (or native) in an activity; and thus it would be more correct to say that there is no specifically scientific talent in the sense of a *mere* natural endowment. Now, imagination *has* in it a mode of instinct-like productiveness, inasmuch as the essential plasticity and sensuousness of the work of art must be subjectively present in the artist as natural disposition and natural impulse, and, considering that it is unconscious operation, must belong to the natural element in man, as well as to the rational. Of course, natural capacity leaves room for other elements in talent and genius, for artistic production is just as much of a spiritual and self-conscious nature; we can but say that its spirituality must, somehow, have an element of natural, plastic, and formative tendency. For this reason, though nearly everyone can reach a certain point in an art, yet, in order to go beyond this point, with which the art in the strict sense begins, it is impossible to dispense with native artistic talent of the highest order.

Considered as a natural endowment, moreover, such talent reveals itself for the most part in early youth, and is manifested in the impelling restlessness that busies itself, with vivacity and industry, in creating shapes in some particular sensuous medium and in seizing on this species of utterance and communication as the only one, or as the chief and the most suitable one. And thus, too, a precocious technical facility, that up to a certain grade of attainment is without effort, is a sign of natural talent. A sculptor finds everything transmute itself into shapes, and he soon begins to take up the clay and model it. And, speaking generally, whatever men of such talents have in their imagination, whatever rouses and moves their inner nature, turns at once into shape, drawing, melody, or poem.

Thirdly, and to conclude: the *content* of art is also in some respects borrowed from the sensuous, from nature; or, in any case, even if the content is of a spiritual kind, it can only be seized and fixed by representing the spiritual fact, such as human relations, in the shape of phenomena with external reality.

3. The question then arises, what the interest or the *end* is which man proposes to himself when he reproduces such a content in the form of works of art. This was the third point of view which we set before us with reference to the work of art, and the closer discussion of which will finally make the transition to the actual and true conception of art.

If in this aspect we glance at the common consciousness, a current idea which may occur to us is:

(*a*) The principle of the *imitation of nature*. According to this view the essential purpose of art consists in imitation, in the sense of a facility in copying natural forms as they exist in a way that corresponds precisely to them; and the success of such a representation, exactly corresponding to nature, is supposed to be what affords complete satisfaction.

This definition contains, prima facie, nothing beyond the purely formal aim that whatever already exists in the external world, just *as* it is therein, is now to be made a second time by man as a copy of the former, as well as he can do it with the means at his command. But we may at once regard this repetition as a *superfluous* labour, seeing that the things which pictures, theatrical representations, etc., imitate and represent—animals, natural scenes, incidents in human life—are before us in other cases already, in our own gardens or our own houses, or in cases within our closer or more remote circle of acquaintance. And, looking more closely, we may regard this superfluous labour as a presumptuous sport which comes far short of nature. For art is restricted in its means of representation; and can produce only *one-sided* deceptions—for instance, a semblance of reality addressed to one sense only; and, in fact, it invariably gives rise, if it rests in the formal purpose of *mere imitation,* to a mere parody of life instead of a genuine vitality. Just so the Turks, being Mohammedans, tolerate, as is well known, no pictures copied from men or the like; and when James Bruce, on his journey to Abyssinia, showed paintings of fish to a Turk, the man was amazed at first, but soon enough made answer: "If this fish shall rise up against you on the last day, and say, 'You have created for me a body, but no living soul,' how will you defend yourself against such an accusation?" The prophet, moreover, it is recorded in the Sunna, said to the two women, Ommi Habiba and Ommi Selma, who told him of pictures in Ethiopian churches, "These pictures will accuse their authors on the day of judgment!"

There are, no doubt, as well, examples of completely deceptive imitation. Zeuxis' painted grapes have from antiquity downward been taken to be the triumph of this principle of the imitation of nature, because the story is that living doves pecked at them. We might add to this ancient example the modern one of Büttner's monkey, which bit in pieces a painted cockchafer in Rösel's "Diversions of the Insect World" and was pardoned by his master, in spite of his having thereby spoilt a beautiful copy of this valuable work, because of this proof of the excellence of the pictures. But when we reflect on these and similar instances, it must at once occur to us that, in place of commending works of art because they have *actually* deceived *even* pigeons and monkeys, we ought simply to censure the people who mean to exalt a work of art by predicating, as its highest and ultimate quality, so poor an effect as this. In general, we may sum up by saying that, as a matter of mere imitation, art cannot maintain a rivalry with nature, and, if it tries, must look like a worm trying to crawl after an elephant.

Considering the unvarying failure—comparative failure, at least—of imitation when contrasted with the original in nature, there remains as end nothing beyond our pleasure in the sleight of hand which can produce something so like nature. And it is doubtless open to man to be pleased at producing over again what is already present in its own right, by his labour, skill, and industry. But enjoyment and admiration, even of this kind, naturally grow frigid or chilled precisely in proportion to the resemblance of the copy to the natural type, or are even converted into tedium and repugnance. There are portraits which, as has been wittily said, are sickeningly like; and Kant adduces another instance relative to this pleasure in imitation as such, viz. that we soon grow tired of a man—and there are such men—who is able to mimic the nightingale's strain quite perfectly; and as soon as it is discovered that a man is producing the notes, we are at once weary of the song. We then recognize in it nothing but a conjuring trick, neither the free production of nature nor a work of art; for we expect from the free productive capacity of human beings something quite other than such music as this, which only interests us when, as is the case with the nightingale's note, it gushes forth from the creature's own vitality without special purpose, and yet recalls the utterance of human feeling. In general, such delight at our skill in mimicking can be but limited, and it becomes man better to take delight in what he produces out of himself. In this sense the invention of any unimportant and technical product has the higher value, and man may be prouder of having invented the hammer, the nail, and so forth, than of achieving feats of mimicry. For this fervour of abstract copying is to be compared to the feat of the man who had taught himself to throw lentils through a small opening without missing. He displayed this skill of his before Alexander, and Alexander presented him with a bushel of lentils as a reward for his frivolous and meaningless art.

Moreover, seeing that the principle of imitation is purely formal, to make it the end has the result that *objective beauty* itself disappears. For the question is in that case no longer *of what nature* that is which is to be copied, but only whether it is *correctly* copied. The object and content of the beautiful comes then to be regarded as a matter of entire indifference. That is to say, if we go outside the principle and speak of a difference of beauty and ugliness in considering beasts, men, landscapes, actions, or characters, this must nevertheless, in presence of the maxim in question, be set down as a distinction that does not belong particularly to art, for which nothing is left but abstract imitation. In this case the above-mentioned lack of criterion in dealing with the endless forms of nature reduces us, as regards the selection of objects and their distinction in beauty and ugliness, to subjective *taste* as an ultimate fact, which accepts no rule and admits of no discussion. And, in fact, if in selecting objects for representation we start from what *men* think beautiful or ugly, and therefore deserving artistic imitation—that is, from their taste—then all circles of natural objects open to us, and not one of them will be likely to fail of a patron.

Among men, for instance, it is the case that at any rate every bridegroom thinks his bride beautiful, and indeed, perhaps, he alone; though not, it may be, every husband his wife; and that subjective taste for such beauty has no fixed rule one may hold to be the good fortune of both parties. If we, moreover, look quite beyond individuals and their accidental taste, to the taste of nations, this again is full of extreme diversity and contrast. How often we hear it said that a European beauty would not please a Chinese or even a Hottentot, insofar as the Chinaman has quite a different conception of beauty from the Negro, and the Negro in turn from the European, and so forth. Indeed, if we look at the works of art of those extra-European peoples—their images of the gods, for instance—which their fancy has originated as venerable and sublime, they may appear to us as the most gruesome idols, and their music may sound to our ears as the most horrible noise; while they, on their side, will regard our sculptures, paintings, and musical productions as trivial or ugly.

But even if we abstract from an objective principle of art, and if beauty is to be based on subjective and individual taste, we shall still soon find on the side of art itself that the imitation of nature, which certainly appeared to be a universal principle and one guaranteed by high authority, is at any rate not to be accepted in this universal and merely abstract form. For if we look at the different arts it will at once be admitted that even if painting and sculpture represent objects which appear like those of nature, or the type of which is essentially borrowed from nature, yet works of architecture on the other hand—and architecture belongs to the fine arts—and the productions of poetry, in as far as they do not confine themselves to mere description, are by no means to be called imitations of nature. At least, if we desired to maintain the principle as valid in the case of these latter arts, we should have to make a long circuit by conditioning the proposition in various ways, and reducing the so-called truth at any rate to probability. But if we admitted probability we should again be met by a great difficulty in determining what is probable and what is not; and still, moreover, one would neither consent nor find it possible to exclude from poetry all wholly arbitrary and completely original imaginations.

The end of art must, therefore, lie in something different from the purely formal imitation of what we find given, which in any case can bring to the birth only *tricks* and not *works* of art. It is, indeed, an element essential to the work of art to have natural shapes for its foundation, seeing that its representation is in the medium of external and therefore of natural phenomena. In painting, for instance, it is an important study to know how to copy with precision the colours in their relations to one another, the effects of light, reflections, etc., and, no less, the forms and figures of objects down to their subtlest characteristics. It is in this respect chiefly that the principle of naturalism in general and of copying nature has recovered its influence in modern times. Its aim is to recall an art which has grown feeble and indistinct to the vigour and crispness of nature, or, again, to invoke against the purely arbitrary and artificial conventionalism, as unnatural as it was inartistic, into which art had strayed, the uniform, direct, and solidly coherent sequences of nature. But however true it is that there is something right in this endeavour from one point of view, yet still the naturalism at which it aims is not as such the substantive and primary concern that underlies fine art. And, therefore, although external appearance in the shape of natural reality constitutes an essential condition of art, yet, nevertheless, neither is the given natural world its *rule,* nor is the mere imitation of external appearances *as* external its *end.*

(*b*) The further question then arises, What *is* the true content of art, and with what aim is this content to be presented? On this subject our consciousness supplies us with the common opinion that it is the task and aim of art to bring in contact with our sense, our feeling, our inspiration, *all* that finds a place in the mind of man. Art, it is thought, should realize in us that familiar saying, *Homo sum: humani nihil a me alienum puto.* Its aim is therefore placed in arousing and animating the slumbering emotions, inclinations, and passions; in filling the *heart,* in forcing the human being, whether cultured or uncultured, to feel the whole range of what man's soul in its inmost and secret corners has power to experience and to create, and all that is able to move and to stir the human breast in its depths and in its manifold aspects and possibilities; to present as a delight to emotion and to perception all that the mind possesses of real and lofty in its thought and in the Idea—all the splendour of the noble, the eternal, and the true; and no less to make intelligible misfortune and misery, wickedness and crime; to make men realize the inmost nature of all that is shocking and horrible, as also of all pleasure and delight; and, finally, to set imagination roving in idle toyings of fancy, and luxuriating in the seductive spells of sense-stimulating visions. This endlessly varied content, it is held, art is bound to embrace, partly in order to complete the natural experience in which our external existence consists, and partly with the general aim of provoking the passions of our nature, both in order that the experiences of life may not leave us unmoved and because we desire to attain to a receptivity that welcomes all phenomena.

Now, such a stimulus is not given in this sphere by actual experience itself, but can only come by the semblance thereof, by art, that is, deceptively substituting its creations for reality. The possibility of this deception by means of artistic semblance rests on the fact that all reality must, for man, traverse the medium of perception and ideas and cannot otherwise penetrate the feelings and the will. In this process it is quite irrelevant whether his attention is claimed by immediate external reality, or whether this effect is produced by another means—that is, by images, symbols, and ideas, containing or representing *the content* of reality. Man can frame to himself ideas of things that are not actual as though they were actual. Hence it is all the same to our feelings whether external reality or only the semblance of it is the means of bringing in contact with us a situation, a relation, or the import of a life. Either mode suffices to awaken our response to its burden, in grief and in rejoicing, in pathos and in horror, and in traversing the emotions and the passions of wrath, hatred, compassion, of anxiety, fear, love, reverence, and admiration, or of the desire of honour and of fame.

This awakening of all feelings in us, the dragging of the heart through the whole significance of life, the realization of all such inner movements by means of a presented exterior consisting merely in deception—all this was what, from the point of view which we have been considering, constituted the peculiar and pre-eminent power of art.

Now, as this mode of treatment credits art with the vocation of impressing on the heart and on the imagination good and bad alike, and of strengthening man to the noblest, as of enervating him to the most sensuous and selfish emotions, it follows that the task set before art is still purely formal, and so it would have no certain purpose, but would merely furnish the empty form for every possible kind of significance and content.

(*c*) It is a fact that art does include this formal side, in that it has power to present every possible subject matter in artistic dress before perception and feeling, just exactly as argumentative reflection has the power of manipulating all possible objects and modes of action, and of furnishing them with reasons and justifications. But when we admit so great a variety of content we are at once met by the remark that the manifold feelings and ideas, which art aims at provoking or reinforcing, intersect and contradict, and by mutual interference cancel one another. Indeed, in this aspect, in so far as art inspires men to directly opposite emotions, it only magnifies the contradiction of our feelings and passions, and either sets them staggering like Bacchantes, or passes into sophistry and scepticism, in the same way as argumentation. This diversity of the material of art itself compels us, therefore, not to be content with so formal an aim for it, seeing that rationality forces its way into this wild diversity and demands to see the emergence of a higher and more universal purpose from these elements in spite of their self-contradiction, and to be assured of its being attained. Just in the same way the state and the social life of men are, of course, credited with the purpose that in them *all* human capacities and *all* individual powers are to be developed and to find utterance in *all* directions and with *all* tendencies. But in opposition to so formal a view there at once arises the question in what *unity* these manifold formations must be comprehended, and what *single end* they must have for their fundamental idea and ultimate purpose.

As such an end, reflection soon suggests the notion that art has the capacity and the function of mitigating the fierceness of the desires.

In respect to this first idea, we have only to ascertain in what feature peculiar to art it is that the capacity lies of eliminating brutality and taming and educating the impulses, desires, and passions. Brutality in general has its reason in a direct selfishness of the impulses, which go to work right away, and exclusively for the satisfaction of their concupiscence. Now, desire is most savage and imperious in proportion as, being isolated and narrow, it occupies the *whole man,* so that he does not retain the power of separating himself as a universal being from this determinateness and of becoming aware of himself as universal. Even if the man in such a case says, "The passion is stronger than I," it is true that the abstract I is then separated for consciousness from the particular passion; but still only in a formal way, inasmuch as this separation is only made in order to pronounce that, against the power of the passion, the I as such is of no account whatever. The savageness of passion consists, therefore, in the oneness of the I as universal with the limited content of its desires, so that the man has no will outside this particular passion.

Now, such brutality and untamed violence of passion is softened through art, to begin with, by the mere fact that it brings before the man as an idea what in such a state he feels and does. And even if art restricts itself to merely setting up pictures of the passions before the mind's eye, or even if it were actually to flatter them, still this is by itself enough to have a softening power, inasmuch as the man is thereby at least *made aware* of what, apart from such presentation, he simply is. For then the man observes his impulses and inclinations, and whereas before they bore him on without power of reflection, he now sees them outside himself, and begins already to be free from them, in so far as they form an object which he contrasts with himself. Hence it may frequently be the case with the artist that when attacked by grief he softens

and weakens the intensity of his own feelings in its effect on his own mind by
representing it in art. Tears, even, are enough to bring comfort; the man who
to begin with is utterly sunk and concentrated in grief is able thus, at any rate,
to utter his inner state in a direct fashion. Still more of a relief, however, is the
utterance of what is within in words, images, pictures, sounds, and shapes. For
this reason it was a good old custom at deaths and funerals to appoint wailing
women, in order to bring the grief before the mind in its utterance. Manifestations of sympathy, too, hold up the content of a man's misfortune to his view;
when it is much talked about he is forced to reflect upon it and is thereby
relieved. And so it has always been held that to weep or to speak one's fill is a
means to obtain freedom from the oppressive weight of care, or at least to find
momentary relief for the heart. Hence the mitigation of the violence of passion
has for its universal reason that man is released from his immediate sunkenness in a feeling, and becomes conscious of it as of something external to him,
towards which he must now enter into an *ideal* relation.

Art, by means of its representations, while remaining within the sensuous
sphere, delivers man at the same time from the power of sensuousness. Of
course we may often hear those favourite phrases about man's duty being to
remain in immediate oneness with nature, but such oneness in its abstraction
is simply and solely coarseness and savagery; and art, in the very process of
dissolving this oneness for man, is raising him with gentle hand above and
away from mere sunkenness in nature. Man's mode of occupying himself with
works of art is always purely contemplative, and educates thereby, in the first
place, no doubt, merely attention to the representations themselves, but then,
going beyond this, it cultivates attention to their significance, the power of
comparison with other contents, and receptivity for the general consideration
of them, and for the points of view which it involves.

To the above there attaches itself in natural connection the second
characteristic which has been ascribed to art as its essential purpose, viz. the
purification of the passions, instruction, and *moral* perfecting. For the
characteristic that art was to bridle savageness and educate the passions
remained quite abstract and general, so that a question must again arise about
a *determinate* kind and an essential *end* of this education.

The doctrine of the purification of passion suffers indeed under the same
defect as the above doctrine of the mitigation of the desires; yet, when more
closely looked at, it at any rate arrives at the point of accentuating the fact that
the representations of art may be held to lack a standard by which their worth
or unworthiness could be measured. This standard simply means their
effectiveness in separating pure from impure in the passions. It therefore
requires a content that has capacity to exercise this purifying power, and, in as
far as the production of such an effect is taken to constitute the substantive
end of art, it must follow that the purifying content must be brought before
consciousness in its *universality* and *essentiality*.

In this latter aspect the end of art has been pronounced to be that it should
teach. Thus, on the one side, the peculiar character of art would consist in the
movement of the emotions and in the satisfaction which lies in this movement,

even in fear, compassion, in painful pathos and shock—that is to say, in the satisfying engagement of the emotions and passions, and to that extent in a satisfaction, entertainment, and delight in the objects of art, in their representation and effect. But, on the other side, this purpose (of art) is held to find its higher standard only in its instructiveness, in the *fabula docet,* and thus in the useful influence which the work of art succeeds in exerting on the subject. In this respect the Horatian adage, *Et prodesse volunt et delectare poetae* ("Poets aim at utility and entertainment alike"), contains, concentrated in a few words, all that has subsequently been elaborated in infinite degrees and diluted into the uttermost extreme of insipidity as a doctrine of art. As regards such instruction we have, then, to ask whether it is meant to be directly or indirectly, explicitly or implicitly contained in the work of art.

If, speaking generally, we are concerned about a purpose which is universal and not contingent, it follows that this purpose, considering the essentially spiritual nature of art, cannot but be itself spiritual, and indeed, moreover, one which is not contingent, but actual in its nature and for its own sake. Such a purpose in relation to teaching could only consist in bringing before consciousness, by help of the work of art, a really and explicitly significant spiritual content. From this point of view it is to be asserted that the higher art ranks itself, the more it is bound to admit into itself such a content as this, and that only in the essence of such a content can it find the standard which determines whether what is expressed is appropriate or inappropriate. Art has been, in fact, the first *instructress* of peoples.

But the purpose of instruction may be treated as *purpose,* to such a degree that the universal nature of the represented content is doomed to be exhibited and expounded directly and obviously as abstract proposition, prosaic reflection, or general theorem, and not merely in an indirect way in the concrete form of a work of *art,* becomes a mere otiose accessory, a husk which is expressly pronounced to be mere husk, a semblance expressly pronounced to be mere semblance. But thereby the very nature of the work of art is distorted. For the work of art ought to bring a content before the mind's eye, not in its generality as such, but with this generality made absolutely individual and sensuously particularized. If the work of art does not proceed from this principle but sets in relief its generalized aspect with the purpose of abstract instruction, then the imaginative and sensuous aspect is only an external and superfluous adornment, and the work of art is a thing divided against itself, in which form and content no longer appear as grown into one. In that case the sensuously individual and the spiritually general are become external to one another.

And further, if the purpose of art is limited to this *didactic* utility, then its other aspect—that of pleasure, entertainment, and delight—is pronounced to be in itself *unessential,* and ought to have its substance merely in the utility of the teaching on which it is attendant. But this amounts to pronouncing that art does not bear its vocation and purpose in itself and that its conception is rooted in something else, to which it is a *means*. Art is, in this case, only one among the several means which prove useful and are applied for the purpose of instruction. This brings us to the boundary at which art is made no longer to be an end on its own merits, seeing that it is degraded into a mere toy of entertainment or a mere means of instruction.

This boundary becomes most sharply marked when a question is raised, in its turn, about a supreme end and aim for the sake of which the passions are to be purified and men are to be instructed. This aim has often, in modern times, been declared to be *moral* improvement, and the aim of art has been placed in the function of preparing the inclinations and impulses for moral perfection, and of leading them to this goal. This idea combines purification with instruction, inasmuch as art is, by communicating an insight into genuine moral goodness—that is, by instruction—at the same time to incite to purification, and in this way alone to bring about the improvement of mankind as its useful purpose and supreme goal.

Regarding art in reference to moral improvement, the same has prima facie to be said as about the didactic purpose. We may readily grant that art must not as a principle take for its aim the immoral and its furtherance. But it is one thing to take immorality for the express aim of representation, and another to abstain from taking morality. Every genuine work of art may have a good moral drawn from it, but, of course, in doing so much depends on interpretation and on him who draws the moral. Thus one may hear the most immoral representations defended by saying that we must know evil, or sin, in order to act morally; and, conversely, it has been said that the portrayal of Mary Magdalene, the beautiful sinner who afterwards repented, has seduced many into sin, because art makes it look so beautiful to repent, and you must sin before you can repent.

But the doctrine of moral improvement, if consistently carried out, goes in general yet further. It would not be satisfied with the possibility of extracting a moral from a work of art by interpretation, but it would, on the contrary, display the moral instruction as the substantive purpose of the work of art, and, indeed, would actually admit to portrayal none but moral subjects, moral characters, actions, and incidents. For art has the choice among its subjects, in contradistinction to history or the sciences which have their subject matter fixed for them.

In order that we may be able to form a thoroughly adequate estimate of the idea that the aim of art is moral from this point of view, we must inquire first of all for the definite standpoint of the morality on which this doctrine is based. If we look closely at the standpoint of morality as we have to understand it in the best sense at the present day, we soon find that its conception does not immediately coincide with what apart from it we are in the habit of calling in a general way virtue, respectability, uprightness, etc. To be respectable and virtuous is not enough to make a man moral. Morality involves *reflection* and the definite consciousness of that which duty prescribes, and acting out of such a prior consciousness. Duty itself is the law of the will, which man nevertheless lays down freely out of his own self and then is supposed to determine himself to this duty for duty's and its fulfilment's sake, by doing good solely from the conviction which he has attained that it is the good.

Now this law, the duty which is chosen for duty's sake to be the guide of action, out of free conviction and the inner conscience, and is then acted upon, is, taken by itself, the abstract universal of the will, and is the direct antithesis of nature, the sensuous impulses, the self-seeking interests, the passions, and of all that is comprehensively entitled the feelings and the heart. In this antagonism the one side is regarded as *negativing* the other; and, seeing that both are present as antagonists within the subject (person), he has, as determining himself out of himself, the choice of following the one or the other. But, according to the view under discussion, a *moral* aspect is acquired by such a decision, and by the act performed in accordance with it, only through the free conviction of duty on the one hand, and, on the other hand, through the conquest, not only of the particular or separate will, of the natural motives, inclinations, passions, etc., but also through that of the nobler emotions and the higher impulses. For the modern moralistic view starts from the fixed antithesis of the will in its spiritual universality to its sensuous natural particularity, and consists not in the completed reconciliation of these contrasted sides, but in their conflict with one another, which involves the requirement that the impulses which conflict with duty ought to yield to it.

This antithesis does not merely display itself for our consciousness, in the limited region of moral action; but also emerges as a fundamental distinction and antagonism between that which is real essentially and in its own right, and that which is external reality and existence. Formulated in the abstract, it is the contrast of the universal and particular, when the former is explicitly fixed over against the latter, just as the latter is over against the former. More concretely, it appears in nature as the opposition of the abstract law against the abundance of individual phenomena, each having its own character. Or it appears in the mind, as the sensuous and spiritual in man, as the battle of the spirit against the flesh, of duty for duty's sake, the cold command, with the individual interest, the warm feelings, the sensuous inclinations and impulses, the individual disposition as such; as the hard conflict of inward freedom and of natural necessity. Further, as the contradiction of the dead conception—empty in itself—compared with full concrete vitality, or of theory and subjective thought contrasted with objective existence and experience.

These are antitheses which have not been invented, either by the subtlety of reflection or by the pedantry of philosophy, but which have from all time and in manifold forms preoccupied and disquieted the human consciousness, although it was modern culture that elaborated them most distinctly and forced them up to the point of most unbending contradiction. Intellectual culture and the modern play of understanding create in man this contrast, which makes him an amphibious animal, inasmuch as it sets him to live in two contradictory worlds at once; so that even consciousness wanders back and forward in this contradiction, and, shuttlecocked from side to side, is unable to satisfy itself *as* itself on the one side as on the other. For, on the one side, we see man a prisoner in common reality and earthly temporality, oppressed by want and poverty, hard driven by nature, entangled in matter, in sensuous aims and their enjoyments. On the other side, he exalts himself to eternal ideas, to a realm of thought and freedom, imposes on himself as a *will* universal laws and attributions, strips the world of its living and flourishing reality and dissolves it into abstractions, inasmuch as the mind is put upon vindicating its rights and its dignity simply by denying the rights of nature and maltreating it, thereby retaliating the oppression and violence which itself has experienced from nature.

Such a discrepancy in life and consciousness involves for modern culture and its understanding the demand that the contradiction should be resolved. Yet the understanding cannot release itself from the fixity of these antitheses. The solution, therefore, remains for consciousness a mere *ought,* and the present and reality only stir themselves in the unrest of a perpetual to and fro, which seeks a reconciliation without finding it. Then the question arises of whether such a many-sided and fundamental opposition, which never gets beyond a mere ought and a postulated solution, can be the genuine and complete truth, and, in general, the supreme purpose. If the culture of the world has fallen into such a contradiction, it becomes the task of philosophy to undo or cancel it, i.e. to show that neither the one alternative in its abstraction nor the other in similar one-sidedness possesses truth, but that they are essentially self-dissolving; that truth only lies in the conciliation and mediation of the two, and that this mediation is no mere postulate, but is in its nature and in reality accomplished and always self-accomplishing.

This intuition agrees directly with the natural faith and will, which always has present to the mind's eye precisely this resolved antithesis, and in action makes it its purpose and achieves it. All that philosophy does is to furnish a reflective insight into the essence of the antithesis in as far as it shows that what constitutes truth is merely the resolution of this antithesis, and that not in the sense that the conflict and its aspects in any way *are not,* but in the sense that they *are, in reconciliation.*

(*d*) Now, as an ultimate aim implied a higher standpoint in the case of moral improvement, we shall have to vindicate this higher standpoint for art no less than for morals. Thereby we at once lay aside the false position, which has already been remarked upon, that art has to serve as a means for moral ends, and to conduce to the moral end of the world, as such, by instruction and moral improvement, and thereby has its substantive aim, not in itself, but in something else. If, therefore, we now continue to speak of an aim or purpose, we must, in the first instance, get rid of the perverse idea, which, in asking, "What is the aim?" retains the accessory meaning of the question, "What is the *use?*" The perverseness of this lies in the point that the work of art would then be regarded as aspiring to something else which is set before consciousness as the essential and as what ought to be; so that then the work of art would only have value as a useful instrument in the realization of an end having substantive importance *outside* the sphere of art. Against this it is necessary to maintain that art has the vocation of revealing *the truth* in the form of sensuous artistic shape, of representing the reconciled antithesis just de-scribed, and, therefore, has its purpose in itself, in this representation and revelation. For other objects, such as instruction, purification, improvement, pecuniary gain, endeavour after fame and honour, have nothing to do with the work of art as such and do not determine its conception.

It is from this point of view, into which *reflective* consideration of the matter resolves itself, that we have to apprehend the idea of art in its inner necessity, as indeed it was from this point of view, historically speaking, that the true appreciation and understanding of art took its origin. For that antithesis, of which we spoke, made itself felt not only within general reflective culture but no less in philosophy as such, and it was not till philosophy discovered how to overcome this antithesis absolutely that it grasped its own conception and, just in as far as it did so, the conception of nature and of art.

Hence this point of view, as it is the reawakening of philosophy in general, so also is the reawakening of the science of art; and, indeed, it is this reawakening to which alone Aesthetics as a science owes its true origin, and art its higher estimation. . . .

William Wordsworth

1770–1850

William Wordsworth, the son of an attorney, was born at Cockermouth, Cumberland, on April 7, 1770. He was orphaned as a young child and placed under the guardianship of uncles. After attending a local grammar school, Wordsworth went to St. John's College, Cambridge, and graduated without distinction in 1791. Strongly drawn to France and the Revolutionary cause, he soon left for Blois and Orléans. There he fell in love with a young girl, Annette Vallon, who eventually bore him a daughter, but lack of funds and family disapproval prevented their marriage. Wordsworth soon became severely disillusioned by the bloody turn of events in France, and in December 1792 he returned to England.

The following year Wordsworth published two poetical works, *An Evening Walk* and *Descriptive Sketches,* written before his sojourn in France. But he remained in emotional turmoil for several years as he tried to establish a tranquil mode of existence and to come to terms with his disappointment over the French Revolution. This struggle is recounted in *The Prelude,* a long autobiographical poem that Wordsworth worked on throughout much of his adult life. In October 1795 Wordsworth moved to a cottage of his own in Dorset with his beloved sister, Dorothy, who remained a source of affection and support throughout his life.

Wordsworth's meeting with Coleridge in the summer of 1795, and the beginning of their lifelong friendship and literary association, was a significant factor in Wordsworth's rejuvenation. Each poet encouraged the other, while Dorothy acted as a catalyst in their relationship. When Coleridge settled in Somerset, both Wordsworths came to live nearby, at Alfoxden, where they spent the year 1797–98.

The *Lyrical Ballads,* published anonymously in 1798, was the product of this year of intense association. All but four of the poems are by Wordsworth, but Coleridge's "Ancient Mariner" was a major contribution. A second edition appeared in January 1801 under Wordsworth's name alone although Coleridge's contributions were still included. The famous Preface was also, according to Coleridge, "half a child of my own brain," but later in *Biographia Literaria* he criticized several of the ideas which it set forth.

During the winter of 1798–99 the three friends went to Germany. Believing that Wordsworth was destined to compose the first great philosophical poem and to take his place in the English literary tradition alongside Shakespeare and Milton, Coleridge encouraged his friend to write. Isolated in the little town of Goslar that winter, Wordsworth began work on what he envisioned as a long narrative poem to be entitled *The Recluse.* In fact, he was beginning to write *The Prelude,* originally intended as a mere overture to the longer work, but which absorbed him for the rest of his life. In Germany he also wrote the "Lucy" series, a famous group of lyrics that includes "She Dwelt Among Untrodden Ways."

Following their return to England, Wordsworth and his sister took up residence at Dove Cottage, Grasmere, in late 1799; here Wordsworth established a quiet domestic routine of walking, study, and writing, pleasantly interrupted from time to time by the appearance of friends and admirers, including Coleridge. In 1802 he brought his bride, Mary Hutchinson, to the cottage. After the birth of several children they moved to Rydal Mount in 1813, and this became Wordsworth's home for the remainder of his life.

The Excursion, a long narrative poem also conceived as part of the never-to-be-completed *Recluse,* was published in 1814, and was considered Wordsworth's major work during his lifetime. Wordsworth had completed one version of *The Prelude* in 1805, but its revision absorbed him for the remainder of his life. Only following his death—on April 23, 1850—was it published. It is now regarded as his masterpiece, and as one of the greatest long poems in English.

LYRICAL BALLADS

PREFACE

1800

The First Volume of these Poems has already been submitted to general perusal. It was published, as an experiment which, I hoped, might be of some use to ascertain, how far, by fitting to metrical arrangement a selection of the real language of men in a state of vivid sensation, that sort of pleasure and that quantity of pleasure may be imparted, which a Poet may rationally endeavour to impart.

I had formed no very inaccurate estimate of the probable effect of those Poems: I flattered myself that they who should be pleased with them would read them with more than common pleasure: and on the other hand I was well aware that by those who should dislike them they would be read with more than common dislike. The result has differed from my expectation in this only, that I have pleased a greater number, than I ventured to hope I should please.

For the sake of variety and from a consciousness of my own weakness I was induced to request the assistance of a Friend, who furnished me with the Poems of the *Ancient Mariner,* the *Foster-Mother's Tale,* the *Nightingale,* the *Dungeon,* and the Poem entitled *Love.* I should not, however, have requested this assistance, had I not believed that the poems of my Friend would in a great measure have the same tendency as my own, and that, though there would be found a difference, there would be found no discordance in the colours of our style; as our opinions on the subject of poetry do almost entirely coincide.

Several of my Friends are anxious for the success of these Poems from a belief, that if the views, with which they were composed, were indeed realized, a class of Poetry would be produced, well adapted to interest mankind permanently, and not unimportant in the multiplicity and in the quality of its moral relations: and on this account they have advised me to prefix a systematic defence of the theory, upon which the poems were written. But I was unwilling to undertake the task, because I knew that on this occasion the Reader would look coldly upon my arguments, since I might be suspected of having been principally influenced by the selfish and foolish hope of *reasoning* him into an approbation of these particular Poems: and I was still more unwilling to undertake the task, because adequately to display my opinions and fully to enforce my arguments would require a space wholly dispropor-tionate to the nature of a preface. For to treat the subject with the clearness and coherence, of which I believe it susceptible, it would be necessary to give a full account of the present state of the public taste in this country, and to determine how far this taste is healthy or depraved; which again could not be determined, without pointing out, in what manner language and the human mind act and react on each other, and without retracing the revolutions not of literature alone but likewise of society itself. I have therefore altogether declined to enter regularly upon this defence; yet I am sensible, that there would be some impropriety in abruptly obtruding upon the Public, without a few words of introduction, Poems so materially different from those, upon which general approbation is at present bestowed.

It is supposed, that by the act of writing in verse an Author makes a formal engagement that he will gratify certain known habits of association, that he not only thus apprizes the Reader that certain classes of ideas and expressions will be found in his book, but that others will be carefully excluded. This exponent or symbol held forth by metrical language must in different æras of literature have excited very different expectations: for example, in the age of Catullus, Terence and Lucretia, and that of Statius or Claudian, and in our own country, in the age of Shakespeare and Beaumont and Fletcher, and that of Donne and Cowley, or Dryden, or Pope. I will not take upon me to determine the exact import of the promise which by the act of writing in verse an Author in the present day makes to his Reader; but I am certain it will appear to many persons that I have not fulfilled the terms of an engagement thus voluntarily contracted. I hope therefore the Reader will not censure me, if I attempt to state what I have proposed to myself to perform, and also, (as far as the limits of a preface will permit) to explain some of the chief reasons which have determined me in the choice of my purpose: that at least he may be spared any unpleasant feeling of disappointment, and that I myself may be protected from the most dishonorable accusation which can be brought against an Author, namely, that of an indolence which prevents him from endeavouring to ascertain what is his duty, or, when his duty is ascertained prevents him from performing it.

The principal object then which I proposed to myself in these Poems was to make the incidents of common life interesting by tracing in them, truly though not ostentatiously, the primary laws of our nature: chiefly as far as regards the manner in which we associate ideas in a state of excitement. Low and rustic life was generally chosen because in that situation the essential passions of the heart find a better soil in which they can attain their maturity, are less under restraint, and speak a plainer and more emphatic language; because in that situation our elementary feelings exist in a state of greater simplicity and consequently may be more accurately contemplated and more forcibly communicated; because the manners of rural life germinate from those elementary feelings; and from the necessary character of rural occupations are more easily comprehended; and are more durable; and lastly, because in that situation the passions of men are incorporated with the beautiful and permanent forms of nature. The language too of these men is adopted (purified indeed from what appear to be its real defects, from all lasting and rational causes of dislike or disgust) because such men hourly communicate with the best objects from which the best part of language is originally derived; and because, from their rank in society and the sameness and narrow circle of their intercourse, being less under the action of social vanity they convey their feelings and notions in simple and unelaborated expressions. Accordingly such a language arising out of repeated experience and regular feelings is a more permanent and a far more philosophical language than that which is frequently substituted for it by Poets, who think that they are conferring honour upon themselves and their art in proportion as they separate themselves from the sympathies of men, and indulge in arbitrary and capricious habits of expression in order to furnish food for fickle tastes and fickle appetites of their own creation.

I cannot be insensible of the present outcry against the triviality and meanness both of thought and language, which some of my contemporaries have occasionally introduced into their metrical compositions; and I acknowledge that this defect where it exists, is more dishonorable to the Writer's own character than false refinement or arbitrary innovation, though I should contend at the same time that it is far less pernicious in the sum of its consequences. From such verses the Poems in these volumes will be found distinguished at least by one mark of difference, that each of them has a worthy *purpose*. Not that I mean to say, that I always began to write with a distinct purpose formally conceived; but I believe that my habits of meditation have so formed my feelings, as that my descriptions of such objects as strongly excite those feelings, will be found to carry along with them a *purpose*. If in this opinion I am mistaken I can have little right to the name of a Poet. For all good poetry is the spontaneous overflow of powerful feelings; but though this be true, Poems to which any value can be attached, were never produced on any variety of subjects but by a man who being possessed of more than usual organic sensibility had also thought long and deeply. For our continued influxes of feeling are modified and directed by our thoughts, which are indeed the representatives of all our past feelings; and as by contemplating the relation of these general representatives to each other, we discover what is really important to men, so by the repetition and continuance of this act feelings connected with important subjects will be nourished, till at length, if we be originally possessed of much organic sensibility, such habits of mind will be produced that by obeying blindly and mechanically the impulses of those habits we shall describe objects and utter sentiments of such a nature and in such connection with each other, that the understanding of the being to whom we address ourselves, if he be in a healthful state of association, must necessarily be in some degree enlightened, his taste exalted, and his affections ameliorated.

I have said that each of these poems has a purpose. I have also informed my Reader what this purpose will be found principally to be: namely to illustrate the manner in which our feelings and ideas are associated in a state of excitement. But speaking in less general language, it is to follow the fluxes and refluxes of the mind when agitated by the great and simple affections of our nature. This object I have endeavoured in these short essays to attain by various means; by tracing the maternal passion through many of its more subtle windings, as in the poems of the *Idiot Boy* and the *Mad Mother;* by accompanying the last struggles of a human being at the approach of death, cleaving in solitude to life and society, as in the Poem of the *Forsaken Indian;* by shewing, as in the Stanzas entitled *We Are Seven,* the perplexity and obscurity which in childhood attend our notion of death, or rather our utter inability to admit that notion; or by displaying the strength of fraternal, or to speak more philosophically, of moral attachment when early associated with the great and beautiful objects of nature, as in *The Brothers;* or, as in the Incident of *Simon Lee,* by placing my Reader in the way of receiving from ordinary moral sensations another and more salutary impression than we are accustomed to receive from them. It has also been part of my general purpose to attempt to sketch characters under the influence of less impassioned feelings, as in the *Old Man Travelling, The Two Thieves,* &c. characters of which the elements are simple, belonging rather to nature than to manners, such as exist now and will probably always exist, and which from their constitution may be distinctly and profitably contemplated. I will not abuse the indulgence of my Reader by dwelling longer upon this subject; but it is proper that I should mention one other circumstance which distinguishes these Poems from the popular Poetry of the day; it is this, that the feeling therein developed gives importance to the action and situation and not the action and situation to the feeling. My meaning will be rendered perfectly intelligible by referring my Reader to the Poems entitled *Poor Susan* and the *Childless Father,* particularly to the last Stanza of the latter Poem.

I will not suffer a sense of false modesty to prevent me from asserting, that I point my Reader's attention to this mark of distinction far less for the sake of these particular Poems than from the general importance of the subject. The subject is indeed important! For the human mind is capable of excitement without the application of gross and violent stimulants; and he must have a very faint perception of its beauty and dignity who does not know this, and who does not further know that one being is elevated above another in proportion as he possesses this capability. It has therefore appeared to me that to endeavour to produce or enlarge this capability is one of the best services in which, at any period, a Writer can be engaged; but this service, excellent at all times, is especially so at the present day. For a multitude of causes unknown to former times are now acting with a combined force to blunt the discriminating powers of the mind, and unfitting it for all voluntary exertion to reduce it to a state of almost savage torpor. The most effective of these causes are the great national events which are daily taking place, and the encreasing accumulation of men in cities, where the uniformity of their occupations produces a craving for extraordinary incident which the rapid communication of intelligence hourly gratifies. To this tendency of life and manners the literature and theatrical exhibitions of the country have conformed themselves. The invaluable works of our elder writers, I had almost said the works of Shakespear and Milton, are driven into neglect by frantic novels, sickly and stupid German Tragedies, and deluges of idle and extravagant stories in verse.— When I think upon this degrading thirst after outrageous stimulation I am almost ashamed to have spoken of the feeble effort with which I have endeavoured to counteract it; and reflecting upon the magnitude of the general evil, I should be oppressed with no dishonorable melancholy, had I not a deep impression of certain inherent and indestructible qualities of the human mind, and likewise of certain powers in the great and permanent objects that act upon it which are equally inherent and indestructible; and did I not further add to this impression a belief that the time is approaching when the evil will be systematically opposed by men of greater powers and with far more distinguished success.

Having dwelt thus long on the subjects and aim of these Poems, I shall request the Reader's permission to apprize him of a few circumstances relating to their *style,* in order, among other reasons, that I may not be censured for not having performed what I never attempted. Except in a very few instances the Reader will find no personifications of abstract ideas in these volumes, not that I mean to censure such personifications: they may be well fitted for certain sorts of composition, but in these Poems I propose to myself to imitate, and, as far as possible, to adopt the very language of men, and I do not find that such personifications make any regular or natural part of that language. I wish to keep my Reader in the company of flesh and blood, persuaded that by so doing I shall interest him. Not but that I believe that others who pursue a different track may interest him likewise: I do not interfere with their claim, I only wish to prefer a different claim of my own. There will also be found in these volumes little of what is usually called poetic diction; I have taken as much pains to avoid it as others ordinarily take to produce it; this I have done for the reason already alleged, to bring my language near to the language of men, and further, because the pleasure which I have proposed to myself to impart is of a kind very different from that which is supposed by many persons to be the proper object of poetry. I do not know how without being culpably particular I can give my Reader a more exact notion of the style in which I wished these poems to be written than by informing him that I have at all times endeavoured to look steadily at my subject, consequently I hope it will be found that there is in these Poems little falsehood of description, and that my ideas are expressed in language fitted to their respective importance. Something I must have gained by this practice, as it is friendly to one property of all good poetry, namely good sense; but it has necessarily cut me off from a large portion of phrases and figures of speech which from father to son have long been regarded as the common inheritance of Poets. I have also thought it expedient to restrict myself still further, having abstained from the use of many expressions, in themselves proper and beautiful, but which have been foolishly repeated by bad Poets till such feelings of disgust are connected with them as it is scarcely possible by any art of association to overpower.

If in a Poem there should be found a series of lines, or even a single line, in which the language, though naturally arranged and according to the strict laws of metre, does not differ from that of prose, there is a numerous class of critics who, when they stumble upon these prosaisms as they call them, imagine that they have made a notable discovery, and exult over the Poet as over a man ignorant of his own profession. Now these men would establish a canon of criticism which the Reader will conclude he must utterly reject if he wishes to be pleased with these volumes. And it would be a most easy task to prove to him that not only the language of a large portion of every good poem, even of the most elevated character, must necessarily, except with reference to the metre, in no respect differ from that of good prose, but likewise that some of the most interesting parts of the best poems will be found to be strictly the language of prose when prose is well written. The truth of this assertion might be demonstrated by innumerable passages from almost all the poetical writings, even of Milton himself. I have not space for much quotation; but, to illustrate the subject in a general manner, I will here adduce a short composition of Gray, who was at the head of those who by their reasonings have attempted to widen the space of separation betwixt Prose and Metrical composition, and was more than any other man curiously elaborate in the structure of his own poetic diction.

> In vain to me the smiling mornings shine,
> And reddening Phoebus lifts his golden fire:
> The birds in vain their amorous descant join,
> Or chearful fields resume their green attire:
> These ears alas! for other notes repine;
> *A different object do these eyes require;*
> *My lonely anguish melts no heart but mine;*
> *And in my breast the imperfect joys expire;*
> Yet Morning smiles the busy race to cheer,
> And new-born pleasure brings to happier men;
> The fields to all their wonted tribute bear;
> To warm their little loves the birds complain.
> *I fruitless mourn to him that cannot hear*
> *And weep the more because I weep in vain.*

It will easily be perceived that the only part of this Sonnet which is of any value is the lines printed in Italics: it is equally obvious that except in the rhyme, and in the use of the single word "fruitless" for fruitlessly, which is so far a defect, the language of these lines does in no respect differ from that of prose.

Is there then, it will be asked, no essential difference between the language of prose and metrical composition? I answer that there neither is nor can be any essential difference. We are fond of tracing the resemblance between Poetry and Painting, and, accordingly, we call them Sisters: but where shall we find bonds of connection sufficiently strict to typify the affinity betwixt metrical and prose composition? They both speak by and to the same organs; the bodies in which both of them are clothed may be said to be of the same substance, their affections are kindred and almost identical, not necessarily differing even in degree; Poetry sheds no tears "such as Angels weep," but natural and human tears; she can boast of no celestial Ichor that distinguishes her vital juices from those of prose; the same human blood circulates through the veins of them both.

If it be affirmed that rhyme and metrical arrangement of themselves constitute a distinction which overturns what I have been saying on the strict affinity of metrical language with that of prose, and paves the way for other distinctions which the mind voluntarily admits, I answer that the distinction of rhyme and metre is regular and uniform, and not, like that which is produced by what is usually called poetic diction, arbitrary and subject to infinite caprices upon which no calculation whatever can be made. In the one case the Reader is utterly at the mercy of the Poet respecting what imagery or diction he may choose to connect with the passion, whereas in the other the metre obeys certain laws, to which the Poet and Reader both willingly submit because they are certain, and because no interference is made by them with the passion but such as the concurring testimony of ages has shewn to heighten and improve the pleasure which co-exists with it.

It will now be proper to answer an obvious question, namely, why, professing these opinions have I written in verse? To this in the first place I reply, because, however I may have restricted myself, there is still left open to me what confessedly constitutes the most valuable object of all writing whether in prose or verse, the great and universal passions of men, the most general and interesting of their occupations, and the entire world of nature, from which I am at liberty to supply myself with endless combinations of forms and imagery. Now, granting for a moment that whatever is interesting in these objects may be as vividly described in prose, why am I to be condemned if to such description I have endeavoured to superadd the charm which by the consent of all nations is acknowledged to exist in metrical language? To this it will be answered, that a very small part of the pleasure given by Poetry depends upon the metre, and that it is injudicious to write in metre unless it be accompanied with the other artificial distinctions of style with which metre is usually accompanied, and that by such deviation more will be lost from the shock which will be thereby given to the Reader's associations than will be counterbalanced by any pleasure which he can derive from the general power of numbers. In answer to those who thus contend for the necessity of accompanying metre with certain appropriate colours of style in order to the accomplishment of its appropriate end, and who also, in my opinion, greatly under-rate the power of metre in itself, it might perhaps be almost sufficient to observe that poems are extant, written upon more humble subjects, and in a more naked and simple style than what I have aimed at, which poems have continued to give pleasure from generation to generation. Now, if nakedness and simplicity be a defect, the fact here mentioned affords a strong presumption that poems somewhat less naked and simple are capable of affording pleasure at the present day; and all that I am now attempting is to justify myself for having written under the impression of this belief.

But I might point out various causes why, when the style is manly, and the subject of some importance, words metrically arranged will long continue to impart such a pleasure to mankind as he who is sensible of the extent of that pleasure will be desirous to impart. The end of Poetry is to produce excitement in coexistence with an over-balance of pleasure. Now, by the supposition, excitement is an unusual and irregular state of the mind; ideas and feelings do not in that state succeed each other in accustomed order. But if the words by which this excitement is produced are in themselves powerful, or the images and feelings have an undue proportion of pain connected with them, there is some danger that the excitement may be carried beyond its proper bounds. Now the co-presence of something regular, something to which the mind has been accustomed when in an unexcited or a less excited state, cannot but have great efficacy in tempering and restraining the passion by an intertexture of ordinary feeling. This may be illustrated by appealing to the Reader's own experience of the reluctance with which he comes to the re-perusal of the distressful parts of Clarissa Harlowe, or the Gamester. While Shakespeare's writings, in the most pathetic scenes, never act upon us as pathetic beyond the bounds of pleasure—an effect which is in a great degree to be ascribed to small, but continual and regular impulses of pleasurable surprise from the metrical arrangement.—On the other hand (what it must be allowed will much more frequently happen) if the Poet's words should be incommensurate with the passion, and inadequate to raise the Reader to a height of desirable excitement, then, (unless the Poet's choice of his metre has been grossly injudicious) in the feelings of pleasure which the Reader has been accustomed to connect with metre in general, and in the feeling, whether chearful or melancholy, which he has been accustomed to connect with that particular movement of metre, there will be found something which will greatly contribute to impart passion to the words, and to effect the complex end which the Poet proposes to himself.

If I had undertaken a systematic defence of the theory upon which these poems are written, it would have been my duty to develope the various causes upon which the pleasure received from metrical language depends. Among the chief of these causes is to be reckoned a principle which must be well known to those who have made any of the Arts the object of accurate reflection; I mean the pleasure which the mind derives from the perception of similitude in dissimilitude. This principle is the great spring of the activity of our minds and their chief feeder. From this principle the direction of the sexual appetite, and all the passions connected with it take their origin: It is the life of our ordinary conversation; and upon the accuracy with which similitude in dissimilitude, and dissimilitude in similitude are perceived, depend our taste and our moral feelings. It would not have been a useless employment to have applied this principle to the consideration of metre, and to have shewn that metre is hence enabled to afford much pleasure, and to have pointed out in what manner that pleasure is produced. But my limits will not permit me to enter upon this subject, and I must content myself with a general summary.

I have said that Poetry is the spontaneous overflow of powerful feelings: it takes its origin from emotion recollected in tranquillity: the emotion is contemplated till by a species of reaction the tranquillity gradually disappears, and an emotion, similar to that which was before the subject of contemplation, is gradually produced, and does itself actually exist in the mind. In this mood successful composition generally begins, and in a mood similar to this it is carried on; but the emotion, of whatever kind and in whatever degree, from various causes is qualified by various pleasures, so that in describing any passions whatsoever, which are voluntarily described, the mind will upon the whole be in a state of enjoyment. Now if Nature be thus cautious in preserving in a state of enjoyment a being thus employed, the Poet ought to profit by the lesson thus held forth to him, and ought especially to take care, that whatever passions he communicates to his Reader, those passions, if his Reader's mind be sound and vigorous, should always be accompanied with an overbalance of pleasure. Now the music of harmonious metrical language, the sense of difficulty overcome, and the blind association of pleasure which has been previously received from works of rhyme or metre of the same or similar construction, all these imperceptibly make up a complex feeling of delight, which is of the most important use in tempering the painful feeling which will always be found intermingled with powerful descriptions of the deeper passions. This effect is always produced in pathetic and impassioned poetry; while in lighter compositions the ease and gracefulness with which the Poet manages his numbers are themselves confessedly a principal source of the gratification of the Reader. I might perhaps include all which it is *necessary* to say upon this subject by affirming what few persons will deny, that of two descriptions either of passions, manners, or characters, each of them equally well executed, the one in prose and the other in verse, the verse will be read a hundred times where the prose is read once. We see that Pope by the power of verse alone, has contrived to render the plainest common sense interesting, and even frequently to invest it with the appearance of passion. In consequence of these convictions I related in metre the Tale of *Goody Blake* and *Harry Gill,* which is one of the rudest of this collection. I wished to draw attention to the truth that the power of the human imagination is sufficient to produce such changes even in our physical nature as might almost appear miraculous. The truth is an important one; the fact (for it is a *fact*) is a valuable illustration of it. And I have the satisfaction of knowing that it has been communicated to many hundreds of people who would never have heard of it, had it not been narrated as a Ballad, and in a more impressive metre than is usual in Ballads.

Having thus adverted to a few of the reasons why I have written in verse, and why I have chosen subjects from common life, and endeavoured to bring my language near to the real language of men, if I have been too minute in pleading my own cause, I have at the same time been treating a subject of general interest; and it is for this reason that I request the Reader's permission to add a few words with reference solely to these particular poems, and to some defects which will probably be found in them. I am sensible that my associations must have sometimes been particular instead of general, and that, consequently, giving to things a false importance, sometimes from diseased impulses I may have written upon unworthy subjects; but I am less apprehensive on this account, than that my language may frequently have suffered from those arbitrary connections of feelings and ideas with particular words, from which no man can altogether protect himself. Hence I have no doubt that in some instances feelings even of the ludicrous may be given to my Readers by expressions which appeared to me tender and pathetic. Such faulty expressions, were I convinced they were faulty at present, and that they must necessarily continue to be so, I would willingly take all reasonable pains to correct. But it is dangerous to make these alterations on the simple authority of a few individuals, or even of certain classes of men; for where the understanding of an Author is not convinced, or his feelings altered, this cannot be done without great injury to himself: for his own feelings are his stay and support, and if he sets them aside in one instance, he may be induced to repeat this act till his mind loses all confidence in itself and becomes utterly debilitated. To this it may be added, that the Reader ought never to forget that he is himself exposed to the same errors as the Poet, and perhaps in a much greater degree: for there can be no presumption in saying that it is not probable he will be so well acquainted with the various stages of meaning through which words have passed, or with the fickleness or stability of the relations of particular ideas to each other; and above all, since he is so much less interested in the subject, he may decide lightly and carelessly.

Long as I have detained my Reader, I hope he will permit me to caution him against a mode of false criticism which has been applied to Poetry in which the language closely resembles that of life and nature. Such verses have been triumphed over in parodies of which Dr. Johnson's Stanza is a fair specimen.

> "I put my hat upon my head,
> And walk'd into the Strand,
> And there I met another man
> Whose hat was in his hand."

Immediately under these lines I will place one of the most justly admired stanzas of the "*Babes* in the Wood."

> "These pretty Babes with hand in hand
> Went wandering up and down;
> But never more they saw the Man
> Approaching from the Town."

In both of these stanzas the words, and the order of the words, in no respect differ from the most unimpassioned conversation. There are words in both, for example, "the Strand," and "the Town," connected with none but the most familiar ideas; yet the one stanza we admit as admirable, and the other as a fair example of the superlatively contemptible. Whence arises this difference? Not from the metre, not from the language, not from the order of the words; but the *matter* expressed in Dr. Johnson's stanza is contemptible. The proper method of treating trivial and simple verses to which Dr. Johnson's stanza would be a fair parallelism is not to say this is a bad kind of poetry, or this is not poetry, but this wants sense; it is neither interesting in itself, nor can *lead* to any thing interesting; the images neither originate in that sane state of feeling which arises out of thought, nor can excite thought or feeling in the Reader. This is the only sensible manner of dealing with such verses: Why trouble yourself about the species till you have previously decided upon the genus? Why take pains to prove that an Ape is not a Newton when it is self-evident that he is not a man?

I have one request to make of my Reader, which is, that in judging these Poems he would decide by his own feelings genuinely, and not by reflection upon what will probably be the judgment of others. How common is it to hear a person say, "I myself do not object to this style of composition or this or that expression, but to such and such classes of people it will appear mean or ludicrous." This mode of criticism so destructive of all sound unadulterated judgment is almost universal: I have therefore to request that the Reader would abide independently by his own feelings, and that if he finds himself affected he would not suffer such conjectures to interfere with his pleasure.

If an Author by any single composition has impressed us with respect for his talents, it is useful to consider this as affording a presumption, that, on other occasions where we have been displeased, he nevertheless may not have written ill or absurdly; and, further, to give him so much credit for this one composition as may induce us to review what has displeased us with more care than we should otherwise have bestowed upon it. This is not only an act of justice, but in our decisions upon poetry especially, may conduce in a high degree to the improvement of our own taste: for an *accurate* taste in Poetry and in all the other arts, as Sir Joshua Reynolds has observed, is an *acquired* talent, which can only be produced by thought and a long continued intercourse with the best models of composition. This is mentioned not with so ridiculous a purpose as to prevent the most inexperienced Reader from judging for himself, (I have already said that I wish him to judge for himself;) but merely to temper the rashness of decision, and to suggest that if Poetry be a subject on which much time has not been bestowed, the judgment may be erroneous, and that in many cases it necessarily will be so.

I know that nothing would have so effectually contributed to further the end which I have in view as to have shewn of what kind the pleasure is, and how the pleasure is produced which is confessedly produced by metrical composition essentially different from what I have here endeavoured to recommend; for the Reader will say that he has been pleased by such composition and what can I do more for him? The power of any art is limited and he will suspect that if I propose to furnish him with new friends it is only upon condition of his abandoning his old friends. Besides, as I have said, the Reader is himself conscious of the pleasure which he has received from such composition, composition to which he has peculiarly attached the endearing name of Poetry; and all men feel an habitual gratitude, and something of an honorable bigotry for the objects which have long continued to please them: we not only wish to be pleased, but to be pleased in that particular way in which we have been accustomed to be pleased. There is a host of arguments in these feelings; and I should be the less able to combat them successfully, as I am willing to allow, that, in order entirely to enjoy the Poetry which I am recommending, it would be necessary to give up much of what is ordinarily enjoyed. But would my limits have permitted me to point out how this pleasure is produced, I might have removed many obstacles, and assisted my Reader in perceiving that the powers of language are not so limited as he may suppose; and that it is possible that poetry may give other enjoyments, of a purer, more lasting, and more exquisite nature. But this part of my subject I have been obliged altogether to omit: as it has been less my present aim to prove that the interest excited by some other kinds of poetry is less vivid, and less worthy of the nobler powers of the mind, than to offer reasons for presuming, that, if the object which I have proposed to myself were adequately attained, a species of poetry would be produced, which is genuine poetry; in its nature well adapted to interest mankind permanently, and likewise important in the multiplicity and quality of its moral relations.

From what has been said, and from a perusal of the Poems, the Reader will be able clearly to perceive the object which I have proposed to myself: he will determine how far I have attained this object; and, what is a much more important question, whether it be worth attaining; and upon the decision of these two questions will rest my claim to the approbation of the public.

LYRICAL BALLADS

PREFACE

1802

The first Volume of these Poems has already been submitted to general perusal. It was published, as an experiment, which, I hoped, might be of some use to ascertain, how far, by fitting to metrical arrangement a selection of the real language of men in a state of vivid sensation, that sort of pleasure and that quantity of pleasure may be imparted, which a Poet may rationally endeavour to impart.

I had formed no very inaccurate estimate of the probable effect of those Poems: I flattered myself that they who should be pleased with them would read them with more than common pleasure: and, on the other hand, I was well aware, that by those who should dislike them they would be read with more than common dislike. The result has differed from my expectation in this only, that I have pleased a greater number, than I ventured to hope I should please.

For the sake of variety, and from a consciousness of my own weakness, I was induced to request the assistance of a Friend, who furnished me with the Poems of the *Ancient Mariner,* the *Foster-Mother's Tale,* the *Nightingale,* and the Poem entitled *Love.* I should not, however, have requested this assistance, had I not believed that the Poems of my Friend would in a great measure have the same tendency as my own, and that, though there would be found a difference, there would be found no discordance in the colours of our style; as our opinions on the subject of poetry do almost entirely coincide.

Several of my Friends are anxious for the success of these Poems from a belief, that, if the views with which they were composed were indeed realized, a class of Poetry would be produced, well adapted to interest mankind permanently, and not unimportant in the multiplicity, and in the quality of its moral relations: and on this account they have advised me to prefix a systematic defence of the theory upon which the poems were written. But I was unwilling to undertake the task, because I knew that on this occasion the Reader would look coldly upon my arguments, since I might be suspected of having been principally influenced by the selfish and foolish hope of *reasoning* him into an approbation of these particular Poems: and I was still more unwilling to undertake the task, because, adequately to display my opinions, and fully to enforce my arguments, would require a space wholly disproportionate to the nature of a preface. For to treat the subject with the clearness and coherence, of which I believe it susceptible, it would be necessary to give a full account of the present state of the public taste in this country, and to determine how far this taste is healthy or depraved; which, again, could not be determined, without pointing out, in what manner language and the human mind act and re-act on each other, and without retracing the revolutions, not of literature alone, but likewise of society itself. I have therefore altogether declined to enter regularly upon this defence; yet I am sensible, that there would be some impropriety in abruptly obtruding upon the Public, without a few words of introduction, Poems so materially different from those, upon which general approbation is at present bestowed.

It is supposed, that by the act of writing in verse an Author makes a formal engagement that he will gratify certain known habits of association; that he not only thus apprizes the Reader that certain classes of ideas and expressions will be found in his book, but that others will be carefully excluded. This exponent or symbol held forth by metrical language must in different æras of literature have excited very different expectations: for example, in the age of Catullus, Terence and Lucretius, and that of Statius or Claudian; and in our own country, in the age of Shakespeare and Beaumont and Fletcher, and that of Donne and Cowley, or Dryden, or Pope. I will not take upon me to determine the exact import of the promise which by the act of writing in verse an Author, in the present day, makes to his Reader; but I am certain, it will appear to many persons that I have not fulfilled the terms of an engagement thus voluntarily contracted. They who have been accustomed to the gaudiness and inane phraseology of many modern writers, if they persist in reading this book to its conclusion, will, no doubt, frequently have to struggle with feelings of strangeness and aukwardness: they will look round for poetry, and will be induced to inquire by what species of courtesy these attempts can be permitted to assume that title. I hope therefore the Reader will not censure me, if I attempt to state what I have proposed to myself to perform; and also, (as far as the limits of a preface will permit) to explain some of the chief reasons which have determined me in the choice of my purpose: that at least he may be spared any unpleasant feeling of disappointment, and that I myself may be protected from the most dishonourable accusation which can be brought against an Author, namely, that of an indolence which prevents him from endeavouring to ascertain what is his duty, or, when his duty is ascertained, prevents him from performing it.

The principal object, then, which I proposed to myself in these Poems was to choose incidents and situations from common life, and to relate or describe them, throughout, as far as was possible, in a selection of language really used by men; and, at the same time, to throw over them a certain colouring of imagination, whereby ordinary things should be presented to the mind in an unusual way; and, further, and above all, to make these incidents and situations interesting by tracing in them, truly though not ostentatiously, the primary laws of our nature: chiefly, as far as regards the manner in which we associate ideas in a state of excitement. Low and rustic life was generally chosen, because in that condition, the essential passions of the heart find a better soil in which they can attain their maturity, are less under restraint, and speak a plainer and more emphatic language; because in that condition of life our elementary feelings co-exist in a state of greater simplicity, and, conse-

quently, may be more accurately contemplated, and more forcibly communicated; because the manners of rural life germinate from those elementary
feelings; and, from the necessary character of rural occupations, are more
easily comprehended; and are more durable; and lastly, because in that
condition the passions of men are incorporated with the beautiful and
permanent forms of nature. The language, too, of these men is adopted
(purified indeed from what appear to be its real defects, from all lasting and
rational causes of dislike or disgust) because such men hourly communicate
with the best objects from which the best part of language is originally derived;
and because, from their rank in society and the sameness and narrow circle of
their intercourse, being less under the influence of social vanity they convey
their feelings and notions in simple and unelaborated expressions. Accordingly, such a language, arising out of repeated experience and regular feelings,
is a more permanent, and a far more philosophical language, than that which
is frequently substituted for it by Poets, who think that they are conferring
honour upon themselves and their art, in proportion as they separate themselves from the sympathies of men, and indulge in arbitrary and capricious
habits of expression, in order to furnish food for fickle tastes, and fickle
appetites, of their own creation.

I cannot, however, be insensible of the present outcry against the
triviality and meanness both of thought and language, which some of my
contemporaries have occasionally introduced into their metrical compositions;
and I acknowledge that this defect, where it exists, is more dishonorable to
the Writer's own character than false refinement or arbitrary innovation,
though I should contend at the same time that it is far less pernicious in the
sum of its consequences. From such verses the Poems in these volumes will
be found distinguished at least by one mark of difference, that each of them
has a worthy *purpose*. Not that I mean to say, that I always began to write
with a distinct purpose formally conceived; but I believe that my habits of
meditation have so formed my feelings, as that my descriptions of such
objects as strongly excite those feelings, will be found to carry along with
them a *purpose*. If in this opinion I am mistaken, I can have little right to the
name of a Poet. For all good poetry is the spontaneous overflow of powerful
feelings: but though this be true, Poems to which any value can be attached,
were never produced on any variety of subjects but by a man, who being
possessed of more than usual organic sensibility, had also thought long and
deeply. For our continued influxes of feeling are modified and directed by our
thoughts, which are indeed the representatives of all our past feelings; and, as
by contemplating the relation of these general representatives to each other
we discover what is really important to men, so, by the repetition and
continuance of this act, our feelings will be connected with important
subjects, till at length, if we be originally possessed of much sensibility, such
habits of mind will be produced, that, by obeying blindly and mechanically the
impulses of those habits, we shall describe objects, and utter sentiments, of
such a nature and in such connection with each other, that the understanding
of the being to whom we address ourselves, if he be in a healthful state of

association, must necessarily be in some degree enlightened, and his affections ameliorated.

I have said that each of these poems has a purpose. I have also informed my Reader what this purpose will be found principally to be: namely, to illustrate the manner in which our feelings and ideas are associated in a state of excitement. But, speaking in language somewhat more appropriate, it is to follow the fluxes and refluxes of the mind when agitated by the great and simple affections of our nature. This object I have endeavoured in these short essays to attain by various means; by tracing the maternal passion through many of its more subtile windings, as in the poems of the *Idiot Boy* and the *Mad Mother;* by accompanying the last struggles of a human being, at the approach of death, cleaving in solitude to life and society, as in the Poem of the *Forsaken indian;* by showing, as in the Stanzas entitled *We Are Seven,* the perplexity and obscurity which in childhood attend our notion of death, or rather our utter inability to admit that notion; or by displaying the strength of fraternal, or to speak more philosophically, of moral attachment when early associated with the great and beautiful objects of nature, as in *The Brothers;* or, as in the Incident of *Simon Lee,* by placing my Reader in the way of receiving from ordinary moral sensations another and more salutary impression than we are accustomed to receive from them. It has also been part of my general purpose to attempt to sketch characters under the influence of less impassioned feelings, as in the *Two April Mornings, The Fountain, The Old Man Travelling, The Two Thieves,* &c. characters of which the elements are simple, belonging rather to nature than to manners, such as exist now, and will probably always exist, and which from their constitution may be distinctly and profitably contemplated. I will not abuse the indulgence of my Reader by dwelling longer upon this subject; but it is proper that I should mention one other circumstance which distinguishes these Poems from the popular Poetry of the day; it is this, that the feeling therein developed gives importance to the action and situation, and not the action and situation to the feeling. My meaning will be rendered perfectly intelligible by referring my Reader to the Poems entitled *Poor Susan* and the *Childless Father,* particularly to the last Stanza of the latter Poem.

I will not suffer a sense of false modesty to prevent me from asserting, that I point my Reader's attention to this mark of distinction, far less for the sake of these particular Poems than from the general importance of the subject. The subject is indeed important! For the human mind is capable of being excited without the application of gross and violent stimulants; and he must have a very faint perception of its beauty and dignity who does not know this, and who does not further know, that one being is elevated above another, in proportion as he possesses this capability. It has therefore appeared to me, that to endeavour to produce or enlarge this capability is one of the best services in which, at any period, a Writer can be engaged; but this service, excellent at all times, is especially so at the present day. For a multitude of causes, unknown to former times, are now acting with a combined force to blunt the discriminating powers of the mind, and unfitting it for all voluntary exertion to reduce it to a state of almost savage torpor. The most effective of these causes are the great national events which are daily taking place, and the increasing accumulation of men in cities, where the uniformity of their occupations produces a craving for extraordinary incident, which the rapid communication of intelligence hourly gratifies. To this tendency of life and manners the literature and theatrical exhibitions of the country have conformed them-selves. The invaluable works of our elder writers, I had almost said the works of Shakespeare and Milton, are driven into neglect by frantic novels, sickly and stupid German Tragedies, and deluges of idle and extravagant stories in verse.—When I think upon this degrading thirst after outrageous stimulation, I am almost ashamed to have spoken of the feeble effort with which I have endeavoured to counteract it; and, reflecting upon the magnitude of the general evil, I should be oppressed with no dishonorable melancholy, had I not a deep impression of certain inherent and indestructible qualities of the human mind, and likewise of certain powers in the great and permanent objects that act upon it, which are equally inherent and indestructible; and did I not further add to this impression a belief, that the time is approaching when the evil will be systematically opposed, by men of greater powers, and with far more distinguished success.

Having dwelt thus long on the subjects and aim of these Poems, I shall request the Reader's permission to apprize him of a few circumstances relating to their *style*, in order, among other reasons, that I may not be censured for not having performed what I never attempted. The Reader will find that person-ifications of abstract ideas rarely occur in these volumes; and, I hope, are utterly rejected as an ordinary device to elevate the style, and raise it above prose. I have proposed to myself to imitate, and, as far as is possible, to adopt the very language of men; and assuredly such personifications do not make any natural or regular part of that language. They are, indeed, a figure of speech occasionally prompted by passion, and I have made use of them as such; but I have endeavoured utterly to reject them as a mechanical device of style, or as a family language which Writers in metre seem to lay claim to by prescription. I have wished to keep my Reader in the company of flesh and blood, persuaded that by so doing I shall interest him. I am, however, well aware that others who pursue a different track may interest him likewise; I do not interfere with their claim, I only wish to prefer a different claim of my own. There will also be found in these volumes little of what is usually called poetic diction; I have taken as much pains to avoid it as others ordinarily take to produce it; this I have done for the reason already alleged, to bring my language near to the language of men, and further, because the pleasure which I have proposed to myself to impart is of a kind very different from that which is supposed by many persons to be the proper object of poetry. I do not know how, without being culpably particular, I can give my Reader a more exact notion of the style in which I wished these poems to be written, than by informing him that I have at all times endeavoured to look steadily at my subject, consequently, I hope that there is in these Poems little falsehood of description, and that my ideas are expressed in language fitted to their respective importance. Something I must have gained by this practice, as it is friendly to one property of all good poetry, namely good sense; but it has necessarily cut me off from a large portion of phrases and figures of speech which from father to son have long been regarded as the common inheritance of Poets. I have also thought it expedient to restrict myself still further, having abstained from the use of many expressions, in themselves proper and beautiful, but which have been foolishly repeated by bad Poets, till such feelings of disgust are connected with them as it is scarcely possible by any art of association to overpower.

If in a poem there should be found a series of lines, or even a single line, in which the language, though naturally arranged, and according to the strict laws of metre, does not differ from that of prose, there is a numerous class of critics, who, when they stumble upon these prosaisms, as they call them, imagine that they have made a notable discovery, and exult over the Poet as over a man ignorant of his own profession. Now these men would establish a canon of criticism which the Reader will conclude he must utterly reject, if he wishes to be pleased with these volumes. And it would be a most easy task to prove to him, that not only the language of a large portion of every good poem, even of the most elevated character, must necessarily, except with reference to the metre, in no respect differ from that of good prose, but likewise that some of the most interesting parts of the best poems will be found to be strictly the language of prose, when prose is well written. The truth of this assertion might be demonstrated by innumerable passages from almost all the poetical writings, even of Milton himself. I have not space for much quotation; but, to illustrate the subject in a general manner, I will here adduce a short composition of Gray, who was at the head of those who, by their reasonings, have attempted to widen the space of separation betwixt Prose and Metrical composition, and was more than any other man curiously elaborate in the structure of his own poetic diction.

> In vain to me the smiling mornings shine,
> And reddening Phoebus lifts his golden fire:
> The birds in vain their amorous descant join,
> Or cheerful fields resume their green attire.
> These ears, alas! for other notes repine;
> *A different object do these eyes require;*
> *My lonely anguish melts no heart but mine;*
> *And in my breast the imperfect joys expire;*
> Yet morning smiles the busy race to cheer,
> And new-born pleasure brings to happier men;
> The fields to all their wonted tribute bear;
> To warm their little loves the birds complain.
> *I fruitless mourn to him that cannot hear,*
> *And weep the more because I weep in vain.*

It will easily be perceived that the only part of this Sonnet which is of any value is the lines printed in Italics: it is equally obvious, that, except in the rhyme, and in the use of the single word "fruitless" for fruitlessly, which is so far a defect, the language of these lines does in no respect differ from that of prose.

By the foregoing quotation I have shown that the language of Prose may yet be well adapted to Poetry; and I have previously asserted that a large portion of the language of every good poem can in no respect differ from that of good Prose. I will go further. I do not doubt that it may be safely affirmed, that there neither is, nor can be, any essential difference between the language of prose and metrical composition. We are fond of tracing the resemblance between Poetry and Painting, and, accordingly, we call them Sisters: but where shall we find bonds of connection sufficiently strict to typify the affinity betwixt metrical and prose composition? They both speak by and to the same organs; the bodies in which both of them are clothed may be said to be of the same substance, their affections are kindred, and almost identical, not necessarily differing even in degree; Poetry sheds no tears "such as Angels weep," but natural and human tears; she can boast of no celestial Ichor that distinguishes her vital juices from those of prose; the same human blood circulates through the veins of them both.

If it be affirmed that rhyme and metrical arrangement of themselves constitute a distinction which overturns what I have been saying on the strict affinity of metrical language with that of prose, and paves the way for other artificial distinctions which the mind voluntarily admits, I answer that the language of such Poetry as I am recommending is, as far as is possible, a selection of the language really spoken by men; that this selection, wherever it is made with true taste and feeling, will of itself form a distinction far greater than would at first be imagined, and will entirely separate the composition from the vulgarity and meanness of ordinary life; and, if metre be superadded thereto, I believe that a dissimilitude will be produced altogether sufficient for the gratification of a rational mind. What other distinction would we have? Whence is it to come? And where is it to exist? Not, surely, where the Poet speaks through the mouths of his characters: it cannot be necessary here, either for elevation of style, or any of its supposed ornaments; for, if the Poet's subject be judiciously chosen, it will naturally, and upon fit occasion, lead him to passions the language of which, if selected truly and judiciously, must necessarily be dignified and variegated, and alive with metaphors and figures. I forbear to speak of an incongruity which would shock the intelligent Reader, should the Poet interweave any foreign splendour of his own with that which the passion naturally suggests: it is sufficient to say that such addition is unnecessary. And, surely, it is more probable that those passages, which with propriety abound with metaphors and figures, will have their due effect, if, upon other occasions where the passions are of a milder character, the style also be subdued and temperate.

But, as the pleasure which I hope to give by the Poems I now present to the Reader must depend entirely on just notions upon this subject, and, as it is in itself of the highest importance to our taste and moral feelings, I cannot content myself with these detached remarks. And if, in what I am about to say, it shall appear to some that my labour is unnecessary, and that I am like a man fighting a battle without enemies, I would remind such persons that, whatever may be the language outwardly holden by men, a practical faith in the opinions which I am wishing to establish is almost unknown. If my conclusions are admitted, and carried as far as they must be carried if admitted at all, our judgments concerning the works of the greatest Poets both ancient and modern will be far different from what they are at present, both when we praise, and when we censure: and our moral feelings influencing, and influenced by these judgments will, I believe, be corrected and purified.

Taking up the subject, then, upon general grounds, I ask what is meant by the word Poet? What is a Poet? To whom does he address himself? And what language is to be expected from him? He is a man speaking to men: a man, it is true, endued with more lively sensibility, more enthusiasm and tenderness, who has a greater knowledge of human nature, and a more comprehensive soul, than are supposed to be common among mankind; a man pleased with his own passions and volitions, and who rejoices more than other men in the spirit of life that is in him; delighting to contemplate similar volitions and passions as manifested in the goings-on of the Universe, and habitually impelled to create them where he does not find them. To these qualities he has added a disposition to be affected more than other men by absent things as if they were present; an ability of conjuring up in himself passions, which are indeed far from being the same as those produced by real events, yet (especially in those parts of the general sympathy which are pleasing and delightful) do more nearly resemble the passions produced by real events, than any thing which, from the motions of their own minds merely, other men are accustomed to feel in themselves; whence, and from practice, he has acquired a greater readiness and power in expressing what he thinks and feels, and especially those thoughts and feelings which, by his own choice, or from the structure of his own mind, arise in him without immediate external excitement.

But, whatever portion of this faculty we may suppose even the greatest Poet to possess, there cannot be a doubt but that the language which it will suggest to him, must, in liveliness and truth, fall far short of that which is uttered by men in real life, under the actual pressure of those passions, certain shadows of which the Poet thus produces, or feels to be produced, in himself. However exalted a notion we would wish to cherish of the character of a Poet, it is obvious, that, while he describes and imitates passions, his situation is altogether slavish and mechanical, compared with the freedom and power of real and substantial action and suffering. So that it will be the wish of the Poet to bring his feelings near to those of the persons whose feelings he describes, nay, for short spaces of time perhaps, to let himself slip into an entire delusion, and even confound and identify his own feelings with theirs; modifying only the language which is thus suggested to him, by a consideration that he describes for a particular purpose, that of giving pleasure. Here, then, he will apply the principle on which I have so much insisted, namely, that of selection; on this he will depend for removing what would otherwise be painful or disgusting in the passion; he will feel that there is no necessity to trick out or to elevate nature: and, the more industriously he applies this principle, the deeper will be his faith that no words, which his fancy or imagination can suggest, will be to be compared with those which are the emanations of reality and truth.

But it may be said by those who do not object to the general spirit of these remarks, that, as it is impossible for the Poet to produce upon all occasions language as exquisitely fitted for the passion as that which the real passion itself suggests, it is proper that he should consider himself as in the situation of a translator, who deems himself justified when he substitutes excellences of another kind for those which are unattainable by him; and endeavours occasionally to surpass his original, in order to make some amends for the general inferiority to which he feels that he must submit. But this would be to encourage idleness and unmanly despair. Further, it is the language of men who speak of what they do not understand; who talk of Poetry as of a matter of amusement and idle pleasure; who will converse with us as gravely about a *taste* for Poetry, as they express it, as if it were a thing as indifferent as a taste for Rope-dancing, or Frontiniac or Sherry. Aristotle, I have been told, hath said, that Poetry is the most philosophic of all writing: it is so: its object is truth, not individual and local, but general, and operative; not standing upon external testimony, but carried alive into the heart by passion; truth which is its own testimony, which gives strength and divinity to the tribunal to which it appeals, and receives them from the same tribunal. Poetry is the image of man and nature. The obstacles which stand in the way of the fidelity of the Biographer and Historian, and of their consequent utility, are incalculably greater than those which are to be encountered by the Poet who has an adequate notion of the dignity of his art. The Poet writes under one restriction only, namely, that of the necessity of giving immediate pleasure to a human Being possessed of that information which may be expected from him, not as a lawyer, a physician, a mariner, an astronomer or a natural philosopher, but as a Man. Except this one restriction, there is no object standing between the Poet and the image of things; between this, and the Biographer and Historian there are a thousand.

Nor let this necessity of producing immediate pleasure be considered as a degradation of the Poet's art. It is far otherwise. It is an acknowledgment of the beauty of the universe, an acknowledgment the more sincere, because it is not formal, but indirect; it is a task light and easy to him who looks at the world in the spirit of love: further, it is a homage paid to the native and naked dignity of man, to the grand elementary principle of pleasure, by which he knows, and feels, and lives, and moves. We have no sympathy but what is propagated by pleasure: I would not be misunderstood; but wherever we sympathize with pain it will be found that the sympathy is produced and carried on by subtle combinations with pleasure. We have no knowledge, that is, no general principles drawn from the contemplation of particular facts, but what has been built up by pleasure, and exists in us by pleasure alone. The Man of Science, the Chemist and Mathematician, whatever difficulties and disgusts they may have had to struggle with, know and feel this. However painful may be the objects with which the Anatomist's knowledge is connected, he feels that his knowledge is pleasure; and where he has no pleasure he has no knowledge. What then does the Poet? He considers man and the objects that surround him as acting and re-acting upon each other, so as to produce an infinite complexity of pain and pleasure; he considers man in his own nature and in his ordinary life as contemplating this with a certain quantity of immediate knowledge, with certain convictions, intuitions, and deductions which by habit become of the nature of intuitions; he considers him as looking upon this complex scene of ideas and sensations, and finding every where objects that immediately excite in him sympathies which, from the necessities of his nature, are accompanied by an overbalance of enjoyment.

To this knowledge which all men carry about with them, and to these sympathies in which without any other discipline than that of our daily life we are fitted to take delight, the Poet principally directs his attention. He considers man and nature as essentially adapted to each other, and the mind of man as naturally the mirror of the fairest and most interesting qualities of nature. And thus the Poet, prompted by this feeling of pleasure which accompanies him through the whole course of his studies, converses with general nature with affections akin to those, which, through labour and length of time, the Man of Science has raised up in himself, by conversing with those particular parts of nature which are the objects of his studies. The knowledge both of the Poet and the Man of Science is pleasure; but the knowledge of the one cleaves to us as a necessary part of our existence, our natural and unalienable inheritance; the other is a personal and individual acquisition, slow to come to us, and by no habitual and direct sympathy connecting us with our fellow-beings. The Man of Science seeks truth as a remote and unknown benefactor; he cherishes and loves it in his solitude: the Poet, singing a song in which all human beings join with him, rejoices in the presence of truth as our visible friend and hourly companion. Poetry is the breath and finer spirit of all knowledge; it is the impassioned expression which is in the countenance of all Science. Emphatically may it be said of the Poet, as Shakespeare hath said of man, "that he looks before and after." He is the rock of defence of human nature; an upholder and preserver, carrying every where with him relationship and love. In spite of difference of soil and climate, of language and manners, of laws and customs, in spite of things silently gone out of mind and things violently destroyed, the Poet binds together by passion and knowledge the vast empire of human society, as it is spread over the whole earth, and over all time. The objects of the Poet's thoughts are every where; though the eyes and senses of man are, it is true, his favourite guides, yet he will follow wheresoever he can find an atmosphere of sensation in which to move his wings. Poetry is the first and last of all knowledge—it is as immortal as the heart of man. If the labours of Men of Science should ever create any material revolution, direct or indirect, in our condition, and in the impressions which we habitually receive, the Poet will sleep then no more than at present, but he will be ready to follow the steps of the Man of Science, not only in those general indirect effects, but he will be at his side, carrying sensation into the midst of the objects of the Science itself. The remotest discoveries of the Chemist, the Botanist, or Mineralogist, will be as proper objects of the Poet's art as any upon which it can be employed, if the time should ever come when these things shall be familiar to us, and the relations under which they are contemplated by the followers of these respective Sciences shall be manifestly and palpably material to us as enjoying and suffering beings. If the time should ever come when what is now called Science, thus familiarized to men, shall be ready to put on, as it were, a form of flesh and blood, the Poet will lend his divine spirit to aid the transfiguration, and will welcome the Being thus produced, as a dear and genuine inmate of the household of man.—It is not, then, to be supposed that any one, who holds that sublime notion of Poetry which I have attempted to convey, will break in upon the sanctity and truth of his pictures by transitory and accidental ornaments, and endeavour to excite admiration of himself by arts, the necessity of which must manifestly depend upon the assumed meanness of his subject.

What I have thus far said applies to Poetry in general; but especially to those parts of composition where the Poet speaks through the mouths of his characters; and upon this point it appears to have such weight that I will conclude, there are few persons of good sense, who would not allow that the dramatic parts of composition are defective, in proportion as they deviate from the real language of nature, and are coloured by a diction of the Poet's own, either peculiar to him as an individual Poet, or belonging simply to Poets in general, to a body of men who, from the circumstance of their compositions being in metre, it is expected will employ a particular language.

It is not, then, in the dramatic parts of composition that we look for this distinction of language; but still it may be proper and necessary where the Poet speaks to us in his own person and character. To this I answer by referring my Reader to the description which I have before given of a Poet. Among the qualities which I have enumerated as principally conducing to form a Poet, is implied nothing differing in kind from other men, but only in degree. The sum of what I have there said is, that the Poet is chiefly distinguished from other men by a greater promptness to think and feel without immediate external excitement, and a greater power in expressing such thoughts and feelings as are produced in him in that manner. But these passions and thoughts and feelings are the general passions and thoughts and feelings of men. And with what are they connected? Undoubtedly with our moral sentiments and animal sensations, and with the causes which excite these; with the operations of the elements and the appearances of the visible universe; with storm and sun-shine, with the revolutions of the seasons, with cold and heat, with loss of friends and kindred, with injuries and resentments, gratitude and hope, with fear and sorrow. These, and the like, are the sensations and objects which the Poet describes, as they are the sensations of other men, and the objects which interest them. The Poet thinks and feels in the spirit of the passions of men. How, then, can his language differ in any material degree from that of all other men who feel vividly and see clearly? It might be *proved* that it is impossible.

But supposing that this were not the case, the Poet might then be allowed to use a peculiar language when expressing his feelings for his own gratification, or that of men like himself. But Poets do not write for Poets alone, but for men. Unless therefore we are advocates for that admiration which depends upon ignorance, and that pleasure which arises from hearing what we do not understand, the Poet must descend from this supposed height, and, in order to excite rational sympathy, he must express himself as other men express themselves. To this it may be added, that while he is only selecting from the real language of men, or, which amounts to the same thing, composing accurately in the spirit of such selection, he is treading upon safe ground, and we know what we are to expect from him. Our feelings are the same with respect to metre; for, as it may be proper to remind the Reader, the distinction of metre is regular and uniform, and not like that which is produced by what is usually called poetic diction, arbitrary, and subject to infinite caprices upon which no calculation whatever can be made. In the one case, the Reader is utterly at the mercy of the Poet respecting what imagery or diction he may choose to connect with the passion, whereas, in the other, the metre obeys certain laws, to which the Poet and Reader both willingly submit because they are certain, and because no interference is made by them with the passion but such as the concurring testimony of ages has shown to heighten and improve the pleasure which co-exists with it.

It will now be proper to answer an obvious question, namely, Why, professing these opinions, have I written in verse? To this, in addition to such answer as is included in what I have already said, I reply in the first place, Because, however I may have restricted myself, there is still left open to me what confessedly constitutes the most valuable object of all writing, whether in prose or verse, the great and universal passions of men, the most general and interesting of their occupations, and the entire world of nature, from which I am at liberty to supply myself with endless combinations of forms and imagery. Now, supposing for a moment that whatever is interesting in these objects may be as vividly described in prose, why am I to be condemned, if to such description I have endeavoured to superadd the charm which, by the consent of all nations, is acknowledged to exist in metrical language? To this, by such as are unconvinced by what I have already said, it may be answered, that a very small part of the pleasure given by Poetry depends upon the metre, and that it is injudicious to write in metre, unless it be accompanied with the other artificial distinctions of style with which metre is usually accompanied, and that by such deviation more will be lost from the shock which will be thereby given to the Reader's associations, than will be counterbalanced by any pleasure which he can derive from the general power of numbers. In answer to those who still contend for the necessity of accompanying metre with certain appropriate colours of style in order to the accomplishment of its appropriate end, and who also, in my opinion, greatly under-rate the power of metre in itself, it might perhaps, as far as relates to these Poems, have been almost sufficient to observe, that poems are extant, written upon more humble subjects, and in a more naked and simple style than I have aimed at, which poems have continued to give pleasure from generation to generation. Now, if nakedness and simplicity be a defect, the fact here mentioned affords a strong presumption that poems somewhat less naked and simple are capable of affording pleasure at the present day; and, what I wished *chiefly* to attempt, at present, was to justify myself for having written under the impression of this belief.

But I might point out various causes why, when the style is manly, and the subject of some importance, words metrically arranged will long continue to impart such a pleasure to mankind as he who is sensible of the extent of that pleasure will be desirous to impart. The end of Poetry is to produce excitement in coexistence with an over-balance of pleasure. Now, by the supposition, excitement is an unusual and irregular state of the mind; ideas and feelings do not in that state succeed each other in accustomed order. But, if the words by which this excitement is produced are in themselves powerful, or the images and feelings have an undue proportion of pain connected with them, there is some danger that the excitement may be carried beyond its proper bounds. Now the co-presence of something regular, something to which the mind has been accustomed in various moods and in a less excited state, cannot but have great efficacy in tempering and restraining the passion by an intertexture of ordinary feeling, and of feeling not strictly and necessarily connected with the passion. This is unquestionably true, and hence, though the opinion will at first appear paradoxical, from the tendency of metre to divest language in a certain degree of its reality, and thus to throw a sort of half consciousness of unsubstantial existence over the whole composition, there can be little doubt but that more pathetic situations and sentiments, that is, those which have a greater proportion of pain connected with them, may be endured in metrical composition, especially in rhyme, than in prose. The metre of the old ballads is very artless; yet they contain many passages which would illustrate this opinion, and, I hope, if the following Poems be attentively perused, similar instances will be found in them. This opinion may be further illustrated by appealing to the Reader's own experience of the reluctance with which he comes to the re-perusal of the distressful parts of Clarissa Harlowe, or the Gamester. While Shakespeare's writings, in the most pathetic scenes, never act upon us as pathetic beyond the bounds of pleasure—an effect which, in a much greater degree than might at first be imagined, is to be ascribed to small, but continual and regular impulses of pleasurable surprise from the metrical arrangement.—On the other hand (what it must be allowed will much more frequently happen) if the Poet's words should be incommensurate with the passion, and inadequate to raise the Reader to a height of desirable excitement, then, (unless the Poet's choice of his metre has been grossly injudicious) in the feelings of pleasure which the Reader has been accustomed to connect with metre in general, and in the feeling, whether cheerful or melancholy, which he has been accustomed to connect with that particular movement of metre, there will be found something which will greatly contribute to impart passion to the words, and to effect the complex end which the Poet proposes to himself.

If I had undertaken a systematic defence of the theory upon which these poems are written, it would have been my duty to develope the various causes upon which the pleasure received from metrical language depends. Among the chief of these causes is to be reckoned a principle which must be well known to those who have made any of the Arts the object of accurate reflection; I mean the pleasure which the mind derives from the perception of similitude in dissimilitude. This principle is the great spring of the activity of our minds, and their chief feeder. From this principle the direction of the sexual appetite, and all the passions connected with it, take their origin: it is the life of our ordinary conversation; and upon the accuracy with which similitude in dissimilitude, and dissimilitude in similitude are perceived, depend our taste and our moral feelings. It would not have been a useless employment to have applied this principle to the consideration of metre, and to have shown that metre is hence enabled to afford much pleasure, and to have pointed out in what manner that pleasure is produced. But my limits will not permit me to enter upon this subject, and I must content myself with a general summary.

I have said that Poetry is the spontaneous overflow of powerful feelings: it takes its origin from emotion recollected in tranquillity: the emotion is contemplated till by a species of reaction the tranquillity gradually disappears, and an emotion, kindred to that which was before the subject of contempla- tion, is gradually produced, and does itself actually exist in the mind. In this mood successful composition generally begins, and in a mood similar to this it is carried on; but the emotion, of whatever kind and in whatever degree, from various causes is qualified by various pleasures, so that in describing any passions whatsoever, which are voluntarily described, the mind will upon the whole be in a state of enjoyment. Now, if Nature be thus cautious in preserving in a state of enjoyment a being thus employed, the Poet ought to profit by the lesson thus held forth to him, and ought especially to take care, that whatever passions he communicates to his Reader, those passions, if his Reader's mind be sound and vigorous, should always be accompanied with an overbalance of pleasure. Now the music of harmonious metrical language, the sense of difficulty overcome, and the blind association of pleasure which has been previously received from works of rhyme or metre of the same or similar construction, an indistinct perception perpetually renewed of language closely resembling that of real life, and yet, in the circumstance of metre, differing from it so widely, all these imperceptibly make up a complex feeling of delight, which is of the most important use in tempering the painful feeling which will always be found intermingled with powerful descriptions of the deeper passions. This effect is always produced in pathetic and impassioned poetry; while, in lighter compositions, the ease and gracefulness with which the Poet manages his numbers are themselves confessedly a principal source of the gratification of the Reader. I might perhaps include all which it is *necessary* to say upon this subject by affirming, what few persons will deny, that, of two descriptions, either of passions, manners, or characters, each of them equally well executed, the one in prose and the other in verse, the verse will be read a hundred times where the prose is read once. We see that Pope, by the power of verse alone, has contrived to render the plainest common sense interesting, and even frequently to invest it with the appearance of passion. In consequence of these convictions I related in metre the Tale of *Goody Blake and Harry Gill,* which is one of the rudest of this collection. I wished to draw attention to the truth, that the power of the human imagination is sufficient to produce such changes even in our physical nature as might almost appear miraculous. The truth is an important one; the fact (for it is a *fact*) is a valuable illustration of it. And I have the satisfaction of knowing that it has been communicated to many hundreds of people who would never have heard of it, had it not been narrated as a Ballad, and in a more impressive metre than is usual in Ballads.

Having thus explained a few of the reasons why I have written in verse, and why I have chosen subjects from common life, and endeavoured to bring my language near to the real language of men, if I have been too minute in pleading my own cause, I have at the same time been treating a subject of general interest; and it is for this reason that I request the Reader's permission to add a few words with reference solely to these particular poems, and to some defects which will probably be found in them. I am sensible that my associations must have sometimes been particular instead of general, and that, consequently, giving to things a false importance, sometimes from diseased impulses I may have written upon unworthy subjects; but I am less apprehensive on this account, than that my language may frequently have suffered from those arbitrary connections of feelings and ideas with particular words and phrases, from which no man can altogether protect himself. Hence I have no doubt, that, in some instances, feelings even of the ludicrous may be given to my Readers by expressions which appeared to me tender and pathetic. Such faulty expressions, were I convinced they were faulty at present, and that they must necessarily continue to be so, I would willingly take all reasonable pains to correct. But it is dangerous to make these alterations on the simple authority of a few individuals, or even of certain classes of men; for where the understanding of an Author is not convinced, or his feelings altered, this cannot be done without great injury to himself: for his own feelings are his stay and support, and, if he sets them aside in one instance, he may be induced to repeat this act till his mind loses all confidence in itself, and becomes utterly debilitated. To this it may be added, that the Reader ought never to forget that he is himself exposed to the same errors as the Poet, and perhaps in a much greater degree: for there can be no presumption in saying, that it is not probable he will be so well acquainted with the various stages of meaning through which words have passed, or with the fickleness or stability of the relations of particular ideas to each other; and above all, since he is so much less interested in the subject, he may decide lightly and carelessly.

Long as I have detained my Reader, I hope he will permit me to caution him against a mode of false criticism which has been applied to Poetry in which the language closely resembles that of life and nature. Such verses have been triumphed over in parodies of which Dr. Johnson's stanza is a fair specimen.

> "I put my hat upon my head,
> And walk'd into the Strand,
> And there I met another man
> Whose hat was in his hand."

Immediately under these lines I will place one of the most justly admired stanzas of the "*Babes* in the Wood."

> "These pretty Babes with hand in hand
> Went wandering up and down;
> But never more they saw the Man
> Approaching from the Town."

In both these stanzas the words, and the order of the words, in no respect differ from the most unimpassioned conversation. There are words in both, for example, "the Strand," and "the Town," connected with none but the most familiar ideas; yet the one stanza we admit as admirable, and the other as a fair example of the superlatively contemptible. Whence arises this difference? Not from the metre, not from the language, not from the order of the words; but the *matter* expressed in Dr. Johnson's stanza is contemptible. The proper method of treating trivial and simple verses, to which Dr. Johnson's stanza would be a fair parallelism, is not to say, This is a bad kind of poetry, or This is not poetry; but This wants sense; it is neither interesting in itself, nor can *lead* to any thing interesting; the images neither originate in that sane state of feeling which arises out of thought, nor can excite thought or feeling in the Reader. This is the only sensible manner of dealing with such verses. Why trouble yourself about the species till you have previously decided upon the genus? Why take pains to prove that an ape is not a Newton, when it is self-evident that he is not a man?

I have one request to make of my Reader, which is, that in judging these Poems he would decide by his own feelings genuinely, and not by reflection upon what will probably be the judgment of others. How common is it to hear a person say, "I myself do not object to this style of composition, or this or that expression, but to such and such classes of people it will appear mean or ludicrous." This mode of criticism, so destructive of all sound unadulterated judgment, is almost universal: I have therefore to request, that the Reader would abide independently by his own feelings, and that if he finds himself affected he would not suffer such conjectures to interfere with his pleasure.

If an Author by any single composition has impressed us with respect for his talents, it is useful to consider this as affording a presumption, that, on other occasions where we have been displeased, he nevertheless may not have written ill or absurdly; and, further, to give him so much credit for this one composition as may induce us to review what has displeased us with more care than we should otherwise have bestowed upon it. This is not only an act of justice, but, in our decisions upon poetry especially, may conduce in a high degree to the improvement of our own taste: for an *accurate* taste in poetry, and in all the other arts, as Sir Joshua Reynolds has observed, is an *acquired* talent, which can only be produced by thought, and a long continued intercourse with the best models of composition. This is mentioned, not with so ridiculous a purpose as to prevent the most inexperienced Reader from judging for himself, (I have already said that I wish him to judge for himself;) but merely to temper the rashness of decision, and to suggest, that, if Poetry be a subject on which much time has not been bestowed, the judgment may be erroneous; and that in many cases it necessarily will be so.

I know that nothing would have so effectually contributed to further the end which I have in view, as to have shown of what kind the pleasure is, and how that pleasure is produced, which is confessedly produced by metrical composition essentially different from that which I have here endeavoured to recommend: for the Reader will say that he has been pleased by such composition; and what can I do more for him? The power of any art is limited; and he will suspect, that, if I propose to furnish him with new friends, it is only upon condition of his abandoning his old friends. Besides, as I have said, the Reader is himself conscious of the pleasure which he has received from such composition, composition to which he has peculiarly attached the endearing name of Poetry; and all men feel an habitual gratitude, and something of an honorable bigotry for the objects which have long continued to please them; we not only wish to be pleased, but to be pleased in that particular way in which we have been accustomed to be pleased. There is a host of arguments in these feelings; and I should be the less able to combat them successfully, as I am willing to allow, that, in order entirely to enjoy the Poetry which I am recommending, it would be necessary to give up much of what is ordinarily enjoyed. But, would my limits have permitted me to point out how this pleasure is produced, I might have removed many obstacles, and assisted my Reader in perceiving that the powers of language are not so limited as he may suppose; and that it is possible that poetry may give other enjoyments, of a purer, more lasting, and more exquisite nature. This part of my subject I have not altogether neglected; but it has been less my present aim to prove, that the interest excited by some other kinds of poetry is less vivid, and less worthy of the nobler powers of the mind, than to offer reasons for presuming, that, if the object which I have proposed to myself were adequately attained, a species of poetry would be produced, which is genuine poetry; in its nature well adapted to interest mankind permanently, and likewise important in the multiplicity and quality of its moral relations.

From what has been said, and from a perusal of the Poems, the Reader will be able clearly to perceive the object which I have proposed to myself: he will determine how far I have attained this object; and, what is a much more important question, whether it be worth attaining: and upon the decision of these two questions will rest my claim to the approbation of the public.

Appendix to the Preface

1802

As perhaps I have no right to expect from a Reader of an Introduction to a volume of Poems that attentive perusal without which it is impossible, imperfectly as I have been compelled to express my meaning, that what I have said in the Preface should throughout be fully understood, I am the more anxious to give an exact notion of the sense in which I use the phrase *poetic diction;* and for this purpose I will here add a few words concerning the origin of the phraseology which I have condemned under that name.—The earliest Poets of all nations generally wrote from passion excited by real events; they wrote naturally, and as men: feeling powerfully as they did, their language was daring, and figurative. In succeeding times, Poets, and men ambitious of the fame of Poets, perceiving the influence of such language, and desirous of producing the same effect, without having the same animating passion, set themselves to a mechanical adoption of those figures of speech, and made use of them, sometimes with propriety, but much more frequently applied them to feelings and ideas with which they had no natural connection whatsoever. A language was thus insensibly produced, differing materially from the real language of men in *any situation.* The Reader or Hearer of this distorted language found himself in a perturbed and unusual state of mind: when affected by the genuine language of passion he had been in a perturbed and unusual state of mind also: in both cases he was willing that his common judgment and understanding should be laid asleep, and he had no instinctive and infallible perception of the true to make him reject the false; the one served as a passport for the other. The agitation and confusion of mind were in both cases delightful, and no wonder if he confounded the one with the other, and believed them both to be produced by the same, or similar causes. Besides, the Poet spake to him in the character of a man to be looked up to, a man of genius and authority. Thus, and from a variety of other causes, this distorted language was received with admiration; and Poets, it is probable, who had before contented themselves for the most part with misapplying only expressions which at first had been dictated by real passion, carried the abuse still further, and introduced phrases composed apparently in the spirit of the original figurative language of passion, yet altogether of their own invention, and distinguished by various degrees of wanton deviation from good sense and nature.

It is indeed true that the language of the earliest Poets was felt to differ materially from ordinary language, because it was the language of extraordinary occasions; but it was really spoken by men, language which the Poet himself had uttered when he had been affected by the events which he described, or which he had heard uttered by those around him. To this language it is probable that metre of some sort or other was early superadded. This separated the genuine language of Poetry still further from common life, so that whoever read or heard the poems of these earliest Poets felt himself moved in a way in which he had not been accustomed to be moved in real life, and by causes manifestly different from those which acted upon him in real life. This was the great temptation to all the corruptions which have followed: under the protection of this feeling succeeding Poets constructed a phraseology which had one thing, it is true, in common with the genuine language of poetry, namely, that it was not heard in ordinary conversation; that it was unusual. But the first Poets, as I have said, spake a language which, though unusual, was still the language of men. This circumstance, however, was disregarded by their successors; they found that they could please by easier means: they became proud of a language which they themselves had invented, and which was uttered only by themselves; and, with the spirit of a fraternity, they arrogated it to themselves as their own. In process of time metre became a symbol or promise of this unusual language, and whoever took upon him to write in metre, according as he possessed more or less of true poetic genius, introduced less or more of this adulterated phraseology into his compositions, and the true and the false became so inseparably interwoven that the taste of men was gradually perverted; and this language was received as a natural language; and at length, by the influence of books upon men, did to a certain degree really become so. Abuses of this kind were imported from one nation to another, and with the progress of refinement this diction became daily more and more corrupt, thrusting out of sight the plain humanities of nature by a motley masquerade of tricks, quaintnesses, hieroglyphics, and enigmas.

It would be highly interesting to point out the causes of the pleasure given by this extravagant and absurd language: but this is not the place; it depends upon a great variety of causes, but upon none perhaps more than its influence in impressing a notion of the peculiarity and exaltation of the Poet's character, and in flattering the Reader's self-love by bringing him nearer to a sympathy with that character; an effect which is accomplished by unsettling ordinary habits of thinking, and thus assisting the Reader to approach to that perturbed and dizzy state of mind in which if he does not find himself, he imagines that he is *balked* of a peculiar enjoyment which poetry can, and ought to bestow.

The sonnet which I have quoted from Gray, in the Preface, except the lines printed in Italics, consists of little else but this diction, though not of the worst kind; and indeed, if I may be permitted to say so, it is far too common in the best writers, both antient and modern. Perhaps I can in no way, by positive example, more easily give my Reader a notion of what I mean by the phrase *poetic diction* than by referring him to a comparison between the metrical paraphrases which we have of passages in the old and new Testament, and those passages as they exist in our common Translation. See Pope's "Messiah" throughout, Prior's "Did sweeter sounds adorn my flowing tongue," &c. &c. "Though I speak with the tongues of men and of angels," &c. &c. See 1st Corinthians, chapter xiiith. By way of immediate example, take the following of Dr. Johnson:

> "Turn on the prudent Ant thy heedless eyes,
> Observe her labours, Sluggard, and be wise;
> No stern command, no monitory voice,
> Prescribes her duties, or directs her choice;
> Yet, timely provident, she hastes away
> To snatch the blessings of a plenteous day;
> When fruitful Summer loads the teeming plain,
> She crops the harvest and she stores the grain.
> How long shall sloth usurp thy useless hours,
> Unnerve thy vigour, and enchain thy powers?
> While artful shades thy downy couch enclose,
> And soft solicitation courts repose,
> Amidst the drowsy charms of dull delight,
> Year chases year with unremitted flight,
> Till want now following, fraudulent and slow,
> Shall spring to seize thee, like an ambushed foe."

From this hubbub of words pass to the original. "Go to the Ant, thou Sluggard, consider her ways, and be wise: which having no guide, overseer, or ruler, provideth her meat in the summer, and gathereth her food in the harvest. How long wilt thou sleep, O Sluggard? when wilt thou arise out of thy sleep? Yet a little sleep, a little slumber, a little folding of the hands to sleep. So shall thy poverty come as one that travaileth, and thy want as an armed man." Proverbs, chap. vith.

One more quotation and I have done. It is from Cowper's verses supposed to be written by Alexander Selkirk:

> "Religion! what treasure untold
> Resides in that heavenly word!
> More precious than silver and gold,
> Or all that this earth can afford.
> But the sound of the church-going bell
> These valleys and rocks never heard,
> Ne'er sighed at the sound of a knell,
> Or smiled when a sabbath appeared.
> Ye winds, that have made me your sport,
> Convey to this desolate shore
> Some cordial endearing report
> Of a land I must visit no more.
> My Friends, do they now and then send
> A wish or a thought after me?
> O tell me I yet have a friend,
> Though a friend I am never to see."

I have quoted this passage as an instance of three different styles of composition. The first four lines are poorly expressed; some Critics would call the language prosaic; the fact is, it would be bad prose, so bad, that it is scarcely worse in metre. The epithet "church-going" applied to a bell, and that by so chaste a writer as Cowper, is an instance of the strange abuses which Poets have introduced into their language till they and their Readers take them as matters of course, if they do not single them out expressly as objects of admiration. The two lines "Ne'er sigh'd at the sound," &c. are, in my opinion, an instance of the language of passion wrested from its proper use, and, from the mere circumstance of the composition being in metre, applied upon an occasion that does not justify such violent expressions; and I should condemn the passage, though perhaps few Readers will agree with me, as vicious poetic diction. The last stanza is throughout admirably expressed: it would be equally good whether in prose or verse, except that the Reader has an exquisite pleasure in seeing such natural language so naturally connected with metre. The beauty of this stanza tempts me here to add a sentiment which ought to be the pervading spirit of a system, detached parts of which have been imperfectly explained in the Preface,—namely, that in proportion as ideas and feelings are valuable, whether the composition be in prose or in verse, they require and exact one and the same language.

ESSAY,

SUPPLEMENTARY TO THE PREFACE

1815

By this time, I trust that the judicious Reader, who has now first become acquainted with these poems, is persuaded that a very senseless outcry has been raised against them and their Author.—Casually, and very rarely only, do I see any periodical publication, except a daily newspaper; but I am not wholly unacquainted with the spirit in which my most active and persevering Adversaries have maintained their hostility; nor with the impudent falsehoods and base artifices to which they have had recourse. These, as implying a consciousness on their parts that attacks honestly and fairly conducted would be unavailing, could not but have been regarded by me with triumph; had they been accompanied with such display of talents and information as might give weight to the opinions of the Writers, whether favourable or unfavourable. But the ignorance of those who have chosen to stand forth as my enemies, as far as I am acquainted with their enmity, has unfortunately been still more gross than their disingenuousness, and their incompetence more flagrant than their malice. The effect in the eyes of the discerning is indeed ludicrous: yet, contemptible as such men are, in return for the forced compliment paid me by their long-continued notice (which, as I have appeared so rarely before the public, no one can say has been solicited) I entreat them to spare themselves. The lash, which they are aiming at my productions, does, in fact, only fall on phantoms of their own brain; which, I grant, I am innocently instrumental in raising.—By what fatality the orb of my genius (for genius none of them seem to deny me) acts upon these men like the moon upon a certain description of patients, it would be irksome to inquire; nor would it consist with the respect which I owe myself to take further notice of opponents whom I internally despise.

With the young, of both sexes, Poetry is, like love, a passion; but, for much the greater part of those who have been proud of its power over their minds, a necessity soon arises of breaking the pleasing bondage; or it relaxes of itself;—the thoughts being occupied in domestic cares, or the time engrossed by business. Poetry then becomes only an occasional recreation; while to those whose existence passes away in a course of fashionable pleasure it is a species of luxurious amusement.—In middle and declining age, a scattered number of serious persons resort to poetry, as to religion, for a protection against the pressure of trivial employments, and as a consolation for the afflictions of life. And lastly, there are many, who, having been enamoured of this art, in their youth, have found leisure, after youth was spent, to cultivate general literature; in which poetry has continued to be comprehended *as a study*.

Into the above Classes the Readers of poetry may be divided; Critics abound in them all; but from the last only can opinions be collected of absolute value, and worthy to be depended upon, as prophetic of the destiny of a new work. The young, who in nothing can escape delusion, are especially subject to it in their intercourse with poetry. The cause, not so obvious as the fact is unquestionable, is the same as that from which erroneous judgments in this art, in the minds of men of all ages, chiefly proceed; but upon Youth it operates with peculiar force. The appropriate business of poetry (which, nevertheless, if genuine is as permanent as pure science) her appropriate employment, her privilege and her *duty,* is to treat of things not as they *are,* but as they *appear;* not as they exist in themselves, but as they *seem* to exist to the *senses* and to the *passions.* What a world of delusion does this acknowledged principle prepare for the inexperienced! what temptations to go astray are here held forth for those whose thoughts have been little disciplined by the understanding, and whose feelings revolt from the sway of reason!—When a juvenile Reader is in the height of his rapture with some vicious passage, should experience throw in doubts, or common-sense suggest suspicions, a lurking consciousness that the realities of the Muse are but shows, and that her liveliest excitements are raised by transient shocks of conflicting feeling and successive assemblages of contradictory thoughts—is ever at hand to justify extravagance, and to sanction absurdity. But, it may be asked, as these illusions are unavoidable, and no doubt eminently useful to the mind as a process, what good can be gained by making observations the tendency of which is to diminish the confidence of youth in its feelings, and thus to abridge its innocent and even profitable pleasures? The reproach implied in the question could not be warded off, if Youth were incapable of being delighted with what is truly excellent; or if these errors always terminated of themselves in due season. But, with the majority, though their force be abated, they continue through life. Moreover, the fire of youth is too vivacious an element to be extinguished or damped by a philosophical remark; and, while there is no danger that what has been said will be injurious or painful to the ardent and the confident, it may prove beneficial to those who, being enthusiastic, are, at the same time, modest and ingenuous. The intimation may unite with their own misgivings to regulate their sensibility, and to bring in, sooner than it would otherwise have arrived, a more discreet and sound judgment.

If it should excite wonder that men of ability, in later life, whose understandings have been rendered acute by practice in affairs, should be so easily and so far imposed upon when they happen to take up a new work in verse, this appears to be the cause;—that, having discontinued their attention to poetry, whatever progress may have been made in other departments of knowledge, they have not, as to this art, advanced in true discernment beyond the age of youth. If then a new poem falls in their way, whose attractions are of that kind which would have enraptured them during the heat of youth, the judgment not being improved to a degree that they shall be disgusted, they are dazzled; and prize and cherish the faults for having had power to make the present time vanish before them, and to throw the mind back, as by enchantment, into the happiest season of life. As they read, powers seem to be revived, passions are regenerated, and pleasures restored. The Book was probably taken up after an escape from the burthen of business, and with a wish to forget the world, and all its vexations and anxieties. Having obtained this wish, and so much more, it is natural that they should make report as they have felt.

If Men of mature age, through want of practice, be thus easily beguiled into admiration of absurdities, extravagances, and misplaced ornaments, thinking it proper that their understandings should enjoy a holiday, while they are unbending their minds with verse, it may be expected that such Readers will resemble their former selves also in strength of prejudice, and an inaptitude to be moved by the unostentatious beauties of a pure style. In the higher poetry, an enlightened Critic chiefly looks for a reflexion of the wisdom of the heart and the grandeur of the imagination. Wherever these appear, simplicity accompanies them; Magnificence herself, when legitimate, depending upon a simplicity of her own, to regulate her ornaments. But it is a well known property of human nature that our estimates are ever governed by comparisons, of which we are conscious with various degrees of distinctness. Is it not, then, inevitable (confining these observations to the effects of style merely) that an eye, accustomed to the glaring hues of diction by which such Readers are caught and excited, will for the most part be rather repelled than attracted by an original Work the coloring of which is disposed according to a pure and refined scheme of harmony? It is in the fine arts as in the affairs of life, no man can *serve* (i.e. obey with zeal and fidelity) two Masters.

As Poetry is most just to its own divine origin when it administers the comforts and breathes the spirit of religion, they who have learned to perceive this truth, and who betake themselves to reading verse for sacred purposes, must be preserved from numerous illusions to which the two Classes of Readers, whom we have been considering, are liable. But, as the mind grows serious from the weight of life, the range of its passions is contracted accordingly; and its sympathies become so exclusive that many species of high excellence wholly escape, or but languidly excite, its notice. Besides, Men who read from religious or moral inclinations, even when the subject is of that kind which they approve, are beset with misconceptions and mistakes peculiar to themselves. Attaching so much importance to the truths which interest them, they are prone to overrate the Authors by whom these truths are expressed and enforced. They come prepared to impart so much passion to the Poet's language, that they remain unconscious how little, in fact, they receive from it. And, on the other hand, religious faith is to him who holds it so momentous a thing, and error appears to be attended with such tremendous consequences, that, if opinions touching upon religion occur which the Reader condemns, he not only cannot sympathize with them however animated the expression, but there is, for the most part, an end put to all satisfaction and enjoyment. Love, if it before existed, is converted into dislike; and the heart of the Reader is set against the Author and his book.—To these excesses, they, who from their professions ought to be the most guarded against them, are perhaps the most liable; I mean those sects whose religion, being from the calculating understanding, is cold and formal. For when Christianity, the religion of humility, is founded upon the proudest quality of our nature, what can be expected but contradictions? Accordingly, believers of this cast are at one time contemptuous; at another, being troubled as they are and must be with inward misgivings, they are jealous and suspicious;—and at all seasons, they are under temptation to supply, by the heat with which they defend their tenets, the animation which is wanting to the constitution of the religion itself.

Faith was given to man that his affections, detached from the treasures of time, might be inclined to settle upon those of eternity:—the elevation of his nature, which this habit produces on earth, being to him a presumptive evidence of a future state of existence; and giving him a title to partake of its holiness. The religious man values what he sees chiefly as an "imperfect shadowing forth" of what he is incapable of seeing. The concerns of religion refer to indefinite objects, and are too weighty for the mind to support them without relieving itself by resting a great part of the burthen upon words and symbols. The commerce between Man and his Maker cannot be carried on but by a process where much is represented in little, and the infinite Being accommodates himself to a finite capacity. In all this may be perceived the affinities between religion and poetry;—between religion—making up the deficiencies of reason by faith, and poetry—passionate for the instructon of reason; between religion—whose element is infinitude, and whose ultimate trust is the supreme of things, submitting herself to circumscription and reconciled to substitutions; and poetry—etherial and transcendant, yet incapable to sustain her existence without sensuous incarnation. In this community of nature may be perceived also the lurking incitements of kindred error;—so that we shall find that no poetry has been more subject to distortion, than that species the argument and scope of which is religious; and no lovers of the art have gone further astray than the pious and the devout.

Whither then shall we turn for that union of qualifications which must necessarily exist before the decisions of a critic can be of absolute value? For a mind at once poetical and philosophical; for a critic whose affections are as free and kindly as the spirit of society, and whose understanding is severe as that of dispassionate government? Where are we to look for that initiatory composure of mind which no selfishness can disturb? For a natural sensibility that has been tutored into correctness without losing any thing of its quickness; and for active faculties capable of answering the demands which an Author of original imagination shall make upon them,—associated with a judgment that cannot be duped into admiration by aught that is unworthy of it?—Among those and those only, who, never having suffered their youthful love of poetry to remit much of its force, have applied, to the consideration of the laws of this art, the best power of their understandings. At the same time it must be observed—that, as this Class comprehends the only judgments which are trust-worthy, so does it include the most erroneous and perverse. For to be mis-taught is worse than to be untaught; and no perverseness equals that which is supported by system, no errors are so difficult to root out as those which the understanding has pledged its credit to uphold. In this Class are contained Censors, who, if they be pleased with what is good, are pleased with it only by imperfect glimpses, and upon false principles; who, should they generalize rightly to a certain point, are sure to suffer for it in the end;—who, if they stumble upon a sound rule, are fettered by misapplying it, or by straining it too far; being incapable of perceiving when it ought to yield to one of higher order. In it are found Critics too petulant to be passive to a genuine Poet, and too feeble to grapple with him; Men, who take upon them to report of the course which *he* holds whom they are utterly unable to accompany,— confounded if he turn quick upon the wing, dismayed if he soar steadily into "the region";—Men of palsied imaginations and indurated hearts; in whose minds all healthy action is languid,—who, therefore, feed as the many direct them, or with the many, are greedy after vicious provocatives;—Judges, whose censure is auspicious, and whose praise ominous! In this Class meet together the two extremes of best and worst.

The observations presented in the foregoing series, are of too ungracious a nature to have been made without reluctance; and were it only on this account I would invite the Reader to try them by the test of comprehensive experience. If the number of judges who can be confidently relied upon be in reality so small, it ought to follow that partial notice only, or neglect, perhaps long continued, or attention wholly inadequate to their merits—must have been the fate of most works in the higher departments of poetry; and that, on the other hand, numerous productions have blazed into popularity, and have passed away, leaving scarcely a trace behind them:—it will be, further, found that when Authors have at length raised themselves into general admiration and maintained their ground, errors and prejudices have prevailed concerning their genius and their works, which the few who are conscious of those errors and prejudices would deplore; if they were not recompensed by perceiving that there are select Spirits for whom it is ordained that their fame shall be in the world an existence like that of Virtue, which owes its being to the struggles it makes, and its vigour to the enemies whom it provokes;—a vivacious quality ever doomed to meet with opposition, and still triumphing over it; and, from the nature of its dominion, incapable of being brought to the sad conclusion of Alexander, when he wept that there were no more worlds for him to conquer.

Let us take a hasty retrospect of the poetical literature of this Country for the greater part of the last two Centuries, and see if the facts correspond with these inferences.

Who is there that can now endure to read the "Creation" of Dubartas? Yet all Europe once resounded with his praise; he was caressed by Kings; and, when his Poem was translated into our language, the Faery Queen faded before it. The name of Spenser, whose genius is of a higher order than even that of Ariosto, is at this day scarcely known beyond the limits of the British Isles. And, if the value of his works is to be estimated from the attention now paid to them by his Countrymen, compared with that which they bestow on those of other writers, it must be pronounced small indeed.

> "The laurel, meed of mighty Conquerors
> And Poets *sage*"—

are his own words; but his wisdom has, in this particular, been his worst enemy; while, its opposite, whether in the shape of folly or madness, has been their best friend. But he was a great power; and bears a high name: the laurel has been awarded to him.

A Dramatic Author, if he write for the Stage, must adapt himself to the taste of the Audience, or they will not endure him; accordingly the mighty genius of Shakespeare was listened to. The People were delighted; but I am not sufficiently versed in Stage antiquities to determine whether they did not flock as eagerly to the representation of many pieces of contemporary Authors, wholly undeserving to appear upon the same boards. Had there been a formal contest for superiority among dramatic Writers, that Shakespeare, like his predecessors Sophocles and Euripides, would have often been subject to the mortification of seeing the prize adjudged to sorry competitors, becomes too probable when we reflect that the Admirers of Settle and Shadwell were, in a later age, as numerous, and reckoned as respectable in point of talent as those of Dryden. At all events, that Shakespeare stooped to accommodate himself to the People, is sufficiently apparent; and one of the most striking proofs of his almost omnipotent genius, is, that he could turn to such glorious purpose those materials which the prepossessions of the age compelled him to make use of. Yet even this marvellous skill appears not to have been enough to prevent his rivals from having some advantage over him in public estimation; else how can we account for passages and scenes that exist in his works, unless upon a supposition that some of the grossest of them, a fact which in my own mind I have no doubt of, were foisted in by the Players, for the gratification of the many?

But that his Works, whatever might be their reception upon the stage, made little impression upon the ruling Intellects of the time, may be inferred from the fact that Lord Bacon, in his multifarious writings, no where either quotes or alludes to him.—His dramatic excellence enabled him to resume possession of the stage after the Restoration; but Dryden tells us that in his time two of Beaumont's and Fletcher's Plays was acted for one of Shakespeare's. And so faint and limited was the perception of the poetic beauties of his dramas in the time of Pope, that, in his Edition of the Plays, with a view of rendering to the general Reader a necessary service, he printed between inverted commas those passages which he thought most worthy of notice.

At this day, the French Critics have abated nothing of their aversion to this darling of our Nation: "the English with their Buffon de Shakespeare" is as familiar an expression among them as in the time of Voltaire. Baron Grimm is the only French writer who seems to have perceived his infinite superiority to the first names of the French Theatre; an advantage which the Parisian Critic owed to his German blood and German education. The most enlightened Italians, though well acquainted with our language, are wholly incompetent to measure the proportions of Shakespeare. The Germans only, of foreign nations, are approaching towards a knowledge and feeling of what he is. In some respects they have acquired a superiority over the fellow-countrymen of the Poet; for among us it is a current, I might say, an established opinion that Shakespeare is justly praised when he is pronounced to be "a wild irregular genius, in whom great faults are compensated by great beauties." How long may it be before this misconception passes away, and it becomes universally acknowledged that the judgment of Shakespeare in the selection of his materials, and in the manner in which he has made them, heterogeneous as they often are, constitute a unity of their own, and contribute all to one great end, is not less admirable than his imagination, his invention, and his intuitive knowledge of human Nature!

There is extant a small Volume of miscellaneous Poems in which Shakespeare expresses his own feelings in his own Person. It is not difficult to conceive that the Editor, George Stevens, should have been insensible to the beauties of one portion of that Volume, the Sonnets; though there is not a part of the writings of this Poet where is found in an equal compass a greater number of exquisite feelings felicitously expressed. But, from regard to the Critic's own credit, he would not have ventured to talk of an act of parliament not being strong enough to compel the perusal of these, or any production of Shakespeare, if he had not known that the people of England were ignorant of the treasures contained in those little pieces; and if he had not, moreover, shared the too common propensity of human nature to exult over a supposed fall into the mire of a genius whom he had been compelled to regard with admiration, as an inmate of the celestial regions,—"there sitting where he durst not soar."

Nine years before the death of Shakespeare, Milton was born; and early in life he published several small poems, which, though on their first appearance they were praised by a few of the judicious, were afterwards neglected to that degree that Pope, in his youth, could pilfer from them without danger of detection.—Whether these poems are at this day justly appreciated I will not undertake to decide: nor would it imply a severe reflection upon the mass of Readers to suppose the contrary; seeing that a Man of the acknowledged genius of Voss, the German Poet, could suffer their spirit to evaporate; and could change their character, as is done in the translation made by him of the most popular of those pieces. At all events it is certain that these Poems of Milton are now much read, and loudly praised; yet were they little heard of till more than 150 years after their publication; and of the Sonnets, Dr. Johnson, as appears from Boswell's Life of him, was in the habit of thinking and speaking as contemptuously as Stevens wrote upon those of Shakespeare.

About the time when the Pindaric Odes of Cowley and his imitators, and the productions of that class of curious thinkers whom Dr. Johnson has strangely styled Metaphysical Poets, were beginning to lose something of that extravagant admiration which they had excited, the Paradise Lost made its appearance. "Fit audience find though few," was the petition addressed by the Poet to his inspiring Muse. I have said elsewhere that he gained more than he asked; this I believe to be true; but Dr. Johnson has fallen into a gross mistake when he attempts to prove, by the sale of the work, that Milton's Countrymen were "*just* to it" upon its first appearance. Thirteen hundred Copies were sold in two years; an uncommon example, he asserts, of the prevalence of genius in opposition to so much recent enmity as Milton's public conduct had excited. But be it remembered that, if Milton's political and religious opinions, and the manner in which he announced them, had raised him many enemies, they had procured him numerous friends; who, as all personal danger was passed away at the time of publication, would be eager to procure the master-work of a Man whom they revered, and whom they would be proud of praising. The demand did not immediately increase; "for," says Dr. Johnson, "many more Readers" (he means Persons in the habit of reading poetry) "than were supplied at first the nation did not afford." How careless must a writer be who can make this assertion in the face of so many existing title pages to belie it! Turning to my own shelves, I find the folio of Cowley, 7th Edition, 1681. A book near it is Flatman's Poems, 4th Edition, 1686; Waller, 5th Edition, same date. The Poems of Norris of Bemerton not long after went, I believe, through nine Editions. What further demand there might be for these works I do not know, but I well remember, that 25 Years ago, the Bookseller's stalls in London swarmed with the folios of Cowley. This is not mentioned in disparagement of that able writer and amiable Man; but merely to shew—that, if Milton's work was not more read, it was not because readers did not exist at the time. Only 3000 copies of the Paradise Lost sold in 11 Years; and the Nation, says Dr. Johnson, had been satisfied from 1623 to 1644, that is 41 Years, with only two Editions of the Works of Shakespeare; which probably did not together make 1000 Copies; facts adduced by the critic to prove the "paucity of Readers."— There were Readers in multitudes; but their money went for other purposes, as their admiration was fixed elsewhere. We are authorized, then, to affirm that the reception of the Paradise Lost, and the slow progress of its fame, are proofs as striking as can be desired that the positions which I am attempting to establish are not erroneous.—How amusing to shape to one's self such a critique as a Wit of Charles's days, or a Lord of the Miscellanies, or trading Journalist, of King William's time, would have brought forth, if he had set his faculties industriously to work upon this Poem, every where impregnated with *original* excellence!

So strange indeed are the obliquities of admiration, that they whose opinions are much influenced by authority will often be tempted to think that there are no fixed principles in human nature for this art to rest upon. I have been honoured by being permitted to peruse in MS. a tract composed between the period of the Revolution and the close of that Century. It is the Work of an English Peer of high accomplishments, its object to form the character and direct the studies of his Son. Perhaps no where does a more beautiful treatise of the kind exist. The good sense and wisdom of the thoughts, the delicacy of the feelings, and the charm of the style, are, throughout, equally conspicuous. Yet the Author, selecting among the Poets of his own Country those whom he deems most worthy of his son's perusal, particularizes only Lord Rochester, Sir John Denham, and Cowley. Writing about the same time, Shaftsbury, an Author at present unjustly depreciated, describes the English Muses as only yet lisping in their Cradles.

The arts by which Pope, soon afterwards, contrived to procure to himself a more general and a higher reputation than perhaps any English Poet ever attained during his life-time, are known to the judicious. And as well known is it to them, that the undue exertion of these arts, is the cause why Pope has for some time held a rank in literature, to which, if he had not been seduced by an over-love of immediate popularity, and had confided more in his native genius, he never could have descended. He bewitched the nation by his melody, and dazzled it by his polished style, and was himself blinded by his own success. Having wandered from humanity in his Eclogues with boyish inexperience, the praise, which these compositions obtained, tempted him into a belief that nature was not to be trusted, at least in pastoral Poetry. To prove this by example, he put his friend Gay upon writing those Eclogues which the Author intended to be burlesque. The Instigator of the work, and his Admirers, could perceive in them nothing but what was ridiculous. Nevertheless, though these Poems contain some odious and even detestable passages, the effect, as Dr. Johnson well observes, "of reality and truth became conspicuous even when the intention was to shew them grovelling and degrading." These Pastorals, ludicrous to those who prided themselves upon their refinement, in spite of those disgusting passages "became popular, and were read with delight as just representations of rural manners and occupations."

Something less than 60 years after the publication of the Paradise Lost appeared Thomson's Winter; which was speedily followed by his other Seasons. It is a work of inspiration; much of it is written from himself, and nobly from himself. How was it received? "It was no sooner read," says one of his contemporary Biographers, "than universally admired: those only excepted who had not been used to feel, or to look for any thing in poetry, beyond a *point* of satirical or epigrammatic wit, a smart *antithesis* richly trimmed with rhyme, or the softness of an *elegiac* complaint. To such his manly classical spirit could not readily commend itself; till, after a more attentive perusal, they had got the better of their prejudices, and either acquired or affected a truer taste. A few others stood aloof, merely because they had long before fixed the articles of their poetical creed, and resigned themselves to an absolute despair of ever seeing any thing new and original. These were somewhat mortified to find their notions disturbed by the appearance of a poet, who seemed to owe nothing but to nature and his own genius. But, in a short time, the applause became unanimous; every one wondering how so many pictures, and pictures so familiar, should have moved them but faintly to what they felt in his descriptions. His digressions too, the overflowings of a tender benevolent heart, charmed the reader no less; leaving him in doubt, whether he should more admire the Poet or love the Man."

This case appears to bear strongly against us:—but we must distinguish between wonder and legitimate admiration. The subject of the work is the changes produced in the appearances of nature by the revolution of the year: and, by undertaking to write in verse, Thomson pledged himself to treat his subject as became a Poet. Now it is remarkable that, excepting a passage or two in the Windsor Forest of Pope, and some delightful pictures in the Poems

of Lady Winchelsea, the Poetry of the period intervening between the publication of the Paradise Lost and the Seasons does not contain a single new
image of external nature; and scarcely presents a familiar one from which it
can be inferred that the eye of the Poet had been steadily fixed upon his object,
much less that his feelings had urged him to work upon it in the spirit of
genuine imagination. To what a low state knowledge of the most obvious and
important phenomena had sunk, is evident from the style in which Dryden has
executed a description of Night in one of his Tragedies, and Pope his
translation of the celebrated moon-light scene in the Iliad. A blind man, in the
habit of attending accurately to descriptions casually dropped from the lips of
those around him, might easily depict these appearances with more truth.
Dryden's lines are vague, bombastic, and senseless; those of Pope, though he
had Homer to guide him, are throughout false and contradictory. The verses of
Dryden, once highly celebrated, are forgotten; those of Pope still retain their
hold upon public estimation,—nay, there is not a passage of descriptive poetry,
which at this day finds so many and such ardent admirers. Strange to think of
an Enthusiast, as may have been the case with thousands, reciting those
verses under the cope of a moon-light sky, without having his raptures in the
least disturbed by a suspicion of their absurdity.—If these two distinguished
Writers could habitually think that the visible universe was of so little consequence to a Poet, that it was scarcely necessary for him to cast his eyes upon
it, we may be assured that those passages of the elder Poets which faithfully
and poetically describe the phenomena of nature, were not at that time holden
in much estimation, and that there was little accurate attention paid to these
appearances.

   Wonder is the natural product of Ignorance; and as the soil was *in such
good condition* at the time of the publication of the Seasons, the crop was
doubtless abundant. Neither individuals nor nations become corrupt all at
once, nor are they enlightened in a moment. Thomson was an inspired Poet,
but he could not work miracles; in cases where the art of seeing had in some
degree been learned, the teacher would further the proficiency of his pupils,
but he could do little *more*, though so far does vanity assist men in acts of
self-deception that many would often fancy they recognized a likeness when
they knew nothing of the original. Having shewn that much of what his
Biographer deemed genuine admiration must in fact have been blind wonder-
ment,—how is the rest to be accounted for?—Thomson was fortunate in the
very title of his Poem, which seemed to bring it home to the prepared
sympathies of every one: in the next place, notwithstanding his high powers,
he writes a vicious style; and his false ornaments are exactly of that kind which
would be most likely to strike the undiscerning. He likewise abounds with
sentimental common-places, that from the manner in which they were
brought forward bore an imposing air of novelty. In any well-used Copy of the
Seasons the Book generally opens of itself with the rhapsody on love, or with
one of the stories, (perhaps Damon and Musidora); these also are prominent in
our Collections of Extracts; and are the parts of his Works which, after all,
were probably most efficient in first recommending the Author to general

notice. Pope, repaying praises which he had received, and wishing to extol him to the highest, only styles him "an elegant and philosophical Poet"; nor are we able to collect any unquestionable proofs that the true characteristics of Thomson's genius as an imaginative Poet were perceived, till the elder Warton, almost 40 Years after the publication of the Seasons, pointed them out by a note in his Essay on the life and writings of Pope. In the Castle of Indolence (of which Gray speaks so coldly) these characteristics were almost as conspicuously displayed, and in verse more harmonious and diction more pure. Yet that fine Poem was neglected on its appearance, and is at this day the delight only of a Few!

When Thomson died, Collins breathed his regrets into an Elegiac Poem, in which he pronounces a poetical curse upon *him* who should regard with insensibility the place where the Poet's remains were deposited. The Poems of the mourner himself have now passed through innumerable Editions, and are universally known; but if, when Collins died, the same kind of imprecation had been pronounced by a surviving admirer, small is the number whom it would not have comprehended. The notice which his poems attained during his life-time was so small, and of course the sale so insignificant, that not long before his death he deemed it right to repay to the Bookseller the sum which he had advanced for them, and threw the Edition into the fire.

Next in importance to the Seasons of Thomson, though at considerable distance from that work in order of time, come the Reliques of Ancient English Poetry; collected, new-modelled, and in many instances (if such a contradiction in terms may be used) composed, by the editor, Dr. Percy. This Work did not steal silently into the world, as is evident from the number of legendary tales, which appeared not long after its publication; and which were modelled, as the Authors persuaded themselves, after the old Ballad. The Compilation was however ill-suited to the then existing taste of City society; and Dr. Johnson, mid the little senate to which he gave laws, was not sparing in his exertions to make it an object of contempt. The Critic triumphed, the legendary imitators were deservedly disregarded, and, as undeservedly, their ill-imitated models sank, in this Country, into temporary neglect; while Burger, and other able Writers of Germany, were translating, or imitating, these Reliques, and composing, with the aid of inspiration thence derived, Poems, which are the delight of the German nation. Dr. Percy was so abashed by the ridicule flung upon his labours from the ignorance and insensibility of the Persons with whom he lived, that, though while he was writing under a mask he had not wanted resolution to follow his genius into the regions of true simplicity and genuine pathos, (as is evinced by the exquisite ballad of Sir Cauline and by many other pieces) yet, when he appeared in his own person and character as a poetical writer, he adopted, as in the tale of the Hermit of Warkworth, a diction scarcely in any one of its features distinguishable from the vague, the glossy, and unfeeling language of his day. I mention this remarkable fact with regret, esteeming the genius of Dr. Percy in this kind of writing superior to that of any other man by whom, in modern times, it has been cultivated. That even Burger, (to whom Klopstock gave, in my hearing, a commendation which he denied to Goethe and Schiller, pronouncing him to be a genuine Poet, and one of the few among the Germans whose works would last) had not the fine sensibility of Percy, might be shewn from many passages, in which he has deserted his original only to go astray. For example:

> Now daye was gone, and night was come,
> And all were fast asleepe,
> All, save the Ladye Emmeline,
> Who sate in her bowre to weepe:
>
> And soone shee heard her true Love's voice
> Low whispering at the walle,
> Awake, awake, my deare Ladye,
> 'Tis I thy true-love call.

Which is thus tricked out and dilated,

> Als nun die Nacht Gebirg' und Thal
> Vermummt in Rabenschatten,
> Und Hochburgs Lampen über-all
> Schon ausgeflimmert hatten,
> Und alles tief entschlafen war;
> Doch nur das Fraulein immerdar,
> Voll Fieberangst, noch wachte,
> Und seinen Ritter dachte:
> Da horch! Ein süsser Liebeston
> Kam leis empor geflogen.
> "Ho, Trudchen, ho! Da bin ich schon!
> Frisch auf! Dich angezogen!"

But from humble ballads we must ascend to heroics.

All hail Macpherson! hail to thee, Sire of Ossian! The Phantom was begotten by the snug embrace of an impudent Highlander upon a cloud of tradition—it travelled southward, where it was greeted with acclamation, and the thin Consistence took its course through Europe, upon the breath of popular applause. The Editor of the "Reliques" had indirectly preferred a claim to the praise of invention by not concealing that his supplementary labours were considerable: how selfish his conduct contrasted with that of the disinterested Gael, who, like Lear, gives his kingdom away, and is content to become a pensioner upon his own issue for a beggarly pittance!—Open this far-famed Book!—I have done so at random, and the beginning of the "Epic Poem Temora," in 8 Books, presents itself. "The blue waves of Ullin roll in light. The green hills are covered with day. Trees shake their dusky heads in the breeze. Grey torrents pour their noisy streams. Two green hills with aged oaks surround a narrow plain. The blue course of a stream is there. On its banks stood Cairbar of Atha. His spear supports the king; the red eyes of his fear are sad. Cormac rises on his soul with all his ghastly wounds." Precious memorandums from the pocket-book of the blind Ossian!

If it be unbecoming, as I acknowledge that for the most part it is, to speak disrespectfully of Works that have enjoyed for a length of time a widely spread reputation, without at the same time producing irrefragable proofs of their unworthiness, let me be forgiven upon this occasion.—Having had the good fortune to be born and reared in a mountainous Country, from my very childhood I have felt the falsehood that pervades the volumes imposed upon the World under the name of Ossian. From what I saw with my own eyes, I knew that the imagery was spurious. In nature every thing is distinct, yet nothing defined into absolute independent singleness. In Macpherson's work it is exactly the reverse; every thing (that is not stolen) is in this manner defined, insulated, dislocated, deadened,—yet nothing distinct. It will always be so when words are substituted for things. To say that the characters never could exist, that the manners are impossible, and that a dream has more substance than the whole state of society, as there depicted, is doing nothing more than pronouncing a censure which Macpherson defied; when, with the steeps of Morven before his eyes, he could talk so familiarly of his Car-borne heroes;—Of Morven, which, if one may judge from its appearance at the distance of a few miles, contains scarcely an acre of ground sufficiently accommodating for a sledge to be trailed along its surface.—Mr. Malcolm Laing has ably shewn that the diction of this pretended translation is a motley assembly from all quarters; but he is so fond of making out parallel passages as to call poor Macpherson to account for his very *"ands"* and his *"buts!"* and he has weakened his argument by conducting it as if he thought that every striking resemblance was a *conscious* plagiarism. It is enough that the coincidences are too remarkable for its being probable or possible that they could arise in different minds without communication between them. Now as the Translators of the Bible, Shakespeare, Milton, and Pope, could not be indebted to Macpherson, it follows that he must have owed his fine feathers to them; unless we are prepared gravely to assert, with Madame de Stael, that many of the characteristic beauties of our most celebrated English Poets, are derived from the ancient Fingallian; in which case the modern translator would have been but giving back to Ossian his own.—It is consistent that Lucien Buonaparte, who could censure Milton for having surrounded Satan in the infernal regions with courtly and regal splendour, should pronounce the modern Ossian to be the glory of Scotland;—a Country that has produced a Dunbar, a Buchanan, a Thomson, and a Burns! These opinions are of ill omen for the Epic ambition of him who has given them to the world.

Yet, much as these pretended treasures of antiquity have been admired, they have been wholly uninfluential upon the literature of the Country. No succeeding Writer appears to have caught from them a ray of inspiration; no Author in the least distinguished, has ventured formally to imitate them— except the Boy, Chatterton, on their first appearance. He had perceived, from the successful trials which he himself had made in literary forgery, how few critics were able to distinguish between a real ancient medal and a counterfeit of modern manufacture; and he set himself to the work of filling a Magazine with *Saxon poems,*—counterparts of those of Ossian, as like his as one of his misty stars is to another. This incapability to amalgamate with the literature of the Island, is, in my estimation, a decisive proof that the book is essentially unnatural; nor should I require any other to demonstrate it to be a forgery, audacious as worthless.—Contrast, in this respect, the effect of Macpherson's publication with the Reliques of Percy, so unassuming, so modest in their pretensions!—I have already stated how much Germany is indebted to this latter work; and for our own Country, its Poetry has been absolutely redeemed by it. I do not think that there is an able Writer in verse of the present day who would not be proud to acknowledge his obligations to the Reliques; I know that it is so with my friends; and, for myself, I am happy in this occasion to make a public avowal of my own.

Dr. Johnson, more fortunate in his contempt of the labours of Macpherson than those of his modest friend, was solicited not long after to furnish Prefaces biographical and critical for some of the most eminent English Poets. The Booksellers took upon themselves to make the collection; they referred probably to the most popular miscellanies, and, unquestionably, to their Books of accounts; and decided upon the claim of Authors to be admitted into a body of the most Eminent, from the familiarity of their names with the readers of that day, and by the profits, which, from the sale of his works, each had brought and was bringing to the Trade. The Editor was allowed a limited exercise of discretion, and the Authors whom he recommended are scarcely to be mentioned without a smile. We open the volume of Prefatory Lives, and to our astonishment the *first* name we find is that of Cowley!—What is become of the Morning-star of English Poetry? Where is the bright Elizabethan Constellation? Or, if Names are more acceptable than images, where is the ever-to-be-honoured Chaucer? where is Spenser? where Sydney? and lastly where he, whose rights as a Poet, contradistinguished from those which he is universally allowed to possess as a Dramatist, we have vindicated, where Shakespeare?—These, and a multitude of others not unworthy to be placed near them, their contemporaries and successors, we have *not*. But in their stead, we have (could better be expected when precedence was to be settled by an abstract of reputation at any given period made as in the case before us?) we have Roscommon, and Stepney, and Phillips, and Walsh, and Smith, and Duke, and King, and Spratt—Halifax, Granville, Sheffield, Congreve, Broome, and other reputed Magnates; Writers in metre utterly worthless and useless, except for occasions like the present, when their productions are referred to as evidence what a small quantity of brain is necessary to procure a considerable stock of admiration, provided the aspirant will accommodate himself to the likings and fashions of his day.

As I do not mean to bring down this retrospect to our own times, it may with propriety be closed at the era of this distinguished event. From the literature of other ages and countries, proofs equally cogent might have been adduced that the opinions announced in the former part of this Essay are founded upon truth. It was not an agreeable office, not a prudent undertaking, to declare them, but their importance seemed to render it a duty. It may still be asked, where lies the particular relation of what has been said to these

Volumes?—The question will be easily answered by the discerning Reader who is old enough to remember the taste that was prevalent when some of these Poems were first published, 17 years ago; who has also observed to what degree the Poetry of this Island has since that period been coloured by them; and who is further aware of the unremitting hostility with which, upon some principle or other, they have each and all been opposed. A sketch of my own notion of the constitution of Fame, has been given; and, as far as concerns myself, I have cause to be satisfied. The love, the admiration, the indifference, the slight, the aversion, and even the contempt, with which these Poems have been received, knowing, as I do, the source within my own mind, from which they have proceeded, and the labour and pains, which, when labour and pains appeared needful, have been bestowed upon them,—must all, if I think consistently, be received as pledges and tokens, bearing the same general impression though widely different in value;—they are all proofs that for the present time I have not laboured in vain; and afford assurances, more or less authentic, that the products of my industry will endure.

If there be one conclusion more forcibly pressed upon us than another by the review which has been given of the fortunes and fate of Poetical Works, it is this,—that every Author, as far as he is great and at the same time *original*, has had the task of *creating* the taste by which he is to be enjoyed: so has it been, so will it continue to be. This remark was long since made to me by the philosophical Friend for the separation of whose Poems from my own I have previously expressed my regret. The predecessors of an original Genius of a high order will have smoothed the way for all that he has in common with them;—and much he will have in common; but, for what is peculiarly his own, he will be called upon to clear and often to shape his own road:—he will be in the condition of Hannibal among the Alps.

And where lies the real difficulty of creating that taste by which a truly original Poet is to be relished? Is it in breaking the bonds of custom, in overcoming the prejudices of false refinement, and displacing the aversions of inexperience? Or, if he labour for an object which here and elsewhere I have proposed to myself, does it consist in divesting the Reader of the pride that induces him to dwell upon those points wherein Men differ from each other, to the exclusion of those in which all Men are alike, or the same; and in making him ashamed of the vanity that renders him insensible of the appropriate excellence which civil arrangements, less unjust than might appear, and Nature illimitable in her bounty, have conferred on Men who stand below him in the scale of society? Finally, does it lie in establishing that dominion over the spirits of Readers by which they are to be humbled and humanized, in order that they may be purified and exalted?

If these ends are to be attained by the mere communication of *knowledge*, it does *not* lie here.—TASTE, I would remind the Reader, like IMAGINATION, is a word which has been forced to extend its services far beyond the point to which philosophy would have confined them. It is a metaphor, taken from a *passive* sense of the human body, and transferred to things which are in their essence *not* passive,—to intellectual *acts* and *operations*. The word, imagination, has been overstrained, from impulses honourable to mankind, to meet the demands of the faculty which is perhaps the noblest of our nature. In the instance of taste, the process has been reversed; and from the prevalence of dispositions at once injurious and discreditable,—being no other than that selfishness which is the child of apathy,—which, as Nations decline in productive and creative power, makes them value themselves upon a presumed refinement of judging. Poverty of language is the primary cause of the use which we make of the word, imagination; but the word, Taste, has been stretched to the sense which it bears in modern Europe by habits of self-conceit, inducing that inversion in the order of things whereby a passive faculty is made paramount among the faculties conversant with the fine arts. Proportion and congruity, the requisite knowledge being supposed, are subjects upon which taste may be trusted; it is competent to this office;—for in its intercourse with these the mind is *passive,* and is affected painfully or pleasurably as by an instinct. But the profound and the exquisite in feeling, the lofty and universal in thought and imagination; or in ordinary language the pathetic and the sublime;—are neither of them, accurately speaking, objects of a faculty which could ever without a sinking in the spirit of Nations have been designated by the metaphor—*Taste.* And why? Because without the exertion of a co-operating *power* in the mind of the Reader, there can be no adequate sympathy with either of these emotions: without this auxiliar impulse elevated or profound passion cannot exist.

Passion, it must be observed, is derived from a word which signifies, *suffering;* but the connection which suffering has with effort, with exertion, and *action,* is immediate and inseparable. How strikingly is this property of human nature exhibited by the fact, that, in popular language, to be in a passion, is to be angry!—But,

> "Anger in hasty *words* or *blows*
> Itself discharges on its foes."

To be moved, then, by a passion, is to be excited, often to external, and always to internal, effort; whether for the continuance and strengthening of the passion, or for its suppression, accordingly as the course which it takes may be painful or pleasurable. If the latter, the soul must contribute to its support, or it never becomes vivid,—and soon languishes, and dies. And this brings us to the point. If every great Poet with whose writings men are familiar, in the highest exercise of his genius, before he can be thoroughly enjoyed, has to call forth and to communicate *power,* this service, in a still greater degree, falls upon an original Writer, at his first appearance in the world.—Of genius the only proof is, the act of doing well what is worthy to be done, and what was never done before: Of genius, in the fine arts, the only infallible sign is the widening the sphere of human sensibility, for the delight, honor, and benefit of human nature. Genius is the introduction of a new element into the intellectual universe: or, if that be not allowed, it is the application of powers to objects on which they had not before been exercised, or the employment of them in such a manner as to produce effects hitherto unknown. What is all this but an advance, or a conquest, made by the soul of the Poet? Is it to be supposed that the Reader can make progress of this kind, like an Indian Prince or General—stretched on his Palanquin, and borne by his Slaves? No, he is invigorated and inspirited by his Leader, in order that he may exert himself, for he cannot proceed in quiescence, he cannot be carried like a dead weight. Therefore to create taste is to call forth and bestow power, of which knowledge is the effect; and *there* lies the true difficulty.

As the pathetic participates of an *animal* sensation, it might seem—that, if the springs of this emotion were genuine, all men, possessed of competent knowledge of the facts and circumstances, would be instantaneously affected. And, doubtless, in the works of every true Poet will be found passages of that species of excellence, which is proved by effects immediate and universal. But there are emotions of the pathetic that are simple and direct, and others—that are complex and revolutionary; some—to which the heart yields with gentleness, others,—against which it struggles with pride: these varieties are infinite as the combinations of circumstance and the constitutions of character. Remember, also, that the medium through which, in poetry, the heart is to be affected—is language; a thing subject to endless fluctuations and arbitrary associations. The genius of the Poet melts these down for his purpose; but they retain their shape and quality to him who is not capable of exerting, within his own mind, a corresponding energy. There is also a meditative, as well as a human, pathos; an enthusiastic, as well as an ordinary, sorrow; a sadness that has its seat in the depths of reason, to which the mind cannot sink gently of itself—but to which it must descend by treading the steps of thought. And for the sublime,—if we consider what are the cares that occupy the passing day, and how remote is the practice and the course of life from the sources of sublimity, in the soul of Man, can it be wondered that there is little existing preparation for a Poet charged with a new mission to extend its kingdom, and to augment and spread its enjoyments?

Away, then, with the senseless iteration of the word, *popular,* applied to new works in Poetry, as if there were no test of excellence in this first of the fine arts but that all Men should run after its productions, as if urged by an appetite, or constrained by a spell!—The qualities of writing best fitted for eager reception are either such as startle the world into attention by their audacity and extravagance; or they are chiefly of a superficial kind, lying upon the surfaces of manners; or arising out of a selection and arrangement of incidents, by which the mind is kept upon the stretch of curiosity, and the fancy amused without the trouble of thought. But in every thing which is to send the soul into herself, to be admonished of her weakness or to be made conscious of her power;—wherever life and nature are described as operated upon by the creative or abstracting virtue of the imagination; wherever the instinctive wisdom of antiquity and her heroic passions uniting, in the heart of the Poet, with the meditative wisdom of later ages, have produced that accord of sublimated humanity, which is at once a history of the remote past and a prophetic annunciation of the remotest future, *there,* the Poet must reconcile himself for a season to few and scattered hearers.—Grand thoughts, (and Shakespeare must often have sighed over this truth) as they are most naturally and most fitly conceived in solitude, so can they not be brought forth in the midst of plaudits without some violation of their sanctity. Go to a silent exhibition of the productions of the Sister Art, and be convinced that the qualities which dazzle at first sight, and kindle the admiration of the multitude, are essentially different from those by which permanent influence is secured. Let us not shrink from following up these principles as far as they will carry us, and conclude with observing—that there never has been a period, and perhaps never will be, in which vicious poetry, of some kind or other, has not excited more zealous admiration, and been far more generally read, than good; but this advantage attends the good, that the *individual,* as well as the species, survives from age to age: whereas, of the depraved, though the species be immortal the individual quickly *perishes;* the object of present admiration vanishes, being supplanted by some other as easily produced; which, though no better, brings with it at least the irritation of novelty,—with adaptation, more or less skilful, to the changing humours of the majority of those who are most at leisure to regard poetical works when they first solicit their attention.

Is it the result of the whole that, in the opinion of the Writer, the judgment of the People is not to be respected? The thought is most injurious; and could the charge be brought against him, he would repel it with indignation. The People have already been justified, and their eulogium pronounced by implication, when it was said, above—that, of *good* Poetry, the *individual,* as well as the species, *survives*. And how does it survive but through the People? what preserves it but their intellect and their wisdom?

> "—Past and future, are the wings
> On whose support, harmoniously conjoined,
> Moves the great Spirit of human knowledge—"

The voice that issues from this Spirit, is that Vox populi which the Deity inspires. Foolish must he be who can mistake for this a local acclamation, or a transitory outcry—transitory though it be for years, local though from a Nation. Still more lamentable is his error, who can believe that there is any thing of divine infallibility in the clamour of that small though loud portion of the community, ever governed by factitious influence, which, under the name of the PUBLIC, passes itself, upon the unthinking, for the PEOPLE. Towards the Public, the Writer hopes that he feels as much deference as it is intitled to: but to the People, philosophically characterized, and to the embodied spirit of their knowledge, so far as it exists and moves, at the present, faithfully supported by its two wings, the past and the future, his devout respect, his reverence, is due. He offers it willingly and readily; and, this done, takes leave of his Readers, by assuring them—that, if he were not persuaded that the Contents of these Volumes, and the Work to which they are subsidiary, evinced something of the "Vision and the Faculty divine"; and that, both in words and things, they will operate in their degree, to extend the domain of sensibility for the delight, the honor, and the benefit of human nature, notwithstanding the many happy hours which he has employed in their composition, and the manifold comforts and enjoyments they have procured to him, he would not, if a wish could do it, save them from immediate destruction;—from becoming at this moment, to the world, as a thing that had never been.

Sir Walter Scott

1771–1832

Sir Walter Scott was born on August 15, 1771, in Edinburgh, the son of a solicitor and a descendant of colorful Scottish forebears. His childhood was divided between his home in Edinburgh and long stays with his relatives in the Border country. At a young age he displayed the remarkable power of memory which distinguished him throughout his life. Educated locally, he read widely and developed fluency in Latin before entering Old College, Edinburgh, in 1783. Three years later he began a law apprenticeship with his father, and in 1788 he began the study of law as well as history and philosophy at the university. Scott was a sociable, cheerful man. He seems also to have been genuinely modest, even in his virtually unparalleled success as a novelist.

In July 1792 Scott qualified as an advocate and began the practice of law. He was to be involved in the legal profession to some extent for the rest of his life, but it was never his chief concern. He loved to ramble in the countryside, acquainting himself with rural people and collecting their ballads, and he began reading the works of the German Romantics as well as English Gothic novels. His first publications were translations of German ballads and a play by Goethe, but they attracted little notice.

Following his marriage in 1797, Scott and his wife settled first in Edinburgh, then at a cottage on the River Esk. His first major work, *The Minstrelsy of the Scottish Border,* was published in three volumes in 1802–1803. This ballad collection was heavily edited by Scott, who sought to "restore" many of the ballads to what he believed to be their original form. In his long, strongly patriotic Preface to the collection, Scott justified his "improvements," many of which resulted in impressive poems, although Scott's tampering was derided by later scholars. In the Preface Scott also set forth his views on the relationship of literature to history, and he expressed his strong desire to preserve Scottish tradition, its "manners and character," which he saw as "daily melting and dissolving into those of her sister and ally" (England).

Scott had by this time established his own literary circle, which included James Hogg, William Laidlaw, and Lady Anne Hamilton, and, receiving an appointment to a sheriffship, moved to Ashiestiel, on the banks of the Tweed. After publishing an edition of the medieval romance *Sir Tristrem* in 1804, in which he included verses of his own, Scott turned to the composition of an original, full-length narrative poem, *The Lay of the Last Minstrel,* which appeared in 1805. *The Lay* was an immediate success and ran into many editions. Over the next ten years he published many narrative poems, including *Marmion, The Lady of the Lake, Rokeby,* and *The Lord of the Isles.*

Scott found himself the center of Edinburgh society. Appointed clerk of session, he moved to the country estate of Abbotsford and built a country house there. He also became a partner in the Ballantyne printing firm that eventually turned publisher, bringing out many of his works, which now included essays as well as poetry. He also edited the works of other writers, publishing a nineteen-volume edition of Swift and an eighteen-volume edition of Dryden.

Scott's first historical novel—he is considered the founder of the genre—was *Waverley*, published anonymously in 1814. This novel was an enormous popular success. It was followed over the next decade by many equally popular works of historical fiction, including *Guy Mannering, Old Mortality, The Heart of Midlothian, Rob Roy,* and *Ivanhoe*. Scott's fictions made use of a variety of historical settings: the recent Scottish past, the Middle Ages of England, France and Germany, as well as Palestine at the time of the Crusades. These adventures were essentially romantic re-tellings of the deeds of knights-at-arms, but Scott also described the lives of "ordinary people" in some detail. This "folk" aspect of Scott's work influenced later nineteenth century realists.

In the last years of his life Scott suffered from failing health. Despite the popularity of his novels, Scott's publishing business ran into great debt due to financial crisis in Scotland. Refusing to declare bankruptcy, Scott stoically attempted to write himself out of debt. As a result, most of his later popular novels were of inferior quality, but he wrote two substantial nonfiction works, *The Life of Napoleon* (1827) and *Tales of a Grandfather* (1828), a collection of stories from Scottish history. Scott died on September 21, 1832, at Abbotsford. His numerous works, reprinted in several editions throughout the nineteenth century, made a fortune for his creditors.

Introductory Remarks
on Popular Poetry

The Introduction originally prefixed to *The Minstrelsy of the Scottish Border* was rather of a historical than a literary nature; and the remarks which follow have been added, to afford the general reader some information upon the character of Ballad Poetry.

It would be throwing away words to prove, what all must admit, the general taste and propensity of nations in their early state, to cultivate some species of rude poetry. When the organs and faculties of a primitive race have developed themselves, each for its proper and necessary use, there is a natural tendency to employ them in a more refined and regulated manner for purposes of amusement. The savage, after proving the activity of his limbs in the chase or the battle, trains them to more measured movements, to dance at the festivals of his tribe, or to perform obeisance before the altars of his deity. From the same impulse, he is disposed to refine the ordinary speech which forms the vehicle of social communication betwixt him and his brethren, until, by a more ornate diction, modulated by certain rules of rhythm, cadence, assonance of termination, or recurrence of sound or letter, he obtains a dialect more solemn in expression, to record the laws or exploits of his tribe, or more sweet in sound, in which to plead his own cause to his mistress.

This primeval poetry must have one general character in all nations, both as to its merits and its imperfections. The earlier poets have the advantage, and it is not a small one, of having the first choice out of the stock of materials which are proper to the art; and thus they compel later authors, if they would avoid slavishly imitating the fathers of verse, into various devices, often more ingenious than elegant, that they may establish, if not an absolute claim to originality, at least a visible distinction betwixt themselves and their predecessors. Thus it happens, that early poets almost uniformly display a bold, rude, original cast of genius and expression. They have walked at free-will, and with unconstrained steps, along the wilds of Parnassus, while their followers move with constrained gestures and forced attitudes, in order to avoid placing their feet where their predecessors have stepped before them. The first bard who compared his hero to a lion, struck a bold and congenial note, though the simile, in a nation of hunters, be a very obvious one; but every subsequent poet who shall use it, must either struggle hard to give his lion, as heralds say, with a *difference,* or lie under the imputation of being a servile imitator.

It is not probable that, by any researches of modern times, we shall ever reach back to an earlier model of poetry than Homer; but as there lived heroes before Agamemnon, so, unquestionably, poets existed before the immortal Bard who gave the King of kings his fame; and he whom all civilised nations now acknowledge as the Father of Poetry, must have himself looked back to an ancestry of poetical predecessors, and is only held original because we know not from whom he copied. Indeed, though much must be ascribed to the riches of his own individual genius, the poetry of Homer argues a degree of perfection in an art which practice had already rendered regular, and concerning which his frequent mention of the bards, or chanters of poetry, indicates plainly that it was studied by many, and known and admired by all.

It is indeed easily discovered, that the qualities necessary for composing such poems are not the portion of every man in the tribe; that the bard, to reach excellence in his art, must possess something more than a full command of words and phrases, and the knack of arranging them in such form as ancient examples have fixed upon as the recognised structure of national verse. The tribe speedily became sensible that, besides this degree of mechanical facility, which (like making what are called at school nonsense verses) may be attained by dint of memory and practice, much higher qualifications are demanded. A keen and active power of observation, capable of perceiving at a glance the leading circumstances from which the incident described derives its character; quick and powerful feelings, to enable the bard to comprehend and delineate those of the actors in his piece; and a command of language, alternatively soft and elevated, and suited to express the conceptions which he had formed in his mind, are all necessary to eminence in poetical art.

Above all, to attain the highest point of his profession, the poet must have that original power of embodying and detailing circumstances, which can place before the eyes of others a scene which only exists in his own imagination. This last high and creative faculty, namely, that of impressing the mind of the hearers with scenes and sentiments having no existence save through their art, has procured for the bards of Greece the term of Ποιητής, which, as it singularly happens, is literally translated by the Scottish epithet for the same class of persons, whom they term the *Makers*. The French phrase of Trouvers, or Troubadours, namely, the Finders, or Inventors, has the same reference to the quality of original conception and invention proper to the poetical art, and without which it can hardly be said to exist to any pleasing or useful purpose.

The mere arrangement of words into poetical rhythm, or combining them according to a technical rule or measure, is so closely connected with the art of music, that an alliance between these two fine arts is very soon closely formed. It is fruitless to inquire which of them has been first invented, since doubtless the precedence is accidental; and it signifies little whether the musician adapts verses to a rude tune, or whether the primitive poet, in reciting his productions, falls naturally into a chant or song. With this additional accomplishment, the poet becomes ἀοιδός, or the man of song, and his character is complete when the additional accompaniment of a lute or harp is added to his vocal performance.

Here, therefore, we have the history of early poetry in all nations. But it is evident that, though poetry seems a plant proper to almost all soils, yet not only is it of various kinds, according to the climate and country in which it has its origin, but the poetry of different nations differs still more widely in the degree of excellence which it attains. This must depend in some measure, no doubt, on the temper and manners of the people, or their proximity to those spirit-stirring events which are naturally selected as the subject of poetry, and on the more comprehensive or energetic character of the language spoken by the tribe. But the progress of the art is far more dependent upon the rise of some highly-gifted individual, possessing in a pre-eminent and uncommon degree the powers demanded, whose talents influence the taste of a whole nation, and entail on their posterity and language a character almost indelibly sacred. In this respect Homer stands alone and unrivalled, as a light from whose lamp the genius of successive ages, and of distant nations, has caught fire and illumination; and who, though the early poet of a rude age, has purchased for the era he has celebrated, so much reverence, that, not daring to bestow on it the term of barbarous, we distinguish it as the heroic period.

No other poet (sacred and inspired authors excepted) ever did, or ever will possess the same influence over posterity, in so many distant lands, as has been acquired by the blind old man of Chios; yet we are assured that his works, collected by the pious care of Pisistratus, who caused to be united into their present form those divine poems, would otherwise, if preserved at all, have appeared to succeeding generations in the humble state of a collection of detached ballads, connected only as referring to the same age, the same general subjects, and the same cycle of heroes, like the metrical poems of the Cid in Spain, or of Robin Hood in England.

In other countries less favoured, either in language or in picturesque incident, it cannot be supposed that even the genius of Homer could have soared to such exclusive eminence, since he must at once have been deprived of the subjects and themes so well adapted for his muse, and of the lofty, melodious, and flexible language in which he recorded them. Other nations, during the formation of their ancient poetry, wanted the genius of Homer, as well as his picturesque scenery and lofty language. Yet the investigation of the early poetry of every nation, even the rudest, carries with it an object of curiosity and interest. It is a chapter in the history of the childhood of society, and its resemblance to, or dissimilarity from, the popular rhymes of other nations in the same stage, must needs illustrate the ancient history of states; their slower or swifter progress towards civilisation; their gradual or more rapid adoption of manners, sentiments, and religion. The study, therefore, of lays rescued from the gulf of oblivion, must in every case possess considerable interest for the moral philosopher and general historian.

The historian of an individual nation is equally or more deeply interested in the researches into popular poetry, since he must not disdain to gather from the tradition conveyed in ancient ditties and ballads, the information necessary to confirm or correct intelligence collected from more certain sources. And although the poets were a fabling race from the very beginning of time, and so much addicted to exaggeration, that their accounts are seldom to be relied on without corroborative evidence, yet instances frequently occur where the statements of poetical tradition are unexpectedly confirmed.

To the lovers and admirers of poetry as an art, it cannot be uninteresting to have a glimpse of the National Muse in her cradle, or to hear her babbling the earliest attempts at the formation of the tuneful sounds with which she was afterwards to charm posterity. And I may venture to add, that among poetry, which, however rude, was a gift of Nature's first-fruits, even a reader of refined taste will find his patience rewarded, by passages in which the rude minstrel rises into sublimity or melts into pathos. These were the merits which induced the classical Addison to write an elaborate commentary upon the ballad of 'Chevy Chase,' and which roused, like the sound of a trumpet, the heroic blood of Sir Philip Sidney.

It is true that passages of this high character occur seldom; for during the infancy of the art of poetry, the bards have been generally satisifed with a rude and careless expression of their sentiments; and even when a more felicitous expression, or loftier numbers, have been dictated by the enthusiasm of the composition, the advantage came unsought for, and perhaps unnoticed, either by the minstrel or the audience.

Another cause contributed to the tenuity of thought and poverty of expression, by which old ballads are too often distinguished. The apparent simplicity of the ballad stanza carried with it a strong temptation to loose and trivial composition. The collections of rhymes, accumulated by the earliest of the craft, appear to have been considered as forming a joint stock for the common use of the profession; and not mere rhymes only, but verses and stanzas, have been used as common property, so as to give an appearance of sameness and crudity to the whole series of popular poetry. Such, for instance, is the salutation so often repeated:

> Now Heaven thee save, thou brave young knight,
> Now Heaven thee save and see.

And such the usual expression for taking counsel with:

> Rede me, rede me, brother dear,
> My rede shall rise at thee.

Such also is the unvaried account of the rose and the brier, which are said to spring out of the grave of the hero and heroine of the metrical legends, with little effort at a variation of the expressions in which the incident is prescriptively told. The least acquaintance with the subject will recall a great number of commonplace verses, which each ballad-maker has unceremoniously appropriated to himself, thereby greatly facilitating his own task, and at the same time degrading his art by his slovenly use of over-scutched phrases. From the same indolence, the balladmongers of most nations have availed themselves of every opportunity of prolonging their pieces, of the same kind, without the labour of actual composition. If a message is to be delivered, the poet saves himself a little trouble by using exactly the same words in which it was originally couched, to secure its being transmitted to the person for whose ear it was intended. The bards of ruder climes, and less favoured languages, may indeed claim the countenance of Homer for such repetitions; but whilst, in the Father of Poetry, they give the reader an opportunity to pause, and look back upon the enchanted ground over which they have travelled, they afford nothing to the modern bard, save facilitating the power of stupefying the audience with stanzas of dull and tedious iteration.

Another cause of the flatness and insipidity, which is the great imperfection of ballad poetry, is to be ascribed less to the compositions in their original state, when rehearsed by their *authors,* than to the ignorance and errors of the reciters or transcribers, by whom they have been transmitted to us. The more popular the composition of an ancient poet, or *Maker,* became, the greater chance there was of its being corrupted; for a poem transmitted through a number of reciters, like a book reprinted in a multitude of editions, incurs the risk of impertinent interpolations from the conceit of one rehearser, unintelligible blunders from the stupidity of another, and omissions equally to be regretted, from the want of memory in a third. This sort of injury is felt very early, and the reader will find a curious instance in the Introduction to the romance of *Sir Tristrem.* Robert de Brunne there complains, that though the romance of *Sir Tristrem* was the best which had ever been made, if it could be recited as composed by the author, Thomas of Erceldoune; yet that it was written in such an ornate style of language, and such a difficult strain of versification, as to lose all value in the mouths of ordinary minstrels, who could scarcely repeat one stanza without omitting some part of it, and marring, consequently, both the sense and the rhythm of the passage. This deterioration could not be limited to one author alone; others must have suffered from the same cause, in the same or a greater degree. Nay, we are authorised to conclude, that in proportion to the care bestowed by the author upon any poem, to attain what his age might suppose to be the highest graces of poetry, the greater was the damage which it sustained by the inaccuracy of reciters, or their desire to humble both the sense and diction of the poem to their powers of recollection, and the comprehension of a vulgar audience. It cannot be expected that compositions subjected in this way to mutilation and corruption, should continue to present their original sense or diction; and the accuracy of our editions of popular poetry, unless in the rare event of recovering original or early copies, is lessened in proportion.

But the chance of these corruptions is incalculably increased, when we consider that the ballads have been, not in one, but innumerable instances of transmission, liable to similar alterations, through a long course of centuries, during which they have been handed from one ignorant reciter to another, each discarding whatever original words or phrases time or fashion had, in his opinion, rendered obsolete, and substituting anachronisms by expressions taken from the customs of his own day. And here it may be remarked, that the desire of the reciter to be intelligible, however natural and laudable, has been one of the greatest causes of the deterioration of ancient poetry. The minstrel who endeavoured to recite with fidelity the words of the author, might indeed fall into errors of sound and sense, and substitute corruptions for words he did not understand. But the ingenuity of a skilful critic could often, in that case, revive and restore the original meaning, while the corrupted words became, in such cases, a warrant for the authenticity of the whole poem.

In general, however, the later reciters appear to have been far less desirous to speak the author's words, than to introduce amendments and new readings of their own, which have always produced the effect of modernising, and usually that of degrading and vulgarising, the rugged sense and spirit of the antique minstrel. Thus, undergoing from age to age a gradual process of alteration and recomposition, our popular and oral minstrelsy has lost, in a great measure, its original appearance; and the strong touches by which it had been formerly characterised, have been generally smoothed down and destroyed by a process similar to that by which a coin, passing from hand to hand, loses in circulation all the finer marks of the impress.

The very fine ballad of 'Chevy Chase' is an example of this degrading species of alchymy, by which the ore of antiquity is deteriorated and adulterated. While Addison, in an age which had never attained to popular poetry, wrote his classical criticism on that ballad, he naturally took for his text the ordinary stall copy, although he might and ought to have suspected that a ditty couched in the language nearly of his own time could not be the same with that which Sir Philip Sidney, more than one hundred years before, had spoken of as being 'evil apparelled in the dust and cobwebs of an uncivilised age.' The venerable Bishop Percy was the first to correct this mistake, by producing a copy of the song, as old, at least, as the reign of Henry VII., bearing the name of the author, or transcriber, Richard Sheale. But even the Rev. Editor himself fell under the mistake of supposing the modern 'Chevy Chase' to be a new copy of the original ballad, expressly modernised by some one later bard. On the contrary, the current version is now universally allowed to have been produced by the gradual alterations of numerous reciters, during two centuries, in the course of which the ballad has been gradually moulded into a composition bearing only a general resemblance to the original—expressing the same events and sentiments in much smoother language, and more flowing and easy versification; but losing in poetical fire and energy, and in the vigour and pithiness of the expression, a great deal more than it has gained in suavity of diction. Thus:

> The Percy owt of Northumberland,
>   And a vowe to God mayd he,
> That he wolde hunt in the mountayns,
>   Off Cheviot within dayes thre,
> In the mauger of doughty Dougles
>   And all that ever with him be,

becomes:

> The stout earl of Northumberland
>   A vow to God did make,
> His pleasure in the Scottish woods
>   Three summer days to take, etc.

From this, and other examples of the same kind, of which many might be quoted, we must often expect to find the remains of Minstrel poetry, composed originally for the courts of princes and halls of nobles, disguised in the more modern and vulgar dialect in which they have been of late sung to the frequenters of the rustic ale-bench. It is unnecessary to mention more than one other remarkable and humbling instance, printed in the curious collection entitled *A Ballad Book,* where we find, in the words of the ingenious editor, a stupid ballad printed as it was sung in Annandale, founded on the well-known story of the Prince of Salerno's daughter, but with the uncouth change of Dysmal for Ghismonda, and Guiscard transformed into a greasy kitchen-boy.

To what base uses may we not return!

Sometimes a still more material and systematic difference appears between the poems of antiquity, as they were originally composed, and as they now exist. This occurs in cases where the longer metrical romances, which were in fashion during the middle ages, were reduced to shorter compositions, in order that they might be chanted before an inferior audience. A ballad, for example, of Thomas of Erceldoune, and his intrigues with the Queen of Faery Land, is, or has been, long current in Teviotdale, and other parts of Scotland. Two ancient copies of a poem or romance on the same subject, and containing very often the same words and turns of expression, are preserved in the libraries of Lincoln and Peterborough. We are left to conjecture whether the originals of such ballads have been gradually contracted into their modern shape by the impatience of later audiences, combined with the lack of memory displayed by modern reciters, or whether, in particular cases, some ballad-maker may have actually set himself to work to retrench the old details of the minstrels, and regularly and systematically to modernise, and if the phrase be permitted, to balladise, a metrical romance. We are assured, however, that 'Roswal and Lilian' was sung through the streets of Edinburgh two generations since; and we know that the romance of 'Sir Eger, Sir Grime, and Sir Greysteil' had also its own particular chant, or tune. The stall copies of both these romances, as they now exist, are very much abbreviated, and probably exhibit them when they were undergoing, or had nearly undergone, the process of being cut down into ballads.

Taking into consideration the various indirect channels by which the popular poetry of our ancestors has been transmitted to their posterity, it is nothing surprising that it should reach us in a mutilated and degraded state, and that it should little correspond with the ideas we are apt to form of the first productions of national genius; nay, it is more to be wondered at that we possess so many ballads of considerable merit, than that the much greater number of them which must have once existed should have perished before our time.

Having given this brief account of ballad poetry in general, the purpose of the present prefatory remarks will be accomplished, by shortly noticing the popular poetry of Scotland, and some of the efforts which have been made to collect and illustrate it.

It is now generally admitted that the Scots and Picts, however differing otherwise, were each by descent a Celtic race; that they advanced in a course of victory somewhat farther than the present frontier between England and Scotland, and about the end of the eleventh century subdued and rendered tributary the Britons of Strathcluyd, who were also a Celtic race like themselves. Excepting, therefore, the provinces of Berwickshire and the Lothians, which were chiefly inhabited by an Anglo-Saxon population, the whole of Scotland was peopled by different tribes of the same aboriginal race—a race passionately addicted to music, as appears from the kindred Celtic nations of Irish, Welsh, and Scottish, preserving each to this day a style and character of music peculiar to their own country, though all three bear marks of general resemblance to each other. That of Scotland, in particular, is early noticed and extolled by ancient authors, and its remains, to which the natives are passionately attached, are still found to afford pleasure even to those who cultivate the art upon a more refined and varied system.

This skill in music did not, of course, exist without a corresponding degree of talent for a species of poetry, adapted to the habits of the country, celebrating the victories of triumphant clans, pouring forth lamentations over fallen heroes, and recording such marvellous adventures as were calculated to amuse individual families around their household fires, or the whole tribe when regaling in the hall of the chief. It happened, however, singularly enough, that while the music continued to be Celtic in its general measure, the language of Scotland, most commonly spoken, began to be that of their neighbours the English, introduced by the multitude of Saxons who thronged to the court of Malcolm Canmore and his successors; by the crowds of prisoners of war, whom the repeated ravages of the Scots in Northumberland carried off as slaves to their country; by the influence of the inhabitants of the richest and most populous provinces in Scotland, Berwickshire, namely, and the Lothians, over the more mountainous; lastly, by the superiority which a language like the Anglo-Saxon, considerably refined, long since reduced to writing, and capable of expressing the wants, wishes, and sentiments of the speakers, must have possessed over the jargon of various tribes of Irish and British origin, limited and contracted in every varying dialect, and differing, at the same time, from each other. This superiority being considered, and a fair length of time being allowed, it is no wonder that, while the Scottish people retained their Celtic music, and many of their Celtic customs, together with their Celtic dynasty, they should nevertheless have adopted throughout the Lowlands, the Saxon language, while in the Highlands they retained the Celtic dialect, along with the dress, arms, manners, and government of their fathers.

There was, for a time, a solemn national recognisance that the Saxon language and poetry had not originally been that of the royal family. For at the coronations of the kings of Scotland, previous to Alexander III., it was a part of the solemnity, that a Celtic bard stepped forth, so soon as the king assumed his seat upon the fated stone, and recited the genealogy of the monarch in Celtic verse, setting forth his descent, and the right which he had by birth to occupy the place of sovereignty. For a time, no doubt, the Celtic songs and poems remained current in the Lowlands, while any remnant of the language yet lasted. The Gaelic or Irish bards, we are also aware, occasionally strolled into the Lowlands, where their music might be received with favour, even after the recitation was no longer understood. But though these aboriginal poets showed themselves at festivals and other places of public resort, it does not appear that, as in Homer's time, they were honoured with high places at the board, and savoury morsels of the chine; but they seem rather to have been accounted fit company for the feigned fools and sturdy beggars, with which they were ranked by a Scottish statute.

Time was necessary wholly to eradicate one language and introduce another; but it is remarkable that, at the death of Alexander the Third, the last Scottish king of the pure Celtic race, the popular lament for his death was composed in Scoto-English, and, though closely resembling the modern dialect, is the earliest example we have of that language, whether in prose or poetry. About the same time flourished the celebrated Thomas the Rhymer, whose poem, written in English, or Lowland Scottish, with the most anxious attention both to versification and alliteration, forms, even as it now exists, a very curious specimen of the early romance. Such complicated construction was greatly too concise for the public ear, which is best amused by a looser diction, in which numerous repetitions and prolonged descriptions enable the comprehension of the audience to keep up with the voice of the singer or reciter, and supply the gaps which in general must have taken place, either through a failure of attention in the hearers, or of voice and distinct enunciation on the part of the minstrel.

The usual stanza which was selected as the most natural to the language and the sweetest to the ear, after the complex system of the more courtly measures, used by Thomas of Erceldoune, was laid aside, was that which, when originally introduced, we very often find arranged in two lines, thus:

> Earl Douglas on his milk-white steed, most like a baron bold,
> Rode foremost of his company, whose armour shone like gold;

but which, after being divided into four, constitutes what is now generally called the ballad stanza:

> Earl Douglas on his milk-white steed,
> Most like a baron bold,
> Rode foremost of his company,
> Whose armour shone like gold.

The breaking of the lines contains a plainer intimation how the stanza ought to be read, than every one could gather from the original mode of writing out the poem, where the position of the cæsura, or inflection of voice, is left to the individual's own taste. This was sometimes exchanged for a stanza of six lines, the third and sixth rhyming together. For works of more importance and pretension, a more complicated versification was still retained, and may be found in the tale of 'Ralph Coilzear,' the 'Adventures of Arthur at the Tarn-Wathelyn,' 'Sir Gawain,' and 'Sir Gologras,' and other scarce romances. A specimen of this structure of verse has been handed down to our times in the stanza of 'Christ Kirk on the Green,' transmitted by King James I. to Allan Ramsay and to Burns. The excessive passion for alliteration, which formed a rule of the Saxon poetry, was also retained in the Scottish poems of a more elevated character, though the more ordinary minstrels and ballad-makers threw off the restraint.

The varieties of stanza thus adopted for popular poetry were not, we may easily suppose, left long unemployed. In frontier regions, where men are continually engaged in active enterprise, betwixt the task of defending themselves and annoying their neighbours, they may be said to live in an atmosphere of danger, the excitation of which is peculiarly favourable to the encouragement of poetry. Hence, the expressions of Lesly the historian, quoted in the following Introduction, in which he paints the delight taken by the Borderers in their peculiar species of music, and the rhyming ballads in which they celebrated the feats of their ancestors, or recorded their own ingenious stratagems in predatory warfare. In the same Introduction the reader will find the reasons alleged why the taste for song was and must have been longer preserved on the Border than in the interior of the country.

Having thus made some remarks on early poetry in general, and on that of Scotland in particular, the Editor's purpose is, to mention the fate of some previous attempts to collect ballad poetry, and the principles of selection and publication which have been adopted by various editors of learning and information; and although the present work chiefly regards the Ballads of Scotland, yet the investigation must necessarily include some of the principal collections among the English also.

Of manuscript records of ancient ballads, very few have been yet discovered. It is probable that the minstrels, seldom knowing either how to read or write, trusted to their well-exercised memories. Nor was it a difficult task to acquire a sufficient stock-in-trade for their purpose, since the Editor has not only known many persons capable of retaining a very large collection of legendary lore of this kind, but there was a period in his own life, when a memory that ought to have been charged with more valuable matter, enabled him to recollect as many of these old songs as would have occupied several days in the recitation.

The press, however, at length superseded the necessity of such exertions of recollection, and sheaves of ballads issued from it weekly, for the amuse-ment of the sojourners at the ale-house, and the lovers of poetry in grange and hall, where such of the audience as could not read, had at least read unto them. These fugitive leaves, generally printed upon broadsides, or in small miscel-lanies called Garlands, and circulating amongst persons of loose and careless habits—so far as books were concerned—were subject to destruction from many causes; and as the editions in the early age of printing were probably much limited, even those published as chap-books in the early part of the eighteenth century, are rarely met with.

Some persons, however, seem to have had what their contemporaries probably thought the bizarre taste of gathering and preserving collections of this fugitive poetry. Hence the great body of ballads in the Pepysian collection at Cambridge, made by that Secretary Pepys, whose Diary is so very amusing; and hence the still more valuable deposit, in three volumes folio, in which the late Duke John of Roxburghe took so much pleasure, that he was often found enlarging it with fresh acquisitions, which he pasted in and registered with his own hand.

The first attempt, however, to reprint a collection of ballads for a class of readers distinct from those for whose use the stall copies were intended, was that of an anonymous editor of three 12mo volumes, which appeared in London, with engravings. These volumes came out in various years in the beginning of the eighteenth century. The editor writes with some flippancy, but with the air of a person superior to the ordinary drudgery of a mere collector. His work appears to have been got up at considerable expense, and the general introductions and historical illustrations which are prefixed to the various ballads, are written with an accuracy of which such a subject had not till then been deemed worthy. The principal part of the collection consists of stall-ballads, neither possessing much poetical merit, nor any particular rarity or curiosity. Still, this original Miscellany holds a considerable value amongst collectors; and as the three volumes—being published at different times—are seldom found together, they sell for a high price when complete.

We may now turn our eyes to Scotland, where the facility of the dialect, which cuts off the consonants in the termination of the words, so as greatly to simplify the task of rhyming, and the habits, dispositions, and manners of the people, were of old so favourable to the composition of ballad poetry, that, had the Scottish songs been preserved, there is no doubt a very curious history might have been composed by means of minstrelsy only, from the reign of Alexander III. in 1285, down to the close of the Civil Wars in 1745. That materials for such a collection existed cannot be disputed, since the Scottish historians often refer to old ballads as authorities for general tradition. But their regular preservation was not to be hoped for or expected. Successive garlands of song sprung, flourished, faded, and were forgotten in their turn; and the names of a few specimens are only preserved, to show us how abundant the display of these wild-flowers had been.

Like the natural free gifts of Flora, these poetical garlands can only be successfully sought for where the land is uncultivated; and civilisation and increase of learning are sure to banish them, as the plough of the agriculturist bears down the mountain daisy. Yet it is to be recorded with some interest, that the earliest surviving specimen of the Scottish press is a Miscellany of Millar and Chapman, which preserves a considerable fund of Scottish popular poetry, and, among other things, no bad specimen of the feats of Robin Hood, 'the English ballad-maker's joy,' and whose renown seems to have been as freshly preserved in the north as on the southern shores of the Tweed. There were probably several collections of Scottish ballads and metrical pieces during the seventeenth century. A very fine one, belonging to Lord Montagu, perished in the fire which consumed Ditton House, about twenty years ago.

James Watson, in 1706, published at Edinburgh a miscellaneous collection in three parts, containing some ancient poetry. But the first editor who seems to have made a determined effort to preserve our ancient popular poetry, was the well-known Allan Ramsay in his *Evergreen,* containing chiefly extracts from the ancient Scottish Makers, whose poems have been preserved in the Bannatyne Manuscript, but exhibiting amongst them some popular ballads. Amongst these is the 'Battle of Harlaw,' apparently from a modernised copy, being apparently the most ancient Scottish historical ballad of any length now in existence. He also inserted in the same collection the genuine Scottish Border ballad of 'Johnnie Armstrong,' copied from the recitation of a descendant of the unfortunate hero, in the sixth generation. This poet also included in the *Evergreen* 'Hardyknute,' which, though evidently modern, is a most spirited and beautiful imitation of the ancient ballad. In a subsequent collection of lyrical pieces, called the *Tea-Table Miscellany,* Allan Ramsay inserted several old ballads, such as 'Cruel Barbara Allan,' 'The Bonnie Earl of Murray,' 'There came a Ghost to Margaret's Door,' and two or three others. But his unhappy plan of writing new words to old tunes, without at the same time preserving the ancient verses, led him, with the assistance of 'some ingenious young gentlemen,' to throw aside many originals, the preservation of which would have been much more interesting than anything which has been substituted in their stead.

In fine, the task of collecting and illustrating ancient popular poetry, whether in England or Scotland, was never executed by a competent person, possessing the necessary powers of selection and annotation, till it was undertaken by Dr. Percy, afterwards Bishop of Dromore in Ireland. This reverend gentleman, himself a poet, and ranking high among the literati of the day, commanding access to the individuals and institutions which could best afford him materials, gave the public the result of his researches in a work entitled *Reliques of Ancient English Poetry,* in three volumes, published in London 1765, which has since gone through four editions. The taste with which the materials were chosen, the extreme felicity with which they were illustrated, the display at once of antiquarian knowledge and classical reading which the collection indicated, render it difficult to imitate, and impossible to excel, a work which must always be held among the first of its class in point of merit, though not actually the foremost in point of time. But neither the high character of the work, nor the rank and respectability of the author, could protect him or his labours from the invidious attacks of criticism.

The most formidable of these were directed by Joseph Ritson, a man of acute observation, profound research, and great labour. These valuable attributes were unhappily combined with an eager irritability of temper, which induced him to treat antiquarian trifles with the same seriousness which men of the world reserve for matters of importance, and disposed him to drive controversies into personal quarrels, by neglecting, in literary debate, the courtesies of ordinary society. It ought to be said, however, by one who knew him well, that this irritability of disposition was a constitutional and physical infirmity; and that Ritson's extreme attachment to the severity of truth corresponded to the rigour of his criticisms upon the labours of others. He seems to have attacked Bishop Percy with the greater animosity, as bearing no good-will to the hierarchy, in which that prelate held a distinguished place.

Ritson's criticism, in which there was too much horse-play, was grounded on two points of accusation. The first regarded Dr. Percy's definition of the order and office of minstrels, which Ritson considered as designedly overcharged, for the sake of giving an undue importance to his subject. The second objection respected the liberties which Dr. Percy had taken with his materials, in adding to, retrenching, and improving them, so as to bring them nearer to the taste of his own period. We will take some brief notice of both topics.

First, Dr. Percy, in the first edition of his work, certainly laid himself open to the charge of having given an inaccurate, and somewhat exaggerated, account of the English minstrels, whom he defined to be an 'order of men in the middle ages, who subsisted by the arts of poetry and music, and sung to the harp the verses which they themselves "composed."' The reverend editor of the *Reliques* produced in support of this definition many curious quotations, to show that in many instances the persons of these minstrels had been honoured and respected, their performances applauded and rewarded by the great and the courtly, and their craft imitated by princes themselves.

Against both these propositions Ritson made a determined opposition. He contended, and probably with justice, that the minstrels were not necessarily poets, or in the regular habit of composing the verses which they sung to the harp; and indeed, that the word *minstrel,* in its ordinary acceptation, meant no more than musician.

Dr. Percy, from an amended edition of his 'Essay on Minstrelsy,' prefixed to the fourth edition of the *Reliques of Ancient Poetry,* seems to have been, to a certain point, convinced by the critic's reasoning; for he has extended the definition impugned by Ritson, and the minstrels are thus described as singing verses 'composed by themselves or *others.*' This we apprehend to be a tenable position; for, as on the one hand it seems too broad an averment to say that all minstrels were by profession poets, so on the other it is extravagant to affirm that men who were constantly in the habit of reciting verse, should not frequently have acquired that of composing it, especially when their bread depended on giving pleasure; and to have the power of producing novelty is a great step towards that desirable end. No unprejudiced reader, therefore, can have any hesitation in adopting Bishop Percy's definition of the minstrels and their occupation, as qualified in the fourth edition of his Essay, implying that they were sometimes poets, sometimes the mere reciters of the poetry of others.

On the critic's second proposition, Dr. Percy successfully showed that at no period of history was the word minstrel applied to instrumental music exclusively; and he has produced sufficient evidence that the talents of the profession were as frequently employed in chanting or reciting poetry as in playing the mere tunes. There is the appearance of distinction being some-times made between minstrel recitations and minstrelsy of music alone; and we may add a curious instance to those quoted by the Bishop. It is from the singular ballad respecting Thomas of Erceldoune, which announces the proposition that *tongue* is chief of minstrelsy.

We may also notice that the word minstrel, being in fact derived from the Minné-singer of the Germans, means, in its primary sense, one who *sings* of *love,* a sense totally inapplicable to a mere instrumental musician.

A second general point on which Dr. Percy was fiercely attacked by Mr. Ritson was also one on which both the parties might claim the right to sing *Te Deum.* It respected the rank or *status* which was held by the minstrels in society during the Middle Ages. On this, the editor of the *Reliques of Ancient Poetry* had produced the most satisfactory evidence that, at the courts of the Anglo-Norman princes, the professors of the gay science were the favourite solacers of the leisure hours of princes, who did not themselves disdain to share their tuneful labours, and imitate their compositions. Mr. Ritson replied to this with great ingenuity, arguing, that such instances of respect paid to French minstrels reciting in their native language in the court of Norman monarchs, though held in Britain, argued nothing in favour of English artists professing the same trade, and of whose compositions, and not of those existing in the French language, Dr. Percy professed to form his collection. The reason of the distinction betwixt the respectability of the French minstrels and the degradation of the same class of men in England, Mr. Ritson plausibly alleged to be, that the English language, a mixed speech betwixt Anglo-Saxon and Norman-French, was not known at the court of the Anglo-Norman kings until the reign of Edward III.; and that, therefore, until a very late period, and when the lays of minstrelsy were going out of fashion, English performers in that capacity must have confined the exercise of their talents to the amusement of the vulgar. Now, as it must be conceded to Mr. Ritson that almost all the English metrical romances which have been preserved till the present day are translated from the French, it may also be allowed that a class of men employed chiefly in rendering into English the works of others, could not hold so high a station as those who aspired to original composition; and so far the critic has the best of the dispute. But Mr. Ritson has over-driven his argument, since there was assuredly a period in English history when the national minstrels, writing in the national dialect, were, in proportion to their merit in their calling, held in honour and respect.

Thomas the Rhymer, for example, a minstrel who flourished in the end of the twelfth century, was not only a man of talent in his art, but of some rank in society; the companion of nobles, and himself a man of landed property. He and his contemporary, Kendal, wrote, as we are assured by Robert de Brunne, in a passage already alluded to, a kind of English, which was designed 'for pride and nobleye,' and not for such inferior persons as Robert himself addressed, and to whose comprehension he avowedly lowered his language and structure of versification. There existed, therefore, during the time of this historian, a more refined dialect of the English language, used by such composers of popular poetry as moved in a higher circle; and there can be no doubt that, while their productions were held in such high esteem, the authors must have been honoured in proportion.

The education bestowed upon James I. of Scotland, when brought up under the charge of Henry IV., comprehended both music and the art of vernacular poetry; in other words, minstrelsy in both branches. That poetry, of which the King left several specimens, was, as is well known, English; nor is it to be supposed that a prince, upon whose education such sedulous care was bestowed, would have been instructed in an art which, if we are to believe Mr. Ritson, was degraded to the last degree, and discreditable to its professors. The same argument is strengthened by the poetical exercises of the Duke of Orleans, in English, written during his captivity after the battle of Agincourt. It could not be supposed that the noble prisoner was to solace his hours of imprisonment with a degrading and vulgar species of composition.

We could produce other instances to show that this acute critic has carried his argument considerably too far. But we prefer taking a general view of the subject, which seems to explain clearly how contradictory evidence should exist on it, and why instances of great personal respect to individual minstrels, and a high esteem of the art, are quite reconcilable with much contempt thrown on the order at large.

All professors of the fine arts—all those who contribute, not to the necessities of life, but to the enjoyments of society, hold their professional respectability by the severe tenure of exhibiting excellence in their department. We are well enough satisfied with the tradesman who goes through his task in a workmanlike manner, nor are we disposed to look down upon the divine, the lawyer, or the physician, unless they display gross ignorance of their profession: we hold it enough that if they do not possess the highest knowledge of their respective sciences, they can at least instruct us on the points we desire to know. But

> *Mediocribus esse poetis*
> *Non dî, non homines, non concessere columnæ.*

The same is true respecting the professors of painting, of sculpture, of music, and the fine arts in general. If they exhibit paramount excellence, no situation in society is too high for them which their manners enable them to fill; if they fall short of the highest point of aim, they degenerate into sign-painters, stone-cutters, common crowders, doggerel rhymers, and so forth—the most contemptible of mankind. The reason of this is evident. Men must be satisfied with such a supply of their actual wants as can be obtained in the circumstances, and should an individual want a coat, he must employ the village tailor, if Stultze is not to be had. But if he seeks for delight, the case is quite different; and he that cannot hear Pasta or Sontag, would be little solaced for the absence of these sirens by the strain of a crack-voiced ballad-singer. Nay, on the contrary, the offer of such inadequate compensation would only be regarded as an insult, and resented accordingly.

The theatre affords the most appropriate example of what we mean. The first circles in society are open to persons eminently distinguished in the drama; and their rewards are, in proportion to those who profess the useful arts, incalculably higher. But those who lag in the rear of the dramatic art are proportionally poorer and more degraded than those who are the lowest of a useful trade or profession. These instances will enable us readily to explain why the greater part of the minstrels, practising their profession in scenes of vulgar mirth and debauchery, humbling their art to please the ears of drunken clowns, and living with the dissipation natural to men whose precarious subsistence is, according to the ordinary phrase, from hand to mouth only, should fall under general contempt, while the *stars* of the profession, to use a modern phrase, looked down on them from the distant empyrean, as the planets do upon those shooting exhalations arising from gross vapours in the nether atmosphere.

The debate, therefore, resembles the apologue of the gold and silver shield. Dr. Percy looked on the minstrel in the palmy and exalted state to which, no doubt, many were elevated by their talents, like those who possess excellence in the fine arts in the present day; and Ritson considered the reverse of the medal, when the poor and wandering glee-man was glad to purchase his bread by singing his ballads at the ale-house, wearing a fantastic habit, and latterly sinking into a mere crowder upon an untuned fiddle, accompanying his rude strains with a ruder ditty, the helpless associate of drunken revellers, and marvellously afraid of the constable and parish-beadle. The difference betwixt the extreme positions of the highest and lowest in such a profession cannot be more marked than that which separated David Garrick or John Kemble from the outcasts of a strolling company, exposed to penury, indigence, and prosecution according to law.

There was still another and more important subject of debate between Dr. Percy and his hostile critic. The former, as a poet and a man of taste, was tempted to take such freedoms with his original ballads as might enable him to please a more critical age than that in which they were composed. Words were thus altered, phrases improved, and whole verses were inserted or omitted at pleasure. Such freedoms were specially taken with the poems published from a folio manuscript in Dr. Percy's own possession, very curious from the miscellaneous nature of its contents, but, unfortunately, having many of the leaves mutilated, and injured in other respects, by the gross carelessness and ignorance of the transcriber. Anxious to avail himself of the treasures which this manuscript contained, the editor of the *Reliques* did not hesitate to repair and renovate the songs which he drew from this corrupted yet curious source, and to accommodate them with such emendations as might recommend them to the modern taste.

For these liberties with his subject, Ritson censured Dr. Percy in the most uncompromising terms, accused him, in violent language, of interpolation and forgery, and insinuated that there existed no such thing *in rerum natura* as that folio manuscript, so often referred to as the authority of originals inserted in the *Reliques*. In this charge, the eagerness of Ritson again betrayed him farther than judgment and discretion, as well as courtesy, warranted. It is, no doubt, highly desirable that the text of ancient poetry should be given untouched and uncorrupted. But this is a point which did not occur to the editor of the *Reliques* in 1765, whose object it was to win the favour of the public, at a period when the great difficulty was not how to secure the very words of old ballads, but how to arrest attention upon the subject at all. That great and important service to national literature would probably never have been attained without the work of Dr. Percy; a work which first fixed the consideration of general readers on ancient poetry, and made it worth while to inquire how far its graces were really antique, or how far derived from the taste with which the publication had been superintended and revised. The object of Dr. Percy was certainly intimated in several parts of his work, where he ingenuously acknowledges that certain ballads have received emendations, and that others are not of pure and unmixed antiquity; that the beginning of some and the end of others have been supplied; and, upon the whole, that he has in many instances decorated the ancient ballads with the graces of a more refined period.

This system is so distinctly intimated, that if there be any critic still of opinion, like poor Ritson, whose morbid temperament led him to such a conclusion, that the crime of literary imitation is equal to that of commercial forgery, he ought to recollect that guilt, in the latter case, does not exist without a corresponding charge of uttering the forged document, or causing it to be uttered, as genuine, without which the mere imitation is not culpable, at least not criminally so. This quality is totally awanting in the accusation so roughly brought against Dr. Percy, who avowedly indulged in such alterations and improvements upon his materials as might adapt them to the taste of an age not otherwise disposed to bestow its attention on them.

We have to add that, in the fourth edition of the *Reliques,* Mr. Thomas Percy of St. John's College, Oxford, pleading the cause of his uncle with the most gentlemanlike moderation, and with every respect to Mr. Ritson's science and talents, has combated the critic's opinion, without any attempt to retort his injurious language.

It would be now, no doubt, desirable to have had some more distinct account of Dr. Percy's folio manuscript and its contents; and Mr. Thomas Percy, accordingly, gives the original of 'The Marriage of Sir Gawain,' and collates it with the copy published in a complete state by his uncle, who has on this occasion given entire rein to his own fancy, though the rude origin of most of his ideas is to be found in the old ballad. There is also given a copy of that elegant metrical tale, 'The Child of Elle,' as it exists in the folio manuscript, which goes far to show it has derived all its beauties from Dr. Percy's poetical powers. Judging from the two specimens, we can easily conceive why the Reverent Editor of the *Reliques* should have declined, by the production of the folio manuscript, to furnish his severe Aristarch with weapons against him, which he was sure would be unsparingly used. Yet it is certain the manuscript contains much that is really excellent, though mutilated and sophisticated. A copy of the fine ballad of 'Sir Caulin' is found in a Scottish shape, under the name of 'King Malcolm and Sir Colvin,' in Buchan's *North Country Ballads,* to be presently mentioned. It is, therefore, unquestionably ancient, though possibly retouched, and perhaps with the addition of a second part, of which the Scottish copy has no vestiges. It would be desirable to know exactly to what extent Dr. Percy had used the licence of an editor in these and other cases; and certainly, at this period, would be only a degree of justice due to his memory.

On the whole, we may dismiss the *Reliques of Ancient Poetry* with the praise and censure conferred on it by a gentleman, himself a valuable labourer in the vineyard of antiquities: 'It is the most elegant compilation of the early poetry that has ever appeared in any age or country. But it must be frankly added that so numerous are the alterations and corrections that the severe antiquary, who desires to see the old English ballads in a genuine state, must consult a more accurate edition than this celebrated work.'

Of Ritson's own talents as an editor of ancient poetry, we shall have occasion to speak hereafter. The first collector who followed the example of Dr. Percy was Mr. T. Evans, bookseller, father of the gentleman we have just quoted. His *Old Ballads, Historical and Narrative, with some of modern date,* appeared in two volumes in 1777, and were eminently successful. In 1784 a second edition appeared, extending the work to four volumes. In this collection many ballads found acceptance, which Bishop Percy had not considered as possessing sufficient merit to claim admittance into the *Reliques.* The 8vo *Miscellany* of 1723 yielded a great part of the materials. The collection of Evans contained several modern pieces of great merit, which are not to be found elsewhere, and which are understood to be the production of William Julius Mickle, translator of the *Lusiad,* though they were never claimed by him, nor received among his works. Amongst them is the elegiac poem of 'Cumnor Hall,' which suggested the fictitious narrative entitled *Kenilworth.* 'The Red-Cross Knight,' also by Mickle, which has furnished words for a beautiful glee, first occurred in the same collection. As Mickle with a vein of great facility united a power of verbal melody which might have been envied by bards of much greater renown, he must be considered as very successful in those efforts, if the ballads be regarded as avowedly modern. If they are to be judged of as accurate imitations of ancient poetry, they have less merit; the deception being only maintained by a huge store of double consonants, strewed at random into ordinary words, resembling the real fashion of antiquity as little as the niches, turrets, and tracery of plaster stuck upon a modern front. In the year 1810, the four volumes of 1784 were republished by Mr. R. H. Evans, the son of the original editor, with very considerable alterations and additions. In this last edition, the more ordinary modern ballads were judiciously retrenched in number, and large and valuable additions made to the ancient part of the collection. Being in some measure a supplement to the *Reliques of Ancient Poetry,* this miscellany cannot be dispensed with on the shelves of any bibliomaniac who may choose to emulate Captain Cox of Coventry, the prototype of all collectors of popular poetry.

While Dr. Percy was setting the example for a classical publication of ancient English poetry, the late David Herd was, in modest retirement, compiling a collection of Scottish songs, which he has happily described as 'the poetry and music of the heart.' The first part of his miscellany contains heroic and historical ballads, of which there is a respectable and well-chosen selection. Mr. Herd, an accountant, as the profession is called in Edinburgh, was known and generally esteemed for his shrewd, manly common sense and antiquarian science, mixed with much good-nature and great modesty. His hardy and antique mould of countenance, and his venerable grizzled locks, procured him, amongst his acquaintance, the name of Graysteil. His original collection of songs, in one volume, appeared in 1769; an enlarged one, in two volumes, came out in 1776. A publication of the same kind, being Herd's book still more enlarged, was printed for Lawrie and Symington in 1791. Some modern additions occur in this later work, of which by far the most valuable were two fine imitations of the Scottish ballad, by the gifted author of the *Man of Feeling*—(now, alas! no more)—called 'Duncan' and 'Kenneth.'

John Pinkerton, a man of considerable learning and some severity as well as acuteness of disposition, was now endeavouring to force himself into public attention, and his collection of *Select Ballads,* London, 1783, contains sufficient evidence that he understood, in an extensive sense, Horace's maxim, *quidlibet audendi.* As he was possessed of considerable powers of poetry, though not equal to what he was willing to take credit for, he was resolved to enrich his collection with all the novelty and interest which it could derive from a liberal insertion of pieces dressed in the garb of antiquity, but equipped from the wardrobe of the editor's imagination. With a boldness, suggested perhaps by the success of Mr. Macpherson, he included, within a collection amounting to only twenty-one tragic ballads, no less than five, of which he afterwards owned himself to have been altogether, or in great part, the author. The most remarkable article in this miscellany was a second part to the noble ballad of 'Hardy Knute,' which has some good verses. It labours, however, under this great defect, that, in order to append his own conclusion to the original tale, Mr. Pinkerton found himself under the necessity of altering the leading circumstance in the old ballad, which would have rendered his catastrophe inapplicable. With such licence, to write continuations and conclusions would be no difficult task. In the second volume of the *Select Ballads,* consisting of comic pieces, a list of fifty-two articles contained nine written entirely by the editor himself. Of the manner in which these supposititious compositions are executed, it may be briefly stated that they are the work of a scholar much better acquainted with ancient books and manuscripts than with oral tradition and popular legends. The poetry smells of the lamp; and it may be truly said, that if ever a ballad had existed in such quaint language as the author employs, it could never have been so popular as to be preserved by oral tradition. The glossary displays a much greater acquaintance with learned lexicons than with the familiar dialect still spoken by the Lowland Scottish, and it is, of course, full of errors. Neither was Mr. Pinkerton more happy in the way of conjectural illustration. He chose to fix on Sir John Bruce of Kinross the paternity of the ballad of 'Hardy Knute,' and of the fine poem called 'The Vision.' The first is due to Mrs. Halket of Wardlaw, the second to Allan Ramsay, although, it must be owned, it is of a character superior to his ordinary poetry. Sir John Bruce was a brave, blunt soldier, who made no pretence whatever to literature, though his daughter, Mrs. Bruce of

Arnot, had much talent, a circumstance which may, perhaps, have misled the antiquary.

Mr. Pinkerton read a sort of recantation, in a List of Scottish Poets, prefixed to a Selection of Poems from the Maitland Manuscript, vol. i., 1786, in which he acknowledges, as his own composition, the pieces of spurious antiquity included in his *Select Ballads,* with a coolness which, when his subsequent invectives against others who had taken similar liberties is considered, infers as much audacity as the studied and laboured defence of obscenity with which he disgraced the same pages.

In the meantime, Joseph Ritson, a man of diligence and acumen equal to those of Pinkerton, but of the most laudable accuracy and fidelity as an editor, was engaged in various publications respecting poetical antiquities, in which he employed profound research. A select collection of English Songs was compiled by him, with great care and considerable taste, and published at London, 1783. A new edition of this has appeared since Ritson's death, sanctioned by the name of the learned and indefatigable antiquary, Thomas Park, and augmented with many original pieces, and some which Ritson had prepared for publication.

Ritson's Collection of Songs was followed by a curious volume, entitled *Ancient Songs from the Time of Henry III. to the Revolution,* 1790; *Pieces of Ancient Popular Poetry,* 1792; and *A Collection of Scottish Songs, with the genuine music,* London, 1794. This last is a genuine, but rather meagre collection of Caledonian popular songs. Next year Mr. Ritson published *Robin Hood,* 2 vols., 1795, being 'A Collection of all the Ancient Poems, Songs, and Ballads now extant, relative to that celebrated Outlaw.' This work is a notable illustration of the excellences and defects of Mr. Ritson's system. It is almost impossible to conceive so much zeal, research, and industry bestowed on a subject of antiquity. There scarcely occurs a phrase or word relating to Robin Hood, whether in history or poetry, in law books, in ancient proverbs, or common parlance, but it is here collected and explained. At the same time, the extreme fidelity of the editor seems driven to excess, when we find him pertinaciously retaining all the numerous and gross errors which repeated recitations have introduced into the text, and regarding it as a sacred duty to prefer the worst to the better readings, as if their inferiority was a security for their being genuine. In short, when Ritson copied from rare books, or ancient manuscripts, there could not be a more accurate editor; when taking his authority from oral tradition, and judging between two recited copies, he was apt to consider the worst as most genuine, as if a poem was not more likely to be deteriorated than improved by passing through the mouths of many reciters. In the Ballads of Robin Hood, this superstitious scrupulosity was specially to be regretted, as it tended to enlarge the collection with a great number of doggerel compositions, which are all copies of each other, turning on the same idea of Bold Robin meeting with a shepherd, a tinker, a mendicant, a tanner, etc., etc., by each and all of whom he is soundly thrashed, and all of whom he receives into his band. The tradition which avers it was the brave outlaw's custom to try a bout at quarter-staff with his young recruits, might indeed have authorised one or two such tales, but the greater part ought to have been rejected as modern imitations of the most paltry kind, composed probably about the age of James I. of England. By adopting this spurious trash as part of Robin Hood's history, he is represented as the best cudgelled hero, Don Quixote excepted, that ever was celebrated in prose or rhyme. Ritson also published several garlands of North Country songs.

Looking on this eminent antiquary's labours in a general point of view, we may deprecate the eagerness and severity of his prejudices, and fell surprise that he should have shown so much irritability of disposition on such a topic as a collection of old ballads, which certainly have little in them to affect the passions; and we may be sometimes provoked at the pertinacity with which he has preferred bad readings to good. But while industry, research, and antiquarian learning are recommendations to works of this nature, few editors will ever be found so competent to the task as Joseph Ritson. It must also be added to his praise, that although not willing to yield his opinion rashly, yet if he saw reason to believe that he had been mistaken in any fact or argument, he resigned his own opinion with a candour equal to the warmth with which he defended himself while confident he was in the right. Many of his works are now almost out of print, and an edition of them in common orthography, and altering the bizarre spelling and character which his prejudices induced the author to adopt, would be, to antiquaries, an acceptable present.

We have now given a hasty account of various collections of popular poetry during the eighteenth century; we have only further to observe, that, in the present century, this species of lore has been sedulously cultivated. The present Collection first appeared in 1802, in two volumes, and what may appear a singular coincidence, it was the first work printed by Mr. James Ballantyne (then residing at Kelso), as it was the first serious demand which the present author made on the patience of the public. The *Border Minstrelsy*, augmented by a third volume, came to a second edition in 1803. In 1803 Mr. John Grahame Dalzell, to whom his country is obliged for his antiquarian labours, published *Scottish Poems of the Sixteenth Century*, which, among other subjects of interest, contains a curious contemporary ballad of 'Belrinnes,' which has some stanzas of considerable merit.

The year 1806 was distinguished by the appearance of '*Popular Ballads and Songs, from Traditions, Manuscripts, and Scarce Editions, with Translations of Similar Pieces from the Ancient Danish Language, and a few Originals by the Editor,* Robert Jamieson, A.M. and F.A.S.' This work, which was not greeted by the public with the attention it deserved, opened a new discovery regarding the original source of Scottish ballads. Mr. Jamieson's extensive acquaintance with the Scandinavian literature enabled him to detect not only a general similarity betwixt these and the Danish ballads preserved in the *Kempe Viser,* an early collection of heroic ballads in that language, but to demonstrate that, in many cases, the stories and songs were distinctly the same, a circumstance which no antiquary had hitherto so much as suspected. Mr. Jamieson's annotations are also very valuable, and preserve some curious illustrations of the old poets. His imitations, though he is not entirely free from the affectation of using rather too many obsolete words, are generally highly interesting. The work fills an important place in the collections of those who are addicted to this branch of antiquarian study.

Mr. John Finlay, a poet whose career was cut short by a premature death, published a short collection of *Scottish Historical and Romantic Ballads,* in 1808. The beauty of some imitations of the old Scottish ballad, with the good sense, learning, and modesty of the preliminary dissertations, must make all admirers of ancient lore regret the early loss of this accomplished young man.

Various valuable collections of ancient ballad poetry have appeared of late years, some of which are illustrated with learning and acuteness, as those of Mr. Motherwell and Mr. Kinloch intimate much taste and feeling for this species of literature. Nor is there any want of editions of ballads, less designed for public sale, than to preserve floating pieces of minstrelsy which are in immediate danger of perishing. Several of those, edited, as we have occasion to know, by men of distinguished talent, have appeared in a smaller form and more limited edition, and must soon be among the *introuvables* of Scottish typography.

We would particularise a duodecimo, under the modest title of a *Ballad Book*, without place or date annexed, which indicates, by a few notes only, the capacity which the editor possesses for supplying the most extensive and ingenious illustrations upon antiquarian subjects. Most of the ballads are of a comic character, and some of them admirable specimens of Scottish dry humour. Another collection which calls for particular distinction, is in the same size, or nearly so, and bears the same title with the preceding one, the date being Edinburgh, 1827. But the contents are announced as containing the budget, or stock-in-trade, of an old Aberdeenshire minstrel, the very last, probably, of the race, who, according to Percy's definition of the profession, sung his own compositions, and those of others, through the capital of the country, and other towns in that country of gentlemen. This man's name was Charles Leslie, but he was known more generally by the nickname of Mussel-mou'd Charlie, from a singular projection of his under lip. His death was thus announced in the newspapers for October 1792:—'Died at Old Rain, in Aberdeenshire, aged one hundred and four years, Charles Leslie, a hawker, or ballad-singer, well known in that country by the name of Mussel-mou'd Charlie. He followed his occupation till within a few weeks of his death.' Charlie was a devoted Jacobite, and so popular in Aberdeen, that he enjoyed in that city a sort of monopoly of the minstrel calling, no other person being allowed, under any pretence, to chant ballads on the causeway, or plane-stanes, of 'the brave burgh.' Like the former collection, most of Mussel-mou'd Charlie's songs were of a jocose character.

But the most extensive and valuable additions which have been of late made to this branch of ancient literature are the collections of Mr. Peter Buchan of Peterhead, a person of indefatigable research in that department, and whose industry has been crowned with the most successful results. This is partly owing to the country where Mr. Buchan resides, which, full as it is of minstrel relics, has been but little ransacked by any former collectors; so that, while it is a very rare event south of the Tay, to recover any ballad having a claim to antiquity, which has not been examined and republished in some one or other of our collections of ancient poetry, those of Aberdeenshire have been comparatively little attended to. The present Editor was the first to solicit attention to those northern songs, in consequence of a collection of ballads communicated to him by his late respected friend, Lord Woodhouselee. Mr. Jamieson, in his collections of *Songs and Ballads*, being himself a native of Morayshire, was able to push this inquiry much farther, and at the same time, by doing so, to illustrate his theory of the connection between the ancient Scottish and Danish ballads, upon which the publication of Mr. Buchan throws much light. It is, indeed, the most complete collection of the kind which has yet appeared.

Of the originality of the ballads in Mr. Buchan's collection we do not entertain the slightest doubt. Several (we may instance the curious tale of 'The Two Magicians') are translated from the Norse, and Mr. Buchan is probably unacquainted with the originals. Others refer to points of history, with which the editor does not seem to be familiar. It is out of no disrespect to this laborious and useful antiquary, that we observe his prose composition is rather florid, and forms, in this respect, a strong contrast to the extreme simplicity of the ballads, which gives us the most distinct assurance that he has delivered the latter to the public in the shape in which he found them. Accordingly, we have never seen any collection of Scottish poetry appearing, from internal evidence, so decidedly and indubitably original. It is perhaps a pity that Mr. Buchan did not remove some obvious errors and corruptions; but, in truth, though their remaining on record is an injury to the effect of the ballads, in point of composition, it is, in some degree, a proof of their authenticity. Besides, although the exertion of this editorial privilege, of selecting readings, is an advantage to the ballads themselves, we are contented rather to take the whole in their present, though imperfect state, than that the least doubt should be thrown upon them, by amendments or alterations, which might render their authenticity doubtful. The historical poems, we observe, are few and of no remote date. That of the 'Bridge of Dee' is amongst the oldest, and there are others referring to the times of the Covenanters. Some, indeed, are composed on still more recent events; as the marriage of the mother of the late illustrious Byron, and a catastrophe of still later occurrence, 'The Death of Leith-Hall.'

As we wish to interest the admirers of ancient minstrel lore in this curious collection, we shall only add, that, on occasion of a new edition, we would recommend to Mr. Buchan to leave out a number of songs which he has only inserted because they are varied, sometimes for the worse, from sets which have appeared in other publications. This restriction would make considerable room for such as, old though they be, possess to this age all the grace of novelty.

To these notices of late collections of Scottish Ballads, we ought to add some remarks on the very curious '*Ancient Legendary Tales,* printed chiefly from Original Sources, edited by the Rev. Charles Henry Hartshorne, M.A., 1829.' The editor of this unostentatious work has done his duty to the public with much labour and care, and made the admirers of this species of poetry acquainted with very many ancient legendary poems, which were hitherto unpublished and very little known. It increases the value of the collection that many of them are of a comic turn, a species of composition more rare, and, from its necessary allusion to domestic manners, more curious and interesting, than the serious class of Romances.

We have thus, in a cursory manner, gone through the history of English and Scottish popular poetry, and noticed the principal collections which have been formed from time to time of such compositions, and the principles on which the editors have proceeded. It is manifest that, of late, the public attention has been so much turned to the subject by men of research and talent, that we may well hope to retrieve from oblivion as much of our ancient poetry as there is now any possibility of recovering.

Another important part of our task consists in giving some account of the modern imitation of the English Ballad, a species of literary labour which the author has himself pursued with some success. Our remarks on this species of composition are prefixed to the fourth volume of the present edition.

"Novalis"

1772–1801

"Novalis" was the pseudonym of Georg Friedrich Philipp von Hardenberg, who was born on May 2, 1772, on his father's estate in Prussian Saxony. His family belonged to the Protestant nobility of Lower Saxony and had called themselves *de Novali* since the thirteenth century. He studied law at Jena and at Leipzig, where he became a friend of Schiller and Friedrich von Schlegel, and was introduced to the writings of Kant and Fichte. He completed his studies in philosophy, history, and law at Wittenberg, then held positions in local government while continuing to read widely, concentrating particularly on the natural sciences.

In 1795 he became engaged to the fourteen-year-old Sophie von Kühn, whose death two years later prompted his composition of *Hymnen an die Nacht* (1800), six prose poems interspersed with verse that celebrate death as a higher form of life in the presence of God. Two collections of fragments, *Blutenstaub* (1798) and *Glauben und Liebe* (1798), represent his attempts to unite poetry, philosophy, and science in an allegorical interpretation of the world. Novalis' two novels, again both fragments, are *Die Lehringe zu Sais* (1798) and *Heinrich von Ofterdingen* (1799–1800), the latter his most important work. Set in the Middle Ages, it depicts the poet von Ofterdingen (believed by Novalis and his Romantic contemporaries to be the author of the *Niebelungenlied*) as transforming the world through the power of his imagination.

Novalis's writing had a considerable influence on the later Romantics and the Symbolists. He died of tuberculosis at Weissenfels on March 25, 1801.

Selected Aphorisms

FROM

POLLEN

1. Imagination represents the afterlife either on high or in the depths or in metempsychosis. We dream of journeys through the universe, but is the universe not within us? We do not realize the profundities of our spirits. Inward is the direction of the mystic path. Within us or nowhere is eternity with its worlds of past and future. The external world is the world of shadows; it casts its shadow into the realm of light. Now it may well seem to us dark within, lonely, formless. But how very differently we will think when this darkness is past and the shadow-body has moved away. We shall enjoy more than ever: for our spirits have known privation.

2. Darwin makes the remark that we are less dazzled by the light upon awakening if we have been dreaming about visible objects. Blessed, then, are they who have already dreamed here about seeing. They will more readily be able to bear the glory of the other world.

3. How can a human being have sense for anything if he does not have the germ of it within himself? Whatever I am to understand must develop organically within me; and whatever I seem to be learning is only a feeding, an incitement to the organism.

4. The seat of the soul is where the inner world and the outer world meet. Where they overlap, it is in every point of the overlap.

5. The sense of shame is the awareness of profanation. Friendship, love, and piety must be treated with secrecy. Only in rare and intimate moments should we speak of them, reaching silent agreements upon them. Many things are too delicate to be thought about, many more too delicate for discussing.

6. Self-expression is the source of all abasement, just as, contrariwise, it is the basis for all true elevation. The first step is introspection—exclusive contemplation of the self. But whoever stops there goes only half way. The second step must be genuine observation outward—spontaneous, sober observation of the external world.

7. A man will never achieve anything excellent in the way of representation so long as he wishes to represent nothing more than his own experiences, his own favorite objects, so long as he cannot bring himself to study with diligence and to represent at his leisure an object wholly foreign and wholly uninteresting to him. One who would portray must be able to portray anything, must want to portray anything. Thus is developed the lofty style of representation so much admired, and rightly so, of Goethe.

8. The highest goal of development is to gain control of one's transcendental

self, to become equal to the ego of the ego. All the less surprising is the lack of complete sense and understanding for others. Without total self-understanding no one will ever really learn to understand others.

9. In serene souls there is no wit. Wit indicates a disturbed equilibrium. It is the result of a disturbance and at the same time the means of regaining balance. Passion possesses the sharpest wit. Genuinely social wit is without bite. There is a variety of the latter which is nothing but magical play of colors amid higher spheres. The situation of the dissolution of all relationships, despair, or spiritual death, is the most frightfully witty of all.

10. Can anything be said in favor of the recently so much abused average man? Does not the greatest strength belong to durable mediocrity? And is man supposed to be anything more than one of the *populo*?

11. Wherever a genuine propensity to reflection prevails, not merely for the thinking of this or that thought, there there is progrediency. A great many learned people do not have this propensity. They have learned how to deduce and conclude, as a shoemaker has learned how to make shoes, without ever having hit upon the idea of taking the trouble to find the basis for their thoughts. And yet salvation lies upon no other path. With many people this propensity lasts only for a time. It waxes and wanes, very often with the years, often with the discovery of a *system which they sought only in order to be absolved from further trouble of reflection.*

12. Every beloved object is the mid-point of a Paradise.

13. Wit, as a principle of affinities, is simultaneously the *menstruum universale*. Witty combinations are, e.g., Jew and cosmopolite, childhood and wisdom, banditry and nobility, virtue and hetaera-ship, abundance and want of critical judgment in naïveté, and so on *ad infinitum.*

14. Social impulse is organizational impulse. By virtue of this spiritual assimilation a good society will often develop out of quite ordinary components, around a man of intelligence.

15. The best thing in the sciences is their philosophical ingredient—like life in an organic body. Dephilosophize the sciences and what is left? Earth, air, and water.

16. Law courts, theatres, court, church, government, public assemblies, academies, directorial boards, etc., are, as it were, the special internal organs of the mystic state-individual.

17. All accidents of our lives are materials out of which we can make whatever we like. One who has much intelligence will make much of his life. Every acquaintance, every incident might, for a thoroughly gifted person, become the first link of an infinite series, the beginning of an unending novel.

18. The noble mercantile spirit, the true big business, flourished only in the Middle Ages, most particularly at the time of the German Hansa. The Medici,

the Fuggers, were merchants as they should be. All our merchants, not excepting the Hopes and the Teppers, are nothing but tradesmen.

19. A translation is either grammatical, or transformative, or mythic.

Mythic translations are translations in the grand manner. They portray the pure and perfect character of the individual art work. They do not give us the actual art work, but its ideal. There still does not exist a total model of such. But in the spirit of many criticisms and descriptions of art works there are lively traces of such to be found. They need a head in which poetic intelligence and philosophical intelligence have interpenetrated to their fullest extent. Greek mythology is in part such a translation of a national religion. The modern Madonna is also such a myth.

Grammatical translations are translations in the usual sense. They require much erudition—but only discursive capabilities.

To the transformative translations belongs, if they are to be genuine, the highest poetic spirit. They verge slightly on travesty—like Bürger's Homer in iambs, Pope's Homer, French translations in general. The true translator of this sort must in fact be the artist himself and be able to present the idea of the whole this way or that way at will. He must be the poet's poet and thus be able to allow him to speak in accordance with his own idea and at the same time in accordance with the poet's idea. The genius of mankind stands in a similar relationship to each individual person.

Not only books, but everything can be translated in these three manners.

20. Where children are, there is the Golden Age.

21. The more limited a system is, the more it will please the worldly wise. Thus the system of the materialists, the doctrine of Helvetius and of Locke as well, have had the greatest success among that class. Even now Kant still finds more adherents than Fichte.

22. The art of writing books has not yet been invented. But it is on the point of being invented. Fragments of this sort are literary seed-grain. There may be, to be sure, many a dead kernel among them—but if only a few spring up. . . .

23. If the spirit sanctifies, every real book is a Bible.

24. Describing human beings has hitherto been impossible because it was not known what a human being was. Once it is known what a human being is, it will be possible to describe individuals in genuine genetic fashion. Anyone who holds fragments of this sort to the letter may be an honorable man—only, he shouldn't call himself a poet. Must we be always circumspect? He who is too old for enthusiasm, let him avoid youthful gatherings. Now there are literary saturnalia. The more motley life is, the better.

25. Do we perhaps require so much strength and exertion for common and ordinary things because nothing is more uncommon, more out-of-the-ordinary for the actual human creature than dreary routine?

26. We are close to waking when we dream that we are dreaming.

27. Reviewers are literary policemen. Doctors belong among the policemen. Hence the need for critical journals that treat authors professionally by medicine and by surgery and that do not merely track down the disease and with malicious pleasure announce it. Previous methods of cure were largely barbaric. Genuine policing is not just defensive and polemical against the evil at hand, but seeks to improve the sick installation.

FROM

MISCELLANEOUS FRAGMENTS

1. The raw discursive thinker is a scholastic. The true scholastic is a mystical subtilizer. Out of logical atoms he builds his universe—he annihilates all living nature in order to put an artifice of thought in its place. His objective is an infinite automaton. Opposed to him is the raw intuitive thinker. He is a mystical macrologue. He hates rules and fixed forms. A wild, violent life prevails in Nature—everything is alive. No laws—arbitrariness and miracles everywhere. He is purely dynamic.

2. Every person who consists of several persons is a person raised to a higher power—or a genius. . . .

3. Lessing saw too sharply and in so doing lost the feeling for the unclear totality, the magical view of objects together in multiple lighting and shadow.

4. Klopstock's works seem to be mostly free translations and arrangements of an unknown poet by a very talented but unpoetical philologist.

5. The artist stands on mankind like a statue on its pedestal.

6. Lyric poetry is for heroes, it makes heroes. Narrative poetry is for human beings. Heroes are lyric, human beings are narrative, genius is dramatic. Man is lyric, woman is narrative, marriage is dramatic.

7. Only an artist can divine the meaning of life.

8. The system of morality must become the system of Nature. All sickness is like sin in the sense that it is a transcendency. Our sicknesses are all phenomena of a heightened sensation that is seeking to pass over into higher powers. When man tried to become God, he sinned. Sicknesses of plants are animalizations, sicknesses of animals are rationalizations, sicknesses of stones are vegetizations. Should not each stone and animal correspond to a particular plant? Plants are dead stones, animals are dead plants.

9. Anyone seeking God will find Him everywhere.

10. Nothing is more accessible to the mind than the infinite.

11. Seasons, times of day, lives and destinies, are all, strikingly enough, thoroughly rhythmical, metrical, according to a beat. In all trades and arts, in

all machines, in organic bodies, in our daily functions, everywhere: rhythm, meter, beat, melody. Anything we do with a certain skill, we do rhythmically without being aware of it. Rhythm is found everywhere. All mechanisms are metrical, rhythmical. There must be more to this. Could it be simply the influence of laziness?

12. Who has declared the Bible completed? Should the Bible not be still in the process of growth?

13. Every wrong action, every unworthy emotion is infidelity to the Beloved, an adultery.

14. There is only one temple in the world and that is the human body. Nothing is more sacred than that noble form.

15. Spinoza is a man drunk with God.

16. Man is a sun and his senses are his planets.

17. The more personal, local, temporal, particularized a poem is, the nearer it stands to the *centrum* of poetry. A poem must be completely inexhaustible, like a human being or a good proverb.

18. If God could become man, then He can also become stone, plant, animal, and element, and perhaps in this way there is a continuous redemption in Nature.

19. Dreams are extremely important for the psychologist—and for the historian of human races. Dreams have contributed very much to the culture and development of mankind. Hence, rightly, the former great respect for dreams.

20. A character is a fully developed will.

21. Language is Delphi.

22. Republic is the *fluidum deferens* of youth. Where young people are, there is republic.

23. With marriage the system alters. The married man desires order, security, and peace—he wants to live as a family in a family, in an orderly household: he seeks true monarchy.

Friedrich von Schlegel

1772–1829

Friedrich von Schlegel was born in Hanover on March 10, 1772, a younger brother of A. W. von Schlegel, who achieved fame through his German translations of Shakespeare. Friedrich studied law, then philosophy, art, and the classics at Göttingen and Leipzig. Greek philosophy and culture were essential, he believed, to a complete education, a view he put forth in *Über das Studium der griechischen Poesie* (1797) and the *Geschichte der Poesie der Griechen und Romer* (1798). In 1796 Friedrich joined his brother in Jena, and two years later they began publishing the *Athenaeum,* a quarterly review which soon became an influential voice in the Romantic movement.

Friedrich von Schlegel's view of poetry combines a belief in the organic process of nature with the classical notion of universal and ultimate values. The aim of poetry, in his view, is to present that which is eternal and unchanging, but the eternal can be seen only through the veil of concrete nature. In order to reveal the universal in what is present and actual, poetry must be produced from within the traditions of a particular nation or culture. Strongly influenced by the thought of J. G. Fichte, Schlegel believed that modern poetry had to be simultaneously philosophical, mythological, ironic, and religious. His famous review of *Wilhelm Meister* in the *Athenäum* praised Goethe's work as prototypically Romantic.

Schlegel taught briefly at the University of Jena, then went to Paris in 1802 with a daughter of Moses Mendelssohn, whom he married two years later. In Paris he studied Sanskrit and composed the first study of Indo-German linguistics, *Über die Sprache und Weisheit der Inder* (1808). In 1808 he and his wife converted to Catholicism; at this point, his Romanticism underwent a fundamental change. He began to espouse the ideals of medieval Christendom, and called for a new construction of society, based upon the social order of the Middle Ages (wherein the Church stood at the center of public life and thought). He developed this concept in a series of lectures he gave in Vienna between 1810 and 1812.

Much of the remainder of his life was devoted to conservative political activity. In 1820 he became editor of the right-wing Catholic paper *Concordia;* an attack in the paper by him on the Romanticism he had formerly espoused led to an irreconcilable breach with his brother. He died in Dresden on January 12, 1829.

THE ATHENAEUM

About no subject is there less philosophizing than about philosophy. (1.)

3. Kant introduced the concept of the negative into philosophy. Would it not also be worthwhile to try to introduce the concept of the positive into philosophy?

5. What is called good society is usually nothing but a mosaic of polished caricatures.

10. Duty is for Kant the One and All. Out of the duty of gratitude, he claims, one has to defend and esteem the ancients; and only out of duty has he become a great man.

16. If the essence of cynicism consists in preferring nature to art, virtue to beauty and science; in not bothering about the letter—to which the Stoic strictly adheres—but in looking up to the spirit of things; in absolute contempt of all economic values and political splendor, and in courageous defence of the rights of independent freedom; then Christianity would be nothing but universal cynicism.

19. The surest method of being incomprehensible or, moveover, to be misunderstood is to use words in their original sense; especially words from the ancient languages.

22. A project is the subjective germ of a developing object. A perfect project should simultaneously be entirely subjective and entirely objective—an indivisible and living individual. As to its origin, it should be entirely subjective, original, and possible only in this mind; as to its character, entirely objective, physical, and morally necessary. The sense for projects—which could be called aphorisms of the future—differs from the sense for aphorisms of the past only in direction, progressive in the former and regressive in the latter. The essential thing is the ability to idealize and realize matters immediately and simultaneously, to complete them and carry them out partly within oneself. Since the word transcendental refers precisely to the unification and separation of the ideal and the real, one could easily say that the sense for aphorisms and projects is the transcendental part of the historical spirit.

24. Many works of the ancients have become fragments. Many works of the moderns are fragments at the time of their origin.

25. The German national character is a favorite subject of character experts, probably because the less mature a nation, the more she is an object of criticism and not of history.

27. Like Leibniz's possible worlds, most men are only equally entitled pretenders to existence. There are few existences.

29. Witty inspirations are the proverbs of the educated.

31. Prudishness is pretense of innocence without innocence. Women have to remain prudish as long as men are sentimental, dense, and evil enough to demand of them eternal innocence and lack of education. For innocence is the only thing which can ennoble lack of education.

32. One should have wit, but not wish to have it; otherwise there will be witticism, the Alexandrian style of wit.

34. Almost all marriages are only concubinages, liaisons, or rather provisional attempts, remote approximations of real marriage. The true nature of marriage does not conform to the paradoxes of this or that system, but rather according to all canonical and secular laws that more than one person should become only one. This ought to warrant the least possible infringement of free will, which certainly has a right to be consulted when the question at issue is whether one is to be an individual or only the integral part of a common personality; it is even hard to see what legitimate argument can be raised against a *marriage à quatre*. But if the state must insist on holding together those attempts at marriage that have failed, it is actually obstructing marriage, for its cause would be advanced by new and possibly more successful attempts.

37. Many a witty inspiration is like the surprising reunion of befriended thoughts after a long separation.

39. Most thoughts are only profiles of thoughts. They must be inverted and synthesized with their antipodes. Thus many philosophical writings become very interesting which would not have been so otherwise.

42. Good drama must be drastic.

43. Philosophy still moves too much straight ahead, and is not yet cyclical enough.

44. Every philosophical review ought to be a philosophy of reviews at the same time.

49. Women are treated as unjustly in poetry as in life. The feminine ones are not idealistic, and the idealistic, not feminine.

50. True love should be, according to its origin, entirely arbitrary and entirely accidental at the same time; it should seem both necessary and free; in keeping with its nature, however, it should be both destiny and virtue and appear as a mystery and a miracle.

51. The naive is what is or appears to be natural, individual, or classical to the point of irony or to the point of continuous alternation of self-creation and self-destruction. If it is only instinct, then it is childlike, childish, or silly; if it is only intention, it becomes affectation. The naive which is simultaneously beautiful, poetic, and idealistic, must be both intention and instinct. The essence of intention, in this sense, is freedom. Consciousness is far from intention. There is a certain enamoured contemplation of one's own natural-

ness or silliness which itself is unspeakably silly. Intention does not necessarily require a profound calculation or plan. Even Homeric naiveté is not merely instinct: there is at least as much intention in it as in the gracefulness of loving children or innocent girls. Even if Homer did not have particular intentions, his poetry and the actual authoress of his poetry, nature, does have intention.

53. It is equally deadly for a mind to have a system or to have none. Therefore it will have to decide to combine both.

54. One can only become a philosopher, but not be one. As soon as one believes he is a philosopher, he stops being one.

56. Since philosophy now criticizes everything it comes across, a critique of philosophy would be nothing more than a just reprisal.

61. The few existing writings against Kantian philosophy are the most important documents in the case history of sound common sense.

62. Publication is to thinking as confinement is to the first kiss.

63. Every uneducated person is a caricature of himself.

64. The obsession with moderation is the spirit of castrated narrowmindedness.

66. When the author has no idea as to what to reply to the critic, he then likes to say: you cannot do it better anyway. This is the same as if a dogmatic philosopher would reproach a sceptic for not being able to devise a system.

74. In the corrupt linguistic usage, verisimilitude means as much as "nearly true" or "somewhat true," or something that once could become true. But by its very composition, the word cannot mean all this. What appears to be true, does not have to be true even in the smallest degree: and yet it must appear positive. Verisimilitude is the object of intelligence, of the ability to distinguish among the possible consequences of free actions the real ones, and it is something entirely subjective. That which some logicians have called and tried to calculate as verisimilitude is possibility.

77. A dialogue is a chain or a wreath of aphorisms. A correspondence is a dialogue on an enlarged scale, and memorabilia are a system of aphorisms. As yet there is nothing which is aphoristic in matter and form, altogether subjective and individual, simultaneously completely objective, and a necessary part in the system of all sciences.

80. The historian is a prophet looking backward.

82. Philosophical demonstrations are demonstrations in the sense of military language. Philosophical deductions are no better than those of politics: in the sciences, too, one first takes possession of an area and demonstrates one's claim to it later on. We can apply to definitions what Chamfort said about the friends we have in the world. There are three kinds of explanations in science: explanations which throw a light upon, or give a hint at a matter; explanations

which do not explain anything; and explanations which obscure everything. Good definitions cannot be made off-hand, but ought to occur to us spontaneously. A definition which is not witty is worth nothing, and for every individual there is an infinite number of real definitions. The necessary formalities of this artificial philosophy degenerate into protocol and luxury. Their aim and value consist in proving virtuosity to be legitimate, like the bravura-arias of singers and the Latin writing of the philologists. It must be admitted, however, that their rhetorical effect is not bad. The main thing, however, is to know something and to say it. The attempt to prove or even to explain it is quite superfluous in most cases. The categorical style of the twelve commandments and the thetical method through which purely speculative facts are presented without any veil, any attentuation, and any artificial disguise as texts for studying and symphilosophizing are most appropriate for enlightened natural philosophy. If both are to be done equally well, there is doubtless more difficulty in stating something than in explaining it. There are plenty of demonstrations excellent in their form which prove to be false and trivial statements. Leibniz stated and Wolff proved. Enough said.

84. Considered subjectively, philosophy always begins in the middle, like an epic poem.

87. The most important thing in love is the sense for one another, and the highest thing, the faith in one another. Devotion is the expression of that faith, and pleasure can revive and enhance that sense, even if not create it, as is commonly thought. Therefore, sensuality can delude bad persons for a short time into thinking they could love each other.

89. Criticism is the only substitute for the equally impossible moral mathematics and science of propriety sought for in vain by many a philosopher.

90. The subject of history is the gradual realization of all that is practically necessary.

93. The doctrine of the spirit and the letter of things is interesting for the following reason among others; that it could bring in touch philosophy and philology.

96. Whoever does not philosophize for the sake of philosophy, but rather uses philosophy as a means, is a sophist.

102. Women have no sense at all for art, yet indeed for poetry. They have no talent for science, yet for philosophy. By no means do they lack speculation and inner vision of the infinite, but only the power of abstraction which can be learned so much more easily.

108. Beautiful is that which is simultaneously attractive and sublime.

111. The lessons of a novel ought to be of such a character that they are communicable only as a whole and cannot be proved singularly or exhausted analytically. Otherwise the rhetorical form would be far more preferable.

113. A classification is a definition comprising a system of definitions.

114. A definition of poetry can only determine what poetry should be and not what poetry actually was and is; otherwise the most concise formula would be: Poetry is that which at some time and some place was thus named.

116. Romantic poetry is a progressive universal poetry. Its mission is not merely to reunite all separate genres of poetry and to put poetry in touch with philosophy and rhetorics. It will, and should, now mingle and now amalgamate poetry and prose, genius and criticism, the poetry of art and the poetry of nature, render poetry living and social, and life and society poetic, poetize wit, fill and saturate the forms of art with solid cultural material of every kind, and inspire them with vibrations of humor. It embraces everything poetic, from the greatest system of art which, in turn, includes many systems, down to the sigh, the kiss, which the musing child breathes forth in artless song. It can lose itself in what it represents to such a degree that one might think its one and only goal were the characterization of poetic individuals of every type; and yet no form has thus far arisen appropriate to expressing the author's mind so perfectly, so that artists who just wanted to write a novel have by coincidence described themselves. Romantic poetry alone can, like the epic, become a mirror of the entire surrounding world, a picture of its age. And yet, it too can soar, free from all real and ideal interests, on the wings of poetic reflection, midway between the work and the artist. It can even exponentiate this reflection and multiply it as in an endless series of mirrors. It is capable of the highest and the most universal education; not only by creating from within, but also from without, since it organizes in similar fashion all parts of what is destined to become a whole; thus, a view is opened to an endlessly developing classicism. Among the arts Romantic poetry is what wit is to philosophy, and what society, association, friendship, and love are in life. Other types of poetry are completed and can now be entirely analyzed. The Romantic type of poetry is still becoming; indeed, its peculiar essence is that it is always becoming and that it can never be completed. It cannot be exhausted by any theory, and only a divinatory criticism might dare to characterize its ideal. It alone is infinite, as it alone is free; and as its first law it recognizes that the arbitrariness of the poet endures no law above him. The Romantic genre of poetry is the only one which is more than a genre, and which is, as it were, poetry itself: for in a certain sense all poetry is or should be Romantic.

117. Those works whose ideal has not as much living reality and, as it were, personality as the beloved one or a friend had better remain unwritten. They would at least never become works of art.

124. If one writes or reads novels from the point of view of psychology, it is very inconsistent and petty to want to shy away from even the slowest and most detailed analysis of the most unnatural lusts, gruesome tortures, shocking infamy, and disgusting sensual or spiritual impotence.

125. Perhaps a completely new epoch of sciences and arts would arise, if symphilosophy and sympoetry became so universal and intimate that it would no longer be unusual if several characters who complement each other would

produce common works. Sometimes one can scarcely resist the idea that two minds might actually belong together like separate halves, and that only in union could they be what they might be. Were there an art of fusing individuals, or could postulating criticism do somewhat more than just postulate—and there are everywhere so many indications for this—then I should like to see Jean Paul and Peter Leberecht [Ludwig Tieck] fused. The latter has precisely everything the former lacks. The fusion of Jean Paul's grotesque talent and Peter Leberecht's fantastic education would produce an excellent Romantic poet.

139. From the Romantic point of view, also the modifications of poetry, even the eccentric and monstrous ones, have their value as raw material and preliminary exercises of universality, provided they contain something, if only they are original.

146. As the novel permeates all modern poetry, thus tinges satire—which through all transformations always remained among the Romans a classical universal poetry, a social poetry from and for the center of the cultured universe—all Roman poetry, even the whole of Roman literature, and establishes, as it were, its tone. One has to have loved and understood Horace's satires for a long time in order to have a sense for that which is the most urbane, original, and beautiful in the prose of a Cicero, Caesar, or Suetonius. These are the eternal fountainheads of urbanity.

155. The rude cosmopolitan attempts of the Carthaginians and other peoples of classical antiquity, compared to the political universality of the Romans, appear like the natural poetry of uncivilized nations compared to the classical art of the Greeks. Only the Romans were content with the spirit of despotism and despised its letter; they alone had naive tyrants.

166. The genuine talent of the poetic Tacitus was to characterize nations and ages, to depict the great in a grand style. In historical portraits, however, the critical Suetonius is the greater master.

196. Pure autobiographies are written either by neurotics who are fascinated by their ego, as in Rousseau's case; or by authors of a robust artistic or adventuresome self-love, such as Benvenuto Cellini; or by born historians who regard themselves only as material for historic art; or by women who also coquette with posterity; or by pedantic minds who want to bring even the most minute things in order before they die and cannot let themselves leave the world without commentaries. Autobiographies can also be regarded as mere plaidoyers before the public. Another great group among the autobiographers is formed by the autopseusts.

206. An aphorism ought to be entirely isolated from the surrounding world like a little work of art and complete in itself like a hedgehog.

216. The French Revolution, Fichte's *Theory of Knowledge,* and Goethe's *Wilhelm Meister* are the three greatest tendencies of the age. Whoever takes offence at this combination, and whoever does not consider a revolution

important unless it is blatant and palpable, has not yet risen to the lofty and broad vantage point of the history of mankind. Even in our meager histories of culture, which usually resemble a collection of variants accompanied by a running commentary whose classical text has been lost, many a little book of which the noisy rabble scarcely took notice in its time, plays a greater role than did all this rabble.

220. If wit is the principle and organ of universal philosophy, and if philosophy is nothing but the spirit of universality, that is, the science of all perpetually mixing and separating sciences, a logical chemistry, as it were: then that absolute, enthusiastic, and completely material wit is of infinite value and dignity, in which Bacon was one of the first, and Leibniz one of the greatest virtuosos, both leaders in the art of scholastic prose. The most important scientific discoveries are *bon mots* in their genre. They are this by virtue of the astonishing accident of their origin, the combinatory character of thought, and the baroque quality of their casual expression. In their substance, however, they are indeed much more than the mere expectation of a purely poetic wit which resolves itself into nothing. The best are *échappées de vue* into infinity. Leibniz's whole philosophy consists of some aphorisms and projects which are witty in this sense. Kant, the Copernicus of philosophy, has by his nature perhaps more of this syncretistic spirit and critical wit than Leibniz: his situation, however, as well as his education, is not so witty; his ideas have the same destiny as popular tunes: the Kantians sang them to death; thus, one is easily inclined to do him an injustice and to consider him less witty than he really is. To be sure, philosophy is in good condition only if it must no longer wait for and expect inspirations of genius, but can progress steadily with a sure method by enthusiastic strength and the art of genius. But shall we disregard the few still existing products of synthesizing genius only because the combinatory art and science does not yet exist? And how could it exist as long as we are still spelling most of the sciences as if we were sixth-grade boys flattering ourselves that we have achieved our goal if we can decline and conjugate in one of the numerous dialects of philosophy—without hitherto knowing anything about syntax, or how to construct even the smallest sentences?

222. The revolutionary desire to realize God's kingdom on earth is the elastic point of progressive development and the beginning of modern history. Whatever is without relationship to God's kingdom, is for it only incidental.

233. Religion is usually nothing but a supplement to or even a substitute for education, and nothing is religious in the strict sense which is not a product of freedom. Thus one can say: The freer, the more religious; and the more education, the less religion.

234. To maintain that there is only one mediator is very one-sided and presumptuous. For the perfect Christian—and in this regard the unique Spinoza comes nearest to being one—everything should be a mediator.

238. There is a poetry whose One and All is the relationship of the ideal and the

real: it should thus be called transcendental poetry according to the analogy of the technical language of philosophy. It begins in the form of satire with the absolute disparity of ideality and reality, it hovers in their midst in the form of the elegy, and it ends in the form of the idyll with the absolute identity of both. But we should not care for a transcendental philosophy unless it were critical, unless it portrayed the producer along with the product, unless it embraced in its system of transcendental thoughts a characterization of transcendental thinking: in the same way, that poetry which is not infrequently encountered in modern poets should combine those transcendental materials and preliminary exercises for a poetic theory of the creative power with the artistic reflection and beautiful self-mirroring, which is present in Pindar, the lyric fragments of the Greeks, the ancient elegy: and among the moderns, in Goethe: thus this poetry should portray itself with each of its portrayals; everywhere and at the same time, it should be poetry and the poetry of poetry.

247. Dante's prophetic poem is the only system of transcendental poetry and still the highest of its kind. Shakespeare's universality is like the focus of Romantic art. Goethe's purely poetic poetry is the most complete poetry of poetry. This is the great triad of modern poetry, the innermost and most sacred sphere among all the narrower and wider spheres constituting the critical selection of the classics of modern literature.

248. Singular great men are not so isolated among the Greeks and the Romans. They had fewer men of genius, but more geniality. Everything Classical is of genius. The entire antiquity is a genius, the only genius that without exaggeration can be called absolutely great, unique, and unattainable.

255. The more poetry becomes knowledge, the more it also becomes art. If poetry is to become art, and if the artist is to have a thorough knowledge and scholarship of his means and goals, their hindrances and subjects, he has to philosophize about his art. If he is to become not only an inventor and worker, but also an expert in his field, and also be able to understand his fellow-citizens in the realm of art, he must also become a philologist.

259.—A. Aphorisms, you maintain, are the true form of the universal philosophy. The form does not matter. What, however, can these aphorisms achieve and be for the greatest and most serious concern of mankind, the perfection of knowledge?—B. Nothing but Lessing's salt against decay, perhaps a cynical *lanx satura* in the classical style of Lucilius and Horace, or even *fermenta cognitionis* for the critical philosophy, marginal notes to the text of the age.

262. Every good man progressively becomes God. To become God, to be man, and to educate oneself, are expressions that are synonymous.

268. A so-called happy marriage corresponds to love as a correct poem to an improvised song.

299. With respect to ingenious subconsciousness, I think, philosophers might well rival poets.

300. When reason and unreason come into contact, an electrical shock occurs. This is called polemics.

305. Intention to the point of irony and having the arbitrary appearance of self-destruction is as naive as instinct to the point of irony. As the naive plays with the contradictions of theory and practice, so the grotesque plays with the odd displacements of form and matter; it likes the air of the casual and odd and flirts with absolute caprice. Humor deals with being and not being; its peculiar essence is reflection. Hence, its kinship with elegy and with everything transcendental; hence, also, its arrogance and its affinity to the mysticism of wit. As genius is necessary for the naive, grave and pure beauty is necessary for humor. Preferably it hovers over lightly and clearly flowing rhapsodies of philosophy or poetry and flees from heavy bulks as well as from incoherent fragments.

344. To philosophize is to seek omniscience together.

365. Mathematics is, as it were, a sensuous logic, and relates to philosophy as do the arts, music, and plastic art to poetry.

366. Reason is mechanical, wit chemical, and genius organic spirit.

367. Authors are often thought to be insulted by comparing them to manu-facturers. Yet should not the true author also be a manufacturer? Should he not devote his entire life to the business of molding literary materials into forms which in a grand manner are practical and useful? We would wish many a bungler a small part of that diligence and care which we hardly appreciate in the most common implements.

395. In true prose everything must be underlined.

DIALOGUE ON POETRY

Poetry befriends and binds with unseverable ties the hearts of all those who love it. Even though in their own lives they may pursue the most diverse ends, may feel contempt for what the other holds most sacred, may fail to appreciate or to communicate with one another, and remain in all other realms strangers forever; in poetry through a higher magic power, they are united and at peace. Each Muse seeks and finds another, and all streams of poetry flow together into the one vast sea.

There is only one reason, and for everyone it remains the same; but just as every man has his own nature and his own love, so does he bear within him his own poetry which must and should remain his own as surely as he is himself, as surely as there is anything original in him. And he must not allow himself to be robbed of his own being, his innermost strength by a criticism that wishes to purge and purify him into a stereotype without spirit and without sense. Fools attempt that who do not know what they are about. But the sublime discipline of genuine criticism should teach the lover of poetry how he ought to form his inner self. Above all it should teach him to grasp every other independent form of poetry in its classical power and abundance, so that the flower and kernel of other minds may become a sustenance and seed for his own imagination.

Never will the mind that knows the orgies of the true Muse journey on this road to the very end, nor will he presume to have reached it; for never will he be able to quench a longing which is eternally regenerated out of the abundance of gratifications. The world of poetry is as infinite and inexhaustible as the riches of animating nature with her plants, animals, and formations of every type, shape, and color. Nor are the artificial or natural products which bear the form and name of poems easily included under the most inclusive term. And what are they, compared with the unformed and unconscious poetry which stirs in the plant and shines in the light, smiles in a child, gleams in the flower of youth, and glows in the loving bosom of women? This, however, is the primeval poetry without which there would be no poetry of words. Indeed, there is and never has been for us humans any other object or source of activity and joy but that one poem of the godhead the earth, of which we, too, are part and flower. We are able to perceive the music of the universe and to understand the beauty of the poem because a part of the poet, a spark of his creative spirit, lives in us and never ceases to glow with secret force deep under the ashes of our self-induced unreason.

It is not necessary for anyone to sustain and propagate poetry through clever speeches and precepts, or, especially, to try to produce it, invent it, establish it, and impose upon it restrictive laws as the theory of poetics would like to. Just as the core of the earth adorned itself with formations and growths,

369

just as life sprang forth of itself from the deep and everything was filled with beings merrily multiplying; even so, poetry bursts forth spontaneously from the invisible primordial power of mankind when the warming ray of the divine sun shines on it and fertilizes it. Only through form and color can man recreate his own creation, and thus one cannot really speak of poetry except in the language of poetry.

Everyone's view of poetry is true and good as far as that view itself is poetry. But since one's poetry is limited, just because it is one's own, so one's view of poetry must of necessity be limited. The mind cannot bear this; no doubt because, without knowing it, it nevertheless does know that no man is merely man, but that at the same time he can and should be genuinely and truly all mankind. Therefore, man, in reaching out time and again beyond himself to seek and find the complement of his innermost being in the depths of another, is certain to return ever to himself. The play of communicating and approaching is the business and the force of life; absolute perfection exists only in death.

Therefore, the poet cannot be satisfied with leaving behind in lasting works the expression of his unique poetry as it was native to him and which he acquired by education. He must strive continually to expand his poetry and his view of poetry, and to approximate the loftiest possibility of it on earth by endeavoring in the most specific way to integrate his part with the entire body of poetry: deadening generalizations result in just the opposite.

He can do this when he has found the center point through communication with those who have found theirs from a different side, in a different way. Love needs a responding love. Indeed, for the true poet communication, even with those who only play on the colorful surface, can be beneficial and instructive. He is a sociable being.

For there has always been a great attraction in speaking about poetry with poets and the poetically-minded. Many such conversations I have never forgotten; in the case of others I do not know exactly what belongs to my imagination and what to my memory; much in them is true, other things are invented. Such, too, is the present dialogue. It is intended to set against one another quite divergent opinions, each of them capable of shedding new light upon the infinite spirit of poetry from an individual standpoint, each of them striving to penetrate from a different angle into the real heart of the matter. It was my interest in this many-sidedness that made me resolve to communicate publicly things that I had observed in a circle of friends and had considered at first only in relation to them—to communicate these things to all those who feel a love in their own hearts and who, by virtue of the fullness of life within them, are disposed to be initiated into the sacred mysteries of nature and poetry.

Amalia and Camilla were just getting involved in an increasingly lively discussion about a new play, when two of the expected friends, whom we shall call Marcus and Antonio, joined the company, laughing loudly. After the two had arrived, the company, accustomed to gather at Amalia's for free and gay pursuit of their mutual inclination, was as complete as it usually was. Without premeditation or rule, it usually happened that poetry was the subject, the occasion, the center of their gathering. —Until now, one or another of them would read a play or some other work, about which there would be a good deal of talk and many good and fine things would be said. Soon, however, everyone sensed something missing in this kind of conversation. Amalia was the first to observe this and to see how it might be remedied. She thought the friends did not realize clearly enough the diversity of their views. Because of this, true exchange became confused and some remained silent who otherwise might have talked. Each, or perhaps at first only one who felt most inclined, should speak from the bottom of his heart his thoughts about poetry or about a part, an aspect of it, or better still, write them down, so that they would have the opinion of each in black and white. Camilla enthusiastically agreed with her friend, so that for once there would be a change from the eternal reading. Only then, she said, would the battle become quite hot, which it must be, for otherwise there was no hope for eternal peace.

The friends approved of the suggestion and immediately went to work. Even Lothario, who usually said and argued the least and often remained silent for hours, not letting himself be disturbed in his dignified calm no matter what the others might say and argue, appeared to take the liveliest interest and even promised to read something. The interest grew with the work and preparations, the ladies made a festive occasion of it. Finally a day was set when each would read his contribution. All these circumstances heightened their attention more than usual, while the tone of their conversation remained as natural and easy as was their wont.

Camilla described and praised with much enthusiasm a play which had been given the day before. Amalia, on the other hand, found fault with it and maintained that there was no trace of art in it or, indeed, of meaning. Her friend readily agreed; but, she said, it was at any rate wild and lively, or at least good actors who were in a good mood could make it so. —If they are really good actors, said Andrea, as he glanced at his manuscript and at the door to see if the missing friends would be coming soon; if they are really good actors, they must lose their good mood at being asked to recreate the mood of the poet.— My friend, replied Amalia, your good mood makes you a poet. The fact that such playwrights are called poets is itself a fiction, and is actually much worse than for the players to call themselves or let themselves be called artists. —Let us have our way, too, said Antonio, siding obviously with Camilla. If for once by a happy chance a spark of life, joy, and wit develops among the common masses, let us rather acknowledge it than always keep telling ourselves how common the common masses are. —This is just what the argument is about, said Amalia. Nothing happened in the play we are talking about except what happens there every day, a good deal of nonsense. Thereupon, she began to quote examples, but soon was asked to stop, for indeed, they proved only too well what they were intended to prove.

Camilla retorted that this did not affect her, for she had not particularly paid attention to the speeches and expressions of the characters in the plays.

—She was asked what it was she had paid attention to, since it was not an operetta. —To the external appearance, she replied, which I let take the place of a light music for me. Then she praised one of the more sophisticated actresses, described her manners, her beautiful clothes, and expressed surprise that such a thing as our theater could be taken so seriously. As a rule, almost everything in it is common; but even in life, which after all affects us even more, the common often makes a very romantic and pleasant appearance. —Almost everything is common as a rule, said Lothario. This is quite correct. Certainly we should not go as frequently to a place where one is fortunate if he does not suffer from crowds, disagreeable odors, or unpleasant neighbors. Once a learned man was asked for an inscription for the theater. I would suggest this: Come, wanderer, and behold utmost triviality. This would be true in most cases.

Here the conversation was interrupted by the arrival of the friends. Had they been present, the argument might have assumed a different direction and developed other complications; for Marcus did not think this way about the theater and could not give up hope that something would yet come of it.

They entered the gathering, as we said, laughing without restraint, and from the last words which could be heard, one could gather that their conversation was about the so-called classical poets of the English. A few things more were said about this subject. Antonio, who occasionally liked to introduce polemical ideas into the conversation although he rarely led it, asserted that the basic principles of English criticism and enthusiasm should be sought in Smith's *On National Wealth*.[1] They were only too glad when they could carry another classic to their public treasure. Just as every book on that island became an essay after it had lain its proper time, in the same manner every writer became a classic. For the same reason and in the same way, they were just as proud of making the best scissors as of making the best poetry. Such an Englishman reads his Shakespeare no differently than he does Pope,[2] Dryden,[3] or whoever else might be a classic; he does no more thinking while reading one than the other. —Marcus declared that the Golden Age was only a modern disease that every nation had to go through, as a child had to have smallpox. —Therefore, one ought to try to decrease the power of the disease through inoculation, said Antonio. Ludovico, who with his revolutionary philosophy pursued annihilation on a grand scale, began to talk of a *system of false poetry* that he wanted to present, which raged and still rages to some extent in this age, especially with the English and the French. The deep, basic connection of all those false trends harmonizing so beautifully, complementing each other, and meeting each other half way in a friendly fashion, he thought as peculiar and instructive as it was amusing and grotesque. His only wish was to be able to write verse, for only in a comic poem could he do properly what he had in mind. He wanted to say more about it, but the ladies interrupted him and asked Andrea to commence; otherwise there would be no end to forewords. Afterwards they could talk and argue all the more. Andrea opened his manuscript and read.

EPOCHS OF LITERATURE

Wherever living spirit appears captured in a formed letter, there is art, there is division, material to be overcome, and tools to be used; there is a plan and laws of execution. This is why we see the masters of poetry striving so vigorously to form it in the most manifold way. Poetry is an art, and when it yet was not, it had to become so. And when it becomes art, it excites in those who truly love it a strong desire to know it, to comprehend the intention of the master, to grasp the nature of the work, the origin of the school, and to discover the process of its development. Art is based on knowledge, and the discipline of art is its history.

It is an essential quality of all art to follow closely what has already been formed. Therefore, history goes back from generation to generation, from phase to phase, always farther back into antiquity, to its original source.

For the modern generation, for Europe, this source resides in Greece, and for the Greeks and their poetry it was Homer and the old school of the Homerids.[4] This was the inexhaustible source of the poetry which in every respect was capable of being formed, a mighty stream of representation in which waves of life rush against one another, a peaceful ocean where the fullness of the earth and the splendor of the heavens are amiably reflected. Just as the sages sought the beginning of nature in water, so does the oldest poetry manifest itself in fluid form.

The body of legends and songs grouped itself around two different focal points. On the one hand there is a great, common undertaking, an onrush of power and discord, the glory of the bravest; and on the other hand the abundance of the sensuous, the new, strange, and charming, the happiness of a family, a paragon of most versatile ingenuity, the way he succeeds in returning home in spite of difficulties. This original division prepared and shaped what we call the *Iliad* and *Odyssey* and whatever else found in this grouping a firm foothold and thus was preserved for posterity, rather than other songs of the same time.

In the growth of Homeric poetry, we see analogically the development of all poetry. But the roots of it are concealed from our eyes, and the flower and branches of the plant arise with incomprehensible beauty from the night of antiquity. This enticingly formed chaos is the seed from which the world of ancient poetry was organized.

The epic form declined rapidly. In its place there arose, even among the Ionians,[5] the art of the iambics, which in both theme and treatment was the direct opposite of mythic poetry. For this reason the iambics became the second focal point of Greek poetry, and along with it the elegy, whose changes and transformations are almost as manifold as those of the epic.

What the poetry of Archilochos[6] was, we must guess not only from the fragments, information, and imitation in Horace's[7] *Epodes*, but also from the analogy with the comedy of Aristophanes,[8] and even the more distant analogy with Roman satire. We have no other material to fill the largest gap in the history of art. Yet everyone willing to reflect does realize that it is a permanent feature of the highest poetry to burst out in holy wrath and express its full power even in the strangest material, that is, everyday reality.

These are the sources of Greek poetry, its basis and beginning. The most beautiful flower includes the lyrical, choral, tragic, and comic works of the Dorians,[9] Aeolians,[10] and Athenians from Alcman[11] and Sappho[12] to Aristophanes. What remained from this truly golden age in the best genres of poetry bears the mark of a more or less beautiful or great style, the mark of the lively power of enthusiasm, and the formation of art in divine harmony.

The whole rests on the firm foundation of ancient poetry, one and indivisible by virtue of the joyously solemn life of free men and the holy power of the ancient gods.

First lyric poetry with its music of beautiful emotions joined iambic poetry, which reflects the violence of passion, and the elegiac where the changing moods in the play of life appear so alive that they can be taken for love and hate; emotions which moved the peaceful chaos of Homeric poetry to new forms and creations. The choral songs, on the other hand, gravitated more toward the heroic spirit of the epic, and like it were differentiated so naturally according to the prevalence either of moral seriousness or of sacred freedom in the disposition and mood of the people. What Eros inspired in Sappho breathed music. And just as Pindar's[13] dignity is mellowed by the merry charm of gymnastic games, so did the dithyrambs, we assume, imitate exuberantly the most daring beauties of orchestration.

The founders of the art of tragedy found their material and their prototypes in the epic. Just as the epic developed parody within itself, so did the same masters who invented tragedy delight in the invention of satyrical plays.

Simultaneously with sculpture, there originated a new genre similar to it in the power of form and the laws of structure.

From the union of parody and the old iambic poetry there arose, in contrast to tragedy, comedy, which abounds in the highest kind of mimicry that is possible only in words.

Whereas in tragedy actions and events, characteristic features, and passion were harmoniously ordered and formed out of a given legend into a beautiful system; here, a lavish abundance of ingenuity was boldly cast as a rhapsody, with deep understanding in seeming incoherence.

Both kinds of Attic drama intruded most effectively into life through their relationship to the ideal of both great forms, in which the highest and only life appears, the life of man among men. Enthusiasm for the Republic is found in the works of Aeschylus[14] and Aristophanes, and a lofty prototype of a beautiful family in the heroic conditions of ancient times is at the basis of Sophocles'[15] art.

Whereas Aeschylus is the eternal prototype of austere greatness and unrefined enthusiasm, and Sophocles is a model of harmonious perfection; Euripides[16] already shows that unfathomable delicacy possible only in a decadent artist, and his poetry is often only the most ingenious recitation.

This original body of Greek poetry—the old epic, iambic poetry, the elegy, festive songs and plays—is poetry itself. Everything that follows up to our own times is remnant, echo, isolated presentiment, approximation, and return to that highest Olympus of poetry.

For the sake of completeness I must mention that the first sources and prototypes of the didactic poem—the interrelationship of poetry and philosophy—are also to be looked for in this period when the old forms flourished: in the nature-inspired hymns of the mysteries, in the ingenious teachings of the gnomes of social morality, in the universal poems of Empedocles[17] and other poet-philosophers, and perhaps in the symposia where philosophical dialogue and its presentation are entirely transformed into poetry.

Such singularly great minds like Sappho, Pindar, Aeschylus, Sophocles, and Aristophanes have never reappeared. There were still, however, ingenious virtuosi of genius like Philoxenos[18] who characterize the state of disintegration and fermentation, which is the transition from the great poetry of ideas to the precious, learned poetry of the Greeks. The center of this latter poetry was Alexandria.[19] Yet not only here did there flourish a classical Pleiades of tragic poets; on the Attic stage, too, there shone a score of virtuosi. Yet even though the poets were making numerous attempts in all genres to imitate and transform each ancient form, this occurred primarily in the dramatic genre, where what remained of this period's inventive spirit expressed itself through a rich abundance of the most ingenious and often peculiar new combinations and compounds, partly in seriousness, partly in parody. However, this genre did not go beyond the ornamental, the witty, and the artificial, as was also true of the other genres among which we mention only the idyll as a peculiar form of the period, a form, however, whose distinctiveness resides almost exclusively in its formlessness. In the rhythm, in many a turn of its language and the manner of presentation it follows to some extent the epic style. The plot and dialogue follow the Doric single-scene mimes taken from social life with its local color, and in the antistrophic songs the idyl follows the artless songs of the shepherds. Its erotic spirit is like that of the elegy and the epigram of that time, when this spirit invaded even the epic works. Many of those, to be sure, were epic in form only, and the artist wanted to show in the didactic genre that his art could successfully deal with even the most difficult and driest material. On the other hand, some wrote on mythological themes to prove that they knew even the rarest and could regenerate and refine even the oldest and best-developed forms. Or they simply played in ornate parodies with only seemingly real objects. In general the poetry of that age spent itself either in the artificiality of the form, or in the sensuous charm of the material that was current even in the new Attic comedy; but the most sensual of those were lost.

But even when the possibilities of imitation were exhausted, they were satisfied with making new wreaths of old flowers; thus anthologies close the period of Greek poetry.

The Romans had only a short outburst of poetry, during which they energetically struggled and strove to appropriate the art of their models. They received these models first from the Alexandrians; therefore, the erotic and learned elements dominate in their works and, where art is concerned, these elements must remain the vantage point from which their art is to be appreciated. For the man of sense lets every production remain in its own sphere, and judges it only according to its own ideal. To be sure, Horace appears interesting in any form, and in vain would we look for a man of this Roman's stature among the later Greeks. But this general interest in him is more a romantic one than a judgment of his art, which can rank him high only in satire. It is a splendid phenomenon when Roman vigor and Greek art become one to the point of coalescence. Thus Propertius[20] created a great universe by means of the most learned art; the stream of fervent love flowed powerfully from his sincere heart. He can console us for the loss of the Greek elegiac poets, as Lucretius[21] does for the loss of Empedocles.

For the course of a few generations everybody in Rome wanted to write poetry and everybody believed he had to court the Muses and help them along. And this the Romans called their Golden Age of poetry. It was like a barren flower in the making of that nation. The moderns have followed them; what occurred under Augustus[22] and Maecenas[23] prefigured Italy's cinquecent-ists.[24] Louis XIV[25] tried to force the same spiritual renaissance in France; the English, too, agreed to consider the taste during Queen Anne's[26] reign as best. Henceforth, no nation wanted to remain without its Golden Age; each following age was even emptier and worse than the one before and what the Germans finally imagine to be their Golden Age, the dignity of this presenta-tion prohibits from a more accurate description.

I am returning to the Romans. They had, as was said, only one attack of poetry, which in fact was always alien to them. Only the poetry of urbanity was natural to them, and only with satire did they enrich the realm of art. Under each master their satire assumed a new form, now by emulating the grand old style of Roman social life and wit, now by imitating the classical daring of Archilochos and of ancient comedy. Or it shaped the carefree lightness of an improvisor into the clean elegance of a correct Greek, or it returned in the stoical manner and the purest style to the great old way of the nation, or again it gave way to the fervor of hate. Through satire there appears in new splendor what survives of the urbanity of eternal Rome in Catullus[27] and Martial,[28] and otherwise remains isolated and scattered. The satire affords us a Roman vantage point for the achievements of the Roman spirit.

After the force of poetry had subsided as quickly as it had come, man's spirit took a new direction: art disappeared in the clash of the old world and the new, and more than a millenium had passed before a great poet arose in the Occident again. He who among the Romans had rhetorical talent devoted himself to legal matters, and if he was a Greek he gave popular lectures about various kinds of philosophy. The Romans were satisfied with merely preserv-ing old treasures of any kind, collecting and mixing them, abridging and spoiling them. As in the other branches of education, also in poetry there was only rarely a trace of originality, isolated and without emphasis. Nowhere was there an artist, no classical work in such a long time. On the other hand, religious invention and inspiration was all the more lively: in the creation of a new religion, in the attempts at transforming the old, in mystical philosophy must we seek the energy of that time which in this respect was great: it was a border area of culture, a fertile chaos leading to a new order of things, the true Middle Ages.

A pure fountainhead of new heroic poetry flowed across Europe with the appearance of the Teutons. And when the wild energy of Gothic poetry merged through the influence of the Arabs with the echoes of the charming fairy tales of the Orient, there flourished on the southern coast of the Mediterranean a merry trade of inventors of lovely songs and unusual stories which also spread, now in this form, now in that, along with the Latin saints' legends, worldly romances, praising love and arms.

Catholic hierarchy had meanwhile come of age; jurisprudence and theology allowed a certain return to antiquity. The great Dante,[29] sacred founder and father of modern poetry, entered this path, uniting religion and poetry. From the ancestors of the nation he learned to condense the most peculiar and unusual, the most sacred and the sweetest in the vernacular into classical dignity and power, thus ennobling the Provençal art of rhyming. And since he was not fortunate enough to go back to the very sources, the Romans indirectly could stimulate the general idea of a great work of ordered structure. Powerfully he seized upon this idea and concentrated in *one* center the energy of his inventive spirit and in *one* immense poem embraced in his strong arms his nation and his age, the church and the empire, wisdom and revelation, nature and God's kingdom. The poem was a selection of the finest and the most infamous he had seen, of the greatest and the most peculiar he could invent; it was the most candid presentation of himself and his friends, the most glorious glorification of his beloved; everything was true to fact and truthful in the realm of the visible, and full of secret meaning and relation to the invisible.

Petrarch[30] gave the canzone and the sonnet perfection and beauty. His songs are the essence of his life and a spirit animates and forms them into one indivisible work: eternal Rome on earth and the Madonna in heaven as reflection of the only Laura[31] of his heart symbolize and capture in beautiful freedom the spiritual unity of his entire poetry. His feeling, as it were, created the language of love and even after centuries is valued by all men of nobility. In the same way Boccaccio's[32] mind established for the poets of every nation an inexhaustible source of peculiar, mostly true, and very thoroughly elaborated stories, which through their power of expression and the excellent structure of his periods raised the narrative language of conversation to a solid foundation for the prose of the novel. As strict as is Petrarch in purity of love, just so earthly is the talent of Boccaccio, who preferred to console all charming women rather than to worship one. Through joyful grace and sociable jest, Boccaccio succeeded in being original in the canzone even after Petrarch, more than the latter did in his attempt to approximate the great Dante's vision and terzinas.

These three are the pillars of the old style of modern art; the connoisseur should appreciate their value; to the feeling of the amateur, however, it is precisely the best and most original in them which remains difficult or at least foreign.

Having sprung from such sources, the stream of poetry in the fortunate Italian nation could not run dry again. These founders, to be sure, left behind no school but merely imitators; quite soon, however, there originated a new species. The form and manner of the creation of poetry which now again had become art were applied to the themes of adventure in the books of chivalry, and in this way came into being the Italian Romance, originally meant for public reading, changing either blatantly or subtly with a touch of sociable wit and intellectual spice the miraculous stories of old into the grotesque. But this grotesque is, even in Ariosto,[33] only isolated and not to be found in the whole of his work which scarcely deserves the name; like Boiardo[34] he embellished the romance with novellas and, according to the spirit of his age, with beautiful devices derived from the ancients, achieved a great deal of grace in the art of the stanza. Through this excellence and his clear understanding, he surpasses his predecessor; the abundance of clear images and a felicitous mixture of jest and seriousness make him a master and prototype in facile narrative and sensuous fantasies. The attempt to elevate the romance through a weighty subject and classical language to the dignity of the ancient epic—which was envisaged as the masterpiece of masterpieces for the nation and, because of its allegorical meaning, as especially for the scholars—no matter how often undertaken, remained only an attempt that missed the mark. In an entirely new way, but applicable only once, Guarini[35] succeeded in *Il Pastor Fido*, the greatest, indeed the only masterpiece of the Italians after those great ones, to fuse the romantic spirit and classical form in most beautiful harmony, and thus gave the sonnet new vigor and charm.

The art history of the Spaniards, who were most intimately familiar with the poetry of the Italians, and of the English, who had at that time a very receptive sense for the romantic elements which might have come their way even second hand, culminated in the art of two men, Cervantes[36] and Shakespeare, who were so great that everything else in comparison with them appears as merely preparatory, explicatory, and complementary circumstance. The fullness of their works and the gradual ascent of their boundless spirit would alone be material for a story of its own. We merely wish to point to the thread of the story, to discern the chief divisions of the entire work, and at least to see some definite points and the general course of development.

When Cervantes took up the pen after he could no longer wield the sword, he composed the *Galatea*, a wonderfully great composition of undying music of the imagination and love: the most delicate and lovely of all novels. In addition he also composed many works which dominated the stage and were as worthy as the divine *Numancia* of the old tragic style. This was the first great period of his poetry; its characteristic was sublime beauty, serious but lovely.

The chief work in his second manner is the first part of *Don Quixote*, where fantastic wit and a lavish abundance of daring ideas prevail. In the same spirit and around the same time he also composed many of his novellas, especially the comic ones. In the last years of his life he gave in to the prevailing taste in drama, and for this reason treated it with negligence. Also, in the second part of *Don Quixote* he took into consideration critical judgment. However, it was up to him to please himself and with unfathomed understanding to fashion the material of the second part—which everywhere bears the stamp of the first and thus constitutes one work consisting of two separate and fused parts—an opus which, as it were, contemplates itself. He wrote the great *Pérsiles* with a thoughtful art in an earnest, dark manner, according to his own idea of the novel of Heliodorus.[37] What else he wanted to create—presumably in the genre of the books of chivalry and of the dramatized novel—as well as completing the second part of *La Galatea* was prevented by his death.

The Spanish prose in the books of chivalry before Cervantes was antiquated in a beautiful manner, flourishing in the pastoral novel and in the romantic drama imitating artless life sharply and exactly in the language of everyday. The most lovely forms for tender songs, full of music and thoughtful dallying, and the romance, devised to tell with nobility and simplicity, seriously and with truth, a noble and moving old story, were at home in that country for ages. For Shakespeare the way was prepared to a lesser degree, almost exclusively through the colorful variety of the English theater. Now scholars, now actors, noblemen, and court fools worked for the theater, where mystery plays from the childhood of drama or old English farces alternated with patriotic histories and other subjects in every form and manner, but there was nothing that we would call art. Yet it was a fortunate circumstance for both the effectiveness and even the thoroughness of the theater that the actors had to work early for a stage which was not designed for exterior appearance, and that in the historical drama the monotony of theme directed the writer's and the viewer's attention to the form.

Shakespeare's earliest works must be seen in the same light in which the connoisseur admires the antiquities of Italian painting. They are without perspective and other perfections but they are thorough, great, and show good sense, and in their genre only the works in the best manner by the same master are superior to them. We include here *Locrinus*,[38] whose tragic pathos in the Gothic dialect is glaringly fused with robust old English gaiety and the divine *Pericles*,[39] and other works of art by that only master which were denied the authenticity against all history because of the madness of shallow critics or their own stupidity. We assume that these productions are earlier than *Adonis*[40] and the sonnets since there is no trace in them of that sweet and lovely form, nor of the lofty spirit that breathes more or less in all the later plays of the poet, especially in those of the greatest perfection. Love, friendship, and noble company, according to his own account, brought about a beautiful revolution in his spirit. His knowledge of the delicate poems of Spenser,[41] the favorite of the elegant set, gave sustenance to his new romantic *élan,* and he might have induced Shakespeare to read the novellas which now, more often than before, he transformed, reconstructed, and dramatized in a fantastically charming manner with a profound understanding of the stage. This development extended also to the historical plays, giving them more fullness, grace, and wit, and inspired all his plays with the romantic spirit which most properly characterizes them in connection with profound thoroughness, and constitutes them as a romantic basis for the modern drama which is durable enough for ages to come.

Of the novellas first to be dramatized, we mention only *Romeo*[42] and *Love's Labour's Lost*[43] as the loftiest points of his youthful imagination, being closest to *Adonis* and the sonnets. In the three plays about Henry VI and Richard III we discern a steady transition from the older and not yet romanticized manner to a great one. To this group Shakespeare added the histories of Richard II through Henry V,[44] and this work is the peak of his power. In *Macbeth* and in *Lear*[45] we witness the signposts of his manly maturity, and *Hamlet*[46] vacillates insolubly in the transition between the novella and what these tragedies are. In the last period we mention the *Tempest, Othello*,[47] and the Roman plays;[48] there is infinitely much understanding in them, but already something of the coldness of age.

After the death of those great men, the beautiful imagination vanished in their countries. Strangely enough, philosophy—hitherto unpolished—developed into an art, and excited and monopolized the enthusiasm of brilliant men. In poetry, on the other hand, there were, to be sure, from Lope de Vega[49] to Gozzi,[50] some appreciable virtuosi, but no poets, and even those only for the stage. Moreover, the multitude of wrong tendencies was increasing in all learned and popular genres and forms all the time. Out of superficial abstractions and rationalizations, out of misunderstood antiquity and mediocre talent, there arose in France a comprehensive and coherent system of false poetry which rested on an equally false theory of literature; and from here this sickly mental malady of so-called good taste spread over all the countries of Europe. The French and English established their various golden ages and carefully selected, as worthy representatives of their nations in the Pantheon of fame, a number of classics from among the writers who, all of them, do not deserve mention in a history of art.

Meanwhile, even here there remained a tradition whose contention was to return to the ancients and to nature, and this spark caught fire with the Germans after they had gone through almost all their models. Winckelmann[51] taught that antiquity was to be viewed as a whole, and was the first to demonstrate how to establish an art through the history of its genesis. Goethe's universality gently reflected the poetry of almost all nations and ages, an inexhaustibly instructive set of works, studies, sketches, fragments, and experiments in every genre and in the most varied forms. Philosophy arrived in a few daring steps to the point where it could comprehend itself and the spirit of man, in whose depths it was bound to discover the primordial source of the imagination and the ideal of beauty, and thus was compelled to recognize poetry, whose essence and existence it had not even suspected. Philosophy and poetry, the two most sublime powers in man, which even in Athens in the period of their highest fruition were effective only in isolation, now intermingle in perpetual interaction in order to stimulate and develop each other. Translation of poets and imitation of their rhythms have become an art, and criticism a discipline which annihilated old errors and opened new vistas in the knowledge of antiquity, whose background reveals a perfect history of poetry.

Nothing further is required but that the Germans continue using these methods, that they follow the example set by Goethe, explore the forms of art back to their sources in order to be able to revive or combine them, and that they go back to the origins of their own language and poetry, and release the old power, the sublime spirit which lies dormant, unrecognized, in the documents of the fatherland's prehistory, from the song of the Nibelungs[52] to Fleming[53] and Weckherlin.[54] Thus poetry—which in no nation was so excellent and originally developed—beginning as a heroic legend, then becoming a pastime of the knights, and finally a trade of the citizens—will be and will remain in this nation a basic discipline of true scholars and an effective art of ingenious poets.

Camilla. You have hardly mentioned the French at all.

Andrea. It happened without particular intention; I found no reason to do so.

Antonio. He could have shown us by that example how a nation can be great without any poetry.

Camilla. And also he could have shown how one lives without poetry.

Ludovico. Through this underhand trick he indirectly anticipated my polemical work on the theory of false poetry.

Andrea. This will be altogether up to you; I have in this way subtly announced what you intended to do.

Lothario. While talking about the transition from poetry to philosophy and from philosophy to poetry, you mentioned Plato as a poet (may the Muse reward you for it), and I listened also for the name of Tacitus.[55] This cultured perfection of style, this sterling and clear representation which we find in the great histories of antiquity should serve the poet as a prototype. I am convinced that this great quality can still be of use.

Marcus. Or perhaps used in an entirely new way.

Amalia. If it goes on like this, before too long one thing after another will be transformed into poetry. Is, then, everything poetry?

Lothario. Every art and every discipline that functions through language, when exercised as an art for its own sake and when it achieves its highest summit, appears as poetry.

Ludovico. And every art or discipline which does not manifest its nature through language possesses an invisible spirit: and that is poetry.

Marcus. I agree with almost all your points. I only wish you had shown more consideration for the various kinds of poetry; or, to express it better, I wish a more explicit theory of the kinds of poetry had developed from your presentation.

Andrea. In my talk I wanted to keep entirely within the limits of history.

Ludovico. You could even have invoked philosophy. At least I have not encountered in any system the original contrast of poetry as I have in your juxtaposition of the epic and iambic modes.

Andrea. This juxtaposition is altogether of a historical nature.

Lothario. It is quite natural if poetry originated in such a grandiose manner as in that fortunate country, that it manifests itself in a twofold manner. Poetry either creates a world of its own or allies itself with the external world, which in the beginning does not happen through idealizing it, but in a harsh and hostile manner. This is how I explain to myself the epic and iambic genres.

Amalia. I always shudder when I open a book where the imagination and its works are classified under headings.

Marcus. No one expects you to read such despicable books. Yet, a theory of genres is just what we lack. And what else can it be but a classification which at the same time would be a history and theory of literature?

Ludovico. Such a theory would elucidate for us how and in what way the imagination of a fictitious poet—who, being a prototype, would be the poet's poet—by means of its activity and through it necessarily must limit and divide itself.

Amalia. But how can such an artificial creation serve poetry?

Lothario. Actually, Amalia, until now you have very little reason to complain to your friends about the artificial nature of poetry. Many other things have to occur if poetry is really to become an artificial creation.

Marcus. Without division, creation does not take place; and creation is the quintessence of art. Therefore you will have to recognize these classifications at least as means.

Amalia. These means often become an end in themselves, and they always remain a dangerous, roundabout way which much too frequently kills the sense for the highest things before the goal is reached.

Ludovico. The right sense cannot be killed.

Amalia. But what means and for what goal? A goal is real if one can reach it immediately or never. Each free spirit should seize the ideal directly and surrender to the haromony which he will find in himself as soon as he looks for it there.

Ludovico. The inward vision can become clearer to itself and quite vivid only through externalized representation.

Marcus. And representation is the task of art, no matter what you say.

Antonio. One should also treat poetry as an art. It is of little use to consider it such in a critical history if the poets themselves are not artists and masters capable of creating with sure tools, for a certain purpose, in whatever manner.

Marcus. And why should they not? Certainly, they must and will. Of most importance are the definite purpose and the separation through which alone the work of art receives form and becomes complete in itself. The imagination of the poet should not spend itself in a chaotic generalization of poetry, but each work should have a thoroughly definite character according to form and genre.

Antonio. You are again aiming at your theory of genres. I wish you were done with it.

Lothario. Our friend is not to blame even if he returns to that problem time and again. The theory of genres would then be the true aesthetics of literature. In the individual case I often found confirmed what I already knew in general: that the principles of rhythm and even of the rhymed syllables are based on music; what is of essential importance for the delineation of characters, situations, and passions—their very spirit—may also be present in the visual arts. Even diction, though directly connected with the very nature of poetry, is related through poetry to rhetoric. The genres are actually poetry itself.

Marcus. Even a concise theory of poetry would leave many things undone or, actually, everything. There is no want of doctrines and theories postulating that poetry should become an art and how this should come about. Does poetry, however, become and art because of this? This could happen only in a practical manner if several poets united to found a school of poetry where the master would take his apprentice to task and pester him thoroughly as in the other arts, but who would leave him as heritage a solid foundation worked out in the sweat of his brow. Then the successors, having an advantage from the start, might continue to build on this basis with ever greater magnificence and daring, in order ultimately to move with freedom and ease on the proudest heights.

Andrea. The realm of poetry is invisible. If only you do not pay attention to its external form, you will find in its history a school of poetry greater than in any other art. The masters of all ages and nations have paved a way for us and left for us an immense capital. To show this as briefly as possible was the purpose of my lecture.

Antonio. Even among us and nearby there is no want of examples of a master who, perhaps without knowing or intending it, tremendously prepared the way for his successors. Even though the poetry of Voss[56] has long since lost its importance, his merit as translator and linguist, through which with ineffable energy and endurance he cleared a new area for cultivation, will shine even more brightly, the more his endeavors will be surpassed by better ones. Then one will appreciate that only through former words were new and better ones made possible.

Marcus. The ancients also had schools of poetry in the most specific sense. And I will not deny that I cherish the hope that this is still possible. What is more feasible and at the same time more desirable than a thorough instruction in the art of meter? The theater cannot become worthwhile until a poet is in charge of it in its entirety and many work for it in the same spirit. I am merely hinting at some paths to the possibility of carrying out my idea. Indeed, it could be the goal of my ambition to unite such a school, and thus to foster a basic knowledge of at least some kinds and means of poetry.

Amalia. Again, why only kinds and means? Why not the entire and indivisible poetry? Our friend cannot leave his old vice. He must always separate and divide, where only the whole in its undivided power can be effective and satisfying. And I hope you do not intend to found your school altogether alone.

Camilla. Otherwise he might remain his only pupil, if he alone wants to be master. We at least are not willing to become pupils in that way.

Antonio. Certainly not. You shall not be ruled despotically by a single individual, my dear friend. We should all have the opportunity to instruct you. We all intend to be masters and pupils at the same time; now master, now pupil as it happens. For me the latter will most frequently be true. Yet I would be ready to enter a defensive and offensive alliance of and for poetry, if only I could envisage the feasibility of such an art school.

Ludovico. Reality would be the best judge.

Antonio. But first it should be investigated and settled whether or not poetry can be taught and learned at all.

Lothario. At least it will become clear that human wit and art can lure it from darkness into day. Nevertheless it will remain a miracle, you may say what you wish.

Ludovico. So it is. Poetry is the finest branch of magic, and the isolated individual cannot rise up to magic. But where any human instinct functions in alliance with human spirit there is magical power. On this power I rely; I feel the spirit hovering amidst our friends; I live not in the hope but in the certainty of a new dawn of a new poetry. The rest is here on these pages, if this is the time for it.

Antonio. Let us hear it. I hope we shall find in what you are about to offer a contrast to Andrea's "Epochs of Literature." Thus we shall be able to use one view and force as lever for the others and discuss both the more freely and incisively, and again return to the greatest problem whether or not poetry can be taught and learned.

Camilla. It is well that you put an end to it. You want to teach everything and have not even mastered the vocabulary you are using; I would be inclined to constitute myself chairman and bring order into the discussion.

Antonio. Later we shall keep order, and in an emergency appeal to you. But now let us listen.

Ludovico. What I have to offer and consider timely for a discussion is a

TALK ON MYTHOLOGY

Considering your serious reverence for art, I wish to challenge you, my friends, to ask yourselves this question: should the force of inspiration also in poetry continue to split up and, when it has exhausted itself by struggling against the hostile element, end up in lonely silence? Are the most sacred things always to remain nameless and formless, and be left in darkness to chance? Is love indeed invincible, and is there an art worthy of the name if it does not have the power to bind the spirit of love with its magic word, to make the spirit of love follow and obey it, and to inspire its beautiful creations in accordance with its necessary freedom?

You above all others must know what I mean. You yourselves have written poetry, and while doing so you must often have felt the absence of a firm basis for your activity, a matrix, a sky, a living atmosphere.

The modern poet must create all these things from within himself, and many have done it splendidly; up to now, however, each poet separately and each work from its very beginning, like a new creation out of nothing.

I will go right to the point. Our poetry, I maintain, lacks a focal point, such as mythology was for the ancients; and one could summarize all the essentials in which modern poetry is inferior to the ancient in these words: We have no mythology. But, I add, we are close to obtaining one or, rather, it is time that we earnestly work together to create one.

For it will come to us by an entirely opposite way from that of previous ages, which was everywhere the first flower of youthful imagination, directly joining and imitating what was most immediate and vital in the sensuous world. The new mythology, in contrast, must be forged from the deepest depths of the spirit; it must be the most artful of all works of art, for it must encompass all the others; a new bed and vessel for the ancient, eternal fountainhead of poetry, and even the infinite poem concealing the seeds of all other poems.

You may well smile at this mystical poem and the disorder that might originate from the abundance of poetic creations. But the highest beauty, indeed the highest order is yet only that of chaos, namely of such a one that waits only for the touch of love to unfold as a harmonious world, of such a chaos as the ancient mythology and poetry were. For mythology and poetry are one and inseparable. All poems of antiquity join one to the other, till from ever increasing masses and members the whole is formed. Everything interpenetrates everything else, and everywhere there is one and the same spirit, only expressed differently. And thus it is truly no empty image to say: Ancient poetry is a single, indivisible, and perfect poem. Why should what has once been not come alive again? In a different way, to be sure. And why not in a more beautiful, a greater way?

I plead with you only not to give in to disbelief in the possibility of a new mythology. Doubts from all sides and in all directions would be welcome, so that the investigation may become that much more free and rich. And now lend my conjectures an attentive ear. More than conjectures, considering the situation of the matter, I cannot hope to offer. But I hope that these conjectures through you yourselves will become truths. For if you want to employ them in such a way, they are to a certain extent suggestions for experiments.

If a new mythology can emerge only from the innermost depths of the spirit and develop only from itself, then we find a very significant hint and a noteworthy confirmation of what we are searching for in that great phenomenon of our age, in idealism. Idealism originated in just this way, from nothing as it were, and now it has constituted itself in the spiritual sphere as a firm point from which the creative energy of man can safely expand, developing in all directions, without losing itself or the possibility of return. All disciplines and all arts will be seized by the great revolution. You can see it already at work in physics where idealism erupted of its own before it was touched by the magic wand of philosophy. And this wonderful, great fact can at the same time be a hint for you of the secret correspondence and inner unity of the age. Idealism—from a practical view nothing other than the spirit of that revolution—and its great maxims which we are to practice and propagate from our own energy and freedom; this idealism, considered theoretically, as great as it manifests itself at this point, is yet only a part, a branch, a mode of expression of the phenomenon of all phenomena: that mankind struggles with all its power to find its own center. It must, as things are, either perish or be rejuvenated. What is more probable, and what does one not hope for from such an age of rejuvenation? Remote antiquity will become alive again, and the remotest future of culture will announce itself in auguries. Yet this is not what matters to me at this point, for I do not want to pass over anything but to lead you step by step to the certainty of the most sacred mysteries. Just as it is the nature of spirit to determine itself and in perennial alternation to expand and return to itself, and as every thought is nothing but the result of such an activity; so is the same process generally discernible in every form of idealism, which itself is but a recognition of this very law. The new life, intensified by this recognition, manifests its secret energy in the most splendid manner through the infinite abundance of new ideas, general comprehensibility, and lively efficacy. Naturally this phenomenon assumes a different form in each individual; this is why success must often fall short of expectation. But our expectations cannot be disappointed in what the necessary laws allow us to expect for the development as a whole. Idealism in any form must transcend itself in one way or another, in order to be able to return to itself and remain what it is. Therefore, there must and will arise from the matrix of idealism a new and equally infinite realism, and idealism will not only by analogy of its genesis be an example of the new mythology, but it will indirectly become its very source. Traces of a similar tendency you can now observe almost everywhere, especially in physics where nothing is more needed than a mythological view of nature.

I, too, have long borne in me the ideal of such a realism, and if it has not yet found expression, it was merely because I am still searching for an organ for communicating it. And yet I know that I can find it only in poetry, for in the form of philosophy and especially of systematic philosophy realism can never again appear. But even considering a general tradition, it is to be expected that this new realism, since it must be of idealistic origin and must hover as it were over an idealistic ground, will emerge as poetry which indeed is to be based on the harmony of the ideal and real.

Spinoza,[57] it seems to me, has an identical fate as the good old Saturn of the fable. The new gods pulled down the sublime one from the lofty throne of knowledge. He faded back into the solemn obscurity of the imagination; there he lives and now dwells with the other Titans in dignified exile. Keep him here! Let his memories of the old mastery melt away in the song of the Muses into a soft longing. Let him put away the militant attire of systematic philosophy and share the dwelling in the temple of new poetry with Homer and Dante, joining the household gods and friends of every god-inspired poet.

Indeed, I barely comprehend how one can be a poet without admiring Spinoza, loving him, and becoming entirely his. In the invention of details your own imagination is rich enough; to stimulate it, to excite it to activity, and to provide it with nourishment there is nothing better than the creations of other artists. In Spinoza, however, you will find the beginning and end of all imagination, the general basis on which all individual creation rests; and especially the separation of the original, the eternal aspect of imagination from the individual and the typical must be very welcome to you. Seize the opportunity and observe. You are granted a profound view into the innermost workshop of poetry. Spinoza's feeling is of the same kind as his imagination. It is not a sensitivity to this or that nor a passion that smolders and dies again, but a clear fragrance that hovers invisibly visible over the whole; everywhere eternal longing finds an accord from the depths of the simple work which in calm greatness breathes the spirit of original love.

And is not this soft reflection of the godhead in man the actual soul, the kindling spark of all poetry? Mere representation of man, passions, and actions does not truly amount to anything, as little as using artificial forms does, even if you shuffle and turn over the old stuff together millions of times. That is only the visible, the external body, for when the soul has been extinguished what is left is only the lifeless corpse of poetry. When that spark of inspiration breaks out in works, however, a new phenomenon stands before us, alive and in the beautiful glory of light and love.

And what else is any wonderful mythology but hieroglyphic expression of sourrounding nature in this transfigured form of imagination and love?

Mythology has one great advantage. What usually escapes our consciousness can here be perceived and held fast through the senses and spirit like the soul in the body surrounding it, through which it shines into our eye and speaks to our ear.

This is the crucial point: that in regard to the sublime we do not entirely depend on our emotions. To be sure, he whose emotions have run dry, in him they will nowhere spring forth; this is a well-known truth which I am not in the least inclined to oppose. But we should take part everywhere in what is already formed. We should develop, kindle, and nourish the sublime through contact with the same in kind, the similar, or if of equal stature the hostile; in a word, give it form. If the sublime, however, is incapable of being intentionally created, then let us give up any claims to a free art of ideas, for it would be an empty name.

Mythology is such a work of art created by nature. In its texture the sublime is really formed; everything is relation and metamorphosis, conformed and transformed, and this conformation and transformation is its peculiar process, its inner life and method, if I may say so.

Here I find a great similarity with the marvelous wit of romatic poetry which does not manifest itself in individual conceptions but in the structure of the whole, and which was so often pointed out by our friend for the works of Cervantes and Shakespeare. Indeed, this artfully ordered confusion, this charming symmetry of contradictions, this wonderfully perennial alteration of enthusiasm and irony which lives even in the smallest parts of the whole, seem to me to be an indirect mythology themselves. The organization is the same, and certainly the arabesque is the oldest and most original form of human imagination. Neither this wit nor a mythology can exist without something original and inimitable which is absolutely irreducible, and in which after all the transformations its original character and creative energy are still dimly visible, where the naive profundity permits the semblance of the absurd and of madness, of simplicity and foolishness, to shimmer through. For this is the beginning of all poetry, to cancel the progression and laws of rationally thinking reason, and to transplant us once again into the beautiful confusion of imagination, into the original chaos of human nature, for which I know as yet no more beautiful symbol than the motley throng of the ancient gods.

Why won't you arise and revive those splendid forms of great antiquity? Try for once to see the old mythology, steeped in Spinoza and in those views which present-day physics must excite in every thinking person, and everything will appear to you in new splendor and vitality.

But to accelerate the genesis of the new mythology, the other mythologies must also be reawakened according to the measure of their profundity, their beauty, and their form. If only the treasures of the Orient were as accessible to us as those of Antiquity. What new source of poetry could then flow from India if a few German artists with their catholicity and profundity of mind, with the genius for translation which is their own, had the opportunity which a nation growing ever more dull and brutal barely knows how to use. In the Orient we must look for the most sublime form of the Romantic, and only when we can draw from the source, perhaps will the semblance of southern passion which we find so charming in Spanish poetry appear to us occidental and sparse.

In general, one must be able to press toward the goal by more than one way. Let each pursue his own in joyful confidence, in the most individual manner; for nowhere has the right of individuality more validity—provided individuality is what this word defines: indivisible unity and an inner and vital coherence—than here where the sublime is at issue. From this standpoint I would not hesitate to say that the true value, indeed the virtue of man is his originality.

And if I place so much emphasis on Spinoza, it is indeed not from any subjective preference (I have expressly omitted the objects of such a preference) or to establish him as master of a new autocracy, but because I could demonstrate by this example in a most striking and illuminating way my ideas about the value and dignity of mysticism and its relation to poetry. Because of his objectivity in this respect, I chose him as a representative of all the others. This is the way I reason. Just as the *Theory of Knowledge*,[58] in the view of those who have not noticed the infinitude and eternal abundance of idealism, remains a perfect form, a general system for all knowledge, so, too, is Spinoza in a similar way the general basis and support for every individual kind of mysticism. And this, in my opinion, even those who have no special understanding of either mysticism or of Spinoza will readily acknowledge.

I cannot conclude without urging once more the study of physics, from whose dynamic paradoxes the most sacred revelations of nature are now bursting forth in all directions.

And thus let us, by light and life, hesitate no longer, but accelerate, each according to his own mind, that great development to which we were called. Be worthy of the greatness of the age and the fog will vanish from your eyes; and there will be light before you. All thinking is a divining, but man is only now beginning to realize his divining power. What immense expansion will this power experience, and especially now! It seems to me that he who could understand the age—that is, those great principles of general rejuvenation and of eternal revolution—would be able to succeed in grasping the poles of mankind, to recognize and to know the activity of the first men as well as the nature of the Golden Age which is to come. Then the empty chatter would stop and man would become conscious of what he is: he would understand the earth and the sun.

This is what I mean by the new mythology.

Antonio. During your lecture I remembered two remarks which I have often had to listen to and which now have become far clearer than before. The idealists assured me on all occasions that Spinoza, to be sure, is good, but thoroughly incomprehensible. In the critical writings, on the other hand, I found that every work of a genius is clear to the eye, but always remains hidden to the understanding. According to your view these pronouncements belong together, and I sincerely delight in their unintended symmetry.

Lothario. I would like to take our friend to task for seeming to mention physics so exclusively although he tacitly based everything on history, which, as much as physics, could be the real source of his mythology, that is, if we can use this old name of physics for something that as yet does not even exist. Your view of the age, by the way, is of a nature which in my opinion deserves the name of a historical view.

Ludovico. One begins at the point where one notices the first traces of life. And now that is in physics.

Marcus. Your tempo was a bit fast. For specific points I frequently would have to ask you to assist me with commentaries. In general, however, your theory gave me a new outlook on the didactic or, as our philologist calls it, the didascalic genre. I realize now how this crux of all previous classifications necessarily belongs to poetry. For the nature of poetry as a higher, idealistic view of things, of man as well, and of nature is incontestable. It is understandable that it can be of advantage to isolate this essential part of the whole in the process of education.

Antonio. I cannot consider didactic poetry as an actual genre, as I cannot the romantic. Every poem should actually be romantic as well as didactic, in that broader sense of the word where it describes the general tendency in its deep and infinite sense. We make this demand everywhere, without using the name. Even in the quite popular genres, as for instance in drama, we demand irony; we demand that events, men, in short the play of life, be taken as play and be represented as such. This seems to us the most essential point, and what does it not all contain? We are concerned only with the meaning of the whole; and things which individually excite, move, occupy, and delight our sense, our hearts, understanding, and imagination seem to us to be only a sign, a means for viewing the whole at the moment when we rise to such a view.

Lothario. All the sacred plays of art are only a remote imitation of the infinite play of the universe, the work of art which eternally creates itself anew.

Ludovico. In other words, all beauty is allegory. The sublime, because it is unutterable, can be expressed only allegorically.

Lothario. The innermost mysteries of all the arts and all knowledge are therefore a possession of poetry. Everything has emerged from it and must flow back to it. In an ideal condition of mankind, there would be only poetry; the arts and knowledge would then be one. In our condition only the true poet would be an ideal man and a universal artist.

Antonio. Or the communication and representation of all the arts and knowledge cannot exist without a poetic component.

Ludovico. I am of Lothario's opinion that the energy of all the arts and knowledge meets at one central point, and I hope by the gods to be able to obtain nourishment for your enthusiasm even from mathematics and to kindle your spirit by its wonders. I preferred physics also for the reason that the connection here is most visible. Physics cannot conduct an experiment without a hypothesis, and every hypothesis, even the most limited, if systematically thought through, leads to hypotheses of the whole, and depends on such hypotheses even if without the conscious knowledge of the person who uses them. It is in fact wonderful how physics—as soon as it is concerned not with technical purposes but with general results—without knowing it gets into cosmogony, astrology, theosophy, or whatever you wish to call it, in short, into a mystic discipline of the whole.

Marcus. And do you suppose Plato did not know as much about it as Spinoza, whom I simply cannot stomach because of his barbaric form?

Antonio. Even if Plato were—which he is not—as objective in this respect as Spinoza; yet it was better that our friend chose the latter to show us the fountainhead of poetry in the mysteries of realism, just because in Spinoza a poetry of form is inconceivable. For Plato, on the other hand, the form of presentation and its pefection and beauty are not means, but on the contrary a goal in itself. Strictly speaking, his form is for that reason already thoroughly poetic.

Ludovico. I said myself in the talk that I brought in Spinoza only as a representative. Had I wanted to deal with it more extensively, I would also have talked about the great Jakob Böhme.[59]

Antonio. With whom you could also have demonstrated whether the Christian ideas about the universe look worse than the old ones which you want to reintroduce.

Andrea. I beg you to honor the old gods.

Lothario. And I ask you to remember the Eleusinian mysteries. I wish I had put my thoughts about it on paper, so that I could present them to you in the order and detail befitting the dignity and importance of the subject. Only through the extant mysteries have I come to understand the meaning of the ancient gods. I would like to think that the view of nature prevalent there would illuminate many things for present-day scholars, if they were ready for it. The most daring and powerful, indeed I am tempted to say the wildest and most enraged expression of realism is the best. Remind me, Ludovico, at least to show you the Orphic fragment which starts with the bisexuality of Zeus.

Marcus. I remember a hint in Winckelmann from which I would assume that he values this fragment as much as you do.

Camilla. Would it be possible for you, Ludovico, to present for us in a beautiful form the philosophy of Spinoza; or even better, your own view of what you call realism?

Marcus. I would prefer the latter.

Ludovico. He who has in mind something like it, could do it and would want to do it only in the manner of Dante. Like him, he would have to have in his mind and heart only *one* poem, and often he would despair whether it can be expressed at all. Were he to succeed, however, he would have done enough.

Andrea. You have set a worthy prototype. Certainly Dante is the only one who, altogether alone, under certain favorable and innumerable adverse circumstances, through his own gigantic power, invented and formed a kind of mythology as was possible at that time.

Lothario. Actually, every work should be a new revelation of nature. Only by being individual and universal does a work become *the work*. Only in this way does it differ from studies.

Antonio. And yet I could mention to you studies which at the same time are works, in your sense of the word.

Marcus. And do not poems which are meant to have an external effect, as for instance excellent plays, without being mystical and comprehensive, differ already by their objectivity from studies which at first deal only with the inner development of the artist and which only prepare his ultimate goal, the objective external effectiveness?

Lothario. If they are simply good plays, they are only a means to an end; they lack independence and inner perfection for which I simply cannot find another word but the work, which for this reason I would like to keep exclusively for this purpose. In comparison with what Ludovico has in mind, drama is only applied poetry. And yet what I call a work in my sense of the word can well be in an individual case objective and dramatic in your sense too.

Andrea. In this way, among the ancient genres only in the epic would a work in your great sense of the word be possible.

Lothario. This is a remark which is correct as far as in the epic genre the one work is usually also the only one. The tragic and comic works of the ancients, on the other hand, are only variations, different expressions of one and the same ideal. As far as the systematic and proportionate formation is concerned, structure and organization, they remain the best models and, if I may say so, are the works among the works.

Antonio. What I have to contribute to the symposium is somewhat lighter fare. Amalia has already forgiven me and allowed me to direct my instructions that were intended only for her to the entire group. . . .

Andrea. I am glad that in the essay you have given there finally began to be discussed what to me seems the highest of all questions concerning the art of poetry. Namely, that of the union of ancient and modern: under which conditions it is possible, to what extent it is advisable. Let us try to get at the bottom of this problem!

Ludovico. I would protest against the limitations and vote for the unconditional union. The spirit of poetry is indivisible and everywhere it is the same.

Lothario. The spirit, to be sure! Here I would like to apply the division into spirit and letter. What you have presented or at least alluded to in your talk on mythology is, if you wish, the spirit of poetry. You can certainly not object when I consider meter and things of this sort, indeed even characters, plot, and what is connected with it, as the letter. In the spirit your unconditional union of ancient and modern may take place, and our friend only pointed out this kind to us. This is not the case in the letter of poetry. The ancient rhythm, for example, and the rhymed syllabic meter will always remain in contrast. A third, a middle possibility between those two does not exist.

Andrea. I, too, have often realized that the treatment of characters and passions by the ancients and the moderns is plainly different. With the former they are ideally conceived and graphically executed. With the latter the character either is really historical or is constructed as if he were; the execution, on the other hand, is more picturesque and in the manner of a portrait.

Antonio. If so, strangely enough, you would have to count diction, which actually should be the center of all the letter, with the spirit of poetry. For although that general dualism manifests itself even here in its extremes, and on the whole its character is in contrast with the old, sensuous and our own abstract language; yet there are to be found quite a few transitions from one area into the other; and I do not see why there could not be many more of those, although no complete union were possible.

Ludovico. And I do not see why we cling to the word only, to the letter of the letter, and for the sake of pleasing it do not want to acknowledge that language stands nearer to the spirit of poetry than do its other means. Language, as originally conceived, is identical with allegory, the first direct instrument of magic.

Lothario. One will find in Dante, Shakespeare, and other great authors passages and expressions which considered as they stand bear the entire stamp of the greatest uniqueness; they stand nearer to the spirit of the originator than other organs of poetry ever could.

Antonio. I object in the essay on Goethe only that its judgments are expressed somewhat too dictatorially. It could be that there are others as clever as you are who have a thoroughly different view of one thing and another.

Marcus. I admit willingly that I only said it as it appears to me, after having inquired most honestly, mindful of those maxims of art and education to which on the whole we all agree.

Antonio. This agreement may well be only very relative.

Marcus. Be that as it may. A true aesthetic judgment, you will grant me, a formed and thoroughly complete view of a work is always a critical fact, if I may say so. But it is also only a fact and for this very reason it is a futile task to want to motivate it, lest the motive itself contains a new fact or a more accurate definition of the former. Or, too, as for the external effect where nothing else is left but to show that we do have a discipline, without which aesthetic judgment would not be possible; this discipline, however, is so little an aesthetic judgment that we see it all too often only as being most strikingly the absolute opposite of all art and all judgment. Exhibition of skill among friends is out of place; ultimately there can be no other claim in any communication, no matter how artfully prepared, of an aesthetic judgment, but the invitation to everyone to formulate clearly and determine strictly, so that the communicated impression is worth the trouble of his reflecting whether he can agree with it and, in such a case, of his recognizing it voluntarily and readily.

Antonio. And even when we do not agree, in the end it is a matter of one saying: I love the sweet. No, says the other, quite the contrary, I prefer the bitter.

Lothario. About some details this may be said, and yet a knowledge in the matters of art remains a strong possibility. And I think that if that historical view were developed more completely, and if one could succeed in setting up the principles of poetry in the way our philosophical friend has tried to, then the art of poetry would have a foundation lacking neither in firmness nor compass.

Marcus. Do not forget the model which is so essential for orienting us in the present, and which at the same time constantly reminds us to rise up to the past and work for a better future. Let us at least keep that basis and remain true to the model.

Lothario. A worthy resolution against which there is nothing to be said. And certainly we will learn more and more in this way to understand each other with regard to the essential.

Antonio. Therefore we can now wish nothing more but that we may find in ourselves ideas for poems and then the laudable ability to create according to these ideas.

Ludovico. Do you perhaps consider it impossible to construct future poems *a priori?*

Antonio. Give me ideas for poems and I make bold to give this ability to you.

Lothario. You may be right, in your sense of the word, to consider as impossible what you are saying. Yet I myself from my own experience know the opposite. I may say that a few times the success corresponded to my expectation of a certain poem: such correspondence in this or that area of art may at first be necessary or at least possible.

Andrea. If you have this talent you will be able to tell me, too, whether we may ever hope to get ancient tragedies again.

Lothario. I welcome it in jest as well as seriously that you challenged me not to speak only about the opinion of others but to contribute at least one thing to the symposium from my own conviction. Only when the mysteries and mythology are rejuvenated by the spirit of physics, will it be possible to write tragedies in which everything is ancient, and which yet would be certain to capture the sense of the age through the meaning. Greater compass and greater variety of external form would be allowed, indeed advisable, approximately in the way they really did occur in many secondary species and variations of the ancient tragedy.

Marcus. Trimeters can be formed in our language as excellently as hexameters. But the choral syllabic meters, I am afraid, are an insoluble difficulty.

Camilla. Why should the content be entirely mythological and not historical as well?

Lothario. Because with a historic subject we postulate a modern treatment of characters, which is entirely at odds with the spirit of antiquity. Against the ancient or romantic tragedy the artist would get the worst of it in one way or another.

Camilla. Thus I hope that you will count Niobe among the mythological subjects.

Marcus. I would much rather ask for a Prometheus.

Antonio. And I would humbly suggest the old fable of Apollo and Marsyas. It seems to me very timely. Or more properly, it is probably always timely in any well-composed literature.

NOTES

1. Smith, Adam (1723–1790). Scottish political economist; professor of logic and moral philosophy at Glasgow. Many contributions to ethics; his chief work is *The Wealth of Nations.*

2. Pope, Alexander (1688–1744). English poet and translator of the Homeric epics. Chief works: *The Rape of the Lock; The Dunciad; Essays on Man.*

3. Dryden, John (1631–1700). English poet, dramatist, translator, and prose writer. Representative of English classicism. Important as literary critic and theorist (*Essay on Dramatic Poesy,* 1668). Chief works: *Astraea Redux; The Rival Ladies; Marriage à la Mode; Ode for St. Cecilia's Day;* and dozens of plays, satires, odes, and fine lyrical poems.

4. Homerids. A poetic guild on the island of Chios; they considered Homer as their founder.

5. Ionians. Ancient Greek tribe in Asia Minor.

6. Archilochos (early 7th century B.C.). A Greek poet. He is the first writer of iambic trimeters and trochaic tetrameters.

7. Horace (Quintus Horatius Flaccus) (65–8 B.C.). Latin poet. Chief works: *Epodes, Satires, Epistles, Ars Poetica,* and three books of *Odes.*

8. Aristophanes (c. 445–c. 385 B.C.). The supreme poet of Athenian Old Comedy. Chief works: *The Frogs, The Birds,* and *The Clouds.*

9. Dorians. A race which invaded Greece about the 12th century B.C. and settled in Doris.

10. Aeolians. Greek tribes of Thessaly and Boeotia.

11. Alcman (7th century B.C.). Greek lyric poet. Extant fragments of songs for choruses.

12. Sappho (fl. 612 B.C.). Greek poetess. Her songs include hymns to the gods and marriage songs written in simple and direct style.

13. Pindar (518–c. 438 B.C.). Greek lyric poet. Famous for his odes in celebration of victors in the Olympic Games.

14. Aeschylus (525–c. 456 B.C.). Athenian tragic poet. Chief works: *The Persians; Oresteia; Seven Against Thebes;* and *Prometheus Bound.*

15. Sophocles (496–406 B.C.). Athenian tragic poet. Seven plays survived; most important are: *Antigone; Oedipus Tyrannus; Electra;* and *Oedipus at Colonus.*

16. Euripides (485–406 B.C.). Athenian tragic poet. Nineteen plays survived. Most important: *Medea; Hippolytus; Electra;* and *Bacchae.*

17. Empedocles (mid-5th century B.C.). Greek philosopher and poet. Lengthy fragments survive, mostly from his chief work, *On Nature.*

18. Philoxenos (436–380 B.C.). Greek lyric poet. His chief work is the dithyramb *Cyclops.*

19. Alexandria. Important cultural center in the Middle Ages. Poets of the Alexandrian period 323–120 B.C.

20. Propertius, Sextus (c. 54/50–16 B.C.). Latin poet. Melancholic love poetry contained in four books of elegies.

21. Lucretius Carus, Titus (c. 100/90–c. 55/53 B.C.). Latin philosopher-poet. His main work, *De Rerum Natura,* is an exposition of the physical system of Epicurus.

22. Augustus (Gaius Julius Caesar Octavianus) (63 B.C.–A.D. 14). First Roman Emperor. The Roman Augustan Age was the most fruitful era of Latin literature.

23. Maecenas, Gaius Cilnius (c. 74/64 B.C.–8 B.C.). Roman statesman and patron of letters.

24. Cinquecentists. Artists and poets of the Italian Renaissance, specifically, the 15th century. Most important representatives in literature are Ariosto and Tasso.

25. Louis XIV (1638–1715). King of France. The arts and literature flourished during his reign.

26. Anne Stuart (1665–1714). Queen of England. No great names in English literature, many minor poets. Typical representative is Alexander Pope, see note 2.

27. Catullus, Gaius Valerius (c. 84–c. 54 B.C.). The greatest Latin lyric poet. His work is characterized by a deep sincerity, tenderness, and intensity of feeling.

28. Martial (Marcus Valerius Martialis) (c. A.D. 40–c. 104). Latin poet. Very prolific and versatile.

29. Dante Alighieri (1265–1321). The greatest Italian poet. Chief works: *The Divine Comedy; The New Life; On Monarchy.*

30. Petrarch (Petrarca), Francesco (1304–1374). Italian poet and humanist. Love poems glorifying Laura, patriotic odes, and poetry including other themes. Since the Renaissance he has been called "the Father of the Italian Language."

31. Laura, Petrarch's beloved.

32. Boccaccio, Giovanni (1313–1375). Italian storyteller and poet. First biographer of Dante. His main work is *The Decameron.*

33. Ariosto, Lodovico (1474–1533). Italian poet and dramatist. Best known for his masterpiece, *Orlando Furioso.*

34. Boiardo, Matteo Maria (1434–1494). Italian poet. His greatest work is *Orlando Innamorato,* to which Ariosto's *Orlando Furioso* is a sequel.

35. Guarini, Giovanni Battista (1538–1612). Italian poet. His fame derives from the pastoral drama *Il Pastor Fido.*

36. Cervantes Saavedra, Miguel de (1547–1616). Spanish novelist, dramatist, and poet. His principal works are the novel *Don Quixote de la Mancha;* the pastoral romance

La Galatea; and eight plays; one of them, *Numancia,* was praised for patriotic reasons. *Pérsiles* was published posthumously.

37. Heliodorus (3rd century A.D.?). Greek writer, best known for his *Aethiopica* or romance of Theagenes and Charicleia.

38. *Locrinus.* A pseudo-Shakespearean tragedy of love and war in old Britain. Anonymous.

39. *Pericles.* Tragedy by Shakespeare.

40. *Adonis (Venus and Adonis).* A narrative poem by Shakespeare.

41. Spenser, Edmund (c. 1552–1599). English poet. His most ambitious work is *The Faerie Queene.*

42. *Romeo (Romeo and Juliet).* An early tragedy by Shakespeare.

43. *Love's Labour's Lost.* A comedy by Shakespeare.

44. *Richard II; Henry V.* Two of Shakespeare's Histories.

45. *Macbeth; King Lear.* Tragedies by Shakespeare.

46. *Hamlet.* A tragedy by Shakespeare.

47. *Tempest; Othello.* A drama and a tragedy by Shakespeare.

48. Roman Plays. Shakespeare's plays based on Roman history: *Titus Andronicus; Coriolanus; Julius Caesar;* and *Anthony and Cleopatra.*

49. Vega Carpio, Lope Felix de (1562–1635). Spanish dramatist, poet, and novelist. Better known for a large number of successful productions than for any masterpieces; among those, comedies, dramas, and tragedies.

50. Gozzi, Gaspare, Conte (1713–1786). Italian journalist, poet, and prose writer.

51. Winckelmann, Johann Joachim (1717–1768). German archeologist and art historian. He was the founder of the German classical revival, which accepted his views and values.

52. *Nibelungenlied.* A Middle High German narrative poem (c. 1200). One of the most popular and celebrated monuments of older German literature.

53. Fleming, Paul (1609–1640). German poet. One of the few of his age whose work shows any inner development: the progress from petrarchistic lyric to individual poetic expression.

54. Weckherlin, Georg Rudolf (1584–1653). German poet. An early representative of German Baroque poetry.

55. Tacitus, Gaius Cornelius (c. A.D. 55–c. 117). Roman historian. Tacitus' major works are the *Histories* and the *Annals.* Important for German historiography is his *Germania.*

56. Voss, Johann Heinrich (1751–1826). German poet and translator. First influenced by Rousseau and Klopstock, he then turns to the classics, translating Homer. He invented the rural idyll in hexameters (*Luise*).

57. Spinoza, Benedict (Baruch) de (1632–1677). Philosopher of Portuguese origin who lived in the Netherlands. Main work: *Ethics.* Spinoza is the most prominent representative of a pantheistic philosophy. His doctrine found a revival in Germany at the end of the eighteenth century. The so-called "objective," or "realistic" turn toward nature of authors like Schelling, Goethe, Schleiermacher, Novalis, and Schlegel is influenced by "Spinozistic" pantheism.

58. *Theory of Knowledge.* Title of Fichte's main work (first edition, 1794). In this book Fichte expounded his doctrine of the Ego, as the only reality. In a dialectical process, by limiting itself, the Ego creates the Non-Ego as its opposite: the world of experience, through which the Ego asserts its freedom.

59. Böhme, Jakob (1575–1624). German philosopher and mystic, especially influential in German and European Romanticism.

Samuel Taylor Coleridge

1772–1834

Samuel Taylor Coleridge was born at Ottery St. Mary, Devon, on October 21, 1772, the son of a scholar and parson who died when his son was seven. Young Coleridge was educated as a charity pupil at Christ's Hospital, then attended Jesus College, Cambridge, but left in 1794 without taking a degree. From an early age he was unconventional, imaginative, and extremely gregarious, supporting idealistic causes with ardor.

After leaving Cambridge, Coleridge and his friend Robert Southey began lecturing together, first in an attempt to interest others in founding a utopian community in America, and then on a variety of social, political, and theological topics. The association with Southey ended after several years, but as a consequence of the friendship Coleridge was persuaded by his friend to marry Sara Fricker, and the union proved unhappy.

About this time Coleridge began publishing occasional poems in local periodicals, and his literary interests soon led, in the autumn of 1795, to his meeting with William Wordsworth. Coleridge's first collection, *Poems on Various Subjects*, was published in 1796, and a second edition appeared in 1797. At this time he also wrote "Kubla Khan" and began work on "The Ancient Mariner." In 1798 Thomas and John Wedgwood, famous potters, began acting as his patrons, paying him an annuity of 150 pounds annually with the hope that he would be able to devote himself more freely to writing. This temporary rescue from financial worry and his intimacy with Wordsworth and his sister helped Coleridge to finish "The Ancient Mariner" and to write a number of other poems, including "Frost at Midnight" and "Christabel." His collaboration with Wordsworth resulted in the anonymous publication of the *Lyrical Ballads* in 1798, which included "The Ancient Mariner," three other poems by Coleridge, and nineteen by Wordsworth. Later that year he went with Wordsworth and his sister to Germany, where they spent the winter, Coleridge enrolling at the University of Göttingen to study language and philosophy. Upon his return he traveled in Devon with Southey, visited the Lake District, secured a job as a writer for the *Morning Post,* and began a translation of Schiller's *Wallenstein.*

In 1800 the Coleridges settled near the Wordsworths in the Lake District, but the differences between the two men grew painful to Coleridge. The relatively ascetic Wordsworth was happily married, prosperous, and apparently writing effortlessly; the indulgent and effusive Coleridge was tormented by personal anxieties, domestic strife, and great physical pain which made him dependent upon opium. Seeking separation from an uncomfortable situation, Coleridge went to Malta in 1804, where he spent several years as an aide to the governor. He then traveled in Italy before returning to England in August 1806. He had by this time formally separated from his wife, and the Wedgwood's annuity had been given over to Mrs. Coleridge and her relatives. For several years Coleridge lived an unsettled life, trying to earn a living by writing for various periodicals, and publishing *The Friend*, a journal of his own literary, social, and philosophical criticism. At this time he also fell in love with Sara Hutchinson, Wordsworth's sister-in-law, but could never marry her because of his opposition to divorce.

A turn in Coleridge's fortunes came in 1807 when he was invited to give a series of lectures on poetry at the Royal Institution. They appear to have been uneven in quality, in part because of Coleridge's ill-health, but a second series, on Shakespeare and Milton, given in the winter of 1811–12, was widely praised. And in January 1813 Coleridge's play *Osorio*, now rewritten as *Remorse* with a prologue by Charles Lamb, began a long and successful run on Drury Lane. For the next several years Coleridge lived with friends around Bristol and lectured on Shakespeare and other subjects. Most significantly, in 1814, he began to dictate the *Biographia Literaria*, his major critical work, to his friend John Morgan.

Following his move to Highgate in 1816—it was to be his home for the remainder of his life—and with continual encouragement from his friends, Coleridge over the next two years published *Christabel; The Statesman's Manual; or the Bible the Best Guide to Political Skill and Foresight;* several collections of poetry; a series of pamphlets in support of the Factory Acts; and most important, the *Biographia Literaria. Aids to Reflection*, published in 1825, made him well-known to American Transcendentalists and led to his being dubbed in England the "Oracle of Highgate." Several collected editions of his poems were published in his last years, and *The Constitution of Church and State*, his last prose work, appeared four years before his death, on July 25, 1834.

Coleridge stands out as one of the greatest, most catholic minds in the history of English literature. He held men of the stature of Keats, Carlyle, and Emerson, in awe of his torrential conversation. Perhaps the best brief estimation of Coleridge was offered by his friend Wordsworth soon after his death; "he was the most *wonderful* man I ever knew—wonderful for the originality of his mind, and the power he possessed of throwing out in profusion grand central truths from which might be evolved the most comprehensive systems."

ANIMA POETAE

Our quaint metaphysical opinions, in an hour of anguish, are like playthings by the bedside of a child deadly sick.

The elder languages were fitter for poetry because they expressed only prominent ideas with clearness, the others but darkly. . . . Poetry gives most pleasure when only generally and not perfectly understood. It was so by me with Gray's "Bard" and Collins' Odes. The "Bard" once intoxicated me, and now I read it without pleasure. From this cause it is that what I call metaphysical poetry gives me so much delight.

Poetry which excites us to artificial feelings makes us callous to real ones.

The immoveableness of all things through which so many men were moving—a harsh contrast compared with the universal motion, the harmonious system of motions in the country, and everywhere in Nature. In the dim light London appeared to be a huge place of sepulchres through which hosts of spirits were gliding.

Not only words, as far as relates to speaking, but the knowledge of words as distinct component parts, which we learn by learning to read—what an immense effect it must have on our reasoning faculties! Logical in opposition to real.

Hot-headed men confuse, your cool-headed gentry jumble. The man of warm feelings only produces order and true connection.

To *think* of a thing is different from to *perceive* it, as "to walk" is from to "feel the ground under you"; perhaps in the same way too—namely, a succession of perceptions accompanied by a sense of *nisus* and purpose.

Materialists unwilling to admit the mysterious element of our nature make it all mysterious—nothing mysterious in nerves, eyes, etc., but that nerves think, etc.! Stir up the sediment into the transparent water, and so make all opaque.

> —and the deep power of Joy
> We see into the Life of Things.

By deep feeling we make our *ideas dim*, and this is what we mean by our life, ourselves. I think of the wall—it is before me a distinct image. Here I necessarily think of the *idea* and the thinking *I* as two distinct and opposite things. Now let me think of *myself,* of the thinking being. The idea becomes dim, whatever it be—so dim that I know not what it is; but the feeling is deep and steady, and this I call *I*—identifying the percipient and the perceived.

Hartley, looking out of my study window, fixed his eyes steadily and for some time on the opposite prospect and said, "Will yon mountains *always* be?" I shewed him the whole magnificent prospect in a looking-glass, and held it up, so that the whole was like a canopy or ceiling over his head, and he struggled to express himself concerning the difference between the thing and the image almost with convulsive effort. I never before saw such an abstract of *thinking* as a pure act and energy—of thinking as distinguished from thought.

Quaere, whether or no too great definiteness of terms in any language may not consume too much of the vital and idea-creating force in distinct, clear, full-made images, and so prevent originality. For original might be distinguished from positive thought.

Metaphysics make all one's thoughts equally corrosive on the body, by introducing a habit of making momently and common thought the subject of uncommon interest and intellectual energy.

The unspeakable comfort to a good man's mind, nay, even to a criminal, to be *understood*—to have some one that understands one—and who does not feel that, on earth, no one does? The hope of this, always more or less disappointed—gives the passion to friendship.

Hartley, at Mr. Clarkson's, sent for a candle. The *seems* made him miserable. "What do you mean, my love?" "The seems, the seems. What seems to be and is not, men and faces, and I do not (know) what, ugly, and sometimes pretty, and these turn ugly, and they seem when my eyes are open and worse when they are shut—and the candle cures the *seems*."

We imagine ourselves discoverers, and that we have struck a light, when, in reality, at most, we have but snuffed a candle.

The great federal republic of the universe.

The rocks and stones put on a vital resemblance and life itself seemed, thereby, to forego its restlessness, to anticipate in its own nature an infinite repose, and to become, as it were, compatible with immoveability.

"He who cannot wait for his reward has, in reality, not earned it." These words I uttered in a dream, in which a lecture I was giving—a very profound one, as I thought—was not listened to, but I was quizzed.

A smile, as foreign or alien to, as detached from the gloom of the countenance, as I have seen a small spot of light travel slowly and sadly along the mountain's breast, when all beside has been dark with the storm.

The sunny mist, the luminous gloom of Plato.

Nothing affects me much at the moment it happens. It either stupifies me, and I, perhaps, look at a merry-make and dance-the-hay of flies, or listen entirely to the loud click of the great clock, or I am simply indifferent, not without some sense of philosophical self-complacency. For a thing at the moment is but a thing of the moment; it must be taken up into the mind, diffuse itself through the whole multitude of shapes and thoughts, not one of which it leaves untinged, between (not one of) which and it some new thought is not engendered. Now this is a work of time, but the body feels it quicker with me.

What is it that I employ my metaphysics on? To perplex our clearest notions and living moral instincts? To extinguish the light of love and of conscience, to put out the life of arbitrement, to make myself and others *worthless, soulless, Godless*? No, to expose the folly and the legerdemain of those who have thus abused the blessed organ of language, to support all old and venerable truths, to support, to kindle, to project, to make the reason spread light over our feelings, to make our feelings diffuse vital warmth through our reason—these are my objects and these my subjects. Is this the metaphysic that bad spirits in hell delight in?

My nature requires another nature for its support, and reposes only in another from the necessary indigence of its being. Intensely similar yet not the same (must that other be); or, may I venture to say, the same indeed, but dissimilar, as the same breath sent with the same force, the same pauses, and the same melody pre-imaged in the mind, into the flute and the clarion shall be the same *soul diversely incarnate.*

Abstruse reasoning is to the inductions of common sense what reaping is to delving. But the implements with which we reap, how are they gained? by delving. Besides, what is common sense now was abstract reasoning with earlier ages.

The soul within the body—can I, any way, compare this to the reflection of the fire seen through my window on the solid wall, seeming, of course, within the solid wall, as deep within as the distance of the fire from the wall. I fear I can make nothing out of it; but why do I always hurry away from any interesting thought to do something uninteresting? As, for instance, when this thought struck me, I turned off my attention suddenly and went to look for the copy of Wolff which I had missed. Is it a cowardice of all deep feeling, even though pleasurable? or is it laziness? or is it something less obvious than either? Is it connected with my epistolary embarrassments?

I have only to shut my eyes to feel how ignorant I am whence these forms and coloured forms, and colours distinguishable beyond what I can distinguish, derive their birth. These varying and infinite co-present colours, what are they? I ask, to what do they belong in my waking remembrance? and almost never receive an answer. Only I perceive and know that whatever I change, in any part of me, produces some change in these eye-spectra; as, for instance, if I press my legs or change sides.

There are thoughts that seem to give me a power over my own life. I could kill myself by persevering in the thought. Mem., to describe as accurately as may be the approximating symptoms.

This evening, and indeed all this day, I ought to have been reading and filling the margins of Malthus.

I had begun and found it pleasant. Why did I neglect it? Because I ought not to have done this. The same applies to the reading and writing of letters, essays, etc. Surely this is well worth a serious analysis, that, by understanding, I may attempt to heal it. For it is a deep and wide disease in my moral nature, at once elm-and-oak-rooted. Is it love of liberty, of spontaneity or what? These all express, but do not explain the fact.

After I had got into bed last night I said to myself that I had been pompously enunciating as a difficulty, a problem of easy and common solution—viz., that it was the effect of association. From infancy up to manhood, under parents, schoolmasters, inspectors, etc., our pleasures and pleasant self-chosen pursuits (self-chosen because pleasant, and not originally pleasant because self-chosen) have been forcibly interrupted, and dull, unintelligible rudiments, or painful tasks imposed upon us instead. Now all duty is felt as a *command,* and every command is of the nature of an offence. Duty, therefore, by the law of association being felt as a command from without, would naturally call up the sensation of the pain roused from the commands of parents and schoolmasters. But I awoke this morning at half-past one, and as soon as disease permitted me to think at all, the shallowness and sophistry of this solution flashed upon me at once. I saw that the phenomenon occurred far, far too early: I have observed it in infants of two or three months old, and in Hartley I have seen it turned up and layed bare to the unarmed eye of the merest common sense. The fact is that interruption of itself is painful, because and as far as it acts as *disruption.* And thus without any reference to or distinct recollection of my former theory I saw great reason to attribute the effect, wholly, to the streamy nature of the associative faculty, and the more, as it is evident that they labour under this defect who are most reverie-ish and streamy—Hartley, for instance, and myself. This seems to me no common corroboration of my former thought on the origin of moral evil in general.

It is related by D. Unzer, an authority wholly to be relied on, that an *ohrwurm* (earwig) cut in half ate its own hinder part! Will it be the reverse with Great Britain and America?

One travels along with the lines of a mountain. Years ago I wanted to make Wordsworth sensible of this. How fine is Keswick vale! Would I repose, my soul lies and is quiet upon the broad level vale. Would it act? it darts up into the mountain-top like a kite, and like a chamois-goat runs along the ridge—or like a boy that makes a sport on the road of running along a wall or narrow fence!

One of the most noticeable and fruitful facts in psychology is the modification of the same feeling by difference of form. The Heaven lifts up my soul, the sight of the ocean seems to widen it. We feel the same force at work, but the difference, whether in mind or body that we should feel in actual travelling horizontally or in direct ascent, *that* we feel in fancy. For what are our feelings of this kind but a motion imagined, (together) with the feelings that would accompany that motion, (but) less distinguished, more blended, more rapid, more confused, and, thereby, co-adunated? Just as white is the very emblem of one in being the confusion of all.

How opposite to nature and the fact to talk of the "one moment" of Hume, of our whole being an aggregate of successive single sensations! Who ever felt a single sensation? Is not every one at the same moment conscious that there co-exist a thousand others, a darker shade, or less light, even as when I fix my attention on a white house or a grey bare hill or rather long ridge that runs out of sight each way (how often I want the German *unübersekbar!*) (untranslatable)—the pretended sight-sensation, is it anything more than the light-point in every picture either of nature or of a good painter? and, again, subordinately, in every component part of the picture? And what is a moment? Succession with interspace? Absurdity! It is evidently only the *licht-punct* in the indivisible undivided duration.

There are two sorts of talkative fellows whom it would be injurious to confound, and I, S. T. Coleridge, am the latter. The first sort is of those who use five hundred words more than needs to express an idea—that is not my case. Few men, I will be bold to say, put more meaning into their words than I, or choose them more deliberately and discriminately. The second sort is of those who use five hundred more ideas, images, reasons, etc., than there is any need of to arrive at their object, till the only object arrived at is that the mind's eye of the bystander is dazzled with colours succeeding so rapidly as to leave one vague impression that there has been a great blaze of colours all about something. Now this is my case, and a grievous fault it is. My illustrations swallow up my thesis. I feel too intensely the omnipresence of all in each, platonically speaking; or, psychologically, my brain- fibres, or the spiritual light which abides in the brain-marrow, as visible light appears to do in sundry rotten mackerel and other *smashy* matters, is of too general an affinity with all things, and though it perceives the *difference* of things, yet is eternally pursuing the likenesses, or, rather, that which is common (between them). Bring me two things that seem the very same, and then I am quick enough (not only) to show the difference, even to hair-splitting, but to go on from circle to circle till I break against the shore of my hearers' patience, or have my concentricals dashed to nothing by a snore. That is my ordinary mishap. At Malta, however, no one can charge me with one or the other. I have earned the general character of being a quiet well-meaning man, rather dull indeed! and who would have thought that he had been a *poet!* "O, a very wretched poetaster, ma'am! As to the reviews, 'tis well known he half-ruined himself in paying cleverer fellows than himself to write them," etc.

How far might one imagine all the theory of association out of a system of growth, by applying to the brain and soul what we know of an embryo? One tiny particle combines with another its like, and, so, lengthens and thickens, and this is, at once, memory and increasing vividness of impression. One might make a very amusing allegory of an embryo soul up to birth! Try! it is promising! You have not above three hundred volumes to write before you come to it, and as you write, perhaps, a volume once in ten years, you have ample time.

My dear fellow! never be ashamed of scheming—you can't think of living less than 4000 years, and that would nearly suffice for your present schemes. To be sure, if they go on in the same ratio to the performance, then a small difficulty arises; but never mind! look at the bright side always and die in a dream! Oh!

In the preface of my metaphysical works, I should say—"Once for all, read Kant, Fichte, etc., and then you will trace, or, if you are on the hunt, track me." Why, then, not acknowledge your obligations step by step? Because I could not do so in a multitude of glaring resemblances without a lie, for they had been mine, formed and full-formed, before I had ever heard of these writers, because to have fixed on the particular instances in which I have really been indebted to these writers would have been hard, if possible, to me who read for truth and self-satisfaction, and not to make a book, and who always rejoiced and was jubilant when I found my own ideas well expressed by others—and, lastly, let me say, because (I am proud, perhaps, but) I seem to know that much of the *matter* remains my own, and that the *soul* is mine. I fear not him for a critic who can confound a fellow-thinker with a compiler.

In all processes of the understanding the shortest way will be discovered the last; and this, perhaps, while it constitutes the great advantage of having a teacher to put us on the shortest road at the first, yet sometimes occasions a difficulty in the comprehension, inasmuch as the longest way is more near to the existing state of the mind, nearer to what if left to myself, on starting the thought, I should have thought next. The shortest way gives me the *knowledge* best, but the longest makes me more *knowing.*

If one thought leads to another, so often does it blot out another. This I find when having lain musing on my sofa, a number of interesting thoughts having suggested themselves, I conquer my bodily indolence, and rise to record them in these books, alas! my only confidants. The first thought leads me on indeed to new ones; but nothing but the faint memory of having had these remains of the other, which had been even more interesting to me. I do not know whether this be an idiosyncrasy, a peculiar disease, of *my* particular memory—but so it is with *me*—my thoughts crowd each other to death.

The first man of science was he who looked into a thing, not to learn whether it could furnish him with food, or shelter, or weapons, or tools, or ornaments, or *playwiths,* but who sought to know it for the gratification of *knowing;* while he that first sought to *know* in order to *be* was the first philosopher. I have read of two rivers passing through the same lake, yet all the way preserving their streams visibly distinct—if I mistake not, the Rhone and the Adar, through the Lake of Geneva. In a far finer distinction, yet in a subtler union, such, for the contemplative mind, are the streams of knowing and being. The lake is formed by the two streams in man and nature as it exists in and for man; and up this lake the philosopher sails on the junction-line of the constituent streams, still pushing upward and sounding as he goes, towards the common fountain-head of both, the mysterious source whose being is knowledge, whose knowledge is being—the adorable I AM IN THAT I AM.

BIOGRAPHIA LITERARIA

Chapter XIII

O Adam, One Almighty is, from whom
All things proceed, and up to him return,
If not depraved from good: created all
Such to perfection, one first nature all,
Indued with various forms, various degrees
Of substance, and, in things that live, of life;
But more refin'd, more spirituous and pure,
As nearer to him plac'd, or nearer tending,
Each in their several active spheres assign'd,
Till body up to spirit work, in bounds
Proportion'd to each kind. So from the root
Springs lighter the green stalk, from thence the leaves
More airy: last the bright consummate flower
Spirits odorous breathes. Flowers and their fruit,
Man's nourishment, by gradual scale sublim'd,
To *vital* spirits aspire: to *animal:*
To *intellectual!*—give both life and sense,
Fancy and understanding; whence the soul
REASON receives, and reason is her *being,*
Discursive or intuitive.

PAR. LOST. b. V.

"Sane si res corporales nil nisi materiale continerent, verissime dicerentur in fluxu consistere neque habere substantiale quicquam, quemadmodum et Platonici olim recte agnovere.—Hinc igitur, præter purè mathematica et phantasiæ subjecta, collegi quædam metaphysica solâque mente perceptibilia, esse admittenda: et massæ materiali *principium* quoddam superius et, ut sic dicam, *formale* addendum: quandoquidem omnes veritates rerum corporearum ex solis axiomatibus logisticis et geometricis, nempe de magno et parvo, toto et parte, figura et situ, colligi non possint; sed alia de causa et effectu, *actioneque* et *passione,* accedere debeant, quibus ordinis rerum rationes salventur. Id principium rerum, an ἐντελεχείαν an vim appellemus, non refert, modó meminerimus, per solam *Virium* notionem intelligibiliter explicari."

LEIBNITZ: *Op.* T. II. P. II. *p.* 53—T. III. *p.* 321.

Σέβομαι Νοερῶν
Κρυφίαν τάξιν·
Χώρει ΤΙ ΜΕΣΟΝ

Οὐ καταχυθέν.
Synesii *Hymn*.
III. l. 231.

Des Cartes, speaking as a naturalist, and in imitation of Archimedes, said, give me matter and motion and I will construct you the universe. We must of course understand him to have meant.: I will render the construction of the universe intelligible. In the same sense the transcendental philosopher says; grant me a nature having two contrary forces, the one of which tends to expand infinitely, while the other strives to apprehend or *find* itself in this infinity, and I will cause the world of intelligences with the whole system of their representations to rise up before you. Every other science presupposes intelligence as already existing and complete: the philosopher contemplates it in its growth, and as it were represents its history to the mind from its birth to its maturity.

The venerable Sage of Koenigsberg has preceded the march of this master-thought as an effective pioneer in his essay on the introduction of negative quantities into philosophy, published 1763. In this he has shown, that instead of assailing the science of mathematics by metaphysics, as Berkeley did in his Analyst, or of sophisticating it, as Wolf did, by the vain attempt of deducing the first principles of geometry from supposed deeper grounds of ontology, it behoved the metaphysician rather to examine whether the only province of knowledge, which man has succeeded in erecting into a pure science, might not furnish materials, or at least hints, for establishing and pacifying the unsettled, warring, and embroiled domain of philosophy. An imitation of the mathematical *method* had indeed been attempted with no better success than attended the essay of David to wear the armour of Saul. Another use however is possible and of far greater promise, namely, the actual application of the positions which had so wonderfully enlarged the discoveries of geometry, mutatis mutandis, to philosophical subjects. Kant having briefly illustrated the utility of such an attempt in the questions of space, motion, and infinitely small quantities, as employed by the mathematician, proceeds to the idea of negative quantities and the transfer of them to metaphysical investigation. Opposites, he well observes, are of two kinds, either logical, that is, such as are absolutely incompatible; or real, without being contradictory. The former he denominates Nihil negativum irrepræsentabile, the connection of which produces nonsense. A body in motion is something—Aliquid cogitabile; but a body, at one and the same time in motion and not in motion, is nothing, or, at most, air articulated into nonsense. But a motory force of a body in one direction, and an equal force of the same body in an opposite direction is not incompatible, and the result, namely, rest, is real and representable. For the purposes of mathematical calculus it is indifferent which force we term negative, and which positive, and consequently we appropriate the latter to that, which happens to be the principal object in our thoughts. Thus if a man's capital be ten and his debts eight, the subtraction will be the same, whether we call the capital negative debt, or the debt negative capital. But in as much as the latter stands practically in reference to the former, we of course represent the sum as 10–8. It is equally clear that two equal forces acting in opposite directions, both being finite and each distinguished from the other by its direction only, must neutralize or reduce each other to inaction. Now the transcendental philosophy demands; first, that two forces should be conceived which counteract each other by their essential nature; not only not in consequence of the accidental direction of each, but as prior to all direction, nay, as the primary forces from which the conditions of all possible directions are derivative and deducible: secondly, that these forces should be assumed to be both alike infinite, both alike indestructible. The problem will then be to discover the result or product of two such forces, as distinguished from the result of those forces which are finite, and derive their difference solely from the circumstance of their direction. When we have formed a scheme or outline of these two different kinds of force, and of their different results by the process of discursive reasoning, it will then remain for us to elevate the Thesis from notional to actual, by contemplating intuitively this one power with its two inherent indestructible yet counteracting forces, and the results or generations to which their inter-penetration gives existence, in the living principle and in the process of our own self-consciousness. By what instrument this is possible the solution itself will discover, at the same time that it will reveal to and for whom it is possible. Non omnia possumus omnes. There is a philosophic no less than a poetic genius, which is differenced from the highest perfection of talent, not by degree but by kind.

The counteraction then of the two assumed forces does not depend on their meeting from opposite directions; the power which acts in them is indestructible; it is therefore inexhaustibly re-ebullient; and as something must be the result of these two forces, both alike infinite, and both alike indestructible; and as rest or neutralization cannot be this result; no other conception is possible, but that the product must be a tertium aliquid, or finite generation. Consequently this conception is necessary. Now this tertium aliquid can be no other than an inter-penetration of the counteracting powers, partaking of both.

Thus far had the work been transcribed for the press, when I received the following letter from a friend, whose practical judgement I have had ample reason to estimate and revere, and whose taste and sensibility preclude all the excuses which my self-love might possibly have prompted me to set up in plea against the decision of advisers of equal good sense, but with less tact and feeling.

"*Dear C.*

"*You ask my opinion concerning your Chapter on the Imagination, both as to the impressions it made on myself, and as to those which I think it will make on the* PUBLIC, *i.e. that part of the public, who, from the title of the work and from its forming a sort of introduction to a volume of poems, are likely to constitute the great majority of your readers.*

"*As to myself, and stating in the first place the effect on my* understanding, *your opinions and method of argument were not only so* new *to me, but so directly the reverse of all I had ever been accustomed to consider as truth, that even if I had comprehended your premises sufficiently to have admitted them, and had seen the necessity of your conclusions, I should still have been in that state of mind, which in your note p. 52, 53. you have so ingeniously evolved, as the antithesis to that in which a man is, when he makes a* bull. *In your own words I should have felt as if I had been standing on my head.*

"*The effect on my* feelings, *on the other hand, I cannot better represent, than by supposing myself to have known only our light airy modern chapels of ease, and then for the first time to have been placed, and left alone, in one of our largest Gothic cathedrals in a gusty moonlight night of autumn. 'Now in glimmer, and now in gloom;' often in palpable darkness not without a chilly sensation of terror; then suddenly emerging into broad yet visionary lights with coloured shadows of fantastic shapes, yet all decked with holy insignia and mystic symbols; and ever and anon coming out full upon pictures and stone-work images of great men, with whose* names *I was familiar, but which looked upon me with countenances and an expression, the most dissimilar to all I had been in the habit of connecting with those names. Those whom I had been taught to venerate as almost superhuman in magnitude of intellect, I found perched in little fretwork niches, as grotesque dwarfs; while the grotesques, in my hitherto belief, stood guarding the high altar with all the characters of Apotheosis. In short, what I had supposed substances were thinned away into shadows, while everywhere shadows were deepened into substances:*

     'If substance may be call'd what shadow seem'd,
     For each seem'd either!'
                                     Milton.

    "*Yet after all, I could not but repeat the lines which you had quoted from a MS. poem of your own in the* Friend, *and applied to a work of Mr. Wordsworth's though with a few of the words altered:*

     'An orphic tale indeed,
    A tale *obscure* of high and passionate thoughts
    To a *strange* music chaunted!'

    "*Be assured, however, that I look forward anxiously to your great book on the* constructive philosophy, *which you have promised and announced: and that I will do my best to understand it. Only I will not promise to descend into the dark cave of Trophonius with you, there to rub my own eyes, in order to* make *the sparks and figured flashes, which I am required to see.*

    "*So much for myself. But as for the* Public, *I do not hesitate a moment in advising and urging you to withdraw the Chapter from the present work, and to reserve it for your announced treatises on the Logos or communicative intellect in Man and Deity. First, because, imperfectly as I understand the present Chapter, I see clearly that you have done too much, and yet not enough. You have been obliged to omit so many links, from the necessity of compression, that what remains, looks (if I may recur to my former illustration) like the fragments of the winding steps of an old ruined tower. Secondly, a still stronger argument (at least one that I am sure will be more forcible with you) is, that your readers will have both right and reason to complain of you. This Chapter, which cannot, when it is printed, amount to so little as an hundred pages, will of necessity greatly increase the expense of the work; and every reader who, like myself, is neither prepared nor perhaps calculated for the study of so abstruse a subject so abstrusely treated, will, as I have before hinted, be almost entitled to accuse you of a sort of imposition on him. For who, he might truly observe, could from your title-page, viz.* My Literary Life and Opinions, *published too as introductory to a volume of miscellaneous poems, have anticipated, or even conjectured, a long treatise on ideal Realism which holds the same relation in abstruseness to Plotinus, as Plotinus does to Plato. It will be well, if already you have not too much of metaphysical disquisition in your work, though as the larger part of the disquisition is historical, it will doubtless be both interesting and instructive to many to whose* unprepared *minds your speculations on the esemplastic power would be utterly unintelligible. Be assured, if you do publish this Chapter in the present work, you will be reminded of Bishop Berkeley's Siris, announced as an Essay on Tar-water, which beginning with Tar ends with the Trinity, the omne scibile forming the interspace. I say in the* present *work. In that greater work to which you have devoted so many years, and study so intense and various, it will be in its proper place. Your prospectus will have described and announced both its contents and their nature; and if any persons purchase it, who feel no interest in the subjects of which it treats, they will have themselves only to blame.*

"I could add to these arguments one derived from pecuniary motives, and particularly from the probable effects on the sale *of your present publication; but they would weigh little with you compared with the preceding. Besides, I have long observed, that arguments drawn from your own personal interests more often act on you as narcotics than as stimulants, and that in money concerns you have some small portion of pig-nature in your moral idiosyncracy, and, like these amiable creatures, must occasionally be pulled backward from the boat in order to make you enter it. All success attend you, for if hard thinking and hard reading are merits, you have deserved it.*

"Your affectionate, &c."

In consequence of this very judicious letter, which produced complete conviction on my mind, I shall content myself for the present with stating the main result of the Chapter, which I have reserved for that future publication, a detailed prospectus of which the reader will find at the close of the second volume.

The IMAGINATION then, I consider either as primary, or secondary. The primary IMAGINATION I hold to be the living Power and prime Agent of all human Perception, and as a repetition in the finite mind of the eternal act of creation in the infinite I AM. The secondary Imagination I consider as an echo of the former, co-existing with the conscious will, yet still as identical with the primary in the *kind* of its agency, and differing only in *degree,* and in the *mode* of its operation. It dissolves, diffuses, dissipates, in order to re-create; or where this process is rendered impossible, yet still at all events it struggles to idealize and to unify. It is essentially *vital,* even as all objects (*as* objects) are essentially fixed and dead.

FANCY, on the contrary, has no other counters to play with, but fixities and definites. The Fancy is indeed no other than a mode of Memory emancipated from the order of time and space; while it is blended with, and modified by that empirical phenomenon of the will, which we express by the word CHOICE. But equally with the ordinary memory the Fancy must receive all its materials ready made from the law of association.

Whatever more than this, I shall think it fit to declare concerning the powers and privileges of the imagination in the present work, will be found in the critical essay on the uses of the Supernatural in poetry, and the principles that regulate its introduction: which the reader will find prefixed to the poem of *The Ancient Mariner.*

Chapter XIV

During the first year that Mr. Wordsworth and I were neighbours, our conversations turned frequently on the two cardinal points of poetry, the power of exciting the sympathy of the reader by a faithful adherence to the truth of nature, and the power of giving the interest of novelty by the modifying colors of imagination. The sudden charm, which accidents of light and shade, which moon-light or sun-set diffused over a known and familiar landscape, appeared to represent the practicability of combining both. These are the poetry of nature. The thought suggested itself (to which of us I do not recollect) that a series of poems might be composed of two sorts. In the one, the incidents and agents were to be, in part at least, supernatural; and the excellence aimed at was to consist in the interesting of the affections by the dramatic truth of such emotions, as would naturally accompany such situations, supposing them real. And real in *this* sense they have been to every human being who, from whatever source of delusion, has at any time believed himself under super-natural agency. For the second class, subjects were to be chosen from ordinary life; the characters and incidents were to be such, as will be found in every village and its vicinity, where there is a meditative and feeling mind to seek after them, or to notice them, when they present themselves.

In this idea originated the plan of the "Lyrical Ballads"; in which it was agreed, that my endeavours should be directed to persons and characters supernatural, or at least romantic; yet so as to transfer from our inward nature a human interest and a semblance of truth sufficient to procure for these shadows of imagination that willing suspension of disbelief for the moment, which constitutes poetic faith. Mr. Wordsworth, on the other hand, was to propose to himself as his object, to give the charm of novelty to things of every day, and to excite a feeling analogous to the supernatural, by awakening the mind's attention from the lethargy of custom, and directing it to the loveliness and the wonders of the world before us; an inexhaustible treasure, but for which, in consequence of the film of familiarity and selfish solicitude we have eyes, yet see not, ears that hear not, and hearts that neither feel nor understand.

With this view I wrote "The Ancient Mariner," and was preparing among other poems, "The Dark Ladie," and the "Christabel," in which I should have more nearly realized my ideal, than I had done in my first attempt. But Mr. Wordsworth's industry had proved so much more successful, and the number of his poems so much greater, that my compositions, instead of forming a balance, appeared rather an interpolation of heterogeneous matter. Mr. Wordsworth added two or three poems written in his own character, in the impassioned, lofty, and sustained diction, which is characteristic of his genius. In this form the "Lyrical Ballads" were published; and were presented by him, as an *experiment,* whether subjects, which from their nature rejected the usual ornaments and extra-colloquial style of poems in general, might not be so managed in the language of ordinary life as to produce the pleasureable interest, which it is the peculiar business of poetry to impart. To the second edition he added a preface of considerable length; in which, notwithstanding some passages of apparently a contrary import, he was understood to contend for the extension of this style to poetry of all kinds, and to reject as vicious and indefensible all phrases and forms of style that were not included in what he (unfortunately, I think, adopting an equivocal expression) called the language of *real* life. From this preface, prefixed to poems in which it was impossible to deny the presence of original genius, however mistaken its direction might be deemed, arose the whole long-continued controversy. For from the conjunction of perceived power with supposed heresy I explain the inveteracy and in some instances, I grieve to say, the acrimonious passions, with which the controversy has been conducted by the assailants.

Had Mr. Wordsworth's poems been the silly, the childish things, which they were for a long time described as being; had they been really distinguished from the compositions of other poets merely by meanness of language and inanity of thought; had they indeed contained nothing more than what is found in the parodies and pretended imitations of them; they must have sunk at once, a dead weight, into the slough of oblivion, and have dragged the preface along with them. But year after year increased the number of Mr. Wordsworth's admirers. They were found too not in the lower classes of the reading public, but chiefly among young men of strong sensibility and meditative minds; and their admiration (inflamed perhaps in some degree by opposition) was distinguished by its intensity, I might almost say, by its *religious* fervor. These facts, and the intellectual energy of the author, which was more or less consciously felt, where it was outwardly and even boisterously denied, meeting with sentiments of aversion to his opinions, and of alarm at their consequences, produced an eddy of criticism, which would of itself have borne up the poems by the violence with which it whirled them round and round. With many parts of this preface, in the sense attributed to them, and which the words undoubtedly seem to authorize, I never concurred; but on the contrary objected to them as erroneous in principle, and as contradictory (in appearance at least) both to other parts of the same preface, and to the author's own practice in the greater number of the poems themselves. Mr. Wordsworth in his recent collection has, I find, degraded this prefatory disquisition to the end of his second volume, to be read or not at the reader's choice. But he has not, as far as I can discover, announced any change in his poetic creed. At all events, considering it as the source of a controversy, in which I have been honored more than I deserve by the frequent conjunction of my name with his, I think it expedient to declare once for all, in what points I coincide with his opinions, and in what points I altogether differ. But in order to render myself intelligible I must previously, in as few words as possible, explain my ideas, first, of a POEM; and secondly, of POETRY itself, in *kind,* and in *essence.*

The office of philosophical *disquisition* consists in just *distinction;* while it is the privilege of the philosopher to preserve himself constantly aware, that distinction is not division. In order to obtain adequate notions of any truth, we must intellectually separate its distinguishable parts; and this is the technical *process* of philosophy. But having so done, we must then restore them in our conceptions to the unity, in which they actually co-exist; and this is the *result* of philosophy. A poem contains the same elements as a prose composition; the difference therefore must consist in a different combination of them, in consequence of a different object being proposed. According to the difference of the object will be the difference of the combination. It is possible, that the object may be merely to facilitate the recollection of any given facts or observations by artificial arrangement; and the composition will be a poem, merely because it is distinguished from prose by metre, or by rhyme, or by both conjointly. In this, the lowest sense, a man might attribute the name of a poem to the well-known enumeration of the days in the several months;

> Thirty days hath September,
> April, June, and November,

and others of the same class and purpose. And as a particular pleasure is found in anticipating the recurrence of sounds and quantities, all compositions that have this charm superadded, whatever be their contents, *may* be entitled poems.

So much for the superficial *form.* A difference of object and contents supplies an additional ground of distinction. The immediate purpose may be the communication of truths; either of truth absolute and demonstrable, as in works of science; or of facts experienced and recorded, as in history. Pleasure, and that of the highest and most permanent kind, may *result* from the *attainment* of the end; but it is not itself the immediate end. In other works the communication of pleasure may be the immediate purpose; and though truth, either moral or intellectual, ought to be the *ultimate* end, yet this will distinguish the character of the author, not the class to which the work belongs. Blest indeed is that state of society, in which the immediate purpose would be baffled by the perversion of the proper ultimate end; in which no charm of diction or imagery could exempt the Bathyllus even of an Anacreon, or the Alexis of Virgil, from disgust and aversion!

But the communication of pleasure may be the immediate object of a work not metrically composed; and that object may have been in a high degree attained, as in novels and romances. Would then the mere superaddition of metre, with or without rhyme, entitle *these* to the name of poems? The answer is, that nothing can permanently please, which does not contain in itself the reason why it is so, and not otherwise. If metre be superadded, all other parts must be made consonant with it. They must be such, as to justify the perpetual and distinct attention to each part, which an exact correspondent recurrence of accent and sound are calculated to excite. The final definition then, so deduced, may be thus worded. A poem is that species of composition, which is opposed to works of science, by proposing for its *immediate* object pleasure, not truth; and from all other species (having *this* object in common with it) it is discriminated by proposing to itself such delight from the *whole,* as is compatible with a distinct gratification from each component *part.*

Controversy is not seldom excited in consequence of the disputants attaching each a different meaning to the same word; and in few instances has this been more striking, than in disputes concerning the present subject. If a man chooses to call every composition a poem, which is rhyme, or measure, or both, I must leave his opinion uncontroverted. The distinction is at least competent to characterize the writer's intention. If it were subjoined, that the whole is likewise entertaining or affecting, as a tale, or as a series of interesting reflections, I of course admit this as another fit ingredient of a poem, and an additional merit. But if the definition sought for be that of a *legitimate* poem, I answer, it must be one, the parts of which mutually support and explain each other; all in their proportion harmonizing with, and supporting the purpose and known influences of metrical arrangement. The philosophic critics of all ages coincide with the ultimate judgement of all countries, in equally denying the praises of a just poem, on the one hand, to a series of striking lines or distiches, each of which, absorbing the whole attention of the reader to itself, disjoins it from its context, and makes it a separate whole, instead of an harmonizing part; and on the other hand, to an unsustained composition, from which the reader collects rapidly the general result, unattracted by the component parts. The reader should be carried forward, not merely or chiefly by the mechanical impulse of curiosity, or by a restless desire to arrive at the final solution; but by the pleasureable activity of mind excited by the at-tractions of the journey itself. Like the motion of a serpent, which the Egyptians made the emblem of intellectual power; or like the path of sound through the air; at every step he pauses and half recedes, and from the retrogressive movement collects the force which again carries him onward.

"Præcipitandus est *liber* spiritus," says Petronius Arbiter most happily. The epithet, *liber,* here balances the preceding verb; and it is not easy to conceive more meaning condensed in fewer words.

But if this should be admitted as a satisfactory character of a poem, we have still to seek for a definition of poetry. The writings of Plato, and Bishop Taylor, and the "Theoria Sacra" of Burnet, furnish undeniable proofs that poetry of the highest kind may exist without metre, and even without the contra-distinguishing objects of a poem. The first chapter of Isaiah (indeed a very large portion of the whole book) is poetry in the most emphatic sense; yet it would be not less irrational than strange to assert, that pleasure, and not truth, was the immediate object of the prophet. In short, whatever *specific* import we attach to the word, poetry, there will be found involved in it, as a necessary consequence, that a poem of any length neither can be, or ought to be, all poetry. Yet if an harmonious whole is to be produced, the remaining parts must be preserved *in keeping* with the poetry; and this can be no otherwise effected than by such a studied selection and artificial arrangement, as will partake of *one,* though not a *peculiar* property of poetry. And this again can be no other than the property of exciting a more continuous and equal attention than the language of prose aims at, whether colloquial or written.

My own conclusions on the nature of poetry, in the strictest use of the word, have been in part anticipated in the preceding disquisition on the fancy and imagination. What is poetry? is so nearly the same question with, what is a poet? that the answer to the one is involved in the solution of the other. For it is a distinction resulting from the poetic genius itself, which sustains and modifies the images, thoughts, and emotions of the poet's own mind.

The poet, described in *ideal* perfection, brings the whole soul of man into activity, with the subordination of its faculties to each other, according to their relative worth and dignity. He diffuses a tone and spirit of unity, that blends, and (as it were) *fuses,* each into each, by that synthetic and magical power, to which we have exclusively appropriated the name of imagination. This power, first put in action by the will and understanding, and retained under their irremissive, though gentle and unnoticed, controul *(laxis effertur habenis)* reveals itself in the balance or reconciliation of opposite or discordant qualities: of sameness, with difference; of the general, with the concrete; the idea, with the image; the individual, with the representative; the sense of novelty and freshness, with old and familiar objects; a more than usual state of emotion, with more than usual order; judgement ever awake and steady self-possession, with enthusiasm and feeling profound or vehement; and while it blends and harmonizes the natural and the artificial, still subordinates art to nature; the manner to the matter; and our admiration of the poet to our sympathy with the poetry. "Doubtless," as Sir John Davies observes of the soul (and his words may with slight alteration be applied, and even more appropriately, to the poetic IMAGINATION)

> Doubtless this could not be, but that she turns
>   Bodies to spirit by sublimation strange,

As fire converts to fire the things it burns,
    As we our food into our nature change.
From their gross matter she abstracts their forms,
    And draws a kind of quintessence from things;
Which to her proper nature she transforms,
    To bear them light on her celestial wings.
Thus does she, when from individual states
    She doth abstract the universal kinds;
Which then re-clothed in divers names and fates
    Steal access through our senses to our minds.

Finally, GOOD SENSE is the BODY of poetic genius, FANCY its DRAPERY, MOTION its LIFE, and IMAGINATION the SOUL that is everywhere, and in each; and forms all into one graceful and intelligent whole.

Chapter XVII

As far then as Mr. Wordsworth in his preface contended, and most ably contended, for a reformation in our poetic diction, as far as he has evinced the truth of passion, and the *dramatic* propriety of those figures and metaphors in the original poets, which, stripped of their justifying reasons, and converted into mere artifices of connection or ornament, constitute the characteristic falsity in the poetic style of the moderns; and as far as he has, with equal acuteness and clearness pointed out the process by which this change was effected, and the resemblances between that state into which the reader's mind is thrown by the pleasureable confusion of thought from an unaccustomed train of words and images; and that state which is induced by the natural language of empassioned feeling; he undertook a useful task, and deserves all praise, both for the attempt and for the execution. The provocations to this remonstrance in behalf of truth and nature were still of perpetual recurrence before and after the publication of this preface. I cannot likewise but add, that the comparison of such poems of merit, as have been given to the public within the last ten or twelve years, with the majority of those produced previously to the appearance of that preface, leave no doubt on my mind, that Mr. Wordsworth is fully justified in believing his efforts to have been by no means ineffectual. Not only in the verses of those who have professed their admiration of his genius, but even of those who have distinguished themselves by hostility to his theory, and depreciation of his writings, are the impressions of his principles plainly visible. It is possible, that with these principles others may have been blended, which are not equally evident; and some which are unsteady and subvertible from the narrowness or imperfection of their basis. But it is more than possible, that these errors of defect or exaggeration, by kindling and feeding the controversy, may have conduced not only to the wider propagation of the accompanying truths, but that, by their frequent presentation to the mind in an excited state, they may have won for them a more permanent and practical result. A man will borrow a part from his opponent the more easily, if he feels himself justified in continuing to reject a part. While there remain important points in which he can still feel himself in the right, in which he still finds firm footing for continued resistance, he will gradually adopt those opinions, which were the least remote from his own convictions, as not less congruous with his own theory than with that which he reprobates. In like manner with a kind of instinctive prudence, he will abandon by little and little his weakest posts, till at length he seems to forget that they had ever belonged to him, or affects to consider them at most as accidental and "petty annexments," the removal of which leaves the citadel unhurt and unendangered.

My own differences from certain supposed parts of Mr. Wordsworth's theory ground themselves on the assumption, that his words had been rightly interpreted, as purporting that the proper diction for poetry in general consists altogether in a language taken, with due exceptions, from the mouths of men in real life, a language which actually constitutes the natural conversation of men under the influence of natural feelings. My objection is, first, that in *any* sense this rule is applicable only to *certain* classes of poetry; secondly, that even to these classes it is not applicable, except in such a sense, as hath never by any one (as far as I know or have read) been denied or doubted; and lastly, that as far as, and in that degree in which it is *practicable,* yet as a *rule* it is useless, if not injurious, and therefore either need not, or ought not to be practised. The poet informs his reader, that he had generally chosen *low and rustic* life; but not *as* low and rustic, or in order to repeat that pleasure of doubtful moral effect, which persons of elevated rank and of superior refinement oftentimes derive from a happy *imitation* of the rude unpolished manners and discourse of their inferiors. For the pleasure so derived may be traced to three exciting causes. The first is the naturalness, in *fact,* of the things represented. The second is the apparent naturalness of the *representation,* as raised and qualified by an imperceptible infusion of the author's own knowledge and talent, which infusion does, indeed, constitute it an *imitation* as distinguished from a mere *copy*. The third cause may be found in the reader's conscious feeling of his superiority awakened by the contrast presented to him; even as for the same purpose the kings and great barons of yore retained sometimes *actual* clowns and fools, but more frequently shrewd and witty fellows in that *character*. These, however, were not Mr. Wordsworth's objects. *He* chose low and rustic life, "because in that condition the essential passions of the heart find a better soil, in which they can attain their maturity, are less under restraint, and speak a plainer and more emphatic language; because in that condition of life our elementary feelings coexist in a state of greater simplicity, and consequently may be more accurately contemplated, and more forcibly communicated; because the manners of rural life germinate from those elementary feelings; and from the necessary character of rural occupations are more easily comprehended, and are more durable; and lastly, because in that condition the passions of men are incorporated with the beautiful and permanent forms of nature."

Now it is clear to me, that in the most interesting of the poems, in which the author is more or less dramatic, as "the Brothers," "Michael," "Ruth," "the Mad Mother," &c., the persons introduced are by no means taken *from low or rustic life* in the common acceptation of those words; and it is not less clear, that the sentiments and language, as far as they can be conceived to have been really transferred from the minds and conversation of such persons, are attributable to causes and circumstances not necessarily connected with "their occupations and abode." The thoughts, feelings, language, and manners of the shepherd-farmers in the vales of Cumberland and Westmoreland, as far as they are actually adopted in those poems, may be accounted for from causes, which will and do produce the same results in *every* state of life, whether in town or country. As the two principal I rank that INDEPENDENCE, which raises a man above servitude, or daily toil for the profit of others, yet not above the necessity of industry and a frugal simplicity of domestic life; and the accompanying unambitious, but solid and religious, EDUCATION, which has rendered few books familiar, but the Bible, and the liturgy or hymn book. To this latter cause, indeed, which is so far *accidental*, that it is the blessing of particular countries and a particular age, not the product of particular places or employments, the poet owes the show of probability, that his personages might really feel, think, and talk with any tolerable resemblance to his representation. It is an excellent remark of Dr. Henry More's, (Enthusiasmus triumphatus, Sec. XXXV.), that "a man of confined education, but of good parts, by constant reading of the Bible will naturally form a more winning and commanding rhetoric than those that are learned; the intermixture of tongues and of artificial phrases debasing *their* style."

It is, moreover, to be considered that to the formation of healthy feelings, and a reflecting mind, *negations* involve impediments not less formidable than sophistication and vicious intermixture. I am convinced, that for the human soul to prosper in rustic life a certain vantage-ground is pre-requisite. It is not every man that is likely to be improved by a country life or by country labors. Education, or original sensibility, or both, must pre-exist, if the changes, forms, and incidents of nature are to prove a sufficient stimulant. And where these are not sufficient, the mind contracts and hardens by want of stimulants: and the man becomes selfish, sensual, gross, and hard-hearted. Let the management of the POOR LAWS in Liverpool, Manchester, or Bristol be compared with the ordinary dispensation of the poor rates in agricultural villages, where the *farmers* are the overseers and guardians of the poor. If my own experience have not been particularly unfortunate, as well as that of the many respectable country clergymen with whom I have conversed on the subject, the result would engender more than scepticism concerning the desireable influences of low and rustic life in and for itself. Whatever may be concluded on the other side, from the stronger local attachments and enter-prising spirit of the Swiss, and other mountaineers, applies to a particular mode of pastoral life, under forms of property that permit and beget manners truly republican, not to rustic life in general, or to the absence of artificial cultivation. On the contrary the mountaineers, whose manners have been so often eulogized, are in general better educated and greater readers than men of equal rank elsewhere. But where this is not the case, as among the peasantry of North Wales, the ancient mountains, with all their terrors and all their glories, are pictures to the blind, and music to the deaf.

I should not have entered so much into detail upon this passage, but here seems to be the point, to which all the lines of difference converge as to their source and centre. (I mean, as far as, and in whatever respect, my poetic creed *does* differ from the doctrines promulged in this preface.) I adopt with full faith the principle of Aristotle, that poetry as poetry is essentially *ideal,* that it avoids and excludes all *accident;* that its apparent individualities of rank, character, or occupation must be *representative* of a class; and that the *persons* of poetry must be clothed with *generic* attributes, with the *common* attributes of the class: not with such as one gifted individual might *possibly* possess, but such as from his situation it is most probable beforehand that he *would* possess. If my premises are right and my deductions legitimate, it follows that there can be no *poetic* medium between the swains of Theocritus and those of an imaginary golden age.

The characters of the vicar and the shepherd-mariner in the poem of *The Brothers,* that of the shepherd of Greenhead Ghyll in the *Michael,* have all the verisimilitude and representative quality, that the purposes of poetry can require. They are persons of a known and abiding class, and their manners and sentiments the natural product of circumstances common to the class. Take *Michael* for instance:

> An old man stout of heart, and strong of limb:
> His bodily frame had been from youth to age
> Of an unusual strength: his mind was keen,
> Intense, and frugal, apt for all affairs,
> And in his shepherd's calling he was prompt
> And watchful more than ordinary men.
> Hence he had learnt the meaning of all winds,
> Of blasts of every tone; and oftentimes
> When others heeded not, he heard the South
> Make subterraneous music, like the noise
> Of bagpipers on distant Highland hills.
> The shepherd, at such warning, of his flock
> Bethought him, and he to himself would say,
> The winds are now devising work for me!
> And truly at all times the storm, that drives
> The traveller to a shelter, summon'd him
> Up to the mountains. He had been alone
> Amid the heart of many thousand mists,
> That came to him and left him on the heights.
> So liv'd he, till his eightieth year was pass'd.

And grossly that man errs, who should suppose
That the green vallies, and the streams and rocks,
Were things indifferent to the shepherd's thoughts.
Fields, where with chearful spirits he had breath'd
The common air; the hills, which he so oft
Had climb'd with vigorous steps; which had impress'd
So many incidents upon his mind
Of hardship, skill or courage, joy or fear;
Which, like a book, preserved the memory
Of the dumb animals, whom he had sav'd,
Had fed or shelter'd, linking to such acts,
So grateful in themselves, the certainty
Of honorable gain; these fields, these hills
Which were his living being, even more
Than his own blood—what could they less? had laid
Strong hold on his affections, were to him
A pleasureable feeling of blind love,
The pleasure which there is in life itself.

On the other hand, in the poems which are pitched at a lower note, as the *Harry Gill, Idiot Boy,* the *feelings* are those of human nature in general; though the poet has judiciously laid the *scene* in the country, in order to place *himself* in the vicinity of interesting images, without the necessity of ascribing a sentimental perception of their beauty to the persons of his drama. In the *Idiot Boy,* indeed, the mother's character is not so much a real and native product of a "situation where the essential passions of the heart find a better soil, in which they can attain their maturity and speak a plainer and more emphatic language," as it is an impersonation of an instinct abandoned by judgement. Hence the two following charges seem to me not wholly ground-less: at least, they are the only plausible objections, which I have heard to that fine poem. The one is, that the author has not, in the poem itself, taken sufficient care to preclude from the reader's fancy the disgusting images of *ordinary morbid idiocy,* which yet it was by no means his intention to represent. He has even by the "burr, burr, burr," uncounteracted by any preceding description of the boy's beauty, assisted in recalling them. The other is, that the idiocy of the *boy* is so evenly balanced by the folly of the *mother,* as to present to the general reader rather a laughable burlesque on the blindness of anile dotage, than an analytic display of maternal affection in its ordinary workings.

In the *Thorn* the poet himself acknowledges in a note the necessity of an introductory poem, in which he should have pourtrayed the character of the person from whom the words of the poem are supposed to proceed: a superstitious man moderately imaginative, of slow faculties and deep feelings, "a captain of a small trading vessel, for example, who, being past the middle age of life, had retired upon an annuity, or small independent income, to some village or country town of which he was not a native, or in which he had not been accustomed to live. Such men having nothing to do become credulous and talkative from indolence." But in a poem, still more in a lyric poem (and the NURSE in Shakespeare's Romeo and Juliet alone prevents me from extending the remark even to dramatic *poetry*, if indeed the Nurse itself can be deemed altogether a case in point) it is not possible to imitate truly a dull and garrulous discourser, without repeating the effects of dullness and garrulity. However this may be, I dare assert, that the parts (and these form the far larger portion of the whole) which might as well or still better have proceeded from the poet's own imagination, and have been spoken in his own character, are those which have given, and which will continue to give, universal delight; and that the passages exclusively appropriate to the supposed narrator, such as the last couplet of the third stanza; the seven last lines of the tenth; and the five following stanzas, with the exception of the four admirable lines at the commencement of the fourteenth, are felt by many unprejudiced and unsophisticated hearts, as sudden and unpleasant sinkings from the height to which the poet had previously lifted them, and to which he again re-elevates both himself and his reader.

If then I am compelled to doubt the theory, by which the choice of *characters* was to be directed, not only *à priori*, from grounds of reason, but both from the few instances in which the poet himself *need* be supposed to have been governed by it, and from the comparative inferiority of those instances; still more must I hesitate in my assent to the sentence which immediately follows the former citation; and which I can neither admit as particular fact, or as general rule. "The language too of these men is adopted (purified indeed from what appear to be its real defects, from all lasting and rational causes of dislike or disgust) because such men hourly communicate with the best objects from which the best part of language is originally derived; and because, from their rank in society and the sameness and narrow circle of their intercourse, being less under the action of social vanity, they convey their feelings and notions in simple and unelaborated expressions." To this I reply; that a rustic's language, purified from all provincialism and grossness, and so far reconstructed as to be made consistent with the rules of grammar (which are in essence no other than the laws of universal logic, applied to psychological materials) will not differ from the language of any other man of commonsense, however learned or refined he may be, except as far as the notions, which the rustic has to convey, are fewer and more indiscriminate. This will become still clearer, if we add the consideration (equally important though less obvious) that the rustic, from the more imperfect developement of his faculties, and from the lower state of their cultivation, aims almost solely to convey *insulated facts*, either those of his scanty experience or his traditional belief; while the educated man chiefly seeks to discover and express those *connections* of things, or those relative *bearings* of fact to fact, from which some more or less general law is deducible. For *facts* are valuable to a wise man, chiefly as they lead to the discovery of the indwelling *law*, which is the true *being* of things, the sole solution of their modes of existence, and in the knowledge of which consists our dignity and our power.

As little can I agree with the assertion, that from the objects with which the rustic hourly communicates the best part of language is formed. For first, if to communicate with an object implies such an acquaintance with it, as renders it capable of being discriminately reflected on; the distinct knowledge of an uneducated rustic would furnish a very scanty vocabulary. The few things, and modes of action, requisite for his bodily conveniences, would alone be individualized; while all the rest of nature would be expressed by a small number of confused general terms. Secondly, I deny that the words and combinations of words derived from the objects, with which the rustic is familiar, whether with distinct or confused knowledge, can be justly said to form the *best* part of language. It is more than probable, that many classes of the brute creation possess discriminating sounds, by which they can convey to each other notices of such objects as concern their food, shelter, or safety. Yet we hesitate to call the aggregate of such sounds a language, otherwise than metaphorically. The best part of human language, properly so called, is derived from reflection on the acts of the mind itself. It is formed by a voluntary appropriation of fixed symbols to internal acts, to processes and results of imagination, the greater part of which have no place in the consciousness of uneducated man; though in civilized society, by imitation and passive remembrance of what they hear from their religious instructors and other superiors, the most uneducated share in the harvest which they neither sowed or reaped. If the history of the phrases in hourly currency among our peasants were traced, a person not previously aware of the fact would be surprised at finding so large a number, which three or four centuries ago were the exclusive property of the universities and the schools; and, at the commencement of the Reformation, had been transferred from the school to the pulpit, and thus gradually passed into common life. The extreme difficulty, and often the impossibility, of finding words for the simplest moral and intellectual processes of the languages of uncivilized tribes has proved perhaps the weightiest obstacle to the progress of our most zealous and adroit missionaries. Yet these tribes are surrounded by the same nature as our peasants are; but in still more impressive forms; and they are, moreover, obliged to *particularize* many more of them. When, therefore, Mr. Wordsworth adds, "accordingly, such a language" (meaning, as before, the language of rustic life purified from provincialism) "arising out of repeated experience and regular feelings, is a more permanent, and a far more philosophical language, than that which is frequently substituted for it by poets, who think they are conferring honor upon themselves and their art in proportion as they indulge in arbitrary and capricious habits of expression:" it may be answered, that the language, which he has in view, can be attributed to rustics with no greater right, than the style of Hooker or Bacon to Tom Brown or Sir Roger L'Estrange. Doubtless, if what is peculiar to each were omitted in each, the result must needs be the same. Further, that the poet, who uses an illogical diction, or a style fitted to excite only the low and changeable pleasure of wonder by means of groundless novelty, substitutes a language of *folly* and *vanity,* not for that of the *rustic,* but for that of *good sense* and *natural feeling.*

Here let me be permitted to remind the reader, that the positions, which I controvert, are contained in the sentences—"*a selection of the* REAL *language of men;*"—"*the language of these men*" (i.e. men in low and rustic life) "*I propose to myself to imitate, and, as far as is possible, to adopt the very language of men.*" "*Between the language of prose and that of metrical composition, there neither is, nor can be any essential difference.*" It is against these exclusively that my opposition is directed.

I object, in the very first instance, to an equivocation in the use of the word "real." Every man's language varies, according to the extent of his knowledge, the activity of his faculties, and the depth or quickness of his feelings. Every man's language has, first, its *individualities;* secondly, the common properties of the *class* to which he belongs; and thirdly, words and phrases of *universal* use. The language of Hooker, Bacon, Bishop Taylor, and Burke differs from the common language of the learned class only by the superior number and novelty of the thoughts and relations which they had to convey. The language of Algernon Sidney differs not at all from that, which every well-educated gentleman would wish to write, and (with due allowances for the undeliberateness, and less connected train, of thinking natural and proper to conversation) such as he would wish to talk. Neither one nor the other differ half so much from the general language of cultivated society, as the language of Mr. Wordsworth's homeliest composition differs from that of a common peasant. For "real" therefore, we must substitute *ordinary,* or *lingua communis.* And this, we have proved, is no more to be found in the phraseology of low and rustic life than in that of any other class. Omit the peculiarities of each, and the result of course must be common to all. And assuredly the omissions and changes to be made in the language of rustics, before it could be transferred to any species of poem, except the drama or other professed imitation, are at least as numerous and weighty, as would be required in adapting to the same purpose the ordinary language of tradesmen and manufacturers. Not to mention, that the language so highly extolled by Mr. Wordsworth varies in every county, nay in every village, according to the accidental character of the clergyman, the existence or nonexistence of schools; or even, perhaps, as the exciseman, publican, or barber, happen to be, or not to be, zealous politicians, and readers of the weekly newspaper *pro bono publico.* Anterior to cultivation, the lingua communis of every country, as Dante has well observed, exists every where in parts, and no where as a whole.

Neither is the case rendered at all more tenable by the addition of the words, *in a state of excitement.* For the nature of a man's words, where he is strongly affected by joy, grief, or anger, must necessarily depend on the number and quality of the general truths, conceptions and images, and of the words expressing them, with which his mind had been previously stored. For the property of passion is not to *create;* but to set in increased activity. At least, whatever new connections of thoughts or images, or (which is equally, if not more than equally, the appropriate effect of strong excitement) whatever generalizations of truth or experience, the heat of passion may produce; yet the terms of their conveyance must have pre-existed in his former conversations, and are only collected and crowded together by the unusual stimulation. It is indeed very possible to adopt in a poem the unmeaning repetitions, habitual phrases, and other blank counters, which an unfurnished or confused understanding interposes at short intervals, in order to keep hold of his subject, which is still slipping from him, and to give him time for recollection; or in mere aid of vacancy, as in the scanty companies of a country stage the same player pops backwards and forwards, in order to prevent the appearance of empty spaces, in the procession of Macbeth, or Henry VIIIth. But what assistance to the poet, or ornament to the poem, these can supply, I am at a loss to conjecture. Nothing assuredly can differ either in origin or in mode more widely from the *apparent* tautologies of intense and turbulent feeling, in which the passion is greater and of longer endurance than to be exhausted or satisfied by a single representation of the image or incident exciting it. Such repetitions I admit to be a beauty of the highest kind; as illustrated by Mr. Wordsworth himself from the song of Deborah. *"At her feet he bowed, he fell, he lay down; at her feet he bowed, he fell; where he bowed, there he fell down dead."*

Chapter XVIII

I conclude, therefore, that the attempt is impracticable; and that, were it not impracticable, it would still be useless. For the very power of making the selection implies the previous possession of the language selected. Or where can the poet have lived? And by what rules could he direct his choice, which would not have enabled him to select and arrange his words by the light of his own judgement? We do not adopt the language of a class by the mere adoption of such words exclusively, as that class would use, or at least understand; but likewise by following the *order*, in which the words of such men are wont to succeed each other. Now this order, in the intercourse of uneducated men, is distinguished from the diction of their superiors in knowledge and power, by the greater *disjunction* and *separation* in the component parts of that, whatever it be, which they wish to communicate. There is a want of that prospectiveness of mind, that *surview*, which enables a man to foresee the whole of what he is to convey, appertaining to any one point; and by this means so to subordinate and arrange the different parts according to their relative importance, as to convey it at once, and as an organized whole.

Now I will take the first stanza, on which I have chanced to open, in the Lyrical Ballads. It is one the most simple and the least peculiar in its language.

> In distant countries have I been,
> And yet I have not often seen
> A healthy man, a man full grown,
> Weep in the public roads alone.

> But such a one, on English ground,
> And in the broad highway, I met;
> Along the broad highway he came.
> His cheeks with tears were wet:
> Sturdy he seem'd, though he was sad:
> And in his arms a lamb he had.

The words here are doubtless such as are current in all ranks of life; and of course not less so in the hamlet and cottage than in the shop, manufactory, college, or palace. But is this the *order*, in which the rustic would have placed the words? I am grievously deceived, if the following less *compact* mode of commencing the same tale be not a far more faithful copy. "I have been in a many parts, far and near, and I don't know that I ever saw before a man crying by himself in the public road; a grown man I mean, that was neither sick nor hurt," &c., &c. But when I turn to the following stanza in "The Thorn":

> At all times of the day and night
> This wretched woman thither goes,
> And she is known to every star,
> And every wind that blows:
> And there, beside the thorn, she sits,
> When the blue day-light's in the skies;
> And when the whirlwind's on the hill,
> Or frosty air is keen and still;
> And to herself she cries,
> Oh misery! Oh misery!
> Oh woe is me! Oh misery!

and compare this with the language of ordinary men; or with that which I can conceive at all likely to proceed, in *real* life, from *such* a narrator, as is supposed in the note to the poem; compare it either in the succession of the images or of the sentences; I am reminded of the sublime prayer and hymn of praise, which Milton, in opposition to an established liturgy, presents as a fair *specimen* of common extemporary devotion, and such as we might expect to hear from every self-inspired minister of a conventicle! And I reflect with delight, how little a mere theory, though of his own workmanship, interferes with the processes of genuine imagination in a man of true poetic genius, who possesses, as Mr. Wordsworth, if ever man did, most assuredly does possess,

THE VISION AND THE FACULTY DIVINE

One point then alone remains, but that the most important; its examination having been, indeed, my chief inducement for the preceding inquisition. *"There neither is or can be any essential difference between the language of prose and metrical composition."* Such is Mr. Wordsworth's assertion. Now prose itself, at least in all argumentative and consecutive works, differs, and ought to differ, from the language of conversation; even as reading ought to differ from talking. Unless therefore the difference denied be that of the mere *words,* as materials common to all styles of writing, and not of the *style* itself in the universally admitted sense of the term, it might be naturally presumed that there must exist a still greater between the ordonnance of poetic composition and that of prose, than is expected to distinguish prose from ordinary conversation.

There are not, indeed, examples wanting in the history of literature, of apparent paradoxes that have summoned the public wonder as new and startling truths, but which on examination have shrunk into tame and harmless *truisms;* as the eyes of a cat, seen in the dark, have been mistaken for flames of fire. But Mr. Wordsworth is among the last men, to whom a delusion of this kind would be attributed by anyone, who had enjoyed the slightest opportunity of understanding his mind and character. Where an objection has been anticipated by such an author as natural, his answer to it must needs be interpreted in some sense which either is, or has been, or is capable of being controverted. My object then must be to discover some other meaning for the term *"essential difference"* in this place, exclusive of the indistinction and community of the words themselves. For whether there ought to exist a class of words in the English, in any degree resembling the poetic dialect of the Greek and Italian, is a question of very subordinate importance. The number of such words would be small indeed, in our language; and even in the Italian and Greek, they consist not so much of different words, as of slight differences in the *forms* of declining and conjugating the same words; forms, doubtless, which having been, at some period more or less remote, the common grammatic flexions of some tribe or province, had been accidentally appropriated to poetry by the general admiration of certain master intellects, the first established lights of inspiration, to whom that dialect happened to be native.

Essence, in its primary signification, means the principle of *individuation,* the inmost principle of the possibility of any thing, as that particular thing. It is equivalent to the *idea* of a thing, when ever we use the word, idea, with philosophic precision. Existence, on the other hand, is distinguished from essence, by the superinduction of *reality.* Thus we speak of the essence, and essential properties of a circle; but we do not therefore assert, that any thing, which really exists, is mathematically circular. Thus too, without any tautology we contend for the *existence* of the Supreme Being; that is, for a reality correspondent to the idea. There is, next, a *secondary* use of the word essence, in which it signifies the point or ground of contra-distinction between two modifications of the same substance or subject. Thus we should be allowed to say, that the style of architecture of Westminster Abbey is *essentially* different from that of St. Paul's, even though both had been built with blocks cut into the same form, and from the same quarry. Only in this latter sense of the term must it have been *denied* by Mr. Wordsworth (for in this sense alone is it *affirmed* by the general opinion) that the language of poetry (i.e. the formal construction, or architecture, of the words and phrases) is *essentially* different from that of prose. Now the burthen of the proof lies with the oppugner, not with the supporters of the common belief. Mr. Wordsworth, in consequence, assigns as the proof of his position, "that not only the language of a large portion of every good poem, even of the most elevated character, must necessarily, except with reference to the metre, in no respect differ from that of good prose, but likewise that some of the most interesting parts of the best poems will be found to be strictly the language of prose, when prose is well written. The truth of this assertion might be demonstrated by innumerable passages from almost all the poetical writings even of Milton himself." He then quotes Gray's sonnet—

> In vain to me the smiling mornings shine,
> And reddening Phœbus lifts his golden fire;
> The birds in vain their amorous descant join,
> Or chearful fields resume their green attire.
> These ears, alas! for other notes repine;
> *A different object do these eyes require;*
> *My lonely anguish melts no heart but mine;*
> *And in my breast the imperfect joys expire.*
> Yet morning smiles the busy race to cheer,
> And newborn pleasure brings to happier men:
> The fields to all their wonted tribute bear,
> To warm their little loves the birds complain.
> *I fruitless mourn to him that cannot hear,*
> *And weep the more because I weep in vain,*

and adds the following remark:—"It will easily be perceived, that the only part of this Sonnet, which is of any value, is the lines printed in italics. It is equally obvious, that, except in the rhyme, and in the use of the single word 'fruitless' for 'fruitlessly,' which is so far a defect, the language of these lines does in no respect differ from that of prose."

An idealist defending his system by the fact, that when asleep we often believe ourselves awake, was well answered by his plain neighbour, "Ah, but when awake do we ever believe ourselves asleep?"—Things identical must be convertible. The preceding passage seems to rest on a similar sophism. For the question is not, whether there may not occur in prose an order of words, which would be equally proper in a poem; nor whether there are not beautiful lines and sentences of frequent occurrence in good poems, which would be equally becoming as well as beautiful in good prose; for neither the one nor the other has ever been either denied or doubted by any one. The true question must be, whether there are not modes of expression, a *construction*, and an *order* of sentences, which are in their fit and natural place in a serious prose composition, but would be disproportionate and heterogeneous in metrical poetry; and, vice versa, whether in the language of a serious poem there may not be an arrangement both of words and sentences, and a use and selection of (what are called) *figures of speech*, both as to their kind, their frequency, and their occasions, which on a subject of equal weight would be vicious and alien in correct and manly prose. I contend that in both cases this unfitness of each for the place of the other frequently will and ought to exist.

And first from the *origin* of metre. This I would trace to the balance in the mind effected by that spontaneous effort which strives to hold in check the workings of passion. It might be easily explained likewise in what manner this salutary antagonism is assisted by the very state, which it counteracts; and how this balance of antagonists became organized into *metre* (in the usual acceptation of that term) by a supervening act of the will and judgement, consciously and for the foreseen purpose of pleasure. Assuming these principles, as the data of our argument, we deduce from them two legitimate conditions, which the critic is entitled to expect in every metrical work. First, that, as the *elements* of metre owe their existence to a state of increased excitement, so the metre itself should be accompanied by the natural language of excitement. Secondly, that as these elements are formed into metre *artificially*, by a *voluntary* act, with the design and for the purpose of blending *delight* with emotion, so the traces of present *volition* should throughout the metrical language be proportionately discernible. Now these two conditions must be reconciled and co-present. There must be not only a partnership, but a union; an interpenetration of passion and of will, of *spontaneous* impulse and of *voluntary* purpose. Again, this union can be manifested only in a frequency of forms and figures of speech (originally the offspring of passion, but now the adopted children of power) greater than would be desired or endured, where the emotion is not voluntarily encouraged and kept up for the sake of that pleasure, which such emotion, so tempered and mastered by the will, is found capable of communicating. It not only dictates, but of itself tends to produce, a more frequent employment of picturesque and vivifying language, than would be natural in any other case, in which there did not exist, as there does in the present, a previous and well understood, though tacit, *compact* between the poet and his reader, that the latter is entitled to expect, and the former bound to supply, this species and degree of pleasureable excitement. We may in some measure apply to this union the answer of *Polixenes*, in the Winter's Tale, to *Perdita's* neglect of the streaked gilly-flowers, because she had heard it said,

> There is an art which, in their piedness, shares
> With great creating nature.
>   *Pol:* Say there be;
> Yet nature is made better by no mean,
> But nature makes that mean; so, ev'n that art,
> Which, you say, adds to nature, is an art,
> That nature makes. You see, sweet maid, we marry
> *A gentler scyon to the wildest stock;*
> And make conceive a bark of ruder kind
> By bud of nobler race. This is an art,
> Which does mend nature—change it rather; but
> The art itself is nature.

Secondly, I argue from the EFFECTS of metre. As far as metre acts in and for itself, it tends to increase the vivacity and susceptibility both of the general feelings and of the attention. This effect it produces by the continued excitement of surprize, and by the quick reciprocations of curiosity still gratified and still re-excited, which are too slight indeed to be at any one moment objects of distinct consciousness, yet become considerable in their aggregate influence. As a medicated atmosphere, or as wine during animated conversation; they act powerfully, though themselves unnoticed. Where, therefore, correspondent food and appropriate matter are not provided for the attention and feelings thus roused, there must needs be a disappointment felt; like that of leaping in the dark from the last step of a stair-case, when we had prepared our muscles for a leap of three or four.

The discussion on the powers of metre in the preface is highly ingenious and touches at all points on truth. But I cannot find any statement of its powers considered abstractly and separately. On the contrary Mr. Wordsworth seems always to estimate metre by the powers, which it exerts during (and, as I think in *consequence of*) its combination with other elements of poetry. Thus the previous difficulty is left unanswered, *what* the elements are, with which it must be combined in order to produce its own effects to any pleasureable purpose. Double and tri-syllable rhymes, indeed, form a lower species of wit, and, attended to exclusively for their own sake, may become a source of momentary amusement; as in poor Smart's distich to the Welsh 'Squire who had promised him a hare:

> Tell me, thou son of great Cadwallader!
> Hast sent the hare? or hast thou swallow'd her

But for any *poetic* purposes, metre resembles (if the aptness of the simile may excuse its meanness) yeast, worthless or disagreeable by itself, but giving vivacity and spirit to the liquor with which it is proportionally combined.

The reference to the "Children in the Wood," by no means satisfies my judgement. We all willingly throw ourselves back for awhile into the feelings of our childhood. This ballad, therefore, we read under such recollections of our own childish feelings, as would equally endear to us poems, which Mr. Wordsworth himself would regard as faulty in the opposite extreme of gaudy and technical ornament. Before the invention of printing, and in a still greater degree, before the introduction of writing, metre, especially *alliterative* metre (whether alliterative at the beginning of the words, as in "Pierce Plouman," or at the end as in rhymes) possessed an independent value as assisting the recollection, and consequently the preservation, of *any* series of truths or incidents. But I am not convinced by the collation of facts, that the "Children in the Wood" owes either its preservation, or its popularity, to its metrical form. Mr. Marshal's repository affords a number of tales in prose inferior in pathos and general merit, some of as old a date, and many as widely popular. *"Tom Hickathrift," "Jack the Giant-killer," "Goody Two-shoes,"* and *"Little Red Riding-hood"* are formidable rivals. And that they have continued in prose, cannot be fairly explained by the assumption, that the comparative meanness of their thoughts and images precluded even the humblest forms of metre. The scene of *Goody Two-shoes* in the church is perfectly susceptible of metrical narration; and, among the Θαύματα θαυμαστότατα even of the present age, I do not recollect a more astonishing image than that of the *"whole rookery, that flew out of the giant's beard,"* scared by the tremendous voice, with which this monster answered the challenge of the heroic *Tom Hickathrift!*

If from these we turn to compositions universally and independently of all early associations, beloved and admired; would *"The Maria," "The Monk,"* or *"The Poor Man's Ass"* of Sterne, be read with more delight, or have a better chance of immortality, had they without any change in the diction been composed in rhyme, than in their present state? If I am not grossly mistaken, the general reply would be in the negative. Nay, I will confess, that, in Mr. Wordsworth's own volumes, the *"Anecdote For Fathers," "Simon Lee," "Alice Fell," "The Beggars,"* and *"The Sailor's Mother,"* notwithstanding the beauties which are to be found in each of them where the poet interposes the music of his own thoughts, would have been more delightful to me in prose, told and managed, as by Mr. Wordsworth they would have been, in a moral essay, or pedestrian tour.

Metre in itself is simply a stimulant of the attention, and therefore excites the question: Why is the attention to be thus stimulated? Now the question cannot be answered by the pleasure of the metre itself: for this we have shown to be *conditional*, and dependent on the appropriateness of the thoughts and expressions, to which the metrical form is superadded. Neither can I conceive any other answer that can be rationally given, short of this: I write in metre, because I am about to use a language different from that of prose. Besides, where the language is not such, how interesting soever the reflections are, that are capable of being drawn by a philosophic mind from the thoughts or incidents of the poem, the metre itself must often become feeble. Take the last three stanzas of THE SAILOR'S MOTHER, for instance. If I could for a moment abstract from the effect produced on the author's feelings, as a man, by the incident at the time of its real occurrence, I would dare appeal to his own judgement, whether in the *metre* itself he found a sufficient reason for *their* being written *metrically?*

> And, thus continuing, she said,
> I had a son, who many a day
> Sailed on the seas; but he is dead;
> In Denmark he was cast away:
> And I have travelled far as Hull, to see
> What clothes he might have left, or other property.
>
> The bird and cage they both were his:
> 'Twas my son's bird; and neat and trim
> He kept it: many voyages
> This singing-bird hath gone with him,
> When last he sailed he left the bird behind;
> As it might be, perhaps, from bodings of his mind.

> He to a fellow-lodger's care
> Had left it, to be watched and fed,
> Till he came back again; and there
> I found it when my son was dead;
> And now, God help me for my little wit!
> I trail it with me, Sir! he took so much delight in it.

If disproportioning the emphasis we read these stanzas so as to make the rhymes perceptible, even *tri-syllable* rhymes could scarcely produce an equal sense of oddity and strangeness, as we feel here in finding *rhymes at all* in sentences so exclusively colloquial. I would further ask whether, but for that visionary state, into which the figure of the woman and the susceptibility of his own genius had placed the poet's imagination, (a state, which spreads its influence and coloring over all, that co-exists with the exciting cause, and in which

> The simplest, and the most familiar things
> Gain a strange power of spreading awe around them

I would ask the poet whether he would not have felt an abrupt downfall in these verses from the preceding stanza?

> The ancient spirit is not dead;
> Old times, thought I, are breathing there;
> Proud was I that my country bred
> Such strength, a dignity so fair:
> She begged an alms, like one in poor estate;
> I looked at her again, nor did my pride abate.

It must not be omitted, and is besides worthy of notice, that those stanzas furnish the only fair instance that I have been able to discover in all Mr. Wordsworth's writings, of an *actual* adoption, or true imitation, of the *real* and *very* language of *low and rustic life,* freed from provincialisms.

Thirdly, I deduce the position from all the causes elsewhere assigned, which render metre the proper form of poetry, and poetry imperfect and defective without metre. Metre therefore having been connected with *poetry* most often and by a peculiar fitness, whatever else is combined with *metre* must, though it be not itself *essentially* poetic, have nevertheless some property in common with poetry, as an intermedium of affinity, a sort (if I may dare borrow a well-known phrase from technical chemistry) of *mordaunt* between it and the superadded metre. Now poetry, Mr. Wordsworth truly affirms, does always imply PASSION: which word must be here understood in its general sense, as an excited state of the feelings and faculties. And as every passion has its proper pulse, so will it likewise have its characteristic modes of expression. But where there exists that degree of genius and talent which entitles a writer to aim at the honors of a poet, the very *act* of poetic composition *itself* is, and is *allowed* to imply and to produce, an unusual state of excitement, which of course justifies and demands a correspondent difference of language, as truly, though not perhaps in as marked a degree, as the excitement of love, fear, rage, or jealousy. The vividness of the descriptions or declamations in Donne or Dryden is as much and as often derived from the force and fervor of the describer, as from the reflections, forms or incidents, which constitute their subject and materials. The wheels take fire from the mere rapidity of their motion. To what extent, and under what modifications, this may be admitted to act, I shall attempt to define in an after remark on Mr. Wordsworth's reply to this objection, or rather on his objection to this reply, as already anticipated in his preface.

Fourthly, and as intimately connected with this, if not the same argument in a more general form, I adduce the high spiritual instinct of the human being impelling us to seek unity by harmonious adjustment, and thus establishing the principle, that *all* the parts of an organized whole must be assimilated to the more *important* and *essential* parts. This and the preceding arguments may be strengthened by the reflection, that the composition of a poem is among the *imitative* arts; and that imitation, as opposed to copying, consists either in the interfusion of the SAME throughout the radically DIFFERENT, or of the different throughout a base radically the same.

Lastly, I appeal to the practice of the best poets, of all countries and in all ages, as *authorizing* the opinion (*deduced* from all the foregoing) that in every import of the word ESSENTIAL, while would not here involve a mere truism, there may be, is, and ought to be an *essential* difference between the language of prose and of metrical composition.

In Mr. Wordsworth's criticism of Gray's Sonnet, the readers' sympathy with his praise or blame of the different parts is taken for granted rather perhaps too easily. He has not, at least, attempted to win or compel it by argumentative analysis. In *my* conception at least, the lines rejected as of no value do, with the exception of the two first, differ as much and as little from the language of common life, as those which he has printed in italics as possessing genuine excellence. Of the five lines thus honourably distinguished, two of them differ from prose, even more widely than the lines which either precede or follow, in the *position* of the words.

> A *different object do these eyes require;*
> My lonely anguish melts no heart but mine;
> *And in my breast the imperfect joys expire.*

But were it otherwise, what would this prove, but a truth, of which no man ever doubted? Videlicet, that there are sentences, which would be equally in their place both in verse and prose. Assuredly it does not prove the point, which alone requires proof; namely, that there are not passages, which would suit the one and not suit the other. The first line of this sonnet is distinguished from the ordinary language of men by the epithet to morning. (For we will set aside, at present, the consideration, that the particular word "*smiling*" is hackneyed and (as it involves a sort of personification) not quite congruous with the common and material attribute of *shining*.) And, doubtless, this adjunction of epithets for the purpose of additional description, where no particular attention is demanded for the quality of the thing, would be noticed as giving a poetic cast to a man's conversation. Should the sportsman exclaim, *"Come boys! the rosy morning calls you up,"* he will be supposed to have some song in his head. But no one suspects this, when he says, "A wet morning shall not confine us to our beds." This then is either a defect in poetry, or it is not. Whoever should decide in the *affirmative,* I would request him to re-peruse any one poem of any confessedly great poet from Homer to Milton, or from Æschylus to Shakespeare; and to strike out (in thought I mean) every instance of this kind. If the number of these fancied erasures did not startle him; or if he continued to deem the work improved by their total omission; he must advance reasons of no ordinary strength and evidence, reasons grounded in the essence of human nature. Otherwise, I should not hesitate to consider him as a man not so much *proof against* all authority, as *dead to* it.

The second line,

> And reddening Phœbus lifts his golden fire;

has indeed almost as many faults as words. But then it is a bad line, not because the language is distinct from that of prose; but because it conveys incongruous images, because it confounds the cause and the effect, the real *thing* with the personified *representative* of the thing; in short, because it differs from the language of GOOD SENSE! That the "Phœbus" is hackneyed, and a schoolboy image, is an *accidental* fault, dependent on the age in which the author wrote, and not deduced from the nature of the thing. That it is part of an exploded mythology, is an objection more deeply grounded. Yet when the torch of ancient learning was re-kindled, so cheering were its beams, that our eldest poets, cut off by Christianity from all *accredited* machinery, and deprived of all *acknowledged* guardians and symbols of the great objects of nature, were naturally induced to adopt, as a *poetic* language, those fabulous personages, those forms of the supernatural in nature, which had given them such dear delight in the poems of their great masters. Nay, even at this day what scholar of genial taste will not so far sympathize with them, as to read with pleasure in Petrarch, Chaucer, or Spenser, what he would perhaps condemn as puerile in a modern poet?

I remember no poet, whose writings would safelier stand the test of Mr. Wordsworth's theory, than Spenser. Yet will Mr. Wordsworth say, that the style of the following stanza is either undistinguished from prose, and the language of ordinary life? Or that it is vicious, and that the stanzas are *blots* in the "Faery Queen"?

> By this the northern waggoner had set
> His sevenfold teme behind the steadfast starre,
> That was in ocean waves yet never wet,
> But firme is fixt, and sendeth light from farre
> To all that in the wild deep wandering are:
> And chearful chanticleer with his note shrill

Had warned once that Phœbus' fiery carre
In haste was climbing up the easterne hill,
Full envious that night so long his roome did fill.
Book I. Can. 2. St. 2.

At last the golden orientall gate
Of greatest heaven gan to open fayre,
And Phœbus fresh, as brydegrome to his mate,
Came dauncing forth, shaking his deawie hayre,
And hurl'd his glist'ring beams through gloomy ayre:
Which when the wakeful elfe perceived, streightway
He started up, and did him selfe prepayre
In sun-bright armes and battailous array;
For with that pagan proud he combat will that day.
B. I. Can. 5. St. 2.

On the contrary to how many passages, both in hymn books and in blank verse poems, could I, (were it not invidious), direct the reader's attention, the style of which is most *unpoetic, because,* and only because, it is the style of *prose*? He will not suppose me capable of having in my mind such verses, as

I put my hat upon my head
And walk'd into the Strand;
And there I met another man,
Whose hat was in his hand.

To such specimens it would indeed be a fair and full reply, that these lines are not bad, because they are *unpoetic;* but because they are empty of all sense and feeling; and that it were an idle attempt to prove that an ape is not a Newton, when it is evident that he is not a man. But the sense shall be good and weighty, the language correct and dignified, the subject interesting and treated with feeling; and yet the style shall, notwithstanding all these merits, be justly blamable as *prosaic,* and solely because the words and the order of the words would find their appropriate place in prose, but are not suitable to *metrical* composition. The "Civil Wars" of Daniel is an instructive, and even interesting work; but take the following stanzas (and from the hundred instances which abound I might probably have selected others far more striking):

And to the end we may with better ease
Discern the true discourse, vouchsafe to shew
What were the times foregoing near to these,
That these we may with better profit know.
Tell how the world fell into this disease;
And how so great distemperature did grow;
So shall we see with what degrees it came;
How things at full do soon wax out of frame.

> Ten kings had from the Norman conqu'ror reign'd
> With intermixt and variable fate,
> When England to her greatest height attain'd
> Of power, dominion, glory, wealth, and state;
> After it had with much ado sustain'd
> The violence of princes, with debate
> For titles and the often mutinies
> Of nobles for their ancient liberties.
>
> For first, the Norman, conqu'ring all by might,
> By might was forc'd to keep what he had got;
> Mixing our customs and the form of right
> With foreign constitutions he had brought;
> Mast'ring the mighty, humbling the poorer wight,
> By all severest means that could be wrought;
> And, making the succession doubtful, rent
> His new-got state, and left it turbulent.
>
> *B. I. St. VII. VIII. & IX.*

Will it be contended on the one side, that these lines are mean and senseless? Or on the other, that they are not prosaic, and for *that* reason unpoetic? This poet's well-merited epithet is that of the *"well-languaged Daniel";* but likewise, and by the consent of his contemporaries no less than of all succeeding critics, the "prosaic Daniel." Yet those, who thus designate this wise and amiable writer, from the frequent incorrespondency of his diction to his metre in the majority of his compositions, not only deem them valuable and interesting on other accounts; but willingly admit, that there are to be found throughout his poems, and especially in his *Epistles* and in his *Hymen's Triumph,* many and exquisite specimens of that style which, as the *neutral ground* of prose and verse, is common to both. A fine and almost faultless extract, eminent, as for other beauties, so for its perfection in this species of diction, may be seen in Lamb's Dramatic Specimens, &c., a work of various interest from the nature of the selections themselves, (all from the plays of Shakespeare's contemporaries), and deriving a high additional value from the notes, which are full of just and original criticism, expressed with all the freshness of originality.

Among the possible effects of practical adherence to a theory, that aims to *identify* the style of prose and verse, (if it does not indeed claim for the latter a yet nearer resemblance to the average style of men in the vivâ voce intercourse of real life) we might anticipate the following as not the least likely to occur. It will happen, as I have indeed before observed, that the metre itself, the sole acknowledged difference, will occasionally become metre to the eye only. The existence of *prosaisms,* and that they detract from the merit of a poem, *must* at length be conceded, when a number of successive lines can be rendered, even to the most delicate ear, unrecognizable as verse, or as having even been intended for verse, by simply transcribing them as prose; when, if the poem be in blank verse, this can be effected without any alteration, or at most by merely restoring one or two words to their proper places, from which they have been transplanted for no assignable cause or reason but that of the author's convenience; but, if it be in rhyme, by the mere exchange of the final word of each line for some other of the same meaning, equally appropriate, dignified, and euphonic.

The answer or objection in the preface to the anticipated remark "that metre paves the way to other distinctions," is contained in the following words. "The distinction of rhyme and metre is voluntary and uniform, and not, like that produced by (what is called) poetic diction, arbitrary, and subject to infinite caprices, upon which no calculation whatever can be made. In the one case the reader is utterly at the mercy of the poet respecting what imagery or diction he may choose to connect with the passion." But is this a *poet*, of whom a poet is speaking? No surely! rather of a fool or madman: or at best of a vain or ignorant phantast! And might not brains so wild and so deficient make just the same havock with rhymes and metres, as they are supposed to effect with modes and figures of speech? How is the reader at the *mercy* of such men? If he continue to read their nonsense, is it not his own fault? The ultimate end of criticism is much more to establish the principles of writing, than to furnish *rules* how to pass judgement on what has been written by others; if indeed it were possible that the two could be separated. But if it be asked, by what principles the poet is to regulate his own style, if he do not adhere closely to the sort and order of words which he hears in the market, wake, high-road, or plough-field? I reply; by principles, the ignorance or neglect of which would convict him of being no *poet*, but a silly or presumptuous usurper of the name! By the principles of grammar, logic, psychology! In one word by such a knowledge of the facts, material and spiritual, that most appertain to his art, as, if it have been governed and applied by *good sense*, and rendered instinctive by habit, becomes the representative and reward of our past conscious reasonings, insights, and conclusions, and acquires the name of Taste. By what *rule* that does not leave the reader at the poet's mercy, and the poet at his own, is the latter to distinguish between the language suitable to *suppressed*, and the language, which is characteristic of *indulged*, anger? Or between that of rage and that of jealousy? Is it obtained by wandering about in search of angry or jealous people in uncultivated society, in order to copy their words? Or not far rather by the power of imagination proceeding upon the *all in each* of human nature? By *meditation*, rather than by *observation*? And by the latter in consequence only of the former? As eyes, for which the former has pre-determined their field of vision, and to which, as to *its* organ, it communicates a microscopic power? There is not, I firmly believe, a man now living, who has, from his own inward experience, a clearer intuition, than Mr. Wordsworth himself, that the last mentioned are the true sources of *genial* discrimination. Through the same process and by the same creative agency will the poet distinguish the degree and kind of the excitement produced by the very act of poetic composition. As intuitively will he know, what differences of style it at once inspires and justifies; what intermixture of conscious volition is natural to that state; and in what instances such figures and colors of speech degenerate into mere creatures of an arbitrary purpose, cold technical artifices of ornament or connection. For, even as truth is its own light and evidence, discovering at once itself and falsehood, so is it the prerogative of poetic genius to distinguish by parental instinct its proper offspring from the changelings, which the gnomes of vanity or the fairies of fashion may have laid in its cradle or called by its names. Could a rule be given from *without*, poetry would cease to be poetry, and sink into a mechanical art. It would be μόρφωσις, not ποίησις. The *rules* of the IMAGINATION are themselves the very powers of growth and production. The *words*, to which they are reducible, present only the outlines and external appearance of the fruit. A deceptive counterfeit of the superficial form and colors may be elaborated; but the marble peach feels cold and heavy, and *children* only put it to their mouths. We find no difficulty in admitting as excellent, and the legitimate language of poetic fervor self-impassioned, Donne's apostrophe to the Sun in the second stanza of his "Progress of the Soul":

> Thee, eye of heaven! this great soul envies not:
> By thy male force is all, we have, begot.
> In the first East thou now beginn'st to shine,
> Suck'st early balm and island spices there,
> And wilt anon in thy loose-rein'd career
> At Tagus, Po, Seine, Thames, and Danow dine,
> And see at night this western world of mine:
> Yet hast thou not more nations seen than she,
> Who before thee one day began to be,
> And, thy frail light being quench'd, shall long, long outlive thee!

Or the next stanza but one:

> Great destiny, the commissary of God,
> That hast mark'd out a path and period
> For ev'ry thing! Who, where we offspring took,
> Our ways and ends see'st at one instant: thou
> Knot of all causes! Thou, whose changeless brow
> Ne'er smiles or frowns! O! vouchsafe thou to look,
> And shew my story in thy eternal book, &c.

As little difficulty do we find in excluding from the honors of unaffected warmth and elevation the madness prepense of pseudo-poesy, or the startling *hysteric* of weakness over-exerting itself, which bursts on the unprepared reader in sundry odes and apostrophes to abstract terms. Such are the Odes to Jealousy, to Hope, to Oblivion, and the like, in Dodsley's collection and the magazines of that day, which seldom fail to remind me of an Oxford copy of verses on the two Suttons, commencing with

> INOCULATION, heavenly maid! descend!

It is not to be denied that men of undoubted talents, and even poets of true, though not of first-rate, genius, have from a mistaken theory deluded both themselves and others in the opposite extreme. I once read to a company of sensible and well-educated women the introductory period of Cowley's preface to his *"Pindaric Odes, written in imitation of the style and manner of the odes of Pindar."* "If, (says Cowley), a man should undertake to translate Pindar, word for word, it would be thought that one madman had translated another; as may appear, when he, that understands not the original, reads the verbal traduction of him into Latin prose, than which nothing seems more raving." I then proceeded with his own free version of the second Olympic, composed for the charitable purpose of *rationalizing* the Theban Eagle.

> Queen of all harmonious things,
> Dancing words and speaking strings,
> What God, what hero, wilt thou sing?
> What happy man to equal glories bring?
> Begin, begin thy noble choice,
> And let the hills around reflect the image of thy voice.
> Pisa does to Jove belong,
> Jove and Pisa claim thy song.
> The fair first-fruits of war, th' Olympic games,
> Alcides offer'd up to Jove;
> Alcides too thy strings may move!
> But, oh! what man to join with these can worthy prove?
> Join Theron boldly to their sacred names;
> Theron the next honor claims;
> Theron to no man gives place,
> Is first in Pisa's and in Virtue's race;
> Theron there, and he alone,
> Ev'n his own swift forefathers has outgone.

One of the company exclaimed, with the full assent of the rest, that if the original were madder than this, it must be incurably mad. I then translated the ode from the Greek, and as nearly as possible, word for word; and the impression was, that in the general movement of the periods, in the form of the connections and transitions, and in the sober majesty of lofty sense, it apeared to them to approach more nearly, than any other poetry they had heard, to the style of our Bible in the prophetic books. The first strophe will suffice as a specimen:

> Ye harp-controuling hymns! (or) ye hymns the sovereigns of harps!
> What God? what Hero?
> What Man shall we celebrate?
> Truly Pisa indeed is of Jove,
> But the Olympiad (or the Olympic games) did Hercules establish,
> The first-fruits of the spoils of war.
> But Theron for the four-horsed car,
> That bore victory to him,
> It behoves us now to voice aloud:

> The Just, the Hospitable,
> The Bulwark of Agrigentum,
> Of renowned fathers
> The Flower, even him
> Who preserves his native city erect and safe.

But are such rhetorical caprices condemnable only for their deviation from the language of real life? and are they by no other means to be precluded, but by the rejection of all distinctions between prose and verse, save that of metre? Surely good sense, and a moderate insight into the constitution of the human mind, would be amply sufficient to prove, that such language and such combinations are the native produce neither of the fancy nor of the imagination; that their operation consists in the excitement of surprise by the juxta-position and *apparent* reconciliation of widely different or incompatible things. As when, for instance, the hills are made to reflect the image of a *voice*. Surely, no unusual taste is requisite to see clearly, that this compulsory juxta-position is not produced by the presentation of impressive or delightful forms to the inward vision, nor by any sympathy with the modifying powers with which the genius of the poet had united and inspirited all the objects of his thought; that it is therefore a species of *wit*, a pure work of the *will*, and implies a leisure and self-possession both of thought and of feeling, incompatible with the steady fervor of a mind possessed and filled with the grandeur of its subject. To sum up the whole in one sentence. When a poem, or a part of a poem, shall be adduced, which is evidently vicious in the figures and contexture of its style, yet for the condemnation of which no reason can be assigned, except that it differs from the style in which men actually converse, then, and not till then, can I hold this theory to be either plausible, or practicable, or capable of furnishing either rule, guidance, or precaution, that might not, more easily and more safely, as well as more naturally, have been deduced in the author's own mind from considerations of grammar, logic, and the truth and nature of things, confirmed by the authority of works, whose fame is not of ONE country nor of ONE age.

Chapter XXII

If Mr. Wordsworth have set forth principles of poetry which his arguments are insufficient to support, let him and those who have adopted his sentiments be set right by the confutation of these arguments, and by the substitution of more philosophical principles. And still let the due credit be given to the portion and importance of the truths, which are blended with his theory; truths, the too exclusive attention to which had occasioned its errors, by tempting him to carry those truths beyond their proper limits. If his mistaken theory have at all influenced his poetic compositions, let the effects be pointed out, and the instances given. But let it likewise be shown, how far the influence has acted; whether diffusively, or only by starts; whether the number and importance of the poems and passages thus infected be great or trifling compared with the sound portion; and lastly, whether they are inwoven into the texture of his works, or are loose and separable. The result of such a trial would evince beyond a doubt, what it is high time to announce decisively and aloud, that the *supposed* characteristics of Mr. Wordsworth's poetry, whether admired or reprobated; whether they are simplicity or simpleness; faithful adherence to essential nature, or wilful selections from human nature of its meanest forms and under the least attractive associations; are as little the *real* characteristics of his poetry at large, as of his genius and the constitution of his mind.

In a comparatively small number of poems he chose to try an experiment; and this experiment we will suppose to have failed. Yet even in these poems it is impossible not to perceive that the natural *tendency* of the poet's mind is to great objects and elevated conceptions. The poem entitled "Fidelity" is for the greater part written in language, as unraised and naked as any perhaps in the two volumes. Yet take the following stanza and compare it with the preceding stanzas of the same poem.

> There sometimes doth a leaping fish
> Send through the tarn a lonely cheer;
> The crags repeat the raven's croak,
> In symphony austere;
> Thither the rainbow comes—the cloud—
> And mists that spread the flying shroud;
> And sun-beams; and the sounding blast,
> That if it could would hurry past;
> But that enormous barrier binds it fast.

Or compare the four last lines of the concluding stanza with the former half.

> Yes, proof was plain that since the day
> On which the traveller thus had died,
> The dog had watched about the spot,
> Or by his master's side
> *How nourish'd there through such long time*
> *He knows, who gave that love sublime,*
> *And gave that strength of feeling, great*
> *Above all human estimate!*

Can any candid and intelligent mind hesitate in determining, which of these best represents the tendency and native character of the poet's genius? Will he not decide that the one was written because the poet *would* so write, and the other because he could not so entirely repress the force and grandeur of his mind, but that he must in some part or other of *every* composition write otherwise? In short, that his only disease is the being out of his element; like the swan, that, having amused himself, for a while, with crushing the weeds on the river's bank, soon returns to his own majestic movements on its reflecting and sustaining surface. Let it be observed that I am here supposing the imagined judge, to whom I appeal, to have already decided against the poet's theory, as far as it is different from the principles of the art, generally acknowledged.

I cannot here enter into a detailed examination of Mr. Wordsworth's works; but I will attempt to give the main results of my own judgement, after an acquaintance of many years, and repeated perusals. And though, to appreciate the defects of a great mind it is necessary to understand previously its characteristic excellences, yet I have already expressed myself with sufficient fulness, to preclude most of the ill effects that might arise from my pursuing a contrary arrangement. I will therefore commence with what I deem the prominent *defects* of his poems hitherto published.

The first *characteristic, though only occasional* defect, which I appear to myself to find in these poems is the INCONSTANCY of the *style*. Under this name I refer to the sudden and unprepared transitions from lines or sentences of peculiar felicity (at all events striking and original) to a style, not only unimpassioned but undistinguished. He sinks too often and too abruptly to that style, which I should place in the second division of language, dividing it into the three species; *first,* that which is peculiar to poetry; *second,* that which is only proper in prose; and *third,* the neutral or common to both. There have been works, such as Cowley's Essay on Cromwell, in which prose and verse are intermixed (not as in the Consolation of Boetius, or the Argenis of Barclay, by the insertion of poems supposed to have been spoken or composed on occasions previously related in prose, but) the poet passing from one to the other, as the nature of the thoughts or his own feelings dictated. Yet this mode of composition does not satisfy a cultivated taste. There is something unpleasant in the being thus obliged to alternate states of feeling so dissimilar, and this too in a species of writing, the pleasure from which is in part derived from the preparation and previous expectation of the reader. A portion of that awkwardness is felt which hangs upon the introduction of songs in our modern comic operas; and to prevent which the judicious Metastasio (as to whose exquisite *taste* there can be no hesitation, whatever doubts may be entertained as to his *poetic genius*) uniformly placed the ARIA at the end of the scene, at the same time that he almost always raises and impassions the style of the recitative immediately preceding. Even in real life, the difference is great and evident between words used as the *arbitrary marks* of thought, our smooth market-coin of intercourse, with the image and superscription worn out by currency; and those which convey pictures either borrowed from *one* outward object to enliven and particularize some *other;* or used allegorically to body forth the inward state of the person speaking; or such as are at least the exponents of his peculiar turn and unusual extent of faculty. So much so indeed, that in the social circles of private life we often find a striking use of the latter put a stop to the general flow of conversation, and by the excitement arising from concentered attention produce a sort of damp and interruption for some minutes after. But in the perusal of works of literary *art*, we *prepare* ourselves for such language; and the business of the writer, like that of a painter whose subject requires unusual splendor and prominence, is so to raise the lower and neutral tints, that what in a different style would be the *commanding* colors, are here used as the means of that gentle *degradation* requisite in order to produce the effect of a *whole*. Where this is not achieved in a poem, the metre merely reminds the reader of his claims in order to disappoint them; and where this defect occurs frequently, his feelings are alternately startled by anticlimax and hyperclimax.

I refer the reader to the exquisite stanzas cited for another purpose from the blind Highland Boy; and then annex, as being in my opinion instances of this *disharmony* in style, the two following:

> And one, the rarest, was a shell,
> Which he, poor child, had studied well:
> The shell of a green turtle, thin
> And hollow;—you might sit therein,
>   It was so wide, and deep.
>
> Our Highland Boy oft visited
> The house which held this prize; and, led
> By choice or chance, did thither come
> One day, when no one was at home,
>   And found the door unbarred.

Or page 172, vol. I.

> 'Tis gone—forgotten—*let me do*
> *My best*. There was a smile or two—
> I can remember them, I see
> The smiles worth all the world to me.
> Dear Baby, I must lay thee down:
> Thou troublest me with strange alarms;
> Smiles has thou, sweet ones of thine own;
> I cannot keep thee in my arms;
> For they confound me: *as it is,*
> I have forgot those smiles of his!

Or page 269, vol. I.

> Thou hast a nest, for thy love and thy rest,
> And though little troubled with sloth
> Drunken lark! thou would'st be loth
> To be such a traveller as I.
>   Happy, happy liver!
> *With a soul as strong as a mountain river*
> *Pouring out praise to th'Almighty giver!*
> Joy and jollity be with us both!

> Hearing thee or else some other,
> As merry a brother
> I on the earth will go plodding on
> By myself chearfully till the day is done.

The incongruity, which I appear to find in this passage, is that of the two noble lines in italics with the preceding and following. So vol. II. page 30.

> Close by a pond, upon the further side,
> He stood alone; a minute's space, I guess,
> I watch'd him, he continuing motionless:
> To the pool's further margin then I drew,
> He being all the while before me full in view.

Compare this with the repetition of the same image, in the next stanza but two.

> And, still as I drew near with gentle pace,
> Beside the little pond or moorish flood
> Motionless as a cloud the old man stood,
> That heareth not the loud winds as they call,
> And moveth altogether, if it move at all.

Or lastly, the second of the three following stanzas, compared both with the first and the third.

> My former thoughts returned; the fear that kills;
> And hope that is unwilling to be fed;
> Cold, pain, and labour, and all fleshly ills;
> And mighty poets in their misery dead.
> But now, perplex'd by what the old man had said,
> My question eagerly did I renew,
> 'How is it that you live, and what is it you do?'
>
> He with a smile did then his words repeat;
> And said, that gathering leeches far and wide
> He travell'd; stirring thus about his feet
> The waters of the ponds where they abide.
> 'Once I could meet with them on every side,
> But they have dwindled long by slow decay;
> Yet still I persevere, and find them where I may.'
>
> While he was talking thus, the lonely place,
> The old man's shape, and speech, all troubled me:
> In my mind's eye I seemed to see him pace
> About the weary moors continually,
> Wandering about alone and silently.

Indeed this fine poem is *especially* characteristic of the author. There is scarce a defect or excellence in his writings of which it would not present a specimen. But it would be unjust not to repeat that this defect is only occasional. From a careful reperusal of the two volumes of poems, I doubt whether the objectionable passages would amount in the whole to one hundred lines; not the eighth part of the number of pages. In the *Excursion* the feeling of incongruity is seldom excited by the diction of any passage considered in itself, but by the sudden superiority of some other passage forming the context.

The second defect I can generalize with tolerable accuracy, if the reader will pardon an uncouth and new-coined word. There is, I should say, not seldom a *matter-of-factness* in certain poems. This may be divided into, *first,* a laborious minuteness and fidelity in the representation of objects, and their positions, as they appeared to the poet himself; *secondly,* the insertion of accidental circumstances, in order to the full explanation of his living characters, their dispositions and actions; which circumstances might be necessary to establish the probability of a statement in real life, where nothing is taken for granted by the hearer; but appear superfluous in poetry, where the reader is willing to believe for his own sake. To this *accidentality* I object, as contravening the essence of poetry, which Aristotle pronounces to be σπουδ- αιότατον χαὶ φιλοσοφώτατον γένος, the most intense, weighty and philosophical product of human art; adding, as the *reason,* that it is the most catholic and abstract. The following passage from Davenant's prefatory letter to Hobbes well expresses this truth. "When I considered the actions which I meant to describe, (those inferring the persons), I was again persuaded rather to choose those of a former age, than the present; and in a century so far removed, as might preserve me from their improper examinations, who know not the requisites of a poem, nor how much pleasure they lose, (and even the pleasures of heroic poesy are not unprofitable), who take away the liberty of a poet, and fetter his feet in the shackles of an historian. For why should a poet doubt in story to mend the intrigues of fortune by more delightful conveyances of probable fictions, because austere historians have entered into bond to truth? An obligation, which were in poets as foolish and unnecessary, as in the bondage of false martyrs, who lie in chains for a mistaken opinion. *But by this I would imply, that truth narrative and past is the idol of historians, (who worship a dead thing), and truth operative, and by effects continually alive, is the mistress of poets, who hath not her existence in matter, but in reason.*"

For this minute accuracy in the painting of local imagery, the lines in the *Excursion*, pp. 96, 97, and 98, may be taken, if not as a striking instance, yet as an illustration of my meaning. It must be some strong motive (as, for instance, that the description was necessary to the intelligibility of the tale) which could induce me to describe in a number of verses what a draughtsman could present to the eye with incomparably greater satisfaction by half a dozen strokes of his pencil, or the painter with as many touches of his brush. Such descriptions too often occasion in the mind of a reader, who is determined to understand his author, a feeling of labor, not very dissimilar to that, with which he would construct a diagram, line by line, for a long geometrical proposition. It seems to be like taking the pieces of a dissected map out of its box. We first look at one part, and then at another, then join and dove-tail them; and when the successive acts of attention have been completed, there is a retrogressive effort of mind to behold it as a whole. The poet should paint to the imagination, not to the fancy; and I know no happier case to exemplify the distinction between these two faculties. Masterpieces of the former mode of poetic painting abound in the writings of Milton, ex. gr.

> The fig-tree; not that kind for fruit renown'd,
> But such as at this day, to Indians known,
> In Malabar or Decan spreads her arms
> Branching so broad and long, that in the ground
> The bended twigs take root, *and daughters grow*
> *About the mother tree, a pillar'd shade*
> *High over-arch'd, and* ECHOING WALKS BETWEEN:
> *There oft the Indian Herdsman, shunning heat,*
> *Shelters in cool, and tends his pasturing herds*
> *At loop holes cut through thickest shade.*
>   MILTON *P. L.* 9. 1100.

This is *creation* rather than *painting,* or if painting, yet such, and with such co-presence of the whole picture flash'd at once upon the eye, as the sun paints in a camera obscura. But the poet must likewise understand and command what Bacon calls the *vestigia communia* of the senses, the latency of all in each, and more especially as by a magical *penna duplex,* the excitement of vision by sound and the exponents of sound. Thus *The Echoing Walks Between,* may be almost said to reverse the fable in tradition of the head of Memnon, in the Egyptian statue. Such may be deservedly entitled the *creative words* in the world of imagination.

The second division respects an apparent minute adherence to *matter-of-fact* in characters and incidents; *a biographical* attention to probability, and an *anxiety* of explanation and retrospect. Under this head I shall deliver, with no feigned diffidence, the results of my best reflection on the great point of controversy between Mr. Wordsworth and his objectors; namely, on THE CHOICE OF HIS CHARACTERS. I have already declared and, I trust, justified, my utter dissent from the mode of argument which his critics have hitherto employed. To *their* question, Why did you chuse such a character, or a character from such a rank of life? the poet might in my opinion fairly retort: why with the conception of my character did you make wilful choice of mean or ludicrous associations not furnished by me, but supplied from your own sickly and fastidious feelings? How was it, indeed, probable, that such arguments could have any weight with an author, whose plan, whose guiding principle, and main object it was to attack and subdue that state of association, which leads us to place the chief value on those things in which man DIFFERS from man, and to forget or disregard the high dignities, which belong to HUMAN NATURE, the sense and the feeling, which *may* be, and *ought* to be, found in *all* ranks? The feelings with which, as Christians, we contemplate a mixed congregation rising or kneeling before their common Maker: Mr. Wordsworth would have us entertain at *all* times, as men, and as readers; and by the excitement of this lofty, yet prideless impartiality in *poetry,* he might hope to have encouraged its continuance in *real life*. The praise of good men be his! In real life, and, I trust, even in my imagination, I honor a virtuous and wise man, without reference to the presence or absence of artificial advantages. Whether in the person of an armed baron, a laurel'd bard, &c., or of an old pedlar, or still older leech-gatherer, the same qualities of head and heart must claim the same reverence. And even in poetry I am not conscious, that I have ever suffered my feelings to be disturbed or offended by any thoughts or images, which the poet himself has not presented.

But yet I object nevertheless and for the following reasons. First, because the object in view, as an *immediate* object, belongs to the moral philosopher, and would be pursued, not only more appropriately, but in my opinion with far greater probability of success, in sermons or moral essays, than in an elevated poem. It seems, indeed, to destroy the main fundamental distinction, not only between a poem and prose, but even between philosophy and works of fiction, inasmuch as it proposes *truth* for its immediate object, instead of *pleasure*. Now till the blessed time shall come, when truth itself shall be pleasure, and both shall be so united, as to be distinguishable in words only, not in feeling, it will remain the poet's office to proceed upon that state of association, which actually exists as *general;* instead of attempting first to *make* it what it ought to be, and then to let the pleasure follow. But here is unfortunately a small *Hysteron-Proteron*. For the communication of pleasure is the introductory means by which alone the poet must expect to moralize his readers. Secondly: though I were to admit, for a moment, *this* argument to be groundless: yet how is the moral effect to be produced, by merely attaching the name of some low profession to powers which are *least* likely, and to qualities which are assuredly not *more* likely, to be found in it? The poet, speaking in his own person, may at once delight and improve us by sentiments, which teach us the independence of goodness, of wisdom, and even of genius, on the favors of fortune. And having made a due reverence before the throne of Antonine, he may bow with equal awe before Epictetus among his fellow-slaves—

> and rejoice
> In the plain presence of his dignity.

Who is not at once delighted and improved, when the POET Wordsworth himself exclaims,

> O many are the poets that are sown
> By Nature; man endowed with highest gifts,
> The vision and the faculty divine,
> Yet wanting the accomplishment of verse,
> Nor having e'er, as life advanced, been led
> By circumstance to take unto the height
> The measure of themselves, these favor'd beings,

> All but a scatter'd few, live out their time
> Husbanding that which they possess within,
> And go to the grave unthought of. Strongest minds
> Are often those of whom the noisy world
> Hears least.
>
> EXCURSION, B. I.

To use a colloquial phrase, such sentiments, in such language, do one's heart good; though I for my part, have not the fullest faith in the *truth* of the observation. On the contrary I believe the instances to be exceedingly rare; and should feel almost as strong an objection to introduce such a character in a poetic fiction, as a pair of black swans on a lake in a fancy-landscape. When I think how many, and how much better books than Homer, or even than Herodotus, Pindar or Æschylus, could have read, are in the power of almost every man, in a country where almost every man is instructed to read and write; and how restless, how difficultly hidden, the powers of genius are; and yet find even in situations the most favorable, according to Mr. Wordsworth, for the formation of a pure and poetic language; in situations which ensure familiarity with the grandest objects of the imagination; but *one Burns,* among the shepherds of *Scotland,* and not a single poet of humble life among those of *English* lakes and mountains; I conclude, that POETIC GENIUS is not only a very delicate but a very rare plant.

But be this as it may, the feelings with which

> I think of CHATTERTON, the marvellous boy,
> The sleepless soul, that perished in his pride;
> Of BURNS, that walk'd in glory and in joy
> Behind his plough upon the mountain-side—

are widely different from those with which I should read a *poem,* where the author, having occasion for the character of a poet and a philosopher in the fable of his narration, had chosen to make him a *chimney-sweeper;* and then, in order to remove all doubts on the subject, had *invented* an account of his birth, parentage and education, with all the strange and fortunate accidents which had concurred in making him at once poet, philosopher, and sweep! Nothing but biography can justify this. If it be admissible even in a *Novel,* it must be one in the manner of De Foe's, that were meant to pass for histories, not in the manner of Fielding's: in the life of Moll Flanders, or Colonel Jack, not in a Tom Jones, or even a Joseph Andrews. Much less then can it be legitimately introduced in a *poem,* the characters of which, amid the strongest individualization, must still remain representative. The precepts of Horace, on this point, are grounded on the nature both of poetry and of the human mind. They are not more peremptory, than wise and prudent. For in the first place a deviation from them perplexes the reader's feelings, and all the circumstances, which are feigned in order to make such accidents less improbable, divide and disquiet his faith, rather than aid and support it. Spite of all attempts, the fiction *will* appear, and unfortunately not as *fictitious* but as *false*. The reader not only *knows*, that the sentiments and language are the poet's own, and his own too in his *artificial* character, *as poet;* but by the fruitless endeavours to make him think the contrary, he is not even suffered to *forget* it. The effect is similar to that produced by an epic poet, when the fable and the characters are *derived* from Scripture history, as in the *Messiah* of *Klopstock,* or in *Cumberland's Calvary;* and not merely *suggested* by it, as in the Paradise Lost of Milton. That *illusion*, contra-distinguished from *delusion,* that *negative* faith, which simply permits the images presented to work by their own force, without either denial or affirmation of their real existence by the judgement, is rendered impossible by their immediate neighbourhood to words and facts of known and absolute truth. A faith, which transcends even historic belief, must absolutely *put out* this mere poetic Analogon of faith, as the summer sun is said to extinguish our household fires, when it shines full upon them. What would otherwise have been yielded to as pleasing fiction, is repelled as revolting falsehood. The effect produced in this latter case by the solemn belief of the reader, is in a less degree brought about in the instances, to which I have been objecting, by the baffled attempts of the author to *make* him believe.

Add to all the foregoing the seeming uselessness both of the project and of the anecdotes from which it is to derive support. Is there one word, for instance, attributed to the pedlar in the EXCURSION, characteristic of a *pedlar*? One sentiment, that might not more plausibly, even without the aid of any previous explanation, have proceeded from any wise and beneficent old man, of a rank or profession in which the language of learning and refinement are natural and to be expected? Need the rank have been at all particularized, where nothing follows which the knowledge of that rank is to explain or illustrate? When on the contrary this information renders the man's language, feelings, sentiments, and information a riddle, which must itself be solved by episodes of anecdote? Finally when this, and this alone, could have induced a genuine *poet* to inweave in a poem of the loftiest style, and on subjects the loftiest and of most universal interest, such minute matters of fact, (not unlike those furnished for the obituary of a magazine by the friends of some obscure *ornament of society lately deceased* in some obscure town), as

> Among the hills of Athol he was born:
> There, on a small hereditary farm,
> An unproductive slip of rugged ground,
> His Father dwelt; and died in poverty;
> While he, whose lowly fortune I retrace,
> The youngest of three sons, was yet a babe,
> A little one—unconscious of their loss.
> But, ere he had outgrown his infant days,
> His widowed mother, for a second mate,
> Espoused the teacher of the Village School;
> Who on her offspring zealously bestowed
> Needful instruction. . . .

>From his sixth year, the Boy of whom I speak,
>In summer tended cattle on the hills;
>But, through the inclement and the perilous days
>Of long-continuing winter, he repaired
>To his step-father's school,—&c.

For all the admirable passages interposed in this narration, might, with trifling alterations, have been far more appropriately, and with far greater verisimilitude, told of a poet in the character of a poet; and without incurring another defect which I shall now mention, and a sufficient illustration of which will have been here anticipated.

Third; an undue predilection for the *dramatic* form in certain poems, from which one or other of two evils result. Either the thoughts and diction are different from that of the poet, and then there arises an incongruity of style; or they are the same and indistinguishable, and then it presents a species of ventriloquism, where two are represented as talking, while in truth one man only speaks.

The fourth class of defects is closely connected with the former; but yet are such as arise likewise from an intensity of feeling disproportionate to *such* knowledge and value of the objects described, as can be fairly anticipated of men in general, even of the most cultivated classes; and with which therefore few only, and those few particularly circumstanced, can be supposed to sympathize. In this class, I comprise occasional prolixity, repetition, and an eddying, instead of progression, of thought. As instances, see pages 27, 28, and 62 of the Poems, Vol. I. and the first eighty lines of the Sixth Book of the *Excursion*.

Fifth and last; thoughts and images too great for the subject. This is an approximation to what might be called *mental* bombast, as distinguished from verbal: for, as in the latter there is a disproportion of the expressions to the thoughts, so in this there is a disproportion of thought to the circumstance and occasion. This, by the bye, is a fault of which none but a man of genius is capable. It is the awkwardness and strength of Hercules with the distaff of Omphale.

It is a well-known fact, that bright colors in motion both make and leave the strongest impressions on the eye. Nothing is more likely too, than that a vivid image or visual spectrum, thus originated, may become the link of association in recalling the feelings and images that had accompanied the original impression. But if we describe this in such lines, as

>They flash upon that inward eye,
>Which is the bliss of solitude!

in what words shall we describe the joy of retrospection, when the images and virtuous actions of a whole well-spent life, pass before that conscience which is indeed the *inward* eye: which is indeed *"the bliss of solitude"*? Assuredly we seem to sink most abruptly, not to say burlesquely, and almost as in a *medly*, from this couplet to—

> And then my heart with pleasure fills,
> And dances with the *daffodils*.
>   Vol. I. p. 320.

The second instance is from Vol. II. page 12, where the poet, having gone out for a day's tour of pleasure, meets early in the morning with a knot of *gypsies,* who had pitched their blanket-tents and straw-beds, together with their children and asses, in some field by the road-side. At the close of the day on his return our tourist found them in the same place. "Twelve hours," says he,

> Twelve hours, twelve bounteous hours are gone, while I
> Have been a traveller under open sky,
> Much witnessing of change and cheer,
> Yet as I left I find them here!

Whereat the poet, without seeming to reflect that the poor tawny wanderers might probably have been tramping for weeks together through road and lane, over moor and mountain, and consequently must have been right glad to rest themselves, their children and cattle, for one whole day; and overlooking the obvious truth, that such repose might be quite as necessary for *them,* as a walk of the same continuance was pleasing or healthful for the more fortunate poet; expresses his indignation in a series of lines, the diction and imagery of which would have been rather above, than below the mark, had they been applied to the immense empire of China improgressive for thirty centuries:

> The weary SUN betook himself to rest:—
> —Then issued VESPER from the fulgent west,
> Outshining, like a visible God,
> The glorious path in which he trod!
> And now, ascending, after one dark hour,
> And one night's diminution of her power,
> Behold the mighty MOON! this way
> She looks, as if at them—but they
> Regard not her:—oh, better wrong and strife,
> Better vain deeds or evil than such life!
> The silent HEAVENS have goings on:
> The STARS have tasks!—but *these* have none!

The last instance of this defect (for I know no other than these already cited) is from the Ode, page 351, Vol. II., where, speaking of a child, "a six years' darling of a pigmy size," he thus addresses him:

> Thou best philosopher, who yet dost keep
> Thy heritage! Thou eye among the blind,
> That, deaf and silent, read'st the eternal deep,
> Haunted for ever by the Eternal Mind,—

> Mighty Prophet! Seer blest!
> On whom those truths do rest,
> Which we are toiling all our lives to find!
> Thou, over whom thy immortality
> Broods like the day, a master o'er the slave,
> A presence that is not to be put by!

Now here, not to stop at the daring spirit of metaphor which connects the epithets "deaf and silent," with the apostrophized *eye:* or (if we are to refer it to the preceding word, philosopher) the faulty and equivocal syntax of the passage; and without examining the propriety of making a "master *brood* o'er a slave," or the *day* brood *at all;* we will merely ask, what does all this mean? In what sense is a child of that age a *philosopher*? In what sense does he *read* "the eternal deep"? In what sense is he declared to be *"for ever haunted"* by the Supreme Being? or so inspired as to deserve the splendid titles of a *mighty prophet,* a *blessed seer*? By reflection? by knowledge? by conscious intuition? or by *any* form or modification of consciousness? These would be tidings indeed; but such as would presuppose an immediate revelation to the inspired communicator, and require miracles to authenticate his inspiration. Children at this age give us no such information of themselves; and at what time were we dipped in the Lethe, which has produced such utter oblivion of a state so godlike? There are many of us that still possess some remembrances, more or less distinct, respecting themselves at six years old; pity that the worthless straws only should float, while treasures, compared with which all the mines of Golconda and Mexico were but straws, should be absorbed by some unknown gulf into some unknown abyss.

But if this be too wild and exorbitant to be suspected as having been the poet's meaning; if these mysterious gifts, faculties, and operations, are *not* accompanied with consciousness; who *else* is conscious of them? or how can it be called the child, if it be no part of the child's conscious being? For aught I know, the thinking Spirit within me may be *substantially* one with the principle of life, and of vital operation. For aught I know, it might be employed as a secondary agent in the marvellous organization and organic movements of my body. But, surely, it would be strange language to say, that *I* construct my *heart!* or that *I* propel the finer influences through my *nerves!* or that *I* compress my brain, and draw the curtains of sleep round my own eyes! Spinoza and Behmen were, on different systems, both Pantheists; and among the ancients there were philosophers, teachers of the EN KAI ΠΑΝ, who not only taught that God was All, but that this All constituted God. Yet not even these would confound the *part, as* a part, with the Whole, *as* the whole. Nay, in no system is the distinction between the individual and God, between the Modification, and the one only Substance, more sharply drawn, than in that of Spinoza. Jacobi indeed relates of Lessing, that, after a conversation with him at the house of the poet, Gleim (the Tyrtæus and Anacreon of the German Parnassus) in which conversation L. had avowed privately to Jacobi his reluctance to admit any *personal* existence of the Supreme Being, or the *possibility* of personality except in a finite Intellect, and while they were sitting at table, a shower of rain came on unexpectedly. Gleim expressed his regret at the circumstance, because they had meant to drink their wine in the garden: upon which Lessing in one of his half-earnest half-joking moods, nodded to Jacobi, and said, "It is *I*, perhaps, that am doing *that*," i.e. *raining!* and J. answered, "or perhaps I"; Gleim contented himself with staring at them both, without asking for any explanation.

So with regard to this passage. In what sense can the magnificent attributes, above quoted, be appropriated to a *child*, which would not make them equally suitable to a *bee*, or a *dog*, or a *field of corn:* or even to a ship, or to the wind and waves that propel it? The omnipresent Spirit works equally in them, as in the child; and the child is equally unconscious of it as they. It cannot surely be, that the four lines, immediately following, are to contain the explanation?

> To whom the grave
> Is but a lonely bed without the sense or sight
> Of day or the warm light,
> A place of thought where we in waiting lie.

Surely, it cannot be that this wonder-rousing apostrophe is but a comment on the little poem, "We are seven"? that the whole meaning of the passage is reducible to the assertion, that a *child,* who by the bye at six years old would have been better instructed in most Christian families, has no other notion of death than that of lying in a dark, cold place? And still, I hope, not as in a *place of thought!* not the frightful notion of lying *awake* in his grave! The analogy between death and sleep is too simple, too natural, to render so horrid a belief possible for children; even had they not been in the habit, as all Christian children are, of hearing the latter term used to express the former. But if the child's belief be only, that "he is not dead, but sleepeth": wherein does it differ from that of his father and mother, or any other adult and instructed person? To form an idea of a thing's becoming nothing; or of nothing becoming a thing; is impossible to all finite beings alike, of whatever age, and however educated or uneducated. Thus it is with splendid paradoxes in general. If the words are taken in the common sense, they convey an absurdity; and if, in contempt of dictionaries and custom, they are so interpreted as to avoid the absurdity, the meaning dwindles into some bald truism. Thus you must at once understand the words *contrary* to their common import, in order to arrive at any *sense;* and *according* to their common import, if you are to receive from them any feeling of *sublimity* or *admiration*.

Though the instances of this defect in Mr. Wordsworth's poems are so few, that for themselves it would have been scarce just to attract the reader's attention toward them; yet I have dwelt on it, and perhaps the more for this very reason. For being so very few, they cannot sensibly detract from the reputation of an author, who is even characterized by the number of profound truths in his writings, which will stand the severest analysis; and yet few as they are, they are exactly those passages which his *blind* admirers would be most likely, and best able, to imitate. But Wordsworth, where he is indeed Wordsworth, may be mimicked by Copyists, he may be plundered by Plagiarists; but he can not be imitated, except by those who are not born to be imitators. For without his depth of feeling and his imaginative power his *sense* would want its vital warmth and peculiarity; and without his strong sense, his *mysticism* would become *sickly*—mere fog, and dimness!

To these defects which, as appears by the extracts, are only occasional, I may oppose, with far less fear of encountering the dissent of any candid and intelligent reader, the following (for the most part correspondent) excellences. First, an austere purity of language both grammatically and logically; in short a perfect appropriateness of the words to the meaning. Of how high value I deem this, and how particularly estimable I hold the example at the present day, has been already stated: and in part too the reasons on which I ground both the moral and intellectual importance of habituating ourselves to a strict accuracy of expression. It is noticeable, how limited an acquaintance with the masterpieces of art will suffice to form a correct and even a sensitive taste, where none but master-pieces have been seen and admired: while on the other hand, the most correct notions, and the widest acquaintance with the works of excellence of all ages and countries, will not perfectly secure us against the contagious familiarity with the far more numerous offspring of tastelessness or of a perverted taste. If this be the case, as it notoriously is, with the arts of music and painting, much more difficult will it be to avoid the infection of multiplied and daily examples in the practice of an art, which uses words, and words only, as its instruments. In poetry, in which every line, every phrase, may pass the ordeal of deliberation and deliberate choice, it is possible, and barely possible, to attain that ultimatum which I have ventured to propose as the infallible test of a blameless style; its *untranslatableness* in words of the same language without injury to the meaning. Be it observed, however, that I include in the *meaning* of a word not only its correspondent object, but likewise all the associations which it recalls. For language is framed to convey not the object alone, but likewise the character, mood and intentions of the person who is representing it. In poetry it *is* practicable to preserve the diction uncorrupted by the affectations and misappropriations, which promiscuous authorship, and reading not promiscuous only because it is disproportionally most conversant with the compositions of the day, have rendered general. Yet even to the poet, composing in his own province, it is an arduous work: and as the result and pledge of a watchful good sense, of fine and luminous distinction, and of complete self-possession, may justly claim all the honor which belongs to an attainment equally difficult and valuable, and the more valuable for being rare. It is at *all* times the proper food of the understanding; but in an age of corrupt eloquence it is both food and antidote.

In prose I doubt whether it be even possible to preserve our style wholly unalloyed by the vicious phraseology which meets us everywhere, from the sermon to the newspaper, from the harangue of the legislator to the speech from the convivial chair, announcing a *toast* or sentiment. Our chains rattle, even while we are complaining of them. The poems of Boetius rise high in our estimation when we compare them with those of his contemporaries, as Sidonius Appollinarius, &c. They might even be referred to a purer age, but that the prose, in which they are set, as jewels in a crown of lead or iron, betrays the true age of the writer. Much however may be effected by education. I believe not only from grounds of reason, but from having in great measure assured myself of the fact by actual though limited experience, that, to a youth led from his first boyhood to investigate the meaning of every word and the reason of its choice and position, Logic presents itself as an old acquaintance under new names.

On some future occasion, more especially demanding such disquisition, I shall attempt to prove the close connection between veracity and habits of mental accuracy; the beneficial after-effects of verbal precision in the preclusion of fanaticism, which masters the feelings more especially by indistinct watchwords; and to display the advantages which language alone, at least which language with incomparably greater ease and certainty than any other means, presents to the instructor of impressing modes of intellectual energy so constantly, so imperceptibly, and as it were by such elements and atoms, as to secure in due time the formation of a second nature. When we reflect, that the cultivation of the judgement is a positive command of the moral law, since the reason can give the *principle* alone, and the conscience bears witness only to the *motive,* while the application and effects must depend on the judgement: when we consider, that the greater part of our success and comfort in life depends on distinguishing the similar from the same, that which is peculiar in each thing from that which it has in common with others, so as still to select the most probable, instead of the merely possible or positively unfit, we shall learn to value earnestly and with a practical seriousness a mean, already prepared for us by nature and society, of teaching the young mind to think well and wisely by the same unremembered process and with the same never forgotten results, as those by which it is taught to speak and converse. Now how much warmer the interest is, how much more genial the feelings of reality and practicability, and thence how much stronger the impulses to imitation are, which a *contemporary* writer, and especially a contemporary *poet*, excites in youth and commencing manhood, has been treated of in the earlier pages of these sketches. I have only to add, that all the praise which is due to the exertion of such influence for a purpose so important, joined with that which must be claimed for the infrequency of the same excellence in the same perfection, belongs in full right to Mr. Wordsworth. I am far however from denying that we have poets whose *general* style possess the same excellence, as Mr. Moore, Lord Byron, Mr. Bowles, and, in all his later and more important works, our laurel-honoring Laureate. But there are none, in whose works I do not appear to myself to find *more* exceptions, than in those of Wordsworth. Quotations or specimens would here be wholly out of place, and must be left for the critic who doubts and would invalidate the justice of this eulogy so applied.

The second characteristic excellence of Mr. W.'s work is: a correspondent weight and sanity of the Thoughts and Sentiments, won—not from books, but—from the poet's own meditative observation. They are *fresh* and have the dew upon them. His muse, at least when in her strength of wing, and when she hovers aloft in her proper element,

> Makes audible a linked lay of truth,
> Of truth profound a sweet continuous lay,
> Not learnt, but native, her own natural notes!
> > > S. T. C.

Even throughout his smaller poems there is scarcely one, which is not rendered valuable by some just and original reflection.

See page 25, vol. 2nd.: or the two following passages in one of his humblest compositions.

> O Reader! had you in your mind
> Such stores as silent thought can bring,
> O gentle Reader! you would find
> A tale in every thing;

and

> I've heard of hearts unkind, kind deeds
> With coldness still returning;
> Alas! the gratitude of men
> Has oftener left me mourning;

or in a still higher strain the six beautiful quatrains, page 134.

> Thus fares it still in our decay:
> And yet the wiser mind
> Mourns less for what age takes away
> Than what it leaves behind.
>
> The Blackbird in the summer trees,
> The Lark upon the hill,
> Let loose their carols when they please,
> Are quiet when they will.
>
> With nature never do *they* wage
> A foolish strife; they see
> A happy youth, and their old age
> Is beautiful and free!
>
> But we are pressed by heavy laws;
> And often, glad no more,
> We wear a face of joy, because
> We have been glad of yore.
>
> If there is one, who need bemoan
> His kindred laid in earth,
> The household hearts that were his own,
> It is the man of mirth.

> My days, my Friend, are almost gone,
> My life has been approved,
> And many love me; but by none
> Am I enough beloved.

or the sonnet on Buonaparte, page 202, vol. 2; or finally (for a volume would scarce suffice to exhaust the instances) the last stanza of the poem on the withered Celandine, vol. 2, p. 212.

> To be a prodigal's favorite—then, worse truth,
> A miser's pensioner—behold our lot!
> O man! that from thy fair and shining youth
> Age might but take the things youth needed not.

Both in respect of this and of the former excellence, Mr. Wordsworth strikingly resembles Samuel Daniel, one of the golden writers of our golden Elizabethan age, now most causelessly neglected: Samuel Daniel, whose diction bears no mark of time, no distinction of age, which has been, and as long as our language shall last, will be so far the language of the to-day and for ever, as that it is more intelligible to us, than the transitory fashions of our own particular age. A similar praise is due to his sentiments. No frequency of perusal can deprive them of their freshness. For though they are brought into the full daylight of every reader's comprehension; yet are they drawn up from depths which few in any age are privileged to visit, into which few in any age have courage or inclination to descend. If Mr. Wordsworth is not equally with Daniel alike intelligible to all readers of average understanding in all passages of his works, the comparative difficulty does not arise from the greater impurity of the ore, but from the nature and uses of the metal. A poem is not necessarily obscure, because it does not aim to be popular. It is enough, if a work be perspicuous to those for whom it is written, and

> Fit audience find, though few.

To the "Ode on the intimation of immortality from recollections of early childhood" the poet might have prefixed the lines which Dante addresses to one of his own Canzoni—

> Canzon, io credo, che saranno radi
> Che tua ragione intendan bene,
> Tanto lor sei faticoso ed alto.
> O lyric song, there will be few, think I,
> Who may thy import understand aright:
> Thou art for *them* so arduous and so high!

But the ode was intended for such readers only as had been accustomed to watch the flux and reflux of their inmost nature, to venture at times into the twilight realms of consciousness, and to feel a deep interest in modes of inmost being, to which they know that the attributes of time and space are inapplicable and alien, but which yet can not be conveyed save in symbols of time and space. For such readers the sense is sufficiently plain, and they will be as little disposed to charge Mr. Wordsworth with believing the Platonic pre-existence in the ordinary interpretation of the words, as I am to believe, that Plato himself ever meant or taught it.

> Πολλά μοι ὑπ᾽ ἀγκῶ-
> νος ὠκέα βέλη
> ἔνδον ἐντὶ φαρέτρας
> φωνᾶντα συνετοῖσιν· ἐς
> δὲ τὸ πᾶν ἑρμηνέων
> χατίζει. σοφὸς ὁ πολ-
> λὰ εἰδὼς φυᾷ.
> μαθόντες δέ, λάβροι
> παγγλωσσία, κόρακες ὣς
> ἄκραντα γαρύετοτ
> Διὸς πρὸς ὄρνιχα θεῖον.

Third (and wherein he soars far above Daniel) the sinewy strength and originality of single lines and paragraphs: the frequent curiosa felicitas of his diction, of which I need not here give specimens, having anticipated them in a preceding page. This beauty, and as eminently characteristic of Wordsworth's poetry, his rudest assailants have felt themselves compelled to acknowledge and admire.

Fourth; the perfect truth of nature in his images and descriptions, as taken immediately from nature, and proving a long and genial intimacy with the very spirit which gives the physiognomic expression to all the works of nature. Like a green field reflected in a calm and perfectly transparent lake, the image is distinguished from the reality only by its greater softness and lustre. Like the moisture or the polish on a pebble, genius neither distorts nor false-colours its objects; but on the contrary brings out many a vein and many a tint, which escapes the eye of common observation, thus raising to the rank of gems what had been often kicked away by the hurrying foot of the traveller on the dusty high road of custom.

Let me refer to the whole description of skating, vol. I., page 42 to 47, especially to the lines

> So through the darkness and the cold we flew,
> And not a voice was idle: with the din
> Meanwhile the precipices rang aloud;
> The leafless trees and every icy crag
> Tinkled like iron; while the distant hills
> Into the tumult sent an alien sound
> Of melancholy, not unnoticed, while the stars
> Eastward were sparkling clear, and in the west
> The orange sky of evening died away.

Or to the poem on the green linnet, vol. I. page 244. What can be more accurate yet more lovely than the two concluding stanzas?

> Upon yon tuft of hazel trees,
> That twinkle to the gusty breeze,
> Behold him perched in ecstasies,
>   Yet seeming still to hover;
> There! where the flutter of his wings
> Upon his back and body flings
> Shadows and sunny glimmerings,
>   That cover him all over.
>
> While thus before my eyes he gleams,
> A brother of the leaves he seems;
> When in a moment forth he teems
>   His little song in gushes:
> As if it pleased him to disdain
> And mock the form which he did feign,
> While he was dancing with the train
>   Of leaves among the bushes.

Or the description of the blue-cap, and of the noon-tide silence, page 284; or the poem to the cuckoo, page 299; or, lastly, though I might multiply the references to ten times the number, to the poem, so completely Wordsworth's, commencing

> Three years she grew in sun and shower,

Fifth: a meditative pathos, a union of deep and subtle thought with sensibility; a sympathy with man as man; the sympathy indeed of a contemplator, rather than a fellow-sufferer or comate, (spectator, haud particeps) but of a contemplator, from whose view no difference of rank conceals the sameness of the nature; no injuries of wind or weather, or toil, or even of ignorance, wholly disguise the human face divine. The superscription and the image of the Creator still remain legible to *him* under the dark lines, with which guilt or calamity had cancelled or cross-barred it. Here the man and the poet lose and find themselves in each other, the one as glorified, the latter as substantiated. In this mild and philosophic pathos, Wordsworth appears to me without a compeer. Such he *is:* so he *writes.* See vol. I. page 134 to 136, or that most affecting composition, the "Affliction of Margaret ——of ——," page 165 to 168, which no mother, and, if I may judge by my own experience, no parent can read without a tear. Or turn to that genuine lyric, in the former edition, entitled "The Mad Mother," page 174 to 178, of which I cannot refrain from quoting two of the stanzas, both of them for their pathos, and the former for the fine transition in the two concluding lines of the stanza, so expressive of that deranged state, in which from the increased sensibility the sufferer's attention is abruptly drawn off by every trifle, and in the same instant plucked back again by the one despotic thought, bringing home with it, by the blending,

fusing power of Imagination and Passion, the alien object to which it had been
so abruptly diverted, no longer an alien but an ally and an inmate.

> Suck, little babe, oh suck again!
> It cools my blood; it cools my brain:
> Thy lips, I feel them, baby! they
> Draw from my heart the pain away.
> Oh! press me with thy little hand;
> It loosens something at my chest:
> About that tight and deadly band
> I feel thy little fingers prest.
> The breeze I see is in the tree!
> It comes to cool my babe and me.
>
> Thy father cares not for my breast,
> 'Tis thine, sweet baby, there to rest,
> 'Tis all thine own!—and, if its hue
> Be changed, that was so fair to view,
> 'Tis fair enough for thee, my dove!
> My beauty, little child, is flown,
> But thou wilt live with me in love;
> And what if my poor cheek be brown?
> 'Tis well for me, thou canst not see
> How pale and wan it else would be.

Last, and pre-eminently, I challenge for this poet the gift of IMAGINATION in
the highest and strictest sense of the word. In the play of *Fancy,* Wordsworth,
to my feelings, is not always graceful, and sometimes *recondite.* The *likeness*
is occasionally too strange, or demands too peculiar a point of view, or is such
as appears the creature of pre-determined research, rather than spontaneous
presentation. Indeed his fancy seldom displays itself, as mere and unmodified
fancy. But in imaginative power, he stands nearest of all modern writers to
Shakespeare and Milton; and yet in a kind perfectly unborrowed and his own.
To employ his own words, which are at once an instance and an illustration, he
does indeed to all thoughts and to all objects

> add the gleam,
> The light that never was, on sea or land,
> The consecration, and the poet's dream.

I shall select a few examples as most obviously manifesting this faculty;
but if I should ever be fortunate enough to render my analysis of imagination,
its origin and characters, thoroughly intelligible to the reader, he will scarcely
open on a page of this poet's works without recognising, more or less, the
presence and the influences of this faculty.

From the poem on the Yew Trees, vol. I. page 303, 304.

> But worthier still of note
> Are those fraternal four of Borrowdale,

Joined in one solemn and capacious grove:
Huge trunks!—and each particular trunk a growth
Of intertwisted fibres serpentine
Up-coiling, and inveterately convolved,—
Not uninformed with phantasy, and looks
That threaten the profane;—a pillared shade,
Upon whose grassless floor of red-brown hue,
By sheddings from the pinal umbrage tinged
Perennially—beneath whose sable roof
Of boughs, as if for festal purpose decked
With unrejoicing berries, ghostly shapes
May meet at noontide—*Fear* and trembling *Hope,*
Silence and *Foresight*—*Death*, the skeleton,
And *Time*, the shadow—there to celebrate,
As in a natural temple scattered o'er
With altars undisturbed of mossy stone,
United worship; or in mute repose
To lie, and listen to the mountain flood
Murmuring from Glaramara's inmost caves.

The effect of the old man's figure in the poem of Resignation and Independence, vol. II. page 33.

While he was talking thus, the lonely place,
The old man's shape, and speech, all troubled me:
In my mind's eye I seemed to see him pace
About the weary moors continually,
Wandering about alone and silently.

Or the 8th, 9th, 19th, 26th, 31st, and 33d, in the collection of miscellaneous sonnets—the sonnet on the subjugation of Switzerland, page 210, or the last ode, from which I especially select the two following stanzas or paragraphs, page 349 to 350.

Our birth is but a sleep and a forgetting;
The soul that rises with us, our life's star,
Hath had elsewhere its setting,
        And cometh from afar.
Not in entire forgetfulness,
And not in utter nakedness,
But trailing clouds of glory do we come
From God, who is our home:
Heaven lies about us in our infancy!
Shades of the prison-house begin to close
        Upon the growing boy;
But he beholds the light, and whence it flows,
        He sees it in his joy!

> The youth who daily further from the East
> Must travel, still is nature's priest,
>   And by the splendid vision
>   Is on his way attended;
> At length the man perceives it die away,
> And fade into the light of common day.

And page 352 to 354 of the same ode.

> O joy that in our embers
> Is something that doth live,
> That nature yet remembers
> What was so fugitive!
> The thought of our past years in me doth breed
> Perpetual benedictions: not indeed
> For that which is most worthy to be blest;
> Delight and liberty, the simple creed
> Of childhood, whether busy or at rest,
> With new-fledged hope still fluttering in his breast:—
> Not for these I raise
> The song of thanks and praise;
> But for those obstinate questionings
> Of sense and outward things,
> Fallings from us, vanishings;
> Blank misgivings of a creature
> Moving about in worlds not realized,
> High instincts, before which our mortal nature
> Did tremble like a guilty thing surprised!
> But for those first affections,
> Those shadowy recollections,
> Which, be they what they may,
> Are yet the fountain light of all our day,
> Are yet a master light of all our seeing;
> Uphold us—cherish—and have power to make
> Our noisy years seem moments in the being
> Of the eternal silence; truths that wake
>   To perish never:
> Which neither listlessness, nor mad endeavour,
> Nor man nor boy,
> Nor all that is at enmity with joy,
> Can utterly abolish or destroy!
> Hence, in a season of calm weather,
> Though inland far we be,
> Our souls have sight of that immortal sea
> Which brought us hither;
> Can in a moment travel thither—

And see the children sport upon the shore,
And hear the mighty waters rolling evermore.

And since it would be unfair to conclude with an extract, which, though highly characteristic, must yet, from the nature of the thoughts and the subject, be interesting, or perhaps intelligible, to but a limited number of readers; I will add, from the poet's last published work, a passage equally Wordsworthian; of the beauty of which, and of the imaginative power displayed therein, there can be but one opinion, and one feeling. See "White Doe," page 5.

Fast the church-yard fills;—anon
Look again and they are gone;
The cluster round the porch, and the folk
Who sate in the shade of the prior's oak!
And scarcely have they disappear'd,
Ere the prelusive hymn is heard;—
With one consent the people rejoice,
Filling the church with a lofty voice!
They sing a service which they feel,
For 'tis the sun-rise of their zeal;
And faith and hope are in their prime
In great Eliza's golden time.

A moment ends the fervent din,
And all is hushed, without and within;
For though the priest, more tranquilly,
Recites the holy liturgy,
The only voice which you can hear
Is the river murmuring near.
When soft!—the dusky trees between,
And down the path through the open green,
Where is no living thing to be seen;
And through yon gateway, where is found,
Beneath the arch with ivy bound,
Free entrance to the church-yard ground;
And right across the verdant sod,
Towards the very house of God;
Comes gliding in with lovely gleam,
Comes gliding in serene and slow,
Soft and silent as a dream,
A solitary doe!
White she is as lily of June,
And beauteous as the silver moon
When out of sight the clouds are driven
And she is left alone in heaven!
Or like a ship some gentle day

> In sunshine sailing far away—
> A glittering ship, that hath the plain
> Of ocean for her own domain. . . .
> What harmonious pensive changes
> Wait upon her as she ranges
> Round and through this pile of state
> Overthrown and desolate!
> Now a step or two her way
> Is through space of open day,
> Where the enamoured sunny light
> Brightens her that was so bright;
> Now doth a delicate shadow fall,
> Falls upon her like a breath,
> From some lofty arch or wall,
> As she passes underneath.

The following analogy will, I am apprehensive, appear dim and fantastic, but in reading Bartram's Travels I could not help transcribing the following lines as a sort of allegory, or connected simile and metaphor of Wordsworth's intellect and genius.—"The soil is a deep, rich, dark mould, on a deep stratum of tenacious clay; and that on a foundation of rocks, which often break through both strata, lifting their back above the surface. The trees which chiefly grow here are the gigantic black oak; magnolia magni-floria; fraxinus excelsior; platane; and a few stately tulip trees." What Mr. Wordsworth *will* produce, it is not for me to prophecy: but I could pronounce with the liveliest convictions what he is capable of producing. It is the *First Genuine Philosophic Poem.* . . .

ON SHAKESPEARE

SHAKESPEARE'S JUDGMENT
EQUAL TO HIS GENIUS

Thus then Shakespeare appears, from his Venus and Adonis and Rape of Lucrece alone, apart from all his great works, to have possessed all the conditions of the true poet. Let me now proceed to destroy, as far as may be in my power, the popular notion that he was a great dramatist by mere instinct, that he grew immortal in his own despite, and sank below men of second or third-rate power, when he attempted aught beside the drama—even as bees construct their cells and manufacture their honey to admirable perfection; but would in vain attempt to build a nest. Now this mode of reconciling a compelled sense of inferiority with a feeling of pride, began in a few pedants, who having read that Sophocles was the great model of tragedy, and Aristotle the infallible dictator of its rules, and finding that the Lear, Hamlet, Othello, and other master-pieces were neither in imitation of Sophocles, nor in obedience to Aristotle,—and not having (with one or two exceptions) the courage to affirm, that the delight which their country received from generation to generation, in defiance of the alterations of circumstances and habits, was wholly groundless,—took upon them, as a happy medium and refuge, to talk of Shakespeare as a sort of beautiful *lusus naturæ*, a delightful monster,— wild, indeed, and without taste or judgment, but like the inspired idiots so much venerated in the East, uttering, amid the strangest follies, the sublimest truths. In nine places out of ten in which I find his awful name mentioned, it is with some epithet of "wild," "irregular," "pure child of nature," &c. If all this be true, we must submit to it; though to a thinking mind it can not but be painful to find any excellence, merely human, thrown out of all human analogy, and thereby leaving us neither rules for imitation, nor motives to imitate;—but if false, it is a dangerous falsehood;—for it affords a refuge to secret self-conceit,—enables a vain man at once to escape his reader's indignation by general swoln panegyrics, and merely by his *ipse dixit* to treat, as contemptible, what he has not intellect enough to comprehend, or soul to feel, without assigning any reason, or referring his opinion to any demonstrative principle; thus leaving Shakespeare as a sort of grand Lama, adored indeed, and his very excrements prized as relics, but with no authority or real influence. I grieve that every late voluminous edition of his works would enable me to substantiate the present charge with a variety of facts, one tenth of which would of themselves exhaust the time allotted to me. Every critic, who has or has not made a collection of black-letter books—in itself a useful and respectable amusement,—puts on the seven-league boots of self-opinion, and strides at once from an illustrator into a supreme judge, and blind and deaf, fills his three-ounce phial at the waters of Niagara; and determines positively the greatness of the cataract to be neither more nor less than his three-ounce phial has been able to receive.

I think this a very serious subject. It is my earnest desire—my passionate endeavor,—to enforce at various times, and by various arguments and instances, the close and reciprocal connection of just taste with pure morality. Without that acquaintance with the heart of man, or that docility and childlike gladness to be made acquainted with it, which those only can have, who dare look at their own hearts—and that with a steadiness which religion only has the power of reconciling with sincere humility;—without this, and the modesty produced by it, I am deeply convinced that no man, however wide his erudition, however patient his antiquarian researches, can possibly understand, or be worthy of understanding, the writings of Shakespeare.

Assuredly that criticism of Shakespeare will alone be genial which is reverential. The Englishman, who, without reverence, a proud and affectionate reverence, can utter the name of William Shakespeare, stands disqualified for the office of critic. He wants one at least of the very senses, the language of which he is to employ, and will discourse at best, but as a blind man, while the whole harmonious creation of light and shade with all its subtle interchange of deepening and dissolving colors rises in silence to the silent *fiat* of the uprising Apollo. However inferior in ability I may be to some who have followed me, I own I am proud that I was the first in time who publicly demonstrated to the full extent of the position, that the supposed irregularity and extravagances of Shakespeare were the mere dreams of a pedantry that arraigned the eagle because it had not the dimensions of the swan. In all the successive courses of lectures delivered by me, since my first attempt at the Royal Institution, it has been, and it still remains, my object, to prove that in all points from the most important to the most minute, the judgment of Shakespeare is commensurate with his genius—nay, that his genius reveals itself in his judgment, as in its most exalted form. And the more gladly do I recur to this subject from the clear conviction, that to judge aright, and with distinct consciousness of the grounds of our judgment, concerning the works of Shakespeare, implies the power and the means of judging rightly of all other works of intellect, those of abstract science alone excepted.

It is a painful truth that not only individuals, but even whole nations, are ofttimes so enslaved to the habits of their education and immediate circumstances, as not to judge disinterestedly even on those subjects, the very pleasure arising from which consists in its disinterestedness, namely, on subjects of taste and polite literature. Instead of deciding concerning their own modes and customs by any rule of reason, nothing appears rational, becoming, or beautiful to them, but what coincides with the peculiarities of their education. In this narrow circle, individuals may attain to exquisite discrimination, as the French critics have done in their own literature; but a true critic can no more be such without placing himself on some central point, from which he may command the whole, that is, some general rule, which, founded in reason, or the faculties common to all men, must therefore apply to each— than an astronomer can explain the movements of the solar system without taking his stand in the sun. And let me remark, that this will not tend to produce despotism, but, on the contrary, true tolerance, in the critic. He will, indeed, require, as the spirit and substance of a work, something true in human nature itself, and independent of all circumstances; but in the mode of applying it, he will estimate genius and judgment according to the felicity with which the imperishable soul of intellect, shall have adapted itself to the age, the place, and the existing manners. The error he will expose, lies in reversing this, and holding up the mere circumstances as perpetual to the utter neglect of the power which can alone animate them. For art can not exist without, or apart from, nature; and what has man of his own to give to his fellow-man, but his own thoughts and feelings, and his observations, so far as they are modified by his own thoughts or feelings?

Let me, then, once more submit this question to minds emancipated alike from national, or party, or sectarian prejudice:—Are the plays of Shakespeare works of rude uncultivated genius, in which the splendor of the parts compensates, if aught can compensate, for the barbarous shapelessness and irregularity of the whole? Or is the form equally admirable with the matter, and the judgment of the great poet, not less deserving our wonder than his genius?—Or, again, to repeat the question in other words:—Is Shakespeare a great dramatic poet on account only of those beauties and excellences which he possesses in common with the ancients, but with diminished claims to our love and honor to the full extent of his differences from them?—Or are these very differences additional proofs of poetic wisdom, at once results and symbols of living power as contrasted with lifeless mechanism—of free and rival originality as contra-distinguished from servile imitation, or, more accurately, a blind copying of effects, instead of a true imitation of the essential principles?—Imagine not that I am about to oppose genius to rules. No! the comparative value of these rules is the very cause to be tried. The spirit of poetry, like all other living powers, must of necessity circumscribe itself by rules, were it only to unite power with beauty. It must embody in order to reveal itself; but a living body is of necessity an organized one; and what is organization but the connection of parts in and for a whole, so that each part is at once end and means?—This is no discovery of criticism;—it is a necessity of the human mind; and all nations have felt and obeyed it, in the invention of metre, and measured sounds, as the vehicle and *involucrum* of poetry—itself a fellow-growth from the same life—even as the bark is to the tree!

No work of true genius dares want its appropriate form, neither indeed is there any danger of this. As it must not, so genius can not, be lawless; for it is even this that constitutes it genius—the power of acting creatively under laws of its own origination. How then comes it that not only single *Zoili*, but whole nations have combined in unhesitating condemnation of our great dramatist, as a sort of African nature, rich in beautiful monsters—as a wild heath where islands of fertility look the greener from the surrounding waste, where the loveliest plants now shine out among unsightly weeds, and now are choked by their parasitic growth, so intertwined that we can not disentangle the weed without snapping the flower?—In this statement I have had no reference to the vulgar abuse of Voltaire, save as far as his charges are coincident with the decisions of Shakespeare's own commentators and (so they would tell you) almost idolatrous admirers. The true ground of the mistake lies in the confounding mechanical regularity with organic form. The form is mechanic, when on any given material we impress a pre-determined form, not necessarily arising out of the properties of the material;—as when to a mass of wet clay we give whatever shape we wish it to retain when hardened. The organic form, on the other hand, is innate; it shapes, as it develops, itself from within, and the fulness of its development is one and the same with the perfection of its outward form. Such as the life is, such is the form. Nature, the prime genial artist, inexhaustible in diverse powers, is equally inexhaustible in forms;—each exterior is the physiognomy of the being within—its true image reflected and thrown out from the concave mirror;—and even such is the appropriate excellence of her chosen poet, of our own Shakespeare—himself a nature humanized, a genial understanding directing self-consciously a power and an implicit wisdom deeper even than our consciousness.

I greatly dislike beauties and selections in general; but as proof positive of his unrivalled excellence, I should like to try Shakespeare by this criterion. Make out your amplest catalogue of all the human faculties, as reason or the moral law, the will, the feeling of the coincidence of the two (a feeling *sui generis et demonstratio demonstrationum*) called the conscience, the understanding or prudence, wit, fancy, imagination, judgment—and then of the objects on which these are to be employed, as the beauties, the terrors, and the seeming caprices of nature, the realities and the capabilities, that is, the actual and the ideal, of the human mind, conceived as an individual or as a social being, as in innocence or in guilt, in a play-paradise, or in a war-field of temptation;—and then compare with Shakespeare under each of these heads all or any of the writers in prose and verse that have ever lived! Who, that is competent to judge, doubts the result?—And ask your own hearts—ask your own common-sense—to conceive the possibility of this man being—I say not, the drunken savage of that wretched socialist, whom Frenchmen, to their shame, have honored before their elder and better worthies—but the anomalous, the wild, the irregular, genius of our daily criticism! What! are we to have miracles in sport?—Or, I speak reverently, does God choose idiots by whom to convey divine truths to man?

SUMMARY OF THE CHARACTERISTICS OF SHAKESPEARE'S DRAMAS

It seems to me that his plays are distinguished from those of all other dramatic poets by the following characteristics:

1. Expectation in preference to surprise. It is like the true reading of the passage—'God said, Let there be light, and there was *light;*'—not there *was* light. As the feeling with which we startle at a shooting star compared with

that of watching the sunrise at the pre-established moment, such and so low is surprise compared with expectation.

2. Signal adherence to the great law of nature, that all opposites tend to attract and temper each other. Passion in Shakespeare generally displays libertinism, but involves morality; and if there are exceptions to this, they are, independently of their intrinsic value, all of them indicative of individual character, and, like the farewell admonitions of the parent, have an end beyond the parental relation. Thus the Countess's beautiful precepts to Bertram, by elevating her character, raise that of Helena her favorite, and soften down the point in her which Shakespeare does not mean us not to see, but to see and to forgive, and at length to justify. And so it is in Polonius, who is the personified memory of wisdom no longer actually possessed. This admirable character is always misrepresented on the stage. Shakespeare never intended to exhibit him as a buffoon; for although it was natural that Hamlet,—a young man of fire and genius, detesting formality, and disliking Polonius on political grounds, as imagining that he had assisted his uncle in his usurpation,—should express himself satirically,—yet this must not be taken as exactly the poet's conception of him. In Polonius a certain induration of character had arisen from long habits of business; but take his advice to Laertes, and Ophelia's reverence for his memory, and we shall see that he was meant to be represented as a statesman somewhat past his faculties—his recollections of life all full of wisdom, and showing a knowledge of human nature, whilst what immediately takes place before him, and escapes from him, is indicative of weakness.

But as in Homer all the deities are in armor, even Venus; so in Shakespeare all the characters are strong. Hence real folly and dulness are made by him the vehicles of wisdom. There is no difficulty for one being a fool to imitate a fool; but to be, remain, and speak like a wise man and a great wit, and yet so as to give a vivid representation of a veritable fool,—*hic labor, hoc opus est*. A drunken constable is not uncommon, nor hard to draw; but see and examine what goes to make up a Dogberry.

3. Keeping at all times in the high road of life. Shakespeare has no innocent adulteries, no interesting incests, no virtuous vice;—he never renders that amiable which religion and reason alike teach us to detest, or clothes impurity in the garb of virtue, like Beaumont and Fletcher, the Kotzebues of the day. Shakespeare's fathers are roused by ingratitude, his husbands stung by unfaithfulness; in him, in short, the affections are wounded in those points in which all may, nay, must, feel. Let the morality of Shakespeare be contrasted with that of the writers of his own, or the succeeding age, or of those of the present day, who boast their superiority in this respect. No one can dispute that the result of such a comparison is altogether in favor of Shakespeare;—even the letters of women of high rank in his age were often coarser than his writings. If he occasionally disgusts a keen sense of delicacy, he never injures the mind; he neither excites, nor flatters passion, in order to degrade the subject of it; he does not use the faulty thing for a faulty purpose, nor carries on warfare against virtue, by causing wickedness to appear as no

wickedness, through the medium of a morbid sympathy with the unfortunate. In Shakespeare vice never walks as in twilight; nothing is purposely out of its place;—he inverts not the order of nature and propriety,—does not make every magistrate a drunkard or glutton, nor every poor man meek, humane, and temperate; he has no benevolent butchers, nor any sentimental rat-catchers.

4. Independence of the dramatic interest on the plot. The interest in the plot is always in fact on account of the characters, not *vice versa*, as in almost all other writers; the plot is a mere canvass and no more. Hence arises the true justification of the same stratagem being used in regard to Benedict and Beatrice,—the vanity in each being alike. Take away from the Much Ado About Nothing all that which is not indispensable to the plot, either as having little to do with it, or, at best, like Dogberry and his comrades, forced into the service, when any other less ingeniously absurd watchmen and night-constables would have answered the mere necessities of the action;—take away Benedict, Beatrice, Dogberry, and the reaction of the former on the character of Hero,— and what will remain? In other writers the main agent of the plot is always the prominent character; in Shakespeare it is so, or is not so, as the character is in itself calculated, or not calculated, to form the plot. Don John is the mainspring of the plot of this play; but he is merely shown and then withdrawn.

5. Independence of the interest on the story as the groundwork of the plot. Hence Shakespeare never took the trouble of inventing stories. It was enough for him to select from those that had been already invented or recorded such as had one or other, or both, of two recommendations, namely, suitableness to his particular purpose, and their being parts of popular tradition,—names of which we had often heard, and of their fortunes, and as to which all we wanted was, to see the man himself. So it is just the man himself, the Lear, the Shylock, the Richard, that Shakespeare makes us for the first time acquainted with. Omit the first scene in Lear, and yet every thing will remain; so the first and second scenes in the Merchant of Venice. Indeed it is universally true.

6. Interfusion of the lyrical—that which in its very essence is poetical—not only with the dramatic, as in the plays of Metastasio, where at the end of the scene comes the *aria* as the *exit* speech of the character,—but also in and through the dramatic. Songs in Shakespeare are introduced as songs only, just as songs are in real life, beautifully as some of them are characteristic of the person who has sung or called for them, as Desdemona's 'Willow,' and Ophelia's wild snatches, and the sweet carollings in As You Like It. But the whole of the Midsummer Night's Dream is one continued specimen of the dramatized lyrical. And observe how exquisitely the dramatic of Hotspur;—

> Marry, and I'm glad on't with all my heart;
> I'd rather be a kitten and cry—mew, &c.

melts away into the lyric of Mortimer;—

> I understand thy looks: that pretty Welsh
> Which thou pourest down from these swelling heavens,

I am too perfect in, &c.

Henry IV. part i. act iii. sc. i.

7. The characters of the *dramatis personæ*, like those in real life, are to be inferred by the reader;—they are not told to him. And it is well worth remarking that Shakespeare's characters, like those in real life, are very commonly misunderstood, and almost always understood by different persons in different ways. The causes are the same in either case. If you take only what the friends of the character say, you may be deceived, and still more so, if that which his enemies say; nay, even the character himself sees himself through the medium of his character, and not exactly as he is. Take all together, not omitting a shrewd hint from the clown or the fool, and perhaps your impression will be right; and you may know whether you have in fact discovered the poet's own idea, by all the speeches receiving light from it, and attesting its reality by reflecting it.

Lastly, in Shakespeare the heterogeneous is united, as it is in nature. You must not suppose a pressure or passion always acting on or in the character!—passion in Shakespeare is that by which the individual is distinguished from others, not that which makes a different kind of him. Shakespeare followed the main march of the human affections. He entered into no analysis of the passions or faiths of men, but assured himself that such and such passions and faiths were grounded in our common nature, and not in the mere accidents of ignorance or disease. This is an important consideration and constitutes our Shakespeare the morning star, the guide and the pioneer, of true philosophy.

ROMEO AND JULIET

In a former lecture I endeavoured to point out the union of the Poet and the Philosopher, or rather the warm embrace between them, in the "Venus and Adonis" and "Lucrece" of Shakespeare. From thence I passed on to "Love's Labours Lost," as the link between his character as a Poet, and his art as a Dramatist; and I shewed that, although in that work the former was still predominant, yet that the germs of his subsequent dramatic power were easily discernible.

I will now, as I promised in my last, proceed to "Romeo and Juliet," not because it is the earliest, or among the earliest of Shakespeare's works of that kind, but because in it are to be found specimens, in degree, of all the excellences which he afterwards displayed in his more perfect dramas, but differing from them in being less forcibly evidenced, and less happily combined: all the parts are more or less present, but they are not united with the same harmony.

There are, however, in "Romeo and Juliet" passages where the poet's whole excellence is evinced, so that nothing superior to them can be met with in the productions of his after years. The main distinction between this play and others is, as I said, that the parts are less happily combined, or to borrow a phrase from the painter, the whole work is less in keeping. Grand portions are produced: we have limbs of giant growth; but the production, as a whole, in which each part gives delight for itself, and the whole, consisting of these delightful parts, communicates the highest intellectual pleasure and satisfaction, is the result of the application of judgment and taste. These are not to be attained but by painful study, and to the sacrifice of the stronger pleasures derived from the dazzling light which a man of genius throws over every circumstance, and where we are chiefly struck by vivid and distinct images. Taste is an attainment after a poet has been disciplined by experience, and has added to genius that talent by which he knows what part of his genius he can make acceptable, and intelligible to the portion of mankind for which he writes.

In my mind it would be a hopeless symptom, as regards genius, if I found a young man with anything like perfect taste. In the earlier works of Shakespeare we have a profusion of double epithets, and sometimes even the coarsest terms are employed, if they convey a more vivid image; but by degrees the associations are connected with the image they are designed to impress, and the poet descends from the ideal into the real world so far as to conjoin both—to give a sphere of active operations to the ideal, and to elevate and refine the real.

In "Romeo and Juliet" the principal characters may be divided into two classes: in one class passion—the passion of love—is drawn and drawn truly, as well as beautifully; but the persons are not individualised farther than as the actor appears on the stage. It is a very just description and development of love, without giving, if I may so express myself, the philosophical history of it—without shewing how the man became acted upon by that particular passion, but leading it through all the incidents of the drama, and rendering it predominant.

Tybalt is, in himself, a common-place personage. And here allow me to remark upon a great distinction between Shakespeare, and all who have written in imitation of him. I know no character in his plays, (unless indeed Pistol be an exception) which can be called the mere portrait of an individual: while the reader feels all the satisfaction arising from individuality, yet that very individual is a sort of class character, and this circumstance renders Shakespeare the poet of all ages.

Tybalt is a man abandoned to his passions—with all the pride of family, only because he thought it belonged to him as a member of that family, and valuing himself highly, simply because he does not care for death. This indifference to death is perhaps more common than any other feeling: men are apt to flatter themselves extravagantly, merely because they possess a quality which it is a disgrace not to have, but which a wise man never puts forward, but when it is necessary.

Jeremy Taylor in one part of his voluminous works, speaking of a great man, says that he was naturally a coward, as indeed most men are, knowing the value of life, but the power of his reason enabled him, when required, to conduct himself with uniform courage and hardihood. The good bishop, perhaps, had in his mind a story, told by one of the ancients, of a Philosopher and a Coxcomb, on board the same ship during a storm: the Coxcomb reviled the Philosopher for betraying marks of fear: "Why are you so frightened? I am not afraid of being drowned: I do not care a farthing for my life."—"You are perfectly right," said the Philosopher, "for your life is not worth a farthing."

Shakespeare never takes pains to make his characters win your esteem, but leaves it to the general command of the passions, and to poetic justice. It is most beautiful to observe, in "Romeo and Juliet," that the characters principally engaged in the incidents are preserved innocent from all that could lower them in our opinion, while the rest of the personages, deserving little interest in themselves, derive it from being instrumental in those situations in which the more important personages develope their thoughts and passions.

Look at Capulet—a worthy, noble-minded old man of high rank, with all the impatience that is likely to accompany it. It is delightful to see all the sensibilities of our nature so exquisitely called forth; as if the poet had the hundred arms of the polypus, and had thrown them out in all directions to catch the predominant feeling. We may see in Capulet the manner in which anger seizes hold of everything that comes in its way, in order to express itself, as in the lines where he reproves Tybalt for his fierceness of behaviour, which led him to wish to insult a Montague, and disturb the merriment.—

> Go to, go to;
> You are a saucy boy. Is't so, indeed?
> This trick may chance to scath you;—I know what.
> You must contrary me! marry, 'tis time.—
> Well said, my hearts!—You are a princox: go:
> Be quiet or—More light, more light!—For shame!
> I'll make you quiet.—What! cheerly, my hearts!
> *Act I., Scene* 5.

The line

> This trick may chance to scath you;—I know what,

was an allusion to the legacy Tybalt might expect; and then, seeing the lights burn dimly, Capulet turns his anger against the servants. Thus we see that no one passion is so predominant, but that it includes all the parts of the character, and the reader never has a mere abstract of a passion, as of wrath or ambition, but the whole man is presented to him—the one predominant passion acting, if I may so say, as the leader of the band to the rest.

It could not be expected that the poet should introduce such a character as Hamlet into every play; but even in those personages, which are subordinate to a hero so eminently philosophical, the passion is at least rendered instructive, and induces the reader to look with a keener eye, and a finer judgment into human nature.

Shakespeare has this advantage over all other dramatists—that he has availed himself of his psychological genius to develope all the minutiæ of the human heart: shewing us the thing that, to common observers, he seems solely intent upon, he makes visible what we should not otherwise have seen: just as, after looking at distant objects through a telescope, when we behold them subsequently with the naked eye, we see them with greater distinctness, and in more detail, than we should otherwise have done.

Mercutio is one of our poet's truly Shakespearean characters; for throughout his plays, but especially in those of the highest order, it is plain that the personages were drawn rather from meditation than from observation, or to speak correctly, more from observation, the child of meditation. It is comparatively easy for a man to go about the world, as if with a pocket-book in his hand, carefully noting down what he sees and hears: by practice he acquires considerable facility in representing what he has observed, himself frequently unconscious of its worth, or its bearings. This is entirely different from the observation of a mind, which, having formed a theory and a system upon its own nature, remarks all things that are examples of its truth, confirming it in that truth, and, above all, enabling it to convey the truths of philosophy, as mere effects derived from, what we may call, the outward watchings of life.

Hence it is that Shakespeare's favourite characters are full of such lively intellect. Mercutio is a man possessing all the elements of a poet: the whole world was, as it were, subject to his law of association. Whenever he wishes to impress anything, all things become his servants for the purpose: all things tell the same tale, and sound in unison. This faculty, moreover, is combined with the manners and feelings of a perfect gentleman, himself utterly unconscious of his powers. By his loss it was contrived that the whole catastrophe of the tragedy should be brought about: it endears him to Romeo, and gives to the death of Mercutio an importance which it could not otherwise have acquired.

I say this in answer to an observation, I think by Dryden, (to which indeed Dr. Johnson has fully replied) that Shakespeare having carried the part of Mercutio as far as he could, till his genius was exhausted, had killed him in the third Act, to get him out of the way. What shallow nonesense! As I have remarked, upon the death of Mercutio the whole catastrophe depends; it is produced by it. The scene in which it occurs serves to show how indifference to any subject but one, and aversion to activity on the part of Romeo, may be overcome and roused to the most resolute and determined conduct. Had not Mercutio been rendered so amiable and so interesting, we could not have felt so strongly the necessity for Romeo's interference, connecting it immediately, and passionately, with the future fortunes of the lover and his mistress.

But what am I to say of the Nurse? We have been told that her character is the mere fruit of observation—that it is like Swift's "Polite Conversation," certainly the most stupendous work of human memory, and of unceasingly active attention to what passes around us, upon record. The Nurse in "Romeo and Juliet" has sometimes been compared to a portrait by Gerard Dow, in which every hair was so exquisitely painted, that it would bear the test of the microscope. Now, I appeal confidently to my hearers whether the closest observation of the manners of one or two old nurses would have enabled Shakespeare to draw this character of admirable generalisation? Surely not. Let any man conjure up in his mind all the qualities and peculiarities that can possibly belong to a nurse, and he will find them in Shakespeare's picture of the old woman: nothing is omitted. This effect is not produced by mere observation. The great prerogative of genius (and Shakespeare felt and availed himself of it) is now to swell itself to the dignity of a god, and now to subdue and keep dormant some part of that lofty nature, and to descend even to the lowest character—to become everything, in fact, but the vicious.

Thus, in the Nurse you have all the garrulity of old age, and all its fondness; for the affection of old age is one of the greatest consolations of humanity. I have often thought what a melancholy world this would be without children, and what an inhuman world without the aged.

You have also in the Nurse the arrogance of ignorance, with the pride of meanness at being connected with a great family. You have the grossness, too, which that situation never removes, though it sometimes suspends it; and, arising from that grossness, the little low vices attendant upon it, which, indeed, in such minds are scarcely vices.—Romeo at one time was the most delightful and excellent young man, and the Nurse all willingness to assist him; but her disposition soon turns in favour of Paris, for whom she professes precisely the same admiration. How wonderfully are these low peculiarities contrasted with a young and pure mind, educated under different circumstances!

Another point ought to be mentioned as characteristic of the ignorance of the Nurse:—it is, that in all her recollections, she assists herself by the remembrance of visual circumstances. The great difference, in this respect, between the cultivated and the uncultivated mind is this—that the cultivated mind will be found to recal the past by certain regular trains of cause and effect; whereas, with the uncultivated mind, the past is recalled wholly by coincident images, or facts which happened at the same time. This position is fully exemplified in the following passages put into the mouth of the Nurse:—

> Even or odd, of all days in the year,
> Come Lammas eve at night shall she be fourteen.
> Susan and she—God rest all Christian souls!—
> Were of an age.—Well, Susan is with God;
> She was too good for me. But, as I said,
> On Lammas eve at night shall she be fourteen;
> That shall she, marry: I remember it well.
> 'Tis since the earthquake now eleven years;
> And she was wean'd,—I never shall forget it,—
> Of all the days of the year, upon that day;
> For I had then laid wormwood to my dug,
> Sitting in the sun under the dove-house wall:
> My lord and you were then at Mantua.—
> Nay, I do bear a brain:—but, as I said,
> When it did taste the wormwood on the nipple
> Of my dug, and felt it bitter, pretty fool,
> To see it tetchy, and fall out with the dug!

> Shake, quoth the dove-house: 'twas no need, I trow,
> To bid me trudge.
> And since that time it is eleven years;
> For then she could stand alone.
> *Act I., Scene 3.*

She afterwards goes on with similar visual impressions, so true to the character.—More is here brought into one portrait than could have been ascertained by one man's mere observation, and without the introduction of a single incongruous point.

I honour, I love, the works of Fielding as much, or perhaps more, than those of any other writer of fiction of that kind: take Fielding in his characters of postillions, landlords, and landladies, waiters, or indeed, of any-body who had come before his eye, and nothing can be more true, more happy, or more humorous; but in all his chief personages, Tom Jones for instance, where Fielding was not directed by observation, where he could not assist himself by the close copying of what he saw, where it is necessary that something should take place, some words be spoken, or some object described, which he could not have witnessed, (his soliloquies for example, or the interview between the hero and Sophia Western before the reconciliation) and I will venture to say, loving and honouring the man and his productions as I do, that nothing can be more forced and unnatural: the language is without vivacity or spirit, the whole matter is incongruous, and totally destitute of psychological truth.

On the other hand, look at Shakespeare: where can any character be produced that does not speak the language of nature? where does he not put into the mouths of his *dramatis personæ*, be they high or low, Kings or Constables, precisely what they must have said? Where, from observation, could he learn the language proper to Sovereigns, Queens, Noblemen or Generals? yet he invariably uses it.—Where, from observation, could he have learned such lines as these, which are put into the mouth of Othello, when he is talking to Iago of Brabantio?

> Let him do his spite:
> My services, which I have done the signiory,
> Shall out-tongue his complaints. 'Tis yet to know,
> Which, when I know that boasting is an honour,
> I shall promulgate, I fetch my life and being
> From men of royal siege; and my demerits
> May speak, unbonneted, to as proud a fortune
> As this that I have reach'd: for know, Iago,
> But that I love the gentle Desdemona,
> I would not my unhoused free condition
> Put into circumscription and confine
> For the sea's worth.
> *Act I., Scene 2.*

I ask where was Shakespeare to observe such language as this? If he did observe it, it was with the inward eye of meditation upon his own nature: for the time, he became Othello, and spoke as Othello, in such circumstances, must have spoken.

Another remark I may make upon "Romeo and Juliet" is, that in this tragedy the poet is not, as I have hinted, entirely blended with the dramatist,— at least, not in the degree to be afterwards noticed in "Lear," "Hamlet," "Othello," or "Macbeth." Capulet and Montague not unfrequently talk a language only belonging to the poet, and not so characteristic of, and peculiar to, the passions of persons in the situations in which they are placed—a mistake, or rather an indistinctness, which many of our later dramatists have carried through the whole of their productions.

When I read the song of Deborah, I never think that she is a poet, although I think the song itself a sublime poem: it is as simple a dithyrambic production as exists in any language; but it is the proper and characteristic effusion of a woman highly elevated by triumph, by the natural hatred of oppressors, and resulting from a bitter sense of wrong: it is a song of exultation on deliverance from these evils, a deliverance accomplished by herself. When she exclaims, "The inhabitants of the villages ceased, they ceased in Israel, until that I, Deborah, arose, that I arose a mother in Israel," it is poetry in the highest sense: we have no reason, however, to suppose that if she had not been agitated by passion, and animated by victory, she would have been able so to express herself; or that if she had been placed in different circumstances, she would have used such language of truth and passion. We are to remember that Shakespeare, not placed under circumstances of excitement, and only wrought upon by his own vivid and vigorous imagination, writes a language that invariably, and intuitively becomes the condition and position of each character.

On the other hand, there is a language not descriptive of passion, not uttered under the influence of it, which is at the same time poetic, and shows a high and active fancy, as when Capulet says to Paris,—

> Such comfort as do lusty young men feel,
> When well-apparell'd April on the heel
> Of limping winter treads, even such delight
> Among fresh female buds, shall you this night
> Inherit at my house.
>
> *Act I., Scene 2.*

Here the poet may be said to speak, rather than the dramatist; and it would be easy to adduce other passages from this play, where Shakespeare, for a moment forgetting the character, utters his own words in his own person.

In my mind, what have often been censured as Shakespeare's conceits are completely justifiable, as belonging to the state, age, or feeling of the individual. Sometimes, when they cannot be vindicated on these grounds, they may well be excused by the taste of his own and of the preceding age; as for instance, in Romeo's speech,

> Here's much to do with hate, but more with love:—
> Why then, O brawling love! O loving hate!
> O anything, of nothing first created!
> O heavy lightness! serious vanity!
> Misshapen chaos of well-seeming forms!
> Feather of lead, bright smoke, cold fire, sick health!
> Still-waking sleep, that is not what it is!
> *Act I., Scene 1.*

I dare not pronounce such passages as these to be absolutely unnatural, not merely because I consider the author a much better judge than I can be, but because I can understand and allow for an effort of the mind, when it would describe what it cannot satisfy itself with the description of, to reconcile opposites and qualify contradictions, leaving a middle state of mind more strictly appropriate to the imagination than any other, when it is, as it were, hovering between images. As soon as it is fixed on one image, it becomes understanding; but while it is unfixed and wavering between them, attaching itself permanently to none, it is imagination. Such is the fine description of Death in Milton:—

> The other shape,
> If shape it might be call'd, that shape had none
> Distinguishable in member, joint, or limb,
> Or substance might be call'd, that shadow seem'd,
> For each seem'd either: black it stood as night;
> Fierce as ten furies, terrible as hell,
> And shook a dreadful dart: what seem'd his head
> The likeness of a kingly crown had on.
> *Paradise Lost,* Book II.

The grandest efforts of poetry are where the imagination is called forth, not to produce a distinct form, but a strong working of the mind, still offering what is still repelled, and again creating what is again rejected; the result being what the poet wishes to impress, namely, the substitution of a sublime feeling of the unimaginable for a mere image. I have sometimes thought that the passage just read might be quoted as exhibiting the narrow limit of painting, as compared with the boundless power of poetry: painting cannot go beyond a certain point; poetry rejects all control, all confinement. Yet we know that sundry painters have attempted pictures of the meeting between Satan and Death at the gates of Hell; and how was Death represented? Not as Milton has described him, but by the most defined thing that can be imagined—a skeleton, the dryest and hardest image that it is possible to discover; which, instead of keeping the mind in a state of activity, reduces it to the merest passivity,—an image, compared with which a square, a triangle, or any other mathematical figure, is a luxuriant fancy.

It is a general but mistaken notion that, because some forms of writing, and some combinations of thought, are not usual, they are not natural; but we are to recollect that the dramatist represents his characters in every situation of life and in every state of mind, and there is no form of language that may not be introduced with effect by a great and judicious poet, and yet be most strictly according to nature. Take punning, for instance, which may be the lowest, but at all events is the most harmless, kind of wit, because it never excites envy. A pun may be a necessary consequence of association: one man, attempting to prove something that was resisted by another, might when agitated by strong feeling, employ a term used by his adversary with a directly contrary meaning to that for which that adversary had resorted to it: it might come into his mind as one way, and sometimes the best, of replying to that adversary. This form of speech is generally produced by a mixture of anger and contempt, and punning is a natural mode of expressing them.

It is my intention to pass over none of the important so-called conceits of Shakespeare, not a few of which are introduced into his later productions with great propriety and effect. We are not to forget, that at the time he lived there was an attempt at, and an affectation of, quaintness and adornment, which emanated from the Court, and against which satire was directed by Shakespeare in the character of Osrick in Hamlet. Among the schoolmen of that age, and earlier, nothing was more common than the use of conceits: it began with the revival of letters, and the bias thus given was very generally felt and acknowledged.

I have in my possession a dictionary of phrases, in which the epithets applied to love, hate, jealousy, and such abstract terms, are arranged; and they consist almost entirely of words taken from Seneca and his imitators, or from the schoolmen, showing perpetual antithesis, and describing the passions by the conjunction and combination of things absolutely irreconcileable. In treating the matter thus, I am aware that I am only palliating the practice in Shakespeare: he ought to have had nothing to do with merely temporary peculiarities: he wrote not for his own only, but for all ages, and so far I admit the use of some of his conceits to be a defect. They detract sometimes from his universality as to time, person, and situation.

If we were able to discover, and to point out the peculiar faults, as well as the peculiar beauties of Shakespeare, it would materially assist us in deciding what authority ought to be attached to certain portions of what are generally called his works. If we met with a play, or certain scenes of a play, in which we could trace neither his defects nor his excellences, we should have the strongest reason for believing that he had had no hand in it. In the case of scenes so circumstanced we might come to the conclusion that they were taken from the older plays, which, in some instances, he reformed or altered, or that they were inserted afterwards by some underhand, in order to please the mob. If a drama by Shakespeare turned out to be too heavy for popular audiences, the clown might be called in to lighten the representation; and if it appeared that what was added was not in Shakespeare's manner, the conclusion would be inevitable, that it was not from Shakespeare's pen.

It remains for me to speak of the hero and heroine, of Romeo and Juliet themselves; and I shall do so with unaffected diffidence, not merely on account of the delicacy, but of the great importance of the subject. I feel that it is impossible to defend Shakespeare from the most cruel of all charges,—that he is an immoral writer—without entering fully into his mode of pourtraying female characters, and of displaying the passion of love. It seems to me, that he has done both with greater perfection than any other writer of the known world, perhaps with the single exception of Milton in his delineation of Eve.

When I have heard it said, or seen it stated, that Shakespeare wrote for man, but the gentle Fletcher for woman, it has always given me something like acute pain, because to me it seems to do the greatest injustice to Shakespeare: when, too, I remember how much character is formed by what we read, I cannot look upon it as a light question, to be passed over as a mere amusement, like a game of cards or chess. I never have been able to tame down my mind to think poetry a sport, or an occupation for idle hours.

Perhaps there is no more sure criterion of refinement in moral character, of the purity of intellectual intention, and of the deep conviction and perfect sense of what our own nature really is in all its combinations, than the different definitions different men would give of love. I will not detain you by stating the various known definitions, some of which it may be better not to repeat: I will rather give you one of my own, which, I apprehend, is equally free from the extravagance of pretended Platonism (which, like other things which super-moralise, is sure to demoralise) and from its grosser opposite.

Consider myself and my fellow-men as a sort of link between heaven and earth, being composed of body and soul, with power to reason and to will, and with that perpetual aspiration which tells us that this is ours for a while, but it is not ourselves; considering man, I say, in this two-fold character, yet united in one person, I conceive that there can be no correct definition of love which does not correspond with our being, and with that subordination of one part to another which constitutes our perfection. I would say therefore that—

"Love is a desire of the whole being to be united to some thing, or some being, felt necessary to its completeness, by the most perfect means that nature permits, and reason dictates."

It is inevitable to every noble mind, whether man or woman, to feel itself, of itself, imperfect and insufficient, not as an animal only, but as a moral being. How wonderfully, then, has Providence contrived for us, by making that which is necessary to us a step in our exaltation to a higher and nobler state! The Creator has ordained that one should possess qualities which the other has not, and the union of both is the most complete ideal of human character. In everything the blending of the similar with the dissimilar is the secret of all pure delight. Who shall dare to stand alone, and vaunt himself, in himself, sufficient? In poetry it is the blending of passion with order that constitutes perfection: this is still more the case in morals, and more than all in the exclusive attachment of the sexes.

True it is, that the world and its business may be carried on without marriage; but it is so evident that Providence intended man (the only animal of all climates, and whose reason is preeminent over instinct) to be the master of the world, that marriage, or the knitting together of society by the tenderest, yet firmest ties, seems ordained to render him capable of maintaining his superiority over the brute creation. Man alone has been privileged to clothe himself, and to do all things so as to make him, as it were, a secondary creator of himself, and of his own happiness or misery: in this, as in all, the image of the Deity is impressed upon him.

Providence, then, has not left us to prudence only; for the power of calculation, which prudence implies, cannot have existed, but in a state which pre-supposes marriage. If God has done this, shall we suppose that he has given us no moral sense, no yearning, which is something more than animal, to secure that, without which man might form a herd, but could not be a society? The very idea seems to breathe absurdity.

From this union arise the paternal, filial, brotherly and sisterly relations of life; and every state is but a family magnified. All the operations of mind, in short, all that distinguishes us from brutes, originate in the more perfect state of domestic life.—One infallible criterion in forming an opinion of a man is the reverence in which he holds women. Plato has said, that in this way we rise from sensuality to affection, from affection to love, and from love to the pure intellectual delight by which we become worthy to conceive that infinite in ourselves, without which it is impossible for man to believe in a God. In a word, the grandest and most delightful of all promises has been expressed to us by this practical state—our marriage with the Redeemer of mankind.

I might safely appeal to every man who hears me, who in youth has been accustomed to abandon himself to his animal passions, whether when he first really fell in love, the earliest symptom was not a complete change in his manners, a contempt and a hatred of himself for having excused his conduct by asserting, that he acted according to the dictates of nature, that his vices were the inevitable consequences of youth, and that his passions at that period of life could not be conquered? The surest friend of chastity is love: it leads us, not to sink the mind in the body, but to draw up the body to the mind—the immortal part of our nature. See how contrasted in this respect are some portions of the works of writers, whom I need not name, with other portions of the same works: the ebullitions of comic humour have at times, by a lamentable confusion, been made the means of debasing our nature, while at other times, even in the same volume, we are happy to notice the utmost purity, such as the purity of love, which above all other qualities renders us most pure and lovely.

Love is not, like hunger, a mere selfish appetite: it is an associative quality. The hungry savage is nothing but an animal, thinking only of the satisfaction of his stomach: what is the first effect of love, but to associate the feeling with every object in nature? the trees whisper, the roses exhale their perfumes, the nightingales sing, nay the very skies smile in unison with the feeling of true and pure love. It gives to every object in nature a power of the heart, without which it would indeed be spiritless.

Shakespeare has described this passion in various states and stages, beginning, as was most natural, with love in the young. Does he open his play by making Romeo and Juliet in love at first sight—at the first glimpse, as any ordinary thinker would do? Certainly not: he knew what he was about, and how he was to accomplish what he was about: he was to develope the whole passion, and he commences with the first elements—that sense of imperfection, that yearning to combine itself with something lovely. Romeo became enamoured of the idea he had formed in his own mind, and then, as it were, christened the first real being of the contrary sex as endowed with the perfections he desired. He appears to be in love with Rosaline; but, in truth, he is in love only with his own idea. He felt that necessity of being beloved which no noble mind can be without. Then our poet, our poet who so well knew human nature, introduces Romeo to Juliet, and makes it not only a violent, but a permanent love—a point for which Shakespeare has been ridiculed by the ignorant and unthinking. Romeo is first represented in a state most susceptible of love, and then, seeing Juliet, he took and retained the infection.

This brings me to observe upon a characteristic of Shakespeare, which belongs to a man of profound thought and high genius. It has been too much the custom, when anything that happened in his dramas could not easily be explained by the few words the poet has employed, to pass it idly over, and to say that it is beyond our reach, and beyond the power of philosophy—a sort of terra incognita for discoverers—a great ocean to be hereafter explored. Others have treated such passages as hints and glimpses of something now nonexistent, as the sacred fragments of an ancient and ruined temple, all the portions of which are beautiful, although their particular relation to each other is unknown. Shakespeare knew the human mind, and its most minute and intimate workings, and he never introduces a word, or a thought, in vain or out of place: if we do not understand him, it is our own fault or the fault of copyists and typographers; but study, and the possession of some small stock of the knowledge by which he worked, will enable us often to detect and explain his meaning. He never wrote at random, or hit upon points of character and conduct by chance; and the smallest fragment of his mind not unfrequently gives a clue to a most perfect, regular, and consistent whole.

As I may not have another opportunity, the introduction of Friar Laurence into this tragedy enables me to remark upon the different manner in which Shakespeare has treated the priestly character, as compared with other writers. In Beaumont and Fletcher priests are represented as a vulgar mockery; and, as in others of their dramatic personages, the errors of a few are mistaken for the demeanour of the many: but in Shakespeare they always carry with them our love and respect. He made no injurious abstracts: he took no copies from the worst parts of our nature; and, like the rest, his characters of priests are truly drawn from the general body.

It may strike some as singular, that throughout all his productions he has never introduced the passion of avarice. The truth is, that it belongs only to particular parts of our nature, and is prevalent only in particular states of society; hence it could not, and cannot, be permanent. The Miser of Molière and Plautus is now looked upon as a species of madman, and avarice as a species of madness. Elwes, of whom everybody has heard, was an individual influenced by an insane condition of mind; but, as a passion, avarice has disappeared. How admirably, then, did Shakespeare foresee, that if he drew such a character it could not be permanent! he drew characters which would always be natural, and therefore permanent, inasmuch as they were not dependent upon accidental circumstances.

There is not one of the plays of Shakespeare that is built upon anything but the best and surest foundation; the characters must be permanent—permanent while men continue men,—because they stand upon what is absolutely necessary to our existence. This cannot be said even of some of the most famous authors of antiquity. Take the capital tragedies of Orestes, or of the husband of Jocasta: great as was the genius of the writers, these dramas have an obvious fault, and the fault lies at the very root of the action. In Œdipus a man is represented oppressed by fate for a crime of which he was not morally guilty; and while we read we are obliged to say to ourselves, that in those days they considered actions without reference to the real guilt of the persons.

There is no character in Shakespeare in which envy is pourtrayed, with one solitary exception—Cassius, in "Julius Cæsar"; yet even there the vice is not hateful, inasmuch as it is counter-balanced by a number of excellent qualities and virtues. The poet leads the reader to suppose that it is rather something constitutional, something derived from his parents, something that he cannot avoid, and not something that he has himself acquired; thus throwing the blame from the will of man to some inevitable circumstance, and leading us to suppose that it is hardly to be looked upon as one of those passions that actually debase the mind.

Whenever love is described as of a serious nature, and much more when it is to lead to a tragical result, it depends upon a law of the mind, which, I believe, I shall hereafter be able to make intelligible, and which would not only justify Shakespeare, but show an analogy to all his other characters.

HAMLET

The seeming inconsistencies in the conduct and character of Hamlet have long exercised the conjectural ingenuity of critics; and, as we are always loth to suppose that the cause of defective apprehension is in ourselves, the mystery has been too commonly explained by the very easy process of setting it down as in fact inexplicable, and by resolving the phenomenon into a misgrowth or *lusus* of the capricious and irregular genius of Shakespeare. The shallow and stupid arrogance of these vulgar and indolent decisions I would fain do my best to expose. I believe the character of Hamlet may be traced to Shakespeare's deep and accurate science in mental philosophy. Indeed, that this character must have some connection with the common fundamental laws of our nature may be assumed from the fact, that Hamlet has been the darling of every country in which the literature of England has been fostered. In order to understand him, it is essential that we should reflect on the constitution of our own minds. Man is distinguished from the brute animals in proportion as thought prevails over sense: but in the healthy processes of the mind, a balance is constantly maintained between the impressions from outward objects and the inward operations of the intellect:—for if there be an overbalance in the contemplative faculty, man thereby becomes the creature of mere meditation, and loses his natural power of action. Now one of Shakespeare's modes of creating characters is, to conceive any one intellectual or moral faculty in morbid excess, and then to place himself, Shakespeare, thus mutilated or diseased, under given circumstances. In Hamlet he seems to have wished to exemplify the moral necessity of a due balance between our attention to the objects of our senses, and our meditation on the workings of our minds,—an *equilibrium* between the real and the imaginary worlds. In Hamlet this balance is disturbed: his thoughts, and the images of his fancy, are far more vivid than his actual perceptions, and his very perceptions, instantly passing through the *medium* of his contemplations, acquire, as they pass, a form and a color not naturally their own. Hence we see a great, an almost enormous, intellectual activity, and a proportionate aversion to real action, consequent upon it, with all its symptoms and accompanying qualities. This character Shakespeare places in circumstances, under which it is obliged to act on the spur of the moment:—Hamlet is brave and careless of death; but he vacillates from sensibility, and procrastinates from thought, and loses the power of action in the energy of resolve. Thus it is that this tragedy presents a direct contrast to that of Macbeth; the one proceeds with the utmost slowness, the other with a crowded and breathless rapidity.

The effect of this overbalance of the imaginative power is beautifully illustrated in the everlasting broodings and superfluous activities of Hamlet's mind, which, unseated from its healthy relation, is constantly occupied with the world within, and abstracted from the world without,—giving substance to shadows, and throwing a mist over all common-place actualities. It is the nature of thought to be indefinite;—definiteness belongs to external imagery alone. Hence it is that the sense of sublimity arises, not from the sight of an outward object, but from the beholder's reflection upon it;—not from the sensuous impression, but from the imaginative reflex. Few have seen a celebrated waterfall without feeling something akin to disappointment: it is only subsequently that the image comes back full into the mind, and brings with it a train of grand or beautiful associations. Hamlet feels this; his senses are in a state of trance, and he looks upon external things as hieroglyphics. His soliloquy—

Oh! that this too, too solid flesh would melt, &c.

springs from that craving after the indefinite—for that which is not—which most easily besets men of genius; and the self-delusion common to this temper of mind is finely exemplified in the character which Hamlet gives of himself:—

It can not be
But I am pigeon-livered, and lack gall
To make oppression bitter.

He mistakes the seeing his chains for the breaking of them, delays action till action is of no use, and dies the victim of mere circumstance and accident.

There is a great significancy in the names of Shakespeare's plays. In the Twelfth Night, Midsummer Night's Dream, As You Like It, and Winter's Tale, the total effect is produced by a co-ordination of the characters as in a wreath of flowers. But in Coriolanus, Lear, Romeo and Juliet, Hamlet, Othello, &c., the effect arises from the subordination of all to one, either as the prominent person, or the principal object. Cymbeline is the only exception; and even that has its advantages in preparing the audience for the chaos of time, place, and costume, by throwing the date back into a fabulous king's reign.

But as of more importance, so more striking, is the judgment displayed by our truly dramatic poet, as well as poet of the drama, in the management of his first scenes. With the single exception of Cymbeline, they either place before us at one glance both the past and the future in some effect, which implies the continuance and full agency of its cause, as in the feuds and party-spirit of the servants of the two houses in the first scene of Romeo and Juliet; or in the degrading passion for shows and public spectacles, and the overwhelming attachment for the newest successful war-chief in the Roman people, already become a populace, contrasted with the jealousy of the nobles in Julius Cæsar;—or they at once commence the action so as to excite a curiosity for the explanation in the following scenes, as in the storm of wind and waves, and the boatswain in the Tempest, instead of anticipating our curiosity, as in most other first scenes, and in too many other first acts;—or they act, by contrast of diction suited to the characters, at once to heighten the effect, and yet to give a naturalness to the language and rhythm of the principal personages, either as that of Prospero and Miranda by the appropriate lowness of the style,—or as in King John, by the equally appropriate stateliness of official harangues or nar-ratives, so that the after blank verse seems to belong to the rank and quality of the speakers, and not to the poet;—or they strike at once the key-note, and give the predominant spirit of the play, as in the Twelfth Night and in Macbeth;—or finally, the first scene comprises all these advantages at once, as in Hamlet.

Compare the easy language of common life, in which this drama com-mences, with the direful music and wild wayward rhythm and abrupt lyrics of the opening of Macbeth. The tone is quite familiar;—there is no poetic description of night, no elaborate information conveyed by one speaker to another of what both had immediately before their senses—(such as the first distich in Addison's Cato, which is a translation into poetry of 'Past four o'clock and a dark morning!');—and yet nothing bordering on the comic on the one hand, nor any striving of the intellect on the other. It is precisely the language of sensation among men who feared no charge of effeminacy for feeling what they had no want of resolution to bear. Yet the armor, the dead silence, the watchfulness that first interrupts it, the welcome relief of the guard, the cold, the broken expressions of compelled attention to bodily feelings still under control—all excellently accord with, and prepare for, the after gradual rise into tragedy;—but, above all, into a tragedy, the interest of which is as eminently *ad et apud intra*, as that of Macbeth is directly *ad extra*.

In all the best attested stories of ghosts and visions, as in that of Brutus, of Archbishop Cranmer, that of Benvenuto Cellini recorded by himself, and the vision of Galileo communicated by him to his favorite pupil Torricelli, the ghost-seers were in a state of cold or chilling damp from without, and of anxiety inwardly. It has been with all of them as with Francisco on his guard,—alone, in the depth and silence of the night;—'twas bitter cold, and they were sick at heart, and *not a mouse stirring.*' The attention to minute sounds,—naturally associated with the recollection of minute objects, and the more familiar and trifling, the more impressive from the unusualness of their producing any impression at all—gives a philosophic pertinency to this last image; but it has likewise its dramatic use and purpose. For its commonness in ordinary conversation tends to produce the sense of reality, and at once hides the poet, and yet approximates the reader or spectator to that state in which the highest poetry will appear, and in its component parts, though not in the whole composition, really is, the language of nature. If I should not speak it, I feel that I should be thinking it;—the voice only is the poet's,—the words are my own. That Shakespeare meant to put an effect in the actor's power in the very first words—'Who's there?'—is evident from the impatience expressed by the startled Francisco in the words that follow—'Nay, answer me: stand and unfold yourself.' A brave man is never so peremptory, as when he fears that he is afraid. Observe the gradual transition from the silence and the still recent habit of listening in Francisco's—'I think I hear them'—to the more cheerful call out, which a good actor would observe, in the—'Stand ho! Who is there?' Bernardo's inquiry after Horatio, and the repetition of his name and in his own presence indicate a respect or an eagerness that implies him as one of the persons who are in the foreground; and the skepticism attributed to him,—

> Horatio says, 'tis but our fantasy;
> And will not let belief take hold of him—

prepares us for Hamlet's after-eulogy on him as one whose blood and judgment were happily commingled. The actor should also be careful to distinguish the expectation and gladness of Bernardo's 'Welcome, Horatio!' from the mere courtesy of his 'Welcome, good Marcellus!'

Now observe the admirable indefiniteness of the first opening out of the occasion of all this anxiety. The preparation informative of the audience is just as much as was precisely necessary, and no more;—it begins with the uncertainty appertaining to a question:—

> *Mar.* What! has *this thing* appeared again to-night?—

Even the word 'again' has its *credibilizing* effect. Then Horatio, the representative of the ignorance of the audience, not himself, but by Marcellus to Bernardo, anticipates the common solution—''tis but our fantasy!' upon which Marcellus rises into

> This dreaded sight, twice seen of us—

which immediately afterwards becomes 'this apparition,' and that, too, an intelligent spirit, that is, to be spoken to! Then comes the confirmation of Horatio's disbelief;—

Tush! tush! 'twill not appear!—

and the silence, with which the scene opened, is again restored in the shivering feeling of Horatio sitting down, at such a time, and with the two eye-witnesses, to hear a story of a ghost, and that, too, of a ghost which had appeared twice before at the very same hour. In the deep feeling which Bernardo has of the solemn nature of what he is about to relate, he makes an effort to master his own imaginative terrors by an elevation of style,—itself a continuation of the effort,—and by turning off from the apparition, as from something which would force him too deeply into himself, to the outward objects, the realities of nature, which had accompanied it:—

> *Ber.* Last night of all,
> When yon same star, that's westward from the pole,
> Had made his course to illume that part of heaven
> Where now it burns, Marcellus and myself,
> The bell then beating one—

This passage seems to contradict the critical law that what is told, makes a faint impression compared with what is beholden; for it does indeed convey to the mind more than the eye can see; whilst the interruption of the narrative at the very moment when we are most intensely listening for the sequel, and have our thoughts diverted from the dreaded sight in expectation of the desired, yet almost dreaded, tale—this gives all the suddenness and surprise of the original appearance;—

> *Mar.* Peace, break thee off; look, where it comes again!—

Note the judgment displayed in having the two persons present, who, as having seen the Ghost before, are naturally eager in confirming their former opinions,—whilst the skeptic is silent, and after having been twice addressed by his friends, answers with two hasty syllables—'Most like,'—and a confession of horror:—

> It harrows me with fear and wonder.

O heaven! words are wasted on those who feel, and to those who do not feel the exquisite judgment of Shakespeare in this scene, what can be said?—Hume himself could not but have had faith in this Ghost dramatically, let his anti-ghostism have been as strong as Samson against other ghosts less powerfully raised.
Act i. sc. 1.

> *Mar.* Good now, sit down, and tell me, he that knows
> Why this same strict and most observant watch, &c.

How delightfully natural is the transition to the retrospective narrative! And observe, upon the Ghost's reappearance, how much Horatio's courage is increased by having translated the late individual spectator into general thought and past experience,—and the sympathy of Marcellus and Bernardo with his patriotic surmises in daring to strike at the Ghost; whilst in a moment, upon its vanishing the former solemn awe-stricken feeling returns upon them:—

> We do it wrong, being so majestical,
> To offer it the show of violence.—

Ib. Horatio's speech:—

> I have heard,
> The cock, that is the trumpet to the morn,
> Doth with his lofty and shrill sounding throat
> Awake the god of day, &c.

No Addison could be more careful to be poetical in diction than Shakespeare in providing the grounds and sources of its propriety. But how to elevate a thing almost mean by its familiarity, young poets may learn in this treatment of the cock-crow.

Ib. Horatio's speech:—

> And, by my advice,
> Let us impart what we have seen to-night
> Unto young Hamlet; for, upon my life,
> The spirit, dumb to us, will speak to him.

Note the unobtrusive and yet fully adequate mode of introducing the main character, 'young Hamlet,' upon whom is transferred all the interest excited for the acts and concerns of the king his father.

Ib. sc. 2. The audience are now relieved by a change of scene to the royal court, in order that Hamlet may not have to take up the leavings of exhaustion. In the king's speech, observe the set and pedantically antithetic form of the sentences when touching that which galled the heels of conscience,—the strain of undignified rhetoric,—and yet in what follows concerning the public weal, a certain appropriate majesty. Indeed was he not a royal brother?—

Ib. King's speech:—

> And now, Laertes, what's the news with you? &c.

Thus with great art Shakespeare introduces a most important, but still subordinate character first, Laertes, who is yet thus graciously treated in consequence of the assistance given to the election of the late king's brother instead of his son by Polonius.

Ib.

> *Ham.* A little more than kin, and less than kind.
> *King.* How is it that the clouds still hang on you?
> *Ham.* Not so, my lord, I am too much i' the sun.

Hamlet opens his mouth with a playing on words, the complete absence of which throughout characterizes Macbeth. This playing on words may be attributed to many causes or motives, as either to an exuberant activity of mind, as in the higher comedy of Shakespeare generally;—or to an imitation of it as a mere fashion, as if it were said—'Is not this better than groaning?'—or to a contemptuous exultation in minds vulgarized and overset by their success, as in the poetic instance of Milton's Devils in the battle;—or it is the language of resentment, as is familiar to every one who has witnessed the quarrels of the lower orders, where there is invariably a profusion of punning invective, whence, perhaps, nicknames have in a considerable degree sprung up;—or it is the language of suppressed passion, and especially of a hardly smothered personal dislike. The first and last of these combine in Hamlet's case; and I have little doubt that Farmer is right in supposing the equivocation carried on in the expression 'too much i' the sun,' or son.

Ib.

> *Ham.* Ay, madam, it is common.

Here observe Hamlet's delicacy to his mother, and how the suppression prepares him for the overflow in the next speech, in which his character is more developed by bringing forward his aversion to externals, and which betrays his habit of brooding over the world within him, coupled with a prodigality of beautiful words, which are the half-embodyings of thought, and are more than thought, and have an outness, a reality *sui generis,* and yet contain their correspondence and shadowy affinity to the images and movements within. Note also Hamlet's silence to the long speech of the king which follows, and his respectful, but general, answer to his mother.

Ib. Hamlet's first soliloquy:—

> O, that this too too solid flesh would melt,
> Thaw, and resolve itself into a dew! &c.

This *tædium vitæ* is a common oppression on minds cast in the Hamlet mould, and is caused by disproportionate mental exertion, which necessitates exhaustion of bodily feeling. Where there is a just coincidence of external and internal action, pleasure is always the result; but where the former is deficient, and the mind's appetency of the ideal is unchecked, realities will seem cold and unmoving. In such cases, passion combines itself with the indefinite alone. In this mood of his mind the relation of the appearance of his father's spirit in arms is made all at once to Hamlet:—it is—Horatio's speech, in particular—a perfect model of the true style of dramatic narrative;—the purest poetry, and yet in the most natural language, equally remote from the inkhorn and the plough.

Ib. sc. 3. This scene must be regarded as one of Shakespeare's lyric movements in the play, and the skill with which it is interwoven with the dramatic parts is peculiarly an excellence of our poet. You experience the sensation of a pause without the sense of a stop. You will observe in Ophelia's short and general answer to the long speech of Laertes the natural careless-ness of innocence, which can not think such a code of cautions and prudences necessary to its own preservation.

Ib. Speech of Polonius:—(in Stockdale's edition.)

> Or (not to crack the wind of the poor phrase)
> Wronging it thus, you'll tender me a fool.

I suspect this 'wronging' is here used much in the same sense as 'wringing' or 'wrenching;' and that the parenthesis should be extended to 'thus.'

Ib. Speech of Polonius:—

> How prodigal the soul
> Lends the tongue vows:—these blazes, daughter, &c.

A spondee has, I doubt not, dropped out of the text. Either insert 'Go to' after 'vows;'—

> Lends the tongue vows: Go to, these blazes, daughter—

or read

> Lends the tongue vows:—These blazes, daughter, mark you—

Shakespeare never introduces a catalectic line without intending an equiva-lent to the foot omitted in the pauses, or the dwelling emphasis, or the diffused retardation. I do not, however, deny that a good actor might by employing the last-mentioned means, namely, the retardation, or solemn knowing drawl, supply the missing spondee with good effect. But I do not believe that in this or any other of the foregoing speeches of Polonius, Shakespeare meant to bring out the senility or weakness of that personage's mind. In the great ever-recurring dangers and duties of life, where to distinguish the fit objects for the application of the maxims collected by the experience of a long life, requires no fineness of tact, as in the admonitions to his son and daughter, Polonius is uniformly made respectable. But if an actor were even capable of catching these shades in the character, the pit and the gallery would be malcontent at their exhibition. It is to Hamlet that Polonius is, and is meant to be, contemptible, because in inwardness and uncontrollable activity of movement, Hamlet's mind is the logical contrary to that of Polonius, and besides, as I have observed before, Hamlet dislikes the man as false to his true allegiance in the matter of the succession to the crown.

Ib. sc. 4. The unimportant conversation with which this scene opens is a proof of Shakespeare's minute knowledge of human nature. It is a well-established fact, that on the brink of any serious enterprise, or event of moment, men almost invariably endeavor to elude the pressure of their own thoughts by turning aside to trivial objects and familiar circumstances: thus this dialogue on the platform begins with remarks on the coldness of the air, and inquiries, obliquely connected, indeed, with the expected hour of the visitation, but thrown out in a seeming vacuity of topics, as to the striking of the clock and so forth. The same desire to escape from the impending thought is carried on in Hamlet's account of, and moralizing on, the Danish custom of wassailing: he runs off from the particular to the universal, and in his repugnance to personal and individual concerns, escapes, as it were, from himself in generalizations, and smothers the impatience and uneasy feelings of the moment in abstract reasoning. Besides this, another purpose is answered;—for by thus entangling the attention of the audience in the nice distinctions and parenthetical sentences of this speech of Hamlet's, Shakespeare takes them completely by surprise on the appearance of the Ghost, which comes upon them in all the suddenness of its visionary character. Indeed, no modern writer would have dared, like Shakespeare, to have preceded this last visitation by two distinct appearances,—or could have contrived that the third should rise upon the former two in impressiveness and solemnity of interest.

But in addition to all the other excellences of Hamlet's speech concerning the wassel-music—so finely revealing the predominant idealism, the ratiocinative meditativeness, of his character—it has the advantage of giving nature and probability to the impassioned continuity of the speech instantly directed to the Ghost. The *momentum* had been given to his mental activity; the full current of the thoughts and words had set in, and the very forgetfulness, in the fervor of his augmentation, of the purpose for which he was there, aided in preventing the appearance from benumbing the mind. Consequently, it acted as a new impulse,—a sudden stroke which increased the velocity of the body already in motion, whilst it altered the direction. The co-presence of Horatio, Marcellus, and Bernardo is most judiciously contrived; for it renders the courage of Hamlet and his impetuous eloquence perfectly intelligible. The knowledge,—the unthought of consciousness,—the sensation,—of human auditors—of flesh and blood sympathists—acts as a support and a stimulation *a tergo*, while the front of the mind, the whole consciousness of the speaker, is filled, yea, absorbed, by the apparition. Add too, that the apparition itself has by its previous appearances been brought nearer to a thing of this world. This accrescence of objectivity in a Ghost that yet retains all its ghostly attributes and fearful subjectivity, is truly wonderful.

Ib. sc. 5. Hamlet's speech:—

> O all you host of heaven! O earth! What else?
> And shall I couple hell?—

I remember nothing equal to this burst unless it be the first speech of Prometheus in the Greek Drama, after the exit of Vulcan and the two Afrites. But Shakespeare alone could have produced the vow of Hamlet to make his memory a blank of all maxims and generalized truths, that 'observation had copied there,'—followed immediately by the speaker noting down the generalized fact,

> That one may smile, and smile, and be a villain!

Ib.

> *Mar.* Hillo, ho, ho, my lord!
> *Ham.* Hillo, ho, ho, boy! come bird, come, &c.

This part of the scene after Hamlet's interview with the Ghost has been charged with an improbable eccentricity. But the truth is, that after the mind has been stretched beyond its usual pitch and tone, it must either sink into exhaustion and inanity, or seek relief by change. It is thus well known, that persons conversant in deeds of cruelty contrive to escape from conscience by connecting something of the ludicrous with them, and by inventing grotesque terms and a certain technical phraseology to disguise the horror of their practices. Indeed, paradoxical as it may appear, the terrible by a law of the human mind always touches on the verge of the ludicrous. Both arise from the perception of something out of the common order of things—something, in fact, out of its place; and if from this we can abstract danger, the uncommonness will alone remain, and the sense of the ridiculous be excited. The close alliance of these opposites—they are not contraries—appears from the circumstance, that laughter is equally the expression of extreme anguish and horror as of joy: as there are tears of sorrow and tears of joy, so is there a laugh of terror and a laugh of merriment. These complex causes will naturally have produced in Hamlet the disposition to escape from his own feelings of the overwhelming and supernatural by a wild transition to the ludicrous,—a sort of cunning bravado, bordering on the flights of delirium. For you may, perhaps, observe that Hamlet's wildness is but half false; he plays that subtle trick of pretending to act only when he is very near really being what he acts.

The subterraneous speeches of the Ghost are hardly defensible:—but I would call your attention to the characteristic difference between this Ghost, as a superstition connected with the most mysterious truths of revealed religion,—and Shakespeare's consequent reverence in his treatment of it,—and the foul earthly witcheries and wild language in Macbeth.

Act ii. sc. 1. Polonius and Reynaldo.

In all things dependent on, or rather made up of, fine address, the manner is no more or otherwise rememberable than the light motions, steps, and gestures of youth and health. But this is almost everything:—no wonder, therefore, if that which can be put down by rule in the memory should appear to us as mere poring, maudlin, cunning,—slyness blinking through the watery eye of superannuation. So in this admirable scene, Polonius, who is throughout the skeleton of his own former skill and statecraft, hunts the trail of policy at a dead scent, supplied by the weak fever-smell in his own nostrils.

Ib. sc. 2. Speech of Polonius:—

> My liege, and madam, to expostulate, &c.

Warburton's note.

Then as to the jingles, and play on words, let us but look into the sermons of Dr. Donne (the wittiest man of that age), and we shall find them full of this vein.

I have, and that most carefully, read Dr. Donne's sermons, and find none of these jingles. The great art of an orator—to make whatever he talks of appear of importance—this, indeed, Donne has effected with consummate skill.
Ib.

> *Ham*. Excellent well;
> You are a fishmonger.

That is, you are sent to fish out this secret. This is Hamlet's own meaning.
Ib.

> *Ham*. For if the sun breeds maggots in a dead dog,
> Being a god, kissing carrion—

These purposely obscure lines, I rather think, refer to some thought in Hamlet's mind, contrasting the lovely daughter with such a tedious old fool, her father, as he, Hamlet, represents Polonius to himself:—'Why, fool as he is, he is some degrees in rank above a dead dog's carcass; and if the sun, being a god that kisses carrion, can raise life out of a dead dog,—why may not good fortune, that favors fools, have raised a lovely girl out of this dead-alive old fool?' Warburton is often led astray, in his interpretations, by his attention to general positions without the due Shakespearean reference to what is probably passing in the mind of his speaker, characteristic, and expository of his particular character and present mood. The subsequent passage,—

> O Jephtha, judge of Israel! what a treasure hadst thou.

is confirmatory of my view of these lines.
Ib.

> *Ham*. You can not, Sir, take from me any thing that I will more willingly part withal; except my life, except my life, except my life.

This repetition strikes me as most admirable.
Ib.

> *Ham*. Then are our beggars, bodies; and our monarchs, and outstretched heroes, the beggars' shadows.

I do not understand this; and Shakespeare seems to have intended the meaning not to be more than snatched at:—'By my fay, I can not reason!'
Ib.

> The rugged Pyrrhus—he whose sable arms, &c.

This admirable substitution of the epic for the dramatic, giving such a reality to the impassioned dramatic diction of Shakespeare's own dialogue, and authorized too, by the actual style of the tragedies before his time (Porrex and Ferrex, Titus Andronicus, &c.), is well worthy of notice. The fancy, that a burlesque was intended, sinks below criticism: the lines, as epic narrative, are superb.

In the thoughts, and even in the separate parts of the diction, this description is highly poetical: in truth, taken by itself, that is its fault that it is too poetical!—the language of lyric vehemence and epic pomp, and not of the drama. But if Shakespeare had made the diction truly dramatic, where would have been the contrast between Hamlet and the play in Hamlet?

Ib.

> had seen the *mobled* queen, &c.

A mob-cap is still a word in common use for a morning-cap, which conceals the whole head of hair, and passes under the chin. It is nearly the same as the night-cap, that is, it is an imitation of it, so as to answer the purpose ('I am not drest for company'), and yet reconciling it with neatness and perfect purity.

Ib. Hamlet's soliloquy:—

> O, what a rogue and peasant slave am I! &c.

This is Shakespeare's own attestation to the truth of the idea of Hamlet which I have before put forth.

Ib.

> The spirit that I have seen,
> May be a devil: and the devil hath power
> To assume a pleasing shape; yea, and, perhaps
> Out of my weakness, and my melancholy,
> (As he is very potent with such spirits)
> Abuses me to damn me.

See Sir Thomas Brown:—

I believe——that those apparitions and ghosts of departed persons are not the wandering souls of men, but the unquiet walks of devils, prompting and suggesting us unto mischief, blood, and villany, instilling and stealing into our hearts, that the blessed spirits are not at rest in their graves, but wander solicitous of the affairs of the world. *Relig. Med.* pt. i. sec. 37.

Act iii. sc. 1. Hamlet's soliloquy:—

> To be, or not to be, that is the question, &c.

This speech is of absolutely universal interest,—and yet to which of all Shakespeare's characters could it have been appropriately given but to Hamlet? For Jaques it would have been too deep, and for Iago too habitual a communion with the heart; which in every man belongs, or ought to belong, to all mankind.

Ib.

> That undiscover'd country, from whose bourne
> No traveller returns.—

Theobald's note in defence of the supposed contradiction of this in the apparition of the Ghost.

O miserable defender! If it be necessary to remove the apparent contradiction,—if it be not rather a great beauty,—surely it were easy to say, that no traveller returns to this world, as to his home or abiding-place.

Ib.

> *Ham.* Ha, ha! are you honest?
> *Oph.* My lord?
> *Ham.* Are you fair?

Here it is evident that the penetrating Hamlet perceives, from the strange and forced manner of Ophelia, that the sweet girl was not acting a part of her own, but was a decoy; and his after-speeches are not so much directed to her as to the listeners and spies. Such a discovery in a mood so anxious and irritable accounts for a certain harshness in him;—and yet a wild upworking of love, sporting with opposites in a wilful self-tormenting strain of irony, is perceptible throughout. 'I did love you once;'—'I lov'd you not;'—and particularly in his enumeration of the faults of the sex from which Ophelia is so free, that the mere freedom therefrom constitutes her character. Note Shakespeare's charm of composing the female character by the absence of characters, that is, marks and out-jottings.

Ib. Hamlet's speech:—

> I say, we will have no more marriages: those that are married already, all but one, shall live: the rest shall keep as they are.

Observe this dallying with the inward purpose, characteristic of one who had not brought his mind to the steady acting point. He would fain sting the uncle's mind;—but to stab his body!—The soliloquy of Ophelia, which follows, is the perfection of love—so exquisitely unselfish!

Ib. sc. 2. This dialogue of Hamlet with the players is one of the happiest instances of Shakespeare's power of diversifying the scene while he is carrying on the plot.

Ib.

> *Ham.* My lord, you play'd once i' the university, you say? (*To Polonius.*)

To have kept Hamlet's love for Ophelia before the audience in any direct form, would have made a breach in the unity of the interest;—but yet to the thoughtful reader it is suggested by his spite to poor Polonius, whom he can not let rest.

Ib. The style of the interlude here is distinguished from the real dialogue by rhyme, as in the first interview with the players by epic verse.

Ib.

> *Ros*. My lord, you once did love me.
> *Ham*. So I do still, by these pickers and stealers.

I never heard an actor give this word 'so' its proper emphasis. Shakespeare's meaning is—'lov'd you? Hum!—*so* I do still,' &c. There has been no change in my opinion:—I think as ill of you as I did. Else Hamlet tells an ignoble falsehood, and a useless one, as the last speech to Guildenstern— 'Why, look you now,' &c.—proves.

Ib. Hamlet's soliloquy:—

> Now could I drink hot blood,
> And do such business as the bitter day
> Would quake to look on.

The utmost at which Hamlet arrives, is a disposition, a mood, to do something;—but what to do, is still left undecided, while every word he utters tends to betray his disguise. Yet observe how perfectly equal to any call of the moment is Hamlet, let it only not be for the future.

Ib. sc. 4. Speech of Polonius. Polonius's volunteer obtrusion of himself into this business, while it is appropriate to his character, still itching after former importance, removes all likelihood that Hamlet should suspect his presence, and prevents us from making his death injure Hamlet in our opinion.

Ib. The king's speech:—

> O, my offence is rank, it smells to heaven, &c.

This speech well marks the difference between crime and guilt of habit. The conscience here is still admitted to audience. Nay, even as an audible soliloquy, it is far less improbable than is supposed by such as have watched men only in the beaten road of their feelings. But the final—'all may be well!' is remarkable;—the degree of merit attributed by the self-flattering soul to its own struggle, though baffled, and to the indefinite half-promise, half-command, to persevere in religious duties. The solution is in the divine *medium* of the Christian doctrine of expiation:—not what you have done, but what you are, must determine.

Ib. Hamlet's speech:—

> Now might I do it, pat, now he is praying:
> And now I'll do it:—And so he goes to heaven:
> And so am I revenged? That would be scann'd, &c.

Dr. Johnson's mistaking of the marks of reluctance and procrastination for impetuous, horror-striking fiendishness!—Of such importance is it to understand the germ of a character. But the interval taken by Hamlet's speech is truly awful! And then—

> My words fly up, my thoughts remain below:
> Words, without thoughts, never to heaven go,—

O what a lesson concerning the essential difference between wishing and willing, and the folly of all motive-mongering, while the individual self remains!

Ib. sc. 4.

> *Ham.* A bloody deed;—almost as bad, good mother,
> As kill a king, and marry with his brother.
> *Queen.* As kill a king?

I confess that Shakespeare has left the character of the Queen in an unpleasant perplexity. Was she, or was she not, conscious of the fratricide?

Act iv. sc. 2.

> *Ros.* Take you me for a sponge, my lord?
> *Ham.* Ay, Sir; that soaks up the King's countenance, his rewards his authorities, &c.

Hamlet's madness is made to consist in the free utterance of all the thoughts that had passed through his mind before;—in fact, in telling home-truths.

Act iv. sc. 5. Ophelia's singing. O, note the conjunction here of these two thoughts that had never subsisted in disjunction, the love for Hamlet, and her filial love, with the guileless floating on the surface of her pure imagination of the cautions so lately expressed, and the fears not too delicately avowed, by her father and brother, concerning the dangers to which her honor lay exposed. Thought, affliction, passion, murder itself—she turns to favor and prettiness. This play of association is instanced in the close:—

> My brother shall know of it, and I thank you for your good counsel.

Ib. Gentleman's speech:—

> And as the world were now but to begin
> Antiquity forgot, custom not known,
> The ratifiers and props of every ward—
> They cry, &c.

Fearful and self-suspicious as I always feel, when I seem to see an error of judgment in Shakespeare, yet I can not reconcile the cool, and, as Warburton calls it, 'rational and consequential,' reflection in these lines with the anonymousness, or the alarm, of this Gentleman or Messenger, as he is called in other editions.

Ib. King's speech:—

> There's such divinity doth hedge a king,
> That treason can but peep to what it would,
> Acts little of his will.

Proof, as indeed all else is, that Shakespeare never intended us to see the King with Hamlet's eyes; though, I suspect, the managers have long done so.
Ib. Speech of Laertes:—

> To hell, allegiance! vows, to the blackest devil!

> Laertes is a *good* character, but, &c.
>   WARBURTON.

Mercy on Warburton's notion of goodness! Please to refer to the seventh scene of this act:—

> I will do it;
> And for this purpose I'll anoint my sword, &c.

uttered by Laertes after the King's description of Hamlet;—

> He being remiss,
> Most generous, and free from all contriving,
> Will not peruse the foils.

Yet I acknowledge that Shakespeare evidently wishes, as much as possible, to spare the character of Laertes,—to break the extreme turpitude of his consent to become an agent and accomplice of the King's treachery;—and to this end he re-introduces Ophelia at the close of this scene to afford a probable stimulus of passion in her brother.
Ib. sc. 6. Hamlet's capture by the pirates. This is almost the only play of Shakespeare, in which mere accidents, independent of all will, form an essential part of the plot;—but here how judiciously in keeping with the character of the over-meditative Hamlet, ever at last determined by accident or by a fit of passion?
Ib. sc. 7. Note how the King first awakens Laertes's vanity by praising the reporter, and then gratifies it by the report itself and finally points it by—

> Sir, this report of his
> Did Hamlet so envenom with his envy!—

Ib. King's speech:—

> For goodness, growing to a *pleurisy*,
> Dies in his own too much.

Theobald's note from Warburton, who conjectures 'plethory.'
I rather think that Shakespeare meant 'pleurisy,' but involved in it the thought of *plethora*, as supposing pleurisy to arise from too much blood; otherwise I can not explain the following line—

> And then this *should* is like a spendthrift sigh,
> That hurts by easing.

In a stitch in the side every one must have heaved a sigh that 'hurt by easing.'

Since writing the above I feel confirmed that 'pleurisy' is the right word; for I find that in the old medical dictionaries the pleurisy is often called the 'plethory.'

> *Queen.* Your sister's drown'd, Laertes.
> *Laer.* Drown'd! O, where?

That Laertes might be excused in some degree for not cooling, the Act concludes with the affecting death of Ophelia,—who in the beginning lay like a little projection of land into a lake or stream, covered with spray-flowers, quietly reflected in the quiet waters, but at length is undermined or loosened, and becomes a fairy isle, and after a brief vagrancy sinks almost without an eddy!

Act v. sc. 1. O, the rich contrast between the Clowns and Hamlet, as two extremes! You see in the former the mockery of logic, and a traditional wit valued, like truth, for its antiquity, and treasured up, like a tune, for use.

Ib. sc. 1 and 2. Shakespeare seems to mean all Hamlet's character to be brought together before his final disappearance from the scene;—his meditative excess in the grave-digging, his yielding to passion with Laertes, his love for Ophelia blazing out, his tendency to generalize on all occasions in the dialogue with Horatio, his fine gentlemanly manners with Osrick, and his and Shakespeare's own fondness for presentiment:

> But thou would'st not think, how ill all's here about my heart: but
> it is no matter.

MILTON

If we divide the period from the accession of Elizabeth to the Protectorate of Cromwell into two unequal portions, the first ending with the death of James I., the other comprehending the reign of Charles and the brief glories of the Republic, we are forcibly struck with a difference in the character of the illustrious actors, by whom each period is rendered severally memorable. Or rather, the difference in the characters of the great men in each period, leads us to make this division. Eminent as the intellectual powers were that were displayed in both; yet in the number of great men, in the various sorts of excellence, and not merely in the variety but almost diversity of talents united in the same individual, the age of Charles falls short of its predecessor; and the stars of the Parliament, keen as their radiance was, in fulness and richness of lustre, yield to the constellation at the court of Elizabeth;—which can only be paralleled by Greece in her brightest moment, when the titles of the poet, the philosopher, the historian, the statesman, and the general not seldom formed a garland round the same head, as in the instances of our Sidneys and Raleighs. But then, on the other hand, there was a vehemence of will, an enthusiasm of principle, a depth and an earnestness of spirit, which the charms of individual fame and personal aggrandizement could not pacify,—an aspiration after reality, permanence, and general good,—in short, a moral grandeur in the latter period, with which the low intrigues, Machiavellic maxims, and selfish and servile ambition of the former, stand in painful contrast.

The causes of this it belongs not to the present occasion to detail at length; but a mere allusion to the quick succession of revolutions in religion, breeding a political indifference in the mass of men to religion itself, the enormous increase of the royal power in consequence of the humiliation of the nobility and the clergy—the transference of the papal authority to the crown,—the unfixed state of Elizabeth's own opinions, whose inclinations were as popish as her interests were protestant—the controversial extravagance and practical imbecility of her successor—will help to explain the former period; and the persecutions that had given a life-and-soul interest to the disputes so imprudently fostered by James,—the ardor of a conscious increase of power in the commons, and the greater austerity of manners and maxims, the natural product and most formidable weapon of religious disputation, not merely in conjunction, but in closest combination, with newly-awakened political and republican zeal, these perhaps account for the character of the latter æra.

In the close of the former period, and during the bloom of the latter, the poet Milton was educated and formed; and he survived the latter, and all the fond hopes and aspirations which had been its life; and so in evil days, standing as the representative of the combined excellence of both periods, he produced the Paradise Lost as by an after-throe of nature. "There are some persons" (observes a divine, a contemporary of Milton's), "of whom the grace of God takes early hold, and the good spirit inhabiting them, carries them on in an even constancy through innocence into virtue, their Christianity bearing equal date with their manhood, and reason and religion, like warp and woof, running together, make up one web of a wise and exemplary life. This (he adds) is a most happy case, wherever it happens; for, besides that there is no sweeter or more lovely thing on earth than the early buds of piety, which drew from our Saviour signal affection to the beloved disciple, it is better to have no wound than to experience the most sovereign balsam, which, if it work a cure, yet usually leaves a scar behind." Although it was and is my intention to defer the consideration of Milton's own character to the conclusion of this Lecture, yet I could not prevail on myself to approach the Paradise Lost without impressing on your minds the conditions under which such a work was in fact producible at all, the original genius having been assumed as the immediate agent and efficient cause; and these conditions I find in the character of the times and in his own character. The age in which the foundations of his mind were laid, was congenial to it as one golden æra of profound erudition and individual genius;—that in which the superstructure was carried up, was no less favorable to it by a sternness of discipline and a show of self-control, highly flattering to the imaginative dignity of an heir of fame, and which won Milton over from the dear-loved delights of academic groves and cathedral aisles to the anti-prelatic party. It acted on him too, no doubt, and modified his studies by a characteristic controversial spirit (his presentation of God is tinted with it)— a spirit not less busy indeed in political than in theological and ecclesiastical dispute, but carrying on the former almost always, more or less, in the guise of the latter. And so far as Pope's censure of our poet—that he makes God the Father a school divine—is just, we must attribute it to the character of his age, from which the men of genius, who escaped, escaped by a worse disease, the licentious indifference of a Frenchified court.

Such was the *nidus* or soil which constituted, in the strict sense of the word, the circumstances of Milton's mind. In his mind itself there were purity and piety absolute; an imagination to which neither the past nor the present were interesting, except as far as they called forth and enlivened the great ideal, in which and for which he lived; a keen love of truth, which, after many weary pursuits, found a harbor in the sublime listening to the still voice in his own spirit, and as keen a love of his country, which, after a disappointment still more depressive, expanded and soared into a love of man as a probationer of immortality. These were, these alone could be, the conditions under which such a work as the Paradise Lost could be conceived and accomplished. By a life-long study Milton had known—

> What was of use to know,
> What best to say could say, to do had done.
> His actions to his words agreed, his words
> To his large heart gave utterance due, his heart
> Contain'd of good, wise, fair, the perfect shape;

And he left the imperishable total, as a bequest to the ages coming, in the *Paradise Lost*.

Difficult as I shall find it to turn over these leaves without catching some passage, which would tempt me to stop, I propose to consider, 1st, the general plan and arrangement of the work; 2dly, the subject with its difficulties and advantages;—3dly, the poet's object, the spirit in the letter, the ἐνθύμιον ἐν μύθῳ, the true school-divinity; and lastly, the characteristic excellencies of the poem, in what they consist, and by what means they were produced.

1. As to the plan and ordonnance of the Poem.

Compare it with the Iliad, many of the books of which might change places without any injury to the thread of the story. Indeed, I doubt the original existence of the Iliad as one poem; it seems more probable that it was put together about the time of the Pisistratidæ. The Iliad—and, more or less, all epic poems, the subjects of which are taken from history—have no rounded conclusion; they remain, after all, but single chapters from the volume of history, although they are ornamental chapters. Consider the exquisite simplicity of the Paradise Lost. It and it alone really possesses a beginning, a middle, and an end; it has the totality of the poem as distinguished from the *ab ovo* birth and parentage, or straight line, of history.

2. As to the subject.

In Homer, the supposed importance of the subject, as the first effort of confederated Greece, is an after-thought of the critics; and the interest, such as it is, derived from the events themselves, as distinguished from the manner of representing them, is very languid to all but Greeks. It is a Greek poem. The superiority of the Paradise Lost is obvious in this respect, that the interest transcends the limits of a nation. But we do not generally dwell on this excellence of the Paradise Lost, because it seems attributable to Christianity itself;—yet in fact the interest is wider than Christendom, and comprehends the Jewish and Mohammedan worlds;—nay, still further, inasmuch as it represents the origin of evil, and the combat of evil and good, it contains matter of deep interest to all mankind, as forming the basis of all religion, and the true occasion of all philosophy whatsoever.

The FALL of man is the subject; Satan is the cause; man's blissful state the immediate object of his enmity and attack; man is warned by an angel who gives him an account of all that was requisite to be known, to make the warning at once intelligible and awful, then the temptation ensues, and the Fall; then the immediate sensible consequence; then the consolation, wherein an angel presents a vision of the history of man with the ultimate triumph of the Redeemer. Nothing is touched in this vision but what is of general interest in religion; any thing else would have been improper.

The inferiority of Klopstock's Messiah is inexpressible. I admit the prerogative of poetic feeling, and poetic faith; but I can not suspend the judgment even for a moment. A poem may in one sense be a dream, but it must be a waking dream. In Milton you have a religious faith combined with the moral nature; it is an efflux; you go along with it. In Klopstock there is a wilfulness; he makes things so and so. The feigned speeches and events in the

Messiah shock us like falsehoods; but nothing of that sort is felt in the Paradise Lost, in which no particulars, at least very few indeed, are touched which can come into collision or juxtaposition with recorded matter.

But notwithstanding the advantages in Milton's subject, there were concomitant insuperable difficulties, and Milton has exhibited marvellous skill in keeping most of them out of sight. High poetry is the translation of reality into the ideal under the predicament of succession of time only. The poet is an historian, upon condition of moral power being the only force in the universe. The very grandeur of his subject ministered a difficulty to Milton. The statement of a being of high intellect, warring against the supreme Being, seems to contradict the idea of a supreme Being. Milton precludes our feeling this, as much as possible, by keeping the peculiar attributes of divinity less in sight, making them to a certain extent allegorical only. Again poetry implies the language of excitement; yet how to reconcile such language with God! Hence Milton confines the poetic passion in God's speeches to the language of Scripture; and once only allows the *passio vera,* or *quasi humana* to appear, in the passage, where the Father contemplates his own likeness in the Son before the battle:—

> Go then, thou Mightiest, in thy Father's might,
> Ascend my chariot, guide the rapid wheels
> That shake Heaven's basis, bring forth all my war,
> My bow and thunder; my almighty arms
> Gird on, and sword upon thy puissant thigh;
> Pursue these sons of darkness, drive them out
> From all Heaven's bounds into the utter deep:
> There let them learn, as likes them, to despise
> God and Messiah his anointed king.
>
> B. vi. v. 710.

3. As to Milton's object:

It was to justify the ways of God to man! The controversial spirit observable in many parts of the poem, especially in God's speeches, is immediately attributable to the great controversy of that age, the origination of evil. The Arminians considered it a mere calamity. The Calvinists took away all human will. Milton asserted the will, but declared for the enslavement of the will out of an act of the will itself. There are three powers in us, which distinguish us from the beasts that perish:—1, reason; 2, the power of viewing universal truth; and 3, the power of contracting universal truth into particulars. Religion is the will in the reason, and love in the will.

The character of Satan is pride and sensual indulgence, finding in self the sole motive of action. It is the character so often seen *in little* on the political stage. It exhibits all the restlessness, temerity, and cunning which have marked the mighty hunters of mankind from Nimrod to Napoleon. The common fascination of men is, that these great men, as they are called, must act from some great motive. Milton has carefully marked in his Satan the intense selfishness, the alcohol of egotism, which would rather reign in hell than serve in heaven. To place this lust of self in opposition to denial of self or duty, and to show what exertions it would make, and what pains endure to accomplish its end, is Milton's particular object in the character of Satan. But around this character he has thrown a singularity of daring, a grandeur of sufferance, and a ruined splendor, which constitute the very height of poetic sublimity.

Lastly, as to the execution:—

The language and versification of the Paradise Lost are peculiar in being so much more necessarily correspondent to each than those in any other poem or poet. The connection of the sentences and the position of the words are exquisitely artificial; but the position is rather according to the logic of passion or universal logic, than to the logic of grammar. Milton attempted to make the English language obey the logic of passion, as perfectly as the Greek and Latin. Hence the occasional harshness in the construction.

Sublimity is the pre-eminent characteristic of the Paradise Lost. It is not an arithmetical sublime like Klopstock's, whose rule always is to treat what we might think large as contemptibly small. Klopstock mistakes bigness for greatness. There is a greatness arising from images of effort and daring, and also from those of moral endurance; in Milton both are united. The fallen angels are human passions, invested with a dramatic reality.

The apostrophe to light at the commencement of the third book is particularly beautiful as an intermediate link between Hell and Heaven; and observe, how the second and third book support the subjective character of the poem. In all modern poetry in Christendom there is an under consciousness of a sinful nature, a fleeting away of external things, the mind or subject greater than the object, the reflective character predominant. In the Paradise Lost the sublimest parts are the revelations of Milton's own mind, producing itself and evolving its own greatness; and this is so truly so, that when that which is merely entertaining for its objective beauty is introduced, it at first seems a discord.

In the description of Paradise itself, you have Milton's sunny side as a man; here his descriptive powers are exercised to the utmost, and he draws deep upon his Italian resources. In the description of Eve, and throughout this part of the poem, the poet is predominant over the theologian. Dress is the symbol of the Fall, but the mark of intellect; and the metaphysics of dress are, the hiding what is not symbolic and displaying by discrimination what is. The love of Adam and Eve in Paradise is of the highest merit—not phantomatic, and yet removed from every thing degrading. It is the sentiment of one rational being towards another made tender by a specific difference in that which is essentially the same in both; it is a union of opposites, a giving and receiving mutually of the permanent in either, a completion of each in the other.

Milton is not a picturesque, but a musical, poet; although he has this merit, that the object chosen by him for any particular foreground always remains prominent to the end, enriched, but not encumbered, by the opulence of descriptive details furnished by an exhaustless imagination. I wish the

Paradise Lost were more carefully read and studied than I can see any ground for believing it is, especially those parts which, from the habit of always looking for a story in poetry, are scarcely read at all,—as for example, Adam's vision of future events in the 11th and 12th books. No one can rise from the perusal of this immortal poem without a deep sense of the grandeur and the purity of Milton's soul, or without feeling how susceptible of domestic enjoyments he really was, notwithstanding the discomforts which actually resulted from an apparently unhappy choice in marriage. He was, as every truly great poet has ever been, a good man; but finding it impossible to realize his own aspirations, either in religion or politics, or society, he gave up his heart to the living spirit and light within him, and avenged himself on the world by enriching it with this record of his own transcendent ideal.

Francis Jeffrey

1773–1850

Francis Jeffrey, later Lord Jeffrey, was born in Edinburgh on October 23, 1773, and was educated at the universities of Glasgow and Edinburgh and at Queen's College, Oxford. He was admitted to the Scottish bar in 1794 but soon realized that his Whig politics might seriously impede his advancement in the legal profession. Sydney suggested to Jeffrey that they and some of their mutual friends join together to publish a critical periodical, and the result of their collaboration was the *Edinburgh Review*. The first issue appeared in October 1802 to rave reviews. The first three issues were under the editorship of Smith; Jeffrey assumed the role in 1803, and edited and wrote for the *Review* until 1829.

Despite his forebodings, Jeffrey's legal career prospered. During his years as editor of the *Review* he was also acquiring a reputation as an advocate. He was elected lord rector of Glasgow University in 1820 and dean of the faculty of advocates in 1829. As a member of the House of Commons he introduced the Scottish Reform Bill of 1831, and in 1834 became a judge, assuming the title of Lord Jeffrey. He died in Edinburgh on January 26, 1850.

The *Edinburgh Review* exerted a substantial influence throughout the English-speaking world in the nineteenth century. It was the first literary periodical to solicit high-quality articles from knowledgeable contributors who were well compensated for their efforts, breaking the tradition of hiring underpaid hack writers. The *Review* was known for trenchant, often savage, criticism. Jeffrey himself, a frequent contributor, was later dismissed by many as a reactionary who attacked the Romantics, Wordsworth especially, because he was incapable of understanding the greatness of their works. Nevertheless, modern scholars find his essays an invaluable resource for discovering the attitudes of contemporary critics toward the early Romantics.

WORDSWORTH'S "POEMS"

This author is known to belong to a certain brotherhood of poets, who have haunted for some years about the Lakes of Cumberland; and is generally looked upon, we believe, as the purest model of the excellences and peculiarities of the school which they have been labouring to establish. Of the general merits of that school, we have had occasion to express our opinion pretty fully, in more places than one, and even to make some allusion to the former publications of the writer now before us. We are glad, however, to have found an opportunity of attending somewhat more particularly to his pretensions.

The Lyrical Ballads were unquestionably popular; and, we have no hesitation in saying, deservedly popular; for in spite of their occasional vulgarity, affectation, and silliness, they were undoubtedly characterised by a strong spirit of originality, of pathos, and natural feeling; and recommended to all good minds by the clear impression which they bore of the amiable dispositions and virtuous principles of the author. By the help of these qualities, they were enabled, not only to recommend themselves to the indulgence of many judicious readers, but even to beget among a pretty numerous class of persons, a sort of admiration of the very defects by which they were attended. It was upon this account chiefly, that we thought it necessary to set ourselves against this alarming innovation. Childishness, conceit, and affectation, are not of themselves very popular or attractive; and though mere novelty has sometimes been found sufficient to give them a temporary currency, we should have had no fear of their prevailing to any dangerous extent, if they had been graced with no more seductive accompaniments. It was precisely because the perverseness and bad taste of this new school was combined with a great deal of genius and of laudable feeling, that we were afraid of their spreading and gaining ground among us, and that we entered into the discussion with a degree of zeal and animosity which some might think unreasonable towards authors, to whom so much merit had been conceded. There were times and moods indeed, in which we were led to suspect ourselves of unjustifiable severity, and to doubt, whether a sense of public duty had not carried us rather too far in reprobation of errors, that seemed to be atoned for, by excellences of no vulgar description. At other times, the magnitude of these errors—the disgusting absurdities into which they led their feebler admirers, and the derision and contempt which they drew from the more fastidious, even upon the merits with which they were associated, made us wonder more than ever at the perversity by which they were retained, and regret that we had not declared ourselves against them with still more formidable and decided hostility.

In this temper of mind, we read the *annonce* of Mr. Wordsworth's publication with a good deal of interest and expectation, and opened his volumes with greater anxiety, than he or his admirers will probably give us credit for. We have been greatly disappointed certainly as to the quality of the poetry; but we doubt whether the publication has afforded so much satisfaction to any other of his readers:—it has freed us from all doubt or hesitation as to the justice of our former censures, and has brought the matter to a test, which we cannot help hoping may be convincing to the author himself.

Mr. Wordsworth, we think, has now brought the question, as to the merit of his new school of poetry, to a very fair and decisive issue. The volumes before us are much more strongly marked by all its peculiarities than any former publication of the fraternity. In our apprehension, they are, on this very account, infinitely less interesting or meritorious; but it belongs to the public, and not to us, to decide upon their merit, and we will confess, that so strong is our conviction of their obvious inferiority, and the grounds of it, that we are willing for once to wave our right of appealing to posterity, and to take the judgment of the present generation of readers, and even of Mr. Wordsworth's former admirers, as conclusive on this occasion. If these volumes, which have all the benefit of the author's former popularity, turn out to be nearly as popular as the lyrical ballads—if they sell nearly to the same extent—or are quoted and imitated among half as many individuals, we shall admit that Mr. Wordsworth has come much nearer the truth in his judgment of what constitutes the charm of poetry, than we had previously imagined—and shall institute a more serious and respectful inquiry into his principles of composition than we have yet thought necessary. On the other hand,—if this little work, selected from the compositions of five maturer years, and written avowedly for the purpose of exalting a system, which has already excited a good deal of attention, should be generally rejected by those whose prepossessions were in its favour, there is room to hope, not only that the system itself will meet with no more encouragement, but even that the author will be persuaded to abandon a plan of writing, which defrauds his industry and talents of their natural reward.

Putting ourselves thus upon our country, we certainly look for a verdict against this publication; and have little doubt indeed of the result, upon a fair consideration of the evidence contained in these volumes.—To accelerate that result, and to give a general view of the evidence, to those into whose hands the record may not have already fallen, we must now make a few observations and extracts.

We shall not resume any of the particular discussions by which we formerly attempted to ascertain the value of the improvements which this new school has effected in poetry; but shall lay the grounds of our opposition, for this time, a little more broadly. The end of poetry, we take it, is to please—and the name, we think, is strictly applicable to every metrical composition from which we receive pleasure, without any laborious exercise of the understanding. This pleasure, may, in general, be analyzed into three parts—that which we receive from the excitement of Passion or emotion—that which is derived from the play of Imagination, or the easy exercise of Reason—and that which depends on the character and qualities of the Diction. The two first are the vital and primary springs of poetical delight, and can scarcely require explanation to any one. The last has been alternately overrated and undervalued by the professors of the poetical art, and is in such low estimation with the author now before us and his associates, that it is necessary to say a few words in explanation of it.

One great beauty of diction exists only for those who have some degree of scholarship or critical skill. This is what depends on the exquisite *propriety* of the words employed, and the delicacy with which they are adapted to the meaning which is to be expressed. Many of the finest passages in Virgil and Pope derive their principal charm from the fine propriety of their diction. Another source of beauty, which extends only to the more instructed class of readers, is that which consists in the judicious or happy application of expressions which have been sanctified by the use of famous writers, or which bear the stamp of a simple or venerable antiquity. There are other beauties of diction, however, which are perceptible by all—the beauties of sweet sound and pleasant associations. The melody of words and verses is indifferent to no reader of poetry; but the chief recommendation of poetical language is certainly derived from those general associations, which give it a character of dignity or elegance, sublimity or tenderness. Every one knows that there are low and mean expressions, as well as lofty and grave ones; and that some words bear the impression of coarseness and vulgarity, as clearly as others do of refinement and affection. We do not mean, of course, to say any thing in defence of the hackneyed common-places of ordinary versemen. Whatever might have been the original character of these unlucky phrases, they are now associated with nothing but ideas of schoolboy imbecility and vulgar affectation. But what we do maintain is, that much of the most popular poetry in the world owes its celebrity chiefly to the beauty of its diction; and that no poetry can be long or generally acceptable, the language of which is coarse, inelegant or infantine.

From this great source of pleasure, we think the readers of Mr. Wordsworth are in a great measure cut off. His diction has no where any pretensions to elegance or dignity; and he has scarcely ever condescended to give the grace of correctness or melody to his versification. If it were merely slovenly and neglected, however, all this might be endured. Strong sense and powerful feeling will ennoble any expressions; or, at least, no one who is capable of estimating those higher merits, will be disposed to mark these little defects. But, in good truth, no man, now-a-days, composes verses for publication with a slovenly neglect of their language. It is a fine and laborious manufacture, which can scarcely ever be made in a hurry; and the faults which it has, may, for the most part, be set down to bad taste or incapacity, rather than to carelessness or oversight. With Mr. Wordsworth and his friends, it is plain that their peculiarities of diction are things of choice, and not of accident. They write as they do, upon principle and system; and it evidently costs them much pains to keep *down* to the standard which they have proposed to themselves. They are, to the full, as much mannerists, too, as the poetasters who ring changes on the common-places of magazine versification; and all the difference between them is, that they borrow their phrases from a different and a scantier *gradus ad Parnassum*. If they were, indeed, to discard all imitation and set phraseology, and to bring in no words merely for show or for metre,—as much, perhaps, might be gained in freedom and originality, as would infallibly be lost in allusion and authority; but, in point of fact, the new poets are just as great borrowers as the old; only that, instead of borrowing from the more popular passages of their illustrious predecessors, they have preferred furnishing themselves from vulgar ballads and plebeian nurseries.

Their peculiarities of diction alone, are enough, perhaps, to render them ridiculous; but the author before us really seems anxious to court this literary martydom by a device still more infallible,—we mean, that of connecting his most lofty, tender, or impassioned conceptions, with objects and incidents, which the greater part of his readers will probably persist in thinking low, silly, or uninteresting. Whether this is done from affectation and conceit alone, or whether it may not arise, in some measure, from the self-illusion of a mind of extraordinary sensibility, habituated to solitary meditation, we cannot undertake to determine. It is possible enough, we allow, that the sight of a friend's garden-spade, or a sparrow's nest, or a man gathering leeches, might really have suggested to such a mind a train of powerful impressions and interesting reflections; but it is certain, that, to most minds, such associations will always appear forced, strained, and unnatural; and that the composition in which it is attempted to exhibit them, will always have the air of parody, or ludicrous and affected singularity. All the world laughs at Elegiac stanzas to a sucking-pig—a Hymn on Washing-day—Sonnets to one's grandmother—or Pindarics on gooseberry-pye; and yet, we are afraid, it will not be quite easy to convince Mr. Wordsworth, that the same ridicule must infallibly attach to most of the pathetic pieces in these volumes. . . .

When we look at these, and many still finer passages, in the writings of this author, it is impossible not to feel a mixture of indignation and compassion, at that strange infatuation which has bound him up from the fair exercise of his talents, and withheld from the public the many excellent productions that would otherwise have taken the place of the trash now before us. Even in the worst of these productions, there are, no doubt, occasional little traits of delicate feeling and original fancy; but these are quite lost and obscured in the mass of childishness and insipidity with which they are incorporated; nor can any thing give us a more melancholy view of the debasing effects of this miserable theory, than that it has given ordinary men a right to wonder at the folly and presumption of a man gifted like Mr. Wordsworth, and made him appear, in his second avowed publication, like a bad imitator of the worst of his former productions.

We venture to hope, that there is now an end of this folly; and that, like other follies, it will be found to have cured itself by the extravagances resulting from its unbridled indulgence. In this point of view, the publication of the volumes before us may ultimately be of service to the good cause of literature. Many a generous rebel, it is said, has been reclaimed to his allegiance by the spectacle of lawless outrage and excess presented in the conduct of the insurgents; and we think there is every reason to hope, that the lamentable consequences which have resulted from Mr. Wordsworth's open violation of the established laws of poetry, will operate as a wholesome warning to those who might otherwise have been seduced by his example, and be the means of restoring to that ancient and venerable code its due honour and authority.

"THE EXCURSION"

This will never do! It bears no doubt the stamp of the author's heart and fancy: But unfortunately not half so visibly as that of his peculiar system. His former poems were intended to recommend that system, and to bespeak favour for it by the individual merit;—but this, we suspect, must be recommended by the system—and can only expect to succeed where it has been previously established. It is longer, weaker, and tamer, than any of Mr. Wordsworth's other productions; with less boldness of originality, and less even of that extreme simplicity and lowliness of tone which wavered so prettily, in the Lyrical Ballads, between silliness and pathos. We have imitations of Cowper, and even of Milton here; engrafted on the natural drawl of the Lakers—and all diluted into harmony by that profuse and irrepressible wordiness which deluges all the blank verse of this school of poetry, and lubricates and weakens the whole structure of their style.

Though it fairly fills four hundred and twenty good quarto pages, without note, vignette, or any sort of extraneous assistance, it is stated in the title—with something of an imprudent candour—to be but 'a portion' of a larger work; and in the preface, where an attempt is rather unsuccessfully made to explain the whole design, it is still more rashly disclosed, that it is but '*a part of the second part*, of a *long* and laborious work'—which is to consist of three parts!

What Mr. Wordsworth's ideas of length are, we have no means of accurately judging: But we cannot help suspecting that they are liberal, to a degree that will alarm the weakness of most modern readers. As far as we can gather from the preface, the entire poem—or one of them, (for we really are not sure whether there is to be one or two,) is of a biographical nature; and is to contain the history of the author's mind, and of the origin and progress of his poetical powers, up to the period when they were sufficiently matured to qualify him for the great work on which he has been so long employed. Now, the quarto before us contains an account of one of his youthful rambles in the vales of Cumberland, and occupies precisely the period of three days! So that, by the use of a very powerful *calculus,* some estimate may be formed of the probable extent of the entire biography.

This small specimen, however, and the statements with which it is prefaced, have been sufficient to set our minds at rest in one particular. The case of Mr. Wordsworth, we perceive, is now manifestly hopeless; and we give him up as altogether incurable, and beyond the power of criticism. We cannot indeed altogether omit taking precautions now and then against the spreading of the malady;—but for himself, though we shall watch the progress of his symptoms as a matter of professional curiosity and instruction, we really think it right not to harass him any longer with nauseous remedies,—but rather to throw in cordials and lenitives, and wait in patience for the natural termination of the disorder. In order to justify this desertion of our patient, however, it is proper to state why we despair of the success of a more active practice.

A man who has been for twenty years at work on such matter as is now before us, and who comes complacently forward with a whole quarto of it, after all the admonitions he has received, cannot reasonably be expected to 'change his hand, or check his pride,' upon the suggestion of far weightier monitors than we can pretend to be. Inveterate habit must now have given a kind of sanctity to the errors of early taste; and the very powers of which we lament the perversion, have probably become incapable of any other application. The very quantity, too, that he has written, and is at this moment working up for publication upon the old pattern, makes it amost hopeless to look for any change of it. All this is so much capital already sunk in the concern; which must be sacrificed if that be abandoned: and no man likes to give up for lost the time and talent and labour which he has embodied in any permanent production. We were not previously aware of these obstacles to Mr. Wordsworth's conversion; and, considering the peculiarities of his former writings merely as the result of certain wanton and capricious experiments on public taste and indulgence, conceived it to be our duty to discourage their repetition by all the means in our power. We now see clearly, however, how the case stands;—and, making up our minds, though with the most sincere pain and reluctance, to consider him as finally lost to the good cause of poetry, shall endeavour to be thankful for the occasional gleams of tenderness and beauty which the natural force of his imagination and affections must still shed over all his productions,—and to which we shall ever turn with delight, in spite of the affectation and mysticism and prolixity, with which they are so abundantly contrasted.

Long habits of seclusion, and an excessive ambition of originality, can alone account for the disproportion which seems to exist between this author's taste and his genius; or for the devotion with which he has sacrificed so many precious gifts at the shrine of those paltry idols which he has set up for himself among his lakes and his mountains. Solitary musings, amidst such scenes, might no doubt be expected to nurse up the mind to the majesty of poetical conception,—(though it is remarkable, that all the greater poets lived, or had lived, in the full current of society):—But the collision of equal minds,—the admonition of prevailing impressions—seems necessary to reduce its redundancies, and repress that tendency to extravagance or puerility, into which the self-indulgence and self-admiration of genius is so apt to be betrayed, when it is allowed to wanton, without awe or restraint, in the triumph and delight of its own intoxication. That its flights should be graceful and glorious in the eyes of men, it seems almost to be necessary that they should be made in the consciousness that men's eyes are to behold them,—and that the inward transport and vigour by which they are inspired, should be tempered by an occasional reference to what will be thought of them by those ultimate dispensers of glory. An habitual and general knowledge of the few settled and permanent maxims, which form the canon of general taste in all large and polished societies—a certain tact, which informs us at once that many things, which we still love and are moved by in secret, must necessarily be despised as childish, or derided as absurd, in all such societies—though it will not stand in the place of genius, seems necessary to the success of its exertions; and though it will never enable any one to produce the higher beauties of art, can alone secure the talent which does produce them from errors that must render it useless. Those who have most of the talent, however, commonly acquire this knowledge with the greatest facility;—and if Mr. Wordsworth, instead of confining himself almost entirely to the society of the dalesmen and cottagers, and little children, who form the subjects of his book, had condescended to mingle a little more with the people that were to read and judge of it, we cannot help thinking that its texture might have been considerably improved: At least it appears to us to be absolutely impossible, that any one who had lived or mixed familiarly with men of literature and ordinary judgment in poetry, (of course we exclude the coadjutors and disciples of his own school,) could ever have fallen into such gross faults, or so long mistaken them for beauties. His first essays we looked upon in a good degree as poetical paradoxes,—maintained experimentally, in order to display talent, and court notoriety;—and so maintained, with no more serious belief in their truth, than is usually generated by an ingenious and animated defence of other paradoxes. But when we find that he has been for twenty years exclusively employed upon articles of this very fabric, and that he has still enough of raw material on hand to keep him so employed for twenty years to come, we cannot refuse him the justice of believing that he is a sincere convert to his own system, and must ascribe the peculiarities of his composition, not to any transient affectation, or accidental caprice of imagination, but to a settled perversity of taste or understanding, which has been fostered, if not altogether created, by the circumstances to which we have alluded.

The volume before us, if we were to describe it very shortly, we should characterise as a tissue of moral and devotional ravings, in which innumerable changes are rung upon a few very simple and familiar ideas:—But with such an accompaniment of long words, long sentences, and unwieldy phrases—and such a hubbub of strained raptures and fantastical sublimities, that it is often difficult for the most skilful and attentive student to obtain a glimpse of the author's meaning—and altogether impossible for an ordinary reader to conjecture what he is about. Moral and religious enthusiasm, though undoubtedly poetical emotions, are at the same time but dangerous inspirers of poetry; nothing being so apt to run into interminable dulness or mellifluous extravagance, without giving the unfortunate author the slightest intimation of his danger. His laudable zeal for the efficacy of his preachments, he very naturally mistakes for the ardour of poetical inspiration;—and, while dealing out the high words and glowing phrases which are so readily supplied by themes of this description, can scarcely avoid believing that he is eminently original and impressive:—All sorts of commonplace notions and expressions are sanctified in his eyes, by the sublime ends for which they are employed; and the mystical verbiage of the Methodist pulpit is repeated, till the speaker entertains no doubt that he is the chosen organ of divine truth and persuasion.

But if such be the common hazards of seeking inspiration from those potent fountains, it may easily be conceived what chance Mr. Wordsworth had of escaping their enchantment,—with his natural propensities to wordiness, and his unlucky habit of debasing pathos with vulgarity. The fact accordingly is, that in this production he is more obscure that a Pindaric poet of the seventeenth century; and more verbose 'than even himself of yore;' while the wilfulness with which he persists in choosing his examples of intellectual dignity and tenderness exclusively from the lowest ranks of society, will be sufficiently apparent, from the circumstance of his having thought fit to make his chief prolocutor in this poetical dialogue, and chief advocate of Providence and Virtue, *an old Scotch Pedlar*—retired indeed from business—but still rambling about in his former haunts, and gossiping among his old customers, without his pack on his shoulders. The other persons of the drama are, a retired military chaplain, who has grown half an atheist and half a misanthrope—the wife of an unprosperous weaver—a servant girl with her natural child—a parish pauper, and one or two other personages of equal rank and dignity.

The character of the work is decidedly didactic; and more than nine tenths of it are occupied with a species of dialogue, or rather a series of long sermons or harangues which pass between the pedlar, the author, the old chaplain, and a worthy vicar, who entertains the whole party at dinner on the last day of their excursion. The incidents which occur in the course of it are as few and trifling as can well be imagined;—and those which the different speakers narrate in the course of their discourses, are introduced rather to illustrate their arguments or opinions, than for any interest they are supposed to possess of their own.—The doctrine which the work is intended to enforce, we are by no means certain that we have discovered. In so far as we can collect, however, it seems to be neither more nor less than the old familiar one, that a firm belief in the providence of a wise and beneficent Being must be our great stay and support under all afflictions and perplexities upon earth—and that there are indications of his power and goodness in all the aspects of the visible universe, whether living or inanimate—every part of which should therefore be regarded with love and reverence, as exponents of those great attributes. We can testify, at least, that these salutary and important truths are inculcated at far greater length, and with more repetitions, than in any ten volumes of sermons that we ever perused. It is also maintained, with equal conciseness and originality, that there is frequently much good sense, as well as much enjoyment, in the humbler conditions of life; and that, in spite of great vices and abuses, there is a reasonable allowance both of happiness and goodness in society at large. If there be any deeper or more recondite doctrines in Mr. Wordsworth's book, we must confess that they have escaped us;—and, convinced as we are of the truth and soundness of those to which we have alluded, we cannot help thinking that they might have been better enforced with less parade and prolixity. His effusions on what may be called the physiognomy of external nature, or its moral and theological expression, are eminently fantastic, obscure, and affected.

[Jeffrey proceeds to summarize the poem, with comments on what he considers intolerable in it. Extracts, largely uncomprehended, follow. The critic continues:]

These examples, we perceive, are not very well chosen—but we have not leisure to improve the selection; and, such as they are, they may serve to give the reader a notion of the sort of merit which we meant to illustrate by their citation. When we look back to them, indeed, and to the other passages which we have now extracted, we feel half inclined to rescind the severe sentence which we passed on the work at the beginning:—But when we look into the work itself, we perceive that it cannot be rescinded. Nobody can be more disposed to do justice to the great powers of Mr. Wordsworth than we are; and, from the first time that he came before us, down to the present moment, we have uniformly testified in their favour, and assigned indeed our high sense of their value as the chief ground of the bitterness with which we resented their perversion. That perversion, however, is now far more visible than their original dignity; and while we collect the fragments, it is impossible not to mourn over the ruins from which we are condemned to pick them. If any one should doubt of the existence of such a perversion, or be disposed to dispute about the instances we have hastily brought forward, we would just beg leave to refer him to the general plan and character of the poem now before us. Why should Mr. Wordsworth have made his hero a superannuated Pedlar? What but the most wretched affectation, or provoking perversity of taste, could induce any one to place his chosen advocate of wisdom and virtue in so absurd and fantastic a condition? Did Mr. Wordsworth really imagine, that his favourite doctrines were likely to gain any thing in point of effect or authority by being put into the mouth of a person accustomed to higgle about tape, or brass sleeve-buttons? Or is it not plain that, independent of the ridicule and disgust which such a personification must excite in many of his readers, its adoption exposes his work throughout to the charge of revolting incongruity, and utter disregard of probability or nature? For, after he has thus wilfully debased his moral teacher by a low occupation, is there one word that he puts into his mouth, or one sentiment of which he makes him the organ, that has the most remote reference to that occupation? Is there any thing in his learned, abstract, and logical harangues, that savours of the calling that is ascribed to him? Are any of their materials such as a pedlar could possibly have dealt in? Are the manners, the diction, the sentiments, in any, the very smallest degree, accommodated to a person in that condition? or are they not eminently and conspicuously such as could not by possibility belong to it? A man who went about selling flannel and pocket-handkerchiefs in this lofty diction, would soon frighten away all his customers; and would infallibly pass either for a madman, or for some learned and affected gentleman, who, in a frolic, had taken up a character which he was peculiarly ill qualified for supporting.

The absurdity in this case, we think, is palpable and glaring: but it is exactly of the same nature with that which infects the whole substance of the work—a puerile ambition of singularity engrafted on an unlucky predilection for truisms; and an affected passion for simplicity and humble life, most awkwardly combined with a taste for mystical refinements, and all the gorgeousness of obscure phraseology. His taste for simplicity is evinced by sprinkling up and down his interminable declamations a few descriptions of baby-houses, and of old hats with wet brims; and his amiable partiality for humble life, by assuring us that a wordy rhetorician, who talks about Thebes, and allegorizes all the heathen mythology, was once a pedlar—and making him break in upon his magnificent orations with two or three awkward notices of something that he had seen when selling winter raiment about the country—or of the changes in the state of society, which had almost annihilated his former calling.

"ENDYMION" AND "LAMIA"

W e had never happened to see either of these volumes till very lately—and
have been exceedingly struck with the genius they display, and the spirit of
poetry which breathes through all their extravagance. That imitation of our
older writers, and especially of our older dramatists, to which we cannot help
flattering ourselves that we have somewhat contributed, has brought on, as it
were, a second spring in our poetry;—and few of its blossoms are either more
profuse of sweetness, or richer in promise, that this which is now before us.
Mr. Keats, we understand, is still a very young man; and his whole works,
indeed, bear evidence enough of the fact. They are full of extravagance and
irregularity, rash attempts at originality, interminable wanderings, and excessive obscurity. They manifestly require, therefore, all the indulgence that can
be claimed for a first attempt:—But we think it no less plain that they deserve
it: For they are flushed all over with the rich lights of fancy; and so coloured
and bestrewn with the flowers of poetry, that even while perplexed and
bewildered in their labyrinths, it is impossible to resist the intoxication of their
sweetness, or to shut our hearts to the enchantments they so lavishly present.
The models upon which he has formed himself, in the Endymion, the earliest
and by much the most considerable of his poems, are obviously The Faithful
Shepherdess of Fletcher, and The Sad Shepherd of Ben Jonson;—the exquisite metres and inspired diction of which he has copied with great boldness and
fidelity—and, like his great originals, has also contrived to impart to the whole
piece that true rural and poetical air—which breathes only in them, and in
Theocritus—which is at once homely and majestic, luxurious and rude, and
sets before us the genuine sights and sounds and smells of the country, with
all the magic and grace of Elysium. His subject has the disadvantage of being
Mythological; and in this respect, as well as on account of the raised and
rapturous tone it consequently assumes, his poem, it may be thought, would be
better compared to the Comus and the Arcades of Milton, of which, also, there
are many traces of imitation. The great distinction, however, between him and
these divine authors, is, that imagination in them is subordinate to reason and
judgment, while, with him, it is paramount and supreme—that their ornaments and images are employed to embellish and recommend just sentiments,
engaging incidents, and natural characters, while his are poured out without
measure or restraint, and with no apparent design but to unburden the breast
of the author, and give vent to the overflowing vein of his fancy. The thin and
scanty tissue of his story is merely the light framework on which his florid
wreaths are suspended; and while his imaginations go rambling and entangling themselves every where, like wild honeysuckles, all idea of sober reason,
and plan, and consistency, is utterly forgotten, and 'strangled in their waste
fertility.' A great part of the work, indeed, is written in the strangest and most
fantastical manner than can be imagined. It seems as if the author had

517

ventured every thing that occurred to him in the shape of a glittering image or striking expression—taken the first word that presented itself to make up a rhyme, and then made that word the germ of a new cluster of images—a hint for a new excursion of the fancy—and so wandered on, equally forgetful whence he came, and heedless whither he was going, till he had covered his pages with an interminable arabesque of connected and incongruous figures, that multiplied as they extended, and were only harmonised by the brightness of their tints, and the graces of their forms. In this rash and headlong career he has of course many lapses and failures. There is no work, accordingly, from which a malicious critic could cull more matter for ridicule, or select more obscure, unnatural, or absurd passages. But we do not take *that* to be our office;—and must beg leave, on the contrary, to say, that any one who, on this account, would represent the whole poem as despicable, must either have no notion of poetry, or no regard to truth.

It is, in truth, at least as full of genius as of absurdity; and he who does not find a great deal in it to admire and to give delight, cannot in his heart see much beauty in the two exquisite dramas to which we have already alluded; or find any great pleasure in some of the finest creations of Milton and Shakespeare. There are very many such persons, we verily believe, even among the reading and judicious part of the community—correct scholars, we have no doubt, many of them, and, it may be, very classical composers in prose and in verse—but utterly ignorant, on our view of the matter, of the true genius of English poetry, and incapable of estimating its appropriate and most exquisite beauties. With that spirit we have no hesitation in saying that Mr. Keats is deeply imbued—and of those beauties he has presented us with many striking examples. We are very much inclined indeed to add, that we do not know any book which we would sooner employ as a test to ascertain whether any one had in him a native relish for poetry, and a genuine sensibility to its intrinsic charm. The greater and more distinguished poets of our country have so much else in them, to gratify other tastes and propensities, that they are pretty sure to captivate and amuse those to whom their poetry may be but an hindrance and obstruction, as well as those to whom it constitutes their chief attraction. The interest of the stories they tell—the vivacity of the characters they delineate—the weight and force of the maxims and sentiments in which they abound—the very pathos, and wit and humour they display, which may all and each of them exist apart from their poetry, and independent of it, are quite sufficient to account for their popularity, without referring much to that still higher gift, by which they subdue to their enchantments those whose souls are truly attuned to the finer impulses of poetry. It is only, therefore, where those other recommendations are wanting, or exist in a weaker degree, that the true force of the attraction, exercised by the pure poetry with which they are so often combined, can be fairly appreciated:—where, without much incident or many characters, and with little wit, wisdom, or arrangement, a number of bright pictures are presented to the imagination, and a fine feeling expressed of those mysterious relations by which visible external things are assimilated with inward thoughts and emotions, and become the images and exponents of all passions and affections. To an unpoetical reader such passages will generally appear mere raving and absurdity—and to this censure a very great part of the volumes before us will certainly be exposed, with this class of readers. Even in the judgment of a fitter audience, however, it must we fear, be admitted, that, besides the riot and extravagance of his fancy, the scope and substance of Mr. Keats's poetry is rather too dreamy and abstracted to excite the strongest interest, or to sustain the attention through a work of any great compass or extent. He deals too much with shadowy and incomprehensible beings, and is too constantly rapt into an extramundane Elysium, to command a lasting interest with ordinary mortals—and must employ the agency of more varied and coarser emotions, if he wishes to take rank with the enduring poets of this or of former generations. There is something very curious, too, we think, in the way in which he, and Mr. Barry Cornwall also, have dealt with the Pagan mythology, of which they have made so much use in their poetry. Instead of presenting its imaginary persons under the trite and vulgar traits that belong to them in the ordinary systems, little more is borrowed from these than the general conception of their condition and relations; and an original character and distinct individuality is then bestowed upon them, which has all the merit of invention, and all the grace and attraction of the fictions on which it is engrafted. The ancients, though they probably did not stand in any great awe of their deities, have yet abstained very much from any minute or dramatic representation of their feelings and affections. In Hesiod and Homer, they are broadly delineated by some of their actions and adventures, and introduced to us merely as the agents in those particular transactions; while in the Hymns, from those ascribed to Orpheus and Homer, down to those of Callimachus, we have little but pompous epithets and invocations, with a flattering commemoration of their most famous exploits—and are never allowed to enter into their bosoms, or follow out the train of their feelings, with the presumption of our human sympathy. Except the love-song of the Cyclops to his Sea Nymph in Theocritus—the Lamentation of Venus for Adonis in Moschus—and the more recent Legend of Apuleius, we scarcely recollect a passage in all the writings of antiquity in which the passions of an immortal are fairly disclosed to the scrutiny and observation of men. The author before us, however, and some of his contemporaries, have dealt differently with the subject;—and, sheltering the violence of the fiction under the ancient traditionary fable, have in reality created and imagined an entire new set of characters; and brought closely and minutely before us the loves and sorrows and perplexities of beings, with whose names and supernatural attributes we had long been familiar, without any sense or feeling of their personal character. We have more than doubts of the fitness of such personages to maintain a permanent interest with the modern public;—but the way in which they are here managed certainly gives them the best chance that now remains for them; and, at all events, it cannot be denied that the effect is striking and graceful.

FROM

THE STATE OF MODERN POETRY

W e have been rather in an odd state for some years, we think, both as to Poets and Poetry. Since the death of Lord Byron there has been no king in Israel; and none of his former competitors now seem inclined to push their pretensions to the vacant throne. Scott, and Moore, and Southey, appear to have nearly renounced verse, and finally taken service with the Muses of prose:—Crabbe, and Coleridge, and Wordsworth, we fear, are burnt out:—and Campbell and Rogers repose under their laurels, and, contented each with his own elegant little domain, seem but little disposed either to extend its boundaries, or to add new provinces to their rule. Yet we cannot say either that this indifference may be accounted for by the impoverished state of the kingdom whose sovereignty is thus in abeyance, or that the *interregnum* has as yet given rise to any notable disorders. On the contrary, we do not remember a time when it would have been a prouder distinction to be at the head of English poetry, or when the power which every man has to do what is good in his own eyes, seemed less in danger of being abused. Three poets of great promise have indeed been lost, 'in the morn and liquid dew of their youth'—in Kirke White, in Keats, and in Pollok; and a powerful, though more uncertain genius extinguished, less prematurely, in Shelley. Yet there still survive writers of great talents and attraction. The elegance, the tenderness, the feminine sweetness of Felicia Hemans—the classical copiousness of Milman—the facility and graceful fancy of Hunt, though defrauded of half its praise by carelessness and presumption—and, besides many others, the glowing pencil and gorgeous profusion of the author more immediately before us.

There is no want, then, of poetry among us at the present day; nor even of very good and agreeable poetry. But there are no miracles of the art— nothing that marks its descent from 'the highest heaven of invention'— nothing visibly destined to inherit immortality. Speaking very generally, we would say, that our poets never showed a better or less narrow taste, or a juster relish of what is truly excellent in the models that lie before them, and yet have seldom been more deficient in the powers of creative genius; or rather, perhaps, that with an unexampled command over the raw materials of poetry, and a true sense of their value, they have rarely been so much wanting in the skill to work them up to advantage—in the power of attaching human interests to sparkling fancies, making splendid descriptions subservient to intelligible purposes, or fixing the fine and fugitive spirit of poetry in some tangible texture of exalted reason or sympathetic emotion. The improvement in all departments is no doubt immense, since the days when Hoole and Hayley were thought great poets. But it is not quite clear to us, that the fervid and florid Romeos of

520

the present day, may not be gathered, in no very long course of years, to the capacious tomb of these same ancient Capulets. They are but shadows, we fear, that have no independent or substantial existence—and though reflected from grand and beautiful originals, have but little chance to maintain their place in the eyes of the many generations by whom those originals will yet be worshipped—but who will probably prefer, each in their turn, shadows of their own creating.

The present age, we think, has an hundred times more poetry, and more true taste for poetry, than that which immediately preceded it,—and of which, reckoning its duration from the extinction of the last of Queen Anne's wits down to about thirty odd years ago, we take leave to say that it was, beyond all dispute, the most unpoetical age in the annals of this or any other considerable nation. Nothing, indeed, can be conceived more dreary and sterile than the aspect of our national poetry from the time of Pope and Thomson, down to that of Burns and Cowper. With the exception of a few cold and scattered lights— Gray, Goldsmith, Warton, Mason, and Johnson—men of sense and eloquence occasionally exercising themselves in poetry out of scholar-like ambition, but not poets in any genuine sense of the word—the whole horizon was dark, silent, and blank; or only presented objects upon which it is now impossible to look seriously without shame. These were the happy days of Pye and Whitehead—of Hoole and of Hayley—and then, throughout the admiring land, resounded the mighty names of Jerningham and Jage, of Edwards, of Murphy, of Moore, and of others whom we cannot but feel it is a baseness to remember.

The first man who broke 'the numbing spell' was Cowper,—(for Burns was not generally known till long after,)—and, though less highly gifted than several who came after him, this great praise should always be remembered in his epitaph. He is entitled, in our estimation, to a still greater praise; and that is, to the praise of absolute and entire originality. Whatever he added to the resources of English poetry, was drawn directly from the fountains of his own genius, or the stores of his own observation. He was a copyist of no style—a restorer of no style; and did not, like the eminent men who succeeded him, merely recall the age to the treasures it had almost forgotten, open up anew a vein that had been long buried in rubbish, or revive a strain which had already delighted the ears of a more aspiring generation. That this, however, was the case with the poets who immediately followed, cannot, we think, be reasonably doubted; and the mere statement of the fact, seems to us sufficiently to explain the present state of our poetry—its strength and its weakness—its good taste and its deficient power—its resemblance to works that can never die—and its own obvious liability to the accidents of mortality.

It has advanced beyond the preceding age, simply by going back to one still older; and has put *its* poverty to shame only by unlocking the hoards of a remoter ancestor. It has reformed merely by restoring; and innovated by a systematic recurrence to the models of antiquity. Scott went back as far as to the Romances of Chivalry: and the poets of the lakes to the humbler and more pathetic simplicity of our early ballads; and both, and all who have since adventured in poetry, have drawn, without measure or disguise, from the living springs of Shakespeare and Spenser, and the other immortal writers who adorned the glorious era of Elizabeth and James.

It is impossible to value more highly than we do the benefits of this restoration. It is a great thing to have rendered the public once more familiar with these mighty geniuses—and, if we must be copyists, there is nothing certainly that deserves so well to be copied. The consequence, accordingly, has been, that, even in our least inspired writers, we can again reckon upon freedom and variety of style, some sparks of fancy, some traits of nature, and some echo, however feeble, of that sweet melody of rhythm and of diction, which must linger for ever in every ear which has once drank in the music of Shakespeare; while, in authors of greater vigour, we are sure to meet also with gorgeous descriptions and splendid imagery, tender sentiments expressed in simple words, and vehement passions pouring themselves out in fearless and eloquent declamation.

But with all this, it is but too true that we have still a feeling that we are glorying but in secondhand finery and counterfeit inspiration; and that the poets of the present day, though they have not only Taste enough to admire, but skill also to imitate, the great masters of an earlier generation, have not inherited the Genius that could have enabled them either to have written as they wrote, or even to have come up, without their example, to the level of their own imitations. The heroes of our modern poetry, indeed, are little better, as we take it, than the heroes of the modern theatres—attired, no doubt, in the exact costume of the persons they represent, and wielding their gorgeous antique arms with an exact imitation of heroic movements and deportment— nay, even evincing in their tones and gestures, a full sense of inward nobleness and dignity—and yet palpably unfit to engage in any feat of actual prowess, and incapable, in their own persons, even of conceiving what they have been so well taught to personate. We feel, in short, that our modern poetry is substantially derivative, and, as geologists say of our present earth, of secondary formation—made up of the *debris* of a former world, and composed, in its loftiest and most solid parts, of the fragments of things far more lofty and solid.

The consequence, accordingly, is, that we have abundance of admirable descriptions, ingenious similitudes, and elaborate imitations—but little invention, little direct or overwhelming passion, and little natural simplicity. On the contrary, every thing almost now resolves into description,—descriptions not only of actions and external objects, but of characters, and emotions, and the signs and accompaniments of emotion—and all given at full length, ostentatious, elaborate, and highly finished, even in their counterfeit carelessness and disorder. But no sudden unconscious bursts, either of nature or of passion—no casual flashes of fancy, no slight passing intimations of deep but latent emotions, no rash darings of untutored genius, soaring proudly up into the infinite unknown! The chief fault, however, is the want of subject and of matter—the absence of real persons, intelligible interests, and conceivable incidents, to which all this splendid apparatus of rhetoric and fancy may attach itself, and thus get a purpose and a meaning, which it never can possess without them. To satisfy a rational being, even in his most sensitive mood, we require not only a just representation of passion in the abstract, but also that it shall be embodied in some individual person whom we can understand and sympathize with—and cannot long be persuaded to admire splendid images and ingenious allusions which bear upon no comprehensible object, and seem to be introduced for no other purpose than to be admired.

Without going the full length of the mathematician, who could see no beauty in poetry because it *proved* nothing, we cannot think it quite unreasonable to insist on knowing a little what it is about; and must be permitted to hold it a good objection to the very finest composition, that it gives us no distinct conceptions, either of character, of action, of passion, or of the author's design in laying it before us. Now this, we think, is undeniably the prevailing fault of our modern poets. What they do best is description—in a story certainly they do not excel—their pathos is too often overstrained and rhetorical, and their reflections mystical and bombastic. The great want, however, as we have already said, is the want of solid subject, and of persons who can be supposed to have existed. There is plenty of splendid drapery and magnificent localities—but nobody to put on the one, or to inhabit and vivify the other. Instead of living persons, we have commonly little else than mere puppets or academy figures—and very frequently are obliged to be contented with scenes of still life altogether—with gorgeous dresses tossed into glittering heaps, or suspended in dazzling files—and enchanted solitudes, where we wait in vain for some beings like ourselves, to animate its beauties with their loves, or to aggravate its horrors by their contentions.

The consequence of all this is, that modern poems, with great beauty of diction, much excellent description, and very considerable displays of taste and imagination, are generally languid, obscure, and tiresome. Short pieces, however, it should be admitted, are frequently very delightful—elegant in composition, sweet and touching in sentiment, and just and felicitous in expressing the most delicate shades both of character and emotion. Where a single scene, thought, or person, is to be represented, the improved taste of the age, and its general familiarity with beautiful poetry, will generally ensure, from our better artists, not only a creditable, but a very excellent production. What used to be true of *female* poets only, is now true of all. We have not wings, it would seem, for a long flight—and the larger works of those who pleased us most with their small ones, scarcely ever fail of exhibiting the very defects from which we should have thought them most secure—and turn out insipid, verbose, and artificial, like their neighbours. In little poems, in short, which do not require any choice or management of subject, we succeed very well; but where a story is to be told, and an interest to be sustained, through a considerable train of incidents and variety of characters, our want of vigour and originality is but too apt to become apparent; and is only the more conspicuous from our skilful and familiar use of that inspired diction, and those poetical materials which we have derived from the mighty masters to whose vigour and originality they were subservient, and on whose genius they waited but as 'servile ministers.'

Henry Crabb Robinson

1775–1867

Henry Crabb Robinson was born at Bury St. Edmunds, Suffolk, on May 13, 1775. In 1796 he moved to London to study law, was called to the bar in 1813, and practiced on the Norfolk circuit until 1828. Meanwhile, having inherited a small private income, he traveled to Germany in 1800 and met with leading literary figures of the period, including Goethe, Schiller, Herder, and Mme. de Staël (whom he helped to gather materials for her influential book *De l'Allemagne*). Returning to England in 1805, Robinson became an active disseminator of German literary and philosophical ideas. He also wrote for *The Times*, helped to found the University of London, and was an active opponent of slavery.

Robinson was on close terms with the English Romantics, including Coleridge, Wordsworth, and Blake. His diaries, more than one hundred volumes of which survive, provide revealing accounts of Blake in his last years as well as glimpses of other literary and political figures. His lengthy correspondence with William and Dorothy Wordsworth, whom he visited frequently at Rydal Mount, has also been preserved. He died in London on February 5, 1867.

REMINISCENCES OF BLAKE

1810

I was amusing myself this Spring by writing an account of the insane poet & painter engraver, *Blake*. Perthes of Hamburg had written to me asking me to send him an article for a new German Magazine entitled *Vaterländische Annalen* wh. he was abt to set up. And Dr. Malkin having in the memoirs of his son given an acct of this extraordinary genius with Specimens of his poems, I resolved out of these to compile a paper. And this I did, & the paper was translated by Dr. Julius, who many years afterwards introduced himself to me as my translator. It appears in the single number of the 2d. vol. of the *Vaterländische Annalen*. For it was at this time that Buonaparte united Hamburg to the French Empire, on wh. Perthes manfully gave up the Magazine, saying, as he had no longer a Vaterland, there cd. be no *Vaterländische Annalen*. But before I drew up this paper, I went to see a Gallery of Blake's paintings, wh. were exhibited by his brother, a hosier in Carnaby Market; the entrance was 2/6, catalogue included. I was deeply interested by the Catalogue as well as by the pictures. I took 4, telling the brother I hoped he wd. let me come in again. He said, 'Oh! as often as you please.' I dare say such a thing had never happened before or did afterwards.

I afterwards became acquainted with Blake & will postpone till hereafter what I have to relate of this extraordinary character, whose life has since been written very inadequately by Allan Cunningham in his Lives of the English artists . . .

1825–1827

It was at the latter end of the year 1825 that I put in writing my recollections of this remarkable man. The larger portion are under the date of the 10th of Decr. He died in the year 1827. I have therefore now revised what I wrote on the 10th of Decr. & afterwards, & without any attempt to reduce to order or make consistent the wild & strange, strange rhapsodies uttered by this insane man of genius, thinking it better to put down what I find as it occurs, tho' I am aware of the objection that may justly be made to the recording the ravings of insanity in which it may be said there can be found no principle, as there is no ascertainable law of mental association wh. is obeyed; & from wh. therefore nothing can be learned.

This would be perfectly true of *mere* madness, but does not apply to that form of insanity or lunacy called Monomania, & may be disregarded in a case like the present in which the subject of the remark was unquestionably what a German wd. call a *"Verunglückter Genie"* whose theosophic dreams bear a close resemblance to those of *Swedenborg;* whose genius as an artist was praised by no less men than *Flaxman & Fuseli*, & whose poems were thought worthy republication by the biographer of *Swedenborg, Wilkinson*, & of which Wordsworth said, after reading a number, "They were the 'Songs of Innocence & Experience,' showing the two opposite states of the human soul." There is no doubt this poor man was mad, but there is something in the madness of this man which interests me more than the sanity of Lord Byron or Walter Scott!—

The German painter Götzenberger, (a man indeed who ought not to be named *after the others* as an authority for my writing abt Blake) said on his returning to Germany about the time at which I am now arrived, "I saw in England many men of talents, but only 3 men of Genius, Coleridge, Flaxman & Blake, & of these Blake was the greatest." I do not mean to intimate my assent to this opinion, nor to do more than supply such materials as my intercourse with him furnishes to an uncritical narrative, to wh. I shall confine myself. I have written a few sentences in these reminiscences already, those of the year 1810. I had not then begun the regular journal which I afterwards kept. I will therefore go over the ground again & introduce these recollections of 1825 by a reference to the slight knowledge I had of him before, & what occasioned my taking an interest in him, not caring to repeat what Cunningham has recorded of him in the volume of his Lives of the British Painters, &c. &c. except thus much. It appears that he was born [on 28th November 1757]. *Dr. Malkin* our Bury Grammar School Head Master published in the year 1806 a memoir of a very precocious child who died [blank in MS.] years old, & he prefixed to the Memoir an engraving of a portrait of him by Blake, & in the vol. he gave an acct. of Blake as a painter & poet & printed some specimens of his poems, viz. *The Tiger* & ballads & mystical lyrical poems, all of a wild character, & M[alkin] gave an account of visions wh. Blake related to his acquaintance. I knew that Flaxman thought highly of him, & tho' he did not venture to extol him as a genuine Seer, yet he did not join in the ordinary derision of him as a madman. Without having seen him, yet I had already conceived a high opinion of him, & thought he wd. furnish matter for a paper interesting to Germans. And therefore when *Fred. Perthes* the patriotic publisher at Hamburg wrote to me in 1810, requesting me to give him an article for his Patriotische Annalen, I thought I cd. do no better than send him a paper on Blake . . .

Lamb was delighted with the Catalogue, especially with the description of a painting afterwards engraved, & connected with wh. is an anecdote that unexplained wd. reflect discredit on a most amiable & excellent man, but wh. Flaxman considered to have been the wilful act of *Stod[d]art*. It was after the friends of Blake had circulated a subscription paper for an engraving of his *Canterbury Pilgrims* that *Stod[d]art* was made a party to an engraving of a painting of the same subject by himself. Stoddart's work is well-known: Blake's is known by very few. Lamb preferred it greatly to Stoddart's & declared that Blake's description was the finest criticism he had ever read of Chaucer's poem.

In this Catalogue, Blake writes of himself in the most outrageous language, says "This artist defies all competition in colouring," that none can beat him, for none can beat the Holy Ghost; that he & Raphael & Michael Angelo were under the divine influence, while Corregio & Titian worshipped a lascivious & therefore cruel devil, Rubens a proud devil &c. He declared, speaking of colour, Titian's men to be of leather & his women of chalk, & ascribed his own perfection in colouring to the advantage he enjoyed in seeing daily the primitive men walking in their native nakedness in the mountains of Wales.—There were about 30 oil paintings, the colouring excessively dark & high, the veins black & the colour of the primitive men very like that of the red Indians. In his estimation they wd. probably be the primitive men. Many of his designs were unconscious imitations. This appears also in his published works,—the designs to *Blair's Grave,* wh. Fuseli & Schiavonetti highly extolled, & in his designs to illustrate *Job* published after his death for the benefit of his widow.

To this Catalogue & to the printed poems, the small pamphlet wh. appeared in 1783, the edition put forth by Wilkinson, 'The Songs of Innocence,' other works &c already mentioned, to wh. I have to add the first two books of Young's Night Thoughts, & Allan Cumberland's Life of him, I now refer, & will confine myself to the memorandums I took of his conversation. I . . . for the first time dined in his company at the Aders'. . . . He was then 68 years of age. He had a broad, pale face, a large full eye with a benignant expression; at the same time a look of languor except when excited, & then he had an air of inspiration, but not such as without a previous acquaintance with him, or attending to *what* he said, would suggest the notion that he was insane. There was nothing *wild* about his look & though very ready to be drawn out to the assertion of his favourite ideas, yet with no warmth as if he wanted to make proselytes. Indeed one of the peculiar features of his scheme as far as it was consistent was indifference & a very extraordinary degree of tolerance & satisfaction with what had taken place, a sort of pious & humble optimism, not the scornful optimism of *Candide*. But at the same time that he was very ready to praise he seemed incapable of envy, as he was of discontent. He warmly praised some composition of Mrs Aders. . . .

On the 17th I called on him in his house in Fountains Court in the Strand. The interview was a short one, & what I saw was more remarkable than what I heard. He was at work engraving in a small bedroom, light & looking out on a mean yard—everythg. in the room squalid, & indicating poverty except himself. And there was a natural gentility about, & an insensibility to the seeming poverty which quite removed the impression. Besides, his linen was clean, his hand white & his air quite unembarrassed when he begged me to sit down, as if he were in a palace. There was but one chair in the room besides that on wh. he sat. On my putting my hand to it, I found that it would have fallen to pieces if I had lifted it. So, as if I had been a Sybarite, I said with a smile, 'Will you let me indulge myself?' And I sat on the bed and near him. And during my short stay there was nothing in him that betrayed that he was aware of what to other persons might have been even offensive, not in his person, but in all about him.

His wife I saw at this time, & she seemed to be the very woman to make him happy. She had been formed by him. Indeed otherwise she cd. not have lived with him. Notwithstanding her dress, wh. was poor & dirty, she had a good expression in her countenance—& with a dark eye, had remains of beauty in her youth. She had that virtue of virtues in a wife, an implicit reverence of her husband. It is quite certain that she believed in all his visions, & on one occasion, not this day, speaking of his visions she said, 'You know dear, the first time you saw God was when you were 4 years old. And he put his head to the window & set you ascreaming.' In a word, she was formed on the Miltonic model, & like the first wife, Eve, worshipped God in her husband, he being to her what God was to him. Vide Milton's Par. Lost, passim.

He was making designs or engraving, I forget which—Cary's Dante was before [him]. He shewed me some of his designs from Dante of which I do not presume to speak. They were too much above me. But Götzenberger, whom I afterwds. took to see them expressed the highest admiration of them. They are in the hands of *Linnell*, the painter, & it has been suggested, are reserved by him for publication when Blake may have become an object of interest to a greater number than he can be at this age . . .

1826. On the 24th I called a second time on him, & on this occasion it was that I read to him *Wordsworth's Ode* on the supposed pre-existent state, & the subject of W.'s religious character was discussed when we met on the 18th of Feb. & the 12th of May. I will here bring together W. Blake's declaratns. concerning W. & set down his marginalia in the 8vo. edit. A.D. 1815. Vol. I. I had been in the habit when reading this marvellous Ode to friends, to omit one or two passages, especially that beginning

But there's a tree, of many one

lest I shd. be rendered ridiculous, being unable to explain precisely *what* I admired—not that I acknowledged this to be a fair test. But with Blake I cd. fear nothing of the kind, & it was this very Stanza wh. threw him almost into an hysterical rapture. His delight in W.'s poetry was intense. Nor did it seem less notwithstanding by the reproaches he continually cast on W. for his imputed worship of nature, wh. in the mind of Blake constituted Atheism.

The combn. of the warmest praise with imputations which from another wd. assume the most serious character & the liberty he took to interpret as he pleased, rendered it as difficult to be offended as to reason with him. The eloquent descriptions of Nature in W.'s poems were conclusive proof of atheism, for whoever believes in Nature said B. disbelieves in God. For Nature is the work of the Devil. On my obtaining from him the declaration that the Bible was the work of God, I referred to the commencement of Genesis "In the beginning God created the Heaven & the Earth." But I gained nothing by this, for I was triumphantly told that this God was not Jehovah, but the Elohim, & the doctrine of the Gnostics repeated with sufficient consistency to silence one so unlearned as myself.

I lent him the 8vo. ed. of 2 vols. of W.'s poems wh. he had in his possession at the time of his death. They were sent me then. I did not recognise the pencil notes he made in them to be his for some time, & was on the point of rubbing them out, under that impression when I made the discovery. The following are found in the 5th Vol.:—In the fly-leaf under the words Poems referring to the Period of Childhood.

"I see in Wordsw. the natural man rising up agst. the spiritual man continually & then he is no poet, but a heathen philosopher at Enmity agst. all true poetry or inspiration." Under the first poem

> And I cd. wish my days to be
> Bound each to each by natural piety

he had written "There is no such thing as natural piety because the natural man is at enmity with God." p. 43 under the verses to H. C. six years old. "This is all in the highest degree imaginative & equal to any poet, but not superior. I cannot think that real poets have any competition. None are greatest in the Kingdom of God. It is so in Poetry." page 44 "On the influence of natural objects." at the bottom of the page: "Natural objects always did & now do weaken, deaden & obliterate Imagination in me. W. must know that what he writes valuable is not to be found in Nature. Read Michael Angelo's Sonnet, Vol. 2, p. 179."—that is the one beginning

> No mortal object did these eyes behold
> When first they met the placid light of thine.

It is remarkable that Blake whose judgements were in most points so very singular, on one subject closely connected with W.'s poetical reputation should have taken a very commonplace view. Over the heading of the "Essay supplementary to the Preface" at the end of the vol. he wrote "I do not know who wrote these Prefaces: they are very mischievous & direct contrary to W.'s own practice" (p. 341). This is not the defence of his own style in opposition to what is called Poetic Diction, but a sort of historic vindication of the *unpopular* poets. On Macpherson, p. 364. W. wrote with the severity with wh. all great writers have written of him. Blake's comment below was:—"I believe both Macpherson & Chatterton, that what they say is ancient is so." & in the following page: "I own myself an admirer of Ossian equally with any other poet whatever, Rowley & Chatterton also." And at the end of this Essay he wrote "It appears to me as if the last paragraph beginning 'Is it the result of the whole' & it [?] was written by another hand & mind from the rest of these Prefaces: they are the opinions of [blank in MS.] landscape painter. Imagination is the divine vision not of the World, nor of Man, nor from Man as he is a natural man, but only as he is a spiritual Man. Imagination has nothing to do with Memory." . . .

In the No.: of the Gents. Magazine for last Jan. [1852] there is a letter by *Cromek* to Blake, printed in order to convict B[lake] of selfishness. It cannot possibly be substantially true. I may elsewhere notice it. . . .

It was, I believe on the 7th of December that I saw him last. I had just heard of the death of Flaxman, a man whom he professed to admire, & was curious how he wd. receive the intelligence. It was as I expected. He had been ill during the summer, & he said with a smile, 'I thought I shd. have gone first.' He then said, 'I cannot think of death as more than the going out of one room into another.' And Flaxman was no longer thought of. He relapsed into his ordinary train of thinking. Indeed I had by this time learned that there was nothing to be gained by frequent intercourse, & therefore it was that after this interview I was not anxious to be frequent in my visits. This day he said, 'Men are born with an Angel & a Devil.' This he himself interpreted as Soul & Body. And as I have long since said of the strange sayings of a man who enjoys a high reputation "It is more in the language than the thoughts that the singularity is to be looked for." And this day he spoke of the Old Testament as if it were the Evil Element. "Christ, he said, took much after his Mother & in so far he was one of the worst of men." On my asking him for an instance, he referred to his turning the money changers out of the temple—he had no right to do that. He digressed into a condemnation of those who sit in judgment on others. "I have never known a very bad man who had not somethg. very good abt him." Speaking of the Atonement in the ordinary Calvinistic sense, he said "It is a horrible doctrine; if another pay your debt, I do not forgive it." I have no account of any other call, but this is probably an omission. I took Götzenberger to see him & he met the Masqueriers in my Chambers. Masquerier was not the man to meet him. He could not humour B. nor understand the peculiar sense in wh. B. was to be recd.

1827. My journal of this year contains nothing abt Blake. But in Jan. 1828 Barron Field & myself called on Mrs. Blake. The poor old lady was more affected than I expected she would be at the sight of me. She spoke of her husband as dying like an Angel. She informed us that she was going to live with Linnell as his housekeeper, & we understood that she would live with him. And he, as it were, to farm her services & take all she had. The Engravings of Job were his already. Chaucer's Canterbury Pilgrims were hers. I took 2 copies; one I gave to C. Lamb. Barron Field took a proof.

Mrs. Blake died within a few years. And since Blake's death Linnell has not found the market. I took for granted he would seek for Blake's works. Wilkinson printed a small edition of his poems including the "Songs of Innocence & Experience" a few years ago. And Monkton Milne talks of printing an edition. I have a few coloured engravings, but B[lake] is still an object of interest exclusively to men of imaginative taste & psychological curiosity. I doubt much whether these Memoirs will be of any use to this small class.

I have been reading since the life of Blake by Allan Cunningham Vol. II, p. 143 of his Lives of the Painters. It recognises perhaps more of Blake's merit than might have been expected of a Scotch realist.

REMINISCENCES

COLERIDGE, WORDSWORTH, LAMB, &c.

I have a distinct recollection of reading the Monthly Review of the 1st. vol. of Coleridge's poems before I went abroad in 1800 & of the delight the extracts gave me, & my friend Mrs. Clarkson having become intimate with him, he [became] an object of interest with me from my return from Germany in 1805. And when he delivered lectures in the year 1808, Mrs Clarkson engaged me to interest myself in his lectures I needed no persuasion. I did hear some of his lectures that year but I had then engagements wh. put it out of my power to attend them regularly, but I wrote to her two letters in that year wh. she preserved & wh. have been printed by Mrs. Henry Coleridge in her vol. of Notes & Lectures on Shakespear. Pickering. 1849. They give me no pleasure in the perusal, but there was such a want of materials for the account Mrs. C[oleridge] wished to give of her father's lectures that she thought it worth while to print even these. But at the time of my attending these lectures I had no personal acquaintance with C. I have a letter from him written in May 1808, sending me an order to hear his lectures in wh. he says: "Nothing but endless interruptions & the necessity of dining out far oftener than is either good for me or pleasant to me, joined with the reluctance to move (partly from exhaustion by company I cannot keep out, for one cannot dare not be always 'not at home' or 'very particularly engaged,' & the last very often will not serve my turn) these added to my bread & cheese employments + my lectures which are—bread & cheese, i.e. a very losing bargain in a pecuniary view, have prevented me day after day from returning your kind calls. Piu vorrei piu non posso. In the mean time I have left your name with the old woman & the attendants in the office as one to whom I am always at home when I am at home. For Wordsworth has taught me to desire your acquaintance & to esteem you . . . & need I add that anyone so much regarded by Mrs. C[larkson], (whom I love even as my very own sister, whose Love for me, with Wordsworth's sister, wife & wife's sister form almost the only happiness I have on earth) can ever be indifferent to . . . &c. &c. &c. S. T. C."

Yet I find among my papers two 8vo. pages being minutes of C.'s lecture, Feb. 5, 1808 wh. I may not here refer to because they contain nothing personal.

It was not till 1811 that I kept anything like a diary. I am about to make extracts from it & I will extract from it & from the few letters I find from or concerning C. what I think worth preserving, & so set it apart among my Reminiscences.

It has since occurred to me that it will be more convenient if I combine in one continuous article all my reminiscences of Coleridge, Wordsworth, & Lamb. They all belong to one class & comprehend notices of Men of Genius, who tho' of a very different kind, were friends to each other, and besides, I became acquainted with them through the same friend Mrs. Clarkson. I may perhaps, not as their equal by any means, also insert what I have to say of their very excellent friend & an admirable writer, Southey, & also their enemy Hazlitt—in short all of this set or clique as they for some time were considered.

I begin these minutes after I had written the year 1810 & all the preceding, at which time my acquaintance with all of them had commenced & I have already written about them, but my former reminiscences are not in my possession. I therefore begin with the year 1811, & shall take chronologically what I find in my Diary.

Jan. 8. I soon found that tho' C. Lamb was a warm lover of Wordsw.'s poetry yet that he thought Coleridge the greater man. He preferred *The Ancient Mariner* to anything W. had written. Among W.'s poems, L. praised *Hart Leap Well*, not *The Leech-Gatherer*—also the *Sonnets*. He urged agst. Wordsw. what lies essentially in his *subjective* poetry, that W. cannot, like Shakesp[eare], become everything he pleases.

I had written thus far when I found a few pages written in Novr. & December 1810 devoted entirely to Coleridge. I will transfer the substance of them to this paper.

14*th Nov.* Saw Coleridge for the first time in private at Charles Lamb's. A short interview which allowed of little opportunity for the display of his peculiar powers. He related to us that Jeffrey, the Editor of *The Edinb. Review* had lately called on him & assured him that he was a great admirer of Wordsworth's poetry, that his *Lyrical Ballads* were always on his table &c; That he, (W.) had been attacked in the Rev[iew] only because the Errors of Men of Genius ought to be exposed. Jeffrey, he [C.] added was towards me even flattering: he was like a schoolboy who, having tried his man & been thrashed, becomes contentedly a fag.

Jeffrey spoke of Campbell to Coleridge, who had also been visited by him & whom C[oleridge] called 'a chicken-breasted fellow.' 'Camp., said J. is my intimate friend, but he is sadly envious. You outshone him in conversation & I am sure he therefore hates you thoroughly.'

15*th Nov. at Lamb's.* Coler., his friend Morgan, M. Burney &c. &c. C. spoke with warm praise of Wordsw: but blamed him for attaching himself to the low in his desire to avoid the artificial in genteel life. He should have recollected that verse being the language of passion required a style raised in harmony with it. One asks why tales so simple were not in prose. He 'with malice prepense' cast his reflexion on objects that do not naturally excite it. In the *Gypsies* for instance, had the whole world stood idle, more powerful considerations need not have been brought to expose the evil, than are brought forward on their account.

Of *Kant* he spoke in high praise. In his "Himmel-system" he combined the genius of Newton & Burnet. He praised the *Träume eines Geistersehers*, would translate his *Sublime & Beautiful* & thought the *Kritik der Urtheilskraft* the most astonishing of his works.

Fichte & *Schelling* he said will be found at last wrong where they have left their master, towards whom they shewd ingratitude. *Fichte* a great logician, Schelling perhaps a greater man. Schelling's *System* resolves itself into fanaticism not better than that of Jakob Böhmen.

C. had known *Tieck* at Rome but was not aware of his eminence as a poet. He conceded to *Goethe* universal talent, but felt his want of *moral life,* the defect of his poetry. *Schiller* he spoke more kindly of. He quoted "Nimmer, dass glaubt mir, erscheinen die Götter" (N.B. He has translated it). He censured the Graecomanie of S.'s last dramas.

Jean Paul. He said that J.P's wit consisted not in pointing out analogies in themselves striking, but in finding unexpected analogies. You admire, not the things combined, but the act of combination. And he applied this to *Windham.* N. B. It did not occur to me then to remark as it does now, that this is the character of *all* wit, & that that wh. he contrasted with it as a different kind of wit, is not wit, but acuteness.

He made an elaborate distinction between Fancy & Imagination. The excess of fancy is delirium, of imagn., mania. Fancy is the arbitrary bringing together of things that lie remote & forming them into a Unity: the materials lie ready for the fancy which acts by a sort of juxtaposition. On the other hand the Imagination under some excitement generates & produces a form of its own. The 'Seas of Milk & Ships of Amber' (? Belvidera) he quoted as fanciful delirium. As a sort of disease of imagination he related what occurred to himself. He had been watching intensely the motions of a kite among the mountains of Westmoreland, when he, on a sudden, saw two kites in an opposite direction. This illusion lasted some time. At last he discovered that the two kites were the fluttering branches of a tree beyond a wall.

18th Nov. At Godwin's. Northcote, the Dawes etc. Coleridge made himself very merry at the expense of *Fuseli,* whom he always called *Fuzzle* or *Fuzly.* He told a story of Fuseli's being on a visit at Liverpool at a time when unfortunately he had to divide the attention of the public with a Prussian soldier who had excited great notice by his enormous powers of eating, & the annoyance was aggravated by persons persisting to consider the soldier as his countryman. He spent his last evening at Dr. Crompton's, when *Roscoe* (whose visitor F. was) took an opportunity to give a hint to the party that no one shd. mention the glutton. The admonition unfortunately was not heard by a lady who, turning to the great Academician & lecturer, said, 'Well Sir, your countryman has been surpassing himself.' 'Madam,' growled the irritated artist, 'the fellow is no countryman of mine.' 'Why, he is a foreigner. Have you not heard what he has been doing? He has eaten a live cat.' 'A live cat,' everyone repeated, except Fuseli whose rage was roused by the exclamation of Mrs. Currie, a lady famous for her blunders. 'Dear me! Mr. Fuseli, that is a fine subject for your pencil.' '*My* pencil, Madam?' 'To be sure, Sir. The *horrible* is your *forte,* you know.' 'You mean the *terrible,* Madam,' he replied with an assumed composure, at the same time muttering between his teeth, 'if a silly woman could mean anything.'

December 20th. Met Coleridge by accident with Cha. & Mary Lamb. As I entered, he was apparently arguing in favour of Christianity. At the same time contending that Miracles were not an essential in the Christian System, he insisted that they were not brought forward as proofs; that miracles were acknowledged as having been performed by others as well as the true believers. Pharaoe's magicians wrought miracles also, tho' those of Moses were more powerful. In the New Testamt. the appeal is made to the knowl. which the believer has of the truths of his religion, not to the wonders wrought to make him believe.

Of *Jesus Christ* he asserted that he was a Platonic philosopher, & when Christ spoke of his identity with the Father, he spoke in a Spinosistic or Pantheistic sense, accordg to which he could truly say that his transcendental sense was *one* with God, while his empirical sense retained its finite nature.

I related the argument of Wieland's Agathodæmon (who represents J[esus] C[hrist]—like the Pythagorean *Apollonius,* a philanthropic impostor). C. dissented from this representation. He was convinced that J. C. felt the truth of all he affirmed & knew that he was inspired. But on my remarking that, in a certain sense, everyone who utters a truth may be said to be inspired, C. assented to this & afterwards named *Fox* & other of the Quakers, Mad. *Guyon,* St. *Theresa* &c. as being *also* inspired.

On my suggesting in the form of a question, That an eternal & absolute truth, like those of religion, could not be *proved* by an accidental fact of history, he at once assented, & declared it to be inadvisable to ground the belief of Christianity on historic evidence: He went so far as to affirm that religious belief is an act not of the understanding but of the will. To become a believer, one must love the doctrine & must resolve with passion to believe, Not sit down coolly to enquire whether he shd. believe or no. Notwithstanding the sceptical tendency of such opinions, he added that accepting as he did Christianity in its spirit in conformity with his own philosophy, he was content for the sake of its divine truths to receive as articles of faith, the miracles of the New Testament, taken in their literal sense. *N. B.* It occurs to me now that I perhaps ought to have written instead of *receive as articles of faith, leave undisputed.* I am reminded in writing this of one of the famous Pensées of Pascal which Jacobi quotes repeatedly. I cite from memory. "It is this which distinguishes spiritual from material truths. You must believe the first before you can understand them. You must understand the last before you can believe them.

Coleridge added to this warm praise of Spinoza, Jacobi on Spinoza, Schiller *Über die Sendung Moses* etc., & he assented to a remark of mine that the error of Spinoza seems to be the attempting to reduce to demonstration what was matter of faith.

A talk abt. Shakespear[e]. C. Lamb spoke with admiration of *Love's Labour[s] Lost, Mids[ummer] Night's Dream.* Coler[idge] did not concur. But they agreed in this, that not a line of *Titus Andronicus* could have been written by Shakesp[eare], wh. Lamb ascribed to Marlowe from its resemblance to *The Jew of Malta.*

Dec. 23d. Coleridge at Collier's. Coleridge exhibited his inconsistency by beginning with praising the K[ing] Geo[rge] III, to whose firmness he said we were indebted for our not yielding to the French. Yet being pressed, he admitted that the King was an enemy to the Americans, & a friend to the Slave Trade, & also that another system of government might have saved the country from infinite misery. So that the poor old K[ing] had at last nothing left him but his personal morals & their influence on the upper classes.

This day his chief talk was on Shakesp[eare]. The leading ideas are those that have been published recently by Mrs. Coler[idge] & my notes are of less value. I shall therefore abridge them. The one thought which he this eveng. expressed in different ways was, that Shakesp. meant in his *Iago* & in his *Rich[ard] III* to exhibit the pride of intellect & the same in *Falstaff,* but at the same time to show the superiority of moral sense over mere intellect. (See the Lectures. Vol. I, pp. 187, 257.) *Falstaff* had more intellect than the *Prince* & did not think it was possible for the Prince to escape from his influence, but the higher moral charr. of the Prince raises him above his insidious companion. Of *R.* 3 he wrote but little. He found it a stock play & wrote merely what expressed R's character—certainly not the scene with Qu. Anne. In *Pericles* we see how Sh. handled a piece he had to refit for representation. He began with indifference, only now & then putting in a word, but interesting himself in his subj[ec]t, the last two acts are almost altogether by him.

Hamlet he considered in a point of view which seems to agree very well with that taken in *Wilhelm Meister*. H[amlet] said C., is one whose internal images *(ideal)* are so vivid, that all actual objects are faint & dead to him; hence his soliloquies on the nature of man, his disregard of life & hence his vacillations & convulsive energies. I remarked that it seemed to me unaccountable why Sh. did not make Hamlet destroy himself. C. said that S. meant to show that even such a character was forced to be the slave of chance—a salutary moral lesson. He remained to the last inept & immovable; not even the spirit of his father could rouse him to action.

Milton. He spoke of Milton as decidedly an aristocrat & an enemy to popular elections. His works have only one exceptional passage—his vindication of Cromwell's purging the House of Commons. The execution of *Par[adise] Regained* is superior to that of *Par[adise] Lost,* & that is all Milton meant in giving it a preference to the *Par[adise] Lost*. C. took occasion to assert his approbn. of the death of Charles.

Hartley. Of Hartley's doctrine of assocn. This is as old as Aristotle. Hartley understood it better when he reached the 2d. vol. of his great work & would not rest the evidce of Christy. on it. 'Thought,' said C., 'is a breaking thro the law of Association. They who wd. build everything on association are too apt to leave out of account the things associated.

Taylor's *Holy Living & Holy Dying* he declared to be a perfect poem in its details. Its rhythm may be compared with the *Night Thoughts*.

As usual he spoke with contempt of *Locke's Essay*. It led to the destruction of metaphysical science by encouraging the unlearned to think that with good sense they might dispense with study. The popularity of *Locke's Essay* he ascribed to his political position: he was the advocate of the new dynasty agst the old & as a religious writer, agst the Infidel, tho' he was but an Arian. And the *national* vanity was gratified. He & Newton were pitted agst Leibnitz. It was to lessen Leibnitz that Voltaire set up Locke. He assented to my remark that Atheism might be demonstrated out of Locke. He praised Stillingfleet as the opponent of Locke's *Essay*.

1811. I now resume from my journal.

Jan. 23d. I met *Coleridge* with Rickman, Morgan &c. at C. Lamb's. The conversation was on politics & on no subject did I like him so little. He was very vehement agst. granting to the Irish even equal civil rights because then they would claim equal power. The Cath[olic] spirit, said C., is incorrigible. The priests wd. claim the tithes & require to have their religion established. 'I would not give equal power to 3 millions of barbarians.' I replied 'I wd. give them equal rights because they could not convert their rights into power without ceasing to be barbarians.' C. said he wd. hang every Irishman who refused to be considered as an Englishman. I denied that a Union forced on the nation agst their will could have a magical influence on them. I tried to draw a parallel bet. the relation of the Italians to the French, & that of the Irish to the English, wh. C. denied to be valid. The Italians, he said, are not inferior to the French as the Irish are to the English. The original conquest of Irel[and], he said, by England, was for their benefit. They wd. otherwise have been a nest of pirates.

Coler. & Rickman both justified the expense of our civil jurisprudence. Lawyers, said C., are now what the clergy race were, the depositories of intellect. It is no evil that they shd. form a rich, powerful & honoured body. Cheap law makes lawyers base & the whole nation litigious. This, he sd., was seen in Sicily.

29th Jan. With Coler. at Rickman's. He talked on the Drama & Shakesp. He contrasted, as he did afterwards in his lectures, the Greek with the Shakesp. drama: Shakesp. fools supplied the place of the Greek chorus; both represented a passionless spectator.

Coleridge & Rickman both abused the Reformers, but Coler. notwithst[andin]g expressed his contempt for Pitt. The alarm of 1793 was a panic of property which misled the Engl. government into a series of blunders wh. laid the foundation of French dominion.

He justified the Usury Laws agt. Bentham. By generating a contempt for usurers, many were deterred from becoming mere money-lenders. Genoa fell because their merchants were changed into usurers. "In money loans one party is in sorrow. In the traffic of merchandise, both parties gain & rejoice." Of criminal law he said that its object is not merely to prevent mischievous acts: it is to be a moral instructor.

13th March. With Coler. who called on me. He spoke abt. a translation I had made of a German tale & I shd. have been flattered had he spoken in the same way of the writing of a stranger, but Coler. like all kind-hearted men, has a pleasure in giving pleasure.

Speaking of Southey today, he said S. was not competent to appreciate Spanish poetry; he wanted modifying power. He was a jewel setter; whatever he found to his taste he formed it into, or made it the ornament of a story.

March 24. A call on Coler. He expatiated largely on the powerful effect of brotherly & sisterly love in the formn. of char[acte]r. Certain peculiarities in his wife, Mrs. Southey, Mrs. Lovell he ascribed to their having no brother. I recollect too, but it was on some other occasion, his saying that he envied Wordsworth his having had a sister & that his own character had suffered from the want of a sister. To-day he also spoke of *incest*. The universal horror he ascribed not to *instinct* (if I mistake not *Southey,* he said, believed in the *instinct*). He was of opinion that fatal consequences had been found to follow from the intercourse. And therefore a religious horror had been industriously excited by priests—he spoke of novelty as exciting, & of habitual presence as represssing desire.

March 29. With Coler. at Hazlitt's. Before Lamb came, Coler. praised his *serious* conversation & Hazlitt ascribed his puns to *humility.*

C. in his abuse of the Scotch, said, Edinb[urgh] is a talking town & the Edinb. Rev. is a concentration of all the smartness of all Scotland. When, in an Edinb. Conversazione, a spark is elicited, it is instantly caught, preserved, & brought to the Rev[iew]. He denied humour to the nation.

Of *Rogers* he said that he was the slave of public opinion. He at first eulogised Bloomfield, but when the world neglected him, he neglected him too.

Abstraction was spoken of. Hazlitt sd. he had learned from painting how hard it is to have an idea of an individual object. At first we have only a general idea, that is, vague, broken, imperfect. On my saying that this is all generally meant by *general* idea, Hazlitt said he had no other. Coler. said, 'We cannot bring an individual object under a class with[ou]t having a previous notion of the class.' This, by the bye, is Kantian logic, tho in my journal I perceive I was not aware of this.

Mar. 30. With Coler. & Hazlitt at Lamb's. Coler. spoke with a kindness of Godwin wh. gratified me. G., it was said, was wounded by Southey's Rev[iew] of his *Life of Chaucer* in the *Annual Review.* S.'s severity he ascribed to the habit of reviewing. He did not justify the rev[iew] but said its severity proceeded from the great purity of S.'s own mind. 'Such men are *blunt* in their moral feelings,' sd. C., probably meaning that their distribution of praise & blame wanted delicacy. C. said, 'S. sd. of my poetry, that I was a Dutch imitator of the Germans.' He sd. he mentioned this, not because he was offended by it, but to show how S. could speak *even* of him.

As to Godwin, C. spoke indignantly of those who from being extravag[an]t admirers became revilers. Tobin was one of these & Montagu another. There is, after all, in G., sd. C., more than I was at one time willing to admit, tho' not so much as his admirers fancied. He himself had declaimed agst. G. openly but visited him notwithstanding. He did not approve of the language of Wordsworth altogether concerning G. On my remarking that I had learned to hate Helvetius & Mirabeau, but retained much of my love for G., the distinction was acquiesced in.

We spoke of national antipathies. C. said, but playfully, 'When I say *a Scotch rascal,* I lay the emphasis on Scotch, as if the infamy was in that.' C.

abused the Irish, but has no dislike to Jews or Turks. This reminds me that I *once* heard Coler. say: 'When I have been asked to subscribe to a society for converting Jews to Xtnty, I have been accustomed to say, 'I have no money for any Charity, but if I had, I wd. subscribe to make them first *good* Jews & then it wd. be time to make good Christians of them.'

At this time Hazlitt was in vain striving to become a portrait painter. He had obtained the patronage of Clarkson, who said he had heard he was more able to paint like Titian than any living painter. Someone had said that his portrait of Lamb had a Titianesque air about it, & certainly this is the only painting of H. I ever saw with pleasure. He made a portrait of my brother wh. he knew to be bad & gave up reluctantly. It was destroyed. He painted Mr. Howel's portrait—a strong likeness, but a coarse picture. He was therefore driven to become a writer, & being in this not altogether unsuccessful, he managed to live, but in constant difficulties: hence his morbid views of society, & his *Jacobin* character, as described by Burke at the commencement of his Reflexions on the French Revolution.

26th April. With Lamb; Coler. there. He was violent in his censure of a book by William Taylor of Norwich, wh. has for its second title '*Who was the Father of Jesus Christ,*' the author's speculative opinion being that Zachariah, the High Priest was the Father. C. contended that such a book ought to be prosecuted for its indecency, it being an insult to the feelings of the community at large. The book exists, & I need give no account of it here. My friend Ant. Robinson admired it & urged Pople to publish it. P. asked my opinion of the publicn. as a mere question of prudence. It was, that without the offensive title, the book might be safely printed. No one would think of it. But if prosecuted, there would be a conviction. The book was never advertised & never read. It is very extravagant & absurd. Roberts (Taylor's biographer) has given me a copy.

On the 6th of June, met Coler. at the Exhibition. He drew my attention to the 'vigorous impotence" of Fuseli, especially in his *Macbeth*. 'The prominent witch,' said C., 'is smelling a stink.' C. spoke of painting as one of the lost arts. Some time after, C., speaking of a great picture by West, said, 'In this picture are a number of figures, each of which is painted as it might have been if it had been a single figure, no one figure having any relation to or influencing any other figure, & tho' they ought to be under each a light of its own, yet each figure looks as if it were in the open-air.' He explained the *ideal* beauty to be that wh. is common to all of a class, taking from each individual that wh. is accidental to him.

It was at the same time, the 11th of June, that C. made some strong remarks on a most excellent man whom he professed to admire, even in making strictures that might be thought to depreciate him—Mr. Clarkson. 'I have long,' said C., 'looked on him rather as an abstraction than as an individual who is to be loved because he returns the love men bear to their equals. Clarkson is incapable of loving any except those to whom he has been a benefactor. He is so accustomed to *serve* that he cannot love those whose happiness he can no longer promote. As others are benevolent from vanity, he is made vain by beneficence.' 'Many years ago I called him the moral steam engine, the giant with one idea. I am sorry that the reverence I feel for him as an abstract is in danger of being weakened. The abstract is deteriorating.' This par[ticu]lar remark was occasioned by Cl. having joined the Jacobins in signing a requisition for a reform meeting. This C. cd. not forgive.

I frequently saw Coler. this summer & was made privy to an incident which need no longer be kept a secret. C. was then a contributor to the Courier & wrote an article on the *Duke of York,* which was printed on Friday, the 5th of July. But the Govt. got scent of it & therefore, by the interference of Mr. Arbuthnot of the Treasury, after about 2000 copies had been printed, it was suppressed. This offended C. who would gladly have transferred his services to the *Times.* I spoke abt. him to Walter, but Fraser was then firmly established & no other hand was required for the highest department. I have found a paper in Col.s hand wh. has a reference to this affair. It states what service he was willing to give; such as attending 6 hrs a day & writing so many articles per week. One paragraph only has any significance, because it shows the state of his mind. 'The above, always supposing the paper to be truly independent (1st) of the Administration (2) of the Palace Yard & that its fundamental principle is, the due proportion of political power to Property, joined with the removal of all obstacles to the free circulation & transfer of Property & all artificial facilitations of its natural tendency to accumulate in large & growing masses.'

I met Southey several times this summer. I dined with him once at John Thelwall's in spite of the now wide departure of the poet from the politics of the lecturer, wh. he once himself professed. On the 24th of July, Southey spoke with high admiration of the genius of Blake, both as poet & painter, but deemed him mad. Blake, he said, spoke of his Visions with diffidence as if he did not expect to be believed. S. also spoke of his friend *W. S. Landor* with high admiration, whose *Gebir* is all but a mad poem, but who is not mad in life. Southey spoke with great admiration of Wordsworth but blamed his not publishing his great poem on his own life. 'He has a sort of *miserly* feeling towards his poems as if they would cease to be *his* if they were published.' He praised W.'s pamphlet on the war very highly & allowed but *one* fault in him— that he overrated some of his own poems.

He spoke with feeling of Coler. & his infirmities. With a strong sense of duty he has neglected it in every relation of life.

28*th July.* An evening at Morgan's, Kensington, where Southey & Coler. were. Coleridge, of Klopstock, said he was a compound of everything bad in Young, Harvey & Richardson. Praised Lamb's *Essay on Hogarth.* He said there were *wrongers* as well as *writers* on subjects. A walk home with Southey alone. Southey on forms of government, said—A republic is in itself the best form of government, as a sundial is the most perfect instrument to ascertain the time of day, but as the Sun will not always shine we have invented clocks. If men had always the sun of reason to enlighten them we should not want artificial forms of government. On *Spain,* Southey was, (as his works show) an enthusiast. He said "A Jacobin revoln. must purify the country before it can come to any good. Catholicism is a bar to all reforms. In the Cortes $\frac{9}{10}$ are bigoted Papists, 1/10 Jacobin atheists." Of Thelwall he said, "*John* is a very good-hearted man, but a consummate coxcomb. We ought never to forget that he was once as near being hanged as possible & there is great merit in that." He spoke highly of *Blanco White*. He begged me to try & prevent any more articles appearing against him in the Times.

3d of August. Using the word "poor Col.," tho coupled with expression of my admiration, *Lamb* seriously reproved me. "I hate *poor* applied to *such* a man," & referred to a similar sentiment uttered by Ben Jonson of Bacon.

Aug. 7. A chat with Coleridge at Lamb's. I omit an interesting anecdote C. related of his son Hartley, because I have sent it to Derwent Col. & it probably will be printed. I can at any time add it. [H.C.R. adds note:—] Vide the Life by Der. Col.

20th Oct. With Col. at Collier's. He spoke both of Scott & Southey as poets in very low terms. Of Scott he said that when you strike out all the interesting *names* of places &c., you will find nothing left. Yet he did not set Southey above him. He spoke of his own poems with seeming disesteem. He publd. his 1st vol. from poverty: he wanted £20. On the first publicn. of his poems he was accused of writing in an inflated & bombastic style; now he is ranked with those who are accused of a false simplicity. He was asked to repeat from *Christabel* but was unable to recollect the words. This I had witnessed once before.

[There follows a note in shorthand, which reads:—] Both times he was affected by liquor.

[Note added in margin] I heard C. say "I have been ill with liquor, but I was never intoxicated. Liquor affects my stomach, not my head." Sed quaere.

1811. C. *Lamb* wrote this year for children a version of the nursery tale of *Prince Dorus*. I mention this because it is not in his collected works, & like 2 vols. of *Poems for Children*, likely to be lost. I this year tried to persuade him to make a new version of the old tale of *Reynard the Fox*. He said he was sure it wd. not succeed. 'Sense for humour,' said L. 'is extinct. No satire but personal satire will succeed.' Many, many years afterwards I prevailed with Sam. Naylor to modernise Reynard, & it has succeeded.

21 June. A pleasant party at Collier's. Lamb in high spirits. One pun from him at least successful. Punsters being abused & the old joke repeated that he who puns will pick a pocket, someone said: Punsters themselves have no pockets. 'No' said Lamb, they carry only a *ridicule*.

Coleridge this winter delivered a course of 15 lectures on Milton & Shakespeare, in Fleet St., wh. I attended. To me they were less interesting than they would otherwise have been, because, having lately been much in his company, the leading ideas were familiar to me. The difference was not great between his conversation, wh. was a sort of lecturing, & soliloquising, & his lectures wh. were colloquial, & in which, as he was himself aware, it was impossible for him to be methodical, & those hearers who enjoyed him most, probably enjoyed most his digressions. The same subjects haunted his mind for many years so that I do not doubt that on comparing my scanty notes with those on Shakesp. publd. lately by Mrs. H. Coleridge, I shd. find a great resemblance. A report of these lectures appeared occasionally in the Morning Chronicle from J. P. Collier. With difficulty I obtained permission from Walter to insert a paragraph in the Times. The only condition of its appearance was that it shd. be cold & dry. Here it is: "*From a Correspondent.* Mr Coleridge commenced yesterday evening his long announced lectures on the principles of poetry. To those who consider poetry in no other light than as a most *entertaining* species of comp[ositio]n., this Gentleman's mode of enquiring into its principles may want attraction. Unlike most professional critics on works of taste his great object appears to be to exhibit in poetry the principles of moral wisdom & the laws of our intellectual nature, wh. form the basis of social existence. In the introductory lecture delivered last night, Mr. C. deduced the causes of false criticism on works of imagn., from circumstances wh. may hitherto have been thought to stand in no very close connection with our literary habits viz: the excessive stimulus produced by the wonderful political events of the age;—the facilities afforded to general & indiscriminate reading; the rage for public speaking & the habit consequently induced of requiring instantaneous intelligibility; periodical criticism wh. teaches those to fancy they can judge who ought to be content to learn; the increase of cities wh. has put an end to the old fashioned village-gossiping, & substituted literary small-talk in its place; & the improved habits of domestic life & higher purity of moral feelings wh. in relation to the drama have produced effects unfavourable to the exertion of poetic talent or of judgment. From such topics it will be seen that Mr. Coleridge is original in his views. On all occasions indeed, he shews himself to be a man who really thinks & feels for himself; & in the development of his moral philosophy, something may be expected from him very different from critics in general on Shakespeare, Milton & our other national poets. However serious the design of Mr. C's lectures, in the execution he shows himself by no means destitute of the talents of humour, irony & satire."

18*th Nov.* My journal remarks, what indeed I had too often occasion to repeat, that C. was ever referring to what he had done & to what he was to do, & so overlooked what he ought then to have been doing.

24*th Nov.* A visit to C. at Hammersmith with Rough. Today I noticed his antithetical comparn. of the fine arts one with another, quite Schellingian. He incidentally gave to Calderon the fancy & the imagination of Shakespear[e] without his philosophy.

Lecture II. No note.

Lecture III. ,,   ,, *IV* Ditto.

Lecture V. . . .

Lecture VI. . . .

The 7*th Lecture* my journal praises as incomparably the best, & refers to a report of it which I sent to & which appeared in the Morning Chronicle.

Lecture VIII. . . . I lost several lectures going into the country & on my return I renewed my attendance.

In a letter by me to Mrs. Clarkson of the 13th of Decr., I thus characterised these lectures: 'As evidences of splendid talent. . . . '

The concluding lectures were of the same kind & produced the same comment. They were but indifferently attended, & scoffers were not infrequently among the number. Among my personal acquaintance not a few, I always took a lady with me, & among the ladies he had many admirers. . . . One eveng. I saw *Rogers* there, & with him was Lord Byron. He was wrapped up, but I recognised his club-foot & his countenance & general appearance.

Whilst these lectures were going on, Hazlitt too commenced a course on *The History of Eng. Philosophy* at the Russell Institution. 1812. On the 14th of Jan. he commenced & his delivery was so very bad, his lecture being read v. rapidly, & the subject also was so unsuited to a lecture, that tho' the matter was sensible, yet it gave no pleasure, & Stoddart's remonstrances & those of other friends had nearly caused him to break down entirely & give up the course. But he recovered greatly his self-possession & his voice & could read slow[ly] & very much improved, & so he remained an occasional lecturer all his life.

May. At this time appeared in the Quart. Rev. a brutal attack on Lamb in the review of Weber's edition of Ford's works, calling him a *poor maniac*. Barron Field remonstrated with Murray, who protested that he had never heard of Miss L.'s calamity & Gifford, the editor, made the same declaration. The author was [blank in MS.] That C.L. had for an instant only been in confinement was not known to myself or to the rest of C.L.s friends until the recent disclosure in Talfourd's Final Memorials. It was this brutal attack wh. occasioned & justified Lamb's sonnet, *St Crispin to Mr Gifford*, a happy jeu d'esprit.

To this date belongs one of the most felicitous of Coleridge's satirical strokes. His connection with the Courier newspaper & Stuart, its proprietor, is well-known & belongs to C.'s history. The character of Stuart too is well-known. It was after Stuart's desertion of the popular cause & he [*sic* when?] underwent the suspicion of being involved in a famous stock-jobbing forgery of the *Eclair* a French paper that I heard C. praise Stuart warmly. I cd. not help interposing with questions founded on these circumstances. Coler. at length became excited & made a convulsive movement of his lip, preceding the coming joke. "Why, if I'm pressed as to Dan's strict honesty, which I don't wish to be, I shd. say: Dan's a Scotchman who is content to get rid of the itch when he can afford to wear clean linen. Such men form a class!"

It was in the month of May that Wordsworth came to London & spent several weeks here. I had now an opportunity of seeing much of him & also of rendering a service both to him & Coleridge, by being mediator between them & healing what at one time threatened to become an incurable wound in their friendship. W. had with very kind intentions, given Basil Montagu a hint of C.'s unfortunate habits which B.M. repeated with unwarrantable exaggerations. The *excess* was denied by W. What he did say was *justified,* & the friends forgave each other. The reconciliation was the easier because, tho' unfriendly words had been uttered by them of each other, yet they were warm admirers of each others genius & most ungrudgingly professed that admiration while, on the contrary, neither of them thought very highly of Southey's poetical genius, tho' his personal character & his talents as a prose writer & literator [sic] were very highly estimated.

Coler. was at all times a profuse eulogist of Wordsworth's poems but always with qualifications & even with objections to W.'s diction & style, which indeed he has printed. And he was *passionate* in his professions of *love* to him as a man, but these professions expressed but the feeling of the moment. Wordsworth's words might be considered as announcing his permanent convictions. It was delightful to hear Wordsworth speak of himself, when alone with him & he was under no apprehension of being misunderstood & consequently [mis]represented. He said, of wh. I have a note at this very time, that he was convinced he could never make his poems a source of emolument to him & being then independent, he was content. "If men are to become better," he said, "the poems will sooner or later find admirers: If society is not to advance in civilisation it would be wretched selfishness to deplore any want of personal reputation. The approbation of a few compensates for the want of popularity. But no one," said he, "has completely understood me—not even Coleridge. He is not happy enough. I am myself one of the happiest of men & no man who lives a life of constant bustle & whose happiness depends on the opinions of others can possibly comprehend the best of my poems."

But W. was loud in his praise of the powers of C.'s mind wh. he said were greater than those of any man he ever knew. From such a man under favourable influences anything might be hoped for. His genius he thought great, but his talents he thought still greater & it is in the union of so much genius with so much talent that he thought C. surpassed all other men. W., in a digression, remarked of himself that he had comparatively but little talent: genius was his peculiar faculty.

If (of which there can be no doubt) genius is properly creation & production from within & talent is the faculty of appropriation from without and assimilation, then Genius & Talent will be given respectively in a larger proportion to Wordsw. & Coleridge.

13th May. A dinner with the Wordsws. at Serjt Roughs. W. S. *Landor* was spoken of. I then knew nothing of him but he was praised by W. for a forthcoming tragedy. Walter Scott was mentioned. W. allowed him little merit, the secret of his popularity lying in the vulgarity of his conceptions which the million can at once comprehend. And of Wilson, whom the Edinb. Rev[iewer]s. had most disingenuously set above Words. W. did not hesitate to say 'Wilson's poems are an attenuation of mine. He owes everythg. to me & this he acknowledges to me in private, but he ought to have said it to the public also.' That this attenuation constituted the merit of Wilson in the eyes of the Edinb. Rev., I have no doubt. Wordsworth's best poems were too highly seasoned with poetry for the Scotch taste. These Reviewers' over-praise of Wilson might therefore be to a degree honest & merely the effect of want of taste, but as the Edin. Rev. was already pledged agst the Lake School, personal ill-will had begun to mix with their want of feeling & they were glad to have an opportunity of conceding all they felt they *must* concede in favour of that school, giving the benefit not to Wordsw. but to his pupil, his imitator & his diluter, (Bar. Field called Wilson '*Wordsworth & Water*') & so obtain credit for candour in admissions which were only another mode of giving effect to ill-will.

I will not anticipate what properly belongs to a later period & say all that I wish to say of *Wilson*. He became after this the editor of Blackwood's Magazine & under his editorship appeared the most contemptuous depreciation of Wordsw. & also very warm praise. I told Wordsw. that it was reported Wilson wrote *all* the articles. W. intimated that he thought Wilson capable of doing so. Tho' Wilson had a residence near Rydal they were never intimate. But there was no open breach between them. Wordsw. related to me—this also I relate by way of anticipation—that when Wilson was a candidate for the professorship of Moral Philosophy in the Univ. of Edinb., Wil. applied to Wordsw. for a testimonial. Words. repeated to me the one he sent—I quote from memory. It imported that if a delicate perception of all the subtleties of Ethics as a science & ability in developing what he thought & making it intelligible & impressing it on others constituted the qualification, he knew no one more highly qualified than Wilson. The testimonial was sent in & Wilson became & I believe, still is, the professor.

I will continue my Anticipation & say here all that occurs to me about the Edin. Rev. wh. I do the more readily because these Reminiscences will probably not be brought down so low as to include what I wish to say.

The scornful treatment of my friends *Wordsw. Lamb* &c &c always incensed me agst the Edin. Rev. W. always tho[ught] that he was robbed of his just fame & consequently of his just emolument by the Edinb. Rev. & many years afterwds he told Serjt. Talfourd that he might say to his friend Mr. Jeffrey that but for *him*, (J.), Wordsw. would have gone to Rome twenty years before he did. Talfourd never reported to W. what J. replied to this. Nor did he to me but he told me this,—That he obtained from J. a frank confession that he was conscious he was wrong in the Judgement he had formed of *Lamb*, whom he *then* admired. But he adhered to his original judgment of Wordsw. & could acquire no taste for him more than he had at first. This is evidenced by the reprinting in the collected papers even of the silly review of the *Rejected Addresses* in wh. the tale of Nancy Lake is declared to be 'rather a favo[u]rble specimen' of W. W. I believe no one of the articles on Lamb are [sic] retained.

I once only met Jeffrey by dining with him at Talfourd's. I managed to introduce the subject & obtained from him the strange assertion: "I was always an admirer of Wordsworth." "Indeed," I answered, "The Edinb. Rev. had a strange way of expressing admiration." But Jeffrey intimated the same sort of thing to Coleridge. Such declarations are worse than foolish.

To go back to this dinner at Rough's. Doctor W[ordsworth]. was there. He & Rough were old College friends, & they retained a regard for each other. The Dr. & I sparred about the Bible Society to which he was fiercely & at the same time plausibly opposed. I in vain attempted then, as I have often done since, to urge on High-Churchmen a coalition with Rationalistic Dissenters agt. the Evangelical churchm[en] & the Calvinistic Dissenters. W. W. on the contrary thought the Church had more to fear from the Latitudinarians than from the Methodistic party on the bench of bishops.

The same Eveng. W. accompanied me to Chas. Aiken's where were Mrs Barbauld, all the Aikens & the peculiar friends of the A[iken]s. There was a conscious want of perfect harmony between Wordsw. & the U[nitarian] rational party, as well as the Orthodox party. But he gave his hand cordially to James Montgomery & *all* were eager to get near him. The homage was involuntary. He had not then expressed the esteem for Mrs. Barb. wh. he late in life avowed. At this time W. was accustomed to express something like bitterness towards both Mrs. B. & Dr. Aiken on account of their critical Editions of the poets, by which they intercepted, he said, the natural judgments of unaffected readers. This eveng. Wordsw. gave offence by suggesting that possibly Sir Francis Burdett's violent speeches might have suggested to Bellingham the murdering Percival, saying that when men conceived the idea of committing a horrid act, they tried to conceal the enormity from themselves by fancying a laudable motive. He was rudely opposed by the younger Roscoe. He s[ai]d Sir Fr. B.'s was a constitutional speech. "What were the people to do who were starving?" "Not murder people," said W., "unless they mean to eat their hearts." He wished to see more of Montgomery & liked Mr. & Mrs. Chas. Aiken. Of the others he said nothing.

At this time Coler. had gone out of his way to attack Mrs. Barbauld in his last lecture in Fleet St.

31*st May.* An interesting day, being early at Hamond's, Hampstead, where I met Wordsw. & then with a party at Mr. Carr's. Wordsw also there. I abridge from notes. I found W. engaged in defending his own poetry. [This] he was in the habit of doing & this is to be said in justification of his so doing, that he was systematically depreciated in the Edinb. Rev., & the Quart. Rev. either dared not or did not wish to defend him. Talfourd was the first in minor journals to write in his praise & in private circles, individuals, who like myself, were his defenders, became butts of ridicule. He was driven to be his own advocate. At Hamond's was one of the *Millers,* a clergyman (to be mentioned on some other occasion) a cousin of Hamond. He estimated W.'s poems chiefly for the purity of their moral. W. on the other hand, valued them only according to the powers of mind they presupposed in the writer or excited in the hearer. He spoke with contempt of Campbell & analysed with effect the celebrated passage in *The Pleasures of Hope,* "Where Andes, Giant of the Western Star" declaring it to be a jumble of discordant images, which, like Gray's ridiculous image of the Bard's beard, 'streaming like a Meteor in the troubled air' had been stolen without effect from a line by Milton in wh. a spear is for its brightness compared to a Meteor.

W. also expatiated on his fears lest a social war would arise between the poor & the rich, and [sic] the danger of which is aggravated by the vast extension of the manufacturing system. This was a topic wh. at this time haunted alike both Wordsw. & Southey. Now that 36 years have elapsed not only the danger has increased but the war has actually broken out & as an evidence that men now distinctly perceive the fact, in France a word has been applied, not invented, wh. expresses by implication the fact. Society is divided into *proprietaires* & *proletaires*. And here we have an incessant controversy carried on by our political economists who discuss the respective claims of *labour* & of *capital*. Hamond urged that the masters would keep Servants in order, but agst this it was remarked that the extent to wh. manufactures were carried was such as to destroy the ancient personal influence of Master over Servant.

Words. also defended earnestly the Church Establishment & was not disconcerted by a laugh raised agst him because having before said he wd. shed his blood for the Chruch, he confessed that he could not say *when* he had been in a church in his own country. 'All our ministers are so vile.' The mischief of allowing the clergy to depend on the caprice of the mob he thought more than outweighed all the evils that arise out of an establishment & in this I agreed with him.

The same day I dined with Wordsw. at Mr. Carr's. Walter Scott & his wife were spoken of, Mrs. W. S. not favourably by either Davy or Wordsw. Joanna Baillie, however, gave her this good word: 'When I visited her I thought I saw a great deal to like: she seemed to look up to & admire her husband. She was obliging to her guests. The children were well-bred & the house in capital order. She had some smart roses in her cap & I did not like her the worse for that.'—Pollock was there, but he was less in harmony with the poet than Burrell. It was said of him by Burrell "he was a hard-headed man, a Senior Wrangler who thought that ev.thg. was to be done by the head alone & without the heart." Yet I ought to add that the sayer of this is now a very old bachelor occupying a 2d. floor in Gray's Inn & he of whom it was said has been the husband of two wives & the father of more than 20 children—mostly alive now. And he is now the Lord Chief Baron.

1812. *4th June*. Wordsw. at this time lent me *Peter Bell* wh. I read in M.S. with great delight, but not without some disapprobation. It contained one passage so very exceptionable that I ventured to beg him to expunge it. He said: 'Lady Beaumont has advised me to leave it out too. I will see whether I ought not to leave it out. When it did at last appear,—I was abroad at the time— I read a contemptuous rev[iew] in the Times with no other extract than this same passage, the very worst to my taste that ever Wordsworth wrote. It is now expunged & therefore may not be known to the next generation of Wordsworth's readers. Its place is supplied by a picture as wild but not as ridiculous. I will copy it as an illustration of what a man who lives much alone & feeds on his own fancies may bring himself to compose. Peter Bell, looking into a pool of water:

> A startling sight
> Meets him beneath the shadowy trees.
> Is it a fiend that to a stake
> Of fire his desperate self is tethering?
>   Etc., etc.
> Is it a party in a parlour

> Crammed just as they on earth were crammed,
> Some sipping punch, some sipping tea,
> But as you by their faces see
> All silent and all damned?

Mrs. Bas[il] Montagu told me that she had no doubt she suggested this image to W. by relating to him an anecdote. A person walking in a friend's garden, looking in at a window, saw a company of ladies sitting near the window with countenances *fixed*. In an instant he was aware of their condition & broke the window. He saved them from incipient suffocation.

Lamb did not object to this rejected stanza. He said: 'It is full of imagn.' No doubt of that, & what if it were? But tho' he did not object to that passage, he disliked the whole poem. He saw nothing good in it: he objected that the narrative is slow. My journal adds: 'as if that were not the *art* of the poet.' I might have said that to object to the poet a want of progress is as absurd as to object to the dancer that he does not get on. In both alike the object is to give delight by not getting on.

6th June. I had the satisfaction of introduc[in]g W. to my friend *Ant. Robinson* & of perceiving that they duly appreciated each other. W. had been pleased with a letter by Ant. Robinson on his *Convention of Cintra*, who, he said, had better understood him than I had in my review of it in the *London Review*. This honesty in W. pleased me.

On an earlier eveng. spent with W. at Morgan's with whom Coler[idge] lived, W. eulogised Burns for his poetical apology for drunkenness in his introduction to *Tam O'Shanter*. He also praised the conclusion of *Death & Dr. Hornbrook,* wh. he compared with the abrupt termination of the conflict between Gabriel & Satan in Milton. My journal adds: This remark did not bring its own evidence with it.

During this time Coler. delivered a course of 5 lectures on poetry &c at Willis's Rooms—a mere genteel audience, of course. I heard them all. They suggested little or no observation.

Coler. was sadly annoyed by the necessity of thus appealing to the kindness of his friends. He at this time repeated to me an epigram of wh. I recollect only the point. 'I fell asleep & I fancied I was surrounded by my friends who made me marvellous fine promises. I awoke & found these promises as much a dream as if they had been actually made.'

11th June. An unexpected call from W. He had received the information of the death of a dau[ghte]r (Catharine) of the age of 4 & he was going down immediately to Wales to Mrs. W. He seemed deeply affected. I called with him on *a Mr. De Quincey*, a friend who had been lately in Westmoreland & was much attached to the little child. De Qu. burst into tears on seeing Mr. W. as if *he* had been the father. Miss Wordsw. had written to him. This was the first time I had seen De Qu. I had heard of him only as a literary friend of W. of whose talents as a writer W. thought highly. He has since acquired celebrity as the *Opium Eater* & has lived a sad example of the wretchedness that attends the life of a man of superior intellect whose conduct is the sport of ill-regulated passions. His history is a curious one. He was the son of a widow lady at Bristol who may, for aught I know, be still living—a lady of fortune. De Qu. had, I believe, an independent income, at least he was brought up to no profession & after he left Oxford devoted himself passionately to literature. He became an ardent admirer of the Lake poets in his youth & Cottle has in his *Memoirs* related how, when De Quincey was very young, he enquired of C[ottle] whether Coleridge was not, (as he suspected) very poor, & whether £300 would not be acceptable to him & gave the money on an affirmative answer to these questions.

Here I will digressively state that when Cottle was preparing his *Memoirs* for the press he was requested by Coleridge's friends to withhold this fact from the public, because it was thght. De Q. had by his subsequent conduct cancelled the obligation. Cottle referring the question to me, I was decidedly of opinion that the fact ought not to be withheld.—De Q. took a residence near Grasmere where he became intimate with the poets. Here I formed an acquaintance with him. While residing here De Qu. became connected with the daughter of a Statesman, a small freeholder—so they are called in the Northern Counties.—It was not till after he had had several children by her, & that to the knowledge of the whole neighbourhood, that he married her. When this marriage took place he expected that Mrs. Wordsworth & the other ladies of W.'s house would visit her. This they declined doing & in consequence De Quincey's friendship turned to gall & from being the enthusiastic follower, he became the enemy of W., depreciating his works & in his writings, where he could not but praise the poet, he reviled the man. Living without any profitable occupation & unable to convert literature into a means of subsistence, he sank into poverty & drew down the worthy family of the poor wife into his own abyss of misery. They looked up to him as a *Gentleman* & he made his father-in-law sell his little estate for his benefit & father & family were brought literally to the parish.

I cannot follow his history in all its details. I used occasionally to see him in London. For some years I was the depository of a large collection of books which were kept in my chambers to save warehouse rent, till they were sold to supply his wants. They were classical works & I believe of value. His *Confessions of an Opium Eater* acquired celebrity, but it is the only work of his which did. He became an unsuccessful hanger-on [of] the booksellers & took up his residence in Scotland: in London he c[oul]d not possibly maintain himself. I saw him occasionally there as a shiftless man. He had a wretchedly invalid countenance: his skin looked like mother-of-pearl. He had a very delicate hand & a voice more soft than a woman's, but his conversation was highly intelligent & interesting. He was *near* being a very attractive man, as he was always an object of compassion. I have not seen him for many years & as a writer, it is only in periodicals that I am acquainted with him. He wore out the patience of Blackwood & of the Edinb. Rev., obtaining from the publishers prepayment for papers wh., being paid for, were not to be had. It has been latterly only in *Tait's Magazine* that I have read his papers, & Tait, I hear, never pays till he has the article in hand. Those wh. I have read with most interest have been the papers entitled "*Autobiography of the Opium Eater*, & these are rendered entertaining because they are full of anecdotes of the great poets of the Lakes. But to create this interest, he has had recourse to the most unworthy expedients. Outraging all decency, he betrays private confidence without the slightest scruple, relating the most confidential conversations, even reporting the unkind words uttered by one friend to another & utterly regardless of all delicacy. I was with Wordsw. one day when the advertisement of one of his papers was read. He said with great earnestness: 'I beg that no friend of mine will ever tell me a word of the contents of those papers' & I dare say he was substantially obeyed. It was a year or two afterw[ard]s (for these papers went on for a long time & were very amusing) however, that I ventured to say: 'I cannot help telling one thing De Q. says in his last number in [these] very words—that Mrs. W. is a better wife than you deserve.' 'Did he say that?' W. exclaimed in a tone of unusual vehemence, 'Did he say that? That is *so* true that I can forgive him almost anything else he says.' Yet writing of Mrs. W. in terms of the most extravagant eulogy, he could not refrain from concluding: '*But she squints.*'

Materials of this kind must be limited & local & temporary politics also will fail & therfore I have not been surprised when I have heard anecdotes of the extreme distress to wh. De Qu. has been reduced. It has been such, & at the same time so little confidence has been felt in his management of money that I have heard that Wilson, Jeffrey & other of the literary aristocracy of Edinburgh have been accustomed to send joints of meat & other articles for the house. By this time probably his children have been provided for by her [their?] relations & I have heard that his eldest daughter has proved a very clever & also morally a well-conducted person & yet of this same girl I heard an anecdote related which, if correct in all its parts, would have made one tremble at the thought of what she would become. *Many* years ago I heard Captain Hamilton relate this story: One day when this child was so young that no one could think her capable of understanding what was said, two sheriff's officers came into the room in wh. her father was, & one of them presenting a writ said: 'I arrest you, Sir.' De Qu. took the writ & said coolly: 'Oh, you are mistaken, Sir. This writ is against my brother. My name is Charles, not Thomas.' The men said he was called Thomas by ev. one, but De Q. was confident. So one of them stept out into the kitchen to the servant. 'What's your master's name, Betty?' 'Charles, Sir,' with a curtsey. The little girl had slipped out of the room & told her to say so if she should be asked by either of the men. One is glad to repeat that she is now said to be highly esteemed.

Aug. 4th. From Mrs. Morgan &c. with whom Coleridge then lived I heard some anecdotes related of his childhood wh. are worth comparing with the printed accounts. 'His father was a clergyman at Ottery St. Mary's, Devon. & he had pupils. On his death Buller, who was probably already a judge? & who had been a pupil of C.'s father, went to see the widow & made an offer of his patronage for the youngest child, Samuel. He was in consequence taken to London & it was expected he would have a presentation to the Charterhouse. He was however sent by Buller to the Blue Coat School. His family were proud

& considered this a degradation. They refused to notice the boy in the school. His brothers would not let him go to them in his school-dress & he refused to go in any other even when he might have gone. He used to dine with Buller on the Sundays, but one day there being company, the Blue Coat boy was sent to dine at the Second Table, & though but *nine* years old he would not go again. Thus he lost his only friend & having no one to shew him any kindness, his childhood passed away in wretchedness. This made him a good scholar, for he had always his book in hand, that he might forget his misery.'

Copied from my journal.

13*th Augt.* A long tête-à-tête with Coleridge wh. I availed myself of by shewing him some new scenes to *Faust* & endeavouring to infuse into him a higher & juster sense of Goethe's pre-eminence. I succeeded but partially. He was not pleased with the first scenes in Faust & objected that Mephistofeles is not a Character. I urged that Meph. was not intended to be a character. He is the representative of the human race or rather an abstraction of certain qualities in man & to this he had no reply. He deemed *Mahomet's Gesang* an imitation of Stolberg's *Felsenstrom.* But what is the allegory or import of the *Felsenstrom?* He was not however offended by *the Prologue in Heaven* to *Faust* tho' a parody on Job. He said of Job: "This incomparable poem has been absurdly interpreted. Job far from being the most patient was the most impatient of men. He was rewarded for his impatience. His integrity & sincerity had their recompense because he was superior to the hypocrisy of his friends."

Coler: praised *Wallenstein* but imputed to Schiller a sort of *Ventriloquism* in poetry. Wordsworth's *Ruth,* said Col:, has the same fault as it stands now, tho' originally W. had not put sentiments into the mouth of the Lover wh. are now there & wh. would better become the poet. He praised Schelling more than he had done before; said, "he appears greatest in his last work on *Freiheit,* tho' *his* is the philosophy of Jakob Böhme."

He had been reading *Lear* again. The Fool he thought unlike all Sh's other Fools; one of the profoundest & most astonishing of all his characters.

20*th Augt.* Another evening with Coleridge at Capt. Burney's. I copy as a statem[en]t of my own impression what I wrote in my journal—not that I think my impressions either true or valuable:—"He afterwards made many remarks on the doctrine of the Trinity from which I could gather only that he was very desirous to be orthodox, to indulge in all the subtleties & refinements of metaphysics & yet conform with the popular religion. That he is consciously excited by any unworthy suggestion or grossly insincere I do not believe, but that he deceives himself. He repeated a droll poem by himself founded on the raising of devils by repeating formularies of Hebrew words. He considered the most plausible objection to Christianity to be that there is an unfulfilled prophecy in Christ's not having appeared among the Jews, wh. the early Christians expected. But this too may be answered."

Nov. 3d. Col. commenced a course of lectures on Belles Lettres at the Surrey Institution and [sic] which were continued down to the 26th of January. As the novelty of these lectures had worn off & I was familiar with his opinions;

they attracted less attention from me, or I was become more lazy for I have made very few remarks on them. The audience at the Russell Institution were much more evangelical than at the other lecture rooms & sometimes C[oleridge] flattered the religious opinions of his hearers & at other times ran counter to them. Almost the only note I made on this course of lectures was the following:—

1813 *Jan. 26th*. Heard Col's concluding lecture. . . .

On the 23d. of January was performed Coleridge's *Remorse*, the single drama which he was able to introduce on the stage. It was with great difficulty that he succeeded in having it performed at Drury Lane. He complained of ill-treatment from Sheridan who slandered it in Company. He told me that Sheridan had said that in the original copy there was in the famous Cave Scene:—

Drip, drip, drip! there's nothing here but dripping.

However there was every disposition to do justice to it on the stage, nor were the public unfavo[u]rably disposed towards it. . . . It would be out of place in me to play the critic, nor need much be said. It would be acknowledged by the friends & enemies of Col. that the poetical merits of this play are greater than its dramatic merits & for this very palpable cause, that his poetical mind is as undramatical as Wordsworth's & Lord Byron's. . . .

1813. I saw but little either of Coleridge or any of the poets &c. this year. I was honestly trying to become a lawyer.

On the 2d. of Feby. I accompanied Aders to see Coleridge. He spoke of Goethe with more favour than usual to my German friend. Without meaning to impute insincerity to C. I may observe that he had a need of sympathy & therefore preferably said what he knew would please, not what would displease. He was not a good disputant. He said that if he seemed to depreciate Goethe it was because he compared him with the greatest of poets; that he tho[ugh]t Goethe had from a sort of caprice underrated the talent which in his youth he had so eminently displayed in his *Werter,* that of exhibiting men in a state of exalted sensibility. In after life he delighted in representing objects of pure beauty not objects of desire & passion—rather as statues or paintings. Therefore he called Goethe *picturesque.*

Lessing's *Laocoon* he declared to be unequal, in parts contradictory, his examples destroying his theory.

Reinecke Fuchs. The moral of this piece is that if there be a conflict between dull, blundering knaves such as Isegrim & Bruin, the Wolf & the Bear & a complete, clever scoundrel like Reynard the Fox, Reynard is entitled to victory. It is the prize due to his talents & poor imbecile creatures like the hare & the hens must perish, & as this is the constitution of nature, they do not excite our sympathy. My journal adds: "I never before heard him argue in favour of Buonaparte." He accused Schlegel of one-sidedness in his excessive admiration of Shakespeare.

29th April. Even my visits to Lamb were become rare. This evening I was there & with *Hazlitt,* whose recent appointmt. as a Reporter on the Chronicle paper placed him, as he flattered himself, in a state of ease. The necessaries of life were supplied to him.

Poets are accused of being insensible to each other's merits. Hamond 18*th Oct.* told me to-day that he had seen a letter from Walter Scott stating that he had declined the laureateship in favour of Southey, saying: "I am the more popular now, but posterity will enquire most abt. Southey." And Southey showed the same freedom from jealousy towards Wordsworth. He told Hamond that *The Recluse* was to be published this season & that it wd. establish Wordsworth as the first poet of his age & country. W.'s *Excursion* did appear, but instead of the critical world acknowledging its merits, the Edin. Rev. wrote its most scornful review. "This will never do" was its dictatorial commencement.

30*th Dec.* with Lamb, Hazlitt &c at Rickman's. *Rickman* produced one of Chatterton's forgeries. In one M.S. there were seventeen kinds of little *ee's.* "This must be modern," said Lamb, "& written by one of the Mob of Gentlemen who write with ease."

1814. This year also is nearly a blank as concerns the poets; none of them did I see except Lamb, & with him my meetings were become seldom. His card-parties were held but once a month. I had however the gratification of making the Lambs known to the Aikens & the consequences were that I substituted in the place of disrespect, kindness on the part of Lamb towards the Aikens & the Aikens made known their admiration. This evening we spent at Dr. Aiken's. C. Lamb was infinitely amusing, telling a droll story of an India House clerk accused of eating man's flesh & remarking that among cannibals those who rejected the favourite dish would be called Misanthropists.

Of those I consider as the appendages to the poets I also saw but little. In February De Quincey came to London, but I found his company wearisome. He appeared to me then to be the mere admirer of Wordsw. having nothing of his own, in wh. I did him wrong. But he was certainly cold & dry & wanted all power of conversation. I saw Hazlitt a little. He was put into spirits by being allowed to write in the Edinb. Rev. thro' the introduction of Lady Mac[k]intosh, after having been, as he fancied, ungratefully & insolently dismissed from the Chronicle by Perry. He printed afterwards in some fugitive paper, that Walter was the only newspaper proprietor who treated his writers as gentlemen. Perry, he complained to me, treated them as menials.

The publication of *The Excursion* this year was an epoch in Wordsworth's literary life, but suggests nothing here.

1816. This year my personal acquaintance with Wordsworth & Southey was improved by a journey in the North. I lament to perceive that as my means of knowledge advance, my power of profiting by those means seems to decline. Is it that my curiosity being blunted, I became inattentive or that I had less to note down because I was already familiar with what was said? It was in Septr. that I went to Mr Wordsworth, introducing to him young Torlonia, the son of the rich Roman banker, & his travelling tutor Mr. Walter, & MrW[ordsworth] delighted in pointing out the beauties of his home & neighbourhood to the strangers. I was on this occasion impressed by the enviable state of his family & of his circumstances, his distributorship of the stamps relieving him from all anxiety abt. their present support tho' not their future welfare.

On the 9th of Septr. I introduced my companions to the Laureat[e]. A pleasant eveng. with him, Nash, Westall junr., Mrs S[outhey] & her 2 sisters, Miss Barker &c. Our conversation on politics was very sad. Southey while he confessed that Ferdinand VII wanted generosity, nevertheless asserted that in his severe measures he acted *defensively*. Under the constitution the reformers proposed, he wd. have been at once dethroned.

In England & indeed all Europe, he anticipated a *servile war* & he expected a convulsion in 3 years. I deemed him then as I now believe he was, an honest alarmist. My diary describes Hartley Coleridge as a foreign Jew boy. Coleridge's daughter I was much pleased with. Of the three sisters, Mrs. Coleridge was the least agreeable.

On the 11th of Septr. I set out with Mr. Wordsw. from Keswick on a business journey, he having, as Executor to his brother the lawyer, to sell some of his property. We went first to *Cockermouth*. He rode & I walked. To render some of his poems intelligible, he related the occasion of their composition. I shd. be tempted to state some of these, but I will wait for the Life in which a collection of such notes is to appear. I will compare the future vol[ume] with my diary of the journey, p. 33.

At Cockermouth I had a singular illustration of the *maxim* 'A prophet is without honour in his own country.' Mr. Hutton the solicitor employed to sell some houses, a very gentlemanly & seemingly intelligent man, asked me once: 'Is it true,—as I have heard it reported—that Mr. W. ever wrote any verses?' I accompanied W. to *Calderbridge* & *Ravenglass* &c.

I saw Southey again & we renewed our political conversation. The point on wh. Southey & Wordsworth differed most was on the law of the Press. S. wd. have punished a second political libel with transportation. W[ordsworth] was unwilling to restrain the press.

On this journey I saw several times *De Quincey*. He was already become the bitter enemy of Words: & for no better reason, as far as I cd. perceive, than that the Ws. wd. not shelter by their patronage, the woman he had married after he had disgraced her, as I have already said. On this journey I became tired of his company, & I regretted having accepted of his hospitality as he had a claim of a return. I had no doubt that De Qu. felt in like manner tired of me & all cordiality between us from that time ceased. This did not of course prevent his making troublesome applications to me when he sunk into absolute poverty, but in that state men care not of whom they borrow or beg. De Qu. tho' he spoke with obvious dislike of Wordsw. as a man, & vehemently agst. Coler: yet eulogised their genius. Of Southey he spoke lowly as a poet. Indeed he appeared to be a sort of Pococurante, abusing all the German great men, *Goethe, Schiller,* &c.—Tho' intimate with Wilson he did not praise his poetry.

During this year my acquaintance continued with Godwin but I was brought to a more close observation of his character as developed under the sad circumstances into which he was brought by imprudence if not recklessness. Early in the year he had visited Wordsworth & left him with feelings of great bitterness. Their diverging political affections separated them. Wordsworth perhaps carried too far his forbearance of the renewed abuses & corruptions of the restored Monarchs, because he thought any evil they could inflict under a domestic government would be slight compared with the utter slavery which would have prevailed over Europe had Buonaparte ultimately triumphed, while such men as *Godwin & Hazlitt* were ready to love Buonaparte as the enemy of their enemies. My diary of May 28. 1816. has this paragraph:— "Europe was rising morally & intellectually when the French Revolution after promising to advance the world rapidly in its progress towards perfection, suddenly, by the woeful turn it took, threw the age back in its expectations, almost in its wishes, till at last from alarm & anxiety, even zealous reformers were glad to compromise the cause of freedom & purchase national independence & political liberty at the expense of civil liberty in France, in Italy & most intensely did I rejoice at the counter-revolution. I had also rejoiced when a boy at the Revolution & am ashamed of neither sentiment & I shall not be ashamed tho' the Bourbon shd. become as vile as any of the sovereigns wh. France was cursed with under the ancestors of Louis XVIII; & tho' the promises of liberty made to the Germans by their Sovereigns shd. all be broken & tho' Italy & Spain shd. relapse into the deepest horrors of papal superstition. To rejoice in immediate good is permitted to us. The immediate is often alone our scope of action & observation."—I then thought that my friends in general erred either in loving or hating too indiscriminately the then objects of their political attachment or antipathy.

It was during this year, Dec. 15, 1816, that *Shelley* attached himself to *Mary Godwin* which led to events that acquired a sad & memorable notoriety. Mrs. Godwin consulted me on the state in wh. Shelley then (Dec. 25th) was with both his wife & the Godwin family. Mrs. Godwin accused Mrs. Shelley of being guilty of adultery & alleged this as an excuse for S.'s conduct. I had no confidence in Mrs. G.'s veracity, nor on her word alone could I believe that Mrs S. was enceinte when she was found drowned by an act of suicide. I learned that all the children of Godwin & Mrs. G. justified the conduct of Mary G. in eloping with Shelley, but I believe Godwin himself did not sanction the act & that it grieved him. But he was under too great pecuniary obligations to Shelley to be able to interfere vigorously.

A few weeks before this was written the death of Mrs Shelley was announced. She was a woman of great ability. Wordsworth especially admired her taste in poetry. He praised her Lives of the Italian poets in the Cabinet Library.

During this year Coleridge was residing with Gil[l]man at Highgate who had generously taken him under his charge. I used now & then to go and see him at Gil[l]man's but I went seldom for I thought the Gil[l]mans treated me with rudeness & this happened to Lamb also. On the 14th of July I took Ch. Becher to see C. when Coler. amused me by declaring that he had years before

Goethe discovered his theory of colours, wh. by diverting his attention to other subjects, Southey had prevented his publishing. And on my intimating that I heard that others had lately announced a like system, C. naïvely remarked that he was very free in communicating his thoughts in conversation. It was this day that Lamb joined us & Gil[l]man came in & assumed an air as if he meant it to express: "Now Gentlemen, it is time for you to go." We took the hint & went & Lamb said he would never call again.

On the 21st of Decr. I accompanied Cargill to Coleridge when we found he had been very ill, but he was able to expatiate eloquently on the distinction bet. fancy & imagination. Fancy he called memory without judgement. See his Lay Sermon. He spoke of German literature; praised Steffens & lamented the Romanism of the Schlegels & Tieck. He spoke of Hazlitt's attacks on him with unexpected moderation but complained of Lamb's toleration of him, to whom Hazlitt was indebted for what had been thought original ideas in him, & who violated private confidence so outrageously. He was pleased at being told that H. had been knocked down lately by John Lamb, Charles L.'s brother.

I heard Mary Lamb say, after I had cut him for a cause I will now state: 'You are rich in friends. We cannot afford to cast off our friends because they are not all we wish,' & I have heard Lamb say: 'Hazlitt does bad actions without being a bad man.'

It was on Sunday, the 22d of Dec., the day after this conversation with Coleridge, that I broke altogether with Hazlitt. I had read in the morning's *Examiner*, a paper, manifestly by H., abusing Wordsworth for his writings in favour of the King, I rather think especially the sonnet express[in]g the wish that the king could be restored for an instant to his faculties in order to be aware of the victory gained by the nation over Buonaparte. "I recollected," he said,—(I quote from memory)—"hearing this gent[leman] say 'I shd. wish to see every member of the Ho[use] of Commons hanged.' I put in a word in favour of Cha. Fox & Sheridan. But he said: no. There is not one of them fit to live. And then he referred to what he called their tergiversation." This eveng I took tea at Basil Montagu's. Hazlitt on coming in, offered me his hand wh. I refused. And during the evening I took an opportunity to say: Nothing shd. induce me to continue an acquaintance with the writer of an article in to-day's *Examiner*. Hazlitt said coolly: I am not in the habit of defending everything I write. I do not say that all I have written is just. And on my especially remarking on the breach of confidence, he said: It may be indelicate, but I must write an article every week, & I have not time to be delicate. On which I repeated the anecdote of the French minister to the libeller: 'Je n'en vois pas la necessité.' He then made a distinction: I would never take advantage of a slip in a man's conversation, who might say *once* what was not his real habitual opinion & a repetition would be a substantial falsehood. But what I published was an often repeated sentiment, not said to me alone but many. And such things might be repeated. I replied: One aggravation is wanting in this case & your vindication amounts to this: 'Tho' I won't lye, I will betray.' He said he thought it useful to expose persons who would otherwise gain credit by canting. I admitted that the attack on Southey's *Carmen Nuptiale* was unexceptionable & he said he still believed Southey was an honest man.

After this evening I never to my recollection exchanged a word with Hazlitt. I often met him at Lamb's but we never spoke. He lived 12 years afterwards & many years before his death he said to Mary Lamb: 'Robinson cuts me, but in spite of that I shall always have a kind feeling towards him, for he was the first person that ever found out there was anything in me.' That is true, for when I became acquainted with him at Bury, he was living with his elder brother a miniature painter. And I admired him when no one else thought anythg. of him & before he had printed anythg. but wh. by the bye I have said before.

1817. In the summer of 1817 Ludwig Tieck, the first of the romantic school of poetry in Germany, came to England. His object was to inspect M.S.S. & rare copies of ancient dramas in our public libraries, it being his boast that he had read every accessible printed drama before & contemporaneous with Shakespeare. He was also desirous of seeing Coleridge, whose reputation both as a poet & critic had reached Germany. On the 24th of June, Mr. Green & I accompanied him to Highgate where Mr. Gil[l]man joined us. C. of course was the talker & L. T. is a good listener. However he did talk & abt. religion. He professed Catholicism, but it was of a harmless kind, for while he said that the people in Catholic countries would be without their religion, he admitted that England owed its greatness to the Reformation & he said that the Catholic system requires Protest[antis]m to keep it in order—precisely what Mrs. Barbauld says of the Church & Dissent. He spoke with great love of Goethe but called the *Prologue to Faust* impious (Goethe to me said: How innocent that is!) T. lamented Goethe's want of religion & said his later works are loquacious. C. read some of his own poems & T. seemed impressed by his eloquence.

On the 29th, I accomp[anie]d T. to Godwin to whom he was very complimentary on account of his works.

Speaking on a future occasion of Coleridge, Tieck said he had herrliche Ideen abt Shakesp[eare] but did not estimate highly his formal criticisms. His conversation he admired & said there was much poetry in *Christabel*. He spoke favourably of Strutt's & Lord Chedworth's remarks on Shakesp:. Of Ben Jonson he praised expecially *The Silent Woman* (wh. he has translated.) *The Fox & The Alchemist, The Devil is an Ass* & *Bartholomew Fair* perhaps his best. Of German literature he did not speak very favourably. He despised his imitators who had become perhaps more popular than himself, such as *Fouqué*. But *Solger* [?] he praised highly.—I shall have to write of Tieck anno 1829 if these Reminiscences ever reach so far.

In December I had a call from Wordsworth & the ladies. We talked abt. Coleridge who had before consulted with me abt. the expediency of prosecuting the Edin. Magazine for a libel, wh. the Wordsworths agreed with me in thinking inadvisable. The publisher had applied to W. to write in his Magazine & had inserted both eulogistic & abusive articles. W. wrote to him coolly not to trouble himself abt. him, W., as he could make no return in kind.

On the 30th I spent the eveng. at Lamb's where I found two parties congregated round the two poets, but Coler. had a thicker mass than W. C. was rambling in his peculiar way to Monkhouse who listened attentively & Manning, who smiled, as my journal remarks, as if he thought that C. shd. not metaphysicise on what he knew nothing abt.   (probably early in 1851.)

27*th Dec.* I was gratified to-day by hearing Col. eloquently expatiating on the necessity of protecting Hone for the sake of English law. He derided the lawyer's definition of a libel wh. looks only to tendency & disregards intention. *Tilbrook* related a droll anecdote. *Southey* received a letter from a stranger in Essex, with a fee, requesting him to write an acrostic on the name Rebecca Rankin. He was addressing the lady but had a rival who beat him at verse-making. S. did not send the money back, & distributed the money in buying blankets for some poor women at Keswick.

1818. 17*th Feb.* This day attended two courses of lectures on the poets, one from Hazlitt, one from Coleridge. Neither seems to have pleased me. My journal remarks on the recklessness of Hazlitt who, to a party mostly of Saints at the Surrey Institution, was all but obscene in his notice of Prior, quoting his unseemly verses agst. Blackmore, & eulogised Voltaire. Of Coleridge I was led to remark that his mind seemed confined within a narrow circle of ideas, wh. he was ever repeating, but wh. he had not the power of adapting to the popular taste.
On the 24th of Feb. I attended in like manner two lectures from the same men. Hazlitt was so vulgarly abusive of Wordsworth that I lost my temper & hissed & attacked him with a violence I afterwards regretted to the persons near me, tho' I said nothing but the truth. Coleridge confirmed the apprehension that these lectures wd. not add to his fame.

1819. In the year 1819 I either did not see at all or saw to no purpose either of the great poets. My journal does not mention anythg. concerning them except that it notices a very unfavourable judgment of *Peter Bell* by Charles Lamb whose judgment against those he loved might be fairly taken. He loved Wordsworth, tho' not so intensely as Coleridge, but he denied him the faculty of story-telling & he deemed *Peter Bell* one of W.'s poorest works & the *Introduction* childish. I wonder that he did not perceive the exquisite beauty of much in the Introduction.
1820. In the year 1820 I saw much both of Wordsworth & Southey. With W. I took a journey thro' Switzerland, & I have written a brief notice of that journey. I was mortified by observing that it records nothing of W. worth recollecting till I recollected it could not be otherwise, for we were always in motion & W.'s mind was devoted exclusively to the observation of the scenes around him. His *Memorials* shew the objects that attracted his notice.
Southey I also saw on a particular occasion—the papers of my poor friend Hamond which were given to him but wh. he transferred to me. I have in

speaking of Hamond noticed Southey's participation in this sad history, therefore I shall have but little to say, I expect, of the poets this year.

9th May. Southey at bk.fast with me & afterwards we walked together to Wapping on Hamond's business. On our walk he repeated to me his unpublished hexameters & he had the power to make them agreeable in recital;—less unpleasant by far than his naked opinions. He expressed his regret that the King of France did not on his second return put to death some 16 marshalls & other great men by martial law or without any trial whatever. Public opinion, he said, would justify the violence. He affirmed that before 20 years the excesses of the popular writers wd. put an end to every free press in Europe. Now if time be not of the essence of such predictions, Southey may be in the right after all, for now after 30 years it looks more likely than ever that what he foretold will take place.

29th October. Leigh Hunt hardly belongs to this set & I very seldom saw him at Lamb's, yet I remark in my journal to-day: "Read the *Indicator* to-day. There is a spirit of enjoyment in this little book which gives a charm to it. Hunt is the very opposite of Hazlitt in loving everything. He catches the sunny side of all things & excepting a few antipathies, mostly abstractions, lo! everything is beautiful."

Wordsworth was in London a considerable time after our Swiss tour & in good plight. My journal has this note: "18*th Nov*. At Monkhouse's to dinner with the Wordsw.s, Lambs, Mr. Kenyon. W. in excellent mood: his improved & improving mildness & tolerance must very much conciliate all who know him."

8th Dec. Read the beginning of Keats's *Hyperion*. My journal says: "A poem of great promise. There are a wildness, power & originality in this young poet which, if his perilous journey to Italy do not destroy him, promise to place him at the head of the poets of the next generation. Lamb places him next to Wordsworth, not meaning any comparison. They are dissimilar."

1821. The year 1821 supplies nothing to my recollections of the poets & their literary friends. I was at Ambleside on my return from Scotland, only for a short time, but I was happy to find that with Words. & his family my acquaintance had improved to friendship.

1822. In the Jan. of this year 1822 I first saw Hartley Coleridge. He made on me the impression that he was an unpleasant youth, but endowed with qualities wh. would one day confer distinction. Now I look back on him with admiration & compassion.

In the spring of this year Hazlitt & his wife went into Scotland & Mary Lamb told me for what purpose they went before the act was perpetrated. They are gone, she said, & this was on the 9th of April, in order that Mrs. H. should obtain a divorce by proving adultery agst her husband & then he is to marry the daughter of the house in wh. he lodges!!! In fact Hazlitt did obtain the required divorce, in order to obtain wh. his wife was obliged to swear there was no collusion!!! On his return, the girl refused him. She was the daughter of my old tailor, Walker, & sister of the present Mrs. Robert Roscoe, a very respectable woman. W. Hazlitt made this sad adventure the subject of a little book, the worst he ever wrote, thoroughly bad, *The New Pygmalion*. He afterwards married a widow, for wh. he was liable to transporation, according to the case of The King *v.* Lolly.

Some time after the marriage, John Collier met Hazlitt in the street & wished him joy. "You may well wish me joy," said H. "She has £300 a year & is not so bad neither." But the £300 per annum did not last. His wife became tired of him, & the money being in her own hands & she finding that he had no hold upon him [her?] left him. H. lived a wretched life & died in extreme poverty. I may hereafter say more about him.

Godwin was this year a source of trouble to me. My early admiration of his works led me to form an acquaintance with him which I regretted but from wh. I did not withdraw till I had suffered largely both substantially & in spirits. His pecuniary distresses seemed to have entirely blunted his moral sense. In the June of this year he lost the benefit he had derived from occupying a house which was the subject of litigation. As two claimed he wd. pay rent to neither & he could not be made to see that there was anythg. wrong in his so doing. He did not refuse from prudence bona fide but he thought he might fairly profit by the litigation. It was a piece of good luck. At last he had to pay arrears of rent, costs of action &c. Being in great want & C. Lamb having lent him £50, I could not refuse him £30. Soon after a subscription was opened. I put down my £30 as an already paid subscription & when I ultimately declined all further intercourse with him, I used in jest to say I owed him £20, as I considered £50 wd. be my ultimate loss. What provoked me to abandon all further participation in his affairs was this—that several hundred pounds having been with difficulty raised to rescue him from prison & the money being paid in the assurance that he was thereby set at liberty, the very next day after the payment he was arrested again. Such a man could not be helped I thought, & it was a relief to me when I had courage to take & keep the resolution & tho' he lived many years afterwards, I did not renew my acquaintance. When this *last* occurrence took place I do not exactly recollect.

Among the worst features of Godwin's mind was an utter insensibility to kindness. He considered all acts of beneficence as a debt to his intellect. On this occasion Walter Scott sent £10 but his name was not to be published. This offended him. Had he not been so severely pressed, he wd. have returned the money & refused to acknowledge the gift, leaving that to the Committee. This indeed I do not censure.

21st Dec. Aders, through me, obtained the acquaintance of Coleridge of wh. he was reasonably vain. This day there was a splendid dinner & C. was the star. He talked freely of Wordsworth. He had not seen the last published works, but he spoke less favourably of the later than he did of the earlier works. He reproached W. with a vulgar attachment to orthodoxy in its literal sense. "The later portions of *The Excursion* are distinguishable from the earlier, & I can," said Col., "from internal evidence separate the one from the other." He accused

W. of a disregard to the mechanism of his verse & insinuated a decline of his faculties. This judgment I thought to proceed from a feeling of personal unkindness.

I was more willing to concur in what C. said of Southey. He spoke depreciatingly of Southey's politics, declaring him to be morally an independent, intellectually a dependent man.

1823. I also introduced to the Aders, the Wordsworths & Lambs as well as Flaxmans. Aders's possession of a fine collection of old pictures & his musical connections & the talents of himself & Mrs. A. enabled them to acquire a large acquaintance, wh. otherwise it wd. have been difficult for them to do. On the 5th of April there was a large musical party in Euston Sq. at wh. Wordsw[orth] & Coleridge were present & I noticed a great diversity in their enjoyment of music. Coleridge's was very lively & openly expressed. Wordsw. sat retired & was silent, with his face covered. Some thought he was asleep. He *might* pass over to sleep after enjoyment. He declared himself highly gratified & indeed came to the party after he had declined the invitation. Flaxman, who was also there, confessed that he could not endure fine music *long:* it exhausted him. So it might be with Wordsworth.

On the *4th of April* I was one of a party at dinner at Monkhouse's, concerning which there is a letter in Talfourd's *Letters of Lamb,* Vol. II p. 95, to Bernard Barton. Lamb says of this party: "I dined in Parnassus with Words., Col:, Rogers & Tom Moore; half the poetry of England constellated & clustered in Gloucester Place. Coler[idge] was in his finest vein of talk—had all the talk. . . . We did not quaff Hippocrene last night." The short letter is in Lamb's charming style. I have this to add. It is a pity indeed to put water to wine, but there is no help for it. I and Mr. Gil[l]man were the only unpoetical men at table besides the Amphitryon. My journal says: "Our party consisted of W., Col. L., M. & R., 5 poets of very unequal worth & most disproprotionate popularity whom the public would arrange probably in the very inverse order except that it wd. place Moore above Rogers. Coler[idge] alone displayed any of his peculiar talent. He talked much & well. I have not for years seen him in such excellent health & spirits. His subjects, metaphysical criticisms on words. He talked chiefly to Wordsw[orth]. Rogers occasionally let fall a remark. Moore seemed conscious of his inferiority. He was very attentive to Col. but seemed also to relish L. whom he sat next. L. was in a happy frame: kept himself within bounds & was only cheerful at last." This seems at variance with his own letter for he complains of headache & did not go to Aders' party. I have a very distinct recollection of more than I put in my journal, as is often the case. For instance I can add this with confidence. Lamb sat next Tom Moore & when he was sufficiently touched with wine to be very amusing, I overheard him say with a hiccough, "Mr. Moore, let me drink a glass of wine with you," suiting the word to the action. "Hitherto Mr. Moore I have had an antipathy to you; but now that I have seen you I shall like you ever after." Some years after I mentioned this to Moore: he recollected the fact but not Lamb's amusing manner. It occurred to me at the time that Moore felt, if not his inferiority, at least that his talent was of another sort. For many years he had been the most brilliant man of his company. In anecdotes, small talk & especially in singing, he was supreme; but he was no match for Coleridge in his vein; as little could he feel Lamb's humour.

April 4. 1823 [This is a subsequent addition pasted on the back of pp. 48–55] "Dined at Mr. Monkhouse's, a gentleman I had never seen before, on Wordsworth's invitation, who lives there whenever he comes to town. A singular party, Coleridge, Rogers, Wordsworth & wife, Charles Lamb, the hero at present of the London Magazine, & his sister (the poor woman who went mad with him in the diligence on the way to Paris) & a Mr. Robinson, one of the minora sidera of this constellation of the Lakes, the host himself, a Mæcenas of the school, contributing nothing but good dinners & silence. Charles Lamb, a clever fellow certainly, but full of villainous & abortive puns which he miscarries of every minute. Some excellent things however have come from him, & his friend Robinson mentioned to me not a bad one. On Robinson's receiving his first brief, he called on Lamb to tell him of it. I suppose, said Lamb, you addressed that line of Milton's [sic] to it: 'Thou first best [great] cause *least* understood.' There follow a number of puns & anecdotes by Coleridge & Lamb."

The Rev[iewers] Athen. April 23. 1853. introduce the above extract with the remark: "The tone of it we do not like" & add at the end that they shd. like to see Lamb's account of the same dinner & after-dinner table-talk.

2d. May. I dined with Coleridge at Mr. Green's in Lincoln's Inn Fields. C. was the only talker, but, says my journal "he did not talk his best. He repeated one of his own jokes by wh. he offended a Methodist lady at the whist table by calling for her *last trump* & confessing that though he always thought her an angel, he did not before consider her to be an *arch-angel*."

This year arose the quarrel between Lamb & Southey of which I need say nothing because it is fully stated in the *Letters* of Lamb, among which Lamb's *Elia* letter appears. Southey told me that Lamb had written to him afterwards a letter of deep contrition for that letter. There is nothing more likely than that Lamb shd. express a great deal more sorrow than it was right in him to feel. I may add as to that same Elia letter that I felt flattered by the being singled with the other of Lamb's friends under the initials of my name. I mention it as an anecdote which shows that L.'s reputation was spread even among lawyers, that a 4 guinea brief was brought to me by an attorney, an entire stranger, at the following Assizes by direction of another attorney, also a stranger who knew nothing more of me that that I was Elia's H. C. R. This letter of Lamb's has higher merits in my eyes than any kindness towards me. His praises of Leigh Hunt & Hazlitt were most generous by wh. he wilfully exposed himself to obloquy, & towards Hazlitt especially, because he & Hazlitt were at that time not on friendly terms. Indeed Hazlitt was always putting the friendship of all who knew him to a severe trial, such as few could sustain as well as Lamb— the most kind, generous & self-sacrificing of men.

It is but fair that I shd. add that in Blackwood's Magazine for November there is a humorous attack on Lamb for his letter to Southey, which my journal says "is not ill-done," tho' I could not have been pleased at a note to the passage—"H. C. R. unwearied in every service of a friend"—the note being:—"Correspondent & caricaturist of Wordsworth."

1824. The year 1824 does not supply many materials to my reminiscences of the poets & that connection.

5*th Mar*. In March I was at Lamb's with Monkhouse when a religious conversation arose between them. My journal notices the strong anti-religious language of Lamb, & at the same time I am convinced, as it justly remarks, that Lamb was a man of *"natural piety"* & that his supposed anti-religious language was in fact directed solely agst the dogmatism of systematic theology. He has the spirit of devotion in his heart & the organ of theosophy in his skull.

The Wordsworths were in London this spring when I saw them frequently with the Lambs, Aders, & Flaxmans, all of whom I had brought together.

19*th April* at Monkhouse's I met Wordsw[orth] & Ed. Irving together. W. stated that the pressing difficulty on his mind had always been to reconcile the prescience of the Almighty with accountability in man. I stated mine to be the incompatibility of final & absolute evil with the Divine supremacy. Irving did not pretend to answer either objection. He was no metaphysician he said, & knew no more of God than was revealed. This did not meet but evaded the difficulty. The poet he felt to be too great to be angry with & he seemed to take no offence even with me.

3*d. June*. A large party at Green's, where, in spite of the dancers, Coleridge was willing to metaphysicise. He declaimed this eveng on the growing hypocrisy of the age & the attempt to put down liberality of speculation. Sir Humphrey Davy had joined that party & they were patronising Granville Penn's attack on geology as anti-Christian! They consider the modern theory of a deluge anti-Mosaic. Where should the dove pick up a leaf? &c. &c. C. displeased me by speaking bitterly of Schlegel & Ludwig Tieck, abusing Tieck in the style of Schelling. The atheist, said Coleridge, seeks only an infinite cause. The spurious divine is content with a mere personal will which is the death of all reason. The philosophic theologian unites them—but *how*, he did not say. C. declared German philosophy to be in a state of rapid deterioration. When did he write the passages from Schelling published as his own in his Biog. Literaria?

10*th June* I went with C. L. to Highgate, self-invited. My journal says "A rich evening at Gil[l]man's. The Greens, Collins R.A., the Aders & a Mr. Taylor, a young man of talents in the Colonial Office." This must have been Henry Taylor, the future author of *Philip van Arteveld*, my present acquaintance. Coler., says my journal, "talked his best & his superiority above Irving the more apparent because they seemed to think alike. He dwelt on the internal evidence of Xtnty, insisting on its supplying the wants of our nature. Coler. as his daughter now confesses, holding as of no value, the *historical* evidence of Xtnty. "The Advocatus Diaboli of the eveng. was Mr. Taylor," says my journal, who, if that acct. be correct, with verbal acuteness & in a very gentlemanly tone, but over-confidently, set up Mahomet as enjoying his own internal conviction & as having improved the condition of mankind. Lamb asked him whether he came in a turban or a hat. There was also a Mr. Chance who irritated Irving so that Irving said in anger: 'Sir, I reject the whole bundle of your opinions.' But I thought Mr. Chance had only words: Irving smelt Antinomianism in them.

Coleridge was unfriendly to the Germans, & called Herder a coxcomb, setting Schiller above Goethe, granting the great poet only the merit of exquisite taste & denying him principle. It requires great modification & great qualification to render this just. There is something of truth in such assertions, but they are more false than true.

Irving on our walk home spoke of a friend who had translated *Wilhelm Meister* & said of him: "We do not sympathise on religious sentiment." This was *Carlyle* whom he did not name. But, continued I[rving] 'When I perceive there is a sincere searching after truth, I think I like a person the better for not having found it.' Probably, says my journal, he suspected I was a doubter. On this same walk Lamb spoke of his friend Manning as the most wonderful man he had ever known,—greater than Coleridge or Wordsworth. Yet he had done nothing, & tho' he travelled in China that produced nothing. Him I knew afterwards—an interesting man, but nothing more.

6th July. Tea at Lamb's. There was a party, Hessey the publisher among them—Giving a somewhat overdone description from De Quincey, the opium-eater's lips, of his sufferings, Lamb remarked that he ought to choose as his publishers *Pain & Fuss* (Payne & Foss, who, by the bye, were not publishers). Clare, the shepherd poet was there, a feeble man, but he was ill, & Elton the translator from the classics, who looked more like a hunter than a poet.

Probably an anecdote belongs to *this* year, tho' I have not found it in my journal & have but an imperfect recollection of it. The incident was amusing when it occurred. *Words.* & *Lady Morgan* were invited to dine at I forget whose house. The poet would on no account take her downstairs, & he disturbed the table arrangements by placing himself at the bottom when her ladyship was at the top. She was either unobserving of his conduct or resolved to show him she did not care for it, for she sent the servant to get him to drink a glass of wine with her. His look was as solemn as if it had been a death summons. This I saw. I was told she asked her neighbour, "Has not Mr. Words. written some poems?"

1825. I did not see any of my north-country friends this year, that is 1825, & therefore this year wd. have been a blank in the annals of my poetically minded friends but for my frequent visits to dear Ch. L On the 10th of Feb. I saw in Lamb's chambers, says my journal, "a forward, talking young man" introduced to Lamb as his great admirer. "He will be a pleasant man enough when the obtrusiveness of youth is worn away a little." Now this same man, viz Harrison Ainsworth, is the author of numerous popular romances of the class of Spanish Beggar & Bandit tales, constituting the old daily literature. They have been & are still popular tho' of the most mischievous kind, his heroes being generally banditti or highwaymen or political characters of a deplorable notoriety—a man therefore who could not venture to stand a ballot at the Athenæum.

It is barely within the field assigned to this chapter to mention that I this year succeeded in inducing a barrister going to India to take as his clerk a son of John Hazlitt, W. Hatzlitt's very inferior brother, which occasioned Talfourd's ill-naturedly telling me that I had more pleasure in serving disagreeable than agreeable people. I do not know what has become of this lad. He was a smart lad & was doing well for a number of years.

An important incident in Lamb's life, tho' in the end not so happy for him as he anticipated, was his obtaining his discharge with a pension of almost £400 a year from the India House. This he announced to me by a note put into my letter box:—"I have left the India House. D—time. I'm all for eternity." He was rather more than 50 years of age. I found him & his sister in high spirits when I called to wish them joy on the 22d of April. "I never saw him so calmly cheerful" says my journal, "as he seemed then." It is notorious this did not last. In the autumn this joy was already somewhat abated when I found the parodist Hone with him, to whom he rendered great kindness by supplying him with articles for his "Every Day Book" wh. are however known to the readers of Lamb—especially his *Selections from the Ancient Dramatists made at the British Museum*. These were afterwards collected & published in two small volumes. I sent these *Selections from the Ancient Dramatists* to Ludw. Tieck. He said of them "Sie sind aus meinem Herzen geschrieben.—They are written out of my heart." The remark was made as well of the criticism as of the text.

1826. This too was an unproductive year. The poets from the North did not come to London. My chief correspondence with Wordsworth arose out of his dissatisfaction with his publishers the Longmans, from whom he had obtained scarcely anything in all his life. He had so little acquaintance with the business part of literature that he even applied to one so ignorant as myself to negotiate with a publisher for him. I had neither the acquaintance with persons nor familiarity with business to qualify me for the undertaking, & was therefore of no use to him. On this subject I saw several times Alaric Watts, who had undertaken this for Wordsworth. But ultimately he did nothing, except, I believe in publishing some small pieces in an *Annual* of wh. he was editor. Wordsworth was averse to let anything of his appear in these poor imitations of the German *Musen-Almanachs*, but I believe somethg. of his was so published by A. Watts. I fear that neither poet nor editor was satisfied with the result.

In May I was in company with *Sam: Rogers*, with whom I was becoming acquainted. He praised Wordsworth but lamented his obstinacy in adhering to tasteless peculiarities. There was at this time a current anecdote that Rogers once said to Wordsworth "If you wd. let me edit your poems & give me leave to omit some half dozen & make a few trifling alterations, I wd. engage you shd. be as popular a poet as any living," & that W. answered: "I am much obliged to you Mr. Rogers; I am a poor man but I wd. rather remain as I am."

In May I was engaged reading Coleridge's *Aids to Reflexion*, that beautiful *composition*, in the special sense of being compounded of the production of the Scotch Archbishop *Leighton* & himself. I compared it to an ancient statue, said to be made of ivory & gold, likening the portion belonging to the Abp. to the ivory, & that of the poet to the gold. Coler. somewhere admits that, musing over Leighton's text, he was not always able to distinguish what was properly his own from what was consciously derived from his master. J.J. Taylor quotes this & hints that this might be the case with St. John in his old age when writing his Gospel. On first reading these *Aids*, I remarked that his, Coleridge's philosophy was his own, his religion that of the vulgar. This [is] in my journal. Might I not more truly have said that Col. was not unwilling in one publication to write both *eso*terically & *exo*terically? I also at first considered this as an attempt to express Kantian principles in the English language & adapt it to popular religious sentiment.

15*th June*. With the Montagus & Irving at Highgate. In my journal I wrote "Col. eloquent as usual but I never took a note of his conversation wh. was not a caput mortuum, tho' there was still the sense of a glorious spirit having been active. Irving not brilliant, but gloomy in his denunciatn. of God's vengeance for the irreligion of the country." The only thing he at this time said wh. I heard with satisfaction was his confession that Coleridge had convinced him that he was a Bibliolatrist. Of Irving I have elsewhere written. Coleridge at a later period of his life declared I. to be mad in the juridical use of the word. He had been unsettled by excessive flattery stimulating exorbitant vanity.

1827 was a more entire blank than the preceding as to all personal intercourse with Wordsworth &c. except that I had become a correspondent with Miss Wordsw., his sister, & my letters as well to her as the rest of the family were preserved & returned to me on his death. My short accounts of my journeys were thought good by him from their condensation & some of these may be worth preserving.

1828. This year I became acquainted with *Quillinan*, who was then the friend & became afterwards the son-in-law of Wordsworth. He was then the friend only of *Dora* Wordsworth to whose care his wife had, at her death, entrusted the educn. of her children in Protestant principles, Qu. being a Catholic & having undertaken on his marriage to bring up his daughters, if any, Protestant. The sons were to be brought up Catholics. He had only daughters. Qu. most scrupulously kept his word, but he informed me not long before his death that his wife was inclined to pass over to the Rom. Cath. Church wh. he wd. not encourage. His attachment to the R. C. Church of wh. he made a boast, was of a very slight texture. By the knavery of Sir Egerton Bridges, his son, & the son's attorney, Qu: was involved in sad litigation by wh. however his character did not suffer except on account of manifest indiscretion, but wh. wd. have made a beggar of him if he had not been a beggar before. W. visited Qu. this year & in the summer I saw him several times. He approved of my leaving the bar & if I had needed to be confirmed in my resolution his approbation wd. have sufficed. I was not a little gratified by hearing that, at Saml. Rogers', he declared me to be the wisest barrister he had ever known.

I may here digressively refer to a very curious note on this subject contained in *W. S. Landor's* "Pericles & Aspasia" in wh. W. S. L. in the midst of a bitter attack on the American *N. P. Willis* reproached him (very absurdly by the bye) for disrespect towards Mr. R.——who is praised for this same act. In fact W. S.

L's well-intended but ill-executed compliment is really more objectionable than the American letter giving an account of a bk.fast in my chambers.

28th May. A dinner at Quillinan's who was desirous to gratify some of his military friends with the sight of two poets. He had been a Hussar as was recollected to his disadvantage by a contemptuous critic of his poems in the Athenæum. There was a Colonel Miller, a man of a fine military air without any swagger, who had distinguished himself in the Peruvian army; *Kenyon,* then designated as the friend of Wordsworth & Southey, an American lady, a Miss Douglas, of whom W. said: 'She is anxious to see famous people & talk herself.' Southey was there, sadly out of humour at the Cath[olic] Emancipation then going on, but restrained by being in the house of a Romanist. During this visit to London, Wordsw. indulged the hope to accompany me to Italy wh. he executed 9 years afterwards when the activity of his mind was abated. He wd. have required the permission of the Govt. He at this time stated that, including a life annuity of £100 from Sir Geo. Beaumont, but subject to the maintenance of his sister, he had £400 per ann independently of his office income.

3d. June. Wordsworth brought *Hills* to bk.fast with me. I shd. say, mentioning Hills, that he was a great friend of John Wordsworth & a warm admirer of the poet wh. brought us acquainted. He for a time fluctuated between law & literature. Ultimately he decided in favour of a literary life—that is bookish indolence. He met on a steam-boat a Quaker family & fell in love with the young lady of the party, Wordsworth's poetry being the seductive medium—a pure & idealised *Galiotto.* They married; he lived abroad where he died also many years ago. He published a metrical translation of *Faust* wh. he gave me, but it acquired no reputation. He was happy in his wife, but used to complain of her family, especially brothers, for having over-reached him in money matters. He used to speak bitterly of Quakers as a body, as if slyness & selfishness were their characteristic qualities.

During this year Lamb & his sister were living on Enfield Green near a small inn. My occasional visits were acceptable to them & I had a bin at the inn. I introduced them to Relph but tho' they & he alike wanted society yet they had too little in common to be companionable. When I went, whatever the hour of the day, Dumbee Whist was resorted to. Lamb had no other occupation than the reading of old books & occasionally writing verse to wh. he was becoming less apt & less inclined. My visits to the Lambs in this their solitude & a few letters between Miss Wordsworth & myself constituted all my intercourse with them before my journey to Italy wh. changed for a time my habits & occupations.

1829. At this time I used to see Moxon in whom C. Lamb took an active interest & whom he induced to marry their adopted child Miss Isola. At this time too, in 1829, I found Lamb anxious to serve Martin Burney, who by his injudicious call to the bar & habits of indulgence had brought himself to a state of great want. Through Rickman & Alsager he was able sometimes to procure employment for Martin, to whom he was attached & who, notwithstanding his infirmities, was an object of tender interest.

William Hazlitt

1778–1830

William Hazlitt was born at Maidstone, Kent, on April 10, 1778, the fourth child of a Unitarian preacher. Following his birth, the family lived briefly in Ireland and then in America, returning to England in 1787 and settling in Shropshire. In his childhood Hazlitt was known as an exceedingly happy child, but his personality underwent a noticeable transformation in adolescence, and as an adult he was considered sullen and often unapproachable. Coleridge, for one, called him "singularly repulsive—brow-hanging, shoe-contemplative, strange."

Hazlitt read widely as a child and thereby laid the foundation in literature and philosophy that he was to use in his writing. But writing did not come easily to Hazlitt, who pursued a career as a painter for several years, studying at the Louvre before the war forced his return to England in 1803. An accomplished portrait painter, he was encouraged by Wordsworth, Coleridge, and Charles Lamb—whose portrait by Hazlitt hangs in the National Portrait Gallery—to continue in that career. But in 1805 he turned his attention to philosophy and published his first book, *On the Principles of Human Action*. Other book-length essays followed on various political and philosophical topics. In 1808 Hazlitt married, and he and his wife settled at Winterslow, Salisbury Plain, where he lived off and on for the remainder of his life.

A period of failure followed his marriage. He tried working on several literary projects, including an English grammar, and he briefly returned to painting in order to support his growing family. By the end of 1811, however, he was penniless and believed himself a failure as both painter and writer. Nevertheless, he forced himself to give a series of lectures on philosophy in London, and got a job reporting for the *Morning Chronicle*. By 1813 he was an established drama critic and journalist, contributing to a number of periodicals. Collections of his essays were later published as *The Round Table* (two volumes, 1817), *Characters of Shakespeare's Plays* (1817); and *A View of the English Stage* (1818). The defeat of his longtime idol, Napoleon, however, was a heavy blow for Hazlitt, who reportedly turned to drink in his sorrow. Heavy drinking and ill-health accentuated his disagreeableness, and he engaged in frequent quarrels with his friends, both in and out of print.

Despite these setbacks Hazlitt continued to lecture, concentrating on English writers; these were published as *On the English Poets* (1818) and *On the English Comic Writers* (1819). In 1819 he delivered his last lectures, on literature in the Elizabethan Age, and thenceforth concentrated on essays for various journals, including the *London Magazine,* which he also edited temporarily. Much of his writing was done at his country home at Winterslow, where he lived alone following a separation and later divorce from his wife.

Hazlitt's most famous collections of essays were published in the 1820s: *Table Talk* (1821); *The Spirit of the Age* (1825); and *The Plain Speaker* (1826); other volumes were later collected by his son and published posthumously. Hazlitt's work falls into three categories: the familiar essay, which, along with those of Lamb and Hunt, established a model for writers in the Victorian Age; social criticism which reflected his political liberalism; and literary criticism, which is now regarded as some of the finest in the language.

ON COMMON-PLACE
CRITICS

"Nor can I think what thoughts they can conceive."

We have already given some account of common-place people; we shall in this number attempt a description of another class of the community, who may be called (by way of distinction) common-place critics. The former are a set of people who have no opinions of their own, and do not pretend to have any; the latter are a set of people who have no opinions of their own, but who affect to have one upon every subject you can mention. The former are a very honest, good sort of people, who are contented to pass for what they are; the latter are a very pragmatical, troublesome sort of people, who would pass for what they are not, and try to put off their common-place notions in all companies and on all subjects, as something of their own. They are of both species, the grave and the gay; and it is hard to say which is the most tiresome.

A common-place critic has something to say upon every occasion, and he always tells you either what is not true, or what you knew before, or what is not worth knowing. He is a person who thinks by proxy, and talks by rote. He differs with you, not because he thinks you are in the wrong, but because he thinks somebody else will think so. Nay, it would be well if he stopped here; but he will undertake to misrepresent you, and will set you right, not only in opinions which you have, but in those which you may be supposed to have. Thus, if you say that *Bottom* the weaver is a character that has not had justice done to it, he shakes his head, is afraid you will be thought extravagant, and wonders you should think the *Midsummer Night's Dream* the finest of all Shakespear's plays. He judges of matters of taste and reasoning as he does of dress and fashion, by the prevailing tone of good company; and you would as soon persuade him to give up any sentiment that is current there, as to wear the hind part of his coat before. By the best company, of which he is perpetually talking, he means persons who live on their own estates, and other people's ideas. By the opinion of the world, to which he pays and expects you to pay great deference, he means that of a little circle of his own, where he hears and is heard. Again, *good sense* is a phrase constantly in his mouth, by which he does not mean his own sense or that of anybody else, but the opinions of a number of persons who have agreed to take their opinions on trust from others. If any one observes that there is something better than common sense, viz. *uncommon* sense, he thinks this a bad joke. If you object to the opinions of the majority, as often arising from ignorance or prejudice, he appeals from them to the sensible and well-informed; and if you say that there may be other persons as sensible and well-informed as himself and his friends, he smiles at your presumption. If you attempt to prove anything to him, it is in vain, for he is not thinking of what you say, but of what will be thought of it. The stronger your reasons, the more incorrigible he thinks you; and looks upon any attempt to expose his gratuitous assumptions as the wandering of a disordered imagination. His notions are like plaster figures cast in a mould, as brittle as they are hollow; but they will break before you can make them give way. In fact, he is the representative of a large part of the community, the shallow, the vain, and indolent, of those who have time to talk, and are not bound to think; and he considers any deviation from the select forms of common-place, or the accredited language of conventional impertinence, as compromising the authority under which he acts in his diplomatic capacity. It is wonderful how this class of people agree with one another; how they herd together in all their opinions; what a tact they have for folly; what an instinct for absurdity; what a sympathy in sentiment; how they find one another out by infallible signs, like Freemasons! The secret of this unanimity and strict accord is, that not any one of them ever admits any opinion that can cost the least effort of mind in arriving at, or of courage in declaring it. Folly is as consistent with itself as wisdom: there is a certain level of thought and sentiment, which the weakest minds, as well as the strongest, find out as best adapted to them; and you as regularly come to the same conclusions, by looking no farther than the surface, as if you dug to the centre of the earth! You know beforehand what a critic of this class will say on almost every subject the first time he sees you, the next time, the time after that, and so on to the end of the chapter. The following list of his opinions may be relied on:—It is pretty certain that before you have been in the room with him ten minutes, he will give you to understand that Shakespear was a great but irregular genius. Again, he thinks it a question whether any one of his plays, if brought out now for the first time, would succeed. He thinks that *Macbeth* would be the most likely, from the music which has been since introduced into it. He has some doubts as to the superiority of the French school over us in tragedy, and observes, that Hume and Adam Smith were both of that opinion. He thinks Milton's pedantry a great blemish in his writings, and that *Paradise Lost* has many prosaic passages in it. He conceives that genius does not always imply taste, and that wit and judgment are very different faculties. He considers Dr. Johnson as a great critic and moralist, and that his Dictionary was a work of prodigious erudition and vast industry; but that some of the anecdotes of him in Boswell are trifling. He conceives that Mr. Locke was a very original and profound thinker. He thinks Gibbon's style vigorous but florid. He wonders that the author of *Junius* was never found out. He thinks Pope's translation of the *Iliad* an improvement on the simplicity of the original, which was necessary to fit it to the taste of modern readers. He thinks there is a great deal of grossness in the old comedies; and that there has been a great improvement in the morals of the higher classes since the reign of Charles II. He thinks the reign of Queen Anne the golden period of our literature; but that, upon the whole, we have no English writer equal to Voltaire. He speaks of Boccaccio as a very licentious writer, and thinks the wit in Rabelais quite extravagant, though he never read either of them. He cannot get through Spenser's *Fairy Queen,* and pronounces all allegorical poetry tedious. He prefers Smollett to Fielding, and discovers more knowledge of the world in *Gil Blas* than in *Don Quixote*. Richardson he thinks very minute and tedious. He thinks the French Revolution has done a great deal of harm to the cause of liberty; and blames Buonaparte for being so ambitious. He reads the *Edinburgh* and *Quarterly Reviews*, and thinks as they do. He is shy of having an opinion on a new actor or a new singer; for the public do not always agree with the newspapers. He thinks that the moderns have great advantages over the ancients in many respects. He thinks Jeremy Bentham a greater man than Aristotle. He can see no reason why artists of the present day should not paint as well as Raphael or Titian. For instance, he thinks there is something very elegant and classical in Mr. Westall's drawings. He has no doubt that Sir Joshua Reynolds's Lectures were written by Burke. He considers Horne Tooke's account of the conjunction *That* very ingenious, and holds that no writer can be called elegant who uses the present for the subjunctive mood, who says, *If it is* for *If it be*. He thinks Hogarth a great master of low, comic humour; and Cobbett a coarse, vulgar writer. He often talks of men of liberal education, and men without education, as if that made much difference. He judges of people by their pretensions; and pays attention to their opinions according to their dress and rank in life. If he meets with a fool, he does not find him out; and if he meets with any one wiser than himself, he does not know what to make of him. He thinks that manners are of great consequence to the common intercourse of life. He thinks it difficult to prove the existence of any such thing as original genius, or to fix a general standard of taste. He does not think it possible to define what wit is. In religion, his opinions are liberal. He considers all enthusiasm as a degree of madness, particularly to be guarded against by young minds; and believes that truth lies in the middle, between the extremes of right and wrong. He thinks that the object of poetry is to please; and that astronomy is a very pleasing and useful study. He thinks all this, and a great deal more, that amounts to nothing. We wonder we have remembered one half of it.

> For true no-meaning puzzles more than wit.

Though he has an aversion to all new ideas, he likes all new plans and matters-of-fact; the new Schools for All, the Penitentiary, the New Bedlam, the new Steam-Boats, the Gas-Lights, the new Patent Blacking; everything of that sort, but the Bible Society. The Society for the Suppression of Vice he thinks a great nuisance, as every honest man must.

In a word, a common-place critic is the pedant of polite conversation. He refers to the opinion of Lord M. or Lady G. with the same air of significance that the learned pedant does to the authority of Cicero or Virgil; retails the wisdom of the day, as the anecdote-monger does the wit; and carries about with him the sentiments of people of a certain respectability in life, as the dancing-master does their air, or their valets their clothes.

ON POETRY IN GENERAL

The best general notion that I can give of poetry is, that it is the natural impression of any object or event, by its vividness exciting an involuntary movement of imagination and passion, and producing, by sympathy, a certain modulation of the voice, or sounds, expressing it.

In treating of poetry, I shall speak first of the subject-matter of it, next of the forms of expression to which it gives birth, and afterwards of its connection with harmony of sound.

Poetry is the language of the imagination and the passions. It relates to whatever gives immediate pleasure or pain to the human mind. It comes home to the bosoms and businesses of men; for nothing but what so comes home to them in the most general and intelligible shape, can be a subject for poetry. Poetry is the universal language which the heart holds with nature and itself. He who has a contempt for poetry, cannot have much respect for himself, or for anything else. It is not a mere frivolous accomplishment, (as some persons have been led to imagine), the trifling amusement of a few idle readers or leisure hours—it has been the study and delight of mankind in all ages. Many people suppose that poetry is something to be found only in books, contained in lines of ten syllables, with like endings: but wherever there is a sense of beauty, or power, or harmony, as in the motion of a wave of the sea, in the growth of a flower that "spreads its sweet leaves to the air, and dedicates its beauty to the sun,"—*there* is poetry, in its birth. If history is a grave study, poetry may be said to be a graver: its materials lie deeper, and are spread wider. History treats, for the most part, of the cumbrous and unwieldy masses of things, the empty cases in which the affairs of the world are packed, under the heads of intrigue or war, in different states, and from century to century: but there is no thought or feeling that can have entered into the mind of man, which he would be eager to communicate to others, or which they would listen to with delight, that is not a fit subject for poetry. It is not a branch of authorship: it is "the stuff of which our life is made." The rest is "mere oblivion," a dead letter: for all that is worth remembering in life, is the poetry of it. Fear is poetry, hope is poetry, love is poetry, hatred is poetry; contempt, jealousy, remorse, admiration, wonder, pity, despair, or madness, are all poetry. Poetry is that fine particle within us, that expands, rarefies, refines, raises our whole being: without it "man's life is poor as beast's." Man is a poetical animal: and those of us who do not study the principles of poetry, act upon them all our lives, like Molière's *Bourgeois Gentilhomme*, who had always spoken prose without knowing it. The child is a poet in fact, when he first plays at hide-and-seek, or repeats the story of Jack the Giant-killer; the shepherd-boy is a poet, when he first crowns his mistress with a garland of flowers; the countryman, when he stops to look at the rainbow; the city-apprentice, when he gazes after the Lord-Mayor's show; the miser, when he hugs his gold; the courtier, who builds his hopes upon a smile; the savage, who paints his idol with blood; the slave, who worships a tyrant, or the tyrant, who fancies himself a god;—the vain, the ambitious, the proud, the choleric man, the hero and the coward, the beggar and the king, the rich and the poor, the young and the old, all live in a world of their own making; and the poet does no more than describe what all the others think and act. If his art is folly and madness, it is folly and madness at second hand. "There is warrant for it." Poets alone have not "such seething brains, such shaping fantasies, that apprehend more than cooler reason" can.

> The lunatic, the lover, and the poet
> Are of imagination all compact.
> One sees more devils than vast hell can hold:
> The madman. While the lover, all as frantic,
> Sees Helen's beauty in a brow of Egypt.
> The poet's eye in a fine frenzy rolling,
> Doth glance from heav'n to earth, from earth to heav'n;
> And as imagination bodies forth
> The forms of things unknown, the poet's pen
> Turns them to shape, and gives to airy nothing
> A local habitation and a name.
> Such tricks hath strong imagination.

If poetry is a dream, the business of life is much the same. If it is a fiction, made up of what we wish things to be, and fancy that they are, because we wish them so, there is no other nor better reality. Ariosto has described the loves of Angelica and Medoro: but was not Medoro, who carved the name of his mistress on the barks of trees, as much enamoured of her charms as he? Homer has celebrated the anger of Achilles: but was not the hero as mad as the poet? Plato banished the poets from his Commonwealth, lest their descriptions of the natural man should spoil his mathematical man, who was to be without passions and affections, who was neither to laugh nor weep, to feel sorrow nor anger, to be cast down nor elated by anything. This was a chimera, however, which never existed but in the brain of the inventor; and Homer's poetical world has outlived Plato's philosophical Republic.

Poetry then is an imitation of Nature, but the imagination and the passions are a part of man's nature. We shape things according to our wishes and fancies, without poetry; but poetry is the most emphatical language that can be found for those creations of the mind "which ecstasy is very cunning in." Neither a mere description of natural objects, nor a mere delineation of natural feelings, however distinct or forcible, constitutes the ultimate end and aim of poetry, without the heightenings of the imagination. The light of poetry is not only a direct but also a reflected light, that while it shews us the object, throws a sparkling radiance on all around it: the flame of the passions, communicated to the imagination, reveals to us, as with a flash of lightning, the inmost recesses of thought, and penetrates our whole being. Poetry represents forms chiefly as they suggest other forms; feelings, as they suggest forms or other feelings. Poetry puts a spirit of life and motion into the universe. It describes the flowing, not the fixed. It does not define the limits of sense, or analyse the distinctions of understanding, but signifies the excess of the imagination beyond the actual or ordinary impression of any object or feeling. The poetical impression of any object is that uneasy, exquisite sense of beauty or power that cannot be contained within itself; that is impatient of all limit; that (as flame bends to flame) strives to link itself to some other image of kindred beauty or grandeur; to enshrine itself, as it were, in the highest forms of fancy, and to relieve the aching sense of pleasure by expressing it in the boldest manner, and by the most striking examples of the same quality in other instances. Poetry, according to Lord Bacon, for this reason, "has something divine in it, because it raises the mind and hurries it into sublimity, by conforming the shows of things to the desires of the soul, instead of subjecting the soul to external things, as reason and history do." It is strictly the language of the imagination; and the imagination is that faculty which represents objects, not as they are in themselves, but as they are moulded by other thoughts and feelings, into an infinite variety of shapes and combinations of power. This language is not the less true to nature, because it is false in point of fact; but so much the more true and natural, if it conveys the impression which the object under the influence of passion makes on the mind. Let an object, for instance, be presented to the senses in a state of agitation or fear—and the imagination will distort or magnify the object, and convert it into the likeness of whatever is most proper to encourage the fear. "Our eyes are made the fools" of our other faculties. This is the universal law of the imagination,

> That if it would but apprehend some joy,
> It comprehends some bringer of that joy:
> Or in the night imagining some fear,
> How easy is each bush suppos'd a bear!

When Iachimo says of Imogen,

> The flame o' th' taper
> Bows towards her, and would under-peep her lids
> To see the enclosed lights

this passionate interpretation of the motion of the flame to accord with the speaker's own feelings, is true poetry. The lover, equally with the poet, speaks of the auburn tresses of his mistress as locks of shining gold, because the least tinge of yellow in the hair, has, from novelty and a sense of personal beauty, a more lustrous effect to the imagination than the purest gold. We compare a man of gigantic stature to a tower: not that he is anything like so large, but because the excess of his size beyond what we are accustomed to expect, or the usual size of things of the same class, produces by contrast a greater feeling of magnitude and ponderous strength than another object of ten times the same dimensions. The intensity of the feeling makes up for the disproportion of the objects. Things are equal to the imagination, which have the power of affecting the mind with an equal degree of terror, admiration, delight, or love. When Lear calls upon the heavens to avenge his cause, "for they are old like him," there is nothing extravagant or impious in this sublime identification of his age with theirs; for there is no other image which could do justice to the agonizing sense of his wrongs and his despair!

Poetry is the high-wrought enthusiasm of fancy and feeling. As in describing natural objects, it impregnates sensible impressions with the forms of fancy, so it describes the feelings of pleasure or pain, by blending them with the strongest movements of passion, and the most striking forms of nature. Tragic poetry, which is the most impassioned species of it, strives to carry on the feeling to the utmost point of sublimity or pathos, by all the force of comparison or contrast; loses the sense of present suffering in the imaginary exaggeration of it; exhausts the terror or pity by an unlimited indulgence of it; grapples with impossibilities in its desperate impatience of restraint; throws us back upon the past, forward into the future; brings every moment of our being or object of nature in startling review before us; and in the rapid whirl of events, lifts us from the depths of woe to the highest contemplations on human life. When Lear says of Edgar, "Nothing but his unkind daughters could have brought him to this;" what a bewildered amazement, what a wrench of the imagination, that cannot be brought to conceive of any other cause of misery than that which has bowed it down, and absorbs all other sorrow in its own! His sorrow, like a flood, supplies the sources of all other sorrow. Again, when he exclaims in the mad scene, "The little dogs and all, Tray, Blanche, and Sweetheart, see, they bark at me!" it is passion lending occasion to imagination to make every creature in league against him, conjuring up ingratitude and insult in their least looked-for and most galling shapes, searching every thread and fibre of his heart, and finding out the last remaining image of respect or attachment in the bottom of his breast, only to torture and kill it! In like manner, the "So I am" of Cordelia gushes from her heart like a torrent of tears, relieving it of a weight of love and of supposed ingratitude, which had pressed upon it for years. What a fine return of the passion upon itself is that in Othello—with what a mingled agony of regret and despair he clings to the last traces of departed happiness—when he exclaims,

> Oh now, for ever
> Farewel the tranquil mind. Farewel content;
> Farewel the plumed troops and the big war,
> That make ambition virtue! Oh farewel!
> Farewel the neighing steed, and the shrill trump,
> The spirit-stirring drum, th' ear-piercing fife,
> The royal banner, and all quality,
> Pride, pomp, and circumstance of glorious war:
> And O you mortal engines, whose rude throats
> Th' immortal Jove's dread clamours counterfeit,
> Farewel! Othello's occupation's gone!

How his passion lashes itself up and swells and rages like a tide in its sounding course, when in answer to the doubts expressed of his returning love, he says,

> Never, Iago. Like to the Pontic sea,
> Whose icy current and compulsive course
> Ne'er feels retiring ebb, but keeps due on
> To the Propontic and the Hellespont:
> Even so my bloody thoughts, with violent pace,
> Shall ne'er look back, ne'er ebb to humble love,
> Till that a capable and wide revenge
> Swallow them up.

The climax of his expostulation afterwards with Desdemona is at that line,

> But there where I had garner'd up my heart,
> To be discarded thence!

One mode in which the dramatic exhibition of passion excites our sympathy without raising our disgust is, that in proportion as it sharpens the edge of calamity and disappointment, it strengthens the desire of good. It enhances our consciousness of the blessing, by making us sensible of the magnitude of the loss. The storm of passion lays bare and shews us the rich depths of the human soul: the whole of our existence, the sum total of our passions and pursuits, of that which we desire and that which we dread, is brought before us by contrast; the action and re-action are equal; the keenness of immediate suffering only gives us a more intense aspiration after, and a more intimate participation with the antagonist world of good; makes us drink deeper of the cup of human life; tugs at the heart-strings; loosens the pressure about them; and calls the springs of thought and feeling into play with tenfold force.

Impassioned poetry is an emanation of the moral and intellectual part of our nature, as well as of the sensitive—of the desire to know, the will to act, and the power to feel; and ought to appeal to these different parts of our constitution, in order to be perfect. The domestic or prose tragedy, which is thought to be the most natural, is in this sense the least so, because it appeals almost exclusively to one of these faculties, our sensibility. The tragedies of Moore and Lillo, for this reason, however affecting at the time, oppress and lie like a dead weight upon the mind, a load of misery which it is unable to throw off; the tragedy of Shakspeare, which is true poetry, stirs our inmost affections; abstracts evil from itself by combining it with all the forms of imagination, and with the deepest workings of the heart, and rouses the whole man within us.

The pleasure, however, derived from tragic poetry, is not anything peculiar to it as poetry, as a fictitious and fanciful thing. It is not an anomaly of the imagination. It has its source and ground-work in the common love of strong excitement. As Mr. Burke observes, people flock to see a tragedy; but if there were a public execution in the next street, the theatre would very soon be empty. It is not then the difference between fiction and reality that solves the difficulty. Children are satisfied with the stories of ghosts and witches in plain prose: nor do the hawkers of full, true, and particular accounts of murders and executions about the streets, find it necessary to have them turned into penny ballads, before they can dispose of these interesting and authentic documents. The grave politician drives a thriving trade of abuse and calumnies poured out against those whom he makes his enemies for no other end than that he may live by them. The popular preacher makes less frequent mention of heaven than of hell. Oaths and nicknames are only a more vulgar sort of poetry or rhetoric. We are as fond of indulging our violent passions as of reading a description of those of others. We are as prone to make a torment of our fears, as to luxuriate in our hopes of good. If it be asked, Why we do so? the best answer will be, Because we cannot help it. The sense of power is as strong a principle in the mind as the love of pleasure. Objects of terror and pity exercise the same despotic control over it as those of love or beauty. It is as natural to hate as to love, to despise as to admire, to express our hatred or contempt, as our love or admiration.

> Masterless passion sways us to the mood
> Of what it likes or loathes.

Not that we like what we loathe; but we like to indulge our hatred and scorn of it; to dwell upon it, to exasperate our idea of it by every refinement of ingenuity and extravagance of illustration; to make it a bugbear to ourselves, to point it out to others in all the splendour of deformity, to embody it to the senses, to stigmatize it by name, to grapple with it in thought, in action, to sharpen our intellect, to arm our will against it, to know the worst we have to contend with, and to contend with it to the utmost. Poetry is only the highest eloquence of passion, the most vivid form of expression that can be given to our conception of anything, whether pleasurable or painful, mean or dignified, delightful or distressing. It is the perfect coincidence of the image and the words with the feeling we have, and of which we cannot get rid in any other way, that gives an instant "satisfaction to the thought." This is equally the origin of wit and fancy, of comedy and tragedy, of the sublime and pathetic. When Pope says of the Lord Mayor's show,—

> Now night descending, the proud scene is o'er,
> But lives in Settle's numbers one day more!

—when Collins makes Danger, "with limbs of giant mould,"

> Throw him on the steep
> Of some loose hanging rock asleep:

when Lear calls out in extreme anguish,

> Ingratitude, thou marble-hearted fiend,
> How much more hideous shew'st in a child
> Than the sea-monster!

—the passion of contempt in the one case, of terror in the other, and of indignation in the last, is perfectly satisfied. We see the thing ourselves, and shew it to others as we feel it to exist, and as, in spite of ourselves, we are compelled to think of it. The imagination, by thus embodying and turning them to shape, gives an obvious relief to the indistinct and importunate cravings of the will.—We do not wish the thing to be so; but we wish it to appear such as it is. For knowledge is conscious power; and the mind is no longer, in this case, the dupe, though it may be the victim of vice or folly.

Poetry is in all its shapes the language of the imagination and the passions, of fancy and will. Nothing, therefore, can be more absurd than the outcry which has been sometimes raised by frigid and pedantic critics, for reducing the langauge of poetry to the standard of common sense and reason: for the end and use of poetry, "both at the first and now, was and is to hold the mirror up to nature," seen through the medium of passion and imagination, not divested of that medium by means of literal truth or abstract reason. The painter of history might as well be required to represent the face of a person who has just trod upon a serpent with the still-life expression of a common portrait, as the poet to describe the most striking and vivid impressions which things can be supposed to make upon the mind, in the langauge of common conversation. Let who will strip nature of the colours and the shapes of fancy, the poet is not bound to do so; the impressions of common sense and strong imagination, that is, of passion and indifference, cannot be the same, and they must have a separate language to do justice to either. Objects must strike differently upon the mind, independently of what they are in themselves, as long as we have a different interest in them, as we see them in a different point of view, nearer or at a greater distance (morally or physically speaking), from novelty, from old acquaintance, from our ignorance of them, from our fear of their consequences, from contrast, from unexpected likeness. We can no more take away the faculty of the imagination, than we can see all objects without light or shade. Some things must dazzle us by their preternatural light; others must hold us in suspense, and tempt our curiosity to explore their obscurity. Those who would dispel these various illusions, to give us their drab-coloured creation in their stead, are not very wise. Let the naturalist, if he will, catch the glow-worm, carry it home with him in a box, and find it next morning nothing but a little grey worm; let the poet or the lover of poetry visit it at evening, when beneath the scented hawthorn and the crescent moon it has built itself a palace of emerald light. This is also one part of nature, one appearance which the glow-worm presents, and that not the least interesting; so poetry is one part of the history of the human mind, though it is neither science nor philosophy. It cannot be concealed, however, that the progress of knowledge and refinement has a tendency to circumscribe the limits of the imagination, and to clip the wings of poetry. The province of the imagination is principally visionary, the unknown and undefined: the understanding restores things to their natural boundaries, and strips them of their fanciful pretensions. Hence the history of religious and poetical enthusiasm is much the same; and both have received a sensible shock from the progress of experimental philosophy. It is the undefined and uncommon that gives birth and scope to the imagination; we can only fancy what we do not know. As in looking into the mazes of a tangled wood we fill them with what shapes we please, with ravenous beasts, with caverns vast, and drear enchantments, so in our ignorance of the world about us, we make gods or devils of the first object we see, and set no bounds to the wilful suggestions of our hopes and fears.

> And visions, as poetic eyes avow,
> Hang on each leaf and cling to every bough.

There can never be another Jacob's dream. Since that time, the heavens have gone farther off, and grown astronomical. They have become averse to the imagination, nor will they return to us on the squares of the distances, or on Doctor Chalmers's Discourses. Rembrandt's picture brings the matter nearer to us.—It is not only the progress of mechanical knowledge, but the necessary advances of civilization that are unfavourable to the spirit of poetry. We not only stand in less awe of the preternatural world, but we can calculate more surely, and look with more indifference, upon the regular routine of this. The heroes of the fabulous ages rid the world of monsters and giants. At present we are less exposed to the vicissitudes of good or evil, to the incursions of wild beasts or "bandit fierce," or to the unmitigated fury of the elements. The time has been that "our fell of hair would at a dismal treatise rouse and stir as life were in it." But the police spoils all; and we now hardly so much as dream of a midnight murder. *Macbeth* is only tolerated in this country for the sake of the music; and in the United States of America, where the philosophical principles of government are carried still farther in theory and practice, we find that the *Beggar's Opera* is hooted from the stage. Society, by degrees, is constructed into a machine that carries us safely and insipidly from one end of life to the other, in a very comfortable prose style.

> Obscurity her curtain round them drew,
> And siren Sloth a dull quietus sung.

The remarks which have been here made, would, in some measure, lead to a solution of the question of the comparative merits of painting and poetry. I do not mean to give any preference, but it should seem that the argument which has been sometimes set up, that painting must affect the imagination more strongly, because it represents the image more distinctly, is not well founded. We may assume without much temerity, that poetry is more poetical than painting. When artists or connoisseurs talk on stilts about the poetry of painting, they shew that they know little about poetry, and have little love for the art. Painting gives the object itself; poetry what it implies. Painting embodies what a thing contains in itself; poetry suggests what exists out of it, in any manner connected with it. But this last is the proper province of the imagination. Again, as it relates to passion, painting gives the event, poetry the progress of events: but it is during the progress, in the interval of expectation and suspense, while our hopes and fears are strained to the highest pitch of breathless agony, that the pinch of the interest lies.

> Between the acting of a dreadful thing
> And the first motion, all the interim is
> Like a phantasma or a hideous dream.
> The mortal instruments are then in council;
> And the state of man, like to a little kingdom,
> Suffers then the nature of an insurrection.

But by the time that the picture is painted, all is over. Faces are the best part of a picture; but even faces are not what we chiefly remember in what interests us most.—But it may be asked then, Is there anything better than Claude Lorraine's landscapes, than Titian's portraits, than Raphael's cartoons, or the Greek statues? Of the two first I shall say nothing, as they are evidently picturesque, rather than imaginative. Raphael's cartoons are certainly the finest comments that ever were made on the Scriptures. Would their effect be the same if we were not acquainted with the text? But the New Testatment existed before the cartoons. There is one subject of which there is no cartoon, Christ washing the feet of the disciples the night before his death. But that chapter does not need a commentary! It is for want of some such resting place for the imagination that the Greek statues are little else than specious forms. They are marble to the touch and to the heart. They have not an informing principle within them. In their faultless excellence they appear sufficient to themselves. By their beauty they are raised above the frailties of passion or suffering. By their beauty they are deified. But they are not objects of religious faith to us, and their forms are a reproach to common humanity. They seem to have no sympathy with us, and not to want our admiration.

Poetry in its matter and form is natural imagery or feeling, combined with passion and fancy. In its mode of conveyance, it combines the ordinary use of language with musical expression. There is a question of long standing, in what the essence of poetry consists; or what it is that determines why one set of ideas should be expressed in prose, another in verse. Milton has told us his idea of poetry in a single line—

> Thoughts that voluntary move
> Harmonious numbers.

As there are certain sounds that excite certain movements, and the song and dance go together, so there are, no doubt, certain thoughts that lead to certain tones of voice, or modulations of sound, and change "the words of Mercury into the songs of Apollo." There is a striking instance of this adaptation of the movement of sound and rhythm to the subject, in Spenser's description of the Satyrs accompanying Una to the cave of Sylvanus.

> So from the ground she fearless doth arise
> And walketh forth without suspect of crime.

> They, all as glad as birds of joyous prime,
>   Thence lead her forth, about her dancing round,
> Shouting and singing all a shepherd's rhyme;
>   And with green branches strewing all the ground,
> Do worship her as queen with olive garland crown'd.
>
> And all the way their merry pipes they sound,
>   That all the woods and doubled echoes ring;
> And with their horned feet do wear the ground,
>   Leaping like wanton kids in pleasant spring;
> So towards old Sylvanus they her bring,
>   Who with the noise awaked, cometh out.
>   *Faery Queen*, b.i., c. vi.

On the contrary, there is nothing either musical or natural in the ordinary construction of language. It is a thing altogether arbitrary and conventional. Neither in the sounds themselves, which are the voluntary signs of certain ideas, nor in their grammatical arrangements in common speech, is there any principle of natural imitation, or correspondence to the individual ideas, or to the tone of feeling with which they are conveyed to others. The jerks, the breaks, the inequalities, and harshnesses of prose, are fatal to the flow of a poetical imagination, as a jolting road or a stumbling horse disturbs the reverie of an absent man. But poetry makes these odds all even. It is the music of language, answering to the music of the mind, untying as it were "the secret soul of harmony." Wherever any object takes such a hold of the mind as to make us dwell upon it, and brood over it, melting the heart in tenderness, or kindling it to a sentiment of enthusiasm;—wherever a movement of imagination or passion is impressed on the mind, by which it seeks to prolong and repeat the emotion, to bring all other objects into accord with it, and to give the same movement of harmony, sustained and continuous, or gradually varied according to the occasion, to the sounds that express it—this is poetry. The musical in sound is the sustained and continuous; the musical in thought is the sustained and continuous also. There is a near connection between music and deep-rooted passion. Mad people sing. As often as articulation passes naturally into intonation, there poetry begins. Where one idea gives a tone and colour to others, where one feeling melts others into it, there can be no reason why the same principle should not be extended to the sounds by which the voice utters these emotions of the soul, and blends syllables and lines into each other. It is to supply the inherent defect of harmony in the customary mechanism of language, to make the sound an echo to the sense, when the sense becomes a sort of echo to itself—to mingle the tide of verse, "the golden cadences of poetry," with the tide of feeling, flowing and murmuring as it flows—in short, to take the language of the imagination from off the ground, and enable it to spread its wings where it may indulge its own impulses—

> Sailing with supreme dominion
> Through the azure deep of air

without being stopped, or fretted, or diverted with the abruptness and petty obstacles, and discordant flats and sharps of prose, that poetry was invented. It is to common language, what springs are to a carriage, or wings to feet. In ordinary speech we arrive at a certain harmony by the modulations of the voice: in poetry the same thing is done systematically by a regular collocation of syllables. It has been well observed, that every one who declaims warmly, or grows intent upon a subject, rises into a sort of blank verse or measured prose. The merchant, as described in Chaucer, went on his way "sounding always the increase of his winning." Every prose-writer has more or less of rhythmical adaptation, except poets, who, when deprived of the regular mechanism of verse, seem to have no principle of modulation left in their writings.

An excuse might be made for rhyme in the same manner. It is but fair that the ear should linger on the sounds that delight it, or avail itself of the same brilliant coincidence and unexpected recurrence of syllables, that have been displayed in the invention and collocation of images. It is allowed that rhyme assists the memory; and that a man of wit and shrewdness has been heard to say, that the only four good lines of poetry are the well-known ones which tell the number of days in the months of the year.

> Thirty days hath September, etc.

But if the jingle of names assists the memory, may it not also quicken the fancy? and there are other things worth having at our fingers' ends, besides the contents of the almanac.—Pope's versification is tiresome, from its excessive sweetness and uniformity. Shakspeare's blank verse is the perfection of dramatic dialogue.

All is not poetry that passes for such: nor does verse make the whole difference between poetry and prose. The *Iliad* does not cease to be poetry in a literal translation; and Addison's *Campaign* has been very properly denominated a Gazette in rhyme. Common prose differs from poetry, as treating for the most part either of such trite, familiar, and irksome matters of fact, as convey no extraordinary impulse to the imagination, or else of such difficult and laborious processes of the understanding, as do not admit of the wayward or violent movements either of the imagination or the passions.

I will mention three works which come as near to poetry as possible without absolutely being so, namely, the *Pilgrim's Progress*, *Robinson Crusoe*, and the *Tales of Boccaccio*. Chaucer and Dryden have translated some of the last into English rhyme, but the essence and power of poetry was there before. That which lifts the spirit above the earth, which draws the soul out of itself with indescribable longings, is poetry in kind, and generally fit to become so in name, by being "married to immortal verse." If it is of the essence of poetry to strike and fix the imagination, whether we will or no, to make the eye of childhood glisten with the starting tear, to be never thought of afterwards with indifference, John Bunyan and Daniel Defoe may be permitted to pass for poets in their way. The mixture of fancy and reality in the *Pilgrim's Progress* was never equalled in any allegory. His pilgrims walk above the earth, and yet are on it. What zeal, what beauty, what truth of fiction! What deep feeling in the description of Christian's swimming across the water at last, and in the picture of the Shining Ones within the gates, with wings at their backs and garlands on their heads, who are to wipe all tears from his eyes! The writer's genius, though not "dipped in dews of Castalie," was baptised with the Holy Spirit and with fire. The prints in this book are no small part of it. If the confinement of Philoctetes in the island of Lemnos was a subject for the most beautiful of all the Greek tragedies, what shall we say to Robinson Crusoe in his? Take the speech of the Greek hero on leaving his cave, beautiful as it is, and compare it with the reflections of the English adventurer in his solitary place of confinement. The thoughts of home, and of all from which he is for ever cut off, swell and press against his bosom, as the heaving ocean rolls its ceaseless tide against the rocky shore, and the very beatings of his heart become audible in the eternal silence that surrounds him. Thus he says:

> As I walked about, either in my hunting, or for viewing the country, the anguish of my soul at my condition would break out upon me on a sudden, and my very heart would die within me to think of the woods, the mountains, the deserts I was in; and how I was a prisoner, locked up with the eternal bars and bolts of the ocean, in an uninhabited wilderness, without redemption. In the midst of the greatest composures of my mind, this would break out upon me like a storm, and make me wring my hands, and weep like a child. Sometimes it would take me in the middle of my work, and I would immediately sit down and sigh, and look upon the ground for an hour or two together, and this was still worse to me, for if I could burst into tears or vent myself in words, it would go off, and the grief having exhausted itself would abate   P. 50.

The story of his adventures would not make a poem like the *Odyssey,* it is true; but the relator had the true genius of a poet. It has been made a question whether Richardson's romances are poetry; and the answer perhaps is, that they are not poetry, because they are not romance. The interest is worked up to an inconceivable height; but it is by an infinite number of little things, by incessant labour and calls upon the attention, by a repetition of blows that have no rebound in them. The sympathy excited is not a voluntary contribution, but a tax. Nothing is unforced and spontaneous. There is a want of elasticity and motion. The story does not "give an echo to the seat where love is throned." The heart does not answer of itself like a chord in music. The fancy does not run on before the writer with breathless expectation, but is dragged along with an infinite number of pins and wheels, like those with which the Lilliputians dragged Gulliver pinioned to the royal palace.—Sir Charles Grandison is a coxcomb. What sort of a figure would he cut, translated into an epic poem, by the side of Achilles? Clarissa, the divine Clarissa, is too interesting by half. She is interesting in her ruffles, in her gloves, her samplers, her aunts and uncles—she is interesting in all that is uninteresting. Such things, however intensely they may be brought home to us, are not conductors to the imagination. There is infinite truth and feeling in Richardson; but it is extracted from a *caput mortuum* of circumstances: it does not evaporate of itself. His poetical genius is like Ariel confined in a pinetree, and requires an artificial process to let it out. Shakespeare says—

> Our poesy is as a gum
> Which issues whence 'tis nourished, our gentle flame
> Provokes itself, and like the current flies
> Each bound it chafes.

I shall conclude this general account with some remarks on four of the principal works of poetry in the world, at different periods of history—Homer, the Bible, Dante, and let me add, Ossian. In Homer, the principle of action or life is predominant; in the Bible, the principle of faith and the idea of Providence; Dante is a personification of blind will; and in Ossian we see the decay of life, and the lag end of the world. Homer's poetry is the heroic: it is full of life and action: it is bright as the day, strong as a river. In the vigour of his intellect, he grapples with all the objects of nature, and enters into all the relations of social life. He saw many countries, and the manners of many men; and he has brought them all together in his poem. He describes his heroes going to battle with a prodigality of life, arising from an exuberance of animal spirits: we see them before us, their number, and their order of battle, poured out upon the plain "all plumed like estriches, like eagles newly bathed, wanton as goats, wild as young bulls, youthful as May, and gorgeous as the sun at midsummer," covered with glittering armour, with dust and blood; while the Gods quaff their nectar in golden cups, or mingle in the fray; and the old men assembled on the walls of Troy rise up with reverence as Helen passes by them. The multitude of things in Homer is wonderful; their splendour, their truth, their force, and variety. His poetry is, like his religion, the poetry of number and form: he describes the bodies as well as the souls of men.

The poetry of the Bible is that of imagination and of faith: it is abstract and disembodied: it is not the poetry of form, but of power; not of multitude, but of immensity. It does not divide into many, but aggrandizes into one. Its ideas of Nature are like its ideas of God. It is not the poetry of social life, but of solitude: each man seems alone in the world, with the original forms of nature, the rocks, the earth, and the sky. It is not the poetry of action or heroic enterprise, but of faith in a supreme Providence, and resignation to the power that governs the universe. As the idea of God was removed farther from humanity, and a scattered polytheism, it became more profound and intense, as it became more universal, for the Infinite is present to everything: "If we fly into the uttermost parts of the earth, it is there also; if we turn to the east or the west, we cannot escape from it." Man is thus aggrandized in the image of his Maker. The history of the patriarchs is of this kind; they are founders of a chosen race of people, the inheritors of the earth; they exist in the generations which are to come after them. Their poetry, like their religious creed, is vast, unformed, obscure, and infinite; a vision is upon it—an invisible hand is suspended over it. The spirit of the Christian religion consists in the glory hereafter to be revealed; but in the Hebrew dispensation, Providence took an immediate share in the affairs of this life. Jacob's dream arose out of this intimate communion between heaven and earth: it was this that let down, in the sight of the youthful patriarch, a golden ladder from the sky to the earth, with angels ascending and descending upon it, and shed a light upon the lonely place, which can never pass away. The story of Ruth, again, is as if all the depth of natural affection in the human race was involved in her breast. There are descriptions in the book of Job more prodigal of imagery, more intense in passion, than anything in Homer, as that of the state of his prosperity, and of the vision that came upon him by night. The metaphors in the Old Testament are more boldly figurative. Things were collected more into masses, and gave a greater *momentum* to the imagination.

Dante was the father of modern poetry, and he may therefore claim a place in this connection. His poem is the first great step from Gothic darkness and barbarism; and the struggle of thought in it to burst the thraldom in which the human mind had been so long held, is felt in every page. He stood bewildered, not appalled, on that dark shore which separates the ancient and the modern world; and saw the glories of antiquity dawning through the abyss of time, while revelation opened its passage to the other world. He was lost in wonder at what had been done before him, and he dared to emulate it. Dante seems to have been indebted to the Bible for the gloomy tone of his mind, as well as for the prophetic fury which exalts and kindles his poetry; but he is utterly unlike Homer. His genius is not a sparkling flame, but the sullen heat of a furnace. He is power, passion, self-will personified. In all that relates to the descriptive or fanciful part of poetry, he bears no comparison to many who had gone before, or who have come after him; but there is a gloomy abstraction in his conceptions, which lies like a dead weight upon the mind; a benumbing stupor, a breathless awe, from the intensity of the impression; a terrible obscurity, like that which oppresses us in dreams; an identity of interest, which moulds every object to its own purposes, and clothes all things with the passions and imaginations of the human soul,—that make amends for all other deficiencies. The immediate objects he presents to the mind are not much in themselves, they want grandeur, beauty, and order; but they become every-thing by the force of the character he impresses upon them. His mind lends its own power to the objects which it contemplates, instead of borrowing it from them. He takes advantage even of the nakedness and dreary vacuity of his subject. His imagination peoples the shades of death, and broods over the silent air. He is the severest of all writers, the most hard and impenetrable, the most opposite to the flowery and glittering; who relies most on his own power, and the sense of it in others, and who leaves most room to the imagination of his readers. Dante's only endeavour is to interest; and he interests by exciting our sympathy with the emotion by which he is himself possessed. He does not place before us the objects by which that emotion has been created; but he seizes on the attention, by shewing us the effect they produce on his feelings;

and his poetry accordingly gives the same thrilling and overwhelming sensation, which is caught by gazing on the face of a person who has seen some object of horror. The improbability of the events, the abruptness and monotony in the *Inferno,* are excessive: but the interest never flags, from the continued earnestness of the author's mind. Dante's great power is in combining internal feelings with external objects. Thus the gate of hell, on which that withering inscription is written, seems to be endowed with speech and consciousness, and to utter its dread warning, not without a sense of mortal woes. This author habitually unites the absolutely local and individual with the greatest wildness and mysticism. In the midst of the obscure and shadowy regions of the lower world, a tomb suddenly rises up with the inscription, "I am the tomb of Pope Anastasius the Sixth": and half the personages whom he has crowded into the *Inferno* are his own acquaintance. All this, perhaps, tends to heighten the effect by the bold intermixture of realities, and by an appeal, as it were, to the individual knowledge and experience of the reader. He affords few subjects for picture. There is, indeed, one gigantic one, that of count Ugolino, of which Michael Angelo made a bas-relief, and which Sir Joshua Reynolds ought not to have painted.

Another writer whom I shall mention last, and whom I cannot persuade myself to think a mere modern in the groundwork, is Ossian. He is a feeling and a name that can never be destroyed in the minds of his readers. As Homer is the first vigour and lustihood, Ossian is the decay and old age of poetry. He lives only in the recollection and regret of the past. There is one impression which he conveys more entirely than all other poets, namely, the sense of privation, the loss of all things, of friends, of good name, of country—he is even without God in the world. He converses only with the spirits of the departed; with the motionless and silent clouds. The cold moonlight sheds its faint lustre on his head; the fox peeps out of the ruined tower; the thistle waves its beard to the wandering gale; and the strings of his harp seem, as the hand of age, as the tale of other times, passes over them, to sigh and rustle like the dry reeds in the winter's wind! The feeling of cheerless desolation, of the loss of the pith and sap of existence, of the annihilation of the substance, and the clinging to the shadow of all things as in a mock-embrace, is here perfect. In this way, the lamentation of Selma for the loss of Salgar is the finest of all. If it were indeed possible to shew that this writer was nothing, it would only be another instance of mutability, another blank made, another void left in the heart, another confirmation of that feeling which makes him so often complain, "Roll on, ye dark brown years, ye bring no joy on your wing to Ossian!"

ON FAMILIAR STYLE

It is not easy to write a familiar style. Many people mistake a familiar for a vulgar style, and suppose that to write without affectation is to write at random. On the contrary, there is nothing that requires more precision, and, if I may so say, purity of expression, than the style I am speaking of. It utterly rejects not only all unmeaning pomp, but all low, cant phrases, and loose, unconnected, *slipshod* allusions. It is not to take the first word that offers, but the best word in common use; it is not to throw words together in any combinations we please, but to follow and avail ourselves of the true idiom of the language. To write a genuine familiar or truly English style, is to write as any one would speak in common conversation who had a thorough command and choice of words, or who could discourse with ease, force, and perspicuity, setting aside all pedantic and oratorical flourishes. Or, to give another illustration, to write naturally is the same thing in regard to common conversation as to read naturally is in regard to common speech. It does not follow that it is an easy thing to give the true accent and inflection to the words you utter, because you do not attempt to rise above the level of ordinary life and colloquial speaking. You do not assume, indeed, the solemnity of the pulpit, or the tone of stage-declamation; neither are you at liberty to gabble on at a venture, without emphasis or discretion, or to resort to vulgar dialect or clownish pronunciation. You must steer a middle course. You are tied down to a given and appropriate articulation, which is determined by the habitual associations between sense and sound, and which you can only hit by entering into the author's meaning, as you must find the proper words and style to express yourself by fixing your thoughts on the subject you have to write about. Any one may mouth out a passage with a theatrical cadence, or get upon stilts to tell his thoughts; but to write or speak with propriety and simplicity is a more difficult task. Thus it is easy to affect a pompous style, to use a word twice as big as the thing you want to express: it is not so easy to pitch upon the very word that exactly fits it. Out of eight or ten words equally common, equally intelligible, with nearly equal pretensions, it is a matter of some nicety and discrimination to pick out the very one the preferableness of which is scarcely perceptible, but decisive. The reason why I object to Dr. Johnson's style is that there is no discrimination, no selection, no variety in it. He uses none but "tall, opaque words," taken from the "first row of the rubric"—words with the greatest number of syllables, or Latin phrases with merely English terminations. If a fine style depended on this sort of arbitrary pretension, it would be fair to judge of an author's elegance by the measurement of his words and the substitution of foreign circumlocutions (with no precise associations) for the mother-tongue. How simple is it to be dignified without ease, to be pompous without meaning! Surely, it is but a mechanical rule for avoiding what is low, to be always pedantic and affected. It is clear you cannot use a vulgar English word if you never use a common English word at all. A fine tact is shewn in adhering to those which are perfectly common, and yet never falling into any expressions which are debased by disgusting circumstances, or which owe their significa-tion and point to technical or professional allusions. A truly natural or familiar style can never be quaint or vulgar, for this reason, that it is of universal force and applicability, and that quaintness and vulgarity arise out of the immediate connection of certain words with coarse and disagreeable, or with confined ideas. The last form what we understand by *cant* or *slang* phrases.—To give an example of what is not very clear in the general statement. I should say that the phrase *To cut with a knife*, or *To cut a piece of wood*, is perfectly free from vulgarity, because it is perfectly common; but to *cut an acquaintance* is not quite unexceptionable, because it is not perfectly common or intelligible, and has hardly yet escaped out of the limits of slang phraseology. I should hardly, therefore, use the word in this sense without putting it in italics as a license of expression, to be received *cum grano salis*. All provincial or bye-phrases come under the same mark of reprobation—all such as the writer transfers to the page from his fireside or a particular *coterie*, or that he invents for his own sole use and convenience. I conceive that words are like money, not the worse for being common, but that it is the stamp of custom alone that gives them circulation or value. I am fastidious in this respect, and would almost as soon coin the currency of the realm as counterfeit the King's English. I never invented or gave a new and unauthorised meaning to any word but one single one (the term *impersonal* applied to feelings), and that was in an abstruse metaphysical discussion to express a very difficult distinction. I have been (I know) loudly accused of revelling in vulgarisms and broken English. I cannot speak to that point; but so far I plead guilty to the determined use of acknowledged idioms and common elliptical expressions. I am not sure that the critics in question know the one from the other, that is, can distinguish any medium between formal pedantry and the most barbarous solecism. As an author I endeavour to employ plain words and popular modes of construction, as, were I a chapman and dealer, I should common weights and measures.

The proper force of words lies not in the words themselves, but in their application. A word may be a fine-sounding word, of an unusual length, and very imposing from its learning and novelty, and yet in the connection in which it is introduced may be quite pointless and irrelevant. It is not pomp or pretension, but the adaptation of the expression to the idea, that clenches a writer's meaning:—as it is not the size or glossiness of the materials, but their being fitted each to its place, that gives strength to the arch; or as the pegs and nails are as necessary to the support of the building as the larger timbers, and more so than the mere shewy, unsubstantial ornaments. I hate anything that occupies more space than it is worth. I hate to see a load of band-boxes go along the street, and I hate to see a parcel of big words without anything in them. A person who does not deliberately dispose of all his thoughts alike in cumbrous draperies and flimsy disguises, may strike out twenty varieties of familiar every-day language, each coming somewhat nearer to the feeling he wants to convey, and at last not hit upon that particular and only one which may be said to be identical with the exact impression in his mind. This would seem to shew that Mr. Cobbett is hardly right in saying that the first word that occurs is always the best. It may be a very good one; and yet a better may present itself on reflection or from time to time. It should be suggested naturally, however, and spontaneously, from a fresh and lively conception of the subject. We seldom succeed by trying at improvement, or by merely substituting one word for another that we are not satisfied with, as we cannot recollect the name of a place or person by merely plaguing ourselves about it. We wander farther from the point by persisting in a wrong scent; but it starts up accidentally in the memory when we least expected it, by touching some link in the chain of previous association.

There are those who hoard up and make a cautious display of nothing but rich and rare phraseology—ancient medals, obscure coins, and Spanish pieces of eight. They are very curious to inspect, but I myself would neither offer nor take them in the course of exchange. A sprinkling of archaisms is not amiss, but a tissue of obsolete expressions is more fit *for keep than wear*. I do not say I would not use any phrase that had been brought into fashion before the middle or the end of the last century, but I should be shy of using any that had not been employed by any approved author during the whole of that time. Words, like clothes, get old-fashioned, or mean and ridiculous, when they have been for some time laid aside. Mr. Lamb is the only imitator of old English style I can read with pleasure; and he is so thoroughly imbued with the spirit of his authors that the idea of imitation is almost done away. There is an inward unction, a marrowy vein, both in the thought and feeling, an intuition, deep and lively, of his subject, that carries off any quaintness or awkwardness arising from an antiquated style and dress. The matter is completely his own, though the manner is assumed. Perhaps his ideas are altogether so marked and individual as to require their point and pungency to be neutralised by the affectation of a singular but traditional form of conveyance. Tricked out in the prevailing costume, they would probably seem more startling and out of the way. The old English authors, Burton, Fuller, Coryate, Sir Thomas Browne, are a kind of mediators between us and the more eccentric and whimsical modern, reconciling us to his peculiarities. I do not, however, know how far this is the case or not, till he condescends to write like one of us. I must confess that what I like best of his papers under the signature of Elia (still I do not presume, amidst such excellence, to decide what is most excellent) is the account of "Mrs. Battle's Opinions on Whist," which is also the most free from obsolete allusions and turns of expression—

A well of native English undefiled.

To those acquainted with his admired prototypes, these *Essays* of the ingenious and highly gifted author have the same sort of charm and relish that Erasmus's *Colloquies* or a fine piece of modern Latin have to the classical scholar. Certainly, I do not know any borrowed pencil that has more power or felicity of execution than the one of which I have here been speaking.

It is as easy to write a gaudy style without ideas as it is to spread a pallet of shewy colours or to smear in a flaunting transparency. "What do you read?" "Words, words, words."—"What is the matter?" "*Nothing*," it might be answered. The florid style is the reverse of the familiar. The last is employed as an unvarnished medium to convey ideas; the first is resorted to as a spangled veil to conceal the want of them. When there is nothing to be set down but words, it costs little to have them fine. Look through the dictionary, and cull out a *florilegium*, rival the *tulippomania. Rouge* high enough, and never mind the natural complexion. The vulgar, who are not in the secret, will admire the look of preternatural health and vigour; and the fashionable, who regard only appearances, will be delighted with the imposition. Keep to your sounding generalities, your tinkling phrases, and all will be well. Swell out an unmeaning truism to a perfect tympany of style. A thought, a distinction is the rock on which all this brittle cargo of verbiage splits at once. Such writers have merely *verbal* imaginations, that retain nothing but words. Or their puny thoughts have dragon-wings, all green and gold. They soar far above the vulgar failing of the *Sermo humi obrepens*—their most ordinary speech is never short of an hyperbole, splendid, imposing, vague, incomprehensible, magniloquent, a cento of sounding common-places. If some of us, whose "ambition is more lowly," pry a little too narrowly into nooks and corners to pick up a number of "unconsidered trifles," they never once direct their eyes or lift their hands to seize on any but the most gorgeous, tarnished, thread-bare, patchwork set of phrases, the left-off finery of poetic extravagance, transmitted down through successive generations of barren pretenders. If they criticise actors and actresses, a huddled phantasmagoria of feathers, spangles, floods of light, and oceans of sound float before their morbid sense, which they paint in the style of Ancient Pistol. Not a glimpse can you get of the merits or defects of the performers: they are hidden in a profusion of barbarous epithets and wilful rhodomontade. Our hypercritics are not thinking of these little fantoccini beings—

That strut and fret their hour upon the stage

but of tall phantoms of words, abstractions, *genera* and *species*, sweeping clauses, periods that unite the Poles, forced alliterations, astounding antitheses—

And on their pens *Fustian* sits plumed.

If they describe kings and queens, it is an Eastern pageant. The Coronation at either House is nothing to it. We get at four repeated images—a curtain, a throne, a sceptre, and a foot-stool. These are with them the wardrobe of a lofty imagination; and they turn their servile strains to servile uses. Do we read a description of pictures? It is not a reflection of tones and hues which "nature's own sweet and cunning hand laid on," but piles of precious stones, rubies, pearls, emeralds, Golconda's mines, and all the blazonry of art. Such persons are in fact besotted with words, and their brains are turned with the glittering but empty and sterile phantoms of things. Personifications, capital letters, seas of sunbeams, visions of glory, shining inscriptions, the figures of a transparency, Britannia with her shield, or Hope leaning on an anchor, make up their stock-in-trade. They may be considered as *hieroglyphical* writers. Images stand out in their minds isolated and important merely in themselves, without any ground-work of feeling—there is no context in their imaginations. Words affect them in the same way, by the mere sound, that is, by their possible, not by their actual application to the subject in hand. They are fascinated by first appearances, and have no sense of consequences. Nothing more is meant by them than meets the ear: they understand or feel nothing more than meets their eye. The web and texture of the universe, and of the heart of man, is a mystery to them: they have no faculty that strikes a chord in unison with it. They cannot get beyond the daubings of fancy, the varnish of sentiment. Objects are not linked to feelings, words to things, but images revolve in splendid mockery, words represent themselves in their strange rhapsodies. The categories of such a mind are pride and ignorance—pride in outside show, to which they sacrifice everything, and ignorance of the true worth and hidden structure both of words and things. With a sovereign contempt for what is familiar and natural, they are the slaves of vulgar affectation—of a routine of high-flown phrases. Scorning to imitate realities, they are unable to invent anything, to strike out one original idea. They are not copyists of nature, it is true; but they are the poorest of all plagiarists, the plagiarists of words. All is far-fetched, dear bought, artificial, oriental in subject and allusion; all is mechanical, conventional, vapid, formal, pedantic in style and execution. They startle and confound the understanding of the reader by the remoteness and obscurity of their illustrations; they soothe the ear by the monotony of the same everlasting round of circuitous metaphors. They are the *mock-school* in poetry and prose. They flounder about between fustian in expression and bathos in sentiment. They tantalise the fancy, but never reach the head nor touch the heart. Their Temple of Fame is like a shadowy structure raised by Dulness to Vanity, or like Cowper's description of the Empress of Russia's palace of ice, "as worthless as in show 'twas glittering"—

It smiled, and it was cold!

ON THE PROSE STYLE
OF POETS

Do you read or sing? If you sing, you sing very ill.

I have but an indifferent opinion of the prose-style of poets: not that it is not sometimes good, nay, excellent; but it is never the better, and generally the worse, from the habit of writing verse. Poets are winged animals, and can cleave the air, like birds, with ease to themselves and delight to the beholders; but like those "feathered, two-legged things," when they light upon the ground of prose and matter-of-fact, they seem not to have the same use of their feet.

What is a little extraordinary, there is a want of *rhythmus* and cadence in what they write without the help of metrical rules. Like persons who have been accustomed to sing to music, they are at a loss in the absence of the habitual accompaniment and guide to their judgment. Their style halts, totters, is loose, disjointed, and without expressive pauses or rapid movements. The measured cadence and regular *sing-song* of rhyme or blank verse have destroyed, as it were, their natural ear for the mere characteristic harmony which ought to subsist between the sound and the sense. I should almost guess the Author of *Waverley* to be a writer of ambling verses from the desultory vacillation and want of firmness in the march of his style. There is neither *momentum* nor elasticity in it; I mean as to the *score*, or effect upon the ear. He has improved since in his other works: to be sure, he has had practice enough. Poets either get into this incoherent, undetermined, shuffling style, made up of "unpleasing flats and sharps," of unaccountable starts and pauses, of doubtful odds and ends, flirted about like straws in a gust of wind; or, to avoid it and steady themselves, mount into a sustained and measured prose (like the translation of Ossian's *Poems*, or some parts of Shaftesbury's *Characteristics*) which is more odious still, and as bad as being at sea in a calm. Dr. Johnson's style (particularly in his *Rambler*) is not free from the last objection. There is a tune in it, a mechanical recurrence of the same rise and fall in the clauses of his sentences, independent of any reference to the meaning of the text, or progress or inflection of the sense. There is the alternate roll of his cumbrous cargo of words; his periods complete their revolutions at certain stated intervals, let the matter be longer or shorter, rough or smooth, round or square, different or the same. This monotonous and balanced mode of composition may be compared to that species of portrait-painting which prevailed about a century ago, in which each face was cast in a regular and preconceived mould. The eye-brows were arched mathematically as if with a pair of compasses, and the distances between the nose and mouth, the forehead and chin, determined according to a "fore-gone conclusion," and the features of the identical individual were afterwards accommodated to them, how they could!

Horne Tooke used to maintain that no one could write a good prose style, who was not accustomed to express himself *vivâ voce,* or to talk in company.

He argued that this was the fault of Addison's prose, and that its smooth, equable uniformity, and want of sharpness and spirit, arose from his not having familiarised his ear to the sound of his own voice, or at least only among his friends and admirers, where there was but little collision, dramatic fluctuation, or sudden contrariety of opinion to provoke animated discussion, and give birth to different intonations and lively transitions of speech. His style (in this view of it) was not indented, nor did it project from the surface. There was no stress laid on one word more than another—it did not hurry on or stop short, or sink or swell with the occasion: it was throughout equally insipid, flowing, and harmonious, and had the effect of a studied recitation rather than of a natural discourse. This would not have happened (so the Member for Old Sarum contended) had Addison laid himself out to argue at his club, or to speak in public; for then his ear would have caught the necessary modulations of sound arising out of the feeling of the moment, and he would have transferred them unconsciously to paper. Much might be said on both sides of this question: but Mr. Tooke was himself an unintentional confirmation of his own argument; for the tone of his written compositions is as flat and unraised as his manner of speaking was hard and dry. Of the poet it is said by some one, that

> He murmurs by the running brooks
> A music sweeter than their own.

On the contrary, the celebrated person just alluded to might be said to grind the sentences between his teeth which he afterwards committed to paper, and threw out crusts to the critics, or *bon-mots* to the Electors of Westminster (as we throw bones to the dogs) without altering a muscle, and without the smallest tremulousness of voice or eye! I certainly so far agree with the above theory as to conceive that no style is worth a farthing that is not calculated to be read out, or that is not allied to spirited conversation: but I at the same time think the process of modulation and inflection may be quite as complete, or more so, without the external enunciation; and that an author had better try the effect of his sentences on his stomach than on his ear. He may be deceived by the last, not by the first. No person, I imagine, can dictate a good style, or spout his own compositions with impunity. In the former case, he will flounder on before the sense or words are ready, sooner than suspend his voice in air; and in the latter, he can supply what intonation he pleases, without consulting his readers. Parliamentary speeches sometimes read well aloud; but we do not find, when such persons sit down to write, that the prose-style of public speakers and great orators is the best, most natural, or varied of all others. It has almost always either a professional twang, a mechanical rounding off, or else is stunted and unequal. Charles Fox was the most rapid and even *hurried* of speakers; but his written style halts and creeps slowly along the ground. A speaker is necessarily kept within bounds in expressing certain things, or in pronouncing a certain number of words, by the limits of the breath or power of respiration: certain sounds are observed to join in harmoniously or happily with others: an emphatic phrase must not be placed where the power of utterance is enfeebled or exhausted, etc. All this must be attended to in writing (and will be so unconsciously by a practised hand), or there will be *hiatus in manuscriptis*. The words must be so arranged, in order to make an efficient readable style, as "to come trippingly off the tongue." Hence it seems that there is a natural measure of prose in the feeling of the subject and the power of expression in the voice, as there is an artificial one of verse in the number and co-ordination of the syllables; and I conceive that the trammels of the last do not (where they have been long worn) greatly assist the freedom or the exactness of the first.

Again, in poetry, from the restraints in many respects, a greater number of inversions, or a latitude in the transposition of words is allowed, which is not conformable to the strict laws of prose. Consequently, a poet will be at a loss, and flounder about for the common or (as we understand it) *natural* order of words in prose composition. Dr. Johnson endeavoured to give an air of dignity and novelty to his diction by affecting the order of words usual in poetry. Milton's prose has not only this drawback, but it has also the disadvantage of being formed on a classic model. It is like a fine translation from the Latin; and indeed, he wrote originally in Latin. The frequency of epithets and ornaments, too, is a resource for which the poet finds it difficult to obtain an equivalent. A direct, or simple prose-style seems to him bald and flat; and instead of forcing an interest in the subject by severity of description and reasoning, he is repelled from it altogether by the absence of those obvious and meretricious allurements by which his senses and his imagination have been hitherto stimulated and dazzled. Thus there is often at the same time a want of splendour and a want of energy in what he writes, without the invocation of the Muse—*invita Minerva*. It is like setting a rope-dancer to perform a tumbler's tricks—the hardness of the ground jars his nerves; or it is the same thing as a painter's attempting to carve a block of marble for the first time—the coldness chills him, the colourless uniformity distracts him, the precision of form demanded disheartens him. So in prose-writing, the severity of composition required damps the enthusiasm, and cuts off the resources of the poet. He is looking for beauty, when he should be seeking for truth; and aims at pleasure, which he can only communicate by increasing the sense of power in the reader. The poet spreads the colours of fancy, the illusions of his own mind, round every object, *ad libitum;* the prose-writer is compelled to extract his materials patiently and bit by bit, from his subject. What he adds of ornament, what he borrows from the pencil, must be sparing, and judiciously inserted. The first pretends to nothing but the immediate indulgence of his feelings: the last has a remote practical purpose. The one strolls out into the adjoining fields or groves to gather flowers: the other has a journey to go, sometimes through dirty roads, and at others through untrodden and difficult ways. It is this effeminacy, this immersion in sensual ideas, or craving after continual excitement, that spoils the poet for his prose-tasks. He cannot wait till the effect comes of itself, or arises out of the occasion: he must force it upon all occasions, or his spirit droops and flags under a supposed imputation of dulness. He can never drift with the current, but is always hoisting sail, and has his streamers flying. He has got a striking simile on hand; he *lugs* it in with the first opportunity, and with little connexion, and so defeats his object. He has a story to tell: he tells it in the first page, and where it would come in well, has nothing to say; like Goldsmith, who having to wait upon a Noble Lord, was so full of himself and of the figure he should make, that he addressed a set speech, which he had studied for the occasion, to his Lordship's butler, and had just ended as the nobleman made his appearance. The prose-ornaments of the poet are frequently beautiful in themselves, but do not assist the subject. They are pleasing excrescences—hindrances, not helps in an argument. The reason is, his embellishments in his own walk grow out of the subject by natural association; that is, beauty gives birth to kindred beauty, grandeur leads the mind on to greater grandeur. But in treating a common subject, the link is truth, force of illustration, weight of argument, not a graceful harmony in the immediate ideas; and hence the obvious and habitual clue which before guided him is gone, and he hangs on his patch-work, tinsel finery at random, in despair, without propriety, and without effect. The poetical prose-writer stops to describe an object, if he admires it, or thinks it will bear to be dwelt on: the genuine prose-writer only alludes to or characterizes it in passing, and with reference to his subject. The prose-writer is master of his materials: the poet is the slave of his style. Everything showy, everything extraneous tempts him, and he reposes idly on it: he is bent on pleasure, not on business. He aims at effect, at captivating the reader, and yet is contented with commonplace ornaments, rather than none. Indeed, this last result must necessarily follow, where there is an ambition to shine, without the effort to dig for jewels in the mine of truth. The habits of a poet's mind are not those of industry or research: his images come to him, he does not go to them; and in prose-subjects, and dry matters of fact and close reasoning, the natural stimulus that at other times warms and rouses, deserts him altogether. He sees no unhallowed visions, he is inspired by no daydreams. All is tame, literal, and barren, without the Nine. Nor does he collect his strength to strike fire from the flint by the sharpness of collision, by the eagerness of his blows. He gathers roses, he steals colours from the rainbow. He lives on nectar and ambrosia. He "treads the primrose path of dalliance," or ascends "the highest heaven of invention," or falls flat to the ground. *He is nothing, if not fanciful!*

I shall proceed to explain these remarks, as well as I can, by a few instances in point.

It has always appeared to me that the most perfect prose-style, the most powerful, the most dazzling, the most daring, that which went the nearest to the verge of poetry, and yet never fell over, was Burke's. It has the solidity, and sparkling effect of the diamond: all other *fine writing* is like French paste or Bristol-stones in the comparison. Burke's style is airy, flighty, adventurous, but it never loses sight of the subject; nay, is always in contact with, and derives its increased or varying impulse from it. It may be said to pass yawning gulfs "on the unstedfast footing of a spear": still it has an actual resting-place and tangible support under it—it is not suspended on nothing. It differs from poetry, as I conceive, like the chamois from the eagle: it climbs to an almost equal height, touches upon a cloud, overlooks a precipice, is picturesque, sublime—but all the while, instead of soaring through the air, it stands upon a rocky cliff, clambers up by abrupt and intricate ways, and browzes on the roughest bark, or crops the tender flower. The principle which guides his pen is truth, not beauty—not pleasure, but power. He has no choice, no selection of subject to flatter the reader's idle taste, or assist his own fancy: he must take what comes, and make the most of it. He works the most striking effects out of the most unpromising materials, by the mere activity of his mind. He rises with the lofty, descends with the mean, luxuriates in beauty, gloats over deformity. It is all the same to him, so that he loses no particle of the exact, characteristic, extreme impression of the thing he writes about, and that he communicates this to the reader, after exhausting every possible mode of illustration, plain or abstracted, figurative or literal. Whatever stamps the original image more distinctly on the mind, is welcome. The nature of his task precludes continual beauty; but it does not preclude continual ingenuity, force, originality. He had to treat of political questions, mixed modes, abstract ideas, and his fancy (or poetry, if you will) was ingrafted on these artificially, and as it might sometimes be thought, violently, instead of growing naturally out of them, as it would spring of its own accord from individual objects and feelings. There is a resistance in the *matter* to the illustration applied to it—the concrete and abstract are hardly co-ordinate; and therefore it is that, when the first difficulty is overcome, they must agree more closely in the essential qualities, in order that the coincidence may be complete. Otherwise, it is good for nothing; and you justly charge the author's style with being loose, vague, flaccid, and imbecile. The poet has been said

> To make us heirs
> Of truth and pure delight in endless lays.

Not so the prose-writer, who always mingles clay with his gold, and often separates truth from mere pleasure. He can only arrive at the last through the first. In poetry, one pleasing or striking image obviously suggests another: the increasing the sense of beauty or grandeur is the principle of composition: in prose, the professed object is to impart conviction, and nothing can be admitted by way of ornament or relief, that does not add new force or clearness to the original conception. The two classes of ideas brought together by the orator or impassioned prose-writer, to wit, the general subject and the particular image, are so far incompatible, and the identity must be more strict, more marked, more determinate, to make them coalesce to any practical purpose. Every word should be a blow: every thought should instantly grapple with its fellow. There must be a weight, a precision, a conformity from association in the tropes and figures of animated prose to fit them to their place in the argument, and make them *tell,* which may be dispensed with in poetry, where there is something much more congenial between the subject-matter and the illustration—

Like beauty making beautiful old rime!

What can be more remote, for instance, and at the same time more apposite, more *the same*, than the following comparison of the English Constitution to "the proud Keep of Windsor," in the celebrated *Letter to a Noble Lord?*

"Such are *their* ideas; such *their* religion, and such *their* law. But as to *our* country and *our* race, as long as the well-compacted structure of our church and state, the sanctuary, the holy of holies of that ancient law, defended by reverence, defended by power—a fortress at once and a temple—shall stand inviolate on the brow of the British Sion; as long as the British Monarchy—not more limited than fenced by the orders of the State—shall, like the proud Keep of Windsor, rising in the majesty of proportion, and girt with the double belt of its kindred and coeval towers; as long as this awful structure shall oversee and guard the subjected land, so long the mounds and dykes of the low, fat, Bedford level will have nothing to fear from all the pickaxes of all the levellers of France. As long as our Sovereign Lord the King, and his faithful subjects, the Lords and Commons of this realm—the triple cord which no man can break; the solemn, sworn, constitutional frank-pledge of this nation; the firm guarantees of each other's being, and each other's rights; the joint and several securities, each in its place and order, for every kind, and every quality of property and of dignity—As long as these endure, so long the Duke of Bedford is safe: and we are all safe together—the high from the blights of envy and the spoliations of rapacity; the low from the iron hand of oppression and the insolent spurn of contempt. Amen! and so be it: and so it will be,

> Dum domus Æneæ Capitoli immobile saxum
> Accolet; imperiumque pater Romanus habebit."

Nothing can well be more impracticable to a simile than the vague and complicated idea which is here embodied in one; yet how finely, how nobly it stands out, in natural grandeur, in royal state, with double barriers round it to answer for its identity, with "buttress, frieze, and coigne of 'vantage" for the imagination to "make its pendant bed and procreant cradle," till the idea is confounded with the object representing it—the wonder of a kingdom; and then how striking, how determined the descent, "at one fell swoop," to the "low, fat, Bedford level!" Poetry would have been bound to maintain a certain decorum, a regular balance between these two ideas; sterling prose throws aside all such idle respect to appearances, and with its pen, like a sword, "sharp and sweet," lays open the naked truth! The poet's Muse is like a mistress, whom we keep only while she is young and beautiful, *durante bene placito;* the Muse of prose is like a wife, whom we take during life, *for better, for worse.* Burke's execution, like that of all good prose, savours of the texture of what he describes, and his pen slides or drags over the ground of his subject, like the painter's pencil. The most rigid fidelity and the most fanciful extravagance meet, and are reconciled in his pages. I never pass Windsor but I think of this passage in Burke, and hardly know to which I am indebted most for enriching my moral sense, that or the fine picturesque stanza in Gray,

> From Windsor's heights the expanse below
> Of mead, of lawn, of wood survey,

I might mention that the so-much-admired description in one of the India speeches, of Hyder Ally's army (I think it is) which "now hung like a cloud upon the mountain, and now burst upon the plain like a thunder-bolt," would do equally well for poetry or prose. It is a bold and striking illustration of a naturally impressive object. This is not the case with the Abbé Sieyès's far-famed "pigeon-holes," nor with the comparison of the Duke of Bedford to "the Leviathan, tumbling about his unwieldy bulk in the ocean of royal bounty." Nothing here saves the description but the force of the invective; the startling truth, the vehemence, the remoteness, the aptitude, the perfect peculiarity and coincidence of the allusion. No writer would ever have thought of it but himself; no reader can ever forget it. What is there in common, one might say, between a Peer of the Realm, and "that sea-beast," of those

> Created hugest that swim the ocean-stream?

Yet Burke has knit the two ideas together, and no man can put them asunder. No matter how slight and precarious the connexion, the length of line it is necessary for the fancy to give out in keeping hold of the object on which it has fastened, he seems to have "put his hook in the nostrils" of this enormous creature of the crown, that empurples all its track through the glittering expanse of a profound and restless imagination!

In looking into the *Iris* of last week, I find the following passages, in an article on the death of Lord Castlereagh:

"The splendour of Majesty leaving the British metropolis, careering along the ocean, and landing in the capital of the North, is distinguished only by glimpses through the dense array of clouds in which Death hid himself, while he struck down to the dust the stateliest courtier near the throne, and the broken train of which pursues and crosses the Royal progress wherever its glories are presented to the eye of imagination. . . .

"The same indefatigable mind—a mind of all work—which thus ruled the Continent with a rod of iron, the sword—within the walls of the House of Commons ruled a more distracted region with a more subtle and finely-tempered weapon, the tongue; and truly, if this *was* the only weapon his Lordship wielded there, where he had daily to encounter, and frequently almost alone, enemies more formidable than Buonaparte, it must be acknowledged that he achieved greater victories than Demosthenes or Cicero ever gained in far more easy fields of strife; nay, he wrought miracles of speech, outvying those miracles of song, which Orpheus is said to have performed, when not only men and brutes, but rocks, woods, and mountains, followed the sound of his voice and lyre. . . .

"But there was a worm at the root of the gourd that flourished over his head in the brightest sunshine of a court; both perished in a night, and in the morning, that which had been his glory and his shadow, covered him like a shroud; while the corpse, notwithstanding all his honours, and titles, and offices, lay unmoved in the place where it fell, till a judgment had been passed upon him, which the poorest peasant escapes when he dies in the ordinary course of nature."

This, it must be confessed, is very unlike Burke: yet Mr. Montgomery is a very pleasing poet, and a strenuous politician. The whole is *travelling out of the record*, and to no sort of purpose. The author is constantly getting away from the impression of his subject, to envelop himself in a cloud of images, which weaken and perplex, instead of adding force and clearness to it. Provided he is figurative, he does not care how commonplace or irrelevant the figures are, and he wanders on, delighted in a labyrinth of words, like a truant school-boy, who is only glad to have escaped from his task. He has a very slight hold of his subject, and is tempted to let it go for any fallacious ornament of style. How obscure and circuitous is the allusion to "the clouds in which Death hid himself, to strike down the stateliest courtier near the throne!" How hackneyed is the reference to Demosthenes and Cicero, and how utterly quaint and unmeaning is the ringing the changes upon Orpheus and his train of men, beasts, woods, rocks, and mountains in connexion with Lord Castlereagh! But he is better pleased with this classical fable than with the death of the Noble Peer, and delights to dwell upon it, to however little use. So he is glad to take advantage of the scriptural idea of a gourd; not to enforce, but as a relief to his reflections; and points his conclusion with a puling sort of common-place—that a peasant, who dies a natural death, has no Coroner's Inquest to sit upon him. All these are the faults of the ordinary poetical style. Poets think they are bound, by the tenour of their indentures to the Muses, to "elevate and surprise" in every line; and not having the usual resources in common or abstracted subjects, aspire to the end without the means. They make, or pretend, an extraordinary interest where there is none. They are ambitious, vain, and indolent—more busy in preparing idle ornaments, which they take their chance of bringing in somehow or other, than intent on eliciting truths by fair and honest inquiry. It should seem as if they considered prose as a sort of waiting-maid to poetry, that could only be expected to wear her mistress's cast-off finery. Poets have been said to succeed best in fiction; and the account here given may in part explain the reason. That is to say, they must choose their own subject, in such a manner as to afford them continual opportunities of appealing to the senses and exciting the fancy. Dry details, abstruse speculations do not give scope to vividness of description; and, as they cannot bear to be considered dull, they become too often affected, extravagant, and insipid.

I am indebted to Mr. Coleridge for the comparison of poetic prose to the second-hand finery of a lady's-maid (just made use of). He himself is an instance of his own observation, and (what is even worse) of the opposite fault—an affectation of quaintness and originality. With bits of tarnished lace and worthless frippery, he assumes a sweeping oriental costume, or borrows the stiff dresses of our ancestors, or starts an eccentric fashion of his own. He is swelling and turgid—everlastingly aiming to be greater than his subject; filling his fancy with fumes and vapours in the pangs and throes of miraculous parturition, and bringing forth only *still-births*. He has an incessant craving, as it were, to exalt every idea into a metaphor, to expand every sentiment into a lengthened mystery, voluminous and vast, confused and cloudy. His style is not succinct, but incumbered with a train of words and images that have no practical, and only a possible relation to one another—that add to its stateliness, but impede its march. One of his sentences winds its "forlorn way obscure" over the page like a patriarchal procession with camels laden, wreathed turbans, household wealth, the whole riches of the author's mind poured out upon the barren waste of his subject. The palm-tree spreads its sterile branches overhead, and the land of promise is seen in the distance. All this is owing to his wishing to overdo everything— to make something more out of everything than it is, or than it is worth. The simple truth does not satisfy him—no direct proposition fills up the moulds of his understanding. All is foreign, far-fetched, irrelevant, laboured, unproductive. To read one of his disquisitions is like hearing the variations to a piece of music without the score. Or, to vary the simile, he is not like a man going a journey by the stage-coach along the high-road, but is always getting into a balloon, and mounting into the air, above the plain ground of prose. Whether he soars to the empyrean, or dives to the centre (as he sometimes does), it is equally to get away from the question before him, and to prove that he owes everything to his own mind. His object is to invent; he scorns to imitate. The business of prose is the contrary. But Mr. Coleridge is a poet, and his thoughts are free.

I think the poet-laureate is a much better prose-writer. His style has an antique quaintness, with a modern familiarity. He has just a sufficient sprinkling of *archaisms*, of allusions to old Fuller, and Burton, and Latimer, to set off or qualify the smart flippant tone of his apologies for existing abuses, or the ready, galling virulence of his personal invectives. Mr. Southey is a faithful historian, and no inefficient partisan. In the former character, his mind is tenacious of facts; and in the latter, his spleen and jealousy prevent the "extravagant and erring spirit" of the poet from losing itself in Fancy's endless maze. He "stoops to *earth*," at least, and prostitutes his pen to some purpose (not at the same time losing his own soul, and gaining nothing by it)—and he vilifies Reform, and praises the reign of George III in good set terms, in a straightforward, intelligible, practical, pointed way. He is not buoyed up by conscious power out of the reach of common apprehensions, but makes the most of the obvious advantages he possesses. You may complain of a pettiness and petulance of manner, but certainly there is no want of spirit or facility of execution. He does not waste powder and shot in the air, but loads his piece, takes a level aim, and hits his mark. One would say (though his Muse is ambidexter) that he wrote prose with his right hand; there is nothing awkward, circuitous, or feeble in it. "The words of Mercury are harsh after the songs of Apollo": but this would not apply to him. His prose-lucubrations are pleasanter reading than his poetry. Indeed, he is equally practised and voluminous in both; and it is no improbable conjecture, that Mr. Southey may have had some idea of rivalling the reputation of Voltaire in the extent, the spirit, and the versatility of his productions in prose and verse, except that he has written no tragedies but *Wat Tyler!*

To my taste, the Author of *Rimini,* and Editor of the *Examiner,* is among the best and least corrupted of our poetical prose-writers. In his light but well-supported columns we find the raciness, the sharpness, and sparkling effect of poetry, with little that is extravagant or far-fetched, and no turgidity or pompous pretension. Perhaps there is too much the appearance of relaxation and trifling (as if he had escaped the shackles of rhyme), a caprice, a levity, and a disposition to innovate in words and ideas. Still the genuine master-spirit of the prose-writer is there; the tone of lively, sensible conversation; and this may in part arise from the author's being himself an animated talker. Mr. Hunt wants something of the heat and earnestness of the political partisan; but his familiar and miscellaneous papers have all the ease, grace, and point of the best style of Essay-writing. Many of his effusions in the *Indicator* shew, that if he had devoted himself exclusively to that mode of writing, he inherits more of the spirit of Steele than any man since his time.

Lord Byron's prose is bad; that is to say, heavy, laboured, and coarse: he tries to knock some one down with the butt-end of every line, which defeats his object—and the style of the Author of *Waverley* (if he comes fairly into this discussion) as mere style, is villainous. It is pretty plain he is a poet; for the sound of names runs mechanically in his ears, and he rings the changes unconsciously on the same words in a sentence, like the same rhymes in a couplet.

Not to spin out this discussion too much, I would conclude by observing, that some of the old English prose-writers (who were not poets) are the best, and, at the same time, the most *poetical* in the favourable sense. Among these we may reckon some of the old divines, and Jeremy Taylor at the head of them. There is a flush like the dawn over his writings; the sweetness of the rose, the freshness of the morning dew. There is a softness in his style, proceeding from the tenderness of his heart: but his head is firm, and his hand is free. His materials are as finely wrought up as they are original and attractive in themselves. Milton's prose-style savours too much of poetry, and, as I have already hinted, of an imitation of the Latin. Dryden's is perfectly unexceptionable, and a model, in simplicity, strength, and perspicuity, for the subjects he treated of.

ON THE DIFFERENCE BETWEEN WRITING AND SPEAKING

> Some minds are proportioned to that which may be dispatched at once, or within a short return of time: others to that which begins afar off, and is to be won with length of pursuit.
>
> BACON.

It is a common observation, that few persons can be found who speak and write equally well. Not only is it obvious that the two faculties do not always go together in the same proportions: but they are not usually in direct opposition to each other. We find that the greatest authors often make the worst company in the world; and again, some of the liveliest fellows imaginable in conversation, or extempore speaking, seem to lose all their vivacity and spirit the moment they set pen to paper. For this a greater degree of quickness or slowness of parts, education, habit, temper, turn of mind, and a variety of collateral and predisposing causes are necessary to account. The subject is at least curious, and worthy of an attempt to explain it. I shall endeavour to illustrate the difference by familiar examples rather than by analytical reasonings. The philosopher of old was not unwise who defined motion by getting up and walking.

The great leading distinction between writing and speaking is, that more time is allowed for the one than the other; and hence different faculties are required for, and different objects attained by, each. He is properly the best speaker who can collect together the greatest number of apposite ideas at a moment's warning: he is properly the best writer who can give utterance to the greatest quantity of valuable knowledge in the course of his whole life. The chief requisite for the one, then, appears to be quickness and facility of perception—for the other, patience of soul, and a power increasing with the difficulties it has to master. He cannot be denied to be an expert speaker, a lively companion, who is never at a loss for something to say on every occasion or subject that offers: he, by the same rule, will make a respectable writer, who, by dint of study, can find out anything good to say upon any one point that has not been touched upon before, or who, by asking for time, can give the most complete and comprehensive view of any question. The one must be done off-hand, at a single blow: the other can only be done by a repetition of blows, by having time to think and do better. In speaking, less is required of you, if you only do it at once, with grace and spirit: in writing, you stipulate for all that you are capable of, but you have the choice of your own time and subject. You do not expect from the manufacturer the same despatch in executing an order that you do from a shopman or warehouseman. The difference of *quicker* and *slower*, however, is not all: that is merely a difference of comparison in doing the same thing. But the writer and speaker have to do things essentially different. Besides habit, and greater or less facility, there is also a certain reach of capacity, a certain depth or shallowness, grossness or refinement of intellect, which marks out the distinction between those whose chief ambition is to shine by producing an immediate effect, or who are thrown back, by a natural bias, on the severer researches of thought and study.

We see persons of that standard or texture of mind that they can do nothing, but on the spur of the occasion: if they have time to deliberate, they are lost. There are others who have no resource, who cannot advance a step by any efforts or assistance, beyond a successful arrangement of commonplaces: but these they have always at command, at everybody's service. There is [Fletcher?]—meet him where you will in the street, he has his topic ready to discharge in the same breath with the customary forms of salutations; he is hand and glove with it; on it goes and off, and he manages it like Wart his caliver.

> Hear him but reason in divinity,
> And, all-admiring, with an inward wish
> You would desire that he were made a prelate.
> Let him but talk of any state-affair,
> You'd say it had been all in all his study.
> Turn him to any cause of policy,
> The Gordian knot of it he will unloose,
> Familiar as his garter. When he speaks,
> The air, a charter'd libertine, stands still—

but, ere you have time to answer him, he is off like a shot, to repeat the same rounded, fluent observations to others:—a perfect master of the sentences, a walking polemic wound up for the day, a smartly bound political pocketbook! Set the same person to write a common paragraph, and he cannot get through it for very weariness: ask him a question, ever so little out of the common road, and he stares you in the face. What does all this bustle, animation, plausibility, and command of words amount to? A lively flow of animal spirits, a good deal of confidence, a communicative turn, and a tolerably tenacious memory with respect to floating opinions and current phrases. Beyond the routine of the daily newspapers and coffeehouse criticism, such persons do not venture to think at all: or if they did, it would be so much the worse for them, for they would only be perplexed in the attempt, and would perform their part in the mechanism of society with so much the less alacrity and easy volubility.

The most dashing orator I ever heard is the flattest writer I ever read. In speaking, he was like a volcano vomiting out *lava;* in writing, he is like a volcano burnt out. Nothing but the dry cinders, the hard shell remains. The tongues of flame, with which, in haranguing a mixed assembly, he used to illuminate his subject, and almost scorched up the panting air, do not appear painted on the margin of his works. He was the model of a flashy, powerful demagogue—a madman blest with a fit audience. He was possessed, infuriated with the patriotic *mania;* he seemed to rend and tear the rotten carcase of corruption with the remorseless, indecent rage of a wild beast: he mourned over the bleeding body of his country, like another Antony over the dead body of Cæsar, as if he would "move the very stones of Rome to rise and mutiny": he pointed to the "Persian abodes, the glittering temples" of oppression and luxury, with prophetic exultation; and like another Helen, had almost fired another Troy! The lightning of national indignation flashed from his eye; the workings of the popular mind were seen labouring in his bosom: it writhed and swelled with its rank "fraught of aspics' tongues," and the poison frothed over at his lips. Thus qualified, he "wielded at will the fierce democracy, and fulmin'd over" an area of souls, of no mean circumference. He who might be said to have "roared you in the ears of the groundlings an 'twere any lion, aggravates his voice" on paper, "like any sucking-dove." It is not merely that the same individual cannot sit down quietly in his closet, and produce the same, or a correspondent effect—that what he delivers over to the compositor is tame, and trite, and tedious—that he cannot by any means, as it were, "create a soul under the ribs of death"—but sit down yourself, and read one of these very popular and electrical effusions (for they have been published), and you would not believe it to be the same! The thunder-and-lightning mixture of the orator turns out a mere drab-coloured suit in the person of the prose-writer. We wonder at the change, and think there must be some mistake, some leger-de-main trick played off upon us, by which what before appeared so fine now appears to be so worthless. The deception took place *before;* now it is removed. "Bottom! thou art translated!" might be placed as a motto under most collections of printed speeches that I have had the good fortune to meet with, whether originally addressed to the people, the senate, or the bar. Burke's and Windham's form an exception: Mr. Coleridge's *Conciones ad Populum* do not, any more than Mr. Thelwall's *Tribune.* What we read is the same: what we hear and see is different—"the self-same words, but *not* to the self-same tune." The orator's vehemence of gesture, the loudness of the voice, the speaking eye, the conscious attitude, the inexplicable dumb show and noise,—all "those brave sublunary things that made his raptures clear,"—are no longer there, and without these he is nothing;—his "fire and air" turn to puddle and ditch-water, and the God of eloquence and of our idolatry sinks into a common mortal, or an image of lead, with a few labels, nicknames, and party watch-words stuck in his mouth. The truth is, that these always made up the stock of his intellectual wealth; but a certain exaggeration and extravagance of *manner* covered the nakedness and swelled out the emptiness of the *matter:* the sympathy of angry multitudes with an impassioned theatrical declaimer supplied the place of argument or wit; while the physical animation and ardour of the speaker evaporated in "sound and fury, signifying nothing," and leaving no trace behind it. A popular speaker (such as I have been here describing) is like a vulgar actor off the stage—take away his cue, and he has nothing to say for himself. Or he is so accustomed to the intoxication of popular applause, that without that stimulus he has no motive or power of exertion left—neither imagination, understanding, liveliness, common sense, words, or ideas—he is fairly cleared out; and in the intervals of sober reason, is the dullest and most imbecile of all mortals.

An orator can hardly get beyond *commonplaces:* if he does, he gets beyond his hearers. The most successful speakers, even in the House of Commons, have not been the best scholars or the finest writers—neither those who took the most profound views of their subject, nor who adorned it with the most original fancy, or the richest combinations of language. Those speeches that in general told the best at the time, are not now readable. What were the materials of which they were chiefly composed? An imposing detail of passing events, a formal display of official documents, an appeal to established maxims, an echo of popular clamour, some worn-out metaphor newly vamped-up,—some hackneyed argument used for the hundredth, nay thousandth time, to fall in with the interests, the passions, or prejudices of listening and devoted admirers;—some truth or falsehood, repeated as the Shibboleth of party time out of mind, which gathers strength from sympathy as it spreads, because it is understood or assented to by the million, and finds, in the increased action of the minds of numbers, the weight and force of an instinct. A COMMON-PLACE does not leave the mind "sceptical, puzzled, and undecided in the moment of action":—"it gives a body to opinion, and a permanence to fugitive belief." It operates mechanically, and opens an instantaneous and infallible communication between the hearer and speaker. A set of cant-phrases, arranged in sounding sentences, and pronounced "with good emphasis and discretion," keep the gross and irritable humours of an audience in constant fermentation; and levy no tax on the understanding. To give a reason for anything is to breed a doubt of it, which doubt you may not remove in the sequel; either because your reason may not be a good one, or because the person to whom it is addressed may not be able to comprehend it, or because *others* may not be able to comprehend it. He who offers to go into the grounds of an acknowledged axiom, risks the unanimity of the company "by most admired disorder," as he who digs to the foundation of a building to shew its solidity, risks its falling. But a common-place is enshrined in its own unquestioned evidence, and constitutes its own immortal basis. Nature, it has been said, abhors a *vacuum;* and the House of Commons, it might be said, hates everything but a common-place! Mr. Burke did not often shock the prejudices of the House: he endeavoured to *account for them*, to "lay the flattering unction" of philosophy "to their souls." They could not endure him. Yet he did not attempt this by dry argument alone; he called to his aid the flowers of poetical fiction, and strewed the most dazzling colours of language over the Standing Orders of the House. It was a double offence to them—an aggravation of the encroachments of his genius. They would rather "hear a cat mew or an axle-tree grate," than hear a man talk philosophy by the hour—

> Not harsh and crabbed, as dull fools suppose,
> But musical as is Apollo's lute,
> And a perpetual feast of nectar'd sweets,
> Where no crude surfeit reigns.

He was emphatically called the *Dinner-Bell*. They went out by shoals when he began to speak. They coughed and shuffled him down. While he was uttering some of the finest observations (to speak in compass) that ever were delivered in that House, they walked out, not as the beasts came out of the ark, by twos and by threes, but in droves and companies of tens, of dozens, and scores! Oh! it is "the heaviest stone which melancholy can throw at a man," when you are in the middle of a delicate speculation to see "a robusteous periwig-pated fellow" deliberately take up his hat and walk out. But what effect could Burke's finest observations be expected to have on the House of Commons in their corporate capacity? On the supposition that they were original, refined, comprehensive, his auditors had never heard, and assuredly they had never thought of them before: how then should they know that they were good or bad, till they had time to consider better of it, or till they were told what to think? In the meantime, their effect would be to stop the question: they were blanks in the debate: they could at best only be laid aside and left *ad referendum*. What would it signify if four or five persons, at the utmost, felt their full force and fascinating power the instant they were delivered? They would be utterly unintelligible to nine-tenths of the persons present, and their impression upon any particular individual, more knowing than the rest, would be involuntarily paralysed by the torpedo touch of the elbow of a country-gentleman or city-orator. There is a reaction in insensibility as well as in enthusiasm; and men in society judge not by their own convictions, but by sympathy with others. In reading, we may go over the page again, whenever anything new or questionable "gives us pause": besides we are by ourselves, and it is *a word to the wise*. We are not afraid of understanding too much, and being called upon to unriddle. In hearing, we are (saving the mark!) in the company of fools; and time presses. Was the debate to be suspended while Mr. Fox or Mr. Windham took this or that Honourable Member aside, to explain to them *that fine observation* of Mr. Burke's, and to watch over the new birth of their understandings, the dawn of this new light! If we were to wait till Noble Lords and Honourable Gentlemen were inspired with a relish for abstruse thinking, and a taste for the loftier flights of fancy, the business of this great nation would shortly be at a stand. No: it is too much to ask that our good things should be duly appreciated by the first person we meet, or in the next minute after their disclosure; if the world are a little, a very little, the wiser or better for them a century hence, it is full as much as can be modestly expected! The impression of anything delivered in a large assembly must be comparatively null and void, unless you not only understand and feel its value yourself, but are conscious that it is felt and understood by the meanest capacity present. Till that is the case, the speaker is in your power, not you in his. The eloquence that is effectual and irresistible must stir the inert mass of prejudice, and pierce the opaquest shadows of ignorance. Corporate bodies move slow in the progress of intellect, for this reason, that they must keep back, like convoys, for the heaviest sailing vessels under their charge. The sinews of the wisest councils are, after all, impudence and interest: the most enlightened bodies are often but slaves of the weakest intellects they reckon among them,

and the best-intentioned are but tools of the greatest hypocrites and knaves.—
To conclude what I had to say on the character of Mr. Burke's parliamentary
style, I will just give an instance of what I mean in affirming that it was too
recondite for his hearers; and it shall be even in so obvious a thing as a
quotation. Speaking of the newfangled French Constitution, and in particular
of the King (Louis XVI) as the chief power in form and appearance only, he
repeated the famous lines in Milton describing Death, and concluded with
peculiar emphasis,

> What *seem'd* its head,
> The *likeness* of a kingly crown had on.

The person who heard him make the speech said, that if ever a poet's
language had been finely applied by an orator to express his thoughts and
make out his purpose, it was in this instance. The passage, I believe, is not in
his reported speeches; and I should think, in all likelihood, it "fell still-born"
from his lips; while one of Mr. Canning's well-thumbed quotations out of Virgil
would electrify the Treasury Benches, and be echoed by all the politicians of
his own standing, and the tyros of his own school, from Lord Liverpool in the
Upper down to Mr. William Ward in the Lower House.

Mr. Burke was an author before he was a Member of Parliament: he
ascended to that practical eminence from "the platform" of his literary
pursuits. He walked out of his study into the House. But he never became a
thorough-bred debater. He was not "native to that element," nor was he ever
"subdued to the quality" of that motley crew of knights, citizens, and
burgesses. The late Lord Chatham was made for, and by it. He seemed to vault
into his seat there, like Hotspur, with the exclamation in his mouth—"that
Roan shall be my throne." Or he sprang out of the genius of the House of
Commons, like Pallas from the head of Jupiter, completely armed. He assumed
an ascendancy there from the very port and stature of his mind—from his
aspiring and fiery temperament. He vanquished, because he could not yield.
He controlled the purposes of others, because he was strong in his own
obdurate self-will. He convinced his followers by never doubting himself. He
did not argue, but assert; he took what he chose for granted, instead of making
a question of it. He was not a dealer in *moot-points*. He seized on some
stronghold in the argument, and held it fast with a convulsive grasp—or
wrested the weapons out of his adversaries' hands by main force. He entered
the lists like a gladiator. He made political controversy a combat of personal
skill and courage. He was not for wasting time in long-winded discussions with
his opponents, but tried to disarm them by a word, by a glance of his eye, so
that they should not dare to contradict or confront him again. He did not
wheedle, or palliate, or circumvent, or make a studied appeal to the reason or
the passions—he *dictated* his opinions to the House of Commons. "He spoke
as one having authority, and not as the Scribes." But if he did not produce such
an effect either by reason or imagination, how did he produce it? The principle
by which he exerted his influence over others (and it is a principle of which

some speakers that I might mention seem not to have an idea, even in possibility) was sympathy. He himself evidently had a strong possession of his subject, a thorough conviction, an intense interest; and this communicated itself from his *manner,* from the tones of his voice, from his commanding attitudes and eager gestures, instinctively and unavoidably to his hearers. His will was surcharged with electrical matter like a Voltaic battery; and all who stood within its reach felt the full force of the shock. Zeal will do more than knowledge. To say the truth, there is little knowledge,—no ingenuity, no parade of individual details, not much attempt at general argument, neither wit nor fancy in his speeches—but there are a few plain truths told home: whatever he says, he does not mince the matter, but clenches it in the most unequivocal manner, and with the fullest sense of its importance, in clear, short, pithy old English sentences. The most obvious things, as he puts them, read like axioms—so that he appears, as it were, the genius of common sense personified; and in turning to his speeches you fancy that you have met with (at least) one honest statesman! Lord Chatham commenced his career in the intrigues of a camp and the bustle of a mess-room; where he probably learnt that the way to govern others is to make your will your warrant, and your word a law. If he had spent the early part of his life, like Mr. Burke, in writing a treatise on the *Sublime and Beautiful,* and in dreaming over the abstract nature and causes of things, he would never have taken the lead he did in the British Senate.

Both Mr. Fox and Mr. Pitt (though as opposite to each other as possible) were essentially speakers, not authors, in their mode of oratory. Beyond the moment, beyond the occasion, beyond the immediate power shewn, astonishing as that was, there was little remarkable or worth preserving in their speeches. There is no thought in them that implies a habit of deep and refined reflection (more than we are accustomed ordinarily to find in people of education); there is no knowledge that does not lie within the reach of obvious and mechanical search; and as to the powers of language, the chief miracle is, that a source of words so apt, forcible, and well-arranged, so copious and unfailing, should have been found constantly open to express their ideas without any previous preparation. Considered as written style, they are not far out of the common course of things; and perhaps it is assuming too much, and making the wonder greater than it is, with a very natural love of indulging our admiration of extraordinary persons, when we conceive that parliamentary speeches are in general delivered without any previous preparation. They do not, it is true, allow of preparation at the moment, but they have the preparation of the preceding night, and of the night before that, and of nights, weeks, months, and years of the same endless drudgery and routine, in going over the same subjects, argued (with some paltry difference) on the same grounds. *Practice makes perfect.* He who has got a speech by heart on any particular occasion, cannot be much gravelled for lack of matter on any similar occasion in future. Not only are the topics the same; the very same phrases—whole batches of them,—are served up as the Order of the Day; the same parliamentary bead-roll of grave impertinence is twanged off, in full cadence, by the Honourable Member or his Learned and Honourable Friend; and the well-known, voluminous, calculable periods roll over the drowsy ears of the auditors, almost before they are delivered from the vapid tongue that utters them! It may appear, at first sight, that here are a number of persons got together, picked out from the whole nation, who can speak at all times upon all subjects in the most exemplary manner; but the fact is, they only repeat the same things over and over on the same subjects,—and they obtain credit for general capacity and ready wit, like Chaucer's Monk, who, by having three words of Latin always in his mouth, passed for a great scholar.

> A few termes coude he, two or three,
> That he had learned out of som decree;
> No wonder is, he herd it all the day.

Try them on any other subject *out of doors*, and see how soon the extempore wit and wisdom "will halt for it." See how few of those who have distinguished themselves *in* the House of Commons have done anything *out of it;* how few that have, shine *there!* Read over the collections of old Debates, twenty, forty, eighty, a hundred years ago; they are the same *mutatis mutandis,* as those of yesterday. You wonder to see how little has been added; you grieve that so little has been lost. Even in their own favourite topics, how much are they to seek! They still talk gravely of the Sinking Fund in St. Stephen's Chapel, which has been for some time exploded as a juggle by Mr. Place of Charing-Cross; and a few of the principles of Adam Smith, which every one else had been acquainted with long since, are just now beginning to dawn on the collective understanding of the two Houses of Parliament. Instead of an exuberance of sumptuous matter, you have the same meagre standing dishes for every day in the year. You must serve an apprenticeship to a want of originality, to a suspension of thought and feeling. You are in a go-cart of prejudices, in a regularly constructed machine of pretexts and precedents; you are not only to wear the livery of other men's thoughts, but there is a House-of-Commons jargon which must be used for everything. A man of simplicity and independence of mind cannot easily reconcile himself to all this formality and mummery; yet woe to him that shall attempt to discard it! You can no more move against the stream of custom than you can make head against a crowd of people; the mob of lords and gentlemen will not let you speak or think but as they do. You are hemmed in, stifled, pinioned, pressed to death,—and if you make one false step, are "trampled under the hoofs of a swinish multitude!" Talk of mobs! Is there any body of people that has this character in a more consummate degree than the House of Commons? Is there any set of men that determines more by acclamation, and less by deliberation and individual conviction?—that is moved more *en masse,* in its aggregate capacity, as brute force and physical number?—that judges with more Midas ears, blind and sordid, without discrimination of right and wrong? The greatest test of courage I can conceive, is to speak truth in the House of Commons. I have heard Sir Francis Burdett say things there which I could not enough admire; and which he could not have ventured upon saying, if, besides his honesty, he had not been a man of fortune, of family, of character,—aye, and a very good-looking man into the bargain! Dr. Johnson had a wish to try his hand in the House of Commons. An elephant might as well have been introduced there, in all the forms: Sir William Curtis makes a better figure. Either he or the Speaker (Onslow) must have resigned. The orbit of his intellect was not the one in which the intellect of the House moved by ancient privilege. *His* common-places were not *their* common-places. Even Horne Tooke failed, with all his *tact*, his self-possession, his ready talent, and his long practice at the hustings. He had weapons of his own, with which he wished to make play, and did not lay his hand upon the established levers for wielding the House of Commons. A succession of dry, sharp-pointed sayings, which come in excellently well in the pauses or quick turns of conversation, do not make a speech. A series of drops is not a stream. Besides, he had been in the practice of rallying his guests and tampering with his subject; and this ironical tone did not suit his new situation. He had been used to "give his own little Senate laws," and when he found the resistance of the great one more than he could manage, he shrunk back from the attempt, disheartened and powerless. It is nothing that a man can talk (the better, the worse it is for him) unless he can talk in trammels; he must be drilled into the regiment; he must not run out of the course! The worse thing a man can do is to set up for a wit there—or rather (I should say) for a humorist—to say odd out-of-the-way things, to ape a character, to play the clown or the wag in the House. This is the very forlorn hope of a parliamentary ambition. They may tolerate it till they know what you are at, but no longer. It may succeed once or twice, but the third time you will be sure to break your neck. They know nothing of you, or your whims, nor have they time to look at a puppet-show. "They look only at the stop-watch, my Lord!" We have seen a very lively sally of this sort which failed lately. The House of Commons is the last place where a man will draw admiration by making a jest of his own character. But if he has a mind to make a jest of humanity, of liberty, and of common sense and decency, he will succeed well enough!

The only person who ever "hit the House between wind and water" in this way,—who made sport for the Members, and kept his own dignity (in our time at least), was Mr. Windham. He carried on the traffic in parliamentary conundrums and enigmas with great *éclat* for more than one season. He mixed up a vein of characteristic eccentricity with a succession of far-fetched and curious speculations, very pleasantly. Extremes meet; and Mr. Windham overcame the obstinate attachment of his hearers to fixed opinions by the force of paradoxes. He startled his bed-rid audience effectually. A paradox was a treat to them, on the score of novelty at least; "the sight of one," according to the Scotch proverb, "was good for sore eyes." So Mr. Windham humoured them in the thing for once. He took all sorts of commonly-received doctrines and notions (with an understood reserve)—reversed them, and set up a fanciful theory of his own instead. The changes were like those in a pantomime. Ask the first old woman you meet her opinion on any subject, and you could get at the statesman's; for his would be just the contrary. He would be wiser than the old woman at any rate. If a thing had been thought cruel, he would prove that it was humane; if barbarous, manly; if wise, foolish; if sense, nonsense. His creed was the antithesis of common sense, loyalty excepted. Economy he could turn into ridicule, "as a saving of cheese-parings and candle-ends";—and total failure was with him "negative success." He had no occasion, in thus setting up for original thinking, to inquire into the truth or falsehood of any proposition, but to ascertain whether it was currently believed in, and then to contradict it point-blank. He made the vulgar prejudices of others "servile ministers" to his own solecism. It was not easy always to say whether he was in jest or earnest—but he contrived to hitch his extravagances into the midst of some grave debate; the House had their laugh for nothing; the question got into shape again, and Mr. Windham was allowed to have been more *brilliant* than ever.

Mr. Windham was, I have heard, a silent man in company. Indeed his whole style was an artificial and studied imitation, or capricious caricature of Burke's bold, natural, discursive manner. This did not imply much spontaneous power or fertility of invention; he was an intellectual posture-master, rather than a man of real elasticity and vigour of mind. Mr. Pitt was also, I believe, somewhat taciturn and reserved. There was nothing clearly in the subject-matter of his speeches to connect with the ordinary topics of discourse, or with any given aspect of human life. One would expect him to be quite as much in the clouds as the automaton chess-player or the last new Opera-singer. Mr. Fox said little in private, and complained that in writing he had no style. So (to compare great things with small) Jack Davies, the unrivalled racket-player, never said anything at all in company, and was what is understood by a modest man. When the racket was out of his hand, his occupation, his delight, his glory—that which he excelled all mankind in—was gone! So when Mr. Fox had no longer to keep up the ball of debate, with the floor of Saint Stephen's for a stage, and the world for spectators of the game, it is hardly to be wondered at that he felt a little at a loss—without his usual train of subjects, the same crowd of associations, the same spirit of competition, or stimulus to extraordinary exertion. The excitement of leading in the House of Commons (which, in addition to the immediate attention and applause that follows, is a sort of whispering gallery to all Europe) must act upon the brain like brandy or laudanum upon the stomach; and must, in most cases, produce the same debilitating effects afterwards. A man's faculties must be quite exhausted, his virtue gone out of him. That any one accustomed all his life to the tributary roar of applause from the great council of the nation, should think of dieting himself with the prospect of posthumous fame as an author, is like offering a confirmed dram-drinker a glass of fair water for his morning's draught. Charles Fox is not to be blamed for having written an indifferent history of James II, but for having written a history at all. It was not his business to write a history—his business was *not to have made any more Coalitions!* But he found writing so dull, he thought it better to be a colleague of Lord Grenville! He did not want style (to say so is nonsense, because the style of his speeches was just and fine)—he wanted a sounding-board in the ear of posterity to try his periods upon. If he had gone to the House of Commons in the morning, and tried to make a speech fasting, when there was nobody to hear him, he might have been equally disconcerted at his want of style. The habit of speaking is the habit of being heard, and of wanting to be heard; the habit of writing is the habit of thinking aloud, but without the help of an echo. The orator sees his subject in the eager looks of his auditors; and feels doubly conscious, doubly impressed with it in the glow of their sympathy; the author can only look for encouragement in a blank piece of paper. The orator feels the impulse of popular enthusiasm,

like proud seas under him:

the only Pegasus the writer has to boast, is the hobby-horse of his own thoughts and fancies. How is he to get on, then? From the lash of necessity. We accordingly see persons of rank and fortune continually volunteer into the service of oratory—and the State; but we have few authors who are not paid by the sheet! I myself have heard Charles Fox engaged in familiar conversation. It was in the Louvre. He was describing the pictures to two persons that were with him. He spoke rapidly, but very unaffectedly. I remember his saying—"All those blues and greens and reds are the Guercinos; you may know them by the colours." He set Opie right as to Domenichino's Saint Jerome. "You will find," he said, "though you may not be struck with it at first, that there is a great deal of truth and good sense in that picture." There was a person at one time a good deal with Mr. Fox, who, when the opinion of the latter was asked on any subject, very frequently interposed to give the answer. This sort of tantalizing interruption was ingeniously enough compared by some one, to walking up Ludgate-hill, and having the spire of St. Martin's constantly getting in your way, when you wished to see the dome of St. Paul's! Burke, it is said, conversed as he spoke in public, and as he wrote. He was communicative, diffuse, magnificent. "What is the use," said Mr. Fox to a friend, "of Sheridan's trying to swell himself out in this manner, like the frog in the fable?"—alluding to his speech on Warren Hastings's trial. "It is very well for Burke to express himself in that figurative way. It is natural to him; he talks so to his wife, to his servants, to his children; but as for Sheridan, he either never opens his mouth at all, or if he does, it is to utter some joke. It is out of the question for him to affect these *Orientalisms*." Burke once came into Sir Joshua Reynolds's painting-room, when one of his pupils was sitting for one of the sons of Count Ugolino; this gentleman was personally introduced to him;—"Ah! then," said Burke, "I find that Mr. N[orthcote] has not only a head that would do for Titian to paint, but is himself a painter." At another time, he came in when Goldsmith was there, and poured forth such a torrent of violent personal abuse against the King, that they got to high words, and Goldsmith threatened to leave the room if he did not desist. Goldsmith bore testimony to his powers of conversation. Speaking of Johnson, he said, "Does he wind into a subject like a serpent, as Burke does?" With respect to his facility in composition, there are contradictory accounts. It has been stated by some, that he wrote out a plain sketch first, like a sort of dead colouring, and added the ornaments and tropes afterwards. I have been assured by a person who had the best means of knowing, that the *Letter to a Noble Lord* (the most rapid, impetuous, glancing, and sportive of all his works) was printed off, and the proof sent to him: and that it was returned to the printing-office with so many alterations and passages interlined, that the compositors refused to correct it as it was—took the whole matter in pieces, and re-set the copy. This looks like elaboration and after-thought. It was also one of Burke's latest compositions. A regularly bred speaker would have made up his mind beforehand; but Burke's mind being, as originally constituted and by its first bias, that of an author, never became set. It was in further search and progress. It had an internal spring left. It was not tied down to the printer's form. It could still project itself into new beauties, and explore strange regions from the unwearied impulse of its own delight or curiosity. Perhaps among the passages interlined, in this case, were the description of the Duke of Bedford, as "the Leviathan among all the creatures of the crown,"—the *catalogue raisonnée* of the Abbé Sieyes's pigeon-holes,—or the comparison of the English Monarchy to "the proud keep of Windsor, with its double belt of kindred and coeval towers." Were these to be given up? If he had had to make his defence of his pension in the House of Lords, they would not have been ready in time, it appears; and, besides, would have been too difficult of execution on the spot: a speaker must not set his heart on such forbidden fruit. But Mr. Burke was an author, and the press did not "shut the gates of *genius* on mankind." A set of oratorical flourishes, indeed, is soon exhausted, and is generally all that the extempore speaker can safely aspire to. Not so with the resources of art or nature, which are inexhaustible, and which the writer has time to seek out, to embody, and to fit into shape and use, if he has the strength, the courage, and patience to do so.

There is then a certain range of thought and expression beyond the regular rhetorical routine, on which the author, to vindicate his title, must trench somewhat freely. The proof that this is understood to be so, is, that what is called an oratorical style is exploded from all good writing; that we immediately lay down an article, even in a common newspaper, in which such phrases occur as "the Angel of Reform," "the drooping Genius of Albion"; and that a very brilliant speech at a loyal dinner-party makes a very flimsy, insipid pamphlet. The orator has to get up for a certain occasion a striking compilation of partial topics, which, "to leave no rubs or botches in the work," must be pretty familiar as well as palatable to his hearers; and in doing this, he may avail himself of all the resources of an artificial memory. The writer must be original, or he is nothing. He is not to take up with ready-made goods; for he has time allowed him to create his own materials, to make novel combinations of thought and fancy, to contend with unforeseen difficulties of style and execution, while we look on, and admire the growing work in secret and at leisure. There is a degree of finishing as well as of solid strength in writing which is not to be got at every day, and we can wait for perfection. The author owes a debt to truth and nature which he cannot satisfy at sight, but he has pawned his head on redeeming it. It is not a string of clap-traps to answer a temporary or party-purpose,—violent, vulgar, and illiberal,—but general and lasting truth that we require at his hands. We go to him as pupils, not as partisans. We have a right to expect from him profounder views of things; finer observations; more ingenious illustrations; happier and bolder expressions. He is to give the choice and picked results of a whole life of study; what he has struck out in his most felicitous moods, has treasured up with most pride, has laboured to bring to light with most anxiety and confidence of success. He may turn a period in his head fifty different ways, so that it comes out smooth and round at last. He may have caught a glimpse of a simile, and it may have vanished again: let him be on the watch for it, as the idle boy watches for the lurking-place of the adder. We can wait. He is not satisfied with a reason he has offered for something: let him wait till he finds a better reason. There is some word, some phrase, some idiom that expresses a particular idea better than any other, but he cannot for the life of him recollect it: let him wait till he does. Is it strange that among twenty thousand words in the English language, the one of all others that he most needs should have escaped him? There are more things in nature than there are words in the English language, and he must not expect to lay rash hands on them all at once.

> Learn to *write* slow: all other graces
> Will follow in their proper places.

You allow a writer a year to think of a subject; he should not put you off with a truism at last. You allow him a year more to find out words for his thoughts; he should not give us an echo of all the fine things that have been said a hundred times. All authors, however, are not so squeamish; but take up with words and ideas as they find them delivered down to them. Happy are they who write Latin verses!—who copy the style of Dr. Johnson!—who hold up the phrase of ancient Pistol! They do not trouble themselves with those hair-breadth distinctions of thought or meaning that puzzle nicer heads;—let us leave them to their repose! A person in habits of composition often hesitates in conversation for a particular word: it is because he is in search of the best word, and *that* he cannot hit upon. In writing he would stop till it came. It is not true, however, that the scholar could avail himself of a more ordinary word if he chose, or readily acquire a command of ordinary language; for his associations are habitually intense, not vague and shallow; and words occur to him only as *tallies* to certain modifications of feeling. They are links in the chain of thought. His imagination is fastidious, and rejects all those that are "of no mark or likelihood." Certain words are in his mind indissolubly wedded to certain things; and none are admitted at the *levée* of his thoughts but those of which the banns have been solemnized with scrupulous propriety. Again, the student finds a stimulus to literary exertion, not in the immediate *éclat* of his undertaking, but in the difficulty of his subject, and the progressive nature of his task. He is not wound up to a sudden and extraordinary effort of presence of mind; but is for ever awake to the silent influxes of things, and his life is one long labour. Are there no sweeteners of his toil? No reflections, in the absence of popular applause or social indulgence, to cheer him on his way? Let the reader judge. *His* pleasure is the counterpart of, and borrowed from the same source as the writer's. A man does not read out of vanity, nor in company, but to amuse his own thoughts. If the reader, from disinterested and merely intellectual motives, relishes an author's "fancies and good nights," the last may be supposed to have relished them no less. If he laughs at a joke, the inventor chuckled over it to the full as much. If he is delighted with a phrase, he may be sure the writer jumped at it; if he is pleased to cull a straggling flower from the page, he may believe that it was plucked with no less fondness from the face of nature. Does he fasten, with gathering brow and looks intent, on some difficult speculation? He may be convinced that the writer thought it a fine thing to split his brain in solving so curious a problem, and to publish his discovery to the world. There is some satisfaction in the contemplation of power; there is also a little pride in the conscious possession of it. With what pleasure do we read books! If authors could but feel this, or remember what they themselves once felt, they would need no other temptation to persevere.

To conclude this account with what perhaps I ought to have set out with,—a definition of the character of an author. There are persons who in society, in public intercourse, feel no excitement,

Dull as the lake that slumbers in the storm,

but who, when left alone, can lash themselves into a foam. They are never less alone than when alone. Mount them on a dinner-table, and they have nothing to say; shut them up in a room by themselves, and they are inspired. They are "made fierce with dark keeping." In revenge for being tongue-tied, a torrent of words flows from their pens, and the storm which was so long collecting comes down apace. It never rains but it pours. Is not this strange, unaccountable? Not at all so. They have a real interest, a real knowledge of the subject, and they cannot summon up all that interest, or bring all that knowledge to bear, while they have anything else to attend to. Till they can do justice to the feeling they have, they can do nothing. For this they look into their own minds, not in the faces of a gaping multitude. What they would say (if they could) does not lie at the orifices of the mouth ready for delivery, but is wrapped in the folds of the heart and registered in the chambers of the brain. In the sacred cause of truth that stirs them, they would put their whole strength, their whole being into requisition; and as it implies a greater effort to drag their words and ideas from their lurking-places, so there is no end when they are once set in motion. The whole of a man's thoughts and feelings cannot lie on the surface, made up for use; but the whole must be a greater quantity, a mightier power, if they could be got at, layer under layer, and brought into play by the levers of imagination and reflection. Such a person then sees farther and feels deeper than most others. He plucks up an argument by the roots, he tears out the very heart of his subject. He has more pride in conquering the difficulties of a question, than vanity in courting the favour of an audience. He wishes to satisfy himself before he pretends to enlighten the public. He takes an interest in things in the abstract more than by common consent. Nature is his mistress, truth his idol. The contemplation of a pure idea is the ruling passion of his breast. The intervention of other people's notions, the being the immediate object of their censure or their praise, puts him out. What will tell, what will produce an effect, he cares little about; and therefore he produces the greatest. The *personal* is to him an impertinence; so he conceals himself and writes. Solitude "becomes his glittering bride, and airy thoughts his children." Such a one is a true author; and not a member of any Debating Club, or Dilettanti Society whatever!

BYRON AND WORDSWORTH

I am much surprised at Lord Byron's haste to return a volume of Spenser, which was lent him by Mr. Hunt, and at his apparent indifference to the progress and (if he pleased) *advancement* of poetry up to the present day. Did he really think that all genius was concentred in his own time, or in his own bosom? With his pride of ancestry, had he no curiosity to explore the heraldry of intellect? or did he regard the Muse as an upstart—a mere modern *blue-stocking* and fine lady? I am afraid that high birth and station, instead of being (as Mr. Burke predicates,) 'a cure for a narrow and selfish mind,' only make a man more full of himself, and, instead of enlarging and refining his views, impatient of any but the most inordinate and immediate stimulus. I do not recollect in all Lord Byron's writings, a single recurrence to a feeling or object that had ever excited an interest before; there is no display of natural affection—no twining of the heart round any object: all is the restless and disjointed effect of first impressions, of novelty, contrast, surprise, grotesque costume, or sullen grandeur. *His* beauties are the *houris* of Paradise, the favourites of a seraglio, the changing visions of a feverish dream. His poetry, it is true, is stately and dazzling, arched like a rainbow, of bright and lovely hues, painted on the cloud of his own gloomy temper—perhaps to disappear as soon! It is easy to account for the antipathy between him and Mr. Wordsworth. Mr. Wordsworth's poetical mistress is a Pamela; Lord Byron's an Eastern princess or a Moorish maid. It is the extrinsic, the uncommon that captivates him, and all the rest he holds in sovereign contempt. This is the obvious result of pampered luxury and high-born sentiments. The mind, like the palace in which it has been brought up, admits none but new and costly furniture. From a scorn of homely simplicity, and a surfeit of the artificial, it has but one resource left in exotic manners and preternatural effect. So we see in novels, written by ladies of quality, all the marvellous allurements of a fairy tale, jewels, quarries of diamonds, giants, magicians, condors and ogres. The author of the Lyrical Ballads describes the lichen on the rock, the withered fern, with some peculiar feeling that he has about them: the author of Childe Harold describes the stately cypress, or the fallen column, with the feeling that every schoolboy has about them. The world is a grown schoolboy, and relishes the latter most. When Rousseau called out—*'Ah! voila de la pervenche!'* in a transport of joy at sight of the periwinkle, because he had first seen this little blue flower in company with Madame Warens thirty years before, I cannot help thinking, that any astonishment expressed at the sight of a palm-tree, or even of Pompey's Pillar, is vulgar compared to this! Lord Byron, when he does not saunter down Bond-street, goes into the East: when he is not occupied with the passing topic, he goes back two thousand years, at one poetic, gigantic stride! But instead of the sweeping mutations of empire, and the vast lapses of duration, shrunk up into an antithesis, commend me to the 'slow and creeping foot of time,' in the commencement of Ivanhoe, where the jester and the swine-herd watch the sun going down behind the low-stunted trees of the forest, and their loitering and impatience make the summer's day seem so long, that we wonder how we have ever got to the end of the six hundred years that have passed since! That where the face of nature has changed, time should have rolled on its course, is but a common-place discovery; but that where all seems the same, (the long rank grass, and the stunted oaks, and the innocent pastoral landscape,) all should have changed—this is to me the burthen and the mystery. The ruined pile is a memento and a monument to him that reared it—oblivion has here done but half its work; but what yearnings, what vain conflicts with its fate come over the soul in the other case, which makes man seem like a grasshopper—an insect of the hour, and all that he is, or that others have been—nothing!

THE SPIRIT OF THE AGE

MR. WORDSWORTH

Mr. Wordsworth's genius is a pure emanation of the Spirit of the Age. Had he lived in any other period of the world, he would never have been heard of. As it is, he has some difficulty to contend with the hebetude of his intellect, and the meanness of his subject. With him 'lowliness is young ambition's ladder': but he finds it a toil to climb in this way the steep of Fame. His homely Muse can hardly raise her wing from the ground, nor spread her hidden glories to the sun. He has 'no figures nor no fantasies, which busy *passion* draws in the brains of men': neither the gorgeous machinery of mythologic lore, nor the splendid colours of poetic diction. His style is vernacular: he delivers household truths. He sees nothing loftier than human hopes; nothing deeper than the human heart. This he probes, this he tampers with, this he poises, with all its incalculable weight of thought and feeling, in his hands; and at the same time calms the throbbing pulses of his own heart, by keeping his eye ever fixed on the face of nature. If he can make the lifeblood flow from the wounded breast, this is the living colouring with which he paints his verse: if he can assuage the pain or close up the wound with the balm of solitary musing, or the healing power of plants and herbs and 'skyey influences,' this is the sole triumph of his art. He takes the simplest elements of nature and of the human mind, the mere abstract conditions inseparable from our being, and tries to compound a new system of poetry from them; and has perhaps succeeded as well as any one could. '*Nihil humani a me alienum puto*'—is the motto of his works. He thinks nothing low or indifferent of which this can be affirmed: every thing that professes to be more than this, that is not an absolute essence of truth and feeling, he holds to be vitiated, false, and spurious. In a word, his poetry is founded on setting up an opposition (and pushing it to the utmost length) between the natural and the artificial; between the spirit of humanity, and the spirit of fashion and of the world!

It is one of the innovations of the time. It partakes of, and is carried along with, the revolutionary movement of our age: the political changes of the day were the model on which he formed and conducted his poetical experiments. His Muse (it cannot be denied, and without this we cannot explain its character at all) is a levelling one. It proceeds on a principle of equality, and strives to reduce all things to the same standard. It is distinguished by a proud humility. It relies upon its own resources, and disdains external show and relief. It takes the commonest events and objects, as a test to prove that nature is always interesting from its inherent truth and beauty, without any of the ornaments of dress or pomp of circumstances to set it off. Hence the unaccountable mixture of seeming simplicity and real abstruseness in the *Lyrical Ballads*. Fools have laughed at, wise men scarcely understand them. He takes a subject or a story merely as pegs or loops to hang thought and feeling on; the incidents are trifling, in proportion to his contempt for imposing appearances; the reflections are profound, according to the gravity and the aspiring pretensions of his mind.

His popular, inartificial style gets rid (at a blow) of all the trappings of verse, of all the high places of poetry: 'the cloud-capt towers, the solemn temples, the gorgeous palaces,' are swept to the ground, and 'like the baseless fabric of a vision, leave not a wrack behind.' All the traditions of learning, all the superstitions of age, are obliterated and effaced. We begin *de novo*, on a *tabula rasa* of poetry. The purple pall, the nodding plume of tragedy are exploded as mere pantomime and trick, to return to the simplicity of truth and nature. Kings, queens, priests, nobles, the altar and the throne, the distinctions of rank, birth, wealth, power, 'the judge's robe, the marshal's truncheon, the ceremony that to great ones 'longs,' are not to be found here. The author tramples on the pride of art with greater pride. The Ode and Epode, the Strophe and the Antistrophe, he laughs to scorn. The harp of Homer, the trump of Pindar and of Alcæus are still. The decencies of costume, the decorations of vanity are stripped off without mercy as barbarous, idle, and Gothic. The jewels in the crisped hair, the diadem on the polished brow are thought meretricious, theatrical, vulgar; and nothing contents his fastidious taste beyond a simple garland of flowers. Neither does he avail himself of the advantages which nature or accident holds out to him. He chooses to have his subject a foil to his invention, to owe nothing but to himself. He gathers manna in the wilderness, he strikes the barren rock for the gushing moisture. He elevates the mean by the strength of his own aspirations; he clothes the naked with beauty and grandeur from the stores of his own recollections. No cypress grove loads his verse with funeral pomp: but his imagination lends 'a sense of joy

> To the bare trees and mountains bare,
> And grass in the green field.'

No storm, no shipwreck startles us by its horrors: but the rainbow lifts its head in the cloud, and the breeze sighs through the withered fern. No sad vicissitude of fate, no overwhelming catastrophe in nature deforms his page: but the dew-drop glitters on the bending flower, the tear collects in the glistening eye.

> Beneath the hills, along the flowery vales,
> The generations are prepared; the pangs,
> The internal pangs are ready; the dread strife
> Of poor humanity's afflicted will,
> Struggling in vain with ruthless destiny.

As the lark ascends from its low bed on fluttering wing, and salutes the morning skies; so Mr. Wordsworth's unpretending Muse, in russet guise, scales the summits of reflection, while it makes the round earth its footstool, and its home!

Possibly a good deal of this may be regarded as the effect of disappointed views and an inverted ambition. Prevented by native pride and indolence from climbing the ascent of learning or greatness, taught by political opinions to say to the vain pomp and glory of the world, 'I hate ye,' seeing the path of classical and artificial poetry blocked up by the cumbrous ornaments of style and turgid *commonplaces,* so that nothing more could be achieved in that direction but by the most ridiculous bombast or the tamest servility; he has turned back partly from the bias of his mind, partly perhaps from a judicious policy—has struck into the sequestered vale of humble life, sought out the Muse among sheep-cotes and hamlets and the peasant's mountain-haunts, has discarded all the tinsel pageantry of verse, and endeavoured (not in vain) to aggrandise the trivial and add the charm of novelty to the familiar. No one has shown the same imagination in raising trifles into importance: no one has displayed the same pathos in treating of the simplest feelings of the heart. Reserved, yet haughty, having no unruly or violent passions, (or those passions having been early suppressed,) Mr. Wordsworth has passed his life in solitary musing, or in daily converse with the face of nature. He exemplifies in an eminent degree the power of *association;* for his poetry has no other source or character. He has dwelt among pastoral scenes, till each object has become connected with a thousand feelings, a link in the chain of thought, a fibre of his own heart. Every one is by habit and familiarity strongly attached to the place of his birth, or to objects that recall the most pleasing and eventful circumstances of his life. But to the author of the *Lyrical Ballads,* nature is a kind of home; and he may be said to take a personal interest in the universe. There is no image so insignificant that it has not in some mood or other found the way into his heart: no sound that does not awaken the memory of other years.—

> To him the meanest flower that blows can give
> Thoughts that do often lie too deep for tears.

The daisy looks up to him with sparkling eye as an old acquaintance: the cuckoo haunts him with sounds of early youth not to be expressed: a linnet's nest startles him with boyish delight: an old withered thorn is weighed down with a heap of recollections: a grey cloak, seen on some wild moor, torn by the wind, or drenched in the rain, afterwards becomes an object of imagination to him: even the lichens on the rock have a life and being in his thoughts. He has described all these objects in a way and with an intensity of feeling that no one else had done before him, and has given a new view or aspect of nature. He is in this sense the most original poet now living, and the one whose writings could the least be spared: for they have no substitute elsewhere. The vulgar do not read them, the learned, who see all things through books, do not understand them, the great despise, the fashionable may ridicule them: but the author has created himself an interest in the heart of the retired and lonely student of nature, which can never die. Persons of this class will still continue to feel what he has felt: he has expressed what they might in vain wish to express, except with glistening eye and faltering tongue! There is a lofty philosophic tone, a thoughtful humanity, infused into his pastoral vein. Remote from the passions and events of the great world, he has communicated interest and dignity to the primal movements of the heart of man, and ingrafted his own conscious reflections on the casual thoughts of hinds and shepherds. Nursed amidst the grandeur of mountain scenery, he has stooped to have a nearer view of the daisy under his feet, or plucked a branch of white-thorn from the spray: but in describing it, his mind seems imbued with the majesty and solemnity of the objects around him—the tall rock lifts its head in the erectness of his spirit; the cataract roars in the sound of his verse; and in its dim and mysterious meaning, the mists seem to gather in the hollows of Helvellyn, and the forked Skiddaw hovers in the distance. There is little mention of mountainous scenery in Mr. Wordsworth's poetry; but by internal evidence one might be almost sure that it was written in a mountainous country, from its bareness, its simplicity, its loftiness and its depth!

His later philosophic productions have a somewhat different character. They are a departure from, a dereliction of his first principles. They are classical and courtly. They are polished in style, without being gaudy; dignified in subject, without affectation. They seem to have been composed not in a cottage at Grasmere, but among the half-inspired groves and stately recollections of Cole-Orton. We might allude in particular, for examples of what we mean, to the lines on a Picture by Claude Lorraine, and to the exquisite poem, entitled *Laodamia*. The last of these breathes the pure spirit of the finest fragments of antiquity—the sweetness, the gravity, the strength, the beauty and the languor of death—

Calm contemplation and majestic pains.

Its glossy brilliancy arises from the perfection of the finishing, like that of careful sculpture, not from gaudy colouring—the texture of the thoughts has the smoothness and solidity of marble. It is a poem that might be read aloud in Elysium, and the spirits of departed heroes and sages would gather round to listen to it! Mr. Wordsworth's philosophic poetry, with a less glowing aspect and less tumult in the veins than Lord Byron's on similar occasions, bends a calmer and keener eye on mortality; the impression, if less vivid, is more pleasing and permanent; and we confess it (perhaps it is a want of taste and proper feeling) that there are lines and poems of our author's, that we think of ten times for once that we recur to any of Lord Byron's. Or if there are any of the latter's writings, that we can dwell upon in the same way, that is, as lasting and heart-felt sentiments, it is when laying aside his usual pomp and pretension, he descends with Mr. Wordsworth to the common ground of a disinterested humanity. It may be considered as characteristic of our poet's writings, that they either make no impression on the mind at all, seem mere *nonsense-verses*, or that they leave a mark behind them that never wears out. They either

Fall blunted from the indurated breast—

without any perceptible result, or they absorb it like a passion. To one class of readers he appears sublime, to another (and we fear the largest) ridiculous. He has probably realised Milton's wish,—'and fit audience found, though few'; but we suspect he is not reconciled to the alternative. There are delightful passages in the EXCURSION, both of natural description and of inspired reflection (passages of the latter kind that in the sound of the thoughts and of the swelling language resemble heavenly symphonies, mournful *requiems* over the grave of human hopes); but we must add, in justice and in sincerity, that we think it impossible that this work should ever become popular, even in the same degree as the *Lyrical Ballads*. It affects a system without having any intelligible clue to one; and instead of unfolding a principle in various and striking lights, repeats the same conclusions till they become flat and insipid. Mr. Wordsworth's mind is obtuse, except as it is the organ and the receptacle of accumulated feelings: it is not analytic, but synthetic; it is reflecting, rather than theoretical. The EXCURSION, we believe, fell still-born from the press. There was something abortive, and clumsy, and ill-judged in the attempt. It was long and laboured. The personages, for the most part, were low, the fare rustic: the plan raised expectations which were not fulfilled, and the effect was like being ushered into a stately hall and invited to sit down to a splendid banquet in the company of clowns, and with nothing but successive courses of apple-dumplings served up. It was not even *toujours perdrix!*

Mr. Wordsworth, in his person, is above the middle size, with marked features, and an air somewhat stately and Quixotic. He reminds one of some of Holbein's heads, grave, saturnine, with a slight indication of sly humour, kept under by the manners of the age or by the pretensions of the person. He has a peculiar sweetness in his smile, and great depth and manliness and a rugged harmony, in the tones of his voice. His manner of reading his own poetry is particularly imposing; and in his favourite passages his eye beams with preternatural lustre, and the meaning labours slowly up from his swelling breast. No one who has seen him at these moments could go away with an impression that he was a 'man of no mark or likelihood.' Perhaps the comment of his face and voice is necessary to convey a full idea of his poetry. His language may not be intelligible, but his manner is not to be mistaken. It is clear that he is either mad or inspired. In company, even in a *tête-à-tête*, Mr. Wordsworth is often silent, indolent, and reserved. If he is become verbose and oracular of late years, he was not so in his better days. He threw out a bold or an indifferent remark without either effort or pretension, and relapsed into musing again. He shone most (because he seemed most roused and animated) in reciting his own poetry, or in talking about it. He sometimes gave striking views of his feelings and trains of association in composing certain passages; or if one did not always understand his distinctions, still there was no want of interest—there was a latent meaning worth inquiring into, like a vein of ore that one cannot exactly hit upon at the moment, but of which there are sure indications. His standard of poetry is high and severe, almost to exclusiveness. He admits of nothing below, scarcely of any thing above himself. It is fine to hear him talk of the way in which certain subjects should have been treated by eminent poets, according to his notions of the art. Thus he finds fault with Dryden's description of Bacchus in the *Alexander's Feast*, as if he were a mere good-looking youth, or boon companion—

> Flushed with a purple grace,
> He shows his honest face—

instead of representing the God returning from the conquest of India, crowned with vine-leaves, and drawn by panthers, and followed by troops of satyrs, of wild men and animals that he had tamed. You would think, in hearing him speak on this subject, that you saw Titian's picture of the meeting of *Bacchus and Ariadne*—so classic were his conceptions, so glowing his style. Milton is his great idol, and he sometimes dares to compare himself with him. His Sonnets, indeed, have something of the same high-raised tone and prophetic spirit. Chaucer is another prime favourite of his, and he has been at the pains to modernize some of the Canterbury Tales. Those persons who look upon Mr. Wordsworth as a merely puerile writer, must be rather at a loss to account for his strong predilection for such geniuses as Dante and Michael Angelo. We do not think our author has any very cordial sympathy with Shakespear. How should he? Shakespear was the least of an egotist of any body in the world. He does not much relish the variety and scope of dramatic composition. 'He hates those interlocutions between Lucius and Caius.' Yet Mr. Wordsworth himself wrote a tragedy when he was young; and we have heard the following energetic lines quoted from it, as put into the mouth of a person smit with remorse for some rash crime:

> ———Action is momentary,
> The motion of a muscle this way or that;
> Suffering is long, obscure, and infinite!

Perhaps for want of light and shade, and the unshackled spirit of the drama, this performance was never brought forward. Our critic has a great dislike to Gray, and a fondness for Thomson and Collins. It is mortifying to hear him speak of Pope and Dryden, whom, because they have been supposed to have all the possible excellences of poetry, he will allow to have none. Nothing, however, can be fairer, or more amusing, than the way in which he sometimes exposes the unmeaning verbiage of modern poetry. Thus, in the beginning of Dr. Johnson's *Vanity of Human Wishes*—

> Let observation with extensive view
> Survey mankind from China to Peru—

he says there is a total want of imagination accompanying the words, the same idea is repeated three times under the disguise of a different phraseology: it comes to this—'let *observation*, with extensive *observation*, *observe* mankind'; or take away the first line, and the second,

> Survey mankind from China to Peru,

literally conveys the whole. Mr. Wordsworth is, we must say, a perfect Drawcansir as to prose writers. He complains of the dry reasoners and matter-of-fact people for their want of *passion;* and he is jealous of the rhetorical declaimers and rhapsodists as trenching on the province of poetry. He condemns all French writers (as well of poetry as prose) in the lump. His list in this way is indeed small. He approves of Walton's Angler, Paley, and some other writers of an inoffensive modesty of pretension. He also likes books of voyages and travels, and Robinson Crusoe. In art, he greatly esteems Bewick's woodcuts, and Waterloo's sylvan etchings. But he sometimes takes a higher tone, and gives his mind fair play. We have known him enlarge with a noble intelligence and enthusiasm on Nicolas Poussin's fine landscape-compositions, pointing out the unity of design that pervades them, the superintending mind, the imaginative principle that brings all to bear on the same end; and declaring he would not give a rush for any landscape that did not express the time of day, the climate, the period of the world it was meant to illustrate, or had not this character of *wholeness* in it. His eye also does justice to Rembrandt's fine and masterly effects. In the way in which that artist works something out of nothing, and transforms the stump of a tree, a common figure into an *ideal* object, by the gorgeous light and shade thrown upon it, he perceives an analogy to his own mode of investing the minute details of nature with an atmosphere of sentiment; and in pronouncing Rembrandt to be a man of genius, feels that he strengthens his own claim to the title. It has been said of Mr. Wordsworth, that 'he hates conchology, that he hates the Venus of Medicis.' But these, we hope, are mere epigrams and *jeux-d' esprit,* as far from truth as they are free from malice; a sort of running satire or critical clenches—

> Where one for sense and one for rhyme
> Is quite sufficient at one time.

We think, however, that if Mr. Wordsworth had been a more liberal and candid critic, he would have been a more sterling writer. If a greater number of sources of pleasure had been open to him, he would have communicated pleasure to the world more frequently. Had he been less fastidious in pronouncing sentence on the works of others, his own would have been received more favourably, and treated more leniently. The current of his feelings is deep, but narrow; the range of his understanding is lofty and aspiring rather than discursive. The force, the originality, the absolute truth and identity with which he feels some things, makes him indifferent to so many others. The simplicity and enthusiasm of his feelings, with respect to nature, renders him bigotted and intolerant in his judgments of men and things. But it happens to him, as to others, that his strength lies in his weakness; and perhaps we have no right to complain. We might get rid of the cynic and the egotist, and find in his stead a commonplace man. We should 'take the good the Gods provide us': a fine and original vein of poetry is not one of their most contemptible gifts, and the rest is scarcely worth thinking of, except as it may be a mortification to those who expect perfection from human nature; or who have been idle enough at some period of their lives, to deify men of genius as possessing claims above it. But this is a chord that jars, and we shall not dwell upon it.

Lord Byron we have called, according to the old proverb, 'the spoiled child of fortune': Mr. Wordsworth might plead, in mitigation of some peculiarities, that he is 'the spoiled child of disappointment.' We are convinced, if he had been early a popular poet, he would have borne his honours meekly, and would have been a person of great *bonhommie* and frankness of disposition. But the sense of injustice and of undeserved ridicule sours the temper and narrows the views. To have produced works of genius, and to find them neglected or treated with scorn, is one of the heaviest trials of human patience. We exaggerate our own merits when they are denied by others, and are apt to grudge and cavil at every particle of praise bestowed on those to whom we feel a conscious superiority. In mere self-defence we turn against the world, when it turns against us; brood over the undeserved slights we receive; and thus the genial current of the soul is stopped, or vents itself in effusions of petulance and self-conceit. Mr. Wordsworth has thought too much of contemporary critics and criticism; and less than he ought of the award of posterity, and of the opinion, we do not say of private friends, but of those who were made so by their admiration of his genius. He did not court popularity by a conformity to established models, and he ought not to have been surprised that his originality was not understood as a matter of course. He has *gnawed too much on the bridle;* and has often thrown out crusts to the critics, in mere defiance or as a point of honour when he was challenged, which otherwise his own good sense would have withheld. We suspect that Mr. Wordsworth's feelings are a little morbid in this respect, or that he resents censure more than he is gratified by praise. Otherwise, the tide has turned much in his favour of late years—he has a large body of determined partisans—and is at present sufficiently in request with the public to save or relieve him from the last necessity to which a man of genius can be reduced—that of becoming the God of his own idolatry!

MR. COLERIDGE

The present is an age of talkers, and not of doers; and the reason is, that the world is growing old. We are so far advanced in the Arts and Sciences, that we live in retrospect, and doat on past achievements. The accumulation of knowledge has been so great, that we are lost in wonder at the height it has reached, instead of attempting to climb or add to it; while the variety of objects distracts and dazzles the looker-on. What *niche* remains unoccupied? What path untried? What is the use of doing anything, unless we could do better than all those who have gone before us? What hope is there of this? We are like those who have been to see some noble monument of art, who are content to admire without thinking of rivalling it; or like guests after a feast, who praise the hospitality of the donor 'and thank the bounteous Pan'—perhaps carrying away some trifling fragments; or like the spectators of a mighty battle, who still hear its sound afar off, and the clashing of armour and the neighing of the war-horse and the shout of victory is in their ears, like the rushing of innumerable waters!

Mr. Coleridge has 'a mind reflecting ages past'; his voice is like the echo of the congregated roar of the 'dark rearward and abyss' of thought. He who has seen a mouldering tower by the side of a chrystal lake, hid by the mist, but glittering in the wave below, may conceive the dim, gleaming, uncertain intelligence of his eye: he who has marked the evening clouds uprolled (a world of vapours), has seen the picture of his mind, unearthly, unsubstantial, with gorgeous tints and ever-varying forms—

> That which was now a horse, even with a thought
> The rack dislimns, and makes it indistinct
> As water is in water.

Our author's mind is (as he himself might express it) *tangential*. There is no subject on which he has not touched, none on which he has rested. With an understanding fertile, subtle, expansive, 'quick, forgetive, apprehensive,' beyond all living precedent, few traces of it will perhaps remain. He lends himself to all impressions alike; he gives up his mind and liberty of thought to none. He is a general lover of art and science, and wedded to no one in particular. He pursues knowledge as a mistress, with outstretched hands and winged speed; but as he is about to embrace her, his Daphne turns—alas! not to a laurel! Hardly a speculation has been left on record from the earliest time, but it is loosely folded up in Mr. Coleridge's memory, like a rich, but somewhat tattered piece of tapestry: we might add (with more seeming than real extravagance), that scarce a thought can pass through the mind of man, but its sound has at some time or other passed over his head with rustling pinions. On whatever question or author you speak, he is prepared to take up the theme with advantage—from Peter Abelard down to Thomas Moore, from the subtlest metaphysics to the politics of the *Courier*. There is no man of genius, in whose praise he descants, but the critic seems to stand above the author, and 'what in him is weak, to strengthen, what is low, to raise and support': nor is there any work of genius that does not come out of his hands like an illuminated Missal, sparkling even in its defects. If Mr. Coleridge had not been the most impressive talker of his age, he would probably have been the finest writer; but he lays down his pen to make sure of an auditor, and mortgages the admiration of posterity for the stare of an idler. If he had not been a poet, he would have been a powerful logician; if he had not dipped his wing in the Unitarian controversy, he might have soared to the very summit of fancy. But in writing verse, he is trying to subject the Muse to *transcendental* theories: in his abstract reasoning, he misses his way by strewing it with flowers. All that he has done of moment, he had done twenty years ago: since then, he may be said to have lived on the sound of his own voice. Mr. Coleridge is too rich in intellectual wealth, to need to task himself to any drudgery: he has only to draw the sliders of his imagination, and a thousand subjects expand before him, startling him with their brilliancy, or losing themselves in endless obscurity—

> And by the force of blear illusion,
> They draw him on to his confusion.

What is the little he could add to the stock, compared with the countless stores that lie about him, that he should stoop to pick up a name, or to polish an idle fancy? He walks abroad in the majesty of an universal understanding, eyeing the 'rich strond,' or golden sky above him, and 'goes sounding on his way,' in eloquent accents, uncompelled and free!

Persons of the greatest capacity are often those, who for this reason do the least; for surveying themselves from the highest point of view, amidst the infinite variety of the universe, their own share in it seems trifling, and scarce worth a thought, and they prefer the contemplation of all that is, or has been, or can be, to the making a coil about doing what, when done, is no better than vanity. It is hard to concentrate all our attention and efforts on one pursuit, except from ignorance of others; and without this concentration of our faculties, no great progress can be made in any one thing. It is not merely that the mind is not capable of the effort; it does not think the effort worth making. Action is one; but thought is manifold. He whose restless eye glances through the wide compass of nature and art, will not consent to have 'his own nothings monstered': but he must do this, before he can give his whole soul to them. The mind, after 'letting contemplation have its fill,' or

> Sailing with supreme dominion
> Through the azure deep of air,

sinks down on the ground, breathless, exhausted, powerless, inactive; or if it must have some vent to its feelings, seeks the most easy and obvious; is soothed by friendly flattery, lulled by the murmur of immediate applause, thinks as it were aloud, and babbles in its dreams! A scholar (so to speak) is a more disinterested and abstracted character than a mere author. The first looks at the numberless volumes of a library, and says, 'All these are mine': the other points to a single volume (perhaps it may be an immortal one) and says, 'My name is written on the back of it.' This is a puny and groveling ambition, beneath the lofty amplitude of Mr. Coleridge's mind. No, he revolves in his wayward soul, or utters to the passing wind, or discourses to his own shadow, things mightier and more various!—Let us draw the curtain, and unlock the shrine.

Learning rocked him in his cradle, and while yet a child,

> He lisped in numbers, for the numbers came.

At sixteen he wrote his *Ode on Chatterton*, and he still reverts to that period with delight, not so much as it relates to himself (for that string of his own early promise of fame rather jars than otherwise) but as exemplifying the youth of a poet. Mr. Coleridge talks of himself, without being an egotist, for in him the individual is always merged in the abstract and general. He distinguished himself at school and at the University by his knowledge of the classics, and gained several prizes for Greek epigrams. How many men are there (great scholars, celebrated names in literature) who having done the same thing in their youth, have no other idea all the rest of their lives but of this achievement, of a fellowship and dinner, and who, installed in academic honours, would look down on our author as a mere strolling bard! At Christ's Hospital, where he was brought up, he was the idol of those among his schoolfellows, who mingled with their bookish studies the music of thought and of humanity; and he was usually attended round the cloisters by a group of these (inspiring and inspired) whose hearts, even then, burnt within them as he talked, and where the sounds yet linger to mock Elia on his way, still turning pensive to the past! One of the finest and rarest parts of Mr. Coleridge's conversation, is when he expatiates on the Greek tragedians (not that he is not well acquainted, when he pleases, with the epic poets, or the philosophers, or orators, or historians of antiquity)—on the subtle reasonings and melting pathos of Euripides, on the harmonious gracefulness of Sophocles, tuning his love-laboured song, like sweetest warblings from a sacred grove; on the high-wrought trumpet-tongued eloquence of Æschylus, whose Prometheus, above all, is like an Ode to Fate, and a pleading with Providence, his thoughts being let loose as his body is chained on his solitary rock, and his afflicted will (the emblem of mortality)

> Struggling in vain with ruthless destiny.

As the impassioned critic speaks and rises in his theme, you would think you heard the voice of the Man hated by the Gods, contending with the wild winds as they roar, and his eye glitters with the spirit of Antiquity!

Next, he was engaged with Hartley's tribes of mind, 'etherial braid, thought-woven,'—and he busied himself for a year or two with vibrations and vibratiuncles and the great law of association that binds all things in its mystic chain, and the doctrine of Necessity (the mild teacher of Charity) and the Millennium, anticipative of a life to come—and he plunged deep into the controversy on Matter and Spirit, and, as an escape from Dr. Priestley's Materialism, where he felt himself imprisoned by the logician's spell, like Ariel in the cloven pine-tree, he became suddenly enamoured of Bishop Berkeley's fairyworld, and used in all companies to build the universe, like a brave poetical fiction, of fine words—and he was deep-read in Malebranche, and in Cudworth's Intellectual System (a huge pile of learning, unwieldy, enormous) and in Lord Brook's hieroglyphic theories, and in Bishop Butler's Sermons, and in the Duchess of Newcastle's fantastic folios, and in Clarke and South and Tillotson, and all the fine thinkers and masculine reasoners of that age—and Leibnitz's *Pre-Established Harmony* reared its arch above his head, like the rainbow in the cloud, covenanting with the hopes of man—and then he fell plump, ten thousand fathoms down (but his wings saved him harmless) into the *hortus siccus* of Dissent, where he pared religion down to the standard of reason and stripped faith of mystery, and preached Christ crucified and the Unity of the Godhead, and so dwelt for a while in the spirit with John Huss and Jerome of Prague and Socinus and old John Zisca, and ran through Neal's History of the Puritans, and Calamy's Non-Conformists' Memorial, having like thoughts and passions with them—but then Spinoza became his God, and he took up the vast chain of being in his hand, and the round world became the centre and the soul of all things in some shadowy sense, forlorn of meaning, and around him he beheld the living traces and the sky-pointing proportions of the mighty Pan—but poetry redeemed him from this spectral philosophy, and he bathed his heart in beauty, and gazed at the golden light of heaven, and drank of the spirit of the universe, and wandered at eve by fairy-stream or fountain,

> When he saw nought but beauty,
> When he heard the voice of that Almighty One
> In every breeze that blew, or wave that murmured—

and wedded with truth in Plato's shade, and in the writings of Proclus and Plotinus saw the ideas of things in the eternal mind, and unfolded all mysteries with the Schoolmen and fathomed the depths of Duns Scotus and Thomas Aquinas, and entered the third heaven with Jacob Behmen, and walked hand in hand with Swedenborg through the pavilions of the New Jerusalem, and sung his faith in the promise and in the word in his *Religious Musings*—and lowering himself from that dizzy height, poised himself on Milton's wings, and spread out his thoughts in charity with the glad prose of Jeremy Taylor, and wept over Bowles's Sonnets, and studied Cowper's blank verse, and betook himself to Thomson's Castle of Indolence, and sported with the wits of Charles the Second's days and of Queen Anne, and relished Swift's style and that of the John Bull (Arbuthnot's we mean, not Mr. Croker's), and dallied with the British Essayists and Novelists, and knew all qualities of more modern writers with a learned spirit, Johnson, and Goldsmith, and Junius, and Burke, and Godwin, and the Sorrows of Werther, and Jean Jacques Rousseau, and Voltaire, and Marivaux, and Crebillon, and thousands more—now 'laughed with Rabelais in his easy chair' or pointed to Hogarth, or afterwards dwelt on Claude's classic scenes, or spoke with rapture of Raphael, and compared the women at Rome to figures that had walked out of his pictures, or visited the Oratory of Pisa, and described the works of Giotto and Ghirlandaio and Massaccio, and gave the moral of the picture of the Triumph of Death, where the beggars and the wretched invoke his dreadful dart, but the rich and mighty of the earth quail and shrink before it; and in that land of siren sights and sounds, saw a dance of peasant girls, and was charmed with lutes and gondolas,—or wandered into Germany and lost himself in the labyrinths of the Hartz Forest and of the Kantean philosophy, and amongst the cabalistic names of Fichté and Schelling and Lessing, and God knows who—this was long after, but all the former while, he had nerved his heart and filled his eyes with tears, as he hailed the rising orb of liberty, since quenched in darkness and in blood, and had kindled his affections at the blaze of the French Revolution, and sang for joy when the towers of the Bastile and the proud places of the insolent and the oppressor fell, and would have floated his bark, freighted with fondest fancies, across the Atlantic wave with Southey and others to seek for peace and freedom—

> In Philarmonia's undivided dale!

Alas! 'Frailty, thy name is *Genius!*'—What is become of all this mighty heap of hope, of thought, of learning, and humanity? It has ended in swallowing doses of oblivion and in writing paragraphs in the *Courier.*—Such and so little is the mind of man!

It was not to be supposed that Mr. Coleridge could keep on at the rate he set off; he could not realize all he knew or thought, and less could not fix his desultory ambition; other stimulants supplied the place, and kept up the intoxicating dream, the fever and the madness of his early impressions. Liberty (the philosopher's and the poet's bride) had fallen a victim, meanwhile, to the murderous practices of the hag, Legitimacy. Proscribed by court-hirelings, too romantic for the herd of vulgar politicians, our enthusiast stood at bay, and at last turned on the pivot of a subtle casuistry to the *unclean side:* but his discursive reason would not let him trammel himself into a poet-laureate or stamp-distributor, and he stopped, ere he had quite passed that well-known 'bourne from whence no traveller returns'—and so has sunk into torpid, uneasy repose, tantalized by useless resources, haunted by vain imaginings, his lips idly moving, but his heart for ever still, or, as the shattered chords vibrate of themselves, making melancholy music to the ear of memory! Such is the fate of genius in an age, when in the unequal contest with sovereign wrong, every man is ground to powder who is not either a born slave, or who does not willingly and at once offer up the yearnings of humanity and the dictates of reason as a welcome sacrifice to besotted prejudice and loathsome power.

Of all Mr. Coleridge's productions, the *Ancient Mariner* is the only one that we could with confidence put into any person's hands, on whom we wished to impress a favourable idea of his extraordinary powers. Let whatever other objections be made to it, it is unquestionably a work of genius—of wild, irregular, overwhelming imagination, and has that rich, varied movement in the verse, which gives a distant idea of the lofty or changeful tones of Mr. Coleridge's voice. In the *Christabel,* there is one splendid passage on divided friendship. The *Translation of Schiller's Wallenstein* is also a masterly production in its kind, faithful and spirited. Among his smaller pieces there are occasional bursts of pathos and fancy, equal to what we might expect from him; but these form the exception, and not the rule. Such, for instance, is his affecting Sonnet to the author of the Robbers.

> Schiller! that hour I would have wish'd to die,
>   If through the shudd'ring midnight I had sent
>   From the dark dungeon of the tower time-rent,

That fearful voice, a famish'd father's cry—
That in no after-moment aught less vast
 Might stamp me mortal! A triumphant shout
 Black horror scream'd, and all her goblin rout
From the more with'ring scene diminish'd pass'd.
Ah! Bard tremendous in sublimity!
 Could I behold thee in thy loftier mood,
Wand'ring at eve, with finely frenzied eye,
 Beneath some vast old tempest-swinging wood!
 Awhile, with mute awe gazing, I would brood,
Then weep aloud in a wild ecstasy.

His Tragedy, entitled *Remorse*, is full of beautiful and striking passages, but it does not place the author in the first rank of dramatic writers. But if Mr. Coleridge's works do not place him in that rank, they injure instead of conveying a just idea of the man, for he himself is certainly in the first class of general intellect.

If our author's poetry is inferior to his conversation, his prose is utterly abortive. Hardly a gleam is to be found in it of the brilliancy and richness of those stores of thought and language that he pours out incessantly, when they are lost like drops of water in the ground. The principal work, in which he has attempted to embody his general views of things, is the FRIEND, of which, though it contains some noble passages and fine trains of thought, prolixity and obscurity are the most frequent characteristics.

No two persons can be conceived more opposite in character or genius than the subject of the present and of the preceding sketch. Mr. Godwin, with less natural capacity, and with fewer acquired advantages, by concentrating his mind on some given object, and doing what he had to do with all his might, has accomplished much, and will leave more than one monument of a powerful intellect behind him; Mr. Coleridge, by dissipating his, and dallying with every subject by turns, has done little or nothing to justify to the world or to posterity, the high opinion which all who have ever heard him converse, or known him intimately, with one accord entertain of him. Mr. Godwin's faculties have kept at home, and plied their task in the workshop of the brain, diligently and effectually: Mr. Coleridge's have gossiped away their time, and gadded about from house to house, as if life's business were to melt the hours in listless talk. Mr. Godwin is intent on a subject, only as it concerns himself and his reputation; he works it out as a matter of duty, and discards from his mind whatever does not forward his main object as impertinent and vain. Mr. Coleridge, on the other hand, delights in nothing but episodes and digressions, neglects whatever he undertakes to perform, and can act only on spontaneous impulses, without object or method. 'He cannot be constrained by mastery.' While he should be occupied with a given pursuit, he is thinking of a thousand other things; a thousand tastes, a thousand objects tempt him, and distract his mind, which keeps open house, and entertains all comers; and after being fatigued and amused with morning calls from idle visitors, finds the day consumed and its business unconcluded. Mr. Godwin, on the contrary, is somewhat exclusive and unsocial in his habits of mind, entertains no company but what he gives his whole time and attention to, and wisely writes over the doors of his understanding, his fancy, and his senses—'No admittance except on business.' He has none of that fastidious refinement and false delicacy, which might lead him to balance between the endless variety of modern attainments. He does not throw away his life (nor a single half-hour of it) in adjusting the claims of different accomplishments, and in choosing between them or making himself master of them all. He sets about his task, (whatever it may be) and goes through it with spirit and fortitude. He has the happiness to think an author the greatest character in the world, and himself the greatest author in it. Mr. Coleridge, in writing an harmonious stanza, would stop to consider whether there was not more grace and beauty in a *Pas de trois,* and would not proceed till he had resolved this question by a chain of metaphysical reasoning without end. Not so Mr. Godwin. That is best to him, which he can do best. He does not waste himself in vain aspirations and effeminate sympathies. He is blind, deaf, insensible to all but the trump of Fame. Plays, operas, painting, music, ball-rooms, wealth, fashion, titles, lords, ladies, touch him not—all these are no more to him than to the magician in his cell, and he writes on to the end of the chapter, through good report and evil report. *Pingo in eternitatem*—is his motto. He neither envies nor admires what others are, but is contented to be what he is, and strives to do the utmost he can. Mr. Coleridge has flirted with the Muses as with a set of mistresses: Mr. Godwin has been married twice, to Reason and to Fancy, and has to boast no short-lived progeny by each. So to speak, he has *valves* belonging to his mind, to regulate the quantity of gas admitted into it, so that like the bare, unsightly, but well-compacted steam-vessel, it cuts its liquid way, and arrives at its promised end: while Mr. Coleridge's bark, 'taught with the little nautilus to sail,' the sport of every breath, dancing to every wave,

> Youth at its prow, and Pleasure at its helm,

flutters its gaudy pennons in the air, glitters in the sun, but we wait in vain to hear of its arrival in the destined harbour. Mr. Godwin, with less variety and vividness, with less subtlety and susceptibility both of thought and feeling, has had firmer nerves, a more determined purpose, a more comprehensive grasp of his subject, and the results are as we find them. Each has met with his reward: for justice has, after all, been done to the pretensions of each; and we must, in all cases, use means to ends!

It was a misfortune to any man of talent to be born in the latter end of the last century. Genius stopped the way of Legitimacy, and therefore it was to be abated, crushed, or set aside as a nuisance. The spirit of the monarchy was at variance with the spirit of the age. The flame of liberty, the light of intellect, was to be extinguished with the sword—or with slander, whose edge is sharper than the sword. The war between power and reason was carried on by the first of these abroad—by the last at home. No quarter was given (then or now) by the Government-critics, the authorised censors of the press, to those who followed the dictates of independence, who listened to the voice of the tempter, Fancy. Instead of gathering fruits and flowers, immortal fruits and amaranthine flowers, they soon found themselves beset not only by a host of prejudices, but assailed with all the engines of power, by nicknames, by lies, by all the arts of malice, interest and hypocrisy, without the possibility of their defending themselves 'from the pelting of the pitiless storm,' that poured down upon them from the strong-holds of corruption and authority. The philosophers, the dry abstract reasoners, submitted to this reverse pretty well, and armed themselves with patience 'as with triple steel,' to bear discomfiture, persecution, and disgrace. But the poets, the creatures of sympathy, could not stand the frowns both of king and people. They did not like to be shut out when places and pensions, when the critic's praises, and the laurel-wreath were about to be distributed. They did not stomach being *sent to Coventry*, and Mr. Coleridge sounded a retreat for them by the help of casuistry, and a musical voice.—'His words were hollow, but they pleased the ear' of his friends of the Lake School, who turned back disgusted and panic-struck from the dry desert of unpopularity, like Hassan the camel-driver,

> And curs'd the hour, and curs'd the luckless day,
> When first from Shiraz' walls they bent their way.

They are safely inclosed there, but Mr. Coleridge did not enter with them; pitching his tent upon the barren waste without, and having no abiding place nor city of refuge!

SIR WALTER SCOTT

Sir Walter Scott is undoubtedly the most popular writer of the age—the 'lord of the ascendant' for the time being. He is just half what the human intellect is capable of being: if you take the universe, and divide it into two parts, he knows all that it *has been;* and that it *is to be* is nothing to him. His is a mind brooding over antiquity—scorning 'the present ignorant time.' He is 'laudator temporis acti'—a *'prophesier* of things past.' The old world is to him a crowded map; the new one a dull, hateful blank. He dotes on all well-authenticated superstitions; he shudders at the shadow of innovation. His retentiveness of memory, his accumulated weight of interested prejudice or romantic association have overlaid his other faculties. The cells of his memory are vast, various, full even to bursting with life and motion; his speculative understanding is empty, flaccid, poor, and dead. His mind receives and treasures up every thing brought to it by tradition or custom—it does not project itself beyond this into the world unknown, but mechanically shrinks back as from the edge of a precipice. The land of pure reason is to his apprehension like *Van Dieman's Land;*—barren, miserable, distant, a place of exile, the dreary abode of savages, convicts, and adventurers. Sir Walter would make a bad hand of a description of the *Millennium,* unless he could lay the scene in Scotland five hundred years ago, and then he would want facts and worm-eaten parchments to support his drooping style. Our historical novelist firmly thinks that nothing *is* but what *has been*—that the moral world stands still, as the material one was supposed to do of old—and that we can never get beyond the point where we actually are without utter destruction, though every thing changes and will change from what it was three hundred years ago to what it is now,—from what it is now to all that the bigoted admirer of the good old times most dreads and hates!

It is long since we read, and long since we thought of our author's poetry. It would probably have gone out of date with the immediate occasion, even if he himself had not contrived to banish it from our recollection. It is not to be denied that it had great merit, both of an obvious and intrinsic kind. It abounded in vivid descriptions, in spirited action, in smooth and flowing versification. But it wanted *character*. It was 'poetry of no mark or likelihood.' It slid out of the mind as soon as read, like a river; and would have been forgotten, but that the public curiosity was fed with ever new supplies from the same teeming liquid source. It is not every man that can write six quarto volumes in verse, that are caught up with avidity, even by fastidious judges. But what a difference between *their* popularity and that of the Scotch Novels! It is true, the public read and admired the *Lay of the Last Minstrel, Marmion,* and so on, and each individual was contented to read and admire because the public did so: but with regard to the prose-works of the same (supposed) author, it is quite *another-guess* sort of thing. Here every one stands forward to applaud on his own ground, would be thought to go before the public opinion, is eager to extol his favourite characters louder, to understand them better than every body else, and has his own scale of comparative excellence for each work, supported by nothing but his own enthusiastic and fearless convictions. It must be amusing to the *Author of Waverley* to hear his readers and admirers (and are not these the same thing?) quarrelling which of his novels is the best, opposing character to character, quoting passage against passage, striving to surpass each other in the extravagance of their encomiums, and yet unable to settle the precedence, or to do the author's writings justice—so various, so equal, so transcendant are their merits! His volumes of poetry were received as fashionable and well-dressed acquaintances: we are ready to tear the others in pieces as old friends. There was something meretricious in Sir Walter's ballad-rhymes; and like those who keep opera *figurantes,* we were willing to have our admiration shared, and our taste confirmed by the town: but the Novels are like the betrothed of our hearts, bone of our bone, and flesh of our flesh, and we are jealous that any one should be as much delighted or as thoroughly acquainted with their beauties as ourselves. For which of his poetical heroines would the reader break a lance so soon as for Jeanie Deans? What *Lady of the Lake* can compare with the beautiful Rebecca? We believe the late Mr. John Scott went to his death-bed (though a painful and premature one) with some degree of satisfaction, inasmuch as he had penned the most elaborate panegyric on the *Scotch Novels* that had as yet appeared!—The *Epics* are not poems, so much as metrical romances. There is a glittering veil of verse thrown over the features of nature and of old romance. The deep incisions into character are 'skinned and filmed over'—the details are lost or shaped into flimsy and insipid decorum; and the truth of feeling and of circumstance is translated into a tinkling sound, a tinsel *common-place*. It must be owned, there is a power in true poetry that lifts the mind from the ground of reality to a higher sphere, that penetrates the inert, scattered, incoherent materials presented to it, and by a force and inspiration of its own, melts and moulds them into sublimity and beauty. But Sir Walter (we contend, under correction) has not this creative impulse, this plastic power, this capacity of reacting on his first impressions. He is a learned, a literal, a *matter-of-fact* expounder of truth or fable: he does not soar above and look down upon his subject, imparting his own lofty views and feelings to his descriptions of nature—he relies upon it, is raised by it, is one with it, or he is nothing. A poet is essentially a *maker;* that is, he must atone for what he loses in individuality and local resemblance by the energies and resources of his own mind. The writer of whom we speak is deficient in these last. He has either not the faculty or not the will to impregnate his subject by an effort of pure invention. The execution also is much upon a par with the more ephemeral effusions of the press. It is light, agreeable, effeminate, diffuse. Sir Walter's Muse is a *Modern Antique*. The smooth, glossy texture of his verse contrasts happily with the quaint, uncouth, rugged materials of which it is composed; and takes away any appearance of heaviness or harshness from the body of local traditions and obsolete costume. We see grim knights and iron armour; but then they are woven in silk with a careless, delicate hand, and have the softness of flowers. The poet's figures might be compared to old tapestries copied on the finest velvet:—they are not like Raphael's *Cartoons*, but they are very like Mr. Westall's drawings, which accompany, and are intended to illustrate them. This facility and grace of execution is the more remarkable, as a story goes that not long before the appearance of the *Lay of the Last Minstrel* Sir Walter (then Mr.) Scott, having, in the company of a friend, to cross the Firth of Forth in a ferry-boat, they proposed to beguile the time by writing a number of verses on a given subject, and that at the end of an hour's hard study, they found they had produced only six lines between them. 'It is plain,' said the unconscious author to his fellow-labourer, 'that you and I need never think of getting our living by writing poetry!' In a year or so after this, he set to work, and poured out quarto upon quarto, as if they had been drops of water. As to the rest, and compared with true and great poets, our Scottish Minstrel is but 'a metre balladmonger.' We would rather have written one song of Burns, or a single passage in Lord Byron's *Heaven and Earth*, or one of Wordsworth's 'fancies and good-nights,' than all his epics. What is he to Spenser, over whose immortal, ever-amiable verse beauty hovers and trembles, and who has shed the purple light of Fancy, from his ambrosial wings, over all nature? What is there of the might of Milton, whose head is canopied in the blue serene, and who takes us to sit with him there? What is there (in his ambling rhymes) of the deep pathos of Chaucer? Or of the o'er-informing power of Shakespear, whose eye, watching alike the minutest traces of characters and the strongest movements of passion, 'glances from heaven to earth, from earth to heaven,' and with the lambent flame of genius, playing round each object, lights up the universe in a robe of its own radiance? Sir Walter has no voluntary power of combination: all his associations (as we said before) are those of habit or of tradition. He is a mere narrative and descriptive poet, garrulous of the old time. The definition of his poetry is a pleasing superficiality.

Not so of his NOVELS AND ROMANCES. There we turn over a new leaf—another and the same—the same in matter, but in form, in power how different! The author of Waverley has got rid of the tagging of rhymes, the eking out of syllables, the supplying of epithets, the colours of style, the grouping of his characters, and the regular march of events, and comes to the point at once, and strikes at the heart of his subject, without dismay and without disguise. His poetry was a lady's waiting-maid, dressed out in cast-off finery: his prose is a beautiful, rustic nymph, that, like Dorothea in Don Quixote, when she is surprised with dishevelled tresses bathing her naked feet in the brook, looks round her, abashed at the admiration her charms have excited! The grand secret of the author's success in these latter productions is that he has completely got rid of the trammels of authorship; and torn off at one rent (as Lord Peter got rid of so many yards of lace in the *Tale of a Tub*) all the ornaments of fine writing and worn-out sentimentality. All is fresh, as from the hand of nature: but going a century or two back and laying the scene in a remote and uncultivated district, all becomes new and startling in the present advanced period.—Highland manners, characters, scenery, superstitions, Northern dialect and costume, the wars, the religion, and politics of the sixteenth and seventeenth centuries, give a charming and wholesome relief to the fastidious refinement and 'over-laboured lassitude' of modern readers, like the effect of plunging a nervous valetudinarian into a cold-bath. The *Scotch Novels*, for this reason, are not so much admired in Scotland as in England. The contrast, the transition is less striking. From the top of the Calton Hill, the inhabitants of 'Auld Reekie' can descry, or fancy they descry the peaks of Ben Lomond and the waving outline of Rob Roy's country: we who live at the southern extremity of the island can only catch a glimpse of the billowy scene in the descriptions of the Author of Waverley. The mountain air is most bracing to our languid nerves, and it is brought us in ship-loads from the neighbourhood of Abbot's-Ford. There is another circumstance to be taken into the account. In Edinburgh there is a little opposition and something of the spirit of cabal between the partisans of works proceeding from Mr. Constable's and Mr. Blackwood's shops. Mr. Constable gives the highest prices; but being the Whig bookseller, it is grudged that he should do so. An attempt is therefore made to transfer a certain share of popularity to the second-rate Scotch novels, 'the embryo fry, the little airy of *ricketty* children,' issuing through Mr. Blackwood's shop-door. This operates a diversion, which does not affect us here. The Author of Waverley wears the palm of legendary lore alone. Sir Walter may, indeed, surfeit us: his imitators make us sick! It may be asked, it has been asked, 'Have we no materials for romance in

England? Must we look to Scotland for a supply of whatever is original and striking in this kind?' And we answer—'Yes!' Every foot of soil is with us worked up: nearly every movement of the social machine is calculable. We have no room left for violent catastrophes; for grotesque quaintnesses; for wizard spells. The last skirts of ignorance and barbarism are seen hovering (in Sir Walter's pages) over the Border. We have, it is true, gipsies in this country as well as at the Cairn of Derncleugh: but they live under clipped hedges, and repose in camp-beds, and do not perch on crags, like eagles, or take shelter, like sea-mews, in basaltic subterranean caverns. We have heaths with rude heaps of stones upon them: but no existing superstition converts them into the Geese of Micklestane-Moor, or sees a Black Dwarf groping among them. We have sects in religion: but the only thing sublime or ridiculous in that way is Mr. Irving, the Caledonian preacher, who 'comes like a satyr staring from the woods, and yet speaks like an orator!' We had a Parson Adams not quite a hundred years ago—a Sir Roger de Coverley rather more than a hundred! Even Sir Walter is ordinarily obliged to pitch his angle (strong as the hook is) a hundred miles to the North of the 'Modern Athens' or a century back. His last work, indeed, is mystical, is romantic in nothing but the title-page. Instead of 'a holy-water sprinkle dipped in dew,' he has given us a fashionable watering-place—and we see what he has made of it. He must not come down from his fastnesses in traditional barbarism and native rusticity; the level, the littleness, the frippery of modern civilization will undo him as it has undone us!

Sir Walter has found out (oh, rare discovery) that facts are better than fiction; that there is no romance like the romance of real life; and that if we can but arrive at what men feel, do, and say in striking and singular situations, the result will be 'more lively, audible, and full of vent,' than the fine-spun cobwebs of the brain. With reverence be it spoken, he is like the man who having to imitate the squeaking of a pig upon the stage, brought the animal under his coat with him. Our author has conjured up the actual people he has to deal with, or as much as he could get of them, in 'their habits as they lived.' He has ransacked old chronicles, and poured the contents upon his page; he has squeezed out musty records; he has consulted wayfaring pilgrims, bed-rid sibyls; he has invoked the spirits of the air; he has conversed with the living and the dead, and let them tell their story their own way; and by borrowing of others, has enriched his own genius with everlasting variety, truth, and freedom. He has taken his materials from the original, authentic sources, in large concrete masses, and not tampered with or too much frittered them away. He is only the amanuensis of truth and history. It is impossible to say how fine his writings in consequence are, unless we could describe how fine nature is. All that portion of the history of his country that he has touched upon (wide as the scope is) the manners, the personages, the events, the scenery, lives over again in his volumes. Nothing is wanting—the illusion is complete. There is a hurtling in the air, a trampling of feet upon the ground, as these perfect representations of human character or fanciful belief come thronging back upon our imaginations. We will merely recall a few of the subjects of his pencil to the reader's recollection; for nothing we could add, by way of note or commendation, could make the impression more vivid.

There is (first and foremost, because the earliest of our acquaintance) the Baron of Bradwardine, stately, kind-hearted, whimsical, pedantic; and Flora MacIvor (whom even *we* forgive for her Jacobitism), the fierce Vich Ian Vohr, and Evan Dhu, constant in death, and Davie Gellatly roasting his eggs or turning his rhymes with restless volubility, and the two stag-hounds that met Waverley, as fine as ever Titian painted, or Paul Veronese:—then there is old Balfour of Burley, brandishing his sword and his Bible with fire-eyed fury, trying a fall with the insolent, gigantic Bothwell at the 'Change-house, and vanquishing him at the noble battle of Loudon-hill; there is Bothwell himself, drawn to the life, proud, cruel, selfish, profligate, but with the love-letters of the gentle Alice (written thirty years before), and his verses to her memory, found in his pocket after his death: in the same volume of *Old Mortality* is that lone figure, like a figure in Scripture, of the woman sitting on the stone at the turning to the mountain, to warn Burley that there is a lion in his path; and the fawning Claverhouse, beautiful as a panther, smooth-looking, blood-spotted; and the fanatics, Macbriar and Mucklewrath, crazed with zeal and sufferings; and the inflexible Morton, and the faithful Edith, who refused to 'give her hand to another while her heart was with her lover in the deep and dead sea.' And in *The Heart of Mid Lothian* we have Effie Deans (that sweet, faded flower) and Jeanie, her more than sister, and old David Deans, the patriarch of St. Leonard's Crags, and Butler, and Dumbiedikes, eloquent in his silence, and Mr. Bartoline Saddle-tree and his prudent helpmate, and Porteous swinging in the wind, and Madge Wildfire, full of finery and madness, and her ghastly mother.—Again, there is Meg Merrilies, standing on her rock, stretched on her bier with 'her head to the east,' and Dirk Hatterick (equal to Shakespear's Master Barnardine), and Glossin, the soul of an attorney, and Dandy Dinmont, with his terrier-pack and his pony Dumple, and the fiery Colonel Mannering, and the modish old counsellor Pleydell, and Dominie Sampson, and Rob Roy (like the eagle in his eyry), and Baillie Nicol Jarvie, and the inimitable Major Galbraith, and Rashleigh Osbaldistone, and Die Vernon, the best of secret-keepers; and in the *Antiquary,* the ingenious and abstruse Mr. Jonathan Oldbuck, and the old beadsman Edie Ochiltree, and that preternatural figure of old Edith Elspeith, a living shadow, in whom the lamp of life had been long extinguished, had it not been fed by remorse and 'thick-coming' recollections; and that striking picture of the effects of feudal tyranny and fiendish pride, the unhappy Earl of Glenallan; and the Black Dwarf, and his friend Habby of the Heughfoot (the cheerful hunter), and his cousin Grace Armstrong, fresh and laughing like the morning; and the *Children of the Mist,* and the baying of the blood-hound that tracks their steps at a distance (the hollow echoes are in our ears now), and Amy and her hapless love, and the villain Varney, and the deep voice of George of Douglas—and the immoveable Balafre, and Master Oliver the Barber in Quentin Durward—and the quaint humour of the Fortunes of Nigel, and the comic spirit of Peveril of the Peak—and the fine old English romance of

Ivanhoe. What a list of names! What a host of associations! What a thing is human life! What a power is that of genius! What a world of thought and feeling is thus rescued from oblivion! How many hours of heartfelt satisfaction has our author given to the gay and thoughtless! How many sad hearts has he soothed in pain and solitude! It is no wonder that the public repay with lengthened applause and gratitude the pleasure they receive. He writes as fast as they can read, and he does not write himself down. He is always in the public eye, and we do not tire of him. His worst is better than any other person's best. His *back-grounds* (and his later works are little else but back-grounds capitally made out) are more attractive than the principal figures and most complicated actions of other writers. His works (taken together) are almost like a new edition of human nature. This is indeed to be an author!

The political bearing of the *Scotch Novels* has been a considerable recommendation to them. They are a relief to the mind, rarefied as it has been with modern philosophy, and heated with ultra-radicalism. At a time also, when we bid fair to revive the principles of the Stuarts, it is interesting to bring us acquainted with their persons and misfortunes. The candour of Sir Walter's historic pen levels our bristling prejudices on this score, and sees fair play between Roundheads and Cavaliers, between Protestant and Papist. He is a writer reconciling all the diversities of human nature to the reader. He does not enter into the distinctions of hostile sects or parties, but treats of the strength or the infirmity of the human mind, of the virtues or vices of the human breast, as they are to be found blended in the whole race of mankind. Nothing can show more handsomely or be more gallantly executed. There was a talk at one time that our author was about to take Guy Faux for the subject of one of his novels, in order to put a more liberal and humane construction on the Gunpowder Plot than our 'No Popery' prejudices have hitherto permitted. Sir Walter is a professed *clarifier* of the age from the vulgar and still lurking old-English antipathy to Popery and Slavery. Through some odd process of *servile* logic, it should seem, that in restoring the claims of the Stuarts by the courtesy of romance, the House of Brunswick are more firmly seated in point of fact, and the Bourbons, by collateral reasoning, become legitimate! In any other point of view, we cannot possibly conceive how Sir Walter imagines 'he has done something to revive the declining spirit of loyalty' by these novels. His loyalty is founded on *would-be* treason: he props the actual throne by the shadow of rebellion. Does he really think of making us enamoured of the 'good old times' by the faithful and harrowing portraits he has drawn of them? Would he carry us back to the early stages of barbarism, of clanship, of the feudal system as 'a consummation devoutly to be wished?' Is he infatuated enough, or does he so dote and drivel over his own slothful and self-willed prejudices, as to believe that he will make a single convert to the beauty of Legitimacy, that is, of lawless power and savage bigotry, when he himself is obliged to apologise for the horrors he describes, and even render his descriptions credible to the modern reader by referring to the authentic history of these delectable times? He is indeed so besotted as to the moral of his own story, that he has even the blindness to go out of his way to have a fling at *flints* and *dungs* (the contemptible ingredients, as he would have us believe, of a modern rabble) at the very time when he is describing a mob of the twelfth century—a mob (one should think) after the writer's own heart, without one particle of modern philosophy or revolutionary politics in their composition, who were to a man, to a hair, just what priests, and kings, and nobles *let* them be, and who were collected to witness (a spectacle proper to the times) the burning of the lovely Rebecca at a stake for a sorceress, because she was a Jewess, beautiful and innocent, and the consequent victim of insane bigotry and unbridled profligacy. And it is at this moment (when the heart is kindled and bursting with indignation at the revolting abuses of self-constituted power) that Sir Walter *stops the press* to have a sneer at the people, and to put a spoke (as he thinks) in the wheel of upstart innovation! This is what he calls, 'backing his friends'—it is thus he administers charms and philtres to our love of Legitimacy, makes us conceive a horror of all reform, civil, political, or religious, and would fain put down the *Spirit of the Age.* The author of Waverley might just as well get up and make a speech at a dinner at Edinburgh, abusing Mr. Mac-Adam for his improvements in the roads, on the ground that they were nearly *impassable* in many places 'sixty years since'; or object to Mr. Peel's *Police-Bill,* by insisting that Hounslow-Heath was formerly a scene of greater interest and terror to highwaymen and travellers, and cut a greater figure in the Newgate Calendar than it does at present.—Oh! Wickliff, Luther, Hampden, Sidney, Somers, mistaken Whigs, and thoughtless Reformers in religion and politics, and all ye, whether poets or philosophers, heroes or sages, inventors of arts or sciences, patriots, benefactors of the human race, enlighteners and civilisers of the world, who have (so far) reduced opinion to reason, and power to law, who are the cause that we no longer burn witches and heretics at slow fires, that the thumb-screws are no longer applied by ghastly, smiling judges, to extort confession of imputed crimes from sufferers for conscience sake; that men are no longer strung up like acorns on trees without judge or jury, or hunted like wild beasts through thickets and glens, who have abated the cruelty of priests, the pride of nobles, the divinity of kings in former times; to whom we owe it, that we no longer wear round our necks the collar of Gurth the swineherd, and of Wamba the jester; that the castles of great lords are no longer the dens of banditti, from whence they issue with fire and sword, to lay waste the land; that we no longer expire in loathsome dungeons without knowing the cause, or have our right hands struck off for raising them in self-defence against wanton insult; that we can sleep without fear of being burnt in our beds, or travel without making our wills; that no Amy Robsarts are thrown down trap-doors by Richard Varneys with impunity; that no Red Reiver of Westburn-Flat sets fire to peaceful cottages; that no Claverhouse signs cold-blooded death-warrants in sport; that we have no Tristan the Hermit, or Petit-André, crawling near us, like spiders, and making our flesh creep, and our hearts sicken within us at every moment of our lives—ye who have produced this change in the face of nature and society, return to earth once more, and beg pardon of Sir Walter and his patrons, who sigh at not being able to undo all that you have done! Leaving this question, there are two other remarks which we wished to make on the Novels. The one was, to express our admiration of the good-nature of the mottos, in which the author has taken occasion to remember and quote almost every living author (whether illustrious or obscure) but himself—an indirect argument in favour of the general opinion as to the source from which they spring—and the other was, to hint our astonishment at the innumerable and incessant instances of bad and slovenly English in them, more, we believe, than in any other works now printed. We should think the writer could not possibly read the manuscript after he has once written it, or overlook the press.

If there were a writer, who 'born for the universe'—

> Narrow'd his mind,
> And to party gave up what was meant for mankind

who, from the height of his genius looking abroad into nature, and scanning the recesses of the human heart, 'winked and shut his apprehension up' to every thought or purpose that tended to the future good of mankind—who, raised by affluence, the reward of successful industry, and by the voice of fame above the want of any but the most honourable patronage, stooped to the unworthy arts of adulation, and abetted the views of the great with the pettifogging feelings of the meanest dependant on office—who, having secured the admiration of the public (with the probable reversion of immortality), showed no respect for himself, for that genius that had raised him to distinction, for that nature which he trampled under foot—who, amiable, frank, friendly, manly in private life, was seized with the dotage of age and the fury of a woman, the instant politics were concerned—who reserved all his candour and comprehensiveness of view for history, and vented his littleness, pique, resentment, bigotry, and intolerance on his contemporaries—who took the wrong side, and defended it by unfair means—who, the moment his own interest or the prejudices of others interfered, seemed to forget all that was due to the pride of intellect, to the sense of manhood—who, praised, admired by men of all parties alike, repaid the public liberality by striking a secret and envenomed blow at the reputation of every one who was not the ready tool of power—who strewed the slime of rankling malice and mercenary scorn over the bud and promise of genius, because it was not fostered in the hot-bed of corruption, or warped by the trammels of servility—who supported the worst abuses of authority in the worst spirit—who joined a gang of desperadoes to spread calumny, contempt, infamy, wherever they were merited by honesty or talent on a different side—who officiously undertook to decide public questions by private insinuations, to prop the throne by nicknames, and the altar by lies—who being (by common consent), the finest, the most humane and accomplished writer of his age, associated himself with and encouraged the lowest panders of a venal press; deluging, nauseating the public mind with the offal and garbage of Billingsgate abuse and vulgar *slang;* showing no remorse, no relenting or compassion towards the victims of this nefarious and organized system of party-proscription, carried on under the mask of literary criticism and fair discussion, insulting the misfortunes of some, and trampling on the early grave of others—

> Who would not grieve if such a man there be?
> Who would not weep if Atticus were he?

But we believe there is no other age or country of the world (but ours), in which genius could have been so degraded!

THE AGE OF ELIZABETH

LECTURE I

General View of the Subject

The age of Elizabeth was distinguished, beyond, perhaps, any other in our history, by a number of great men, famous in different ways, and whose names have come down to us with unblemished honours; statesmen, warriors, divines, scholars, poets, and philosophers, Raleigh, Drake, Coke, Hooker, and higher and more sounding still, and still more frequent in our mouths, Shakespear, Spenser, Sidney, Bacon, Jonson, Beaumont and Fletcher, men whom fame has eternised in her long and lasting scroll, and who, by their words and acts, were benefactors of their country, and ornaments of human nature. Their attainments of different kinds bore the same general stamp, and it was sterling: what they did, had the mark of their age and country upon it. Perhaps the genius of Great Britain (if I may so speak without offence or flattery), never shone out fuller or brighter, or looked more like itself, than at this period. Our writers and great men had something in them that savoured of the soil from which they grew: they were not French, they were not Dutch, or German, or Greek, or Latin; they were truly English. They did not look out of themselves to see what they should be; they sought for truth and nature, and found it in themselves. There was no tinsel, and but little art; they were not the spoiled children of affectation and refinement, but a bold, vigorous, indepen-dent race of thinkers, with prodigious strength and energy, with none but natural grace, and heartfelt unobtrusive delicacy. They were not at all sophisticated. The mind of their country was great in them, and it prevailed. With their learning and unexampled acquirement, they did not forget that they were men: with all their endeavours after excellence, they did not lay aside the strong original bent and character of their minds. What they performed was chiefly nature's handy-work; and time has claimed it for his own.—To these, however, might be added others not less learned, nor with a scarce less happy vein, but less fortunate in the event, who, though as renowned in their day, have sunk into 'mere oblivion,' and of whom the only record (but that the noblest) is to be found in their works. Their works and their names, 'poor, poor dumb names,' are all that remains of such men as Webster, Deckar, Marston, Marlow, Chapman, Heywood, Middleton, and Rowley! 'How lov'd, how honour'd once avails them not:' though they were the friends and fellow-labourers of Shakespear, sharing his fame and fortunes with him, the rivals of Jonson, and the masters of Beaumont and Fletcher's well-sung woes! They went out one by one unnoticed, like evening lights; or were swallowed up in the headlong torrent of puritanic zeal which succeeded, and swept away every thing in its unsparing course, throwing up the wrecks of taste and genius at

random, and at long fitful intervals, amidst the painted gew-gaws and foreign
frippery of the reign of Charles II. and from which we are only now recovering
the scattered fragments and broken images to erect a temple to true Fame!
How long, before it will be completed?

If I can do any thing to rescue some of these writers from hopeless
obscurity, and to do them right, without prejudice to well-deserved reputation,
I shall have succeeded in what I chiefly propose. I shall not attempt, indeed,
to adjust the spelling, or restore the pointing, as if the genius of poetry lay hid
in errors of the press, but leaving these weightier matters of criticism to those
who are more able and willing to bear the burden, try to bring out their real
beauties to the eager sight, 'draw the curtain of Time, and shew the picture of
Genius,' restraining my own admiration within reasonable bounds!

There is not a lower ambition, a poorer way of thought, than that which
would confine all excellence, or arrogate its final accomplishment to the
present, or modern times. We ordinarily speak and think of those who had the
misfortune to write or live before us, as labouring under very singular
privations and disadvantages in not having the benefit of those improvements
which we have made, as buried in the grossest ignorance, or the slaves 'of
poring pedantry'; and we make a cheap and infallible estimate of their progress
in civilization upon a graduated scale of perfectibility, calculated from the
meridian of our own times. If we have pretty well got rid of the narrow bigotry
that would limit all sense or virtue to our own country, and have fraternized,
like true cosmopolites, with our neighbours and contemporaries, we have
made our self-love amends by letting the generation we live in engross nearly
all our admiration and by pronouncing a sweeping sentence of barbarism and
ignorance on our ancestry backwards, from the commencement (as near as
can be) of the nineteenth, or the latter end of the eighteenth century. From
thence we date a new era, the dawn of our own intellect and that of the world,
like 'the sacred influence of light' glimmering on the confines of Chaos and old
night; new manners rise, and all the cumbrous 'pomp of elder days' vanishes,
and is lost in worse than Gothic darkness. Pavilioned in the glittering pride of
our superficial accomplishments and upstart pretensions, we fancy that every
thing beyond that magic circle is prejudice and error; and all, before the
present enlightened period, but a dull and useless blank in the great map of
time. We are so dazzled with the gloss and novelty of modern discoveries, that
we cannot take into our mind's eye the vast expanse, the lengthened
perspective of human intellect, and a cloud hangs over and conceals its loftiest
monuments, if they are removed to a little distance from us—the cloud of our
own vanity and shortsightedness. The modern sciolist *stultifies* all understanding but his own, and that which he conceives like his own. We think, in
this age of reason and consummation of philosophy, because we knew nothing
twenty or thirty years ago, and began to think then for the first time in our
lives, that the rest of mankind were in the same predicament, and never knew
any thing till we did; that the world had grown old in sloth and ignorance, had
dreamt out its long minority of five thousand years in a dozing state, and that
it first began to wake out of sleep, to rouse itself, and look about it, startled by

the light of our unexpected discoveries, and the noise we made about them. Strange error of our infatuated self-love! Because the clothes we remember to have seen worn when we were children, are now out of fashion, and our grandmothers were then old women, we conceive with magnanimous continuity of reasoning, that it must have been much worse three hundred years before, and that grace, youth, and beauty are things of modern date—as if nature had ever been old, or the sun had first shone on our folly and presumption. Because, in a word, the last generation, when tottering off the stage, were not so active, so sprightly, and so promising as we were, we begin to imagine, that people formerly must have crawled about in a feeble, torpid state, like flies in winter, in a sort of dim twilight of the understanding; 'nor can we think what thoughts they could conceive,' in the absence of all those topics that so agreeably enliven and diversify our conversation and literature, mistaking the imperfection of our knowledge for the defect of their organs, as if it was necessary for us to have a register and certificate of their thoughts, or as if, because they did not see with our eyes, hear with our ears, and understand with our understandings, they could hear, see, and understand nothing. A falser inference could not be drawn, nor one more contrary to the maxims and cautions of a wise humanity. 'Think,' says Shakespear, the prompter of good and true feelings, 'there 's livers out of Britain.' So there have been thinkers, and great and sound ones, before our time. They had the same capacities that we have, sometimes greater motives for their exertion, and, for the most part, the same subject-matter to work upon. What we learn from nature, we may hope to do as well as they; what we learn from them, we may in general expect to do worse.—What is, I think, as likely as any thing to cure us of this overweening admiration of the present, and unmingled contempt for past times, is the looking at the finest old pictures; at Raphael's heads, at Titian's faces, at Claude's landscapes. We have there the evidence of the senses, without the alterations of opinion or disguise of language. We there see the blood circulate through the veins (long before it was known that it did so), the same red and white 'by nature's own sweet and cunning hand laid on,' the same thoughts passing through the mind and seated on the lips, the same blue sky, and glittering sunny vales, 'where Pan, knit with the Graces and the Hours in dance, leads on the eternal spring.' And we begin to feel, that nature and the mind of man are not a thing of yesterday, as we had been led to suppose; and that 'there are more things between heaven and earth, than were ever dreamt of in our philosophy.'—Or grant that we improve, in some respects, in a uniformly progressive ratio, and build, Babel-high, on the foundation of other men's knowledge, as in matters of science and speculative inquiry, where by going often over the same general ground, certain general conclusions have been arrived at, and in the number of persons reasoning on a given subject, truth has at last been hit upon, and long-established error exploded; yet this does not apply to cases of individual power and knowledge, to a million of things beside, in which we are still to seek as much as ever, and in which we can only hope to find, by going to the fountain-head of thought and experience. We are quite wrong in supposing (as we are apt to do), that we can plead an exclusive title to wit and wisdom, to taste and genius, as the net produce and clear reversion of the age we live in, and that all we have to do to be great, is to despise those who have gone before us as nothing.

Or even if we admit a saving clause in this sweeping proscription, and do not make the rule absolute, the very nature of the exceptions shews the spirit in which they are made. We single out one or two striking instances, say Shakespear or Lord Bacon, which we would fain treat as prodigies, and as a marked contrast to the rudeness and barbarism that surrounded them. These we delight to dwell upon and magnify; the praise and wonder we heap upon their shrines, are at the expence of the time in which they lived, and would leave it poor indeed. We make them out something more than human, 'matchless, divine, what we will,' so to make them no rule for their age, and no infringement of the abstract claim to superiority which we set up. Instead of letting them reflect any lustre, or add any credit to the period of history to which they rightfully belong, we only make use of their example to insult and degrade it still more beneath our own level.

It is the present fashion to speak with veneration of old English literature; but the homage we pay to it is more akin to the rites of superstition, than the worship of true religion. Our faith is doubtful; our love cold; our knowledge little or none. We now and then repeat the names of some of the old writers by rote; but we are shy of looking into their works. Though we seem disposed to think highly of them, and to give them every credit for a masculine and original vein of thought, as a matter of literary courtesy and enlargement of taste, we are afraid of coming to the proof, as too great a trial of our candour and patience. We regard the enthusiastic admiration of these obsolete authors, or a desire to make proselytes to a belief in their extraordinary merits, as an amiable weakness, a pleasing delusion; and prepare to listen to some favourite passage, that may be referred to in support of this singular taste, with an incredulous smile; and are in no small pain for the result of the hazardous experiment; feeling much the same awkward condescending disposition to patronise these first crude attempts at poetry and lispings of the Muse, as when a fond parent brings forward a bashful child to make a display of its wit or learning. We hope the best, put a good face on the matter, but are sadly afraid the thing cannot answer.—Dr. Johnson said of these writers generally, that 'they were sought after because they were scarce, and would not have been scarce, had they been much esteemed.' His decision is neither true history nor sound criticism. They were esteemed, and they deserved to be so.

One cause that might be pointed out here, as having contributed to the long-continued neglect of our earlier writers, lies in the very nature of our academic institutions, which unavoidably neutralizes a taste for the productions of native genius, estranges the mind from the history of our own literature, and makes it in each successive age like a book sealed. The Greek and Roman classics are a sort of privileged text-books, the standing order of the day, in a University education, and leave little leisure for a competent acquaintance with, or due admiration of, a whole host of able writers of our own, who are suffered to moulder in obscurity on the shelves of our libraries, with a decent reservation of one or two top-names, that are cried up for form's sake, and to save the national character. Thus we keep a few of these always ready in capitals, and strike off the rest, to prevent the tendency to a superfluous population in the republic of letters; in other words, to prevent the writers from becoming more numerous than the readers. The ancients are become effete in this respect, they no longer increase and multiply; or if they have imitators among us, no one is expected to read, and still less to admire them. It is not possible that the learned professors and the reading public should clash in this way, or necessary for them to use any precautions against each other. But it is not the same with the living languages, where there is danger of being overwhelmed by the crowd of competitors; and pedantry has combined with ignorance to cancel their unsatisfied claims.

We affect to wonder at Shakespear, and one or two more of that period, as solitary instances upon record; whereas it is our own dearth of information that makes the waste; for there is no time more populous of intellect, or more prolific of intellectual wealth, than the one we are speaking of. Shakespear did not look upon himself in this light, as a sort of monster of poetical genius, or on his contemporaries as 'less than smallest dwarfs,' when he speaks with true, not false modesty, of himself and them, and of his wayward thoughts, 'desiring this man's art, and that man's scope.' We fancy that there were no such men, that could either add to or take any thing away from him, but such there were. He indeed overlooks and commands the admiration of posterity, but he does it from the *tableland* of the age in which he lived. He towered above his fellows, 'in shape and gesture proudly eminent'; but he was one of a race of giants, the tallest, the strongest, the most graceful, and beautiful of them; but it was a common and a noble brood. He was not something sacred and aloof from the vulgar herd of men, but shook hands with nature and the circumstances of the time, and is distinguished from his immediate contemporaries, not in kind, but in degree and greater variety of excellence. He did not form a class or species by himself, but belonged to a class or species. His age was necessary to him; nor could he have been wrenched from his place in the edifice of which he was so conspicuous a part, without equal injury to himself and it. Mr. Wordsworth says of Milton, 'that his soul was like a star, and dwelt apart.' This cannot be said with any propriety of Shakespear, who certainly moved in a constellation of bright luminaries, and 'drew after him a third part of the heavens.' If we allow, for argument's sake (or for truth's, which is better), that he was in himself equal to all his competitors put together; yet there was more dramatic excellence in that age than in the whole of the period that has elapsed since. If his contemporaries, with their united strength, would hardly make one Shakespear, certain it is that all his successors would not make half a one. With the exception of a single writer, Otway, and of a single play of his (Venice Preserved), there is nobody in tragedy and dramatic poetry (I do not here speak of comedy) to be compared to the great men of the age of Shakespear, and immediately after. They are a mighty phalanx of kindred spirits closing him round, moving in the same orbit, and impelled by the same causes in their whirling and eccentric career. They had the same faults and the same excellences; the same strength and depth and richness, the same truth of character, passion, imagination, thought and language, thrown, heaped, massed together without careful polishing or exact method, but poured out in unconcerned profusion from the lap of nature and genius in boundless and unrivalled magnificence. The sweetness of Deckar, the thought of Marston, the gravity of Chapman, the grace of Fletcher and his young-eyed wit, Jonson's learned sock, the flowing vein of Middleton, Heywood's ease, the pathos of Webster, and Marlow's deep designs, add a double lustre to the sweetness, thought, gravity, grace, wit, artless nature, copiousness, ease, pathos, and sublime conceptions of Shakespear's Muse. They are indeed the scale by which we can best ascend to the true knowledge and love of him. Our admiration of them does not lessen our relish for him: but, on the contrary, increases and confirms it.—For such an extraordinary combination and development of fancy and genius many causes may be assigned; and we may seek for the chief of them in religion, in politics, in the circumstances of the time, the recent diffusion of letters, in local situation, and in the character of the men who adorned that period, and availed themselves so nobly of the advantages placed within their reach.

I shall here attempt to give a general sketch of these causes, and of the manner in which they operated to mould and stamp the poetry of the country at the period of which I have to treat; independently of incidental and fortuitous causes, for which there is no accounting, but which, after all, have often the greatest share in determining the most important results.

The first cause I shall mention, as contributing to this general effect, was the Reformation, which had just then taken place. This event gave a mighty impulse and increased activity to thought and inquiry, and agitated the inert mass of accumulated prejudices throughout Europe. The effect of the concussion was general; but the shock was greatest in this country. It toppled down the full-grown, intolerable abuses of centuries at a blow; heaved the ground from under the feet of bigotted faith and slavish obedience; and the roar and dashing of opinions, loosened from their accustomed hold, might be heard like the noise of an angry sea, and has never yet subsided. Germany first broke the spell of misbegotten fear, and gave the watch-word; but England joined the shout, and echoed it back with her island voice, from her thousand cliffs and craggy shores, in a longer and a louder strain. With that cry, the genius of Great Britain rose, and threw down the gauntlet to the nations. There was a mighty fermentation: the waters were out; public opinion was in a state of projection. Liberty was held out to all to think and speak the truth. Men's brains were busy; their spirits stirring; their hearts full; and their hands not idle. Their eyes were opened to expect the greatest things, and their ears burned with curiosity and zeal to know the truth, that the truth might make them free. The death-blow which had been struck at scarlet vice and bloated hypocrisy, loosened their tongues, and made the talismans and love-tokens of Popish superstition, with which she had beguiled her followers and committed abominations with the people, fall harmless from their necks.

The translation of the Bible was the chief engine in the great work. It threw open, by a secret spring, the rich treasures of religion and morality, which had been there locked up as in a shrine. It revealed the visions of the prophets, and conveyed the lessons of inspired teachers (such they were thought) to the meanest of the people. It gave them a common interest in the common cause. Their hearts burnt within them as they read. It gave a *mind* to the people, by giving them common subjects of thought and feeling. It cemented their union of character and sentiment: it created endless diversity and collision of opinion. They found objects to employ their faculties, and a motive in the magnitude of the consequences attached to them, to exert the utmost eagerness in the pursuit of truth, and the most daring intrepidity in maintaining it. Religious controversy sharpens the understanding by the subtlety and remoteness of the topics it discusses, and braces the will by their infinite importance. We perceive in the history of this period a nervous masculine intellect. No levity, no feebleness, no indifference; or if there were, it is a relaxation from the intense activity which gives a tone to its general character. But there is a gravity approaching to piety; a seriousness of impression, a conscientious severity of argument, an habitual fervour and enthusiasm in their mode of handling almost every subject. The debates of the schoolmen were sharp and subtle enough; but they wanted interest and grandeur, and were besides confined to a few: they did not affect the general mass of the community. But the Bible was thrown open to all ranks and conditions 'to run and read,' with its wonderful table of contents from Genesis to the Revelations. Every village in England would present the scene so well described in Burns's Cotter's Saturday Night. I cannot think that all this variety and weight of knowledge could be thrown in all at once upon the mind of a people, and not make some impressions upon it, the traces of which might be discerned in the manners and literature of the age. For to leave more disputable points, and take only the historical parts of the Old Testament, or the moral sentiments of the New, there is nothing like them in the power of exciting awe and admiration, or of rivetting sympathy. We see what Milton has made of the account of the Creation, from the manner in which he has treated it, imbued and impregnated with the spirit of the time of which we speak. Or what is there equal (in that romantic interest and patriarchal simplicity which goes to the heart of a country, and rouses it, as it were, from its lair in wastes and wildernesses) equal to the story of Joseph and his Brethren, of Rachael and Laban, of Jacob's Dream, of Ruth and Boaz, the descriptions in the book of Job, the deliverance of the Jews out of Egypt, or the account of their captivity and return from Babylon? There is in all these parts of the Scripture, and numberless more of the same kind, to pass over the Orphic hymns of David, the prophetic denunciations of Isaiah, or the gorgeous visions of Ezekiel, an originality, a vastness of conception, a depth and tenderness of feeling, and a touching simplicity in the mode of narration, which he who does not feel, need be made of no 'penetrable stuff.' There is something in the character of Christ too (leaving religious faith quite out of the question) of more sweetness and majesty, and more likely to work a change in the mind of man, by the contemplation of its idea alone, than any to be found in history, whether actual or feigned. This character is that of a sublime humanity, such as was never seen on earth before, nor since. This shone manifestly both in his words and actions. We see it in his washing the Disciples' feet the night before his death, that unspeakable instance of humility and love, above all art, all meanness, and all pride, and in the leave he took of them on that occasion, 'My peace I give unto you, that peace which the world cannot give, give I unto you'; and in his last commandment, that 'they should love one another.' Who can read the account of his behaviour on the cross, when turning to his mother he said, 'Woman, behold thy son,' and to the Disciple John, 'Behold thy mother,' and 'from that hour that Disciple took her to his own home,' without having his heart smote within him! We see it in his treatment of the woman taken in adultery, and in his excuse for the woman who poured precious ointment on his garment as an offering of devotion and love, which is here all in all. His religion was the religion of the heart. We see it in his discourse with the Disciples as they walked together towards Emmaus, when their hearts burned within them; in his sermon from the Mount, in his parable of the good Samaritan, and in that of the Prodigal Son—in every act and word of his life, a grace, a mildness, a dignity and love, a patience and wisdom worthy of the Son of God. His whole life and being were imbued, steeped in this word, *charity;* it was the spring, the well-head from which every thought and feeling gushed into act; and it was this that breathed a mild glory from his face in that last agony upon the cross, 'when the meek Saviour bowed his head and died,' praying for his enemies. He was the first true teacher of morality; for he alone conceived the idea of a pure humanity. He redeemed man from the worship of that idol, self, and instructed him by precept and example to love his neighbour as himself, to forgive our enemies, to do good to those that curse us and despitefully use us. He taught the love of good for the sake of good, without regard to personal or sinister views, and made the affections of the heart the sole seat of morality, instead of the pride of the understanding or the sternness of the will. In answering the question, 'who is our neighbour?' as one who stands in need of our assistance, and whose wounds we can bind up, he has done more to humanize the thoughts and tame the unruly passions, than all who have tried to reform and benefit mankind. The very idea of abstract benevolence, of the desire to do good because another wants our services, and of regarding the human race as one family, the offspring of one common parent, is hardly to be found in any other code or system. It was 'to the Jews a stumbling block, and to the Greeks foolishness.' The Greeks and Romans never thought of considering others, but as they were Greeks or Romans, as they were bound to them by certain positive ties, or, on the other hand, as separated from them by fiercer antipathies. Their virtues were the virtues of political machines, their vices were the vices of demons, ready to inflict or to endure pain with obdurate and remorseless inflexibility of purpose. But in the Christian religion, 'we perceive a softness coming over the heart of a nation, and the iron scales that fence and harden it, melt and drop off.' It becomes malleable, capable of pity, of forgiveness, of relaxing in its claims, and remitting its power. We strike it, and it does not hurt us: it is not steel or marble, but flesh and blood, clay tempered with tears, and 'soft as sinews of the new-born babe.' The gospel was first preached to the poor, for it consulted their wants and interests, not its own pride and arrogance. It first promulgated the equality of mankind in the community of duties and benefits. It denounced the iniquities of the chief Priests and Pharisees, and declared itself at variance with principalities and powers, for it sympathizes not with the oppressor, but the oppressed. It first abolished slavery, for it did not consider the power of the will to inflict injury, as clothing it with a right to do so. Its law is good, not power. It at the same time tended to wean the mind from the grossness of sense, and a particle of its divine flame was lent to brighten and purify the lamp of love!

There have been persons who, being sceptics as to the divine mission of Christ, have taken an unaccountable prejudice to his doctrines, and have been disposed to deny the merit of his character; but this was not the feeling of the great men in the age of Elizabeth (whatever might be their belief) one of whom says of him, with a boldness equal to its piety:

> The best of men
> That e'er wore earth about him, was a sufferer;
> A soft, meek, patient, humble, tranquil spirit;
> The first true gentleman that ever breathed.

This was old honest Deckar, and the lines ought to embalm his memory to every one who has a sense either of religion, or philosophy, or humanity, or true genius. Nor can I help thinking, that we may discern the traces of the influence exerted by religious faith in the spirit of the poetry of the age of Elizabeth, in the means of exciting terror and pity, in the delineation of the passions of grief, remorse, love, sympathy, the sense of shame, in the fond desires, the longings after immortality, in the heaven of hope, and the abyss of despair it lays open to us.

The literature of this age then, I would say, was strongly influenced (among other causes), first by the spirit of Christianity, and secondly by the spirit of Protestantism.

The effects of the Reformation on politics and philosophy may be seen in the writings and history of the next and of the following ages. They are still at work, and will continue to be so. The effects on the poetry of the time were chiefly confined to the moulding of the character, and giving a powerful impulse to the intellect of the country. The immediate use or application that was made of religion to subjects of imagination and fiction was not (from an obvious ground of separation) so direct or frequent, as that which was made of the classical and romantic literature.

For much about the same time, the rich and fascinating stores of the Greek and Roman mythology, and those of the romantic poetry of Spain and Italy, were eagerly explored by the curious, and thrown open in translations to the admiring gaze of the vulgar. This last circumstance could hardly have afforded so much advantage to the poets of that day, who were themselves, in fact, the translators, as it shews the general curiosity and increasing interest in such subjects, as a prevailing feature of the times. There were translations of Tasso by Fairfax, and of Ariosto by Harrington, of Homer and Hesiod by Chapman, and of Virgil long before, and Ovid soon after; there was Sir Thomas North's translation of Plutarch, of which Shakespear has made such admirable use in his Coriolanus and Julius Cæsar: and Ben Jonson's tragedies of Catiline and Sejanus may themselves be considered as almost literal translations into verse, of Tacitus, Sallust, and Cicero's Orations in his consulship. Boccacio, the divine Boccacio, Petrarch, Dante, the satirist Aretine, Machiavel, Castiglione, and others, were familiar to our writers, and they make occasional mention of some few French authors, as Ronsard and Du Bartas; for the French literature had not at this stage arrived at its Augustan period, and it was the imitation of their literature a century afterwards, when it had arrived at its greatest height (itself copied from the Greek and Latin), that enfeebled and impoverished our own. But of the time that we are considering, it might be said, without much extravagance, that every breath that blew, that every wave that rolled to our shores, brought with it some accession to our knowledge, which was engrafted on the national genius. In fact, all the disposeable materials that had been accumulating for a long period of time, either in our own, or in foreign countries, were now brought together, and required nothing more than to be wrought up, polished, or arranged in striking forms, for ornament and use. To this every inducement prompted, the novelty of the acquisition of knowledge in many cases, the emulation of foreign wits, and of immortal works, the want and the expectation of such works among ourselves, the opportunity and encouragement afforded for their production by leisure and affluence; and, above all, the insatiable desire of the mind beget its own image, and to construct out of itself, and for the delight and admiration of the world and posterity, that excellence of which the idea exists hitherto only in its own breast, and the impression of which it would make as universal as the eye of heaven, the benefit as common as the air we breathe. The first impulse of genius is to create what never existed before: the contemplation of that, which is so created, is sufficient to satisfy the demands of taste; and it is the habitual study and imitation of the original models that takes away the power, and even wish to do the like. Taste limps after genius, and from copying the artificial models, we lose sight of the living principle of nature. It is the effort we make, and the impulse we acquire, in overcoming the first obstacles, that projects us forward; it is the necessity for exertion that makes us conscious of our strength; but this necessity and this impulse once removed, the tide of fancy and enthusiasm, which is at first a running stream, soon settles and crusts into the standing pool of dulness, criticism, and *virtù*.

What also gave an unusual *impetus* to the mind of man at this period, was the discovery of the New World, and the reading of voyages and travels. Green islands and golden sands seemed to arise, as by enchantment, out of the bosom of the watery waste, and invite the cupidity, or wing the imagination of the dreaming speculator. Fairy land was realised in new and unknown worlds. 'Fortunate fields and groves and flowery vales, thrice happy isles,' were found floating 'like those Hesperian gardens famed of old,' beyond Atlantic seas, as dropt from the zenith. The people, the soil, the clime, everything gave unlimited scope to the curiosity of the traveller and reader. Other manners might be said to enlarge the bounds of knowledge, and new mines of wealth were tumbled at our feet. It is from a voyage to the Straits of Magellan that Shakespear has taken the hint of Prospero's Enchanted Island, and of the savage Caliban with his god Setebos. Spenser seems to have had the same feeling in his mind in the production of his Faery Queen, and vindicates his poetic fiction on this very ground of analogy.

> Right well I wote, most might sovereign,
> That all this famous antique history
> Of some the abundance of an idle brain
> Will judged be, and painted forgery,
> Rather than matter of just memory:
> Since none that breatheth living air, doth know
> Where is that happy land of faery
> Which I so much do vaunt, but no where show,
> But vouch antiquities, which nobody can know.
>
> But let that man with better sense avise,
> That of the world least part to us is read:
> And daily how through hardy enterprize
> Many great regions are discovered,
> Which to late age were never mentioned.
> Who ever heard of th' Indian Peru?
> Or who in venturous vessel measured
> The Amazons' huge river, now found true?
> Or fruitfullest Virginia who did ever view?
>
> Yet all these were when no man did them know,
> Yet have from wisest ages hidden been:
> And later times things more unknown shall show.
> Why then should witless man so much misween
> That nothing is but that which he hath seen?
> What if within the moon's fair shining sphere,
> What if in every other star unseen,
> Of other worlds he happily should hear,
> He wonder would much more; yet such to some appear.

Fancy's air-drawn pictures after history's waking dream shewed like clouds over mountains; and from the romance of real life to the idlest fiction, the transition seemed easy.—Shakespear, as well as others of his time, availed himself of the old Chronicles, and of the traditions or fabulous inventions contained in them in such ample measure, and which had not yet been appropriated to the purposes of poetry or the drama. The stage was a new thing; and those who had to supply its demands laid their hands upon whatever came within their reach: they were not particular as to the means, so that they gained the end. Lear is founded upon an old ballad; Othello on an Italian novel; Hamlet on a Danish, and Macbeth on a Scotch tradition: one of which is to be found in Saxo-Grammaticus, and the last in Hollingshed. The Ghost-scenes and the Witches in each, are authenticated in the old Gothic history. There was also this connecting link between the poetry of this age and the supernatural traditions of a former one, that the belief in them was still extant, and in full force and visible operation among the vulgar (to say no more) in the time of our authors. The appalling and wild chimeras of superstition and ignorance, 'those bodiless creations that ecstacy is very cunning in,' were inwoven with existing manners and opinions, and all their effects on the passions of terror or pity might be gathered from common and actual observation—might be discerned in the workings of the face, the expressions of the tongue, the writhings of a troubled conscience. 'Your face, my Thane, is as a book where men may read strange matters.' Midnight and secret murders too, from the imperfect state of the police, were more common; and the ferocious and brutal manners that would stamp the brow of the hardened ruffian or hired assassin, more incorrigible and undisguised. The portraits of Tyrrel and Forrest were, no doubt, done from the life. We find that the ravages of the plague, the destructive rage of fire, the poisoned chalice, lean famine, the serpent's mortal sting, and the fury of wild beasts, were the common topics of their poetry, as they were common occurrences in more remote periods of history. They were the strong ingredients thrown into the cauldron of tragedy, to make it 'thick and slab.' Man's life was (as it appears to me) more full of traps and pit-falls; of hair-breadth accidents by flood and field; more way-laid by sudden and startling evils; it trod on the brink of hope and fear; stumbled upon fate unawares; while the imagination, close behind it, caught at and clung to the shape of danger, or 'snatched a wild and fearful joy' from its escape. The accidents of nature were less provided against; the excesses of the passions and of lawless power were less regulated, and produced more strange and desperate catastrophes. The tales of Boccacio are founded on the great pestilence of Florence, Fletcher the poet died of the plague, and Marlow was stabbed in a tavern quarrel. The strict authority of parents, the inequality of ranks, or the hereditary feuds between different families, made more unhappy loves or matches.

> The course of true love never did run even.

Again, the heroic and martial spirit which breathes in our elder writers, was yet in considerable activity in the reign of Elizabeth. 'The age of chivalry was not then quite gone, nor the glory of Europe extinguished for ever.' Jousts and tournaments were still common with the nobility in England and in foreign countries: Sir Philip Sidney was particularly distinguished for his proficiency in these exercises (and indeed fell a martyr to his ambition as a soldier)—and the gentle Surrey was still more famous, on the same account, just before him. It is true, the general use of firearms gradually superseded the necessity of skill in the sword, or bravery in the person: and as a symptom of the rapid degeneracy in this respect, we find Sir John Suckling soon after boasting of himself as one—

> Who prized black eyes, and a lucky hit
> At bowls, above all the trophies of wit.

It was comparatively an age of peace,

> Like strength reposing on his own right arm;

but the sound of civil combat might still be heard in the distance, the spear glittered to the eye of memory, or the clashing of armour struck on the imagination of the ardent and the young. They were borderers on the savage state, on the times of war and bigotry, though in the lap of arts, of luxury, and knowledge. They stood on the shore and saw the billows rolling after the storm: 'they heard the tumult, and were still.' The manners and out-of-door amusements were more tinctured with a spirit of adventure and romance. The war with wild beasts, &c. was more strenuously kept up in country sports. I do not think we could get from sedentary poets, who had never mingled in the vicissitudes, the dangers, or excitements of the chase, such descriptions of hunting and other athletic games, as are to be found in Shakespear's Midsummer Night's Dream, or Fletcher's Noble Kinsmen.

With respect to the good cheer and hospitable living of those times, I cannot agree with an ingenious and agreeable writer of the present day, that it was general or frequent. The very stress laid upon certain holidays and festivals, shews that they did not keep up the same Saturnalian licence and open house all the year round. They reserved themselves for great occasions, and made the best amends they could, for a year of abstinence and toil by a week of merriment and convivial indulgence. Persons in middle life at this day, who can afford a good dinner every day, do not look forward to it as any particular subject of exultation: the poor peasant, who can only contrive to treat himself to a joint of meat on a Sunday, considers it as an event in the week. So, in the old Cambridge comedy of the Returne from Parnassus, we find this indignant description of the progress of luxury in those days, put into the mouth of one of the speakers.

> Why is 't not strange to see a ragged clerke,
> Some stammell weaver, or some butcher's sonne,
> That scrubb'd a late within a sleeveless gowne,
> When the commencement, like a morrice dance,
> Hath put a bell or two about his legges,
> Created him a sweet cleane gentleman:
> How then he 'gins to follow fashions.
> He whose thin sire dwelt in a smokye roofe,
> Must take tobacco, and must wear a locke.
> His thirsty dad drinkes in a wooden bowle,
> But his sweet self is served in silver plate.
> His hungry sire will scrape you twenty legges

For one good Christmas meal on new year's day,
But his mawe must be capon cramm'd each day.
Act III. Scene 2.

This does not look as if in those days 'it snowed of meat and drink' as a
matter of course throughout the year!—The distinctions of dress, the badges of
different professions, the very signs of the shops, which we have set aside for
written inscriptions over the doors, were, as Mr. Lamb observes, a sort of
visible language to the imagination, and hints for thought. Like the costume of
different foreign nations, they had an immediate striking and picturesque
effect, giving scope to the fancy. The surface of society was embossed with
hieroglyphics, and poetry existed 'in act and complement extern.' The poetry
of former times might be directly taken from real life, as our poetry is taken
from the poetry of former times. Finally, the face of nature, which was the
same glorious object then that it is now, was open to them; and coming first,
they gathered her fairest flowers to live for ever in their verse:—the movements of the human heart were not hid from them, for they had the same
passions as we, only less disguised, and less subject to controul. Deckar has
given an admirable description of a mad-house in one of his plays. But it might
be perhaps objected, that it was only a literal account taken from Bedlam at
that time: and it might be answered, that the old poets took the same method
of describing the passions and fancies of men whom they met at large, which
forms the point of communion between us: for the title of the old play, 'A Mad
World, my Masters,' is hardly yet obsolete; and we are pretty much the same
Bedlam still, perhaps a little better managed, like the real one, and with more
care and humanity shewn to the patients!

Lastly, to conclude this account; what gave a unity and common direction
to all these causes, was the natural genius of the country, which was strong in
these writers in proportion to their strength. We are a nation of islanders, and
we cannot help it; nor mend ourselves if we would. We are something in
ourselves, nothing when we try to ape others. Music and painting are not our
forte: for what we have done in that way has been little, and that borrowed
from others with great difficulty. But we may boast of our poets and
philosophers. That's something. We have had strong heads and sound hearts
among us. Thrown on one side of the world, and left to bustle for ourselves, we
have fought out many a battle for truth and freedom. That is our natural style;
and it were to be wished we had in no instance departed from it. Our situation
has given us a certain cast of thought and character; and our liberty has
enabled us to make the most of it. We are of a stiff clay, not moulded into every
fashion, with stubborn joints not easily bent. We are slow to think, and
therefore impressions do not work upon us till they act in masses. We are not
forward to express our feelings, and therefore they do not come from us till
they force their way in the most impetuous eloquence. Our language is, as it
were, to begin anew, and we make use of the most singular and boldest
combinations to explain ourselves. Our wit comes from us, 'like birdlime,
brains and all.' We pay too little attention to form and method, leave our works

in an unfinished state, but still the materials we work in are solid and of nature's mint; we do not deal in counterfeits. We both under and over-do, but we keep an eye to the prominent features, the main chance. We are more for weight than show; care only about what interests ourselves, instead of trying to impose upon others by plausible appearances, and are obstinate and intractable in not conforming to common rules, by which many arrive at their ends with half the real waste of thought and trouble. We neglect all but the principal object, gather our force to make a great blow, bring it down, and relapse into sluggishness and indifference again. *Materiam superabat opus*, cannot be said of us. We may be accused of grossness, but not of flimsiness; of extravagance, but not of affectation; of want of art and refinement, but not of a want of truth and nature. Our literature, in a word, is Gothic and grotesque; unequal and irregular; not cast in a previous mould, nor of one uniform texture, but of great weight in the whole, and of incomparable value in the best parts. It aims at an excess of beauty or power, hits or misses, and is either very good indeed, or absolutely good for nothing. This character applies in particular to our literature in the age of Elizabeth, which is its best period, before the introduction of a rage for French rules and French models; for whatever may be the value of our own original style of composition, there can be neither offence nor presumption in saying, that it is at least better than our second-hand imitations of others. Our understanding (such as it is, and must remain to be good for any thing) is not a thoroughfare for common places, smooth as the palm of one's hand, but full of knotty points and jutting excrescences, rough, uneven, overgrown with brambles; and I like this aspect of the mind (as some one said of the country), where nature keeps a good deal of the soil in her own hands. Perhaps the genius of our poetry has more of Pan than of Apollo; 'but Pan is a God, Apollo is no more!'

Charles Lamb

1775–1834

Charles Lamb was born in London in 1775, the son of a scrivener. He was educated at Christ's Hospital, where he was a near contemporary of Coleridge and Leigh Hunt. A good student, he read widely and was well liked, but a speech impediment seems to have kept him from pursuing further education at Cambridge and a Church career. He left school at fifteen and took a post as a government clerk, a position that was to become his lifelong occupation.

During his adolescence, Lamb appears to have suffered from an episode of insanity, and although he never had a recurrence of mental illness, he was burdened throughout his life by a fear of madness. His concern was heightened by the fragile mental state of his sister Mary, who had killed their mother during a similar attack in 1796. Henceforth, Charles took Mary under his protection and cared for her for the rest of his life.

Lamb's first notable writing consisted of letters to his friends, beginning with a correspondence he carried on with Coleridge in the 1790s. Perhaps to alleviate the daily drudgery of his job, he soon drew about him a wide circle of friends with whom he corresponded regularly, among them Godwin, Hazlitt, Hood, and the Wordsworths. His letters are highly idiosyncratic, revealing his personal tastes, his habits, the opinions of his friends, and, pre-eminently, his responses to books of all sorts.

Lamb also began writing poems, which were collected by Coleridge and others, and published an Elizabethan-style verse tragedy, *John Woodvil* (1802). In 1807 Lamb and his sister published their *Tales from Shakespeare,* a re-telling for children of some of the plays; it enjoyed wide popularity. The following year he published a selection of what he called "specimens" of Elizabethan dramatists, which brought the work of Shakespeare's lesser-known contemporaries to wide public attention.

Lamb wrote little in the way of formal criticism, and his literary essays display his personal preferences more than any carefully-formulated theory. In "On the Tragedies of Shakespeare," for example, Lamb displays a greater interest in the characters from Shakespeare's dramas than in the plays themselves; he often said that he preferred reading the plays to seeing them enacted. "On the Artificial Comedy of the Last Century" gently rebukes the moralizing critics of the day. Lamb also wrote noteworthy essays on Blake and Hogarth, and in a review of Wordsworth's *Excursion* speaks favorably of his friend's achievement at a time when Wordsworth was receiving little critical support. Lamb's literary tastes are reflected in his letters, in which he speaks with admiration of seventeenth-century poets and prose writers and eighteenth-century novelists. Above all, he enjoyed that writing which depicted life realistically, and voiced his distaste for masques and pastorals.

Beginning in 1820, Lamb became a regular contributor to the newly-founded *London Magazine*, publishing essays under the pseudonym of "Elia." His pieces in the magazine are subjective and discursive, and present his experiences and reflections in a somewhat archaic literary style that echoes seventeenth-century writers such as Browne and Burton. In his later years, the quality of his writing declined somewhat, as did that of the *London Magazine*. Following his retirement from government service in 1825, Lamb moved with his ailing sister to Edmonton, where he died on December 17, 1834.

THE ARTIFICIAL COMEDY
OF THE LAST CENTURY

The artificial Comedy, or Comedy of manners, is quite extinct on our stage. Congreve and Farquhar show their heads once in seven years only, to be exploded and put down instantly. The times cannot bear them. Is it for a few wild speeches, an occasional licence of dialogue? I think not altogether. The business of their dramatic characters will not stand the moral test. We screw everything up to that. Idle gallantry in a fiction, a dream, the passing pageant of an evening, startles us in the same way as the alarming indications of profligacy in a son or ward in real life should startle a parent or guardian. We have no such middle emotions as dramatic interests left. We see a stage libertine playing his loose pranks of two hours' duration, and of no after consequence, with the severe eyes which inspect real vices with their bearings upon two worlds. We are spectators to a plot or intrigue (not reducible in life to the point of strict morality), and take it all for truth. We substitute a real for a dramatic person, and judge him accordingly. We try him in our courts, from which there is no appeal to the *dramatis personæ*, his peers. We have been spoiled with—not sentimental comedy—but a tyrant far more pernicious to our pleasures which has succeeded to it, the exclusive and all-devouring drama of common life; where the moral point is every thing; where, instead of the fictitious half-believed personages of the stage (the phantoms of old comedy), we recognise ourselves, our brothers, aunts, kinsfolk, allies, patrons, enemies,—the same as in life,—with an interest in what is going on so hearty and substantial, that we cannot afford our moral judgment, in its deepest and most vital results, to compromise or slumber for a moment. What is *there* transacting, by no modification is made to affect us in any other manner than the same events or characters would do in our relationships of life. We carry our fire-side concerns to the theatre with us. We do not go thither, like our ancestors, to escape from the pressure of reality, so much as to confirm our experience of it; to make assurance double, and take a bond of fate. We must live our toilsome lives twice over, as it was the mournful privilege of Ulysses to descend twice to the shades. All that neutral ground of character, which stood between vice and virtue; or which in fact was indifferent to neither, where neither properly was called in question; that happy breathing-place from the burthen of a perpetual moral questioning—the sanctuary and quiet Alsatia of hunted casuistry—is broken up and disfranchised, as injurious to the interests of society. The privileges of the place are taken away by law. We dare not dally with images, or names, of wrong. We bark like foolish dogs at shadows. We dread infection from the scenic representation of disorder, and fear a painted pustule. In our anxiety that our morality should not take cold, we wrap it up in a great blanket surtout of precaution against the breeze and sunshine.

I confess for myself that (with no great delinquencies to answer for) I am glad for a season to take an airing beyond the diocese of the strict conscience,—not to live always in the precincts of the law-courts,—but now and then, for a dream-while or so, to imagine a world with no meddling restrictions—to get into recesses, whither the hunter cannot follow me—

> Secret shades
> Of woody Ida's inmost grove,
> While yet there was no fear of Jove.

I come back to my cage and my restraint the fresher and more healthy for it. I wear my shackles more contentedly for having respired the breath of an imaginary freedom. I do not know how it is with others, but I feel the better always for the perusal of one of Congreve's—nay, why should I not add even of Wycherley's—comedies. I am the gayer at least for it; and I could never connect those sports of a witty fancy in any shape with any result to be drawn from them to imitation in real life. They are a world of themselves almost as much as fairy-land. Take one of their characters, male or female (with few exceptions they are alike), and place it in a modern play, and my virtuous indignation shall rise against the profligate wretch as warmly as the Catos of the pit could desire; because in a modern play I am to judge of the right and the wrong. The standard of *police* is the measure of *political justice*. The atmosphere will blight it, it cannot live here. It has got into a moral world, where it has no business, from which it must needs fall headlong; as dizzy, and incapable of making a stand, as a Swedenborgian bad spirit that has wandered unawares into the sphere of one of his Good Men, or Angels. But in its own world do we feel the creature is so very bad? The Fainalls and the Mirabels, the Dorimants and the Lady Touchwoods, in their own sphere, do not offend my moral sense; in fact they do not appeal to it at all. They seem engaged in their proper element. They break through no laws, or conscientious restraints. They know of none. They have got out of Christendom into the land—what shall I call it?—of cuckoldry—the Utopia of gallantry, where pleasure is duty, and the manners perfect freedom. It is altogether a speculative scene of things, which has no reference whatever to the world that is. No good person can be justly offended as a spectator, because no good person suffers on the stage. Judged morally, every character in these plays—the few exceptions only are *mistakes*—is alike essentially vain and worthless. The great art of Congreve is especially shown in this, that he has entirely excluded from his scenes,—some little generosities in the part of Angelica perhaps excepted,—not only anything like a faultless character, but any pretensions to goodness or good feelings whatsoever. Whether he did this designedly, or instinctively, the effect is as happy, as the design (if design) was bold. I used to wonder at the strange power which his Way of the World in particular possesses of interesting you all along in the pursuits of characters, for whom you absolutely care nothing—for you neither hate nor love his personages—and I think it is owing to this very indifference for any, that you endure the whole. He has spread a privation of moral light, I will call it, rather than by the ugly name of palpable darkness, over his creations; and his shadows flit before you without distinction or preference. Had he introduced a good character, a single gush of moral feeling, a revulsion of the judgment to actual life and actual duties, the impertinent Goshen would have only lighted to the discovery of deformities, which now are none, because we think them none.

Translated into real life, the characters of his, and his friend Wycherley's dramas, are profligates and strumpets,—the business of their brief existence, the undivided pursuit of lawless gallantry. No other spring of action, or possible motive of conduct, is recognised; principles which, universally acted upon, must reduce this frame of things to a chaos. But we do them wrong in so translating them. No such effects are produced in *their* world. When we are among them, we are amongst a chaotic people. We are not to judge them by our usages. No reverend institutions are insulted by their proceedings—for they have none among them. No peace of families is violated—for no family ties exist among them. No purity of the marriage bed is stained—for none is supposed to have a being. No deep affections are disquieted, no holy wedlock bands are snapped asunder—for affection's depth and wedded faith are not of the growth of that soil. There is neither right nor wrong,—gratitude or its opposite,—claim or duty,—paternity or sonship. Of what consequence is it to Virtue, or how is she at all concerned about it, whether Sir Simon, or Dapperwit, steal away Miss Martha; or who is the father of Lord Froth's or Sir Paul Pliant's children?

The whole is a passing pageant, where we should sit as unconcerned at the issues, for life or death, as at a battle of the frogs and mice. But, like Don Quixote, we take part against the puppets, and quite as impertinently. We dare not contemplate an Atlantis, a scheme, out of which our coxcomical moral sense is for a little transitory ease excluded. We have not the courage to imagine a state of things for which there is neither reward nor punishment. We cling to the painful necessities of shame and blame. We would indict our very dreams.

Amidst the mortifying circumstances attendant upon growing old, it is something to have seen the School for Scandal in its glory. This comedy grew out of Congreve and Wycherley, but gathered some allays of the sentimental comedy which followed theirs. It is impossible that it should be now *acted*, though it continues, at long intervals, to be announced in the bills. Its hero, when Palmer played it at least, was Joseph Surface. When I remember the gay boldness, the graceful solemn plausibility, the measured step, the insinuating voice—to express it in a word—the downright *acted* villany of the part, so different from the pressure of conscious actual wickedness,—the hypocritical assumption of hypocrisy,—which made Jack so deservedly a favourite in that character, I must needs conclude the present generation of playgoers more virtuous than myself, or more dense. I freely confess that he divided the palm with me with his better brother; that, in fact, I liked him quite as well. Not but there are passages,—like that, for instance, where Joseph is made to refuse a pittance to a poor relation,—incongruities which Sheridan was forced upon by the attempt to join the artificial with the sentimental comedy, either of which must destroy the other—but over these obstructions Jack's manner floated him so lightly, that a refusal from him no more shocked you, than the easy compliance of Charles gave you in reality any pleasure; you got over the paltry question as quickly as you could, to get back into the regions of pure comedy, where no cold moral reigns. The highly artificial manner of Palmer in this character counteracted every disagreeable impression which you might have received from the contrast, supposing them real, between the two brothers. You did not believe in Joseph with the same faith with which you believed in Charles. The latter was a pleasant reality, the former a no less pleasant poetical foil to it. The comedy, I have said, is incongruous; a mixture of Congreve with sentimental incompatibilities: the gaiety upon the whole is buoyant; but it required the consummate art of Palmer to reconcile the discordant elements.

A player with Jack's talents, if we had one now, would not dare to do the part in the same manner. He would instinctively avoid every turn which might tend to unrealise, and so to make the character fascinating. He must take his cue from his spectators, who would expect a bad man and a good man as rigidly opposed to each other as the death-beds of those geniuses are contrasted in the prints, which I am sorry to say have disappeared from the windows of my old friend Carrington Bowles, of St. Paul's Church-yard memory—(an exhibition as venerable as the adjacent cathedral, and almost coeval) of the bad and good man at the hour of death; where the ghastly apprehensions of the former,—and truly the grim phantom with his reality of a toasting-fork is not to be despised,—so finely contrast with the meek complacent kissing of the rod,—taking it in like honey and butter,—with which the latter submits to the scythe of the gentle bleeder, Time, who wields his lancet with the apprehensive finger of a popular young ladies' surgeon. What flesh, like loving grass, would not covet to meet half-way the stroke of such a delicate mower?—John Palmer was twice an actor in this exquisite part. He was playing to you all the while that he was playing upon Sir Peter and his lady. You had the first intimation of a sentiment before it was on his lips. His altered voice was meant to you, and you were to suppose that his fictitious co-flutterers on the stage perceived nothing at all of it. What was it to you if that half reality, the husband, was overreached by the puppetry—or the thin thing (Lady Teazle's reputation) was persuaded it was dying of a plethory? The fortunes of Othello and Desdemona were not concerned in it. Poor Jack has passed from the stage in good time, that he did not live to this our age of seriousness. The pleasant old Teazle *King,* too, is gone in good time. His manner would scarce have passed current in our day. We must love or hate—acquit or condemn—censure or pity—exert our detestable coxcombry of moral judgment upon everything. Joseph Surface, to go down now, must be a downright revolting villain—no compromise—his first appearance must shock and give horror—his specious plausibilities, which the pleasurable faculties of our fathers welcomed with such hearty greetings, knowing that no harm (dramatic harm even) could come, or was meant to come, of them, must inspire a cold and killing aversion. Charles (the real canting person of the scene—for the hypocrisy of Joseph has its ulterior legitimate ends, but his brother's professions of a good heart centre in downright self-satisfaction) must be *loved,* and Joseph *hated.* To balance one disagreeable reality with another, Sir Peter Teazle must be no longer the comic idea of a fretful old bachelor bridegroom, whose teasings (while King acted it) were evidently as much played off at you, as they were meant to concern anybody on the stage,— he must be a real person, capable in law of sustaining an injury—a person towards whom duties are to be acknowledged—the genuine crim.con.antagon- ist of the villanous seducer Joseph. To realise him more, his sufferings under his unfortunate match must have the downright pungency of life—must (or should) make you not mirthful but uncomfortable, just as the same predica- ment would move you in a neighbour or old friend. The delicious scenes which give the play its name and zest, must affect you in the same serious manner as if you heard the reputation of a dear female friend attacked in your real presence. Crabtree and Sir Benjamin—those poor snakes that live but in the sunshine of your mirth—must be ripened by this hot-bed process of realization into asps or amphisbænas; and Mrs. Candour—O! frightful!—become a hooded serpent. Oh! who that remembers Parsons and Dodd—the wasp and butterfly of the School for Scandal—in those two characters; and charming natural Miss Pope, the perfect gentlewoman as distinguished from the fine lady of comedy, in this latter part—would forego the true scenic delight—the escape from life—the oblivion of consequences—the holiday barring out of the pedant Reflection—those Saturnalia of two or three brief hours, well won from the world—to sit instead at one of our modern plays—to have his coward conscience (that forsooth must not be left for a moment) stimulated with perpetual appeals—dulled rather, and blunted, as a faculty without repose must be—and his moral vanity pampered with images of notional justice, notional beneficence, lives saved without the spectators' risk, and fortunes given away that cost the author nothing?

No piece was, perhaps, ever so completely cast in all its parts as this *manager's comedy.* Miss Farren had succeeded to Mrs. Abington in Lady Teazle; and Smith, the original Charles, had retired when I first saw it. The rest of the characters, with very slight exceptions, remained. I remember it was then the fashion to cry down John Kemble, who took the part of Charles after Smith; but, I thought very unjustly. Smith, I fancy was more airy, and took the eye with a certain gaiety of person. He brought with him no sombre recollections of tragedy. He had not to expiate the fault of having pleased beforehand in lofty declamation. He had no sins of Hamlet or of Richard to atone for. His failure in these parts was a passport to success in one of so opposite a tendency. But, as far as I could judge, the weighty sense of Kemble made up for more personal incapacity than he had to answer for. His harshest tones in this part came steeped and dulcified in good-humour. He made his defects a grace. His exact declamatory manner, as he managed it, only served to convey the points of his dialogue with more precision. It seemed to head the shafts to carry them deeper. Not one of his sparkling sentences was lost. I remember minutely how he delivered each in succession, and cannot by any effort imagine how any of them could be altered for the better. No man could deliver brilliant dialogue—the dialogue of Congreve or of Wycherley—because none understood it—half so well as John Kemble. His Valentine, in Love for Love, was, to my recollection, faultless. He flagged sometimes in the intervals of tragic passion. He would slumber over the level parts of an heroic character. His Macbeth has been known to nod. But he always seemed to me to be particularly alive to pointed and witty dialogue. The relaxing levities of tragedy have not been touched by any since him—the playful court-bred spirit in which he condescended to the players in Hamlet—the sportive relief which he threw into the darker shades of Richard—disappeared with him. He had his sluggish moods, his torpors—but they were the halting-stones and resting-place of his tragedy—politic savings, and fetches of the breath—husbandry of the lungs, where nature pointed him to be an economist—rather, I think, than errors of the judgment. They were, at worst, less painful than the eternal tormenting unappeasable vigilance,—the "lidless dragon eyes," of present fashionable tragedy.

Detached Thoughts
On Books and Reading

> To mind the inside of a book is to entertain one's self with the forced
> product of another man's brain. Now I think a man of quality and
> breeding may be much amused with the natural sprouts of his own.
>
> Lord Foppington, in the *Relapse*.

An ingenious acquaintance of my own was so much struck with this bright
sally of his Lordship, that he has left off reading altogether, to the great
improvement of his originality. At the hazard of losing some credit on this
head, I must confess that I dedicate no inconsiderable portion of my time to
other people's thoughts. I dream away my life in others' speculations. I love to
lose myself in other men's minds. When I am not walking, I am reading; I
cannot sit and think. Books think for me.

I have no repugnances. Shaftesbury is not too genteel for me, nor
Jonathan Wild too low. I can read any thing which I call *a book*. There are
things in that shape which I cannot allow for such.

In this catalogue of *books which are no books—biblia a-biblia*—I reckon
Court Calendars, Directories, Pocket-Books, Draught Boards, bound and
lettered on the back, Scientific Treatises, Almanacks, Statutes at Large: the
works of Hume, Gibbon, Robertson, Beattie, Soame Jenyns, and generally, all
those volumes which "no gentleman's library should be without:" the Histories
of Flavius Josephus (that learned Jew), and Paley's Moral Philosophy. With
these exceptions, I can read almost any thing. I bless my stars for a taste so
catholic, so unexcluding.

I confess that it moves my spleen to see these *things in books' clothing*
perched upon shelves, like false saints, usurpers of true shrines, intruders into
the sanctuary, thrusting out the legitimate occupants. To reach down a
well-bound semblance of a volume, and hope it some kind-hearted play-book,
then, opening what "seem its leaves," to come bolt upon a withering Population Essay. To expect a Steele, or a Farquhar, and find—Adam Smith. To view
a well-arranged assortment of blockheaded Encyclopædias (Anglicanas or
Metropolitanas) set out in an array of russia, or morocco, when a tithe of that
good leather would comfortably re-clothe my shivering folios; would renovate
Paracelsus himself, and enable old Raymund Lully to look like himself again in
the world. I never see these impostors, but I long to strip them, to warm my
ragged veterans in their spoils.

To be strong-backed and neat-bound is the desideratum of a volume.
Magnificence comes after. This, when it can be afforded, is not to be lavished
upon all kinds of books indiscriminately. I would not dress a set of Magazines,
for instance, in full suit. The dishabille, or half-binding (with russia backs
ever) is *our* costume. A Shakspeare, or a Milton (unless the first editions), it
were mere foppery to trick out in gay apparel. The possession of them confers

no distinction. The exterior of them (the things themselves being so common), strange to say, raises no sweet emotions, no tickling sense of property in the owner. Thomson's Seasons, again, looks best (I maintain it) a little torn, and dog's-eared. How beautiful to a genuine lover of reading are the sullied leaves, and worn-out appearance, nay the very odour (beyond russia), if we would not forget kind feelings in fastidiousness, of an old "Circulating Library" Tom Jones, or Vicar of Wakefield! How they speak of the thousand thumbs that have turned over their pages with delight!—of the lone sempstress, whom they may have cheered (milliner, or harder-working mantua-maker) after her long day's needle-toil, running far into midnight, when she has snatched an hour, ill spared from sleep, to steep her cares, as in some Lethean cup, in spelling out their enchanting contents! Who would have them a whit less soiled? What better condition could we desire to see them in?

In some respects the better a book is, the less it demands from binding. Fielding, Smollett, Sterne, and all that class of perpetually self-reproductive volumes—Great Nature's Stereotypes—we see them individually perish with less regret, because we know the copies of them to be "eterne." But where a book is at once both good and rare—where the individual is almost the species, and when *that* perishes,

> We know not where is that Promethean torch
> That can its light relumine—

such a book, for instance, as the Life of the Duke of Newcastle, by his Duchess—no casket is rich enough, no casing sufficiently durable, to honour and keep safe such a jewel.

Not only rare volumes of this description, which seem hopeless ever to be reprinted; but old editions of writers, such as Sir Philip Sydney, Bishop Taylor, Milton in his proseworks, Fuller—of whom we *have* reprints, yet the books themselves, though they go about, and are talked of here and there, we know, have not endenizened themselves (nor possibly ever will) in the national heart, so as to become stock books—it is good to possess these in durable and costly covers. I do not care for a First Folio of Shakspeare. I rather prefer the common editions of Rowe and Tonson, without notes, and with *plates*, which, being so execrably bad, serve as maps, or modest remembrancers, to the text; and without pretending to any supposable emulation with it, are so much better than the Shakspeare gallery *engravings*, which *did*. I have a community of feeling with my countrymen about his Plays, and I like those editions of him best, which have been oftenest tumbled about and handled.—On the contrary, I cannot read Beaumont and Fletcher but in Folio. The Octavo editions are painful to look at. I have no sympathy with them. If they were as much read as the current editions of the other poet, I should prefer them in that shape to the older one. I do not know a more heartless sight than the reprint of the Anatomy of Melancholy. What need was there of unearthing the bones of that fantastic old great man, to expose them in a winding-sheet of the newest fashion to modern censure? what hapless stationer could dream of Burton ever becoming popular?—The wretched Malone could not do worse, when he bribed the sexton of Stratford church to let him whitewash the painted effigy of old Shakspeare, which stood there, in rude but lively fashion depicted, to the very colour of the cheek, the eye, the eyebrow, hair, thc vcry dress he used to wear—the only authentic testimony we had, however imperfect, of these curious parts and parcels of him. They covered him over with a coat of white paint. By ——, if I had been a justice of peace for Warwickshire, I would have clapt both commentator and sexton fast in the stocks, for a pair of meddling sacrilegious varlets.

I think I see them at their work—these sapient trouble-tombs.

Shall I be thought fantastical, if I confess, that the names of some of our poets sound sweeter, and have a finer relish to the ear—to mine, at least—than that of Milton or of Shakspeare? It may be, that the latter are more staled and rung upon in common discourse. The sweetest names, and which carry a perfume in the mention, are, Kit Marlowe, Drayton, Drummond of Hawthornden, and Cowley.

Much depends upon *when* and *where* you read a book. In the five or six impatient minutes, before the dinner is quite ready, who would think of taking up the Fairy Queen for a stopgap, or a volume of Bishop Andrewes' sermons?

Milton almost requires a solemn service of music to be played before you enter upon him. But he brings his music, to which, who listens, had need bring docile thoughts, and purged ears.

Winter evenings—the world shut out—with less of ceremony the gentle Shakspeare enters. At such a season, the Tempest, or his own Winter's Tale—

These two poets you cannot avoid reading aloud—to yourself, or (as it chances) to some single person listening. More than one—and it degenerates into an audience.

Books of quick interest, that hurry on for incidents, are for the eye to glide over only. It will not do to read them out. I could never listen to even the better kind of modern novels without extreme irksomeness.

A newspaper, read out, is intolerable. In some of the Bank offices it is the custom (to save so much individual time) for one of the clerks—who is the best scholar—to commence upon the Times, or the Chronicle, and recite its entire contents aloud, *pro bono publico*. With every advantage of lungs and elocution, the effect is singularly vapid. In barbers' shops and public-houses a fellow will get up and spell out a paragraph, which he communicates as some discovery. Another follows with *his* selection. So the entire journal transpires at length by piece-meal. Seldom-readers are slow readers, and, without this expedient, no one in the company would probably ever travel through the contents of a whole paper.

Newspapers always excite curiosity. No one ever lays one down without a feeling of disappointment.

What an eternal time that gentleman in black, at Nando's, keeps the paper! I am sick of hearing the waiter bawling out incessantly, "The Chronicle is in hand, Sir."

Coming in to an inn at night—having ordered your supper—what can be more delightful than to find lying in the window-seat, left there time out of mind by the carelessness of some former guest—two or three numbers of the old Town and Country Magazine, with its amusing *tête-à-tête* pictures—"The Royal Lover and Lady G——;" "The Melting Platonic and the old Beau,"—and such-like antiquated scandal? Would you exchange it—at that time, and in that place—for a better book?

Poor Tobin, who latterly fell blind, did not regret it so much for the weightier kinds of reading—the Paradise Lost, or Comus, he could have *read* to him—but he missed the pleasure of skimming over with his own eye a magazine, or a light pamphlet.

I should not care to be caught in the serious avenues of some cathedral alone, and reading *Candide*.

I do not remember a more whimsical surprise than having been once detected—by a familiar damsel—reclined at my ease upon the grass, on Primrose Hill (her Cythera), reading—*Pamela*. There was nothing in the book to make a man seriously ashamed at the exposure; but as she seated herself down by me, and seemed determined to read in company, I could have wished it had been—any other book. We read on very sociably for a few pages; and, not finding the author much to her taste, she got up, and—went away. Gentle casuist, I leave it to thee to conjecture, whether the blush (for there was one between us) was the property of the nymph or the swain in this dilemma. From me you shall never get the secret.

I am not much a friend to out-of-doors reading. I cannot settle my spirits to it. I knew a Unitarian minister, who was generally to be seen upon Snow-hill (as yet Skinner's-street *was not*), between the hours of ten and eleven in the morning, studying a volume of Lardner. I own this to have been a strain of abstraction beyond my reach. I used to admire how he sidled along, keeping clear of secular contacts. An illiterate encounter with a porter's knot, or a bread-basket, would have quickly put to flight all the theology I am master of, and have left me worse than indifferent to the five points.

There is a class of street-readers, whom I can never contemplate without affection—the poor gentry, who, not having wherewithal to buy or hire a book, filch a little learning at the open stalls—the owner, with his hard eye, casting envious looks at them all the while, and thinking when they will have done. Venturing tenderly, page after page, expecting every moment when he shall interpose his interdict, and yet unable to deny themselves the gratification, they "snatch a fearful joy." Martin B——, in this way, by daily fragments, got through two volumes of Clarissa, when the stall-keeper damped his laudable ambition, by asking him (it was in his younger days) whether he meant to purchase the work. M. declares, that under no circumstance in his life did he ever peruse a book with half the satisfaction which he took in those uneasy snatches. A quaint poetess of our day has moralised upon this subject in two very touching but homely stanzas.

> I saw a boy with eager eye
> Open a book upon a stall,

And read, as he'd devour it all;
  Which when the stall-man did espy,
Soon to the boy I heard him call,
"You Sir, you never buy a book,
Therefore in one you shall not look."
The boy pass'd slowly on, and with a sigh
He wish'd he never had been taught to read,
Then of the old churl's books he should have had no need.
Of sufferings the poor have many,
Which never can the rich annoy:
I soon perceived another boy,
Who look'd as if he had not any
Food, for that day at least—enjoy
The sight of cold meat in a tavern larder.
This boy's case, then thought I, is surely harder,
Thus hungry, longing, thus without a penny,
Beholding choice of dainty-dressed meat:
No wonder if he wish he ne'er had learn'd to eat.

THE TRAGEDIES OF SHAKESPEARE

Considered With Reference
To Their Fitness for Stage Representation

Taking a turn the other day in the Abbey, I was struck with the affected attitude of a figure, which I do not remember to have seen before, and which upon examination proved to be a whole-length of the celebrated Mr. Garrick. Though I would not go so far with some good Catholics abroad as to shut players altogether out of consecrated ground, yet I own I was not a little scandalised at the introduction of theatrical airs and gestures into a place set apart to remind us of the saddest realities. Going nearer, I found inscribed under this harlequin figure the following lines:—

> To paint fair Nature, by divine command,
> Her magic pencil in his glowing hand,
> A Shakspeare rose: then, to expand his fame
> Wide o'er this breathing world, a Garrick came.
> Though sunk in death the forms the Poet drew,
> The Actor's genius made them breathe anew;
> Though, like the bard himself, in night they lay,
> Immortal Garrick call'd them back to day:
> And till Eternity with power sublime
> Shall mark the mortal hour of hoary Time,
> Shakspeare and Garrick like twin-stars shall shine,
> And earth irradiate with a beam divine.

It would be an insult to my readers' understandings to attempt anything like a criticism on this farrago of false thoughts and nonsense. But the reflection it led me into was a kind of wonder, how, from the days of the actor here celebrated to our own, it should have been the fashion to compliment every performer in his turn, that has had the luck to please the town in any of the great characters of Shakspeare, with a notion of possessing a *mind congenial with the poet's;* how people should come thus unaccountably to confound the power of originating poetical images and conceptions with the faculty of being able to read or recite the same when put into words; or what connection that absolute mastery over the heart and soul of man, which a great dramatic poet possesses, has with those low tricks upon the eye and ear, which a player by observing a few general effects, which some common passion, as grief, anger, etc., usually has upon the gestures and exterior, can easily compass. To know the internal workings and movements of a great mind, of an Othello or a Hamlet, for instance, the *when* and the *why* and the *how far* they should be moved; to what pitch a passion is becoming; to give the reins and to pull in the curb exactly at the moment when the drawing in or the slacking is most graceful; seems to demand a reach of intellect of a vastly different extent from that which is employed upon the bare imitation of the signs of these passions in the countenance or gesture, which signs are usually observed to be most lively and emphatic in the weaker sort of minds, and which signs can after all but indicate some passion, as I said before, anger, or grief, generally; but of the motives and grounds of the passion, wherein it differs from the same passion in low and vulgar natures, of these the actor can give no more idea by his face or gesture than the eye (without a metaphor) can speak, or the muscles utter intelligible sounds. But such is the instantaneous nature of the impressions which we take in at the eye and ear at a playhouse, compared with the slow apprehension oftentimes of the understanding in reading, that we are apt not only to sink the play-writer in the consideration which we pay to the actor, but even to identify in our minds in a perverse manner, the actor with the character which he represents. It is difficult for a frequent play-goer to disembarrass the idea of Hamlet from the person and voice of Mr. K. We speak of Lady Macbeth, while we are in reality thinking of Mrs. S. Nor is this confusion incidental alone to unlettered persons, who, not possessing the advantage of reading, are necessarily dependent upon the stage-player for all the pleasure which they can receive from the drama, and to whom the very idea of *what an author is* cannot be made comprehensible without some pain and perplexity of mind: the error is one from which persons otherwise not meanly lettered, find it almost impossible to extricate themselves.

Never let me be so ungrateful as to forget the very high degree of satisfaction which I received some years back from seeing for the first time a tragedy of Shakspeare performed, in which these two great performers sustained the principal parts. It seemed to embody and realise conceptions which had hitherto assumed no distinct shape. But dearly do we pay all our life afterwards for this juvenile pleasure, this sense of distinctness. When the novelty is past, we find to our cost that, instead of realising an idea, we have only materialised and brought down a fine vision to the standard of flesh and blood. We have let go a dream, in quest of an unattainable substance.

How cruelly this operates upon the mind, to have its free conceptions thus cramped and pressed down to the measure of a straitlacing actuality, may be judged from that delightful sensation of freshness, with which we turn to those plays of Shakspeare which have escaped being performed, and to those passages in the acting plays of the same writer which have happily been left out in the performance. How far the very custom of hearing anything *spouted*, withers and blows upon a fine passage, may be seen in those speeches from *Henry the Fifth*, etc., which are current in the mouths of school-boys from their being to be found in *Enfield Speakers*, and such kind of books. I confess myself utterly unable to appreciate that celebrated soliloquy in *Hamlet*, beginning "To be or not to be," or to tell whether it be good, bad, or indifferent, it has been so handled and pawed about by declamatory boys and men, and torn so inhumanly from its living place and principle of continuity in the play, till it is become to me a perfect dead member.

It may seem a paradox, but I cannot help being of opinion that the plays of Shakspeare are less calculated for performance on a stage than those of almost any other dramatist whatever. Their distinguished excellence is a reason that they should be so. There is so much in them, which comes not under the province of acting, with which eye, and tone, and gesture, have nothing to do.

The glory of the scenic art is to personate passion, and the turns of passion; and the more coarse and palpable the passion is, the more hold upon the eyes and ears of the spectators the performer obviously possesses. For this reason, scolding scenes, scenes where two persons talk themselves into a fit of fury, and then in a surprising manner talk themselves out of it again, have always been the most popular upon our stage. And the reason is plain, because the spectators are here most palpably appealed to, they are the proper judges in this war of words, they are the legitimate ring that should be formed round such "intellectual prize-fighters." Talking is the direct object of the imitation here. But in the best dramas, and in Shakspeare above all, how obvious it is, that the form of *speaking,* whether it be in soliloquy or dialogue, is only a medium, and often a highly artificial one, for putting the reader or spectator into possession of that knowledge of the inner structure and workings of mind in a character, which he could otherwise never have arrived at *in that form of composition* by any gift short of intuition. We do here as we do with novels written in the *epistolary form.* How many improprieties, perfect solecisms in letter-writing, do we put up with in "Clarissa" and other books, for the sake of the delight which that form upon the whole gives us.

But the practice of stage representation reduces everything to a controversy of elocution. Every character, from the boisterous blasphemings of Bajazet to the shrinking timidity of womanhood, must play the orator. The love-dialogues of *Romeo and Juliet,* those silversweet sounds of lovers' tongues by night; the more intimate and sacred sweetness of nuptial colloquy between an Othello or a Posthumus with their married wives, all those delicacies which are so delightful in the reading, as when we read of those youthful dalliances in Paradise—

> As beseem'd
> Fair couple link'd in happy nuptial league,
> Alone:

by the inherent fault of stage representation, how are these things sullied and turned from their very nature by being exposed to a large assembly; when such speeches as Imogen addresses to her lord, come drawling out of the mouth of a hired actress, whose courtship, though nominally addressed to the personated Posthumus, is manifestly aimed at the spectators, who are to judge of her endearments and her returns of love.

The character of Hamlet is perhaps that by which, since the days of

Betterton, a succession of popular performers have had the greatest ambition to distinguish themselves. The length of the part may be one of their reasons. But for the character itself, we find it in a play, and therefore we judge it a fit subject of dramatic representation. The play itself abounds in maxims and reflections beyond any other, and therefore we consider it as a proper vehicle for conveying moral instruction. But Hamlet himself—what does he suffer meanwhile by being dragged forth as a public schoolmaster, to give lectures to the crowd! Why, nine parts in ten of what Hamlet does, are transactions between himself and his moral sense, they are the effusions of his solitary musings, which he retires to holes and corners and the most sequestered parts of the palace to pour forth; or rather, they are the silent meditations with which his bosom is bursting, reduced to *words* for the sake of the reader, who must else remain ignorant of what is passing there. These profound sorrows, these light-and-noise-abhorring ruminations, which the tongue scarce dares utter to deaf walls and chambers, how can they be represented by a gesticulating actor, who comes and mouths them out before an audience, making four hundred people his confidants at once? I say not that it is the fault of the actor so to do; he must pronounce them *ore rotundo,* he must accompany them with his eye, he must insinuate them into his auditory by some trick of eye, tone, or gesture, or he fails. *He must be thinking all the while of his appearance, because he knows that all the while the spectators are judging of it.* And this is the way to represent the shy, negligent, retiring Hamlet.

It is true that there is no other mode of conveying a vast quantity of thought and feeling to a great portion of the audience, who otherwise would never learn it for themselves by reading, and the intellectual acquisition gained this way may, for aught I know, be inestimable; but I am not arguing that *Hamlet* should not be acted, but how much *Hamlet* is made another thing by being acted. I have heard much of the wonders which Garrick performed in this part; but as I never saw him, I must have leave to doubt whether the representation of such a character came within the province of his art. Those who tell me of him, speak of his eye, of the magic of his eye, and of his commanding voice: physical properties, vastly desirable in an actor, and without which he can never insinuate meaning into an auditory,—but what have they to do with Hamlet? what have they to do with intellect? In fact, the things aimed at in theatrical representation, are to arrest the spectator's eye upon the form and the gesture, and so to gain a more favourable hearing to what is spoken: it is not what the character is, but how he looks; not what he says, but how he speaks it. I see no reason to think that if the play of Hamlet were written over again by some such writer as Banks or Lillo, retaining the process of the story, but totally omitting all the poetry of it, all the divine features of Shakspeare, his stupendous intellect; and only taking care to give us enough of passionate dialogue, which Banks or Lillo were never at a loss to furnish; I see not how the effect could be much different upon an audience, nor how the actor has it in his power to represent Shakspeare to us differently from his representation of Banks or Lillo. Hamlet would still be a youthful accomplished prince, and must be gracefully personated; he might be puzzled in his mind, wavering in his conduct, seemingly cruel to Ophelia, he might see a ghost, and start at it, and address it kindly when he found it to be his father; all this in the poorest and most homely language of the servilest creeper after nature that ever consulted the palate of an audience; without troubling Shakspeare for the matter; and I see not but there would be room for all the power which an actor has, to display itself. All the passions and changes of passion might remain; for those are much less difficult to write or act than is thought; it is a trick easy to be attained, it is but rising or falling a note or two in the voice, a whisper with a significant foreboding look to announce its approach, and so contagious the counterfeit appearance of any emotion is, that let the words be what they will, the look and tone shall carry it off and make it pass for deep skill in the passions.

It is common for people to talk of Shakspeare's plays being *so natural*, that everybody can understand him. They are natural indeed, they are grounded deep in nature, so deep that the depth of them lies out of the reach of most of us. You shall hear the same persons say that *George Barnwell* is very natural, and *Othello* is very natural, that they are both very deep; and to them they are the same kind of thing. At the one they sit and shed tears, because a good sort of young man is tempted by a naughty woman to commit *a trifling peccadillo*, the murder of an uncle or so, that is all, and so comes to an untimely end, which is *so moving;* and at the other, because a blackamoor in a fit of jealousy kills his innocent white wife: and the odds are that ninety-nine out of a hundred would willingly behold the same catastrophe happen to both the heroes, and have thought the rope more due to Othello than to Barnwell. For of the texture of Othello's mind, the inward construction marvellously laid open with all its strengths and weaknesses, its heroic confidences and its human misgivings, its agonies of hate springing from the depths of love, they see no more than the spectators at a cheaper rate, who pay their pennies apiece to look through the man's telescope in Leicester Fields, see into the inward plot and topography of the moon. Some dim thing or other they see, they see an actor personating a passion, of grief, or anger, for instance, and they recognise it as a copy of the usual external effects of such passions; or at least as being true to *that symbol of the emotion which passes current at the theatre for it,* for it is often no more than that: but of the grounds of the passion, its correspondence to a great or heroic nature, which is the only worthy object of tragedy,—that common auditors know anything of this, or can have any such notions dinned into them by the mere strength of an actor's lungs,—that apprehensions foreign to them should be thus infused into them by storm, I can neither believe, nor understand how it can be possible.

We talk of Shakspeare's admirable observation of life, when we should feel that, not from a petty inquisition into those cheap and everyday characters which surrounded him, as they surround us, but from his own mind, which was, to borrow a phrase of Ben Jonson's, the very "sphere of humanity," he fetched those images of virtue and of knowledge, of which every one of us recognising a part, think we comprehend in our natures the whole; and oftentimes mistake the powers which he positively creates in us for nothing more than indigenous faculties of our own minds, which only waited the application of corresponding virtues in him to return a full and clear echo of the same.

To return to Hamlet.— Among the distinguishing features of that wonderful character, one of the most interesting (yet painful) is that soreness of mind which makes him treat the intrusions of Polonius with harshness, and that asperity which he puts on in his interviews with Ophelia. These tokens of an unhinged mind (if they be not mixed in the latter case with a profound artifice of love, to alienate Ophelia by affected discourtesies, so to prepare her mind for the breaking off of that loving intercourse, which can no longer find a place amidst business so serious as that which he has to do) are parts of his character, which to reconcile with our admiration of Hamlet, the most patient consideration of his situation is no more than necessary; they are what we *forgive afterwards,* and explain by the whole of his character, but *at the time* they are harsh and unpleasant. Yet such is the actor's necessity of giving strong blows to the audience, that I have never seen a player in this character, who did not exaggerate and strain to the utmost these ambiguous features,— these temporary deformities in the character. They make him express a vulgar scorn at Polonius which utterly degrades his gentility, and which no explanation can render palatable; they make him show contempt, and curl up the nose at Ophelia's father,—contempt in its very grossest and most hateful form; but they get applause by it: it is natural, people say; that is, the words are scornful, and the actor expresses scorn, and that they can judge of: but why so much scorn, and of that sort, they never think of asking.

So to Ophelia.—All the Hamlets that I have ever seen, rant and rave at her as if she had committed some great crime, and the audience are highly pleased, because the words of the part are satirical, and they are enforced by the strongest expression of satirical indignation of which the face and voice are capable. But then, whether Hamlet is likely to have put on such brutal appearances to a lady whom he loved so dearly, is never thought on. The truth is, that in all such deep affections as had subsisted between Hamlet and Ophelia, there is a stock of *supererogatory love* (if I may venture to use the expression), which in any great grief of heart, especially where that which preys upon the mind cannot be communicated, confers a kind of indulgence upon the grieved party to express itself, even to its heart's dearest object, in the language of a temporary alienation; but it is not alienation, it is a distraction purely, and so it always makes itself to be felt by that object; it is not anger, but grief assuming the appearance of anger,—love awkwardly counterfeiting hate, as sweet countenances when they try to frown: but such sternness and fierce disgust as Hamlet is made to show, is no counterfeit, but the real face of absolute aversion,—of irreconcilable alienation. It may be said he puts on the madman; but then he should only so far put on this counterfeit lunacy as his own real distraction will give him leave; that is, incompletely, imperfectly; not in that confirmed, practised way, like a master of his art, or as Dame Quickly would say, "like one of those harlotry players."

I mean no disrespect to any actor, but the sort of pleasure which

Shakspeare's plays give in the acting seems to me not at all to differ from that which the audience receive from those of other writers; and, *they being in themselves essentially so different from all others*, I must conclude that there is something in the nature of acting which levels all distinctions. And in fact, who does not speak indifferently of the *Gamester* and of *Macbeth* as fine stage performances, and praise the Mrs. Beverley in the same way as the Lady Macbeth of Mrs. S.? Belvidera, and Calista, and Isabella, and Euphrasia, are they less liked than Imogen, or than Juliet, or than Desdemona? Are they not spoken of and remembered in the same way? Is not the female performer as great (as they call it) in one as in the other? Did not Garrick shine, and was he not ambitious of shining in every drawling tragedy that his wretched day produced,—the productions of the Hills and the Murphys and the Browns,—and shall he have that honour to dwell in our minds for ever as an inseparable concomitant with Shakspeare? A kindred mind! O who can read that affecting sonnet of Shakspeare which alludes to his profession as a player:—

> Oh for my sake do you with Fortune chide,
> The guilty goddess of my harmful deeds,
> That did not better for my life provide
> Than public means which public manners breeds—
> Thence comes it that my name receives a brand;
> And almost thence my nature is subdued
> To what it works in, like the dyer's hand——

Or that other confession;—

> Alas! 'tis true, I have gone here and there,
> And made myself a motley to the view,
> Gored mine own thoughts, sold cheap what is most dear—

Who can read these instances of jealous self-watchfulness in our sweet Shakspeare, and dream of any congeniality between him and one that, by every tradition of him, appears to have been as mere a player as ever existed; to have had his mind tainted with the lowest player's vices,—envy and jealousy, and miserable cravings after applause; one who in the exercise of his profession was jealous even of the women-performers that stood in his way; a manager full of managerial tricks and stratagems and finesse: that any resemblance should be dreamed of between him and Shakspeare,—Shakspeare who, in the plenitude and consciousness of his own powers, could with that noble modesty, which we can neither imitate nor appreciate, express himself thus of his own sense of his own defects:—

> Wishing me like to one more rich in hope,
> Featured like him, like him with friends possess'd:
> Desiring *this man's art, and that man's scope.*

I am almost disposed to deny to Garrick the merits of being an admirer of Shakspeare. A true lover of his excellences he certainly was not; for would any true lover of them have admitted into his matchless scenes such ribald trash as Tate and Cibber, and the rest of them, that

> With their darkness durst affront his light,

have foisted into the acting plays of Shakspeare? I believe it impossible that he could have had a proper reverence for Shakspeare, and have condescended to go through that interpolated scene in *Richard the Third*, in which Richard tries to break his wife's heart by telling her he loves another woman, and says, "if she survives this she is immortal." Yet I doubt not he delivered this vulgar stuff with as much anxiety of emphasis as any of the genuine parts: and for acting, it is as well calculated as any. But we have seen the part of Richard lately produce great fame to an actor by his manner of playing it, and it lets us into the secret of acting, and of popular judgments of Shakspeare derived from acting. Not one of the spectators who have witnessed Mr. C.'s exertions in that part, but has come away with a proper conviction that Richard is a very wicked man, and kills little children in their beds, with something like the pleasure which the giants and ogres in children's books are represented to have taken in that practice; moreover, that he is very close and shrewd, and devilish cunning, for you could see that by his eye.

But is in fact this the impression we have in reading the Richard of Shakspeare? Do we feel anything like disgust, as we do at that butcherlike representation of him that passes for him on the stage? A horror at his crimes blends with the effect which we feel, but how is it qualified, how is it carried off, by the rich intellect which he displays, his resources, his wit, his buoyant spirits, his vast knowledge and insight into characters, the poetry of his part— not an atom of all which is made perceivable in Mr. C.'s way of acting it. Nothing but his crimes, his actions, is visible; they are prominent and staring; the murderer stands out, but where is the lofty genius, the man of vast capacity,—the profound, the witty, accomplished Richard?

The truth is, the Characters of Shakspeare are so much the objects of meditation rather than of interest or curiosity as to their actions, that while we are reading any of his great criminal characters,—Macbeth, Richard, even Iago,—we think not so much of the crimes which they commit, as of the ambition, the aspiring spirit, the intellectual activity, which prompts them to overleap those moral fences. Barnwell is a wretched murderer; there is a certain fitness between his neck and the rope; he is the legitimate heir to the gallows; nobody who thinks at all can think of any alleviating circumstances in his case to make him a fit object of mercy. Or to take an instance from the higher tragedy, what else but a mere assassin is Glenalvon! Do we think of anything but of the crime which he commits, and the rack which he deserves? That is all which we really think about him. Whereas in corresponding characters in Shakspeare so little do the actions comparatively affect us, that while the impulses, the inner mind in all its perverted greatness, solely seems real and is exclusively attended to, the crime is comparatively nothing. But when we see these things represented, the acts which they do are comparatively everything, their impulses nothing. The state of sublime emotion into which we are elevated by those images of night and horror which Macbeth is made to utter, that solemn prelude with which he entertains the time till the bell shall strike which is to call him to murder Duncan,—when we no longer read it in a book, when we have given up that vantage-ground of abstraction which reading possesses over seeing, and come to see a man in his bodily shape before our eyes actually preparing to commit a murder, if the acting be true and impressive, as I have witnessed it in Mr. K.'s performance of that part, the painful anxiety about the act, the natural longing to prevent it while it yet seems unperpetrated, the too close pressing semblance of reality, give a pain and an uneasiness which totally destroy all the delight which the words in the book convey, where the deed doing never presses upon us with the painful sense of presence: it rather seems to belong to history,—to something past and inevitable, if it has anything to do with time at all. The sublime images, the poetry alone, is that which is present to our minds in the reading.

So to see Lear acted,—to see an old man tottering about the stage with a walking-stick, turned out of doors by his daughters in a rainy night, has nothing in it but what is painful and disgusting. We want to take him into shelter and relieve him. That is all the feeling which the acting of Lear ever produced in me. But the Lear of Shakspeare cannot be acted. The contemptible machinery by which they mimic the storm which he goes out in, is not more inadequate to represent the horrors of the real elements, than any actor can be to represent Lear: they might more easily propose to personate the Satan of Milton upon a stage, or one of Michael Angelo's terrible figures. The greatness of Lear is not in corporal dimension, but in intellectual: the explosions of his passion are terrible as a volcano: they are storms turning up and disclosing to the bottom that sea his mind, with all its vast riches. It is his mind which is laid bare. This case of flesh and blood seems too insignificant to be thought on; even as he himself neglects it. On the stage we see nothing but corporal infirmities and weakness, the impotence of rage; while we read it, we see not Lear, but we are Lear,—we are in his mind, we are sustained by a grandeur which baffles the malice of daughters and storms; in the aberrations of his reason, we discover a mighty irregular power of reasoning, immethodised from the ordinary purposes of life, but exerting its powers, as the wind blows where it listeth, at will upon the corruptions and abuses of mankind. What have looks, or tones, to do with that sublime identification of his age with that of the *heavens themselves*, when in his reproaches to them for conniving at the injustice of his children, he reminds them that "they themselves are old"? What gestures shall we appropriate to this? What has the voice or the eye to do with such things? But the play is beyond all art, as the tamperings with it show: it is too hard and stony; it must have love-scenes, and a happy ending. It is not enough that Cordelia is a daughter, she must shine as a lover too. Tate has put his hook in the nostrils of this Leviathan, for Garrick and his followers, the showmen of the scene, to draw the mighty beast about more easily. A happy ending!—as if the living martyrdom that Lear had gone through,—the flaying of his feelings alive, did not make a fair dismissal from the stage of life the only decorous thing for him. If he is to live and be happy after, if he could sustain this world's burden after, why all this pudder and preparation,—why torment us with all this unnecessary sympathy? As if the childish pleasure of getting his gilt robes and sceptre again could tempt him to act over again his misused station,—as if at his years, and with his experience, anything was left but to die.

Lear is essentially impossible to be represented on a stage. But how many dramatic personages are there in Shakspeare, which though more tractable and feasible (if I may so speak) than Lear, yet from some circumstance, some adjunct to their character, are improper to be shown to our bodily eye. *Othello*, for instance. Nothing can be more soothing, more flattering to the nobler parts of our natures, than to read of a young Venetian lady of highest extraction, through the force of love and from a sense of merit in him whom she loved, laying aside every consideration of kindred, and country, and colour, and wedding with a *coal-black Moor*—(for such he is represented, in the imperfect state of knowledge respecting foreign countries in those days, compared with our own, or in compliance with popular notions, though the Moors are now well enough known to be by many shades less unworthy of a white woman's fancy)—it is the perfect triumph of virtue over accidents, of the imagination over the senses. She sees Othello's colour in his mind. But upon the stage, when the imagination is no longer the ruling faculty, but we are left to our poor unassisted senses, I appeal to every one that has seen *Othello* played, whether he did not, on the contrary, sink Othello's mind in his colour; whether he did not find something extremely revolting in the courtship and wedded caresses of Othello and Desdemona; and whether the actual sight of the thing did not over-weigh all that beautiful compromise which we make in reading;—and the reason it should do so is obvious, because there is just so much reality presented to our senses as to give a perception of disagreement, with not enough of belief in the internal motives,—all that which is unseen,—to overpower and reconcile the first and obvious prejudices. What we see upon a stage is body and bodily action; what we are conscious of in reading is almost exclusively the mind, and its movements: and this, I think, may sufficiently account for the very different sort of delight with which the same play so often affects us in the reading and the seeing.

It requires little reflection to perceive, that if those characters in Shakspeare which are within the precincts of nature, have yet something in them which appeals too exclusively to the imagination, to admit of their being made objects to the senses without suffering a change and a diminution,—that still stronger the objection must lie against representing another line of characters, which Shakspeare has introduced to give a wildness and a supernatural elevation to his scenes, as if to remove them still further from that assimilation to common life in which their excellence is vulgarly supposed to consist. When we read the incantations of those terrible beings the Witches in *Macbeth*, though some of the ingredients of their hellish composition savour of the grotesque, yet is the effect upon us other than the most serious and appalling that can be imagined? Do we not feel spell-bound as Macbeth was?

Can any mirth accompany a sense of their presence? We might as well laugh under a consciousness of the principle of Evil himself being truly and really present with us. But attempt to bring these beings on to a stage, and you turn them instantly into so many old women, that men and children are to laugh at. Contrary to the old saying, that "seeing is believing," the sight actually destroys the faith: and the mirth in which we indulge at their expense, when we see these creatures upon a stage, seems to be a sort of indemnification which we make to ourselves for the terror which they put us in when reading made them an object of belief,—when we surrendered up our reason to the poet, as children to their nurses and their elders; and we laugh at our fears, as children who thought they saw something in the dark, triumph when the bringing in of a candle discovers the vanity of their fears. For this exposure of supernatural agents upon a stage is truly bringing in a candle to expose their own delusiveness. It is the solitary taper and the book that generates a faith in these terrors: a ghost by chandelier light, and in good company, deceives no spectators,—a ghost that can be measured by the eye, and his human dimensions made out at leisure. The sight of a well-lighted house, and a well-dressed audience, shall arm the most nervous child against any apprehensions: as Tom Brown says of the impenetrable skin of Achilles with his impenetrable armour over it, "Bully Dawson would have fought the devil with such advantages."

Much has been said, and deservedly, in reprobation of the vile mixture which Dryden has thrown into the *Tempest:* doubtless without some such vicious alloy, the impure ears of that age would never have sate out to hear so much innocence of love as is contained in the sweet courtship of Ferdinand and Miranda. But is the *Tempest* of Shakspeare at all a subject for stage representation? It is one thing to read of an enchanter, and to believe the wondrous tale while we are reading it; but to have a conjuror brought before us in his conjuring-gown, with his spirits about him, which none but himself and some hundred of favoured spectators before the curtain are supposed to see, involves such a quantity of the *hateful incredible,* that all our reverence for the author cannot hinder us from perceiving such gross attempts upon the senses to be in the highest degree childish and inefficient. Spirits and fairies cannot be represented, they cannot even be painted,—they can only be believed. But the elaborate and anxious provision of scenery, which the luxury of the age demands, in these cases works a quite contrary effect to what is intended. That which in comedy, or plays of familiar life, adds so much to the life of the imitation, in plays which appeal to the higher faculties, positively destroys the illusion which it is introduced to aid. A parlour or a drawing-room,—a library opening into a garden,—a garden with an alcove in it,—a street, or the piazza of Covent Garden does well enough in a scene; we are content to give as much credit to it as it demands; or rather, we think little about it,—it is little more than reading at the top of a page, "Scene, a Garden"; we do not imagine ourselves there, but we readily admit the imitation of familiar objects. But to think by the help of painted trees and caverns, which we know to be painted, to transport our minds to Prospero, and his island and his lonely cell; or by the aid of a fiddle dexterously thrown in, in an interval of speaking, to make us believe that we hear those supernatural noises of which the isle was full:—the Orrery Lecturer at the Haymarket might as well hope, by his musical glasses cleverly stationed out of sight behind his apparatus, to make us believe that we do indeed hear the crystal spheres ring out that chime, which if it were to inwrap our fancy long, Milton thinks,

> Time would run back and fetch the age of gold,
> And speckled vanity
> Would sicken soon and die,
> And leprous Sin would melt from earthly mould;
> Yea Hell itself would pass away,
> And leave its dolorous mansions to the peering day.

The Garden of Eden, with our first parents in it, is not more impossible to be shown on a stage, than the Enchanted Isle, with its no less interesting and innocent first settlers.

The subject of Scenery is closely connected with that of the Dresses, which are so anxiously attended to on our stage. I remember the last time I saw *Macbeth* played, the discrepancy I felt at the changes of garment which he varied,—the shiftings and re-shiftings, like a Romish priest at mass. The luxury of stage-improvements, and the importunity of the public eye, require this. The coronation robe of the Scottish monarch was fairly a counterpart to that which our King wears when he goes to the Parliament-house,—just so full and cumbersome, and set out with ermine and pearls. And if things must be represented, I see not what to find fault with in this. But in reading, what robe are we conscious of? Some dim images of royalty—a crown and sceptre, may float before our eyes, but who shall describe the fashion of it? Do we see in our mind's eye what Webb or any other robe-maker could pattern? This is the inevitable consequence of imitating everything, to make all things natural. Whereas the reading of a tragedy is a fine abstraction. It presents to the fancy just so much of external appearances as to make us feel that we are among flesh and blood, while by far the greater and better part of our imagination is employed upon the thoughts and internal machinery of the character. But in acting, scenery, dress, the most contemptible things, call upon us to judge of their naturalness.

Perhaps it would be no bad similitude, to liken the pleasure which we take in seeing one of these fine plays acted, compared with that quiet delight which we find in the reading of it, to the different feelings with which a reviewer, and a man that is not a reviewer, reads a fine poem. The accursed critical habit,— the being called upon to judge and pronounce, must make it quite a different thing to the former. In seeing these plays acted, we are affected just as judges. When Hamlet compares the two pictures of Gertrude's first and second husband, who wants to see the pictures? But in the acting, a miniature must be lugged out; which we know not to be the picture, but only to shew how finely a miniature may be represented. This shewing of everything, levels all things: it makes tricks, bows, and curtseys, of importance. Mrs. S. never got more fame by anything than by the manner in which she dismisses the guests in the banquet-scene in *Macbeth:* it is as much remembered as any of her thrilling tones or impressive looks. But does such a trifle as this enter into the imaginations of the reader of that wild and wonderful scene? Does not the mind dismiss the feasters as rapidly as it can? Does it care about the gracefulness of the doing it? But by acting, and judging of acting, all these non-essentials are raised into an importance, injurious to the main interest of the play.

I have confined my observations to the tragic parts of Shakspeare. It would be no very difficult task to extend the inquiry to his comedies; and to show why Falstaff, Shallow, Sir Hugh Evans, and the rest are equally incompatible with stage representation. The length to which this Essay has run, will make it, I am afraid, sufficiently distasteful to the Amateurs of the Theatre, without going any deeper into the subject at present.

CHARACTERS

OF DRAMATIC WRITERS,
CONTEMPORARY WITH SHAKSPEARE

When I selected for publication, in 1808, Specimens of English Dramatic Poets who lived about the time of Shakspeare, the kind of extracts which I was anxious to give were, not so much passages of wit and humour, though the old plays are rich in such, as scenes of passion, sometimes of the deepest quality, interesting situations, serious descriptions, that which is more nearly allied to poetry than to wit, and to tragic rather than to comic poetry. The plays which I made choice of were, with few exceptions, such as treat of human life and manners, rather than masques and Arcadian pastorals, with their train of abstractions, unimpassioned deities, passionate mortals—Claius, and Medorus, and Amintas, and Amarillis. My leading design was, to illustrate what may be called the moral sense of our ancestors. To shew in what manner they felt, when they placed themselves by the power of imagination in trying circumstances, in the conflicts of duty and passion, or the strife of contending duties; what sort of loves and enmities theirs were; how their griefs were tempered, and their full-swoln joys abated: how much of Shakspeare shines in the great men his contemporaries, and how far in his divine mind and manners he surpassed them and all mankind. I was also desirous to bring together some of the most admired scenes of Fletcher and Massinger, in the estimation of the world the only dramatic poets of that age entitled to be considered after Shakspeare, and, by exhibiting them in the same volume with the more impressive scenes of old Marlowe, Heywood, Tourneur, Webster, Ford, and others, to shew what we had slighted, while beyond all proportion we had been crying up one or two favourite names. From the desultory criticisms which accompanied that publication I have selected a few which I thought would best stand by themselves, as requiring least immediate reference to the play or passage by which they were suggested.

Christopher Marlowe

Lust's Dominion, or the Lascivious Queen.—This tragedy is in King Cambyses' vein; rape, and murder, and superlatives; "huffing braggart puft lines," such as the play-writers anterior to Shakspeare are full of, and Pistol but coldly imitates.

Tamburlaine the Great, or the Scythian Shepherd.—The lunes of Tamburlaine are perfect midsummer madness. Nebuchadnezzar's are mere modest pretensions compared with the thundering vaunts of this Scythian

Shepherd. He comes in, drawn by conquered kings, and reproaches these *pampered jades of Asia* that they can *draw but twenty miles a day*. Till I saw this passage with my own eyes, I never believed that it was any thing more than a pleasant burlesque of mine ancient's. But I can assure my readers that it is soberly set down in a play, which their ancestors took to be serious.

Edward the Second.—In a very different style from mighty *Tamburlaine* is the tragedy of *Edward the Second*. The reluctant pangs of abdicating royalty in Edward furnished hints which Shakspeare scarcely improved in his *Richard the Second;* and the death-scene of Marlowe's king moves pity and terror beyond any scene ancient or modern with which I am acquainted.

The Rich Jew of Malta.—Marlowe's Jew does not approach so near to Shakspeare's as his Edward the Second does to Richard the Second. Barabas is a mere monster brought in with a large painted nose to please the rabble. He kills in sport, poisons whole nunneries, invents infernal machines. He is just such an exhibition as a century or two earlier might have been played before the Londoners "by the royal command," when a general pillage and massacre of the Hebrews had been previously resolved on in the cabinet. It is curious to see a superstition wearing out. The idea of a Jew, which our pious ancestors contemplated with so much horror, has nothing in it now revolting. We have tamed the claws of the beast, and pared its nails, and now we take it to our arms, fondle it, write plays to flatter it; it is visited by princes, affects a taste, patronises the arts, and is the only liberal and gentlemanlike thing in Christendom.

Doctor Faustus.—The growing horrors of Faustus' last scene are awfully marked by the hours and half-hours as they expire, and bring him nearer and nearer to the exactment of his dire compact. It is indeed an agony and a fearful colluctation. Marlowe is said to have been tainted with atheistical positions, to have denied God and the Trinity. To such a genius the history of Faustus must have been delectable food: to wander in fields where curiosity is forbidden to go, to approach the dark gulf near enough to look in, to be busied in speculations which are the rottenest part of the core of the fruit that fell from the tree of knowledge. Barabas the Jew, and Faustus the conjurer, are offsprings of a mind which at least delighted to dally with interdicted subjects. They both talk a language which a believer would have been tender of putting into the mouth of a character though but in fiction. But the holiest minds have sometimes not thought it reprehensible to counterfeit impiety in the person of another, to bring Vice upon the stage speaking her own dialect; and, themselves being armed with an unction of self-confident impunity, have not scrupled to handle and touch that familiarly which would be death to others. Milton in the person of Satan has started speculations hardier than any which the feeble armoury of the atheist ever furnished; and the precise, strait-laced Richardson has strengthened Vice, from the mouth of Lovelace, with entangling sophistries and abstruse pleas against her adversary Virtue, which Sedley, Villiers, and Rochester wanted depth of libertinism enough to have invented.

Thomas Decker

Old Fortunatus.—The humour of a frantic lover, in the scene where Orleans to his friend Galloway defends the passion with which himself, being a prisoner in the English king's court, is enamoured to frenzy of the king's daughter Agripyna, is done to the life. Orleans is as passionate an inamorata as any which Shakspeare ever drew. He is just such another adept in Love's reasons. The sober people of the world are with him

A swarm of fools
Crowding together to be counted wise.

He talks "pure Biron and Romeo," he is almost as poetical as they, quite as philosophical, only a little madder. After all, Love's sectaries are a reason unto themselves. We have gone retrograde to the noble heresy, since the days when Sidney proselyted our nation to this mixed health and disease; the kindliest symptom, yet the most alarming crisis in the ticklish state of youth; the nourisher and the destroyer of hopeful wits; the mother of twin births, wisdom and folly, valour and weakness; the servitude above freedom; the gentle mind's religion; the liberal superstition.

The Honest Whore.—There is in the second part of this play, where Bellafront, a reclaimed harlot, recounts some of the miseries of her profession, a simple picture of honour and shame, contrasted without violence, and expressed without immodesty, which is worth all the *strong lines* against the harlot's profession with which both parts of this play are offensively crowded. A satirist is always to be suspected who, to make vice odious, dwells upon all its acts and minutest circumstances with a sort of relish and retrospective fondness. But so near are the boundaries of panegyric and invective, that a worn-out sinner is sometimes found to make the best declaimer against sin. The same high-seasoned descriptions, which in his unregenerate state served but to inflame his appetites, in his new province of a moralist will serve him, a little turned, to expose the enormity of those appetites in other men. When Cervantes with such proficiency of fondness dwells upon the Don's library, who sees not that he has been a great reader of books of knight-errantry— perhaps was at some time of his life in danger of falling into those very extravagances which he ridiculed so happily in his hero?

John Marston

Antonio and Mellida.—The situation of Andrugio and Lucio, in the first part of this tragedy, where Andrugio Duke of Genoa banished his country, with the loss of a son supposed drowned, is cast upon the territory of his mortal enemy the Duke of Venice, with no attendants but Lucio an old nobleman, and a page—resembles that of Lear and Kent in that king's distresses. Andrugio, like Lear, manifests a kinglike impatience, a turbulent greatness, an affected resignation. The enemies which he enters lists to combat, "Despair and mighty

Grief and sharp Impatience," and the forces which he brings to vanquish them, "cornets of horse," etc., are in the boldest style of allegory. They are such a "race of mourners" as the "infection of sorrows loud" in the intellect might beget on some "pregnant cloud" in the imagination. The prologue to the second part, for its passionate earnestness, and for the tragic note of preparation which it sounds, might have preceded one of those old tales of Thebes or Pelops' line, which Milton has so highly commended, as free from the common error of the poets in his day, of "intermixing comic stuff with tragic sadness and gravity, brought in without discretion corruptly to gratify the people." It is as solemn a preparative as the "warning voice which he who saw the Apocalypse heard cry."

What you Will.—O I shall ne'er forget how he went cloath'd. Act I. Scene I.—To judge of the liberality of these notions of dress, we must advert to the days of Gresham, and the consternation which a phenomenon habited like the merchant here described would have excited among the flat round caps and cloth stockings upon 'Change, when those "original arguments or tokens of a citizen's vocation were in fashion, not more for thrift and usefulness than for distinction and grace." The blank uniformity to which all professional distinctions in apparel have been long hastening, is one instance of the decay of symbols among us, which, whether it has contributed or not to make us a more intellectual, has certainly made us a less imaginative people. Shakspeare knew the force of signs: a "malignant and a turban'd Turk." This "mealcap miller," says the author of *God's Revenge against Murder*, to express his indignation at an atrocious outrage committed by the miller Pierot upon the person of the fair Marieta.

Author Unknown

The Merry Devil of Edmonton.—The scene in this delightful comedy, in which Jerningham, "with the true feeling of a zealous friend," touches the griefs of Mounchensey, seems written to make the reader happy. Few of our dramatists or novelists have attended enough to this. They torture and wound us abundantly. They are economists only in delight. Nothing can be finer, more gentlemanlike, and nobler, than the conversation and compliments of these young men. How delicious is Raymond Mounchensey's forgetting, in his fears, that Jerningham has a "Saint in Essex"; and how sweetly his friend reminds him! I wish it could be ascertained, which there is some grounds for believing, that Michael Drayton was the author of this piece. It would add a worthy appendage to the renown of that Panegyrist of my native Earth; who has gone over her soil, in his Polyolbion, with the fidelity of a herald, and the painful love of a son; who has not left a rivulet, so narrow that it may be stept over, without honourable mention; and has animated hills and streams with life and passion beyond the dreams of old mythology.

Thomas Heywood

A Woman Killed with Kindness.—Heywood is a sort of *prose* Shakspeare.

His scenes are to the full as natural and affecting. But we miss *the poet,* that which in Shakspeare always appears out and above the surface of *the nature.* Heywood's characters in this play, for instance, his country gentlemen, etc., are exactly what we see, but of the best kind of what we see, in life. Shakspeare makes us believe, while we are among his lovely creations, that they are nothing but what we are familiar with, as in dreams new things seem old; but we awake, and sigh for the difference.

The English Traveller.—Heywood's preface to this play is interesting, as it shews the heroic indifference about the opinion of posterity, which some of these great writers seem to have felt. There is a magnanimity in authorship as in everything else. His ambition seems to have been confined to the pleasure of hearing the players speak his lines while he lived. It does not appear that he ever contemplated the possibility of being read by after ages. What a slender pittance of fame was motive sufficient to the production of such plays as the *English Traveller,* the *Challenge for Beauty,* and the *Woman Killed with Kindness!* Posterity is bound to take care that a writer loses nothing by such a noble modesty.

Thomas Middleton and William Rowley

A Fair Quarrel.—The insipid levelling morality to which the modern stage is tied down, would not admit of such admirable passions as these scenes are filled with. A puritanical obtuseness of sentiment, a stupid infantile goodness, is creeping among us, instead of the vigorous passions, and virtues clad in flesh and blood, with which the old dramatists present us. Those noble and liberal casuists could discern in the differences, the quarrels, the animosities of men, a beauty and truth of moral feeling, no less than in the everlastingly inculcated duties of forgiveness and atonement. With us, all is hypocritical meekness. A reconciliation-scene, be the occasion never so absurd, never fails of applause. Our audiences come to the theatre to be complimented on their goodness. They compare notes with the amiable characters in the play, and find a wonderful sympathy of disposition between them. We have a common stock of dramatic morality, out of which a writer may be supplied without the trouble of copying it from originals within his own breast. To know the boundaries of honour, to be judiciously valiant, to have a temperance which shall beget a smoothness in the angry swellings of youth, to esteem life as nothing when the sacred reputation of a parent is to be defended, yet to shake and tremble under a pious cowardice when that ark of an honest confidence is found to be frail and tottering, to feel the true blows of a real disgrace blunting that sword which the imaginary strokes of a supposed false imputation had put so keen an edge upon but lately: to do, or to imagine this done in a feigned story, asks something more of a moral sense, somewhat a greater delicacy of perception in questions of right and wrong, than goes to the writing of two or three hackneyed sentences about the laws of honour as opposed to the laws of the land, or a commonplace against duelling. Yet such things would stand a writer nowadays in far better stead than Captain Agar and his conscientious honour; and he would be considered as a far better teacher of morality than old Rowley or Middleton, if they were living.

William Rowley

A New Wonder; A Woman Never Vext.—The old play-writers are distinguished by an honest boldness of exhibition, they shew everything without being ashamed. If a reverse in fortune is to be exhibited, they fairly bring us to the prison-grate and the alms-basket. A poor man on our stage is always a gentleman, he may be known by a peculiar neatness of apparel, and by wearing black. Our delicacy in fact forbids the dramatising of distress at all. It is never shewn in its essential properties; it appears but as the adjunct of some virtue, as something which is to be relieved, from the approbation of which relief the spectators are to derive a certain soothing of self-referred satisfaction. We turn away from the real essences of things to hunt after their relative shadows, moral duties; whereas, if the truth of things were fairly represented, the relative duties might be safely trusted to themselves, and moral philosophy lose the name of a science.

Thomas Middleton

The Witch.—Though some resemblance may be traced between the charms in *Macbeth,* and the incantations in this play, which is supposed to have preceded it, this coincidence will not detract much from the originality of Shakspeare. His witches are distinguished from the witches of Middleton by essential differences. These are creatures to whom man or woman, plotting some dire mischief, might resort for occasional consultation. Those originate deeds of blood, and begin bad impulses to men. From the moment that their eyes first meet with Macbeth's, he is spell-bound. That meeting sways his destiny. He can never break the fascination. These witches can hurt the body, those have power over the soul. Hecate in Middleton has a son, a low buffoon: the hags of Shakspeare have neither child of their own, nor seem to be descended from any parent. They are foul anomalies, of whom we know not whence they are sprung, nor whether they have beginning or ending. As they are without human passions, so they seem to be without human relations. They come with thunder and lightning, and vanish to airy music. This is all we know of them. Except Hecate, they have no *names;* which heightens their mysteriousness. The names, and some of the properties, which the other author has given to his hags, excite smiles. The Weïrd Sisters are serious things. Their presence cannot co-exist with mirth. But, in a lesser degree, the witches of Middleton are fine creations. Their power, too, is, in some measure, over the mind. They raise jars, jealousies, strifes, "like a thick scurf" over life.

William Rowley.—Thomas Decker.— John Ford, etc.

The Witch of Edmonton.—Mother Sawyer, in this wild play, differs from the hags of both Middleton and Shakspeare. She is the plain traditional old woman witch of our ancestors; poor, deformed, and ignorant; the terror of villages, herself amenable to a justice. That should be a hardy sheriff, with the power of the county at his heels, that would lay hands upon the Weïrd Sisters. They are of another jurisdiction. But upon the common and received opinion, the author (or authors) have engrafted strong fancy. There is something frightfully earnest in her invocations to the Familiar.

Cyril Tourneur

The Revengers' Tragedy.—The reality and life of the dialogue, in which Vindici and Hippolito first tempt their mother, and then threaten her with death for consenting to the dishonour of their sister, passes any scenical illusion I ever felt. I never read it but my ears tingle, and I feel a hot blush overspread my cheeks, as if I were presently about to proclaim such malefactions of myself as the brothers here rebuke in their unnatural parent, in words more keen and dagger-like than those which Hamlet speaks to his mother. Such power has the passion of shame truly personated, not only to strike guilty creatures unto the soul, but to "appal" even those that are "free."

John Webster

The Duchess of Malfy.—All the several parts of the dreadful apparatus with which the death of the Duchess is ushered in, the waxen images which counterfeit death, the wild masque of madmen, the tomb-maker, the bellman, the living person's dirge, the mortification by degrees,—are not more remote from the conceptions of ordinary vengeance, than the strange character of suffering which they seem to bring upon their victim is out of the imagination of ordinary poets. As they are not like inflictions of this life, so her language seems not of this world. She has lived among horrors till she is become "native and endowed unto that element." She speaks the dialect of despair; her tongue has a smatch of Tartarus and the souls in bale. To move a horror skilfully, to touch a soul to the quick, to lay upon fear as much as it can bear, to wean and weary a life till it is ready to drop, and then step in with mortal instruments to take its last forfeit: this only a Webster can do. Inferior geniuses may "upon horror's head horrors accumulate," but they cannot do this. They mistake quantity for quality; they "terrify babes with painted devils"; but they know not how a soul is to be moved. Their terrors want dignity, their affrightments are without decorum.

The White Devil, or Vittoria Corombona.—This White Devil of Italy sets off a bad cause so speciously, and pleads with such an innocence-resembling boldness, that we seem to see that matchless beauty of her face which inspires such gay confidence into her, and are ready to expect, when she has done her pleadings, that her very judges, her accusers, the grave ambassadors who sit as spectators, and all the court, will rise and make proffer to defend her in spite of the utmost conviction of her guilt; as the Shepherds in *Don Quixote* make proffer to follow the beautiful Shepherdess Marcela, "without making any profit of her manifest resolution made there in their hearing."

> So sweet and lovely does she make the shame,
> Which, like a canker in the fragrant rose,
> Does spot the beauty of her budding name!

I never saw anything like the funeral dirge in this play, for the death of Marcello, except the ditty which reminds Ferdinand of his drowned father in the *Tempest*. As that is of the water, watery; so this is of the earth, earthy. Both have that intenseness of feeling, which seems to resolve itself into the element which it contemplates.

In a note on the *Spanish Tragedy* in the Specimens, I have said that there is nothing in the undoubted plays of Jonson which would authorise us to suppose that he could have supplied the additions to *Hieronymo*. I suspected the agency of some more potent spirit. I thought that Webster might have furnished them. They seemed full of that wild, solemn, preternatural cast of grief which bewilders us in the Duchess of Malfy. On second consideration, I think this a hasty criticism. They are more like the overflowing griefs and talking distraction of Titus Andronicus. The sorrows of the Duchess set inward; if she talks, it is little more than soliloquy imitating conversation in a kind of bravery.

John Ford

The Broken Heart.—I do not know where to find, in any play, a catastrophe so grand, so solemn, and so surprising as in this. This is indeed, according to Milton, to describe high passions and high actions. The fortitude of the Spartan boy, who let a beast gnaw out his bowels till he died without expressing a groan, is a faint bodily image of this dilaceration of the spirit, and exenteration of the inmost mind, which Calantha, with a holy violence against her nature, keeps closely covered, till the last duties of a wife and a queen are fulfilled. Stories of martyrdom are but of chains and the stake; a little bodily suffering. These torments

> On the purest spirits prey,
> As on entrails, joints, and limbs,
> With answerable pains, but more intense.

What a noble thing is the soul in its strengths and in its weaknesses! Who would be less weak than Calantha? Who can be so strong? The expression of this transcendent scene almost bears us in imagination to Calvary and the Cross; and we seem to perceive some analogy between the scenical sufferings which we are here contemplating, and the real agonies of that final completion to which we dare no more than hint a reference. Ford was of the first order of poets. He sought for sublimity, not by parcels, in metaphors or visible images, but directly where she has her full residence in the heart of man; in the actions and sufferings of the greatest minds. There is a grandeur of the soul above mountains, seas, and the elements. Even in the poor perverted reason of Giovanni and Annabella, in the play which stands at the head of the modern collection of the works of this author, we discern traces of that fiery particle, which, in the irregular starting from out the road of beaten action, discovers something of a right line even in obliquity, and shews hints of an improveable greatness in the lowest descents and degradations of our nature.

Fulke Greville, Lord Brooke

Alaham, Mustapha.—The two tragedies of Lord Brooke, printed among his poems, might with more propriety have been termed political treatises than plays. Their author has strangely contrived to make passion, character, and interest, of the higher order, subservient to the expression of state dogmas and mysteries. He is nine parts Machiavel and Tacitus, for one part Sophocles or Seneca. In this writer's estimate of the powers of the mind, the understanding must have held a most tyrannical pre-eminence. Whether we look into his plays, or his most passionate love-poems, we shall find all frozen and made rigid with intellect. The finest movements of the human heart, the utmost grandeur of which the soul is capable, are essentially comprised in the actions and speeches of Cælica and Camena. Shakspeare, who seems to have had a peculiar delight in contemplating womanly perfection, whom for his many sweet images of female excellence all women are in an especial manner bound to love, has not raised the ideal of the female character higher than Lord Brooke, in these two women, has done. But it requires a study equivalent to the learning of a new language to understand their meaning when they speak. It is indeed hard to hit:

> Much like thy riddle, Samson, in one day
> Or seven though one should musing sit.

It is as if a being of pure intellect should take upon him to express the emotions of our sensitive natures. There would be all knowledge, but sympathetic expressions would be wanting.

Ben Jonson

The Case is Altered.—The passion for wealth has worn out much of its grossness in tract of time. Our ancestors certainly conceived of money as able to confer a distinct gratification in itself, not considered simply as a symbol of wealth. The old poets, when they introduce a miser, make him address his gold as his mistress; as something to be seen, felt, and hugged; as capable of satisfying two of the senses at least. The substitution of a thin, unsatisfying medium in the place of the good old tangible metal, has made avarice quite a

Platonic affection in comparison with the seeing, touching, and handling pleasures of the old Chrysophilites. A bank note can no more satisfy the touch of a true sensualist in this passion, than Creusa could return her husband's embrace in the shades. See the Cave of Mammon in Spenser; Barabas' contemplation of his wealth in the *Rich Jew of Malta;* Luke's raptures in the *City Madam;* the idolatry and absolute gold-worship of the miser Jaques in this early comic production of Ben Jonson's. Above all hear Guzman, in that excellent old translation of the *Spanish Rogue,* expatiate on the "ruddy cheeks of your golden ruddocks, your Spanish pistolets, your plump and full-faced Portuguese, and your clear-skinned pieces of eight of Castile," which he and his fellows the beggars kept secret to themselves, and did privately enjoy in a plentiful manner. "For to have them, to pay them away, is not to enjoy them; to enjoy them, is to have them lying by us; having no other need of them than to use them for the clearing of the eye-sight, and the comforting of our senses. These we did carry about with us, sewing them in some patches of our doublets near unto the heart, and as close to the skin as we could handsomely quilt them in, holding them to be restorative."

Poetaster.—This Roman play seems written to confute those enemies of Ben in his own days and ours, who have said that he made a pedantical use of his learning. He has here revived the whole Court of Augustus, by a learned spell. We are admitted to the society of the illustrious dead. Virgil, Horace, Ovid, Tibullus, converse in our own tongue more finely and poetically than they were used to express themselves in their native Latin. Nothing can be imagined more elegant, refined, and court-like, than the scenes between this Louis the Fourteenth of antiquity and his literati. The whole essence and secret of that kind of intercourse is contained therein. The economical liberality by which greatness, seeming to waive some part of its prerogative, takes care to lose none of the essentials; the prudential liberties of an inferior, which flatter by commanded boldness and soothe with complimentary sincerity. These, and a thousand beautiful passages from his *New Inn,* his *Cynthia's Revels,* and from those numerous court-masques and entertainments which he was in the daily habit of furnishing, might be adduced to shew the poetical fancy and elegance of mind of the supposed rugged old bard.

Alchemist.—The judgment is perfectly overwhelmed by the torrent of images, words, and book-knowledge, with which Epicure Mammon (Act II. Scene 2) confounds and stuns his incredulous hearer. They come pouring out like the successive falls of Nilus. They "doubly redouble strokes upon the foe." Description outstrides proof. We are made to believe effects before we have testimony for their causes. If there is no one image which attains the height of the sublime, yet the confluence and assemblage of them all produces a result equal to the grandest poetry. The huge Xerxean army countervails against single Achilles. Epicure Mammon is the most determined offspring of its author. It has the whole "matter and copy of the father—eye, nose, lip, the trick of his frown." It is just such a swaggerer as contemporaries have described old Ben to be. Meercraft, Bobadil, the Host of the New Inn, have all his image and superscription. But Mammon is arrogant pretension personified.

Sir Samson Legend, in *Love for Love,* is such another lying, overbearing character, but he does not come up to Epicure Mammon. What a "towering bravery" there is in his sensuality! he affects no pleasure under a Sultan. It is as if "Egypt with Assyria strove in luxury."

George Chapman

Bussy D'Ambois, Byron's Conspiracy, Byron's Tragedy, etc. etc.—Webster has happily characterised the "full and heightened style" of Chapman, who, of all the English play-writers, perhaps approaches nearest to Shakspeare in the descriptive and didactic, in passages which are less purely dramatic. He could not go out of himself, as Shakspeare could shift at pleasure, to inform and animate other existences, but in himself he had an eye to perceive and a soul to embrace all forms and modes of being. He would have made a great epic poet, if indeed he has not abundantly shewn himself to be one; for his Homer is not so properly a translation as the stories of Achilles and Ulysses rewritten. The earnestness and passion which he has put into every part of these poems, would be incredible to a reader of mere modern translations. His almost Greek zeal for the glory of his heroes can only be paralleled by that fierce spirit of Hebrew bigotry, with which Milton, as if personating one of the zealots of the old law, clothed himself when he sat down to paint the acts of Samson against the uncircumcised. The great obstacle to Chapman's translations being read, is their unconquerable quaintness. He pours out in the same breath the most just and natural, and the most violent and crude expressions. He seems to grasp at whatever words come first to hand while the enthusiasm is upon him, as if all other must be inadequate to the divine meaning. But passion (the all in all in poetry) is everywhere present, raising the low, dignifying the mean, and putting sense into the absurd. He makes his readers glow, weep, tremble, take any affection which he pleases, be moved by words, or in spite of them, be disgusted and overcome their disgust.

Francis Beaumont.—John Fletcher.

Maid's Tragedy.—One characteristic of the excellent old poets is, their being able to bestow grace upon subjects which naturally do not seem susceptible of any. I will mention two instances. Zelmane in the *Arcadia* of Sidney, and Helena in the *All's Well that Ends Well* of Shakspeare. What can be more unpromising at first sight, than the idea of a young man disguising himself in woman's attire, and passing himself off for a woman among women; and that for a long space of time? Yet Sir Philip has preserved so matchless a decorum, that neither does Pyrocles' manhood suffer any stain for the effeminacy of Zelmane, nor is the respect due to the princesses at all diminished when the deception comes to be known. In the sweetly constituted mind of Sir Philip Sidney, it seems as if no ugly thought or unhandsome meditation could find a harbour. He turned all that he touched into images of honour and virtue. Helena in Shakspeare is a young woman seeking a man in marriage. The ordinary rules of courtship are reversed, the habitual feelings are crossed. Yet with such exquisite address this dangerous subject is handled, that Helena's forwardness loses her no honour; delicacy dispenses with its laws in her favour, and nature, in her single case, seems content to suffer a sweet violation. Aspatia, in the *Maid's Tragedy,* is a character equally difficult, with Helena, of being managed with grace. She too is a slighted woman, refused by the man who had once engaged to marry her. Yet it is artfully contrived, that while we pity we respect her, and she descends without degradation. Such wonders true poetry and passion can do, to confer dignity upon subjects which do not seem capable of it. But Aspatia must not be compared at all points with Helena; she does not so absolutely predominate over her situation but she suffers some diminution, some abatement of the full lustre of the female character, which Helena never does. Her character has many degrees of sweetness, some of delicacy; but it has weakness, which, if we do not despise, we are sorry for. After all, Beaumont and Fletcher were but an inferior sort of Shakspeares and Sidneys.

Philaster.—The character of Bellario must have been extremely popular in its day. For many years after the date of *Philaster's* first exhibition on the stage, scarce a play can be found without one of these women pages in it, following in the train of some pre-engaged lover, calling on the gods to bless her happy rival (his mistress), whom no doubt she secretly curses in her heart, giving rise to many pretty *equivoques* by the way on the confusion of sex, and either made happy at last by some surprising turn of fate, or dismissed with the joint pity of the lovers and the audience. Donne has a copy of verses to his mistress, dissuading her from a resolution which she seems to have taken up from some of these scenical representations, of following him abroad as a page. It is so earnest, so weighty, so rich in poetry, in sense, in wit, and pathos, that it deserves to be read as a solemn close in future to all such sickly fancies as he there deprecates.

John Fletcher

Thierry and Theodoret.—The scene where Ordella offers her life a sacrifice, that the king of France may not be childless, I have always considered as the finest in all Fletcher, and Ordella to be the most perfect notion of the female heroic character, next to Calantha in the *Broken Heart.* She is a piece of sainted nature. Yet noble as the whole passage is, it must be confessed that the manner of it, compared with Shakspeare's finest scenes, is faint and languid. Its motion is circular, not progressive. Each line revolves on itself in a sort of separate orbit. They do not join into one another like a running-hand. Fletcher's ideas moved slow; his versification, though sweet, is tedious, it stops at every turn; he lays line upon line, making up one after the other, adding image to image so deliberately, that we see their junctures. Shakspeare mingles everything, runs line into line, embarrasses sentences and metaphors; before one idea has burst its shell, another is hatched and clamorous for disclosure. Another striking difference between Fletcher and Shakspeare, is the fondness of the former for unnatural and violent situations.

He seems to have thought that nothing great could be produced in an ordinary way. The chief incidents in some of his most admired tragedies shew this. Shakspeare had nothing of this contortion in his mind, none of that craving after violent situations, and flights of strained and improbable virtue, which I think always betrays an imperfect moral sensibility. The wit of Fletcher is excellent, like his serious scenes, but there is something strained and farfetched in both. He is too mistrustful of Nature, he always goes a little on one side of her. Shakspeare chose her without a reserve: and had riches, power, understanding, and length of days, with her, for a dowry.

Faithful Shepherdess.—If all the parts of this delightful pastoral had been in unison with its many innocent scenes and sweet lyric intermixtures, it had been a poem fit to view with *Comus* or the *Arcadia,* to have been put into the hands of boys and virgins, to have made matter for young dreams, like the loves of Hermia and Lysander. But a spot is on the face of this Diana. Nothing short of infatuation could have driven Fletcher upon mixing with this "blessedness" such an ugly deformity as Cloe, the wanton shepherdess! If Cloe was meant to set off Clorin by contrast, Fletcher should have known that such weeds by juxtaposition do not set off, but kill sweet flowers.

Philip Massinger.—Thomas Decker.

The Virgin Martyr.—This play has some beauties of so very high an order, that with all my respect for Massinger, I do not think he had poetical enthusiasm capable of rising up to them. His associate Decker, who wrote *Old Fortunatus,* has poetry enough for anything. The very impurities which obtrude themselves among the sweet pieties of this play, like Satan among the Sons of Heaven, have a strength of contrast, a raciness, and a glow, in them, which are beyond Massinger. They are to the religion of the rest what Caliban is to Miranda.

Philip Massinger.—Thomas Middleton.
—William Rowley.

Old Law.—There is an exquisiteness of moral sensibility, making one's eyes to gush out tears of delight, and a poetical strangeness in the circumstances of this sweet tragi-comedy, which are unlike anything in the dramas which Massinger wrote alone. The pathos is of a subtler edge. Middleton and Rowley, who assisted in it, had both of them finer geniuses than their associate.

James Shirley

Claims a place amongst the worthies of this period, not so much for any transcendent talent in himself, as that he was the last of a great race, all of whom spoke nearly the same language, and had a set of moral feelings and notions in common. A new language, and quite a new turn of tragic and comic interest, came in with the Restoration.

On the Death of
Coleridge

When I heard of the death of Coleridge, it was without grief. It seemed to me that he long had been on the confines of the next world,—that he had a hunger for eternity. I grieved then that I could not grieve. But, since, I feel how great a part he was of me. His great and dear spirit haunts me. I cannot think a thought, I cannot make a criticism on men and books, without an ineffectual turning and reference to him. He was the proof and touchstone of all my cogitations. He was a Grecian (or in the first form) at Christ's Hospital, where I was Deputy-Grecian; and the same subordination and deference to him I have preserved through a life-long acquaintance. Great in his writings, he was greatest in his conversation. In him was disproved that old maxim, that we should allow every one his share of talk. He would talk from morn to dewy eve, nor cease till far midnight; yet who ever would interrupt him? who would obstruct that continuous flow of converse, fetched from Helicon or Zion? He had the tact of making the unintelligible seem plain. Many who read the abstruser parts of his "Friend" would complain that his words did not answer to his spoken wisdom. They were identical. But he had a tone in oral delivery which seemed to convey sense to those who were otherwise imperfect recipients. He was my fifty-years-old friend without a dissension. Never saw I his likeness, nor probably the world can see again. I seem to love the house he died at more passionately than when he lived. I love the faithful Gillmans more than while they exercised their virtues towards him living. What was his mansion is consecrated to me a chapel.

BIBLIOGRAPHY

GENERAL

Abrams, M. H. *The Mirror and the Lamp: Romantic Theory and the Critical Tradition.* Oxford: Oxford University Press, 1953.

———. *Natural Supernaturalism.* New York: Norton, 1971.

———, ed. *English Romantic Poetry: Modern Essays in Criticism.* Second Edition. New York: Oxford University Press, 1975.

———. *The Correspondent Breeze: Essays on English Romanticism.* New York: Norton, 1984.

Alford, Steven E. *Irony and the Logic of the Romantic Imagination.* New York: Lang, 1984.

Bloom, Harold, ed. *Romanticism and Consciousness: Essays in Criticism.* New York: Norton, 1970.

———. *The Ringers in the Tower: Studies in Romantic Tradition.* Chicago: University of Chicago Press, 1971.

———. *The Visionary Company.* Ithaca: Cornell University Press, 1971.

———. *Anxiety of Influence; A Theory of Poetry.* New York: Oxford University Press, 1973.

———. *Poetry and Repression: Revisionism from Blake to Stevens.* New Haven: Yale University Press, 1976.

———. *Deconstruction and Criticism.* New York: Seabury Press, 1979.

———. *Agon: Towards a Theory of Revisionism.* New York: Oxford University Press, 1982.

———. *The Breaking of the Vessels.* (The Wellek Library Lectures.) Chicago: The University of Chicago Press, 1982.

Brantley, Richard E. *Locke, Wesley and the Method of English Romanticism.* Gainesville: University of Florida Press, 1984.

Brisman, Leslie. *Romantic Origins.* Ithaca: Cornell University Press, 1978.

Brown, Marshall. *The Shape of German Romanticism.* Ithaca: Cornell University Press, 1979.

Bush, Douglas. *Mythology and the Romantic Tradition in English Poetry.* New York: Norton, 1969.

Cantor, Paul A. *Creature and Creator: Myth-Making and English Romanticism.* New York: Cambridge University Press, 1984.

Cooke, Michael G. *The Romantic Will.* New Haven: Yale University Press, 1976.

———. *Acts of Inclusion: Studies Bearing on an Elementary Theory of Romanticism.* New Haven: Yale University Press, 1979.

De Man, Paul. *The Rhetoric of Romanticism.* New York: Columbia University Press, 1984.

Eliot, T. S. *Selected Essays.* New York: Harcourt, Brace & World, 1964.

Engelberg, Karsten, ed. *The Romantic Heritage: A Collection of Critical Essays.* Copenhagen: University of Copenhagen, 1983.

Fletcher, Ian, ed. *Romantic Mythologies.* New York: Barnes & Noble, 1967.

Fry, Paul. *The Poet's Calling in the English Ode.* New Haven: Yale University Press, 1980.

Frye, Northrop. *Fables of Identity: Studies in Poetic Mythology.* New York: Harcourt, Brace & World, 1963.

———, ed. *Romanticism Reconsidered.* New York: Columbia University Press, 1963.

———. *The Secular Scripture: A Study of the Structure of Romance.* Cambridge, Mass.: Harvard University Press, 1976.

————. *A Study of English Romanticism*. New York: Random House, 1968. Reprint: Chicago: University of Chicago Press, 1983.

Furst, Lilian R. *The Contours of European Romanticism*. Lincoln: University of Nebraska Press, 1980.

Hagstrum, Jean H. *The Romantic Body*. Knoxville: University of Tennessee Press, 1985.

Hilles, Frederick W.; and Bloom, Harold, eds. *From Sensibility to Romanticism: Essays Presented to Frederick A. Pottle*. New York: Oxford University Press, 1965.

Hoagwood, Terence Alex. *Prophecy and the Philosophy of Mind: Tradition of Blake and Shelley*. University of Alabama Press, 1985.

Homans, Margaret. *Women Writers and Poetic Identity*. Princeton: Princeton University Press, 1980.

Houtchens, Carolyn Washburn; and Houtchens, Lawrence Huston, eds. *The English Romantic Poets and Essayists: A Review of Research and Criticism*. Revised ed. New York: New York University Press, 1966.

Jones, Howard M. *Revolution and Romanticism*. Cambridge, Mass.: Harvard University Press, 1974.

Jordon, Frank, ed. *The English Romantic Poets: A Review of Research and Criticism*. New York: MLA, 1972.

Knight, G. Wilson. *Studies in the Poetry of Vision*. New York: Oxford University Press, 1941.

Kumar, Shiv K. *British Romantic Poets: Recent Revaluations*. New York: New York University Press, 1966.

Lipking, Lawrence, ed. *High Romantic Argument: Essays for M.H. Abrams*. Ithaca: Cornell University Press, 1981.

Lobb, Edward. *T.S. Eliot and the Romantic Critical Tradition*. London and Boston: Routledge & Kegan Paul, 1981.

Newlyn, Lucy. *Coleridge, Wordsworth and the Language of Allusion*. Oxford, New York: Oxford University Press, 1986.

Piper, H.W. *The Romantic Universe: Pantheism and the Concept of Imagination in the English Romantic Poets*. University of London: Athlone Press, 1962.

Prickett, Stephen, ed. *The Romantics*. New York: Holmes and Meier, 1981.

Rajan, Tilottamna. *Dark Interpreter: The Discourse of Romanticism*. Ithaca: Cornell University Press, 1980.

Redpath, Theodore. *The Young Romantic and Critical Opinion*. New York: St. Martin's Press, 1973.

Reed, Arden, ed. *Romanticism and Language*. Ithaca: Cornell University Press, 1984.

Reed, Walter L. *Meditations on the Hero: A Study of the Romantic Hero in Nineteenth-Century Fiction*. New Haven: Yale University Press, 1974.

Reiman, Donald H., ed. and introd. *The Romantics Reviewed, 1793–1830: A Collection in Depth of Periodical Reviews of the English Romantic Writers*. New York: Garland Press, 1972.

————. *English Romantic Poetry, 1800–1835: A Guide to Information Sources*. Detroit: Gale Press, 1979.

Schapiro, Barbara A. *The Romantic Mother: Narcissistic Patterns in Romantic Poetry*. Baltimore: Johns Hopkins University Press, 1983.

Simpson, David. *Irony and Authority in Romantic Poetry*. Totowa, N.J.: Rowman & Littlefield, 1979.

Studies in Romanticism, 1961–

Taylor, Anya. *Magic and English Romanticism.* Athens, Georgia: The University of
     Georgia Press, 1979.
Thorslev, Peter L. *Romantic Contraries: Freedom Versus Destiny.* New Haven: Yale
     University Press, 1984.
Thurley, Geoffrey. *The Romantic Predicament.* London: Macmillan, 1983. New York:
     St. Martin's Press, 1984.
Vogler, Thomas A. *Preludes to Vision: The Epic Venture in Blake, Wordsworth, Keats,
     and Hart Crane.* Berkeley: University of California Press, 1971.
Webster, Sarah McKim. "Circumscription and the Female in the Early Romantics."
     Philological Quarterly 61 (Winter 1982): 51–70.
Weiskel, Thomas. *The Romantic Sublime: Studies in the Structure and Psychology of
     Transcendence.* Baltimore: Johns Hopkins University Press, 1976.
Woodring, Carl. *Politics in English Romantic Poetry.* Cambridge, Mass.: Harvard
     University Press, 1970.
The Wordsworth Circle, 1970–1981.

IMMANUEL KANT

Beck, Lewis White. *Essays on Kant and Hume.* New Haven: Yale University Press,
     1978.
Bernstein, John Andrew. *Shaftesbury, Rousseau, and Kant: An Introduction to the
     Conflict Between Aesthetic and Moral Values in Modern Thought.* Rutherford,
     N.J.: Fairleigh Dickinson University Press, 1980.
Cassirer, Ernst. *Rousseau, Kant and Goethe: Two Essays.* Translated by James
     Gutman, Paul Oskar Kristeller, and John Herman Randall, Jr. Princeton:
     Princeton University Press, 1945.
Cohen, Ted and Guyer, Paul, eds. *Essays on Kant's Aesthetics.* Chicago: University of
     Chicago Press, 1982.
Coleman, Francis X. *The Harmony of Reason: A Study in Kant's Aesthetics.* Pitts-
     burgh: University of Pittsburgh Press, 1974.
Crawford, Donald W. *Kant's Aesthetic Theory.* Madison: University of Wisconsin Press,
     1974.
Finlay, J. N. *Kant and the Transcendental Object: A Hermeneutic Study.* Oxford:
     Clarendon Press, 1981.
Gadamer, Hans-Georg. *Truth and Method.* New York: The Seabury Press, 1975.
Guyer, Paul. *Kant and the Claims of Taste.* Cambridge, Mass.: Harvard University
     Press, 1979.
Handy, William J. *Kant and the Southern New Critics.* Austin: University of Texas
     Press, 1963.
Hendel, Charles William. *The Philosophy of Kant and Our Modern World; Four
     Lectures.* New York: Liberal Arts Press, 1957.
Kivy, Peter. *The Seventh Sense.* New York: Burt Franklin & Co., 1976.
Knox, Israel. *The Aesthetic Theories of Kant, Hegel, and Schopenhauer.* New York:
     Humanities Press, 1958.
Nahun, Milton C. *The Artist as Creator: An Essay on Human Freedom.* Baltimore:
     Johns Hopkins University Press, 1956.
Podro, Michael. *The Manifold in Perception: Theories of Art from Kant to Hildebrand.*
     Oxford-Warburg Studies. Oxford: Clarendon Press, 1972.

Schaper, Eva. *Studies in Kant's Aesthetics*. Edinburgh: Edinburgh University Press, 1979.

Warnock, Mary. *Imagination*. Berkeley and Los Angeles: University of California Press, 1976.

Wellek, Rene. *Immanuel Kant in England*. Princeton: Princeton University Press, 1931.

GOTTHOLD LESSING

Allison, Henry E. *Lessing and the Enlightenment; His Philosophy of Religion and its Relation to Eighteenth Century Thought*. Ann Arbor: University of Michigan Press, 1966.

Brown, Francis Andrew. *Gotthold Ephraim Lessing*. New York: Twayne, 1971.

Garland, Henry Bernard. *Lessing, the Founder of Modern German Literature*. London: Macmillan, 1962.

Graham, Ilse. *Goethe and Lessing: The Wellsprings of Creation*. London: Elek, 1973.

Heller, Peter. *Dialectics and Nihilism; Essays on Lessing, Nietzsche, Mann, and Kafka*. Amherst: University of Massachusetts Press, 1966.

Lanport, F. J. *Lessing and the Drama*. Oxford: Clarendon Press, 1981.

Mehring, Franz. *The Lessing Legend*. Translated by A.S. Grogan. New York: Critics Group, 1938.

Metzger, Michael M. *Lessing and the Language of Comedy*. The Hague: Mouton, 1966.

Robertson, John George. *Lessing's Dramatic Theory*. Bronx, N.Y.: B. Blom, 1965. Reprint of 1939 Edition.

Schmitz, Frederich Joseph. *The Problem of Individualism and the Crisis in the Lives of Lessing and Hamann*. Berkeley: University of California Press, 1944.

Schneider, Reinhold. *Lessing's Drama*. Munchen: K. Alber, 1948.

Wessel, Leonard P. *G.E. Lessing's Theology, a Study in the Problematic Nature of the Enlightenment*. The Hague: Mouton, 1977.

JOHANN VON GOETHE

Boyd, James. *Goethe's Knowledge of English Literature*. Oxford: Clarendon Press, 1932.

Boyesen, Hjalmar Hjorth. *Essays in German Literature*. Freeport, N.Y.: Books for Libraries Press, 1972.

Bruford, Walter Horace. *Culture and Society in Classical Weimar, 1775–1806*. London: Cambridge University Press, 1962.

Burckhardt, Sigurd. *The Drama of Language: Essays on Goethe and Kleist*. Baltimore: Johns Hopkins University Press, 1970.

Butler, Eliza Marian. *Byron and Goethe; Analysis of a Passion*. London: Bowes and Bowes, 1956.

Calvert, George Henry. *Coleridge, Shelley, Goethe*. Folcroft, Penn.: Folcroft Press, 1970.

Cassirer, Ernst. *Rousseau, Kant, Goethe; Two Essays*. Translated by James Gutmann, Paul Oskar Kristeller, and John Herman Randall, Jr. Princeton: Princeton University Press, 1970.

Croce, Benedetto. *Goethe*. London: Methuen, 1923.

Dieckmann, Liselotte. *Johann Wolfgang von Goethe*. New York: Twayne, 1974.

Dowden, Edward. *New Studies in Literature*. London: Kegan Paul, Trench, Trubner & Co., Ltd., 1895.

Eissler, Kurt Robert. *Goethe: A Psychological Study*. Detroit: Wayne State University Press, 1963.

Fairley, Barker. *Goethe as Revealed in His Poetry*. New York, Ungar, 1963.

———. *A Study of Goethe*. Oxford: Clarendon Press, 1947.

Friedenthal, Richard. *Goethe, His Life and Times*. Cleveland: World Publishing Co., 1965.

Goethe, Johann Wolfgang von. *The Autobiography of Johann Wolfgang von Goethe*. Translated by John Oxenford. New York: Horizon Press, 1969.

Gray, Ronald P. *Goethe: A Critical Introduction*. London: Cambridge University Press, 1967.

———. *Goethe the Alchemist: A Study of Alchemical Symbolism in Goethe's Literary and Scientific Works*. Cambridge: Cambridge University Press, 1952.

Gundolf, Friedrich. *Goethe*. New York: AMS Press, 1971.

Lukacs, Gyorgy. *Goethe and His Age*. Translated by Robert Anchor. London: Merlin Press, 1968.

Mann, Thomas. *Freud, Goethe, Wagner*. New York: Knopf, 1977.

———. *Three Essays*. Translated by H.T. Lowe-Porter. New York: Knopf, 1929.

Masson, David. *The Three Deals: Luther's, Milton's, and Goethe's*. Folcroft, Penn.: Folcroft Press, 1969.

Needles, George Henry. *Goethe and Scott*. Toronto: Oxford University Press, 1950.

Robertson, John George. *Goethe and the 20th Century*. Cambridge: Cambridge University Press, 1912. New York: Haskell House, 1972.

Rolland, Romain. *Goethe and Beethoven*. Translated by G.A. Pfister and E.S. Kemp. New York: Harper, 1931.

Rose, William. *Men, Myths, and Movements in German Literature; a Volume of Historical and Critical Papers*. Port Washington, N.Y.: Kennikat Press, 1964.

Schweitzer, Albert. *Goethe; Four Studies*. Translated by C.R. Joy. Boston: Beacon Press, 1949.

Van Abbi, Derek Maurice. *Goethe: New Perspectives on a Writer and His Time*. London: Allen and Unwin, 1972.

Victor, Karl. *Goethe, the Poet*. Translated by Moses Hadas. Cambridge, Mass.: Harvard University Press, 1949.

———. *Goethe, the Thinker*. Translated by Bayard Q. Morgan. Cambridge, Mass.: Harvard University Press, 1950.

Weinberg, Kurt. *The Figure of Faust in Valery and Goethe: An Exegesis of Man Faust*. Princeton: Princeton University Press, 1976.

JOHANN G. HERDER

Barnand, F. *Herder's Social and Political Thought, from Enlightenment to Nationalism*. Oxford: Clarendon Press, 1965.

Berlin, Isaiah. *Vico and Herder: Two Studies in the History of Ideas*. New York: Viking Press, 1976.

Clark, Robert Thomas. *Herder: His Life and Thought*. Berkeley: University of California Press, 1955.

Ergang, Robert Reinhold. *Herder and the Foundations of German Nationalism*. New York: Octagon Books, 1966.

Fugate, Joe K. *The Psychological Basis of Herder's Aesthetics.* The Hague: Mouton, 1966.

Mayo, Robert S. *Herder and the Beginnings of Comparative Literature.* Chapel Hill: University of North Carolina Press, 1969.

Schizk, Edgar B. *Metaphorical Organicism in Herder's Early Works; A Study of the Relation of Herder's Literary Idiom to His World View.* The Hague: Mouton, 1971.

Wells, G. *Herder and After; A Study in the Development of Sociology.* The Hague: Mouton, 1971.

WILLIAM BLAKE

Ault, Donald D. *Visionary Physics: Blake's Response to Newton.* Chicago: University of Chicago Press, 1974.

Beer, John B. *Blake's Humanism.* New York: Barnes & Noble, 1968.

— ——. *Blake's Visionary Universe.* New York: Barnes & Noble, 1969.

Bentley, G. E., Jr., ed. *William Blake: The Critical Heritage.* London: Routledge & Kegan Paul, 1975.

Bentley, Gerald Endes. *A Blake Bibliography.* Minneapolis: University of Minnesota Press, 1964.

Bloom, Harold. *Blake's Apocalypse; A Study in Poetic Argument.* Garden City, N.Y.: Doubleday, 1965.

Bronowski, Jacob. *William Blake and the Age of Revolution.* London: Routledge & Kegan Paul, 1972.

Chesterton, G. K. *William Blake.* London: Duckworth & Co., 1920.

Crehan, A. S. *Blake in Context.* Dublin: Gill & Macmillan, 1984.

Damon, Samuel Foster. *A Blake Dictionary: The Ideas and Symbols of William Blake.* Providence: Brown University Press, 1965.

Deen, Leonard W. *Conversing in Paradise: Poetic Genius and Indentity-as-Community in Blake's Los.* Columbia: University of Missouri Press, 1983.

DiSalvo, Jackie. *War of Titans: Blake's Critique of Milton and the Politics of Religion.* Philadelphia: University of Pennsylvania Press, 1983.

Erdman, David V; and Grant, John E.; eds. *Blake's Visionary Forms Dramatic.* Princeton: Princeton University Press, 1970.

Frosch, Thomas R. *The Awakening of Albion: The Renovation of the Body in the Poetry of William Blake.* Ithaca: Cornell University Press, 1974.

Frye, Northrup, ed. *Blake; A Collection of Critical Essays.* Englewood Cliffs, N.J.: Prentice-Hall, 1966.

———. *Fearful Symmetry; A Study of William Blake.* Boston: Beacon Press, 1962.

Holloway, John. *Blake: The Lyric Poetry.* London: Edward Arnold, 1968.

Howard, John. *Blake's Milton: A Study in the Selfhood.* Rutherford N.J.: Fairleigh Dickinson University Press, 1976.

Jackson, Wallace. *The Probable and the Marvellous: Blake, Wordsworth, and the 18th Century Critical Tradition.* Athens: University of Georgia Press, 1978.

Johnson, Mary Lynn; and Grant, John E.; eds. *Blake's Poetry and Designs.* (A Norton Critical Edition.) New York: Norton, 1979. Rutherford, N.J.: Fairleigh Dickinson University Press, 1984.

Keynes, Geoffrey Langdon. *Blake Studies; Notes on His Life and Works.* London: R. Hart-Davis, 1949.

Korteling, Jacomina. *Mysticism in Blake and Wordsworth.* New York: Haskell House, 1966.

Levenberger, Peter. *William Blake's Esemplastic Power: A Study of William Blake's Myth of Unification*. Zurich: Juris-Verlag, 1978.

Mellor, Anne Kosklawetz. *Blake's Human Form Divine*. Berkeley: University of California Press, 1974.

Morton, Arthur Leslie. *The Everlasting Gospel; A Study in the Sources of William Blake*. Folcroft, Penn.: Folcroft Library Editions, 1974.

Paley, Morton D. *Energy and the Imagination: A Study of the Development of Blake's Thought*. Oxford: Clarendon Press, 1970.

——, and Phillips, Michael. *William Blake: Essays in Honour of Sir Geoffrey Keynes*. Oxford: Clarendon Press, 1973.

Rudd, Margaret. *Organized Innocence; The Story of Blake's Prophetic Books*. London: Routledge & Kegan Paul, 1956.

Saurat, Denis. *Blake and Modern Thought*. New York: Russell & Russell, 1964.

Scholz, Joachim J. *Blake and Novalis: A Comparison of Romanticism's High Arguments*. Frankfurt am Main: Pern, 1978.

Tannenbaum, Leslie. *Biblical Tradition in Blake's Early Prophecies: The Great Code of Art*. Princeton: Princeton University Press, 1982.

Webster, Brenda. *Blake's Prophetic Psychology*. London: Macmillan, 1983.

FRIEDRICH SCHILLER

Boyesen, Hjalmar Hjorth. *Essays on German Literature*. Freeport, N.Y.: Books for Libraries Press, 1972.

——. *Goethe and Schiller; Their Lives and Works*. New York: C. Scribner's Sons, 1882.

Carlyle, Thomas. *The Life of Friedrich Schiller*. London: Taylor, 1825.

Dewhurst, Kenneth, and Reeves, Nigel, eds. *Friedrich Schiller: Medicine Psychology and Literature*. Oxford: Sandford Publications, 1978.

Ellis, John Martin. *Schiller's Kalliasburck and the Study of His Aesthetic Theory*. The Hague: Mouton, 1969.

Ewer, Frederic. *The Prestige of Schiller in England*. New York: Columbia University Press, 1932.

Frey, John R. *Schiller 1759/1959; Commemorative American Studies*. Urbana: University of Illinois Press, 1959.

Garland, Henry Birrand. *Schiller*. New York: McBride, 1950.

Ives, Margaret C. *The Analogue of Harmony: Some Reflections on Schiller's Philosophical Essays*. Pittsburgh, Penn.: Duquesne University Press, 1970.

Kaufmann, Friedrich Wilhelm. *Schiller, Poet of Philosophical Idealism*. Oberlin, O.: The Academy Press, 1942.

Kerry, Stanley Sephton. *Schiller's Writing on Aesthetics*. Manchester: English University Press, 1961.

Kostka, Edward K. *Schiller in Russian Literature*. Philadelphia: University of Pennsylvania Press, 1965.

Mainland, William Faulkner. *Schiller and the Changing Past*. London: Heinemann, 1957.

Mann, Thomas. *Last Essays*. Translated by Richard & Clara Winston and Tania & James Stern. New York: Knopf, 1959.

Meakin, Annette M. *Goethe and Schiller; 1785–1805; The Story of a Friendship*. London: F. Griffiths, 1932.

Miller, Ronald D. *Schiller and the Ideal of Freedom*. Oxford: Clarendon Press, 1970.

Norman, Frederick. *Schiller; Bicentenary Lectures*. London: Institute of German Languages and Literatures, University of London, 1960.

Rea, Thomas. *Schiller's Dramas and Poems in England*. London: Unwin, 1906.

Regin, Deric Worgenvort. *Freedom and Dignity; The Historical and Philosophical Thought of Schiller*. The Hague: M. Nijhoff, 1965.

Stahl, Ernst Ludwig. *Friedrich Schiller's Drama; Theory and Practice*. Oxford: Clarendon Press, 1954.

Williamson, Elizabeth Mary. *Schiller; Poet or Philosopher*. Oxford: Clarendon Press, 1961.

Witte, William. *Schiller*. Oxford: Blackwell, 1949.

———. *Schiller and Burns and Other Essays*. Oxford: Blackwell, 1959.

MADAME DE STAËL

Andrews, Wayne. *Germaine; a Portrait of Madame de Staël*. New York: Atheneum, 1963.

Furst, Lillian R. "Mme de Staël's *De l'Allemagne:* A Misleading Intermediary." *Orbis Litterarum* 31 (1976): 43–58.

Gutwirth, Madelyne. *Madame de Staël, Novelist: The Emergence of the Artist as Woman*. Urbana: University of Illinois Press, 1978.

Hawkins, Richmond Laurin. *Madame de Staël and the United States*. Cambridge, Mass.: Harvard University Press, 1930.

Herold, S. Christopher. *Mistress to an Age; A Life of Madame de Staël*. Indianapolis: Bobbs-Merrill Co., 1958.

Levaillant, Maurice. *The Passionate Exiles; Madame de Staël and Madame Récamier*. Translated by Malcolm Barnes. New York: Farrar, Straus and Cudahy, 1955.

Porter, Laurence M. "The Emergence of a Romantic Style: From *De La Litterature* to *De l'Allemagne*." In *Authors and Their Centuries*, edited by Phillip Crant. Columbia: University of South Carolina Press, 1973.

Postgate, Helen Belle. *Madame de Staël*. New York: Twayne Publishers, 1968.

West, Anthony. *Mortal Wounds*. New York: McGraw-Hill, 1973.

Whitford, Robert Calum. *Madame de Staël's Literary Reputation in English*. Urbana: University of Illinois, 1918.

G.W.F. HEGEL

Berry, Christopher J. *Hume, Hegel, and Human Nature*. The Hague: M. Nijhoff, 1982.

Butler, Clark. *G.W.F. Hegel*. Boston: Twayne, 1977.

Caird, Edward. *Hegel*. New York: AMS Press, 1972.

Cook, David J. *Language in the Philosophy of Hegel*. The Hague: Mouton, 1973.

Cooper, Barry. *The End of History: An Essay on Modern Hegelianism*. Toronto: University of Toronto Press, 1984.

Croce, Benedetto. *What is Living and What is Dead of the Philosophy of Hegel*. Translated by Douglas Ainslie. New York: Russell & Russell, 1969.

Derrida, Jacques. *Margins of Philosophy*. Translated by Alan Bass. Chicago: University of Chicago Press, 1982.

Dupre, Louis K. *The Philosophical Foundations of Marxism*. New York: Harcourt, Brace & World, 1966.

Flaccus, Louis William. *Artists and Thinkers*. Freeport, N.Y.: Books for Libraries Press, 1967.

Gadaner, Hans-Georg. *Hegel's Dialectics: His Hermeneutical Studies*. Translated by Christopher Smith. New Haven: Yale University Press, 1976.

Heidegger, Martin. *Hegel's Concept of Experience*. New York: Harper & Row, 1970.

Kaufmann, Walter Arnold. *Hegel; Reinterpretation*. Garden City, N.Y.: Doubleday, 1965.

Lowith, Karth. *From Hegel to Nietzsche: The Revolution in Nineteenth-Century Thought*. Translated from the German by David E. Green. New York: Holt, Rinehart, & Winston, 1964.

Lukacs, Gyorgy. *The Young Hegel: Studies in the Relation Between Economics and Dialectics*. Translated by Audrey Livingstone. Cambridge, Mass.: M.I.T. Press, 1975.

Marcuse, Herbert. *Reason and Revolution; Hegel and the Rise of Social Theory*. Boston: Beacon Press, 1960.

Nauen, Franz Gabriel. *Revolution, Idealism, and Human Freedom: Schilling, Holderlin, Hegel and the Crisis of Early German Idealism*. The Hague: Nijhoff, 1971.

Ortega y Gasset, Jose. *Kant, Hegel, Dilthey*. Madrid: Revista de Occidente, 1958.

Plant, Raymond. *Hegel: An Introduction*. Oxford: Blackwell, 1983.

Soll, Ivan. *An Introduction to Hegel's Metaphysics*. Chicago: University of Chicago Press, 1969.

Toews, John Edward. *Hegelianism: The Path Toward Dialectical Humanism, 1805–1841*. New York: Cambridge University Press, 1980.

WILLIAM WORDSWORTH

Abrams, M.H., ed. *Wordsworth: A Collection of Critical Essays*. Englewood Cliffs, N.J.: Prentice-Hall, 1972.

Averill, James H. *Wordsworth and the Poetry of Human Suffering*. Ithaca: Cornell University Press, 1980.

Bauer, Neil S. *William Wordsworth: A Reference Guide to British Criticism, 1793–1899*. Boston: G.K. Hall, 1978.

Beer, John Bernard. *Wordsworth and the Human Heart*. New York: Columbia University Press, 1978.

———. *Wordsworth in Time*. London: Faber, 1979.

Bloom, Harold, ed. *William Wordsworth*. New York: Chelsea House, 1985.

Brantley, Richard E. *Wordsworth's "Natural Methodism."* New Haven: Yale University Press, 1975.

Chandler, James K. *Wordsworth's Second Nature: A Study of the Poetry of Politics*. Chicago: University of Chicago Press, 1981.

Cosgrove, Brian. *Wordsworth and the Poetry of Self-Sufficiency: A Study of the Poetic Development, 1796–1814*. (SSEL, Romantic Reassessment, 93). Salzburg: University of Salzburg, 1982.

Durrant, Geoffrey. *Wordsworth and the Great System: A Study of Wordsworth's Poetic Universe*. New York: Cambridge University Press, 1970.

Gill, Stephen, ed. *William Wordsworth*. New York: Oxford University Press, 1984.

Hartman, Geoffrey H., ed. *New Perspectives on Coleridge and Wordsworth: Selected Papers from the English Institute*. New York: Columbia University Press, 1972.

Havens, Raymond Dexter. *The Mind of a Poet*. Baltimore: Johns Hopkins University Press, 1941.

Hearn, Ronald B. et al., eds. *Wordsworthian Criticism since 1952: A Bibliography*. Salzburg: Inst. fur Ang. Sprache & Lit., University of Salzburg, 1978.

Jackson, Wallace. *The Probable and the Marvelous: Blake, Wordsworth, and the 18th-Century Critical Tradition*. Athens: University of Georgia Press, 1978.

Jacobus, Mary. *Tradition and Experiment in Wordsworth's "Lyrical Ballads" (1798)*. Oxford: Clarendon Press, 1976.

McConnel, Frank D. *The Confessional Imagination: A Reading of Wordsworth's "Prelude."* Baltimore: Johns Hopkins University Press, 1974.

McFarland, Thomas. *Romanticism and the Forms of Ruin: Wordsworth, Coleridge, and the Modalities of Fragmentation*. Princeton: Princeton University Press, 1981.

Onorato, Richard. *The Character of the Poet: Wordsworth in "The Prelude."* Princeton: Princeton University Press, 1971.

Parrish, Stephen Maxfield. *The Art of the "Lyrical Ballads."* Cambridge, Mass.: Harvard University Press, 1973.

———, ed. *"The Prelude," 1798–1799*. Ithaca: Cornell University Press.

Reed, Mark. *Wordsworth: The Chronology of the Middle Years, 1800–1815*. Cambridge, Mass.: Harvard University Press, 1975.

Simpson, David. *Wordsworth and the Figurings of the Real*. London: Macmillan, 1982.

Stam, David H. *Wordsworthian Criticism, 1964–1973: An Annotated Bibliography*. New York: The New York Public Library & Readex Books, 1974.

Watson, J. R. *Wordsworth's Vital Soul: The Sacred and the Profane in Wordsworth's Poetry*. London: Macmillan, 1982.

Wlecke, Albert O. *Wordsworth and the Sublime*. Berkeley: University of California Press, 1973.

Woodring, Carl. *Wordsworth*. Boston: Houghton Mifflin, 1965.

Wordsworth, Jonathan. *William Wordsworth: The Borders of Vision*. Oxford: Clarendon Press, 1982.

———, Abrams, M.H.; Gill, Stephen; eds. *"The Prelude" 1799, 1805, 1850*. New York: Norton, 1979.

SIR WALTER SCOTT

Alexander, J. H., and Hewitt, David, eds. *Scott and His Influence*. Association for Scottish Literary Studies, Occasional Papers. Aberdeen: University of Aberdeen, 1983.

Anderson, W. E. K., ed. *The Journal of Sir Walter Scott*. Oxford: Clarendon Press, 1972.

Bold, Alan, ed. *Sir Walter Scott: The Long Forgotten Melody*. Totowa, N.J.: Barnes & Noble, 1983.

Cockshut, A. O. J. *The Achievement of Walter Scott*. New York: New York University Press, 1969.

Curry, Kenneth. *Sir Walter Scott's "Edinburgh Annual Register."* Knoxville: University of Tennessee Press, 1977.

Dickson, Nicholas. *Bible in Waverley; or, Sir Walter Scott's Use of the Sacred Scriptures*. Folcroft, Penn.: Folcroft Library Editions, 1979.

Hartveit, Lars. *Dream Within a Dream: A Thematic Approach to Scott's Vision of Fictional Reality*. New York: Humanities Press, 1979.

Hayden, John O., ed. *Scott: The Critical Heritage*. New York: Barnes & Noble, 1970.

Hewitt, David, ed. *Scott on Himself: A Selection of the Autobiographical Writings of Sir Walter Scott.* New York: Columbia University Press, 1981.

Johnson, Edgar. *Sir Walter Scott: The Great Unknown.* New York: Macmillan, 1970.

Jordan, Frank. "Scott and Wordsworth; or Reading Scott Well." *The Wordsworth Circle.* 4 (1973): 112–23.

McMaster, Graham. *Scott and Society.* Cambridge: Cambridge University Press, 1982.

Mayhead, Robin. *Walter Scott.* Cambridge: Cambridge University Press, 1973.

Millgate, Jane. *Walter Scott: The Making of the Novelist.* Toronto: University of Toronto Press, 1984.

Shaw, Harry E. *The Forms of Historical Fiction: Sir Walter Scott and His Successors.* Ithaca: Cornell University Press, 1983.

Walker, Eric G. *Scott's Fiction and the Picturesque.* Salzburg: Institut für Anglistik and Amerikanistik, University of Salzburg, 1982.

Whitmore, Daniel. "Scott's Indebtedness to the German Romantics: *Ivanhoe* Reconsidered." *The Wordsworth Circle* 15 (1984): 72–73.

Wilson, A. N. *The Laird of Abbotsford: A View of Sir Walter Scott.* Oxford: Oxford University Press, 1980.

NOVALIS

Birrell, Gordon. *The Boundless Present: Space and Time in the Literary Fairy Tales of Novalis and Tieck.* Chapel Hill: University of North Carolina Press, 1979.

Dalke, Robert. *Novalis "Subjects."* Canton, N.Y.: Institute of Further Studies, 1973.

Friedrichsmeyer, Sara. *The Androgyne in Early German Romanticism: Friedrich Schlegel, Novalis and the Metaphysics of Love.* New York: Lang, 1983.

Hannah, Richard W. *The Fichtean Dynamic of Novalis' Poetics.* Bern: Lang, 1981.

Haywood, Bruce. *Novalis; The Veil of Imagery.* The Hague: Mouton, 1959.

Malsch, Sara Ann. *The Image of Martin Luther in the Writings of Novalis and Friedrich Schlegel: The Speculative Vision of History and Religion.* Bern: Lang, 1974.

Massey, Marilyn Chapin. *Feminine Soul: The Fate of an Ideal.* Boston: Beacon, 1985.

Molnar, Geza von. *Novalis "Fichte Studies"; The Foundations of His Aesthetics.* The Hague: Mouton, 1970.

Neubauer, John. *Bifocal Vision: Novalis' Philosophy of Nature and Disease.* Chapel Hill: The University of North Carolina Press, 1971.

———. *Novalis.* Boston: Twayne, 1980.

Scholz, Joachim J. *Blake and Novalis: A Comparison of Romanticism's High Arguments.* Bern: Lang, 1978.

FRIEDRICH SCHLEGEL

Eichner, Hans. *Friedrich Schlegel.* New York: Twayne, 1970.

Friedrichsmeyer, Sara. *The Androgyne in Early German Romanticism: Friedrich Schlegel, Novalis and the Metaphysics of Love.* New York: Lang, 1983.

Goslee, Nancy M. "Pure Stream from a Troubled Source: Byron, Schlegel and Prometheus." *The Byron Journal* 10 (1982): 20–36.

Higonnet, Margaret R. "Friedrich Schlegel on Lessing: Criticism as the Mother of Poets." *Lessing Yearbook* 2 (1979): 83–103.

Malsch, Sara Ann. *The Image of Martin Luther in the Writings of Novalis and*

Friedrich Schlegel: The Speculative Vision of History and Religion. Bern: Lang, 1974.

Peter, Klaus. *Friedrich Schlegel*. (Sammlung Metzler, 171.) Stuttgart: Metzler, 1978.

Stoljar, Margaret. *Athenaeum: A Critical Commentary*. Bern: Lang, 1973.

SAMUEL TAYLOR COLERIDGE

Barfield, Owen. *What Coleridge Thought*. Middletown, Conn.: Wesleyan University Press, 1971.

Barth, J. Robert. *The Symbolic Imagination: Coleridge and the Romantic Tradition*. Princeton: Princeton University Press, 1977.

Beer, John, ed. *Coleridge's Variety: Bicentenary Studies*. With an introduction by L.C. Knights. London: Macmillan, 1974. Pittsburgh: University of Pittsburgh Press, 1975.

———. *Coleridge's Poetic Intelligence*. New York: Barnes & Noble, 1977.

Bloom, Harold. *Figures of Capable Imagination*. New York: Seabury Press, 1976.

Boulger, James D., ed. *Twentieth-Century Interpretations of "The Rime of the Ancient Mariner."* Englewood Cliffs, N.J.: Prentice-Hall, 1969.

Brett, R. L., ed. *S.T. Coleridge*. London: Bell, 1971. Athens: Ohio University Press, 1972.

Burke, Kenneth. *Language as Symbolic Action: Essays on Life, Literature, and Method*. Berkeley: University of California Press, 1966.

Christensen, Jerome. *Coleridge's Blessed Machine of Language*. Ithaca: Cornell University Press, 1981.

Coburn, Kathleen, ed. *Inquiring Spirit: A New Presentation of Coleridge from His Published and Unpublished Prose Writings*. Revised edition. Toronto: University of Toronto Press, 1979.

———, ed. *Experience into Thought: Perspectives in the Coleridge Notebooks*. Toronto: University of Toronto Press, 1979.

Corrigan, Timothy. *Coleridge, Language and Criticism*. Athens: University of Georgia Press, 1982.

Crawford, Walter B.; Lauterbach, Edward S.; Crawford, Ann M.; eds. *Samuel Taylor Coleridge: An Annotated Bibliography of Criticism and Scholarship, II: 1900–1939 (With Additional Entries for 1795–1899)*. Boston: G.K. Hall, 1983.

Hamilton, Paul. *Coleridge's Poetics*. Stanford: Stanford University Press, 1983.

Happel, Stephen. *Coleridge's Religious Imagination*. 3 vols. Salzburg: University of Salzburg, 1983.

Harding, Anthony John. *Coleridge and the Idea of Love: Aspects of Relationship in Coleridge's Thought and Writing*. London: Cambridge University Press, 1974.

Hartman, Geoffrey H., ed. *New Perspectives on Coleridge and Wordsworth: Selected Papers from the English Institute*. New York: Columbia University Press, 1972.

Jackson, J. R. de J., ed. *Coleridge: The Critical Heritage*. New York: Barnes & Noble, 1970.

Kessler, Edward. *Coleridge's Metaphors of Being*. Princeton: Princeton University Press, 1979.

Levere, Trevor H. *Poetry Realized in Nature: Samuel Taylor Coleridge and Early Nineteenth-Century Science*. Cambridge: Cambridge University Press, 1981.

McFarland, Thomas. *Coleridge and the Pantheist Tradition*. Oxford: Clarendon Press, 1969.

———. *Romanticism and the Forms of Ruin: Wordsworth, Coleridge, and Modalities of Fragmentation*. Princeton: Princeton University Press, 1981.

Milton, Mary Lee Taylor. *The Poetry of Samuel Taylor Coleridge: An Annotated Bibliography of Criticism, 1935–1970.* New York: Garland Publishing, 1981.

Modiano, Raimonda. *Coleridge and the Concept of Nature.* Tallahassee: Florida State University Press, 1985.

Parker, Reeve. *Coleridge's Meditative Art.* Ithaca: Cornell University Press, 1975.

Prickett, Stephen. *Wordsworth and Coleridge: "The Lyrical Ballads."* London: Arnold, 1975.

———. *Romanticism and Religion: The Tradition of Coleridge and Wordsworth on the Victorian Church.* Cambridge: Cambridge University Press, 1976.

Stevenson, Warren. *Nimbus of Glory: A Study of Coleridge's Three Great Poems.* Atlantic Highlands, N.J.: Humanities Press, 1983.

Sultana, Donald, ed. *New Approaches to Coleridge: Biographical and Critical Essays.* London: Vision, 1981. Totowa, N.J.: Barnes & Noble, 1981.

Wallace, Catherine Miles. *The Design of "Biographia Literaria."* London: George Allen & Unwin, 1983.

Wheeler, Kathleen. *Sources, Processes and Methods in Coleridge's "Biographia Literaria."* Cambridge: Cambridge University Press, 1980.

FRANCIS JEFFREY

Chapman, Gerald Webster, ed. *Literary Criticism in England: 1660–1800.* New York: Knopf, 1966.

Flynn, Philip. *Francis Jeffrey.* Newark: University of Delaware Press, 1978.

Grieg, James. *Francis Jeffrey of the "Edinburgh Review."* Edinburgh: Oliver & Boyd, 1948.

Morgan, Peter. "Principles and Perspectives in Jeffrey's Criticism." *Studies in Scottish Literature* 4 (1967): 179–93.

———. "Francis Jeffrey as Epistolary Critic." *Studies in Scottish Literature* 17 (1982): 116–34.

———, ed. *Jeffrey's Criticism: A Selection.* Edinburgh: Scottish Academic Press, 1983.

Noyes, Russell. *Wordsworth and Jeffrey in Controversy.* Bloomington: Indiana University Press, 1941.

Pitrie, David W. "Francis Jeffrey and Religion: Excerpts from His 1799–1800 Commonplace Book." *Eighteenth-Century Life* 8 (1982): 97–107.

HENRY CRABB ROBINSON

Behler, Diana I. "Henry Crabb Robinson as a Mediator of Early German Romanticism to England." *Arcadia* 12 (1977): 117–55.

———. "Henry Crabb Robinson as a Mediator of Lessing and Herder to England." *Lessing Yearbook* 7 (1984): 105–26.

Brown, Eluned, ed. *The London Theatre 1811–1866: Selections from the Diary of Henry Crabb Robinson.* London: Society for Theatre Research, 1966.

Hudson, Derek, ed. *The Diary of Henry Crabb Robinson: An Abridgement.* London: Oxford University Press, 1967.

Morley, Edith J., ed. *The Correspondence of Henry Crabb Robinson with the Wordsworth Circle (1808–1866).* Oxford: Clarendon Press, 1927.

———. *The Life and Times of Henry Crabb Robinson.* London: J.M. Dent & Sons, Ltd., 1935.

Norman, Frederick. *Henry Crabb Robinson and Goethe.* London: A. Moring, Ltd., 1930–31.

Steinberg, S.H. "The Correspondent of *The Times* in Hamburg-Altona in 1807." *Festschrift Percy Ernst Schramm,* vol. 2, pp. 26–47. Wiesbaden: Franz Steiner, 1964.

Wellens, Oskar. "Henry Crabb Robinson, Reviewer of Wordsworth, Coleridge, and Byron in the *Critical Review:* Some New Attributions." *Bulletin of Research in the Humanities* 84 (1981): 98–120.

WILLIAM HAZLITT

Albrecht, William P. *Hazlitt and the Creative Imagination.* Lawrence: University of Kansas Press, 1965.

——. "Hazlitt Studies, 1963–1972." *The Wordsworth Circle* 6 (1975): 67–79.

——. "The Originality of Hazlitt's Essays." *The Yale Review* 72 (1983): 366–84.

——. *Hazlitt: The Mind of a Critic.* New York: Oxford University Press, 1984.

Foot, Michael. "Hazlitt's Revenge on the Lakers." *The Wordsworth Circle* 14 (1983): 61–68.

Houck, James A. *William Hazlitt: A Reference Guide.* Boston: G.K. Hall, 1977.

——. "Byron and William Hazlitt." In *Lord Byron and His Contemporaries: Essays from the Sixth International Byron Seminar,* edited by Charles Robinson. Newark: University of Delaware Press, 1982.

Keynes, Geoffrey. *Bibliography of William Hazlitt.* Second Edition, revised. Charlottesville: University Press of Virginia, 1981.

Kinnaird, John. *William Hazlitt: Critic of Power.* New York: Columbia University Press, 1978.

Mahoney, John L. *The Logic of Passion: The Literary Criticism of William Hazlitt.* New York: Fordham University Press, 1981.

Misra, J. B. "Hazlitt and Wordsworth: 'On Going a Journey' in the Light of Wordsworth's Poetry." *CIEFL Bulletin* 2 (1975): 83–97.

Park, Roy. *Hazlitt and the Spirit of the Age: Abstraction and Critical Theory.* Oxford: Clarendon Press, 1971.

Patterson, Charles I., Jr. "Hazlitt's Criticism in Retrospect." *Studies in English Literature, 1500–1900* 21 (1981): 647–63.

Ready, Robert. "Flat Realities: Hazlitt on Biography." *Prose Studies* 5 (1982): 309–17.

Sikes, Herschel M., ed. *The Letters of William Hazlitt.* New York: New York University Press, 1978.

Wordle, Ralph M. *Hazlitt.* Lincoln: University of Nebraska Press, 1971.

CHARLES LAMB

Barnett, George L. *Charles Lamb.* Boston: G.K. Hall, 1976.

Bate, Jonathan. "Lamb on Shakespeare." *Charles Lamb Bulletin* 51 (1985): 76–85.

Cecil, David. *A Portrait of Charles Lamb.* London: Constable, 1983.

Coldwell, Jean. "The Playgoer as Critic: Charles Lamb on Shakespeare's Character." *Shakespeare Quarterly* 26: 184–95.

Courtney, Winifred F. *Young Charles Lamb 1775–1802.* New York: New York University Press, 1982.

Frank, Robert. *Don't Call Me Gentle Charles! An Essay on Lamb's Essays of Elia*. Corvallis: Oregon State University Press, 1976.

Heller, Janet Ruth. "Charles Lamb and the Reader of Drama." *Charles Lamb Bulletin* 42 (1983): 25–36.

Morrs, Edwin W., Jr., ed. *The Letters of Charles and Mary Anne Lamb*. Ithaca: Cornell University Press, 1977.

Park, Roy. "Lamb, Shakespeare and the Stage." *Shakespeare Quarterly* 33 (1982): 164–77.

———, ed. *Lamb as Critic*. London: Routledge & Kegan Paul. Lincoln: University of Nebraska Press, 1980.

Prance, Claude A. *Companion to Charles Lamb. A Guide to People and Places; 1760–1847*. London: Mansell Publishing Ltd., 1983.

Randel, Fred U. *The World of Elia: Charles Lamb's Essayistic Romanticism*. Port Washington, N.Y.: Kennikat Press, 1975.

Robson, Mark B. "Charles Lamb: The Dramatist and Drama Critic." *Publication of the Arkansas Philological Association* 2 (1985):75–89.

Wedd, Mary P. "Lamb as a Critic of Wordsworth." *Charles Lamb Bulletin* 41 (1983): 1–16.

Acknowledgments

IMMANUEL KANT

The selections from "The Beautiful and the Sublime," translated by Carl J. Friedrich, are taken from *Immanuel Kant's Moral and Political Writings*, edited by Carl J. Friedrich, copyright © 1949 by Random House, Inc. Reprinted by permission.

The "Transcendental Aesthetic," translated by John Watson, is taken from *The Philosophy of Kant*, edited by John Watson, published by Macmillan & Co. (New York), 1894.

GOTTHOLD LESSING

The selections from "Laokoon," translated by E.C. Beasley and Helen Zimmern, are taken from *The Selected Prose Works of G.E. Lessing*, edited by Edward Bell, published by George Bell & Sons (London), 1890.

JOHANN VON GOETHE

"Ancient and Modern" and "On Criticism" (both translated by J.E. Spingarn); the "Supplement to Aristotle's *Poetics*" and "Shakespeare ad Infinitum" (both translated by Randolph S. Bourne); and the selections from the "Conversations with Eckermann" (translated by John Oxenford) are all taken from *Goethe's Literary Essays*, edited by J.E. Spingarn, copyright © 1921 by Harcourt, Brace & Co. Reprinted by permission.

JOHANN GOTTFRIED HERDER

The selections from "On the Origin of Language," translated by Alexander Gode, are taken from *Two Essays on the Origins of Language*, copyright © 1966 by The University of Chicago. Reprinted by permission.

WILLIAM BLAKE

The Blake selections are taken from *The Complete Writings of William Blake*, edited by Geoffrey Keynes, copyright © 1957 by Random House, Inc. Reprinted by permission.

FRIEDRICH VON SCHILLER

The Schiller selections, translated by Theodore Martin and R.D. Boylan, are taken from *The Works of Friedrich von Schiller*, published by The Aldus Press (London), 1902.

MADAME DE STAËL

The selections from "Germany," translated by O.W. Wight, are taken from *Germany*, edited by O.W. Wight, published by Houghton, Mifflin & Co. (Boston), 1887.

G.W.F. HEGEL

The selections from "On Art," translated by Bernard Bosanquet, are taken from *The Introduction to Hegel's Philosophy of Fine Art*, published by Routledge & Kegan Paul, Ltd. (London), 1905.

SIR WALTER SCOTT

"Introductory Remarks on Popular Poetry" is taken from *Minstrelsy of the Scottish Border*, edited by T.F. Henderson, published by Charles Scribner's Sons (New York), 1902.

WILLIAM WORDSWORTH

The Wordsworth selections are taken from *Literary Criticism of William Wordsworth*, edited by Paul M. Zall, copyright © 1966 by University of Nebraska Press. Reprinted by permission.

NOVALIS

The "Selected Aphorisms," translated by Charles E. Passage, are taken from *Hymns to the Night and Other Selected Writings*, edited by Charles E. Passage, copyright © 1960 by The Liberal Arts Press, Inc. Reprinted by permission.

FRIEDRICH SCHLEGEL

The Schlegel selections, translated by Ernst Behler and Roman Struc, are taken from *Dialogue on Poetry and Literary Aphorisms*, edited by Ernst Behler and Roman Struc, copyright © 1968 by Pennsylvania State University. Reprinted by permission.

SAMUEL TAYLOR COLERIDGE

The selections from "Anima Poetae" are taken from *The Portable Coleridge*, edited by I.A. Richards, copyright © 1950 by The Viking Press, Inc. Reprinted by permission.

"Shakespeare's Judgement Equal to His Genius," "Characteristics of Shakespeare's Drama," "Hamlet," "Romeo and Juliet," "Milton," and the selections from the "Biographia Literaria" are taken from *Selected Poetry and Prose of*

Coleridge, edited by Donald A. Stauffer, copyright © 1951 by Random House, Inc. Reprinted by permission.

FRANCIS JEFFREY

The Jeffrey selections are taken from *Jeffrey's Criticism,* edited by Peter F. Morgan, copyright © 1983 by Peter F. Morgan. Reprinted by permission.

HENRY CRABB ROBINSON

The "Reminiscences of Coleridge, Wordsworth and Lamb" and the selections from the "Reminiscences of Blake" are taken from *Blake, Coleridge, Wordsworth, Lamb, Etc.,* edited by Edith J. Morley, copyright © 1922 by Longmans, Green & Co. Reprinted by permission.

WILLIAM HAZLITT

"On Commonplace Criticism," "On Poetry in General," "On Familiar Style," "On the Prose Style of Poets," and "On the Difference Between Writing and Speaking" are taken from *The Selected Essays of William Hazlitt,* edited by Geoffrey Keynes, copyright © 1930 by Random House, Inc. Reprinted by permission.

"Byron and Wordsworth" and "The Age of Elizabeth: A General View" are taken from The Collected Works of William Hazlitt, edited by A.R. Waller and Arnold Glover, published by McClure, Phillips & Co. (New York), 1902.

The selections from *The Spirit of the Age* ("Mr. Wordsworth," "Mr. Coleridge," and "Sir Walter Scott") are taken from *Lectures on the English Poets and the Spirit of the Age,* edited by Catherine MacDonald Maclean, published by J.M. Dent & Sons (London), 1910.

CHARLES LAMB

"On the Artificial Comedy of the Last Century" and "Detached Thoughts on Books and Reading" are taken from *The Works of Charles Lamb,* published by Edward Moxon (London), 1840.

"On the Death of Coleridge," "The Tragedies of Shakespeare," and "The Characters of Dramatic Writers Contemporary with Shakespeare" are taken from *The Life and Works of Charles Lamb,* published by Macmillan & Co. (London), 1899.